THE
TOOLS
AND
TECHNIQUES
OF

7th Edition

Estate Planning

1988

- Stephan R. Leimberg

- Stephen N. Kandell

- Herbert L. Levy

- Ralph Gano Miller

- Morey S. Rosenbloom

NATIONAL UNDERWRITER

The National Underwriter Co. • 420 East 4th St. • Cincinnati, OH 45202

Library of Congress Catalog Card Number 88-61369

ISBN 0-87218-461-7

published by

NULAW SERVICES

a department of

THE NATIONAL UNDERWRITER COMPANY

Copyright © 1977, 1979, 1980, 1982, 1983, 1985, 1987, 1989
The National Underwriter Company
420 East Fourth Street
Cincinnati, Ohio 45202

Seventh Edition

Printed in the United States of America

DEDICATION

To our parents and our children

and others

whom we love,

who have taught us —

and from whom

we will learn so much more.

And to our friend and co-author,

Herbert L. Levy,

whom we deeply miss.

ABOUT THE AUTHORS

Stephan R. Leimberg

Stephan R. Leimberg designed the format for and is the principal author of this text. He has served on the faculty of The American College since 1971 and is currently Professor of Taxation and Estate Planning. He has been granted the B.A. degree by Temple University, a J.D. by the Temple University School of Law, and holds the CLU designation. Mr. Leimberg is a Lecturer in Law at both the Tax Masters of Temple University School of Law and in its M.B.A. Program, as well as an adjunct professor in the Tax Masters Program at Widener University.

Professor Leimberg is on the Board of Advisors of the Bureau of National Affairs—Tax Management—Financial Planning, and Commerce Clearing House's Financial and Estate Planning Advisory Board. He is the co-chairman, with Sidney Kess, of the National Conference on Financial Planning.

His books include *Keeping Your Money*, published by John Wiley and Company, and *The Executor's Manual*, published by Doubleday.

Other books include *Federal Income Taxation*, Warren, Gorham and Lamont; *Introduction to Estate Administration in Pennsylvania*, The Pennsylvania Bar Institute; and *Money and Retirement*, Addison-Wesley Publishing Co.

Mr. Leimberg is the Editor and Publisher of *Think About It*, a monthly newsletter on income, estate, and gift taxes relating to Insurance, Business and Estate Planning, published by many Associations of Life Underwriters, CLU Chapters, and insurance companies.

Professor Leimberg has been a main platform speaker at both the Million Dollar Round Table annual meeting and the Top of the Table and has appeared before numerous estate planning councils, Life Underwriters Associations, life insurance companies, and study groups. He has also addressed the International Association of Financial Planners, the State Bars of Texas, Wisconsin and Oklahoma, the Pennsylvania Bar Institute Basic Legal Practice Course, numerous CPA societies, and has been a featured speaker at three workshops of the National Aeronautics and Space Administration. He appeared as an expert witness on IRAs before a subcommittee of the House Ways and Means Committee of the United States House of Representatives.

Professor Leimberg has also spoken at the N.Y.U. Tax Institute, The Southern California Tax and Estate Planning Forum, the Notre Dame Law School Estate Planning Institute, and at the Annual Meeting of the National Association of Estate Planning Councils.

Leimberg has served on the Board of Directors of the Philadelphia CLU chapter, the Philadelphia Estate Planning Council, and was a Director of the Delaware Valley Chapter of the International Association for Financial Planning, Inc.

Herbert L. Levy

Herbert L. Levy was, before his death in December, 1982, in the private practice of law in Allentown, Pa. He was graduated from City University of New York (B.S. in accounting, 1964), St. John's University School of Law (J.D. 1966) and New York University School of Law (LL.M. in taxation, 1967) where he served as Tax Editor of the N.Y.U. *Tax Law Review.*

He was co-author of *Introduction to Estates and Trusts Practice in the Commonwealth of Pennsylvania* (7 editions).

Mr. Levy instructed the American College's Advanced Estate Planning Course and was a frequent lecturer on estate planning and taxation.

Stephen N. Kandell

Stephen N. Kandell is a CLU (1973) and the Director of Estate and Business Analysis, Leonard Day Agency, Manufacturers Life, Philadelphia, Pa. He attended City College of New York (B.B.A. 1964) and completed his legal training at New York University School of Law (J.D. 1967 and LL.M. 1968). Mr. Kandell has lectured before various groups on estate planning and taxation.

Morey S. Rosenbloom

Morey S. Rosenbloom is a partner in the Philadelphia, Pennsylvania law firm of Blank, Rome, Comisky & McCauley. He graduated from Temple University School of Law and served as a legal assistant to the then Chief Justice, John C. Bell, of the Supreme Court of the Commonwealth of Pennsylvania.

Mr. Rosenbloom is a lecturer in law at the Law School at Temple University and an instructor of the American College Advanced Estate Planning Course.

He has lectured at numerous seminars on the topic of estate and business planning to various legal, banking, insurance and estate planning groups throughout the country.

Mr. Rosenbloom has co-authored several publications, including *Practical Will Drafting, Computing The Federal Estate Tax, The Wait and See Buy-Sell* and *Funding Corporate Buy-Sell Agreements With Life Insurance*.

Ralph Gano Miller

Ralph Gano Miller is a member of the California Bar and a cum laude graduate of Stanford University with a BA and Masters Degree in Business Administration. He is a summa cum laude graduate of the University of San Diego Law School.

Mr. Miller is a CPA and author of over 15 law review and journal articles on various estate planning tools and techniques. He has served as a member of the Board of Regents of the University of San Diego Law School, and as a professor of federal income taxation and gift and estate taxation at the California Western Law School.

He was a founding member of the Independent Board of Trustees of the California Western University Law School. He is an instructor of the Advanced Estate Planning Course of the CLU program and has spoken at many tax institutes, including the New York University and University of Southern California Tax Institutes.

He is a member of the American Bar Association Sections on Taxation and Real Property, Probate and Trust Law and served as Chairman of the Administrative Law Section.

Mr. Miller has served as Chairman, Section of Taxation, of the San Diego County Bar Association's Section on Taxation and Real Property, Probate and Trust Law. He served as President of the Southern California Estate Planning Council.

He is past Chairman of the Taxation Advisory Commission, Board of Legal Specialization for the State Bar of California, and is a certified specialist in tax law in California. He also served as a member of the Board of Legal Specialization.

Mr. Miller is the President of the Ralph Gano Miller Professional Law Corporation.

ACKNOWLEDGMENTS

We wish to thank The American College, which graciously permitted us to use some of the forms, worksheets, and articles developed for its *Advanced Estate Planning* courses. We highly recommend its book on the Tax Reform Act of 1986, *The Financial Services Professional's Guide to the Tax Reform Act of 1986* and *The Financial Services Professional's Guide to the State of the Art: 1989*, from which we have liberally borrowed for information on TRA '86, TRA '87, and TAMRA '88.

Many of the new Appendix chapters were coauthored by Elkins Park, PA attorney Charles K. Plotnik. Our thanks to attorney Charles K. Plotnik, who also coauthored an excellent book and cassette on estate planning for paralegals and clients, *Keeping Your Money*, for his highly practical commentary.

We would like to express our appreciation to Financial Data Corporation for allowing us to use its updated (version 4.0) NumberCruncher I, financial planning TOOLKIT, and Graphpak computer illustrations throughout this seventh edition. Information on these products, which have been designed to follow almost all the mathematical computations in this book and our companion texts, *The Tools and Techniques of Financial Planning* (third edition) and *The Tools and Techniques of Employee Benefits and Retirement Planning*, can be ordered by calling 1-800-654-2227 or 215-525-6957.

Finally, we applaud S. Samuel Scoville, J.D., CLU, and the following members of his fine staff at The National Underwriter Company for their technical assistance in the production of this edition and in their heroic efforts in updating this text for TAMRA '88: Alice Whaling Fossett, LL.B., CLU; Garry L. Baumgartner, J.D., CLU; Deborah A. Tabacco, J.D., CLU, ChFC; Darlene K. Chandler, J.D., CLU; William J. Wagner, J.D., LL.M; and April A. Kestel, J.D.

PREFACE TO THE SECOND EDITION

Professor George Cooper, in a brilliant article in the March 1977 *Columbia Law Review,* shocked attorneys and other members of the estate planning team by commenting on the current federal estate tax as a "voluntary" tax. He then quoted Professor A. James Casner who said, "In fact, we haven't got an estate tax, what we have, you pay an estate tax if you want to; if you don't want to you don't have to."

Professor Cooper proves his point by discussing methods for freezing estates, creating tax exempt wealth, and disposing of wealth already accumulated.

Tools and Techniques, 2d edition, is designed to provide the fastest possible means of acquainting the student or general practitioner with every major planning device mentioned in Professor Cooper's article — and many others.

To accomplish this goal, we have added chapters on recapitalizations, charitable contributions, disclaimers, deferred payments of federal estate taxes, powers of appointment, survivor's income benefit ("death benefit only" plans), and incorporation. Additionally, the discussions of installment sales, retirement plans, private annuities, life insurance, trusts, and many other key topics have been expanded.

Updating continued even as typesetting of the second edition progressed, enabling us to reflect in the revisions not only the Revenue Act of 1978, but also a number of 1979 cases and rulings. A summary of major income, estate, and gift tax provisions of the Revenue Act of 1978 has also been added.

A new dimension to *Tools and Techniques* was added with the introduction of "Issues And Implications In Community Property States" — for most chapters. This means that *Tools and Techniques* is now an even more valuable guide for practitioners in Arizona, California, Idaho, Louisiana, Nevada, New Mexico, Texas and Washington. (Because it is impossible to discuss thoroughly the laws of all eight states, focus has been placed on California's property laws. General principles of community property law are discussed within the California framework in the Introduction. Although many of these principles will be universally applicable, it is important to review the laws of your own state rather than relying solely on the text discussion.)

Tools and Techniques was originally designed as a basic practice manual for the Pennsylvania Bar Institute — and is still used by that organization. Since then we have attempted to expand its applicability to all members of the estate planning team. From its conception in 1975 *Tools and Techniques* has been used extensively in law schools, M.B.A. programs, CLU and CPA classes, and trust school sessions on estate planning. To further expand the utility and practicality of *Tools and Techniques 2d Edition* for the trust officer, attorney, accountant, and life insurance agent, the authors now include three practicing attorneys, Herbert Levy, Ralph Gano Miller, Jr., and Morey S. Rosenbloom. Three authors, Stephen Kandell, Herbert Levy, and Ralph Gano Miller, Jr. have earned the Master of Laws (LL.M.) degree. Mr. Miller is a CPA and Stephen Kandell is a CLU and advanced underwriting consultant for a major life insurance company.

The authors are fortunate to have received substantial technical and copy editing assistance on this second edition by S. Samuel Scoville, J.D., CLU, and the following editorial staff members of the Advanced Sales Reference Service Department of The National Underwriter Company: Alice W. Fossett, LL.B., CLU, Garry L. Baumgartner, J.D., and Rita C. Bell, editorial assistant.

We express our thanks to our secretaries, Mrs. Carol Fenon, Mrs. Alicia M. Howard, Ms. Mary Ann Ritter, Mrs. Mary Jo Kopczynski, Ms. Denise Temponi, Mrs. Jessie Torelli, and to Ms. Hattie M. Darien and Ms. Kathy E. Bretz of the Pennsylvania Bar Institute staff for the many, many hours spent typing and retyping copy.

S.R.L.
H.L.L.
S.N.K.
M.S.R.
R.G.M., Jr.

PREFACE TO THE THIRD EDITION

Rampant inflation coupled with economic unrest has awakened the financial fears and threatened the psychological security of our clients throughout the country. Fast changing tax laws have increased not only in complexity but also in number. This has made it almost impossible for the general practitioner to master or even stay abreast of the most recent estate planning tools and techniques.

This third edition is designed to accomplish two major objectives: update and expand. With the assistance of S. Samuel Scoville, JD, CLU, and members of his staff, Alice W. Fossett, JD, CLU, and Garry L. Baumgartner, JD, the authors of "Tools and Techniques" have updated every page of the second edition to encompass the repeal of carryover basis, the Technical Corrections Act of 1979, and all pivotal cases, regulations, and rulings up to the date of this printing in late 1980. [Ed.Note: With the second printing of the third edition, Chapter 15, "Installment Sales," was revised to reflect the Installment Sales Revision Act of 1980. The House-passed version of that legislation had been merely summarized in the first printing.]

This substantially expanded edition now includes information on the computation of the federal estate tax, valuation of assets for gift and estate tax purposes, how basis is determined, interest-free loans, family partnerships, powers of attorney, medical expense reimbursement plans, and the Orphans' Exclusion.

New data gathering forms have been added that should prove especially useful for clients who live in — or move to or from — community property states. Worksheets to perform liquidity needs and computations are also included. A thorough explanation of the Tax Reform Act of 1976 now precedes the explanation of the Revenue Act of 1978, providing perspective and background on the interaction of our current gift and estate tax systems.

The growing popularity of "Tools and Techniques of Estate Planning" has been most gratifying. The book is now widely used by a number of bar associations, CPA groups, CLUs, and trust departments throughout the country. Many law schools, MBA programs, CLU and CPA classes and trust schools are using "Tools and Techniques" as a textbook.

It is our intention through this third edition to continue to provide a highly readable, accurate, and creative source of information that will show how to freeze the growth in estates, create tax exempt wealth, and dispose of wealth already accumulated.

S.R.L.
H.L.L.
S.N.K.
M.S.R.
R.G.M.

PREFACE TO THE FOURTH EDITION

"The average estate owner no longer needs to worry about estate planning after the passage of ERTA, The Economic Recovery Tax Act." This is a statement many so-called financial planners have been making in newspapers and magazine articles since the passage of the Act on August 13, 1981. The truth is, nothing could be further from the truth. Careful comprehensive planning of every estate is now more important than ever.

Clearly, ERTA does contain many provisions which can substantially reduce the federal estate tax payable at death and make the payment of the tax burden easier to handle. *Tools and Techniques* has been completely revised to reflect all of the major ERTA income, estate, and gift tax provisions affecting the estate planner. But the complacency occasioned by a careless perusal of the Act is misplaced for a number of reasons.

First, many of the most favorable tax relief provisions (e.g., income and estate and gift tax rate reductions, increased unified credit and indexing of income tax rates) are "phased in" and will not fully benefit anyone for many years.

Second, since some of the tax relief provisions (e.g., increase in unified credit and special use valuation maximum limits) are not indexed, unchecked inflation may wipe out or severely reduce their real advantage.

Third, some of the provisions (e.g., the reduction in top estate tax rates) affect only the super wealthy and will not benefit most clients.

Fourth, the much ballyhooed unlimited gift and estate tax marital deductions are "revise or forfeit" provisions. They aren't automatic and may be lost unless a client revises his will and trust. In some cases the $10,000 annual exclusion will not be allowed unless a new Crummey trust is drawn.

Fifth, the cost of living has not diminished; it has increased — substantially! An often forgotten but quite essential part of estate planning involves the creation of capital for income replacement when the key bread winner dies. More — not less — capital will be needed than ever before.

Sixth, and most essential, is what estate planning is all about: People. ERTA makes it possible more than ever before to customize an estate plan in order to efficiently and effectively accomplish a client's objectives. But although greater numbers of choices are possible, they must be offered to and chosen by the client. Reliance on state law or on previous dispositive tools or techniques will not suffice.

One chapter of Tools and Techniques has been deleted (The Orphans' Deduction); most others have been expanded and all have been updated to the date of publication. A substantial explanation and commentary on the implications of ERTA can be found in Appendix D following discussions of the Tax Reform Act of 1976 and the Revenue Act of 1978. New forms have been added throughout the book to assist in computing federal estate tax qualification for Section 6166 Installment Payouts and Section 303 Stock Redemptions. An extensive discussion on the Federal Gift Tax has been added as Appendix D.

We appreciate the faith and trust of the many law schools, bar associations, CLU, CFP, and CPA groups, banks, insurance companies, and other financial service institutions that have adopted *Tools and Techniques* in their educational programs. We promise to continue to maintain and increase the accuracy, readability, and creativity of *Tools and Techniques* in the 80's.

Stephan R. Leimberg
Herbert L. Levy
Stephen N. Kandell
Ralph Gano Miller
Morey S. Rosenbloom

PREFACE TO THE FIFTH EDITION

"Change" — next to the word, "new," followed by "tax law" — it's probably the most repeated word in our profession. This is the fifth major change in *Tools and Techniques*. Since 1975, when the book was written for use by lawyers in the legal practice course of the Pennsylvania Bar Association, over 80,000 copies have been purchased. The book has grown in size from 140 pages to over 400. This totally up-dated fifth edition contains several completely new chapters and many have been signifiantly expanded.

Tools and Techniques is used in the Tax Masters Programs of many law and business schools, as a main text by the prestigious College of Financial Planning as part of the CFP program, and by hundreds of insurance companies as a major part of their training programs. *Tools and Techniques* — along with *Tax Facts* — comprise the mainstay of the sophisticated life insurance agent's estate planning library.

We expect that there will be many more editions of *Tools and Techniques* in the future. Each edition is an attempt to create an easier to read, more accurate, comprehensive, and useful device to help planners better serve their clients. We have been assisted in this goal by S. Samuel Scoville, J.D., CLU and the following members of his staff: Alice Whaling Fossett, LL.B., CLU; Garry L. Baumgartner, J.D., CLU; Stephen Von Wahlde, J.D.; Deborah A. Tabacco, J.D.; Rita C. Bell, Assistant to the Editor. They have helped to make and to keep *Tools and Techniques* the highly respected and utilized book that it is. We express to them our warm appreciation.

Stephan R. Leimberg
Stephen N. Kandell
Morey S. Rosenbloom
Ralph Gano Miller

PREFACE TO THE SIXTH EDITION

The more things change the more they stay the same. Tax Reform—one more time—was here again in 1986. The rules change—the names of the players change—but the goals and objectives are the same. As estate planners, we are still trying, ten years and over 150,000 copies after our first edition came off the press, to help people help people.

The big buzzwords of the year are GRITs, Splits, and RITs. Read all about it and read it here first. Yes, Virginia, there is a Santa Claus if you are willing to plan. And, No, there is still no free lunch in the tax law. For every "gimmie" there's a "gotcha"—a cost. Some of our old standbys (such as the short term trust) are gone. But we have new ways of handling new laws to solve old problems (and we still have old ways of handling old laws to solve old problems).

One change that runs throughout the book is the repeal of the 60% deduction for net long term capital gains. For taxable years beginning after 1986, net capital gains are fully taxable, and in many places we refer simply to gain taxed at ordinary income rates. Know, however, that taxpayers must continue to categorize gain as either capital or ordinary, and as either short-term or long-term. The structure for determining net capital gains and losses remains unchanged in order to facilitate reinstatement of a capital gains rate differential if there is a future tax rate increase. Also, in certain contexts, such as planning for charitable giving of long-term capital gain property (see chapter 2), or in computing the tax elements of payments made under an installment sale (chapter 15) or a private annuity (chapter 21), the distinction is very important.

As we reviewed the fifth edition and started our revision, we came across many names in the hundreds of hypotheticals throughout TOOLS AND TECHNIQUES. Thinly disguised, these names are often our friends, business acquaintances, or relatives. Some have died, some have become disabled, some have lost fortunes, some have gained fortunes. Some single friends have married, and some married friends are single. Some over the last ten years have been living out their lives according to very steady, consistent, and long planned patterns, while others are now in places, positions, and circumstances they couldn't have dreamed they'd be in ten years ago.

It sounds corny (some of the best things in life are corny, so I make no apologies), but we've seen the human drama unfold throughout our pages over the last five editions. We've seen most of the tools and techniques we've written about are real and true and actually work. More importantly, we've talked to thousands of planners throughout the country who have been using these ideas successfully.

Ideas are like products: get a good one and you want to sell it to everyone you meet. The enthusiasm's great, but no one idea or product will work with everyone, or work with anyone every time. As times change, so must the concepts. There's more information in TOOLS AND TECHNIQUES than ever before. And now there's even a companion text for financial planners, TOOLS AND TECHNIQUES OF FINANCIAL PLANNING.

But the goals have not changed. People now, as was the case ten years ago, and as will be ten years into the future, will want to solve the financial problems in their L.I.V.E.S. So before you begin to focus on the over 30 chapters of solutions, take a few minutes to ponder the goals our clients want to meet and the pitfalls they want to avoid:

L. — LACK OF LIQUIDITY (Without adequate cash to pay death taxes and other estate settlement costs, our clients' most precious assets are often sacrificed in forced sales.)

I. — IMPROPER DISPOSITION OF ASSETS (The wrong assets too often end up going to the wrong person at the wrong time in the wrong manner.)

I. — INFLATION (Without adequate diversification, the buying power of a working lifetime often diminishes to an insufficiency.)

I. — INADEQUATE INCOME AND CAPITAL (In the event of death, disability, retirement, and special needs, the difference between dignity and despair may be adequacy of financial resources.)

V. — VALUE—THE NEED TO STABILIZE AND MAXIMIZE (One of the first tasks in estate planning is to protect and make best use of the assets the client already has.)

E. — EXCESSIVE TRANSFER COSTS (Most people will pay too darn much in taxes and other expenses to transfer financial security.)

S. — SPECIAL NEEDS (Providing for those people and organizations that we love and who can't care for themselves may be the most important task of the planner.)

No, not much has really changed in the last ten years since Herb Levy and I wrote the first edition. In fact, the basic principle upon which we wrote was actually written thousands of years before we were born:

"IF I AM NOT FOR MYSELF, WHO WILL BE FOR ME?

BEING ONLY FOR MYSELF, WHAT AM I?

IF NOT NOW, WHEN?"

My coauthors and I invite you to share in our knowledge and experience—and to give us feedback, so that we can make the seventh edition more useful to you.

Stephan R. Leimberg

PREFACE TO THE SEVENTH EDITION

"Half-life of knowledge" — an incredibly appropriate phrase for estate and financial planners to consider when wondering why it has been necessary to produce seven editions of the same book since 1976, when the first edition was printed. The 1986 "Tax Reform" Act, coupled with the last second (December 22) tax law change of 1987, the Omnibus Budget Reconciliation Act and the Technical and Miscellaneous Revenue Act of 1988 (TAMRA), have dashed all hopes that tax law would be allowed to "mature" before additional Congressional tinkering. Planners must help clients make immediate decisions that may affect hundreds of thousands and in some cases millions of dollars. So last year's information just isn't good enough any more. In fact, it's downright dangerous. That's why a seventh edition was urgently needed.

Wealthy clients (look for the tax law of the not too distant future to be lowering the definition of "wealthy") can be hurt most by the changes reflected in this text. Five forces (see KEEPING WEALTH IN THE FAMILY; THE ALMOST IMPOSSIBLE DREAM, in Appendix D) make it difficult or almost impossible (for those who do not begin to plan immediately) to keep wealth in the family and pass it down one or two generations. These five forces (the freezing of 55 percent rates, the new 5 percent add-on estate tax, the almost new generation-skipping transfer tax, the almost new 15 percent excise tax on "excess" accumulations, and the new Code section 2036(c)) amount to nothing less than a draconian and confiscatory system that could eventually change the economic environment of our country. This cruel combination of forces attacks business owners and professionals especially hard.

Many clients (and some poorly informed planners) will tend to ignore or not fully appreciate the combined impact of these five forces, or the urgency of taking decisive action to lessen their impact. They will pay a heavy price for their inaction. Conscientious planners will realize that even clients whose estates seem completely protected by the present unified credit will soon be exposed to one or more of the ravages of the "five horsemen."

On one level, choice is easier now than ever: Do nothing and allow the federal government to be your major beneficiary. (Top estate tax rates are 55 percent, which, together with the 5 percent add-on, total 60 percent, which, when added to the 15 percent excise estate tax can result in a 75 percent top tax — unless the client's named beneficiary is a grandchild, in which case, a 55 percent generation skipping transfer tax must be added.)

On another level, the answer to the question, "Well, what should I do?" is more difficult than ever. The labyrinth-like interweaving of constantly mutating Code sections is made even more hairpullingly complex by regulations which, if and when they appear, arrive too late and in too voluminous and confusing an array. Moreover, many times the regulations don't seem to follow the Code at all (witness the computation of the excess accumulations tax as described in the Code compared with the process described in the regulations). This of course makes the planner's task more difficult and more hazardous from a malpractice standpoint.

The bottom line is that knowledge is more fleeting, and therefore up to date practical information is more precious. A knowledgeable planner will soon be worth his weight (even before dieting) in gold. We hope that this seventh edition will help you help others. We welcome your comments on how the eighth edition can be even more useful to you.

Stephan R. Leimberg

INTRODUCTION AND BIBLIOGRAPHY

Estate planning is a fascinating subject. No two problems are ever quite the same and no perfect answers or well-established rules exist to solve problems. Estate planning is not merely planning to save or reduce taxes during lifetime or at death; it is far more complex because a person and his or her relationship with property and other people is involved.

There is no easy way to learn estate planning. The field is vast and covers not only income, estate, and gift tax law but involves many facets of corporate, probate, estate, trust, and securities law as well.

The essential concern is to ascertain all the facts, whether they may seem material or relevant at the time. From those facts you must then recognize and clearly state the problems. Then the real challenge begins: finding or creating the appropriate solutions.

A good library of up-to-date texts, tapes and articles is essential. The following is a list of some of the books and information sources we have found useful: (It is extremely important to check with the publisher to see if the version you are purchasing or using is the most recent version and if it encompasses all of the major tax law changes.)

Bittker and Eustice, *Federal Income Taxation of Corporations and Shareholders*, (Student Edition), Warren, Gorham and Lamont

Bureau of National Affairs, *Tax Management Income, Estates, Gifts and Trusts Portfolios*

Bureau of National Affairs, *Tax Management Financial Planning Service*

Casner, *Estate Planning*, Little, Brown and Co.

Commerce Clearing House, Inc., *Federal Tax Articles*

Commerce Clearing House, Inc., *Financial and Estate Planning Reporter*

Commerce Clearing House, Inc., *Inheritance Estate and Gift Tax Reporter*

Ferguson, Freeland and Stephens, *Federal Income Taxation and Estates and Beneficiaries*, Little, Brown and Co.

Harris, *Handling Federal Estate and Gift Taxes*, Bancroft Whitney

Helfert, *Techniques of Financial Analysis*, Dow, Jones, Irwin, Inc.

Hendrickson, *Interstate and International Estate Planning*, Practicing Law Institute

Herz and Baller, *Business Acquisitions: Planning and Practice*, Practicing Law Institute

Kahn and Colson, *Federal Taxation of Estates and Trusts*, ALI-ABA

Leimberg, Satinsky, Ivers, Krader, and Parker, *The Federal Income Tax Law*, Warren, Gorham, and Lamont

Mertens, *Law of Federal Gift and Estate Taxation*, Lofit Publications, Inc.

Mertens, *Law of Federal Income Taxation*, Callahan and Co.

Nossaman and Wyatt, *Trust Administration and Taxation*, Matthew Bender and Co.

Plotnick and Leimberg, *The Executor's Manual*, Doubleday and Company

Plotnik and Leimberg, *Keeping Your Money*, John Wiley & Co.

Prentice-Hall, *Tax Ideas*

Number Cruncher I, Financial Data Corporation

Rabkin and Johnson, *Current Legal Forms With Tax Analysis*, Matthew Bender and Co.

Rabkin and Johnson, *Federal Income Gift and Estate Taxation*, Matthew Bender and Co.

Sellin, *New York University Institute on Federal Taxation*, Matthew Bender and Co.

Stephens, Maxfield and Lind, *Federal Estate and Gift Taxation*, Warren, Gorham and Lamont

Stoeber, *Tax Planning Techniques for the Closely Held Corporation*, The National Underwriter Company

Tax Facts 1 and 2, The National Underwriter Company

Warren and Surrey, *Federal Estate and Gift Taxation*, Foundation Press

Weisz, *Supertrust III*, Farnsworth Publishing Company

White and Chasman, *Business Insurance*, Prentice-Hall

We highly recommend tax services such as Prentice-Hall, Research Institute of America, and Commerce Clearing House. These services are most useful. The Advanced Sales Reference Service, published by The National Underwriter Company, has a strong following within the life insurance industry. Additionally, journals such as the *Journal of Taxation, Tax Law Review,Taxes, Taxation for Lawyers, Estate Planning, Taxation for Accountants, Trusts and Estates, Financial Planning Magazine, The Practical Lawyer*, and *The CLU Journal* are highly useful.

One of the best tools for "Keeping Current" is a quarterly cassette service of the same name available from the American Society of Chartered Life Underwriters.

A service that specializes in the taxation and uses of life insurance in business and estate planning is *Think About It*, a monthly newsletter used extensively by life underwriters associations and insurance companies throughout the country.

Keep in mind that TOOLS AND TECHNIQUES is a survey text. It is not meant to be a detailed examination of any one particular area. We have tried to design the text to give you enough familiarity with an area so that when doing research, you will have an initial understanding of that area.

Because no single text can replace broad, substantive courses in estate and gift taxation planning coupled with a case study approach, we strongly recommend the two-part Advanced Estate Planning Course of The American College. Helpful background and supplementary technical reading may be found in the *Advanced Sales Reference Service*, referred to earlier. References to "ASRS" appearing immediately above "Footnote References" at the ends of chapters are to this service.

PRINCIPLES OF COMMUNITY PROPERTY LAW

Arizona, California, Idaho, Louisiana, Nevada, New Mexico, Texas, Washington, and Wisconsin all use some form of the community property system in establishing the legal relationship between a husband and wife. The general theory is that the husband and wife form a partnership and that property acquired during marriage by the labor and skill of either belongs to both. Community property laws originate from the community property system of Spain, transplanted in turn to Mexico and California.

Community property laws have significant effects on the legal relationships between spouses who reside or formerly resided in one of the eight community property states. To help illustrate those effects, sections have been added to various chapters discussing community property implications and issues relating to the chapter's subject matter.

In many respects, the laws of the community property states are different. Focus will be placed on California's community property laws. Thus, *while general principles should be noted, the community property laws of a particular state should be reviewed before relying on any discussion.*

California law generally defines community property to be all real property situated in California and all personal property wherever situated acquired during marriage, other than separate property, by a married person while domiciled in California. The husband and wife have equal interests in all community property.

California law generally defines separate property as (1) property owned by either spouse before marriage, (2) property acquired after marriage by gift, devise, bequest or descent, (3) in certain respects, the rents, issues and profits of separate property and (4) property acquired during marriage with the proceeds of separate property. Separate property is owned solely by the spouse who originally acquired it.

California law provides, however, that if the spouses separate, their respective earnings and profits accruing after the date of separation are their separate property. Thus, it is not an absolute rule that earnings during marriage in California are community property. The spouses may also alter the normal community property rules by agreement.

Many married couples move into California, having accumulated property in separate property states. In these situations, some of the property may be characterized under California law as quasi-community property.

Quasi-community property is all real or personal property, wherever situated, which would have been community property if the spouses had acquired the property while living in California. Quasi-community property is treated as separate property of the acquiring spouse for all purposes other than division on divorce or upon the death of the acquiring spouse. In the event of divorce or the death of the acquiring spouse, quasi-community property is treated similarly to community property (except that only real property situated in California is treated as quasi-community property in the event of a division on death of the acquiring spouse). As quasi-community property rights apply only to division on divorce or upon the death of the acquiring spouse, the property will retain its separate property character if the non-acquiring spouse dies first.

Courts in several community property states, especially California, have also found that non-married couples can expressly or impliedly agree to apply community property principles to earnings and accumulations during their relationship. In some cases, one "partner" has proven such an agreement over the denial of the other. Although the non-married couple may feel uncomfortable discussing property rights, in many situations major problems could be avoided by an appropriate agreement.

CONTENTS

Appendix A

Appendix B

Appendix C

Appendix D

Appendix E

Chapter 1

BUY-SELL (BUSINESS CONTINUATION) AGREEMENT

WHAT IS IT?

A business purchase agreement is an arrangement for the disposition of a business interest in the event of the owner's death, disability, retirement, or upon withdrawal from the business at some earlier time. Business purchase agreements can take a number of forms:

(1) an agreement between the business itself and the individual owners (a stock redemption agreement);

(2) an agreement between the individual owners (a cross-purchase or "criss-cross" agreement);

(3) an agreement between the individual owners and key person, family member, or outside individual (a "third-party" business buy-out agreement); and

(4) a combination of the foregoing.

The most common types of business purchase agreements are the stock redemption plan (often called a stock retirement plan) and the cross-purchase plan. The distinguishing feature of the redemption agreement is that the corporation itself agrees to purchase (redeem) the stock of the withdrawing or deceased stockholder. In a cross-purchase plan the individuals agree between or among themselves to purchase the interest of a withdrawing or deceased stockholder.

WHEN IS THE USE OF SUCH A DEVICE INDICATED?

1. When a guaranteed market must be created for the sale of a business interest in the event of death, disability, or retirement.

2. When it is necessary or desirable to "peg" the value of the business for federal and state death tax purposes. See page 477 for an explanation of new Code section 2036(c) and the estate tax implications of a buy-sell agreement.

3. When a shareholder would be unable or unwilling to continue running the business with the family of a deceased co-stockholder.

4. When the business involves a high amount of financial risk for the family of a deceased shareholder and it is desirable to convert the business interest into cash at his or her death.

5. When it is necessary or desirable to prevent all or part of the business from falling into the hands of "outsiders."

WHAT ARE THE REQUIREMENTS?

A written agreement is drawn stating the purchase price, terms, and funding arrangements. The agreement obligates the retiring or disabled owner or owner's estate to sell the business either (a) to the business itself, or (b) to the surviving owner(s). Occasionally an agreement combines the two types of obligations and will give the individuals an option to purchase the stock but provide that if they fail to exercise the option, then the corporation must purchase the stock.

The stock agreement specifies the event triggering the respective obligations. Generally that event is the death, disability, or the retirement of the owner. Valuation should be according to book value, a formula value, or some agreed amount.

"Funding" pertains to how the promises under the agreement will be financed. Generally, in a redemption agreement, the business will purchase, own, and be the beneficiary of life and disability income insurance on each person who owns an interest in the business.

In the case of a cross-purchase agreement, the prospective buyer (each business associate) purchases, owns, and is beneficiary of a life and disability income insurance policy on his or her co-owners.

HOW IT IS DONE — AN EXAMPLE

Stock Redemption Plan

Herb and Steve are equal stockholders in a business valued at $100,000. The business purchases $50,000 of life insurance and a policy providing $570 a month of disability insurance on both men.

At Herb's death, his stock passes to his estate. The life insurance proceeds on Herb's life are paid to the business. Then the business pays the cash proceeds to Herb's estate according to the agreement. In return for the cash, Herb's executor transfers the stock to the business. Steve, therefore, ends up with ownership of all the outstanding voting stock (the stock owned by the business itself is not entitled to vote).

Under the buy-sell agreement, should Herb become totally disabled prior to retirement, he would receive his full salary for one year. At the end of a year of total disability, Herb's interest would be sold to the business. The business would pay at least $5,000 (10 percent of $50,000) as a down payment to Herb. The business would also issue Herb a 10-year note (secured by his stock which is placed in an escrow account) for the remaining value of the stock, $45,000. The business would pay 9 percent interest on the note (assuming 9% is the safe harbor rate needed to avoid the unstated interest rules of Code section 483). Thus, Herb would receive approximately $570 a month for 120 months. In order to help pay off the note, the business would receive $570

Tools and Techniques

a month of disability income insurance proceeds from a policy owned by and made payable to the business.

In the event Herb retired, he would sell his stock to the business. The business would pay Herb at least $5,000 (10 percent of $50,000) as a down payment, plus it would give Herb a 10-year note (secured by his stock) for the remaining $45,000. The business would also pay Herb 9 percent interest. Herb, therefore, would receive about $570 a month for 120 months. The cash value of the life insurance policy on Herb's life could be used to help finance the down payment. One limiting factor, in general, is that in many states, the corporation can redeem its stock only to the extent it has earned surplus.

Cross-Purchase Agreement

Assume Herb and Steve are equal stockholders in a business valued at $100,000. Herb purchases a $50,000 life insurance policy and a $570 a month disability income policy on Steve's life. Steve purchases policies in an equal amount on Herb's life.

Assuming Herb dies first, his stock passes to his estate. The insurance proceeds on Herb's life are paid directly to Steve. Steve then pays cash to Herb's estate according to the cross-purchase agreement. In return for the cash, Herb's executor transfers stock to Steve. Therefore, Steve becomes the sole owner of the corporation.

In the event of Herb's disability, he receives his full salary for one year assuming he is totally disabled. At that time, Herb must sell his business interest to Steve. Steve will pay at least $5,000 (10 percent) down payment to Herb. Steve will also give Herb a 10-year note (secured by his stock) for the balance upon which he will pay 9 percent interest. This will provide approximately $570 a month for 120 months. During this time, Steve will be receiving $570 a month of income from a disability income insurance policy purchased on Herb's life which can be used to pay off the note.

At Herb's retirement, Herb will sell his stock to Steve. Steve will pay at least $5,000 (10 percent) down payment to Herb. Steve will also give Herb a 10-year note (secured by his stock) for the $45,000 balance. Interest at 9 percent will be paid so that Herb will receive about $570 a month for 120 months. Steve can use the cash value on the policy he owns on Herb's life to provide the down payment.

WHAT ARE THE TAX IMPLICATIONS?

Stock Redemption Agreements

1. Assuming the corporation is owner and beneficiary of the policy(ies), the value of the insurance on the decedent's life will not be includible (as insurance proceeds per se) in his gross estate for federal estate tax purposes.

However, the insurance proceeds will be considered in valuing the decedent's interest in the business unless there is a valid agreement fixing the price for federal estate tax purposes and the proceeds are excluded from the purchase price under the terms of the agreement.[1]

The agreement will generally establish the value of the business for federal estate tax purposes if: (1) the estate is obligated to sell at the decedent-shareholder's death; (2) the agreement prohibits the shareholder from disposing of his interest during lifetime without first offering it to the corporation at no more than the contract price; (3) the price was fair and adequate at the time the agreement was made and resulted from a bona fide arms-length transaction; and (4) the price must be fixed by the terms of the agreement, or the agreement must contain a formula or method for determining price.[2] Planners must also consider the impact of Code section 2036(c) on buy-sells (see page 477).

2. Life insurance or disability income premiums used to fund the agreement are not deductible by the corporation.[3] On the other hand, death proceeds (or disability income proceeds) will be received by the corporation income tax free.[4] Premiums paid by the corporation will not be taxable income to its shareholders.

3. The biggest potential problem in a corporate stock redemption agreement is the possibility that the redemption will be treated as a dividend distribution. The Internal Revenue Code states the general rule that distributions of money or property in redemption of stock by a corporation will be treated as a dividend (subject to ordinary income taxation to the extent of the corporation's earnings and profits) unless the distribution or redemption meets certain exceptions to the general rule. The most common exception is that a redemption of all of a shareholder's stock (a complete termination of his interest) will not be treated as a dividend.

For example, Herb and Steve, unrelated parties, own stock in a closely held corporation. Herb dies and his stock passes to his estate. The corporation redeems all of Herb's stock from his estate. The result is a total redemption. The distribution will not be subjected to dividend treatment because Herb's estate has given up all control, share of future profits, and share of future assets in the event of a sale or liquidation of the corporation, i.e., Herb's estate has completely terminated its interest.

The favorable tax treatment can be complicated or even thwarted by what is known as "constructive ownership" (attribution) rules.[5] Essentially, the basic constructive ownership rules work as follows:

a. The "estate/beneficiary" attribution rule. Under this rule, stock owned by a beneficiary of an estate is considered constructively (treated for tax purposes as if it were actually) owned by the estate.[6] A redemption of all the stock actually owned by the estate (without a simultaneous redemption of stock owned by a beneficiary) may be considered a partial redemption and may be taxable to the estate as a dividend. The estate is still considered a stockholder since it is deemed to own stock actually owned by the beneficiary.

For example, Herb and Steve are father and son. Herb owns 75 percent of the stock while Steve owns the remaining 25 percent. Steve is a beneficiary under Herb's will. If the corporation redeems only Herb's stock from his executor, the entire amount paid by the corporation for the stock may be treated and taxed as a dividend (to the extent of corporate earnings and profits) because the redemption is *deemed* to be of less than all the stock owned directly or indirectly by the estate. After the redemption, the estate is considered to own *all* the outstanding shares of the corporation since Steve's stock is attributed to (deemed to be owned by) Herb's estate.

In other words, Herb's estate constructively owns the shares actually owned by Herb's son. (It may be possible to avoid the estate/beneficiary attribution rule by "eliminating the beneficiary." If, before the redemption takes place, the son has received all the property to which he is entitled from the estate, no longer has a claim against the estate, and no liabilities of the estate can be assessed against him as a beneficiary, his stock will not be attributed to the estate since he will no longer be considered a beneficiary.)

b. The "family/trust/corporation" attribution rule. Under this rule, an individual is considered to own the stock owned directly or indirectly by or for his or her spouse, children, grandchildren, and parents. Stock owned by certain other parties and entities is also attributed to and from each party or entity in determining whether all the stock has been redeemed.[7] These other parties include:

    (i) A trust and its beneficiaries.

    (ii) A partnership and its partners.

    (iii) A corporation and its shareholders.

There is also the possibility of an incomplete termination as a result of stock being attributed from a close family member to an estate beneficiary and in turn through the estate beneficiary to the estate.

For example, Herb owns 1,000 shares in a closely held corporation. His son, Steve, owns the remaining 500 shares. Herb's widow is the sole beneficiary under Herb's will. Even if the corporation immediately redeems Herb's entire 1,000 shares, the redemption will be treated as less than a compelte redemption and there-

fore may become subject to dividend treatment because Steve's 500 shares are attributed to (treated as if owned by) his mother under the family attribution rules. Then the shares she is deemed to own are in turn considered to be owned by Herb's estate under the estate/beneficiary attribution rules. So even after all the shares Herb actually owned are purchased by the corporation from Herb's estate, his estate is still constructive owner of all the outstanding stock of the corporation. Steve's shares are traced to his mother and from her to Herb's estate.

There is an exception to the family attribution rule. Under certain circumstances, it may be possible to "waive" the family attribution rule (but not the estate or entity rules) and therefore break the "chain" between family members. This "10-year waiver rule" works as follows: In essence, the family attribution rules will not apply if, immediately following the redemption, the stockholder whose stock is redeemed has no interest in the corporation (except as creditor) and agrees not to acquire an interest for 10 years following the redemption, other than by bequest or inheritance.[8]

In the example discussed above, Herb's executor would sell Herb's stock to the corporation. Herb's widow would notify the IRS of her election to waive attribution between her son, Steve, and herself. Since she doesn't own any stock personally and since she has "waived" her right to receive any stock except by bequest or inheritance, when the corporation redeems the stock held by the estate's executor, there is no attribution from Steve to her and then from her to the estate. Therefore, the redemption results in a complete termination of the estate's interest. The proceeds of the redemption, therefore, are not subject to dividend treatment.

Entities such as a corporation, trust, or estate may waive the constructive ownership and break the fictional ownership linkage from a family member who actually owns stock to a beneficiary who does not (but is deemed to own it). The individual who is deemed to own stock must join in the waiver. After the redemption, neither the entity nor the beneficiary may hold an interest in the corporation. They must agree not to acquire such an interest for at least 10 years. They must also agree to notify the IRS if they do acquire such an interest. There is joint and several liability in the event either the entity or the waiving family members acquires a prohibited interest within the 10-year period. The Statute of Limitations remains open during that time for the IRS to levy on any deficiency.

It is important to note that an entity may break the fictional linkage only between family members; it may not waive "entity" attribution, the constructive ownership between a beneficiary and an entity. For example, assume 30 percent of the stock of a corporation is owned

Tools and Techniques

by a trust. Its beneficiaries, Michael, David, and Danny Green, own no stock personally. Debbie Green, the trust beneficiaries' mother, owns 52 percent of the corporation's stock. The remaining stock is held by unrelated employees of the corporation.

Assume the trust sells all of its stock back to the corporation. The redemption is still not complete because the trust's beneficiaries, Michael, David, and Danny, are deemed to own stock owned by their mother through the "family" attribution rule. The stock they are deemed to own is then attributed from them to the trust through the entity attribution rule. So the redemption of stock from the trust would be less than complete. But if the trust and all three brothers waive attribution and break the link connecting the mother's stock to the sons, the redemption would be complete. But what if one or more of the sons actually owned stock in the corporation? In that case the trust could break the link from Debbie Green to her children (the family attribution) but not the link between the children and itself (the entity attribution).

4. A purchase (either through stock redemption or cross-purchase) of a decedent-shareholder's interest generally means that the estate of a decedent will not realize any taxable gain for income tax purposes. The stock purchased from the estate obtains a "stepped-up basis," i.e., a new "cost" in the executor's hands equal to its value for federal estate tax purposes.[9] Since the purchaser generally pays a price equal to the value of the stock at the applicable federal estate tax valuation date, there would not be any gain realized by the estate; the amount paid for the stock equalled the basis of the stock in the hands of the executor.

For example, on January 1, 1970, Herb and Steve each invested $10,000 in a corporation which is worth $100,000 ($50,000 each) at Herb's death. If the corporation paid Herb's estate $50,000 in complete redemption of his stock, there would be no income tax consequences to his estate since the estate's basis in the stock is "stepped up" from $10,000 to $50,000 (the value for death tax purposes) and this was the amount received by the estate under the redemption. The "amount realized" ($50,000) by the estate did not exceed the seller's cost ($50,000) and so there is no taxable gain.

5. Effective for corporate tax years beginning after December 31, 1986 and through December 31, 1989, regular C corporations (not S corporations) will be subject to a 20% alternative minimum tax if certain items of preference income are present. Included in the items of preference income is one half of the amount by which the corporation's adjusted net book income exceeds its alternative minimum taxable income. Essentially, this means that one-half the difference between (a) what the company tells its shareholders it made and (b) what the company tells the IRS it made is subject to a 20% tax.

Although this provision of the 1986 Code is quite complex, it is designed to provide a preference item for purposes of the alternative minimum tax where pre-tax financial statement (book) income exceeds taxable income as adjusted for other tax preferences (alternative minimum taxable income).[10]

Life insurance proceeds, to the extent they exceed the cash surrender value in the policy immediately prior to death, constitute income for purposes of book income (but not for purposes of taxable income). Assume a corporation owned a $1,100,000 policy on the life of a key shareholder. The purpose of the insurance was to redeem his stock when he died. Further, assume the contract has a cash surrender value of $100,000. In the year the $1,100,000 is paid to the corporation, one-half of the excess proceeds, $500,000, would be subject to the 20% alternative minimum tax. So the tax would be, at most, $100,000 (roughly, less than 10% of the face amount).

This tax occurs only when the alternative minimum tax exceeds the corporation's regular corporate income tax. For corporations who pay relatively low taxes and have large key man insurance policies, the potential impact of the alternative minimum tax must be considered.

Corporations have a $40,000 exemption against all preference items. This is reduced by 25% of the amount by which the alternative minimum taxable income exceeds $150,000, but not less than zero.

For tax years beginning after 1989, this particular preference will be determined by reference to the relationship between alternative minimum taxable income and "adjusted current earnings," rather than book income. (See chapter 13.)

6. Since passage of the 1986 Tax Reform Act, the desirability of qualifying a *lifetime* stock redemption as a complete termination or substantially disproportionate redemption of a shareholder's interest so as to avoid dividend treatment is not as essential as it was before the Act *where an individual shareholder has a low basis* in a stock that is to be redeemed. Assume an individual has a $1,000 cost basis in his corporate stock. The fair market value of this stock is presently $1,001,000. If the corporation completely redeems his stock for the $1,001,000, he will realize a $1,000,000 gain on the transaction. Although it is a sale or exchange of a capital asset, the gain will be subject to the 28% rate, resulting in a tax liability of $280,000. (After 1987, there is no longer any special tax treatment for long term capital gains.) If the same redemption were not to come within the rules of Code section 302(b)(3), dealing with a complete termination of a shareholder's interest, and the distribution were considered a dividend, the full $1,001,000 would be taxable as ordinary income. The tax liability of $280,280 is practically the same as if the transaction were considered a sale or exchange.

On the other hand, where the basis of the shareholder's interest is high, the tax treatment to the shareholder is quite different. Assume the shareholder's fair market value of his business interest is $1,000,000. Further assume the shareholder's cost basis is $800,000. If the corporation redeems the stock, and such redemption qualifies as a complete redemption of the shareholder's interest, he will realize gain to the extent of $200,000, since the transaction is a sale or exchange of a capital asset and is not considered a dividend. Assuming a 28% tax bracket, the tax would be $56,000. However, if the transaction is considered a dividend, the full $1,000,000 would be taxable as ordinary income and subject to a $280,000 tax - quite a significant difference.

Keep in mind that in a death-time redemption, the distinction between a sale or exchange and dividend treatment is quite important since the estate of the redeeming stockholder receives a step-up in basis to the fair market value of the stock at the shareholder's death.

Cross-Purchase Agreements

1. The value of life insurance owned on a decedent-shareholder's life by a surviving co-shareholder will not be included in the decedent's estate for federal estate tax purposes. This is because the decedent-shareholder has no incidents of ownership in the policy his co-shareholder owns. However, the value of life insurance the decedent owned at the time of death on the lives of co-shareholders will be includible.[11] (Generally, this is equivalent to the policy's interpolated terminal reserve plus unearned premiums.)

    As with the stock redemption agreement a properly drawn cross-purchase agreement will, generally, be effective in establishing the value of the business for federal estate tax purposes providing: (1) the estate is obligated to sell at the decedent-shareholder's death, (2) there is a lifetime "first offer" provision prohibiting a shareholder from disposing of his or her stock interest without first offering it to the other shareholders at no more than the contract price, (3) the price was fair and adequate when made and resulted from a bona fide arm's length transaction, and (4) the price must be fixed by the terms of the agreement or the agreement must contain a formula or method for determining the price.

2. Life insurance or disability income premiums paid to fund the agreement are not deductible by the co-shareholders. The death proceeds or disability benefits will be received by the respective co-shareholders income tax free.

3. There is no possibility under a cross-purchase agreement that "redemptions" will be treated as dividends and no potential attribution problems since there are no redemptions; there should be no transaction between the corporation and its shareholders in a cross-purchase agreement. By definition, in a cross-purchase plan the entire transaction is between the co-shareholders.

4. As is the case with a stock redemption, if the price paid for the stock is more than its basis (cost) in the selling shareholder's hands, the difference is taxable at ordinary income rates despite the fact that the asset sold is a capital asset.

5. Under a cross-purchase agreement, the surviving shareholder has the advantage of increasing his basis in the company for income tax purposes by the amount of money paid for the stock. This is not available under a stock redemption. This will result in a reduced gain, in the event of a subsequent lifetime sale, to the surviving shareholders.

IMPLICATIONS AND ISSUES IN COMMUNITY PROPERTY STATES

Several problems can arise in connection with buy-sell agreements as a result of community property rights. If all or part of the stock is subject to a buy-sell agreement, careful planning is required (1) to protect against the risk that the shareholder's spouse may predecease the seller and leave the spouse's community property interest in the stock to third parties, (2) to protect against attachment by creditors of the shareholder's spouse, and (3) to protect the agreement from attachment by the stockholder's spouse if the spouse survives the stockholder and seeks to claim his or her community property interest in the stock free of the agreement. If all or part of the stockholder's interest is quasi-community property, care should be taken to protect against the spouse's claim, if he or she survives the stockholder, that he or she is entitled to a community property interest in the stock free of the agreement. Appropriate written consents should be obtained in the above situations.

It is important to determine the nature of the interest held by the stockholder, not only for purposes of determining whether consents need to be obtained and wills reviewed, but also to evaluate the tax consequences. If all of the stock is community property, the community property interest of the stockholder's spouse will be included in the spouse's estate if he or she predeceases the stockholder, and will be excluded from the stockholder's estate if the stockholder dies first. If all of the stock is the separate property of the stockholder, it will be included in the stockholder's estate only (unless he or she passes the stock to the spouse and then dies). If all of the stock is quasi-community property, the stockholder's spouse will have no interest if he or she dies first, and the full value of the stock will be in the stockholder's estate for federal estate tax purposes.

The basis of property acquired from a decedent is subject to a peculiar set of rules.

5

Generally, the basis of property acquired from a decedent is the fair market value of the property at the date of the decedent's death. Revenue Code Section 1014 defines which property is deemed "acquired from a decedent" and therefore subject to these special basis rules. Generally, Section 1014 applies to all property includable in the gross estate.

The surviving spouse is deemed to have acquired her one-half share of the community property from the decedent spouse. This gives the surviving spouse a new basis even though her one-half of the community property was not included or taxed in the decedent spouse's estate. The new basis for the surviving spouse's one-half will therefore be equal to the fair market value of the property at date of death. This rule operates, however, only if the decedent's one-half is fully included in the gross estate. If the property's fair market value is greater than its adjusted income tax basis, the basis will receive a "step-up" free of either estate or income taxes. If the fair market value is less than the adjusted basis, the new basis will actually be a "step-down".

This "step-up" or "step-down" in basis for both spouses' halves of the community property does not apply to property held as joint tenancy or tenancy in common property. Even though the original nature of the property was community property (e.g., a spouse's earnings in a community property state), taking the title as joint tenants or tenants in common will change its nature so that it no longer has the attributes of community property. However, in most states with community property laws, it is possible to re-establish the property as community property by an agreement between the spouses without actually changing the recorded title to the property. As of January 1, 1985, some states, such as California, require such agreements to be in writing.

The ability of the surviving spouse to sell immediately the entire community interest of corporate stock, either under a buy-sell contract to other shareholders or to redeem some or all of it within the scope of Section 303 (avoiding dividend treatment), can often be the most significant estate planning step taken by husband and wife shareholders in community property states!

Problems can occur when attempting to determine whether stock held by a married person in a community property state is community property. A portion of the stock can be separate property and a portion community property. A commom example is a man who owns a business prior to marriage.

Let us examine the setting in which this issue frequently arises. Assume that Mr. Jones owns all of the stock in Jones Manufacturing Company, Inc. The company was incorporated prior to his marriage to Mrs. Jones. At the time of the marriage, the company was worth $100,000. However, during the marriage the value of the company appreciates rapidly. If Mr. Jones dies, will the stock in the company, or, in the alternative, the appreciation in value of the stock, be deemed his separate property or will it be community property?

Court decisions characterizing appreciation in closely-held businesses arise in only three settings: (1) a claim by a creditor that the business should be made available for the payment of a debt, (2) divorce and the division of property pursuant to divorce, and (3) the death of one of the spouses.

Most states use some form of an "apportionment rule" to characterize the increase in value of closely-held business interests during marriage which were originally held as a spouse's separate property. Under the apportionment rule, if one of the spouses invests separate property in a business and conducts that business during the marriage, the resulting projects or increases in value of the business will be apportioned or allocated between the community estate and the spouse's separate estate according to the amount attributable to the spouse's personal efforts on the one hand (inuring to the benefit of the community), and to the capital improvement on the other (inuring to the benefit of the spouse's separate estate).

The possibility of creating such a community property interest in a corporation originally held as the separate property of one spouse can be determined only by a court in the absence of a written agreement. Thus, it is advisable for the spouses to agree, in writing, on the nature of their interests and the proportion of community and separate property.

There are other possible combinations of interest such as combinations of community property and quasi-community property or combinations of separate property and quasi-community property or combinations of all three types of property. In any event, the exact nature of stock ownership and their respective proportions should be identified and agreed upon in writing. In many situations it may be advisable to incorporate the property agreement into the buy-sell agreement.

QUESTIONS AND ANSWERS

Question — Under what situations would a business buy-out by a third party be indicated?

Answer — There are certain situations in which an owner of a business interest is either unwilling or unable to enter into a conventional stock redemption or cross-purchase agreement. Usually, such a business owner will have problems such as estate liquidity, lack of management skills or interest by members of his or her family, or desires the value of the business to be "pegged" for federal estate tax purposes.

A typical example is where an individual has a wife and three children, only one of whom he desires or expects to be able to take over the business. He would like to treat his children as equally as possible. One way he could do this is by entering into a buy-sell agreement with the one child he expects to take over the business. That child will take over the business through the buy-sell agreement. The funds paid by that child to the decedent's executor in return for the business interest could provide the client's widow and remaining children with cash for their living needs and estate settlement costs.

Question — What are some of the various methods of establishing the purchase price of a business?

Answer — The purchase price to be paid for the stock of a shareholder may be set by a variety of methods. One method is to provide for the exact purchase price in advance with the further provision that the parties may change the price at any time upon mutual agreement.

Another method of fixing the price is to use book value based on the company's financial statements.

A third method of valuation is a formula approach. Formula valuation methods are often used to take into account net profits and, to some degree, goodwill. An example would be straight capitalization of the average net profits of the business at a definite rate. For instance, as the NumberCruncher computer illustration below shows, at a 12 percent rate, a business producing average net after-tax profits of $100,000 would be worth about $833,333 using this approach ($100,000 divided by .12). A 50 percent interest in such a business would be worth $416,667, half of $833,333. Combinations of these three methods can also be used. (See Valuation of Assets in Appendix B.)

CAPITALIZATION OF INCOME

INPUT: CAPITALIZATION RATE 0.120
INPUT: ADJUSTED EARNINGS $100,000

EXPECTED RATE OF RETURN	VALUE OF ASSET OR BUSINESS
0.08	$1,250,000
0.09	$1,111,111
0.10	$1,000,000
0.11	$909,091
0.12	$833,333
0.13	$769,231
0.14	$714,286
0.15	$666,667
0.16	$625,000
0.17	$588,235

Question — What can be done if one of the persons involved in a business purchase agreement is uninsurable?

Answer — Life insurance may be used for the insurable stockholders, and for the uninsurable stockholders, a sinking fund method should be used to at least accumulate enough money for a down payment. Often an amount equivalent to the appropriate insurance premium on the uninsurable's life (given his or her age) is deposited into some type of segregated reserve account. Such an account might be invested in bonds, mutual funds, fixed or variable annuity, or merely left in a savings account until the death of the uninsurable.

Typically, the agreement will provide that installment payments covering the remainder of the purchase price can be spread over a relatively long period of time.

Several life insurance companies are offering guaranteed issue type contracts even on those stockholder-employees previously thought to be uninsurable as long as the stockholder-employee is actively at work full time. One type of policy provides that if a death occurs during a certain initial period of time, e.g. 3 years, only premiums paid plus interest are payable as a death benefit. After the initial period the full death benefit is payable. A second type policy provides for a graded death benefit, i.e., one that increases over a period of time to the full death benefit.

Question — Will an agreement giving a surviving stockholder or the corporation an *option* to buy the deceased shareholder's stock usually fix the value of a business interest for federal estate tax purposes?

Answer — Yes, if there is a "first offer" provision and the price was fair and adequate when made. (A "first offer" provision requires the selling shareholder [or his or her executor] to offer the interest to the specified purchaser at an agreed upon price [fixed or set by formula] both during lifetime and after death before offering it to others.) Although the estate must be obligated to sell at death, the survivor(s) or the corporation need not be obligated to buy. An option in their hands would be sufficient. However, agreements involving substantially only family members may be determined not to be made at arm's length and therefore not effective in pegging the value for federal estate tax purposes. But see page 477 for risk of estate tax inclusion under Code section 2036(c).

Question — Assume that there are three stockholders of a corporation and all stockholders have entered into a cross-purchase agreement. One of the stockholders dies and the other two stockholders purchase the decedent's stock using the life insurance proceeds under which the decedent was the insured and the remaining two stockholders were the policyowners.

The decedent's personal representative now owns an insurance policy on the life of each of the surviving shareholders. They purchase their respective policies from the personal representative. Are there any potential tax problems?

Answer — This situation brings into play the "transfer-for-value" rule. This tax trap creates an exception to the general rule that the proceeds of an insurance policy are not subject to federal income tax.

The transfer-for-value rule provides that if insurance policies are transferred for value (no gift has taken place but a consideration has been given for such transfer) then the owner-beneficiary of that policy will have taxable income when the insured dies. The difference between the proceeds of the policy and the sum of (a) the value paid and (b) the premiums paid by the new owner-beneficiary will be taxable as ordinary income.

There are exceptions to the transfer-for-value rule where the transfer for value is made

(1) to the insured (as is the case here),

(2) to a corporation in which the insured is an officer or stockholder,

(3) to a partner of the insured,

(4) to a partnership in which the insured is a partner,

(5) where the new owner's basis (cost) is determined in whole or in part by reference to the transferor's basis, or

(6) where a transfer of a policy or an interest in a policy is made between spouses or between spouses incident to a divorce. For instance, if a divorce decree requires one spouse to transfer a policy to another, the transfer will be considered a nontaxable event which results in a carryover basis in the policy and avoids the transfer for value tax trap.

Question — Assume that there is a stock redemption agreement funded by life insurance. The amount of the life insurance on the date of the death of one of the stockholders exceeds the corporate obligation under the redemption agreement. Are there any tax consequences?

Answer — The proceeds of corporate-owned life insurance will not generally be taxable to the corporation when it receives the same (except for potential exposure to a corporate level alternative minimum tax). However, the earnings and profits of the corporation will be increased by the amount of the proceeds and then reduced when a portion of the proceeds is used to redeem the shares of stock.

If the entire amount of the proceeds has not been used to redeem a decedent-shareholder's interest, there will be a permanent increase in corporate earnings and profits, which means that there should be additional dollars available for the payment of dividends; because of this, the potential exists for imposition of the accumulated earnings tax penalty, as well as dividend treatment on any distribution made by the corporation to its shareholders.

Question — Assume that the parties enter into either a redemption agreement or a cross-purchase agreement. Should anything be done to protect their rights with respect to a possible transfer to third parties?

Answer — The stock certificates owned by the parties to either the redemption agreement or the cross-purchase agreement should bear a legend indicating a restriction on the ability to transfer those shares of stock as a result of the redemption or cross-purchase agreement.

Question — Why is a cross-purchase plan often preferred over a stock redemption arrangement?

Answer — Where a corporation purchases the stock of a withdrawing, disabled, or deceased stockholder, the surviving shareholders cannot increase their basis (cost for purposes of determining gain) by the amount paid. For example, assume Steve, Roberta, and Lee each own an interest in the SRL Corporation worth $100,000. Each invested $10,000 in 1977 when the corporation was formed. If Lee dies and the corporation (pursuant to a fully funded buy-sell agreement) pays his executor $100,000 for his stock, Steve's basis and Roberta's basis remain at $10,000. But if Steve and Roberta had been the purchasers and had each *personally* paid $50,000 to Lee's executor, their individual basis would have increased by that $50,000 amount. The distinction is important because, in this simplified example, the taxable gain on a future sale of Steve's stock or Roberta's stock could be as much as $50,000 less using a cross-purchase arrangement.

It is important to recognize, however, that this does not mean a cross-purchase plan will always be better than a stock redemption. In some cases a stock redemption will be preferred:

(1) The basis increase may be higher when a stock redemption is used if

(a) surviving shareholders intend to retain the stock they own until death, and

(b) there is high appreciation in the value of the stock.

(2) Shareholders will often prefer, for both psychological and cash flow reasons, that corporate dollars be used to pay premiums.

(3) Premium payments by a corporation may be indicated when the corporation is in a lower income tax bracket than the individual shareholders.

(4) Where there are more than 3 shareholders involved, administrative inconvenience and cost generally make corporate-owned life insurance preferable over the multiplicity of policies required in a cross-purchase arrangement. For example, if there were 5 shareholders, 20 separate policies would be required. (The formula for determining the number of policies is $N \times (N - 1)$ with N being the number of shareholders.)

Other factors to consider in deciding between a cross-purchase and stock redemption include:

(1) possibility of dividend treatment because of constructive ownership (attribution) rules in family-owned corporations;

(2) state law restrictions on a corporation's right to purchase its own stock in the absence of sufficient surplus;

(3) transfer-for-value problems at the death of a shareholder if estate-owned policies are transferred to individuals other than the insureds;

(4) stock ownership desired after the purchase occurs;

(5) premium outlay differences due to differences in age and ownership interests between shareholders.

(6) possible alternative minimum tax problems where life insurance is used to fund a stock redemption.

Question — Is there a solution to the dilemma of the cross-purchase vs. stock redemption decision?

Answer — One technique that may avoid or minimize problems inherent in a buy-sell of either the cross-purchase or the stock redemption type is the "Wait and See" (also known as the "option") approach, popularized by attorneys Stephan R. Leimberg and Morey S. Rosenbloom.

Under a "Wait and See" type agreement, the estate of a deceased shareholder is bound to sell at an agreed-upon price or according to a predetermined formula, but the parties *wait* a specified length of time after the death of a shareholder to *see* if—and to what extent—a cross-purchase or stock redemption or combination (perhaps even coordinated with a Section 303 stock redemption) should be used.

The suggested method is for the corporation to have a first option to purchase any or all of a deceased shareholder's interest. Surviving shareholders have a secondary option to purchase any or all stock remaining. If, at this point, some stock still remains in the executor's hands, the corporation is *required* to purchase the entire balance.

Life insurance could be purchased by the corporation, by the surviving shareholders, or by both. (The corporation might, for example, purchase whole life insurance while the shareholders might purchase term insurance.) If the corporation is owner and beneficiary of the insurance it can apply proceeds directly to the extent a stock redemption is indicated or make loans to the extent necessary to shareholders who will be purchasing stock on an individual basis. If life insurance is owned by and payable to shareholders on an individual basis, they could apply proceeds directly to the extent a cross-purchase is indicated or make loans or capital contributions to the corporation to enable it to effect a stock redemption.

The "Wait and See" approach provides an infinite variety of options and a maximum in planning flexibility.

Question — If a cross-purchase agreement funded with life insurance is changed to a stock redemption agreement, and the insurance which was owned by the individuals on each other is transferred to the corporation, will there be any income tax consequences as relates to the insurance?

Answer — No. Changing insurance from a cross-purchase agreement to a stock redemption agreement will not violate the transfer-for-value rule, since policies can be transferred from a stockholder to a corporation of which the insured is a stockholder. This will qualify as an exception to the transfer-for-value rule. Note, however, that the reverse, i.e., change from a stock redemption to a cross-purchase, will be a violation of the transfer-for-value rule if insurance is transferred from the corporation to a stockholder other than the insured.

Question — Can a buy-sell agreement "peg" the value of a business interest for federal gift tax purposes?

Answer — Although an agreement will probably not be controlling for federal gift tax purposes, it should carry strong evidentiary weight as to the business value and will be considered along with other relevant factors. An agreement will probably be successful in establishing value if:

(1) the price (or formula) is reasonable at the time the agreement is signed.

(2) the agreement is negotiated by parties knowledgeable of relevant facts and at arms-length.

(3) the price (or formula) agreed upon is as binding during lifetime as at death, i.e., the lifetime price permitted can't be higher than the sale price at a shareholder's death.

(4) the price is fixed by the terms of the agreement or the agreement contains a formula or method for determining price.

ASRS, Secs. 40 - 43.

Footnote References

Buy-Sell (Business Continuation) Agreement

1. Reg. §20.2031-2(f).
2. Reg. §20.2031-2(h); *May v. McGowan*, 194 F.2d 396, (CA-2, 1952); *Comm'r. v. Child's Estate*, 147, F.2d 368, (CA-3, 1945); *Estate of Mitchell*, 37 BTA 1 (1938). See also Rev. Rul. 59-60, 1959-1 CB 237.
3. IRC Section 264(a)(1).
4. IRC Section 101(a)(1).
5. IRC Sections 302(c)(1); 318.
6. IRC Section 318(a)(3).
7. IRC Sections 318(a)(1); 318(a)(2).
8. IRC Section 302(c)(2).
9. IRC Section 1014.
10. Tax Reform Act of 1986, Section 701, amending IRC Sections 55-57.
11. IRC Section 2033.
12. IRC Section 1014(b)(6).

9

Chapter 2

CHARITABLE CONTRIBUTIONS

WHAT IS IT?

A charitable contribution is a gratuitous transfer of property to charitable, religious, scientific, educational, and other specified organizations. If the donee of the gift falls within categories designated by the law, a charitable deduction may be taken for income, gift, or estate tax purposes.

Charitable contributions have tax value, therefore, because they result in a current income tax reduction, may reduce federal estate taxes, and can be made gift tax free. From the charity's point of view, charitable contributions are also tax favored; the charity itself pays no tax upon the receipt of either a lifetime gift or a bequest and, generally, no income tax is paid by the qualified charity on income earned by donated property.

WHEN IS THE USE OF SUCH A DEVICE INDICATED?

1. When the donor wishes, for nontax reasons, to benefit the charity.
2. When the donor wishes to reduce income or estate taxes by taking advantage of the deductions allowed for such gifts.
3. When the donor would like to achieve both motives described above.

WHAT ARE THE REQUIREMENTS?

1. Charitable contributions are deductible only if they are made to organizations which are "qualified." Examples of "qualified" organizations include nonprofit schools and hospitals, churches and synagogues, the United Fund, Community Chest, YMCA, YMHA, The American Red Cross, the Boy Scouts, Campfire Girls, and the Heart Association.

   A donee will be considered qualified only if it meets three conditions: (a) it must be operated exclusively for religious, charitable, scientific, literary, or educational purposes; or to foster national or international amateur sports competition or to prevent cruelty to children or animals; (b) no part of the organization's earnings can benefit any private shareholder or similar individual; (c) the organization cannot be one disqualified for tax exemption because it attempts to influence legislation or participates in, publishes or distributes statements for, or intervenes in, any political campaign in behalf of any candidate seeking public office. The Internal Revenue Service publishes a list of qualified charities.

2. The second requirement necessary for a charitable contribution deduction is that "property" must be the subject of the gift. Therefore, the value of a taxpayer's time or services, even if contributed to a qualified charity, is not deductible. For example, if a carpenter spent 10 hours building chairs for his church, he could not deduct his normal hourly wage as a charitable contribution. However, he could deduct the cost of materials he purchased and used in producing the finished product.

   A taxpayer who donates the use of his property to a charity has not made a contribution of property. So the rent-free use of an office or even an office building will not be considered a charitable contribution any more than a contribution of personal services.

3. A third requirement for a charitable contribution deduction is that there must in fact be a contribution to the charity in excess of value received by the donor. In some cases the donor will receive a benefit in conjunction with his charitable gift. Such a contribution is deductible only to the extent that the value of the contributed property exceeds any consideration or benefit to the donor. For example, the individual might donate cash to a charity. The charity in turn might pay the donor (and perhaps his survivors) an annuity income for life. Only the difference between the contribution made and the value of a similar commercial annuity would be deductible.

4. The fourth requirement that must be met for a deduction to be allowed is that the gift to charity must actually be paid in cash or other property before the close of the tax year in question. Typically, therefore, even an accrual basis taxpayer must actually pay cash or contribute other property before the close of the tax year in order to receive a deduction.

5. A charitable contribution at death will be deductible regardless of whether it is made by will, by the terms of a life insurance policy, or by gift during the decedent's lifetime in such a manner that the gift will be includible in his gross estate. But the transfer must be made by the decedent, as distinguished from a transfer made by his estate or beneficiaries, in order to be deductible. Therefore, a deduction would not be allowed for a bequest to charity if the bequest requires the approval of a third party.

6. Where the lifetime transfer or bequest to charity is a gift of a "partial interest" (i.e., where the gift will be split between noncharitable and charitable beneficiaries) very strict rules apply. Generally, if a charity's interest in the transfer of property is a remainder interest (the charity

11

receives what remains after the noncharitable income beneficiaries have received income for a specified time), a transfer in trust will qualify only if it is a so-called annuity or unitrust or a pooled income fund. These terms are defined and described below.

7. An appraisal must accompany a tax return showing donations of property valued at over $5,000. Who can be an appraiser? You are qualified to be an appraiser for tax purposes only if (1) you hold yourself out to the public as an appraiser, (2) you are qualified to appraise the particular type of property in question, and (3) you understand that an overstatement of value may lead to the imposition of penalties. Generally, a separate appraisal must be made for each item of property unless similar items are donated in the same year. Partnerships donating property valued at over $5,000 must provide a copy of the appraisal to every partner who receives a proportionate share of the deduction.

All donors must keep cancelled checks, a receipt, or other reliable written records. These documents must show the name of the donee, the date of the contribution, and the amount of the gift. The safest approach is to make the records at the same time you make the gift and have the recipient charity sign a receipt.

HOW IT IS DONE — AN EXAMPLE

A gift to charity is probably one of the simplest estate planning techniques. During lifetime, such a gift can be accomplished merely by writing a check, assigning stock, transferring life insurance policies, signing a deed to real estate, or conveying property to charity in any other normal outright manner. Likewise, at death, gifts to charity can be made by will, by life insurance contract, by employee benefit contract (the death benefits from a pension plan can be paid to charity), or by trust.

WHAT ARE THE TAX IMPLICATIONS?

1. A charitable contribution to a qualified charity reduces current income taxes (assuming the donor itemizes deductions). Since passage of the 1986 Tax Reform Act, charitable contributions will not reduce current income taxes as much as before. Prior to the Act the maximum individual income tax bracket was 50%. After the Act, the top bracket was 38.5% for tax years beginning in 1987, 28% for tax years beginning thereafter. Thus, the income tax savings to an individual making a gift to charity will not be as great.

2. No federal gift taxes are payable on gifts to qualified charities regardless of the size of the gift.

3. Gifts to qualified charities can reduce the federal estate tax and with no limitation on the deduction (i.e., the donor's entire estate can be left to charity and a deduction will be allowed for the entire gift).

4. The charity itself will pay no tax upon the receipt of either a lifetime gift or a bequest.

5. Generally, no income tax will be payable by a qualified charity on income earned by donated property.

6. If an otherwise deductible charitable contribution to a college or university entitles the donor to purchase tickets for athletic events, 80% of the contribution will be deductible.

ISSUES AND IMPLICATIONS IN COMMUNITY PROPERTY STATES

Because of the equal ownership aspect of community property as between a husband and wife, care must be exercised in any creation of a charitable trust which benefits both parties, since taxable transfers may occur.

For example, if community property is used to fund a trust which benefits only one of the spouses, there has been a gift by the other spouse. Conversely, if the separate property of one of the spouses is used to fund a trust which provides for a lifetime benefit for both spouses, there is a recognized gift to the non-contributing spouse. After 1981, the availability of the unlimited marital deduction for federal gift tax purposes eliminates the prior concerns as to federal gift tax. (See Chapter 33.) However, most states do have some form of gift tax and only some have an unlimited gift tax marital deduction. Therefore, state gift tax can still be a problem in these circumstances. If community property is used to fund a trust that provides a lifetime benefit for both spouses, there will be no gift tax consequences.

It is possible for community property to be "split", creating separate interests for each spouse, which could then be used to fund separate charitable trusts, each involving life interests of only the spouse making the gift. Or, one spouse can make a gift with her half of the "split" funds, and the other can use the funds for his own purposes or to pay their joint income tax liability. In order for community property to be "split," an agreement between the parties must be made to that effect. A "split" is essentially a transmutation of community property to separate property, and, since January 1, 1985, such transmutations in some states, such as California, must be in writing.

Generally, the same income, estate and gift tax advantages which are available for gifts of separate property will be available in situations where community property is the subject of a charitable contribution.

QUESTIONS AND ANSWERS

Question — How do you figure the after-tax-savings cost of a charitable contribution?

Answer — The tax savings and after-tax cost can be found as follows:

$$\boxed{\text{Tax Savings} = \text{Amount of deductible gift} \times \text{Effective tax bracket}}$$

For example, a $2,000 gift by a 28 percent taxpayer equals $560 in tax savings. Stated another way, the out-of-pocket cost of the gift equals:

$$\boxed{\text{Amount contributed} - \text{Tax savings}}$$

For instance, the $2,000 gift above less the $560 in tax savings equals the out-of-pocket cost of the gift, $1,440.

Question — How do you determine the amount of an income tax charitable deduction?

Answer — The amount of a charitable contribution deduction that will be allowed for income tax purposes depends on the five following factors, which will be discussed in detail below:

1. *The type of property given away.*
    (a) rent-free occupancy
    (b) cash
    (c) long-term capital gain property
    (d) ordinary income property
    (e) tangible personal property where the use of that property by the donee is related to the exempt functions of the donee, and tangible personal property where the use of that property is unrelated to the exempt purposes of the donee
    (f) future interests in property

(These various types of property will be discussed in detail in the following question.)

2. *The identity of the donee.* Generally, contributions to publicly supported domestic organizations—so-called public charities—are more favorably treated than contributions to foreign organizations or to most private foundations. Cash contributions to public charities, for example, are fully deductible up to 50 percent of a donor's contribution base (adjusted gross income computed without regard to any net operating loss carryback to the taxable year). The deduction for an individual's contributions to most nonpublic (private) charities, regardless of the type of property given away, is limited to the lesser of (a) 30 percent of the taxpayer's contribution base, or (b) 50 percent of his contribution base minus the amount of charitable contribution deductions allowed for contributions to the public-type charities.[1]

For example, if a wealthy individual donates property worth 40 percent of his contribution base (A.G.I.) to a public charity such as the Boy Scouts, his contributions to "30 percent charities" (private charities) are deductible only up to 10 percent of his contribution base.[2] Donations to individuals or to foreign charities (except where allowed by treaty) are not deductible. Twenty (20) percent is the limit, however, for gifts of capital gain property to private nonoperating foundations.

3. *The identity of the contributor.* Individuals are limited to specified percentages of their contribution base if they itemize deductions. A corporation is limited to a deduction based on a percentage of its taxable income.[3]

4. *The amount of property given away.* Both individuals and corporations can carry over excess contributions—contributions above their deductible limit—for up to 5 years.[4]

5. *The place where the contribution is to be used.* As mentioned above, gifts made to United States charities are treated more favorably than gifts to most foreign charities.

Question — How does the type of property interest given to charity affect the income tax limit on deductions and what is the effect of a contribution of a partial interest in property to charity?

Answer — Generally, a charitable contribution of less than a donor's entire interest in property is non-deductible. Gifts of a partial interest in property are deductible only in four very narrowly defined situations:

1. The first is a gift of an undivided portion of the donor's entire interest.[5] For example, if Jesse Verr, a successful businessman, gave his original Ramlo sculpture to the Philadelphia Museum of Art, but agreed with the museum that he could keep it as long as he or his wife lived, no current deduction would be allowed. However, if Jesse gave an undivided one-half interest in the sculpture, i.e., if he gave the museum an immediate, absolute, and complete right of ownership (for display purposes or otherwise) for one-half of each year, he would likely be successful in obtaining a current deduction.[6]

2. The second situation involves a gift of a remainder interest in a personal residence or farm.[7] If Helene Abraham gives a qualified organization her home or farm with the stipulation that she may live there for life, she may take a current income tax deduction for the value of the future gift. This assumes, of course, that the gift is irrevocable.

Tools and Techniques

3. The third circumstance in which a charitable contribution of less than the donor's entire interest could generate a deduction is where the donor makes a gift to a qualified charitable organization of a remainder interest in real property granted solely for conservation purposes.[8]

4. Finally, a gift of a partial interest would be deductible if transferred in trust. This exception allows a charitable deduction for outright transfers of property even if less than the taxpayer's entire interest is transferred. The deduction is allowed to the same extent that a deduction would be allowed had the same property been transferred in trust rather than directly to the charitable organization. Gifts in trust will be discussed in detail in a question that follows.

The chart at Figure 2.1 and the discussion that follows illustrate how each type of property influences the limit on the deduction for an individual who itemizes deductions.

(A) Rent-Free Occupancy

Contributions of a mere right to use property (such as a rent-free lease to the Boy Scouts) are not deductible.[9] This is the situation because, to be deductible, contributions must be made in cash or other property. The mere right to use property is considered neither cash nor other property.[10] The IRS considers a contribution of the right to use property as a contribution of less than the donor's entire interest in the property.

(B) Cash

Where the property is cash (as in a gift of any other type of property), it is necessary to ask, "Who is the donee?" If the donee is a publicly supported charity, the deduction ceiling (column 3) is 50 percent of the individual taxpayer's contribution base (adjusted gross income).[11] A corporation's deduction is limited to 10 percent of its taxable income (with certain adjustments).[12] Regardless of the type of property gifted, a corporation can always take a current deduction of 10 percent of its taxable income (column 4). Likewise, regardless of the

Figure 2.1

CHARITABLE CONTRIBUTION DEDUCTION LIMITATIONS

		PERCENTAGE LIMITATION				
		INDIVIDUAL AS DONOR	CORP. AS DONOR			
Type of Property	Donee†	Adjusted Gross Income	Taxable Income	Individual Carryover	Corporation Carryover	TAX TREATMENT
N(1)	(2)	(3)	(4)	(5)	(6)	(7)
(A) Rent-Free Occupancy or Services	—	—	—	—	—	No Deduction
(B) Cash	Public	50%	10%	5 yrs.	5 yrs.	Full Deduction
(C) Long-Term Capital Gain Property (except for tangible personal property)	Public	30%*	10%	5 yrs.	5 yrs.	Full Deduction for Fair Market Value (Gain is a Tax Preference)
(D) Ordinary Income Property	Public	50%	10%	5 yrs.	5 yrs.	Deduction Limited to Basis‡
(E) Tangible Personal Property (L.T.C.G. Property)						
(1) Use-Related	Public	30%*	10%	5 yrs.	5 yrs.	Full Deduction for Fair Market Value
(2) Use-Unrelated to Exempt Purposes of Donee	Public	50%	10%	5 yrs.	5 yrs.	Deduction Limited to Adjusted Basis
(F) Future Interests in Property*						

* See detailed discussion in text.

† Regardless of the type of property given, the deduction for an individual's contributions to private charities is limited to the lesser of (a) 30 percent of the taxpayer's "contribution base" (roughly the same as adjusted gross income) or (b) 50 percent of the contribution base less any charitable contribution deduction allowed for contributions to public-type charities.

‡ There is an important exception. The deduction for corporate donors (other than S corporations) has a higher limit, basis plus one-half of appreciation in value, where the property is to be used by the donee solely for the care of the ill, the needy, or infants. (See the text below.)

identity of the donee, a corporation may carry over excess contributions for up to five years (column 6).

Contributions by individuals to "public" organizations in excess of the deductible limit for the taxable year may also be carried over (column 5) for a period of up to five years.[13] In other words, excess contributions are not wasted and can be used as itemized deductions in future years. For example, if an individual contributed $20,000 in cash to a synagogue, but his adjusted gross income was only $36,000, he could currently deduct only 50 percent of his adjusted gross income, $18,000. He could, however, carry over the $2,000 excess ($20,000 contribution minus $18,000) to the following year (a five-year carryover is also provided for excess contributions to nonoperating foundations).

A full deduction, up to the percentage limitation of 50 percent of contribution base for individuals who itemize deductions (or 10 percent of taxable income for corporations) is allowed for gifts of cash (column 7).[14]

(C) Long-Term Capital Gain Property

The Tax Reform Act of 1986 retained the technical distinction between capital gains and ordinary income, even though the rates (as of 1989) will be the same. This distinction remains important for charitable gift purposes.

Long-term capital gain property is property which would have produced a long-term capital gain on the date of the gift had it been sold rather than donated to charity. Long-term capital gain property can be divided into two types:

The first type would consist of intangible personal property and all real property. A gift of Xerox stock purchased 11 years ago at $100 a share, now worth $400 a share, would be considered intangible personal long-term capital gain property. Appreciated land held the requisite "long-term" period would be an example of real property properly classified as long-term capital gain property.

The second type of long-term capital gain property is tangible personal property such as a car, a painting, sculpture, an antique, or jewelry. Tangible personal property will be discussed in *Section E*.

Where long-term capital gain property, such as stock held for the requisite period, is given to a "public" donee (column 2), an individual's deduction may not exceed 30 percent of his adjusted gross income (column 3).[15] If his gift exceeds this percentage limitation, he may carry over the deduction for up to five future years (column 5). The full fair market value of the gift is deductible (column 7).[16]

For example, suppose Phil Kay donates stock worth $25,000 to the United Fund. The stock cost him $12,000 when he purchased it four years ago. If his adjusted gross income is $50,000, his maximum contribution deduction is $15,000 (30 percent of $50,000). He will be able to carry over the $10,000 balance and apply that as a deduction against future years' income.

The deduction for long-term capital gains type property is doubly advantageous. First, a person saves the taxes on his potential profit; in the above example, Phil saves the tax on a $13,000 long-term capital gain. Second, he gets a deduction for the full fair market value of the gift. Here it will be $25,000.

But since passage of the Tax Reform Act of 1986, the excess of the value of the capital gain property over its adjusted basis (i.e., the unrealized appreciation) is considered an item of tax preference ($13,000 in the example) for purposes of the alternative minimum tax.[17]

There is an election the taxpayer may want to make in certain situations. The 30 percent limit can be increased to 50 percent if the donor is willing to reduce the value of his gift by his potential gain.[18] The election can be extremely important for a taxpayer whose income fluctuates widely from year to year. It is of particular value when the amount of appreciation is small. For example, the value of a gift of long-term capital gain property with a basis of $980 and a fair market value of $1,000 would be reduced by only $20. In this way, the taxpayer could qualify for the higher 50 percent limitation at the expense of losing only a very small portion of his deduction.

(D) Ordinary Income Property

"Ordinary income property" is an asset that would have resulted in ordinary income (rather than capital gain) on the date of contribution had it been sold at its fair market value rather than contributed.[19] Ordinary income property includes (a) capital assets held less than the requisite long-term period at the time contributed; (b) Section 306 stock (stock acquired in a nontaxable corporate transaction which is treated as ordinary income if sold); (c) works of art, books, letters, and musical compositions, but only if given by the person who created or prepared them or for whom they were prepared; and (d) a businessman's stock in trade and inventory (which would result in ordinary income if sold).

Ordinary income property given to a public charity (column 2) by an individual is deductible subject to a 50 percent of contribution base ceiling. However, generally a taxpayer's deduction is limited to his basis (cost) for the property (column 7).[20] For example, if a famous painter donated one of his paintings worth $25,000 to an art museum, his deduction would be limited to his cost for producing the painting. This means that only the cost for canvas, paint, etc., would be deductible. No deduction would be allowed for the value of his time and talent.

15

A similar situation occurs where Doug Koch owned his National Motors stock for 4 months. (A sale would have resulted in short-term capital gain.) He purchased the stock at a cost of $12,000 and gave it to The American College when it was worth $25,000. Only his cost (basis) is deductible. Therefore, since the property is considered ordinary income property, he will be limited to a charitable deduction of $12,000 even though the property had a fair market value of $25,000 at the time of the gift.

An exception to this rule is provided for ordinary income property given by a corporation to a public charity or private operating foundation for use in its exempt purpose for care of the ill, the needy, or infants.[21]

In situations where this requirement can be met, the allowable deduction for contributions of appreciated ordinary income property is limited to (a) the donor's basis plus (b) one-half the potential gain in the property (but in no event can this deduction exceed twice the basis).[22]

Assume a pharmaceutical corporation donates $11,000 worth of medicine (inventory) to a charity that performs services for ill and infirm individuals. If the basis to the corporation was $5,000, it may deduct $8,000: its $5,000 basis plus one-half the $6,000 potential gain.

Gifts of substantially appreciated ordinary income property should be avoided if possible. Capital assets should be held for the requisite long-term period if that will make it long-term capital gain property (deductible at full fair market value) or left to charity by will so that a full estate tax deduction can be obtained. Alternatively, ordinary income-type property could be left to the donor's children by will. The stepped-up basis they receive in the property after the donor's death will enable them to obtain a larger income tax deduction if they give the property to charity.

(E) Tangible Personal Property

Tangible personal property (which would have produced capital gain if sold) includes cars, jewelry, sculpture, art works, books, etc., but only if created or produced by persons other than the donor.[23] With respect to this type of property, a distinction must be made between (a) gifts that will be used by the donee charity in such a manner that the use of the gift is related to the exempt purposes of the donee and (b) gifts that will not be used by the charity in a manner related to the exempt purposes of the donee.

For example, a gift of a painting (not by the artist) would be "use related" if the painting were donated to a museum which planned to exhibit the painting in its public galleries. The same gift would be "use unrelated" if given to the Red Cross or to the Campfire Girls. It is unlikely that either of these organizations would use the painting as a painting. In all likelihood the art would be sold and the proceeds used for the exempt purposes of the Red Cross or the Campfire Girls. However, it is the gift itself and not the cash or other property that can be obtained for the gift which determines whether the gift is use related or use unrelated.

Another example might be the contribution of a stamp collection to an educational institution. If the stamp collection is placed in the donee organization's library for display and study by students, the use of the donated property is related to the educational purposes constituting the basis of the charitable organization's tax exemption. However, if the stamps were sold, even if the proceeds were used by the organization for educational purposes, the use of the property is an unrelated use.

Howard Levin has a $10,000 adjusted gross income. He contributes a collection of whaling harpoons to the Cape May County Historical Museum for display purposes. The collection cost him $2,000, but on the date of contribution it was worth $10,000. The type of property contributed is tangible personal property. The donee is a public charity and the gift is use related to the exempt purposes of the Museum. Therefore he can deduct up to 30 percent of his contribution base (A.G.I.), $10,000. This figure is $3,000. He gets credit for the full $10,000 contribution so that he will be able to carry over the excess contribution, $7,000, for up to five years (subject to the 30 percent rule each year).

If the gift is use unrelated (i.e., made to a donee whose direct use of the asset is unrelated to the charitable function of the donee) the deductible amount is limited to the donor's basis in the property. This is true for corporations as well as individuals.[24]

(F) Future Interests in Property

A "future interest" is any interest or right that will vest in possession or enjoyment at some time in the future. The term "future interest" includes situations where a donor purports to give tangible personal property to a charitable organization but has made a written or oral agreement with the organization reserving to a noncharitable beneficiary (himself or a member of his immediate family) the right to use, possess, or enjoy the property. For example, suppose Robin Lynn donates a genuine Meccariello photograph to an art museum but arranges with the museum to keep the photograph in her home as long as she lives. The museum has a future interest in the photograph.

One of the basic general rules governing charitable contribution deductions is that contributions must (a) actually be paid, (b) be paid in cash or other property, and (c) be paid before the close of the tax year. Futhermore, generally no deductions are allowed for an outright contribution of less than the donor's entire interest in property.

Since the benefit to the museum—and consequently to the public—was deferred in the gift of the Meccariello photograph, no current tax deduction would be allowed. The implication is that a deduction will not be allowed until the charity receives actual possession or enjoyment of the work of art. The gift of tangible personal property must be complete in the sense that all interest and rights to the possession and enjoyment of the property must vest in the charity. This means that a transfer of a future interest in property to a charity is not deductible until all intervening interests in and rights to possession held by the donor or certain related persons or organizations have expired (or unless the gift is in the form of a future interest in trust which meets the requirements discussed below).

Charitable remainder interests are a form of future interest in which an income interest is given by the donor to someone other than the donor, and at the death of that income beneficiary, the principal goes to a designated charity. An example would be a gift to X for life where the remainder (the princial at the death of X) goes to charity (the "remainderman") upon the death of X (the income beneficiary). A gift "to X for life, remainder to The American College" would be considered a gift of a future interest to The American College.

Question — Why are stocks and bonds often used for charitable gifts?

Answer — Securities such as listed stocks, mutual funds, or bonds are often selected as the subject of a charitable gift because:

(a) They are transferable with minimal cost or delay;

(b) as mentioned above, appreciated securities can be transferred without causing the donor to realize gain on the appreciation and still yield a current deduction measured by the fair market value of the gift;

(c) securities selling below their cost should be sold and the net proceeds donated (this sale-gift procedure can lower the donor's tax);

(d) the donor's spendable income is often increased rather than decreased by the contribution;

(e) a lifetime gift removes appreciating property and may lower death taxes and administration expenses.

Question — What is a charitable remainder trust?

Answer — A distinction must be made between trusts established solely for the benefit of charity (deductible without meeting the requirements below) and trusts which have both charitable and noncharitable beneficiaries. Deduc-

tions for contributions to this second type of trust are measured by the present value of the ultimate gift to charity. If the charity receives income for a specified term and then the corpus goes to the donor's family or some other noncharitable beneficiary, the trust is referred to as a charitable lead trust (discussed in more detail below.) But if noncharitable beneficiaries receive income for a specified period (e.g., "for 10 years" or "for life") and afterwards the charity receives the remaining corpus, the trust is called a charitable remainder trust.

Gifts of a remainder interest in trust generally are deductible only if made in one of three ways: (1) a "fixed annuity" trust, (2) a "unitrust," or (3) a "pooled income fund."[25]

These three permissible forms of trust are an outgrowth of congressional concern over potential abuses of gifts of a remainder interest in trust to charity. For example, suppose Mr. and Mrs. W were a financially secure but childless couple. Mr. W might leave his property to his wife in trust. Mrs. W, according to the terms of the trust, would receive the income for life if she survived her husband. At her death, the principal in the trust would pass to a designated charity. Mr. W would take a current charitable contribution deduction for the present value of the gift which the charity would receive at the death of the income beneficiary. To counteract inflation and provide for contingencies, a clause might be inserted in the trust agreement authorizing an invasion of principal for Mrs. W's benefit.

The potential for abuse was that the principal in the trust was often invested in securities that produced an extremely high income but at the cost of a correspondingly high risk. This situation naturally worked to the detriment of the charitable remainderman. In addition, the ability of the trustee to make substantial invasions of the principal of the trust further increased the likelihood that little, if any, of the original contribution would be received by the charity. The result was a decrease in the value of the charity's remainder interest.

For these reasons, rules were designed to prevent a taxpayer from receiving a current charitable contribution deduction for a gift to charity of a remainder interest in trust which may be substantially in excess of the amount the charity may ultimately receive (because the assumptions used in calculating the value of the remainder interest had little relation to the actual investment policies of the trust).

Pursuant to these rules, deductions are basically limited to situations where the trust specifies (a) a fixed annual *amount* which is to be paid to the noncharitable income beneficiary (an annuity trust), or (b) the amount the income beneficiary will receive in terms of a *fixed percentage* of the value of the trust assets ascertained each

Tools and Techniques

year (a unitrust), or (c) that property contributed by a number of donors is commingled with property transferred by other donors and each beneficiary of an income interest will receive income determined by the rate of return earned by the trust for such year (a pooled income fund).

Question — What is a charitable remainder annuity trust?

Answer — A charitable remainder annuity trust is a trust designed to permit payment of a fixed amount annually to a noncharitable (income) beneficiary with the remainder going to charity.[26]

The donor transfers money or securities to a trust which pays him a fixed dollar amount each year for life. If the income of the trust is insufficient to meet the required annual payment, the difference is paid from capital gains or principal. If the income is greater than the amount required in any given year, the excess is reinvested in trust. The income tax deduction is computed in the year funds are irrevocably placed in trust and is measured by the present value of the charity's right to receive the trust assets at the death of the income beneficiary.

For example, if the donor transferred $100,000 to the trust and retained a $5,000 a year lifetime income, his deduction would depend on his age at his nearest birthday. As Figure 2.2 illustrates, a 55-year-old donor would receive a $59,977 deduction. A 65-year-old would receive a $66,015 deduction for the same contribution.[27]

In order to qualify for income (and estate and gift) tax deductions, the charitable remainder annuity trust must meet a number of tests. The primary requirements are these:

1. A fixed amount or fixed percentage of the initial value of the trust must be payable to the noncharitable beneficiary.

2. This annuity must be not less than an amount equal to 5 percent of the initial fair market value of all the property transferred in trust.

3. The specified amount must be paid at least annually to the beneficiary out of income and/or principal.

4. The trust must be irrevocable and not subject to a power by either the donor, the trustee, or the beneficiary to invade, alter, or amend the trust.

5. The trust must be for the benefit of a named individual or individuals who must be living at the time the property is transferred to the trust. The noncharitable income beneficiaries must be living at the time of the transfer in trust and their interests must be for a term of years not exceeding 20 years, or a life estate.

6. The entire remainder must go to charity.

If all the necessary tests are met, the donor of a charitable remainder annuity trust will be entitled to an income tax deduction limited to the value of the remainder interest.

Question — What is a charitable remainder unitrust?

Answer — A charitable remainder unitrust, like a charitable remainder annuity trust, is basically designed to permit payment of a periodic sum to a noncharitable beneficiary with a remainder to charity.[28] The key distinction is in how the periodic sum is computed.

Figure 2.2

CHARITABLE REMAINDER ANNUITY TRUST — ONE LIFE*	
Age of Donor — Nearest Birthday	55
Amount Transferred in Trust	$100,000
Rate of Annuity (Not Less Than .05)	0.050
Amount of Annuity	$5,000
Factor for Life of One Beneficiary	8.0046
Unadjusted Present Value of Annuity	$40,023
Unadjusted Value of Charity's Interest	$59,977
Deduction as a Percentage of Amount Transferred	0.600
Actual Amount of Charitable Deduction if Annuity is Payable at End of Period:	
Annual	$59,977
Semi-Annual	$59,000
Quarterly	$58,504
Monthly	$58,176
Weekly	$58,048

*Courtesy NumberCruncher Software

It works like this: The donor would irrevocably transfer money or securities to a trustee. In return, the trustee would pay the donor (or other income beneficiary) income from the property for life. The donor could also provide that if he predeceased his spouse, she in turn would receive income from the donated property for life. The donor would receive payments based on a fixed percentage of the fair market value of the assets placed in trust. The assets would be revalued each year.

For example, assume the unitrust provides that the donor is to receive 5 percent of the trust assets each year. If $100,000 were placed in the trust, the donor would receive $5,000 the first year. If the value of the trust increased to $120,000 a year later, the donor would receive 5 percent, $6,000, and so on each year. If the income of the unitrust were insufficient in a given year to pay the stated percentage, capital gains or principal could be used to make up the deficit (but they need not be so used).

Figure 2.3 illustrates that if $250,000 is placed into a trust lasting for the life of a 67 year old person and the annuity rate selected is 9 percent with payments made quarterly, the donor's deduction would be $90,712 (36 percent of the value of the property placed into the trust).

In order to qualify for income (and estate and gift) tax deductions, a charitable remainder unitrust must meet a number of tests, these being the most important:

1. A fixed percentage of the net fair market value of the principal, as revalued annually, must be payable to the noncharitable beneficiary.

2. The percentage payable must be not less than 5 percent of the annual value.

3. The unitrust may provide that the noncharitable beneficiary can receive the lesser of (a) the specified fixed percentage or (b) the trust income for the year, plus any excess trust income to the extent of any deficiency in the prior years by reason of the distribution being limited to the amount of trust income in such years.

4. The noncharitable income beneficiaries must be living at the time of transfer in trust and their interests must be for a term of years not exceeding 20 years, or a life estate.

5. The entire remainder must go to charity.

The tax deductions allowed are the same as in the case of a charitable remainder annuity trust.

The deduction is allowed in the year funds are irrevocably placed in trust. The deduction is measured by the present value at the date of the gift of the charity's right to eventually receive the unitrust's assets. If the donor in the above example were age 70, his charitable deduction (assuming there were no survivor provisions) would be in excess of $102,000.

Question — How can a charitable remainder trust be used to generate estate tax savings?

Answer — The deduction created by the use of a qualified charitable remainder trust is measured by the value of the remainder interest that will pass to charity—using the same tables applied in connection with trusts created during life.

Figure 2.4 shows the federal estate tax savings possible through an inter vivos charitable remainder trust. The "without charitable trust" column shows a widow who makes no provisions for a charitable remainder trust (or

Figure 2.3

CHARITABLE REMAINDER UNITRUST — ONE LIFE*		
Input:	Amount Transferred in Trust	$250,000
Input:	Rate of Annuity (Not Less Than .05)	0.090
Input:	Adjusted Payout Rate Factor Table F(1)*	0.965232
	Adjusted Payout Rate	0.0869
Input:	Factor at Nearest Adjusted Payout Rate Below . . . . 8.687% (Table E†)	0.365900
Input:	Factor at Nearest Adjusted Payout Rate Above . . . . 8.687% (Table E†)	0.35889
	Difference	0.00701
Input:	Adjusted Payout Rate Below . . . . 8.687% Table E†	0.086
Input:	Adjusted Payout Rate Above . . . . 8.687% Table E†	0.088
	Donor's Deduction	$90,712
	Deduction as a Percentage of Amount Transferred	0.363

*Courtesy NumberCruncher Software
† Reg. 1.664-4(b)(5)

Tools and Techniques

outright donation). In this situation her taxable estate is $1,000,000. If the same individual created a charitable remainder trust, her taxable estate would be reduced considerably. In addition, a current income tax deduction would have been obtained for the value of the remainder interest of the property donated.

Figure 2.4

ESTATE TAX SAVINGS USING A CHARITABLE REMAINDER TRUST (assume death occurs in 1989)	Without Charitable Trust	With Charitable Trust
Adjusted Gross Estate	$1,000,000	$1,000,000
Charitable Contribution	————	100,000
Taxable Estate (Tentative Tax Base)	$1,000,000	$900,000
Estate Tax Before Unified Credit	$ 345,800	$ 306,800
Unified Credit	192,800	192,800
Estate Tax after Unified Credit	$ 153,000	$ 114,000
Net Cost of $100,000 Charitable Contribution Is $61,000: $100,000 – $39,000 =	$39,000 Estate Tax Savings	

Question — Can a charitable remainder trust be used to increase the income of a life beneficiary?

Answer — The charitable remainder trust (either annuity or unitrust) can be used to provide income for members of the donor's family in lieu of, or in addition to, the donor. For example, assume Mrs. W is a widow with no children or other close relatives except for her 50-year-old brother. Her estate is worth $1,000,000 after taking into consideration estimated debts and administration expenses. She has been debating whether to leave her estate outright to her brother or provide in her will that it pass to a charitable remainder trust for her late husband's law school with income reserved for her brother's life.

Should Mrs. W die, the remainder gift to the law school—taking into consideration her brother's age—would be worth about 32 percent of the $1,000,000, or $320,000. Figure 2.5 illustrates that the charitable trust will generate $12,340 a year in additional lifetime income for her brother. Furthermore, note that over $123,000 which would otherwise have been paid in estate taxes is instead given to the law school.

Figure 2.5

INCREASE IN INCOME USING CHARITABLE REMAINDER TRUST (assume death occurs in 1989)	Estate Going Outright to Brother	Charitable Trust with Income to Brother
Adjusted Gross Estate	$1,000,000	$1,000,000
Less Charitable Deduction	0	320,000
Taxable Estate (Tentative Tax Base)	1,000,000	680,000
Federal Estate Tax (F.E.T. Less Credit)	153,000	29,600
Capital Remaining to Produce Income for Brother	847,000	970,400
Income Produced at 10%	84,700	97,040
	$12,340 Increase in annual Income	

Question — What is a pooled income fund?

Answer — A pooled income fund is a trust created and maintained by a public charity rather than a private donor.

The illustration at Figure 2.6 is based on a $200,000 contribution made by a 68 year old and a fund rate of return of 9.64 percent. The donor's deduction is $74,839, 37% of the contribution.

The basic requirements are these:

1. The donor must contribute an irrevocable, vested remainder interest to the charitable organization which maintains it.

2. The property transferred by each donor must be commingled with the property transferred by other donors.

3. The fund cannot invest in tax-exempt securities.

4. No donor or income beneficiary can be a trustee.

5. The donor must retain (for himself or one or more named income beneficiaries) a life income interest.

6. Each income beneficiary must be entitled to and receive a pro rata share of the income (annually) based upon the rate of return earned by the fund.

If these tests are met, the donor will be entitled to an income, and gift or estate tax deduction.

Figure 2.6

POOLED INCOME FUND		LIFE OF ONE BENEFICIARY
Input: Amount Transferred in Trust		$200,000
Input: Fund's Yearly Rate of Return		0.0964
Input: Yearly Rate of Return Factor/Table G — Leave 0 if Factor Not Shown		0.000%
Input: Factor at Nearest Adjusted Payout Rate Below	9.637% (Table G)	0.375260
Input: Factor at Nearest Adjusted Payout Rate Above	9.637% (Table G)	0.369500
Difference		0.00576
Input: Adjusted Payout Rate Below	9.637% Table G	9.6%
Input: Adjusted Payout Rate Above	9.637% Table G	9.8%
Donor's Deduction		$74,839
Deduction as a Percentage of Amount Transferred		0.37

Question — What factors should be examined in deciding between an annuity trust and a unitrust?

Answer — The choice between an annuity trust and a unitrust involves a number of considerations. An annuity trust is indicated where simplicity in administration is desired since there is no need for an annual revaluation. (At least 5 percent of the initial fair market value of the trust property must be distributed in the case of an annuity trust, while if a unitrust is used, there must be a distribution of at least 5 percent of the trust's fair market value as redetermined each year.) Furthermore, depending on payout rate, and age of the annuitant, the annuity trust may yield a larger charitable contribution deduction (see example in footnote 27). Generally, if the payout is greater than 10%, the unitrust will produce a larger value for the remainder interest than the annuity trust.

There are, however, a number of disadvantages of an annuity trust when compared with a unitrust. First, inflation may cause a fixed annuity to lose some of its value. Of course, the unitrust may, under adverse circumstances, also fail the income beneficiary. If investment results are poor, the life income beneficiary may experience an absolute loss of income. This will result in both an inflation loss and a diminution of the dollar amount of his annual payment. On the other hand, if the trustee of the unitrust is skillful, he may be able to enhance the value of the principal fund and consequently the dollar amount of the annual payment.

A second disadvantage is caused by regulations which provide that the governing instrument in the case of an annuity trust must prohibit any additional contributions from being made. This is probably to confine the trust to a single valuation date. It therefore becomes impossible to pour over future testamentary bequests into the trust or to have other grantors make inter vivos additions to the already created trust rather than having to set up new trusts for the same purpose. Conversely, regulations specifically permit additional contributions to unitrusts if the governing instruments contains provisions regarding the effect of such an addition upon valuation and the unitrust amount payable.[29] If trust income is less than the required percentage payment in a unitrust, the liquidity problem could be avoided if the noncharitable beneficiary is willing to forgive all or a part of any particular year's payment, an act tantamount to a contribution to the trust.

A third disadvantage of an annuity trust is that the specified annuity must be paid each year regardless of whether or not there is sufficient trust income. If the corpus of the trust were real property, such as an apartment house, and if rents were to fall below the specified annuity plus expenses, the trustee would have to borrow against the property or sell it. However, a unitrust, if the trust instrument so provides, can limit its payout to the income beneficiary to the actual trust income. In later years, if trust income exceeds the percentage regularly distributable, the deficiency could be made up by excess distributions.

Question — What is a charitable lead (income) trust?

Answer — An income tax device that will enable a taxpayer to reduce the tax burden of an unusually high income year is the charitable income trust, also often called the "front-end annuity" trust. He will be allowed a current deduction for the value of the income interest he gives to a charity in trust with the remainder going to a noncharitable beneficiary (or a reversion in the donor). The cost of the large current deduction is that the donor is taxable on the trust income each year under the "grantor trust" provisions of the Code. This means that the grantor *must* be treated as the owner of such interest under Code section 671 in order to obtain a current income tax deduction. Also, the charity must receive either a guaranteed annuity or a fixed percentage of the annual net fair market value of the trust assets.

If for some reason the taxpayer is no longer taxable on the yearly income of the trust, there will be a partial recapture of the previously allowed deduction which must be reported by the taxpayer as income in that year. For example, if the individual contributes the income for five years but dies within three years of this contribution, recapture would be triggered. His income for the year of his death would have to include a recaptured portion of the excessive deduction which he took at the time the trust was established.

The charitable lead trust works like this: The donor transfers income-producing property to a trust. The trust in turn will provide the charity with a guaranteed annuity or annual payments equal to a fixed percentage of the fair market value of the trust property as annually recomputed. At the end of the specified period, the property would be returned to the donor (or go to a noncharitable beneficiary of the donor's choice).

As long as the donor has a reversionary interest in the income or principal of the trust which is greater than 5%, or is otherwise considered the owner of the income

or principal under the grantor trust rules of the Code, he can take an immediate deduction at the inception of the trust. The deduction is based on the present value of the charity's future income rights.

Figure 2.7 is an example of how a charitable income trust can be used where the donor wants property to ultimately go to his daughter. This illustration assumes a donor who has a pregift taxable income of $45,000 and owns $20,000 in securities yielding 5 percent which he wants to eventually transfer to his daughter.

The trust is designed to be a grantor trust. This ensures that the income from the securities held in trust, while payable to the charity, is includible in the donor's income. The donor does not receive an income tax charitable contributions deduction each year of the trust for the income payable to the charity, but he does receive a charitable contributions deduction in the year the trust is funded for the present value of the payments the charity is to receive over the ensuing ten years. He would not receive this deduction unless he were considered owner of the income interest, as described in section 170(f)(2)(B) of the Code.

Question — How can the charitable lead trust be used for estate tax savings?

Answer — As defined above, property is placed in the trust. A fixed amount of the income it produces is paid annually to a charity for a specified period of time (this is the "front-end" or "lead" period). At the end of that time full ownership of the property and the income it produces passes to noncharitable beneficiaries—such as the children or grandchildren of the trust's grantor.

When property is placed in the trust by bequest, an estate tax deduction is allowed for the actuarial value of the front-end annuity interest. An incredible $539,082 estate tax deduction would be allowed if a client left a $1,000,000 bequest in trust to pay $60,000 a year to The American College for 24 years. Stated another way, the deduction could wipe out almost 54 percent of the estate tax liability on trust property; but then—in the 25th year—the property would go intact to the donor's family. And, by properly combining the annuity payout level and the duration of the annuity period, it might be possible to eliminate an even greater amount of estate tax! For example, an annuity payout of 9 percent of the trust's original corpus for 24 years would result in a deduction of $808,623. Furthermore, those same remainder beneficiaries can be named as trustees and therefore control the property they someday will own.

Question — What is a bargain sale and how is it used for charitable purposes?

Answer — The bargain sale is a device used to minimize the out-of-pocket cost of a charitable gift. Prior to the 1969

Figure 2.7

	Direct Gift of Securities to Daughter without Trust	Securities Placed in a 10-Year Charitable Income Trust with Trust Income Payable to College and Remainder to Daughter
Pregift Taxable Income	$45,000	$45,000
Less		
Donated Securities		
Income	$ 1,000	0
Charitable Deduction	0	$12,290
Total Reductions	$ 1,000	$12,290
Postgift Taxable Income	44,000	32,710
Postgift Income Tax		
(joint return-1988 rates)	8,453	5,291
Spendable Income — Year of Gift	36,547	39,709

The present value of the daughter's remainder interest would be $7,710 ($20,000 – [61.45% x $20,000]), even though she would ultimately receive $20,000 worth of securities upon termination of the trust. Under this arrangement, future income from the securities will continue to be taxed to the donor until the termination of trust. Under the direct gift approach, such income would be taxable to the donor's daughter.

Tax Reform Act an individual could sell appreciated property to a charity at his cost. The donor would receive back an amount equal to his investment. In addition, he would obtain a charitable deduction for the appreciation in the property with no tax on his portion.

Under current law, the taxpayer has a taxable gain on the bargain sale because he must allocate his cost basis between the part of the property he sold to the charity and the part he donated.[30] This means the donor pays tax on his pro rata share of the appreciation.

For example, suppose a donor sells property he has owned for several years to his favorite charity. At the date of the sale it was worth $10,000. The sale price is the same as his cost, $4,000. The gift amounts to 6/10 (60 percent) of the property, so he is deemed to have given the charity 60 percent of his $4,000 cost basis, $2,400. This leaves him only the difference, $1,600 of cost, to apply against the $4,000 he received. His long-term capital gain is therefore $2,400.

The $6,000 gift ($10,000 – $4,000) saves him $1,680 in taxes if he is in a 28 percent marginal tax bracket. He also has recovered his $4,000 investment, so his total "recovery" is $5,680. If he is in a 28 percent bracket, his tax will be 28 percent of $2,400, or $672. The net return is $5,008 ($5,680 – $672), and the charity is enriched by $6,000.

Question — How can gifts of closely held stock be used to generate a charitable contribution deduction?

Answer — Several recent court decisions have opened the door to a new charitable contribution deduction tool: the use of closely held stock. The idea is to enable the owner of a closely held corporation to siphon funds from his business free of income tax by making a charitable contribution of his personally owned stock followed by an unrelated redemption of that stock by the corporation.[31] If used properly, the technique may eliminate or reduce the threat of an accumulated earnings tax problem, generate a current income tax deduction for the donor (at no loss of control), and provide cash for the donor's favorite charity with no out-of-pocket outlay.

It works like this. First, the stockholder donates some of his stock to the charitable organization. He receives a charitable contribution deduction measured by the present value of the stock contributed. Then the corporation redeems the stock from the charity. (Had the corporation redeemed the stock directly from the donor, dividend treatment would probably have resulted.)

One use of this device involved a closely held corporation whose controlling shareholder gave a school about 200 shares of his corporation's stock each year. He took an annual deduction for the present value of the gifts, about $25,000.

Tools and Techniques

The terms of the gift provided that the university could not dispose of the shares without first offering them to the corporation at their book value. The corporation was not required to purchase the stock but did have 60 days in which to purchase any stock offered to it.

Within a year or two after the shares were received by the school, they were offered to the corporation which always purchased them. The proceeds of these redemptions were then invested by the school.

It appears that the key elements in the success of this device are that the gifts were, in fact, complete and irrevocable and that there was no formal or informal agreement that the university would offer the stock for redemption or that it would be redeemed. This avoided the obvious attack that the redemptions from the charity were in essence redemptions from the donor and should have been taxed as ordinary income to him.[32]

Retention of substantial rights in the stock given to charity, e.g. voting rights, will result in disallowance of the deduction because the entire interest in the property is not transferred.[33]

Question — Why is life insurance a good way to make charitable contributions?

Answer — Life insurance, like any other property, can be and often is the subject of a gift. In fact, life insurance is a favored means of making charitable contributions for a number of reasons:

First, the death benefit going to charity is guaranteed as long as premiums are paid. This means that the charity will receive an amount which is fixed in value and not subject to the potential downside risks of securities.

Second, life insurance provides an "amplified" gift that can be purchased on the installment plan. Through a relatively small annual cost (premium), a large benefit can be provided for the charity. A large gift can be made without impairing or diluting the control of a family business interest or other investments. Assets earmarked for the donor-insured's family can thus be kept intact.

Third, life insurance is a self-completing gift. If the donor lives, cash values, which can be used by the charity currently, grow constantly from year to year. If the donor becomes disabled, the policy will remain in full force through the waiver-of-premium feature, guaranteeing both the ultimate death benefit to the charity as well as the same cash values and dividend build-up that would have been earned had the insured not become disabled. Even if death occurs after only one deposit, the charity is assured of its full gift.

Fourth, the death proceeds can be received by the designated charity free of federal income and estate taxes, probate and administrative costs and delays, brokerage fees, or other transfer costs. Thus, the charity in fact receives "one hundred cent" dollars. This prompt cash payment should be compared with the payment of a gift to the selected charity under the terms of an individual's will. In that case, probate delays of up to several years are not uncommon.

Fifth, because of the contractual nature of the life insurance contract, large gifts to charity are not subject to attack by disgruntled heirs. Life insurance proceeds also do not run afoul of the so-called mortmain statues which prohibit or limit gifts made within a short time of death.

Finally, a substantial gift may be made with no attending publicity. Since the life insurance proceeds paid to charity can be arranged so that they will not be part of the decedent's probate estate, the proceeds can be paid confidentially. Of course, publicity may be given if desired.

Question — How is the gift of a life insurance policy valued?

Answer — Since the bundle of rights in a life insurance policy can be considered equivalent to property, a gift of a life insurance policy is valued according to the same general tax rules as any other gift of property.

If a life insurance policy was sold at a gain, the gain would be taxed at ordinary income rates. Therefore, a gift of life insurance is a gift of ordinary income property. Assuming the value of the policy (interpolated terminal reserve plus unearned premium on the date of the sale) exceeds the policyholder's net premium payments, the deduction for a gift of a policy is generally limited to the policyholder's basis (cost), i.e., his net premium payments.

For example, suppose an individual assigns a policy on his life to The College for Financial Planning. His charitable contribution deduction is limited to his basis (i.e., his cost in the contract or the value of the policy, if lower). If he paid net premiums of $15,000 but the policy had a value of $18,000, his charitable contribution deduction would be limited to $15,000.

If there would have been no gain if the policy was sold rather than donated, the value of the donated policy would have been equal to its replacement cost at the date of the gift. In other words, if the total net premiums paid exceeded the value of the policy when the individual assigned it (i.e., the policy would not give rise to a gain if sold), the policy is treated as equivalent to cash.

The amount of the deduction is dependent on the replacement cost of the policy. This differs depending on whether the policy in question is (1) a single premium or paid-up policy, (2) a premium-paying policy, or (3) a newly issued policy. The insurance company in question will generally calculate the exact value on IRS Form 712 upon request.

The replacement cost of a single premium or paid-up policy (1) is the single premium the same insurer would charge for a policy of the same amount at the insured's attained age (increased by the value of any dividend credits and reduced by the amount of any loans outstanding).

The replacement cost of a premium-paying policy (2) is the policy's interpolated terminal reserve plus any unearned premium at the date of the gift (again, taking into consideration any dividend credits and outstanding loans).

The replacement cost of a newly issued policy (3) is the gross premium paid by the insured.

A gift of a life insurance policy to charity must, of course, satisfy local requisites of a valid gift. In most states, this means that the donor must have intended to make a present gift of the policy and that he delivered it, actually or constructively, to the charitable donee. An absolute assignment is the clearest way of effectuating the transfer.

Question — Is it possible to obtain a charitable deduction for premium payments if a charity owns a life insurance policy on the donor's life?

Answer — Premium payments are considered gifts of cash and are, therefore, fully and currently deductible as charitable contributions if the charity owns the policy outright.

The donor should send his check directly to the charity and have it pay the premium to the life insurance company in order to insure the most favorable tax results. The canceled check will serve as proof of (1) the fact that a gift was made to the charity,(2) the date the gift was made, and (3) the amount of the gift. It will also assure the donor of a full deduction up to 50 percent of his adjusted gross income. (When an "indirect" gift is made to a charity, the annual deduction limit is lowered to 30 percent of the taxpayer's income. A gift in trust is one such example. Another example of an indirect gift is where premiums on a policy owned by a charity are remitted directly to the life insurance company instead of to the charity itself.)

Question — Is it possible to use life insurance in a way that "balloons" or "swells" the marital deduction?

Answer — Some authorities feel that it is possible for a policy owner to obtain both an immediate income tax deduction and an estate tax advantage through the gift of a life insurance policy to charity. During his life, the policyholder gives a policy on his life to a charity. He transfers all but one of the incidents of ownership to the charitable organization. Thus, the charity would receive the right to surrender the policy, the right to borrow the cash value, etc.[34]

A gift of property (the rights in the policy) is made which gives rise to a current income tax deduction for the fair market value of the policy—the same value that the policy would have for gift tax purposes. The former policyowner may or may not decide to continue to pay premiums on the policy. If he does, in essence he is making additional gifts each year to the charity as the premium is paid.

At his death, because of his retained incident of ownership, the death proceeds should be included in his gross estate. Since the proceeds will be paid to the charity, they will be deducted under Code Section 2055, resulting in a wash. However, if the marital deduction is based on the value of the adjusted gross estate, as was the case prior to the 1981 Economic Recovery Tax Act, the inclusion of the death proceeds should increase the maximum marital deduction by half the amount of the death proceeds. Many estates will continue to use the prior marital deduction limitation of one-half the adjusted gross estate, and will not use the unlimited marital deduction.

The following example illustrates how a larger gross estate could mean a lower federal estate tax. This is the estate tax picture of an individual before using the life insurance gift technique. Assume death occurs in 1989. Further assume the marital deduction is limited to one-half the adjusted gross estate.

Gross Estate		$1,500,000
Less deductions:		
Administration fees Funeral costs, debts		50,000
Adjusted Gross Estate		$1,450,000
Less deductions:		
Marital deduction	$725,000	
Charitable bequest	0	
Total Deductions		$725,000
Taxable Estate (Tentative Tax Base)		$725,000
Federal Estate Tax (after unified credit)		$ 46,250

Now assume the estate owner, using the same marital deduction formula, purchases a $100,000 whole life policy on his own life and names a qualified charity as owner-beneficiary. Certain ownership rights in the policy are restricted so that the insured must consent to their exercise. (This retained power will be discussed in footnote 34.) His new federal estate tax computation would look like this:

Tools and Techniques

Gross Estate		$1,600,000
Less deductions:		
Administrative fees		
Funeral costs, debts		50,000
Adjusted Gross Estate		$1,550,000
Less deductions:		
Marital deduction	775,000	
Charitable bequest	100,000	
Total Deductions		$875,000
Taxable Estate (Tentative Tax Base)		$675,000
Federal Estate Tax		
(after unified credit)		$ 27,750

By increasing the gross estate by $100,000, the estate owner decreases his estate tax by $18,500 ($46,250 – $27,750). This is because in the example given the marital deduction is based on the adjusted gross estate, which is calculated before the deduction for the charitable bequest is taken.

The significance of this technique will be diminished to the extent that an individual wishes to avail himself of the unlimited marital deduction as now permitted by the 1981 Economic Recovery Tax Act. If such individual uses an unlimited marital deduction, he would not have any federal estate tax at his death. Thus, from an estate tax point of view the technique of "swelling" the marital deduction will not achieve any tax savings and will be of no significance unless a formula type marital deduction clause is used which is based on a percentage of the adjusted gross estate.

Another way to "balloon" the estate tax marital deduction might be to establish a charitable trust. The donor will name himself trustee and the trust instrument will give the trustee broad discretion in the selection of the specific qualified charity or charities to be benefited. The trust would be named owner and beneficiary of the insurance proceeds, but the death proceeds should be includible in the gross estate of the donor. This is because he has retained the power, during his lifetime, to affect the beneficial interests of the trust beneficiaries in the life insurance proceeds.

The estate owner (given the same numerical facts and the same marital deduction formula as in the prior illustration) should also realize an income tax benefit during his lifetime. He can deduct the amount of the premium from his gross income within the allowable percentage limits. If it is assumed that net premiums were $3,000 a year and that the estate owner died after 20 years, his total premium outlay would have been $60,000. If he was in the 28 percent income tax bracket, his income tax savings would have been $16,800 over the 20 years. Stated another way, he contributed $100,000 to charity at an after-tax cost of $26,500 ($60,000 premium outlay minus (a) $16,700 estate tax savings and (b) $16,800 income tax savings).[35]

Question — How could life insurance enable a charity to convince a donor to make an immediate gift of land or other property?

Answer — Life insurance can serve as a means of enabling a donor to make a large current gift. For example, an individual is 50 years old, is a widower, and has three children. His adjusted gross estate is about $1 million. One of his assets is a parcel of land with a basis and fair market value of about $200,000. He wants to perpetuate the memory of his late wife through a memorial scholarship fund, but at the same time he does not want to deprive his children of a significant part of his estate.

He can satisfy his overall objective through an immediate gift coupled with the purchase of life insurance to replace the gifted property. Assuming his income is taxed at a top marginal bracket of 28 percent, the arrangement would work like this:

He would contribute the $200,000 parcel of land to his favorite charity immediately. Since the gift is an outright contribution, it will be currently deductible up to 50 percent of his adjusted gross income. (If his income is not high enough to allow him to deduct the entire $200,000 in one year, he could carry over the excess and deduct it against his next 5 years' income.) The $200,000 charitable contribution would result in $56,000 of tax savings, since he is in a 28 percent income tax bracket. He can take this $56,000 that otherwise would have been used to pay taxes and instead make annual gifts of up to $10,000 each to his children. They in turn could purchase a policy on his life and name themselves as owners and beneficiaries.

The chart at Figure 2.8 compares a charitable bequest of the $200,000 parcel of land by will to an immediate lifetime charitable gift of the property coupled with the purchase of life insurance to replace the gifted land. Although the federal estate tax is the same in either situation, the heirs receive $100,000 more by the lifetime gift/insurance purchase technique. Assume death occurs in 1989.

The premium on a $100,000 whole life policy for a male age 50 is only about $3,000 a year; so it will take almost 20 years before the premiums even equal his $56,000 tax savings, the charity has the ownership of the land immediately, and he has provided his children with everything they would have received even if he made no gift. In fact, properly arranged, the policy proceeds will be received free of income, estate tax, inheritance tax, and probate cost. Thus his children could be in better financial condition than if he had waited to make the gift.

Figure 2.8

	BEQUEST OF PROPERTY BY WILL	LIFETIME GIFT OF PROPERTY		BEQUEST OF PROPERTY BY WILL		LIFETIME GIFT OF PROPERTY
Adjusted Gross Estate	$1,000,000	$800,000	Adjusted Gross Estate	$1,000,000		$800,000
		less	Estate Tax (after unified credit)	75,000	less	75,000
Charitable Bequest by Will	200,000	0		925,000		725,000
Taxable Estate (Tentative Tax Base)	$ 800,000	$800,000	Charitable Bequest by Will	200,000	less	0
				725,000		725,000
					plus	
			New Life Insurance	0		100,000
			Passing to Heirs	725,000		825,000
			Advantage of Lifetime Gift	$100,000		

Question — Can a donor obtain a charitable deduction if he splits policy cash values or death benefits between a charity and a family member?

Answer — A life insurance policy can be split into two parts, the protection element and the policy cash value. The protection element, often called the net amount at risk, is the difference between the face amount of the policy and its cash (surrender) value. By splitting the proceeds of a policy between a donor's family and a charity, a donor can provide additional protection for the benefit of his family and at the same time make a meaningful gift to charity.

Note that if a donor attempts to "split dollar" the charitable gift (i.e., to name his personal beneficiary as the recipient of the policy's pure death benefit (the amount at risk) but making the charity owner of the cash value) the IRS will claim that this is a gift of a "partial interest" in property and will disallow a deduction for a portion of the premium payment, or the annual increase in the cash value.[35] The same principle applies where the donor retains an interest in the policy cash value but assigns an interest in the "amount at risk" portion to the charity. The problem is caused by the Code section which provides that a charitable deduction is not allowed for contributions to charity of less than the taxpayer's entire interest in the property.

A gift of the cash value is considered a gift of less than the entire interest in the property regardless of whether the donor retains the right to designate the beneficiary of the risk portion or irrevocably designates the beneficiary before making the gift.[37] Furthermore, if the gift is considered "less than the policyowner's entire interest," disallowance of the gift tax deduction will cause a gift of the policy cash value to be a taxable transfer.[38]

Question — Can group term life insurance be used for charitable contributions?

Answer — Currently, employees must include the cost of group term life insurance coverage over $50,000 in their taxable income. The tax on this economic benefit must be paid with after-tax dollars, which has the effect of reducing the spendable income of the employee.

However, by naming a charity as the beneficiary of group insurance coverage over $50,000, the employee can provide for a gift to charity and at the same time avoid the tax on the economic benefit.

For example, a 63-year-old executive with an average top tax bracket of 28 percent who had $140,000 of coverage would save 28% of $105.30 per month ($1,263.60 annually), or $353.80 annually. The advantage of this technique was significantly enhanced by the introduction of higher group term rates for individuals over age 65 who receive group term insurance on or after January, 1989.

Question — What are some other ways a life insurance policy can be used to generate income or capital for a charity?

Answer — There are a number of additional ways life insurance may be utilized for charitable purposes. Some potential donors are not in a position to turn over to a charity an entire portfolio of life insurance or even a single policy. It is still possible to provide protection for their families and at the same time make periodic cash donations. Annual policy dividends can be paid directly to a specific charity.

Tools and Techniques

The donor could retain control over the disposition of the policy proceeds and the charity's interest in the policy would be limited to the right to receive annual cash dividends. The donation could be for a specified period only, for example, 5, 10, or 15 years. It could be on an unlimited basis but with the insured-owner reserving the right to revoke at anytime. Alternatively, the gift could be made without limitation. As the dividends are paid, they could be taken as deductions.

Alternatively, the dividends from the existing policy could be used to purchase a new policy. The charity, instead of receiving the dividend itself, would be named owner and beneficiary of the policy purchased by the dividend (and perhaps an additional cash donation). The charitable contribution would equal the premium paid.

For example, Scott Kay is a 26-year-old attorney who is married and has one child. On his 21st birthday his father purchased a $50,000 whole life policy for him, which Scott now owns.

Scott would like to make annual contributions to the long-term library building program of his law school but does not feel his income will support additional contributions. He could use the current dividend on his $50,000 policy—which is now in excess of $150 per year—and use that dividend to purchase a policy to be owned by the law school. He could buy over $5,000 of life insurance that would guarantee the law school a sizable gift whether he lived, died, or (assuming he purchased a waiver-of-premium feature) became disabled.

Sometimes an individual will want to make a charitable contribution at death but is concerned with his family's needs. He could name the charity as the revocable beneficiary of a policy on his life so that any time before his death he could change the beneficiary designation to his wife and children. Although he would not qualify for a current income tax deduction, at his death, when the proceeds were paid to the charity, the increase in the marital deduction due to the inclusion of the policy proceeds in his estate—coupled with the charitable deduction—would result in an overall lower estate tax burden assuming the marital deduction is based on a percentage of the adjusted gross estate. Alternatively, a donor could name the charity as contingent or second contingent beneficiary under life insurance protecting his dependents. In this way insurance can serve a dual purpose—it is primarily for the protection of an individual's family but also is a means for providing a potential gift to a charity if conditions should warrant it.

Question — What impact will the Technical and Miscellaneous Revenue Act (TAMRA) of 1988 have on the valuation of charitable deductions?

Answer — Congress was concerned that the tables being used in 1988 and earlier years did not properly reflect either current interest (discount) rates or current mortality experience. It therefore provided that new tables (and/or formulas) reflecting more current interest rates and mortality assumptions should be issued during 1989 by the Treasury. (See page 391 for a more detailed explanation.) If a charitable (income, estate or gift tax) deduction is allowed with respect to a significant part of the property transferred, a client could elect to value the property (a) using an interest rate equal to 120 percent of the federal mid-term rate for the month in which the valuation date falls, or (b) value interests in the property by reference to the federal mid-term rate in effect for either of the two months preceding the valuation date.

ASRS, Secs. 53, ¶¶ 9.1, 20.5(h); 54, ¶¶ 31, 44.5(d); 55,¶¶ 46, 57.10; and 49, ¶¶ 38, 48.2.

Footnote References

Charitable Contributions

1. IRC Sections 170(b)(1)(B), 170(b)(1)(E), 170(c).
2. Reg. §1.170A-8(f).
3. IRC Sections 170(b)(2), 170(d)(2)(A), 170(a)(2), Reg. §1.170A-11.
4. IRC Sections 170(b)(1)(B), 170(d)(1)(A), 170(d)(2).
5. IRC Section 170(f)(3)(B). See also Rev. Rul. 58-260, 1958-1 C.B. 126; Reg. §1.170A-7(a).
6. Reg. §1.170-1(d).
7. IRC Section 170(f)(3)(B)(i).
8. IRC Sections 170(f)(3)(B)(iv), 170(f)(3)(C).
9. IRC Section 170(f)(3)(A); Reg. §1.170A-7(a).
10. IRC Section 170(b)(1).
11. IRC Section 170(b)(1)(E).
12. IRC Sections 170(b)(2), 170(d)(2); Reg. §1.170-1(c).
13. IRC Sections 170(d)(1), 170(b)(1)(B), 170(b)(1)(D)(ii), 170(b)(1)(D)(iii); Reg. §1.170A-10(a).
14. IRC Sections 170(b)(1), 170(d)(1)(A), 170(b)(2), 170(d)(2)(A), 170(a)(2); Regs. §§1.170A-8(b), 1.170A-11.
15. IRC Section 170(b)(1)(C)(i).
16. IRC Sections 170(b)(1)(C)(ii), 170(e)(1).
17. Tax Reform Act of 1986, Section 701, amending IRC Section 57.
18. IRC Sections 170(b)(1)(C)(iii), 170(e)(1)(B); Regs. §§1.170A-8(b), 1.170A-8(d)(2).
19. IRC Section 170(e)(3).
20. IRC Section 170(e)(1)(A); Sen. Rep. P.L. 91-171 (12060).
21. IRC Section 170(e)(3); Tax Reform Act of 1976, Title XXI, Sec. 2135.
22. Joint Committee on Taxation, General Explanation of Tax Reform Act of 1976, H.R. 10612, 94th Congress, P.L. 94-455 (Dec. 29, 1976); IRC Sec. 170(e)(3)(B).
23. IRC Sections 170(e)(1)(B)(i), 170(b)(1)(D)(i), 170(b)(1)(D)(iii); Reg. §1.170A-4.
24. IRC Section 170(e)(1)(B)(i). See Cong. Record, 12-23-69.
25. IRC Sections 170(f)(2)(A), 664. But see discussion of gifts of a partial interest for an exception.
26. IRC Section 664(d)(1). The Tax Reform Act of 1976 provides a measure of relief from the stringent requirements imposed on

charitable remainder trusts by the Reform Act of 1969. The 1976 Code amendment provided an extension to pre-September 21, 1974 charitable remainder trusts and wills providing for such trusts in order to conform to the 1969 estate tax requirements. They had until December 31, 1977, to make the appropriate amendments. Tax Reform Act of 1976, Sec. 1304; IRC Section 2055(e)(3) (added by P.L. 93-483); Reg. §20.2055-2(a).

27. The computation of these amounts and all like amounts hereafter referred to involve the following steps:

For both annuity trust and unitrust computations, age is age at nearest birthday, Reg. §20.2031-10(a)(2), Reg. §1.664-4(b)(4).

In the case of an annuity trust, go to Regulation §20.2031-7(f) Table A (reproduced in Chapter 21, Figure 21.2) determine the value of an annuity at the given age. In the case of a person age 55 this is 8.0046. If the principal sum is $100,000 and the payout is 5 percent, the annuity will be for $5,000: $5,000 × 8.046 = $40,023, the value of the annuity. The value of the remainder is $100,000 (the principal sum) minus the value of the annuity: ($100,000 − $40,023) = $59,977.

In the case of the unitrust, go to Regulation §1.664-4(b)(5), Table E. The value of a remainder interest after a 5 percent unitrust payout at age 55 is .37416. This factor applied to the principal sum of $100,000 is $37,416; the deduction allowed. (The actual payout rate and the adjusted payout rate will vary if adjustment is required under Table F or under Reg. §1.664-4(b)(1). However, these adjustments should not be large enough to be significant for planning purposes.)

It is interesting to note that the value of a charitable remainder interest of a residence in the hands of a noncharitable tenant may be greater for gift tax than income tax purposes because no deduction for depreciation is required for gift tax purposes. Rev. Rul. 76-473, 1976-2 C.B. 306. For recent Revenue Rulings regarding the federal estate tax deduction for charitable remainders, see Revs. Ruls. 76-543, 1976-2 C.B. 287, 76-544, 1976-2 C.B. 288, 76-545, 1976-2 C.B. 289, 76-546, 1976-2 C.B. 290.

28. IRC Section 664(d)(2).

29. Reg. §1.664-3(b).

30. Reg. §1.1011-2.

31. Note that the basic planning principle in these cases (i.e., that the redemption by a corporation of closely held stock from a charity will not be considered a dividend to the individual who donated the stock to the charity in the absence of a prearranged plan) is still useful. *Grove v. Comm.*, 490 F.2d 241 (C.A.-2, 1973); *Dewitt v. U.S.*, 503 F.2d 1406 (Ct. Cl. 1974); *Carrington v. Comm.*, 476 F.2d 704 (C.A.-5, 1973). Although both *Grove* and *Carrington* were decided after 1969, they were decided on the basis of pre-1969 Tax Reform Act law. This is why the retention of a life income by the donor did not cause a loss of the charitable deduction. But under present law, a retention of the life income produced by the donated stock or by the proceeds of a sale of such stock would make the contribution a gift of "less than the donor's entire interest in the contributed property." Such a gift would not qualify for a charitable deduction. See IRS Private Letter Ruling 8123069 where IRS held that appreciated securities used for the redemption of all stock held by the charity would not cause dividend consequences.

32. *Palmer v. Comm.*, 62 TC 684 (1974), aff'd on other grounds, 523 F.2d 1308 (8th Cir. 1975), acq. 1978-1 CB 2. See also TAM 8623007, reaching the same conclusion as *Palmer* on "materially identical" facts. But see TAM 8552009, where controlling

shareholders, H and W, gave nonvoting common stock shares in a family corporation to a qualified charitable trust. The shares were subject to a stock restriction agreement that would not allow the trust to sell the stock to anyone outside the stockholder group without first offering it to the corporation and the other authorized shareholders at a value contained in the agreement. The donors claimed a fair market value for the stock on their income tax return for the year of the gift of $18 million, and later had the corporation redeem the stock from the trust for the same amount. The IRS refused to apply the rationale of the *Palmer* case, above, claiming that the fair market value of the stock at the time of the gift was $32 million and at the time of the redemption was $36 million, and that the gift and the redemption were part of the taxpayers' plan to use the trust as a conduit to make a gift to the remaining stockholders, their descendants, by increasing the value of their descendants' shares and correspondingly decreasing the value of H's and W's shares. The Service characterized the transaction as a redemption by the corporation from H and W of all the ostensibly donated stock, followed by a gift of the proceeds to their descendants.

33. Rev. Rul. 81-282, 1981-2 C.B. 78.

34. One possible flaw in this argument is that the IRS could insist that the taxpayer is giving less than his entire interest in the property. Success with this argument could cause forfeiture of the income tax deduction. Furthermore, the gift tax deductions for charitable contributions could be disallowed. In Rev. Rul. 76-200, 1976-1 C.B. 308, the IRS said that where an insured assigns (even irrevocably) the cash surrender value of a policy to a charity but retains the right to name or change the beneficiary of proceeds in excess of the cash value and assign the balance of the proceeds in excess of the charity's right to the cash value, he has given less than his entire interest (and not an undivided portion of his entire interest). The gift tax deduction was disallowed.

35. The probability of success of this concept was reinforced by Rev. Rul. 72-552, 1972-2 C.B. 43, which stated that the value of inter vivos transfers to a charitable corporation would be includible in the estate of the donor who, as president of the corporation, retained power over the disposition of its funds. The ruling also held that the value was includible in determining the marital deduction allowable and qualified as a charitable deduction. The IRC Section 2036 control retained was the right to select the charitable beneficiaries who would receive the funds of the charitable corporation. By inference, the retention by the policy-owner-donor of the right to choose between two charitable beneficiaries or the right to consent to any change in beneficiary should qualify as an "incident of ownership" under IRC Section 2042 and have the same effect as that discussed in Rev. Rul. 72-552.

Some courts have held that the mere right to change the time or manner of payment of proceeds to the beneficiary (as by electing, changing, or revoking settlement options) is a taxable incident of ownership. *Estate of Lumpkin, Jr. v. Comm'r*, 474 F.2d 1092 (5th Cir. 1973). See also *Eleanor M. Schwager*, 64 T.C. 781 (1975), which held that the right to require written consent to a beneficiary change is an incident of ownership.

36. IRC Section 170(f)(3).

37. Rev. Rul. 76-143, 1976-1 C.B. 63. See also Rev. Rul. 76-1, 1976-1 C.B. 57, which disallowed a deduction for a gift to charity of the annuity portion of a split-life contract.

38. Rev. Rul. 76-200, 1976-1 C.B. 308.

Tools and Techniques

Chapter 3

DEFERRED COMPENSATION (NONQUALIFIED)

WHAT IS IT?

Nonqualified deferred compensation is an arrangement whereby an employer promises to pay an employee in the future for services rendered currently. The plan is generally set up to provide for the employee's salary to be continued over a period of years after retirement and other termination of employment.

These payments are referred to as "deferred" compensation because they represent compensation earned currently but which will not be paid until a future date or event. The term "nonqualified" refers to the fact that the plan does not attempt to meet the stringent coverage and contribution requirements necessary to obtain government approval for qualified pension/profit-sharing tax treatment.

WHEN IS THE USE OF SUCH A DEVICE INDICATED?

1. When a business does not have a government approved ("qualified") retirement plan to offer key employees and would like to provide those key employees with retirement benefits.

2. Where a business has a qualified retirement plan, but would like to provide additional retirement benefits for certain key people over and above those permissible under a qualified plan.

3. Where a highly paid employee or executive would like to defer the taxation on income from peak earning years to a future date when he might be in a lower income tax bracket (usually at retirement).

4. When an executive or other highly paid individual would like to use his employer to, in effect, provide a forced savings program for him and to use such a savings program as a retirement plan.

WHAT ARE THE REQUIREMENTS?

1. In order to successfully defer income tax, an agreement should contain a contingency which may cause the employee to forfeit rights to future payments. As long as an employee's rights are forfeitable, there can be no constructive receipt of income under the agreement.[1]

2. Even if an employee's rights are nonforfeitable, he will not be deemed to have constructive receipt of income if the agreement is entered into before the employee earns the compensation in question and the employer's promise to pay is not secured in any way. This means that the

agreement cannot be formally funded (no interest in a trust or escrowed fund or in a specific asset can be given to the employee without causing the money to be immediately taxable).[2]

However, it is permissible for a corporation to finance its obligation under the agreement by purchasing a life insurance contract, annuities, mutual funds, securities, or a combination of these investment media, without adverse tax consequences to the employee. The assets which will be used to finance the employer's obligation to the employee must remain the unrestricted property of the corporation (subject to the claims of the corporation's creditors). The employee must be given no interest or specific rights in the monies the corporation sets aside to meet its obligation under the agreement.[3]

The Internal Revenue Service has permitted the establishment of so-called "Rabbi Trusts" in conjunction with certain plans of deferred compensation. These trusts enable an employer to transfer funds to an irrevocable grantor trust which satisfies certain criteria (including the requirement that the trust assets remain subject to the claims of the employer's general creditors).[4] Although such a trust can provide protection from loss of benefits (e.g., in the event of a hostile takeover), its real benefit is more psychological, since in the event of employer insolvency or bankruptcy the assets held in trust must be available to the employer's general creditors. (This topic is covered in more detail in our book, *Tools and Techniques of Employee Benefits and Retirement Planning*.)

HOW IT IS DONE — AN EXAMPLE

The selected employee enters into an employment contract with his employer. The contract stipulates that specific payments will be made to the employee or the employee's beneficiaries in the event of death, disability, or retirement. This creates a direct enforceable obligation; the employer must provide the agreed upon benefits. In return for this promise, the selected employee agrees to continue in the service of the company.

The agreement sometimes will obligate the employee to (a) refrain from engaging in any competitive business after retirement, and (b) remain available for consultation purposes after retirement.

Often, the employer will purchase life insurance (alone or in combination with other savings vehicles, such as a fixed or variable annuity or a mutual fund) to provide the required benefits. The business would apply for and own the policy

Tools and Techniques

(or other security) on the life of the employee. The business would pay the premiums and be named the policy beneficiary. The business would completely control and own the policy (as well as any other asset used to finance the employer's obligation under the agreement).

The purpose of the life insurance policy is to provide funds necessary to pay retirement benefits called for under the contract. Policy cash values can be used for this purpose. Alternatively, the policy can be held by the corporation until the employee's death, and the employee can be paid the agreed upon deferred compensation out of other corporate assets. Should the employee die prior to retirement, the life insurance will be received by the corporation and then can be used to provide death benefit payments to the employee's family.

Assume the Krauss Corporation is in a 34 percent federal income tax bracket. The corporation enters into a nonqualified deferred compensation agreement with its president, Robert P. Krauss, who is 45 years old. Krauss agrees to defer a $5,000 a year salary increase. Instead of receiving the $5,000 salary increase currently, the after-tax cost of this raise ($3,300) is applied on Krauss' behalf as the annual premium for a life insurance policy on his life.

The Krauss Corporation then agrees to provide retirement and death benefits as follows: (a) If Krauss dies before retirement, $5,000 a year will be paid to his widow for a period equal to the number of years he was covered under the plan. (b) If he remains with the corporation until retirement at age 65, he will receive $10,000 a year for 10 years, in addition to any other fringe benefits to which he may be entitled.

Because the Krauss Corporation is in a 34 percent marginal tax bracket (plus state income taxes), each $1,000 of benefit payments made to its president (or his widow) would actually cost only $660. Retirement benefits could be paid out of current earnings and the corporation could continue the insurance policy in force until the tax-free death proceeds are received. Alternatively, the cash values of the policy could be used to finance the corporation's obligation under the contract.

A premium of $3,300 would purchase approximately $75,000 of life insurance (life paid up at age 65) for a male age 45. If Krauss died at age 50 after five years' premium payments, the corporation would receive $75,000 of tax free policy proceeds (in addition to dividends and perhaps interest); it would have paid $16,500 in premiums; it is obligated to pay a total of $25,000 ($5,000 a year for five years) to Bob's widow, but its after-tax cost for making such payments is only $16,500 (66% x $25,000). This results in a net gain to the corporation of approximately $42,000 ($75,000 insurance proceeds less $16,500 of premiums and less $16,500 of after-tax cost of such payments).

If Bob Krauss' death occurs at age 75, the corporation receives over $122,000 in death proceeds and dividends; it has paid $66,000 in premiums; it has made lifetime payments of $100,000 ($10,000 a year for 10 years) so its net after tax deduction cost for those deferred compensation payments has been $66,000 ($100,000 minus $100,000 x 34 percent tax) and its total cost to provide the promised benefits is approximately $10,000 ($122,000 insurance proceeds minus $66,000 premiums, minus $66,000 cost of deferred compensation payments).

WHAT ARE THE TAX IMPLICATIONS?

The Employer's Tax Position

1. Premiums paid by the employer are not tax deductible. The life insurance policy is considered an asset of the employer and is, therefore, carried on the books of the employer as such. Therefore, no tax deduction is allowed for payment of the premiums.[5] (No current deduction is allowed for any other funding vehicle as well.)

2. When the executive reaches retirement age, the employer, as owner of the policy, may choose one of the settlement options available under the policy to fulfill its obligation under the plan. In this case, a portion of each installment payment received by the employer would be taxable under the annuity rules.[6] However, if the policy is surrendered and a lump sum payment is received, that portion which exceeds the employer's cost (the net premiums the employer has paid) is treated as ordinary income.[7]

3. At the employee's death, the entire policy proceeds receivable by the employer are generally income tax free.[8] (See paragragh 5 of "What are the Tax Implications" in Chapter 1, Buy-Sell Agreement, for possible alternative minimum tax on proceeds received by a regular C corporation.) If the employee dies before retirement, these proceeds can be used to pay his or her family the agreed upon benefits. If the employee lives beyond retirement and begins to receive deferred compensation, the employer, rather than surrendering the policy at this time, may choose to make benefit payments out of current or accumulated earnings. Therefore, the employer can continue the policy in force until the employee dies. At that time, the death proceeds would be received by the corporation on an income tax free basis.

4. When the benefits are paid by the employer under the deferred compensation plan, either to the employee (after retiring) or to his or her family (on death before retirement), payments by the corporation are deductible assuming that benefits constitute reasonable additional compensation.[9]

5. Another tax break is available to both employers and employees. Deferred compensation payments are generally exempt from FICA (Social Security) and FUTA (unemployment) taxes. The exemption applies whether

these benefits are paid to the employee or to his dependents, so long as the payments are made after termination of employment because of death, disability retirement or retirement after attaining a specified age *and* if made under a plan which covers employees generally or a class or classes of employees.[10] Such payments are not excepted from other income tax requirements. Thus, deferred compensation payments are wages subject to income tax withholding.

For payments made to an employee under a nonqualified deferred compensation program for services performed after 1983, the deferred amounts will be subject to social security tax in the year services are performed or in a later year if there was a substantial risk of forfeiture of the rights to the deferred amounts in the year the services are performed.[11]

In most instances, only those employees who earn in excess of the social security taxable wage base elect to defer compensation and will not, therefore, be affected by the provision in the prior paragraph unless the deferred amount was forfeitable when earned.

The Employee's Tax Position

1. During employment, the employee is not taxed on amounts set aside by the employer to meet its financial obligation. Therefore, if a life insurance policy is purchased on the life of the employee, assuming it is part of the general assets of the employer and is not specifically earmarked for the purpose of carrying out the liabilities under the deferred compensation agreement, premiums paid by the employer will not be taxable to the employee.[12] This same principle applies to a purchase by the employer of an annuity, mutual fund or other savings vehicle to finance its obligation.

2. Benefits received from the deferred compensation plan by the employee (or his family) are taxable at ordinary income rates as received; however, the tax liability may be reduced because benefit payments typically commence at retirement. Although many individuals will be in a lower income tax bracket at retirement, many individuals will not be, since passage of the Tax Reform Act of 1986. As a result of this Act, there are only two income tax brackets - 15% and 28%. A married individual with taxable income in excess of $29,750 will be in the 28% bracket. Prior to passage of this Act, the tax brackets ranged from 11% to 50%.

3. If the employee dies prior to retirement, the first $5,000 of benefits paid to his widow may be excludible from income as an employee's death benefit. (Death benefits under this type of agreement qualify only if the employee's rights to living benefits at the time of death are forfeitable.)

4. The commuted value of benefit payments will be included in the employee's gross estate for federal estate tax purposes. Therefore, the present value of the future income promised to the employee's spouse will be taxable in the employee's estate.[13] This is "income in respect of a decedent" (Section 691 Income) and an income tax deduction will be allowed to the recipient of such income for the additional federal estate tax attributable to the inclusion of the deferred compensation.[14]

But because of the unlimited federal estate tax marital deduction, if the death benefit is payable to the employee's surviving spouse in a qualifying manner, no estate tax will be incurred when the employee dies. (Therefore, no deduction for income in respect of a decedent will be allowed.)

IMPLICATIONS AND ISSUES IN COMMUNITY PROPERTY STATES

As stated previously (see general discussion in Introduction), the earnings of a resident husband or wife are generally treated as community property in the nine community property states. This can cause some problems in the context of non-qualified deferred compensation. A spouse may enter into a deferred compensation arrangement with his or her employer. The deferred amount would be community property if paid currently. If the spouses obtain a divorce or one of the spouses dies, it may be necessary to determine the present value of the deferred amount in order to divide the community assets.

Whether, as regards forfeitable nonqualified deferred compensation rights, there is "property" subject to division in divorce or at death is a preliminary problem, although not one of as much importance now as it was previously under the former reasoning that only "vested" rights could be "property" subject to division. Under the extreme view, there was "property" only if the rights had fully matured and payments were either being presently received or there was a non-forfeitable right to immediate payment. The generally accepted current analysis establishes that there is "property" subject to division even though there is no certainty that compensation will ever be received.

A useful classification of nonqualified deferred compensation rights and pension rights has been suggested: (1) "vested and matured"—a nonforfeitable right to immediate payment; (2) "vested and unmatured"—a nonforfeitable right to payment at some future time, even though the right might terminate on a participant's death prior to retirement; (3) "contingent"—a nonvested accrued right and the contractual right to continue in the plan with, probably, a reasonable expectation of acquiring vested benefits within a relatively short time; and (4) "merely expectancy".

While forfeitable deferred compensation has been treated as a "mere expectancy" and thus of no value in a division of community property, at least one community property state, California, has abandoned this approach in the context of deferred compensation. California courts hold that the present value of deferred compensation can be determined. The fact that the deferred compensation obligation is unsecured and not formally funded would be a significant factor in reducing value. If the benefits are forfeitable, additional reductions in value are appropriate. In many circumstances, it may be appropriate to order a division of deferred compensation as it is paid, rather than requiring a current division. Thus, the spouse who did not earn the deferred compensation may not be paid. He or she presumably would receive a greater amount if the deferred benefit was actually paid (as opposed to 50 percent of a current value discounted for risk factors).

Another aspect commented on elsewhere in *Tools and Techniques,* which also relates to all community property planning, is the danger of signing a so-called "community property agreement" which makes all property owned by both spouses the community property of both of them. For example, assume Dr. Lee Stein, an employee who worked for a national corporation while he was a resident of a separate property state, accrued a substantial deferred compensation benefit. If Lee then moves to a community property state, the deferred compensation benefit already accrued is still his separate property (specifically, "quasi-community property"); if he then signs an agreement making all property of his wife, Ronda, and himself community property, he will be making a taxable gift to Ronda. Because of the nature of the gift, it may be that even the $10,000 annual gift tax exclusion will not be available (since the wife may not be able to dispose of her newly received interest). On the other hand, under post-ERTA law, the transfer should qualify for the unlimited marital deduction; however, the long range tax implications of that deduction should be fully understood (see chapter 33). Moreover, state gift tax laws should still be considered.

Therefore, one should be very careful in entering into such agreements without receiving competent advice from an attorney knowledgeable in both property law and taxation.

QUESTIONS AND ANSWERS

Question — Can a nonqualified deferred compensation plan provide a disability benefit?

Answer — Yes. A plan may be set up to include a disability benefit. There are several ways of providing disability benefits: (1) A disability income policy can be purchased along with the other assets used to finance the employer's obligation under the plan. (2) A disability waiver of premium benefit attached to the life insurance policy will enable the company to cover its liability in the event the employee becomes totally disabled. (3) A combination of these methods can be used. The second approach works like this:

Assuming Bob Krauss, in the example above, became disabled, the money normally set aside for premium payments ($3,300 a year) would not have to be paid since premiums would be waived. The Krauss Corporation would have $5,000 to pay out to the employee since his salary continuation payments by the corporation would be deductible.

Generally, wage continuation payments and disability retirement income payments are fully includible in an employee's gross income. However, under Code Section 22 an employee who is under the age of 65, is retired on disability, and is considered totally and permanently disabled may be entitled to a tax credit for disability retirement income.

Question — What effect does ERISA (the Pension Reform Act of 1974) have on unfunded nonqualified deferred compensation plans?

Answer — Unfunded nonqualified deferred compensation plans for select groups of management or highly compensated individuals are exempt from all requirements except easily complied with disclosure provisions (Part I of the Labor Section). Thus, such plans are not subject to ERISA requirements as to participation, vesting, nondiscrimination, minimum funding, and fiduciary responsibility rules.

The employer can comply with the act by a simple written statement (a letter will do) provided to both the employee and the Secretary of Labor indicating the employer's name, IRS identification number, a declaration of intent to provide the plan for a select group of management or highly compensated employees, a statement of the number of plans and number of employees in each plan, and an indication that, upon request of the Secretary of Labor, the employer will provide a copy of the deferred compensation agreement. This must be done within 120 days of the adoption of a plan.

Question — What is the earliest date the corporation can take a deduction for unfunded deferred compensation payments?

Answer — A corporation cannot take a deduction until it actually makes payments to the employee (or a deceased employee's beneficiary) regardless of whether the corporation is on a cash or accrual basis of accounting.[15]

Question — Can directors' fees be deferred through an unfunded deferred compensation agreement?

Answer — Yes. Individual nonqualified deferred compensation agreements can be made with independent contractors, directors, and even employees of other business organizations. Also, tax-exempt organizations can establish nonqualified deferred compensation plans but generally must comply with the additional requirements of section 457.

Question — If a corporation finances its obligation under a deferred compensation agreement with corporate owned annuity contracts, are there any current adverse tax consequences to the employee or to the employer-corporation?

Answer — There are no current tax consequences to the employee so long as the annuity remains the asset of the corporation and the employee has no interest in the annuity. However, the Tax Reform Act of 1986 made changes affecting the corporation's tax position where an annuity is used to finance the employer's obligation under the agreement. For contributions made after February 28, 1986 to annuity contracts held by a "non natural person," such as a corporation, "the income on the contract" for the tax year of the policyholder is generally treated as ordinary income received by the contract owner for that year.[16]

Question — Is it possible for a nonqualified deferred compensation agreement to trigger a section 2036(c) inclusion?

Answer — Not unless the individual providing the services has engaged in a "valuation freeze" transaction. If the agreement concerns services to be rendered by an individual who holds (or held) a substantial interest in the enterprise for which he renders services and he has engaged as a transferor in a "valuation freeze" transaction as described in Code section 2036(c)(1) (see page 477), the agreement will not, in and of itself, bring into the individual's estate the value of the property involved in the valuation freeze transaction. However, to be certain that the agreement will not trigger a section 2036(c) inclusion, the agreement should meet the following safe harbor rules found in section 2036(c)(7), as added by TAMRA '88, Sec. 3031(b): (1) the agreement must be an arm's length agreement for fair market value (determined at the time services are provided); (2) the agreement must not otherwise involve any change in interests in the enterprise; (3) the agreement must not call for services (say, as a consultant or director) to be rendered after the transfer for a period greater than three years after the date of the transfer (and for this purpose the term of any agreement includes any period for which the agreement may be extended at the option of the individual providing the services); and (4) the performance of the agreement must not be contingent on gross receipts, in-

come, profits, or similar items of the enterprise. (See page 477 et seq. for a more detailed explanation of Code section 2036(c).)

ASRS, Sec. 64

Footnote References

Deferred Compensation (Nonqualified)

1. Regs. §§1.451-1, 1.451-2.
2. Rev. Rul. 60-31, 1960-1 C.B. 174; Rev. Rul. 70-435, 1970-2 C.B. 100. See also IRS Letter Ruling 8439012, where under an executive's deferred compensation plan, his compensation was placed in a trusteed bank account, but his rights were only those of an unsecured general creditor of the company. No income was recognized by the executive as a result of the company's placing the money in the trust account.
3. See also *Comm'r. v. Oates*, 207 F.2d 711 (CA-7, 1953); Rev. Rul. 68-99, 1968-1 C.B. 193; Rev. Rul. 72-25, 1972-1 C.B. 127.
4. Let. Ruls. 8113107 and 8736045.
5. IRC Section 264(a).
6. IRC Section 72.
7. IRC Section 72(e); Reg. §1.72-11(d).
8. IRC Section 101(a).
9. IRC Sections 404(a)(5); 162, 212.
10. Rev. Rul. 78-263, 1978-2 C.B. 252; Rev. Rul. 77-25, 1977-1 C.B. 301.
11. Code Sec. 3121, as amended by P.L. 98-21, Sec. 324, 4 83.
12. Rev. Rul. 68-99, 1968-1 C.B. 193; Rev. Rul. 72-25, 1972-1 C.B. 127.
13. IRC Section 2039(a); *Goodman v. Granger*, 243 F.2d 264 (CA-3,1957).
14. Section 691(c). The income tax deduction for the additional federal estate tax generated by the inclusion of the IRD is as follows:

	Federal estate tax payable (with net 691 income included in the gross estate)
Minus	
	Federal estate tax payable (with no 691 income included in gross estate)
Equals	
	Portion of Federal Estate Tax attributable to 691 items

   Note the planning implication of this computation: To the extent no estate tax is generated by IRD, no income tax deduction will be allowed. So if deferred compensation payments are made to a surviving spouse (or to a marital trust on her behalf), to the extent they qualify for the marital deduction, the 691 income tax deduction is lost.
15. IRC Sections 404(a)(5), 404(d).
16. IRC Section 72(u).

Chapter 4

DISCLAIMERS

WHAT IS IT?

A disclaimer (or renunciation) is an unqualified refusal by a potential beneficiary to accept benefits given through a testamentary or intervivos transfer of property. Most often a disclaimer refers to the refusal by a potential beneficiary to accept a bequest under the terms of a will or trust.

For federal tax purposes, the disclaimant is regarded as never having received the property (that is, for tax purposes it's as if he predeceased the testator). As a result of this consequence, no transfer is considered to have been made *by the disclaimant* for federal gift, estate, or generation-skipping transfer tax purposes.[1]

However, as a consequence of TRA '86, it is possible for a disclaimer to create a generation-skipping transfer (GST) *by someone other than the disclaimant*, where under prior law the disclaimer would not have created such a transfer. This result can occur because under the new GST tax law enacted by TRA '86, a "direct skip" transfer (i.e., a transfer to or for an individual two or more generations younger than the transferor) is a GST subject to the GST tax (if it is also subject to federal estate or gift tax).[2] Under prior law, a direct skip transfer was not a GST for GST tax purposes. The first example below will illustrate how a disclaimer can create such a GST.

The new requirements of federal law, applicable only to transfers creating an interest in the person disclaiming made after December 31, 1976, will apply, for federal estate, gift, and generation skipping transfer tax purposes even if local law does not characterize the refusal as a disclaimer. For these federal tax purposes, the time limits prescribed for a qualified disclaimer should also supersede any time period prescribed by local law. To be fully effective for both state and federal purposes, the disclaimer must also comply with the applicable state law, and may have to meet separate rules for state gift or state death taxes.

WHEN IS THE USE OF SUCH A DEVICE INDICATED?

1. When an individual with children and a large estate in his own right is left a bequest by another individual and this bequest would compound his potential estate tax problem, a disclaimer may be an appropriate estate planning tool. He may wish to disclaim the bequest in favor of the next recipients under the will or trust, very often his children. By making the disclaimer, the disclaimed property will not be included in the parent's estate at his death.

2. Where an individual who is in a high income tax bracket is left a bequest "if he is living otherwise to his children" (who are in lower income tax brackets), a disclaimer can shift the income taxation to the children (assuming they are age 14 or older) if they are the next recipients of the gift under the will or trust.

3. Where an individual wishes to make a tax free gift to the person who would be the next recipient under the will or trust, he can disclaim the property.

4. When property is left to a spouse who doesn't need or want it, she could disclaim the portion she doesn't want and avoid a needless double taxation.

WHAT ARE THE REQUIREMENTS?[3]

1. There must be an irrevocable and unqualified refusal to accept an interest in property.

2. The refusal must be in writing.

3. The writing must be received by the transferor, his legal representative, or the holder of legal title to the property.

4. The refusal must be received no later than nine months after the day on which the transfer creating the interest is made or, if later, nine months after the day on which the donee or beneficiary attains the age of 21.

5. The disclaimer must be made prior to acceptance of the interest or any of its benefits.

6. The interest must pass either to the spouse of the decedent or to a person other than the disclaimant without any direction on the part of the disclaimant. (A valid disclaimer by a surviving spouse may be made even though the interest passes to a trust in which she has an income interest.)

7. The interest disclaimed should be an entire interest, but can be an undivided fractional part of the proposed gift.

HOW IT IS DONE — EXAMPLES

1. Doug Koch, a wealthy client, has four children. An aunt of his just died and, under the terms of her will, named Mr. Koch as recipient of her entire estate if he is alive. If he is deceased when she dies, Mr. Koch's four children are named equally as contingent heirs. Mr. Koch has adequate assets and income to live comfortably, and does not need additional property to compound his already high potential estate tax. By filing in writing an effective "qualified disclaimer" within nine months of his aunt's death, Mr. Koch will be deemed to have

Tools and Techniques

predeceased his aunt for both federal gift and estate tax purposes and his interest in her estate would be distributed to his children under the terms of her will without any federal gift, estate, or GST tax liability to him.

However, if Doug had consulted his estate planner before taking action, the planner might have brought about Doug's reconsideration of his proposed disclaimer by an explanation along these lines: The Code says that if Doug makes a qualified disclaimer, then for federal transfer tax purposes, his interest in his aunt's estate will be treated as if the interest had never been distributed to him. That means her estate will be distributed to whomever local law says will take upon Doug's disclaimer. *If the* distributees are Doug's children (or others in their generation or younger), Doug's disclaimer will have created a direct skip transfer(s) from his aunt to his children. The transfer(s) may or may not attract the GST tax, depending upon how much property is involved and on the extent to which the aunt's $1,000,000 GST exemption is allocated to the transfer(s). If the aunt's estate is in the 55% federal estate tax bracket, the estate tax and the GST tax combined could virtually confiscate the property otherwise going to Doug's children.

2. Mr. Ed Radosh specifically leaves $100,000 to his son with a gift over to his favorite charity if his son disclaims. His son can decide after his father's death whether to accept the bequest and donate the bequest to charity if he wishes and receive an income tax deduction or if it would be more beneficial to disclaim the property in favor of the charity and have the estate receive the charitable deduction.

3. Mr. Jules Einhorn thought that at his death his wife would have ample funds and his son very little. Therefore, he left most of his property to his son with a contingent gift to his wife in the event his son predeceased him. At the time of Mr. Einhorn's death the son was financially well off, but the mother was in dire financial straits. By disclaiming his share and permitting the wife to take, the son not only allowed a better distribution of assets but also may have qualified Mr. Einhorn's estate for a marital deduction due to the transfer of the assets to the surviving spouse. This could result in a substantial saving on federal estate taxes. She could then make gift tax-free transfers to her son using the annual gift tax exclusion and the unified credit.

WHAT ARE THE TAX IMPLICATIONS?

1. A disclaimer of a property interest or a power is not treated as a gift for gift tax purposes.[4]

2. A disclaimed interest in property is not considered to be a transfer by a disclaimant/decedent for estate tax purposes and will not be included in his estate at death as a transfer with a retained life estate.[5]

3. If property is disclaimed by a person in favor of a surviving spouse or charity, the marital or charitable deduction will be permitted provided the property would otherwise qualify for these deductions.[6]

4. Any income received on disclaimed property will be chargeable to the person in whose favor the property was disclaimed.

IMPLICATIONS AND ISSUES IN COMMUNITY PROPERTY STATES

Please refer to the background information on Community Property contained in the Introduction. A qualified disclaimer is taken into account for purposes of the marital deduction. In either a separate property or a community property state, a disclaimer can be expected initially to qualify the estate for the marital deduction or to increase or decrease the deduction if the surviving spouse gains or loses because of the disclaimer.

The availability of the unlimited marital deduction, which applies to both separate and community property, alleviates concerns for future planning in this area. However, different rules apply to the disposition of separate and community property by Will in community property states and therefore it is still important to carefully characterize all of the property interests held by a decedent and his or her spouse to determine if under community property rules a disclaimer is desired or required.

Where the entire community property is subjected to probate (both the decedent's one-half interest and the surviving spouse's one-half interest) upon the death of only one spouse, the surviving spouse should exercise caution to disclaim only the community property interest of the decedent. A disclaimer of both halves would probably result in a taxable gift to the individual who takes as the result of the disclaimers. As mentioned in the Introduction, several types of problems can arise when attempting to determine whether specific property is to be characterized as community, quasi-community or separate.

QUESTIONS AND ANSWERS

Question — Can a beneficiary of a life insurance policy disclaim his interest in the proceeds?

Answer — Yes—such an interest may be disclaimed within nine months of the decedent's death. However, if the beneficiary was an irrevocable beneficiary, the disclaimer most likely must be made within nine months of the beneficiary designation.

Question — Can an interest in jointly held property be disclaimed?

Answer — Yes—if made within nine months of the creation of the gift and before any of the property or its benefits have been accepted by the disclaimant. However, in the event of death, IRS will not recognize a disclaimer of joint property which passes by right of survivorship.[7] If the disclaimant has previously accepted the property interest or any of its benefits, there can be no valid federal disclaimer even though state law authorizes such disclaimers and property is actually distributed in accordance with the state law.

Question — Can an individual after attaining age 21 disclaim property if he has received an interest in the property during his minority?

Answer — The law indicates that an individual can make a "qualified disclaimer" after attaining age 21, if the disclaimer is made within nine months after reaching age 21 and if the other requirements of the law are met. However, the law does not allow a "qualified disclaimer" if benefits have been received from the property prior to the disclaimer.

A beneficiary who is under 21 years of age has until 9 months after his 21st birthday in which to make a qualified disclaimer of his interest in property. Any actions taken with regard to an interest in property by a beneficiary or a custodian prior to the beneficiary's 21st birthday will not be an acceptance by the beneficiary of the interest. For example, a minor who receives dividends on stock prior to the age of 21 will not be deemed to have made an acceptance, assuming he did not accept dividends after attaining age 21. This rule holds even with respect to a gift under the Uniform Gifts to Minors Act or the Uniform Transfers to Minors Act where under the Act custodianship ends and the property is delivered to the donee when he attains age 18.[8]

Question — If a testator dies leaving a trust with income payable to his wife for her lifetime and remainder payable to his children, can the children disclaim their remainder interest after their mother's death?

Answer — Not unless the mother died within nine months of the testator since the disclaimer must be made within nine months of the testator's death since this is when the gift was complete. The children would have to disclaim within this period or, if later, within 9 months of the date the child reaches age 21.

Question — Is a disclaimer valid where a surviving spouse refuses to accept all or a portion of an interest in property passing from a decedent, and, as a result of that refusal, the property passes to a trust in which that spouse has an income interest [such as the typical family (nonmarital "B") trust]?

Answer — A disclaimer will be valid where a spouse refuses an interest in property even if, as a result of that disclaimer, he or she receives an income interest (as long as that income interest does not result from the surviving spouse's direction).

This "Blank Check" post mortem marital deduction planning tool means an estate owner doesn't have to decide how much of his estate should go to a surviving spouse by will. His will can allow that decision to be made by the survivor when more facts are known. All the estate owner's property could be left to the surviving spouse with a provision that any part of the bequest which is disclaimed will be placed in the nonmarital ("by pass") trust. This planning may—in some cases—be preferable to a specific marital formula bequest.

Question — What are some of the other things one considers about the use of a disclaimer?

Answer — Some of the factors to be considered are:

1. If a disclaiming beneficiary is indebted to the estate, the instrument should specify whether the debt may be set off against the alternative takers (who might be the disclaimant's children).[9]

2. A disclaimer of a power may extinguish it; hence, it may be desirable to designate an alternative donee of the power.[10]

3. A disclaimer of a legacy may result in the disclaimed legacy passing to the disclaimant's issue under an anti-lapse statute.[11]

4. A disclaimer could cause a premature "closing" of a class of beneficiaries.[12]

5. It is generally desirable to express a partial disclaimer in the form of a fraction or percentage. A partial disclaimer may be valid only if it represents an "undivided portion of an interest."[13]

6. To guard against the possibility that the disclaimed property may not pass to someone other than the disclaimant (unless it is to a surviving spouse), an alternative taker should be provided for. Further, the statutory schedule may not coincide with the settlor's intent.

7. The instrument should indicate whether a disclaimer accelerates future interests.[14]

Question — What is the effect of a disclaimer if federal requirements are met but state disclaimer laws are not?

Answer — State law is important because it governs property rights, and how and under what conditions and to whom property will pass. It is possible that a person could make a valid disclaimer under Federal Law—say within the nine month statutory period—which would not meet a shorter period required for an effective disclaimer of

Tools and Techniques

property rights under state law. Federal law provides that the disclaimer can be effective if the property passes as the result of the disclaimer to the party who would have received it if the disclaimer had been effective under state law.

ASRS, Secs. 54, ¶44.3(1); 55, ¶57.5(f).

Footnote References

Disclaimers

1. IRC Section 2518(a).
2. IRC Sections 2612(c), 2613(a).
3. IRC 2518(b).
4. IRC 2518(a).

5. See *Brown v. Routzahn*, 63 F.2d 914 (6th Cir.) Cert. denied 290 U.S. 641 (1933).
6. IRC 2056(d)(2), 2055(a).
7. IRS Letter Ruling 7829008.
8. Reg. §25.2518-2(d)(3), (4), Example (11).
9. *Matter of Colacci*, 549 P.2d 1096 (Colo. App. 1976).
10. Schwartz, "Effective Use of Disclaimers," 19 B.C. Law Rev. 551 (1978).
11. *Brannan v. Ely*, 157 Md. 100, 145 Atl. 361 (1929); *Thompson v. Thornton*, 197 Mass. 273, 83 N.E. 880 (1908).
12. See Schwartz, *Future Interests & Estate Planning*, §11.4 (Supp. 1978).
13. Schwartz, "Effective Use of Disclaimers," 19 B.C. Law Rev. 551, 567, 573 (1978).
14. Schwartz, *Future Interests & Estate Planning*, §§11.5-11.9 (Supp. 1978).

Chapter 5

DURABLE POWER OF ATTORNEY

WHAT IS IT?

A Power of Attorney is a written document which enables an individual, the "principal," to designate another person or persons as his "attorney-in-fact," that is, to act on the principal's behalf. The scope of the power can be severely limited ("only to pay my utility bills") or quite broad ("all the legal powers I myself have, including but not limited to the following —").

A "Durable" Power of Attorney is a Power of Attorney which is not terminated by subsequent disability or incapacity of the principal. At this date, all states have recognized some form of Durable Power of Attorney. The vast majority of such states have either enacted in total the Durable Power of Attorney provisions of the Uniform Probate Code (U.P.C.) or have drafted their own statutes in conformity with the provisions of the U.P.C.

The definition of a Durable Power of Attorney, according to the Uniform Probate Code, is:

> "A durable power of attorney is a power of attorney by which a principal designates another his attorney in fact in writing and the writing contains the words 'This power of attorney shall not be affected by subsequent disability or incapacity of the principal, or lapse of time,' or 'This power of attorney shall become effective upon the disability or incapacity of the principal,' or similar words showing the intent of the principal that the authority conferred shall be exercisable notwithstanding the principal's subsequent disability or incapacity, and, unless it states a time of termination, notwithstanding the lapse of time since the execution of the instrument."

WHEN IS THE USE OF SUCH A DEVICE INDICATED?

1. When the principal is elderly and there is a significant chance that he will become senile. The use of a broadly drawn Durable Power of Attorney may negate the necessity of petitioning the local court for appointment of a guardian or conservator to handle the principal's assets.

2. When an individual is suffering from a physical disability or illness, the effect of which could lead to a permanent or long term incapacity.

3. In all situations where an individual desires to provide for the continuity of the management of his or her assets in the event he or she is unable to manage such assets for either a short or long duration of time because of physical or mental incapacity. The Durable Power of Attorney permits the individual, when competent, to make a determination of who will handle his or her affairs.

4. As a temporary and expedient substitute for a living revocable trust. The trust device is more burdensome and possibly much more costly than the Durable Power of Attorney.

5. As an addition to the revocable living trust, to provide flexibility.

WHAT ARE THE REQUIREMENTS?

1. The principal (the one giving the Power) must be of legal age and competent at the time the Power is given.

2. The attorney in fact (the one receiving the Power) must be of legal age at the time the Power is exercised.

3. The Power of Attorney must include the words "this Power of Attorney shall not be affected by subsequent disability or incapacity of the principal" or "this Power of Attorney shall become effective upon the disability or incapacity of the principal" or similar words showing the principal's intent that the authority conferred shall be exercisable regardless of whether or not he or she subsequently becomes disabled or incapacitated.

HOW IS IT DONE?

Assume your client, Joe Mozino, a widower, is on his deathbed on December 28. He could give $10,000 (or less) to each of his 10 great grandchildren, four grandchildren, and each of their four wives. Eighteen donees times $10,000 equals $180,000. If he's alive four days later, on January 1, he could sign another 18 checks for a similar amount. Even if he dies two weeks after making the second round of gifts, a total of $360,000 escapes federal estate taxation. If he's only in the 37 percent estate tax bracket, the savings is $133,200!

The problem is, he may be mentally competent to act—and physically able—on the 28th of December. But if he becomes either physically or mentally incompetent after that date, the estate tax savings he is legally entitled to will be lost unless someone is entitled by state law to act (specifically to make gifts) on his behalf. Joe could name his son, Andrew, his attorney-in-fact and give him the power (in addition to other powers) to make gifts on his behalf. Andrew could draw checks on Joe's account to each of the donees (just as if Joe drew the checks).

An example of a broadly drawn Durable Power of Attorney appears at Figure 5.1.

Figure 5.1

POWER OF ATTORNEY

      KNOW ALL MEN BY THESE PRESENTS, that I, Brett A. Rosenbloom, of Delaware County, Pennsylvania, hereby revoke any general power of attorney that I have heretofore given to any person, and by these Presents do constitute, make and appoint my brother, Eric J. Rosenbloom, of Delaware County, Pennsylvania, my true and lawful attorney.

      1. To ask, demand, sue for, recover and receive all sums of money, debts, goods, merchandise, chattels, effects and things of whatsoever nature or description which are now or hereafter shall be or become owing, due, payable, or belonging to me in or by any right whatsoever, and upon receipt thereof, to make, sign, execute and deliver such receipts, releases or other discharges for the same, respectively, as he shall think fit.

      2. To deposit any moneys which may come into his hands as such attorney with any bank or bankers, either in my or his own name, and any of such money or any other money to which I am entitled which now is or shall be so deposited to withdraw as he shall think fit; to sign mutual savings bank and federal savings and loan association withdrawal orders; to sign and endorse checks payable to my order and to draw, accept, make, endorse, discount, or otherwise deal with any bills of exchange, checks, promissory notes or other commercial or mercantile instruments; to borrow any sum or sums of money on such terms and with such security as he may think fit and for that purpose to execute all notes or other instruments which may be necessary or proper; and to have access to any and all safe deposit boxes registered in my name.

      3. To sell, assign, transfer and dispose of any and all stocks, bonds (including U. S. Savings Bonds), loans, mortgages or other securities registered in my name; and to collect and receipt for all interest and dividends due and payable to me.

      4. To invest in my name in any stock, shares, bonds (including U. S. Treasury Bonds referred to as "flower bonds"), securities or other property, real or personal, as to vary such investments as he, in his sole discretion, may deem best; and to vote at meetings of shareholders or other meetings of any corporation or company and to execute any proxies or other instruments in connection therewith.

      5. To enter into and upon my real estate, and to let, manage, and improve the same or any part thereof, and to repair or otherwise improve or alter, and to insure any buildings thereon; to sell, either at public or private sale or exchange any part or parts of my real estate or personal property for such consideration and upon such terms as he shall think fit, and to execute and deliver good and sufficient deeds or other instruments for the conveyance or transfer of the same, with such covenants of warranty or otherwise as he shall see fit, and to give good and effectual receipts for all or any part of the purchase price or other consideration; and to mortgage my real estate and in connection therewith to execute bonds and warrants and all other necessary instruments and documents.

      6. To contract with any person for leasing for such periods, at such rents and subject to such conditions as he shall see fit, all or any of my said real estate; to give notice to quit to any tenant or occupier thereof; and to receive and recover from all tenants and occupiers thereof or of any part thereof all rents, arrears of rent, and sums of money which now are or shall hereafter become due and payable in respect thereof; and also on non-payment thereof or of any part thereof to take all necessary or proper means and proceedings for determining the tenancy or occupation of such tenants or occupiers, and for ejecting the tenants or occupiers and recovering the possession thereof.

Figure 5.1 cont.

7. To commence, prosecute, discontinue or defend all actions or other legal proceedings pertaining to me or my estate or any part thereof; to settle, compromise, or submit to arbitration any debt, demand or other right or matter due me or concerning my estate as he, in his sole discretion, shall deem best and for such purpose to execute and deliver such releases, discharges or other instruments as he may deem necessary and advisable; and to satisfy mortgages, including the execution of a good and sufficient release, or other discharge of such mortgage.

8. To execute, acknowledge and file all Federal, State and Local tax returns of every kind and nature, including without limitation, income, gift and property tax returns.

9. To engage, employ and dismiss any agents, clerks, servants or other persons as he, in his sole discretion, shall deem necessary and advisable.

10. To convey and transfer any of my property to trustees who shall hold the same for my benefit and/or the benefit of my children and other members of my immediate family upon such trust terms and conditions as to my attorney shall deem desirable.

11. To make gifts to my wife and/or issue upon such terms and conditions as he in his discretion shall determine.

12. In general, to do all other acts, deeds and matters whatsoever in or about my estate, property and affairs as fully and effectually to all intents and purposes as I could do in my own proper person if personally present, giving to my said attorney power to make and substitute under him an attorney or attorneys for all the purposes herein described, hereby ratifying and confirming all that the said attorney or substitute or substitutes shall do therein by virtue of these Presents.

13. In addition to the powers and discretion herein specially given and conferred upon my attorney, and notwithstanding any usage or custom to the contrary, to have the full power, right and authority to do, perform and to cause to be done and performed all such acts, deeds and matters in connection with my property and estate as he, in his sole discretion, shall deem reasonable, necessary and proper, as fully, effectually and absolutely as if he were the absolute owner and possessor thereof.

14. In the event of my disability or incompetency, from whatever cause, this power of attorney shall not thereby be revoked.

IN WITNESS WHEREOF, I have hereunto set my hand and seal this   day of   , 19 .

_____(SEAL)
BRETT A. ROSENBLOOM

STATE OF PENNSYLVANIA:
                        ss.
COUNTY OF DELAWARE

Before me, the undersigned, a Notary Public within and for the County of Delaware, Commonwealth of Pennsylvania, personally appeared Brett A. Rosenbloom, known to me to be the person whose name is subscribed to the within instrument, and acknowledged that he executed the same for the purposes therein contained.

IN WITNESS WHEREOF, I have hereunto set my hand and official seal this   day of   , 19 .

_____
Notary Public

Tools and Techniques

WHAT ARE THE TAX IMPLICATIONS?

The holder of the Durable Power of Attorney, if the Power is broadly drawn, can be given: (1) the right to execute on behalf of the principal all tax returns including income and gift tax returns; (2) the power to make gifts on behalf of the principal (thereby possibly reducing the principal's estate for Federal Estate Tax purposes) and (3) the right to elect to treat gifts made by the competent spouse as split between the competent spouse and the incompetent principal for federal gift tax purposes. Other nontax powers which can be given under a power of attorney include the right to buy or sell real estate, the right to invest in stocks, bonds or other securities, or the right to sue on behalf of the principal.

"Flower Bonds" are government obligations issued by the U.S. Treasury which can generally be purchased at a discount and can be redeemed at par value to pay federal estate taxes if owned by an individual at his death and includible in his estate. ("Flower bonds" are discussed in depth in Chapter 10.)

Due to the relatively low interest rate payable on flower bonds, they are often not purchased until a very short time before death. The Treasury has taken the position that flower bonds purchased pursuant to a Power of Attorney at a time when the principal was incompetent were not purchased by the decedent.[1] The courts in the State of New York have rejected the Treasury position on the basis that under New York law the transaction was only voidable and not void.[2] A *Durable* Power of Attorney which specifically authorizes the purchase of flower bonds should be beyond Treasury attack in all jurisdictions that recognize such Powers.

ISSUES AND IMPLICATIONS IN COMMUNITY PROPERTY STATES

Because community property is owned equally by both husband and wife, many transactions require the signature of both spouses in order to be effective. Particularly in situations where the couple has a community property proprietorship business, the incapacity of one spouse could seriously affect the stability and viability of the business.

Incapacity of one spouse could also prevent the sale of securities or the sale of or even borrowing against real or other property. Because of presumptions of community property status in many instances, title companies and others concerned with the completeness of title transfer usually require the signature (personally or by exercise of a power of attorney) of both spouses even though the property is in the name of only one spouse.

In many cases, a wife will give a power of attorney to her husband if he is the primary manager of the property for the sake of convenience of management. However, consideration should also be given to providing a method of dealing with both halves of the property if either the husband or the wife should suffer any incapacity.

It should be noted that while all states authorize some form of durable power, not all states have adopted the Uniform Durable Power of Attorney provisions.

QUESTIONS AND ANSWERS

Question — How broad can a Durable Power of Attorney be written?

Answer — The extent of the powers conferred by the principal upon the attorney-in-fact are limited only by the desires of the principal. The example of a broad general Power of Attorney shown on pages 40-41 is an attempt by a principal to confer upon the "attorney-in-fact" the right to act to the same extent the principal could have acted if the principal were present and able to act.

Question — What is the duration of a Durable Power of Attorney?

Answer — The Durable Power of Attorney, once properly executed, continues until revoked by the principal or until it terminates by its terms on the death of the principal. However, as a practical matter, many insurance companies and financial institutions attempt not to recognize any Power of Attorney which has been executed more than six months before the date it is presented for use. The obvious purpose of this "rule of convenience" is to make certain that the Power of Attorney is still in full force and effect.

However, the six month rule suggested above should not be applicable to a Durable Power of Attorney. The Durable Power of Attorney by its very nature is designed to cover the situation where the principal becomes incompetent. If, in fact, the principal is incompetent, it would be impossible for the attorney to obtain a freshly dated Power of Attorney.

Question — Can there be more than one attorney-in-fact under a Durable Power of Attorney?

Answer — Yes; however, caution must be taken in drafting the Power of Attorney. If the Power of Attorney merely names John Doe and Mary Roe as the holders of the Power, then both must act together in order for the Power to be operable. If, however, the Power is in favor of, "John Doe *or* Mary Roe, either of them to act in place of the principal," then each person can act independently.

Furthermore, the Power of Attorney can provide for successor "attorneys-in-fact" in the event of the primary attorney's death or inability to serve.

Question — Does a Power of Attorney terminate upon disability?

Answer — A Power of Attorney which is not a "Durable Power of Attorney" terminates upon disability. However, actions taken by the attorney-in-fact when he or she is unaware of the principal's disability are binding upon the principal.

A Durable Power of Attorney by its very definition survives and continues and is not affected by subsequent disability or incapacity of the principal.

Question — Does the death of the principal terminate a Durable Power of Attorney?

Answer — Yes. The death of the principal terminates a Power of Attorney whether or not it is durable. However, as in the case of a Power of Attorney which is not durable, the Durable Power of Attorney permits the attorney-in-fact who has no notice of the death of his principal to continue to act according to and under the Power until the attorney-in-fact learns of the death of the principal.

Question — What is the relationship between the "attorney-in-fact" under a Durable Power of Attorney and a court appointed guardian for the incompetent?

Answer — The Durable Power of Attorney continues in operation after the appointment of a guardian for the incompetent. However, the guardian of the incompetent appointed by the Court has the same rights as the principal and can terminate the Durable Power of Attorney on behalf of his ward, the incompetent.

Footnote References

Durable Power of Attorney

1. See, Treasury Form PD 1782, Application for Redemption at Par of United States Treasury Bonds Eligible for Payment of Federal Estate Tax; Treasury Regulation 306.28(G).
2. *Estate of Watson v. Simon*, 442 F. Supp. 1000 (DC NY 1977), reversed on jurisdictional grounds.

Chapter 6

EMPLOYEE DEATH BENEFIT EXCLUSION

WHAT IS IT?

The Internal Revenue Code allows the estate or other beneficiary of an employee to receive up to $5,000 from the decedent's employer free from income tax. This exclusion applies to the beneficiary of any employee of a corporation, a sole proprietorship, or a partnership.

The income tax exclusion is available regardless of whether the benefit is paid voluntarily or under contract, whether paid directly or to a trust, and whether paid in a lump sum or in installments. The exclusion will be allowed regardless of whether the benefit is paid to a former or to an active employee.

WHEN IS THE USE OF SUCH A DEVICE INDICATED?

1. When an employer desires to reward key officers or long service employees by providing an income tax free fringe benefit.

2. When an employee-stockholder wishes to provide a fringe benefit that will be income tax free to his or her spouse or other beneficiary.

3. When an employee needs additional financial security to provide for his or her family upon death.

WHAT ARE THE REQUIREMENTS?

1. The $5,000 exclusion is not available when an employee has a nonforfeitable right to receive that amount while living. (An exception is made for total distributions made within one taxable year of the recipient under a qualified pension or profit-sharing plan or under some tax-deferred annuity plans.)[1]

2. The $5,000 exclusion is not available for payments under a joint and survivor annuity where the annuity starting date occurs (annuity payments have begun) before the death of the employee.[2]

3. The $5,000 exclusion is not available with respect to interest payments on amounts held by an employer under an agreement to pay interest.[3]

4. The $5,000 exclusion is not available for payments with respect to self-employed individuals except for distributions from a qualified retirement plan made by reason of the employee's death.[4]

HOW IT IS DONE — AN EXAMPLE

Generally, an employer will select one or more key officers, long service employees, or even himself (assuming he is an employee). The business will agree to pay that employee's widow or family a certain amount in the event the employee dies while employed. The employer can provide this benefit entirely on a selective basis and thus can pick and choose the executives, supervisors, or other employees to be covered.

WHAT ARE THE TAX IMPLICATIONS?

1. When benefits are paid out to the widow or family of the deceased employee, those benefits, assuming they are reasonable, will be deductible as a business expense.[5]

2. The first $5,000 paid by (or on behalf of) an employer as a death benefit will be income tax free to the employee's estate or beneficiary.[6]

3. Amounts paid by an employer in excess of $5,000 will usually be taxable as ordinary income since such payments will generally be considered additional compensation for past services rendered by the employee (even if the employer uses tax-free life insurance proceeds to fund the benefit). However, in the case of a purely voluntary payment by an employer, there are some cases in which the amounts in excess of $5,000 have been considered as tax-exempt gifts.[7]

HOW CAN LIFE INSURANCE ENHANCE THIS TOOL?

In many instances, an employer may use a life insurance policy to fund its promise. The corporation would insure the employee and own, pay premiums on, and be named beneficiary of the policy. The policy cash values would grow tax free and are considered a corporate asset.

At the employee's death, the employer would receive the policy proceeds. Once the employer receives the insurance proceeds, it would then pay the promised amount to the beneficiary of the employee. Assuming the payments were reasonable, they would be deductible by the corporation as a business expense. (Amounts in excess of $5,000 will not be deductible if such amounts are considered gifts.)

Premiums for the insurance purchased to fund the agreement are not deductible by the employer.[8] The death proceeds, when received by the employer, will be income tax free.[9]

IMPLICATIONS AND ISSUES IN COMMUNITY PROPERTY STATES

As stated previously in this chapter, the $5,000 employee's death benefit exclusion is not available when the benefit is

Tools and Techniques

nonforfeitable (other than lump sum distributions from a qualified pension or profit sharing plan or some tax deferred annuity plans). If the spouse is the beneficiary of the death benefit, no community property issues would arise. Problems could arise, however, if the spouse were not the beneficiary of the death benefit and did not consent to the designation of beneficiary. A spouse usually cannot be deprived of community property rights without giving consent. The major question then becomes whether the death benefit is community property. The other possible question is whether the Employee Retirement Income Security Act (ERISA) will preempt state law, a possibility that is discounted by many estate planners in this particular situation.

IRS regulations specify that the $5,000 exclusion does not apply to amounts constituting income payable during the employee's life as compensation for services, such as bonuses or uncollected salary, or other amounts which the employee possessed a nonforfeitable right to receive while living (other than distributions from qualified plans).

The rules relating to distributions from qualified plans, which have been previously discussed, will apply to determine whether a benefit payable from a qualified plan is community property.

If, however, the death benefit subject to the $5,000 exclusion is not paid from a qualified plan, difficult issues arise. Where an employer voluntarily makes payment to the survivor of an employee, the payment would not be community property. The employee would have had no property interest or contractual right before his death. In some cases, however, courts have found an implied agreement on the part of the employer to pay the death benefit. Thus, the lack of an express agreement to pay death benefits is not alone sufficient to support a claim that the employer's payment of the death benefit was intended as a gift.

In the absence of a gift, it is likely that the death benefit will be found to be community property. California courts have held that accidental death benefits paid by an employer are community property.

If the death benefit is community property, only one-half of the death benefit would be includable in the employee's gross estate.

QUESTIONS AND ANSWERS

Question — Is the $5,000 exclusion available if the payment is made in installments?

Answer — Generally, the $5,000 exclusion is available whether amounts were paid in a lump sum or in installments.[10] If the death benefit is paid in installments, the $5,000 exclusion will be treated as part or all of the cost basis of the employee. Under the annuity rules, an exclusion ratio is determined. Basically, a fraction is established. The employee's "investment in the contract" is divided

by the "expected return" under the contract. The resulting quotient is the percentage of each payment which may be excluded from gross income. In this case, the surviving spouse or other beneficiary would use $5,000 (or the amount the employer paid if less) as his or her cost or investment in the contract. The expected return would be the total amount estimated to be received under the contract.

Question — Will a deduction be allowed for amounts paid by an employer in excess of $5,000?

Answer — The Internal Revenue Service will examine the specific situation. If facts indicate that the payment was purely a gift or was made to disguise a dividend, the deduction will be denied. For example, if the widow of the employee is a controlling stockholder, the Internal Revenue Service could claim payments are in essence constructive dividends. This would make the entire death benefit, including the first $5,000, taxable to the widow and nondeductible by the corporation.[11]

Question — What are the estate tax ramifications of a voluntary death benefit paid by the employer to the survivor or other beneficiary of a deceased employee?

Answer — Where an employer voluntarily makes payments to the survivor of an employee, there will be no inclusion of those amounts in the employee's estate;[12] however, benefits provided will be includible in the employee's estate if, at the time of his death, the employee was, in fact, receiving, or had an enforceable right to receive, lifetime benefits under a contract or plan.

All rights and benefits which the employee had by reason of his employment (except rights under a qualified pension or profit-sharing plan) are treated as one contract or plan in determining whether the employee had an enforceable right to lifetime payments. Therefore, inclusion of death payments cannot be avoided by providing lifetime benefits under one arrangement and death benefits under another plan.[13]

Even if the employer promised only a pure death benefit and made no promises to pay income during the lifetime of the employee, amounts paid to his widow or other beneficiaries will still be includible in his estate if the employee retained, at the time of his death, power to alter, amend, revoke, or terminate the agreement or change the beneficiary.[14]

Question — If an employee works for two or more employers, can the employee's survivors take two or more $5,000 exclusions?

Answer — No. Each employee is allowed only one $5,000 exclusion regardless of the number of employers or beneficiaries or plans involved.

Question — Can an employer provide a death benefit to more than one beneficiary?

Answer — Yes, but the $5,000 exclusion would have to be divided among the beneficiaries. The apportionment ratio would be:

$$\$5,000 \times \frac{\text{Beneficiary's portion of death benefit}}{\text{Total death benefit payable}}$$

For example, Allan Gart, the president of the Allover Travel Company, died recently. Pursuant to an agreement with Allan, Allover Travel Company pays a total of $20,000 to various members of his family—$10,000 is paid to Allan's widow, $4,000 to Allan's son, and $6,000 to his daughter. These were the only taxable employer-produced death benefits received by Allan's family. The firm was under no obligation to provide Allan with retirement or disability benefits. Figure 6.1 shows Allan's widow received $10,000 out of the $20,000 total death benefit. So she is entitled to exclude an amount equal to ½ of the $5,000 exclusion, $2,500. Allan's son received $4,000 out of the $20,000 total, ⅕ of the total. Therefore, he is entitled to ⅕ of the $5,000 exclusion, $1,000. Allan's daughter is allowed to take the remaining portion of the exclusion ($5,000 – $3,500), $1,500.

Question — Will payments made under the pre-retirement death benefit provisions of a nonqualified deferred compensation program be eligible for the $5,000 exclusion?

Answer — The $5,000 death benefit exclusion can be used against a variety of death benefits, including a death benefit made under a deferred compensation plan for key executives. With some exceptions (as previously noted), the executive must not have had a nonforfeitable right to such amounts while he was alive.

ASRS, Secs. 53, ¶20.4(g); 59, ¶930.3(b); 61, ¶230; 64.

Footnote References
Employee Death Benefit Exclusion

1. IRC Section 101(b)(2).
2. Reg. §1.101-2(b)(2).
3. IRC Section 101(c); Reg. §1.101-3(a).
4. IRC Section 101(b)(3).
5. See *Rubber Associates, Inc.*, 335 F.2d 75 (CA-6, 1964); *Fifth Ave. Coach Lines Inc.*, 31 T.C. 1080 (1958).
6. IRC Section 101(b)(2).
7. The courts, following the rules laid down by the Supreme Court in *Comm'r. v. Duberstein*, 363 U.S. 278 (1960) are divided as to whether the payments are tax free gifts or taxable compensation. Each case is decided on its facts. See *Flarsheim v. U.S.*, 156 F.2d 105 (CA-8, 1946); *Simpson v. U.S.*, 261 F.2d 497 (CA-7, 2958).
8. IRC Section 264(a)(1).
9. IRC Section 101.
10. Reg. §1.101-2(a)(1).
11. See *Lengsfield v. Comm'r.*, 241 F.2d 508 (CA-5, 1957); *Schner-Block Co., Inc. v. Comm'r.*, 329 F.2d 875 (CA-2, 1964) aff'g T.C. Memo 1963-166.
12. *Estate of Barr*, 40 T.C. 227 (1963); *Estate of Albright*, 42 T.C. 643 (1964).
13. Reg. §20.2039-1(b)(2)(Ex. 6).
14. IRC Sections 2036, 2038.

Figure 6.1

COMPUTING THE EMPLOYEE DEATH BENEFIT EXCLUSION				
INPUT:	**REMAINING EXCLUSION**	**$5,000**	**AMOUNT EXCLUDIBLE**	**AMOUNT INCLUDIBLE**
Input:	Payment to Beneficiary 1	$10,000	$2,500	$7,500
Input:	Payment to Beneficiary 2	$4,000	$1,000	$3,000
Input:	Payment to Beneficiary 3	$6,000	$1,500	$4,500
Input:	Payment to Beneficiary 4	$0	$0	$0
Input:	Payment to Beneficiary 5	$0	$0	$0
	Total Death Benefit Payable	$20,000	$5,000	$15,000

Tools and Techniques

Chapter 7

EMPLOYEE STOCK OWNERSHIP PLAN

WHAT IS IT?

An employee stock ownership plan, commonly referred to as an ESOP (the ESOP plan trust is usually called an employee stock ownership trust or ESOT), is technically considered a stock bonus plan and the trust may qualify as a tax-exempt employee trust.[1]

Stock bonus plans are one of the oldest forms of deferred compensation recognized by the Internal Revenue Service. These plans are established by employers to provide benefits similar to those of a profit sharing plan, except that the employer contributions are not necessarily dependent on profits. Benefits may be distributable in the form of the employer's stock.

There are significant advantages to both the employer and the employee which can be derived from the stock bonus plan and, as a result, a significant increase in the use of such plans has occurred in recent years. The Tax Reform Acts of 1984 and 1986 have added provisions to the Internal Revenue Code (discussed below) which make ESOPs even more attractive to both the employer and the employee.

WHEN IS THE USE OF SUCH A DEVICE INDICATED?

An ESOP may be useful:

1. When a shareholder who is a substantial owner of a closely-held business would like to shift his investment, on a tax-deferred basis, into publicly traded securities. Amendments made to the Internal Revenue Code by the Tax Reform Act of 1984 permit tax-free rollover of the proceeds received from the sale of a business to an ESOP, if the proceeds are invested in another business, and are intended to encourage employee stock ownership (see discussion of mechanics under "What Are the Tax Implications", infra).

2. When an employer would like to obtain an income tax deduction with little or no cash outlay. A current deduction is allowed for both employer contributions of cash and for contributions of stock (including stock of the employer company) or other property contributed to the ESOP.[2] A contribution of an employer's stock generates a deduction equal to its fair market value. The sizable deduction reduces cash flow out of the corporation in profit years and in loss years a carry-back is created which might result in a tax refund to the corporation.[3]

3. When an employer wants to create a market for its stock. An ESOP may be able to purchase treasury stock or authorized but unissued stock as well as stock owned by individual shareholders without causing a loss of corporate control by majority shareholders. (But note that if a defined contribution plan—other than a profit sharing plan—is established by an employer whose stock is not readily tradable on an established market and employer stock comprises more than 10 percent of the plan's assets, participating employees must be entitled to exercise voting rights on stock allocated to their account on certain major corporate matters.)

4. When a corporation faces an accumulated earnings threat. An ESOP can be used to take cash out of a corporation and thus reduce the potential for an IRS accumulated earnings tax problem. The reduction in taxable income of the corporation due to deductible contributions lessens the pressure on a corporation to pay dividends which are taxable at ordinary income rates to the recipient and nondeductible to the corporation.

5. When an employer is seeking a way to motivate and compensate long service employees. Since the ultimate value of an employee's ESOP interest is directly related to the value of the employee's stock, increased productivity and corporate growth become an employee concern. ESOPs also provide a means for employees (including shareholder-employees) to supplement social security as well as other corporate-provided retirement benefits.

6. When shareholders have large estates and would like to minimize death taxes and probate costs while increasing estate liquidity. An ESOP may result in substantial savings in federal and state death taxes and probate expenses. The Tax Reform Act of 1986 (TRA '86) allows a deduction from a deceased stockholder's estate for 50 percent of the proceeds, up to the lower of half of the taxable estate or the amount to produce a tax reduction of $750,000, from the estate's sale of employer securities to an ESOP.[4] When a shareholder sells part or all of his personally-owned corporate holdings to an ESOP, future growth on those shares is transferred to plan participants.

7. When a corporation desires to have payment of premiums for life insurance on key employees made from deductible contributions. In appropriate cases, life insurance payments on key employees, who are also shareholders, may be shifted to the ESOP from the corporation, and these premium payments, which are otherwise not deductible to the corporation, effectively become deductible contributions to the ESOP. The insurance policy is an investment of the ESOP and may

51

be the source of liquidity to buy the shareholder's stock at his death.

8. When an employer is seeking a means for financing corporate growth through the use of untaxed dollars. By selling rather than contributing stock to the ESOP, an employer can obtain a large amount of cash. Conversely, if the corporation had borrowed cash from a bank to finance corporate expansion, only interest payments on the loan would be deductible. The principal would have to be repaid with "expensive" (nondeductible) dollars. On the other hand, the corporation will get a deduction for the dollars it then contributes to the ESOP. The ESOP receives these free of tax and uses them (without reduction for income taxes) to repay the bank loan.

WHAT ARE THE REQUIREMENTS?

To qualify for favorable tax treatment, the requirements the ESOP and ESOT must meet include the following:

1. ESOPs meeting certain requirements may distribute benefits in the form of employer stock *or* cash. Participants must be given the right to receive employer stock if they so desire, unless the employer's charter or by-laws restrict the ownership of substantially all outstanding employer stock to employees and/or the ESOP. If ownership is so restricted, a participant need not be given the right to receive employer stock. The participant must then be given the right to receive his benefit in cash. If employer stock is distributed, participants must be given a "put" option for a limited time which allows them to force the employer to purchase the stock at its fair market value.[5] The put option requirement does not apply for tax years beginning after 1981 to a bank which maintains an ESOP if the bank is prohibited by law from redeeming or buying its own stock and participants are given the right to receive their benefits in cash. It appears that an ESOP with no cash distribution option (which would not be typical) is required to give a put option to participants only with respect to employer stock acquired by the plan after December 31, 1979 or acquired with proceeds of a loan obtained from or guaranteed by a disqualified person (unless the stock is readily tradable on an established securities market).

2. The plan must meet requirements pertaining to coverage, nondiscrimination in contributions, nondiscrimination in benefits, nonforfeitable rights on termination, nondiversion of assets, rules regarding forfeitures, and rules relative to the source of contributions. IRS regulations do not allow an ESOP to be integrated with social security contributions. Certain ESOPs in existence on November 1, 1977, with social security integration provisions were "grandfathered" and may be able to continue to use those provisions. As is the case for all qualified retirement plans, an ESOP must be in writing.

3. The trust must be for the exclusive benefit of the employees or their beneficiaries (e.g., the ESOP is not meant as a means of bailing out financially troubled employers).

4. The trust must be a United States trust and not a foreign trust.

5. The cost of employer stock purchased by the trustee must not exceed its fair market value. TRA '86 requires an independent appraisal for all ESOP security transactions.[6]

6. Participants must be entitled to vote employer stock which has been allocated to their accounts if the stock is registered under the Securities Exchange Act of 1934. If the employer's stock is not readily tradable on an established market and more than 10 percent of the plan's assets are invested in employer stock, the plan must give participants voting rights on major corporate issues (generally those involving the approval or disapproval of any corporate merger or consolidation, recapitalization, reclassification, liquidation, dissolution, sale of substantially all assets of a trade or business, or similar transactions) on employer stock acquired after December 31, 1979.[7]

7. Participants who have completed 10 years of participation must be given the opportunity to diversify 25 percent of their account balances at age 55 and an additional 25 percent at age 60. This applies only to stock acquired after December 31, 1986.[8]

8. With respect to distributions attributable to stock acquired after December 31, 1986, the plan must provide that, if the participant elects (and required spousal consent is properly given), the distribution of a participant's account balance will commence within one year after the plan year (1) in which he separates from service by reason of attainment of normal retirement age, disability, or death, or (2) which is the fifth plan year following the plan year in which he otherwise separates from service.[9]

9. The plan must insure that, in the case of certain "qualified sales" (after October 22, 1986) of employer securities by a participant (under Code section 1042) or executor (under Code section 2057) to the ESOP, no portion of the assets of the plan attributable to the securities purchased by the plan may accrue or be allocated for the benefit of (1) the taxpayer who makes the election under Section 1042 (or the decedent whose executor makes the election under Section 2057), (2) any individual who is a member of the family (brother, sister, spouse, ancestor, lineal descendant) of the taxpayer or decedent, or (3) any person who owns, or is considered as owning under the attribution rules of Section 318(a), more than 25% (by number or value) of any class of outstanding stock of the employer or any corporation which is a member of the same controlled group of corporations as is the employer.[10]

HOW IT IS DONE — EXAMPLES

A corporate client has been consistently earning $200,000 per year. The corporation has no pension or profit-sharing plan. The employees are eager to see some type of deferred compensation program instituted. Because of an expansion program, the corporation periodically is in a cash-poor position. The schedule below shows the amount of the increase in corporate working capital by comparing an ESOP with a profit-sharing plan and no deferred compensation plan.

From the comparison, it is clear that establishing an ESOP gives the greatest increase in working capital.

A corporate client needs a new building which will cost approximately $250,000. The only available loans require an amortization of the $250,000 at the rate of $50,000 per year for five years plus interest on the unpaid balance. Using the schedule set forth below, if the corporation established a profit-sharing plan, only $66,000 would be left after taxes on $200,000 of earnings in order to amortize the principal debt and pay the interest. Clearly this would not be enough money. If the corporation had no plan, sufficient monies would be available to amortize the debt and pay the interest although the net worth increase after such payments would be rather small. If an ESOP were established, the ESOP could borrow the $250,000 from the bank (the loan may have to be guaranteed by the corporation) and the ESOP would immediately purchase $250,000 of capital stock from the corporation. The corporation's net working capital would be immediately increased by $250,000. The corporation would then make contributions to the ESOP on an annual basis and the ESOP would repay the bank.

	No Plan	Profit Sharing Plan	ESOP
Earnings Before Tax	$200,000	$200,000	$200,000
Contributions (15% × $600,000 of compensation eligible for coverage)	0	90,000	90,000
Taxable Income	$200,000	$110,000	$110,000
Tax (assume combined federal and state bracket is 40%)	80,000	44,000	44,000
Net Earnings After Taxes	$120,000	$ 66,000	$ 66,000
Net Worth Increase: Net Earnings After Taxes	$120,000	$ 66,000	$ 66,000
Cash from Sale of Capital Stock to ESOP	0	0	90,000
Increase in Working Capital	$120,000	$ 66,000	$156,000

The Deficit Reduction Act of 1984 sought to encourage banks, insurance companies, and corporations actively engaged in the business of lending money to make leveraged ESOP loans by providing a 50 percent exclusion for interest received or accrued on loans to leveraged ESOPs made after July 18, 1984, which were used to acquire employer securities. TRA '86 extends the 50 percent interest exclusion to include security acquisition loans to an ESOP from a mutual fund. TRA '86 also extends the interest exclusion to lenders who refinance security acquisition loans.[11]

A third example for the use of the ESOP is a situation where a majority of the stock of a close corporation is owned by one individual, and his wife and/or children own the balance of the stock. The stock represents a part of the individual's estate, but not "more than 35 percent of his adjusted gross estate" and therefore not enough to qualify for a redemption under Section 303 of the Internal Revenue Code. Additionally, the spouse and/or the children, also shareholders, are beneficiaries of the estate and therefore a redemption of the stock by the corporation would constitute a dividend to the estate (by reason of the attribution rules of section 318 of the Code). Also consider that the corporation may not have sufficient funds to redeem all the shares of stock and certainly any partial redemption would also constitute a dividend.

Creation of the ESOP would establish an entity that could purchase all or any portion of the stock owned by the estate and not create dividend consequences to the estate. Such a purchase would indirectly give rise to a deduction for the corporation, a deduction it would not get if the purchase had been made directly from the estate. Although such a transaction has been given approval by the Internal Revenue Service in at least one private letter ruling, it is advisable to obtain a favorable ruling in advance of the sale.

The Internal Revenue Service has issued revenue procedures[12] with some rather stringent requirements that must be met for an advance ruling.

The fourth example of the use of an ESOP involves the conversion of premiums on nondeductible key individual life insurance into a tax deduction. Assume that a corporation is owned by two or more stockholders equally and the stockholders desire to have a buy-sell agreement (either an entity or cross purchase type) funded by life insurance so that on the death of any one stockholder there will be sufficient monies to purchase or redeem the shares of stock of the decedent and permit the company to continue in business. Payment of the life insurance premiums are normally nondeductible.

If, however, the company established an ESOP and the investment committee directed the ESOP to purchase key individual insurance on the lives of all of the stockholders, then upon the death of any stockholder, the trust being the beneficiary of the life insurance policy, would be entitled to the proceeds and would then be able to use the proceeds and

Tools and Techniques

negotiate with the personal representative of the deceased stockholder for the purchase of the shares of stock at the then fair market value of those shares on the date of the decedent's death. Consideration must be given to the possibility that the ESOP would not be able to acquire the stock which then would leave the proceeds in the plan. An alternative may be to have the corporation continue to own the policies and contribute enough stock to the plan each year to offset the insurance premium tax cost.

Final regulations prohibit an ESOP from buying life insurance with the proceeds of a loan obtained from or guaranteed by a disqualified person. In addition, a leveraged ESOP must not obligate itself to purchase stock at an indefinite future time (although it can be given an option to acquire stock).

WHAT ARE THE TAX IMPLICATIONS?

A corporation is allowed a deduction for contributions made to the ESOP even if it had no profits during the year the contribution was made.[13] The excess deduction might therefore generate a net operating loss carryback with a resulting tax refund.

An employer can generally deduct a contribution to a single ESOP of up to 15 percent of the total compensation paid to all participants in the plan. If the employer deducts less than 15 percent of covered compensation, the difference between the amount which was actually contributed and the amount which could have been deducted may no longer be carried forward and used to increase the deduction limit in future years. The deduction, even with "carryovers", generally cannot exceed 25 percent of covered compensation. TRA '86 eliminated the unused contribution carry forward effective for taxable years beginning after December 31, 1986; unused pre-1987 contribution carryforwards may still be used.[14]

An employer can combine an ESOP of the stock bonus type with a money purchase pension plan (which need not, but can, be an ESOP) to increase its annual deduction to 25 percent of plan participants' compensation.

Special deduction rules apply to plans which have incurred debt to purchase employer stock. An employer may contribute as much as 25 percent of covered compensation to a single ESOP where the contributions are applied to make principal payments on the loan. Additional unlimited deductions are allowed for employer contributions used to pay interest on the loan. Limitations on allocations to employee accounts which apply if more than one-third of contributions are allocated to certain key employees may limit the availability of these special deduction limits in some circumstances.[15]

The employer does not have to make the contribution to the ESOP in stock of the employer. The contribution may be made in cash, any other property, or employer stock. However, a contribution of property may involve a prohibited transaction or other problems which should be carefully examined. Any one of the three contribution media, alone or in combination with the others, will create a deduction to the corporation equal to the cash and the fair market value of the assets being transferred.

If the corporation transfers assets to the ESOP that have appreciated in value, the transfer will constitute a realization of income to the corporation.[16] For example, if the corporation bought stock which grew from $3 to $8 a share, a contribution of that stock would result in a $5 per share gain. This is true on the transfer of all property with the exception of cash and stock of the employer.

The corporation is allowed a special corporate deduction for cash dividends paid with respect to stock held on the dividend record date by an ESOP, provided the dividends (a) are paid directly in cash to participants or their beneficiaries, or (b) are paid indirectly to them through the plan within 90 days after the close of the plan year, or (c) are used to make payments on a loan incurred to purchase qualifying employer securities.[17]

Code section 1042, added by the Tax Reform Act of 1984, provides a major income tax break on sales of stock to an ESOP. Under this section recognition of gain may be deferred on certain sales of closely held stock to an ESOP if (1) such sale would qualify for long term capital gain treatment, (2) after the sale the ESOP owns 30 percent of the total value of the employer securities, *and* (3) within a 15-month period (beginning 3 months prior to the day of sale) "qualified replacement securities" are purchased. A "qualified replacement security" includes corporate stock or bonds issued by a domestic corporation which, for the taxable year of issuance, does not have more than 25 percent of passive investment income. If the cost of the replacement securities is less than the amount of the deferred gain, the difference is currently taxable.[18]

Although it is possible for a shareholder to obtain beneficial nonrecognition of gain on the sale of his shares to an ESOP under Code section 1042, there is a pitfall to avoid. With respect to sales of securities after October 22, 1986, if the ESOP fails to meet the requirements of Code section 409(n) (see paragraph (9) under "What are the Requirements," above), a penalty tax equal to 50% of the amount of any prohibited accrual or allocation will be levied against the plan under Code section 4979A. In addition, the amount of any prohibited accrual or allocation will be treated as if distributed to the individual involved and taxed as such. Up to 5% of the securities purchased by the ESOP in the Section 1042 or 2057 transaction can be allocated to the benefit of lineal descendants of the seller without creating any adverse tax consequences.

Employer contributions are not currently taxable to participating employees. ESOP trust assets grow tax free, even if an employee's rights become nonforfeitable. An employee pays no tax until a distribution is made to him (see the discussion of the tax treatment of distributions in chapter 22).

IMPLICATIONS AND ISSUES IN COMMUNITY PROPERTY STATES

Benefits from qualified plans (pension/profit sharing plans, HR-10 plans, IRAs and ESOPs) are generally held to be community property to the extent contributions are made by or on behalf of a married employee who is a resident of one of the eight community property states (enumerated in the Introduction discussion of community property) during the period of employment.

This rule, while relatively simple to state, can present significant problems when applied to specific situations. The major areas of difficulty are divorce and death of an employee.

There is a question after the enactment of the Employee Retirement Income Security Act of 1974 (ERISA) as to whether community property laws could continue to apply to qualified plan benefits. Some argued that ERISA "preempted" state community property laws. It was also argued that award of a part of an employee's qualified plan benefits to his spouse was an assignment or alienation of benefits prohibited by ERISA. If the courts followed these arguments, spouses in community property states would no longer be entitled to the 50 percent of qualified plan benefits which they had prior to ERISA. Most courts faced with the issue have determined that ERISA does not supersede state community property laws.

There were other problems in connection with the community property aspects of qualified plan benefits which have been resolved by recent legislation. For example, prior to 1972, a spouse's community property interest in his or her spouse's qualified plan benefits was included in his or her gross estate if he or she predeceased the spouse with the qualified plan benefits. Estate taxes were imposed even though the surviving spouse may have had no immediate access to the benefit to provide funds to pay the tax. Unfortunate situations also arose where the appraised "value" of the deceased spouse's community property interest was much greater than the benefit actually received from the plan; for example, when the surviving spouse was less than 100 percent vested and terminated employment soon after his or her spouse's death.

To solve this problem, a provision was added to the Internal Revenue Code in 1972.[19] It provided that the value of any interest a deceased spouse may have in qualified plan benefits due solely to community property laws will not be included in his or her gross estate. However, TRA '86 repealed this provision and thus, the old problems are renewed. The problems of having estate tax imposed with the plan benefits being unavailable to pay the tax, and overvaluing the plan benefits actually received, remain. However, most such benefits go to the surviving spouse and thus are subject to the marital deduction and no federal death tax is due.

The law still provided, however, that if any employee with qualified plan benefits predeceased his or her spouse, and benefits were paid to a beneficiary other than the surviving spouse, the surviving spouse had made a gift of 50 percent of the benefits payable to other beneficiaries (to the extent the benefits were community property). This situation was remedied by the Tax Reform Act of 1976. A provision was added to the Internal Revenue Code to provide that the surviving spouse has not made a gift if benefits are payable to other beneficiaries.[20] TRA '86 repeals this provision. Thus, it may be found that the surviving spouse has made a taxable gift where the participant has directed both community property interests in the benefit to other beneficiaries. However, with the significant rights given to non-participant spouses by the Retirement Equity Act (1984), it is now difficult to have significant plan proceeds distributed without the spouse's permission. Such accidental and unintended taxable gifts, if not within a specific exclusion, can be a problem for persons not aware of the possible trap.

A question arises as to whether a spouse's consent to the designation of a trust as a beneficiary of the employee's plan benefits is a transfer with a retained life estate under Section 2038 of the Internal Revenue Code. If the spouse is a lifetime beneficiary of the trust, care must be exercised to minimize the possibility that the IRS will claim that the spouse's community property share of plan benefits remaining in the trust is subject to federal estate tax upon her death.

The nine community property states have adopted varying positions to deal with the problem of valuing qualified plan benefits for purposes of division in a divorce. Prior to 1976, for example, California courts previously divided only *vested* qualified plan benefits, holding that non-vested benefits were "mere expectancies." Later a 1976 decision of the California Supreme Court overruled the prior position and held that *non-vested* qualified plan benefits were community property assets subject to division in a divorce proceeding. The benefits can be valued using actuarial methods. The court, recognizing that unfairness may result if the benefit does not actually "vest", stated that it may be appropriate in certain situations to divide benefit payments as they are received (rather than fixing a lump sum value at the time of the divorce). Thus, each spouse would share the risk that the full benefit would fail to fully vest.

QUESTIONS AND ANSWERS

Question — What are some problems associated with an ESOP?

Answer — One problem relates to the need for annual revaluation. If the employer's stock is not readily tradable on an established market, an independent appraisal is necessary annually to establish the value of the stock for contribution purposes (if the corporation contributes its stock) or for purposes of determining a proper purchase price (if the ESOP purchases stock from the corporation or from any third party stockholder). This valuation is always subject to question by the Internal Revenue Service and the Department of Labor.

Tools and Techniques

Question — If there are no stock purchases or stock contributions during the year, is an annual appraisal still necessary?

Answer — An annual appraisal is probably still necessary in order to meet the reporting requirements established by ERISA with respect to the current value of the plan assets and the ERISA requirement that the value of a participant's account be determined annually. This information would have to be submitted to the Labor Department, and current value probably could not be determined without such appraisal. If there is a purchase of employer stock by the ESOP trust, the value of the stock would have to be ascertained at the time of purchase. If an ESOP were to pay a price greater than the fair market value of the employer's stock, the investment would be considered improper and might result in a disqualification of the plan.

Question — Are there any provisions of ERISA that do not apply to the ESOP?

Answer — ERISA treats the ESOP as an individual account plan. An individual account plan escapes that part of the ERISA reporting provisions that requires a statement of an actuary and is also exempt from paying plan termination insurance premiums to the Pension Benefit Guaranty Corporation.

Question — Can an ESOP allow "qualified voluntary employee contributions" and nondeductible employee contributions?

Answer — Before TRA '86, participating employees could voluntarily contribute on a nondeductible basis up to 10 percent of compensation (subject to ERISA limits on annual additions). A voluntary deductible contribution of up to $2,000 could have been made to an ESOP (if the plan so provided).

TRA '86 does not permit voluntary deductible contributions to an ESOP.[21] However, TRA '86 does permit voluntary nondeductible contributions to an ESOP as well as to qualified pension, profit sharing, or stock bonus plans. These contributions will be deemed annual additions for maximum contribution purposes and thus, will have the impact of reducing the maximum employer contribution. The contributions will also have to pass a special nondiscrimination test.[22]

Provisions allowing voluntary nondeductible contributions to an ESOP should be approached with caution. Voluntary contributions to an ESOP should not be invested in employer stock unless the employer has complied with applicable federal and state securities requirements.

Question — What is the tax treatment of a distribution of employer stock to a plan participant?

Answer — If employer stock is paid to a plan participant in a lump-sum distribution (as that term is defined in the Internal Revenue Code), any unrealized appreciation on that stock which is not attributable to deductible employee voluntary contributions will not be taxed to the participant until the participant sells the stock.

This unrealized appreciation will be treated as long-term capital gain when the stock is sold. Any appreciation after distribution will be treated as long- or short-term capital gain depending on whether the participant has held the stock for the requisite holding period following the date of distribution. Under TRA '86 there is no deduction allowed for any portion of long-term capital gain realized on sale of stock after 1986, although for tax years beginning in 1987 the maximum tax rate on long-term capital gains was 28%. The cash portion and that portion of the lump sum distribution which is an amount equal to the employer contributions used to purchase stock will be taxed to the participant at the time of distribution subject to TRA '86 15 percent excise tax on distributions over $150,000. This excise tax can be avoided by spreading out distribution payments. (See discussion of the excess distribution and excess accumulation taxes in chapter 22.)

For example, if the individual receives an ESOP distribution of $30,000 cash and employer stock worth $100,000 on the distribution date and if the employer had contributed an amount equal to $70,000 which was used to purchase that stock, then the $30,000 gain will not be taxed to the participant until the securities are sold. But at the date of distribution, the $100,000 will be taxed under the lump-sum distribution rules in effect at the time of distribution.

Amounts attributable to deductible employee contributions are not considered part of a lump sum distribution and are taxed as ordinary income on receipt; any net unrealized appreciation on employer securities attributable to deductible employee contributions is taxed on distribution of the securities, whether or not they are sold.

If the participant or beneficiary of a participant does not take a lump-sum distribution of the cash or employer securities but instead receives the employer securities over a period in excess of one taxable year of the recipient (or beneficiary), the entire amount attributable to the employer contribution, qualified deductible employee voluntary contributions, and any subsequent appreciation on employer stock will be taxed at the ordinary income rate in effect at the time of distribution.

If the employee has made any nondeductible contributions to the ESOP, any unrealized appreciation in the employer stock which is attributable to such contributions will escape taxation until the participant sells the securities. At that time, the entire gain will be taxed.

Question — A participant in an ESOP retires. He receives a distribution of employer stock. Is he under any obligation to sell the stock to the ESOP?

Answer — It seems clear that no prearranged enforceable agreement can exist between the participants of the plan and the ESOP requiring that the participants, upon receipt of the stock distribution from the ESOP, sell those securities back to the ESOP. (ESOPs are allowed by law in order to encourage employers to place capital stock in the hands of employees. An agreement binding the employee to sell the stock back defeats this intent.) Regulations specifically prohibit a "call" option on employer stock acquired with the proceeds of a loan obtained from or guaranteed by a disqualified person.[23]

The IRS has permitted an ESOP to retain a "right of first refusal" on employer stock which is not publicly traded. In other words, if the participant wants to sell the employer stock he has been distributed to a third party, he must first offer it to the employer or the ESOP.[24]

It is possible to have a large number of stockholders with minimal interests in a company as a result of employer-stock distributions from the ESOP. All of these "small" stockholders are entitled to certain information and have certain rights under ERISA, state corporate laws, and state and federal securities laws. This factor tends to act as a deterrent to establishing ESOPs.

Question — Can an ESOP purchase life insurance on the life of a key employee of the corporation?

Answer — The ESOP can purchase life insurance, commonly referred to as "key man" life insurance, on the life of an important employee of the corporation. The ESOP can use monies contributed to it by the corporation to pay the premiums, provided, however, that the amount of dollars used for the purchase of such insurance are limited to ensure that the ESOP meets the requirements of investing primarily in qualifying employer securities. On the death of the key person, the ESOP would be the beneficiary of the life insurance and could then use the proceeds for the purchase of shares of stock from that key person, thereby providing a market for that key person's stock as well as liquidity in that key person's estate.

Question — Assume that there is only one key person in a corporation and that key person owns 100 percent of the stock of the corporation. Is an ESOP an appropriate estate planning tool to use if there is no one in management who wishes to, or who is capable of continuing the business?

Answer — The ESOP probably does not present an appropriate estate planning tool in this situation because the obligation to continue the business would be on the trustee of the ESOP. It would be very difficult to find a trustee willing to take the responsibility for operating the business. As a result of the key person's death, with no one available to properly manage and control the company, the stock would probably substantially decrease in value, if not become worthless.

Question — Can an ESOP be used to purchase the majority of the stock of a corporation from present owners?

Answer — There's no problem with a transfer of ownership from present stockholders to employees through an ESOP purchase of the present owners' stock. But there is a problem if an ESOP is used to buy most of present owners' stock to enable an outsider to obtain effective control by buying only the remaining amount of stock (coupled with control of a majority interest through trusteeship of the ESOP). It appears that the use of ESOP funds by an outsider to acquire the employer is a transaction for that party's personal benefit and not for the benefit of participants and beneficiaries. It therefore violates prudent transaction requirements imposed on fiduciaries and could cause rescission of the sale and restoration to the ESOP of lost profits.[25]

Question — A man entitled to $50,000 from a pension plan dies having designated his adult son as the beneficiary of his plan benefits. Assume the funds are community property. The wife did not consent to the beneficiary designation. Can the wife be deprived of her 50 percent share of the pension benefits by her husband's action? If she did consent, has she made a taxable gift to her son of $25,000?

Answer — In most community property states, the wife cannot be deprived of her community property interest by her husband's unilateral action of naming their son as the sole beneficiary. Thus, she is entitled to $25,000 from the plan. If the plan has already paid the funds to the son, the plan could be liable to the wife. Thus, it is important for plans to verify the existence or nonexistence of community property rights before distributing benefits. If the wife consented to the designation of the son as beneficiary, however, she would have no claim. Under the Tax Reform Act of 1976, even if she permitted the distribution to the son to occur, she would not have made a taxable gift to her son for federal gift tax purposes but might have made one for state gift tax purposes. However, TRA '86 repeals the 1976 provision. Thus, it may be found (for federal gift tax purposes) that the surviving spouse has made a taxable gift to the son.[26] The Retirement Equity Act of 1984 imposes additional restrictions on a married participant's ability to name a beneficiary for plan death benefits other than the surviving spouse. Generally, a qualified plan is now required to pay plan benefits in the form of a "Qualified Pre-retirement Survivor Annuity" for participants dying prior to reaching retirement age and in the form of a "Qualified Joint and Survivor Annuity" for married participants who die af-

Tools and Techniques

ter reaching retirement age. (See Chapter 22 for a more detailed analysis of the Retirement Equity Act of 1984 changes.)

Question — Does an employer contribution in excess of 25 percent of covered compensation to pay interest on a loan obtained by an ESOP to buy employer stock exceed the annual additions limit?

Answer — Employer contributions applied to pay loan interest, and forfeitures of fully leveraged (loaned) employer stock owned by the ESOP are disregarded for purposes of the 25 percent/$30,000 annual additions limit to a participant's account in the ESOP which would otherwise apply. However, this rule applies only if deductible contributions allocated to "highly compensated employees" (as defined in Code section 414(q) — see chapter 22), are not more than one-third of the total contributions.[27]

Question — What types of employer stock qualify as "employer securities" for purposes of an ESOP?

Answer — An ESOP must be designed to invest primarily in "employer securities." Shares of common stock of an employer which are readily tradable on an established securities market are "employer securities." If the employer has no stock which is publicly traded, "employer securities" are shares of common stock issued by the employer with a combination of voting power and dividend rights equal or greater than the classes of common stock of the employer with the greatest voting power and dividend rights. Noncallable preferred stock can be "employer securities" if the preferred stock is convertable at any time into common stock meeting the above requirements, and the conversion price is reasonable.[28]

Question — Can the proceeds of stocks sold by a deceased shareholder's estate to an ESOP be excluded from estate tax?

Answer — Yes. TRA '86 allows a 50 percent deduction from a deceased shareholder's taxable estate due to the estate's sale of employer securities to an ESOP. This deduction is allowed up to a maximum of $750,000. This is an extraordinary estate planning opportunity that is presently scheduled to be available only through 1991.[29]

Although it is possible for an estate to obtain beneficial nonrecognition of gain on the sale of his shares to an ESOP under Code section 2057, there is a pitfall to avoid. With respect to sales of securities after October 22, 1986, if the ESOP fails to meet the requirements of Code section 409(n) (see paragraph (9) under "What are the Requirements," above), adverse tax consequences will result. A penalty tax equal to 50% of the amount of any prohibited accrual or allocation will be levied against the plan under Code section 4979A. And, the amount of any prohibited accrual or allocation will be treated as if distributed to the individual involved and taxed as such.

There is a 50% excise tax on prohibited allocations of employer securities acquired in a transaction involving the tax-deferred sale to an ESOP and the use of proceeds to make an investment in "qualified replacement securities." The same penalty applies to employer securities purchased by the ESOP under the special 50% estate tax deduction for sale of securities to an ESOP.

A prohibited allocation occurs if any of the securities involved go to a 25% or more shareholder or, within 10 years, goes to the seller, or a relative of the seller (with a small exception for permissible allocations to lineal descendants of the seller). This tax is to be paid by the employer and is effective for sales of employer securities after October 22, 1986.[30]

Question — Must participants be given the opportunity to diversify their account balances?

Answer — Yes. TRA '86 provides that participants who have completed 10 years of participation in the ESOP must be given the opportunity to diversify 25 percent of their account balances at age 55 and an additional 25 percent at age 60.[31]

Question — Are pre-age 59½ distributions from ESOPs assessed a 10 percent excise tax?

Answer — Possibly not. Under TRA '86, a pre-age 59½ distribution from an ESOP is exempt from the early distribution excise tax assessed by new TRA '86 provisions if the distribution occurs prior to January 1, 1990 from an ESOP, the distibution is attributable to assets invested in employer stock for the 5-year period preceding the year of distribution, and ESOP requirements are met with respect to such stock during the 5 year period.[32]

Question — What other benefits are available to employers who maintain an ESOP?

Answer — In general, there is a nondeductible 15% (10% for reversions prior to October 21, 1988) excise tax imposed (on the employer) on the amount of any "employer reversion" from a qualified plan. An "employer reversion" is the amount of cash and the fair market value of other property received by an employer as a return of excess assets from an overfunded defined benefit pension plan.[33]

The excise tax on reversions does not apply to transfers to an ESOP of assets from a terminated defined benefit plan, and the amount transferred is not includible in the income of the employer if the following requirements are met:

(1) The transferred assets must be invested in employer securities within 90 days of the transfer, or used to repay loans used to purchase such securities;

(2) To the extent that it does not exceed the dollar limitation on annual additions or, if less, ⅛ of the amount of the transferred assets, the amount trans-

ferred must be allocated under the ESOP to its participants; additional amounts not allocated in the year of transfer must be held in a suspense account and allocated ratably over a period not to exceed 7 years; and

(3) At least one-half of the participants in the plan which produced the reversion are participants in the ESOP as of the close of the first plan year for which the allocation of securities is required.[34]

This unusual exception to the reversion tax is valid only if the transfer of assets is made pursuant to a termination that occurs after March 31, 1985, and before January 1, 1989.[35]

ASRS, Sec. 59, ¶270.1.

Footnote References

Employee Stock Ownership Plan

1. IRC Sections 401, 4975(e)(7); ERISA Sections 407(d)(1), (5) and (6) and 407(e).
2. IRC Sections 404(a)(3), 404(a)(9).
3. IRC Section 172.
4. IRC Section 2057, as added by TRA '86, Section 1172(a).
5. IRC Sections 4975(e)(7), 409(h)(1)(B).
6. ERISA Section 408(e); IRC Section 401(a)(28)(C), as added by TRA '86, Section 1175(a).
7. IRC Section 401(a)(22).
8. IRC Section 401(a)(28)(B), as added by TRA '86, Section 1175(a).
9. IRC Section 409(o), as added by TRA '86, Section 1174(b).
10. IRC. Section 409(n), as added by TRA '86, Section 1854(a).
11. IRC Section 133, as amended by TRA '86, Section 1173(b)(1).
12. Rev. Proc. 77-30, 1977-2 C.B. 539; Rev. Proc. 78-23, 1978-2 C.B. 503.
13. Reg. §1.401-1(b)(iii).
14. IRC Section 404(a)(3)(A), as added by TRA '86, Section 113(a).
15. IRC Section 404(a)(9); IRC Section 415(c)(6)(C).
16. Rev. Rul. 73-345, 1973-2 C.B. 11.
17. IRC Section 404(k), as amended by TRA '86, Section 1173(a).
18. IRC Section 1042.
19. IRC Section 2039(d) (replaced by Section 2039(c) after TRA '84), repealed by TRA '86, Section 185.
20. IRC Section 2517(c), as repealed by TRA '86, Section 1852(e).
21. IRC Section 219(e), as amended by TRA '86, Section 1101(b)(1).
22. IRC Section 401(m).
23. Reg. §54.4975-7(b)(4).
24. Reg. §54.4975-7(b)(9).
25. *Eaves v. Penn.*, 426 F. Supp. 830 (DC Okla. 1976), aff'd 587 F.2d 453 (10th Cir. 1978).
26. See footnote 18.
27. IRC Section 415(c)(6), as amended by TRA '86, Section 1106.
28. IRC Sections 4975(e)(8), 409(l).
29. IRC Section 2057, as added by TRA '86, Section 1172(a).
30. IRC Section 4979A.
31. See footnote 8.
32. IRC Section 72(t)(2)(C), as amended by TAMRA '88, Section 1011A(c).
33. IRC Section 4980(a), (b), and (c)(2)(A).
34. IRC Section 4980(c)(3), as amended by TAMRA '88, Section 1011A(f).
35. IRC Section 4980(c)(3)(E).

Chapter 8

EXTENSIONS OF TIME TO PAY FEDERAL ESTATE TAX

WHAT IS IT?

Generally, the federal estate tax is payable in full within nine months of the date of death.[1] The Internal Revenue Code does provide relief under certain circumstances by allowing an executor to pay the federal estate taxes attributable to the decedent's business over a period of years.

Under Code §6166 the executor in his discretion may elect to pay the federal estate tax (and generation skipping transfer tax) attributable to the decedent's interest in a closely held business in installments over a period of up to 14 years. During the first four years the executor pays only interest on the unpaid tax. Then, in equal annual increments over as many as ten additional years, the executor pays off the principal of the unpaid tax (together with interest on the unpaid balance).

Code §6166 permits a four year deferral of tax followed by a maximum ten year payout of the tax. Roughly speaking, interest is payable at 4 percent on the tax generated by the first $1,000,000 of business value and at the "going rate" on the balance. The "going rate" charged by the IRS varies quarterly. At the time of this printing this rate is 11%, but only a few years ago was as high as 20%.

Section 6166 is available for any estate that qualifies under the rules of the Internal Revenue Code, regardless of the position of the local District Director of the Internal Revenue Service. However, if the estate does not qualify for the 6166 extension, it still may be possible to obtain some extension under an alternative section §6161, which is discretionary with the District Director.

Under §6161, the District Director may extend the period for payment of tax for a period up to ten years beyond the due date of the estate tax return if he finds that there is "reasonable cause" to grant such an extension.

Under §6159 (see final Question and Answer), the Secretary may permit the installment payment of taxes where the Secretary believes it will facilitate payment of such taxes.

WHEN IS THE USE OF SUCH A DEVICE INDICATED?

1. When the estate has insufficient liquidity to pay the estate taxes when due without selling assets at a substantial loss.

2. Where the estate can earn a greater after-tax rate of return than it spends in interest for the deferral privilege.

WHAT ARE THE REQUIREMENTS?

A. §6161

1. A district director may extend the time for payment of the tax shown on the return for a period of up to ten years beyond the due date of the return, upon a showing of "reasonable cause" for the granting of the extension.

2. "Reasonable cause" for the extension is not expressly defined. Each case is examined on an independent factual basis. However, there are certain guidelines used to establish the presence of reasonable cause. These include: (a) inability to marshal assets to pay the estate tax when otherwise due; (b) an estate comprised in substantial part of assets consisting of rights to receive payments in the future, with the estate having insufficient present cash to pay the estate tax and an inability to borrow against these assets except on unreasonable terms; (c) the assets cannot be collected without litigation; or, (d) there are not sufficient funds available, after the exercise of due diligence, with which to pay the tax in a timely fashion.

B. §6166

1. The gross estate must include an interest classified as a "closely held" business, the value of which *exceeds* 35 percent of the adjusted gross estate. In the case of an estate in which the decedent made a gift of property within three years of death, the estate is treated as meeting the more than 35% requirement only if the estate meets such requirement both with and without the application of the three-year inclusion rule of Code section 2035 (see Appendix B, Computing the Federal Estate Tax).[2]

2. Aggregation of various business interests of the decedent is allowed for purposes of meeting the percentage requirement, provided the decedent owned at least 20 percent of the total value of each, and each activity otherwise qualifies as a closely held trade or business.

3. The amount of federal estate or generation skipping transfer tax which may be deferred, i.e., paid in installments, is only that amount of value attributable to the value of the closely held trade or business. The balance of the estate tax or GST tax must be paid at the regular payment date.

61

4. If the estate qualifies under section 6166 and an election is made, the first installment of principal is due not later than five years and nine months from the date of death. Each succeeding installment is to be paid within one year after the previous installment.

    The maximum number of principal installments which may be paid under this provision is ten, thus allowing for payment over a 14-year period (four years interest only, up to 10 more years principal and interest).

    During the 4-year period immediately following death, interest only payments are to be made, with interest being at a beneficial 4 percent rate in relation to the first $1,000,000 value of the closely held business (roughly translated into approximately $345,800 of tax). But this 4 percent amount is reduced by the available credit, as shown in Figure 8.1.

5. To qualify as an interest in a "closely held" business, the interest can be in a sole proprietorship, a partnership, or a corporation. A partnership interest will qualify if 20 percent or more of the total capital interest in the partnership is included in the gross estate, or if the partnership has 15 or fewer partners. Stock in a corporation qualifies if 20 percent or more in value of the voting stock is included in determining the gross estate of the decedent, or the corporation has 15 or fewer shareholders.

    For purposes of the "15 or fewer owners" test, a partnership interest or corporate stock held by another partnership or corporation or by an estate or trust will be treated as if owned proportionately by shareholders, partners, or beneficiaries (the rule applies in the case of trusts only if a beneficiary has a present interest). A partnership interest or stock held by a member of the decedent's family is considered to be owned by the decedent for purposes of the "15 or fewer owners" test. (But if this attribution is necessary to qualify for 6166, the 4 year deferral of tax and the special 4 percent interest rates are forfeited.)

6. In addition, as interpreted by the Service, the definition of a "trade or business" is not as broad in scope as under many other provisions of the Internal Revenue Code. The business must be "actively" carried on and require a "management" function, rather than being of a nature where the taxpayer merely supervises his investment (such as an apartment house), and the investment is the actual capital producing factor.[3]

7. Only *active* business assets are considered for purposes of the "more than 35 percent of adjusted gross estate" test. Only active business assets can be considered in determining the value of the business interest that qualifies for the deferrral. This "active asset" rule which denies installment payment for passive assets applies to all corporations and partnerships. (It does not apply, however, for purposes of determining whether or not an acceleration of the tax will be required.)

HOW IT IS DONE—AN EXAMPLE OF 6166

Dr. Andrea Apter died at a time when the value of her closely held business, a computer center, was $600,000. Her gross estate was $1,000,000. Administrative costs, debts, and expenses totalled $200,000. Federal estate taxes totalled $120,000. The computation to test qualification is directly below. The computation of the 6166 deferral limitation is at Figure 8.1.

Section 6166 (up to 14 year) Installment Payout:

(1) Estate Tax Value of closely held business included in gross estate $600,000

(2) Adjusted Gross Estate $800,000

(3) 35 percent of Adjusted Gross Estate $280,000

If Line 1 exceeds Line 3, the executor can elect to pay that portion of estate taxes attributable to the inclusion of the farm or other closely held business in installments over up to 14 years (first 4 years, no tax due, only interest—up to next 10 years equal annual installments of tax and declining interest on unpaid balance).

Two or more businesses may be aggregated if the decedent held 20 percent or more interest in each such business.

In this example, the decedent's estate could utilize a Section 6166 installment payout. The deferral amount would be computed according to the following formula: (Assume the net estate and GST tax payable after credits is $120,000.)

Computing 6166 Deferral Limitation:

$$\text{Net F.E.T. and G.S.T.T. Payable (after credits)} \times \frac{\text{Value of Includible Closely Held Business Interest}}{\text{Adjusted Gross Estate}}$$

$$\$120,000 \times \frac{\$600,000}{800,000} = \$90,000$$

Therefore, $30,000 of tax ($120,000-$90,000) must be paid immediately.

The figures that follow illustrate how expensive the installment payout can be. The first set of figures (Figure 8.1) follows the Dr. Andrea Apter example and assumes the estate is in a 33% income tax bracket.

Figure 8.1

```
                    SEC. 6166 QUALIFYING TEST

INPUT:      YEAR OF DEATH .............................          1988
INPUT:      ESTATE'S INCOME TAX BRACKET ...............          0.33
INPUT:      PROFIT MARGIN OF BUSINESS .................          0.100
INPUT:      INTEREST RATE ON NON 4% AMOUNT .........          0.110

INPUT:      VALUE OF GROSS ESTATE.....................    $1,000,000

INPUT:      SEC 2053 + 2054 DEDUCTIONS ...............    - $200,000

            ADJUSTED GROSS ESTATE ....................    $  800,000

INPUT:      VALUE OF BUSINESS ........................      $600,000

            35% OF A. G. E............................      $280,000
            ESTATE QUALIFIES IF VALUE OF BUSINESS EXCEEDS
```

SECTION 6166 DEFERRAL LIMITS

```
INPUT:      NET FED ESTATE TAX .......................      $120,000

            AMOUNT THAT CAN BE DEFERRED ..............       $90,000

            TAX THAT MUST BE PAID NOW ................       $30,000
```

COMPUTATION OF FOUR PERCENT AMOUNT

```
            TAX ON ONE MILLION .......................      $345,800

            UNIFIED CREDIT ...........................    - $192,800

            4% AMOUNT (TEST) .........................      $153,000

            TOTAL DEFERABLE TAX ......................       $90,000

            4 PERCENT AMOUNT .........................       $90,000

            NON 4 PERCENT AMOUNT TAXED AT "GOING RATE"           $0
```

COMPUTING AMOUNTS OF PAYMENTS

```
            NUMBER OF INSTALLMENTS ...................            10

            4% PORTION OF EACH INSTALLMENT ...........        $9,000

            BALANCE OF EACH INSTALLMENT ..............            $0

            TOTAL PAYMENTS (PRINCIPAL) ...............        $9,000
```

Tools and Techniques

Figure 8.1

PAYMENT SCHEDULE

BALANCE OF 4% PORTION	YR 1	YR 2	YR 3	YR 4	YR 5	YR 6	YR 7	YR 8	YR 9	YR 10
	$90,000	$90,000	$90,000	$90,000	$81,000	$72,000	$63,000	$54,000	$45,000	$36,000
INTEREST DUE ON 4% PORTION	$3,673	$3,673	$3,673	$3,673	$3,673	$3,305	$2,938	$2,571	$2,204	$1,836
BALANCE OF NON 4% PORTION	$0	$0	$0	$0	$0	$0	$0	$0	$0	$0
INTEREST DUE ON NON 4% PORTION	$0	$0	$0	$0	$0	$0	$0	$0	$0	$0
TOTAL INTEREST EACH YEAR	$3,673	$3,673	$3,673	$3,673	$3,673	$3,305	$2,938	$2,571	$2,204	$1,836
TOTAL PRINCIPAL EACH YEAR	$0	$0	$0	$0	$9,000	$9,000	$9,000	$9,000	$9,000	$9,000
TOTAL INSTALL EACH YEAR	$3,673	$3,673	$3,673	$3,673	$12,673	$12,305	$11,938	$11,571	$11,204	$10,836
TOTAL TAX PRINCIPAL OVER TERM	$90,000									

BALANCE OF 4% PORTION	YR 11	YR 12	YR 13	YR 14	YR 15	
	$27,000	$18,000	$9,000	$0		
INTEREST DUE ON 4% PORTION	$1,469	$1,102	$735	$367	0	TOTAL INTEREST AT 4% $34,891
BALANCE OF NON 4% PORTION	$0	$0	$0	$0		
INTEREST DUE ON NON 4% PORTION	$0	$0	$0	$0		TOTAL INTEREST ON NON 4% PORTION $0
TOTAL INTEREST EACH YEAR	$1,469	$1,102	$735	$367		TOTAL INTEREST $34,891
TOTAL PRINCIPAL EACH YEAR	$9,000	$9,000	$9,000	$9,000		TOTAL PRINCIPAL $90,000
TOTAL INSTALL EACH YEAR	$10,469	$10,102	$9,735	$9,367		TOTAL INSTALLMENTS $124,891

Figure 8.1

ESTATE INCOME TAX BRACKET	0.33
NET COST OF INTEREST	$23,377
COST OF PRINCIPAL	$90,000
TOTAL COST	$113,377
SALES NECESSARY TO PAY FOR INSTALLMENTS:	
DOLLARS IN SALES TO NET 1 CENT	$0.10
SALES TO PAY TOTAL COST	$1,133,769

The second set (Figure 8.2) shows the cost and cash flow for a widower with a $3,000,000 estate and a $2,000,000 business, Sections 2053 and 2054 deductions of $500,000, and an estate income tax bracket of 28 percent. The interest on amounts of unpaid tax in excess of the 4 percent amount are taxed at an assumed 11 percent.

The figures are taken from a computer printout produced by Financial and Estate Planner's NumberCruncher, Financial Data Corporation, Box 601, Bryn Mawr, PA 19010; 1-800-654-2227.

WHAT ARE THE TAX IMPLICATIONS?

1. Interest is payable on the tax which is not paid by the due date of the return.[4] Under Code Section 6166, a special 4 percent interest rate is allowed. This rate is limited to the estate tax attributable to the first $1,000,000 of farm or other closely held business property ($345,800 of tax).[5] (However, as is obvious from Figure 8.1, that $345,800 amount, when reduced by the unified credit as required, was lowered to $153,000 by 1987 and later years.) Amounts of estate tax attributable to value in excess of the $1,000,000 amount bear interest at the regular rate for interest on deferred payments.[6]

Interest rates on the unpaid balance of the tax in excess of the "4 percent" portion are redetermined quarterly so as to be three percentage points over the short-term federal rate. The interest owed is compounded daily. This can make the use of Section 6166 extremely expensive.

2. The interest charged for the deferred tax is a deductible administration expense for estate tax purposes (which reduces the gross estate, thereby reducing the estate tax payable—and also makes it easier to qualify under the percentage requirements).[7] Alternatively, the interest paid each year can be deducted by the executor as an income tax deduction on the estate's income tax return.

IMPLICATIONS AND ISSUES IN COMMUNITY PROPERTY STATES

In general, for purposes of the definition of an interest in a closely held trade or business under §6166, in regard to the 15 owner test of the allowable number of shareholders or partners, the husband and wife are treated as one partner or shareholder if the interest is owned as community property. This also applies if the form of ownership is as joint tenants, tenants by the entirety, or tenants in common.

Figure 8.2

SEC. 6166 QUALIFYING TEST

INPUT:	YEAR OF DEATH	1989
INPUT:	ESTATE'S INCOME TAX BRACKET	0.28
INPUT:	PROFIT MARGIN OF BUSINESS	0.100
INPUT:	INTEREST RATE ON NON 4% AMOUNT	0.110
INPUT:	VALUE OF GROSS ESTATE.	$3,000,000
INPUT:	SEC 2053 + 2054 DEDUCTIONS	– $500,000
	ADJUSTED GROSS ESTATE	$2,500,000
INPUT:	VALUE OF BUSINESS	$2,000,000 (E16)
	35% OF A. G. E..	$875,000 (E18)
	ESTATE QUALIFIES IF E 16 EXCEEDS E 18	

SECTION 6166 DEFERRAL LIMITS

INPUT:	NET FED ESTATE TAX	$1,000,000
	AMOUNT THAT CAN BE DEFERRED	$800,000
	TAX THAT MUST BE PAID NOW	$200,000

COMPUTATION OF FOUR PERCENT AMOUNT

TAX ON ONE MILLION	$345,800
UNIFIED CREDIT	– $192,800
4% AMOUNT (TEST)	$153,000
TOTAL DEFERABLE TAX	$800,000
4 PERCENT AMOUNT	$153,000
NON 4 PERCENT AMOUNT TAXED AT "GOING RATE"	$647,000

COMPUTING AMOUNTS OF PAYMENTS

NUMBER OF INSTALLMENTS	10
4% PORTION OF EACH INSTALLMENT	$15,300
BALANCE OF EACH INSTALLMENT	$64,700
TOTAL PAYMENTS (PRINCIPAL)	$80,000

Figure 8.2

PAYMENT SCHEDULE

	YR 1	YR 2	YR 3	YR 4	YR 5	YR 6	YR 7	YR 8	YR 9	YR 10
BALANCE OF 4% PORTION	$153,000	$153,000	$153,000	$153,000	$137,700	$122,400	$107,100	$91,800	$76,500	$61,200
INTEREST DUE ON 4% PORTION	$6,244	$6,244	$6,244	$6,244	$6,244	$5,619	$4,995	$4,371	$3,746	$3,122
BALANCE OF NON 4% PORTION	$647,000	$647,000	$647,000	$647,000	$582,300	$517,600	$452,900	$388,200	$323,500	$258,800
INTEREST DUE ON NON 4% PORTION	$75,220	$75,220	$75,220	$75,220	$67,698	$60,176	$52,654	$45,132	$37,610	$30,088
TOTAL INTEREST EACH YEAR	$81,464	$81,464	$81,464	$81,464	$73,942	$65,795	$57,649	$49,503	$41,356	$33,210
TOTAL PRINCIPAL EACH YEAR	$0	$0	$0	$0	$80,000	$80,000	$80,000	$80,000	$80,000	$80,000
TOTAL INSTALL EACH YEAR	$81,464	$81,464	$81,464	$81,464	$153,942	$145,795	$137,649	$129,503	$121,356	$113,210
TOTAL TAX PRINCIPAL OVER TERM	$800,000									

	YR 11	YR 12	YR 13	YR 14	YR 15		
BALANCE OF 4% PORTION	$45,900	$30,600	$15,300	$0			
INTEREST DUE ON 4% PORTION	$2,497	$1,873	$1,249	$624	0	TOTAL INTEREST AT 4%	$59,314
BALANCE OF NON 4% PORTION	$194,100	$129,400	$64,700	$0			
INTEREST DUE ON NON 4% PORTION	$22,566	$15,044	$7,522	$0		TOTAL INTEREST ON NON 4% PORTION	$639,370
TOTAL INTEREST EACH YEAR	$25,063	$16,917	$8,771	$624		TOTAL INTEREST	$698,684
TOTAL PRINCIPAL EACH YEAR	$80,000	$80,000	$80,000	$80,000		TOTAL PRINCIPAL	$800,000
TOTAL INSTALL EACH YEAR	$105,063	$96,917	$88,771	$80,624		TOTAL INSTALLMENTS	$1,498,684

Tools and Techniques

Figure 8.2

ESTATE INCOME TAX BRACKET	0.28
NET COST OF INTEREST	$503,052
COST OF PRINCIPAL	$800,000
TOTAL COST	$1,303,052
SALES NECESSARY TO PAY FOR INSTALLMENTS:	
DOLLARS IN SALES TO NET 1 CENT	$0.10
SALES TO PAY TOTAL COST	$13,030,524

QUESTIONS AND ANSWERS

Question — Is a bond required of the executor?

Answer — The IRS can, if it deems necessary, require the executor to post a bond for the payment of the tax. The amount is up to twice the amount of the tax for which an extension is granted. The executor is also liable—personally—for payment of the tax. He can only be discharged if (a) he pays the tax due or (b) furnishes a bond or security for unpaid (but not yet due) taxes.

Question — Is there an alternative to the requirement that the executor post bond?

Answer — The executor can make an election—under 6166—to accept an IRS lien in lieu of the executor's personal liability or bond.[8]

The requirements of the lien (which serves to discharge the executor from personal liability and eliminate the requirement of a bond) are:

(1) The executor—and all parties who have an interest in the property subject to the lien—must file an agreement consenting to the lien.

(2) A person must be designated as agent for the persons who consented to the lien and the estate's beneficiaries.[9]

(3) The Service may require additional lien property if the value of the original property is—or falls below—the total of (a) unpaid taxes and (b) aggregate interest owed.

Question — Once the installment payout period begins, can the IRS terminate it?

Answer — The deferred tax is accelerated (i.e., becomes due immediately) in three situations:

(1) when all or a significant portion of the business is disposed of or liquidated;

(2) interest or installment payments are not made within 6 months of due date; or

(3) if the estate has undistributed net income (there may be an acceleration to that extent).

Question — Why shouldn't an advisor suggest that a client use a Section 6166 installment payout as an alternative to life insurance?

Answer — First, 6166 cannot be relied upon. The mathematical percentage test may be failed or the firm may be considered an asset holding company rather than a trade or business.

Second, Section 6166 does not "create" assets—the right to make installment payments merely postpones the necessity of paying a certain portion of the total estate tax. Interest *added* to the tax increases the total cost substantially.

Where will the money to pay both tax and interest come from? If it comes from the business, it probably will be in the form of a dividend. In any event, *the dollars to make the deferred payments have to come from somewhere—and they will be after-tax (expensive) dollars*. (See the NumberCruncher illustration, Figure 8.1.)

Third, only a portion of the Federal taxes can be deferred in most cases.

Where will the executor find the cash to pay

(a) administrative expenses?

(b) debts?

(c) remaining portion of Federal estate taxes?

(d) state death taxes?

(e) income taxes?

(f) pecuniary bequests?

Fourth, with certain exceptions, successors in interest cannot dispose of the business—or a major portion of it—without triggering an acceleration ("pay it now").

Fifth, the executor may remain personally liable for unpaid taxes during the entire deferral period (or the successors-in-interest have to tie their hands with a special tax lien to assure the IRS that payment will be made).

Sixth, final distribution to beneficiaries may be delayed over an extended period of time. Most beneficiaries will not want to wait for 14 years to receive their full share of the inheritance.

Seventh, since all beneficiaries must sign the elective agreement to discharge the executor from personal liability, guardians may have to be appointed for minors and otherwise incompetent beneficiaries. Such guardians may refuse to sign such an exoneration.

Question — Is there any danger of losing the right to have an extension of time if the estate, as it appears on the estate tax return as filed, qualifies for an extension?

Answer — Yes. The values of the various assets in the estate can be changed upon audit by IRS. It is the ultimately determined values that will control. It is possible that the estate will not meet the 6166 requirements after the IRS increases the value of assets other than the decedent's business.

Question — How is the election made under §6166?

Answer — Notice of election under §6166 must be filed on or before the due date (including any extensions) of the U.S. Estate Tax Return[10] (Form 706). No special form of notice is required and a letter addressed to the IRS setting forth the identity of the taxpayer, the amount of tax to be deferred, the identity of the closely held business and the computation of qualification under the applicable section will suffice.

Question — What if, based upon the value set forth on the U.S. Estate Tax Return, the decedent's interest in the closely held business does not qualify under §6166, but it is possible that after examination by the IRS such interest will qualify?

Answer — If the estate does not qualify for a payout of federal estate taxes on the values returned or if the estate does qualify, but no tax is due on the values returned, the executor can file a "protective election." The "protective election" would set forth the information required under Revenue Ruling 74-499.

Question — In determining the "at least 20 percent" requirement of §6166 for the aggregation of two or more closely held businesses, or whether 20 percent or more of the value of a closely held business is included in the gross estate, can the executor elect to have interests of family members considered as owned by the decedents?

Answer — Yes. The interest of family members can, if elected by the executors, be considered as owned by the decedent in determining the "at least 20 percent" requirements for qualification under §6166.[11] This election is applicable only to a capital interest in a partnership and to stock which is "not readily tradable". If this election is made by the Executor, the five year deferral provision of §6166 is not available and the payout must be spread over a period not to exceed ten years. In addition, the interest rate charged on the payout is at the "going rate" (the 4 percent special rate is not available).

Question — Can holding company stock qualify for installment payout of estate taxes under section 6166?

Answer — "Yes, but." Only the portion of stock of a holding company that directly or indirectly owns stock in a closely held active trade or business (so called "business company") will be treated as stock in the active company and may therefore qualify. To qualify, the "15 or fewer shareholders" or the "20 percent or more" test and the "more than 35 percent" test must be met.

The ability to payout federal estate taxes attributable to holding company stock may come at a significant cost. The executor must agree to forego both the deferral of principal payments and the special four percent interest rate. This adds to the cost of the payout in two important ways: first, the time value of money works against the estate since much more money (the principal of the unpaid estate tax) must be paid much more quickly. Second, the "going" rate is substantially above the special four percent rate, it compounds daily making the true cost higher than it appears, and it is applied to a much larger base.

Question — What additional provision for the payment of taxes in installments was added by TAMRA '88?

Answer — TAMRA '88 added Section 6159 which provides that the Secretary is authorized to enter into written agreements with taxpayers to pay taxes in installments where the Secretary determines that such an agreement will facilitate payment of such taxes. Such an agreement may be modified or terminated by the Secretary if (1) information provided by the taxpayer was inaccurate or incomplete, (2) the Secretary believes that collection of such tax is in jeopardy, (3) the Secretary determines that the financial condition of the taxpayer has changed (in which case 30 days notice to the taxpayer is required, including the reason for such change), (4) the taxpayer fails to make a timely installment payment (or to timely pay any other tax), or (5) the taxpayer fails to provide a financial update as requested by the Secretary.

ASRS, Sec. 54, §44.7.

Tools and Techniques

Footnote References

Deferred Payment of Federal Estate Taxes

1. IRC Sec. 6075(a).
2. IRC Section 2035(d)(4), as added by the Technical Corrections Act of 1982.
3. Treas. Reg. Sec. 20.6166-2(c); Rev. Ruls. 75-365, 1975-2 C.B. 471; 75-366, 1975-2 C.B. 472; 75-367, 1975-2 C.B. 472.
4. IRC Sec. 6601(a) and 6621.
5. IRC Sec. 6601(j).
6. Rev. Rul. 81-260, 1981-44 IRB 19.
7. *Est. of Charles A. Bahr, Sr.*, 68 TC 74 (1977); acq. Rev. Rul. 78-125, 1978-2 C.B. 149.
8. IRC Sec. 6324A.
9. IRC Sec. 6324A(c).
10. Rev. Rul. 74-499, 1974-2 C.B. 397.
11. IRC Secs. 6166(b)(1)(B)(i), 6166(b)(7), 6166(b)(8), 6166(b)(9), 6166(g)(1), 6166(g)(2); TRA '84, Sec. 1021.

Chapter 9

FAMILY PARTNERSHIP

WHAT IS IT?

A family partnership is a partnership which exists between members of a family. ("Family" includes only an individual's spouse, ancestors, lineal descendants, and any trusts established primarily for the benefit of such persons.)[1] If a partnership among family members is a genuine partnership, it will be treated tax wise the same as any other partnership and the same rules will apply.

The family partnership is a technique frequently utilized as a means of shifting the income tax burden from parents to children or other family members.

However, the Tax Reform Act of 1986 has substantially eliminated the benefit of income shifting to children under age 14. For children under age 14, unearned income in excess of $1,000 generally will be taxed at the parent's top marginal rate. Although family partnerships have sometimes been attacked by IRS as being mere tax avoidance schemes that should not be recognized for tax purposes, if the rules for establishing and operating such partnerships are carefully followed, the IRS will recognize the validity of this income shifting device.

The family partnership was also used as a method for "freezing" the value of a client's estate for federal estate tax purposes. This benefit was substantially eliminated by the Revenue Act of 1987 for property transfers after December 17, 1987.[2]

WHEN IS THE USE OF SUCH A DEVICE INDICATED?

1. When it is desired to shift the income tax burden from a parent who is in a high income tax bracket to a child or other relative who is in a lower income tax bracket, thus providing for intra-family income splitting (and therefore tax saving).

   However, after 1986, under the Tax Reform Act of 1986, the federal government will tax the "net unearned income" (generally, unearned income in excess of $1,000) of a child under age 14 at his parents' top tax rate. This applies to unearned income from any source, including gifts made before 1987. As a result, income shifting to children under age 14 will be of limited benefit.

2. Where it is desired to conduct a family business in a form other than the corporate form, a family partnership may be preferable. Operating a business in corporate form may cause tax problems which would not exist if the business were operated in partnership form—e.g., partnerships are not subject to personal holding company,

accumulated earnings and unreasonable compensation problems. In addition, through a family partnership, control may be preserved in the transferor-parent, particularly if the family partnership is run as a limited partnership. In a corporation, control is centralized in a board of directors and voting power generally shifts with a transfer of stock.

3. Where it is desired to create an entity to assist in the transfer of ownership interests to the younger generation without loss of control. Additionally, with restrictions on liquidation of the partnership interests, a substantial discount in estate tax value may also be available.[3]

WHAT ARE THE REQUIREMENTS?

1. There are the following primary requirements for family partnerships to be treated and taxed as such:

   (a) Capital must be a material income-producing factor. This means the partnership's business must require substantial inventories or substantial investment in plant, machinery or other equipment, as contrasted with a personal service partnership.[4]

   (b) In the case of any partnership created by gift, reasonable compensation must be paid to the donor of the partnership interest for services rendered to the partnership. A partnership interest purchased by one family member from another is considered to be created by gift from the seller. The fair market value of that purchased interest is considered the amount of the donated capital.[5]

   (c) The share of income attributable to the donee's interest can't be proportionately greater than that attributable to the donor's interest.[6]

2. The validity of a family partnership is dependent upon the partners "owning" a capital interest. The Code does not spell out what this means. However, the regulations state that the transferee of a partnership interest must be the "real owner" of the capital interest and have dominion and control over that interest.[7]

   The regulations spell out four retained controls (i.e. powers retained by a donor of a family partnership interest) which are of particular significance in showing that a donee lacks true ownership of his interest.[8] These controls include:

   (a) Retaining control of the distribution of income or restricting the amount of such distributions.

(b) Limiting the right of a donee partnership to sell or liquidate his interest in his discretion and without financial detriment.

(c) Retaining control of assets essential to the partnership business.

(d) Retaining management powers inconsistent with normal relationships among partners.

However, retention of control of the business management or of the voting control of the partnership in a manner that is common in ordinary business relationships will not of itself invalidate the partnership if the donee is free to liquidate his or her interest in the partnership at his discretion and without financial detriment. In addition, it is important that the donee have sufficient maturity and understanding so as to be capable of exercising that discretion.[9]

HOW IT IS DONE — AN EXAMPLE

1. Mark Ciarelli, a successful businessman, is married and has two adult children, Irv and Eric. He presently is the sole owner of an unincorporated manufacturing business (Pierz Enterprises) in which both personal services and capital are material income producing factors. The net profits from the business for last year were approximately $200,000 before Mark's salary. Mark files a joint return with his wife Judy. His wife and his children do not have an income of their own. Mark pays himself a salary of $1,000 per week. The net profit of the business after salary was actually $148,000. Since Mark is unincorporated, both the $52,000 salary and the $148,000 net profit are taxable to him.

Mark can minimize his income tax burden by "splitting" the income with his children. He could make a gift of 30% of his business directly to Irv and Eric. Each child would thus receive a 15% interest. (If his children were minors, Mark could place their interest in trust.) A partnership agreement would be drawn up between Mark and his children. Mark would receive a salary of $52,000/year. The balance of the partnership income would be split 70% to Mark, 15% to Irv and 15% to Eric.

Thus, Mark would receive $103,600 (in addition to his salary), and Irv and Eric would each receive $22,200. Mark would be taxed on $52,000 of salary and $103,600 of partnership profit. Irv and Eric would each be taxed on $22,200 of partnership profit.

The net result of this is that $44,400 of income that was previously taxed at Mark's income tax bracket will now be taxed at his children's lower tax brackets (unless the children are under age 14), thus resulting in an immediate income tax saving, by splitting income among several family members. Additionally, if the business continues to appreciate in value, 30% of that apprecia-

tion may be shifted out of Mark's estate thereby reducing future estate taxes.

2. John and Robin Scott own several pieces of improved real property (apartment buildings) worth approximately $14 million. They expect the properties to appreciate significantly in value over the next 10 years. They contribute the properties to a partnership formed between themselves and their two children, Jane and Steve.

If the partnership contains language similar to the recent Tax Court case[10] which limits the rights of a partner to liquidate the partnership after his death, a substantial discount may be available. In that case, the court reasoned that the value of a partnership interest is reduced where you must find someone to buy an interest in a partnership with multiple properties.

WHAT ARE THE TAX IMPLICATIONS?

1. A reasonable allocation of partnership income must be made to the donor partner in recognition of his other services to the partnership.

Where the interests of family members are acquired by gift and/or intra-family sale, a mandatory allocation of the partnership profits in proportion to capital contributed after due allowance has been made for the compensation for services of the donor general partners must be made. For example, if father and son are each 50% partners in a family partnership whose net income for the year is $100,000 and reasonable services for the donor father would be $20,000, the remaining $80,000 would be taxed $40,000 each to the son and the father. This should be in addition to the $20,000 taxed to the father as compensation for services rendered.

If a contributing member has acquired capital from an independent source and not from an intra-family purchase, the mandatory allocations described in the preceeding paragraph will not apply and profit and loss can be allocated in a different manner.

2. The partnership itself does not pay federal income taxes. However, a partnership return must be filed. Each partner pays taxes individually based upon his or her share of partnership income.

3. Generally, no gain or loss will be realized when property is transferred to the family partnership. The basis of the partnership in the contributed property is the same basis the property had in the hands of the contributing partners.

4. Gifts of a partnership interest are subject to gift tax and will likely raise questions regarding the value of the transferred interests similar to those raised by gifts of stock in closely held corporations. The regulations state that the same principles of valuation should apply.[11] The fair market value at the date of the gift is the value for gift tax purposes.

5. A partnership interest owned by a decedent at his or her death is valued in his or her estate at the fair market value at the date of death or the alternate valuation date. The methods of valuation are essentially the same as those used to value stock in a closely held corporation owned by the decedent at death.

   To the extent a partnership interest was given away by a donor, the appreciation from the date of the gift should not be includible in the donor's estate.[12]

6. If at the time of formation of the partnership the value of a child's partnership interest exceeds the child's contribution to the partnership or amounts paid by the child for the partnership interest, there will be a gift from parent to child subject to the gift tax.

IMPLICATIONS AND ISSUES IN COMMUNITY PROPERTY STATES

In Arizona, California, Nevada, New Mexico, and Washington, the income from separate property of one spouse is separate property income. In Texas, Louisiana, Idaho, and Wisconsin, the income from the separate property of one spouse is community property income. It is in the former group of states where the family partnership may require extra vigilance where the partnership was owned before marriage, was given or inherited, or is separate property of one spouse for whatever reason. In such instances, it is necessary to make a distinction between the earnings of the manager (which are probably community property) and the income received from ownership of the partnership interest (which is separate property).

Using the separate property income from the partnership to purchase items which are taken in the names of both spouses creates a taxable gift (with the exception of real property taken as joint tenants). Thus, if the partner-spouse received $80,000 income from a partnership which he had before the present marriage, over and above his wages from the partnership, and if he uses the $80,000 to buy some stock in the name of his present wife and himself, he will have just made a $40,000 taxable gift to her. For such transactions after 1981, this does not create a federal gift tax problem because of the new unlimited marital deduction which applies to both separate and community property (see chapter 33). Depending on state gift tax law, however, it may still create a state gift tax problem.

Another problem frequently encountered in family partnership in community property states is the failure to designate in the partnership agreement whether the partnership is separate property or community property. This failure is a great source of comfort and fees to litigation attorneys in divorce proceedings. This is rather important since the divorce rate has doubled in the last ten years!

An advantage available prior to 1982 in community property states, where each spouse owns half of the interest in their share of the family partnership, is that each could give up to $3,000 interest to each of the children without the requirement for filing a gift tax return and therefore without those items being brought back into the donor's estate in the event of the donor's death within three years of the date of gift. If only one spouse owned the partnership share, typical in a separate property state, a gift of $6,000 to each child could be made by "splitting" the gift with the non-owning spouse, but that would require the filing of a gift tax return and therefore the gift would be brought back into the estate if the donor died within three years.

However, the changes inherent in the 1981 Economic Recovery Tax Act cancelled any significant advantages of the community property partner since it repealed the pertinent provisions of the three year rule in relation to date of death and introduced the unlimited marital deduction for gifts between spouses. It also increased the annual exclusion from $3,000 to $10,000, a change which makes annual gift programs a much more viable means of transferring interests in family partnerships.

QUESTIONS AND ANSWERS

Question — Can a minor hold a partnership interest directly?

Answer — Yes. A minor child will be recognized as a bona fide partner if it is demonstrated that he is competent to manage his own property and to participate in partnership activities. This requires that the minor possess sufficient maturity and experience to assume dominion and control over the interest transferred to him.[13] Ordinarily, however, a minor will not be deemed to possess the requisite maturity and experience, and therefore, generally, as a practical matter, a partnership interest cannot be transferred to a minor directly.

If a minor's interest is transferred to a fiduciary, such as a court appointed guardian, whose conduct is subject to judicial supervision, the minor will be recognized as a partner. Alternatively, a transfer of a partnership interest to an independent trustee will effectively enable a minor to own an interest in a family partnership.

Question — Can a limited family partnership be utilized?

Answer — Yes. The regulations specifically provide for the formation of family limited partnerships.

To form a valid limited family partnership for tax purposes the limited partnership must be organized and conducted under appropriate state law. It is extremely important that the donee of a limited partnership interest have control over his interest so that he or she can govern the destiny of his interest by exercising dominion over it. Dominion and control would not be lost merely because the donee's interest is held in a fiduciary capacity.

Question — What is a partnership capital freeze?

Answer — It is the creation of a new partnership or the restructuring of an existing partnership into at least two classes of partnership interests. A "fixed" or "frozen" partnership interest is one which will have a priority or preferred right to any income distribution as well as have a priority on a liquidation of the partnership. It is similar to a preferred stock interest in a corporation. A "regular" partnership interest is similar to that which exists in a typical partnership. That interest will share in the profits and growth of the partnership, as is the case with the typical partnership interest. It is similar to the common stock interest in a corporation.

The purpose of this technique is to try to freeze the value of the fixed interest for estate tax purposes so that any appreciation from the date of the freeze will be allocable to the regular partnership interest. Typically, the frozen interest will be held by parents and the regular interest will be held by their children.

The use of partnership freezes was effectively eliminated as an estate planning tool by IRC Section 2036(c), added by the Budget Reconciliation Act of 1987. (See page 477.)

As of this writing the IRS will no longer issue advance rulings on partnership allocations where it is intended to freeze the value of a partner's interest in the partnership. This ban will remain in effect until the IRS issues a ruling on the matter.

Question — What are some helpful hints for successfully operating a family partnership?

Answer — 1. There should be a written formal partnership agreement. It should spell out the rights and obligations of the partners.

2. Meticulous business records should be kept.

3. The donor (managing partner) should be paid a reasonable compensation.

4. Distributions to the donee partner should not be used to discharge parental support obligations.

5. If a minor is involved and his interest is held in trust, the trustee should be an independent trustee and not subject to the direct or indirect control of the donor.

6. Assets should actually be transferred to and titled in the name of the partnership.

Footnote References

Family Partnership

1. IRC Section 704(e)(3).
2. IRC Section 2036(c).
3. *Estate of Watts v. Comm'r.*, 51 TCM (CCH) 60 (1985). See also *Estate of Daniel J. Harrison, Jr. v. Comm'r.*, 52 TCM 1306 (1987).
4. Reg. §1.704-1(e)(1)(iv).
5. IRC Section 704(e)(3).
6. IRC Section 704(e)(2).
7. Reg. §1.704-1(e)(2)(i).
8. Reg. §1.704-1(e)(2)(vi).
9. Reg. §1.704-1(e)(2)(ii)(d).
10. See footnote 3.
11. Regs. §§25.2512-2 and 3. See also Rev. Rul. 59-60, 1959-1 C.B. 237 and Rev. Rul. 65-192, 1965-2 C.B. 259.
12. But see IRC Section 2036(c) and Harmon, "Should Partnership Interests Gifted in a Multi-Level Freeze Be Included in the Donor's Gross Estate Under Section 2036?" 64 *Taxes* 741 (November 1986).
13. Regs 1.704-1(e)(2)(viii); *Finlen v. Healy*, 187 F. Supp. 434 (D. Mont. 1960).

Chapter 10

FLOWER BONDS

WHAT IS IT?

Certain United States Treasury obligations (which are traditionally traded at a discount) owned by a decedent at death can be redeemed at par value (plus accrued interest) in payment of federal estate taxes. Although these bonds (often called "flower bonds" because of the engraving of flowers on their reverse side and because they "blossom" at death) can no longer be purchased directly from the federal government, they can be obtained through stock brokers and bank trust departments.

Because these bonds pay interest in the 3 to 4% range, they can typically be purchased at a substantial discount. As interest rates on alternative government bonds rise, these discounts tend to increase. Discounts exceeding 20 percent were not uncommon.

Flower bonds can be used at par value to pay federal estate taxes. The difference between par value and the purchase price provides a way to pay federal estate taxes at a "discount."

WHEN IS THE USE OF SUCH A DEVICE INDICATED?

1. These treasury bonds are useful in any situation in which the client would like to pay federal estate taxes at a discount.
2. This type of treasury bond is a good way to provide needed liquidity in an estate that otherwise is relatively illiquid. (It may be advantageous for an individual to use relatively nonmarketable securities as collateral for a loan and use the borrowed cash to purchase the bonds, rather than to sell securities to purchase the flower bonds.)
3. Flower bonds are a possible alternative to life insurance where the decedent would be highly "rated" for life insurance purposes or is uninsurable. Flower bonds can be obtained even if the decedent is critically ill.

WHAT ARE THE REQUIREMENTS?

1. The bonds must be purchased during the lifetime of the decedent.
2. These bonds must be owned by the decedent at his or her death.[1] However, the bonds may be held in a grantor-type trust, as opposed to being in the decedent's individual name, as long as the trust contains a direction to the trustee to use the bonds for payment of estate taxes.

   In any case, the bonds must have been purchased by the decedent or at his direction. If the bonds are purchased by someone for the decedent, pursuant to a power of attorney given by the decedent, the power of attorney must have been effective under state law on the date of purchase. (See Chapter 5—Durable Power of Attorney.)

HOW IT IS DONE — AN EXAMPLE

Assume that: (1) a federal estate tax of $200,000 will be due; (2) that the estate is approximately in the 37 percent federal estate tax bracket; (3) John Donne, age 60, a widower, is in a 33 percent federal income tax bracket; and (4) Mr. Donne is quite ill and possibly has terminal cancer (therefore, obtaining life insurance on the client's life is out of the question).

Mr. Donne contacts the local office of a nearby trust company. Assume he selects 3-1//2 percent 1990 series bonds issued February 14, 1958. This bond is due February 15, 1990. Assume the price quoted for the series is $73.26 ($732.60 cost to purchase a $1,000 par value flower bond). This means that for a purchase price of $146,520 ($73.26 x 2,000), Mr. Donne's estate can obtain enough bonds to pay $200,000 in federal estate taxes.

The gain (or increased liquidity) thus appears to be $53,480 ($200,000 – $146,520). However, the gain must be reduced by the additional estate taxes generated by the inclusion of the flower bonds in the gross estate at par.[2] The estate tax of 37 percent will reduce the $53,480 gain by $19,788. Therefore, the actual cost of the flower bonds is the purchase price ($146,520) plus the $19,788 federal estate tax on the difference between the purchase price and $200,000 par value.

The following additional example will help illustrate that the true advantage of flower bonds may be less than it appears.

Raymond Fry, an 80-year-old bachelor, has assets worth over $5 million that consist entirely of listed stocks. Although he is not well physically, his mind is alert. His only heir is his grandnephew, Pete Summers. Pete has told his granduncle that certain United States Treasury bonds (often referred to as "flower bonds") could save federal estate taxes. Certain flower bonds with a $1,000 maturity value were selling for $850. Pete suggested that his uncle sell enough of his stock portfolio to purchase flower bonds with a total par value of $1 million. Raymond's marginal estate tax rate is 55 percent. His marginal income tax rate is 28 percent. Assume enough stock to net $850,000 were sold. If the proceeds from the sale, net of any commissions and fees, were $950,000, of which $357,143 were gain, Raymond would have a tax payable of $100,000 ($357,143 x .28). The current yield of flower bonds is 3 percent. See Figure 10.1.

Tools and Techniques

Figure 10.1

FLOWER BONDS — AN ANALYSIS OF THEIR UTILITY

INPUT:	MARGINAL ESTATE TAX RATE	0.55
INPUT:	MARGINAL INCOME TAX RATE	0.28
INPUT:	TAX COST IF ASSETS MUST BE SOLD TO PURCHASE FLOWER BONDS	$ 100,000
INPUT:	PAR VALUE OF FLOWER BONDS	$1,000,000
INPUT:	MARKET VALUE OF FLOWER BONDS	$ 850,000

GROSS INCREASE IN ESTATE ASSETS .... $ 150,000
     Less tax on sale of assets to purchase flower bonds .... $ 100,000
NET INCREASE IN ESTATE ASSETS .... $ 50,000

GROSS INCREASE IN LIQUIDITY VIA FLOWER BONDS .... $ 150,000
    Less —
        tax on sale of assets to buy bonds $100,000
        increase in federal estate tax .... 27,500 $ 127,500
NET INCREASE IN ESTATE ASSETS (OR LIQUIDITY) .... $ 22,500

You should consider that the current yield on the bond during the individual's lifetime will not be anywhere near comparable to the yield on an alternative investment of the same amount of money. However, this will be of little importance if the client is seriously ill or perhaps only a few hours away from death.

It is important to note that the difference between purchase price of the bonds and par value might increase not only the federal estate taxes but also the administration expenses of the estate. Of course, capital gains would be involved if liquidation of other investments were required in order to raise the cash needed to purchase the flower bonds. But, in spite of these factors, buying bonds below par to pay federal estate taxes should be considered in appropriate cases.

WHAT ARE THE TAX IMPLICATIONS?

The tax implications have been discussed above and, as stated, such treasury bonds are redeemable at par (plus accrued interest) only for the purpose of applying the proceeds in payment of the federal estate tax. The essential flaw is that to the extent that these bonds can be used to pay the federal estate tax at par, they must be valued in the estate at not less than par, *whether or not the bonds actually are redeemed to pay the estate tax.*[3] Bonds held in excess of the amount of the estate tax are includible at the market price plus accrued interest.

These obligations are no longer issued by the treasury since the 1971 repeal of Code Section 6312, but millions of dollars of bonds issued before March 3, 1971, are still available.

IMPLICATIONS AND ISSUES IN COMMUNITY PROPERTY STATES

Since one of the primary requirements for use of flower bonds to pay estate taxes is their ownership by the decedent, purchase of the bonds with community funds would necessitate buying twice the amount of bonds needed to pay the tax, in order to have a sufficient amount in the decedent's ownership.

One way to avoid this (where the individual does not have separate funds available for this purpose, and where the estate plan anticipates that federal tax will be paid by design at the death of the first spouse to die) is to effect a "split" of community property, whereby an amount equal to the cost of the bonds is allocated to the spouse and placed in a bank account or other investment as the spouse's sole and separate property, and the other half of the split funds placed in the ill spouse's sole name, in a traceable fashion, and thereafter used to purchase the flower bonds in the ill spouse's sole name. In order to effect a "split," some states, such as California, require the "split" agreement to be in writing (effective January 1, 1985).

Where cash must be borrowed to purchase the bonds, the loan amount, and the obligation to repay, should clearly be documented as being entirely the decedent's.

QUESTIONS AND ANSWERS

Question — How distant a maturity date may be obtained?

Answer — Three and one-half percent bonds are available with a maturity date of November 15, 1998. A list of available bonds, arranged in order of maturity date, follows:[4]

Series	Dated	Due
3-1/2%, 1990	February 14, 1958	February 15, 1990
4-1/4%, 1987-1992	August 15, 1962	August 15, 1992
4%, 1988-1993	January 17, 1963	February 15, 1993
4-1/8%, 1989-1994	April 18, 1963	May 15, 1994
3%, 1995	February 15, 1955	February 15, 1995
3-1/2%, 1998	October 3, 1960	November 5, 1998

Question — Suppose an executor had the right to use all of the estate's flower bonds to pay estate taxes but chose to use only some of them for that purpose and retained the balance. How would the remaining bonds be taxed?

Answer — Where all the bonds could have been used to pay federal estate taxes, their value is par value regardless of whether or not they were actually used for estate tax payment purposes.

Question — What if the estate owned more bonds than were needed to pay the federal estate taxes, so that after paying the taxes the estate still had bonds which were unredeemed. How would these bonds be valued in the estate?

Answer — Those bonds in excess of the amount that could be redeemed at par for estate tax purposes would be valued at fair market value.[5]

Question — What does the executor do if the par value of the bonds is greater than the amount necessary to pay the estate tax due?

Answer — The executor can exchange the bond for others of smaller value. For example, if a $10,000 4-1//4 percent treasury bond (interest payable on May 15 and November 15) was submitted in payment of a federal estate tax liability of $9,500 and the lowest denomination in which such bonds are issued is $500, the bond would be redeemed to the extent of $9,500 par value. It would then be applied toward the payment of the federal estate tax liability and the government would reissue a $500 denomination bond for the portion of the bond that could not be applied to the payment of the tax.

Question — How and where are the bonds submitted for payment of the taxes?

Answer — Flower bonds are not accepted directly by the IRS in payment of the federal estate tax. Instead, the bonds, together with a certified copy of the decedent's death certificate, are submitted to any Federal Reserve Bank or branch or to the Bureau of the Public Debt, Division of Securities Operations, Washington, D.C. 20226. They should be submitted well in advance (at least a month) of the date specified for redemption. The form that

should be used is number PD1782, *Application for Redemption at Par of United States Treasury Bonds Eligible for Payment of Federal Estate Tax.* These forms can be obtained from any Federal Reserve Bank or branch.

Question — What if the federal estate tax was paid in cash, but the flower bonds were later discovered; can the flower bonds still be used?

Answer — If flower bonds are available for payment of the tax, they can be substituted, as long as the substitution occurs before the distribution of the estate or within two years of the date the tax is paid (whichever occurs earlier).

Question — Can flower bonds be purchased with borrowed funds?

Answer — Yes. Also, the interest expense incurred to finance the purchase of flower bonds is deductible for income tax purposes. (However, where the client also holds substantial amounts of tax-exempt bonds, it is likely that the Internal Revenue Service will attempt to disallow the interest deduction.)

Question — Can an executor purchase flower bonds and use them to pay the federal estate tax?

Answer — The bonds can only be redeemed at par to pay federal estate taxes if the decedent owned the bonds at the date of death.

Question — How are flower bonds taxed for state inheritance or estate tax purposes?

Answer — There is no uniform rule for valuing flower bonds for state death tax purposes. Some states, such as Illinois and Montana, value the bonds at fair market value. Other states, such as New York and California, value flower bonds at par. Valuing these bonds at par for state purposes reduces their tax savings potential.

Question — Compared to life insurance as a means of paying death costs at a "discount," what are the disadvantages of flower bonds?

Answer — There are a number of reasons flower bonds should be considered only as a last resort alternative to life insurance

(1) To obtain the discount, the bonds must be owned at death. This means the bonds must be includible in the estate.

A great deal of the advantage of the discount is given up because such bonds are includible in the gross estate—not at the discount price, but at their (higher) par value—to the extent that they are or can be used to pay estate taxes. Estate taxes must be paid on "phantom assets"; i.e., the tax must be paid on a greater amount of property than the decedent actually had the day before he bought the bonds (and

Tools and Techniques

unlike life insurance, there's no way to assign the bonds out of his estate and still obtain the discount).

A recent case involved a situation where an executor used some flower bonds to pay taxes and, thinking he had paid the entire estate tax due, sold the others at the (low) market price. The IRS later assessed a deficiency and included the bonds at par (rather than at their much lower market price) in the decedent's estate. The IRS argued (successfully) that since the bonds *were* available to pay estate taxes when the return was filed they should be includible at par value. In other words, it doesn't matter that the bonds were not actually used to pay the federal estate tax; if they could have been used they must be included at their par value even if the bonds were sold before the deficiency was assessed.[6] To add insult to tax injury, heirs could sue the executor since bonds that could have been used to pay the estate tax at a discount were sold prematurely.

(2) Life insurance is usually not subject to probate; flower bonds usually are.

(3) Life insurance purchased while an individual is in good health results in a "deeper" discount—possibly as much as a 97 percent discount.

(4) Life insurance can be state inheritance tax free; flower bonds can't.

(5) Life insurance can be used to pay state inheritance taxes *and* all other probate and death-related costs; flower bonds can be used at par only to pay federal estate tax costs.

ASRS, Sec. 51.

Footnote References

Flower Bonds

1. See Treasury Dept., Circular No. 300, 4th Rev. Section 306.28(b), 38 F.R. 7083.

2. Rev. Rul. 156, 1953-2 C.B. 253.

3. Rev. Rul. 156, 1953-2 C.B. 253; *Bankers Tr. Co., Exr. v. U.S.*, 284 F.2d 537 (CA-2, 1960), rev'g. D.C., N.Y., 178 F. Supp. 267.

4. A current list of eligible bond issues may be obtained from any Federal Reserve Bank or from the Bureau of Public Debt, Division of Loans & Currency, Treasury Dept., Washington, D.C.

5. Rev. Proc. 69-18, 1969-2 C.B. 300; Rev. Rul. 69-489, 1969-2 C.B. 172.

6. *Estate of Simmie v. Comm.*, 69 T.C. 890 (1978).

Chapter 11

GIFTS

WHAT IS IT?

For gift tax purposes a gift can be broadly defined to include a sale, exchange, or other transfer of property from one person (the donor) to another (the donee) without adequate and full consideration in money or money's worth.

In addition to an outright transfer, gifts can take other forms. For example, the forgiveness of a debt, foregone interest on an intra-family interest-free or below market loan, the assignment of the benefits of an insurance policy, or the transfer of property to a trust can also be considered gifts.[1] Gifts are a major estate planning tool because of their potential for income as well as estate tax savings and for their non-tax advantages.

The gift tax computation itself is explained in greater detail in Appendix B.

WHEN IS THE USE OF SUCH A DEVICE INDICATED?

1. When the donor has an asset which is likely to appreciate in value over a period of time and would like to save estate taxes on the potential growth.

2. When a donor would like to see the donee (an individual, charity, or other organization) benefited by a gift during the donor's life for nontax motives.

3. When the donor would like to reduce probate costs, estate administration expenses, and protect family members from the claims of the client's creditors.

4. When giving away assets other than closely held stock will make it easier to qualify for a Section 303 redemption of stock, a section 6166 installment payout of taxes attributable to a closely held business interest, and a section 2032A special use valuation for certain real property used for farming or closely held business purposes. (This technique works only if the gift is made more than 3 years prior to death.)

5. When the estate owner desires to maximize the marital deduction provisions of the federal estate and gift tax law. He could give his spouse an unlimited amount of property during his lifetime and pay no federal gift tax because of the 100% gift tax marital deduction. It is important to consider any state gift tax laws as well as the federal gift tax.

6. When a high tax bracket property owner wants to reduce the family's income tax load. It is true that by reducing the maximum income tax bracket from 50% to 28% and creating only one additional bracket of 15%, the Tax Reform Act of 1986 discouraged the use of making gifts

for income tax reduction purposes.[2] Nonetheless, by giving income-producing property, the donor may still be able to remove the income it produces from his income tax bracket and subject it to the donee's generally lower income tax bracket.

All *net unearned income* of a child who has not attained age 14 before the close of the taxable year and who has at least one parent alive at the close of the taxable year will be taxed to the child, but not at the child's tax bracket. This applies to *all* net unearned income; the *source* of the assets creating the income, the *date* the income-producing property was transferred, or the *identity* of the transferor is *irrelevant*.

The tax payable by the under age 14 child on net unearned income is essentially the additional amount of tax the parent would have had to pay if the net unearned income of the child were included in the parent's taxable income.

If parents have two or more children with unearned income to be taxed at the parent's marginal tax rate, all of the children's applicable unearned income will be added together and the tax calculated. The tax is then allocated to each child based on the child's pro rata share of unearned income.

The intent of the '86 tax law was to create three stages:

(1) There will be no tax on the first $500 of unearned income because of the child's standard deduction. (The standard deduction offsets *unearned* income first, up to $500. Any remaining standard deduction is then available to offset earned income.)

(2) The next $500 of unearned income will be taxed to the child at the child's bracket.

(3) Unearned income in excess of the first $1,000 will be taxed to the child at the appropriate parent's rate.

A dependent child under age 14 with $1,000 of unearned income is taxed as follows:

Unearned income	$1,000
Standard deduction	– 500
Net unearned income	$ 500
Taxed at child's rate	x 15%
Tax	$ 75

Therefore, even for children under age 14, there is still some income shifting possible.

79

Tools and Techniques

For children age 14 or older, unearned income will be taxed to the child at his own tax bracket.

As Figure 11.1 shows, income shifting can be very successful, even after TRA '86, where a child is age 14 or older.

WHAT ARE THE REQUIREMENTS?

1. There must be a gratuitous transfer or delivery of property.[3]

2. The property which is the subject of the gift must be accepted by the donee.[4] (Of course, when the property is of benefit to the donee, acceptance is seldom an issue.)

3. The gratuitous transfer must divest the donor of control, dominion, and title over the subject matter of the gift.[5]

HOW IT IS DONE — AN EXAMPLE

1. Caroline O'Gara is age 65, married, and owns $20,000 of dividend-paying stock. The stock yields $1,000 annually. Caroline is presently in a 28 percent federal income tax bracket. On the advice of her lawyer, she gives the $20,000 of stock to her 14 year old son. This will have the result of shifting the income tax liability from Caroline, who would have netted only $720 ($1,000 - $280) from the $1,000 dividends (28 percent x $1,000), to her son, James, who will net $925 from the dividends ($1,000 - $75), since James is in a 15 percent federal income tax bracket and is entitled to a $500 standard deduction (so a 15% rate is applied only to the taxable $500), a saving of $205 yearly.

2. Gerald Carter owns an asset which is worth $100,000 today. It is anticipated that the asset will appreciate at the rate of 10 percent per year, i.e., in 10 years it will be worth approximately $260,000. If the property is given away now, the gift tax is computed on the $100,000 (less the annual exclusion if allowable). If the asset is not given away and it becomes part of the estate (ten years from today), the estate tax is computed on approximately $260,000. Thus, a gift made currently removes future appreciation from the estate.

WHAT ARE THE TAX IMPLICATIONS?

1. A gift will remove future appreciation in the property's value from an individual's estate.

2. Gift tax may have to be paid if the value of the gift exceeds the annual exclusion and if the tax exceeds the unified credit available to the donor.[6] (The credits and exemption equivalents are shown below in the Questions and Answers.) If an individual is married and his spouse consents to "split" the gift, the donor spouse will have the $10,000 annual exclusion as well as the unified credit of his spouse in addition to his own.[7] A married individual can give sizable gifts to a spouse with little or no gift tax liability through the gift tax marital deduction discussed below. See QUESTIONS AND ANSWERS concerning the phase-out of the unified credit and graduated tax brackets for large gifts.

3. Dividend or other income generated by the property given will be taxed to the donee rather than the donor (see the discussion above at 6 under the heading "WHEN IS THE USE OF SUCH A DEVICE INDICATED").

Figure 11.1

POST TRA '86 INCOME SHIFTING — CHILD 14 OR OVER

INPUT:	AMOUNT OF INVESTMENT	$20,000
INPUT:	RATE OF RETURN ON INVESTMENT	0.100
INPUT:	YEARS INVESTMENT LASTS	21
INPUT:	PARENT'S COMBINED (FEDERAL AND STATE) TAX BRACKET	0.40
INPUT:	CHILD'S COMBINED (FEDERAL AND STATE) TAX BRACKET	0.20
INPUT:	TRUST'S COMBINED (FEDERAL AND STATE) TAX BRACKET	0.20

	PARENT	CHILD	TRUST
INTEREST INCOME	$2,000	$2,000	$2,000
TAX	$800	$300	$380
AFTER-TAX INCOME	$1,200	$1,700	$1,620
ANNUAL ADVANTAGE		$500	$420
TOTAL SAVINGS OVER 21 YEARS		$35,201	$29,569
TOTAL SAVINGS OVER 26 YEARS		$60,050	$50,836
TOTAL SAVINGS OVER 31 YEARS		$100,069	$84,447

4. ERTA made a change in the method of computing the estate tax that has tax implications for certain wealthy estate owners. The change made was in computing the gift tax on post-1976 gifts. Pre-ERTA law provided that gift taxes actually payable on post-1976 gifts were subtracted from the tentative tax to arrive at the estate tax payable before credits.

The law now provides that the gift tax subtracted from the tentative tax in the estate tax computation is the tax *that would have been payable on such gifts if the tax rate schedule as in effect at decedent's death had been in effect at the time such gifts were made.* Top gift and estate tax rates will be at 55% until 1993, when they will drop to 50%, on gifts or estates in excess of $2,500,000, and will stay at the 50% rate thereafter. Note also that certain ultra large gift or estate tax transfers result in a 5 percent surtax on the portion of the transfer. See table at end of Appendix C.

It is apparent, then, that the estate of a donor who makes gifts in any of the phase-in years in excess of the dollar amount where that year's top rate begins and then dies in a later calendar year will probably pay a larger estate tax than if the gift had not been made. The change in the estate tax computation, then, amounts to a disincentive for wealthy donors to make such gifts during the top tax rate phase-in years.[8]

The tax implications also include state gift tax where applicable, which in many instances can be greater than the federal gift tax, because of the large credit and exemptions currently available under federal gift tax law.

IMPLICATIONS AND ISSUES IN COMMUNITY PROPERTY STATES

All community property states have adopted statutes which to some degree and by different methods grant equal powers of management and control of community property to each spouse. In many states one spouse cannot make a gift of community property without the prior written consent of the other spouse. If one spouse makes a gift of community property to a third person without the consent of the other spouse, the gift is ordinarily voidable rather than void.

The gift can be voided only at the request of the "injured" spouse. The amount of the gift which can be declared void and brought back to the community estate is generally dependent upon whether the community circumstance is still in existence. If the spouses are still married, the entire gift is returned to the community estate. However, if the community has been terminated (e.g., divorce, death), the "injured" spouse has the right to recapture only one-half of the gift. The other half is allowed to remain with the donee. Therefore, it is advisable to obtain both spouses' consent prior to the gift transfer.

In general, gifts of community property have the same benefits as gifts of separate property where the gift is to a third party. However, since each spouse actually "owns" his or her one-half interest in the property, there is no need to "split" the gift. This provides an advantage for persons with community property since each has property and each can give $10,000 without filing a gift tax return.

As to gifts between spouses, a marital deduction is now available for the entire amount of the gift, where one spouse gives his or her community interest in property to the other.

"Accidental gifts" (that is, taxable gifts which were not intended to be events subject to tax) can be created by transfers of title. This is particularly true in community property states where a husband and wife have acquired property in a common law state and then moved to a community property state. An example would be where a husband and wife who have acquired assets by the husband's earnings in a common law state sell their home and other real property and move to a community property state, where they invest their cash in securities in joint tenancy or community property title. The parties have always considered their property as "belonging to both of them" and frequently do not understand that purchasing joint tenancy securities resulted in a gift of one-half the value from the husband to the wife. While the unlimited marital deduction avoids federal gift tax on such transfers, there may be state gift taxes to consider. In addition, any pre-1982 transfers may have caused taxable gifts under the pre-Economic Recovery Tax Act (ERTA) rules (which did tax interspousal transfers), and interest and penalties may well apply to those gifts. Without having filed a gift tax return for the year in question, the statute of limitations does not run and the taxes, interest and penalty must still be faced.

Many states do not impose a gift tax where real property (as opposed to securities or other types of property) is placed in joint tenancy between a husband and wife, unless the spouses elect to have the transfer treated as a gift. However, the separate nature of the property still remains, and if the title is later changed to community property or tenancy in common, or if the property is sold and a mortgage or trust deed is taken back "as joint tenants", a gift will be triggered! This is a real danger-area for persons moving to a community property state with assets earned by one of the spouses.

In addition, some states (Texas, Louisiana, Idaho) consider the income from assets with a separate property nature to be community property. Others (Arizona, California, Nevada, New Mexico, Washington) consider such income to be the separate property of the spouse who actually "owns" the property. Thus, in the latter group of states, income which comes from an asset which one spouse had before marriage or was given to or inherited by the spouse during marriage is the separate property of that spouse.

It is important to maintain in separate accounts the proceeds of sale of one's separate property and any separate property income. Commingling these funds can transmute them into community property of both spouses and can result in a gift, an act which may result in state gift tax being imposed even though no gift was intended, by using those commingled funds to buy something in co-ownership between the spouses.

Aside from any gift tax aspects, with the increasing frequency of divorce, it may be important for ownership reasons to be able to trace separate and community property.

QUESTIONS AND ANSWERS

Question — What annual gift tax exclusions are available to a donor?

Answer — A donor can make, gift tax free, up to $10,000 worth of gifts (other than "future interest" gifts) to any number of persons or parties each year.[9] The total maximum excludible amount is determined by multiplying the number of persons (or organizations) to whom gifts are made by $10,000.

If the donor is married and his or her spouse consents (by signing the donor's gift tax return) to "splitting" the gift, each spouse is deemed to have given half the gift—even though one spouse in actuality made the entire gift. This has the effect of raising the per donee exclusion to $20,000 per year.

An annual exclusion is allowed only for "present interest" gifts and is denied for "future interest" gifts.[10]

A present interest gift is one in which the donee's possession or enjoyment begins at the instant the gift is made. A future interest is any interest which the donee's use, possession, or enjoyment will not begin until some period of time after the gift is made. In a nutshell, if there is any delay, no matter how short, or any possibility, no matter how remote, that the donee's legal right to use, possession, or enjoyment will not begin at the moment the gift is made, the annual exclusion is denied.

Future interests (which do not qualify for the annual exclusion) include:

(1) reversions,

(2) remainders,

(3) any other delayed interest.

A single transfer may actually be two gifts and for tax purposes will have to be split into two parts. One may be a present interest that qualifies for the annual exclusion. The other gift may be a future interest that will not qualify for the annual exclusion. For instance, assume a donor put $100,000 into a trust which provided that "all the income is to go annually to my son for ten years and one day. The remainder is to go to my daughter at the end of that time".

The first gift, the income to the son, would be a present interest. That's because at the moment of the gift the son has the immediate right to the income stream for 10 years and a day. The present value of that right, according to tables published in the regulations, approximately $62,000, would be the gift. If the donor was married and his spouse consented to splitting the gift, the two annual exclusions would total $20,000, so only $42,000 would be taxable.

The second gift, the daughter's right to the capital at the end of ten years and a day, would be a future interest because her right to possession would be delayed. No annual exclusion would be allowed on that portion (worth approximately $38,000).

Question — Can you summarize the requirements for the gift tax annual exclusion?

Answer — The rules regarding the annual exclusion can be summarized as follows:

(1) A gift in trust is a gift to a trust's beneficiaries for purposes of determining how many annual exclusions may be allowed.

(2) The value of an income interest in a trust qualifies for the annual exclusion if the trustee is required to distribute the income annually or more frequently—even if the value of the remainder interest does not qualify.

(3) The gift of an interest that is contingent upon survivorship is a gift of a future interest. For instance, a gift, "to my son for life, then to my daughter for life, then to my brother if he survives me" is really three gifts. The first gift (to the son) is a present interest if the trustee is given no right to accumulate income and all income must be paid at least annually. The other two gifts (to the daughter and brother) are future interest gifts.

(4) A gift is a future interest gift if the donee's enjoyment depends on the exercise of a trustee's discretion. So if a trustee has the right to accumulate income, the gift is a future interest even if the trustee never exercises the right. The nature of the gift (present or future) is ascertained as of the moment of the transfer and is not determined by what the trustee actually does.

(5) A gift must have an ascertainable value to qualify for the exclusion. If the donor or anyone can divert the income from the beneficiary or it is not reasonably possible at the time of the gift to value it, the exclusion may be denied.

Question — Just how valuable is the annual exclusion—and how would you compute it?

Answer — The annual exclusion can be an extremely effective income, estate, and generation skipping transfer tax saving device.

Figure 11.2

ESTATE TAX OR GST TAX ADVANTAGE OF THE GIFT TAX ANNUAL EXCLUSION*

INPUT:	DONOR'S AGE...	40
INPUT:	DONEES' ANNUAL AFTER-TAX RETURN ON GIFTS	0.060
INPUT:	AMOUNT OF UNUSED ANNUAL EXCLUSION...................	$20,000
INPUT:	NUMBER OF DONEES X	5
		$100,000
	DONOR'S LIFE EXPECTANCY (YEARS)...................... X	42.5
	TOTAL AMOUNT OF GIFTS	$4,250,000
INPUT:	DONOR'S PROJECTED ESTATE TAX OR GSTT BRACKET X	0.50
	POTENTIAL ESTATE TAX OR GSTT SAVINGS	$2,125,000
	PROJECTED VALUE OF GIFTS AT LIFE EXPECTANCY	$18,164,489
	POTENTIAL ESTATE TAX OR GSTT SAVINGS IF ANNUAL GIFTS INVESTED BY DONEES AT COMPOUND INTEREST	$9,082,244

*Illustration courtesy of NumberCruncher Hardware

The illustration at Figure 11.2 multiplies the number of donees by the amount of the annual exclusion available for each and then multiplies that amount by the donor's life expectancy according to the government's table in the regulations. This result is then multiplied by the federal estate tax bracket that you have projected the donor will be in at death. The result is the potential federal estate tax savings if none of the annual gifts are invested by the donees.

The illustration then assumes the donees do invest the annual gifts at the specified rate of return (be conservative since this is an after-tax figure). The final result is the potential estate tax savings—the amount that might have gone to the federal government—if no gifts were made.

Question — What is the unified credit against the gift tax?

Answer — The law provides a single tax credit called the "unified" credit, which is a dollar-for-dollar reduction of any gift or estate tax due. The credit was roughly equivalent to an exemption of $175,625 in 1981, scaling up to $600,000 in 1987 and later years.

	Credit	Exemption Equivalent
1977	$ 30,000[12]	$120,667
1978	34,000	134,000
1979	38,000	147,333
1980	42,500	161,563
1981	47,000	175,000
1982	62,800	225,000
1983	79,300	275,000
1984	96,300	325,000
1985	121,800	400,000
1986	155,800	500,000
1987	192,800	600,000

For example, assume Robin Scott and her husband make a $600,000 gift in 1989 to their son. The computation for *each* spouse would be as follows:

Gift (split under section 2513)	$300,000
Annual Exclusion	10,000
Net Gift	290,000
Tax on Net Gift	84,400
Unified Credit	192,800
Net Tax Due	$ 0

To the extent the credit is used during lifetime it will have the effect of reducing the credit available against the estate tax. Thus, for estate tax purposes there will be only a $108,400 ($192,800 − $84,400) credit left for each spouse as of 1987 (see Appendix B, Estate Tax Computation, for details).

Question — What is a "split gift"?

Answer — When a husband or wife makes a gift to a third person, it may be treated as having been made one-half by the husband and one-half by the wife. This is true even though only one spouse actually makes the gift providing the other spouse consents to the gift.[12]

This would cause the gift tax rate to be lower since the unified rates are progressive. For example: A present interest gift of $110,000 (taxable gift of $100,000) made by a single individual would result in a gift tax of $23,800, whereas a $100,000 taxable gift made by a husband and his consenting wife to a third party (such as a child) would result in each being considered to have made a $50,000 taxable gift and the gift tax would be $10,600 each ($21,200 for both). The savings would be $2,600. A gift tax return must be filed in order to be able to split the gift. Only individuals married to each other can consent to split a gift.

Tools and Techniques

It should be noted that gifts by a husband and wife of community property are *not* eligible for any gift splitting.

Question — What is the gift tax marital deduction?

Answer — In computing the amount of a taxable gift, a deduction is allowed for a gift made by a husband to his wife or vice versa. This deduction is unlimited, so one spouse could conceivably give an entire estate to the other spouse without adverse gift tax consequences.

To qualify for this deduction, the donee-spouse must be given the property outright or must have at least the right to the income from the property and a general power of appointment (essentially the right to say "who gets it") over the principal.[13] (Certain so called "Qualified terminable interest" type property which gives the spouse only a life income may also qualify. This planning technique is discussed more thoroughly in the chapter on marital deduction trusts.)

Question — What is the gift tax based on?

Answer — The gift tax is based on the fair market value of the property transferred.[14]

Question — How is a life insurance policy valued for gift tax purposes?

Answer — If a policy is transferred as a gift immediately after purchase, its value for gift tax purposes is the gross premium paid by the donor.

If a person makes a gift of a previously purchased policy, and the policy is a single-premium or paid-up policy, its gift value is the single premium which the issuing company would charge currently for a comparable contract of equal face value on the life of a person who is the insured's age at the time of the gift.

If the gift is of a policy on which further premium payments are payable, its value is the "interpolated terminal reserve" (roughly equivalent to the cash value) and the value of any unearned portion of the last premium.[15] A gift of group term life is measured by the value of the unearned premium at the date of the transfer, so the ideal time to make an assignment of group term life is immediately before the next premium is due.

If the insured is now uninsurable, the value of the policy may be much more than the interpolated terminal reserve value, depending on health circumstances.

Question — Who must file a gift tax return and when must it be filed?

Answer — The donor must file a gift tax return on or before April 15th following the close of the calendar year in which a gift was made exceeding the annual exclusion or a split gift elected. (An extension of time to file the income tax return automatically extends the time for filing gift tax returns.)

Rules for filing of state gift tax returns vary with the different states.

Question — When is the best time to make a gift?

Answer — Like the answer to the question "When is the best time to plant an oak tree?" the answer to this question is, "twenty years ago." The next best time is right now! The $10,000 per donee annual exclusion ($20,000 when a spouse consents) discussed above is noncumulative; either use it or lose it!

Generally, stocks and other assets which fluctuate widely in value should be given away when the market value for that asset is as low as possible.

However, in any decision making as to giving of property, the financial security of the donor, both current and long-term, should be very carefully considered.

Question — What is the best type of property to give away?

Answer — That depends on the circumstances and objectives of the parties. Income-producing property can be good property to give away if the donor is in a higher income tax bracket than the donee. However, the Tax Reform Act of 1986 has somewhat curtailed this income shifting device. See the discussion under the heading "WHEN IS THE USE OF SUCH A DEVICE INDICATED?" at number 6.

Property which is likely to grow substantially in value (such as, life insurance, common stock, antiques and art, or real estate)is also prime property for giving since future appreciation can be removed from the estate and the gift can be made when the gift tax values (and therefore gift tax transfer costs) are lowest.

Property which has already appreciated should be given away if a sale of such property is contemplated and the donee is in a lower income tax bracket than the donor. Property with relatively low gift tax value and high estate tax value (such as life insurance) makes an excellent gift.

Generally, it is not a good idea to give away "loss property" (property which, if sold, would result in a loss) since the donee cannot use the donor's loss. The donor should sell that property, take the deduction for the loss himself, and give away the cash proceeds.

Although stock in a closely held corporation is often thought of as an ideal asset for gift purposes, care must be taken so that not too much stock is given away. The retention of too little closely held stock might cause an estate to fail the various percentage tests which may qualify it for preferential treatment, e.g., 303 redemptions and Sec. 6166 installment payments of the federal estate tax. (See Chapters 8 and 27.)

Another type of property which might be given is property owned by the donor in a state other than his own state of residence, in order to avoid facing an ancillary probate at the time of the donor's death.

Be sure to consider the age, maturity, and experience of the donee in selecting the gift.

Question — Are there certain types of property which should not be given away?

Answer — It is extremely important to focus on the circumstances of the parties (particularly your client) before making a gift. Do not give away any asset if it will reduce the client's standard of living or financially (or psychologically) endanger his "comfort level." Particularly focus on the impact of the gift on the client's income and capital needs (both present and anticipated) as well as on the client's need for liquidity.

Be aware of the effect of gifts of stock or business or farm interests on qualification for favorable tax law breaks under Code sections 303 (partial stock redemptions to pay death taxes — see chapter 27), 2032A (special use valuation of closely held business and farm real property — see Appendix B, Valuation of Assets), and 6166 (extension of time to pay federal estate tax attributable to closely held business interest — see chapter 8).

Perhaps more important than "what" to give is "how." Outright gifts should be made only after a great deal of consideration. A trust or custodial account or some other form of property management arrangement is appropriate where:

(1) the beneficiary is unwilling or unable to invest, manage, or handle the responsibility of the gift;

(2) the beneficiaries are minors or are adults who lack the emotional or intellectual maturity, physical capacity, or technical training to handle large sums of money or securities;

(3) the donor does not want to significantly reduce the beneficiary's financial dependence on the donor;

(4) the property does not lend itself to fragmentation but the donor desires to spread beneficial ownership among a large number of people (for instance, real estate may be more valuable in some instances if it is not subdivided);

(5) the donor wants to limit the class of beneficiaries and prevent the donee from transferring the property to persons outside the donor's family;

(6) the donor wants to treat children or other relatives equally. A donor may own several parcels of property of equal value. If he gives each to different beneficiaries, one may go up and the other may go down in value. But if they are all placed into one trust and each beneficiary is given an equal share, they will all be treated equally.

We recommend that small outright gifts be made over a period of time to allow beneficiaries to handle money

and other assets under the guidance of the donor. Then larger amounts can be placed into trust - again during the donor's lifetime so that the donor can watch how the trustee invests and manages the property. Lifetime gifts give the donor the opportunity to see how both the trustee and the beneficiaries handle assets and make investments. The donor can then make adjustments to his will and other estate planning vehicles accordingly.

Question — How does the donee of property compute gain or loss on that property if it is subsequently sold?

Answer — Where property is received by gift, the donee is generally required to take over the donor's basis in the property (this is often called a substituted or "carryover" basis).

In addition to that, carryover basis is allowed for the federal gift tax attributable to the appreciation element of the gift. The formula for computing this is:

$$\text{Gift Tax} \quad \times \quad \frac{\text{Net Amount of Appreciation}}{\text{Value of Gift}}$$

For instance, assume property worth $100,000 was given to a donee. The donor's basis was $40,000. Gift tax paid on the gift was $18,000. The donee's basis, as shown in the computer printout below, is $50,800.

COMPUTING BASIS OF GIFT PROPERTY

INPUT: F.M.V. OF PROPERTY AT TIME OF GIFT $100,000

INPUT: DONOR'S BASIS (COST) FOR GIFT $40,000

NET APPRECIATION IN VALUE OF GIFT $60,000

INPUT: GIFT TAX PAID $18,000

DONEE'S BASIS $50,800

If the donee sells property at a gain, he must pay income tax on such gain.

For purposes of determining loss, the donee's basis is the lesser of (a) the donor's basis, or (b) the fair market value of the property at the time of the gift.

Question — What is a "net gift" and what are its tax implications?

Answer — A net gift is a gift of property subject to some obligation or encumbrance. Typically, a net gift results when the donee agrees, as a condition of the gift, to pay

Tools and Techniques

gift taxes on the transfer. The "debt" or obligation against the property may exist before the transfer or arise at the time of the gift.

Netting the gift can be an attractive means of transferring property when a donor does not have cash on hand (and does not want to sell other property to raise cash) to pay gift taxes. A net gift is also useful when a donor wants to limit the extent of the gift to its net value.

For gift tax purposes, the gross amount of the gift is reduced by the amount of the gift tax the donee must pay. In other words, the amount of the gift tax which the donee pays reduces the value of the gift and gift tax is computed on the value of the remaining (net) amount. This means that the actual gift tax liability is lowered since the gift taxes paid reduce the value of the taxable gift.

The value of the "net gift" is measured by the fair market value of the property passing from the donor less the amount of any gift tax paid by the donee. In computing the donee's gift tax liability, you must use the donor's unified credit.

The formula used to compute the donee's tax is: Tentative tax ÷ (1.00 + donor's estate tax bracket)

For instance, assume a retired, 66 year old, single donor living almost entirely from the income of $4,000,000 worth of tax-free municipal bonds, who made no prior gifts, made a gift of property worth $1,000,000. The gift was made to his niece on the condition that she pay the federal gift tax. The tentative tax on a gift of $1,000,000 is $153,000 ($345,800 less a $192,800 unified credit). But the gift tax actually payable (computed below on Number Cruncher I software) is $110,072.

Note that the formula is not applicable if the gift is split between the donor and spouse, each of whom is in a different gift tax bracket because either or both have made prior taxable gifts. Quite often, however, you can determine the correct tax bracket by inspection and adjusting for the bracket differential by computing the tentative tax in the correct lower bracket. In other situations you'll have to make trial computations using first the bracket indicated by the tentative taxable gift and then later using the next lower bracket.

If you have difficulty with making the computation, state your facts in a letter to the Commissioner of Internal Revenue (Actuarial Department), Washington, D.C.

For estate tax purposes, only the net amount of the gift will be considered in the estate tax computation as an adjusted taxable gift. The gift tax paid by the donee can be credited against the donor's estate taxes.

A net gift is treated for income tax purposes as a part sale/part gift transaction to the extent the donor is relieved from paying the gift tax liability. To the extent the donor

TRUE TAX ON A NET GIFT*	
INPUT: YEAR OF GIFT	1989
INPUT: TAXABLE GIFT	$1,000,000
GIFT TAX ON GIFT	$345,800
UNIFIED CREDIT	− $192,800
TENTATIVE TAX	$153,000
TRUE TAX ON NET GIFT EQUALS:	
TENTATIVE TAX	
(1.00 + RATE OF TAX) ..	$110,072

*Courtesy of NumberCruncher Software

is relieved of such liability he or she realizes an immediate economic benefit which is taxable.[16] Specifically, net gifts (made after March 4, 1981) will result in income tax to the donor to the extent the gift tax paid by the donee exceeds the donor's basis in the property.

Question — Can gifts made to a dying spouse cut estate taxes and boost up the basis of appreciated property?

Answer — The so-called "reverse gift" technique is still an appealing strategy where one spouse possesses most of the family wealth and the less affluent spouse is about to die. The wealthier spouse makes a gift of low basis assets to the dying spouse. This inclusion steps up the basis of the property and better utilizes the dying spouse's unified credit.

Note that if a decedent acquires appreciated property by gift within one year of decedent's death and that property passes directly or indirectly to the donor (or donor's spouse) from the decedent, the basis of such property is not stepped up. It remains the basis in the hands of the decedent immediately before the decedent's death.[17] But the technique will work if the decedent lives more than one year after the transfer or the property passes from the decedent to a child or some person other than the grantor or the grantor's spouse.

Question — What is the Crummey technique?

Answer — Typically, a gift in trust does not become immediately available to or enjoyable by beneficiaries; it is therefore a gift of a "future" rather than a "present" interest. Only present interest gifts qualify for the $10,000 annual exclusion allowed by the gift tax law.

Crummey (a case decided by the 9th Circuit in 1968) involved an irrevocable life insurance trust in which the beneficiaries were given the right to *demand*—each year—the lesser of (a) $4,000 or (b) the amount of the donor's transfer (usually an amount approximating the life insurance premiums necessary) to the trust. It was held that the beneficiaries' legal right to immediate use and enjoyment of the contributions to the trust made the transfers present interest gifts which qualified for the annual gift tax exclusion. (Most authorities feel that the trust should include a provision giving each beneficiary the right to demand the lesser of $5,000 or the amount of cash transferred to the trust.)

This technique is an important estate planning tool for four reasons:

First, it enables a donor to transfer money into a trust (to enable the trustee to pay life insurance premiums) gift tax free.

Second, the donor's potential estate tax is reduced by eliminating from the estate tax base the entire amount excluded under the $10,000 annual exclusion.

Third, the technique is an ideal method of saving gift tax on gifts in trust to minors and works even if

(1) the minor beneficiary's right to demand immediate distribution of the contributed corpus is specified to be within a limited period of time, such as the calendar year of the gift to the trust,

(2) the beneficiary in fact does not withdraw the amount contributed to the trust and loses the right to withdraw it after the end of the year in which the gift is made,

(3) the minor beneficiary doesn't have a formal guardian.

Fourth, a gift in trust that qualifies for the annual exclusion by reason of a Crummey withdrawal power will also be shielded from the generation-skipping transfer tax is such power holder is given a separate share of the trust.

The effectiveness of the Crummey gift technique and the rules regarding its use will be subject to "clarification" by case law and Revenue Rulings. One such clarification relates to the donee having a reasonable period of time in which to exercise the power to withdraw the funds and sufficient notice of the existence of the creation of the power. These refinements can be dealt with by providing a reasonable period of time for exercise of the power to withdraw (e.g., 30 days) and actual notice to the donee or his or her actual guardian or legal guardian. The restriction imposed by these rules is that the trust should be created (or subsequent gifts made to it) no later than November or perhaps very early December, but not in the last few days of December.

The Crummey trust gift technique has become a very important aspect of estate planning (see chapter 30).

Question — Does the purchase of property in joint names create a taxable gift?

Answer — It depends on the type of property and also the parties involved. Generally, when property is purchased with the funds of one party and the property is titled jointly, a completed gift is made. The most notable exceptions to this are the titling of property jointly between husband and wife (which because of the unlimited marital deduction is not a taxable event), and titling of joint bank accounts and United States Savings Bonds.

In the case of a joint bank account or United States Savings Bonds, a completed gift does not occur until the noncontributing joint owner draws upon the bank account or surrenders part of the bond for cash.[18]

Question — What techniques remain available after TRA '86 to shift wealth and income to children to save taxes?

Answer — There are still many ways to shift both wealth and income and save taxes.

(1) Give a Series EE U.S. Savings Bond that will not mature until after the donee-child is age 14. No tax will be payable until the bond is redeemed. At that time the gain will be taxed at the child's relatively lower tax bracket. Remember that this strategy will not work if the child already owns Series EE bonds and is already reporting each year's interest accrual as income. Once the election to report income currently is made, it is irrevocable.

(2) Give growth stocks (or growth stock mutual funds) which pay little or no current dividends. The child will therefore pay no tax currently and can hold the stock until reaching age 14. Upon a sale the child will be taxed at the child's bracket.

(3) Give *deep discount* tax-free municipal bonds that mature on or after the child's 14th birthday. The bond interest will be tax free to the child and the discount (face less cost basis) will be taxed to the child at the child's bracket when the bond is redeemed at maturity.

(4) Employ your children. Pay them a reasonable salary for work they actually perform. Remember that the new law standard deduction for children is the greater of (a) $500 or (b) *earned* income (up to a 1988 limit of $3,000). Regardless of how much is paid to the child, the business will have a deduction at its tax bracket, and the amount will be taxable to the child at the child's bracket. Furthermore, the child could establish an IRA to shelter income further.

(5) Consider the multiple advantages of a *term of years* charitable remainder trust for children over age 14 — so the income will be taxed to the child, but the grantor will receive an immediate income tax deduction.

(6) In making gifts to children consider support obligation cases such as *Braun*[19] and *Sutliff*[20]. Parents who can with ease meet the support needs of even an adult college-age child may be considered obligated to provide support. If UGMA (Uniform Gifts to Minors Act) or UTMA (Uniform Transfers to Minors Act) custodial funds or Section 2503(c) trust funds are used to send a child to college, will the parent be taxed? Worse yet, do these cases mean that the custodian or the trustee vio-

lates a fiduciary duty by using such funds to pay for a college education when it's the parent's duty (thus making such funds unavailable for the very purpose for which they were intended)?

Assuming the support problems addressed above are not applicable, judicious use of a 2503(c) trust (but not a UGMA of UTMA account) will allow significant income shifting. The trust can accumulate income while the beneficiary is under age 14 and avoid the kiddie tax. Although only the first $5,000 of that income is taxed at the 15 percent rate, it may not be necessary to fund the trust with property generating more than $5,000 of income. This is so because the 2503(c) trust is designed to make distributions of principal and income to meet its funding objectives.

(7) Emphasis should now be placed on *convertible planning*—the use of a *value shift* followed at the appropriate time by an *income shift*. For example, a GRIT (Grantor Retained Income Trust—see chapter 30) retains for a trust grantor the right to all trust income for a specified number of years. At the end of that time all income and principal will go to the grantor's child (who by then will be 14 or older). None of the principal or appreciation will be in the grantor's estate if the grantor survives the trust term. (Consider a saving clause that terminates the trust in favor of the grantor if tax law is changed to provide that a completed gift does not occur until the donor's interest is terminated.) Consider a split interest purchase of property with the child (see chapter 28). The parent buys and keeps an interest (either for life or a specified term of years) while the child buys and keeps the remainder. This can save estate taxes and generate deductions for the parent. The child's purchase money should come from the other parent, a grandparent, or some source other than the owner-parent. (With respect to these value shifting techniques, see page 477 et seq.)

(8) Life insurance and annuity policies that stay within statutory guidelines (ask for written guarantee from home office) of life insurance should be particularly attractive assuming *loading* costs are relatively low and/or backended. This includes universal, variable, and traditional whole life of the single-, annual-, and limited-payment types. In the case of the SPWL (Single Premium Whole Life) the entire single premium paid at purchase starts earning the declared interest rate immediately. The cost of insurance and expenses is recovered by the insurer from the difference between the declared interest rate and the rate the insurer actually earns. If the policy is surrendered, any unrecovered expenses are deducted from the policy's cash values. The owner can obtain cash values at any time by (1) surrender (gain over cost is taxable) or (2) loan (loan interest is probably nondeductible). Interest is charged at about the same rate credited on borrowed sums and is free of cur-

rent tax. Earnings compound free of current taxation. Unlike tax-free municipal bonds there is no market risk and SPWL is highly liquid. A parent can purchase the product on his own life, which makes college education for the children more likely, and the parent does not have to give up control or make a gift.

(9) Concentrate on gift and estate tax saving devices such as the annual exclusion. Parents should consider giving $10,000 to $20,000 a year of non-income-producing assets to a minor's trust or custodial account; the assets could be converted into income-producing assets slowly after the child turns age 14. The fund can be self-liquidating and exhaust itself by the time the child finishes college/graduate school.

(10) If the parent's return shows a loss, will the child's return be affected by it? (The Code is silent.)

(11) The custodial parent is often the mother, who may have less income (and therefore be in a lower tax bracket) than the father. But what about the logistics of tax return disclosure where the father is filing returns and paying tax for the children? (Suppose he doesn't want her to know how much he has put aside for the kids, and she doesn't want to reveal her income or her new husband's income. Furthermore, the filing father cannot prepare the children's returns until the mother prepares her returns.) What about multiple children from multiple marriages? Split custody?

Techniques for funding a child's education are covered in greater detail in our book, *The Tools and Techniques of Financial Planning*, 3rd edition.

Question — Are all gifts, regardless of amount, entitled to the unified credit and the benefit of the graduated gift tax rates?

Answer — No. For gifts made after December 31, 1987, the benefit of the graduated estate and gift tax rates and the benefit of the unified credit will be phased out for large gifts (see rate tables in Appendix C).

This is accomplished by increasing the gift tax by an additional 5% for taxable amounts exceeding $10,000,000 up to $21,040,000 ($18,340,000 in the case of decedents dying after 1992). The additional 5% is imposed until the benefits of the graduated rates and the unified credit are recaptured.[21] The benefits of the graduated rates and the unified credit are, however, fully available for taxable transfers of less than $10,000,000.

Gifts made before January 1, 1988 are counted in determining the amount of the unified credit subject to the phase-out. Thus, even if a gift of $600,000 were made before January 1, 1988, it would be subject to the full 5% rate adjustment on transfers after 1987.

ASRS, Secs. 51 and 55.

Footnote References

Gifts

1. Reg. §25.2511-1(a); IRC Section 7872(f)(3).

2. Tax Reform Act of 1986, Sections 101 and 1411, amending IRC Section 1.

3. Reg. §25.2511-1(c).

4. Reg. §25.2511-1(c).

5. Reg. §25.2511-2(b).

6. IRC Section 2503(b).

7. IRC Section 2513.

8. See Greenberger, "New Method of Computing Taxes May Weaken ERTA Relief," *Trusts and Estates*, November 1981, page 28.

9. IRC Section 2503(b).

10. Reg. §25.2503-3.

11. For gift tax purposes, only $6,000 of the unified credit can be applied to gifts made after December 31, 1976 and before July 1, 1977. IRC Section 2505.

12. Reg. §25.2513-1.

13. IRC Section 2523.

14. IRC Section 2512; Reg. §25.2512-1.

15. Reg. §25.2512-6.

16. See Rev. Rul. 75-12, 1975-1 C.B. 310 for examples of how to compute the net gift. *Diedrich, et. al. v. Comm.*, 82-1 USTC §9419, 50 AFTR2d 82-5054 (S.Ct., 1982), aff'g 643 F.2d 499, 81-1 USTC §9249, 47 AFTR2d 81-977 (CA-8, 1981), rev'g TCM 1979-441.

17. IRC Section 1014(e), added by ERTA.

18. Reg. §25.2511-1(b)(4).

19. *Frederick C. Braun, Jr. v. Comm.*, TC Memo 1984-285.

20. *Sutliff v. Sutliff*, 489 A.2d 764 (Pa. Super. Ct. 1985).

21. IRC Section 2001(c)(3), as amended by the Revenue Act of 1987 and the Pension Protection Act of 1987, Section 10401(b).

Tools and Techniques

Figure 11.3

UNIFIED RATE SCHEDULE FOR ESTATE AND GIFT TAXES

If the amount with respect to which the tentative tax to be computed is	The tentative tax is:
Not over $10,000	18% of such amount.
Over $10,000 but not over $20,000	$1,800 plus 20% of the excess of such amount over $10,000.
Over $20,000 but not over $40,000	$3,800 plus 22% of the excess of such amount over $20,000.
Over $40,000 but not over $60,000	$8,200 plus 24% of the excess of such amount over $40,000.
Over $60,000 but not over $80,000	$13,000 plus 26% of the excess of such amount over $60,000.
Over $80,000 but not over $100,000	$18,200 plus 28% of the excess of such amount over $80,000.
Over $100,000 but not over $150,000	$23,800 plus 30% of the excess of such amount over $100,000.
Over $150,000 but not over $250,000	$38,800 plus 32% of the excess of such amount over $150,000.
Over $250,000 but not over $500,000	$70,800 plus 34% of the excess of such amount over $250,000.
Over $500,000 but not over $750,000	$155,800 plus 37% of the excess of such amount over $500,000.
Over $750,000 but not over $1,000,000	$248,300 plus 39% of the excess of such amount over $750,000.
Over $1,000,000 but not over $1,250,000	$345,800 plus 41% of the excess of such amount over $1,000,000.
Over $1,250,000 but not over $1,500,000	$448,300 plus 43% of the excess of such amount over $1,250,000.
Over $1,500,000 but not over $2,000,000	$555,800 plus 45% of the excess of such amount over $1,500,000.
Over $2,000,000 but not over $2,500,000	$780,800 plus 49% of the excess of such amount over $2,000,000.

For gifts in excess of $2,500,000 see schedules in Appendix C

Figure 11.4

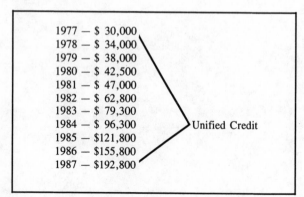

```
1977 — $ 30,000
1978 — $ 34,000
1979 — $ 38,000
1980 — $ 42,500
1981 — $ 47,000
1982 — $ 62,800        Unified Credit
1983 — $ 79,300
1984 — $ 96,300
1985 — $121,800
1986 — $155,800
1987 — $192,800
```

Chapter 12

HR-10 (KEOGH) RETIREMENT PLAN FOR THE SELF-EMPLOYED

WHAT IS IT?

Under an HR-10 (Keogh) plan, a self-employed individual (this term includes a sole proprietor and partners owning 10 percent or more of an interest in a partnership) is allowed to take a tax deduction for money he sets aside to provide for retirement. The HR-10 plan is also a means of providing retirement security for employees working for the self-employed individual.

WHEN IS THE USE OF SUCH A DEVICE INDICATED?

1. When there is a desire on the part of the self-employed to provide personal retirement funds.

2. When there is a desire on the part of the self-employed to provide financial security for the retirement of his or her employees.

3. When the self-employed individual is in a high income tax bracket and would like to defer tax on otherwise currently taxable income.

WHAT ARE THE REQUIREMENTS?

1. Prior to January 1, 1984, an owner-employee (a sole proprietor who owned 100 percent of the business or profession or a partner who owned more than 10 percent of either the capital interest or the profit interest of the partnership) who had full-time employees must have included them in any retirement plan established in which the owner-employee was a participant.

   However, full-time employees with less than three years of service could be excluded. Age could be a basis for exclusion. Likewise, seasonal or part-time employees could also be excluded. A seasonal or part-time individual is one who works less than 1,000 hours during a 12-month period.

   For years beginning after December 31, 1984, HR-10 eligibility rules are the same as those for corporate plans. Full time employees who are below age 21 or who have less than one year of service may be excluded from coverage (the minimum age was reduced from 25).[1]

2. Until 1984, contributions made for covered employees had to be nonforfeitable at the time they were made. Nonforfeitable rights (vested rights) mean that whatever is put into the plan for an employee cannot ever be taken away or lost.[2] (Although contributions were 100 percent vested when made, they need not have been paid immediately to a terminating employee if the terms of the plan permitted the deferral of such payments.) Beginning in 1984, HR-10 plans are treated similar to regular corporate plans. Contributions do not have to be nonforfeitable. A vesting schedule may be established.

3. An HR-10 plan must be in writing.[3] The plan can be described in an individually drafted trust instrument or in a master or prototype plan. A "master plan" refers to a standardized form of plan, with or without a trust, administered by an insurance company or bank acting as the funding medium for purposes of providing benefits on a standardized basis. In a master plan, the sponsoring organization both funds the benefits and administers the plan.

   A "prototype plan" refers to a standardized form of plan which is made available by the sponsoring organization for use without change by a self-employed individual who wishes to adopt such a plan. A prototype plan will not be administered by the sponsoring organization. The employer (the self-employed individual) administers the plan. Internal Revenue Service approval of the plan is generally sought by the sponsoring organization.

   Prior to TEFRA, an HR-10 plan was required to have an institutional trustee, such as a bank or insured credit union. TEFRA repealed this limitation. Thus, the owner-employee maintaining the plan can be the trustee.

4. In addition to the creation of a written instrument, the owner-employee must make a contribution in order to bring the plan into being.

HOW IT IS DONE — AN EXAMPLE

Your client, Marvin Gimpel, is a druggist. He has four full-time employees. Marvin's earned income is $30,000 a year. All his employees have more than one year of service and have attained age 21. Two of his assistants earn $10,000 each, and two other clerks earn $6,000 a year each, a total of $32,000.

Marvin establishes an HR-10 plan. The plan calls for contributions of 10 percent of his earned income to be used to provide a pension for him and contributions of 10 percent of each employee's earnings to provide for their retirements. Since his employees' total salary was $32,000, he would contribute 10 percent of the $32,000 of salary paid to his employees.

Marvin could deduct this entire amount. After making the contribution, however, his own earned income drops to

$26,800 ($30,000 minus his $3,200 contribution). Until 1984, Marvin's contribution to his HR-10 plan would be $2,680 (10% of $26,800). Marvin's total deductions thus would be $5,880. This consists of $3,200 for his employees plus $2,680 for himself. This would reduce his earned income (for federal income tax reporting purposes) to $24,120. However, beginning in 1984, the Tax Equity and Fiscal Responsibility Act of 1982 changed the definition of earned income for a self-employed individual to correspond with the definition of compensation of a common law employee. Earned income is now computed after taking into account amounts contributed by the self-employed individual to the HR-10 plan to the extent a deduction is allowed, not only for his common law employees, but for himself as well. Thus, it appears that a formula will be needed to determine how much he can contribute on his behalf, since you do not know what the contribution will be until after you know how much the earned income is for the self-employed individual, and you do not know what the earned income is until you know what the contribution will be. This change became effective for tax years beginning after December 31, 1983.[4]

WHAT ARE THE TAX IMPLICATIONS?

1. Contributions made on behalf of an owner-employee to an HR-10 plan are deductible from gross income on the owner-employee's federal income tax return.[5] Although substantial parity has been established between HR-10 plans and corporate qualified plans for federal tax purposes, many states allow a lower deduction for contributions to an HR-10 plan. (E.g., until recent conforming legislation, California allowed a maximum deduction of $2,500; it now conforms to federal rules.)

2. The deductible deposits made by an employer are not currently taxable either to the employer himself or to a participating employee. No tax will be paid until benefits are actually received.[6]

3. Income earned by assets in the plan accumulates tax free.[7]

4. A lump-sum distribution receives basically the same tax treatment that a similar distribution would receive from a corporate pension plan.[8]

5. TEFRA limited the exclusion from estate tax for death benefits payable under an HR-10 plan to $100,000, and then the exclusion applied only if the benefit was receivable by any beneficiary (other than the executor) and if payable as an annuity or other than as a lump-sum distribution or if the beneficiary irrevocably elected not to use the special 10-year income averaging.[9]

   However, for years commencing after December 31, 1984, the entire estate tax exclusion has been repealed, so that plan benefits are subject to estate tax like any other asset.[10]

The Tax Reform Act of 1984 contained a provision which permitted individuals who were both in pay status and had made an irrevocable election as to the form of benefit distribution to continue to have the benefit of the estate tax exclusion (the unlimited exclusion for participants in pay status prior to January 1, 1983, or the $100,000 exclusion for participants in pay status prior to January 1, 1985). The Tax Reform Act of 1986 somewhat liberalized the grandfathering provisions. Under the Tax Reform Act of 1986 changes, the participant no longer needs to have been in pay status as of the applicable date. The participant needs only to have separated from service prior to the applicable date and not to have made any change in the form of benefit to be paid.

6. The maximum deductible contribution to a defined contribution plan on behalf of a self-employed individual is limited to the lesser of (a) 25 percent of earned income or (b) $30,000. Under the Tax Reform Act of 1986 (TRA '86) the 25 percent/$30,000 limit is frozen until the defined benefit pension plan limit reaches $120,000, at which time the limit will be increased by reference to the Consumer Price Index.[11] The 25 percent/$30,000 limit does not apply to defined benefit HR-10 plans. Contributions to defined benefit plans are based on actuarial calculations designed to accumulate a reserve large enough to pay the retirement benefits promised by the plan. Under TEFRA and TRA '86 a defined benefit HR-10 plan based on retirement at age 65 can be funded to provide an annual retirement benefit of the lesser of 100 percent of the participant's average compensation for his highest paid three years of participation or $90,000. TRA '86 retains the present law limits and indexes them to the Consumer Price Index ($94,023 for 1988), and conforms the normal retirement age to the Social Security retirement age.[12] If retirement benefits are to commence prior to normal retirement age for receiving full Social Security benefits, the limit is reduced.[13] (For example, in 1987, the $90,000 limit would have been reduced below the previous safe harbor of $75,000 at age 55 to a new maximum annual benefit of approximately $42,000.)

7. Prior to 1987, participants in HR-10 plans could contribute and deduct voluntary employee contributions to such plans. The contribution had to be made in cash and must have been permissible under the terms of the plan. The maximum allowable voluntary employee contribution which could be deducted was the lesser of $2,000 or 100% of compensation (when combined with any contributions made by the individual to an individual retirement plan (IRA) for the same year.) TRA '86 repealed the Code provision providing for deductible voluntary employee contributions.

8. An owner-employee may make additional nondeductible voluntary contributions (like a common law em-

ployee), in addition to his deductible contribution.[14] All such contributions are counted for purposes of the annual additions limitation and must conform to the special nondiscrimination test provided under TRA '86.

9. Until 1984, a 6 percent nondeductible excise tax was imposed on "excess" contributions (above the deductible limits mentioned above) made by self-employed individuals for their own accounts. However, where an HR-10 plan was fully insured, i.e., funded solely through retirement income insurance policies, the owner-employee could *contribute* an amount based on average deductible amounts for the three years immediately preceding the year the last contract under the plan was issued without fear of the excess contributions tax. The deduction, however, was based solely on earned income for the tax year. Between 1984 and TRA '86 there was no excise tax for excess contributions. TRA '86 provides for a 10 percent annual nondeductible excise tax on excess contributions until the excess is eliminated (effective January 1, 1987).[15]

10. Under TEFRA, if an owner-employee was considered a key employee in a top heavy plan, a 10 percent penalty tax was imposed if a distribution occurred prior to attaining age 59½ (this tax was in addition to the normal tax on the distribution). The Tax Reform Act of 1984 eliminated the additional penalty tax on premature distributions to key employees in top heavy plans (see chapter 22), and, instead, imposed the penalty tax on premature distributions to 5-percent owners of the capital or profits interest of the employer, whether or not the plan was top heavy. TRA '86 imposes a 10 percent penalty tax on *all* distributions before attaining age 59½, with certain exceptions (death, divorce, disability, payments made over the participant's life starting from separation from service, and medical expenses).[16]

11. See chapter 22 for a discussion of the excise tax imposed on excess distributions and accumulations in an HR-10 plan.

IMPLICATIONS AND ISSUES IN COMMUNITY PROPERTY STATES

The benefit accumulated in an HR-10 plan for an employee who was married during his participation in the plan while a resident of a community property state belongs equally to the employee and his or her spouse. The employee and spouse can, however, change the normal effect of community property laws by an agreement, such as a pre-nuptial agreement, to the effect that all earnings of the individual will be community property but that contributions to a qualified retirement plan for the employee's benefit will be solely the employee's property. However, the Retirement Equity Act of 1984 limits the ability of a married participant to solely retain plan benefits without the participant's spouse's consent (see Chapter 22).

One frequent issue concerns individuals moving from common law to community property states. For instance, assume a married employee was a resident of a non-community property state for ten years. He and his wife then moved to California where they resided for five years. Contributions were made to an HR-10 plan each year on his behalf throughout the fifteen-year period. What is the status of ownership of benefits accumulated in the plan over the fifteen-year period? The answer is that a portion of the benefits will be community property. Depending on the circumstances, a court may determine the community property portion on the basis of the "contributions made" or the "time" method.

The "contributions made" method would divide the benefits in the proportion of contributions made after moving to the community property state, plus earnings, to the total amount in the plan. The "time" method would divide benefits on the basis of proportionate years of participation in the plan; i.e., one-third of the benefits would be community property.

Each method has advantages and disadvantages. If annual contributions for the employee were greater in the years in which he lived in a community property state, the time method would cause more of the benefits to be separate property than the "contributions made" method. Other methods of dividing community property HR-10 benefits could be used where appropriate.

The non-community property portion of the HR-10 benefit would be the separate property of the employee. In the event of a divorce or the death of the employee, California law provides that certain separate property of the employee be treated as community property for purposes of division on divorce or the employee's death. This separate property is referred to as quasi-community property. Generally, quasi-community property is personal property, wherever situated, and real property situated in California, which would have been community property had the owner acquired it in California. For all purposes other than division on divorce or the employee's death, the benefits remain the employee's separate property. Thus, if the employee's wife predeceases him, her estate will not have any rights to any part of the separate property portion of the HR-10 benefits.

QUESTIONS AND ANSWERS

Question — What is meant by the term "earned income"?

Answer — Earned income is net earnings derived from a self-employed individual's business as a result of personal efforts or personal service rendered as distinguished from investment income. Therefore, inactive owners, such as limited partners, whose income is derived solely from an investment made in the partnership, have no earned income from the firm.

Generally the entire net earnings received by a self-employed individual who is an attorney, an accountant, a physician, or other professional is considered as earned income. "Net earnings" means gross earnings less all allowable business deductions and allowable deductions under Code Sections 404 and 405(c) pertaining to contributions to a qualified plan. These deductions include not only the deductions for common law employees but include deductions for owner-employees as well.

It appears that if deductions for owner-employees must be taken into account before determining such owner-employee's "earned income," an unknown situation presents itself. You can not determine an owner-employee's earned income until you know the allowable contribution for him. You can not determine the allowable contribution until you know his earned income. In some cases an interdependent variable formula will be needed to determine the proper deductible contribution.

But the computation is relatively simple when there are no employees. For example, if the owner-employee's Schedule C earnings are $60,000, multiply by 20 percent to obtain the maximum contribution allowable on his behalf. The figure you arrive at is $12,000. That is the same figure you compute by multiplying his $48,000 net earnings ($60,000 – $12,000) by 25 percent.

Figuring the owner-employee's maximum contribution is not difficult even if there are employees. For instance, assume a payroll of $10,000 for other employees. If you multiply that by 25 percent, you find a $2,500 contribution must be made on behalf of employees. This drops the $60,000 base for determining the owner-employee's contribution in the example above down to $57,500. If you then multiply $57,500 by 20 percent, you arrive at an $11,500 contribution. This is the same as if you found 25 percent of his $46,000 ($57,500 – $11,500) net earnings.

In the case of commercial businessmen and farmers, these individuals can count their entire annual net profit as earned income.

Question — Can an individual who is a full-time corporate employee but who conducts independent consulting work or "moonlights" and receives fees make contributions based on self-employment income?

Answer — Yes. For example, Sel Horvitz, a practicing attorney who teaches three days a week at a local law school and who is participating in the school's tax deferred annuity plan, can still set up an HR-10 plan for himself based on the income earned in private practice. However, there are overall "all plans" limits which may not be exceeded. Sel can also contribute to an IRA up to a maxi-

mum of $2,000 or 100% of his compensation, whichever is lower.

Under TRA '86, a tax deduction may be allowed for single or joint filers with adjusted gross income up to a specified limit[17] (see chapter 14). TRA '86 does permit tax deferred compounding of IRA contributions, even if the contribution to the IRA is not deductible.[18]

Question — Under what circumstances can benefits be paid from an HR-10 plan?

Answer — An HR-10 plan, as well as all corporate qualified plans, must begin distributing benefits by April 1 of the year following the year the employee attains age 70½ or, if later, retires. In plan years beginning after 1984, distributions to 5 percent owners must begin by April 1 following the year of attainment of age 70½, even if the participant is not retired. TRA '86 generally requires all qualified plans to commence distributions by April 1 following the calendar year in which any participant (whether or not retired) attains age 70½ (effective January 1, 1989).[20] The distribution date can be postponed beyond age 70½ for participants who made elections to postpone distributions prior to January 1, 1984 under TEFRA Section 242(b). (See Chapter 22 for other distribution requirements.)

Previously, as long as the participant was not a 5 percent owner of the employer, he could receive distributions at any time without incurring a tax penalty. Under TRA '86, a 10 percent nondeductible tax penalty is imposed on all distributions before the participant attains age 59½, with certain exceptions (death, divorce, disability, payments made over the participant's life starting from separation from service, and medical expenses).[19] (See item 10 under "What Are the Tax Implications?")

TRA '86 replaced a previously available special 10-year forward averaging with 5-year forward averaging unless the participant reached age 50 by January 1, 1986, and uses the 1986 income tax rates.[21] This favorable tax treatment is available only for "lump sum distributions." A distribution will be considered to be made in a "lump-sum" if (a) it is made within one taxable year of the recipient, (b) it consists of the balance of the employee's account, and (c) it occurs under one of the following circumstances:

1. On account of the death of an employee or self-employed person.

2. After the disability of a self-employed person.

3. After an owner-employee or any other employee attains age 59½ (even if employment has not yet terminated).

Question — How may contributions be invested?

Answer — HR-10 plan funds can be invested in life insurance contracts (subject to limitations), mutual funds, variable annuities, government bonds, savings accounts, securities, real estate, etc., or a combination of these funding media.

Question — Can pre-retirement death benefits be provided under an HR-10 plan?

Answer — Yes. Immediate and substantial death benefits can be made available through life insurance to beneficiaries of the owner-employee and other plan participants. These benefits will be received income tax free and can be coordinated with the personal life insurance programs of the participants. (Note, however, that the cash value portion of the death benefit will be subject to income tax.)

Question — If life insurance is used in a plan and paid for by employer contributions to the plan, is any of the premium taxable to the employee?

Answer — The cost of pure insurance is taxable as a current economic benefit. For common law employees the amount the covered person must include is based on government tables. The cost of insurance for a self-employed person is not a deductible contribution. (Pure insurance is the difference between the face amount of the policy, i.e., the death benefit, and the policy's cash value.)[22]

For example, if a $1,000 premium is paid for an ordinary life insurance policy and $150 of the premium represents the cost of pure life insurance, an employee is taxed currently on $150, and an owner-employee cannot deduct the $150.

Any deductible employee contributions which are applied toward the purchase of life insurance will be treated as a distribution in the year so applied.[23]

Question — Many HR-10 plans are "defined contribution plans," i.e., the pension benefit at retirement will be whatever a specified contribution, plus appreciation on the contributions, will earn. Are there other types of plans?

Answer — Yes. There are two alternatives: (1) A defined contribution (profit-sharing) plan can be devised. Contributions in this case would be based on a formula that is applied to the earned income (the profits) of the self-employed individual. (2) A defined benefit plan can also be devised. Under a defined benefit plan a predetermined annual retirement benefit is funded for on an annual basis. A defined benefit formula may have some advantages for the self-employed person over a defined contribution formula. For one, contributions can exceed the 25 percent/$30,000 limits. Second, the proportionate contribution for other employees may be lower than in a defined contribution plan, especially if the other employees are under age 30.

Question — In an HR-10 plan, may employees below a certain age be excluded from coverage?

Answer — Yes, TEFRA repealed the Code section limiting the only eligibility requirements to a 3-year waiting period. An HR-10 plan may now require the same eligibility requirements as a corporate qualified plan (see "Eligibility," Chapter 22, infra).

Question — What must a sole proprietor or partnership do to set up an HR-10 plan?

Answer — To set up an HR-10 plan, a plan that meets the applicable requirements for tax qualification must be executed on or before the last day of the proprietor's or partnership's tax year. Employees must be informed of the plan and contributions must be made within the period required for filing the sole proprietor's or partnership's income tax return (including extensions).

Question — If a self-employed individual contributes less than the maximum allowed in any one year, can he make up the excess in the next tax year?

Answer — Generally, no. Contributions to an HR-10 plan for self employed individuals are allowed only on a year-to-year basis. The law now has no carryover provisions for self-employed individuals. If the amount contributed in a given year was less than the amount allowable, the self-employed individual cannot make it up and contribute more than the limit in the following year. However, before TRA '86, the law did allow carryovers for common law employees. Between TRA '84 and TRA '86, carryovers were permitted for self-employed individuals the same as they were for common law employees. TRA '86 eliminated the carryforward deduction for plan years beginning after December 31, 1986. However, pre-January 1, 1987, unused carryforward amounts will be deductible.[24]

Question — Can an excess contribution be made to an HR-10 plan without penalty?

Answer — No. For years after 1983, HR-10 plans and corporate plans are treated similarly. After 1983 and before TRA '86, employers were able to contribute amounts to such plans in excess of currently deductible amounts. The excess over the amount that was deductible would be carried over into future years. TRA '86 does not permit excess contributions to HR-10 plans or corporate plans. Contributions exceeding the deductible limit are subject to a 10 percent annual nondeductible excise tax until the excess is eliminated.[25]

Question — Can loans be made from an HR-10 plan to an employee without its being treated as a taxable distribution?

Answer — Yes, but only for persons who are not owner-employees. Within certain limits a loan from an HR-10 plan (made after August 13, 1982), which must be repaid within 5 years will not be considered a taxable distribution if it does not exceed the lesser of $50,000 or one-

Tools and Techniques

half of the employee's nonforfeitable accrued benefit under the plan. (A loan of up to $10,000 is allowed, even though more than half the employee's accrued benefit.) For loans made after December 31, 1986, the $50,000 limit will be reduced by the highest outstanding loan balance during the prior 12-month period.[26] This effectively prohibits "rollovers" of loans in excess of $25,000.

The loan should bear a reasonable rate of interest, be adequately secured, provide a reasonable repayment schedule, and be made available on a basis which does not discriminate in favor of employees who are highly-paid.

Note, the 5-year repayment rule does not apply to loans used for residential mortgages.[27] A loan in excess of these prescribed limits would be treated as a taxable distribution.

Generally, loans to "owner-employees" are prohibited transactions and should not be made.

Question — What is a "top heavy" HR-10 plan? Of what significance is the term?

Answer — For plan years beginning after 1983, any plan is a "top heavy" plan if as of the determination date (generally, the last day of the preceding plan year or last day of a new plan's year) the present value of the "key employees" aggregate accrued benefits for a defined benefit plan or the account balances of "key employees" for a defined contribution plan exceed 60 percent of the aggregate accrued benefits or account balances of all employees.[28] Under this definition most HR-10 plans will be considered "top heavy".

A key employee is any employee-participant who, at any time during the plan year or in the 4 preceding plan years, is (or was) an officer, an employee owning one of the ten largest interests in the employer, a more than 5 percent owner, or a more than 1 percent owner earning more than $150,000 a year.[29]

If a plan is considered "top heavy" certain additional requirements must be met. These include:

(1) Rapid Vesting—A top heavy plan must provide for vesting under one of two alternative schedules. One schedule provides any employee with 3 years of service shall be 100 percent vested. The other alternative provides a 6 year graduated schedule beginning after 2 years of service.

(2) Minimum non-integrated contribution or benefit for non-key employees—For a defined contribution plan, the employer generally must contribute for a non-key employee an amount equal to at least 3 percent of that participant's compensation. However, if the key employee uses a percentage for himself which is lower, that percentage may be used.

For a defined benefit plan, the benefit for a non-key employee which must be accrued is at least 2 percent of the employee's average annual compensation multiplied by the employee's years of service with the employer in which a top heavy plan year ends. The minimum benefit however, need not exceed 20 percent of such annual compensation. Years of service before January 1, 1984 need not be counted.

(3) $200,000 cap on compensation (which shall be adjusted by the Secretary of the Treasury beginning after January 1, 1988[30])—If a plan is a "top heavy" plan, only the first $200,000 of compensation (as adjusted) may be taken into account in determining benefits or contributions.

(4) Aggregate limit on benefits and contributions for key employees in a defined benefit and a defined contribution plan—If an employee participates in both types of plans, both of which are top heavy, the sum of the "defined benefit plan fraction" (a fraction based on the portion of the maximum permitted limit for a defined benefit plan the participant has used) and the "defined contribution plan fraction" (a fraction based on the portion of the maximum permitted limit for a defined contribution plan the participant has used) for any year may not exceed 1.0.

The vesting, minimum benefits and limits on compensation requirements do not apply to any employee who is represented by a collective bargaining unit where evidence exists that retirement benefits were the subject of good faith bargaining.

Question — Can plans covering owner-employees be integrated with social security?

Answer — Until January 1, 1984, a modified form of integration was possible only in defined contribution plans where contributions for owner-employees did not exceed one-third of the total amount contributed. The amount of the social security tax paid for employees and the self employment tax for owner-employees was subtracted from each respective contribution.

For plan years beginning after December 31, 1983, the Tax Equity and Fiscal Responsibility Act of 1982 extended the defined contribution HR-10 integration rules to all defined contribution plans, both corporate and noncorporate. A defined contribution plan will be properly integrated with social security if the total contribution for each participant plus the employer's contribution for old age, survivors, and disability insurance (OASDI) bears a uniform relationship to the participant's total or basic or regular rate of compensation. For example, a defined contribution plan would be properly integrated if it provided for contributions of 6.06 percent of 1988 compensation (the employer's tax rate for OASDI for

1988) in excess of $45,000 (the taxable wage base for 1988) and no contributions on the first $45,000.

For plan years beginning after 1988, the contribution rate (%) that applies to compensation above the taxable wage base may not exceed the contribution rate (%) that applies to compensation below the taxable wage base by more than the *lesser of* (1) the rate applied to compensation below the wage base or (2) 5.7% points (or, if greater, the rate of social security tax attributable to old-age insurance).[31] For example, if the plan provides for contributions of 10 percent of pay in excess of the wage base, it would be properly integrated if it provided for contributions of at least 5 percent on pay below the wage base.

If the plan is a "top heavy" plan, the employer generally must contribute on behalf of each non-key participant an amount which is equal to at least 3 percent of his compensation. However, if the employer's maximum contribution rate is less than 3 percent for a key employee that rate may be used.[32]

It appears that defined benefit plans which include owner-employees which, in prior years, could not be integrated, can be integrated in a manner similar to corporate integrated plans as of the effective date of this provision.

ASRS, Sec. 51, Sec. 60.

Footnote References

HR-10

1. IRC Section 410.
2. IRC Section 401(d)(2)(A).
3. ERISA Section 402.
4. IRC Section 401(c)(2).
5. IRC Section 62(7). Contributions on behalf of common law employees are deductible under 404(a).
6. Regs. §1.402(a)-1(a)(1)(i); in tax years beginning before 1982, amounts were subject to tax if they were "available," as well. *Estate of Simmie v. Comm.*, 69 T.C. 890 (1978).
7. IRC Section 501(a).
8. IRC Section 402(e).
9. IRC Section 2039(c), as repealed by TRA '84.
10. IRC Section 2039, as amended by TRA '84, Section 525.
11. IRC Section 415(c)(1)(A), as amended by TRA '86, Section 1106(a).
12. IRC Sections 415(b)(2)(C) and 415(b)(2)(D), as amended by TRA '86, Section 1106(b).
13. Id.
14. TEFRA Section 237, repealing IRC Sections 4972 and 401(d)(5).
15. IRC Section 4979, as added by TRA '86, Section 1117(b).
16. IRC Section 4974, as amended by TRA '86, Section 1121(a).
17. IRC Section 219(g), as added by TRA '86, Section 1101.
18. IRC Section 408(o), as added by TRA '86, Section 1102.
19. IRC Section 401(a)(9)(C), as amended by TRA '86, Section 1121(b).
20. IRC Section 72(t), as added by TRA '86, Section 1123(a).
21. IRC Section 402(e)(1)(C), as amended by TRA '86, Sections 1122(a), (e).
22. IRC Section 404(e).
23. IRC Section 72(o)(3).
24. TEFRA Section 237(a)(1), repealing IRC Section 401(d)(5); IRC Section 404(a)(3)(A), as amended by TRA '86, Section 1131(a).
25. IRC Section 4972, as added by TRA '86, Section 1131(c).
26. IRC Section 72(p)(2)(A), as amended by TRA '86, Section 1134(a).
27. IRC Section 72(p).
28. IRC Section 416(g).
29. IRC Section 416(i).
30. IRC Section 416(d), prior to repeal by TRA '86, Section 1106(d)(3). See also IRC Section 401(a)(17), as amended by TRA '86, Section 1106(d)(1).
31. IRC Section 401(l), as amended by TRA '86, Section 1111(a).
32. IRC Section 416(c).

Chapter 13

INCORPORATION

NOTE: This discussion deals with the general treatment of corporations. In the case of corporations which have elected special status under Subchapter S, different rules may apply. Please refer to Chapter 25.

WHAT IS IT?

There is no formal definition of a corporation under the tax law, as neither the Code nor the regulations expressly define the term. Local law does not control for tax purposes. Under the Code, an organization that has a preponderance of the following elements generally will be taxed as a corporation: (1) associates, (2) limited liability, (3) free transferability of interests, (4) centralized management, (5) continuity of life, and (6) an objective to carry on business and divide the gains therefrom.[1] These terms are explained in the paragraphs which follow.

A corporation must generally have *associates* since it is an inanimate entity that can act only through its board of directors, officers, or agents. These individuals must be bound together for common objectives. However, "one man" corporations may still be recognized as corporations for purposes of federal tax law, provided that the requisite formalities are complied with. Generally, the primary purposes of their association will be the operation of a business for profit.

Limited liability is possessed by an organization that can answer negatively to the question, "Could a creditor of the organization proceed against the individual owners personally in an attempt to satisfy an obligation incurred by the organization?" This is one of the best-known reasons for choosing the corporate form.

If the formalities of corporate procedure are followed, then the corporation is really operating as a business and financial unit entirely separate from its shareholders for tax and most legal purposes. Shareholders will ordinarily not be personally liable for the corporation's debts or other liabilities. (As a practical matter, principal shareholders of small corporations will often be required to cosign a note or give a personal guarantee for the corporation and, therefore, become personally liable for loans to the corporation by banks or other lending institutions. Generally, however, the most a shareholder can lose is his investment in the business.[2])

Free transferability of interest generally means that a member of a corporation can transfer his interest in the profits, assets, and control of the business freely and without restraint. If each member, without the consent of the other members of the organization, can transfer his entire interest to a person who is not a member, there is "free transferability

of interest." It is permissible, however, to impose reasonable restrictions on shareholders to preserve the nature of close corporate membership. These restrictions are often contained in "buy-sell" agreements and facilitate family estate planning with respect to a business interest.[3]

The characteristic of *centralized management* poses the question, "Is the operating authority concentrated in one man or a relatively small class within the group as opposed to the sharing of management decisions commonly found in partnerships?" If any person or group of persons (which does not include all of the members) has continuing, exclusive authority to make the decisions necessary to the management and daily operation of the business, there is centralized management.

The group in which that authority is legally vested is called the board of directors. The board of directors uses its best judgment and independent discretion to determine and execute corporate policies. Although these persons are in fact elected by the shareholders and removable by them for cause (and possibly without cause), the directors are not agents of the shareholders. They are fiduciaries whose duties primarily run to the corporation itself.

It is the board of directors, not the shareholders, who make policy decisions with respect to the products, services, prices, and wages of the company. Likewise, even in the smallest corporation, legally speaking, it is the board of directors which has the right to select, supervise, and remove officers and other personnel. For example, the board of directors, and not the shareholders, fixes compensation and decides on the installation and benefit levels of pension and profit sharing plans, as well as other employee benefits. In short, the supervision and vigilance for the welfare of the entire corporate enterprise is vested in the hands of a very select group.[4]

Continuity of life means that death, disability, incapacity, addition of a new member, or withdrawal of an old member will not cause legal dissolution of the business. If the effect of the death of a member of the firm is the automatic death of the business, a vital element of corporate status is lacking. A corporation is the only form of business enterprise which—theoretically at least—has the advantage of perpetual existence. For example, even the death of a 100 percent stockholder would not cause the legal termination of the business. Practically, speaking, however, without successor management, such a corporation will "die" as quickly as a sole proprietorship. (Some states impose limitations on corporate duration although most jurisdictions allow a corporation to select any period of time desirable.)[5]

WHEN IS THE USE OF SUCH A DEVICE INDICATED?

1. One factor is when a relatively simple and inexpensive means of transferring ownership is desired. It is relatively easy to provide for a new owner's entrance and an old member's exit by merely endorsing shares of stock. This is especially important for gifting to minors.

2. In many instances, the most important factor is when limited liability on the part of the individual owners is desired. The corporation and not its shareholders is responsible for corporate obligations.

3. When a number of fringe benefits are desired. These can be made available through the corporation to its employees. Such benefits are, within limits, tax deductible by the corporation and generally are not currently taxable to the employee—including shareholder-employees. These fringe benefits may include

   (a) pension/profit-sharing plans

   (b) group life insurance

   (c) group health insurance

   (d) disability income coverage

   (e) medical reimbursement plans

   (f) cafeteria plans

   (g) auto and travel costs

4. When other tax-oriented advantages are desired. For instance, assuming a corporation does not have to pay out substantial dividends, the overall tax result may be lower federal income taxes than if the enterprise were run in the form of a sole proprietorship or partnership. It might be easiest to illustrate this point by comparing partnership with corporate tax treatment. If a partnership were formed, owners would be taxed on all the income earned as partners—even if they didn't actually withdraw all partnership earnings from the firm. However, as stockholder-employees, they would be taxed only on salaries (assuming no dividend had to be paid). A lower federal income tax under the corporate form may result because a new tax-paying entity, the corporation, has been created.

   Since the corporation's tax rate may be lower than the individual's tax rate, this income splitting can yield a lower overall current tax. This is especially true on the first $50,000 of corporate income, which is taxed at only a 15% rate. However, as a result of the Tax Reform Act of 1986, the maximum corporate rate is greater than the maximum individual rate. Additionally, it may be more expensive taxwise to be a corporation when it comes down to selling the business. Under the new rules, there may be two taxes as a result of a corporate sale of assets (followed by liquidation) instead of one tax when the seller is a proprietorship or partnership. Thus, if you have assets in the corporation that are likely to appreci-

ate, the income-splitting benefit may be more than offset by the additional taxes.

The rates on corporate taxable income for tax years beginning on and after July 1, 1987 (1988 Corporate Tax Table), including worksheets for computing the tax, are shown below:

1988 CORPORATE TAX TABLE

Taxable Income	Base Amount	Base Tax Owed	% on Excess
0	50,000	0	0.15
50,000	75,000	7,500	0.25
75,000	100,000	13,750	0.34
100,000	335,000	22,250	0.39
335,000	. . . .	113,200	0.34

CORPORATE TAX CALCULATING WORKSHEET

	Example
Step 1: List Taxable Income	$200,000
Step 2: List Base Tax	22,250
Step 3: Compute "Excess" Over Base Amount	$100,000
Step 4: List % on "Excess"	.39
Step 5: Multiply Step 3 x Step 4	39,000
Step 6: Total Steps 2 and 5	61,250

Figure 13.1 compares the tax payable by various entities on $100,000 of taxable income.

Note that graduated rates are denied to personal service corporations. Every dollar of the taxable income of a "qualified personal service corporation" is taxed at a flat rate of 34 percent. The term "qualified personal service corporation" means one in which (a) substantially all of the activities involve the performance of services in the fields of health, law, engineering, architecture, accounting, actuarial science, performing arts, or consulting, and (b) substantially all of the stock of which is held by employees or by their estates.

A corporation can generally declare and pay dividends—as well as salaries—in such a manner as to avoid a "bunching" of income in those years when personal income is highest. On the other hand, if the business were established in the partnership form, the owners would have little control over the receipt and taxation of income. This ability to "time" income is important since, if income can be timed, the ultimate taxes payable can be lowered.

5. When the estate owner wants to entice family members into the business by giving them a stake in the business without giving them control.

Figure 13.1

TAX COMPARISON — 1988*	INPUT: TAX. INCOME	TAX	NET INCOME	MARGINAL RATE	OVERALL RATE
CORPORATE	$100,000	$22,250	$77,750	0.34	0.22
JOINT	$100,000	$25,537	$74,463	0.33	0.26
EXEMPTIONS	1				
SINGLE	$100,000	$28,522	$71,478	0.28	0.29
EXEMPTIONS	1				
SEPARATE	$100,000	$29,269	$70,731	0.33	0.29
EXEMPTIONS	1				
HEAD	$100,000	$26,810	$73,190	0.33	0.27
EXEMPTIONS	1				
TRUST/ESTATE	$100,000	$28,000	$72,000	0.28	0.28

*Illustration Courtesy of NumberCruncher Software.

6. When privacy is desired. The transfer of stock in a closely held corporation is not generally a matter of public record. This makes it possible to shield family financial affairs from public scrutiny.

7. When continuity of operation is important. A corporation may, within limits, legally continue its business with little or no hindrance from the probate court. This makes it possible for corporate officers to make major decisions regarding property which the client has contributed to the corporation without the necessity or delay of the judicial process, and with little or no publicity.

8. When gift tax savings are desired. The transfer of a minority interest in a closely held business may result in a discounted value for gift tax purposes. In other words, transfers of property (via its stock "wrapper") can sometimes be made at discounted values for gift tax purposes.

9. When estate tax savings are desired. Transfers of stock reduce the donor's estate by (1) shifting appreciation in value from donor to donee and (2) shifting income on stock (dividends) to the donee. The stock which is ultimately included in the donor's estate may itself be a minority interest and may therefore (or because of lack of marketability) be valued at a discount.

Disadvantages of the Corporate Form

1. There are a number of additional expenses associated with forming and maintaining a corporation (e.g., attorney fees, accounting fees, corporate supplies, and state incorporation fees).

2. Since the passage of the 1986 Tax Reform Act, the maximum tax rate at the corporate level is higher than the maximum tax rate at the individual level. Thus, for businesses with substantial taxable income, incorporating may increase income taxes. (For a form of corporation that can take advantage of the lower individual rates, see chapter 25, S Corporation.)

3. While some types of income passed through to shareholders are taxed only once (e.g., salaries), dividends are subject to both corporate and shareholder levels of tax.

4. One of the most dramatic disadvantages created by the Tax Reform Act of 1986 was the repeal of the "General Utilities Doctrine." The General Utilities Doctrine essentially avoided a corporation's having to recognize a gain upon a liquidation or sale (followed by a liquidation) of the business. There was generally only one tax at the shareholder level (except for certain recaptures, receivables, etc.).

For example, under the prior rules, if $10,000 were invested by a corporation in a piece of land and the land were worth $100,000 after 10 years, upon liquidation the corporation would be giving the land to the shareholder, and the shareholder would be receiving a $100,000 value in exchange for turning in the stock that cost him, say, $10,000. This would result in a $90,000 capital gain. The corporation generally would not be treated as recognizing any gain. However, the corporation in general was not taxed on any excess of value over the cost the corporation had in the land.

Under the 1986 Tax Reform Act, abolishing the "General Utilities Doctrine," upon liquidation the corporation would be treated as having "sold" the coporate assets and would be taxed on the excess value of the assets over the corporation's basis in the assets. If the corporation had only a $10,000 income tax basis in the land and the land was worth $100,000, then the corporation would first have to recognize a $90,000 gain. Whatever was left after the corporation paid the tax would come out to the shareholder in the liquidation and the shareholder would then be taxed on that receipt, resulting in two taxes to pay.

In general, these rules go into effect for liquidations after December 31, 1986. There is a "grace period" for small corporations (under $5,000,000 in value) that lasts until 1989.

5. In general, you are dealing with a more complex organizational structure and may have to deal with some complex issues (e.g., personal holding company tax, accumulated earnings tax, dividend treatment, collapsible corporation rules).

6. The taxable income of personal service corporations is taxed at a flat rate of 34 percent from the very first dollar. This 34 percent tax eliminates the benefit of the "run up the brackets" for doctors, lawyers, accountants, architects, and other professionals who practice in the corporate form. If the corporation "zeroes out" its taxable income through reasonable salary payments to employee shareholders, there will be no taxable income upon which the IRS can impose the 34 percent tax. But this makes it more likely that the IRS will soon try to disallow deductions for salary payments in a professional service corporation under the "reasonableness" test. In other words, the IRS has a strong incentive to claim that payments made as compensation should be recharacterized as nondeductible dividends to shareholder employees. If the IRS is successful with such an attack, the corporation will then have more income taxable at a 34 percent rate — and then the same dollars will again be taxed to the shareholders upon receipt. One way out of the 34 percent tax trap is to elect S corporation treatment.

HOW IT IS DONE — AN EXAMPLE

Stevens, Roberts, and Lee are engineers who feel they can develop a relatively inexpensive process for manufacturing an aircraft safety component which is in great demand for new jet airliners.

Stevens is a sole proprietor currently engaged in producing aircraft parts. Roberts, a young man who has a postgraduate degree in business administration and an undergraduate degree in engineering, has worked for Stevens for a number of years. He first started as an engineer and almost by accident moved into the firm's sales division. Robert's sales efforts have been so successful that Stevens would like to offer him an interest in a new business venture.

Lee is slightly older than Stevens or Roberts. He is a well-known and highly respected authority in the area of aircraft safety parts. He does quite a bit of consulting work for both government and private enterprise. He met Stevens and Roberts on such a consulting project, and the three men have become good friends. Lee is quite wealthy, and he is interested in keeping both his money and his mind at work.

All three men have something to contribute to a corporation. In return they will want to participate in the control and profits of the business while it is running, or in a distribution of the assets of the business if the corporation's life ends. In other words, they will expect "shares" of the corporation. Assume Stevens will contribute his business (his sole proprietorship). Lee will contribute cash or securities. Roberts wants to contribute his services and a small amount of cash in return for his stock.

Assuming this were the case, here is what might happen: If Lee decides that his contribution to the capital of the corporation will be cash, the stock he receives will normally have a value at the time of the exchange equal to the cash. For example, if he transfers $10,000 of cash to the corporation, he will ordinarily receive back stock with a fair market value of $10,000. Since the value of the stock he receives is no more or less than the value of the cash he transfers to the corporation, he realized neither a gain nor a loss. If he later sells his stock, the cash he paid will determine the basis of his stock. If he realizes $21,000 on the sale of the stock, his gain would be $11,000, the difference between his basis for the stock ($10,000) and the amount he realizes on the sale ($21,000).

Absent provisions in the tax law to the contrary, if any of the three contributed appreciated property to the corporation in return for its stock, a taxable gain would result. But there is an important exception to that general rule.

The exception was designed to encourage the formation of a new corporation. It enables a taxpayer to transfer appreciated property, or even a going business, into a new corporation without the transferor recognizing income on the appreciation at the very time when his other expenses—the expenses involved in the organization and operation of the corporation—are the highest. The exception provides that even if the transferor "realizes" a gain when he transfers appreciated property to his new corporation, he doesn't have to "recognize" gain for tax purposes.[6]

This exception is conditioned on meeting certain basic requirements. It basically states that where a person or persons transfer *property* to a corporation (a) solely in exchange for the corporation's own stock or securities, and (b) the transferor(s) control the corporation immediately after the transfer, no gain will be recognized on the appreciated business or securities contributed to the new corporation. Control generally means ownership of 80 percent or more of the corporation's stock.[7]

The philosophy here is similar to the theory making a like-kind exchange tax free. The transferor who receives stock in exchange for his property has really maintained an interest in the original property. It has merely changed form and now has the physical identity of "stock." This "continuity of interest" concept is a key to nonrecognition of the gain on the appreciated property transferred. [It is important to recognize, however, that for the purposes of corporate law, a shareholder has an undivided interest (shared with all other shareholders) in all corporate property, but that his rights in any specific corporate property (even though originally transferred by him to the corporation in a tax-free exchange) are extremely limited.]

For example, suppose Stevens, who is now operating as a sole proprietor, decides to transfer his going business to the new corporation. If his basis for the sole proprietorship is $10,000, and the fair market value of his business is $50,000 at the time he transfers it to the new corporation, he would probably receive $50,000 worth of stock.

Under the general rule for taxing sales and exchanges, he would realize a $40,000 gain. However, the nonrecognition provision provides that since he received only stock and through that stock controlled the corporation (just as he previously controlled his sole proprietorship), what has happened is really only a substitution of stock certificates for his former physical possession of the property.

This rule is logical since to realize gain there must be a taxable event which usually occurs in the form of a sale, exchange, or other disposition of property. Although technically there may be a sale (a transfer of property in return for money or a promise to pay money) or exchange (a transfer of property in return for other property or services), there has been no exchange in substance. Stevens, in the example, hasn't disposed of his property. He has merely received certificates which evidence that he changed the form of ownership in the original property. This would apply no matter how many people transfer property to the corporation. As long as it was done collectively, if the taxpayers transferring property to the corporation still have both (a) control and (b) interest in the property they originally owned, they would not have to recognize any gain on receipt of the new corporation's stock. Thus, Stevens would not have to recognize the $40,000 gain until and unless he later sells his stock.

Under the assumed facts, if Roberts were to receive stock in the new corporation in exchange for his services, the value of the stock would be currently taxable to him, as stock issued for services is not considered as issued for "property." If Roberts' stock was issued solely for services, it will not be counted in determining whether the transferors of property control the corporation after the exchange.

In addition, care must be taken if the property which is contributed is subject to liabilities in excess of basis, or if short term notes are to be issued by the corporation, as either could destroy the nontaxability of the transfer.

IMPLICATIONS AND ISSUES IN COMMUNITY PROPERTY STATES

Stock purchased by an investor in a corporation will take on the character of the assets used to purchase the stock. Thus, if an individual transfers $1,000 to a corporation in return for stock and that $1,000 consists of community property earn-

ings, the stock itself will be community property. Of course, this result could be altered by a written agreement between the spouse and the investor to treat the stock as property other than community property, or by titling the stock in some other fashion, e.g., as joint tenancy or as the separate property of one spouse.

Upon divorce or death of the stockholder, the community property interest of the spouse will become important. It will be necessary to determine what portion of the stock is community property. As discussed in Chapter 1, a common problem is the situation where a person owned all or most of the stock of a corporation prior to marriage, the person works full time for the corporation, and the value of the corporation increases significantly. A portion of the increase in value of the person's stock may be community property to the extent the increase is attributable to his or her insufficiently rewarded hard work during the marriage, and a portion will be separate property to the extent the increase is the result of the natural increase or earnings of the original stock. The method of valuation cannot be predicted with certainty.

One question which often arises in community property states is the power to manage and control the community property. Until 1975, California law provided that the husband had the management and control over the community property. Under a revision of the community property laws, both spouses now have management power and control over community property. (Similar changes have occurred in the laws of other community property states.) This has implications in connection with the management and control over a corporation. California law provides that a spouse who is operating or managing a business or an interest in a business which is community personal property has the sole management and control of the business or interest. Thus, if an individual owns all the stock in a manufacturing corporation and that individual is also the manager of the business, or a substantial participant in the management of the business, the individual's spouse will not be able to exercise equal control in regard to the management of that business. This allows people to choose business associates and manage a business without regard to the effect of community property laws.

QUESTIONS AND ANSWERS

Question — Why do stockholders often finance business needs by lending money to their corporations rather than by increasing their equity (stock) interest?

Answer — One of the key advantages of operating a business in the corporate form is that many different types of ownership interests in corporations can be created. The interests of any particular investor can be met by creating a security that fits his special needs and desires. This factor facilitates the acquisition of capital. Suppose that in order to acquire working capital and capital for long-term planning the corporation issued bonds. These are written obligations to repay a definite sum of money on a definite date, usually at least 10, and more often 29 or more, years from the date the bond was issued.

Bonds are a favored means of raising corporate capital. One reason for this is that a corporation will obtain a deduction for the interest paid on the indebtedness, but no deduction is allowed for dividends paid on either preferred or common stock. As long as a corporation can earn money at a higher rate (with the cash raised by issuing the bond) than it costs the corporation (in interest necessary to "service the debt"), it usually makes sense for the corporation to borrow money. This is known as "leverage."

Issuance of the bonds generally creates no tax liability to either the corporation or the bondholder. This is because the corporation has merely borrowed money and agreed to return it. Conversely, the bondholders have merely loaned money. When the bond "matures," the principal becomes payable and the bondholders are entitled to a tax-free return of their capital investment. In contrast, the return of equity is a taxable dividend, unless the return can qualify as a stock redemption (which is not a dividend).

A distribution by a corporation with respect to its stock is considered a return on the shareholders' investment and is taxable as a dividend to the extent of corporate earnings and profits—unless the distribution can qualify as a "sale" or "exchange," in which case only the gain in excess of basis is taxable.

Any money bondholders receive in the form of interest, and any money they receive at the maturity of their bonds (after 1987) in excess of their capital investment will be taxed at ordinary income rates. Any excess money received at maturity prior to 1988 may be subject to a more favorable capital gains rate (which was eliminated under the Tax Reform Act of 1986). Receiving money in excess of capital investment can occur when bonds are purchased at a discount but are paid off at face value. (When bonds are *issued* at a discount by the issuing corporation, a bondholder must include a ratable portion of the discount in income each year as the bond matures. For example, if a bond with a par value of $1,000 was issued for $800 and is payable in 10 years, the $200 discount would be included in the taxpayer's income at the rate of $20 a year.)

Another reason bonds are often favored over an increase in equity is that the accumulation of earnings and profits within the corporation to pay debt obligations can be justified more readily than accumulating income to redeem stock. This helps avoid an additional tax on an unreasonable income accumulation.

Question — What is "thin capitalization"?

Answer — Since the interest paid on corporate indebtedness is deductible, the cost of borrowing money through long-term corporate debt is substantially reduced. However, some shareholders attempt to overdo it—they contribute almost no equity investment and characterize almost their entire contribution as debt owed to them by the corporation. This is known as "thin capitalization," since the capital investment is "thin" in relation to the debt, but the "debt" is really disguised stock.

Once the form of the "debt" is disregarded by the IRS and the substance is treated appropriately, corporate deductions for "interest" payments to shareholders are disallowed. Second, receipt of "interest" payments by shareholder-creditors are reclassified and treated as dividends. Third, when the corporation pays off its "debt" to the shareholders, that payment may be taxed as dividend. This means that instead of treating the amount received as a tax-free repayment of a debt, the shareholder-creditor must report the entire distribution as ordinary income. Finally, money which the corporation purportedly was accumulating to pay off the "debt" is now subject to the accumulated earnings tax (which is discussed below). Also, a debt which is reclassified as stock could cause a termination of a Subchapter S election, since a Subchapter S corporation is allowed to have only one class of stock.

To determine if a security should be classified as debt rather than equity, the courts usually examine a number of factors such as: Was there an intention by shareholders to enforce payment of the debt? Was there a debt instrument and did it give the shareholders management or voting rights (like stock)? What was the ratio of debt to equity? A general rule of thumb, subject to variation depending upon the industry, is that if the amount of debt exceeds shareholders' equity by more than four to one, the corporation is thinly capitalized. Basically, the court would examine all the factors relevant to determining if a "loan" by shareholders was in reality more like an ownership interest (stock) than a debtor-creditor relationship.[8]

Keep in mind that, while bonds are a tax-favored means of obtaining corporate funds, frequently a corporation does not want to become obligated to make fixed payments for interest and debt amortization. To avoid a cash flow problem, therefore, corporations often finance long-term operations or investments by common stock, which entail no obligation to pay dividends or preferred stock on which dividend payments can frequently be avoided.

Question — How is a corporation taxed?

Answer — A corporation is taxed as an entity separate from its shareholders. A 15 percent rate is applied to the first

$50,000 of corporate taxable income, a 25 percent rate applies to the next $25,000, a 34 percent rate is levied on the next $25,000, 39 percent on the next $235,000, then 34 percent on any additional taxable income.

The 39 percent tax on income between $100,000 and $335,000 includes a 5 percent add-on tax that is designed to phase out the graduated rates. Corporations with taxable income of $335,000 or more, in effect pay tax at a flat 34 percent rate on all taxable income.

For example, a corporation with $100,000 of taxable income would pay a tax of $22,250 ($50,000 × 15%, plus 25% of $25,000, plus 34% of $25,000). A corporation with $500,000 of taxable income would pay a tax of $170,000 (34% of $500,000). Corporations, like individuals, are liable for a number of other state and local taxes as well. The corporation would report its federal income tax on IRS Form 1120.

Graphically, the return might look like the illustration at Figure 13.2.

Gross income would include such items as profit from sales and receipts from services. It would also include gains on sales or exchanges, income from rent, royalties, interest, and dividends.

A corporation is entitled to two types of deductions; ordinary deductions and special deductions. Ordinary deductions would include compensation of officers and salaries, bonuses, rent payments, charitable contributions, repair expenses, interest paid on indebtedness, casualty losses, deductions for depreciation and amortization of research and experimental costs, advertising, and corporate contributions to pension and profit-sharing plans. A corporation would also receive a carryover deduction for a net operating loss.

Figure 13.2

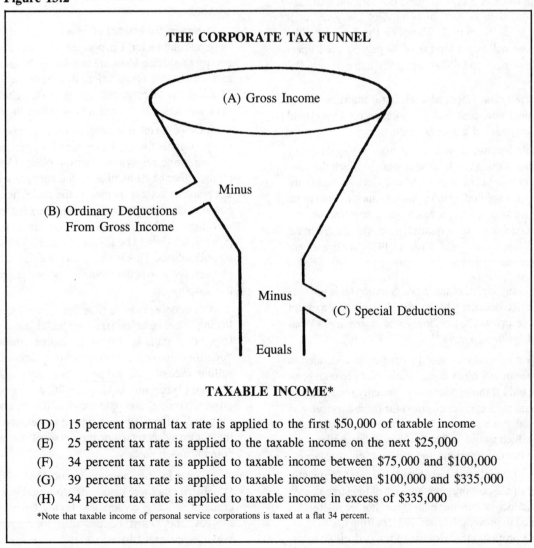

THE CORPORATE TAX FUNNEL

(A) Gross Income

Minus

(B) Ordinary Deductions From Gross Income

Minus

(C) Special Deductions

Equals

TAXABLE INCOME*

(D) 15 percent normal tax rate is applied to the first $50,000 of taxable income

(E) 25 percent tax rate is applied to the taxable income on the next $25,000

(F) 34 percent tax rate is applied to taxable income between $75,000 and $100,000

(G) 39 percent tax rate is applied to taxable income between $100,000 and $335,000

(H) 34 percent tax rate is applied to taxable income in excess of $335,000

*Note that taxable income of personal service corporations is taxed at a flat 34 percent.

Several deductions are classified as "special." One of these items is known as a "dividends received" deduction. Prior law allowed a corporation which owned less than 80 percent of the stock of another corporation to deduct 80 percent of the dividends received. Under current law, there are now three rules:

(1) If the recipient corporation owns less than 20 percent of the voting power and value of stock of the issuing corporation, the 80 percent dividends received deduction is reduced to 70 percent of the amount of the dividend.

(2) If the recipient corporation holds 20 percent or more (up to 79 percent) of the stock of the issuing corporation, the 80 percent dividends received deduction remains at 80 percent.

(3) If the recipient corporation owns 80 percent or more of the stock of the issuing corporation, a 100 percent deduction may apply to dividends received.

The bottom line is that a closely held corporation that holds the stock of a publicly held corporation will likely be entitled to deduct 70 percent of every dollar it receives in the form of dividends on the stock it holds. It therefore will pay a top tax of 39 percent on 30 percent of each dividend dollar, an effective rate of only 11.7 percent.

A corporation might also elect to amortize its organizational cost over five or more years. This would also be considered a special deduction.

Taxable income is what is left after taking ordinary and special deductions. It is the amount to which the various percentage tax rates are applied. Certain credits are then directly applied against this tax, such as corporate overpayments of tax in previous years, payments for estimated taxes (paid on a quarterly basis), and credit on certain foreign taxes paid. Prior to 1986, an investment credit was also allowed.

Question — Many business and estate planning tools are corporate fringe benefits which are deductible to the extent reasonable (as well as ordinary and necessary). What is meant by "reasonable"?

Answer — A corporation would be entitled to a deduction for salaries or any other compensation for personal services, but only if the services were actually rendered and the amount paid as compensation for those services was considered "reasonable." Reasonable means only that amount which would ordinarily be paid for similar services by other corporations under similar circumstances.

This reasonableness test is imposed most frequently on closely held corporations because of the large degree of coincidence of executive and shareholder interest. It is designed to prevent the shareholders from draining off corporate profits in the disguise of tax-deductible salaries. Corporate profits are usually paid out in the form of dividends which are taxable to the shareholders, but nondeductible by the corporation. The portion of the salary considered unreasonable is usually classified as a disguised dividend and, to that extent, the corporation's deduction is disallowed. However, even though that amount may not be deducted by the corporation, it is still taxable as ordinary income to the shareholder-recipient subject to a maximum rate of 33 percent.[9]

Reasonableness is a question of determining the amount that would ordinarily be paid for like services by like enterprises under similar circumstances. Generally, where an executive employee does not own or have options to purchase stock, arm's length bargaining as to the amount of salary is assumed. One element that could be considered in determining reasonableness is the fact that a given individual was not adequately compensated in prior years. Thus, if high compensation in the current year can be attributed to services rendered in prior years, the total current salary might be considered reasonable.

However, the amount of cash compensation is not the only relevant factor. Corporate contributions to pension and profit-sharing plans are considered business expenses and are allowed as deductions as long as the total amount of all forms of compensation paid on behalf of an individual does not exceed a reasonable total.

Some of the other indirect forms of compensation may be: premiums for life insurance; hospitalization; medical care; and salary continuation plans. Costs of these plans, although deductible by the corporation, often do not result in taxable income to the individual. Since the corporation is a separate and distinct tax entity, and since working shareholders would be considered salaried employees, they would be eligible for these forms of indirect compensations. This is true even if they are not only employees, but also officers, directors, and shareholders of the corporation.

An employee may exclude from gross income the following fringe benefits: (1) a "no-additional-cost service" (e.g., free stand-by flights to airline employees); (2) "qualified employee discounts" (e.g., discounts on the selling price of qualified property or services of the employer); (3) certain working condition fringes (e.g., employee parking and athletic facilities); and (4) "de minimis" fringes such as typing of personal letters by the company secretary or the personal use of company copying machines.

In order for the "no-additional-cost services" and the "qualified employee discounts" to be excluded from income of officers, owners and highly compensated employees, they must be provided to employees on a nondiscriminatory basis.

Question — What is the accumulated earnings tax?

Answer — One of the easiest and most common means of financing growth is to accumulate earnings and plow them back into the corporation to purchase new machinery, buildings, and other necessary capital assets. These "plowed-back" earnings and profits begin to add up very quickly. Since the corporate tax rate may be lower than the rate of tax upon the incomes of individual shareholders, they may attempt to use the corporation as a vehicle for reducing taxes by having the corporation retain earnings rather than make taxable distributions in the form of nondeductible dividends.

If a corporation reasonably allows earnings to accumulate in order to fund current or anticipated needs or projects which the corporation has planned, there should not be a problem. However, once earnings are allowed to accumulate beyond the reasonable needs of the business, those earnings may be subject to an additional tax, the accumulated earnings tax.[10]

The accumulated earnings tax is a tax imposed on every corporation which is formed or used for the purpose of avoiding personal income tax with respect to its shareholders by permitting earnings and profits to accumulate instead of being distributed. The purpose of the tax is to discourage the use of a corporation as an accumulation vehicle to shelter its individual stockholders from taxation at personal income tax rates. As a regulative device, the accumulated earnings tax was designed to force the distribution of retained earnings at the point where they no longer serve a legitimate business purpose. Without such a tax on improper accumulations, stockholders could arrange to have dividends paid in years when their incomes were low or they could indefinitely accumulate earnings and profits inside the corporation until the corporation was liquidated.

Accumulations of $250,000 or less will automatically be considered to be for the reasonable needs of the business (this limit is only $150,000 for service corporations in health, law, engineering, architecture, accounting, actuarial science, performing arts, and consulting).[11] However, if a corporation is profitable and begins to accumulate amounts in excess of $250,000, it should be prepared to show a bona fide business reason for not distributing these earnings in the form of dividends.

The accumulated earnings tax is designed to tax only earnings retained beyond the reasonable needs of the business. The question then becomes: "What reasonable needs would a corporation have for accumulating profits?" The regulations state that working capital needs and capital for building expansion or for the replacement of plant or equipment are among the needs that would allow a business to properly accumulate earnings. In addition to these needs, a sinking fund to retire corporate

bonds at maturity has often been found to be a reasonable need to accumulate cash. In other cases, funds set aside to acquire minority interests or quarreling stockholders' interests were also deemed to be retained for reasonable business needs. The Code says that the term "reasonable needs of the business" includes the section 303 redemption needs of the business (see chapter 27), although specific protection from the tax (within limits) is provided only in the corporation tax year in which the stockholder died and in subsequent years.[12] The reasonableness of accumulations in years prior to a year in which the shareholder dies is to be determined solely upon the facts and circumstances existing at the times the accumulations occur.[13]

The accumulated earnings tax rate is 27½ percent on the first $100,000 of "accumulated taxable income" and 38½ percent on the remainder for taxable years prior to December 31, 1988. After this date, the rate is 28 percent on all "accumulated taxable income."

The tax, if applicable, is imposed only on "accumulated taxable income;" an amount which is derived from the taxable income of the corporation for the particular year in question. Thus, the tax does not apply to all of the accumulated earnings and profits of the corporation, but only to the accumulated taxable income of the year or years as to which the tax is asserted.

This tax on a corporation's accumulated taxable income is payable in addition to the regular tax payable by the firm. "Accumulated taxable income" basically means the corporation's taxable income for the year in question with certain adjustments (such as a reduction for federal income taxes paid) minus the sum of (a) distributions from current earnings and profits which the shareholders have reported as ordinary income (dividends paid), (b) amounts from earnings and profits which the shareholders have reported as dividends even though no actual distribution was made (disguised dividends), and (c) the accumulated earnings credit.

In determining whether or not the current year's accumulated taxable income has been retained for the reasonable needs of the business, the availability of prior years' accumulated earnings must also be considered. If past years' accumulations are sufficient to meet current needs (i.e.,this year's business needs) there would be no justification for accumulating current earnings.

There is an accumulated earnings credit; a $250,000 minimum credit in the case of corporations other than service corporations in health, law, engineering, architecture, accounting, actuarial sciences, performing arts, and consulting. These corporations have a $150,000 credit. This takes into consideration earnings from prior years. For example, if prior years' accumulated earnings were in excess of $250,000, there would be no credit. Every

Tools and Techniques

dollar of the current year's accumulated taxable income would be subject to tax unless it could be proven that the income was reasonable.

Question — Will corporate-owned cash value life insurance purchased for key man, split dollar, or deferred compensation financing cause an accumulated earnings tax problem?

Answer — That depends on whether or not the insurance answers a valid corporate business need. There must also be a close correlation between the type of policy and amount of death benefit and the alleged corporate need. Generally, hedging against the loss of a key employee's service because of unexpected death is considered to be a reasonable business need.

Keyman life insurance is insurance which is owned by the corporation insuring the life of a key employee. The purpose of such a policy is to provide a fund at the employee's death which will compensate the corporation for the financial loss resulting from the unavailability of the employee to render services to the corporation. Often, keyman insurance death proceeds are also used to help in finding and compensating a suitable replacement. Therefore, the purchase of life insurance and the earnings used to pay policy premiums should not, per se, be subject to the penalty tax. The point is that it is not the amount, but the purpose of the accumulation, that is important.

The same question often arises as to the effect of a split-dollar plan. If a corporation attempts to prevent taxation of income to shareholders by accumulating its earnings rather than distributing them, the existence or nonexistence of a split-dollar policy will not, by itself, deter the imposition of the tax penalty provided by the law. Conversely, the existence of a split-dollar policy will not, per se, incur the accumulations tax penalty if the corporation is not, in fact, accumulating earnings beyond the reasonable needs of the business.

This section of the Code exists to deter tax evasion and not to prevent a business from operating in a normal businesslike manner. The same principle applies in cases where the corporation has obligated itself to make preretirement death benefits to a key executive under a deferred compensation agreement. An accumulation of corporate earnings to meet obligations under such an agreement is generally considered a reasonable business need (just as the funds accumulated to retire an outstanding corporate bond would be considered reasonable).

A third area where this question often arises is the use of accumulated earnings to provide surplus cash for the redemption of stock. In this case, if the redemption is to be utilized to shift partial or complete control to the remaining shareholders without depleting their personal funds (as for example, where, by shareholder agree-

ment, the corporation will retire shares on the death of a shareholder), it is doubtful that accumulations to reach this result would be found to be a reasonable need. However, if a business purpose can be found, such as an accumulation to purchase the shares of the dissenting minority, then the accumulation may be found to be reasonable. The primary purpose must be a corporate, rather than an individual, benefit from the stock redemption.

Question — What is the personal holding company tax?

Answer — Section 541 of the Internal Revenue Code imposes a tax on companies classified as personal holding companies. Prior to the Tax Reform Act of 1986, the tax was 50 percent. The Act reduces the rate of tax to 28 percent. This reduction in the personal holding company tax is tied to the corresponding reduction in the maximum individual income tax rates. The tax applies to undistributed personal holding company income, and is designed to discourage the use of corporations as "incorporated pocketbooks" wherein income from securities, real property, or personal talents is taxed at corporate rates rather than individual rates.

To be classified as a personal holding company, the corporation must meet both of the following tests: (1) more than 50% of the value of its stock is owned by five or fewer individuals, and (2) at least 60% of its "adjusted ordinary gross income" is "personal holding company income."

"Personal holding company income" consists of (1) passive income, such as rents, royalties, dividends, and interest, and (2) income from personal service contracts under which the corporation is to furnish personal services but the corporation does not have the right to select the individual who will perform the services, and the individual selected by the client owns directly or indirectly 25% or more of the stock in the corporation.

For more on personal holding companies, see chapter 19.

Question — What problems may a "personal service corporation" with only one significant customer face from the Internal Revenue Service where the primary purpose of incorporating was to obtain tax benefits?

Answer — Code section 269A specifically authorizes the IRS to reallocate between an employee-owner of a "personal service corporation" (defined as a corporation whose principal activity is the performance of personal services, with such services substantially performed by employee-owners) and the "personal service corporation" all income, deductions, credits, exclusions and other allowances to the extent necessary to prevent tax avoidance or evasion or to clearly reflect the income of the "personal service corporation" or any of its employee-owners. The authority to reallocate applies only in the event that substantially all of the services of the "personal service corporation" are performed for or on behalf of one other corporation, partnership or other entity and the "personal service corporation" was formed for the principal purpose of avoiding or evading federal income tax by reducing the income of the employee-owner or by securing for him a significant tax benefit not otherwise available. The typical corporation affected by this new law is a corporate partner in a partnership of personal service corporations.[14]

The potential impact of section 269A has been greatly reduced by the parity created between corporate and HR-10 plans, since the tax benefits of a corporate qualified plan are now available to non-corporate entities. Some corporate partners took advantage of legislation provided by TEFRA to liquidate, with the intention of continuing in the partnership as individual partners with the benefit of a Keogh plan.

Question — What is the corporate AMT and how does it affect corporate owned life insurance?

Answer — The corporate AMT (alternative minimum tax) is the excess, if any, of a tentative minimum tax (TMT) over the regular corporate income tax.

The TMT is computed by subtracting an exemption amount ($40,000 phased out by 25 cents for every dollar in excess of a specified amount) from the corporation's alternative minimum taxable income (AMTI), the taxable income of the corporation with certain adjustments (which include upward adjustments for a number of "preference items"). A 20 percent rate is then applied to any excess.

The AMT can be considered a prepayment of the corporation's regular tax because a credit is allowed that reduces the regular tax of the corporation in future years. This credit is equal to the amount by which the regular tax exceeds the current year's TMT.

How does life insurance fit into this tax scheme? One of the preferences that cause an upward adjustment in the AMTI is the "book income" adjustment. This book income adjustment is meant to measure the excess of (a) what the corporation reports to its shareholders as financial statement income over (b) what the coporation reports to IRS as its income subject to the regular corporate tax.

Roughly speaking, the 1989 corporate AMT on such preferences is computed in these steps:

1. Compute the book income.
2. Compute the taxable income.
3. Compute the excess of 1 over 2.
4. Multiply the result of step 3 by .5.
5. Subtract the $40,000 exemption (to the extent allowable).
6. Multiply any remaining amount by 20 percent.

As a rule of thumb, in 1989, a 10 percent tax will be imposed on the excess of book income over taxable income. In 1990 and later years, due to a different method of computing the corporate AMT, a good rule of thumb is that the face amount of life insurance should be increased by about 16%. In actuality, the corporate AMT imposed on life insurance proceeds can be considerably less.

Assume a corporation purchases a $100,000 whole life insurance policy on the life of its owner. The premiums are paid for by the corporation and the proceeds are payable to the corporation. Here are the tax implications:

- The premiums are not tax deductible.
- The proceeds are income tax free (for regular corporate purposes).
- If the premium in a given year exceeds the increase in the policy's cash value (as it usually does in the first few years), to that extent book income will decrease and therefore the corporation's exposure to the AMT will also decrease.
- If the cash value increase in a given year exceeds the premium (as it usually does in older, better policies), the corporation's book income will increase, and so will its exposure to the AMT.
- When the death of the insured occurs, proceeds will typically exceed cash values. To that extent book income increases relative to taxable income, and therefore exposure to the AMT increases.

If the shareholder dies shortly after the policy was purchased and there are no cash values, the entire $100,000 is part of book income. Assuming there was no taxable income, the excess of book income over taxable income will be $100,000, one-half of which is $50,000. This amount will be reduced by the $40,000 exemption (since AMTI does not exceed $150,000, there is no reduction in the exemption). Therefore, only $10,000 will be subject to the tax. At a 20 percent rate the tax will be $2,000, 2 percent of the $100,000 proceeds.

Question — Assuming a corporation will be subject to a corporate AMT, what courses of action should the planner consider?

Answer — There are several ways of dealing with the AMT. The easiest is merely to make up the difference through additional life insurance coverage. The additional premium can be partially funded with the extra income the corporation should have (assuming its tax bracket dropped from pre-TRA '86 levels).

At the prestigious Notre Dame Law School 1987 Tax and Estate Planning Institute, the first speaker, a nationally known tax lawyer and law school professor, speaking to over 300 attorneys and accountants *about life insurance and the new corporate AMT*, said:

> "*Instead of unwinding your redemption agreements . . . I would suggest it would be easier to buy a little more life insurance. Cover the tax*. The purchase of an extra 10 percent of the face amount isn't such a big thing. *It's probably a very good thing for the client to do. . . .*"

The speaker's next statement was even more to the point:

> "*Layer on a little more life insurance. You'll have some very angry clients if they end up paying the AMT and no one brought it up. I worry about that more than anything else . . . . Buying life insurance is a more sensible way of paying the tax than relying on the credit.*"

Employers should be concerned about the new corporate AMT. Their advisors should be concerned about how much additional insurance is needed to replace the insurance lost in taxes. Here's a quick way to calculate the approximate amount of additional insurance needed:

Step 1:	State the face amount before the AMT tax:	<u>$1,000,000.</u>
Step 2:	State the percentage lost due to the AMT: (.07 to .12 before 1990; .13 to .16 1990 and later years)	<u>.10</u>
Step 3:	Subtract the percent lost from 1 (1-.10):	<u>.90</u>
Step 4:	Divide the face amount by the step 3%: ($1,000,000 / .90)	<u>$1,111,111</u>

This amount, $1,111,111, is (roughly) the before-AMT amount necessary for the corporation to net $1,000,000 after the AMT. Conservative planners will round up this amount.

Another alternative to the purchase of more life insurance is an S corporation election. Had the same business elected S status with no taxable income, there would be no tax at either the corporate or individual level, a $2,000 saving.

ASRS, Sec. 43.

Footnote References

Incorporation

1. Reg. §301.7701-2(a).
2. Reg. §301.7701-2(d).
3. Reg. §301.7701-2(e)(2).
4. Reg. §301.7701-2(c).
5. Reg. §301.7701-1(b).
6. IRC Section 351.
7. IRC Section 368(c); Reg. §1.351-1(a)(1).
8. IRC Section 385.
9. IRC Sections 1, 61.
10. IRC Sections 531, 532.
11. IRC Sections 535(c)(2), 535(c)(3).
12. IRC Sections 537(a)(2), 537(b)(1).
13. Reg. §1.537-1(e)(3).
14. IRC Section 269A.

Chapter 14

INDIVIDUAL RETIREMENT PLAN (IRA)

WHAT IS IT?

For years beginning after December 31, 1986, any individual who is not participating in a qualified private or governmental pension plan, profit-sharing plan, HR-10 plan, or tax deferred annuity can set up an individual retirement account (IRA) and take a deduction from gross income equal to the lesser of: (1) $2,000 or (2) 100 percent of compensation (or earned income minus any qualified plan contributions made by him on his behalf, in the case of a self-employed person) includable in his gross income.[1]

If an individual is actively participating in a qualified plan or tax sheltered annuity, a maximum annual contribution of $2,000 can be made to the employer's plan, to an IRA, or as a contribution split in any proportion between the two. After 1986, a deduction will not be available for voluntary employee contributions to qualified plans. Under TRA '86, a tax deduction for this contribution to an IRA is allowed for single filers with adjusted gross income not in excess of $35,000. The deduction is phased out for single filers with incomes of between $25,000 and $35,000.[2] TRA '86 does permit tax-deferred compounding of nondeductible IRA contributions.[3]

An individual who has earnings and who files a joint return with his non-wage-earning spouse can contribute up to the lesser of $2,250 or 100 percent of his compensation for the tax year—reduced in either case by the contributions made for the tax year by him or on his behalf to his own individual retirement plan (other than employer contributions to a simplified employee pension plan)—if he establishes separate IRAs (or IRA subaccounts) for himself and his non-wage-earning spouse. Contributions do not have to be allocated equally to each IRA or IRA subaccount, but at least $250 (and no more than $2,000) must be contributed for the non-working spouse to take advantage of the $2,250 deduction. A deduction for the full amount contributed is permissible if the individual is not actively participating in a qualified plan or tax sheltered annuity. An individual may contribute up to the same limits even if his spouse does work if she elects to be treated as having no compensation for the year. If that is the case, the amount contributed is fully deductible only if neither the individual or his spouse actively participate in an employer's plan.

Under TRA '86, where one or both spouses actively participate in a qualified plan or tax sheltered annuity, a tax deduction is allowed for joint filers with adjusted gross income not in excess of $50,000. The deductions are phased out between $40,000 and $50,000 of joint income.[4]

The Internal Revenue Code also allows certain individuals receiving a distribution from a qualified plan (including pension, profit sharing, stock bonus, or annuity plans) or a tax deferred annuity in the form of a lump sum to "roll over" the distribution within 60 days to an IRA without incurring income tax on the distribution. This tax-free rollover treatment is available to individuals who receive a lump sum distribution from a qualified plan or tax deferred annuity or who receive a distribution of their benefits within one taxable year on account of the termination of a qualified plan. Distributions of accumulated deductible employee contributions which were made to such qualified plans or tax deferred annuities may also be rolled over tax free to an IRA (or in some cases even to another qualified employer plan—if such plan permits). No rollover is permitted for benefits attributable to nondeductible employee contributions made by the individual to the qualified plan.

A participant in a qualified plan may make a tax-free rollover to an IRA of a partial distribution (not qualifying as a lump sum). This rollover of a partial distribution will be permitted if (1) the distribution equals at least 50 percent of the employee's benefits, determined immediately before the distribution, (2) the distribution is not one of a series of periodic payments, (3) the participant elects tax-free rollover treatment at the time of the partial distribution, and (4) for years beginning after 1986, the distribution must be made on account of the employee's death, disability or separation from service. (The second requirement does not apply to distributions after 1986 and before March 31, 1988.) The rollover must be made within 60 days of receipt.[5]

Partial distributions can be rolled over only to an IRA and they cannot be re-rolled over to a second qualified plan. Once a partial distribution is taken, the participant's account in that plan is no longer eligible for tax-favored long term capital gain for pre-1974 plan participation or 5-year forward averaging treatment.

Contributions in the form of "rollovers" are not subject to the 100 percent/$2,000 or $2,250 limits. Partial rollovers of plan benefits to an IRA are allowed. Thus, an employee receiving a $50,000 lump sum benefit attributable to employer contributions could roll over $25,000 to an IRA and incur tax on the remaining $25,000. (The portion of the distribution retained by the individual is not eligible for the special 5-year income averaging provisions and is taxed as ordinary income at the regular rates.) TRA '86 replaces a previously available special 10-year forward averaging with 5-year forward averaging unless the participant reached age 50 by January 1, 1986, and uses the 1986 income tax rates.[6]

Individuals who receive a distribution which includes property can make a bona fide sale of the property and roll over, within the usual sixty day period, all or part of the proceeds to an IRA. It is not necessary to roll over the actual property received.

If a sale of property received in a lump sum distribution is combined with a partial rollover, the resulting tax implications should be carefully considered.

All or part of a lump sum distribution, a distribution made on account of plan termination, or a distribution of accumulated deductible employee contributions made to the surviving spouse of a participant in a qualified plan or tax deferred annuity may be rolled over to an IRA if made within 60 days of receipt. This rollover could have the effect of postponing income taxation of the distribution until after the surviving spouse's death. The rollover preserves any grandfathered federal estate tax exclusion (see item 5 under **WHAT ARE THE TAX IMPLICATIONS?**, below) in the decedent's estate (though not in the surviving spouse's estate), and the rollover acts as an election to forego forward averaging for federal income tax purposes.[7] The Tax Reform Act of 1984 repealed the $100,000 estate tax exclusion for estates of decedents dying after December 31, 1984.[8]

WHEN IS THE USE OF SUCH A DEVICE INDICATED?

1. When your married client or his spouse is covered under a qualified plan and does not make in excess of $50,000. This deduction is phased out for incomes of between $40,000 to $50,000. Even if the contribution is not tax deductible under TRA '86 limits, the earnings will accumulate income tax-free. Additionally, your client should be receiving an income which is not needed by the family to maintain its current standard of living, and which could be put aside for retirement.

2. An IRA is indicated where neither your client nor his (or her) spouse is covered under a qualified plan, but both work. If your client and his spouse are both working, each can have his own IRA and contribute up to the maximum based on his or her respective income assuming both otherwise qualify.

3. An IRA is also indicated where the client is not covered under a plan, has earned income, is married, and his or her spouse has no income from employment.

4. An IRA may also be indicated where an individual has received a distribution from a qualified plan or tax deferred annuity and seeks to avoid current taxation on all or a part of the distribution.

5. Your client may be an employer who does not have any type of qualified retirement plan and would like to establish a plan covering only himself (or herself).

6. Where an individual who files a single return is an active participant in a qualified plan, has an adjusted gross income not in excess of $35,000, and wants to make additional tax deductible voluntary contributions to an IRA. This deduction is phased out for such individuals with incomes of between $25,000 and $35,000 under TRA '86.

WHAT ARE THE REQUIREMENTS?

1. An individual can set aside retirement savings in a variable premium annuity contract, a regular fixed rate annuity contract, or a trusteed or custodial account with a bank, savings and loan, or credit union. Also, it is possible to split total contributions into two IRAs. For example, a part of the permissible contribution could go into a variable premium annuity contract and the balance could be placed into a trusteed bank account.[9]

2. Three parties can make deposits to an IRA. These are the employee himself, the employee's employer, or the employee's union.

3. Annual contributions must be made in cash. Contributions of other property are not permissible (except in the case of "rollovers").[10]

4. The plan must be established and the contribution made within the taxable year for which a deduction is allowed or before the due date (not including extensions) for filing the individual's tax returns for that taxable year. For most taxpayers, the contribution must, therefore, be made by April 15th.

5. The plan must begin to pay a participant's benefit by the April 1st following the calendar year in which the participant reaches age 70½.

6. If a participant dies *after* distributions have begun, any remaining portion of the participant's interest must be distributed at least as rapidly as under the method of distribution being used as of the date of the participant's death. If the participant dies *before* distributions have begun, the entire remaining interest must be distributed within 5 years to the participant's beneficiaries. If the participant's benefit is payable over the life expectancy of the participant's designated beneficiary or a period certain that does not extend beyond the life expectancy of that beneficiary, and distributions begin within one year of the participant's death, then the 5-year rule does not apply. Special rules apply if the surviving spouse is the designated beneficiary.

HOW IT IS DONE — AN EXAMPLE

The IRA should be relatively easy to establish. Banks and insurance companies provide prototype plans. The IRS also provides prototype trusteed and custodial plans. Once an IRA is established all that need be done is to make contributions.

If an employee's earned income is $6,000, the maximum allowable IRA contribution is $2,000 (the lower of $2,000 or 100 percent of includable compensation). If the employee's income were $1,000 the maximum IRA contribution would be $1,000. If his income is $2,250 or greater, he is married, and his spouse has no earned income, then he can contribute an amount up to a maximum of $2,250 (if the couple files jointly) to an IRA for himself and his spouse. However, the contribution for either spouse cannot be more than $2,000.

Tax savings could be substantial. For example, a $2,000 contribution by an individual in a 15 percent bracket would save $300 a year in taxes. A partner in a partnership who did not care to include any other employees in the plan could establish an IRA for himself without having to cover other employees. If the partner's tax bracket were 28 percent, a $2,000 annual IRA contribution would save $560 a year in taxes.

WHAT ARE THE TAX IMPLICATIONS?

1. Money set aside in an IRA is currently deductible from gross income up to the limits specified.[11]

2. The earnings of the IRA account, between the time they are deposited and the time they are received accumulate tax free.[12]

3. An individual must be at least 59½ years old (unless disabled or unless payments are spread over his life expectancy) to receive an IRA payment without tax penalty. The nondeductible penalty tax on a "premature distribution" is 10 percent of the amount of the distribution which is includable in income. Under some circumstances, the total value of the assets of the account may be deemed to be distributed.[13] (An example of this would be where an individual borrows against his IRA.) So, if your client received (or is deemed to have received) a total distribution at age 53 and his account is worth $5,000 at that time, he must pay a $500 nondeductible tax in addition to the regular income tax on the $5,000 distribution.

   Voluntary deductible employee contributions to an employer plan or government plan if distributed (for purposes other than making a rollover) before age 59½ or disability will also be subject to the 10 percent penalty tax.

4. Upon distribution of the funds accumulated in an IRA account, the client will be taxed at ordinary income tax rates.[14] Lump sum distribution tax treatment is not available for distributions from IRAs. It is also not available for distributions of voluntary employee contributions made to an employer or government plan.

   Beginning in 1987, an additional penalty tax of 15% will be imposed if aggregate "retirement" distributions to an individual in a calendar year exceed the greater of (1) $150,000, or (2) $112,500 as adjusted for inflation ($117,529 in 1988). This tax is in addition to any regular income taxes due and applies only to the excess portion of the distribution. All qualified plans and individual retirement plans are aggregated for this additional tax.[15]

5. For estates of decedents dying after 1982 and before 1985, the $100,000 federal estate tax exclusion applicable to a qualified corporate retirement plan is also available for a death benefit payable from an IRA. The Tax Reform Act of 1984 totally eliminated the estate tax exclusion for estates of decedents dying after 1984, unless the participant was receiving benefits prior to January 1, 1985, and had made an irrevocable election as to the form of benefits prior to July 18, 1984. TRA '86 liberalizes this exclusion so that benefits from a participant who separated from service before January 1, 1985, for which the form of payment has been elected will be exempt up to $100,000 (regardless of whether or not he was in pay status), as long as the election is not later changed.

   If an individual dies with an "excess retirement accumulation" he will pay an additional 15% federal estate tax. An "excess retirement accumulation" means the excess (if any) of (A) the value of the individual's interests in qualified plans and individual retirement plans as of the date of death (or alternate valuation date) over (B) the present value of an annual annuity of $112,500, as adjusted by cost of living ($117,529 in 1988), or $150,000, if that is greater, payable over a term certain equal to the individual's life expectancy immediately before his death.[16] For additional information on this tax, see chapter 22.

IMPLICATIONS AND ISSUES IN COMMUNITY PROPERTY STATES

The division of community property interests in qualified plan benefits is becoming an increasingly important factor in divorce proceedings in community property states. In many situations the spouses' respective retirement benefits are their largest assets.

IRAs will undoubtedly be the subject of controversy in many divorce proceedings. To some extent, however, the division of an interest in an IRA should be less difficult than dividing an interest in a qualified corporate plan. All benefits in an IRA must be nonforfeitable. Thus, the problems of valuing nonvested benefits will not be present.

In many cases, each spouse will have his or her own IRA. If the contributions to each IRA were similar, each spouse could agree to keep his own IRA in a divorce settlement. If only one spouse has an IRA or one IRA contains substantially more assets than the other spouse's IRA or spouses with equal IRAs or IRA subaccounts cannot agree to divide their IRA interests equally, significant problems could arise. A spouse may find he or she is obligated to divide an interest in his or her IRA with the other spouse. The obligated spouse may not have sufficient assets outside of the IRA to provide the other spouse with the value of his or her interest. Thus, the obligated spouse may seek a distribution from the IRA to provide funds to settle with his or her spouse. If, however, the spouse with the IRA is under age 59½ and not disabled, the spouse will incur a 10 percent "premature distribution" tax as well as be subject to ordinary income tax on the distribution he or she received (or is deemed to receive). To avoid this undesirable result, the spouses could agree to divide the assets of the IRA after the spouse with the IRA attains age 59½. If an agreement cannot be reached, the spouse with the IRA may be able to persuade a court to postpone division of the IRA until he or she attains age 59½.

An exception provided by the Employee Retirement Income Security Act of 1974 (ERISA) could eliminate the undesirable consequences described above. ERISA provides that the transfer of an individual's interest in an IRA to his or her former spouse under a divorce decree or under a written instrument in connection with the divorce is not a taxable distribution. Thereafter, the IRA will be treated as that of the other spouse. This exception appears to apply only to the transfer of the spouse's entire interest in an IRA. Transfers of partial interests may cause the "premature distribution" tax and ordinary income tax to be imposed.

The question which will arise in such a case is this: A married couple seek a divorce. The husband has an IRA with a balance of $10,000, all of which is community property. Their only major asset is the IRA. The wife does not agree to postpone receipt of her one-half interest until the husband attains age 59½. A court orders the husband to make arrangements to equally divide the assets of the IRA. He is forced to obtain a distribution of the $10,000 prior to his attaining age 59½. Who is responsible for the 10 percent tax on the premature distribution and the ordinary income tax on the distribution, the husband or the husband and wife equally? The answer is, the husband. Code Section 408(g) provides that the penalty tax provisions and ordinary income tax inclusion provisions of Section 408 shall be applied without regard to community property laws. Thus, even though one-half of the assets are the wife's under community property laws, the entire premature distribution will be taxed to the husband. If the court ordered him to pay over $5,000 rather than his net after-tax distribution, he may find that taxes take a major portion of the distribution he does not turn over to his wife.

Tax consequences such as described above should be considered when dividing community property IRA or qualified plan interests. Courts have taken varying approaches to consideration of tax aspects in division of retirement benefits. Some are unwilling to consider tax consequences when dividing retirement benefits. Others, however, have held that tax considerations should be taken into account when dividing retirement benefits in divorce proceedings.

QUESTIONS AND ANSWERS

Question — Can a client borrow from his IRA account?

Answer — No. Borrowing will create a forfeiture of the IRA's tax qualification. Your client will be deemed to have received all the assets in his or her account and must pay ordinary income tax on the amount.[17] In addition, if the client is neither disabled nor 59½ years old at that time, there will also be a 10 percent nondeductible "premature distribution" tax.

Question — How long can an individual wait before beginning to receive distributions from an IRA?

Answer — Distributions do not have to be made until April 1 following the calendar year in which a client reaches age 70½ (of course, payments can begin as early as age 59½ without penalty).[18]

Question — If an individual chooses a particular investment vehicle for his IRA, but later changes his mind, is a shift to another type of investment allowed?

Answer — Yes. It is possible to liquidate an IRA investment and reinvest the proceeds within 60 days in another investment on a tax-free basis. For example, if your client originally purchased mutual funds but later wanted to split his investment between mutual funds and a flexible premium annuity, the change can be made without incurring adverse income tax consequences. This tax-free reinvestment of funds can occur only once each year.

Question — Can an IRA invest in gold coins or stamps?

Answer — If an IRA or any individually directed account under qualified Keogh or corporate retirement plans acquires collectibles, the cost of such collectibles shall be regarded as a current taxable distribution to the plan participant. A collectible is defined as any work of art, any rug or antique, any metal or gem, any stamp or coin, any alcoholic beverage, or any other tangible personal property specified by the IRS. However, TRA '86 permits an exception to this rule for IRA investments in gold or silver coins issued by the United States and purchased after December 31, 1986.[19] TAMRA '88 extended this exception to enable the purchase of coins minted by a state.

Question — A partner owning more than 10 percent of the partnership's capital was a participant in his partnership HR-10 plan. He left the partnership and received the distribution of his retirement plan monies. Can he use a "rollover" IRA? Secondly, assuming he can establish a "rollover" IRA, several years later when he is employed by a corporation which has a retirement plan, can he make a contribution from the "rollover" IRA into the corporate retirement plan?

Answer — The partner can roll over the distribution into a "rollover" IRA. After 1986, he may roll over those monies from the "rollover" IRA into another qualified plan. In prior years, the partner could not roll over those monies from the "rollover" IRA into another qualified plan during the first five years after the original distribution because he was a more-than-five percent owner at the time of the original distribution.[20]

A distribution of voluntary employee contributions which were deductible at the time of contribution may be rolled over to an IRA or to a qualified plan if the plan permits.

Question — Assume an individual established an IRA. He takes distribution prior to age 59½. What are the consequences?

Answer — An individual who receives a distribution from an IRA prior to age 59½ and is not disabled at the time of distribution will generally be subject to a tax of 10 percent of the amount of such distribution which is includable in income, in addition to being required to include the taxable amount of the distribution in income for that taxable year. A third exception to the imposition of the premature distribution penalty is if the distribution from the IRA is one of a series of periodic payments made over the life or life expectancy of the individual.

Question — What's a SEPP?

Answer — SEPPs are Simplified Employee Pension Plans. This is Congress's answer to requests from small "ma and pa" type employers for an alternative to paperwork-infested and complex qualified retirement plans. A SEPP is part HR-10, part employer-sponsored IRA, and part employee-established IRA. (Actually, it's a grown-up IRA account or annuity—no bond purchase plans are permitted.)

Question — How much can be contributed annually to a SEPP?

Answer — Beginning in 1984 the dollar limit on contributions to SEPPs is $30,000. A SEPP is a type of IRA to which an employer can contribute on an employee's behalf. The employee excludes the contribution from gross income up to

   (a) $30,000 or

   (b) 15 percent of compensation (before the SEPP contribution), but

   (c) only the first $200,000 of compensation may be counted. (This $200,000 cap is indexed for inflation ($208,940 in 1988).)

Under TRA '86, employee elective deferrals may be made in any amount up to $7,000, as adjusted for inflation ($7,313 in 1988).[21] Employees are permitted to either elect to have the contribution made to the SEPP or can currently receive the contribution in cash. The elective deferrals are considered wages for Social Security tax purposes.

Question — What are the requirements for a SEPP?

Answer — The essential requirements are

(1) The employer (can be a corporation, partnership, or sole proprietorship) must make a contribution to the plan for each employee age 21 or older who has worked for the employer during at least 3 of the last 5 years. An employer need not contribute on behalf of any employee for a calendar year in which the employee's compensation was less than $300, as adjusted for inflation ($313 in 1988).[22] In the case of elective deferral SEPPs, the employer must have had 25 or fewer eligible employees during the prior taxable year, and at least 50 percent must have elected to contribute to the SEPP.[23]

(2) The employer's contribution can't discriminate in favor of employees who are "highly compensated." It's possible to exclude nonparticipating union employees with respect to whom there is good faith bargaining on retirement benefits and nonresident aliens in considering whether or not contributions are discriminatory in favor of any member of the prohibited class. TRA '86 has set a special nondiscrimination test applicable to salary reduction SEPPs. The deferral percentage for each highly compensated eligible employee cannot exceed the average deferral percentage for all other non-highly compensated eligible employees by more than 125 percent. TRA '86 SEPP provisions apply to taxable years beginning after December 31, 1986.

Employer contributions may be made for an employee who has reached age 70½, unlike the situation with an IRA.

(3) Integration with social security is permitted in a SEPP. Generally, however, contributions have to be a uniform percentage of each covered employee's compensation (e.g., you can't give one employee 10 percent of compensation and give another 15 percent) and only the first $200,000 of an employee's compensation can be considered.) In years beginning after 1988, a limited disparity between the contribution percentages applicable to compensation above and below the social security wage base is permitted. An elective deferral SEPP may not be integrated. Integration is not permitted for a year in which the employer also maintains an integrated pension, profit sharing, or stock bonus plan or tax deferred annuity.

(4) The employee must own the IRA account or annuity. That means 100 percent immediate vesting for all employees. The employer can't tie any strings on the employee's right to keep or withdraw money contributed to the SEPP.

Tools and Techniques

(5) The SEPP has to be in writing. It must spell out

    (a) what an employee has to do to "get a piece of the action" and

    (b) how the "pie is to be sliced," i.e., the manner in which the amount allocated is to be computed.

Question — Can a person participating in some other employer sponsored plan also be covered by a SEPP? Can a person covered by a SEPP take a deduction for an IRA contribution?

Answer — Participants in simplified employee pension plans are permitted to participate in other employer qualified plans. Any contribution by an employer to a SEPP must be aggregated with other contributions by that employer to other qualified plans for purposes of the overall limits on contributions or benefits. A participant can take a deduction for an IRA contribution, under the limits imposed by TRA '86. If a joint filer is covered by a SEPP and does not make in excess of $50,000 he is allowed to make a deductible contribution to an IRA. An individual filer who is covered by a SEPP and does not make in excess of $35,000 is similarly allowed to make deductible contributions to an IRA.

Question — How long does an employer have to make a contribution to a SEPP (and deduct it)?

Answer — In general, the employer must make contributions within 3½ months after the close of the calendar year in order to take the deduction for its tax years in which the calendar year ends. If the employer elects, it may use its taxable year instead of the calendar year. In fact, the plan itself need not be established until such dates.

Question — May a divorced spouse make and deduct contributions to a spousal IRA?

Answer — For pre-1985 years, a divorced spouse for whom a spousal IRA was maintained prior to the divorce was able to make deductible contributions if the spousal IRA was established at least five years before the year the divorce was granted and the former spouse was allowed to deduct contributions to the spousal IRA for at least three of the last five taxable years. The maximum contribution could not exceed the lesser of $1,125 or the sum of the compensation and alimony received by the divorced spouse. For years after 1984, a divorced or legally separated person can make an IRA contribution from taxable alimony or separation payments he or she receives during the year.

Question — Are there special rules for "inherited" IRAs acquired by someone other than a surviving spouse?

Answer — Yes. Inherited IRAs acquired by someone other than a surviving spouse cannot be "rolled over" tax-free and cannot receive tax-free rollovers from other qualified plans or IRAs. No income tax deduction is allowed for amounts contributed to an inherited IRA.

Question — May a contribution be made to an IRA even though it is not deductible?

Answer — Yes. Designated nondeductible contributions may be made on behalf of an individual to an IRA even though he participates in a qualified pension or profit sharing plan. These contributions are intended to provide a tax incentive for retirement savings, and the tax on the earnings on the nondeductible contributions is deferred until withdrawn. The nondeductible limit is the excess of:

(a) The lesser of $2,000 ($2,250 in the case of a spousal IRA) or 100% of compensation over

(b) the amount allowable as a deduction for IRA contributions by active participants.[24]

ASRS, Sec. 62.

Footnote References

Individual Retirement Plan (IRA)

1. IRC Section 219(b). Technically, the initials IRA have a more limited connotation but will be used here to denote any type of individual retirement savings plan.
2. IRC Section 219(g), as added by TRA '86, Section 1101(a).
3. IRC Section 408(o), as added by TRA '86, Section 1102(a).
4. See footnote 2.
5. IRC Section 402(a)(5), as amended by TRA '86, Section 1122(e)(1).
6. IRC Section 402(e)(1)(C), as amended by TRA '86, Section 1122(a).
7. Reg. §§20.2039-4(c), 20.2039-5(c); Let. Rul. 8110967.
8. IRC Section 2039, as amended by TRA '84, Section 525.
9. IRC Sections 408(a); 408(b).
10. IRC Section 408(a)(1).
11. IRC Section 219(a).
12. IRC Section 408(e)(1).
13. IRC Sections 72(t); 408(e)(2).
14. IRC Section 408(d).
15. IRC Section 4980A(a).
16. IRC Section 4980A(d).
17. IRC Section 408(e).
18. IRC Sections 408(a)(6); 408(b)(3).
19. IRC Section 408(m), as amended by TAMRA '88, Section 6057 and TRA '86, Section 1144(a).
20. IRC Section 408(d)(3)(A); IRC Section 405(a)(5)(F), as amended by TAMRA '88, Section 1011A(a)(2).
21. IRC Section 402(g), as added by TRA '86, Section 1105(a).
22. IRC Section 408(k)(6), as added by TRA '86, Section 1108(a).
23. Announcement 80-112, 1980-36 I.R.B. 35; Prop. Reg. §1.408-7(d)(1). IRC Section 408(k)(8), as added by TRA '86, Section 1108(e).
24. IRC Section 408(o)(2)(A).

Chapter 15

INSTALLMENT SALE

WHAT IS IT?

The installment sale is a device for spreading out the taxable gain and thereby deferring the income tax on the sale of property. The key ingredient in an installment sale is that the purchase price will be paid by the buyer in a series of installments over a period of years.

WHEN IS THE USE OF SUCH A DEVICE INDICATED?

1. An installment sale is indicated when a taxpayer wants to sell property to another individual who may not have enough capital to purchase the property outright. The installment sale provides a way, for example, for employees with minimal capital to buy out a business owner who, in return for allowing a long-term payout, may receive a higher price for his business. This device is often used to create a market for a business where none previously existed.

2. An installment sale is indicated where an individual in a high income tax bracket holds substantially appreciated real estate or securities, other than marketable securities. In certain cases, all or a portion of the tax on a sale of such property can be spread over the period of installments.[1]

   One of the big advantages of the installment sale with respect to certain property is that the tax due is prorated over the payment period. This means that the seller will pay the tax due only as actual payments from the sale are received. The seller may be able to shift most of the profit from a high income (high tax) year to a year or years in which he or she is in a lower bracket.

3. The installment sale permits more flexibility than the private annuity, an alternative. The agreement can be made to begin or end whenever the parties involved desire. This eliminates the need to follow a rigid schedule of payments such as is found in a private annuity.

4. An installment sale can be an effective estate freezing device where the sale is between family members and involves rapidly appreciating closely held stock, real estate, or other assets. Used in this manner, the installment sale may serve to freeze the size of an estate subsequent to the sale and thus stabilize the value of the seller's estate for federal estate tax purposes and shift future appreciation to a younger generation. An installment sale to a grandchild for its full fair market value, for example, will avoid the generation-skipping transfer tax and may also avoid any 2036(c) implications. (See the explanation of 2036(c) and installment sales at note 11.).

WHAT ARE THE REQUIREMENTS?

1. A seller of property can defer as much or as little as desired and payments can be set to fit the seller's business or financial needs. The amount of payment received in the year of the sale is irrelevant. A sale for $1,000,000 can qualify even if $500,000 is paid in the year of the sale and the remaining $500,000 (plus interest on the unpaid balance) is paid over the next 5 years.

2. No payment has to be made in the year of the sale. The only requirement is that at least one payment must be made in a taxable year after the year of sale. This means the owner of property can contract to have payments made at the time when it is most advantageous or least disadvantageous. For example, the parties could agree that the entire purchase price for payment of a $1,000,000 parcel of land will be paid 5 years after the sale.

3. No minimum sale price is required.

4. Installment sales treatment is automatic unless the taxpayer elects not to have installment treatment apply.

5. A sale can be made on an installment basis even though the selling price is contingent.

HOW IT IS DONE — AN EXAMPLE

An individual would like to sell property she now owns. Her accountant has explained that a high tax on the inherent gain in the property could consume a substantial portion of her profit. If she receives all of the sale proceeds in the year of sale, the result is that her entire profit will be taxed in one year. So she would like to find a way to reduce or minimize the impact of taxes or defer those taxes.

The installment sale is a possible solution to that problem. By taking advantage of the installment sale provisions of the Internal Revenue Code she may be able to save a great deal of money.[2] Under an installment sale, the title to the property passes immediately from the seller to the buyer. But the distinguishing feature of an installment sale is that the seller does *not* receive a lump sum payment outright. Instead, the seller typically receives the sales price in installments spread out over two or more tax years (although a lump sum payment in a later year will qualify for installment reporting).

For example, if Mrs. Murphey sold land which cost her $50,000 and received $100,000, she'd have a $50,000 gain reportable all in the year of the sale. But if she sells it for $100,000 and agrees to accept $10,000 a year for 10 years (plus appropriate interest on the unpaid balance), she will not have to report the $50,000 gain in the year of the sale. Instead, since her ratio of gross profit ($50,000) to contract price

($100,000) is 50 percent, she'll report $5,000, 50% of each $10,000 payment she receives, as capital gain. (Interest has been ignored here for simplicity.)

To compute the payment, use a hand held financial calculator or computer program. You need to tell the calculator or computer the

(1) interest rate (for semiannual divide annual rate by 2),

(2) number of periods (for semiannual multiply years by 2),

(3) amount to be repaid.

The result will be the annual (or other payment period) payment necessary. For example, to compute the semiannual payment where property worth $100,000 is sold over a 10 year period and the interest rate is .09, input 4.5 (the annual interest rate divided by 2) and press the i (interest) button, input 20 (two payments a year for 10 years) and press the *N* (number of periods) button, and input the present value of the loan, $100,000. Then press the PV (present value) button. Then press "PMT" to compute the $7,687.61 outlay.

NumberCruncher-I and TOOLKIT computer software and other financial planning software can do the computation much more quickly by merely inputting the principal amount, effective interest rate, and number of years.

The rule used to compute the annual gain above is:

Income is realized on each annual payment received in the same proportion the gross profit (selling price less seller's adjusted basis) bears to the total contract price (amount to be received by the seller).

If the sale results in a loss, the installment method may not be used. The loss deduction must be taken in the tax year of the sale.[3]

More technically, for income tax purposes, the installments must be broken into three parts: (a) a return of capital, (b) profit, and (c) interest income.

Interest is segregated from principal payments and taxed as ordinary income. The profit percentage (basically the gain, or difference between the sales price and adjusted basis, expressed as a percentage of the total contract price, exclusive of interest) is applied to each installment payment of principal in order to determine the amount of each payment which is gain. The balance is considered a tax free return of the seller's basis. (See Figure 15.1.)

What if the agreement does not specify an interest charge—or the amount is unreasonably low? This often occurs in intrafamily transactions. These types of sales will be taxed according to what is known as the "unstated interest" rule. Under this rule, the Internal Revenue Service is allowed to "impute" interest (a legal fiction in which all the parties to the transaction are treated as if interest at a statutory rate was paid) (compounded semiannually) unless the parties have agreed to at least a "safe harbor" rate of return on the unpaid balance.[4] In other words a portion of the deferred payments will be treated as interest to both the buyer and seller. For all tax purposes, from the buyer's perspective, that part of a payment which is considered interest does not increase the basis of the property received. However, the buyer may be allowed an interest deduction.

Figure 15.1

Taxation of Seller Under Installment Sale	
A. Recovery of basis (cost element)	Tax free
B. Gain element	Capital gain or ordinary income
C. Interest income	Ordinary income

Computing Tax Free, Gain, and Interest Elements of an Installment Payment		
STEP 1	Segregate interest from payment of principal	
STEP 2	Compute portion of principal payment which is gain	$\dfrac{\text{Total gain}}{\text{Sales price}}$ X principal payment
STEP 3	Compute portion of principal payment which is a return of capital	Principal payment – gain (Step 2)

The following rules should be considered: Interest will not be deductible if it is considered "personal." Generally, this means the interest deduction will be denied (subject to phase-out rules) if the debt was incurred or continued for any reason other than —

(1) for investment purposes (if the property or stock to be purchased is investment property, the interest deduction will be allowed only to the extent of the buyer's investment income, subject to phaseout rules);

(2) to conduct a trade or business (other than the trade or business of performing services as an employee), in which case the interest would be deductible without limit;

(3) as part of the computation of income or loss from a passive investment activity;

(4) to pay estate or generation-skipping transfer taxes in installments under Code sections 6166 or 6161 (there is no limit on the amount of interest deduction in this case); or

(5) as payment on a debt secured by property which at the time the interest is paid or accrued is a qualified residence (this is called "qualified residence interest" and is generally deductible only if the residence in question is the taxpayer's principal residence or a second residence). This deduction is limited to interest on a maximum of $1,000,000 of "acquisition indebtedness" and up to $100,000 of "home equity indebtedness."

Imputed interest is considered only for purposes of the income tax. It does not directly affect the terms of the sale. The imputed interest rules are extremely difficult and will not be discussed at length. The following rules of thumb should be helpful in planning the interest rates that should be built into an installment sale:

(1) There will be no imputed interest problem unless the installment sales contract (a) does not state *any* interest on the unpaid balance, or (b) the specified interest rate is less than the "applicable federal rate" (AFR).

(2) Certain sales of family land to family members require (at the time of this writing) only that the interest rate assumed by the parties be 6 percent or greater if the transaction is for $500,000 or less.

(3) If the transaction does not fall under rule of thumb (1) or (2), and if the selling price is under $2.8 million, interest will be imputed at the lower of (a) 9 percent or (b) the applicable federal rate.

WHAT ARE THE TAX IMPLICATIONS?

1. Many of the income tax ramifications have been mentioned above. Note also that depreciation recapture as well as any investment tax credit recapture is reportable in full in the year of the sale, even if no proceeds from the sale are received in that year.

Also, stock or securities which are traded on an established securities market do not qualify for installment treatment; all payments to be received are treated as received in the year of disposition.

In addition, installment treatment is not allowed for sales of depreciable property to a controlled entity, such as a more than 50% owned partnership or corporation, or trust benefiting the seller or the seller's spouse. All payments to be received are treated as received in the year of disposition.

2. An installment sale will remove the property in question from the transferor-seller's estate, but the present value of any installments due at the seller's death must be included.[5] For instance, if at the date the seller died 10 annual payments remained on an installment sale, and each payment to the estate or its heirs is $12,000, at the IRS's current 10 percent interest assumption, $73,735 would be includible in the seller's gross estate. However, the installment sale still is a valuable estate planning tool since it removes the future appreciation on the property from the transferor-seller's estate without any gift tax implications. For instance, at a 10 percent growth rate, property worth $500,000 when sold in exchange for 10 annual payments would be worth $1,296,871 when the payout was complete.

Additionally, a great deal of the cash proceeds of the sale may be removed from the seller's estate, gift tax free, by maximizing the use of the $10,000 annual exclusion. After receiving payments, the seller could then give back—at his or her whim—all or a portion of the amounts paid.

3. If the seller should die, the estate, or other testamentary beneficiary of the installments due would report the payments in the same way that the decedent would have reported them had he lived.[6] In other words, the allocation of the payments (return of capital, gain, or interest) is not affected by reporting on the installment basis.

There is no step-up in basis at death; however, the testamentary beneficiary of the installments would be entitled to an offsetting income tax deduction to the extent of the estate tax attributable to the installment sale balance which was taxed in the estate.[7]

4. It is important to note the effect of an installment sale on the property's basis for purposes of computing gains and losses and in order to compute the depreciation deduction available to the transferee-buyer. In the case of an installment sale, the transferee-buyer has a new income tax basis for the property; its fair market value at the date of the sale (i.e., the purchase price).[8] The transferee's basis is stepped-up, not carried over, for depreciation purposes.

One result of this stepped-up basis is that (subject to the "second disposition" rules discussed below) a lower bracket family member purchasing the property can sell the property transferred and reinvest the sale proceeds in more liquid or higher yielding assets and probably pay much less in tax on the sale than the transferor-seller would otherwise have had to pay.

An increased basis is of particular advantage in the case of high value, low basis property such as highly appreciated real estate, a portfolio of substantially appreciated stock,or the "founder's stock" in a corporation which has gone public or merged with a publicly held corporation (note, however, that "founder's stock" is subject to rules and regulations of the S.E.C. restricting sale of such stock), or a closely-held corporation, with substantial accumulated earnings, which is about to be liquidated, but which would generate heavy taxation upon liquidation.

For example, if the transferor-seller bought undeveloped nonincome-producing land 10 years ago for $10,000 and it is now worth $100,000, he could sell it to his son for its $100,000 fair market value. The son could then sell the land and purchase mutual funds or other income-producing securities with the proceeds of the sale. If the son received $105,000 for the land, his gain would be only the difference between his $100,000 cost and the amount realized on the sale, $105,000 (i.e., his total gain would be $5,000). He does not have to pay tax on the $90,000 gain his father would have been subject to had he sold the land. The advantage is compounded if the son is in a lower tax bracket than his father.

The overall tax savings is even more dramatic if the father is in a relatively high income tax bracket at the time of the sale but is about to retire. Future payments from son to father spread out the profit and defer taxes. Since the father will probably be in a lower tax bracket after retirement, less of his profits will be lost in the form of taxes.

Special rules apply to installment sales to related parties. Certain "second dispositions" (resales) by a related party purchaser trigger recognition of gain *by the initial seller*. In essence, these rules, stated in more detail below, provide that the original seller's gain on an installment sale will be accelerated if a trustee or other purchaser related to the seller resells the asset within two years of the installment sale (or, in the case of marketable securities, sells at any time).

A resale by a related purchaser (the term "related purchaser" includes brothers and sisters, spouses, ancestors, and lineal descendents—and certain related entities) triggers recognition of gain by the initial seller.

In other words, if property is sold on the installment basis to a related party, and within two years that related party resells the property, the first seller must report — as payments received during the taxable year — any pay-

ments actually received by the related party. This could result in forcing the first seller to report all his gain on the sale before receiving all the payments.

For example, Bob LeClair sells property he bought for $300,000 to Beth, his daughter, for $1,000,000. Bob takes no down payment. The sales price is due in six years. Two days later, Beth sells the property for $1,000,000. She reports no gain because her basis is equal to the $1,000,000 sales price. But Bob will be taxed on his gain in the year Beth sells the asset, because a daughter is a related party for purposes of the "2-year-resale" rule.

The gain is based on his gross profit ratio. It is limited to the extent the amount realized on resale exceeds the actual payments made to the initial seller. Technically, there are three "related purchaser" rules, one applicable to installment sales of property which is not a marketable security, a second applicable to marketable securities, and a third special rule which applies only to installment sales of depreciable property between "closely related" parties.

Rules for Disposition of Property Other than Marketable Securities

The rule for installment sales of property *other* than marketable securities is as follows: If a related purchaser (defined above) disposes of the property he has purchased in an installment sale (in other words if a "second disposition" occurs) before the initial seller (the person who made the "first disposition") has received all the payments he is due under the installment sale, then the amount realized on the second disposition is treated as received—at the time of the second disposition—by the initial seller. For instance, if a mother sells her daughter appreciated land and the daughter immediately resells the land, the mother must report gain.

Fortunately, the gain reportable is limited. Gain, based on her profit percentage, is reportable by the mother only to the extent the daughter receives more in the second disposition than she has already paid her mother. So the initial seller's gain would be accelerated only to the extent additional cash or other property flows into the related group because of the "second disposition."

Although there are no regulations that illustrate mathematically how the second disposition rules apply, it should be as follows:

1. When the related person disposes of the property (the second disposition) before the person making the first disposition receives all payments due from that sale, the first seller is treated as having received the amount actually received by the second (related) seller—at the time of the second disposition. For

example, assume Herb Cheezman bought land for $500,000 and sold it to his son Stephen for $600,000. Assume also that Stephen agreed to pay $60,000 a year for 10 years. (For simplicity, interest is ignored.) In the second year Stephen sells the land to a third party for $1,000,000. Herb is treated as having received $1,000,000 in the second year.

2. There is a limit, however, on the amount Herb must report.

The person making the first disposition (Herb) reports only the amount by which the *lesser of*

A *(1)* the total amount realized with respect to the second disposition by the close of the tax year, (in this example it's $1,000,000)

or *(2)* the total contract price for the first disposition (in our example, $600,000) $600,000

exceeds the total of

B *(1)* the sum of payments actually received with respect to the first disposition (Herb received $60,000×2 years, or $120,000)

plus *(2)* the aggregate sum *deemed* (under the related party — second disposition rules) to have been received from the first disposition for part tax years (here $0) 120,000

So, in this example, Herb would report gain of $480,000

Of course, Stephen would be required to recognize his gain on the sale (i.e., the second disposition)—$1,000,000 (amount realized) minus $600,000 (Stephen's cost basis), or $400,000.

3. Where a second disposition results in recognition of gain to the first seller (Herb), subsequent payments actually received by the first seller from the related purchaser (Stephen) will be tax-free until they have equaled the amount realized as a result of the second disposition.

An important exception to this "second disposition" rule for property other than marketable securities is that if the second disposition occurs more than 2 years after the date of the first sale, it will avoid the resale rules. So, if Stephen waited 2 years and one month before he sold the land, Herb would not realize any gain because of Stephen's disposition. Stephen, of course, would have to report gain based on the difference between the amount he realizes on the sale (assume $1,000,000) and his basis (cost) of $600,000.

Marketable Security Rules

The rule for marketable securities (i.e., any security for which there was a market on an established securities exchange or otherwise) is the same as for other property—with one major difference: there is no 2-year time limit on the "second disposition" rule.

A second disposition—by a related party—could trigger an acceleration regardless of how long after the initial installment sale it is made. The resale rule applies if the property is sold any time prior to the full satisfaction of the installment obligation. So even if Stephen waits 5 years after he buys property from his father, if the subject of that installment sale purchase is marketable stock or bonds, Herb would have to report gain when Stephen makes the sale. (Of course, if Stephen received more in the second disposition than his own cost basis, he would also have to report his gain.)

Note, however, if the stock or securities are traded on an established securities market, installment treatment is not permitted in any event; all payments to be received are treated as received in the year of disposition.

There are four exceptions to both of the "related party"-"second disposition" rules described above:

1. The sale of stock back to the corporation which issued it is not treated as a first disposition. Therefore, a subsequent disposition of the stock by the corporation will not trigger the "second disposition" rule with regard to the sale to the corporation.

2. If property is destroyed by fire, condemned, taken by eminent domain or some other form of compulsory or involuntary conversion such as theft or government seizure, as long as the installment sale was made before this event (or threat or imminence thereof) occurs, the rule will not be applied.

3. No acceleration will occur if the second disposition occurs after the death of either the initial seller or the purchaser.

4. If the IRS can be convinced that neither disposition has income tax avoidance as one of its principal purposes, the resale rules will not apply.

Special Depreciable Property Rule

Installment reporting of taxable income does not apply to any personal or real property depreciation recapture. Recapture of these deductions (so-called Section 1245 and 1250 depreciation recapture) must be reported by a seller in the year of the sale even if any other gain is reported on the installment basis as payments are received.

Since such income must be reported in the year the property is sold, that amount can be added to the seller's basis. It therefore has the effect of reducing the reportable income that must be realized each year.

For instance, Charles Plotnick sells tangible personal property to Nick Martin for $70,000, to be paid in 3 installments. Interest is paid on the unpaid balance at current rates. Assume this is .09. Assume the property originally cost $90,000. It has an adjusted basis of $50,000 at the time of the sale because of depreciation deductions.

Charles must "recapture" his gain (the $20,000 difference between the sales price of $70,000 and his adjusted basis of $50,000). Since he enters the $20,000 of recaptured deductions into income in the year of the sale, he can increase his basis by that $20,000 amount to $70,000 (from $50,000). Since he has a 100 percent basis, he will realize no gain as payments are received.

Payments, exclusive of interest, should be $23,333 which is tax-free as a recovery of basis. But what if he sold the property for $110,000? The gain would be $60,000, the $110,000 amount realized minus his adjusted basis of $50,000. The $40,000 he previously deducted must now be recaptured. Since he must report $40,000, he can add that amount to his $50,000 basis. It now totals $90,000.

Since each payment, exclusive of interest, is $36,667, $30,000 will be tax-free, and the $3,667 balance will be gain.

Note, however, installment treatment is not allowed for sales of depreciable property to a controlled entity, such as a more than 50% owned partnership or corporation, or trust benefiting the seller or the seller's spouse. All payments to be received are treated as received in the year of disposition.

5. TRA '86 significantly affected installment sales in several ways:

    First, the repeal of the long term capital gains deduction will make the sale less appealing for the seller unless the price is raised accordingly (making the intrafamily installment sale or an installment sale of a business to employees much less attractive).

    Second, it has been noted above that, generally, interest on the unpaid balance will be deductible in full only if the debt is properly allocable to investment purposes (and then only to the extent of investment income, subject to phaseout rules) or to business purposes. The loss or curtailment of interest deductions will have a negative impact on intrafamily installment sales (and should shift attention to private annuities).

    Note that TRA '86 bars the use of the installment method if the property in question is publicly traded on an established market. This means gain cannot be deferred on the sale of publicly traded stocks and bonds.

HOW LIFE INSURANCE CAN ENHANCE THIS PLANNING TOOL

Where an individual (or business) transfers property to someone else in return for installment payments, the seller will often purchase insurance on the life (or lives) of the transferee(s) to protect against the potential cessation of payments at the death of the transferee(s). The seller should consider owning, paying premiums on, and being the beneficiary of the policy (the agreed-upon amount of payments made by the purchaser of the property could be increased to provide enough cash to make premium payments).

After the installment sale agreement is signed, the transferee-buyer receives title to the property. This means that the asset itself, as well as any appreciation from the date of the transfer, will be included in the transferee's estate. To provide the liquidity necessary to pay taxes and other death expenses, life insurance is often purchased on the transferee's life by the transferee's spouse, adult children, or on behalf of the transferee's spouse and children by the trustee of an irrevocable trust. The spouse, adult child, or trustee would be the owner, premium payer, and beneficiary of the policy proceeds. In intrafamily transfers, the transferor-seller often will make a gift to the policyholder of enough cash to pay premiums on the insured's life.

A third use of life insurance to improve the benefits of an installment sale is to assure the transferee's family enough cash at his or her death to make the promised installment payments. (Since the property will be in the transferee's estate after the sale, its inclusion could generate substantial estate and inheritance tax problems. This, in turn, creates a need for cash to pay increased death costs and drains the estate of cash to make installment payments.)

If the transferee's spouse, for example, purchases the appropriate amount of insurance on his life, there will be no need to sell or liquidate the transferred asset (perhaps closely held corporate stock) in order to make the agreed upon installment payments. The insurance proceeds can be used to pay death costs, make installment payments, or both.

IMPLICATIONS AND ISSUES IN COMMUNITY PROPERTY STATES

Installment sales by married individuals in community property states often involve real property. In such situations, it is important to ascertain whether the interest in real property is community property. Both spouses should join in any conveyance of community real property. If one spouse does not join in the conveyance of community real property, he or she may be able to void the sale for a specified period (one year from the date of recording of the deed in California). This statute of limitations applies only to land standing in the name of the transferor spouse alone. If the land stands in the name of both spouses, an attempt by either spouse to transfer complete title would be void with respect to the interest of the other spouse. Certain sales to parties who are not aware, in good faith, of the marriage relationship may be incontestable, but such controversies should be avoided.

A purchaser of personal property should also ascertain whether any community property rights are involved. California does not require the written consent of each spouse in connection with the sale of community personal property if the property is sold for "valuable consideration." Exception: Neither spouse can sell, convey, or encumber the furniture, furnishings, or fittings of the home or wearing apparel of the other spouse or minor children without the written consent of the other spouse.

Problems could arise as a result of recent cases regarding joint property rights of non-marital partners. As mentioned in the introduction, some courts have found implied agreements between non-married individuals to treat their property similarly to community property. Caution should be exercised if you are purchasing property from an individual involved in such a relationship. It may be advisable to ask the partner who may have a claim under the recent court decision to convey his or her interest in the property, if any.

Another possibility to consider is the separate sale of each spouse's interest. One spouse could sell his or her interest outright and recognize all of his or her capital gain immediately, while the other spouse sells his or her interest on the installment method and spreads out his or her capital gain. This can reduce capital gain taxes while effectively allowing a greater amount of the sales price to be received in the year of the sale.

QUESTIONS AND ANSWERS

Question — How can the related party rules be avoided?

Answer — For property other than marketable securities where the special depreciable property rule does not apply the related purchaser could hold the property for at least a 2-year period after the sale. The installment obligation could be structured so that no payments need to be made until after the 2-year holding period has lapsed. If the related party was going to sell the property to raise cash to make installment payments, as an alternative the related party could use the property as collateral for a loan to provide funds needed to make installment payments. (The loan must be bona fide and the debtor must continue to bear the economic risk of loss.)

A private annuity could be used—instead of an installment sale—to avoid all three related party rules. Since the installment sales rules do not deal with private annuity arrangements, the transferee should be free to dispose of the transferred property at any time without accelerating the recognition of gain to the transferor.

In any installment sale to a related party the risk of illiquidity of the initial seller in the event of a second disposition by the new owner should be considered. How can this potential problem be overcome? Perhaps the seller might insist on an acceleration clause. This would give the seller the right to demand additional cash payments if the property subject to the installment sale is disposed of before the 2-year waiting period for property other than marketable securities has been met.

It probably would not be advisable to impose formal restrictions on the related purchaser's ability to dispose of the property. Likewise, it probably is not wise to give the seller a legal right to insist that the purchaser must lend him funds to pay a tax imposed on a second disposition. Such contractual restrictions or requirements could be viewed by the IRS as evidence that the entire transaction lacked economic substance.

Question — What type of security can the seller of property under an installment sale require without being taxed on his entire gain in the year of the sale?

Answer — A third party can guarantee payment in the event the buyer defaults. For example, a standby letter of credit that's used as security for a deferred payment sale will not be treated as a payment received on the installment obligation.[9]

But third party notes or other third party obligations that are transferable or marketable prior to default by the installment buyer will be treated as payments to the seller (and therefore taxable in the year received).[10]

Typically, the IRS and the courts will deem funds placed in an escrow account to secure the interest of the seller to be constructively received—and therefore currently taxable in the year of the sale. However, this result is not certain. No presumption of tax avoidance arises merely because the seller requested an installment payout or merely because the buyer was at all times willing to pay the entire purchase price in a lump sum.

The seller is more likely to be successful in avoiding current taxation of escrowed funds if (1) the arrangement serves a legitimate business purpose and (2) the seller continues to look to the contractual obligation of the buyer for payment. An example would be where the escrow arrangement was negotiated in a manner which provided that payments from the escrow account were contingent on the seller's continued adherence to his agreement not to compete. This type of agreement would probably not result in constructive receipt by the seller even if he could control the investment of the money in the escrow account.

Question — What are the income and estate tax implications when the holder of an installment obligation dies?

Answer — The right to receive payments under the obligation is treated as income in respect of a decedent. Thus, payments on the installment obligation are taxable income to the person or entity that receives those payments, as they are received. Payments are taxed in the same manner as they would have been taxed had the seller lived and received payment himself.

For estate tax purposes, the present value of the installment obligation is also includible in the decedent's gross estate. But to reduce the harshness of double taxation, a deduction from income is allowed to the recipient based on the federal estate taxes paid by the decedent's estate attributable to the inclusion of the installment obligation. This is called the section 691 (income in respect of a decedent) deduction.[11]

Question — Is there a problem in arranging an installment sale of property with an existing mortgage upon it?

Answer — Yes. Where property subject to an existing mortgage is sold and the purchaser assumes or takes subject to that mortgage, any debt in excess of the seller's tax basis (cost) will be considered a payment received by the seller in the year of the sale. Any mortgage encumbering the property will be treated as assumed or taken subject to, even though title to the property does not pass in the year of sale and even though the seller remains responsible for payment of the mortgage (as in a "wraparound" mortgage).[12]

Question — What was the "Rushing" technique and is it still viable?

Answer — The "Rushing" technique enabled a donor to obtain installment sale treatment with an asset that is not usually the subject of an installment sale—such as listed stock. It also enabled a person with a large single holding to diversify. It will no longer work where the subject of the sale is a marketable security because of the unlimited time period of the "second disposition" rules for related party transactions. Furthermore, if the stock or securities are traded on an established securities market, installment treatment is not permitted in any event; all payments to be received are treated as received in the year of disposition.

Rushing was a case where the taxpayers owned all the stock in a corporation which was in the final stages of a liquidation. Just before the time limit was reached, they set up irrevocable trusts for their children and placed about $23,000 of assets in each trust. The trusts had an independent corporate trustee. (The donors reserved no administrative powers or beneficial interests. The corporate trustee was given broad powers.)

The taxpayer-donors then sold all their stock in the corporation about to be liquidated to the trusts. They received, in exchange, a small amount of cash and a large installment obligation. The trustee (as sole shareholder of the liquidating corporation) voted to complete the liquidation. It then received all the corporation's assets

(with no taxable gain since it paid full value for the stock). The donors of the trusts claimed installment sale treatment on their gain from the sale of the stock to the trusts.[13]

Thus, *Rushing* seemed to indicate that properly arranged intrafamily sales could result in installment sale treatment. But, as mentioned above, the "Rushing" technique is now unavailable. A resale of marketable securities (which qualified for installment treatment when initially sold) by a party related to the initial seller will trigger gain by the initial seller no matter how long the span between the first and second dispositions. Sales of assets other than marketable securities will not trigger gain by the initial seller if the trust holds the property for longer than 2 years before selling it.

Question — Does the "second disposition" rule mean there are no advantages to a transfer of property (which is not within the special depreciable property rule and not a marketable security) from an individual to an irrevocable trust established for his family in return for installment payments?

Answer — Many advantages still exist, including the following:

(1) Taxation on the gain can be spread over a larger number of years (assuming the trust does not dispose of the property within 2 years, or the trust does not benefit the seller or the seller's spouse if the property is depreciable to the trust). This could lower the applicable total rate considerably.

(2) The family of the seller is more secure from the claims of his creditors.

(3) No gift tax is incurred on the transfer if the stock is sold to the trust at its fair market value.

(4) The trust may have little or no gain on the resale of the asset since it takes as its basis the full purchase price it agreed to pay for the stock. (Of course, the stock may appreciate or decline in value during the 2 years it must be held in order to avoid accelerating the initial seller's gain.)

(5) None of the assets of the trust or income will be includible in the original owner's estate if the trust is irrevocable and he maintains no control. (The present value of future payments remaining on the note would, however, be includible if he died within the installment period. This, in turn, could cause a serious lack of liquidity.)

To obtain this favorable treatment, it is important that

(a) the trustee be completely independent and that the grantor maintain no control over the trustee's actions,

(b) there be prearrangement between the parties requiring the trustee to resell the stock,

(c) the original owner not have a stake in the resale by the trust (i.e., the amount he receives can't be dependent on the amount the trustee receives),

(d) there be a motive—other than tax savings—for the arrangement, and

(e) the "2-year holding rule" be met.

Question — Must there be any down payment in the year of sale to qualify for the installment method of reporting?

Answer — No. There is no requirement that there be any payment in the year of sale. The only requirement of this type is that at least one payment be made in a taxable year after the year in which the property was sold.

Question — Will a bequest of an installment obligation to the obligor avoid tax recognition of the untaxed gain?

Answer — The installment obligation rules can't be circumvented by canceling the obligation during lifetime. Likewise, when an installment seller dies holding an installment obligation, the gain isn't forgiven. Instead, gain is reportable by the seller's estate—or the recipient of the obligation—as payments are made. The amount of gain and character of income realized is the same as the deceased seller would have reported had he or she lived. (Note that death itself does not trigger an acceleration of gain; tax is due only if payments are actually or constructively received or if the obligation is sold.)

Under prior law, it had been argued that if an installment obligation was bequeathed to the purchaser of the property, the interests of the obligor and the obligee "merged." Under this theory, there would be no gain realized because the estate would never realize the unpaid balance.

Current tax law accelerates the unrealized gain when the seller makes a bequest of the obligation to the buyer or his estate cancels the debt. Gain or loss will be recognized to the extent the fair market value of the obligation exceeds the obligation holder's basis. (Where the decedent-seller and the purchaser are related, the fair market value of the obligation can't be less than its face amount.)

If a person forgives an installment obligation in his will, the cancellation is treated as a transfer of the obligation by the decedent's estate. The estate will report the accelerated gain. If a trust or some party other than the decedent held the obligation, the cancellation will be treated as a transfer by that person immediately after the decedent's death.

An installment obligation that becomes unenforceable at the seller's death is treated as if it were cancelled in favor of the obligor.

Question — What is the tax effect where the seller cancels a buyer's obligation to make installments?

Answer — If a seller cancels a buyer's installment obligation (or it becomes unenforceable), the cancellation will be treated as a "disposition" of the obligation. This means the seller must report gain (or loss). The gain (or loss) is measured by the difference between the fair market value of the obligation at the time of its disposition and its basis.

Note that if the seller and buyer are considered "related persons," the fair market value of the obligation will be considered as not less than the face value. For instance, mom sells her summer home in Avalon to her daughter in an installment sale. Mom's basis in the home was $10,000. Her daughter will pay the purchase price, $50,000, in five equal annual $10,000 installments. (Interest is ignored for simplicity.) If mom immediately cancels the daughter's obligation, mom must report gain. Her gain is the difference between the value of what is owed to her, $50,000, and her $10,000 basis. She is also liable for any gift tax on the gift.

A solution would seem to be for mom to forgive, at her whim, and on a year by year basis, all or a portion of each $10,000 payments as it is paid. Her daughter should write a check for the full $10,000 to her. Then, without a prearranged or legally binding plan, she can write her daughter—and son-in-law and each of her grandchildren—checks of $10,000 or under, all of which would be gift tax free (and she could double the amount of each check if her husband joined in on a "split" gift). Mom will recognize gain of $8,000 each of the 5 years, rather than $40,000 in the year of sale.

Question — How is gain computed under installment sales rules where the sales price is not fixed or determinable?

Answer — Often, the price at which property will change hands depends on some contingency. For example, Susan Harmon may sell her stock in the SH Corporation, a closely held business, to her son Mark in return for installment payments. But rather than selling a specific dollar price, the amount may be set as a percentage of the gross profits of the business for each of the next 10 years. The parties may—or may not—put a maximum dollar amount on the selling price.

Installment sales treatment is available even when the actual price can't be determined with precision. If there is a stated maximum selling price, the seller (in this example Susan) can recover basis by means of a "gross profit ratio."[14] This ratio is multiplied by the installment payment (exclusive of interest) to determine the portion of the payment which is gain.

$$\frac{\text{gross profit (realized or to be realized)}}{\text{total contract price (assume this is maximum selling price)}} \times \begin{array}{c}\text{installment}\\\text{payment}\end{array}$$

(The maximum selling price is defined as the largest price which could be paid assuming all contingencies, formulas, etc. operate in the seller's favor.) The seller then reports income on a prorata basis (and recovers his basis over the scheduled payment period in equal annual increments) with respect to each installment payment.

Later, if it is found that the contingency will not be met (and therefore the seller will not actually receive the "maximum" selling price) a recomputation of the seller's income is allowed. The seller may report reduced income (not only in the adjustment year, but in all subsequent years). If the seller reported more income from installment payments in prior years than he or she should have (after the recomputation shows the actual income), the excess is deductible as a loss.

If the sales price is indefinite and no maximum selling price can be determined—but the obligation is payable over a fixed period of time, the seller's basis would be recoverable ratably over that fixed period.[15]

If neither selling price nor payment period can be ascertained with certainty in advance, the arrangement will be closely scrutinized to determine whether there has been a sale or whether the payments, in economic effect, are merely in the nature of rent or royalty income. If it is determined that there has been a sale, the seller's basis will be recovered over 15 years commencing with the date of sale. Any basis not recovered in that time may be carried forward to succeeding years until recovered in full.

Generally, if in any year payments received are less than the basis allocated to that year, the excess basis must be reallocated over the balance of the 15-year period. (A period other than 15 years may be used or required where it is shown that a substantial and inappropriate deferral or acceleration of the recovery of the seller's basis would otherwise result.)

The effect of the contingency sales price rules allowing installment reporting is that taxpayers will now have little justification for treating transactions as "open." (In open transactions a taxpayer can recover his entire cost before reporting any gain—rather than reporting gain ratably.) This "cost recovery" method will now be available only in rare and extraordinary cases involving sales for a contingent price where it's impossible to value a purchaser's obligation to pay a contingent price.

Special rules apply with respect to contingent installment payments for sales of depreciable property to a con-trolled entity, such as a more than 50% owned partnership or corporation. The rules are:

1. Seller's basis is recovered ratably in annual increments if (a) the installment sale is to a controlled entity and (b) it is impossible to reasonably ascertain the fair market value.

2. All noncontingent payments plus the fair market value of contingent payments must be reported in the year of the sale. For instance, assume Tom Miller sells depreciable property to a corporation he controls for no down payment and 10 percent of the net profits from the business for the next 10 years. Assume the fair market value of the promise can be reasonably ascertained to be $200,000. Tom would have to include $200,000 in income in the year of the sale ($0 noncontingent payments plus $200,000 fair market value of contingent payments).

3. The purchaser of the property may not increase his basis in the property by any amount before such time as the seller includes such amount in income.

Question — How soon does a taxpayer have to elect to report payments in installments?

Answer — No election is necessary. Installment sale treatment is automatic for qualifying sales unless an election is made specifying installment sale treatment is not to apply. Although the temporary regulations are not specific as to how such an election is to be made, reporting the entire gain in gross income for the taxable year in which the sale occurs (on or before the due date for filing the tax return—including extensions) will operate as an election that installment sale reporting is not to apply.[16]

Question — When might it be a good idea to forego the installment method of reporting a gain, even though a sale was made on the installment basis?

Answer — If a taxpayer has unrelated losses, he might wish to offset those losses with the gain from the installment sale. He may have unusually low income or high deductions for the year. Thus, he or she would report the full gain in the year of sale even though the sale was an installment sale.

Question — When is interest payable on the unpaid balance of an installment sale deductible by the buyer?

Answer — Interest is deductible only in the period in which that interest is properly allocable. Regardless of how the parties have formed the agreement, the IRS will treat the interest as "constant" (no matter whether the taxpayer is on the cash or accrual method). The service allocates the interest over the term of the contract. The net effect is that the parties must determine the effective interest on a compound interest basis and use that effective rate to compute their interest deductions.

This rule limits both the interest deduction and the interest income to the amount of interest that accrues economically. The compounding period used in determining the effective rate of interest will probably be the same as that called for in the party's agreement.

Question — What changes in the installment sales rules were made by OBRA (The Omnibus Budget Reconciliation Act of 1987) and TAMRA (the Technical and Miscellaneous Revenue Act of 1988)?

Answer — OBRA '87 made two major changes in the treatment of installment sales made by those who do not, in the regular course of their business, make installment sales. One change applies to the sale of nonfarm real property used in the taxpayer's trade or business or that is held for the production of rental income where the property's sales price is greater than $150,000. The complex "proportionate disallowance" rule that made all or much of the gain from an installment sale nondeferrable has been repealed. But under the second change, an interest charge is now imposed on the tax that can be deferred (to the extent that the amount of deferred payments during the year exceed $5 million).

TAMRA '88 expanded the scope of the changes made in 1987, by making them applicable to any installment sales in which the sales price exceeds $150,000 (if the deferred payments for all such sales during the year exceed $5 million).[17] In other words, the interest charge imposed under OBRA '87 now applies to any real or personal property sales (other than farm property) occurring after December 31, 1988, with certain exceptions for binding contracts that were in effect on October 21, 1988.

Footnote References

Installment Sale

1. IRC Section 453.
2. IRC Section 453.
3. Rev. Rul 70-430, 1970-2 C.B. 51.
4. Reg. §1.483-1(c)(2).
5. IRC Section 2033; Reg. §20.2033-1.
6. Reg. §1.691(a)-3.
7. Reg. §1.691(c)-1.
8. IRC Section 1012.
9. Temp. Reg. §15A.453-1(b)(3).
10. Temp. Reg. §15A.453-1(e).
11. An installment sale of stock or of other property to be used in an enterprise will generally not be treated as a retained interest (so as to cause inclusion under 2036(c) of any growth interest given away by a transferor) if the transaction meets certain safe harbor tests. (These tests and a detailed discussion can be found on page 477.)
12. Temp. Reg. §15A.453-1(b)(3)(ii).
13. *Rushing v. Comm.*, 441 F.2d 593 (CA-5, 1971). Note that the IRS has nonacquiesced to *Rushing*. See also *Roberts v. Comm.*, 71 T.C. No. 26 (1978), where the taxpayer was successful using the Rushing technique. The taxpayer showed the court that (1) the grantor gave up control of the trust fund, (2) the trustees invested assets without consulting the grantor, and (3) the transaction was bona fide since the grantor set up the trust with the business purpose of diversifying holdings and for personal reasons.
14. Temp. Reg. §15A.453-1(c)(2).
15. Temp. Reg. §15A.453-1(c)(3).
16. Temp. Reg. §15A.453-1(d)(3).
17. IRC Section 453A, as amended by the Technical and Miscellaneous Revenue Act of 1988.

Tools and Techniques

Chapter 16

INTEREST-FREE AND BELOW MARKET RATE LOANS

WHAT IS IT?

An interest-free or below market rate loan involves the lending of money to a party who is required either to pay no interest or to pay a rate of interest less than that which is currently being charged in the market place.

Most interest-free (or below market rate) loans are made by a corporation to a nonshareholder employee or from a parent to a child or other family member.

The economic advantage of an interest-free (or below market rate) loan lies in the borrower's ability to use either the funds or the interest from the funds.

There are few, if any, tax advantages to an interest-free or below market rate loan, since TRA '86 began the phase-out and eventual denial of all personal (consumer) interest, and limited investment interest deductions to investment income.

WHEN IS THE USE OF SUCH A DEVICE INDICATED?

1. To reduce the estate of the lender to the extent the loan limits future growth in the value of assets and shifts economic wealth to the borrower.

2. As a corporate fringe benefit to enable an employee to purchase a home, provide a child's college education, purchase stock of the employer-corporation, or to pay medical bills.

3. Transfers of income through interest-free or below market rate loans can be used to support parents, provide support for children in school, or to help them purchase a home or business.

WHAT ARE THE REQUIREMENTS?

1. The transaction must constitute a bona fide debt (preferably in writing).

2. If the parties maintain books or records of account, the debt should be entered.

3. There should be a provision in the debt instrument (assuming a no-interest loan is desired) expressly precluding interest, or, in the case of a below market rate loan, stating the interest to be charged.

The keys to success in a loan from a corporation to its employee are:

1. The arrangement must constitute a bona fide debt (preferably a written note containing a reasonable repayment schedule—or a note payable on demand).

2. A demonstrated intent to repay must be evidenced by an agreement between the parties. This is especially important where the loan is to a majority shareholder-employee. Otherwise, the IRS could claim that the "loan" is in fact a disguised dividend.

3. The amount of the loan must be reasonable in relation to the salary of the employee.

It is advisable to avoid situations where the corporation borrows money to make interest-free loans to shareholders. The IRS is likely to treat such transactions as if the real loan was made between the lender and the shareholder. Following that reasoning, interest actually paid by the corporation to the lender could be treated as if the corporation paid a dividend to the shareholder who then paid interest to the lender. This attack is especially likely if the shareholder personally guaranteed the loan to the corporation.[1]

HOW IT IS DONE — EXAMPLES

Your client, Maxine Grayboyes, is a key singer in the industrial productions corporation called, "Off Broad Street." To enable her to purchase a new home, "Off Broad Street" advances, interest-free, $50,000 in return for a demand note.

Terry Halpern is the owner of "Show Time," a magazine devoted to promoting show business and informing people who work for television, radio, theatre groups, and other entertainment vehicles about new and current events. In order to promote a more favorable press image for herself Farrah Fawcelips lent Terry $4,000,000 at 4 percent interest for 8 years. The best deal Terry could have gotten from a local bank would have been 6 percent. Interest-free loans result in taxable gain to the borrower if the funds are used for a purpose that would not give rise to an offsetting interest deduction — for example, if borrowed money were used to purchase tax-exempt bonds.

Rich Marino is the President and one-third shareholder of Trinity Paving Company, Incorporated. Substantial interest-free loans were made by the corporation to him and his brothers, Larry and Tony, who are also shareholders. In order to make these loans, Trinity Paving Company had to carry interest-bearing obligations to third parties. In other words, suppliers to Trinity Paving extended substantial amounts of credit. Rick, Larry, and Tony personally guaranteed these obligations. In this situation, the substance of the transaction is that Trinity Paving is acting as the agent of the three individual taxpayers. It is as if Trinity Paving, on behalf of Rick, Larry, and Tony, obtained loans and then paid interest to the creditors on behalf of the three shareholders. In essence every

Tools and Techniques

time Trinity Paving Company paid interest, those payments (to the extent allocable to its interest-free loans to the shareholders) actually discharged the personal obligations of the shareholders. To the extent that these actual payments were in fact made, the taxpayers are deemed to have received dividend income and made an interest payment.[2]

WHAT ARE THE TAX IMPLICATIONS?

1. The transaction between the corporation and an employee (or an employee-shareholder) must be a bona fide loan. Otherwise, the entire loan may be treated as additional salary or as a disguised dividend.

2. If a corporation actually pays interest on funds it borrows in order to make an interest-free loan to a stockholder, the corporation may be treated as the agent of the stockholder. This would make interest paid by the corporation taxable as a dividend to the stockholder. This problem is particularly acute where a stockholder personally guarantees the corporate loan. However, the stockholder may be entitled to an offsetting interest deduction depending on how the borrowed funds are used.

3. Loans with no interest or below-market rate of interest generally are treated under a legal fiction which considers them as loans bearing a market rate of interest accompanied by a payment or payments from the lender to the borrower. These phantom payments (the difference between what should have been charged and what in fact was charged for the use of the money lent) are characterized in accordance with the substance of the particular transaction. In other words, the IRS might treat the phantom payment from the lender as compensation from a business to an employee, as a dividend from the corporation to its shareholder, or as a gift from the shareholders of the corporation to the borrower.

    Since TRA '86, the borrower can't deduct (subject to a phaseout rule through 1990) personal interest. So with regard to interest actually paid on the loan, the borrower's cost has considerably increased. The bottom line is that interest-free or below-market loans will often result in taxable income to the borrower to the extent of the excess between what they should be paying and what the borrower in fact pays. Still, the interest-free or below-market loan is appealing, even after TRA '86, not as a tax shifting device, but as an economically viable tool for accomplishing personal and business objectives.

4. For a more detailed discussion of personal loans and tax issues, see QUESTIONS AND ANSWERS, below.

IMPLICATIONS AND ISSUES IN COMMUNITY PROPERTY STATES

As discussed in Chapter 11, relating to Gifts (which should be reviewed in conjunction with this Section), some states impose gift taxes on interspousal gifts. The following are some of the potential problem areas which might arise:

If the money lent is the separate property of one spouse (e.g. by that spouse having inherited the funds) a gift can occur between the lending spouses if the demand note is made out in favor of both spouses. The amount of the gift would be one-half of the value of the note (presumably the face amount of note).

A similar gift may be found if the money lent is community property and the demand note received in exchange for the funds names only one spouse. It may be possible to show successfully that the named spouse was holding the note as trustee for the community and a gift avoided, but it creates the opportunity for the taxing authorities to claim that a gift was made and thus creates exposure to either gift tax or legal expense or both in dealing with the problem created.

Another unintended gift could occur if the money were lent to one spouse and then used to purchase assets in the names of both spouses.

Another accidental gift area lies in the repayment of the loan. If the loan is to one spouse and is used to make investments in the name of that spouse, the liability belongs entirely to that spouse. Using community funds or the separate property of the non-borrowing spouse to repay the loan provides the basis for a taxable gift to be recognized.

If the note is called by the lender and the borrower does not have the funds to repay and his spouse or the community does, then a gift can be avoided by the borrower giving to the spouse (or the community) a note for the amount of funds used to repay his obligation.

These problems can be avoided by careful attention to the source of funds for loans and the manner in which investments or repayments are made.

QUESTIONS AND ANSWERS

Question — How can a loan to a key employee be structured in order to tie that employee into the business?

Answer — By making the loan callable upon separation from service or payable in the event of the employee's preretirement death, the corporation can protect its interest. The employee could protect his own estate by purchasing life insurance in the amount of the loan.

Question — What was the effect of recent tax reform acts on interest-free and below-market rate loans?

Answer — Tax law creates a fiction; for income and gift tax purposes the tax law treats interest-free and below market loans as if a specified level of interest was charged and paid—even if it wasn't. In other words, interest is imputed on interest free loans and on other below market rate loans. The amount subjected to gift and income taxation in most cases is the difference between (a) the "statutory rate" and (b) the interest actually payable (if any) under the agreement between the parties. This difference is the "foregone interest".

Under this legal fiction, the borrower is treated as paying the foregone interest to the lender and therefore may take an income tax deduction for the "payment" (but only to the extent the borrower is deemed to have investment income if the interest is considered investment interest; no deduction is allowed, subject to the phaseout rules, for personal interest). The lender will be treated as having received the foregone interest and therefore must report the income "received".

Question — What are the implications of a loan that is treated as a gift?

Answer — If a loan is considered a gift, the lender is treated as if he or she made a gift to the borrower in the amount of the "foregone interest." (See the discussion of term and demand loans below.)

Question — What are the implications if a loan is not a gift?

Answer — The tax characterization of a loan which is not a gift depends on the relationship between the parties. In any case, the IRS will treat the lender as having made a transfer to the borrower in the amount of the "foregone interest".

The Service will probably treat foregone interest as a dividend when the borrower is solely a shareholder (nondeductible by the corporation, taxable as ordinary income to the shareholder, as interest paid by the shareholder, and taxable to the corporation as interest income).

If the borrower is solely an employee, the lender will probably have interest income to the extent of the foregone interest and a corresponding deduction for compensation paid (if reasonable). The borrower will have compensation income, but a deduction for the foregone interest may be denied or limited (see "WHAT ARE THE TAX IMPLICATIONS," No. 3, above).

Question — How will shareholder-employees be treated?

Answer — The Service will likely argue that the foregone interest is a dividend.

Question — How do you compute the amount subject to taxation?

Answer — That depends on two factors: (1) Is the gift tax or is the income tax involved? (2) Is the loan a demand loan or is it a loan for a fixed term, i.e., is it a term loan (including loans with indefinite maturities)?

Demand loans are loans payable in full at any time on the demand of the lender. The amount subject to (both gift and income) tax is the "foregone interest". This foregone interest is measured by the applicable statutory rate specified during each calendar year the loan remains outstanding. This means that from year to year the rate will

change. It also means that the interest income is reportable one year at a time.

A term loan is defined as any loan which is not a demand loan. Taxation of these loans is further broken down according to whether the loan is a "gift loan" or not. A gift loan is a below market loan where the lender intends to make a gift to the borrower in the amount of the foregone interest.

How much interest is foregone in the case of a term loan? Essentially, you find the present value of the interest which should have been charged. You then subtract that amount from the present value of the interest that was in fact charged. The difference is the taxable amount. In calculating present values you must use the statutory discount rate applicable at the time the loan is made.

Where the term loan is not a gift loan (for example, where it is "compensation related", that is, a loan between an employer and an employee or between an independent contractor and the person for whom he performs services), the taxable amount is the present value of the foregone interest for the entire term of the loan. The borrower is deemed to be paying that interest while the lender is deemed to be receiving the interest and is therefore taxed on it. Taxation in the case of a nongift term loan is at a level rate for each year of the loan. (Withholding is not required by an employer on the deemed payment made to an employee arising from a demand or term loan.)

Where the term loan is a gift loan, the amount subject to taxation is found in the same way as a nongift loan. But for gift tax purposes, the entire present value is subject to gift tax in the year of the loan. For income tax purposes, each year's foregone interest is taxed on a year by year basis. The amount, of course, will vary as changes occur in the statutory interest rates.

Question — Are there transactions that will be treated as interest-free or below market rate loans even though they appear to be something else?

Answer — Yes. Congress was concerned with all transactions that in effect were tax avoidance or significant tax shifting schemes. Therefore, many situations which don't look like loans will invoke the below market rules. For example, assume a local country club requires its members to pay a refundable, non-interest-bearing deposit as part of their membership fee. In essence, the member is paying part of the fee with the income that the club earns on the deposit. The IRS could easily apply the rules described above.

Question — What are the exceptions and limitations to the interest-free and below market rate loan rules?

Answer — There are a number of important exceptions:

Tools and Techniques

(1) A loan made to one individual is exempt from both gift and income tax rules if the outstanding balance on the total of all loans made to that person from the lender does not exceed $10,000. Think of this as the "$10,000 and under de minimus rule".

This protection will not apply if the loan is a gift loan and the loan proceeds are used in connection with income producing property. Furthermore, if the loan is a "compensation related" loan or a "corporate shareholder" loan (any loan between a corporation and any shareholder), the protection will not apply if federal tax avoidance is a principal purpose for the loan.

(2) The second exception to the general rules governing interest free and below market rate loans is the "$100,000 and under" rule. This rule provides that where gift loans are made to one person by an individual and the outstanding balances due on the aggregate of the loans made to that person by the lender do not exceed $100,000, the law limits the amount of the "foregone" interest.

The limit is the lower of (a) the statutory rate or (b) the amount earned by the borrower as a result of his investment of the loan proceeds. If the borrower does not earn more than $1,000 in the year, the law treats the parties as if there were no foregone interest.

The $100,000 and under rule applies only if federal tax avoidance is not a principal purpose of the loan.

ASRS: Sec. 53, §20.3(a); Sec. 55, §57.5(b)

Footnote References
Interest-Free and Below Market Rate Loans

1. *Creel v. Comm.*, 72 T.C. 1173 (1979).
2. *Creel*, 72 T.C. 1173 (1979). For other cases on interest-free loans see *Saunders v. U.S.*, 294 F. Supp. 1276, 1282 (D. Hawaii 1968); *Joseph Lupowitz Sons, Inc. v. Comm'r.*, 497 F.2d 862 (3rd Cir. 1974); *Claude J. Lisle et al.*, 35 T.C.M. 140 (1976); *Albert Suttle*, 37 T.C.M. 393 (1978); *Zager*, 72 T.C. 1009 (1979); *William G. Martin*, T.C. Memo 1979-469; *C.S. Williams*, 37 T.C.M. 306 (1978); *Dolese v. U.S.*, 79-2 U.S.T.C. Para. 9540 (10th Cir. 1979).

Chapter 17

LIFE INSURANCE

WHAT IS IT?

Life insurance is a contract under which for a stipulated consideration (a premium), one party (the insurer) agrees to pay the other (the insured), or his or her beneficiary, a defined amount upon the occurrence of death or some other specified event. In essence, life insurance is a contract under which economic protection is provided against the risk of cessation of income due to the insured's death. This definition of life insurance includes accidental death benefits under health insurance policies, whole life, endowment, universal, variable, and term life insurance policies. It encompasses both personally-owned and business-owned policies and includes group coverage as well as individually purchased plans.

WHEN IS THE USE OF SUCH A DEVICE INDICATED?

1. Life insurance is an important estate planning tool to provide cash for the payment of estate and inheritance taxes, debts, administrative costs, and other estate expenses.

2. Life insurance will provide an income for family expenses.

3. Life insurance can be used for special needs such as the payment of college expenses, mortgage balances, or other large capital needs.

4. Life insurance is often used as a credit-building tool; lending institutions and other creditors often use life insurance on a debtor's life as security.

5. Life insurance provides a way to pay federal estate taxes at a "discount." For example, if an individual purchases a $100,000 policy and dies within the first year of a contract (after having paid $1,500 in premiums), $100,000 worth of taxes can be paid at a cost of only $1,500. The difference can be roughly thought of as a discount. Furthermore, properly arranged life insurance owned by a third party who is also named beneficiary can be used to pay estate settlement costs with (1) no probate cost, (2) no inheritance or other state death taxes, (3) no income taxes, (4) no transfer fees, and (5) no federal estate taxes.

WHAT ARE THE VARIOUS TYPES OF LIFE INSURANCE?

1. Term insurance. Under this type of insurance (a) the insured must die before the term expires for which benefits are to be paid; (b) at the expiration of the "term," the insurance protection terminates; (c) initially, the cash outlay for insurance protection is relatively low (the policyowner receives the maximum short term protection for the minimum cash outlay).

There are basically four types of term insurance:

(a) Annual renewable term. This type of policy is renewable each year (regardless of the insured's physical condition) at an increasing premium.

(b) Convertible term. This type of policy may be exchanged without evidence of insurability, i.e., without the insured proving that he is physically and otherwise in a standard class of risks, for a whole life or endowment type of policy.

(c) Decreasing term. A familiar kind of decreasing term is often called "mortgage" insurance. The death benefit decreases over the specified period of time, but the premium generally remains level.

(d) Level term. Here the death benefit remains the same for the entire term of the policy. Generally the premium also remains level.

2. Whole life (permanent) insurance. The major characteristics of whole life insurance are: (a) the premium for a whole life insurance contract remains level throughout the life of the contract; and (b) because of the "reserve" the insurance company needs to maintain a level premium when the insured reaches older ages, certain "cash value" builds up within the contract (this cash value increases annually and can be borrowed by the policyowner or taken as surrender proceeds).

There are basically two types of whole life insurance. The first type is known as straight life, while the second is known as limited payment life. The difference is basically that under a limited payment life policy, premiums are "compressed," i.e., they are payable over a shorter period of time. For example, if a male age 35 purchased a $25,000 straight life policy, the "face amount" (death benefit) would be $25,000. If he purchased a $25,000 20-payment life policy at the same age, the death benefit would be the same and the protection would be provided for as long as the policyowner wanted to keep the policy in force, i.e., it could be kept in force for the insured's life. But because premiums would be compressed into a much smaller period of time (20 annual payments), they would be considerably higher under the limited payment type of plan.

Two other varieties of whole life are: (a) modified life and (b) preferred risk life. A modified life insurance

Tools and Techniques

policy typically provides a given amount of insurance at unusually low premium rates for an initial period (e.g., five years) after issue and then the premium is correspondingly higher for the remainder of the premium period. Modified plans generally have a lower initial cash value than a corresponding face amount of typical straight life would have.

Preferred risk is a type of policy which generally requires that the insured be in above average health. Preferred risk plans are often sold only to professionals or others in low risk occupations or to nonsmokers. Generally, preferred risk policies are sold only in higher amounts (such as $25,000 or greater) and the premiums under such a plan are slightly lower per $1,000 of protection than with standard policies.

3. Endowment insurance. The primary characteristic of endowment insurance is that such a plan pays the face amount (e.g., $25,000) at the sooner of the time of "endowment" (the maturity of the contract) or at the insured's death prior to the endowment date. Endowment policies are basically purchased as a means of forced savings since the protection element is relatively minimal. Various types of endowment policies are often found in pension plans, or personal savings programs. Since the cash value builds up tax free under an endowment policy, such plans are often utilized by individuals in high income tax brackets.

4. Universal life. A universal life policy is interest sensitive life insurance in which the investment, expense, and mortality elements are separately and specifically defined. A contract owner selects a death benefit level. The death benefit may be one that increases over time, coinciding with the increased cash value of the policy (death benefit option II), or, alternatively, the death benefit can remain level regardless of the underlying value changes (death benefit option I). From the premium that is paid, the insurer than deducts a "load" for contractually defined expenses. The remaining premium is then credited toward the contract owner's cash values. Mortality charges are deducted. Interest earned on the remaining cash is then credited at rates based on current investment earnings. (Specific design features will vary from company to company depending on marketing policies and product objectives.) Under this configuration, increased interest rates result in higher cash value levels while increased expense loads and increased mortality charges result in lower cash values. Typically, there is a minimum contractual guarantee as to the interest credited, such as 4 or 4.5%. Mortality costs also have a guarantee through a maximum premium charge for the "pure" cost of the death benefit; however, most companies charge rates lower than the contractually allowed maximum.

There is no such thing as a predetermined "standard" universal life plan; each contract owner selects the level of premium and death benefit desired as well as the length of premium paying period. Significant flexibility in premium payments is possible. Usually a stated minimum premium must be paid the first policy year. But after that the contract owner can vary the amount, the payment date, or frequency of subsequent premiums. (Depending on the amount of the initial premium, additional premiums or premium increases may be limited to stated minimum or maximum levels.) "Stop and go" features allow the discontinuance as well as subsequent resumption of premium payments at any time. (It is not necessary to reinstate the policy to do this.) As long as there is enough cash value to pay the expense (loading) charges and mortality costs, the policy will remain in force. If the cash value falls below that level, the policy will terminate. (Usually there is a 61-day grace period).

Gross premiums are reduced by specified expense charges (as well as mortality costs) to determine the universal life policy's cash value. Expense loads run between 5 and 10 percent of the gross premium and are charged year after year. Additionally, because of greater first year acquisition costs, an extra first year expense may be levied. (This may be factored into the policy as a "per policy" amount, an amount per $1,000 of death benefits, or as a percentage of first year mortality charges. Some companies may spread out the additional first year expenses by increasing the annual percentage of gross premium charges on some minimum amount of cumulative premium and set a lower precentage charge on premiums in excess of that stated minimum amount. Alternatively, rather than increasing expense charges, many insurers are recovering expense and surrender costs through "surrender charges." Upon surrender, the contract owner would receive an amount reduced by a surrender charge, a percentage of the cash value (the longer the policy is held the less is taken out).

Similar to traditional policies, riders such as waiver of premium or accidental death and dismemberment may be added to the basic contract.

5. Variable life. A variable life insurance policy is a relatively new type of insurance policy which resembles a traditional whole life policy with two major distinctions. Both the death benefit payable upon death and the surrender value payable during life are not guaranteed, but can increase or decrease depending upon investment performance of the assets underlying the policy. The death benefit, however, generally, cannot decrease below the initial face amount of the policy, as long as all premiums have been paid. With variable life, you trade the cash surrender value guarantee for the potential of investment growth by directing the overall strategy of your policy's investment program.

The policyowner may allocate the premium, after certain deductions are made, to a particular sub-account held by the insurance company. Among the types of sub-accounts which may be permissible, (depending on the particular company's product) are a Money Market type account, a Growth Stock Account, a Bond Account, a Balanced Fund Account, and a Real Estate Account. And, depending on the insurance company, the choices may be changed several times a year. The death benefit typically, will be adjusted once a year, whereas, the cash value will be adjusted on a daily basis. Premiums are fixed and always remain the same. Since both the surrender value and death benefit can vary, the product is known as variable life.

Among the charges which are deducted from the premium before any investment is made in a sub-account are administrative and sales expenses, any state premium taxes as well as the cost for the mortality element.

The major attractiveness of variable life is that the policyholder can direct where premium dollars are to be invested as contrasted with typical whole life or universal life policies where the policyholder cannot make such direction.

Variable life enjoys the same favorable income tax treatment as other insurance policies. Earnings from the investments are currently income tax deferred. In other words, there is no tax on the internal buildup of cash values until such values are realized by way of surrender, and then only if the surrender value exceeds the policyholder's cost basis, unless the policy is classified as a modified endowment contract. (See question below.) Death benefits, regardless of growth, pass income tax free.

Should a policyholder wish to have access to his cash values and not surrender the policy, he can borrow up to a designated percentage of the cash value (e.g., 90%). Interest, typically, is charged on such loans.

Similar to traditional policies, riders such as waiver of premium or accidental death and dismemberment may be added to the basic contract.

Unlike any other type of insurance, the sale of a variable life insurance product must be accompanied by or preceded by a prospectus approved by the Securities and Exchange Commission.

6. Variable Universal Life. Variable Universal Life is a combination of universal life insurance and variable life insurance. It is like universal life with flexible premiums, adjustable death benefits, policy loan, and partial withdrawal privileges. However, unlike universal life and like variable life, the owner of the life contract and not the insurer decides where the premiums are invested. The alternative accounts where the premiums can be invested are similar to those in the variable life product described above.

Variable Universal Life is a product subject to the rules of the Securities and Exchange Commission and, therefore, requires a prospectus be given to a prospective client before a sale can be made.

7. Survivorship life (joint and survivor life). Survivorship life insurance is a type of life insurance policy which insures two or more people. The policy may be either a whole life or term type of policy. Some companies now also offer an interest sensitive survivorship life insurance policy (e.g., universal life). The death benefit under a survivorship policy is not realized until the last of two or more insured individuals dies (the survivor). At that time the full death benefit is payable to the named beneficiary. Although there are several variations of this type of insurance, most of the policies that are of the whole life variety insure two individuals and provide for an increase in cash values upon the "first death," and, if the policies are participating (dividend paying), also provide for increased dividends. Depending upon the company, the premiums may continue until the survivor's subsequent death or, through a special option, the policy may be paid up at the "first death" and no further premiums would be required.

The policy can insure any two insureds as long as there is an insurable interest. Its use is typically confined to husband-wife, parent-child, or two related business people, such as business owners or key employees. The policy can be considered a very effective tool relieving the federal estate tax burden of those couples who will be subject to such tax and have elected to take maximum advantage of the marital deduction, so that although there will not be any federal estate tax due upon the first spouse's death, there will be tax due at the survivor's death.

The policy may be owned by any party that could own any of the other traditional types of life insurance policy, including an irrevocable trust. There is no requirement that there be joint owners, despite the fact that there are two individuals insured.

8. Single premium whole life. Single premium whole life insurance is a type of limited pay life insurance policy. Unlike traditional whole life policies, however, where premiums are due generally until age 90 or 100, a single premium whole life policy, as the name implies, requires only one premium.

The policyholder purchases a paid-up policy with just one payment rather than paying premiums year after year. For example, a $25,000 single premium might buy a 55-year-old man $75,000 worth of insurance coverage.

Single premium life offers some of the traditional tax advantages that regular whole life policies afford:

Tools and Techniques

1. The money contributed to the policy builds up tax free through policy cash values.

2. The policyholder can borrow those cash values from the policy. Such a loan may trigger income tax consequences if the policy is classified as a modified endowment policy. (See question below.)

3. The proceeds from the policy (the face value, as distinct from the cash surrender value) at the death of the insured go to the beneficiaries completely income tax free and without probate.

4. One of the main characteristics of this type of insurance is that the policy develops immediate cash values. Interest is generally credited based upon some type of "new money" approach, and may be tied into short or long term investments of the particular insurance company. The values that the policy develops can be availed of either through a surrender of the policy or through a policy loan. Many companies allow the policyholder to borrow these values at no interest cost or at a nominal interest cost to the policyholder. For example, if a policyholder borrows $10,000, the insurance company might charge him 8% interest, but that is not his true cost. The company would credit his cash value account with the 8% interest he paid or 7% or 6% depending upon the company. Thus, the true interest cost to borrow would be anywhere from 0% to 2%. The policyholder need never pay back the loan. However, if the contract is classified as a modified endowment contract, borrowing from the policy will likely result in income tax consequences. (See question below.) However, outstanding loans will reduce the death benefit, and interest on the loan is not income tax deductible.

WHAT ARE THE VARIOUS FEATURES OF A LIFE INSURANCE POLICY

The professional should be familiar with the particular life insurance policy's (a) ownership provisions; (b) dividend provisions; and (c) various additional benefits such as the accidental death benefit, disability waiver of premium, and guaranteed insurability (often called insurance of insurability).

The basic ownership rights are the right to name and change the beneficiary, the right to cash in a policy, the right to receive dividends, and the right to dispose of some or all of the policy ownership rights mentioned above. An unconditional sale or gift of all ownership rights in a life insurance policy is known as an "absolute" assignment. When a policy is pledged as collateral for a loan, the assignment is known as a "collateral" assignment.

Dividend provisions are particularly important in small and medium estates. Basically, a dividend is a refund of part of the premiums which the insured has paid to a life insurance company and is the result of the insured's participation in the business fortunes of the policy class to which he or she belongs. The size of the dividend is based on the relative amount of favorable mortality, interest, and "loading" (business cost) experience of the insurance company.

The policyowner can:

(1) take dividends in the form of cash;

(2) use dividends to reduce premiums;

(3) buy paid-up additional insurance (each dividend buys a small single premium policy in addition to the basic plan; no physical examination is required; and this additional insurance is purchased without sales charges or other costs);

(4) leave the dividend with the company to earn (taxable) interest;

(5) purchase one-year term insurance equal to the cash value of the policy;

(6) use dividends to "pay-up" the policy at an earlier than expected date;

(7) use some combination of the above dividend options.

A number of additional benefits can be added (usually by a "rider") to a life insurance policy. For example, an accidental death benefit, for a small extra premium, will be paid in addition to the basic death benefit if death occurs (1) in an accident and (2) before a specified age.

A second additional benefit which can be added is known as "disability waiver of premium." Under this useful benefit, premiums are waived (taken over by the insurance company) after the insured is totally disabled for a period of six months. Generally, most companies will refund any premiums paid during the first six months of disability. Cash values on a whole life policy will continue to grow.

A third additional benefit that can be added and may be advisable when the insured is young is known as "guaranteed insurability" or "insurance of insurability." This benefit allows the insured to purchase additional life insurance at certain specified future dates without evidence of insurability. On the option date, the insured can exercise all, part, or none of the option to purchase additional insurance; but the options are non-cumulative. The rates for the new insurance are those applicable for the age in the year during which the option is exercised. In other words, if an insured waits until he is 35 to exercise an option, he pays the most favorable rates for males age 35.

WHAT ARE THE TAX IMPLICATIONS?

Taxation of Death Benefits

1. Generally, proceeds payable by reason of the insured's death are exempt from income tax.[1] Such death benefit

payments are, therefore, excludible from the gross income of the beneficiary. See paragraph 5 of "What are the Tax Implications" in Chapter 1, Buy-Sell Agreement, for possible alternative minimum tax on proceeds received by a regular C corporation.

2. Where death proceeds are held by the insurance company and the beneficiary receives only the interest (this is known as an "interest only" option), the principal amount, when received, is exempt from income taxes. However, the annual interest earnings are taxable at ordinary income rates to the beneficiary.[2]

3. When the beneficiary chooses to receive death proceeds under a life income or under another option under which payments will be made in installments, the annual interest produced by the death proceeds is taxable to the beneficiary. The balance is recoverable income tax free.[3]

4. As mentioned, generally insurance proceeds paid by reason of the insured's death are excludible from the recipient's gross income. However, where, prior to death a policy or an interest in a policy had been sold or otherwise transferred for valuable consideration, the death proceeds will be exempt only to the extent of (1) the consideration paid by the transferee and (2) the net premiums paid by the transferee after the transfer. The balance of the death proceeds are taxed at ordinary income rates. This is known as the "transfer for value" rule.[4]

For example, Rod Ross purchases a $25,000 policy on his own life. He pays four $500 annual premiums. Then he sells the policy to his son for $2,000. His son now owns a $25,000 policy on Rod's life for which he paid $2,000. Assume that Rod's son pays six additional $500 annual premiums ($3,000) and then Rod dies. At the time of Rod's death, his son would have paid a total of $5,000 for the policy ($2,000 for the policy itself plus $3,000 in premiums). When he receives the $25,000 of proceeds, only his cost, $5,000, will be excludible from income. The remaining $20,000 will be entirely subject to income tax.

The "transfer for value" rule does not apply if the sale or transfer is to (a) the insured, (b) a partner of the insured, (c) a partnership in which the insured is a partner, (d) a corporation of which the insured is a stockholder or officer, or (e) if the transferee's basis is determined in whole or in part by the transferor's basis; slightly oversimplified, if the transfer does not result in a tax basis change. For example, where a policy owned by a partnership is transferred along with other assets to a newly formed corporation as part of a tax free incorporation or where one corporation transfers a policy to another corporation pursuant to a tax free merger or reorganization, the policy does not become subject to the transfer for value rule.[5]

Transfers between spouses made after July 18, 1984 (or December 31, 1983, if the spouses elect) or incident to a divorce, even if for value, come within an exception to the transfer for value rule.[6]

5. The proceeds of a life insurance policy are generally subject to the federal estate tax. Life insurance on the life of a decedent will be includible in the decedent's gross estate (1) if the proceeds are payable to or for the benefit of his or her estate or, (2) if, at the time of death, the insured possessed any incidents of ownership in the policy (such as the right to change the beneficiary, the right to surrender the policy, or the right to obtain a policy loan);[7] or (3) where the policy is transferred by the decedent within three years of his death.[8] Also, the fair market value of a policy (generally the sum of the cash value plus unearned premiums) owned on another person's life is includible in the owner's gross estate.[9]

6. Gifts of life insurance policies or gifts of premium payments may be subject to the federal gift tax. The value of the gift is based on the fair market value of the insurance policy at the time of the gift or in the case of premium payments, the cash amount of the premiums.[10] The gift tax value of a policy can generally be obtained from the insurance company and is measured differently depending upon the type of policy, i.e., term, whole life, etc. See the discussion in chapter 11, Gifts.

Taxation of Premiums and Dividends

1. Premiums for personally owned life insurance are not deductible for income tax purposes. They are considered nondeductible personal expenses unless (a) premiums constitute alimony payments,[11] or (b) premiums are paid on a policy irrevocably assigned to a charity and the insured does not reserve the right to surrender the policy for cash.[12]

2. Life insurance companies generally allow a discount if the premiums are paid one or more years in advance of the due date. The interest increment earned on these prepaid premiums is currently taxable to the policyowner.[13]

3. Dividends paid on participating policies are not taxable income.[14] This is consistent with the definition discussed above, i.e., life insurance policy dividends are generally considered to be a partial return of premiums. However, if dividends are left on deposit with the insurance company and accumulate interest, any interest on the accumulated dividends is taxable to the policyowner at ordinary income rates.[15] Dividends which are used to purchase paid-up additional insurance or one-year term insurance create no income tax liability. They are considered as if they were dividends paid in cash (a return of capital) and then used to buy single premium insurance. Dividends which exceed cost basis in the contract will constitute taxable income.

Taxation of Living Benefits

1. Where the policyowner receives a lump sum cash settlement in excess of the cost of the contract, the difference is considered ordinary income and is taxable in the year the contract matures or is surrendered.[16] The "cost" of the contract is measured by the total premiums paid (excluding premiums paid for accidental death benefits or waiver of premium).[17] The dividend option selected will affect the actual cost or total premiums. For example, if dividends are accumulated or applied to purchase paid-up additional insurance, then the cost of the contract would be the gross premiums paid by the policyowner. However, if dividends are not accumulated or not used to purchase paid-up additional insurance, then the net premiums (gross premiums less dividends received in cash or applied to reduce policy premiums) paid determine the cost of the contract.

2. Often, rather than taking a lump sum, a policyowner will choose to take living benefits of a policy under a "settlement option." Proceeds placed under settlement options (other than the interest option) are taxed under the "annuity rules" of Section 72 of the Internal Revenue Code. Basically, these rules are designed so that the annuitant will not be taxed on the portion of the annuity income which is considered to be a return of premium payments.

   The portion of the annuity income which is considered to be gain is taxable; therefore, each payment is divided into two parts: (1) a nontaxable return of cost, and (2) taxable income.

   To determine which portion of each payment is excludible from gross income and which portion is taxable income, an exclusion ratio or percentage is found. The exclusion ratio is the ratio that the total investment in the contract bears to the total expected return; to find the percentage of each annual payment that is income tax free, divide the investment in the contract (cost) by the expected return.[18] The expected return is the annual payment multiplied by the recipient's life expectancy. (See Table V at Figure 17.1 for multiples representing life expectancy.) The exclusion ratio is then multiplied by each year's total annuity payments to yield the tax-free portion of total payments received during the year. The balance of the payment is taxable as ordinary income.

ISSUES AND IMPLICATIONS IN COMMUNITY PROPERTY STATES

Where community property funds are used to purchase an insurance policy and there has been no agreement otherwise affecting the ownership of the policy, the policy will be owned by the community—and therefore belongs one-half to each spouse.

Thus, if a policy on the husband is community property and the beneficiary is someone other than the spouse, a transfer subject to gift tax will occur when the insured dies and the proceeds are payable to that third person. The amount of the gift will be the wife's one-half interest in the proceeds.

For this reason, careful estate planners note the ownership and beneficiary designations of insurance policies to be able to consider any gift tax problems that may exist. Even payment to a trust of which the surviving spouse is the income beneficiary can result in a gift if the surviving spouse does not have a power under the trust to determine to whom the remainder interest is payable at his or her death. The amount of the gift would be the actuarial value (per IRS Regulations in cases of normal health circumstances of the life tenant) of the remainder interest at the time of the transfer to trust, in the surviving spouse's half of the insurance proceeds.

The main problem in *acquiring* an insurance policy as the separate property of the non-insured spouse is the presumption in most community property states that property acquired during marriage is community property unless proven otherwise. This means that sufficient documentation of the separate property status of the policy must exist so as to overcome the community property presumption. The first step to indicate that an insurance policy is the separate property of one spouse is to name that spouse as owner of the policy. However, more evidence is usually necessary to overcome the presumption, and this requirement varies from state to state.

After the initial acquisition of a new policy as the separate property of one of the spouses or after the conversion of an existing policy into the separate policy of one spouse, the question arises as to what must be done in the future to retain the separate property status of the policy. The answer is dependent upon two different theories found in community property states that deal with the classification of interests in life insurance policies. These theories are known as the "premium tracing" doctrine and the "inception of title" doctrine.

At least two community property states, California and Washington, follow the "premium tracing" doctrine, which states that the classification of the policy as separate or community property depends on the proportion of premium payments made from separate or community funds. Under this doctrine, the classification of the policy is not constant. Therefore, if the policy is initially acquired as separate property, but 10 percent of the premiums are paid with community funds, absent any documentation taken to ensure the separate status of the policy, 10 percent of the proceeds would be community property. Therefore, each spouse would be treated as owning one-half of the 10 percent.

Under the "inception of title" doctrine, which is followed in at least two community property states, Louisiana and Texas, the policy's ownership does not vary depending on

Figure 17.1

Table V — Ordinary Life Annuities One Life — Expected Return Multiples					
Age	Multiple	Age	Multiple	Age	Multiple
5	76.6	42	40.6	79	10.0
6	75.6	43	39.6	80	9.5
7	74.7	44	38.7	81	8.9
8	73.7	45	37.7	82	8.4
9	72.7	46	36.8	83	7.9
10	71.7	47	35.9	84	7.4
11	70.7	48	34.9	85	6.9
12	69.7	49	34.0	86	6.5
13	68.8	50	33.1	87	6.1
14	67.8	51	32.2	88	5.7
15	66.8	52	31.3	89	5.3
16	65.8	53	30.4	90	5.0
17	64.8	54	29.5	91	4.7
18	63.9	55	28.6	92	4.4
19	62.9	56	27.7	93	4.1
20	61.9	57	26.8	94	3.9
21	60.9	58	25.9	95	3.7
22	59.9	59	25.0	96	3.4
23	59.0	60	24.2	97	3.2
24	58.0	61	23.3	98	3.0
25	57.0	62	22.5	99	2.8
26	56.0	63	21.6	100	2.7
27	55.1	64	20.8	101	2.5
28	54.1	65	20.0	102	2.3
29	53.1	66	19.2	103	2.1
30	52.2	67	18.4	104	1.9
31	51.2	68	17.6	105	1.8
32	50.2	69	16.8	106	1.6
33	49.3	70	16.0	107	1.4
34	48.3	71	15.3	108	1.3
35	47.3	72	14.6	109	1.1
36	46.4	73	13.9	110	1.0
37	45.4	74	13.2	111	.9
38	44.4	75	12.5	112	.8
39	43.5	76	11.9	113	.7
40	42.5	77	11.2	114	.6
41	41.5	78	10.6	115	.5

whether premiums are paid with separate or community funds. However, where community funds are used to pay premiums, in the absence of documentation to the contrary, the non-owner spouse will have a right of reimbursement to the extent of one-half of the community funds used to pay the premiums. This right of reimbursement may cause that portion of the proceeds to be includible in the insured spouse's estate.

Therefore, when an insured in a community property state wants to transfer his or her ownership in life insurance policies to his or her spouse, in addition to the transfer by writ-

ten notification to the insurance company, it is wise to also sign a written waiver waiving any further community interest in the policy.

To effect such a waiver of interest, presently and for the future, it is usually best to use the form of "Community Property Waiver" provided by the insuring company. If no such form is available, you may consider using the type of form illustrated at Figure 17.2. It is recommended that such a written waiver contain the following minimum information: (1) a clear identification of the life insurance policy(ies) involved; (2) a statement indicating the parties' intent that the

Tools and Techniques

policy(ies) be held as separate property of one spouse; (3) a clear relinquishment by the other spouse of any community property interest in the policy; (4) and a statement that the payment of any future premiums with community funds shall be treated as a gift of the non-owner-spouse's community interest in those funds to the owner-spouse.

In most cases, even though the insured may be shown on the policy as "Owner" or otherwise indicated as owning the policy, the policy will be considered as community property of the two spouses in the absence of any evidence that there was an agreement between the spouses that it would be his separate property.

A prenuptial agreement can be effective in most states to overcome presumptions of community property and to provide that future premium payments from community property funds will not vest in the community any ownership in the policies on the life of the insured. In view of the increasing frequency of divorce and remarriage, the use of such "prenuptial" agreements is encouraged by most estate planners

to avoid subsequent confusion and possible lawsuits related to the ownership of insurance policies.

One type of insurance policy which remains the separate property of the insured, in spite of having premiums paid with community property earnings, is National Service Life Insurance and Servicemen's Group Life Insurance. These policies, made available by the federal government for persons in the service, have been determined to be incapable of transfer of ownership away from the insured on the basis of federal policy. In some cases, however, the courts of California in divorce and dissolution cases, have frustrated the announced federal intent by awarding community property of equal value to the non-insured spouse. However, the federal policy prevents the transfer of such NSLI policies for purposes of planning for reduction of federal estate taxes. However, only one-half the proceeds are includible in the insured's gross estate for federal estate tax purposes where the premiums have been paid with community property.

For post-1981 estate planning, the availability of the unlimited marital deduction will reduce the incentive to have

Figure 17.2

WAIVER OF COMMUNITY PROPERTY RIGHTS

The undersigned hereby declares that ___he intends to transfer to h____ spouse, _____ , certain policies of life insurance, and that upon said transfer, all rights, privileges and incidents of ownership under any policies so transferred shall be the separate property of said spouse and the undersigned hereby waives any and all community property interest to which ___he may, but for this waiver, hereafter be entitled under the community property laws of California or any other state, province or country.

The undersigned consents to the use of community property funds of h____self and h____ spouse for the payment of any or all premiums and does further agree and declare that any future premium payments on the policies made with community funds shall constitute a gift from the undersigned to h____ said spouse to the extent of h____ interest in the community funds so applied.

Any interest the undersigned may have, now or in the future, as a designated payee of the policies is not affected by this waiver.

This instrument is executed in consideration of natural love and affection and shall be binding upon my heirs, executors, administrators and assigns, and is executed with the intent and knowledge that any interested parties may hence forth act in reliance thereon.

Dated _____

_____
Signature

WITNESSED BY:

_____

---

each spouse own the insurance on the life of the other. In both community and separate property states, more emphasis will be placed on taking advantage of the Unified Credit (as described in the Chapter on Trusts—Marital Deduction) and, where financial security permits, more emphasis will be placed on transfer of insurance from both husband and wife to the next generation, often using irrevocable insurance trusts to keep the insurance and proceeds intact.

QUESTIONS AND ANSWERS

Question — What is "split dollar" life insurance, how does it work, and what are its advantages?

Answer — Split dollar life insurance is an arrangement, typically between an employer and an employee (it can also be used between relatives such as a father and son or grandfather and grandson), under which the cash values, death benefits, and cost (premiums) may be split between the parties.

Under the classical arrangement, the employer pays that part of the annual premium which equals the current year's increase in the cash surrender value of the policy. The employee pays the balance, if any, of the premium. This provides an incentive to key employees, a way by which an employer can reward key individuals on a selective basis, and a means to provide stockholder-employees with substantial insurance at a minimal outlay.

In the event of the insured employee's death the corporation typically gets back the cash value as a death benefit and the insured employee's beneficiary receives the balance of the proceeds. The result of the arrangement is for the employer to have an increasing death benefit and for the employee's beneficiary to have a decreasing death benefit. To maintain the insured-employee's death benefit on a level basis, dividends can be used to purchase an amount of term insurance equal to the cash surrender value of the contract; or, if a universal life policy is used, the death benefit can be increasing.

Furthermore, intrafamily split dollar would enable a son-in-law to purchase insurance on his life that he otherwise might not be able to afford. This way, a father can provide additional financial security for his daughter.

Split dollar can also be used between a corporation and its employee-stockholders. The corporation could split the premium dollars in such a way that the employee-stockholders could be able to afford sizable policies on each others' lives.

Split dollar thus provides an attractive incentive plan; it can be entirely selective; no Internal Revenue Service approval is necessary; and although there is some income tax cost (a so-called P.S. 58 cost which measures the current economic benefit an employee receives when his employer puts up all or a substantial portion of the premium)

that cost is relatively low.[19] (See Figure 17.3.) The split dollar arrangement used creatively can solve a number of estate and business planning problems.

Question — What is a "key man" life insurance policy and how is it taxed?

Answer — A key man life insurance policy is a policy owned by a business which insures the life of a particularly valuable employee for the benefit of a business. It is a good estate planning tool because it provides protection to offset financial loss to a business occurring by reason of the premature death of a valuable employee. Therefore, an employer might want to insure a key man or woman and thereby stabilize and maximize the value of the business interest. Even more common is the situation where the business owner is the key to the success of the business. If the business is to be continued, it should consider insuring the business owner's life.

The business should be the premium payor, owner, and beneficiary of the policy. Proceeds, when received, could be used to offset reduced profits and help pay for replacement of the key individual.

Premiums are not deductible by the corporation or other business entity, but proceeds, when received, will be free of income tax with the possible exception of a corporate level alternative minimum tax.[20] (See chapter 13.)

For federal estate tax purposes, if the insured is a stockholder, the death proceeds will be considered in determining the value of the decendent's stock interest.[21] However, where the insured is controlling stockholder, as long as the corporation is the beneficiary, or the proceeds are paid for the benefit of the corporation (for example, to a corporate creditor), the insurance proceeds will not be separately taxable (as insurance) in the insured's estate.[22] So if the business owner controls only 60 percent of the business, only 60 percent of the insurance—enhanced value of the corporate stock—will be includible in his estate for federal estate tax purposes. Note that if the death proceeds are payable to a personal beneficiary of an insured controlling shareholder (one who owns more than 50 percent of the corporation's stock), the proceeds will be fully includible as life insurance in his estate.

Question — How is group life insurance taxed and how can it be used for estate planning purposes?

Answer — Group life insurance is one of the most effective tools the stockholder-employee of a closely held corporation has for planning his or her personal estate. Likewise, it is extremely useful in planning the estate of an executive or other common law employee. The primary objective of group life insurance is to provide financial security for the employee's family.

Tools and Techniques

Figure 17.3

"P.S. No. 58" RATES

The following rates are used in computing the "cost" of pure life insurance protection that is taxable to the employee.

One Year Term Premiums for $1,000 of Life Insurance Protection

Age	Premium	Age	Premium	Age	Premium
15	$ 1.27	37	$ 3.63	59	$ 19.08
16	1.38	38	3.87	60	20.73
17	1.48	39	4.14	61	22.53
18	1.52	40	4.42	62	24.50
19	1.56	41	4.73	63	26.63
20	1.61	42	5.07	64	28.98
21	1.67	43	5.44	65	31.51
22	1.73	44	5.85	66	34.28
23	1.79	45	6.30	67	37.31
24	1.86	46	6.78	68	40.59
25	1.93	47	7.32	69	44.17
26	2.02	48	7.89	70	48.06
27	2.11	49	8.53	71	52.29
28	2.20	50	9.22	72	56.89
29	2.31	51	9.97	73	61.89
30	2.43	52	10.79	74	67.33
31	2.57	53	11.69	75	73.23
32	2.70	54	12.67	76	79.63
33	2.86	55	13.74	77	86.57
34	3.02	56	14.91	78	94.09
35	3.21	57	16.18	79	102.23
36	3.41	58	17.56	80	111.04
				81	120.57

The rate at insured's attained age is applied to the excess of the amount payable at death over the cash value of the policy at the end of the year.

Generally, the premium payor is the business. The insured or a third party is given a certificate evidencing the insurance. The beneficiary can be anyone (including a trust) designated by the covered employee.

For estate tax purposes, the proceeds of a group life insurance policy are includible in the gross estate of the employee. However, these proceeds can usually be removed from the insured's estate with little or no gift tax cost by an absolute assignment of all incidents of ownership. If a policy is assigned within three years of the insured's death, the entire proceeds will be includible in the gross estate.[23]

The annual gift where a policy has been assigned by the employee to a third party is apparently equal to the premium payments made by the employer.[24]

Group life insurance premiums paid by the corporation are fully deductible as business expenses, subject to the limitation that they are reasonable compensation after considering all other compensation paid that employee.[25] Furthermore, employer-paid premiums are not considered taxable income to the covered employees to the extent the death benefit does not exceed $50,000 (this amount may be lower in some states).[26] The cost of any coverage which exceeds $50,000 of protection is taxable income to the employee. The value of this additional income is measured by the government table shown below.[27] If the employee contributes toward the cost of the insurance, his contribution can be used to offset his tax liability. When the proceeds of group life insurance are received by the insured employee's family, they are not subject to income taxation.[28]

Uniform Premiums for $1,000 of Group Term Life Insurance Protection (Table 1 — Regulation Sec. 1.79-3)

5-Year Age Bracket	Cost — per $1,000 of Protection per Month
Under 30	$ .08
30-34	.09
35-39	.11
40-44	.17
45-49	.29
50-54	.48
55-59	.75
60-64*	1.17

*TAMRA 1988 requires the Treasury to issue revised tables to include rates for age brackets over age 64 with respect to group term life insurance provided after 12-31-88.

Question — What is a salary increase or "selective" pension plan?

Answer — A salary increase pension plan (some call this a "Section 162" plan) is an excellent way to (1) provide benefits where group insurance is either unavailable or inadequate; (2) supplement the benefits of a qualified corporate pension or profit-sharing plan; (3) reward and hold key personnel; and (4) provide estate liquidity for corporate executives.

The corporation pays the premiums on a whole life, universal life, or variable life type policy insuring the selected employee. That employee is named as owner of the policy and designates his own personal beneficiary.

For estate tax purposes, since the policy is owned by the employee who has the right to name the beneficiary, the proceeds will be includible in the employee's gross estate.

The business is able to deduct premiums paid under a "salary increase" pension plan since such premiums are considered additional compensation. The employee must report as ordinary income the amount of premiums paid by the employer under such a plan. When the death proceeds are paid to the insured's personal beneficiary, under this type of plan, they are not subject to income tax.

Advantages of a salary increase plan include:

1. Internal Revenue Service approval is not required.
2. The plan is simple and may be established by the mere signing of an application, acceptance by the insurer of evidence of insurability, and payment of the appropriate premium.
3. The employer is free to choose the employees to include in such a plan.
4. No minimum or maximum number of lives must be covered.
5. The employer can decide how much coverage to provide.
6. The cost of the plan is deductible by the employer.
7. The employee owns and has all rights to the insurance policy.
8. Dividends can be used to reduce the premium outlay or to offset the tax cost of the plan.
9. Cash values of the policy may be used without disqualifying the plan or incurring any tax penalties, provided that the policy is not classified as a modified endowment policy. (See question below) (Interest will be charged on any such loans.)
10. The plan may be discontinued at any time.

Question — What is "Section 79" insurance?

Answer — Section 79 of the Internal Revenue Code deals with the income tax treatment to employees who participate in employer-sponsored group term life insurance plans. The basic advantage of Section 79 insurance is that the premiums paid for the first $50,000 of group term insurance may be provided by the employer without any taxable income being charged to the employee. For term insurance coverage in excess of $50,000, the employee must report an amount based on a government table which is typically less than the actual premium paid. The premiums paid by the employer are generally deductible as part of the group plan.

An option may be given to employees to purchase permanent insurance in addition to or in lieu of all or part of the term insurance. If given, the option must be given to all employees in the same class of employment for plan purposes. The employee purchasing the permanent insurance pays for that portion of the premium representing permanent coverage. His payment is with after-tax dollars. The portion of the premium representing the term insurance coverage is paid for by the employer on a tax deductible basis.

The employer may, however, subject to reasonable compensation considerations, provide a bonus to the employee equal to the cost of the permanent portion of the insurance. If provided by the employer as additional compensation, the bonus is taxable to the employee. The insured-employee (or his or her assignee) is the owner of both the term portion and the permanent portion of the insurance. The employee has all rights to the policy including the rights to any cash surrender values.

The attractiveness of "Section 79" permanent insurance plans has been diminished somewhat by the publication of final regulations to Section 79 of the Code. These regulations, in general, provide that a greater portion of the premium (than previous to the final regulations) must be allocated to the permanent portion of the contract and a lesser portion is to be allocated to the term portion, thus causing a greater share of the premium to be chargeable as income to the employee. In addition, to the extent dividends are used for the employee's benefit they are reportable as income to the employee. Previously they were non-taxable.

Question — Can a split dollar plan be arranged so that the death benefit passing to the beneficiary of a majority shareholder will be estate tax free?

Answer — If the shareholder's spouse—or an irrevocable trust for the benefit of his beneficiaries or any third party—purchases a policy on his life, and then enters into a split dollar agreement with the corporation that prohibits the corporation from taking any action with respect to the policy that might endanger the policyowner's interest, the death benefit can be excludible.

Chances of success in keeping the net amount at risk out of a controlling shareholder's estate are significantly increased if the corporation has no rights to policy values except at the insured's death. The corporation's right at that time should be limited to a recovery of the death proceeds equal to its contributions. The collateral assignment method of split dollar should be used to further evidence the limitation of the corporation's rights.[29]

Question — What is a Crummey Trust and how could it help obtain an annual gift tax exclusion for premiums paid on life insurance held in trust?

Answer — Generally, where a gift is made through a trust which provides for an accumulation of income and for deferred distribution of principal, a contribution to that trust is considered a gift of a future interest and is thus ineligible for the annual gift tax exclusion. The same type of problem is inherent in gift transfers in trust of nonincome producing property such as life insurance.

However, some courts have recognized that a provision in a trust giving the beneficiaries the power to demand immediate possession and enjoyment of principal or income gives rise to a present interest. Cases and rulings based on the Crummey case[30] indicate that giving a non-cumulative right to income to the beneficiary to withdraw the greater of $5,000 or 5 percent of the principal of the trust annually, will make the gift tax exclusion possible.

Question — Can a person achieve estate tax reduction by giving away the ownership of a policy on his life?

Answer — To the extent that one transfers away all of the incidents of ownership and the policy is not payable directly or indirectly to his estate, then the policy will not be included in his estate for federal estate tax purposes, providing that he survives three years past the date of transfer.

Although gifts of insurance made more than three years before death can be effective in reducing the insured's estate for estate tax purposes, it also reduces the ownership rights of an insured during his lifetime, as many insureds have found upon dissolution of a marriage.

Transfer of insurance is subject to gift tax, and therefore one must also consider the value of the policy when making a gift.

Question — Can interest which is paid on funds borrowed to purchase or carry a life insurance contract be deducted on an individual's income tax return?

Answer — The general rule is that a deduction is not allowed for interest paid on indebtedness incurred to purchase or carry life insurance if such insurance is purchased pursuant to a plan which contemplates the systematic direct or indirect borrowing of part or all of the increase in the cash surrender value of such contract. There are four exceptions to this general rule:

(1) **Trade or business exception**—If the indebtedness is incurred in connection with the taxpayer's trade or business, the interest deduction will not be denied.

(2) **$100 a year exception**—The interest deduction will be allowed if the interest on the loan is less than $100 a year.

(3) **The seven-year exception**—An interest deduction will be allowed in spite of the general rule where at least four of the annual premiums due during the first seven years of the contract are paid by means other than direct or indirect borrowing. Therefore, if a policyholder pays *any* four full years' premiums out of the first seven years' premiums due, the interest deduction on policy loans, including interest on loans made during the first seven years, will be allowed.

(4) **The unforeseen event exception**—An interest deduction will be allowed if the indebtedness is incurred as the result of an unforeseen substantial loss of income or unforeseen substantial increase in the taxpayer's financial obligations.[31]

Even if a personally owned policy comes within one of the four just mentioned exceptions to the general rule, only 40% of such interest will be allowed as a deduction in 1988, 20% in 1989, 10% in 1990, and nothing in 1991 and thereafter.

For insurance loans on policies owned by a taxpayer (corporation or other entity) carrying on any trade or business, a deduction will not be allowed for interest on any indebtedness with respect to one or more life insurance policies covering the life of any individual who is an officer, employee, or an individual financially interested in any trade or business carried on by the taxpayer, to the extent the loans aggregate more than $50,000 per insured. However, for a policy owned by such a taxpayer purchased on or before June 20, 1986, if the policy otherwise qualifies for an income tax deduction by coming within one of the four exceptions, interest will continue to be fully tax deductible.[32]

Question — What are the reasons life insurance is often purchased by the trustee of a pension and/or profit-sharing plan?

Answer — Among others, the premium (including any additional rating charge) becomes deductible (as part of the corporation's contribution). The dividend structure of a policy within a pension or profit-sharing plan is generally more favorable than dividends paid on policies owned outside the plan. The death benefits in excess of policy cash value is income tax free, is exempt from the claims of creditors, and is not subject to the 15 percent tax on excess accumulations from qualified plans and IRAs. With some of the newer type policies, such as universal or variable life, favorable returns can also be achieved.

Question — Is there some way to change the beneficiary designation on a number of different policies using a standard form?

Answer — The life insurance industry recently accepted a Standard Change of Beneficiary Form. This form will speed up the handling of routine (about 90 percent of all types of) beneficiary changes and is applicable to almost every life insurance company and almost every life insurance contract.

Instructions for completion of the form (see Figure 17.4) are on the back of each form. The forms are available from the National Association of Life Underwriters, 1922 F. St., N.W., Washington, D.C., 20006 for $2.50 a set. Each set is sufficient to make 33 beneficiary changes.

Question — What is Retired Lives Reserve insurance?

Answer — Retired Lives Reserve is a form of insurance which provides group life insurance benefits for retired employees. Typically, group term insurance products either terminate or are substantially reduced in face amount upon an employee's retirement. A reserve for retired lives overcomes this problem by providing for term insurance even after an employee is retired, at the full face amount.

The employer pays to the insurance company a premium which is allocated to a reserve fund that is later used to provide the protection for retired employees. The reserve, in effect, is a means of pre-funding the post retirement group term premiums for covered employees.[33]

Premiums paid for Retired Lives Reserve are a deductible business expense to the extent they represent reasonable compensation under section 162 of the Code. However, an employer cannot prefund and deduct post-retirement death benefits in excess of amounts that employees may receive on a tax-free basis, which in most instances is $50,000.

Likewise, there is no tax to the employee on the reserve fund contributions while the employee is working.[34]

Retired Lives Reserve insurance is governed under Code section 79 and, therefore, the nondiscrimination rules applicable to group term life insurance, in general, apply.

Question — Will the internal buildup in and the death benefit from a universal life product be treated as favorably as if the contract were a standard life insurance policy?

Answer — "Universal" or "adjustable" life permits the policyholder to change the amount and timing of premiums and the size of the death benefit automatically as the policyholder's needs change. These contracts sometimes allow a policyholder to invest a significant amount of cash without a related increase in the amount of pure insurance in the policy.

Prior to TEFRA and TRA '84, there was confusion—in the case of a policy with a large cash fund and relatively small amount of death protection—as to whether such a contract should be treated as life insurance for tax purposes.

The Tax Reform Act of 1984 provided a comprehensive definition of a life insurance contract for income tax purposes by establishing tests which must be met to keep the death proceeds (and the internal cash buildup) of a universal life policy from being subjected to the federal income tax.[35] Favorable tax treatment will be allowed only if the policy in question satisfies state law definitional requirements of life insurance and also meets one of two Code sanctioned tests (cash value accumulation test or combined guideline premium and cash value corridor test). If these tests are violated at *any* time over the duration of the contract, the contract will *not* be treated as a life insurance policy.

The conclusion to be drawn from the Tax Reform Act of 1984 regarding universal life policies is that such policies will be taxed under traditional level premium life insurance rules if, and only if, such policies meet the tests as spelled out in Code section 7702.

Question — Are cash withdrawals made from a universal life policy taxable as income to the recipient?

Answer — Provided the policy is not classified as a modified endowment contract (see question below), only cash distributions and not policy loans can cause current income

Figure 17.4

Instructions for completion
on reverse side

STANDARD CHANGE OF BENEFICIARY FORM

This form provides for payment
in one sum only.

Name of Insurer
_____

Policy No. (one policy only)   Insured
_____

The undersigned policyowner hereby revokes any previous beneficiary designation and any optional mode of settlement with respect to any death benefit proceeds payable at the death of the Insured. Any such proceeds shall be paid in one sum as follows:

(Check and complete only one of the items numbered 1-5.)

1. ☐ **PRIMARY BENEFICIARY(IES)** — In equal shares to such of:

Full Name	Relationship to Insured	Date of Birth
_____	_____	_____
_____	_____	_____
_____	_____	_____

who may survive the Insured, and if no such beneficiary survives the Insured,
CONTINGENT BENEFICIARY(IES) — In equal shares to such of:

Full Name	Relationship to Insured	Date of Birth
_____	_____	_____
_____	_____	_____
_____	_____	_____

who may survive the Insured.

2. ☐ **SPOUSE PRIMARY BENEFICIARY — CHILDREN CONTINGENT BENEFICIARY**

_____ , spouse of the Insured, if this beneficiary survives the Insured, otherwise in equal shares to the children of the Insured who survive the Insured.

3. ☐ **SPOUSE PRIMARY BENEFICIARY -- CHILDREN BORN OF THE MARRIAGE CONTINGENT BENEFICIARY**

_____ , spouse of the Insured, if this beneficiary survives the Insured, otherwise in equal shares to the children born of the marriage of the Insured and this spouse who survive the Insured.

4. **TRUSTEE(S) AS PRIMARY BENEFICIARY**

_____ of _____ , Trustee(s),
  Name of Trustee(s)   *City and State*

or any successor or successors in trust under written agreement dated _____ , and any amendments thereto, or if the trust is terminated, to the Owner, or the Executors, or Administrators of the Owner.

5. ☐ **INSURED'S ESTATE** — The Executors or Administrators of the Insured.
_____

Either or both of the following may be checked if desired.

6. ☐ **POSTPONEMENT CLAUSE**

In no case shall any payment be made to any beneficiary designated in this form until midnight of the 30th day following the Insured's death, and in the event of the death of a beneficiary during such period, payment shall be made in the same manner as provided in this form had said beneficiary predeceased the Insured. This provision shall not apply to a Trustee.

7. ☐ **CHILDREN'S CLAUSE**

If a child of the Insured predeceases the Insured leaving children who survive the Insured, the share such deceased beneficiary would have received had such beneficiary survived the Insured, shall be paid in equal shares to the surviving children of such deceased beneficiary.

In the event no beneficiary survives the Insured, and if this form or the Policy does not provide otherwise, the proceeds will be paid to the Owner, or the Executors or Administrators of the Owner.

If the Policy requires that a change of beneficiary be endorsed on the Policy, it is requested that the Policy be modified to permit this beneficiary change without endorsement of the Policy.

THIS CHANGE IS SUBJECT TO THE PROVISIONS ON THE REVERSE.

Signed at _____ , this _____ day of _____ , 19 _____
           City and State   *Day*   *Month*   *Year*

_____   _____
        Witness   *Policyowner*

Received and filed with the Insurer

_____   _____
   Authorized Signature   *Date*

---

taxation to the recipient. Where a policyholder reduces the death benefit of a universal life policy, either by switching from an Option II death benefit (increasing death benefit) to an Option I death benefit (level death benefit), or by making a partial surrender, which reduces the face amount of the policy, a new calculation of the policy for the definitional test of life insurance must occur. If the policy has too much cash (after the death benefit reduction), above the maximum allowable under the definitional rules of Code section 7702, the excess must be "forced out" as a distribution.

If the force-out of the cash occurs in years 1 through 5, the policy (after the reduction in the face amount) must meet the guideline premium limitation/cash value corridor test to avoid the forced out distribution from being currently taxed as income to the extent there is a built-in gain in the policy at that time. If the policy after the reduction in face amount meets this test, the cash distributed would be considered a return of basis under the FIFO taxation rules (first in, first out). Only if the amount received exceeded the policyholder's basis would the gain be taxable to the recipient.

If the distribution occurs in policy years 6 through 15, the policy after reduction must meet the corridor percentage limits of Code section 7702. To the extent the cash value exceeds the required amount under this test and is forced out, it is taxable as income to the policyholder to the extent there is a gain in the policy.

For years after the 15th year, the policyholder is taxed on a FIFO basis (no income tax until basis is exceeded).

Provided the policy is not a modified endowment contract, in any year that a cash withdrawal is made and the definitional tests are still met after the withdrawal, any cash withdrawn is taxable only to the extent the amount received in that year and in all previous years exceeds the premiums paid into the contract, i.e., to the extent there is a gain in the contract.[36]

Question — Are distributions such as cash withdrawals or policy loans taxable to the recipient if the policy is classified as a modified endowment contract?

Answer — The Technical and Miscellaneous Revenue Act of 1988 (TAMRA) created a new classification of life insurance policies, termed modified endowment contracts. If a policy falls into this category by failing a test called the seven pay test, distributions from the policy will be taxed less favorably than if the seven pay test is met.

A policy fails the seven pay test if the cumulative amount paid at any time during the first seven years of the contract exceeds the net level premiums that would have been paid during the first seven years if the contract provided for paid-up future benefits. If a material change in the policy's benefits occurs, a new seven year period for testing must begin.

Distributions, including policy loans, from modified endowment contracts are taxed as income first and recovery of basis second, much like distributions from annuity contracts are taxed. Additionally, a penalty tax of 10 percent applies to distribution amounts included in income unless the taxpayer has become disabled, or reached age 59½ or the distribution is part of a series of substantially equal payments made over the taxpayer's life.

With some exceptions, life insurance policies issued on or before June 21, 1988 are grandfathered and not required to comply with the seven pay test.

Question — What is a Reverse Split Dollar Plan?

Answer — It is a split dollar insurance plan wherein the parties to the plan are in reverse roles to the traditional split dollar arrangement. Under a traditional employer-employee plan, an individual owner of a cash value policy is assisted by the corporation in the payment of premiums. The individual pays, as his share of the premium, that amount which pays for the benefits he is receiving (economic benefit or P.S. 58 costs). The balance of the premium is paid by the corporation. The corporation will have an equity interest in the policy equal to its premium paid or cash value. In the event of the employee's death, the corporation receives back its equity interest and the employee's beneficiary receives the balance (risk portion).

Reverse split dollar is just the opposite. The employee owns a policy on his own life. However, the risk portion of the policy is payable to the corporation and can be used for key man protection, stock retirement, or salary continuation. Since the employee owns the policy and all rights and values in the policy, all the corporation is receiving is essentially equivalent to term insurance. The corporation pays for the economic benefit it receives (P.S. 58 costs). Since the corporation is paying only for the pure death benefit, all policy values accrue to the employee. Split dollar is covered in more detail in our book, *The Tools and Techniques of Employee Benefits and Retirement Planning*.

Footnote References

Life Insurance

1. IRC Section 101(a).
2. IRC Section 101(c).
3. IRC Section 101(d)(1)(A), Regs. §1.101-4(a)(1)(i).
4. IRC Section 101(a)(2).
5. IRC Section 101(a)(2).
6. IRC Sections 1041 and 101(b)(2)(A).
7. IRC Section 2042.
8. IRC Section 2035.
9. IRC Section 2033.
10. Regs. §25.2512-6.

11. *Lemuel Alexander Carmichael*, 14 T.C. 1356 (1950), *Estate of Boies C. Hart*, 11 T.C. 16 (1948).

12. See *Eppa Hunton, IV*, 1 T.C. 821 (1943); *Ernest Behrend* 23 B.T.A. 1037 (1931).

13. Rev. Rul. 65-199, 1965-2 C.B. 20.

14. IRC Section 72(e)(1)(B); Regs. §1.72-11(b)(1).

15. Reg. §1.61-7(d).

16. IRC Section 72(e); Regs. §1.72-11(d).

17. IRC Section 72(e)(1)(B).

18. See Regs. §1.72-4.

19. Rev. Rul. 64-328, 1964-2 C.B. 11.

20. IRC Section 101. If the particular insurer publishes rates for individual, initial issue, one-year term policies which are lower than the P.S. 58 rates, these rates may be used in place of the P.S. 58 rates.

21. Regs. §20.2031-2(f).

22. Regs. §20.2042-1(c)(6).

23. Rev. Rul. 69-54, 1969-1 C.B. 221 as modified by Rev. Rul. 72-307, 1972-1 C.B. 307. IRC Section 2035.

24. Rev. Rul. 76-490, 1976-2 C.B. 300.

25. IRC Section 162(a); Reg. §1.264-1.

26. IRC Section 79.

27. Regs. §1.79-3.

28. IRC Section 101.

29. Rev. Rul. 82-145, 1982-2 C.B. 213; Rev. Rul. 76-274, 1976-2 C.B. 278.

30. *D. Clifford Crummey*, 397 F.2d 82 (CA-9, 1968). See also *Harbeck Halstead*, 28 T.C. 1069 (1957), acq. 1958-1 C.B. 5.

31. IRC Section 264.

32. IRC Section 264, as amended by TRA '86, Section 1003.

33. See Rev. Ruls. 69-382, 1969-2 C.B. 28; 69-478, 1969-2 C.B. 29; 73-599, 1973-2 C.B. 40; and 77-92, 1977-1 C.B. 41.

34. IRC Section 79(b)(1).

35. IRC Sections 101(f) and 7702(a).

36. IRC Sections 7702(e) and (f), as amended by TRA '86, Sections 1825(a) and (b).

Chapter 18

MEDICAL EXPENSE REIMBURSEMENT PLAN

WHAT IS IT?

A medical expense reimbursement plan (MERP) is an arrangement provided by an employer (including professional corporations) to reimburse employees for dental expenses, cosmetic surgery, and other medical expenses. Typically, a medical expense reimbursement plan reimburses employees for medical expenses incurred by the employee, his or her spouse, and dependents.

A MERP is used (1) as a substitute for health insurance, (2) as a supplement to provide payments for medical expenses not covered under the company's health insurance plan (such as dental expenses or cosmetic surgery), or (3) to pay for medical expenses in excess of the limits in the company's health insurance plan.

The objective—from a tax standpoint—of a medical expense reimbursement plan is to provide benefits on a tax-free basis to the employee. A corresponding objective is to make such payments tax deductible by the employer.

WHEN IS THE USE OF SUCH A DEVICE INDICATED?

A medical expense reimbursement plan is particularly useful in the following situations:

1. Where a corporation is closely held and family members are the primary or only employees. The medical expense reimbursement plan makes otherwise nondeductible medical expenses deductible.

2. In a professional corporation where the only employee is a professional in a high income tax bracket or where there are few other employees and they are receiving relatively smaller salaries. The medical expense reimbursement plan makes what might otherwise be nondeductible medical expense payments deductible.

3. Where an employer would like to provide significant (and tax favored) benefits to employees beyond those provided by the basic medical coverage already in force.

WHAT ARE THE REQUIREMENTS?

Nondiscrimination

A medical expense reimbursement plan which reimburses an employee for medical expenses incurred for the care of the employee and/or his family must be *non*discriminatory if expected tax benefits for highly compensated employees are to be realized.[1]

Generally speaking, if a plan is considered discriminatory, all or part of the value of the coverage provided to highly compensated employees will be included in their income.[2] Rank and file employees, however, will be entitled to the income tax exclusion in any event.

To be considered nondiscriminatory a plan must satisfy either a three-part eligibility test and a benefits test, or an alternative coverage test.

Eligibility test:

Part 1, the "90%/50% test": At least 90 percent of the employer's nonhighly compensated employees (defined below) must be eligible to participate in the plan. Those who are eligible must qualify for a benefit that is at least 50 percent as valuable as the benefit available to the highly compensated employee who can obtain the most valuable benefit under all health plans of the employer.

Part 2, the "50% test": Nonhighly compensated employees must constitute at least half of the group of employees eligible to participate in the plan. (There is an alternative that will enable small plans with high percentages of highly compensated to qualify. Under this alternative, the plan will be deemed to qualify if the percentage of highly compensated employees eligible to participate is not greater than the percentage of nonhighly compensated employees who are eligible. For instance, if all the employees are eligible to participate, a plan will meet this part of the eligibility test even though it is impossible to satisfy the "50%" test.)

Part 3, the "nondiscriminatory provision" test: A MERP cannot contain a provision that by its terms or otherwise discriminates in favor of highly compensated employees. For instance, if the president of the corporation had a son with a rare blood disease and the plan covered only such a disease, even if technically all employees were eligible for coverage, the plan would fail. A plan can, however, provide benefits based on quantifiable standards. So, it may be possible to have one MERP for salaried and a different MERP for hourly employees.

Benefits test:

Generally, the average value of coverage provided by an employer to nonhighly compensated employees under all health plans must be at least 75% of the average employer-provided benefit received by highly compensated employees.

Alternative test:

MERPs can qualify under an alternative single test that eliminates the need to meet either the eligibility or the benefits test. Under this alternative single test, a plan will qualify if it benefits at least 80% of an employer's nonhighly compen-

149   **Tools and Techniques**

sated employees and it passes the "nondiscriminatory provision" test (the third part of the eligibility test).

Generally, each option or different benefit is treated as a separate plan in testing for discrimination.[3] However, there are detailed rules under which separate plans can be treated as one plan for purposes of certain tests.[4]

If a plan discriminates, a highly compensated employee must include in income his "excess benefit," that is, the excess of the value of his employer provided coverage over the highest benefit under the plan which would be nondiscriminatory. The highest nondiscriminatory benefit is determined by reducing the benefits of highly compensated employees (starting with those having the greatest benefit) until the plan would be nondiscriminatory.[5]

These nondiscrimination rules are effective for plan years beginning in 1989. However, testing of benefits is to be done on the basis of "testing" years, not plan years. A testing year is a 12 month period elected by the employer and designated in the plan. The testing year designated by the employer is required to be the same for all the employer's accident and health plans, but need not be the same as the plan year. In the absence of a designation of a testing year, the testing year will be a calendar year. Generally, the determination of whether a plan is discriminatory for a testing year is made on the basis of the facts as of the "testing day" designated in the plan. The same day must be designated for all health plans of the employer.

It is anticipated that testing in the first year will be based on all health plans providing coverage in the testing year and if a discriminatory excess is determined based on coverage for a part of the year to which section 89 was not yet applicable, the excess would be prorated on the basis of the coverage subject to section 89 for the year.[6]

Continuation of Coverage

An employer's adoption of a plan providing medical care for employees results in an additional and typically unexpected cost due to the passage of the Consolidated Omnibus Budget Reconciliation Act of 1985 (COBRA). COBRA added a requirement that plans providing medical care benefits (that is, benefits of the type which are deductible as medical expenses) must provide continuation of such plan benefits for certain employees and their dependents after termination of employment and certain other qualifying events. There is an exemption for small employers—the COBRA continuation provisions apply for a given year only if the employer had 20 or more employees on a typical business day in the preceding year. Government and church plans are also exempt.

In general, under COBRA the employer must provide the option to continue an employee's existing health plan coverage (including dependent coverage) for 36 months after the following events:

(a) death of the employee

(b) divorce or legal separation of the covered employee (coverage continues for the former spouse and dependents)

(c) the employee's entitlement to Medicare benefits

(d) filing by the employer for Chapter 11 bankruptcy.

(e) a child ceasing to be a dependent for plan purposes

Health plan coverage must be continued for 18 months after the following event:

(a) termination of employment or reduction in hours of employment

Continuation coverage can be terminated before the 36 (or 18) month period ends if

• the employer terminates its health plan for all employees

• the beneficiary fails to pay his or her share of the premium

• the beneficiary becomes covered under another group health plan.

The employer can require the former employee or beneficiary to pay part of the cost of continuation coverage. However, this former employee or beneficiary share can't be more than 102% of the cost to the plan of coverage for similarly situated beneficiaries with respect to whom a qualifying event has not occurred (whether the cost is paid by the employer or employee).

The requirement to provide for continuation of coverage became effective for plan years which began after July 1, 1986. Originally, the penalty for noncompliance with these requirements was disallowance of the employer's deduction. However, for tax years beginning after December 31, 1988, the penalty is, generally, a tax of $100 a day during the period any failure with respect to a qualified beneficiary continues.[7]

Qualification

A MERP must comply with the following qualification requirements:

(1) The plan must be in writing.

(2) The employees' rights must be legally enforceable. This means medical benefits must be reimbursable according to a preestablished formula or rule. If the employee has no right to compel payments because medical expenses are reimbursed arbitrarily at the employer's discretion, the plan will not meet the "legally enforceable" requirement.

(3) Employees must be given reasonable notification of the benefits available to them under the plan.

(4) The plan must be for the exclusive benefit of employees.

(5) The plan must be set up with the intent that it will be maintained indefinitely. Although a plan will not fail to satisfy requirement number (2), above, merely because an employer retains the right to terminate the plan as to claims not yet incurred, it appears that for this "indefinite life" rule, termination of the plan could be considered a violation.

The penalty for failure to comply with these qualification requirements is that all employees must include in income the amount of the employer provided benefits they received (i.e., reimbursements actually made) even if those benefits were specifically excluded from income by some other Code section. Inclusion would be required in the taxable year in which such benefits are received.

HOW IT IS DONE—AN EXAMPLE

Power, Inc. maintains a noncontributory medical expense reimbursement plan as its only form of health coverage for its employees. All employees are covered under the plan. The same benefits are provided for all participants, including dependent care coverage. There are no benefits of a type which can be used by only highly compensated employees and at least 80% of the nonhighly compensated employees have families. This plan will pass the alternative test because 80% of the nonhighly compensated employees are covered and there is no nonquantifiable provision which discriminates in favor of highly compensated employees.

IMPLICATIONS AND ISSUES IN COMMUNITY PROPERTY STATES

No significant difference exists with regard to the application of the medical expense reimbursement law in community property states.

QUESTIONS AND ANSWERS

Question — What is the difference in the tax treatment of employees if a plan does not pass the nondiscrimination tests and if it fails to meet the qualification requirements?

Answer — If the plan is discriminatory, only the excess benefit (that is, discriminatory coverage) is taxable to highly compensated employees. If the plan fails to meet the qualification requirements, all employees are taxed on the value of the benefit (in this case, the reimbursement and services, not the coverage) provided.

Question — Can the nondiscrimination tests be met if all employees are highly compensated?

Answer — Yes. The nondiscrimination rules do not apply to a plan for any year that the only employees are highly compensated employees.

Question — Is a ruling or advance determination letter required?

Answer — No. While no advance rulings are required, it is expected that advance rulings will be available, as in the case of a qualified pension or profit-sharing plan.

Question — If an amount is considered an excess benefit under section 89 and subject to inclusion in the income of the highly compensated individual, *when* is that amount included?

Answer — The amount of the excess benefit is included in the income of the highly compensated individual for the taxable year of that individual in which the "testing" year ends. Thus, if a corporation has designated the 12 month period ending June 30 as its testing year, and the highly compensated individual received an excess benefit in the testing year ending June 30, 1990, he will include that amount in his gross income in his 1990 taxable year.

However, an employer with a testing year that ends after September 30 and on or before December 31 may elect to have the amount included in the employee's income in the employee's tax year following the tax year in which the testing year ended. Thus, if an excess benefit occurs in a testing year ending October 31, 1990, for example, and the employer has made the election, the excess is included in the employee's income for his 1991 tax year. If the employer makes this election, any deduction of the employer attributable to the excess amount is also delayed a year.[8]

Question — Can a one-man professional corporation adopt a very liberal medical reimbursement plan and not come within the discriminatory provisions of the Code?

Answer — Currently, neither the Treasury nor the Internal Revenue Service has directly answered this question. However, it appears that only a unique interpretation of the law would preclude such a plan by a one-man professional corporation. However, the situation with support personnel (i.e. nurses, secretaries, etc.) must be carefully studied. If these people work for a separate entity, such as a partnership, the professional and/or his corporation must not be allowed to be considered to "control" that entity or he may have to include the employees of the separate entity in testing his individual medical expense reimbursement plan for discrimination.

Question — If a statutory employee benefit plan discriminates in favor of highly compensated employees, what is the penalty?

Answer — Any "excess benefit" from a plan that discriminates in favor of "highly compensated employees" will be taxed to such employees. Employers can therefore choose to (a) make such plans nondiscriminatory by bringing in additional employees or by providing employees who are not highly compensated with addition-

Tools and Techniques

al benefits, (b) terminate the plan, or (c) continue the discrimination (the plan will not be disqualified merely because it fails discrimination tests). The employer's deduction is not affected by the discrimination. While the highly compensated employees will pay tax, there is still a benefit to the extent the employer's outlay exceeds the employee's tax cost. However, the employer may be subject to an excise tax if as part of his discriminatory plan he is setting amounts aside to prefund payment of benefits.

The "excess benefit" that will be taxable to highly compensated employees is the excess of the value of the benefit provided that employee over the value that would be nondiscriminatory. The excess is includable even if it would otherwise be excludable under another Code section.

Question — How is "highly compensated employee" defined?

Answer — A "highly compensated employee" is any employee who, during the tax year or the preceding tax year,

(1) owned (directly or by attribution rules) more than 5 percent of the business ("5% owner"), or

(2) received more than $75,000 (as indexed—$78,353 in 1988) from the employer, or

(3) received compensation in excess of $50,000 (as indexed—$52,235 in 1988) from the employer and was a member of the top 20% of employees in terms of pay for the year in question, or

(4) was (at any time) an officer and received more than $45,000 (or, if higher, 50% of the dollar limit for defined benefit pension plan) of annual compensation. If no officer received more than this, the highest paid officer is treated as a highly compensated employee.

An employer who maintained significant business activities in at least two significantly separate geographic areas throughout the year may be able to elect to treat an employee earning $50,000 (indexed) as highly compensated without regard to whether he was a member of the top 20% of employees.

Question — What employees will be excludable for purposes of the eligibility and benefits test?

Answer — The following types of employees can be excluded for purposes of the eligibility and benefits tests:

(1) employees who have not completed at least 6 months of service, or one year in the case of coverage for dental, vision, psychological and orthodontia expenses and elective cosmetic surgery, (or such shorter period as may be specified in the plan);

(2) employees who normally work fewer than six months during any year (or such smaller number of months as may be specified in the plan);

(3) employees who have not attained age 21 (or such lower age as may be specified in the plan);

(4) employees who normally work less than 17½ hours a week (or smaller number if so specified in the plan);

(5) employees covered by a collective bargaining agreement, if such benefits were the subject of good faith bargaining;

(6) nonresident aliens who receive no U.S.-source earned income; and

(7) certain employees who are students employed by educational organizations.

Generally, employees in these categories may not be excluded from consideration unless no employee in that category is eligible under any health plan of the employer. Certain exceptions to this rule apply to employees excluded from a plan because they do not meet minimum age and service requirements.

A special rule permits employers who on a normal working day employ fewer than 10 employees to exclude from testing under the 80% alternative test employees with fewer than 35 hours a week in plan years beginning in 1989 and fewer than 25 hours in 1990 plan years.

Question — What duties are imposed upon employers to comply with the section 89 welfare benefit rules?

Answer — An employer must report separately on Form W-2 any excess benefit paid to a highly compensated employee who participated in a discriminatory plan as well as any amount every employee must include in income because the plan did not comply with the qualification rules.

A nondeductible tax is imposed on employers who fail to report either includable excess benefits or includable income of employees by reason of failure of the plan to comply with qualification rules.

Question — What may the employer deduct?

Answer — The employer may deduct 100 percent of the cost of benefits paid to employees under the plan. Plan administrative expenses, and the cost of any insured stop loss coverage, are also fully deductible. However, deductions can be lost if the plan does not meet the COBRA continuation requirements in tax years beginning before January 1, 1989. (For tax years beginning after December 31, 1988, the penalty is not loss of deduction, but a tax of, generally, $100 a day during the period any failure with respect to a qualified beneficiary continues.)

Deductions for prefunding medical benefits (that is, setting funds aside and deducting amounts for medical benefits to be paid in future years) are limited. Generally, for a given year an employer can deduct expenditures for medical benefits up to a limit equal to the total of (a) the direct costs of the plan for the year—claims paid plus administrative costs, plus (b) contributions to an asset account up to 35% of the preceding year's direct costs.[9] The employer may be subject to an excise tax if such a fund is used in connection with a plan that is discriminatory under section 89.[10]

Question — Is employer provided disability coverage subject to the nondiscrimination requirements of section 89?

Answer — Generally, disability income received under employer provided disability coverage is included in the employee's income when it is received. Consequently, such coverage is not subject to the nondiscrimination requirements of section 89.[11]

Question — What benefits under a MERP are discriminatory in a plan year which began before the Section 89 rules apply?

Answer — A plan may be discriminatory as to coverage or in operation.[12] It is considered discriminatory with respect to coverage unless it benefits 70 percent or more of all employees. Alternatively, if 70 percent of all employees are eligible to be covered, 80 percent of those individuals must in fact participate in coverage.[13] There is a second alternative: coverage may be provided to classes of employees in a manner that does not discriminate in favor of key employees or their families.[14] Since this is not a definite mathematically determinable test, the IRS will determine on a case by case basis under this alternative whether or not there has been discrimination.

Key employees—for purposes of discrimination—are defined as (1) the five highest paid officers, (2) shareholders holding more than 10 percent of the outstanding stock of the corporation, and (3) the highest paid 25 percent of all employees.[15]

If a plan discriminates in coverage, a fraction of payments received will be includable.[16]

$$\frac{\text{Amount reimbursed to } key \text{ employees}}{Total \text{ amount reimbursed to } all \text{ employees}} \times \begin{array}{l}\text{Payment}\\\text{received by}\\\text{given key}\\\text{employees}\end{array}$$

Inclusion depends on the proportion of total payments that went to key employees. This percentage is then multiplied by each key employee's reimbursement. For instance, SRL Corporation's plan fails the coverage requirements. The corporation paid out $10,000 in med-

ical reimbursements, $2,500 of which went to key employees. $2,000 of that went to Ed Staller, a company vice president. Ed must include $500 in income ($2,500/$10,000) × $2,000 = ¼ × $2,000 = $500).

A plan would be considered *discriminatory in operation* if key employees have greater benefits than other employees. This means benefit levels cannot be based on a percentage or proportion of compensation. This is known as the "dollar for dollar" discrimination rule. It is applicable to eligible benefits rather than amounts actually paid. (The mere fact that key employees happen to submit more claims than other employees will not *per se* make the plan discriminatory.)

If the plan discriminates in operation (e.g., a key employee is eligible for twice the benefit anyone else can get), the recipient key employee will have to include the entire amount of excess reimbursement actually received in income—whether or not coverage requirements are met. For example, Dayton Coles, president of the State College Coal Company, received a $1,000 reimbursement for dental coverage, a benefit provided only for him and his family. The entire $1,000 is includable in Dayton's income.

Footnote References
Medical Expense Reimbursement Plan

1. I.R.C. Sec. 89 (however, plans maintained by churches for church employees are not subject to the nondiscrimination requirements, I.R.C. Sec. 89(i)(4))
2. I.R.C. Sec. 89(a)(1)
3. I.R.C. Sec. 89(j)(11)
4. I.R.C. Sec. 89(g)(1)
5. I.R.C. Sec. 89(b)
6. See the Joint Explanation of the Committee of Conference of the Technical and Miscellaneous Revenue Act of 1988, 134 Cong. Rec. No. 151, October 21, 1988, p.11021.
7. I.R.C. Sec. 4980B
8. I.R.C. Sec. 89(a)(2)
9. I.R.C. Secs. 419, 419A
10. I.R.C. Sec. 4976(c)
11. I.R.C. Sec. 89(j)(10)
12. I.R.C. Sec. 105(h)(2), as in effect prior to the effective date of I.R.C. Sec. 89
13. I.R.C. Sec. 105(h)(3)(a)(i), as in effect prior to the effective date of I.R.C. Sec. 89
14. I.R.C. Sec. 105(h)(3)(A)(ii), as in effect prior to the effective date of I.R.C. Sec. 89
15. I.R.C. Sec. 105(h)(5), as in effect prior to the effective date of I.R.C. Sec. 89
16. I.R.C. Sec. 105(h)(7)(B), as in effect prior to the effective date of I.R.C. Sec. 89

Chapter 19

PERSONAL HOLDING COMPANY

WHAT IS IT?

A personal holding company is a corporation which meets two particular tests (and is not specifically excluded from such status).[1] These two tests are: (1) a stock ownership test; and (2) an income test. Both tests must be met in the same taxable year so that it is possible for a corporation to attain personal holding company status in one year and not in the next.

The stock ownership test works like this: The corporation meets the stock ownership requirements if more than 50 percent in value of its outstanding stock is owned directly or indirectly by or for not more than five individuals at any time during the last half of the taxable year.[2] The second test, the income test, is sometimes referred to as the "60 percent" test. If the stock ownership test has been met and at least 60 percent or more of the corporation's adjusted ordinary gross income is personal holding company income (such as dividends, interest, rents, or amounts received in return for a certain type of personal services), the corporation will be classified as a personal holding company.[3]

The personal holding company provisions have generally been thought to be odious since there is a tax of 28%, separate and in addition to the existing corporate tax on specifically defined undistributed income of personal holding companies.[4] However, personal holding company status can be an estate planning tool if arranged properly.

Care should be exercised in the use of personal holding companies based on the repeal of the General Utilities doctrine by the Tax Reform Act of 1986. If assets in the corporation appreciate, generally there will be two taxes created, one at the corporate level (upon a sale of the assets or liquidation of the corporation) and one at the shareholder level (upon a liquidation of the corporation or dividend distribution).

WHEN IS THE USE OF SUCH A DEVICE INDICATED?

1. Where an individual has a large estate consisting of highly appreciated and readily marketable securities and wants to reduce federal estate taxes attributable to those assets.

2. Where an individual would like to reduce the value of his estate through court approved methods for discounts.

3. Where it is desired to achieve the tax savings mentioned above and at the same time allow the owner of the appreciated assets to retain substantial economic control and flexibility in making investment decisions.

WHAT ARE THE REQUIREMENTS?

A corporation is formed by an individual who owns a substantial amount of appreciated securities. He or she transfers a portfolio of common stock of various companies to a newly-formed closely held corporation in return for its stock. This transfer can be accomplished without recognition of any gain. The transfer of assets to a corporation in exchange for its stock and/or securities will not be a taxable event if the transferor controls 80 percent of the voting power and 80 percent of each class of stock immediately after the transfer.[5]

The individual transferring this stock will have a basis (cost for purposes of determining gain or loss) in the new stock equal to the basis in the property transferred to the corporation.[6] Likewise, the corporation will receive the stock or securities transferred to it with the same basis this property had in the individual's hands.[7]

HOW IT IS DONE — EXAMPLES

Denise Lopez, a wealthy investor, purchased shares of Gro-Quick, a closely held corporation, many years ago. These shares are now worth ten times what she paid for them and are continuing to appreciate rapidly. If Denise retains the stock, the shares will be includible in her estate. If she gives them away, she will incur a sizable gift tax. (The taxable portion of any gifts will be considered adjusted taxable gifts and therefore increase the rate at which the taxable estate will be taxed.) Furthermore, some of her beneficiaries are minor children and she does not want to make outright gifts. However, she does not want to use a trust because of certain administrative problems associated with a trust.

Denise forms a corporation and retains 100 percent of its stock. The stock she transfers to the corporation has a fair market value of one million dollars. The corporation is capitalized as follows: $800,000 (fair market value) of non-voting common stock is issued to Denise. In addition, she receives $200,000 worth of voting common stock. (The breakdown is arbitrary and can be varied according to the particular situation.)

Since one of Denise's main objectives is to maintain control while making gifts to limit future appreciation in value of her estate, she retains the voting stock and begins a gifting program with the non-voting common. She gives, over a period of years, the $800,000 worth of non-voting common to family members. This enables her to continue to direct and control the investment program. Because of the unified transfer credit ($600,000) and the annual exclusions ($10,000 per donee per year) the transfer can be made with little or

155

no gift tax cost. Because the non-voting common stock represents most of the right to the financial growth of the business (80%), substantial future appreciation is removed from Denise's estate. For example, if the underlying assets double in value after the gift of the common stock, 80% of that appreciation is realized in the hands of the donees rather than in Denise's hands.

Care should be taken to avoid the application of new §2036(c), which substantially limits the use of estate freezing techniques. (This topic is covered in more detail in Appendix B.) Recapitalization, using preferred and common stock for estate freezes, has effectively been eliminated under this new provision. Additionally, it may be beneficial to use an S corporation as opposed to a C corporation in order to avoid the corporate level tax on appreciation that was created by a repeal of the General Utilities doctrine.

An additional benefit of using a corporation to hold significant assets is the fact that the corporate stock may be worth less than the value of the assets in the coporation. Courts have consistently allowed discounts of 15 percent and more (in one case as much as 55 percent) on the theory that stock of a personal holding company is less attractive to an investor than a similar stock listed on an exchange with ready access to the investing public.

For example, a gift of 100 shares of AT&T is worth more than a gift of shares representing a 10 percent interest in a personal holding company whose only asset is 1,000 shares of AT&T. It is this fact—that an investment in a personal holding company is less desirable than in the underlying shares since the underlying assets can be easily traded in the market while shares in the personal holding company cannot— that is the primary reason for the discount from the net asset value of the underlying shares.[8] Thus, in the example above, Denise's one million dollar portfolio may be valued for estate purposes at considerably less than the one million dollars that the underlying assets are worth. (The value of a gift of less than a controlling interest would be further reduced because of the lack of voting control.)

WHAT ARE THE TAX IMPLICATIONS?

1. As mentioned above, substantial estate and gift tax savings may be possible through "discounts" in the valuation process. (See list of cases in Figure 19.1.)

2. The individual forming the personal holding company can perform bona fide services for it and receive a salary. Assuming salary paid is reasonable, the individual will be taxed at a maximum rate of 33 percent (38.5 percent in 1987) on compensation and that amount will be fully deductible by the corporation. Any "excess" compensation (compensation deemed unreasonable) would be subject to tax at the corporate level (nondeductible) and then taxed at the individual level. Operating expenses may even generate a net operating loss. (Local and state franchise taxes should be considered.)

3. The taxable income of the corporation can be lowered further by providing a working stockholder and working members of his or her family with various fringe benefits. These include a qualified pension or profit-sharing plan. Furthermore, some medical expenses may be deductible. These expenses must be reasonable in view of the services performed by the employee shareholder.

4. A capital loss of a corporation can be carried back up to three years to offset prior income while individuals are not allowed a carryback of losses.

5. There is, of course, a substantial disadvantage if a personal holding company is not properly handled. As in any corporation, there is the potential for double taxation (the first incident when the corporation sells securities and again when the shareholder receives the proceeds or other property as a dividend or on the liquidation of the corporation). However, the potential for double taxation can be minimized or eliminated by carefully controlling the type of investments and expenses incurred.

The other problem is the imposition of state capital stock or franchise tax on the value of the personal holding company stock or on the net income remaining in the corporation each year.

HOW CAN LIFE INSURANCE ENHANCE THIS TOOL?

It is possible to transfer, in addition to other assets, life insurance policies. Thus, an individual would transfer existing life insurance policies (term, whole life, or endowment) having little present value as compared with their face amounts to the personal holding company in exchange for voting common stock. (Alternatively, the company could purchase insurance on the life of the holder of the voting stock.) By then giving non-voting common stock in the holding company to the donee-family members (alternatively, the corporation could sell those family members stock for cash or other property), most of the eventual appreciation due to the death value of the life insurance can be transferred out of the donor-owner's estate.

Since the decedent's executor will have voting control over the personal holding company by virtue of his ownership of the personal holding company voting common stock, that individual could direct the corporation to make a Section 303 stock redemption, thus providing estate liquidity.

IMPLICATIONS AND ISSUES IN COMMUNITY PROPERTY STATES

The particular form of property ownership between spouses holding an interest in a corporation classified as a personal holding company has no particular bearing on meet-

Figure 19.1

PERSONAL HOLDING COMPANY CASES INVOLVING ESTATE TAX DISCOUNTS

Case	Company & Holdings	Shs. to be Valued	Total Shares	Discount Allowed
Celia Waterman 20 TCM 281 (1960)	*Maxcell Corp.* (Apt bldgs)	299	571	30.8%
Lida E. Tompkins Est. 20 TCM 1763 (1961)	*H Street Building Corp.* (Gen'l real estate business, building, contracting and construction)	186	650	32.8%
Drybrough v. U.S. 208 F. Supp. 279 (D.C. Ky 1962)	(5 separate real estate holding companies)			35.0%
Harry S. Leyman 40 TC 100 (1963)	*Leyman Corp.* (Real estate, 2 Buick agencies, parking garages)	2,309	9,400	36.7%
Hamm v. Comm. 325 F.2d 934 (8th Cir. 1963)	*United Properties, Inc.* (Commercial real estate and 10 closely held subsidiaries)	263⅓	1,000	27.2%
Gregg Maxcy Est. 28 TCM 783 (1969) Rev'd on appeal, 441 F.2d 192 (5th Cir. 1971)	*Maxcy Securities, Inc.* (Citrus grove, restaurant, mortgages (1) and accounts receivable (2))	164 / 86	174 / 174	15.0% / 25.0%
Heckscher v. Comm. 63 TC 485 (1975) CCH Dec. 33,023	*Anaheim Realty Co.* (Undeveloped Florida real estate and securities)	2,500	108,675	48.3%
Lloyd R. Smith Est. 9 TCM 907 (1950)	*Smith Investment Co.* (Stock of A O Smith Corp)	408	1,860	22.1%
Bishop Tr. Co. Ltd. v. U.S. 50-1 USTC #10,764 (DC Hawaii 1950)	*Henry P. Baldwin Ltd.* (Stock listed on Honolulu Exchange)	1,861	15,000	32.8%
Goss v. Fitzpatrick 97 F. Supp. 765 (D.C. Conn. 1951)	*Alden M. Young Co.* (Marketable securities; some real estate)	1,900	13,518	42.9%

ing the stock ownership test, by virtue of the family attribution rules. That is, the ownership interest of one's spouse will be attributed back, regardless of whether the spouse's interest is community or separate property.

However, for estate planning purposes, a community property form of ownership is advantageous, as compared to joint tenancy or tenancy in common, because of the "step-up" in the tax basis of both halves of the community property on the death of one spouse.

Of particular importance to estate planners when dealing with a personal holding company is the classification of the income produced by the enterprise, since, in order to meet the "60 percent" test, a significant amount of the income must be classified as personal holding company income (i.e., dividends, interest, rents, etc.).

If the stock ownership is community property, then, absent an agreement to the contrary, the income will also be community property. However, as noted in chapter 9 on Fam-

Tools and Techniques

ily Partnership, in some community property states, if the stock ownership is separate property, this does not necessarily mean that the income produced, or any accretion in value, will also be separate property.

As previously discussed in Chapter 1, if an increase in the value of separate property is attributable to the ability or activity of either spouse, for which the community has not been sufficiently rewarded (e.g., by an appropriate salary), at least a portion of that increase may well be determined to be community property (thereby reducing the gross estate of the original owner-spouse).

In addition, the income produced may be classified as both community and separate property. If one of the spouses invests separate property in a business and conducts that business during marriage, without adequate reward to the community for the spouse's efforts, the resulting profits may be community and separate property in proportion to the amounts attributable to the personal efforts and to capital investment, respectively.

In such circumstance, depending on which spouse dies first, it may be important to be able to show that the profits from, and appreciation in value of, the business are from one (or both) spouse's efforts, rather than merely a natural enhancement in value, in order to spread the increased value between the two estates, and to provide a "step-up" in basis for both halves of the community property at the first death. If the spouse who originally owned the business dies first, then the entire business will receive a "stepped-up" basis regardless of the amount of community property effort.

QUESTIONS AND ANSWERS

Question — How can stock be shifted to children and grandchildren without incurring gift tax costs if the children do not have cash or other property to purchase the stock?

Answer — The parent of a child can lend money directly to his or her children or their custodian or to an irrevocable trust established for their benefit, or guarantee a loan between the child and a third party, such as a bank.[9] The child (or trust) can then purchase stock directly from the corporation for cash. The child could obtain cash to pay back the loan by having the personal holding company declare dividends on the common stock. Even after TRA '86, income shifting from parent to child — and therefore income tax savings — is possible if the child is age 14 or older.

Question — Assuming that personal holding company status is—at some date—considered onerous, how can such classification be avoided?

Answer — As mentioned above, there are two tests—both of which must be met—before a corporation will be classified as a personal holding company. The first requires

that five or fewer shareholders own more than 50 percent of the value of the stock at some time during the last six months of the year. This test can be side-stepped by distributing ownership of shares to unrelated parties or by issuing a second class of stock to unrelated parties in order to dilute ownership value.

The second test requires that personal holding company income be greater than or equal to 60 percent of adjusted ordinary gross income. To avoid this test, property which produces personal holding company income, such as rental property, can be transferred out of the corporation (with potential tax consequences). Conversely, by producing income (active as opposed to passive) within the corporation, the 60 percent test can be avoided. Furthermore, expenses related to adjusted ordinary gross income can be deferred into future periods or a depreciation method can be selected to maximize adjusted ordinary gross income. Finally, if there is a potential personal holding company liability, cash dividends can be paid out during the tax year, post year-end dividends can be paid, consent dividend procedures can be used, deficiency dividend procedures can be used and, as a final alternative, the corporation can be liquidated. (Under TRA '86, the loss of the ability to take a capital gains deduction upon a sale or exchange or liquidation makes the liquidation alternative more expensive. In addition, gain from appreciated property that the corporation distributes will be taxed at the corporate level.) If the corporation does not have any earnings and profits (or declares a dividend to eliminate any) it can elect S corporation status and avoid any personal holding company tax regardless of the level of passive income. Elections after 1986 (1988 for some corporations whose value is less than $5 million) bring into play the built-in gain rules.[10]

Question — Is the personal holding company technique a "sure fire" way to obtain an estate or gift tax valuation discount?

Answer — Not every personal holding company will result in an estate or gift tax discount. In *Estate of Lucretia Davis Jephson*,[11] the value of stock in two personal holding companies that were owned by the decedent was not reduced by a lack of marketability discount. The court in the *Jephson* case held that the proper estate tax value was the net asset value of the companies less the cost involved in liquidating them. Note that the result occurred because the decedent owned 100 percent of both companies and therefore had the unqualified right to liquidate them at any time. Note also that all the assets in both companies were cash or marketable securities, and that neither corporation had any significant liabilities. Planners should use this case as a "how not to do it" guideline.

Footnote References

Personal Holding Company

1. IRC Section 542(c) contains ten types of business entities which are specifically excluded from personal holding company status.

2. IRC Section 542(a)(2). The ownership test pertains to value and not to the number of outstanding shares. Under constructive ownership rules an individual is deemed to own all the stock directly or indirectly owned by or for his or her brothers and sisters, spouse, ancestors, and lineal descendants. Likewise, stock owned directly or indirectly by or for a corporation, partnership, estate, or trust is considered as being owned proportionately by its shareholders, partners, or beneficiaries. IRC Section 544(a).

3. IRC Section 542(a)(1). "Adjusted ordinary gross income" is essentially gross income less gains from sales or other dispositions of capital assets and Section 1231 property, and further reduced by depreciation, certain taxes, interest, and rents attributable to income from certain rents and royalties. IRC Section 543(b).

4. IRC Section 541, as amended by ERTA Sec. 101(d)(2).

5. IRC Sections 351, 368(c); Reg. §1.351-1(b).

6. IRC Section 358(a).

7. IRC Section 362(a).

8. See chart below which illustrates the percentage discounts allowed in a number of personal holding company cases.

9. TRA '84 severely limited the utility of interest-free loans. See IRC Section 7872 and chapter 16 of this book.

10. IRC Section 1374.

11. *Estate of Lucretia Davis Jephson*, 87 T.C. 297 (1986).

Tools and Techniques

Chapter 20

POWER OF APPOINTMENT

WHAT IS IT?

A power of appointment is a right given in a will, trust, or other instrument by one person (the donor) to another (the donee) allowing the donee to name the recipient (appointee) of the donor's property at some future time. Thus, it is the right to dispose of someone else's property and is, therefore, a way to give someone other than the testator or grantor a right to "complete" the provisions of the latter's will or trust. This authority over the disposition of property can provide substantial flexibility in an estate plan and serve as an important tax-saving tool.

WHEN IS THE USE OF SUCH A DEVICE INDICATED?

1. When an estate owner would like someone other than himself to make decisions concerning his property. A power of appointment is a means of providing for an interested, intelligent and informed person who will likely be living and capable of making a wise choice of (a) who should receive trust property, (b) how much income or principal should be allocated to any given individual, and (c) when principal or income should be paid out. Often, delegation of decision-making through a power of appointment is a way to avoid family conflict or confrontation by placing the decision-making responsibility in the hands of an objective (or outside-the-family) party.

2. When the estate owner does not know what the future needs of his intended beneficiaries will be—or even who or how many beneficiaries he will have. The power of appointment makes it possible to postpone the time of decision as to the ultimate disposition of property until a date when all the relevant facts affecting that decision are known.

3. When the estate owner desires to qualify assets for the marital deduction but would like to provide both asset management through a trust and have some right to designate who will receive the property (a gift over to third parties such as children) if the spouse does not exercise the power. (If the estate owner's primary objective is to be sure children or someone other than the surviving spouse receives the principal, rather than a power of appointment, he should consider a "Q.T.I.P." trust, a Qualifying Terminable Interest Property trust which provides the surviving spouse with income for life and then passes principal to the designated remaindermen. This topic is covered in more detail in Chapter 33.)

WHAT ARE THE REQUIREMENTS?

There are no required or "magic" words or phrases for creating a power of appointment. In fact, it is possible to create such a power without even using the word *appoint*. The courts examine whether the words used in the will or trust manifest an intent to create a power. Thus, a power to invade or consume trust corpus is a power of appointment. So, too, is the power to affect the beneficial enjoyment of a trust by altering, amending, revoking or terminating the trust.[1]

A donee might exercise a power by will with specific language such as:

Under the will of my deceased husband, Alan, I have, as to certain property, a power of appointment by will; I, now, in the exercise of that power, appoint the property subject to such power as follows: (Then the exercise of the power would follow.)

Another way to exercise the power (assuming a specific reference to that power is not required for its exercise) would be for the donee to mention powers as part of a general device or bequest.

I bequeath and devise all the residue of my property, real and personal, including any property over which I may have a power of appointment, to _____.

In many states such a general reference to powers of appointment is construed as being sufficient to include that property and in some states the residuary clause need not even refer to powers of appointment to exercise a general power of appointment.

Because of the possibility of confusion and the unintended exercise of a power by the residuary clause in the will of a donee of a power which is exercisable by will, many draftsmen require that the power be exercised by "an instrument other than a will". In this fashion, the donee cannot, intentionally or unintentionally, exercise the power by a will, but instead, must use a separate document.

A *release* of a power is a formal statement that the donee is giving up the power.

A *lapse* is the termination of a power without exercise. Either event may result in inclusion in a donee's estate for federal estate tax purposes, under the same conditions as an exercise; if the donee's property was transferred directly from the donee of a power of appointment to the recipient, would it be includible in the donee's estate? If yes, property subject to the power will be similarly included.

For purposes of trust law, a power of appointment is a "general" one if there are no restrictions on the donee's

Tools and Techniques

choice of appointees. Where there are certain restrictions, then the power is termed a "limited" or "special" power.

A separate categorization of powers of appointment exists with regard to federal estate tax. Regardless of whether there are other restrictions on the possible appointees of the power, the power will be termed a "general" power for purposes of federal estate tax law if it can be appointed in favor of any one or more of the group consisting of the holder of the power, his or her estate, creditors or estate's creditors.[2]

The property owner must decide upon a donee. This person can be anyone who has, under local law, the legal capacity to execute the instrument that must be employed to use the power. For example, if the donor specified that the donee must exercise the power by will, the donee must be old enough to execute a valid will. However, the donee need not necessarily have attained that age at the time of creation of the power.

Once a donee has been selected, that person must follow—precisely—the manner of exercising the power of appointment which the donor specified. This means that if the donor provided the donee with a power to be exercised during lifetime, it cannot be exercised by will (since a will takes effect after death). If the donor had not stated how the power is to be exercised, the donee can use any normal method by which the property subject to the power could be transferred. Therefore, real property could be appointed by deed and stock certificates by endorsement.

In some states, a power of appointment will automatically be exercised—regardless of whether or not the donee has referred to the power—by the residuary clause ("all the rest, residue, and remainder I give . . .") in the donee's will (unless the donee has stated a contrary intent).[3] In many states, if the donee does not exercise the power, the property subject to appointment does not pass to the donee's intestate successors (the donee does not technically own the property for property law purposes, even if he holds a general power of appointment under federal tax law); therefore, it will pass according to the donor's desires if they were expressed in a "gift over," also known as a provision in default of appointment.

HOW IT IS DONE — EXAMPLES

Alan Ferry would like to provide his wife with a power of appointment. He might do this by providing in his will language similar to the following:

Upon the death of my said wife, or, if she shall not survive me, then upon my death, to pay over the principal to such persons (including, but not limited to, my said wife or her estate), and/or corporations, in such estates, interests, and proportions and in such manner, without any restriction or limitation whatsoever, as my said wife may, if she sur-

vives me, appoint by making specific reference to this power in and by her last will duly admitted to probate; or, in default of such appointment, then to divide the principal of the trust, as it shall then exist, into as many equal shares as I shall have children then living and deceased children of mine who shall be survived by issue then living.

This provision would give the wife a "general" power of appointment for purposes of the law of trusts. Additionally, it is a general power for estate tax purposes since it is one in which the donee, Alan's wife, has the power to pass on an interest to anyone including herself or her estate, her creditors, or the creditors of her estate. The example illustrates a "testamentary" power, a power exercisable only by will at the donee's death. If Alan's wife predeceases Alan or dies without effectively exercising her power to appoint, the principal goes to the "takers in default" (of exercise), Alan's children.

Suppose Alan wanted to be sure that his property would be kept intact within his family. He could limit the class to whom his wife could appoint by giving her a limited or "special" power. He might use language such as:

Upon my wife's death, such property shall be distributed to such of my issue and spouses of my issue as she shall appoint by an instrument other than a will making specific reference to this power; and if she shall make no effective appointment, then in equal shares to my children, the issue of any such child who is not then living to take their parent's share, per stirpes. Provided further, that in no event may my wife make any such appointment to herself, her estate, her creditors or the creditors of her estate.

Here, the power is a "special" (or limited) power for trust purposes, and is also not a "general power" for estate tax purposes.

However, if the wife were given the power by her husband to appoint the property to any descendants of the donor's grandfather or the spouses of such descendants, the power would be "special" for trust law purposes, but would be a "general" power for estate tax purposes (since, as a spouse of a descendant of the husband's grandfather, she could include herself within the group of appointees and appoint the property to herself).

For most of our planning purposes, the categorization for estate and gift tax law purposes is more important and we will use that categorization exclusively in the balance of this discussion.

The distinction between a general and a special power has very important tax ramifications which are discussed below.

WHAT ARE THE TAX IMPLICATIONS?

1. The mere existence of a general power of appointment (as considered for federal estate tax purposes) will cause property subject to it to be includible in a donee's estate. (A power granted in a will is generally considered to be created at the testator's death.[4] A power granted in an inter vivos instrument is considered created on the date the agreement becomes effective, usually the date it is executed.)

2. If a general power is exercised or released by a disposition that, if it were a transfer of property owned by the donee, would be includible in the donee's gross estate under the lifetime transfer rules, the property subject to the power will be includible. For example, where a beneficiary of a trust exercised a power to amend a trust by requiring mandatory payment of trust income to himself during his life instead of discretionary payments as provided by the trust, the trust property was included in his gross estate, being in the nature of a transfer of property with a retained life income interest.[5]

3. A release or lapse of a general power is treated the same as if the donee gave property he could have taken personally (or disposed of to the beneficiary of his choice) to the takers in default. For this reason, a release or lapse of a general power may be subject to gift taxation.[6] A qualified disclaimer of a general power of appointment (perhaps to avoid the tax on generation-skipping transfers) will probably avoid the gift tax problem.

   See question and answer following regarding "5 & 5" power, which describes an exception to recognition of a gift under these circumstances.

4. Neither the mere existence of a special power of appointment nor the exercise, release, or lapse of such a right will cause inclusion in the donee's gross estate.

5. No gift tax is attracted by the exercise, release, or lapse of a special power of appointment.

ISSUES AND IMPLICATIONS IN COMMUNITY PROPERTY STATES

Since community property excludes property received by inheritance or gift, it would be very unusual for any property received (or given away by permitting a lapse) to be a community property right initially.

However, a community property agreement (some states require it to be in writing) which was all-inclusive, purporting to have both spouses hold as community property all assets they owned, can have the effect, in some states, of creating a gift by transmuting separate property into community property and thus resulting in a gift of one-half of the value from one spouse to the other. If the agreement can be interpreted as including rights of one spouse under a power of appointment, then the right may become community property, resulting in a gift equal to one-half the value of the right at the time of entering into the agreement. Because of the unlimited marital deduction, no federal gift tax would be triggered.

The more common problem encountered is to have the permitted appointee of the property ask to have the property transferred under the exercise of the power titled in the name of his spouse and himself, as community property, thus creating a gift to the other spouse of one-half the value of the property when the other spouse receives his one-half community interest in what was intended to be the sole property of the permitted appointee under the power. As was mentioned above, the unlimited marital deduction would eliminate any gift tax exposure under federal tax law. However, state gift tax law should be examined to see if any state gift tax would be caused by such event.

Where the holder of a "limited" or "special" power has freedom to choose, among the permitted appointees of a power (e.g., where the power includes "the issue of grantor and spouses of such issue"), then the power may be exercised to give each spouse an undivided interest without any gift involvement. The property could, under these circumstances, be appointed to the spouses as community property, joint tenants or tenants in common (each as to one-half), without any gift being recognized.

QUESTIONS AND ANSWERS

Question — How does the rule against perpetuities affect powers?

Answer — The common law rule against perpetuities states the principle that no interest in property is effective unless it *must* vest—if at all—not later than 21 years (plus, if applicable a gestation period) after some life or lives in being at the time an interest is created. In other words, the measuring period under the rule against perpetuities relates back to the creation of the power. (Some states, such as Pennsylvania, use "wait and see" rules. The interest will be valid *unless* it does not *actually* vest within the appropriate period.) In many states, if the donee *could,* in any fashion, make an appointment of the property under the donor's terms beyond the time period permitted by the Rule, the power is void. (The test is whether the power, by its terms, *will* be exercised within the allowable time period allowed by the Rule.)

Question — Is a power to consume, invade, or appropriate property for the benefit of the donee a general power for federal estate tax purposes if it is limited to an ascertainable standard relating to the health, education, support, or maintenance of the donee-decedent?

Answer — No. This makes such provisions extremely useful estate planning techniques for providing financial flexi-

Tools and Techniques

bility without consequent tax burden.[7] The power over income or corpus or both must be reasonably measurable in terms of the donee's needs for health, education, or support (or any combination of these needs). Maintenance and support mean the same thing and are not limited to bare necessities.

Proper wording is essential; if the holder of a power can use property for his "comfort, welfare, or happiness," the power is general and will cause the property interest to be subject to federal taxation.[8]

Question — Is property includible in a beneficiary's estate if an independent trustee has a discretionary right to make distributions to that person?

Answer — Where the donor gives an independent trustee discretionary authority to invade principal to meet a beneficiary's reasonable needs, that power will not cause property to be includible in the beneficiary's estate.[9] This is yet another way to provide additional security without adverse tax effects.

Question — Is property includible in a donee-decedent's estate where there is a requirement that the donee of a general power of appointment must give notice to the trustee before the exercise takes effect?

Answer — Whether or not the notice has been given before death and whether or not the power has actually been exercised, inclusion will result. The mere existence of a general power created after 1942 will cause inclusion of the property subject to the power.

Question — What is a "5 and 5 power"?

Answer — This is another valuable technique used by estate planners to provide flexibility and financial security for a beneficiary with little or no tax consequence. There is a de minimus rule (a rule that says in essence that for administrative reasons the tax law will ignore small amounts) that provides

> "property subject to a general power will be included in a donee-decedent's estate (or considered a taxable gift) only to the extent that the property which could have been appointed by the exercise of the power the donee allowed to lapse exceeds the greater of (a) $5,000 or (b) 5 percent of the total value of the fund subject to the power as measured at the time of the lapse."[10]

Stated another way, to the extent that a lapse of a general power within a calendar year exceeds the greater of (a) $5,000 or (b) 5 percent of the assets subject to the power, the *excess* is treated as a release of a general power and taxed accordingly. The excess may be treated as a gift subject to gift tax or as a transfer which may subject to estate tax. To make certain that the limits set forth above are not breached, the right of invasion must be made noncumulative.

For example, Brian Gordon was the income beneficiary of a trust with assets of $200,000. The value of the trust remained constant. Brian was also given a noncumulative power (which he did not exercise and which therefore lapsed each year) to withdraw $10,000 of principal a year. On Brian's death, only the $10,000 subject to the power at the time of his death is included in his gross estate. The power that lapsed in prior years can be ignored, since the amount that could be appointed each year did not exceed the greater of $5,000 or 5 percent of the corpus, $200,000.

Jamie Gordon was the income beneficiary of a trust with assets of $80,000. She also had a noncumulative power (which she did not exercise) to withdraw $10,000 of principal a year. At the expiration of each year, Jamie is deemed to have released a general power to the extent of $5,000 (i.e., a $10,000 lapse minus the greater of $5,000 or 5 percent of $80,000 [$4,000]).

Assume that Jamie died in the sixth year of the trust's existence and that the value of the trust assets remained constant at $80,000. Each $5,000 released by Jamie constituted one-sixteenth (5,000/80,000) of the value of the trust assets. Therefore, Jamie's gross estate would include $35,000 on account of this trust. The $35,000 consists of $10,000 on account of the power held by the decedent at the time of her death and $25,000 (i.e., five-sixteenths of the $80,000 value of trust assets equals $25,000) on account of the lapse of the power in each of the five prior years. Each year's lapse is included in the decedent's gross estate to the extent of one-sixteenth of the value of the trust assets because it had the effect of a transfer with a retained life estate.

In addition to the inclusion for estate tax purposes, the failures to exercise the power would result in gifts to the remaindermen of the trust, with the reduction each year by the then value of Jamie's life estate in the lapsed amounts. The relative value of the life estate and remainder interest at each age of the life tenant are shown in the government table reproduced at Figure 21.2 in chapter 21 on Private Annuities.

Question — Can a special (limited) power cause gift tax problems?

Answer — Yes. When an income beneficiary of a trust who also holds a special power of appointment exercises that power during lifetime and in doing so terminates his life interest, there may be a taxable gift. The amount of the gift is the present value of the income interest forfeited by the life tenant-donor. Life income beneficiaries should therefore be careful in exercising a lifetime special power, since the IRS will argue that to the extent the exercise terminates the income interest and that interest goes to someone else, a transfer subject to gift tax has been made.[11]

ASRS: Sec. 46; ¶70; Sec.54,¶44.3(i), Sec. 55, ¶57.5(e);,Sec.58.

Footnote References

Power of Appointment

1. Reg. Sec. 20.2041-1(b)(1).
2. IRC Sec. 2041.
3. Casner, *Estate Planning*, 695, Note 16 (3d edition, 1961, 1977 Supp.).
4. Reg. Secs. 20.2041-1(e), 25.2514-1(e).
5. IRC Sec. 2041(a)(2); Reg. Sec. 20.2041-3(d)(1). See also *Estate of Leo M. Gartland*, 34 T.C. 867 (1960), aff'd 293 F.2d 575 (7th Cir.), cert. den. 368 U.S. 954.
6. IRC Sec. 2514(a) and (b).
7. IRC Sec. 2041(b)(1)(A).
8. Reg. Sec. 20.2041-1(c)(2) and Reg. Sec. 25.2514-1(c)(2). See also Rev. Rul. 77-60, 1977-1 C.B. 282.
9. *Estate of Council*, 65 T.C. 594 (1975).
10. Reg. Secs. 20.2041-3(d)(3), 25.2514-3(c)(4).
11. *Estate of Ruth B. Regester v. Comm.*, 83 T.C. 1 (1984).

Chapter 21

PRIVATE ANNUITY

WHAT IS IT?

A private annuity is an arrangement between two parties, neither of whom is an insurance company. The transferor (annuitant) conveys complete ownership of property to a transferee (obligor, the party obligated to make payments to the person who has transferred the property). The transferee, in turn, promises to make periodic payments to the transferor for a period of time. Usually, this period of time is the transferor's life or, in some cases, the transferor's life plus the life of his or her spouse.

There are basically two types of private annuities, the single life annuity under which payments cease at the death of the annuitant, and the joint and last survivor annuity, in which payments continue until the death of the last survivor, e.g., payments continue as long as either the husband or wife is alive. Generally, since payments under this type of arrangement will continue for a longer period of time than payments under a single life annuity, the amount paid each year will be less than that payable under a single life annuity.

WHEN IS THE USE OF SUCH A DEVICE INDICATED?

1. When your client would like to "spread" gains. For example, your client owns low tax basis property. He needs cash and wants to sell a particular asset but wants to avoid "bunching" gains into a single tax year. Generally, such a client will be in a high income tax bracket. A private annuity will enable him to spread his gain (and therefore defer tax) over a number of years.

   TRA '86 made installment sales difficult and in many cases impossible. First, interest generally will be deductible in an installment sale only to the extent of investment income (assuming the interest is characterized as investment interest). Second, installment sales are barred totally with respect to certain assets, such as publicly traded stock. Private annuities have therefore become more valuable than before as a deferral tool.

2. When your client wishes to retire and shift control of a business to a family member or to a key employee. For example, assume Ed Staller is the sole shareholder of a close corporation. Ed has no heir other than his wife. He has two key employees in the business who are capable of managing it. Ed would like to sell them the business but he is concerned about adequate income upon his retirement. The key employees tell Ed they would like to buy the business but can't afford to pay Ed in a lump sum. Ed could sell all of his stock to the two key employees and in return they could promise to pay him an income for his life (and perhaps for his wife's life). The income would be based on the fair market value of the business.

3. When your client desires to remove a sizable asset, such as a business, from his or her estate for estate tax purposes. For example, Abe Marks is the sole shareholder of a closely-held real estate corporation. He has two daughters who are presently working in the business. He could sell the business to his daughters in return for their agreement to pay an annuity for his life only. This will result in a reduction in Abe's estate (and thus save estate taxes) because the value of the business will be removed from his estate for federal estate tax purposes. At Abe's death, annuity payments cease and neither the close corporation stock nor the promised payments will be in his estate. It is not yet clear whether a private annuity will fit within the safe harbor for debt. But we think the seller in the classic private annuity has not retained an interest in the enterprise and therefore Section 2036(c) should not apply (see page 477).

   The income tax basis received by the daughters for the stock, *after Abe's death*, will be the amount of annuity payments they made to him during his lifetime. Until Abe's death, their basis will be the greater of the amount they paid him or the amount paid plus the present value of all the future payments that will be paid if Abe lives to his life expectancy. Initially, the transferee's basis is equal to the fair market value of the property transferred—assuming no gift is built into the transaction.

4. When your client wishes to obtain a fixed retirement income. For instance, Russ Miller is near retirement age and is a majority shareholder of a close corporation. Presently, his business does not provide pension, profit-sharing, or nonqualified deferred compensation benefits. He would like to retire but depends upon his salary from the business for most of his income. There are key employees present, but they do not have sufficient cash to buy him out. Russ could transfer the business to them in return for their promise to pay him a private annuity. This should yield a higher income than if he sold the business in an installment sale. Furthermore, if the annuity was measured by his lifetime, Russ could be sure he would never outlive the income.

5. When your client owns a large parcel of non-income producing property but is desirous of making it income producing. For example, your client is a widow. Her married son is currently providing $700 a month to support

her. The widow owns real estate which is currently not producing any income, but because of its choice location, is increasing substantially in value. It is expected that the full appreciation in the property will occur over the next 10 years.

A possible solution is for her son to discontinue gifts to his mother and, instead, his mother could transfer the real estate to him in exchange for a monthly lifetime income (say, $750 a month, assuming the present value of the land will support this payment). This will minimize the widow's estate, substantially reduce estate taxes at her death, and, at the same time, give her financial independence. The son becomes the immediate owner of the real estate. The growth in value (and increase in gross estate for tax purposes) will occur in the son's hands and not further increase his mother's estate.

6. When the client's estate is very large and the major or sole heir is a grandchild (or other individual two or more generations below that of the client). Because the private annuity is a sale and not a gift, it will not be subject to the generation-skipping transfer tax.

7. Where the purchaser's objective is to bar others from obtaining the property in question but he can't afford to pay for the asset in a lump sum outright purchase.

WHAT ARE THE REQUIREMENTS?

1. Any type of property can be used. For example, it is possible to transfer a home, undeveloped real estate, stocks, or a business interest. Preferably, the property transferred will be income producing, rapidly appreciating, and will not be subject to depreciation or investment credit recapture or to indebtedness.

2. It is important to ascertain immediately the ability of the obligor to make annuity payments. If the transferee (the obligor) has substantial independent income, then almost any asset can serve as the property to be sold. But, if the transferee has little or no income, then the property sold should be either income producing or at least should be of a type that the obligor can easily and quickly resell or borrow against.[1]

3. It is extremely important that the obligor's promise be unsecured. If the promise of the obligor is secured, a taxable event will occur immediately on a transfer.[1a] This means the annuitant will pay tax on the full amount of the gain. The gain is the difference between the amount realized (the present value of the right to the promised payments) and the transferor's adjusted basis in the property.

4. The transferee (obligor) should be a person not regularly engaged in issuing private annuities.[2] Generally, the obligor would be the natural object of the transferor's (annuitant's) bounty. For example, most private annuities are made between parents and children. The device

may also be useful for transfers between employers and trusted key employees.

5. The annuity amount must be determined by measuring the fair market value of the property. We suggest an appraisal by independent court-recognized appraisal experts shortly before the execution of the private annuity.

6. Your client should be in a high estate tax bracket and should be desirous of reducing his or her estate and providing himself or herself with a lifetime income.

7. An agreement with a trust or corporation which has very few assets may be attacked by the IRS as a sham.

8. Payments must be completely contingent on the life (or lives) of the transferor(s). An agreement providing for a minimum number of payments would not be considered a private annuity.

HOW IT IS DONE — AN EXAMPLE

George Gargas is 65 years old. He owns farmland with a fair market value of $100,000. His basis is only $10,000. He would like to remove the land from his estate and have his son, Bill, own it. He does not, however, want to pay any gift taxes on the transfer.

A private annuity agreement would be drawn stating that the farmland was sold to Bill in return for Bill's promise to pay his father an income for life. At age 65, the father's life expectancy is 20 years (see Figure 21.1).

The annual annuity generated by property worth $100,000 is $14,712. This is arrived at by dividing the fair market value of the property transferred by the present value of an annuity at the appropriate age (6.7970 — see Table A in Figure 21.2.)

Out of the $14,712 he receives each year, Bill's father can exclude a portion ($500) from income. This exclusion applies regardless of how long the father lives if the annuity starting date is before 1987. If the annuity starting date is after 1986, Bill's father could exclude $500 each year only until his basis is recovered.

The exclusion ratio is determined by dividing the father's $10,000 basis in the property by his $294,240 expected return ($14,712 × 20 years). The excludible amount is then found by multiplying this exclusion ratio ($10,000/294,240) by the $14,712 annual payment. (The $500 annual excludible amount can be found directly by dividing the $10,000 basis of the property by the annuitant's 20-year life expectancy.)

The $14,212 balance of each year's annuity payment ($14,712 minus $500) is taxable at ordinary income rates.

WHAT ARE THE TAX IMPLICATIONS?

1. For federal estate tax purposes, where the annuity ceases at the death of the transferor, the value of the property sold to the transferee-obligor in return for his promise to pay the annuity is excludible from the annuitant-transferor's estate. This is because property sold by a

Figure 21.1

Caution: Before using this table, read the explanation of the changes made in the valuation of annuities, life estates, etc. by 1988 legislation, at page 391.

Table V—Ordinary Life Annuities (One Life—Expected Return Multiples)					
Age	**Multiple**	**Age**	**Multiple**	**Age**	**Multiple**
5	76.6	42	40.6	79	10.0
6	75.6	43	39.6	80	9.5
7	74.7	44	38.7	81	8.9
8	73.7	45	37.7	82	8.4
9	72.7	46	36.8	83	7.9
10	71.7	47	35.9	84	7.4
11	70.7	48	34.9	85	6.9
12	69.7	49	34.0	86	6.5
13	68.8	50	33.1	87	6.1
14	67.8	51	32.2	88	5.7
15	66.8	52	31.3	89	5.3
16	65.8	53	30.4	90	5.0
17	64.8	54	29.5	91	4.7
18	63.9	55	28.6	92	4.4
19	62.9	56	27.7	93	4.1
20	61.9	57	26.8	94	3.9
21	60.9	58	25.9	95	3.7
22	59.9	59	25.0	96	3.4
23	59.0	60	24.2	97	3.2
24	58.0	61	23.3	98	3.0
25	57.0	62	22.5	99	2.8
26	56.0	63	21.6	100	2.7
27	55.1	64	20.8	101	2.5
28	54.1	65	20.0	102	2.3
29	53.1	66	19.2	103	2.1
30	52.2	67	18.4	104	1.9
31	51.2	68	17.6	105	1.8
32	50.2	69	16.8	106	1.6
33	49.3	70	16.0	107	1.4
34	48.3	71	15.3	108	1.3
35	47.3	72	14.6	109	1.1
36	46.4	73	13.9	110	1.0
37	45.4	74	13.2	111	.9
38	44.4	75	12.5	112	.8
39	43.5	76	11.9	113	.7
40	42.5	77	11.2	114	.6
41	41.5	78	10.6	115	.5

decedent for full and adequate consideration before death is not taxable in his estate.[3] (See the discussion of Code section 2036(c) in Appendix B.)

Likewise, the value of the promised payment will be excludible. This is because the selling price in a private annuity arrangement is an income which will expire (in the case of a single life annuity) upon the annuitant's death.

Note that this is not the case with a joint and survivor annuity. In a joint and last survivor annuity, payments will continue until the death of the last survivor. So if the annuitant's spouse survives, the present value of fu-

ture payments to her will be includible in the transferor-annuitant's estate (assuming he was sole owner of the property that was transferred in return for the joint and survivor annuity payments).[4] However, because of the unlimited estate tax marital deduction, there would be no federal estate tax.

2. Each annuity payment made by the transferee-obligor to the transferor-annuitant is treated partially as a tax-free return of capital, partially as a capital gain (currently taxed at ordinary rates) and the balance as ordinary income.[5] If the annuity starting date is after 1986, once the transferor-annuitant has recovered his basis, the entire

Tools and Techniques

Figure 21.2

Caution: Before using this table, read the explanation of the changes made in the valuation of annuities, life estates, etc. by 1988 legislation, at page 391.

For estates of decedents dying, or gifts made, after November 30, 1983
Life Estate, Remainder, and Annuity Interests
(Taken from Estate Tax Reg. §20.2031-7 and Gift Tax Reg. §25.2512-5)

TABLE A.—SINGLE LIFE, UNISEX, 10 PERCENT SHOWING THE PRESENT WORTH OF AN ANNUITY, OF A LIFE INTEREST, AND OF A REMAINDER INTEREST

(1) Age	(2) Annuity	(3) Life estate	(4) Remainder
0	9.7188	.97188	.02812
1	9.8988	.98988	.01012
2	9.9017	.99017	.00983
3	9.9008	.99008	.00992
4	9.8981	.98981	.01019
5	9.8938	.98938	.01062
6	9.8884	.98884	.01116
7	9.8822	.98822	.01178
8	9.8748	.98748	.01252
9	9.8663	.98663	.01337
10	9.8565	.98565	.01435
11	9.8453	.98453	.01547
12	9.8329	.98329	.01671
13	9.8198	.98198	.01802
14	9.8066	.98066	.01934
15	9.7937	.97937	.02063
16	9.7815	.97815	.02185
17	9.7700	.97700	.02300
18	9.7590	.97590	.02410
19	9.7480	.97480	.02520
20	9.7365	.97365	.02635
21	9.7245	.97245	.02755
22	9.7120	.97120	.02880
23	9.6986	.96986	.03014
24	9.6841	.96841	.03159
25	9.6678	.96678	.03322
26	9.6495	.96495	.03505
27	9.6290	.96290	.03710
28	9.6062	.96062	.03938
29	9.5813	.95813	.04187
30	9.5543	.95543	.04457
31	9.5254	.95254	.04746
32	9.4942	.94942	.05058
33	9.4608	.94608	.05392
34	9.4250	.94250	.05750
35	9.3868	.93868	.06132
36	9.3460	.93460	.06540
37	9.3026	.93026	.06974
38	9.2567	.92567	.07433
39	9.2083	.92083	.07917
40	9.1571	.91571	.08429
41	9.1030	.91030	.08970
42	9.0457	.90457	.09543
43	8.9855	.89855	.10145
44	8.9221	.89221	.10779
45	8.8558	.88558	.11442
46	8.7863	.87863	.12137
47	8.7137	.87137	.12863
48	8.6374	.86374	.13626
49	8.5578	.85578	.14422
50	8.4743	.84743	.15257
51	8.3874	.83874	.16126
52	8.2969	.82969	.17031
53	8.2028	.82028	.17972
54	8.1054	.81054	.18946

TABLE A.—SINGLE LIFE, UNISEX, 10 PERCENT SHOWING THE PRESENT WORTH OF AN ANNUITY, OF A LIFE INTEREST, AND OF A REMAINDER INTEREST—Continued

(1) Age	(2) Annuity	(3) Life estate	(4) Remainder
55	8.0046	.80046	.19954
56	7.9006	.79006	.20994
57	7.7931	.77931	.22069
58	7.6822	.76822	.23178
59	7.5675	.75675	.24325
60	7.4491	.74491	.25509
61	7.3267	.73267	.26733
62	7.2002	.72002	.27998
63	7.0696	.70696	.29304
64	6.9352	.69352	.30648
65	6.7970	.67970	.32030
66	6.6551	.66551	.33449
67	6.5098	.65098	.34902
68	6.3610	.63610	.36390
69	6.2086	.62086	.37914
70	6.0522	.60522	.39478
71	5.8914	.58914	.41086
72	5.7261	.57261	.42739
73	5.5571	.55571	.44429
74	5.3862	.53862	.46138
75	5.2149	.52149	.47851
76	5.0441	.50441	.49559
77	4.8742	.48742	.51258
78	4.7049	.47049	.52951
79	4.5357	.45357	.54643
80	4.3659	.43659	.56341
81	4.1967	.41967	.58033
82	4.0295	.40295	.59705
83	3.8642	.38642	.61358
84	3.6998	.36998	.63002
85	3.5359	.35359	.64641
86	3.3764	.33764	.66236
87	3.2262	.32262	.67738
88	3.0859	.30859	.69141
89	2.9526	.29526	.70474
90	2.8221	.28221	.71779
91	2.6955	.26955	.73045
92	2.5771	.25571	.74229
93	2.4692	.24692	.75308
94	2.3728	.23728	.76272
95	2.2887	.22887	.77113
96	2.2181	.22181	.77819
97	2.1550	.21550	.78450
98	2.1000	.21000	.79000
99	2.0486	.20486	.79514
100	1.9975	.19975	.80025
101	1.9532	.19532	.80468
102	1.9054	.19054	.80946
103	1.8437	.18437	.81563
104	1.7856	.17856	.82144
105	1.6962	.16962	.83038
106	1.5488	.15488	.84512
107	1.3409	.13409	.86591
108	1.0068	.10068	.89932
109	.4545	.04545	.95455

TABLE B.—TABLE SHOWING THE PRESENT WORTH AT 10 PERCENT OF AN ANNUITY FOR A TERM CERTAIN, OF AN INCOME INTEREST FOR A TERM CERTAIN AND OF A REMAINDER INTEREST POSTPONED FOR A TERM CERTAIN

(1) Number of years	(2) Annuity	(3) Term certain	(4) Remainder
1	.9091	.090909	.909091
2	1.7355	.173554	.826446
3	2.4869	.248685	.751315
4	3.1699	.316987	.683013
5	3.7908	.379079	.620921
6	4.3553	.435526	.564474
7	4.8684	.486842	.513158
8	5.3349	.533493	.466507
9	5.7590	.575902	.424098
10	6.1446	.614457	.385543
11	6.4951	.649506	.350494
12	6.8137	.681369	.318631
13	7.1034	.710336	.289664
14	7.3667	.736669	.263331
15	7.6061	.760608	.239392
16	7.8237	.782371	.217629
17	8.0216	.802155	.197845
18	8.2014	.820141	.179859
19	8.3649	.836492	.163508
20	8.5136	.851356	.148644
21	8.6487	.864869	.135131
22	8.7715	.877154	.122846
23	8.8832	.888322	.111678
24	8.9847	.898474	.101526
25	9.0770	.907704	.092296
26	9.1609	.916095	.083905
27	9.2372	.923722	.076278
28	9.3066	.930657	.069343
29	9.3696	.936961	.063039
30	9.4269	.942691	.057309
31	9.4790	.947901	.052099
32	9.5264	.952638	.047362
33	9.5694	.956943	.043057
34	9.6086	.960857	.039143
35	9.6442	.964416	.035584
36	9.6765	.967651	.032349
37	9.7059	.970592	.029408
38	9.7327	.973265	.026735
39	9.7570	.975696	.024304
40	9.7791	.977905	.022095
41	9.7991	.979914	.020086
42	9.8174	.981740	.018260
43	9.8340	.983400	.016600
44	9.8491	.984909	.015091
45	9.8628	.986281	.013719
46	9.8753	.987528	.012472
47	9.8866	.988662	.011338
48	9.8969	.989693	.010307
49	9.9063	.990630	.009370
50	9.9140	.991481	.008519
51	9.9226	.992256	.007744
52	9.9296	.992960	.007040
53	9.9360	.993600	.006400
54	9.9418	.994182	.005818
55	9.9471	.994711	.005289
56	9.9519	.995191	.004809
57	9.9563	.995629	.004371
58	9.9603	.996026	.003974
59	9.9639	.996387	.003613
60	9.9672	.996716	.003284

Figure 21.3

TAXATION OF SELLER UNDER PRIVATE ANNUITY

A. Recovery of Basis (cost) Element	Tax Free
B. Gain Element	Capital gain (currently taxed at ordinary rates)
C. Income Element	Ordinary income

COMPUTING ANNUAL PAYMENT — TAX FREE, GAIN AND ORDINARY INCOME ELEMENTS

STEP 1.
Compute Annual Payment

$$\frac{\text{F.M.V. of Property Transferred}}{\text{Present Value of Annuity Factor (see Figure 21.2)}}$$

STEP 2.
Compute Exclusion Ratio

$$\frac{\text{Seller's Cost Basis}}{\text{expected return (annual payment x life expectancy)}}$$

STEP 3.
Compute Excludible Amount*

Exclusion ratio x Annual Annuity

STEP 4.
Compute Gain Element
(until total gain recognized)

$$\frac{\text{Present value of annuity minus property's basis}}{\text{life expectancy of annuitant}}$$

STEP 5.
Compute Ordinary Income Element

Annual Payment
  minus sum of (a) excludible amount
  and (b) gain amount

*If annuity starting date is after 1986, amount is excluded only until basis is recovered.

---

payment will be taxed as ordinary income. The obligor is not allowed a deduction for any payments made to the annuitant.[6]

3. There will be no gift if the annual payments made by the obligor to the annuitant are actuarially determined to be equal to the amount of the property sold. However, if the value of the promise made by the transferee-obligor is less than the value of the property transferred, the difference will constitute a gift by the annuitant-transferor.[7] (If the annuity were a joint and survivor annuity, the value of the survivor annuity would be a gift from the transferor. Since it would be a gift of a future interest, it would not qualilfy for the gift tax annual exclusion.[8] If the donee were the transferor's spouse, the gift may qualify for the gift tax marital deduction.[9])

For example, the Internal Revenue Service tables indicate an annuity valuation of 6.7970 for a male or female age 65. If such an individual transfers property with a fair market value of $100,000, a fair exchange would be a life annuity of $14,712 per year ($100,000 divided by 6.7970). But if annuity payments were actually set at, say, $11,000 per year, which has a present value of about $75,000, the difference, $25,000, would constitute a gift from the transferor to the transferee in the year the agreement was signed. But see page 391.

4. The transferee receives a "temporary basis" in the property equal to the value for calculation of the annuity. This provides a means for immediately increasing the basis for depreciation or depletion and can be a very significant benefit. The same basis is available for sale of the property, leaving little, if any, gain to be then taxed.

Tools and Techniques

Figure 21.4

PRIVATE ANNUITIES

If Property Worth $100,000 is Transferred and Annuitant's Basis is $10,000

Annuitant is Age	(1) His life expectancy would be	(2) This yields an annual annuity of	(3) This much is excludible	(4) This much is taxed at ordinary rates	(5) The total expected return is
75	12.5 yrs	$19,176	$800	$18,376	$239,698
70	16 yrs	$16,523	625	15,898	264,367
65	20 yrs	14,712	500	14,212	294,247
60	24.2 yrs	13,424	413	13,011	324,871
55	28.6 yrs	12,493	350	12,143	357,295
	This column is based on life expectancy (See Figure 21.1)	This amount is found by dividing Fair Market Value of property transferred by the present value of an annuity factor at the appropriate age (See Figure 21.2)	This amount is found by dividing the annuitant's basis by his life expectancy	This amount is found by subtracting the excludible portion of each annuity payment from the annual annuity payment (a portion of this amount is gain, i.e. sales price less adjusted basis divided by life expectancy)	This amount is found by multipying the annual annuity column (2) by column (1) life expectancy

However, upon the transferor's death, the basis is adjusted to what the transferee actually paid in annuity payments. If he has retained the property, the only concern for imposition of income tax would be his having depreciated the property below his "adjusted basis". In that event he would realize a gain to the extent of the difference. However, if he had sold the property for a price showing the basis at fair market value and that amount is substantially more than the amount actually paid, the excess will be then immediately taxed to the transferee.

Thus, care should be exercised in making decisions to sell property recently acquired on a private annuity basis.

HOW CAN LIFE INSURANCE ENHANCE THIS TOOL?

The obligation of the transferee must be unsecured. This means that no specific assets are set aside to protect the transferor in case the transferee defaults. But at the death of the transferee-obligor, the obligation passes to his or her estate. The question then arises as to how to eliminate or minimize the possible hardships on the transferee's family and heirs. (The estate of the transferee will still have to continue promised payments for as long as the transferor-annuitant lives.)

Looking at the same problem from another viewpoint, how do you avoid disrupting the financial security of the transferor-annuitant in case the transferee dies before the transferor?

Perhaps the best answer is life insurance. Life insurance can be obtained on the life of the transferee-obligor. It might be owned by and payable to the obligor's spouse (or irrevocable trust for her benefit).

There should be no formal connection between the life insurance and the private annuity; otherwise, the obligation of the transferee might be considered "secured." When the income and estate tax free proceeds are received, the spouse will have cash to (a) continue payments to the transferor, and (b) pay estate taxes caused by the inclusion of the private annuity property in the transferee's estate.[10]

Occasionally, there is a third reason that life insurance may be useful in conjunction with a private annuity. Assume a widow owns a business and has two adult sons and two adult daughters. How can she transfer the business to her sons but at the same time avoid disinheriting her daughters if she does not have considerable other assets?

Life insurance can be used to "equalize" the inheritance. The widow would sell the business to her sons in return for a private annuity. The daughters could be named owners, premium payors, and beneficiaries of a policy (or policies) on their mother's life. Annual gifts by the widow to the daughters could be used to provide premium payments. The widow could obtain the cash to give to her daughters from the private annuity income. When the widow died, each daughter could receive—in the form of tax-free life insurance proceeds—an amount equivalent to what she would have received if the business were divided in four equal shares. (Actually, since the sons are paying their mother for the business, the amount the daughters are to receive might be considerably less than half the value of the business.)

IMPLICATIONS AND ISSUES IN COMMUNITY PROPERTY STATES

In a community property jurisdiction, since the property is owned one-half by each spouse, the practitioner can either arrange a private annuity sale on a joint and survivor annuity basis, or on the basis of a separate annuity contract for each community half of the husband and wife, respectively. If the joint and survivor annuity is used, the total amount payable to the husband and wife is somewhat lower at the beginning than would be the total paid under separate annuities, but that payment remains the same at the death of the first spouse to die. Under the separate annuity approach, at the death of one spouse, the payments to that spouse cease, and the survivor does not have any benefit continuing under the decedent's annuity.

In many instances, practitioners utilize the separate annuity approach to avoid estate taxes at the death of the first spouse to die, since the value of the decedent's community share of the survivor annuity remaining for the surviving spouse would be taxable in the estate of the first to die and would not appear to qualify for the marital deduction.

There are implications in community property states also from the standpoint of the purchaser of the property under a private annuity contract. A typical arrangement is to have a private annuity contract between the parents and a child (rather than a child and his spouse). However, it is unlikely that the property acquired by the child will generate sufficient income to make the private annuity payments. If the child uses his earnings to make up the shortfall, the child's spouse could either be acquiring a community property interest in the property purchased, or could be making a gift to the child as each annuity payment is made. Consideration should be given to this aspect before the annuity contract is entered into.

QUESTIONS AND ANSWERS

Question — What are the alternatives to a private annuity?

Answer — One alternative to a private annuity is the installment sale. However, if an annuitant were to die shortly after the sale took place, the death tax results would differ substantially. Since an installment sale is often evidenced by a series of notes, the present value of those notes would be includible in the estate of the seller. But under the private annuity arrangement where payments are to cease on the death of the annuitant, the entire amount of the transferred property could be excluded from the estate of the annuitant at his or her death.

Another disadvantage of an installment sale is that an installment note bearing interest would cause a sizable portion of each payment in the early years to be considered interest to the seller. Where the subject of the sale is publicly traded stock, the installment sale would not defer taxation. The cost of an installment sale is in many cases higher since investment interest is now deductible only to the extent of investment income if the asset sold was considered an investment.

Question — What basis does the transferee have in the property he now owns?

Answer — In the case of a private annuity, the transferee-obligor has, as his new tax basis, the fair market value of the property which is the actuarial value of future payments.[11] It is because his basis is the fair market value of the property at the time the agreement is executed that the private annuity is so useful. The new owner can immediately sell the property and reinvest the proceeds in more liquid or higher yielding assets. He does not have to worry about tax on gains which the transferor-annuitant would otherwise have had to face. The basis is "stepped-up," not carried over, for purposes of determining the tax on gain if the property is sold or depreciated. This would enable a fully depreciated property (such as an apartment or office building) to receive a new (fair market value) basis for depreciation by the transferee.[12]

(But be aware of potential recapture problems where accelerated depreciation has been used by the transferor.)

Question — What happens to the transferee's basis if the annuitant dies prematurely?

Answer — The transferee may have to readjust his basis or report a gain. If the annuitant dies before the length of his life expectancy according to government tables, the transferee-obligor must make a downward adjustment to his basis for the property. His basis becomes the amount of payments he actually has made. However, if he had sold the property before the annuitant's death, he must report as taxable capital gain the excess of the sales price over the actual annuity payments made.[13]

For example, if the 65-year-old annuitant in the example discussed in the "Tax Implications" section had died after receiving only one annuity payment, and the transferee had sold the property immediately upon receipt, the transferee would have an $85,288 gain ($100,000 minus the single $14,712 annuity payment).

Question — Can the property that will be the subject of the private annuity be placed in escrow as security for the private annuity?

Answer — A promise to pay a private annuity in return for an appreciated security or other asset doesn't cause the transferor-annuitant to realize an immediate gain for only one reason—the value of the buyer's promise to pay is deemed to be too contingent to value. In other words, the annuity rules have been allowed in private annuity situations only because of the uncertainty as to whether or not the one agreeing to make payments will be able to make them as agreed when the time for payment actually arrives.

Where there is any type of security that will be activated to protect the transferor in the event of the transferee's default, a completed sale for tax purposes occurs. This makes the entire gain element taxable immediately rather than taxable ratably over the annuity period.

Question — Can the private annuity be used in situations other than between family members?

Answer — Yes. One possible use for a private annuity lies in the stock redemption area. For example, assume a corporation is owned and operated by an elderly widow and her son-in-law. Each owns 50 percent of the corporation's stock. The corporation's financial health is strong. The widow would like to retire but needs the assurance of a steady income. The son-in-law is in a high income tax bracket but is personally "cash poor."

The corporation could purchase the widow's stock in return for the corporation's promise to pay her an income for life. The transaction would give the son-in-law 100 percent ownership of the corporation. No gift tax would be payable assuming the amount of the annual annuity payment was derived from the appropriate government tables and as the result of an arm's-length transaction.

If the son-in-law had no primary and unconditional personal obligation to purchase the stock, the use of corporate dollars to effect the redemption will not result in a dividend to him. The widow should receive "sale or exchange" treatment if the redemption completely eliminates her interest (attribution rules don't cause problems in this factual situation but extreme care should be taken before a redemption of stock is affected in any family-owned corporation). We recommend that stock redemptions not be effected through private annuities if the seller's life expectancy exceeds 15 years. Longer payout periods may raise IRS suspicion that the seller has received something other than a promise to pay that is unconnected with the business; i.e., the IRS could argue that the seller has retained an equity rather than debt interest. This may also trigger section 2036(c) problems (see page 477).

Question — What happens if the annuitant outlives his life expectancy?

Answer — The transferee must continue to make the annuity payments and such payments continue for the life of the annuitant. That is one of the risks involved in a private annuity; the actual amount to be paid by the transferee may exceed the expected return (the annual payments multiplied by the annuitant's life expectancy).

Question — In a previous example in which an individual transferred property worth $100,000 in return for an annuity of $14,712 per year, the annuitant's expected return in that example was $294,240. If the individual lived for the full 20-year life expectancy, how can it be said that he saved federal estate taxes by transferring property worth $100,000?

Answer — The property transferred is the fair market value of the property on the date of the transfer which in this example occurs 20 years prior to the annuitant's death, according to life expectancy tables. Assuming that the fair market value of the property continues to increase at a net rate of 7 percent per year, on the projected date of the annuitant's death in 20 years, the fair market value of the property would be $386,968.

The entire $294,240 of expected return would not be included in the annuitant's estate since a portion of that amount must be used by the transferor-annuitant to pay tax at ordinary income rates. The annuitant could make sizable gifts to decrease the net amount of cash realized as a result of receiving the annuity payments. In addition, the annuitant will most probably expend the majority of the annuity payments.

Question — If an annuitant lives beyond his life expectancy, what are the tax consequences?

Answer — If the annuity starting date was before 1987, the Internal Revenue Service takes the position that if the annuitant exceeds his life expectancy, he continues to be able to exclude that portion of each payment equal to the recovery of basis. The remainder of each payment will be taxed as ordinary income. However, Code Section 72(b) now provides that where the annuity starting date is after 1986, if an annuitant outlives his life expectancy (and thus has recovered his basis), then the remaining payments will be taxed entirely as ordinary income.

Question — In arranging a private annuity transaction, is it wise to tie the annuity payments to the income generated by the transferred property?

Answer — No. If this is done, the property may be brought back into the transferor's estate at death as a transfer with a retained life estate under Code Section 2036.[14]

Question — Can a joint and survivor private annuity be designed?

Answer — Yes. The advent of an unlimited estate tax marital deduction between spouses makes the joint and survivor annuity a viable planning technique. It has the advantage of providing security for the surviving spouse with no additional federal estate tax cost at either spouse's death (but may trigger state death taxes since most states do not have an unlimited marital deduction). At the time of the exchange, the gift of the survivor annuity may qualify for the gift tax marital deduction as qualified terminable interest property.[15] A second advantage is that the amount payable by the transferee each year is lower than it would be in a single life private annuity. This makes it easier for a purchaser to meet annual obligations under the private annuity.

Question — What effect does the Installment Sales Revision Act of 1980, the Tax Reform Act of 1986, or the 1987 or 1988 tax acts have—if any—on private annuities?

Answer — Although a private annuity can be said to fit within the definition of an installment sale (a disposition of property where at least one payment is to be received after the close of the taxable year in which the disposition occurs), neither law deals specifically with private annuity transactions. According to some authorities, however, the installment sale rules may affect the taxation of private annuities.[16] According to them, a private annuity would literally fall within the definition of a "contingent payment sale" in the Temporary Regulations. It is possible, therefore, that a private annuity could be covered by the rules for an installment agreement that specifies neither a maximum selling price nor a fixed period for payments. If so, the Temporary Regulations would indicate that the basis would have to be recovered over a period of 15 years, unless the taxpayer obtains a ruling permitting a shorter period on the ground that the 15-year period would provide a substantial and inappropriate deferral of recovery of basis. Also, the IRS could require the use of a longer period if the 15-year period would accelerate the recovery of basis.[17]

Using a 15-year period would be advantageous to sellers with a large basis and small potential gains who had actuarial life expectancies greater than 15 years (under age 65). But since the IRS would probably require a longer period if the 15 years would accelerate the taxpayer's recovery of basis, it will probably end up using the taxpayer's life expectancy. A longer period would be advantageous to sellers who have a small basis and a large potential gain.

Aside from the issues involving the period of time over which basis can be recovered, the treatment of a private annuity under the installment sale rules could conceivably be an advantage in some cases. Prior law indicated that the seller under a private annuity arrangement had to report gain immediately when the annuity payments were secured by giving the seller a security interest in the property transferred.[18] Such a rule does not now and never has applied to installment sales.[19] The ability to add security to the private annuity transaction without a loss of income tax advantages would substantially increase its viability.

Potential disadvantages of installment sale treatment would include (1) the application of the second disposition rules; and (2) the rules dealing with cancellations of installment obligations at death.

If the parties could not prove the absence of an income tax avoidance purpose, a resale of the annuity property by the transferee could result in an acceleration of the annuitant-seller's gain if the sale occurred within the statutory time limit. (This would not be the case for a sale to a nonrelated party such as a son-in-law.)

The Service could also argue that at the seller's death, the buyer's obligation to make annuity payments becomes unenforceable. If that is the case, the IRS could treat the obligation as if it were canceled, i.e., cause the gain or loss to be reportable in the final return of the seller. However, it is likely that—at the least—regulations will provide that an annuitant's death is not an event rendering the annuity contract unenforceable.

Although a few authorities feel that private annuities were affected by the Omnibus Budget Reconciliation Act of 1987, we feel that most private annuities were unaffected.

TAMRA (Technical and Miscellaneous Revenue Act) '88 may have made a significant impact on private annuities through its mandate that the Treasury must create up to date tables or formulas for valuing annuities

Tools and Techniques

and other property interests. The exact implications must await release by the government of those tables and formulas. (See page 391 for a more detailed explanation.)

Question — Will the use of a trust automatically cause the loss of the tax benefits of the private annuity?

Answer — No. but it is likely that the IRS will treat property for annuity exchanges involving trusts as if the transaction created a grantor trust rather than a sale. Therefore, all the income of the trust would, if the service is successful, be taxed to the seller (grantor, according to the IRS) as owner.

But this harsh result is neither automatic nor certain. The Ninth Circuit Court of Appeals checks to see if annuity payments are tied to the income of the trust, how payments are calculated, and what role the taxpayer takes in trust investment decisions. Recent cases[20] indicate that client success is most likely where (1) payment is computed by dividing the fair market value of the property by the appropriate annuity factor determined from the government's own tables, (2) the trust is obligated to pay the annuity without regard to the value of the property held in the trust or the income produced by trust assets, and (3) the grantor holds no powers to manage the trust or control the trustee.

ASRS, Sec. 51.

Footnote References

Private Annuity

1. Where a sale is made to children through a private annuity, they or the trustee representing them should have a source of capital or income—other than solely the income from the transferred property—from which to make required payments, otherwise the IRS could argue that the seller's income is in reality inextricably tied to the success of the enterprise, i.e., that he has retained an income interest and therefore Section 2036(c) should apply (see page 477).

1a. *Comm'r. v. Kann*, 174 F.2d 357 (CA-3, 1949); *J. Darsie Lloyd v. Comm'r.*, 33 B.T.A. 905 (1936) acq., 1950-2 C.B. 3; *Estate of Bell v. Comm.*, 60 T.C. 469 (1973); *212 Corp. v. Comm.*, 70 T.C. No. 77 (1978).

2. Rev. Rul. 62-136, 1962-2 C.B. 12.

3. IRC Section 2033; *Fidelity-Philadelphia Trust Co. v. Smith*, 356 U.S. 274 (1958).

4. IRC Sections 2039(a), 2039(b).

5. IRC Section 72; Rev. Rul. 69-74, 1969-1 C.B. 43.

6. *F. A. Gillespie & Sons Co. v. Comm'r.*, 154 F.2d 913 (CA-10, 1946) (cert. den., reh. den.); *Steinbach Kresge Co. v. Sturgess*, 33 F. Supp. 897 (D.C., N.J., 1940).

7. IRC Section 2512(b). To value annuity promise see tables contained in Regs. §25-2512-5. But see also page 391.

8. Reg. §§2.2503 - 3(c), Example (2); Rev. Rul. 70-514, 1970-2 C.B. 198; Let. Rul. 8811017..

9. IRC Section 2523(f)(6), as amended by TAMRA '88.

10. IRC Section 2033.

11. Rev. Rul. 55-119, 1955-1 C.B. 352.

12. Rev. Rul. 55-119, 1955-1 C.B. 352.

13. Rev. Rul. 55-119, 1955-1 C.B. 352.

14. See *Estate of Cornelia B. Schwartz*, 9 T.C. 229, acq.; Rev. Rul. 68-183, 1968-1 C.B. 308.

15. IRC Section 2523(f)(6), as amended by TAMRA '88.

16. See "An Analysis of the Charges Made by the Installment Sales Revision Act of 1980," Emory and Hjorth, *The Journal of Taxation*, February 1981, 66, 71. The effect on private annuities may be even more likely than this article indicates since the disclaimer these authors quote from the "Committee Report" was deleted from the final Senate Report. Also, the Temporary Regulations state that "an installment obligation which is not a fixed amount obligation is a contingent payment obligation." Temp. Reg. Sec. 15A.453-1(d)(2)(iii).

17. Temp. Reg. Sec. 15A.453-1(c)(4).

18. See *Est. of Bell*, 60 T.C. 469 (1973).

19. Generally, the seller can retain a security interest in the property under an installment sale. Reg. Sec. 1.453-4(a). Also, under the new law a third-party guarantee of the buyer's note will not prevent the seller from using the installment method. Code Sec. 453(f)(3). However, if the full proceeds are paid by the buyer into an escrow account, it may not be possible for the seller to use the installment method, unless there are substantial restrictions on the seller's right to receive the amounts in escrow.

20. *LaFarge v. Comm'r*, 689 F.2nd 845 (CA-9, 1982), aff'g in part and rev'g in part 73 T.C. 40 (1979); *Stern v. Comm'r*, (CA-9, Nov. 15, 1984), rev'g and remanding 77 T.C. 614 (1981); *Fabric Estate v. Comm'r*, No. 17536-81, 83 T.C. No. 50, 12/11/84.

For a discussion of the potential impact of Code section 2036(c), the Hydra-like monster created by OBRA, the Omnibus Budget Reconciliation Act of 1987, see page 477.

Chapter 22

PROFIT-SHARING / PENSION PLAN

WHAT IS IT?

A profit-sharing plan, as its name implies, is a plan for sharing employer profits with employees. A profit-sharing plan need not provide a definite, predetermined formula for determining the amount of profits to be shared. However, there must be a definite formula for allocating these profits to each participant. But absent a definite contribution formula, an employer must make recurring and substantial contributions to a profit-sharing plan.[1]

A pension plan is a retirement plan established and maintained by an employer for the benefit of the employer's employees and their beneficiaries. The primary purpose of a pension plan must be to provide benefits for the employees upon their retirement because of age or disability.

WHEN IS THE USE OF SUCH A DEVICE INDICATED?

1. When your client would like to be sure of a steady, adequate, and secure personal retirement income.

2. When your client is in a high income tax bracket and would like to set aside money for retirement on a tax deductible basis.

3. When your client wants to reward long-service employees and provide for their economic welfare after retirement.

4. When your client would like to put his or her business in a better competitive position for attracting, retaining, and eventually retiring personnel.

5. When your client's corporation is about to run into an accumulated earnings tax problem. The corporation would like to "siphon off" some of its earnings and profits and reduce or eliminate the threat of a penalty tax on unreasonably accumulated earnings.

WHAT ARE THE REQUIREMENTS?[2]

(The requirements for pension and profit-sharing plans listed on this page are not exhaustive. For example, other requirements include meeting minimum standards on participation, vesting, and funding.)

1. The plan must be for the exclusive benefit of the corporation's employees.

2. The primary purpose of the plan must be to offer employees a retirement benefit (or, in the case of a profit-sharing plan, provide employees with a share in the company's profits).

3. The plan must not discriminate in favor of highly-compensated employees. Plans which are "top heavy," that is, plans which provide more than 60% of aggregate accumulated benefits or account balances for current key employees, must meet stringent vesting, minimum benefit, and other rules.

4. Contributions to (in the case of a "money-purchase" pension plan and a profit-sharing plan), or benefits from (in the case of a fixed benefit pension plan) a plan may not discriminate in favor of highly-compensated employees.

5. The plan provisions must set forth, in writing, a description of the plan and details of the plan. Furthermore, details of the plan must be communicated to employees.

6. The plan must be permanent. This means the plan must contain no set termination date.

7. The plan *must* require that distributions of the amployee's retirement benefit must begin by April 1 of the year following the year of attainment of age 70½ or, if later, actual retirement. In plan years beginning after 1984, distributions to 5% owners must begin by April 1 following the year of attainment of age 70½, even if the employee hasn't retired. Effective after December 31, 1988, distributions must begin to *all* participants (whether or not retired) by the April 1 following the year of attaining age 70½.

There are two different types of pension plans. The first is known as a fixed or defined benefit plan. Here, definitely determinable retirement benefits are computed using a predetermined benefit formula established when the plan is created. Each employee is promised a specific amount of retirement benefits. The employer's contribution to provide that benefit is based on an actuarial determination of the cost of benefits promised. In other words, contributions are based on benefits and the limits on contributions are based on the benefit they will produce.

A money-purchase pension plan, also known as a defined contribution plan, bases the retirement benefit upon an employer's commitment to make an annual contribution. Benefits are directly dependent upon the length of time an employee participates in the plan and the amount of money contributed on his behalf each year (plus interest and appreciation on such funds). In a money-purchase pension plan, therefore, the employer is not obligated to provide a specific amount of retirement benefits.

A profit-sharing plan is an arrangement by which an employer shares a portion of corporate profits with employees. For years beginning after December 31, 1985, contributions

Tools and Techniques

can be made even if there are no profits. It is a type of defined contribution plan. For all defined contribution plans, the limits on annual contributions to the plans are based on a percentage of salary, which directly limits the contributions. There is no limit to the benefits produced by the plan.

The corporation can distribute these payments currently in the form of cash bonuses, or profits can be shared on a deferred basis through contributions to a profit-sharing plan.

In deferred profit-sharing, contributions are made into an irrevocable trust. Funds then accumulate and are distributed to participants, usually as a retirement benefit, at some later date. Under a profit-sharing plan, participants can also receive benefits in the event of a termination other than retirement, such as death, layoff, or disability.

One strong point often related to a plan in which profits are to be shared is that the employer need not make a contribution in years in which no profits are earned. (A substantial amount of contribution flexibility is also possible in a well-designed pension plan.)

The following comments will discuss the basic principles of eligibility, vesting, contributions, actuarial assumptions, death benefits, retirement age, and social security integration for plans in general. There are special rules for "top heavy" plans which will be covered directly above the heading HOW IT IS DONE — AN EXAMPLE.

Eligibility

A qualified corporate retirement plan may not use an age or service requirement which would exclude any full-time employee who has attained age 21, or who has completed one year of service, whichever is later.[3] If there is 100 percent immediate vesting, a three-year waiting period may be permitted, reduced to a two-year maximum under TRA '86 for plan years beginning after December 31, 1988.[4] Previously, a defined benefit pension plan and target benefit pension plan could exclude any employee who was within five years of the plan's normal retirement age at the time he is hired.[5] This provision has been eliminated by the Omnibus Budget Reconciliation Act (effective for plan years beginning after December 31, 1987).

A plan must be nondiscriminatory in its coverage of employees. (It is permissible to favor rank and file employees.) There are mathematical tests (70 percent/80 percent coverage tests) which, if met, will satisfy the Internal Revenue Code requirements.[6] Alternatively, a plan will qualify if it does not discriminate in favor of shareholders, officers, or highly-paid employees.[7] TRA '86 modifies these requirements. A plan will qualify if the plan benefits at least 70% of the nonhighly compensated employees, or a percentage of nonhighly compensated employees which is at least 70% of the percentage of highly compensated employees benefiting under the plan. Additionally, for plan years beginning after December 31, 1988, each qualified plan must cover, on each day of the plan

year, the lesser of 50 employees or 40% or more of all employees of the employer.[8]

A plan may exclude part-time and seasonal employees, who are those employees who work less than 1,000 hours in a 12-month period.[9] Also, a collective bargaining unit may be excluded if the union prefers not to be covered under a plan and the decision is made as the result of good-faith bargaining.[10]

Vesting

Minimum vesting standards must be met by every plan. Vesting refers to nonforfeitability of benefits by covered employees. The primary rule is that the benefits attributable to employee contributions must always be 100 percent vested.[11]

Benefits attributable to employer contributions must vest no later than under one of three minimum schedules: (a) 5 to 15 year rule—an employee must be at least 25 percent vested in benefits after 5 years of covered service with a graduated increase so that after 15 years of service, the employee is 100 percent vested; (b) 10 year rule—an employee must be 100 percent vested after 10 years of covered service (no vesting is required prior to the 10th year); or (c) rule of 45—any employees who have 5 or more years of covered service must be at least 50 percent vested in benefits at the point where the sum of his or her age and years of covered service equals 45, and thereafter, vesting must continue at the rate of an additional 10 percent per year (however, an employee with 10 years of service must be at least 50 percent vested, regardless of age).[12]

The following chart shows the required vesting percentages under the "5-15 year" rule and the "rule of 45" at various ages and years of service:

Age	Years of Service	Rule of 45	5-15 Rule
35 or Younger	5	0%	25%
	6	0	30
	7	0	35
	8	0	40
	9	0	45
	10	50	50
	11	60	60
	12	70	70
	13	80	80
	14	90	90
	15	100	100
36	5	0	25
	6	0	30
	7	0	35
	8	0	40
	9	50	45
	10	60	50

Age	Years of Service	Rule of 45	5-15 Rule
36	11	70	60
	12	80	70
	13	90	80
	14	100	90
	15		100
37	5	0	25
	6	0	30
	7	0	35
	8	50	40
	9	60	45
	10	70	50
	11	80	60
	12	90	70
	13	100	80
	14		90
	15		100
38	5	0	25
	6	0	30
	7	50	35
	8	60	40
	9	70	45
	10	80	50
	11	90	60
	12	100	70
	13		80
	14		90
	15		100
39	5	0	25
	6	50	30
	7	60	35
	8	70	40
	9	80	45
	10	90	50
	11	100	60
	12		70
	13		80
	14		90
	15		100
40 or Older	5	50	25
	6	60	30
	7	70	35
	8	80	40
	9	90	45
	10	100	50
	11		60
	12		70
	13		80
	14		90
	15		100

Furthermore, the Internal Revenue Service may require more rapid vesting, within limits, in order to prevent discrimination in favor of the prohibited group.

Until recently, a "safe harbor" vesting schedule that would pass IRS approval was the "4-40" schedule shown below. IRS has, however, tried to impose (in many cases) more stringent vesting requirements than the 4-40 schedule. Congress (as of this writing) has voiced its disapproval of such IRS attempts by denying funds for IRS to make this change.

"4-40" Schedule	
Years of Service	Percent Vested
0	0
1	0
2	0
3	0
4	40
5	45
6	50
7	60
8	70
9	80
10	90
11	100

TRA '86 requires full vesting (a) after 5 years or (b) after 7 years under an accelerated graduated vesting schedule for plan years beginning after December 31, 1988.[13]

The following chart shows the required vesting percentages under both methods at various years of service:

Years of Service	(a)	(b)
1	0%	0%
2	0	0
3	0	20
4	0	40
5	100	60
6		80
7		100

The Retirement Equity Act of 1984 (REACT) requires a plan to take into account all years of service (generally 1,000 hours in a plan year) completed after the employee attains age 18 for vesting purposes. Previously, years of service completed prior to age 22 could be disregarded.

Tools and Techniques

Contributions and Benefits

The law imposes certain limitations on contributions and benefits.

Defined Contribution Type Plans—money purchase pension plans, profit sharing plans, stock bonus plans, ESOPs, thrift plans, and target or assumed benefit plans

Defined contribution type pension plans have an annual additions limit equal to the lesser of (a) 25 percent of compensation or (b) $30,000. Under TRA '86, the annual additions limit for contributions to defined contribution plans is frozen until the defined benefit pension plan limit ($94,023 in 1988) reaches $120,000, at which time the limit will be indexed to the Consumer Price Index.[14]

In the case of a profit sharing plan, an employer is allowed a maximum deduction equal to 15 percent of the total compensation of plan participants. An employer can carry payments in excess of that percentage forward (a so-called "carry forward") and obtain a maximum deduction in any year of 25 percent of total compensation based on the current year. TRA '86 eliminated the carryforward deduction for plan years beginning after December 31, 1986. (However, pre-January 1, 1987 unused amounts will be deductible.)[15]

Employees are typically not required to contribute their own funds as a condition of plan participation but plans can provide for voluntary contributions. Thrift plans do require employees to contribute and require the employer to make matching contributions.

Defined contribution plans may be integrated with Social Security based on the Social Security tax (excluding hospital premium) for the current year.

Disabled plan participants (other than a disabled employee who is a member of the prohibited group) can receive the benefit of an employer contribution to a defined contribution plan based on the annualized compensation of the employee during his last year of employment. All such contributions must be immediately 100 percent vested.

Defined Benefit Plan—a plan which provides a fixed or determinable benefit such as 40 percent of an employee's final three years average salary or one percent times final three years average salary times number of years of plan participation or service with the employer

The maximum normal retirement benefit for a new defined benefit plan, with a retirement age of 65 presently, is the lesser of (a) 100 percent of the highest three consecutive years of average compensation, or (b) $90,000. TRA '86 retains these limits, indexed to the Consumer Price Index. The dollar limitation for 1988 is $94,023, as a result of the annual cost-of-living adjustments. The normal retirement age now conforms to the Social Security retirement age. There will be greater restrictions on maximum benefits paid before the Social Security age of retirement.[16]

All plans that were in existence on July 1, 1982 had to be amended no later than the last day of the first plan year beginning after 1983, effective as of the first day of that plan year. (The IRS did extend the amendment date until June 1, 1986 for amendments that incorporated TEFRA, TRA '84, and REA provisions.) The $90,000 limit was effective for years beginning after December 31, 1982. In the case of plans which were in existence on July 1, 1982, if benefits were accrued in excess of $90,000, they do not have to be reduced and can be maintained as the maximum limit instead of $90,000. However, benefits accrued after December 31, 1982 are subject to the $90,000 limit (limit for 1988 is $94,023).

The above limits are based on the annual payment which, with interest compounded until the retirement date of the employee, will create a fund sufficient to provide the described benefit to the employee for his actuarial life expectancy.

The benefit must be reduced pro-rata if the employee has served less than 10 years with his employer. TRA '86 changes the reduction to apply to a participant with less than 10 years of plan participation rather than years of service.[17]

A $10,000 minimum annual benefit may always be provided for an employee who has never been covered by a defined contribution plan maintained by the employer regardless of the rules mentioned above.[18] But this amount must be reduced pro-rata if the employee has served the employer for less than 10 years at retirement. (A grandfather clause in ERISA enables plans in existence on October 2, 1973, to provide an employee with a benefit equal to 100 percent of the pay he or she was receiving on October 2, 1973, regardless of the dollar limitation.)[19]

All the limits above must be actuarially reduced to reflect any post retirement death benefits except in the case of a qualified joint and survivor annuity.

Further reductions must be made in the $90,000 limit where an employee retires before normal retirement age for full Social Security benefits. If retirement benefits are to commence prior to the normal retirement age for full Social Security benefits, the $90,000 limit would be reduced below the previous safe harbor of $75,000 at the rate of approximately 5 percent per year. This reduces age 55 retirement benefits to a new maximum benefit of approximately $42,000.[20] Benefits beginning after age 65 will be increased actuarially based on an assumption of a five percent interest rate (or if lower the rate specified in the plan).

Furthermore, the $90,000/100 percent limit must be reduced if the normal form of retirement is something other than a nonrefund life annuity. For example, a 15 percent reduction would be required if the normal retirement benefit upon which the $90,000/100 percent limit is based is a life annuity with a cash refund. This would drop the maximum limit to $76,500, or 85 percent of the participant's highest three consecutive years of average compensation. In the case of a life annuity with an installment refund, a 10 percent reduction would be required dropping the maximum benefit to $81,000, or 90 percent. With a 20 year certain life annuity, a 30 percent reduction would be required bringing the maximum benefit down to $63,000, or 70 percent. Even a 10 year certain life annuity would require a 10 percent reduction.

Be certain to recognize that all of the dollar limits described above will be increased by 4.47% for 1988 and until a new cost-of-living change is made.

Target or Assumed Benefit Plan—a hybrid between a defined contribution and defined benefit plan in which a "target benefit" is established under the plan for each participant such as 50 percent of an employee's five highest years average salary)

Once the "target benefit" is found, contributions necessary to attain that goal are then actuarially determined based on a conservative interest assumption such as five or six percent and the age of the participant. The plan then becomes a money purchase plan.

The maximum annual addition to the account of a participant in a target benefit plan cannot exceed the lesser of (a) 25 percent of salary or (b) $30,000.

Each participant's account is credited with any investment earnings or gains and losses. This means the actual retirement benefit of a participant under a target benefit plan can be more or less than the actual target itself.

Combination Defined Benefit and Defined Contribution Plans

Often, an employer will cover the same employee with a combination of plans, including a defined benefit pension plan and defined contribution plan, usually a money-purchase pension plan. In this case, each plan must first separately meet the general contribution and benefit limitations mentioned above. Furthermore, the contribution and benefit limitations in both plans must be combined and the resulting fraction must not exceed a combination set for the two plans.[21]

The maximum amount which can be contributed under a combination defined benefit pension plan and defined contribution plan is determined as below. Both types of payments to the plans are deductible as long as the total of the two "fractions" or percentages does not exceed 1.00 or 100%:

Defined Benefit Plan Fraction = Projected Annual Benefit
the lesser of
(1) 1.25 x dollar limit, or
(2) 1.4 x average compensation

Defined Contribution Plan Fraction = Sum of Annual Additions
the sum of the lesser of (for each year of service)
(1) 1.25 x dollar limit, or
(2) 1.4 x 25% of compensation

For example, your client, Herb Chase, earns $40,000 per year. Herb's pension benefit at age 65 under a defined benefit

plan will be $20,000. Twenty thousand dollars is 50 percent of the maximum amount allowed under the rules discussed above relating to defined benefit plans (i.e., the maximum benefit to which Herb could be entitled would be the lesser of $90,000 per year or 100 percent of his $40,000 salary, with the lesser of these being $40,000). In addition to the contribution for his benefit to this defined benefit plan, Herb's account also received $4,000 under a defined contribution plan (money-purchase or profit-sharing). Herb's computation would be as follows (based on no prior years of service with the employer):

Defined Benefit Plan Fraction = $20,000 (Herb's projected annual benefit)
lesser of
(1) 1.25 x $90,000 = $112,500
(2) 1.4 x $40,000 = $56,000

Result: $\frac{\$20,000}{\$56,000}$ = 36%

Defined Contribution Plan Fraction = $4,000 (the annual addition to Herb's account)
lesser of
(1) 1.25 x $30,000 = $37,500
(2) 1.4 x $10,000 = $14,000

Result: $\frac{\$4,000}{\$14,000}$ = 29%

Total combined fraction (36% plus 29%) = 65%

Thus Herb's contributions and benefits do not violate the 100 percent combined plan fraction limitation.

If the defined benefit or defined contribution plan which must be combined is Top Heavy (i.e., 60% of accrued benefits or account balances belong to key employees), the "1.25" in the defined contribution plan and defined benefit plan fractions (regarding dollar limits) will be reduced to "1.0". However, the "1.25" multiplicand can be retained if the following two requirements are met: (1) the plan cannot be "Super Top Heavy" (i.e., the accrued benefits or account balances of key employees cannot exceed 90% of the total benefits for all employees); and (2) the plans must provide additional minimum benefits or contributions for non-key employees (i.e., defined benefit plans must accrue a 3% benefit for each year of service after 1983 and defined contribution plans must have a 4% minimum contribution rate).

The following example shows the possible result where a combination of top heavy plans is involved.

John Smith earns an average salary of $200,000 per year. He is a participant in a defined benefit plan which provides an annual retirement benefit of 45% of salary and a defined contribution plan which provides for an annual contribution of 10% of salary. Both plans are top heavy. John's total com-

Tools and Techniques

bined fraction is determined as follows (based on no prior years of service with the employer):

Defined Benefit Plan Fraction = $90,000 (John's projected annual benefit)

$$\frac{\$90,000}{\text{lesser of}}$$

(1) $1.0 \times \$90,000 = \$90,000$
(2) $1.4 \times \$200,000 = \$280,000$

Result: $\dfrac{\$90,000}{\$90,000} = 1.0$

Defined Contribution Plan Fraction = $20,000 (the annual addition to John's account)

lesser of
(1) $1.0 \times \$30,000 = \$30,000$
(2) $1.4 \times \$50,000 = \$70,000$

Result: $\dfrac{\$20,000}{\$30,000} = .67$

The total combined fraction for John's plans is 1.67, which violates the combined fraction rule, resulting in possible plan disqualification (i.e., loss of tax exempt status). John's problem can be solved only by eliminating the defined contribution plan or by reducing the defined benefit plan benefit by two-thirds.

Deduction of Contributions

In a defined benefit pension plan, an employer can contribute and deduct the amount necessary to pay for the benefits promised. Technically stated, the employer may pay and deduct the plan's "normal cost" plus any amount necessary to amortize liability for benefits earned through the past service of employees. Past service (simplified, past service is the cost of financing benefits credited for past services) liability can be amortized over as few as 10 years (but no more than 30 years).[22]

Generally, the deductible contributions referred to above can be made up to the plan's full-funding limitation. Because the full-funding limitation is determined on the basis of projected benefits, an employer may make deductible contributions, even though the plan's assets are significantly in excess of its termination liability (i.e., amounts that would be owed to participants if the plan were to terminate currently).

The Omnibus Budget Reconciliation Act of 1987 (OBRA '87) modified the full-funding limitation to prevent employers from using a defined benefit plan as a tax-free savings account for funding liabilities that haven't been incurred. For years beginning after 1987, the limitation is the amount by which the lesser of (1) 150% of current liability, or (2) the accrued liability under the plan, exceeds the value of the plan's assets.

In a profit-sharing plan an employer can contribute and deduct a maximum of 15 percent of the total compensation of plan participants (without carry-forwards).[23] A $100,000 covered payroll would therefore yield the right to a $15,000 deductible contribution. In the past, where an employer had paid in less than the allowable 15 percent maximum, it was permissible to carry forward the balance to increase deductions in future years. The maximum deduction allowed, including carryforwards, is 25 percent of covered compensation. As previously indicated, the unused contribution carryforward is eliminated under TRA '86 provisions for plan years beginning after December 31, 1986.[24] Pre-1987 carry-forwards are still available.

Where the employee is utilizing both a pension and profit-sharing plan, the maximum deductible contribution for both plans is the greater of 25 percent of the compensation of covered employees or the contribution required to fund the minimum funding standard. Effective for plan years beginning after December 31, 1986, this deduction limitation is extended to combinations of defined benefit and money purchase plans.[25]

Prior to 1987, employees could deduct "qualified voluntary employee contributions" made to the plan up to a maximum of $2,000 per taxable year or, if less, 100% of his compensation. The plan had to contain special provisions allowing these contributions. TRA '86 repeals those provisions (effective after December 31, 1986).[26] Qualified voluntary employee contributions (made prior to 1987) must be accounted for separately, although separate investment will not be required. No loans to participants or investments in life insurance contracts should be made with plan assets attributable to deductible employee contributions or such action will be considered a distribution. Employees have the alternative of establishing their own Individual Retirement Accounts. (For limitations on the right of an employee who participates in an employer sponsored plan to contribute to an Individual Retirement Account, see chapter 14.)

Actuarial Assumptions

In a defined or fixed benefit pension plan, a conservative estimate should be made as to the rate of return of funds invested in assets other than life insurance. Five to seven percent interest assumptions are typical. Any actual return in excess of the amount assumed must be used to reduce the employer's future contributions.

In a money-purchase plan, the investment experience directly affects the amount a participant will have at retirement. Normally, earnings are allocated to the participant's account in proportion to his or her account balance.

In a profit-sharing plan, the investment experience directly affects the amount in a participant's account. Gains and losses must be allocated proportionately to each individual. Typically, such allocations are made in proportion to the account balances of each participant. At retirement a participant may have more or less than was contributed, depending on the investment experience of the plan.

In the event an employee terminates, under a pension plan (either a fixed benefit plan or a money-purchase plan) the portion of a terminated participant's nonvested account is used to reduce future employer contributions.[27] However, in a profit-sharing plan, the funds in a terminated participant's nonvested account (forfeitures) can be allocated among the accounts of remaining participants on the same basis as the following year's contribution, or can be used to reduce future employer contributions, depending upon what provisions have been made in the plan.[28] TRA '86 provides that effective for plan years beginning after 1985, forfeitures under all defined contribution plans (including money purchase plans) can be used to increase participants' account balances rather than to reduce employer contributions.[29]

Mortality is an important actuarial assumption. In a fixed benefit pension plan, if life insurance is included in the plan, the investment account is generally not used to provide the death benefit. Instead, the investment account that would have gone to the deceased employee had he or she lived is used to reduce future employer contributions to the plan. If life insurance is included in the plan, death proceeds generally go to the employee's beneficiary.

In either a money-purchase pension plan or a profit-sharing plan, the total funds in a participant's account are paid to a beneficiary as a death benefit. This includes the life insurance proceeds as well as any other investments.

Retirement Age

Generally, plans will make provision for normal, early, and late retirement age. Usually, normal retirement age will be age 65.

Mandatory retirement is generally prohibited. Exceptions exist for certain top executives and for good faith occupational requirements.

Previously, employers were not required to accrue additional benefits or pay the actuarial equivalent of normal retirement benefits to employees who chose to work beyond normal retirement age. However, for plan years beginning on or after January 1, 1988, it is unlawful to eliminate the accrual of further benefit credits to an employee's retirement account after the employee attains normal retirement age.

It is also unlawful to exclude an employee from participation in a pension plan even though his age is within 5 years of the age set for normal retirement. Allowance is made, however, for the extension of the normal retirement date for any such late-age-hired person. Most pension plans state that the normal retirement age of participants over age 55 at the time they enter the plan is 10 years from the date of entering the plan.

Early retirement benefits are generally available under a defined benefit plan at an actuarially reduced amount. In a money-purchase plan, the amount of a pension which can be provided with the participant's vested share is what he or she will receive at early retirement. Under a profit-sharing plan, in the case of early retirement, the amount accumulated in a participant's account will be paid generally as a lump sum or as monthly income.

In the case of late retirement, generally, payments prior to actual termination of employment will be made only with the employer's consent. Typically, in a pension plan, benefits are not increased as a result of an employee's late retirement. Usually, the employer will stop making contributions on behalf of a participant at the normal retirement age. (See above with respect to an employer's inability to cease accruals at normal retirement age for plan years beginning on or after January 1, 1988.) However, a higher annuity will still be provided because of the increased age of the participant when payments begin (and the insurance company will have to pay out benefits for a lesser period of time). In the case of a profit-sharing plan, late retirement benefits prior to actual termination of employment are also paid only with the consent of the employer. An employer used to have an option as to whether or not to contribute to the plan on behalf of a participant after normal retirement age. (See above with respect to an employer's inability to cease accruals at normal retirement age for plan years beginning on or after January 1, 1988.)

Social Security Integration

Generally speaking, the benefit structure of Social Security discriminates against the higher-paid employee which usually includes the key shareholders and highly-paid management. Social security benefits replace, relatively speaking, a higher percentage of the lower-paid employee's pre-retirement income. In essence, the business owner is already providing a base pension through contributions to the Social Security system.

Integration of a retirement plan with social security allows an employer to coordinate the benefits provided by social security with those provided by the employer's retirement plan. Through integration, the two benefits combined produce roughly the same proportionate benefit for higher-paid employees as for lower-paid employees.

Integration of a fixed or defined benefit plan can be arranged in one of three basic ways:

(1) Excess plan—the benefit is based on the monthly salary earned by the employee that is in excess of the "covered compensation" for social security purposes. For example, under a 30 percent excess benefit formula, if covered compensation for social security purposes was $12,600, an employee earning $20,000 would receive a retirement benefit based on 30 percent of $7,400 ($20,000 – $12,600), or $2,220 per year.

(2) Step Rate plan—benefits are based on all compensation, but a higher rate is given to compensation

over the "covered compensation" that is credited for social security purposes. For example, the formula might provide for 10 percent of covered compensation plus an additional 40 percent of compensation over $12,600.

(3) Offset plan—the benefit rate is the same for all employees, but is reduced (offset) by a percentage of social security benefits. For example, the formula might provide that all employees will receive 50 percent of average monthly salary, less one-half of their primary social security benefit. TRA '86 restricts the Social Security offset for employees whose wages are below the Social Security wage base (effective for plan years beginning after 1988).[30]

It is also possible to integrate a money-purchase pension plan or a profit-sharing plan. But here integration is on the basis of contributions rather than benefits.

Top Heavy Plans

For plan years beginning in 1984 and thereafter, plans which are considered "top heavy" must meet the basic qualification requirements of other pension plans and in addition meet the following requirements: (1) implement one of two alternative rapid vesting schedules; (2) provide minimum nonintegrated contributions or benefits for plan participants who are non-key employees; (3) limit the amount of a participant's compensation which may be taken into account; and (4) reduce the aggregate limit on contributions and benefits for some key employees.

A plan is considered "top heavy" when more than 60 percent of its aggregate accumulated benefits or account balances is provided to key employees. An employee's status and whether or not a plan is top heavy is determined on a year by year basis. The determination is made on the last day of the preceding plan year for existing plans and on the last day of the first plan year for new plans.

"Key employee" is defined as an employee who, at any time during the plan year or any of the 4 preceding plan years, is (1) an officer of the employer having annual compensation greater than 50 percent of the amount in effect under Code section 415(b)(1)(A) for any such plan year (50% of $94,023 in 1988); (2) 1 of the 10 employees having annual compensation from the employer of more than the limitation in effect under section 415(c)(1)(A) and owning (either personally or applying the constructive ownership provisions of Code section 318) both a more than ½ percent interest and the largest interests in the employer; (3) a 5 percent owner of the employer; or (4) a 1 percent owner of the employer having annual compensation from the employer of more than $150,000.[31]

To be considered an officer for "key employee" purposes, the officer must be an administrative executive who is in regular and continued service. Mere titles do not suffice.

In no event may more than fifty employees be considered as officers under the key employee rule. Special rules apply for smaller employers: If the business (or aggregated group of businesses) has fewer than 500 employees, only 10 percent will be considered officers, but if the business has fewer than 30 employees, at least three officers must be counted.

Each additional qualification requirement will be discussed below in the same order as the normal qualification rules above.

Eligibility

There are no special eligibility requirements for top heavy plans. The same requirements that must be met for any other qualified retirement must be met by top heavy plans.

Vesting

A top heavy plan must meet one of two special vesting rules. The first is a three-year/two-year 100 percent vesting rule. Under this rule an employee who is at least 21 years old and who has completed at least 3 years of service (reduced to 2 years for plan years beginning after 1988) with the employer (or employers) maintaining the plan must be given a nonforfeitable right to 100% of his accrued benefit derived from employer contributions. The second is a six year graded vesting rule. This provides 20 percent vesting at the end of the second year of service and 20 percent in each succeeding year. Full vesting must be attained by the end of the six year period.

Six-year graded vesting	
Years of service	Nonforfeitable percentage
2	20
3	40
4	60
5	80
6 or more	100

Contributions and Benefits

Special limitations on contributions and benefits are imposed where the plan is considered top heavy. Minimum benefits under defined benefit plans must be provided to non-key employees. The benefit accrued during a top heavy year must be at least two percent of average pay for the highest five years for each year of service in which a top heavy plan year ends up to a total of 20 percent of average pay.

In the case of top heavy defined contribution plans, in each year the plan is top heavy, non-key employees must receive minimum contributions of at least three percent of compensation. But if the plan provides the contribution rate of less than three percent for all participants, then instead of the three percent contribution rate, the highest contribution rate percentage on behalf of any key employee can be used (counting only the first $200,000 of compensation).

In determining benefits under a top heavy plan, only the first $200,000 of compensation can be counted, as is the case in non-top heavy plans after 1986. Beginning in 1989, the $200,000 limit will be adjusted annually for inflation. Social Security benefits or contributions can't be counted against the required minimum benefits or contributions.

HOW IT IS DONE — AN EXAMPLE

There are basically three ways an employer places funds into a retirement plan. The first is known as a "fully-insured" plan. Here, the employer places contributions into a funding vehicle of an insurance company, such as a retirement income life insurance contract. The funds usually receive a guarantee as to principal, minimum rate of interest, and annuity purchase rate (the "rate of exchange" at which pension funds can be changed into lifetime payment guarantees). It is the simplest method of investing pension monies.

The second type of investment vehicle is known as the "split funded" plan. Here, the employer places contributions into a trust fund. The trust fund splits contributions into two parts: part of the funds are placed in fixed assets, annuities, and/or life insurance, while the remainder is invested in other investments for diversification. There are principal, interest, and annuity purchase rate guarantees for the funds invested with the insurance company. However, frequently funds invested otherwise have no guarantees of principal or interest, but they may have the advantage of appreciation if invested in equities.

The third type of funding vehicle is known as uninsured. This type of funding implies that the employer contributions are invested solely by investments including equities. Contributions are made by the employer to a trust fund. There are no guarantees as to principal or interest although funds may be applied to buy a guaranteed annuity at normal retirement age. This funding method involves the highest risk because there are no guarantees made by a third party, but in return for the extra risk, this method offers the greatest potential appreciation (or depending upon how the plan is arranged, the lowest possible employer cost).

All three arrangements have advantages and disadvantages. For example, the fully-insured plan guarantees the principal, interest, annuity purchase rates, and expenses. It is the easiest plan to install and administer. The cost and effort of compliance with the Employee Retirement Income Security Act (ERISA) is relatively minimal. A disadvantage is that the growth of dollars in the plan is fixed, and so there is no chance for an equity-type appreciation of funds.

The split funded plan combines guarantees with the possibility of appreciation. The funds invested in insurance contracts obtain guarantees on principal and interest earnings, expense costs, and annuity rates. The side fund is usually invested in growth-oriented securities. Of course, since the side fund is invested in equities, the possibility exists that depreciation in the value of the securities will result in lower benefits for employees (or higher costs for the employer).

The main advantage of a full equity funded approach is that all funds have the possibility of appreciation. If the investment manager is successful, the result will be either reduced cost for the employer or increased benefits for the employees, depending on the type of plan utilized. The disadvantage of this arrangement is that there are no guarantees applied to the funds. Also, if an insurance company is not used, the employer must pay directly for actuarial, administrative, and investment expenses. The cost of hiring private actuarial and administrative services will be higher for small employers in most cases than if an insurer's services were utilized.

WHAT ARE THE INCOME TAX IMPLICATIONS?

1. Within the limits mentioned above, employer contributions to these plans are fully deductible for income tax purposes.[32]

2. Earnings on plan assets accumulate income tax free.[33]

3. Distributions, when paid out in the form of a lump-sum distribution, are taxable as follows:

   (a) The portion of a taxable distribution attributable to years of participation before 1/1/74 is taxed at capital gains rates. This capital gains treatment is phased-out over a five-year period (1987-1991) for taxpayers who did not attain age 50 before January 1, 1986.

   (b) The portion of a taxable distribution attributable to years of participation after 12/31/73 is taxed at ordinary income rates. However, an income averaging provision may be available. TRA '86 provides for 5-year averaging unless the participant reached age 50 by January 1, 1986 and uses the 1986 income tax rates.[34] It can therefore be taxed as ordinary income with special income averaging available. This election applies to distributions made after 1975 in taxable years beginning after 1975. The special income averaging provision cannot be used for the portion of a taxable distribution attributable to deductible employee contributions. Payment of such amounts can be distributed in a different tax year from the balance of the lump sum payment without jeopardizing the special averaging tax treatment given lump sum distributions. See table in Appendix C for the federal tax consequences of a lump sum distribution based on the 1987 and 1988 federal tax rates.

4. An employee generally does not have to include an employer's contribution in gross income even where rights to the benefits in the plan are fully vested (nonforfeitable). Benefits payable under a qualified retirement plan—including deductible employee contributions and earnings on those contributions—are taxed only when

paid to a participant or beneficiary and are not taxed if merely "made available."

However, if life insurance protection is provided under the plan, an employee is considered to have received a distribution each year (a current economic benefit) equal to the portion of the employer's contributions or trust earnings that have been applied during the year to provide pure insurance on the employee's life. This is the so-called "P.S. 58 cost."[35] The employee enters this cost into other income just as if he or she had received a bonus in that amount. Such costs will be recovered income tax free, however, when benefits are received under the contract. (If life insurance is purchased with deductible employee contributions, the amount spent is treated as a distribution.)

When an employee first becomes eligible to receive benefits, those benefits do not have to be paid and immediately rolled over into an IRA to avoid current income taxation. If the plan allows, they can be left in the plan and are not taxed until paid (but if paid to a child or creditor of the employee, they are treated as if paid to the employee).

The plan should place some limits on this deferral of receipt of benefits. IRS regulations require a plan to provide that an employee's election to defer payment of benefits cannot be given effect to the extent it causes his death benefits to be more than "incidental." This generally requires that the present value of benefits projected to be paid to the employee during his lifetime be more than 50 percent of the present value of the total payments to be made to the participant and his beneficiaries.[36]

The Tax Reform Act of 1984 modified the TEFRA provisions which accelerated the rate at which a participant's benefits must be distributed. Under Code section 401(a)(9), as amended by the Tax Reform Act of 1984, a qualified plan must provide that the entire interest of the participant will be distributed over one of the following permissible periods: (1) the life of the participant; (2) the lives of the participant and his or her "designated beneficiary"; (3) a period not extending beyond the life expectancy of the participant; or (4) a period not extending beyond the life expectancy of the participant and his or her "designated beneficiary."[37] A designated beneficiary is generally any individual designated by the participant to receive the balance of his or her benefits remaining at the participant's death.

The chart in Figure 22.1 sets forth the changes which have occurred in the area of plan distributions.

5. An employee who retires and receives periodic payments from the retirement plan is taxed on the receipt of such payments in accordance with the annuity rules. The annuity rules provide for taxation of such payments as ordinary income. If the employee made any nondeductible

contribution to the plan then, if he receives within the first three years of payments the total of such contributions he has made into the plan, all such contributions will be excluded from ordinary income.

If the employee cannot recover his cost within the first three years, the regular annuity rules apply, and an exclusion ratio must be determined. The exclusion ratio is the ratio of the employee's "investment in the contract" (cost) to the employee's "expected return," expressed as follows:

$$\frac{\text{Investment In Contract}}{\text{Expected Return}}$$

The employee's cost or "investment in the contract" is essentially his nondeductible contributions. Where life insurance is included in the plan, it also includes the total of all one year term insurance costs that he has reported as taxable income. The "expected return" is the annual payment the employee will receive multiplied by the employee's life expectancy (see Table, Figure 21.1). (Adjustments must be made for payouts made over differing time periods or where minimum payout guarantees are present.) Once the fraction is determined, it is multiplied by the annual payment. The product is the amount not subject to taxation. The balance of each payment is taxable as ordinary income.

Distributions of deductible employee contributions are also taxable under the annuity rules. TRA '86 eliminated the 3-year basis recovery rule with respect to individuals whose annuity starting date is after July 1, 1986, and replaces it with a pro-rata exclusion ratio for all distributions, as explained above.[38]

6. Under TRA '86, *all* distributions to *all* employees made before the participant attains age 59½ are subject to a 10 percent penalty tax with certain exceptions (death, divorce, disability, payments made over the participant's life starting from separation from service, and medical expenses), and is effective for plan years beginning after December 31, 1986.[39] In years between 1984 and 1987, only distributions to a 5% owner prior to age 59½ were subject to a 10 percent penalty tax, except for those payments made on account of an employee's disability or death.

The chart in Figure 22.1 sets forth the changes which have occurred in the area of premature distribution penalties.

7. TRA '86 added a new 15% tax on the amount of any "excess distributions" made to any individual during any calendar year. This tax applies to all excess distributions made after December 31, 1986, and the individual with respect to whom the excess distributions are made is liable for the tax.[40]

Figure 22.1

	Pre-TEFRA	TEFRA (repealed)	TRA '84 (effective 1/1/85)	TRA '86 (generally for years beginning after 1987)
Time at which distributions are required to begin.	Distributions were not required to begin at any designated time.	Distributions were required to commence at the later of attaining age 70½ or retirement. A Key Employee in a Top-Heavy Plan must commence distributions upon attaining age 70½.	Distributions must begin on the April 1st of the calendar year following the later of attaining age 70½ or retirement, except for a 5% owner of the employer whose benefits must commence on the April 1st following attaining age 70½.	Distributions must commence, for all employees whether or not retired, on April 1 of the calendar year of attaining age 70½ (effective January 1, 1989).*
Amount of benefits which must be distributed during participant's life.	At least 51% of benefits must be distributed during participant's life expectancy.	100% of the benefits must be distributed over the live expectancy of the participant or the participant and his spouse.	100% of the benefits must be distributed over the life expectancy of the participant or the participant and his designated beneficiary. If the designated beneficiary is not the participant's spouse, only the participant's life expectancy can be recalculated annually.	No change from TRA '84
Speed at which benefits must be distributed after participant's death (participant "in pay status", meaning that he or she had started receiving retirement benefits).	None designated.	Remaining benefits must be distributed within 5 years of participant's death unless payments were to be made over life expectancy of participant and spouse.	All remaining benefits must be distributed to the participant's designated beneficiary at least as rapidly as under the method of distribution in effect prior to his death.	No change from TRA '84
Speed at which benefits must be distributed after participant's death (participant *not* in pay status).	None designated.	All benefits must be distributed within 5 years of the participant's death.	The participant's entire interest must be distributed to his designated beneficiary within 5 years after his death. Exceptions exist for payments which were to be made over life expectancy of participant and designated beneficiary.	No change from TRA '84
Penalties for premature distributions.	10% penalty imposed on owner-employees participating in Keogh plans who received a distribution prior to attaining 59½ for any reason other than disability.	10% penalty imposed on distributions for reasons other than disability for all Key Employees under age 59½ who receive distributions of contributions made while the plan was a Top-Heavy Plan.	Effective for years beginning after December 31, 1984, the 10% penalty for pre-59½ distributions for reasons other than disability is extended to distributions made to 5% owners (rather than Key Employees) to the extent the amounts received were contributed while the recipient was a 5% owner.	A 10% penalty is imposed on *all* pre-59½ distributions unless made on account of death, disability, divorce, payments made over life beginning at separation from service, and for certain medical expenses.**

*IRC Section 401(a)(9), as amended by TRA '86, Section 1121 (a).
**IRC Section 72(t), as added by TRA '86, Section 1123(a).

Tools and Techniques

The term "excess distributions" means the aggregate amount of all retirement plan distributions (including IRA distributions) made with respect to any individual during any calendar year to the extent such amount exceeds $150,000. If the retirement distributions of an individual include a lump sum distribution for which he elects special income tax treatment (as in paragraph 3, above), the term "excess distributions" will be applied separately with regard to the lump sum distribution, and the $150,000 limitation is multiplied by 5 for a separate limitation of $750,000.

If the accrued benefit of all retirement plans of an employee exceeded $562,500 as of August 1, 1986, the employee may make an election on Form 5329, to be filed with his 1987 or 1988 income tax return, to have the amount accrued as of August 1, 1986 excluded for purposes of determining the amount of excess distributions tax imposed on his distributions.[41] If the employee elects to "grandfather" the August 1, 1986 balance, the annual $150,000 limitation, discussed above, will be reduced to $112,500 ($117,529, as adjusted for inflation for 1988 and thereafter until the next cost-of-living change is made).

If you think that the 15% excess distributions tax can be avoided by just not making any large distributions from the plan, see the explanation of the new 15% penalty estate tax on "excess accumulations," described below under the heading WHAT ARE THE ESTATE TAX IMPLICATIONS?

8. A beneficiary receiving death benefits from a qualified retirement plan will be taxable on the amount received for income tax purposes either under the lump sum or annuity rules. However, voluntary employee contributions which were deductible are not allowed the relief granted lump sum distributions and are includable in ordinary income. In computing the amount of taxable income the beneficiary must report as a result of the distribution, if the distribution is made in a lump sum and if any portion of the distribution consists of life insurance proceeds for which the employee paid the insurance costs or reported this P.S. 58 cost as taxable income on his return, then the difference between the face amount of the insurance contract and the insurance contract cash value (this difference is called the "pure insurance") passes to the beneficiary free of income tax. Thus, the beneficiary only treats the cash value portion of any death benefit plus any other cash distributions from the plan as income subject to tax.

If, on the other hand, the employee did not pay the insurance cost of the life insurance contract or did not report the cost of such insurance as taxable income, the portion of the insurance proceeds consisting of pure insurance (as defined above) will be considered taxable income to the beneficiary.

9. If the plan participant suffers permanent loss or loss of use of a member or function of the body, or permanent disfigurement, it may be possible for him or her to receive benefits under a qualified plan free of income tax under Code section 105(c). In order for the payment to qualify, the plan must provide 100 percent vesting of benefits if the participant ceases employment due to total and permanent disability, and must also include statutory language from section 105(c) to establish the dual purpose of the plan (i.e., a retirement plan and an "accident and health" plan).

Code section 105 applies to amounts received under "Accident and Health Plans". A qualified plan can serve a dual function of providing retirement benefits and disability benefits. To the extent benefits are provided due to the participant's disability, they will be income tax free if the requirements of section 105(c) are satisfied.

Section 105(c)(2) requires that the disability payment be computed by taking the nature of the injury into account in determining the benefit without regard to the period the employee is absent from work. This requirement may be difficult to satisfy in most pension plan contexts. However, a provision giving the committee discretion to determine disability benefits with reference to the nature of the injury may enable the disabled participant to overcome this hurdle.

WHAT ARE THE ESTATE TAX IMPLICATIONS?

Currently there is no exclusion from the federal estate tax for retirement plan distributions payable at an employee's death. The entire amount attributable to employer contributions is includable in the gross estate of an employee who dies on or after January 1, 1985.

TRA '86 added a second tier estate tax with regard to the estates of decedents dying after December 31, 1986. The new tax is equal to 15% of the decedent's "excess retirement accumulations," and is added to the first tier estate tax. None of the unified credit can be used to offset this new increase in tax. Further, no deductions can reduce the tax. This new tax "penalty for successful investing" may be disruptive to those estate plans which, regardless of the size of the estate, contemplated no estate tax to be due at the death of the first spouse to die. However, TAMRA '88 provides that a surviving spouse who is the beneficiary of all (a de minimis exception is provided) of the decedent spouse's aggregate retirement plans may elect to have the excise tax on excess retirement accumulations not apply at the decedent spouse's death. If the election is made, the decedent spouse's aggregate retirement plans will be treated as those of the surviving spouse for purposes of the excise tax on excess retirement distributions and excess retirement accumulations.

The term "excess retirement accumulation" means the excess (if any) of —

(1) the value of the deceased employee's interests in all qualified employer plans and IRAs as of the date of death (or alternate valuation date, if elected), over

(2) the present value of a single life annuity with annual payments equal to the greater of $117,529 (indexed at the same time and in the same manner as the dollar limitation on annual benefits under a defined benefit pension plan) or $150,000. The $150,000 amount is not available if an election has been made to grandfather accrued benefits accumulated in the plan as of August 1, 1986.

The present value of a single life annuity with annual payments equal to the greater of $117,529 indexed or $150,000 is determined using the interest rate and mortality assumptions prescribed by the Treasury as in effect on the date of death and as if the decedent had not died. TAMRA '88 mandates the Treasury to issue up-to-date tables (or formula) for valuing annuities (see p. 391). Until such tables are issued, the value of the annuity would be based on Table A found in Estate Tax Reg. §20.2031-7(f). This table, reproduced in Appendix B, is based on a 10% return for the life expectancy of the decedent. The worksheet at Figure 22.2 shows the steps in calculating amount of the tax, illustrating a total accumulation of $3 million for a decedent age 55 at death. The table at Figure 22.3 shows the application of the annuity factor at decedent ages from 41 through 99 to the nontaxed amounts, thus facilitating the computation illustrated in the worksheet.

If an election is made to grandfather accrued benefits accumulated in the plan as of August 1, 1986, the present value of a single life annuity with annual payments equal to $117,529 indexed is reduced by the present value of the unrecovered grandfather amount (if any) remaining as of the date of death. If the election is to be made, planners must act quickly; the election must be made by the time the 1988 tax returns are due (including extensions).

Note that excess retirement accumulation does not include life insurance proceeds in excess of cash surrender value.

The credit for estate tax paid on previous transfers does not apply to the excise tax on excess retirement accumulations. Also, no income deduction is allowed with respect to income in respect of a decedent for the excise tax on excess retirement accumulations. However the excise tax on excess retirement accumulations is deductible from the gross estate (for purposes of the first tier tax).

State inheritance tax laws covering distributions from qualified pension and profit-sharing plans vary widely. In Pennsylvania, for example, death benefits are excludible from inheritance taxes as long as such amounts are not available to pay death taxes and other estate expenses; i.e., payments will be state death tax free if payable to a named beneficiary other than the decedent-employee's estate. On the other hand, New Jersey, a neighboring state, taxes retirement plan death benefits payable to any beneficiary other than the deceased employee's spouse, regardless of the manner in which benefits are paid.

Figure 22.2

SIMPLIFIED EXCESS RETIREMENT ACCUMULATIONS WORKSHEET
(Using Reg. Sec. 20.2031-7, Table A)*
©1988, The American College

Step 1. State total accumulation payable. — $3,000,000

Step 2. State annual protected amount ($150,000 or $112,000 indexed). — $ 150,000

Step 3. State assumed age at death. — 55

Step 4. Find discount factor from Reg. Sec. 20.2031-7—Table A. — $ 8.0046

Step 5. Multiply step 2 by step 4 to arrive at total protected amount. — $1,200,690

Step 6. Subtract protected amount (step 5) from step 1 to find amount subject to tax (assumes no grandfathering). — $ 1,799,310

Step 7. Multiply step 6 by .15 to find excess accumulations tax. — $ 269,897

*See pages 390-391

Figure 22.3

PENSION BENEFITS TABLE
1988*

Age	Annuity Factor	$150,000	$117,529	Age	Annuity Factor	$150,000	$117,529
41	9.1030	1,365,450	1,069,867	71	5.8914	883,710	692,410
42	9.0457	1,356,855	1,063,132	72	5.7261	858,915	672,983
43	8.9855	1,347,825	1,056,057	73	5.5571	833,565	653,120
44	8.9221	1,338,315	1,048,606	74	5.3862	807,930	633,035
45	8.8558	1,328,370	1,040,813	75	5.2149	782,235	612,902
46	8.7863	1,317,945	1,032,645	76	5.0441	756,615	592,828
47	8.7137	1,307,055	1,024,113	77	4.8742	731,130	572,860
48	8.6374	1,295,610	1,015,145	78	4.7049	705,735	552,962
49	8.5578	1,283,670	1,005,790	79	4.5357	680,355	533,076
50	8.4743	1,271,145	995,976	80	4.3659	654,885	513,120
51	8.3874	1,258,110	985,763	81	4.1967	629,505	493,234
52	8.2969	1,244,535	975,126	82	4.0295	604,425	473,583
53	8.2028	1,230,420	964,067	83	3.8642	579,630	454,156
54	8.1054	1,215,810	952,620	84	3.6998	554,970	434,834
55	8.0046	1,200,690	940,773	85	3.5359	530,385	415,571
56	7.9006	1,185,090	928,550	86	3.3764	506,460	396,825
57	7.7931	1,168,965	915,915	87	3.2262	483,930	379,172
58	7.6822	1,152,330	902,881	88	3.0859	462,885	362,683
59	7.5675	1,135,125	889,401	89	2.9526	442,890	347,016
60	7.4491	1,117,365	875,485	90	2.8221	423,315	331,679
61	7.3267	1,099,005	861,100	91	2.6955	404,325	316,799
62	7.2002	1,080,030	846,232	92	2.5771	386,565	302,884
63	7.0696	1,060,440	830,883	93	2.4692	370,380	290,203
64	6.9352	1,040,280	815,087	94	2.3728	355,920	278,873
65	6.7970	1,019,550	798,845	95	2.2887	343,305	268,989
66	6.6551	998,265	782,167	96	2.2181	332,715	260,691
67	6.5098	976,470	765,090	97	2.1550	323,250	253,275
68	6.3610	954,150	747,602	98	2.1000	315,000	246,811
69	6.2086	931,290	729,691	99	2.0485	307,275	240,758
70	6.0522	907,830	711,309				

*See pages 390-391.

IMPLICATIONS AND ISSUES IN COMMUNITY PROPERTY STATES

Many community property implications and issues have been discussed in previous chapters. Some additional tax implications should also be mentioned.

The special 5-year averaging method for the ordinary income portion of a lump-sum distribution can cause a significant reduction in taxes which would otherwise be payable. It would appear to be even more beneficial to treat a lump-sum distribution to a married spouse as two equal portions to each spouse (assuming the benefits are community property). The combined taxes on two $25,000 distributions, using the 5-year averaging method, would be significantly less than the tax on a single $50,000 distribution. To avoid this result, ERISA provided that community property laws were to be disregarded when using the 5-year averaging method. The tax will be computed as if only the employee spouse were entitled to the benefit. The spouses can choose to treat the $50,000 distribution (assuming it is community property) as being received in equal portions by each for tax purposes, but they cannot elect the 5-year averaging method.

QUESTIONS AND ANSWERS

Question — Who is a fiduciary and what are the fiduciary responsibility rules established by ERISA (also known as the Pension Reform Act of 1974)?

Answer — A fiduciary is a person who (a) exercises any discretionary authority or discretionary control respecting management of the plan or exercises any authority or control respecting management or disposition of assets; (b) renders investment advice for a fee or other compensation, direct or indirect, with respect to any monies or other property of the plan, or has any authority or responsibility to do so; or (c) has any discretionary authority or discretionary responsibility in the administration of the plan. The term fiduciary also includes persons named by a fiduciary to carry out fiduciary responsibilities (other than trustee responsibilities) under the plan. The Pension Reform Act established rules governing the conduct of fiduciaries and other persons dealing with the plan. The Labor Department administers certain provisions which pertain to rules and remedies similar to those under traditional trust law governing the conduct of fiduciaries.

Specifically, these fiduciary responsibility rules relate to the structure of plan administration, provide general standards of conduct for fiduciaries, and make certain transactions "prohibited transactions" in which plan fiduciaries may not engage. Other provisions which are enforced by the Treasury Department impose an excise tax on certain persons who violate the prohibited transaction rules.

Basically, the Act requires each fiduciary of a plan to act with the care, skill, prudence, and diligence under the circumstances then prevailing that a prudent man acting in a like capacity and familiar with such matters would use in conducting an enterprise of like character and with like aims.

Furthermore, the Act requires that a qualified retirement plan be for the exclusive benefit of the plan's employees and their beneficiaries.[45] Under the "exclusive benefit" umbrella,

(1) the cost of plan assets must not exceed fair market value at the time of purchase;

(2) assets should bring a fair return commensurate with the prevailing rate;

(3) the plan should maintain sufficient liquidity to permit distributions; and

(4) the safeguards and diversity that would be adhered to by a prudent investor must be present.

Question — How does plan termination insurance work?

Answer — The Pension Reform Act established, within the Department of Labor, a public corporation named the Pension Benefit Guaranty Corporation (PBGC). The PBGC is a federal insurance company which provides mandatory plan termination insurance to protect the benefit rights of workers whose defined benefit pension plans go out of existence. As one of its main duties, the corporation administers plan termination insurance for defined benefit pension plans.

The amount insured is limited to the actuarial value of a benefit as a straight life annuity, payable monthly beginning at age 65, equal to the lesser of: (1) one-twelfth of the average compensation paid the participant during the consecutive five year period of his plan participation during which his compensation was highest; or (2) $750 monthly (adjusted to reflect changes in the social security contribution and wage base).

Prior to OBRA '87, premiums for PBGC coverage were $8.50 per participant.[46] OBRA '87 increases the premium, for plan years beginning after December 31, 1987, to the sum of $16.00 plus a new "additional premium." The "additional premium" is calculated by dividing an amount based on the plan's unfunded vested benefits as of the end of the preceding plan year by the number of plan participants at that time. The additional premium will equal $6 per thousand (or fraction thereof) of the plan's unfunded vested benefits as of the end of the preceding plan year. Generally, the aggregate increase in the premium for a participant due to the additional premium won't exceed $34.00.

Question — Can a pension plan make a loan to a participant or plan beneficiary?

Answer — Yes, if the loan is made in accordance with specific provisions in the plan governing such loans, a reasonable charge is made for the use of plan assets, and the loan is adequately secured. Loans must be available to all participants on a reasonably equivalent basis.[47]

After August 13, 1982, TEFRA put limits on tax-free participant borrowing from qualified plans, from tax sheltered annuities, and from plans (qualified and nonqualified) of federal, state, and local governments and their agencies and instrumentalities. TRA '86 did not remove loans to owner employees from the list of prohibited transactions in Code section 4975 and in ERISA.

Under the new rules certain loan transactions are treated as distributions. Loan transactions include: (1) the direct or indirect receipt of a loan, and (2) the assignment (or agreement to assign) or the pledging (or agreement to pledge) of any portion of an employee's interest in a plan.

Two basic rules and two exceptions now apply. The basic rules first:

1. *Loans which are to be repaid within five years.* These loans are taxed as distributions only to the extent that the amount of the loan (together with any other outstanding loans the employee has made from plans with the same employer) exceeds the lesser of (a) $50,000 reduced by the highest outstanding loan balance during the prior 12 months[48], or (b) half of the employee's vested benefits under the employer plans from which he has borrowed (or $10,000, if greater).

Tools and Techniques

2. *Loans which do not have to be repaid within five years.* These loans are fully taxable as distributions. Whether or not a loan must be repaid within five years is ascertained as of the date the loan is made.

Some loans of five years or less may be subsequently extended. The loan balance at the time of the extension is considered a distribution at that time.

If repayment under a "five-year-or-less" loan is not made (so at the end of five years the participant still owes the plan money), any remaining amounts due are considered plan distributions.

"More-than-five-year" loans are not converted to "five-year-or-less" loans or in any other way favorably treated merely because they are repaid in five years or less (regardless of the reason for the early repayments).

Exception 1: *Housing loans.* A loan of more than five years is not treated as a distribution to the extent that it is used by the plan participant to purchase, construct, or substantially rehabilitate a home, apartment, condominium, or mobile home (not used on a transient basis). This exception presumes the dwelling is used (or will be used within a reasonable period of time) as the participant's (or a member of the participant's family) principal residence. TRA '86 limited "more-than-five-year loans" made after December 31, 1986, to those made for the purchase of the participant's principal residence.[49]

Exception 2: *Certain mortgage loans.* Where plan trustees invest a specific percentage or amount of plan assets in residential mortgages or in other types of mortgage investments, such investments are not considered loans as long as the amount lent does not exceed the fair market value of the property the loan was used to purchase. Loans to officers, directors, or owners (or their beneficiaries) are not protected under this exception.

Question — What are the reporting and disclosure requirements of the Act?

Answer — In general, every plan which is not specifically exempted must file certain reports each year. The annual report for plans with 100 or more participants must include an audited financial statement. Annual Reports of defined benefit plans must contain a certified actuarial report. If the plan terminates, additional special reports are required.

The number of participants covered by a plan has no effect on the reporting and disclosure requirements—an annual report must be filed regardless of how many or how few participants are covered. However, where a plan contains less than 100 participants, a simplified report may be authorized.

Furthermore, certain information must be provided to plan participants and beneficiaries. They must be given a summary of the plan written in a manner understand-able by the average participant or beneficiary (Summary Plan Description). Furthermore, beneficiaries and participants can request a status report once a year showing total benefits accrued and nonforfeitable pension benefit rights. Employees who have terminated employment during the plan year must also be given a statement of their deferred vested rights in the plan. Many of these documents become public information and can be inspected.[50]

Question — What is a target benefit pension plan?

Answer — It is a retirement plan under which the required contribution is initially based upon an assumed retirement benefit for each participant, but under which the actual retirement benefit received is based upon the market value of the assets in the individual participant's account at the time of retirement.

Question — What limitations are imposed on a qualified retirement plan regarding the purchase of ordinary life insurance?

Answer — In a profit-sharing plan less than 50 percent of the aggregate employer contributions and forfeitures allocated to each participant's account can be used to purchase ordinary life insurance. If insurance may be purchased only with funds that have been accumulated in the plan for two or more years, the 50 percent rule does not apply. In addition to this requirement, a profit-sharing plan must require the trustee at or before retirement either (a) to convert the policies into cash or (b) to distribute the policies to the employee. A money-purchase plan has the same "less than 50 percent" rule with regard to the purchase of ordinary life insurance.

Life insurance is a permissible purchase in a defined benefit pension plan if it meets either of two tests. The first test is essentially the same as the money-purchase plan test. The alternative test is the "100 to 1" test whereby the insurance is permissible if the insurance amount does not exceed 100 times the expected monthly retirement benefit. For example, if the projected monthly benefit is $1,000, the life insurance can't exceed $100,000.

Question — What is a thrift and savings plan?

Answer — The major characteristic of a thrift and savings plan is that employee-participants must contribute some percentage of compensation to the plan. The employer matches contributions of employees according to some formula. For example, an employer may match each dollar of employee contribution with more or less than $1 of employer contribution. A thrift and savings plan can be tax qualified or can be informal.

A tax qualified thrift and savings plan will result in an employer deduction for contributions to the plan. Employees will not be currently taxed on employer contributions. Both employer and employee contributions will grow tax-free within the plan. When distributions from a qualified thrift and savings plan are made, they are subject to the same rules applicable to other qualified retirement plans. Typically, a thrift and savings plan will require employees to contribute a percentage of compensation in order to participate. It is important when incorporating thrift and savings features in a plan that such required contributions meet the special nondiscrimination test provided under TRA '86.[51] All contributions are counted for purposes of the annual additions limitation.

Contributions made by an employee to a thrift plan which are required as a condition of plan participation or as a condition of obtaining benefits from the employer under the plan will not qualify as qualified voluntary employee contributions.

Question — Can a qualified pension or profit-sharing plan provide for voluntary deductible employee contributions?

Answer — No. Before TRA '86, participating employees could voluntarily contribute on a nondeductible basis up to 10 percent of compensation (subject to ERISA limits on annual additions). Anyone who had earned income, regardless of whether he was an active participant in a qualified plan, could establish an IRA. A voluntary deductible contribution of up to $2,000 could have been made to an employer's plan (if the plan so provided), to an IRA, or as a combination split in any proportion between the two. TRA '86 no longer permits voluntary deductible employee contributions to a qualified plan (effective for plan years beginning after December 31, 1986).[52]

Voluntary nondeductible employee contributions to qualified pension, profit sharing, or stock bonus plans continue to be allowed, providing they meet the special nondiscrimination test provided by TRA '86.[53] Also, 100% of employee contributions, whether voluntary or mandatory, will be included in the annual addition for purposes of the dollar limitation. Accordingly, both employer and employee contributions to a defined contribution plan count toward the $30,000/25% limitation.[54]

Question — What are the advantages of life insurance in a qualified retirement plan?

Answer — There are a number of advantages. These include (1) protection against the premature death of a participant, (2) securing the right to use guaranteed annuity rates at a future retirement date, (3) assurance that insurance can be purchased at original age rates when the participant retires or terminates employment, and (4) in a profit-sharing plan providing key man insurance on the lives of corporate officers or valuable employees for the benefit of the trust and its participants.

Question — Can a qualified pension or profit-sharing plan provide any protection from creditors?

Answer — Yes. ERISA provides that a pension, profit-sharing, or HR-10 plan will not be qualified unless it provides that benefits provided under the plan may not be assigned or alienated, voluntarily or involuntarily. An exception to this rule exists for assignments used to secure plan loans to a participant and voluntary and revocable assignments which do not exceed 10 percent of any benefit payment to a participant, unless the assignment is made for purposes of defraying plan administrative costs.

It is important to note, however, that the anti-alienation provision of ERISA has not prevented some courts from including an owner-employee's interest in plan assets in his bankrupt estate under state law.[55] On the other hand, some states have statutes expressly providing that qualified plan benefits are not subject to attachment, execution or garnishment by creditors and these statutes may provide greater protection than ERISA. California, for example, extends an exemption from attachment, execution and garnishment in bankruptcy proceedings to corporate qualified pension plans.

The Retirement Equity Act of 1984 (REACT) created an additional exception to the ERISA prohibition on assignments and alienation of plan benefits.

The creation, assignment, or recognition of a right to any benefit payable from a plan under a "qualified domestic relations order" (QDRO) is not treated as a prohibited assignment or alienation under ERISA or the Internal Revenue Code, thus allowing enforcement of state QDROs. All qualified retirement plans are now required to provide for the payment of benefits in accordance with the terms of any QDRO.

The term "domestic relations order" means a judgment, decree, or order (including approval of a property settlement agreement) which relates to the provision of child support, alimony payments, or marital property rights to a spouse, former spouse, child or other dependent of a participant, and is made pursuant to state domestic relations law. To be qualified, a domestic relations order must (1) create or recognize the existence of an alternate payee's right to receive all or a portion of the benefits payable with respect to a participant under a plan; (2) clearly specify certain facts (e.g., name and address of participant and alternate payee, amount of benefits to be paid and the number of payments); and (3) not alter the amount or form of benefits under a plan. The term "alternate payee" means any spouse, former spouse, child or other dependent of a participant who is recognized by a domestic relations order as having a right to receive all, or a portion of, a participant's benefits under a plan.

A QDRO can require benefits to be paid to an alternate payee at the participant's earliest retirement age under the plan without regard to whether the participant has separated from service or retired. The REACT exception to the ERISA anti-alienation and assignment provisions went into effect on January 1, 1985.

Question — When does an employee become subject to tax on benefits accruing in a qualified plan?

Answer — An employee or beneficiary of a qualified plan will not be taxed until benefits are received from the plan. For example, even though a participant in a profit-sharing plan has the unrestricted right to make withdrawals of employer or deductible employee contributions, or the earnings on nondeductible employee contributions, there will be no current tax based on constructive receipt. This increases the appeal of making voluntary contributions to qualified plans even where the full amount of such contributions are not tax deductible.

Question — Are there any restrictions on pension or profit sharing plan investments in "collectibles"?

Answer — Yes. The Economic Recovery Tax Act of 1981 added an Internal Revenue Code Subsection which treats investments in "collectibles" after December 31, 1981, by an individually directed account under a qualified plan as a current taxable distribution. Collectibles are defined as (1) art, (2) rugs or antiques, (3) metals or gems, (4) stamps or coins, other than U.S. minted gold and silver coins acquired after 1986, (5) alcoholic beverages, or (6) any other tangible personal property designated as a "collectible" by the Secretary of the Treasury.[56]

Question — Is a qualified plan required to provide a participant's surviving spouse survivor benefits?

Answer — Yes. Under prior law, Internal Revenue Code section 401(a)(11) required a qualified plan that provided for the payment of benefits as a life annuity (either as the normal or alternative form of benefit) to offer a qualified joint and survivor payment option. If a plan's normal form of benefit was a life annuity, then the plan had to automatically provide a qualified joint and survivor annuity unless an election out was made by the participant. A plan not offering a life annuity as a normal form of benefit (e.g., a lump sum as the normal form of benefit) could require a participant to make an affirmative election to receive a qualified joint and survivor annuity.

Under changes made by the Retirement Equity Act of 1984 (REACT), a participant's surviving spouse must be provided "automatic survivor benefits".[57] Defined benefit plans and defined contribution plans are now required to provide automatic survivor benefits (1) in the form of a "qualified joint and survivor annuity", to a vested participant who receives a plan distribution for reasons other than the participant's death (i.e., termination of employment, retirement or disability); and (2) in the form of a "qualified pre-retirement survivor annuity" to

a vested participant who dies before reaching the "annuity starting date" under the plan and who has a surviving spouse.

For automatic survivor coverage purposes, a vested participant means a participant who has a nonforfeitable right to any portion of the accrued benefit or account balance derived from employer contributions, whether or not the participant is still employed by the employer. The term "annuity starting date" means the first day of the first period for which an amount is payable as an annuity (or, in the case of a non-annuity benefit, the first day on which all events have occurred entitling the participant to the benefit).

The automatic survivor coverage rules do not apply to a profit sharing or stock bonus plan if (a) the plan provides that the participant's vested account balance will be paid to his or her surviving spouse (or to a designated beneficiary if there is no surviving spouse or if the surviving spouse gives the proper consent); (b) the participant does not elect payment of benefits in the form of a life annuity; and (c) with respect to the participant, the plan is not a transferee of a plan required to provide automatic survivor benefits.

A "qualified joint and survivor annuity" is an annuity for the life of the participant with a survivor annuity for the life of the spouse that is not less than 50 percent (and not greater than 100 percent) of the amount that is payable during the joint lives of the participant and spouse, and that is the actuarial equivalent of a single life annuity for the life of the participant.

A "qualified pre-retirement survivor annuity" is an annuity for the life of the surviving spouse of the participant with payments to the surviving spouse which are not less than the payments that would have been made under the qualified joint and survivor annuity (or the actuarial equivalent thereof), under the rules set forth in IRC section 417(c).

A qualified joint and survivor annuity and a qualified pre-retirement survivor annuity need not be provided by a plan unless the participant and the surviving spouse have been married throughout the one-year period ending on the earlier of the participant's retirement, disability or the date of the participant's death.

A plan participant may elect not to receive the qualified joint and survivor annuity and/or the qualified pre-retirement survivor annuity at any time during an applicable election period and to receive benefits in another form offered under the plan. The participant is permitted to revoke any such election during the applicable election period. The applicable election period, in the case of a qualified joint and survivor annuity, is the 90 day period ending on the annuity starting date. The applicable election, in the case of a qualified pre-retirement survivor annuity, is a period beginning on the first day of the plan year in which the participant attains age 35 and ending on the date of the participant's death. If the participant separates from service, the applicable election period begins not later than the date of separation.

An election by the participant not to take survivor coverage is effective only if the participant's spouse consents in writing, the consent is witnessed by a plan representative or a notary public, and the spouse's consent acknowledges the effect of the election. Spousal consent is not required if it is established (to the satisfaction of a plan representative) that there is no spouse or that the spouse cannot be located.

The qualified joint and survivor annuity requirements are applicable to all participants under qualified plans who have had one hour or more of service on or after August 23, 1984, and have not begun to receive distributions from the plan prior to January 1, 1985. The qualified pre-retirement survivor annuity provision is applicable to all participants who have had one hour or more of service on or after August 23, 1984, and have not yet reached retirement age under the plan.

Question — Will a plan participant on a one-year leave of absence from work due to a maternity/paternity reason incur a "break-in-service" and therefore cease to participate in the plan?

Answer — No. The Retirement Equity Act of 1984 amended IRC sections 410(a)(5)(E) and 411(a)(6)(E) to provide that an employee who is on a leave of absence for maternity/paternity reasons will not incur a one-year break-in-service for purposes of participation or vesting in the year in which a break would otherwise occur. Maternity/paternity reasons include pregnancy, childbirth, adoption or child caring immediately after childbirth or adoption.

Question — Are there any new taxes to be aware of?

Answer — Generally, there were seven new taxes added to the retirement plan area. Some of these taxes have been discussed elsewhere in this book and will only be referenced here. The new taxes are as follows:

1. A 10% nondeductible excise tax is imposed on the amount of any "employer reversion" from a qualified plan. The tax is increased to 15% for reversions occurring after October 21, 1988.[58] Liability for this tax rests on the employer. An "employer reversion" is the amount of cash and the fair market value of other property received (directly or indirectly) by an employer from a qualified plan. Mistaken excess payments are excluded. For an exception to this reversion tax for the contribution of such reversion to an employee stock ownership plan, see the Question and Answer section of chapter 7, on Employee Stock Ownership Plans.

2. In general, a 10% tax is imposed on the gross amount of early withdrawals (prior to age 59½, death, or disability). There are some exceptions to this tax but it generally applies to the withdrawals of any participant from any "qualified retirement plan."[59] The tax is imposed on the recipient of the distribution regardless of employee or owner status. For this purpose, "qualified retirement plans" include corporate plans and annuities (IRC §§401(a) and 403(a)), KEOGHs, IRAs, and SEPs (IRC §408), and tax-sheltered annuities (IRC §403(b)).

3. There is a 50% nondeductible excise tax on the failure to make a minimum required distribution from the plan. The tax is equal to 50% of the amount by which the minimum required distribution exceeds the actual amount distributed during the taxable year. The tax is imposed on the payee and applies to payments received after 1988. A "waiver" is allowed for "reasonable error" if steps are being taken to pay out the balance due.[60]

4. There is a graduated additional income tax which applies in cases where there is an underpayment of tax due to an overstatement of pension liabilities. The graduated rates of tax range from 10% to 30% depending upon the severity of the overstatement of the pension liability. This tax does not apply if the underpayment for the taxable year due to liability overstatement is less than 150% of the correct valuation. The IRS does maintain discretion to waive the application of this tax under appropriate circumstances.[61]

5. There is a 50% excise tax on prohibited allocations of employer securities acquired in a transaction involving the tax-deferred sale to an ESOP or the purchase of stock from an estate by an ESOP to create an estate tax deduction under IRC §2057. See the Question and Answer section of chapter 7 on Employee Stock Ownership Plans for further details on this tax.[62]

6. There is a 15% tax on the amount of any "excess distributions" made to any individual during any calendar year. This tax applies to distributions made after December 31, 1986. For further explanation of this tax, see Income Tax Implications, above.[63]

7. There is a 15% tax with regard to the estates of decedent dying after December 31, 1986. This new tax is equal to 15% of the decedent's "excess retirement accumulations," and is added to the estate tax. For further explanation of this tax, see Estate Tax Implications, above.[64]

Question — Where a beneficiary designation for a pension plan names the surviving spouse as primary beneficiary, but with an alternate gift to a Family Trust in the event of the death of the surviving spouse before the passage of a reasonable time following the participant's death (e.g., 90 days), or in the event of a disclaimer by the surviving spouse, are there any concerns over restrictions created by the Retirement Equity Act (REA)?

Tools and Techniques

Answer — REA generally provides that all benefits from pension and profit sharing plans, with some exceptions, must be in the form of annuities. If the participant has died, then the general provision under REA is that there be an annuity for the lifetime of the survivor as to at least one-half of the property. Whether the transfer can be made to a trust in lieu of the surviving spouse is something being questioned by a number of practitioners today. Indeed, the REA Book says that the requirements of the Act cannot be met by naming an irrevocable trust as sole beneficiary even though the surviving spouse is the sole beneficiary of the trust and the benefits payable under the trust meet the survivor annuity benefit requirements of the Act.[65]

If the surviving spouse dies, then it may be that REA no longer applies, and any normal transfer can be made and property can go to a trust outright as opposed to being in an annuity form.

On the other hand, the Act seems to lay out clearly the rule that any transfer outside the normal REA rules must be done only on the basis of a written exception being made by the participant and a written waiver by the surviving spouse of any annuity rights. There have been suggestions that payments by pension plans administrators to trusts without such a formal written request and written waiver might cause the trust to be disqualified.

This is an area of the law that is moving very fast and with regard to which a pension law expert should be consulted on beneficiary designations involving large amounts.

The beneficiary designation form reproduced at Figure 22.4 (3 pages) at the end of this chapter is used by Ralph Miller in his California practice and contains language designed to overcome the problems inherent in the law as it presently reads.

ASRS, Sec. 59.

Footnote References

Profit-Sharing/Pension Plan

1. Reg. §1.401-1(b)(2); Rev. Rul. 69-421, Part 2(h), 1969-2 C.B. 59.
2. Regs. §§1.401(a), 1.401-1(b).
3. IRC Section 410(a)(1).
4. IRC Section 410(a)(1)(B), as amended by TRA '86, Section 1113(c).
5. IRC Section 410(a)(2), prior to amendment by OBRA '86, Section 9203(a).
6. IRC Section 410(b)(1)(A), as amended by TRA '86, Section 1112(a).
7. IRC Section 410(b)(1)(B), as amended by TRA '86, Section 1112(a).
8. IRC Section 410(b), as amended by TRA '86, Section 1112(a); IRC Section 401(a)(26).
9. IRC Section 410(a)(1)(A), 410(a)(3)(A).

10. IRC Section 410(b)(3)(A).
11. IRC Section 411(a)(1).
12. IRC Section 411(a)(2).
13. IRC Section 411(a)(2), as amended by TRA '86, Section 1113(a).
14. IRC Section 415(c)(1), as amended by TRA '86, Section 1106(a). IRC Section 415(d)(1), as amended by TRA '86, Section 1106(g)(1).
15. IRC Section 404(a)(3)(A), as amended by TRA '86, Section 1131(a).
16. IRC Section 415(b)(2), as amended by TRA '86, Section 1106(b).
17. IRC Section 415(b)(5), as amended by TRA '86, Section 1106(b)(5).
18. IRC Section 415(b)(4).
19. Employee Retirement Income Security Act of 1974 (ERISA) Section 2004(d)(2).
20. See footnote 16.
21. IRC Section 415(e).
22. IRC Section 404(a)(1).
23. IRC Section 404(a)(3).
24. See footnote 15.
25. IRC Section 404(a)(7), as amended by TRA '86, Section 1131(b).
26. IRC Section 219(e), as amended by TRA '86, Section 1101(b).
27. Reg. §1.401-7.
28. Reg. §1.401-4(a)(1)(iii).
29. IRC Section 401(a)(8), as amended by TRA '86, Section 1119(a).
30. Reg. §1.401-3(e); Rev. Rul. 71-446, 1971-2 C.B. 187 (as modified by Rev. Rul. 72-276, 1972-1 C.B. 111); IRC Section 401(l), as amended by TRA '86, Section 1111(a); Social Security Act, Section 230.
31. IRC Section 416.
32. IRC Sections 404(a)(1), 404(a)(3).
33. IRC Section 501(a).
34. IRC Section 402(e)(1), as amended by TRA '86, Section 1122(a).
35. Reg. §1.72-16(b).
36. Reg. §1.402(a)-1(a)(1)(i); IRC Section 402(a)(1) as amended by ERTA Section 314(c); Reg. §1.401-1(b)(1); Rev. Prop. Reg. §1.401(a)(9)-1; Rul. 72-241, 72-1 C.B. 108.
37. IRC Section 401(a)(9)(A); Prop. Reg. §1.401(a)(9)-1.
38. IRC Section 72(d), as amended by TRA '86, Section 1122(c).
39. IRC Section 72(t).
40. IRC Section 4980A, as amended by TRA '86, Section 1133(a).
41. IRC Section 4980A(c)(5), as amended by TRA '86, Section 1133(a).
42. IRC Section 2039(f), prior to repeal by TRA '84.
43. TIR 1403.
44. IRC Section 2039, as amended by TRA '84.
45. ERISA Section 404.
46. ERISA Sections 4001-4004, 4022(b).
47. ERISA Section 408(b)(1).
48. IRC Section 72(p)(2)(A), as amended by TRA '86, Section 1134(a).
49. IRC Section 72(p)(2)(B), as amended by TRA '86, Section 1134(d).
50. ERISA Section 101-105.
51. IRC Section 401(m). See also Rev. Rul. 80-307, 1980-2 C.B. 136.
52. IRC Section 219(e), as amended by TRA '86, Section 1101(b).
53. IRC Section 401(m).

54. IRC Section 415(c)(2)(B).

55. *In re Goff*, 706 F.2d 574 (5th Cir. 1983); *In re Crenshaw*, 51 BR 554 (Bankr. N.D. Ala. 1985); *In re Daniel*, 771 F.2d 1352 (9th Cir. 1985); *Brooks v. Interfirst Bank, Fort Worth*, 884 F.2d 258 (5th Cir. 1988), rev'g *In re Brooks*, 60 BR 155 (Bankr. N.D. Tex. 1986).

56. IRC Section 408(m).

57. IRC Section 401(a)(11), as amended by the Retirement Equity Act of 1984. IRC Section 417, as added by the Retirement Equity Act of 1984.

58. IRC Section 4980, as amended by the Technical and Miscellaneous Revenue Act of 1988, Section 6069.

59. IRC Section 72(t)(1).

60. IRC Section 4974.

61. IRC Section 6659A.

62. IRC Section 4979A.

63. IRC Section 4981A.

64. IRC Section 4981A(d).

65. Wilf, et al., *The REA Book* (REA Publishing Company: Philadelphia, 1987), Qs I.54 and I.55. Q. I.67 also addresses the question of the surviving spouse's disclaimer of annuity benefits required under REA, pointing out that such a disclaimer may be a prohibited assignment or alienation, in which event payment pursuant to the disclaimer could subject the plan administrator to fiduciary liability and could endanger the qualified status of the plan.

Tools and Techniques

Figure 22.4

DESIGNATION OF BENEFICIARY FOR

_____

_____

_____   _____

Employee's Name   Employee's Soc. Security No.

1. I hereby designate the following, in the order of priority indicated, as the beneficiary to whom (or to which) any such benefit shall be distributed at the death of the participant:

     A. To _____, my spouse, or if my spouse is not then living, or if my spouse disclaims such benefit (as provided in Paragraph 6 below), then in accordance with Paragraph B below.

     B. To the Trustees of the _____, dated _____, hereinafter called the "Family Trust", to be held, managed, administered and distributed according to the terms and provisions thereof.

2. If at the time of death, none of the above beneficiaries survive me or are in existence, then this Plan and Trust share shall be distributed as then provided in the Plan and Trust Agreement.

3. I reserve the right to revoke or change the designation or any of them shown above, but such revocation or change shall be in writing directed to the Committee, and no such revocation or change shall be effective unless and until received by the Committee.

4. Rights of the designated beneficiaries shall be subject to the terms and conditions of the Plan and Trust Agreement and all rules and regulations formulated thereunder.

5. Payment of any credits or funds in the Trust Account to the beneficiary or beneficiaries designated herein shall be a full and complete release and discharge of the Trustee, the Committee and the Employer to the extent of such payment.

6. Disclaimer may be by any method which is effective under the laws of the State of California or by written transfer of the right to receive the death benefit, provided that such transfer meets the requirements of Section 2518(c)(3) of the Internal Revenue Code as is from time to time amended.

7. Any voluntary contribution account benefits shall be distributed according to the terms of this direction and shall be treated as completely separate benefits for the purposes of disclaimer.

8. This beneficiary designation shall not be construed in any way as a revocation of any election I have made pursuant to Section 242(b)(2) of the Internal Revenue Code.

Dated _____

                                           _____

                                           Participant

[See Spousal Consent Over]

Figure 22.4 Cont'd.

<u>TO BE EXECUTED IN THE PRESENCE OF A NOTARY PUBLIC</u>

SPOUSE'S CONSENT TO BENEFICIARY DESIGNATION

CAVEAT: THIS BENEFICIARY DESIGNATION MAY NO LONGER BE VALID ONCE THE PARTIC-
IPANT HAS REACHED HIS OR HER "ANNUITY STARTING DATE" as defined in Section 417 of
the Internal Revenue Code if the participant elects a distribution in a form other
than a qualified joint and survivor annuity unless the participant's spouse at
that time properly completes the consent form shown on page 3 hereto.

I, the spouse of the above-named participant, hereby consent to the above
Beneficiary Designation, which names an individual(s) or entity other than myself
as primary beneficiary of the benefits payable to the participant in the event of
his or her death under the Plan. I hereby waive any rights I may have under federal or state law to receive benefits under the Plan in the form of a qualified
pre-retirement survivor annuity and acknowledge that I am not to be the direct
recipient of any benefits the Plan provides to a participant's "primary beneficiary" (a spouse may be the indirect beneficiary of such benefits in certain circumstances -- such as designation of a family trust as primary beneficiary). I further acknowledge that I am familiar with the financial and legal consequences of
my consent to my spouse's election to waive a qualified pre-retirement survivor
annuity form of benefit.

By my signature below, I am also consenting to any change by my spouse in
designation of beneficiary following the date of this consent.

Dated:_____   _____
                                             Spouse's Signature

            THE SPOUSE'S SIGNATURE MUST BE WITNESSED BY A NOTARY PUBLIC!

STATE OF CALIFORNIA   )
                         : ss.
COUNTY OF SAN DIEGO   )

On this _____ day of _____, 19 _____, before me, a Notary
Public in and for said County and State, personally appeared _____,
personally known to me or proved to me on the basis of satisfactory evidence to be
the person described in and whose name is subscribed to the foregoing instrument,
and executed such instrument before me.

WITNESS my hand and official seal.

                              _____
                                       Notary Public

The Plan Committee hereby accepts the foregoing beneficiary designation.

Dated _____

                         By _____

Figure 22.4 Cont'd.

SPOUSE'S CONSENT TO BENEFICIARY DESIGNATION

(REQUIRED TO BE COMPLETED IN THE NINETY (90) DAY PERIOD PRIOR TO EITHER (1) THE BEGINNING OF RECEIPT OF ANNUITY PAYMENTS; OR (2) IN THE CASE OF NON-ANNUITY BENEFITS, THE FIRST DAY ON WHICH ALL EVENTS HAVE OCCURRED WHICH ENTITLE THE PARTICIPANT TO RECEIVE BENEFITS)

I, the spouse of the above named participant, hereby consent to the above Beneficiary Designation, which names an individual(s) or entity other than myself as primary beneficiary of the benefits payable to the participant in the event of his or her death following his or her election to waive the Qualified Joint and Survivor Annuity form of distribution under the Plan.

I understand that by consenting to my spouse's election to receive benefits in a form other than a Qualified Joint and Survivor Annuity, I am waiving my right to receive a survivor annuity under the Plan and am hereby consent to payment of any death benefits provided by the Plan to the beneficiary designated above by my spouse. I further represent that I have received as much financial information from the Plan and my spouse as I deemed necessary to consent to my spouse's designation of such beneficiary.

By my signature below, I am also consenting to any change by my spouse in designation of beneficiary following the date of this consent.

Dated _____   Name: _____

Address: _____

_____

_____

THE SPOUSE'S SIGNATURE MUST BE WITNESSED BY A NOTARY PUBLIC!

STATE OF CALIFORNIA   )
                         : ss.
COUNTY OF SAN DIEGO   )

On this _____ day of _____, 19 _____, before me, a Notary Public in and for said County and State, personally appeared _____, personally known to me or proved to me on the basis of satisfactory evidence to be the person described in and whose name is subscribed to the foregoing instrument, and executed such instrument before me.

WITNESS my hand and official seal.

_____
Notary Public

[1150]

Chapter 23

RECAPITALIZATION

WHAT IS IT?

A recapitalization in its simplest terms is a reshuffling of the capital structure of a corporation within the corporation's existing framework.[1] A recapitalization involves exchanges of stock or securities for stock or securities. The corporation does not receive any property other than the stock or the securities (or both) that are surrendered as part of the exchange.

Recapitalizations can be accomplished without any exchange. For example, a recapitalization can occur when the Articles of Incorporation of a corporation are amended to change certain features of stock then outstanding or authorized but unissued, such as changing the redemption price for the shares of stock, changing the dividend preference provisions, or changing voting provisions.

WHEN IS THE USE OF SUCH A DEVICE INDICATED?

The following list gives some of the many reasons for considering recapitalizing a corporation.

A recapitalization may be used to:[2]

1. increase the equity interests of younger shareholders;

2. shift control from a majority shareholder to other shareholders;

3. provide more active shareholders with greater voting rights;

4. transfer control to one member of a family while at the same time providing a source of income to another member;

5. effect a gradual shift of control from older to younger shareholders while preserving the older shareholders' interests;

6. provide a key employee with a voice in management through the ownership of voting stock;

7. enable key employees to purchase an equity interest in the corporation at an affordable price;

8. provide for the eventual and gradual withdrawal of a principal shareholder from active management;

9. provide motivation and incentive to younger key employees;

10. provide funding for an employee stock ownership plan (ESOP);

11. increase an existing shareholder's management responsibility;

12. provide a source of income to a shareholder to replace salary upon either retirement or less active role in management;

13. facilitate a redemption or cross-purchase agreement at a lesser price (particularly useful where a shareholder is uninsurable or highly rated and it is impossible or difficult to shift control through a purchase of stock at its current per share price);

14. facilitate a Section 303 redemption without a loss of voting control;

15. improve the financial posture of the corporation by: (a) reducing or eliminating debt; and (b) eliminating interest arrearages;

16. facilitate a disproportionate redemption under Section 302(b)(2); and

17. eliminate minority shareholders through a reverse stock split.

18. save state death taxes through a recapitalization followed by a gift or sale of the growth interest.

WHAT ARE THE REQUIREMENTS?

Nowhere in the Internal Revenue Code is the word "recapitalization" defined. The word recapitalization is included in the term "reorganization." Some examples are set forth in the regulations, but those examples are certainly not all inclusive.[3]

The basic rule is that stock or securities in a corporation must, pursuant to a plan of reorganization, be exchanged *solely* for stock or securities of that corporation. If that rule is followed, then no gain or loss will be recognized on the exchange.[4] An exception exists where the principal amount of securities received exceeds the principal amount of securities surrendered and causes the difference to be taxed as "boot."

"Boot" will normally be taxable to the recipient as ordinary income.[5] It is important to note that there is a difference between the word "stock" and the word "securities" as those words are used in the Internal Revenue Code. Neither word is defined in the Code. The word stock, however, is intended to indicate an ownership interest or equity interest in the corporation. The word securities is intended to indicate indebtedness.

It is significant to note that in a recapitalization, it is not necessary for a stockholder to retain an equity participation in the corporation after the recapitalization. Thus, the continuity of interest rule which is required in other types of reorganizations is not required in a recapitalization.[6] It is

Tools and Techniques

necessary, however, that a business purpose for the recapitalization exist in order for the Internal Revenue Service and the courts to approve the transaction.

Treasury regulations seem to indicate a corporate business purpose rather than a stockholder business purpose must exist. In at least one case the court held that the business purpose was satisfied by looking to the majority shareholders' business purpose rather than the corporate business purpose.[7] It is difficult, however, in a recapitalization to segregate and separate corporate business purpose from shareholder business purpose since most if not all closely held business corporations are run in a manner where business transactions are designed to accommodate shareholder purposes. The Internal Revenue Service has given some recognition to this fact. In two private rulings it approved a recapitalization after finding that the principal purpose of the recapitalization was to accommodate a shareholder's estate plan.[8]

HOW IT IS DONE — AN EXAMPLE

Nick and Jessie own all of the shares of common voting stock of a corporation. Nick would like to shift ownership and control of his voting stock to his son who is going to be taking his place in the business. Nick does not want to pay a gift tax on the transfer. Basically, Nick wants his son to have the benefit of the growth of the future equity in the corporation, since the son will be working in the corporation and contributing to its growth. Jessie is agreeable to such a transaction.

By recapitalizing the corporation and having both Nick and Jessie exchange all of their voting stock for preferred stock and voting common stock, both shareholders receive preferred stock with a face amount and fair market value equal to 90 percent of the value of the common stock exchanged. The remaining common stock received in the exchange would equal the remaining 10 percent value of the stock surrendered. Nick would then gift his common voting stock received in the exchange, over a period of time, to his son. Nick would keep the preferred stock. That stock would be callable by the corporation at a specified price and could therefore help to "freeze" the stock's value at Nick's death. Note that immediately after the exchange, Nick and Jessie still have the same voting control and still share 50 percent each in the equity growth of the corporation. However, Nick will be shifting his share of voting control and that equity growth over a period of time to his son.

WHAT ARE THE TAX IMPLICATIONS?

Tax problems can arise in a recapitalization in three areas: gift tax problems, estate tax problems, and income tax problems.

1. In a closely held corporation, it is easy for an unintentional gift to be made in connection with a recapitaliza-

tion. For instance, a majority stockholder may receive shares of preferred stock with a fair market value in excess of the fair market value of the common stock surrendered. The excess could be considered a dividend. Conversely, if the shareholder surrenders shares of common stock worth more than the fair market value of the preferred stock received, the amount representing any excess could be treated as having been used to make gifts to other shareholders, or to pay compensation, or to satisfy the majority shareholder's obligations."[9]

Estate planners should be conscious of hidden gift tax traps. In one situation, the corporation was recapitalized. The taxpayer exchanged common stock for preferred stock and two classes of common stock, Class A (voting) and Class B (nonvoting). He then gave his children nonvoting common stock (the Class B) and a small portion of the voting (Class A) stock. The preferred stock retained by the taxpayer was entitled to a 7 percent noncumulative dividend, had preference over other classes of stock with respect to declared dividends and assets on liquidation, and was redeemable after the taxpayer's death at the option of the corporation. Dividends were paid on the common stock but not on the preferred. The IRS argued that when the corporation paid dividends on the common, the taxpayer was making a constructive gift to his children, the common stockholders, equal to the 7 percent dividend that should have been paid on the preferred.[10]

Every private letter ruling issued by the Internal Revenue Service relating to recapitalizations contains a caveat. That warning states that a private letter ruling is effective only to the extent that the fair market value of the stock received is substantially equal to the fair market value of the stock surrendered in the exchange. The Internal Revenue Service expresses no opinion as to the tax treatment if there is not an equality in fair market value. The Internal Revenue Service also states that in issuing a ruling it is not making a determination as to the fair market value of the stock, but that the fair market value can be questioned on an examination of the tax return for the year in which the recapitalization took place.

2. Estate tax inclusion will result from the typical recapitalization that is followed by a gift (or sale to family members) of common stock coupled with a retention of preferred stock. The client's estate must include not only the preferred stock retained (Code section 2031) but also the value of the common stock given away. (See page 477.)

There are also less obvious but equally dangerous estate tax traps. For instance, the president and majority shareholder of a corporation was told by a doctor he had terminal cancer. On advice from his attorney he merged his two corporations. After the merger he held a significant amount of the preferred stock with voting rights that expired upon his death. The IRS argued that the value of the voting rights he retained for his lifetime should be considered in valuing the preferred stock he held at the time of his death. The reason is that he had made "a passive transfer" of property to shareholders benefiting from the cessation of voting rights at his death. Those shareholders were his children (who owned the balance of any outstanding stock). The IRS also argued that he had retained a life estate (an indirect right to vote the common stock actually owned by his children) through his retention of the right to vote the preferred stock until his death. At that time, his voting rights in the preferred stock expired and the votes of the common stock held by his children (until then nonvoting) "blossomed into control."[11]

3. Income tax problems can also result from improperly calculating the values of the stock exchanged in a recapitalization. Two possible situations exist: First, in a nonfamily situation the difference in values between the stock exchanged and the stock received could be treated as compensation. Second, in both the family situation and the nonfamily situation, the problems presented by Code sections 305 and 306 must be carefully considered.

Under Section 305, distributions made by a corporation to its shareholders with respect to the corporation's stock are generally considered nontaxable regardless of whether the stock distributed by the corporation is voting stock, nonvoting stock, preferred stock, or common stock.

Section 305 does, however, contain a number of exceptions to the general rule of nontaxability. Those exceptions must be clearly examined since one or more of them may be applicable to the facts in a particular recapitalization. If any of the exceptions do apply, the result may be taxation of the recipient shareholder. (It is also important to examine the Treasury regulations to Section 305 (which contain an exception to the Section 305 exceptions for certain recapitalizations involving single and isolated transactions.)

One must also bear in mind the effect of Code section 306 on any recapitalization. The purpose of section 306 is to prevent a stockholder from removing a corporation's earnings and profits that are 100 percent taxable as a dividend (accumulated earnings and profits) at "sale or exchange" terms (which means only gain is taxable) through the use of preferred stock.

Basically, "section 306 stock" is any stock, other than common stock, issued with respect to common stock and received by a shareholder as a nontaxable stock dividend at a time when the corporation has undistributed post-1913 earnings and profits. It includes stock, other than common stock, received in a nontaxable reorganization, such as in a recapitalization, to the extent the effect was substantially the same as receipt of a stock dividend. If the corporation has no earnings and profits at the time of distribution, the stock distributed will not be section 306 stock.

Section 306 stock bears a "taint." When section 306 stock is disposed of by a stockholder (in all instances other than those covered by specific exceptions), the stockholder will not receive "sale or exchange" tax treatment on that disposition. Instead, the disposition of section 306 stock may cause the entire proceeds to be taxable.

Under one of the exceptions to section 306, if a stockholder dies owning section 306 stock, the taint which attached to that stock would terminate because of the step-up-in-basis rule. Thus, a disposition of the section 306 stock after a stockholder's death (at the estate tax value) would not cause dividend type tax consequences.

Additional exceptions to the rules as to the treatment of amounts realized on section 306 stock provide that section 306 will not apply if: the stock is redeemed as part of a substantially disproportionate or complete redemption (under sections 302(b)(2) or 302(b)(3) of the Code—see chapter 1); the shareholder terminates his entire stock interest (including interests owned by related parties) by selling his stock to an unrelated third party; or the stock is redeemed in a disposition in complete liquidation.

A shareholder can exchange all of his shares of common stock for income paying nonvoting preferred. This often occurs where an individual is nearing retirement and wants to turn control of his business over to a new generation and at the same time provide himself with income. The preferred stock he receives will not be "tainted" as "306" stock if that recapitalization distribution would have been tax free had he received cash instead of preferred stock.

Since the client is giving up his entire voting interest as well as his right to a share in future corporate growth, a cash distribution could be tax free—except where attribution rules apply. Attribution rules may make it impossible to receive the preferred stock without a taint. However, even if there is a "taint," it is still possible for a person to exchange all his common for preferred stock and pay no tax on the exchange. The only effect of the taint is to cause all or most of the amount realized on a subsequent sale or other disposition of that stock to be classified as ordinary income. But it appears that if family attribution rules are used to determine whether the receipt of preferred stock is substantially the same as a dividend, it may be possible to avoid the taint altogether if family attribution can be (and is) waived.

A further question has been one of the interrelationship between Section 306 and Section 303 and which has priority status. (Section 303 was designed as a relief provision permitting a redemption of stock in order to pay death taxes and certain administrative expenses.) Section 306 is inapplicable to the extent that Section 303 applies. Thus, where Section 303 applies, the redemption would be treated as a sale or exchange of an asset (only gain is taxable) instead of being treated as a dividend (which would subject the entire proceeds of the sale to income tax).

Beware of hidden income tax traps:

In one case, the president of a corporation retired. He exchanged 80 shares of common stock for 80 shares of preferred. At that point, the president owned all preferred stock and his son owned all outstanding common stock.

The corporation was required to redeem the preferred stock at the death of a preferred stock shareholder for its $80,000 par value.

The IRS claimed that the fair market value of the preferred stock was really much less than the amount claimed. Therefore, a constructive gift in the amount of the difference had been made between the father and the son.

The IRS also claimed that when the father dies, his estate will be paid $80,000 although the stock is worth much less than that. The difference (minus a "redemption premium," a 10 percent of the issue price penalty to the corporation for premature redemption of preferred stock), argues the IRS, is essentially a dividend. Therefore, the difference between what the stock is worth and what the estate is paid will be taxed as a dividend.

The revenue ruling states that the constructive dividend will be constructively received rateably over the life expectancy of the father (with any constructive dividend not received by death considered to be received at that time).[12]

ISSUES AND IMPLICATIONS IN COMMUNITY PROPERTY STATES

The Introduction and Chapter 1 contain a more complete discussion of community property principles and should be the reference point for consideration of recapitalization issues. In community property states specific attention should be paid to whether the stock holdings involved in any recapitalization are separate, community or quasi-community property. Care is required in determining the character of the stocks to be exchanged and received to be sure that proper consents are obtained and to protect against a spouse's future claim of a community interest. To preclude problems in determination it is advisable for the spouses to agree in writing as to the nature of their interest. A characterization as community could be of significance to a corporate recapitalization where the objective is to transfer control to a younger family generation. If the common shares remaining in the hands of the parents after the recapitalization are community property, each spouse may individually give these shares in increments that qualify for the annual ($10,000 per donee) exclusion from the gift tax. The result is to expedite completion of the transfer before significant appreciation.

While married couples in community property states may hold property in other joint forms, there is a significant advantage to holding as community property. Upon the death of one spouse the basis of the community holdings of the surviving spouse will receive a step-up in basis along with that of the decedent spouse. Thus, Section 306 stock in effect loses its taint at the death of the owner since there is no gain to be taxed as ordinary income.

QUESTIONS AND ANSWERS

Question — Assume a recapitalization will meet the nontax purposes and accomplish a client's estate planning goals. How should one proceed?

Answer — For a recapitalization to be successfully consummated, it is important that an attorney be retained who, after a careful examination of the facts, can make a determination whether a recapitalization would be appropriate. If it is determined that a recapitalization is appropriate and all parties are agreeable, after working out the scheme of the recapitalization, an independent appraisal company should be retained to prepare a valuation report. The attorney should prepare a request for a private letter ruling from the Internal Revenue Service. All documents pertinent to the recapitalization must be prepared in draft form and submitted to the Internal Revenue Service along with the request for the ruling.

Question — Why is valuation required?

Answer — A valuation is necessary in order to assure that the value of the stock received is equal to the value of the stock given up so that no gift, estate, or income tax problem is created. The valuation should be made by an independent appraisal company in order to assure that a true fair market value is ascribed to the stock and that the value can be sustained in court if necessary. Although an attorney or an accountant is capable of placing numbers in valuation formulas, it is appropriate to use a valuation company since such a company has expertise in the specific problem and could be called at a later date as a witness to substantiate the valuation if the Internal Revenue Service chooses to challenge the value and attempt to impose a gift, estate, or income tax.

The IRS will look at the following factors when it values preferred stock: (1) Does the stock pay the same or higher rate of dividends as the high grade preferred stock of a publicly traded company? If the closely held stock is paying a higher rate of interest on debt than the prime rate, it probably should be paying higher dividends than a publicly traded company on its preferred. If it doesn't, the value of the preferred may be less than the amount claimed. (2) Can the company afford to pay the promised dividends and is it in fact making payments? If it can't or doesn't, the value of the preferred is probably overstated. (3) Are corporate assets sufficient to repay preferred stock investors in the event of a liquidation? If they are not, the value of the preferred is probably overstated. (4) Does the preferred stock have voting rights? If it does, the value of the preferred stock may be understated. (5) Is the marketability of the preferred stock restricted by a buy-sell agreement or some other form of covenant? If it is, the value of the preferred stock may be overstated or the agreement may provide a ceiling on the value.[13]

Question — How long does it take for a recapitalization to occur?

Answer — A recapitalization, being an intricate and complex technique, takes a long period of time. Initially, an analysis of an individual's estate must be made and a threshold determination made that a recapitalization would be advisable. Once that determination is accepted, a period of time must take place during which a valuation report and certain accounting statements are prepared. Then the attorney drafts the appropriate reorganization documents and the request for a private letter ruling. Typically, a recapitalization from the time a go ahead is given could take from six months to two years before being consummated.

Question — Is there an alternative to a recapitalization which would not give rise to Section 306 stock if preferred stock were being issued as part of the recapitalization?

Answer — If proper business purposes exist, it is possible for an entirely new corporation to be created and the shares of stock of the existing corporation transferred to the new corporation in return for preferred stock and common voting stock of the new corporation. Such a transfer would take place under the provisions of Code section 351. It is important in such a transaction to also apply for an Internal Revenue Service ruling to the effect that the preferred stock received in the exchange does not constitute Section 306 stock. A valuation report

would still be necessary in this kind of a transaction. This is sometimes called an "estate freeze" when used to transfer control of a corporation to a younger generation while insulating the estate of the parent from future appreciation.

Question — Assume that a recapitalization takes place and the stock received by a shareholder is considered Section 306 stock. Is there any way of avoiding the Section 306 adverse tax consequences on disposition of the stock?

Answer — Section 306(b)(1) provides that if the stock is redeemed and the redemption constitutes a complete termination of the shareholder's interest pursuant to the provisions of Section 302(b)(3), the transaction is treated as a redemption of non-Section 306 stock and thus "sale or exchange" treatment will be available.

Section 306 accords Section 303 priority status. Thus, any gain on Section 306 stock being redeemed to pay estate, inheritance, legacy and succession, or generation-skipping transfer taxes, as well as deductible funeral and administrative expenses, will be taxed as a sale or exchange rather than as a dividend.

ASRS, Sec. 43.

Footnote References

Recapitalization

1. IRC Section 368(a)(1)(E). This is often called an "E" type of reorganization.

2. This list was set forth in Littenberg, "The Use of Recapitalization in Estate Plans Under the 1976 Tax Reform Act, 1978 *S. Cal. Tax Inst.* 722. That article is highly recommended reading since it provides a current, in depth, treatment of the subject of recapitalization.

3. IRC Section 368(a)(1)(E). See also Reg. §1.368-2(e).

4. IRC Section 354.

5. Reg. §1.354-1(b).

6. See Rev. Ruls. 77-415, 1977-2 C.B. 311; 77-479, 1977-2 C.B. 119.

7. *Estate of Parshelsky v. Comm.*, 303 F.2d 14 (C.A.-2, 1962).

8. Letter Rulings 7717007, 8035014.

9. Rev. Rul. 74-269, 1974-1, C.B. 87.

10. IRS Letter Ruling 8403010, September 30, 1983.

11. IRS Letter Ruling 8401006, September 28, 1983; IRC Section 2036.

12. Rev. Rul. 83-119, 1983-2 C.B. 57. See also Rev. Rul. 83-118, 1983-2 C.B. 27, for valuation of preferred stock in a recapitalization.

13. Rev. Rul. 83-118, 1983-2 C.B. 27; Rev. Rul. 83-119, 1983-2 C.B. 57; Rev. Rul. 83-120, 1983-2 C.B. 170.

Chapter 24

REMAINDER INTEREST TRANSACTION (RIT)

WHAT IS IT?

A remainder interest transaction (RIT) is a technique in which a family member sells to some other person a right to receive property at some time in the future. Although the sale (i.e., the legal transfer of property rights and payment of considerations for those rights) is implemented immediately, the property transfer itself does not occur until after the family member's death (or in some cases until after a term of years expires).

Typically, the purchaser pays the seller an amount equal to the actuarial value of the remainder interest as computed under the IRS tables (reproduced in Appendix B). The seller retains the right to use the property or enjoy the income from the property for life. At the seller's death, the remainder purchaser receives the entire property.

Before the Omnibus Budget Reconciliation Act of 1987 (OBRA), there were two major reasons for entering into a RIT: First, when the seller of the remainder interest dies, the remainder purchaser receives the entire property and may have paid only a fraction of the full fair market value for it (this "discount" is particularly large where the seller dies much sooner than his projected life expectancy). Second, the RIT permitted the estate tax free transfer of significant amounts of family wealth at relatively low transfer cost. As such, the RIT, although one of the more aggressive wealth shifting techniques, was one of the most dynamic. Most authorities feel the estate freezing tax elimination advantages of a RIT were lost with the enactment of Code section 2036(c) in OBRA '87. (See the detailed discussion in Appendix B.)

WHEN IS THE USE OF SUCH A DEVICE INDICATED?

1. When the seller wants or needs to retain enjoyment or income or voting rights to particular property for life but shift the remainder to selected others, the remainder interest transaction accomplishes this objective and still enables some tax and other savings.

2. When the remainder purchaser is willing to take a risk that the seller will die before he reaches his life expectancy. For instance, if the seller is age 45, it would cost the purchaser only 11.44 percent to purchase a remainder interest in an asset. So to purchase a remainder interest in a $1,000,000 property owned by a 45 year old, the purchaser would have to pay $114,420. If the seller were to die, say, on the date a 50-year-old's expectation of life terminated, the purchaser, according to the table below, could be said to have profited $38,150 ($152,570-$114,420)

from the transaction. Here are some representative approximate amounts required to purchase a remainder interest in a $1,000,000 property at various ages:

Seller's Age	Amount Payable by Purchaser
45	$114,420
50	152,570
55	199,540
60	255,090
65	320,030
70	394,780
75	478,510
80	563,410
85	646,411

3. Where the seller's life income interest is overvalued because the property is generating income at a rate below the interest rate assumed by government tables.

4. Where the parties anticipate that the RIT property will significantly appreciate in value either because of real appreciation or inflation. Even if the seller outlives projected life expectancy, if the property appreciates fast enough, the purchaser will have achieved a high return on his investment.

5. Where the physical condition of the life tenant is substantially below normal, government actuarial valuation tables must be used in any event (unless the seller is so ill at the time of the sale that death is clearly imminent within 12 months). This favors the purchaser who is likely to receive the remainder more rapidly than expected under IRS mortality tables.[1]

6. Where the parties to the sale of the remainder interest are concerned with assuring that the purchaser and no one else will obtain the property at the seller's death. Since the RIT is a present sale of the future right to possess an asset, the seller can not later give away, sell, or dispose of the property in his will or through intestacy.

7. A RIT prevents a will contest or election against the will with respect to the property in question since it has already passed before a client's death by contract to the purchaser of the remainder interest.

8. Where the parties desire to avoid ancillary administration and reduce probate costs. Since, at the seller's death, the ownership doesn't actually pass to the purchaser (he has owned the future right to it from the time the remainder interest was purchased), it can't be included in the probate estate.

Tools and Techniques

9. The RIT provides privacy since, unlike assets passing through a will or intestacy, the terms of the RIT are documented in a private contract which can be shielded from public scrutiny.

10. Protection from the claims of creditors is available through a RIT. This is especially important to clients in professions that are prone to law suits.

11. In many states the RIT will avoid state estate and inheritance taxes, since technically no property is transferred from a decedent or to a beneficiary at the decedent's death.

WHAT ARE THE REQUIREMENTS?

1. A sales contract must be drawn providing that (a) the seller retains the lifetime use of or income benefits from the RIT property, (b) the purchaser is buying the right to the property at the seller's death no matter when that occurs.

   The agreement should provide that the seller (life tenant) must pay all expenses and charges properly allocable to a life tenant's interest. The seller should be prohibited from pledging or encumbering the property without the prior written consent of the purchaser (remainderman). Likewise, the sales agreement should forbid a sale without the prior written consent of both parties. It should specify that upon a sale, proceeds will be divided between the parties according to their actuarial interests (according to the actuarial tables in the gift tax regulations in effect at that time). The sales agreement should then specify that at the seller's death, the purchaser takes full and absolute control of the property free and clear of the seller's heirs.

2. The parties to the agreement must have a qualified appraiser value the property. The written appraisal, which should be done as close to the execution of the agreement as possible, must represent the fair market value of the asset. (We recommend two appraisals if the numbers involved in the transaction are large). The written appraisal should be incorporated into the sales contract.

3. All actuarial computations should be determined in accordance with government gift tax valuation tables. This should be noted in the sales contract and the procedure for arriving at the remainder interest price should refer to the government's tables.

4. The purchaser should use his own funds (or money acquired from a source other than by gift from the seller—such as a gift from another relative) to pay for the remainder interest. It is possible to pay for the remainder interest in the form of a note rather than cash. In that case it is important that the value of the note be at least equal to the full value of the remainder interest. (In other words be sure the interest rate, security pledged, and other terms of the note are bona fide arm's length and commercially enforceable). It is preferable to arrange for the purchaser to borrow money from an outside source and pay the seller cash rather than to risk an IRS challange that the note is worth less than the true value of the remainder interest purchased.

HOW IT IS DONE — AN EXAMPLE

A 65 year old father sells his son a remainder interest in closely held stock worth $1,000,000. According to the government valuation table (reproduced in Appendix B at Figure B.4a), the actuarial value of $1,000,000 payable at the end of the life expectancy of a 65 year old using a 10 percent discount rate is $320,300. So the son could purchase the future right to the stock when his father dies (no matter when that occurs) for a lump sum of $320,300 payable immediately.

WHAT ARE THE TAX IMPLICATIONS?

1. Since the transfer has been for full and adequate consideration in money or money's worth, there is no gift. Therefore, there is no gift tax payable and no gift tax reporting necessary.[2]

2. To the extent not consumed or given away, any consideration paid by the purchaser to the seller of the remainder interest will be in the seller's estate.

3. The property sold plus any appreciation on the property from the date of the sale may be subject to federal estate taxes even though the seller no longer owns the right to transfer the property at death and holds no strings on it (unless the RIT involves a sale to non-family members, or was deemed given away during life). (See page 477.) Keep in mind that the estate tax inclusion is moot if the client's estate, including the value of RIT property, at death is under $600,000.

4. It is essential, to avoid unexpected gift taxes, that the valuation of the underlying property be not only accurate but also defensible if questioned. The major risk in the RIT technique is that if the Service at some point in the future succeeds in proving that the value of the remainder interest was greater or less than the amount paid for it, it then could claim that the transfer of property was for less than an adequate and full consideration in money or money's worth, i.e., was at least in part a gift. See the explanation of Code Section 2036(c) beginning at page 477 regarding deemed gifts.

   The secret of success is (a) start with at least one, and better yet two, very thorough appraisals from independent and court experienced and academically qualified appraisers (perhaps using the higher of the two); and (b) use the government's own life income-remainder interest tables[6].

5. Basis, on the sale of the remainder interest, is fractionalized.[7] A portion of the basis remains with the life tenant

seller (in the example above with a 65 year old seller, the basis allocated to the remainder, which was sold, would be .32030 times the entire basis). Assuming that the seller's entire basis was, say, $600,000, the seller's basis in the property interest he sold would be $192,180 (.32030 × $600,000).

Gain is the excess of the amount realized in a sale over the seller's adjusted basis. In this example, the seller would recognize a $128,120 gain on the sale, computed as follows:

Sales Price	$320,300
less	
Basis in Remainder	192,180
Gain	$128,120

6. The basis of the purchaser of the remainder interest is equal to the amount paid for the property. In the example above that amount is $320,300.

   If the property is sold during the seller's lifetime, the remainderman realizes a gain equal to the excess of the sales proceeds allocated to the remainder interest (i.e., the amount he realizes from the sale) over his basis. So, following the example above, if the property is sold for $2,000,000 during the lifetime of the seller, say, five years later when the seller is age 70, the respective interests are: life estate—.60522, remainder—.39478. The life tenant receives $1,210,440 (.60522 × $2,000,000). The remainderman receives $789,560 (.39478 × $2,000,000). So the remainderman's gain would be computed as follows:

Sales Price	$789,560
less	
Basis	320,300
Gain	$469,260

   Note that if the life tenant and remainderman jointly sell the property, even if the life tenant continues to hold the proceeds (including the interest that should have gone to the remainderman), the remainderman will be considered to be in constructive receipt of the money and would be currently taxed on it at the time of the sale.[8]

7. When the remainder vests in possession (that is, when the life tenant dies and the remainderman actually receives the property), there should be no taxable event if what is received is property rather than cash.[9]

8. If a remainderman dies during the lifetime of the life tenant, his estate must include the present value of the right to receive the remainder interest. This amount is found by multiplying the value of the property on the date of death by the present value factor at the remain-

derman's age as of the date of death. For example, if the trust assets had appreciated to $5,000,000 by the date of the remainderman's death (assume 10 years after a 60 year old seller sold the remainder interest), the present value of the $5,000,000 would be $1,973,900 (.39478 × $5,000,000).

If the right to the remainder interest is passed outright or in a qualifying manner to the remainderman's surviving spouse, it will qualify for the federal estate tax marital deduction and eliminate federal estate tax on the first death. It would then (to the extent not given away or exhausted) be includible when the second spouse died.

An alternative to passing the remainder interest to the spouse or to a marital trust would be to pay it to a CEBT (credit equivalent bypass trust). Since the remainder increases in value automatically as time passes, passing it to the CEBT leverages the advantage of bypassing the second tax.

There is a special but seldom used Code section which allows the estate to elect to defer payment of the federal estate tax until the remainder vests in possession. (Interest must be paid on the unpaid tax until that date.) This section (6163) could be used if the marital deduction was not available or for any reason was not used.

IMPLICATIONS AND ISSUES IN COMMUNITY PROPERTY STATES

In a community property state if husband and wife both sell a remainder interest, upon the death of either spouse, the decedent spouse's one half community property interest would vest in possession. In other words, the purchaser of the remainder interest would be a tenant in common with the surviving spouse. This, of course, would significantly reduce the income of the surviving spouse. The surviving spouse could seek partition, thereby avoiding any possible conflict with the other tenant(s) in common; however, this would not restore any of the lost income to the surviving spouse.

The possibility of this result should be thought out prior to the RIT's implementation, and if such income would be needed by the surviving spouse, another type of planning device should be utilized.

Would it make sense to use a "LAST TO DIE" RIT that retained the right to the property or its income until the death of the survivor of the spouses? In other words, even after the first spouse dies, the survivor continues to receive income from the property for life. But in a community property state, it appears that this and similar tactics will result in tax disaster. In this instance, the husband will have made a sale to the actual purchaser of the remainder interest but a gift to his wife. On the husband's death, the full value of the transferred property, less an offset for the consideration received from the purchaser, will be included in the husband's estate.[10]

QUESTIONS AND ANSWERS

Question — To avoid the valuation problem (i.e., the IRS argument that the transfer was for less than adequate and full consideration and is therefore a gift), why not use a "savings clause"?

Answer — Some authorities feel that the valuation issue could be solved by providing, "If the IRS determines that the property was undervalued and the seller did not receive full and adequate consideration, then the seller has the right to demand a payment in a lump sum of the difference—with interest payable on the difference to reflect the seller's loss of the use of money he should have been paid."

This tactic sounds good but some scholars think that at the least, a savings clause appears to serve as a red flag. There are many cases in which courts have disregarded the savings clause and held that such clauses are contrary to public policy.

Question — Can the purchaser pay for the remainder interest by paying a private annuity rather than paying a lump sum?

Answer — Yes. This is a device we call the "Private Annuity Time Grab." If annuity payments are determined under the IRS tables (Reg. Sec. 20.2031-7(f), reproduced in Appendix B), this should constitute adequate and full consideration.

The private annuity time grab has no federal estate tax savings advantages, but will accomplish all or most of the nontax objectives described under WHEN IS THE USE OF THIS DEVICE INDICATED? and may save state death taxes as well. It may make an intra-family property transfer possible by transforming a required lump sum payment by the buyer into an actuarially equivalent annual payment. The printout in the next column illustrates a PRIVATE ANNUITY TIME GRAB.

Question — If the property in question is depreciable, who receives depreciation deductions?

Answer — All depreciation on property owned jointly between a life tenant and remainderman must be taken by the life tenant absent a trust agreement to the contrary.[11]

Question — Could a remainder interest owner give away his interest?

Answer — Yes. A gift of a remainder interest to a younger generation beneficiary may be a good planning technique, especially if the seller of the remainder interest is still relatively young. The remainder interest at the time of the gift will have a relatively low value. Yet over the years it will have a steady and almost certain growth in value (even if the underlying property itself merely remains level in value). Remember that by definition a remainder interest is a future interest gift and therefore will not qualify for the gift tax annual exclusion.

PRIVATE ANNUITY TIME GRAB

Input: Annuitant's Age		65
Input: Basis of Property		$400,000
Input: Fair Market Value of Entire Asset		$1,000,000
Remainder Factor at Given Age	X	0.32030
Present Value of Remainder Interest...................		$320,300
P.V. Factor of Annuity at Given Age	X	6.7970
Annual Payment to Purchase Remainder Interest		$47,124

TAX FREE PORTION OF EACH PAYMENT

Basis of Portion Sold	$128,120
Life Expectancy of Transferor Annuitant	20.0
Tax Free Portion of Each Payment Received	$6,406

ORDINARY INCOME PORTION

Annual Payment		$47,124
Less:		
Tax Free Portion ..	$6,406	
Equals		
Ordinary Income Portion .		$40,718

Footnote References

Remainder Interest Transaction (RIT)

1. See Rev. Rul. 80-80, 1980-1 C.B. 194.
2. IRC Section 2512(b).
3. IRS Letter Rulings 7806001, 7837003, 8041098, and 8145012.
4. *Estate of Christ v. Comm.*, 54 TC 493 (1970), aff'd 480 F.2d 171 (9th Cir. 1973); IRS Letter Ruling 8145012.
5. See *Estate of Shafer v. Comm.*, 749 F.2d 1216 (6th Cir. 1984).
6. IRS Letter Ruling 8041098; see explanation of valuation of life estates and remainders at page 390.
7. Reg. §1.61-6(a); see also *Hunter v. Comm.*, 44 TC 109 (1965), and Rev. Rul. 77-413, 1977 CB 298.
8. Rev. Rul. 71-122, 1971-1 CB 224.
9. *Sheppard Holding, Inc. v. U.S.*, Nos. 77-3006, 77-3052, 77-3170, 77-3176 (unpublished opinion, 9th Cir. 1979). The 9th Circuit's decision can't be cited as precedent in the 9th Circuit but can be used in all other jurisdictions. *Sheppard* holds that the receipt of a remainder, *per se*, does not constitute a taxable event.
10. See IRC Section 2036.
11. IRC Section 167(h).

Chapter 25

S CORPORATION

WHAT IS IT?

An "S" corporation (formerly called a Subchapter S or "Tax Option" corporation) is a corporation that has made an election to have its income, deductions, capital gains and losses, charitable contributions, and credits passed through to its shareholders. To a great extent an S corporation is treated for tax purposes similarly to a partnership.

WHEN IS THE USE OF SUCH A DEVICE INDICATED?

1. When your client (currently a sole proprietor or partnership) is entering a new, high risk business, and would like the legal protection against creditors offered by corporate status, but wants to be able to personally deduct losses of the business enterprise if the venture fails. (This same goal can be achieved to a limited degree through the use of Section 1244 stock in a normal corporation.)

   An "S" election enables corporate losses to be passed through the corporation and deducted on the tax returns of the individual shareholders (but only to the extent of the adjusted basis of their stock in the corporation and loans made to the corporation).[1] Thus, losses of an S corporation may be used to offset income earned outside of the business.

2. Where the business, although not inherently risky, has a period of loss during the first years of starting up, the client may elect S corporation status for the early loss years. When the business begins to make a profit, the election may be terminated and future profits taxed to the corporation. The method and other effects of the termination should be carefully planned.

3. When the stockholder(s) would like to take out all corporate income without the normal double taxation on corporate earnings and such payments could not be justified as reasonable compensation. In other words, when S corporation status has been elected, generally there is no tax at the corporate level; typically, income earned by the S corporation is taxed only once, to the individual shareholders, regardless of the amount of income or the services performed, if any, by the shareholders.

   Double taxation has always been a problem when income is earned and then accumulated in a regular ("C") corporation. TRA '86 made the double taxation substantially more onerous. There are four reasons the S corporation passthrough of the corporate level tax is more important than ever after TRA '86 and OBRA '87 (The Omnibus Budget Reconciliation Act of 1987):

a. Corporate tax rates will often exceed individual rates. This is particularly true in the case of professional service corporations, which are taxed at a flat rate of 34% on every dollar of taxable income. No "run up the brackets" is allowed to these corporations.

b. Distributions of the cash proceeds of a sale of appreciated property (assets with a fair market value in excess of their tax basis) of a regular (C) corporation upon its liquidation, or even distributions of the appreciated property itself, will trigger tax both at the corporate and shareholder levels. (Under prior law, the "built-in gains" in corporate assets usually escaped taxation on the corporate level when the assets were sold or distributed in a liquidation or Section 303 distribution even if the corporation had not made an S election.)

c. Corporate gains on capital assets are no longer eligible for a lower capital gains rate. They will therefore be taxed at ordinary rates.

d. The net proceeds of the gain already taxed at the corporate level are again taxed when distributed to shareholders who no longer can take a long term capital gains deduction.

The simplified (it ignores the time value of money) example at Figure 25.1 illustrates one reason so many corporations made an S election late in 1986.

The double taxation problem suffered by regular corporations' shareholders year after year can be alleviated, or in some cases even eliminated, by an increase in shareholders' salaries (thus reducing corporate taxable income).

But this ploy will not work with the potentially huge tax at the time a corporation is liquidated. First, the tax may be many times the normal "doubletax." Second, it is difficult to justify proportionately large salaries in the year the corporation is going out of business. With the loss of the ability to income average, the ultimate tax on a final liquidation could absorb the work product of years of hard work.

4. When the nontax benefits of incorporation are desired, but the individual shareholders are in lower tax brackets than the corporation and they would like the advantage of the tax savings that can be obtained by having the income earned by the corporation taxed directly to them as individuals.

211

Figure 25.1

NON S CORPORATIONS UNDER PRIOR AND NEW LAW		Prior Law	Current Law
Input:	Income Earned and Accumulated	$50,000	$50,000
Input:	Corporate Tax	$8,250	7,500
	Amount Retained by Corporation	$41,750	$42,500
Input:	Tax Rate on Shareholders Upon Distribution of Assets	0.20	0.33
	Tax Payable by Shareholders	$8,350	$14,025
	Total Tax	$16,600	$21,525
Input:	Personal Tax Rate	0.50	0.33
	Probable Tax if S Corporation	$25,000	$16,500
Prior Law	Advantage of C Corporation Status	$8,400	
Curr Law	Advantage of S Corporation Status		$5,025
	Shift in Advantage	$13,425	

5. Where it is desired to spread income among a number of family members, an S corporation is a useful device. By giving stock, the tax on corporate earnings may be shifted to a large number of relatively low tax bracket individuals and taxed at their brackets rather than at the client's bracket (provided they are age 14 or over).[2]

6. When avoidance of the AMT (alternative minimum tax) is desirable.

7. When avoidance of the accumulated earnings tax is desirable.

WHAT ARE THE REQUIREMENTS?

1. The corporation must be a domestic corporation. This means it must be created or organized in the U.S. or one of its states.

2. It must have no more than 35 shareholders.

3. Shareholders must be individuals, estates, or a specific type of trust. Nonresident aliens may not be shareholders.

4. The corporation can have only one class of stock. That means each share must represent equal profit and asset interest with any other share. But it is possible to provide for differences in voting rights among shares of common stock. For instance, there can safely be a "Class A" and a "Class B" voting stock with different terms or powers, as long as both classes are in fact common stock.

A "straight debt instrument" is not considered, for these purposes, a second class of stock. A "straight debt instrument" means a written unconditional promise to pay on demand or on a specified date a sum certain in money so long as: (a) the interest rate (and payment dates) are not contingent on the corporate profits, the discretion of the corporation, or other similar factors, (b) the instrument is not convertible into stock, *and* (c) the creditor is a person, estate or trust eligible to hold S corporation stock. This favorable treatment is not lost merely because the interest rate is dependent upon the prime rate (or a similar factor not related to the debtor corporation).

5. The S corporation cannot be a member of an affiliated group or have an active subsidiary.

HOW IT IS DONE — AN EXAMPLE

There are five equal shareholders of the ABC Corporation which is currently earning profits of $50,000. The federal corporate tax, in 1988 and later years, is $7,500, 15 percent of the first $50,000 of earnings. This means the amount which could be distributed to the S corporation's shareholders is $42,500 ($50,000 – $7,500). Each stockholder's share is $8,500 ($42,500 ÷ 5). Of course, this amount is further reduced by personal taxes. Assuming each owner has outside income and is in approximately a 33 percent tax bracket, individual taxes will be about $2,805. The aggregate income tax on all five individuals' income will be $14,025. In total, the taxes paid are $21,525 ($7,500 of corporate tax plus $14,025 of personal taxes). (The example has been simplified for illustrative purposes.)

Now assume the corporation has elected "S" status. The election, of course, does not change corporate profits, which are still $50,000. However, the $50,000 is now directly through to the shareholders (the character of the income also is passed through) and there is no corporate tax to pay. The net profits subject to distribution are $50,000. Dividing that figure by five, each shareholder's share is $10,000. Personal taxes are therefore increased to $3,300 each. The aggregate tax payable is $16,500.

Taxes Before S Election	Taxes After S Election
$21,525	$16,500

The S election saves $5,025 annually.

WHAT ARE THE TAX IMPLICATIONS?

1. S corporations and their shareholders are taxed under essentially the same rules that apply to partnerships and their partners. Generally, the S corporation doesn't pay federal income tax. Its income (or loss) is passed through directly to its shareholders and therefore avoids the double tax on corporate earnings.

2. Essentially, taxable income of an S corporation is computed as follows:

   Any income that could affect the individual tax liability of a shareholder is passed directly through the corporation to the shareholders. Likewise, any loss, deduction, or credit which could affect the liability of a shareholder is passed through just as if the entity were a partnership. Even tax exempt income such as municipal bond interest or life insurance proceeds is passed through as tax exempt income.

   Shareholders must report or deduct all these "separately treated" items in proportion to their shareholdings. In other words a 10 percent shareholder would be required to report 10 percent of corporation's income, but would be entitled to 10 percent of any corporate earned deductions or credits.

   Typical separately treated items include (1) gains and losses from corporate sales or exchanges of capital assets, and (2) charitable contributions (the corporation's contributions are passed through to shareholders who add them to their own personal contributions in determining the charitable contribution deduction on their own personal returns).

3. Tax exempt interest received by an S corporation retains its tax exempt character and increases the shareholders' basis. If the interest is subsequently distributed, it is not taxable but reduces the shareholders' basis.

4. Excludable interest and dividends are entered into the shareholders' personal returns.

5. Amounts passed through as credits are passed through on a per share per day basis and are claimed by the shareholders on their personal returns.

Figure 25.2

TAX PAYABLE BY ENTITY OR SOLE SHAREHOLDER
C CORPORATION v. S CORPORATION

The chart below compares the tax payable by an entity owned by a sole shareholder who operates as a "C" corporation with the tax the same individual would pay if the corporation had elected S corporation status. It is assumed the shareholder files jointly and does not take earnings and profits out of the C corporation (which would increase the total tax payable and swing the advantage to the S election much more quickly than is apparent in the chart).

Note that the tax savings from the S election occurs once taxable income exceeds a breakeven point of $154,790 and accelerates from there.

Taxable Income	Tax as a C Corporation	Tax as an S Corporation
$ 25,000	$ 3,750	$ 3,750
50,000	7,500	10,133
100,000	22,250	25,538
150,000	41,750	42,037
154,790	43,618	43,618
200,000	61,250	57,092
500,000	170,000	141,092
750,000	255,000	255,000
1,000,000	340,000	281,092
2,000,000	680,000	561,092

6. Allowances for depletion with respect to oil and gas wells are separately computed for each shareholder. Each shareholder must keep records of his basis in each well, and adjust the basis for any depletion taken.

7. Net operating loss is deductible by a shareholder as an ordinary loss in computing adjusted gross income. If it exceeds the shareholder's other income, it can be carried back for three years and then carried forward for up to 15 years. The amount of loss that can be passed through in a given year is limited to the sum of (a) the basis of the shareholder's S corporation stock and (b) the basis of loans he has made to the corporation. However, losses in excess of this sum can be carried forward indefinitely and will be allowed in any subsequent year in which the shareholder has adequate basis in his stock or in debt the corporation owes him.

The corporation's remaining (the nonseparately computed) income, if any, is taxable to the shareholders. Each shareholder reports on Schedule E of his Form 1040 his prorata share. Likewise, each shareholder must report his prorata share of corporate preference items.

All this income must be reported by a shareholder in his taxable year in which, or with which, the corporation's tax year ends. (S corporations are required to use a calendar year for tax accounting purposes, so the tax year of an S corporation ends on December 31, unless a business reason is established for a fiscal year period.) In the case of a deceased shareholder, prorata shares of income attributable to the portion of the corporation's tax year prior to his death are reportable on the final return. Income earned in the balance of the year is reported on the estate's income tax return or on the return of the beneficiary who received the stock.

The prorata shares are determined on a day by day per share basis. This per-share per-day method of prorating income liability also applies where S Corporation stock is sold or given away.

If a corporation has any "net passive income" (income from royalties, rents, dividends, interest, annuities, and gains from stock and securities less allowable deductions connected with those items), it must pay a tax on the lower of (a) the excess net passive income, or (b) its taxable income. The rate of tax is the maximum rate that applies to corporations for that year (currently 34 percent).

Excess net passive income is

$$\frac{\text{Passive investment income}}{\text{Passive investment income}} \times \text{Net Passive Income}$$
(Passive investment income minus 25 percent of gross receipts)

For instance, assume that an S corporation has $200,000 of gross receipts, passive investment income of $100,000, and deductible expenses attributable to that income of $20,000.

Net passive income is $80,000, $100,000 minus $20,000. Excess net passive income is $40,000:

$$\frac{\$100,000 - \$50,000}{\$100,000} \times \$80,000$$

So the tax would be $13,600 (34% × $40,000), assuming the excess net passive income does not exceed the corporation's taxable income for the year.

IMPLICATIONS AND ISSUES IN COMMUNITY PROPERTY STATES

A husband and wife, shareholders of community property stock in an S corporation, both must give their consent to the corporation's election to have its earnings taxed to the shareholders. If retention of the Subchapter S election is desirable, in a situation where an individual is purchasing shares with community property funds, a contract should be entered into with both that individual and his spouse whereby they would agree not to refuse to consent to the election.

The same concern discussed in Chapter 9, dealing with earnings from a separate property investment, should also be considered.

As noted, husband and wife holding stock as community property are counted as only one shareholder. Additionally, community property stock, since half is owned by each spouse, can be more easily given within the scope of the $10,000 annual exclusion without the necessity of filing a gift tax return. However, there is no longer a problem with split gifts within 3 years of death being included in the decedent's estate as a result of the requirement for filing a gift tax return.

QUESTIONS AND ANSWERS

Question — Under what circumstances can the S election be terminated?

Answer — An election of an S corporation will terminate under any of the following circumstances:

(a) Shareholders holding more than 50 percent of the corporation's stock consent to revoke the election. There is no official form; the corporation files a statement with the IRS revoking the election. The termination is effective for the entire taxable year if the revocation is filed on or before the 15th day of the third month of the taxable year; otherwise, the revocation is effective on the first day of the following taxable year. The entrance of a new stockholder cannot revoke an election unless that person owns more than 50 percent of the corporation's stock and that person revokes the election; if no revocation occurs, new shareholders are bound by the same rules that apply to other shareholders.

(b) The corporation fails to satisfy any of the four qualification requirements discussed above under the heading **WHAT ARE THE REQUIREMENTS.** The termination is effective on the day the disqualifying event occurs. For instance, the election ends if the limit on the number of shareholders is exceeded or shares are transferred to an ineligible party. Therefore, a transfer of even one share of S corporation stock to a partnership, corporation, nonresident alien, or nonqualifying trust terminates an election. Likewise, if a second class of stock is issued the election would terminate.

(c) Certain passive income exceeds 25 percent of the corporation's gross receipts for three consecutive tax years and the corporation has accumulated earnings and profits from its days as a "C" (regular) corporation at the end of each such year. This would not be a problem with a newly formed S corporation.

Question — If an S election is terminated, how soon may a new election be made?

Answer — Once terminated, an S election cannot be made again for five years unless the Commissioner of Internal Revenue consents.[3] This will affect those who made elections late in 1986 but decided to void their elections retroactively at their year-end corporate meetings. Those corporations may be barred from making a new S election for 5 years after the date of revocation.

The IRS may waive the effect of an inadvertent termination for any period if the corporation (a) corrects the event that created the termination and (b) agrees, together with all its shareholders, to be treated as if the election had been in effect for that period. (The IRS has been told in the congressional committee report to "be reasonable in granting waivers to avoid inflicting undue hardship on S corporations where the corporation's election has been inadvertently terminated and no tax avoidance results from allowing continued S corporation treatment. For instance, if the election was terminated by the corporation's inadvertent violation of the "one class of stock" requirement but no tax avoidance resulted, the IRS should treat the election as if it never terminated.)

Question — When must an election to be taxed as an S corporation be made by an existing C corporation?

Answer — An "S" election may be made (a) at any time during the entire taxable year prior to the election year, or (b) on or before the 15th day of the 3rd month of the election year. Elections made after that date are treated as made for the next tax year. For instance, for an election to be effective in 1990, a corporation must file the election sometime between January 1, 1989 and March 15, 1990.

An effective election presupposes both that all eligibility requirements are met and that the proper consent from shareholders has been obtained. It is possible to obtain an extension of time to file in certain cases even if a shareholder fails to consent in time.

All shareholders on the day the election is made must consent (on IRS Form 2553 or on a separate consent document). Minors can sign the consent even without legal or natural guardians (or such individuals may consent on behalf of a minor who is unable to act). A decedent's personal representative (executor or administrator) signs on behalf of an estate holding S corporation stock.

Question — How is life insurance owned by an S corporation taxed?

Answer — Key man life insurance premiums are nondeductible. Death proceeds are received income tax free by the corporation and are not subject to either an accumulated earnings tax or an alternative minimum tax. When the proceeds are distributed to the corporation's shareholders, they will be treated in the same manner as any other distributions of separately treated items, i.e., it retains its character as tax free income. If a policy is surrendered during the insured's lifetime or the policy matures, any gain is taxable directly to the corporation's shareholders.

Most advisors recommend that insurance that is indicated be owned on a personal basis. This is because shareholders in an S corporation are currently taxed on corporate income used to purchase nondeductible items such as corporate life insurance, even if there is no actual distribution of cash to pay that tax. For instance, if a corporation pays a $10,000 premium, shareholders of an S corporation are taxed on $10,000 even though they have not received it.

The corporation should pay a deductible bonus to each shareholder, which, after tax, would be sufficient to pay premiums on the appropriate amounts of insurance.

Question — Can an S corporation set up a nonqualified deferred compensation plan?

Answer — A deferred compensation plan can be established by an S corporation. But the tax advantage enjoyed by a conventional corporation is not available. This is because shareholders are taxed directly and immediately on the current taxable income of the corporation, whether or not that income is distributed. Since premiums are not deductible, the outlay for life insurance which is used to finance the corporation's obligation under the deferred compensation plan is immediately taxable to the individual shareholders. A corporation with a $50,000 gross income, $30,000 of deductible expenses, and which pays $5,000 in key man insurance premiums has only $15,000 available for distribution. Yet shareholders are taxed as if they had received $20,000.

Question — How are S corporations treated for fringe benefit purposes?

Answer — S corporations, for purposes of "employee fringe benefits" (Congress did not define this term but it means statutory and non-statutory benefits such as group term and medical benefit insurance) will be treated as partnerships. All shareholders owning more than 2 percent of the stock will be considered partners.

The result is that most shareholder-employees would not be "employees" for purposes of favorable Section 79 group term, medical reimbursement, or other coverage. This results in a loss of the corporation's deduction and taxation of the shareholder-employees.

There was a grandfathering provision which provided that any fringe benefits available on September 28, 1982 by a corporation with S status on that date continued to receive favorable treatment for 5 years (until the first taxable year beginning after December 31, 1987). So S corporations now will be treated as partnerships for purposes of employee benefit plan eligibility and taxation.

Question — Is an outright gift the best way to shift income to a minor child age 14 or older through an S corporation?

Answer — An outright gift of S corporation stock to a minor makes it impossible to exercise any rights with the stock unless a court-appointed guardian is obtained. This is usually expensive, inconvenient, and typically involves a great deal of administrative inflexibility.

An alternative to an outright gift to a minor is a gift to a custodian under the appropriate Uniform Gifts to Minors Act (UGMA). Unfortunately, this device has its limitations.

First, once the minor reaches age 21 (18 in some states), the shares must be distributed. Many clients feel that this age is an inappropriate time to distribute large amounts of money or securities. Most individuals are unwilling to allow a donee-child to obtain unlimited ownership and control at that time.

A second possible problem is that if the minor dies prior to the age at which the shares must be distributed under applicable local law, the likelihood is great that the shares will be returned to the donor through the operation of state intestacy statutes.

The third potential problem is that the custodian may die or become unable to act. Under the Uniform Gifts to Minors Act it is possible that the custodian could name a successor. (Such a successor may be named by the donor when the UGMA account is established or the cus-

todian may name his or her own successor.) Lacking advance preparations, court proceedings may have to be instituted in order to name a successor custodian; a procedure would entail costs and delays.

A grantor trust, one in which the grantor is treated as if he owned trust property for income tax purposes, is eligible to own stock in an S corporation. A grantor trust can hold S corporation stock regardless of whether it is revocable. In fact such a trust can continue as an S corporation shareholder even after the death of the grantor (but only for a limited period of up to 2 years, and even that period is allowed only if the entire corpus of the grantor trust is includible in the grantor's estate. If the entire corpus of the grantor trust is not includible in the gross estate of the grantor, a grantor trust may hold S corporation stock safely for only 60 days.)

The disadvantage of the grantor trust as a receptacle for S corporation stock is obvious: although the stock will not be in the grantor's estate if the trust is irrevocable, its income will be taxed to the grantor (and therefore the ability to shift the tax on income is lost).

Current law enables a modification of a simple trust to be eligible to hold S corporation stock. This modified conventional trust is called the QSCT, the Qualified S Corporation Trust.

Specifically, a QSCT is defined in the Internal Revenue Code as one that

1. owns stock in one or more S corporations (and may hold other types of assets)

2. actually distributes all of its income to one individual (who must be a United States resident or United States citizen)

3. has trust terms requiring that
   (a) there can be only one beneficiary at any given time
   (b) if corpus is distributed during the term of the trust, it can be distributed only to the individual who is at that time the current income beneficiary
   (c) if an income beneficiary dies, the income interest itself will end at that death or upon the earlier termination of the trust
   (d) if the trust ends before the income beneficiary dies, all the assets of the trust must be distributed to that income beneficiary

4. requires an election to be made by the income beneficiary (or the income beneficiary's legal representative) to have the QSCT qualify as such. (Once that election is made, it is irrevocable and can be revoked only if the IRS consents.) That election must be made by each income beneficiary as he or she becomes one. Separate elections must be made if the stock of more than one S corporation is held in the trust.

If the requirements described above are met, the income beneficiary of a QSCT (which can be set up during the grantor's lifetime or by will) is treated as the owner of the stock. The consequence is that any income, as well as any gains or losses, passes directly from the S corporation to the minor beneficiary.

What are the advantages of a QSCT? A gift of S corporation stock can be made to a minor through the trust without incurring the disadvantages of outright ownership. This enables an individual to split income among family members while at the same time eliminating the gift from inclusion in his gross estate. So both income shifting and wealth transfers are possible through the QSCT.

Unlike a custodianship, a QSCT can continue beyond age 18 (or 21) and can last as long as the grantor directed it to last. This means that if the minor dies before the trust terminates, the trust can continue for the lives of a number of successive income beneficiaries and does not have to force trust assets into the estate of the deceased income beneficiary.

Question — What is a Section 678 trust?

Answer — The QSCT is not the only alternative to outright and UGMA gifts. "A nongrantor-owner trust" is an eligible S corporation stock shareholder. The criterion for favorable tax treatment under this type of trust (Section 678 governs, and therefore these nongrantor-owner trusts have come to be called "Section 678 trusts") is that the beneficiary must have unrestricted power "exercisable solely by himself to vest the corpus or the income therefrom in himself." In other words, the beneficiary will be taxed on the income from the S corporation held by the trust if he has the right to take both income and corpus whenever he wants. There must be no restrictions on the beneficiary's right to exercise a withdrawal power.

A Section 678 trust can be created by a parent or grandparent who transfers S corporation stock to it for the benefit of a minor. The minor would be given an unrestricted power to withdraw income or corpus for his own benefit.

Question — How are gifts to QSCTs and Section 678 trusts taxed for gift tax purposes?

Answer — From a gift standpoint, a contribution to either trust will be considered a complete gift. Such gifts can qualify for the $10,000 annual present-interest gift tax exclusion either by meeting the requirements of Section 2503(c) or by including a Crummey withdrawal power.

Question — Will the property in a QSCT or Section 678 trust be includible in the estate of a beneficiary?

Answer — In the case of a QSCT beneficiary, if the beneficiary is given only income rights, assets remaining in the trust at the time of the beneficiary's death will not be includible in his or her estate.

Just the opposite applies in the case of a Section 678 trust. Inclusion is a certainty since, by definition, the beneficiary must be given a general power of appointment (the power of withdrawal) over all or a portion of the trust. Property subject to that power at the time of the beneficiary's death will be includible in his or her estate.

Question — How can a client transfer ownership of a business through an S corporation and at the same time shift income?

Answer — An S corporation is an ideal vehicle to shift both wealth and income to other family members. For instance, assume a doctor, as a sideline, establishes a laboratory or dispensary. He could incorporate the business as an S corporation and give all the shares of the newly formed business to his children (all of whom are 14 or older).

The business would pay no income taxes at the corporate level. The children would pay income taxes on their share of the company's profits (which would otherwise have been taxed to their higher bracket father).

The best type of business for wealth and income shifting purposes is one in which the client performs no services (or the services are only incidental). If the client performs significant services or services which generate all the corporation's income, the IRS is likely to attribute earnings to the client and tax him accordingly. For instance, if the doctor, as a sideline, gives medical lectures for a fee, the S corporation will not be able to shift the tax on income it receives as compensation for his lectures to his children.

Conversely, if income from a passive investment (such as S corporation income from a laboratory run by a person unrelated to the doctor) is channeled to an age 14 or older child, income (and therefore tax) can be shifted without challenge.

It is important to follow formalities. For instance, stockowning children or their guardians should be invited to shareholder meetings.

Question — How have recent tax law changes affected the plurality of S corporations?

Answer — Recent tax law changes have increased the number of S elections for eligible corporations. Reasons an S election is more valuable than ever include:

- TRA '86 changed the relative rate structure making the maximum corporate income tax rates (39 percent) higher than the maximum individual income tax rate (33 percent). The passthrough nature of S corporation taxation provides that business income will be taxed at the lower individual rates.

- TRA '86 repealed the corporate-level exclusion on gains for distributions of property at liquidation. Therefore, the liquidation of a regular (C) corporation will often result in gain at the corporate level and then again at the shareholder level. This will seldom occur in an S corporation liquidation.

- The Omnibus Budget Reconciliation Act of 1987 (OBRA) created a flat tax rate of 34 percent on all taxable income of personal service C corporations. But corporations electing S corporation treatment are generally not subject to any tax at the corporate level, and their shareholders — even professional shareholders — remain entitled to the "run through the brackets" starting with rates as low as 15 percent.

Although the S election is not available for all businesses and is, likewise, not appropriate for every circumstance, a substantial number of closely held corporations can benefit from these tax advantages.

Question — What are the disadvantages of S corporation status?

Answer — Among the drawbacks to S corporation status are that an S corporation

(1) cannot accumulate earnings and profits for capital needs at corporate brackets of 15% on the first $50,000, 25% on the next $25,000, and 34% thereafter;

(2) is limited in its ability to use carryovers (such as, net operating losses or investment tax credits);

(3) is restricted in the fringe benefits it can offer its shareholder-employees (Although the tax law doesn't prohibit the S corporation from offering the benefit, since the shareholder-employee is taxable and the benefit is nondeductible by the corporation, the cost of many fringes is prohibitive.);

(4) is not appropriate as a holding vehicle for certain real estate or other investments.

Additionally, shareholders of an S corporation are prohibited from borrowing from their retirement plans (and will likely have to pay back all loans from such plans before an S election becomes effective).

Question — What is the impact of state law on the decision to elect S corporation treatment?

Answer — A decision to elect S corporation status must consider state tax laws:

(1) Some states do not recognize the S corporation's status for state income tax purposes. There are about 15 jurisdictions that do not currently allow corporate income to be passed through directly to shareholders as it is under federal law. This means the corporation will have to pay tax at the corporate level. This state law refusal to allow "passthrough" treatment may mitigate against a federal S election in states such as New Jersey and Connecticut, and in cities such as Washington, D.C. and New York City.

(2) States tax "passed-through" income at their own rates. Therefore, the reduction of federal tax rates on individuals has not, in many cases, been carried through at the state level.

(3) If the federal income tax base of individuals is used at the state level for computing the state income tax and itemized deductions of a shareholder, an S election may increase the shareholder's state taxable income.

(4) Nonresident shareholders of S corporations typically must pay income tax to the state where the S corporation does business. But if the S corporation is "doing business" in several states, the multiple tax preparations and payments could be burdensome.

(5) Some states require both a federal and a separate state S corporation election. This increases costs and administrative burdens as well as the possibility for unintentional loss of S corporation status. The IRS may not recognize for federal purposes a corporation which was not recognized as such for state purposes. The listing below shows (a) states in which the federal election of S corporation status is recognized, (b) states in which a separate state S corporation election is required, (c) states which do not recognize S corporation elections, and (d) states without an income tax:

(a) *States which recognize a federal election:* Alabama, Alaska, Arizona, Colorado, Delaware, Florida, Georgia, Hawaii, Idaho, Illinois, Iowa, Kansas, Kentucky, Maine, Maryland, Massachusetts, Minnesota, Missouri, Montana, Nebraska, New Mexico, North Dakota, Oklahoma, Ohio, Oregon, Rhode Island, South Carolina, Utah, and West Virginia.

(b) *States which require a state level election:* Arkansas, Florida, Indiana, Mississippi, New York, Pennsylvania, Virginia, and Wisconsin.

(c) *States not recognizing S corporations:* California, Connecticut, District of Columbia, Louisiana, Michigan, New Hampshire, New Jersey, North Carolina, Tennessee, and Vermont.

(d) *States without income tax.* Nevada, South Dakota, Texas, Washington, and Wyoming. Florida has no personal income tax.

Question — How does the TRA '86 tax on liquidations affect S corporations?

Answer — TRA '86 makes liquidating sales and distributions a taxable event for the liquidating corporation. This means the gain on a C corporation will be taxed at both corporate and shareholder levels.

The tax law provides relief from the new tax on liquidations for small closely held corporations, but only if they liquidate prior to 1989. To qualify for this relief, the value of the corporation must be $10,000,000 or less. Furthermore, more than 50% of its stock must be owned and held by 10 or fewer individuals for at least five years. This "relief" is phased out between $5 and $10 million, so that only corporations worth $5 million or less will receive full benefit of the relief exception.

C corporations that convert to S corporations may have a built-in tax time bomb: a tax will be imposed on certain gains of an S corporation if, within 10 years after the S election takes effect, it sells or distributes appreciated assets. The gain that must be recognized in such a situation is limited to the "net recognized net built-in gain" of the corporation at the time it elected S corporation treatment.

This means if a regular corporation elects S corporation status and it liquidates within 10 years, it will typically have to pay a corporate level tax on the amount of appreciation in its assets that existed at the time it made the S election. (The reason that so many corporations scrambled to make an S corporation election by December 31, 1986 was that this time bomb did not apply to elections made by that date, even if the first year as an S corporation was in 1987.) Certain small, closely held corporations can avoid the built in gain problem by making an S election prior to 1989.

Question — How does the corporate alternative minimum tax (AMT) affect corporations that have elected S corporation status?

Answer — TRA '86 imposed a tough corporate alternative minimum tax by adding a number of new preference items. But this tax does not apply to S corporations. This means an S election may result in significant tax saving.

Question — Do the passive loss rules affect S corporations?

Answer — If a shareholder does not materially participate in the business, losses from the business would be considered "passive." They can therefore be used only to offset passive income of the shareholder. Likewise, income received by such a shareholder from the business should be considered "passive" and should therefore offset any passive losses from other investments of the shareholder.

Question — S corporations are allowed only common stock and cannot issue preferred stock. Does this mean an S corporation can never trigger a section 2036(c) estate tax inclusion?

Answer — No, S corporations can safely issue both voting and non-voting common stock. A gift of non-voting common coupled with a retention of the voting stock could fall within the ambit of 2036(c) and cause inclusion of the non-voting stock in the client's estate. (See the explanation of 2036(c) at page 477.)

ASRS, Sec. 43; 53, ¶¶22.5; 59, ¶490.4(b).

Footnote References

S Corporation
1. IRC Sec. 1366(d), Regs. §§1.1374-1(b)(1), 1.1374-1(b)(4).
2. Reg. §1.1373-1.
3. Reg. §1.1372-5(a).

Chapter 26

SALE (GIFT) — LEASEBACK

WHAT IS IT?

A sale-leaseback involves one party selling property (or in the case of a gift-leaseback, giving property) to another party and then leasing back the same property. This type of transaction is usually intended to secure one or more of a number of income and/or estate tax advantages.

WHEN IS THE USE OF SUCH A DEVICE INDICATED?

1. When your client's problem is cash flow; his corporation is "rich" in assets, but is "poor" in cash. The sale of a selected corporate asset and the immediate leaseback of that asset can generate cash without a loss of the use of that asset.

2. When your client earns a large amount of income and is, therefore, in a high income tax bracket. He wants to divert highly taxed income to a member of his family in a lower tax bracket. The hoped-for result is the netting of more after-tax income within the family unit.

3. When your client owns property that is rapidly appreciating and would like to save estate taxes on that future growth.

4. When your client would like to find an alternative to financing business property through a mortgage. Sale-leasebacks have been called "off balance sheet" financing because the lease obligation will often appear as a footnote on the balance sheet rather than as a liability. This should have the effect of increasing his credit standing and ability to borrow money.

WHAT ARE THE REQUIREMENTS?

1. The transaction must have validity to avoid litigation and conflict with the Internal Revenue Service. There must actually be a completed and irrevocable sale (or gift) and a legally enforceable lease agreement.

2. In the case of a sale, the transaction must represent a necessary business operation and not one designed solely and merely to shift income tax responsibility.

3. The terms of the transaction, and especially the amount of the lease payment, must be arrived at in an arms-length, bona fide manner. Any rent or lease amount should be reasonable.

4. If a trustee is involved, the trustee should, in fact, be independent from the grantor of the trust. When the term of the trust is over, trust corpus should not return to the grantor.

5. Under the kiddie tax rules (see chapter 11), to successfully shift taxation to the bracket of a child, that child must be age 14 or over.

The following factors should be considered: (a) Are the lease provisions, especially payments, strictly observed? (b) Does the lessee pay the entire amount of the promised rent? (c) Is the rent reasonable? (d) Was the sale price equivalent to the fair market value of the property?[1]

A positive answer to these questions is necessary for a successful shift of income tax burdens, the attainment of a rental deduction by the lessee, and the protection of 2036(c) estate tax safe harbor provisions for leases (see page 477 et seq.).

If a trust is used, these questions should be asked: (a) Is the trust temporary? (b) Will the property revert to the grantor at the end of a given period (reversionary interest trust)? (c) Is the trust or trustee controlled by the grantor?[2]

The danger factors noted above are particularly important where the transactions are between related parties such as (1) a corporation and its stockholders; (2) husbands and wives; (3) parents and children; (4) grantors using relatives as trustees to create benefits for dependents; (5) affiliated corporations with common stockholders; and (6) taxpayers and foundations created by them.

HOW IT IS DONE — EXAMPLES

Your client, Dennis Raihall, is the president of the Son Ray Corporation. He explains to you that the business is in need of cash. It is on the verge of a break-through in its production process that could double corporate earnings, but it needs money to pay for expensive retooling.

The corporation has a number of valuable assets. One of these assets is selected and sold to the LeClair Corporation. The LeClair Corporation pays Son Ray Corporation the fair market value of the asset and now owns it. Since Son Ray Corporation still needs the asset in its business, it arranges to lease it back from the LeClair Corporation for a reasonable rental price. (It is important that the shareholders of the two corporations are not the same individuals.)

There are a number of types of assets the Son Ray Corporation could have sold: trucks, cars, machinery, equipment, fixtures, office buildings, apartment houses, and other types of real property. Furthermore, professional equipment such

Tools and Techniques

as computers, X-ray machines, etc., are all possibilities. (CAVEAT: Beware of depreciation and investment credit recapture on the sale. Note that gain is both realized and recognized on the corporate level if an appreciated asset is sold.)[3] It is important to make certain that the proposed sale-leaseback is not prohibited by a loan agreement with the firm's bank.

The after-tax proceeds of the sale will give the Son Ray Corporation additional cash and increase its working capital. Assets continue in operation just as they did before the sale. The basic difference is that instead of Son Ray carrying that particular item on its books as an asset, it now leases the property and pays rent for its use. Son Ray will now have the use of a large sum of cash, the after tax proceeds of the sale, which can be used to generate additional profits.

Suppose that Son Ray Corporation owned a factory it built more than 10 years ago at a cost of $200,000. The market value of the property is currently $250,000 (land $50,000, building, $200,000). The Son Ray Corporation has decided not to mortgage the property because the rate of interest it would have to pay is very high, it would not be able to write off payments of principal, and it feels that it could obtain more cash through a sale. Another reason it chose not to mortgage the property was that such a debt would adversely affect its credit standing and ability to borrow additional funds.

The property could be sold for $250,000 and leased back for 10 years with additional options at an annual rental of $30,000. Only the profit on the sale (net proceeds less adjusted basis) would be subject to tax. If an accelerated method of depreciation had been used, deductions taken in prior years may have to be recaptured and reported as additional income received on the sale. Son Ray Corporation now has the balance of the after tax sale proceeds to develop the process that may double overall corporate earnings.

Another way the leaseback arrangement is often utilized is in intrafamily transfers. For example, your client, Mary Jo Kopeznsky, a highly compensated physician, complains about the high income tax burden she faces every year. She wants you to show her how to maximize her family income by minimizing her overall tax burden.

She could transfer (as a gift) business property she owns (such as expensive medical equipment or a professional office building she owns and shares with a number of other professionals) to an irrevocable inter vivos trust established for her 14 year old daughter. The trustee could be a bank or other independent fiduciary. The trust, at a reasonable rental, leases the building back to Doctor Kopeznsky. This means the doctor does not have to move out of her building or lose the use of her equipment. Her daughter is immediately benefited. It is extremely important that there be no preconceived agreement with the trustee as to the amount of rental to be paid or the terms of the lease.

The trust could either distribute the rental income each year to the doctor's daughter or accumulate it for later distribution to her. For example, when her daughter reaches age 18 (and in many states is no longer a minor), trust income or principal might be distributed each year and paid outright and unconditionally to the daughter. If the daughter chose to, she could use the money to pay for her own college education. If, under the applicable state law a parent is not obligated to provide a college education for an adult child, none of the income will be taxable to the high tax bracket mother, even if it is paid directly to the daughter's college.

WHAT ARE THE TAX IMPLICATIONS?

1. In the case of a sale and leaseback, the corporation that sells an asset must pay tax on any gain realized just as in the case of any other sale. Likewise, just as any partnership or corporation that rents property is allowed to take a tax deduction for the cost of the rental, when a sale-leaseback occurs, the fair rental paid by the seller for the use of its previously owned property is completely deductible as an ordinary and necessary business expense.[4]

2. In the case of a gift-leaseback, proper care will enable the donor to receive a double benefit. First, the donor will obtain a business tax deduction for payments of rent. Then, when the rental income is paid to the trust (assuming it is a nongrantor trust), it will generally be taxed to the trust (as long as it is accumulated) or to the donor's child or other trust beneficiary.[5] Ordinarily, the tax bracket of the beneficiary or the trust will be lower than the donor's. The tax savings can provide an excellent means of establishing a college education fund. When income is paid to a minor below age 14, the child will be taxed, but at the parent's top bracket, to the extent the payment exceeds $1,000. There-fore, a recipient child must be 14 or older for the income shift to work.

3. By making an irrevocable gift of an asset (except life insurance transferred by the insured within three years of death), future growth is removed from the client's estate at no additional estate tax cost.

4. There may be gift tax implications if there is an outright gift or if the sales price is less than the property's fair market value.

5. Cost recovery and interest deductions may offset a significant portion of the income from the lease. The lessee will be able to completely deduct the lease payments as an ordinary and necessary business expense. In the case of a sale-leaseback, the lessee would have to report interest income. If the lessee-user acquires the property and subsequently disposes of it, he will be subject to the recapture rules relating to cost recovery deductions, just as if he had been the owner of the property all along.

IMPLICATIONS AND ISSUES IN COMMUNITY PROPERTY STATES

With respect to the sale-leaseback, two aspects are present. Initially, if the sale price is later found to be less than what was the then fair market value, the amount of the gift (undervaluation) is spread between both spouses if the asset was community property. However, many other states' gift taxes have a much lower threshold than federal gift taxes, as to current cash tax payments, and consideration may be given to filing, in the year of the sale-leaseback, a gift tax return based on some other gift, thus possibly starting any statute of limitation periods to begin to run as to any subsequent imposition of a gift tax deficiency, including interest and penalties.

The second concern is making sure that valid legal title has passed. The new California statutory scheme, for example, grants the right to the management and control of community property to either spouse, with certain exceptions. With respect to the lease, mortgage or transfer of real property, both spouses must join in executing the conveying instrument, and practitioners should obtain both signatures for any transfer (including the gift) of any asset.

QUESTIONS AND ANSWERS

Question — In the case of a gift-leaseback, what are the basic prerequisites?

Answer — Where a donor transfers an office building or other income producing assets to a trust for a child and then leases it back:

(1) The donor cannot retain substantially the same control over the property as he or she did before the gift was made.

(2) The leaseback must be in writing and must provide for a reasonable rental (get an appraisal).

(3) The leaseback, as distinguished from the gift in trust, must have a bona fide business purpose.[6]

(4) The trust must have an independent trustee unrelated to the grantor.[7]

Question — What does the Internal Revenue Service look at in the case of sale-leaseback between related parties?

Answer — Basically, the Internal Revenue Service is trying to determine whether the transaction is genuine or merely structured as a sale. If the transaction is, in reality, a disguised loan, at best only part of the "rental" payments will be deductible because they will be considered payments of interest and principal. Only the interest portion can be taken as a tax deduction.[8] Assuming the interest is considered "investment interest," it will be deductible, but only to the extent the taxpayer has investment income. Interest will be deductible without limit if it is considered "business interest." The characterization will be determined case by case, based on the facts and circumstances.

Alternatively, if the transaction is considered a sale, the seller-lessee has to pay a tax on any gain realized. If the property is leased for business purposes, he will be able to deduct his payment under the lease as rent.

The buyer-lessor also would be concerned with the distinction. In the case of a bona fide sale, the buyer-lessor may take depreciation or cost recovery (under the Accelerated Cost Recovery System for assets placed in service after 1980) deductions to the extent of the portion of the purchase price which is allocable to buildings or improvements and be entitled to a deduction for all expenses relating to the maintenance and operation of the property.[9] However, if the Internal Revenue Service treats the transaction as a loan, the buyer will not be entitled to these deductions. This is because the buyer will be considered as a mere mortgagee rather than as owner of the property.

If the transaction is considered a sale, the next question is whether or not the sale price is equal to the fair market value of the property. If the sale price is less than the fair market value of the property transferred, the difference may be considered a gift. This may result in a gift tax being imposed on the seller-lessee.

Question — How can the transaction be structured to minimize an Internal Revenue Service challenge that the arrangement is in reality a loan?

Answer — If possible, the transaction should be structured so that it falls within the safe harbor set up under the Economic Recovery Tax Act of 1981. To qualify, the lessor must be a corporation other than a Subchapter S corporation, the lessor must have a minimum "at risk" investment of 10% of the adjusted basis of the property at all times, and the term of the lease, including extensions, must not exceed certain limits. The property must be leased within three months of its acquisition or, in the case of a sale-leaseback, it must be purchased by the lessor within three months of the lessee's acquisition for a price not in excess of the adjusted basis of the property in the hands of the lessee.

If the safe harbor test cannot be utilized then the transaction should have economic reality. In this regard, all the significant burdens and benefits of ownership should be transferred to the new owner. The parties should assume their obligations as lessee and lessor, respectively. The sale price of the property should be fair and reasonable in light of current market conditions and sales of comparable properties. Financial arrangements must be reasonable.

The transaction should not force a "buy-back." If there is a compulsory repurchase option, the seller is in virtually the same position he would have been in had he mortgaged the property rather than selling it and leasing it back. If a buy-back provision is included, the terms

Tools and Techniques

must be arranged and the amount of the purchase price computed as a result of arms-length bargaining.

The buyer must receive the benefit of any appreciation in value. A final factor generally examined is the application of rent toward the repurchase price. The rental price paid by the lessee should be realistic. It should closely approximate rentals for comparable property and comparable facilities. If part of the rent is to be applied to a repurchase price, the Internal Revenue Service might claim that such payments are in reality disguised payments of interest rather than payments for the use of the property.[10]

Question — What is the primary economic disadvantage to funding through a sale-leaseback rather than a mortgage?

Answer — The primary drawback is the loss of the residual value of the property at the termination of the lease. This drawback can be minimized through a repurchase option or option(s) to renew the lease over the expected life of the property.

Question — What terms should be specified in the lease that may help sustain an equal bargaining position between the donor and the trustee?

Answer —

A. Set rent at current market rates (obtain at least one outside appraisal expert's opinion).

B. Provide for a single year lease term that must be renegotiated each year.

C. Place the property on the open market for lease (the higher the rental the grantor actually pays, the greater the overall tax shift). Note, however, that to the extent rents are deemed "excessive," they might be disallowed as deductions.

D. Provide that lease payments are made "as a condition to the continued use or possession of the premises."

E. Trustee should establish—and strictly enforce—a payment schedule. (Where payments were made randomly, in different amounts, at the client's convenience, and not according to a schedule determined by the trustee, it was held that the grantor failed to relinquish total control over trust property.)

Question — In what situations will the grantor be taxed on trust income?

Answer — The grantor will be taxed on trust income:

1. if he or his spouse has retained a reversionary interest;

2. if he retains power to control beneficial enjoyment;

3. if he retains certain administrative powers;

4. if he retains the power to revoke the trust;

5. if the income is used to pay support and maintenance to a person whom the grantor is legally obligated to support;

6. if the income can be distributed or accumulated to the grantor or his spouse without the approval of an adverse party.

Note that avoiding these situations does not per se assure a rental deduction. These situations concern only the issue of "Is there a valid trust?" and "To whom is the income taxable?" Although the two issues are concurrently operative, they are treated by the IRS as mutually exclusive.

One possible solution is to have someone other than the client fund the trust. For instance, the client's spouse could put cash into an irrevocable trust for the couple's children. The trust could use that cash to purchase assets owned solely by the client in his own name. The trust could then lease the assets to the client's corporation.

Question — What are the best types of property to use in a gift-leaseback?

Answer — The best types of property are *tangible* assets used in the client's trade, business, or profession, such as: land, depreciated buildings (beware of recapture), office equipment (such as computers, word processors, photocopiers), library, trucks and machinery, and other tangibles and office accoutrements needed in business.

Question — Will *cash* work in a gift-leaseback?

Answer — A client *could* fund the trust with cash. The trustee could then acquire new equipment and lease it to the grantor or the grantor's corporation or purchase equipment from the grantor and then lease it back. (Note that some authorities feel the "transfer of cash" method is more vulnerable to IRS attack than the "transfer of property" method where the cash is used to buy property already owned by the grantor.)

Question — Is geographical location of the taxpayer a consideration in planning a transfer and leaseback arrangement?

Answer — It is with respect to your client's chances of prevailing in litigation with the IRS. The chart at Figure 26.1, "Your Odds in the Circuits," lets you see at a glance where the outlook is favorable, unfavorable, or chancy.

ASRS, Sec. 51.

Footnote References

Sale (Gift)—Leaseback

1. See Rev. Rul. 55-540, 1955-2 C.B. 39; Rev. Proc. 75-21, 1975-1 C.B. 715, as modified by Rev. Proc. 79-48, 1979-2 C.B. 529, *Estate of Franklin*, 64 T.C. 752 (1975), *Narver v. Comm.*, 76 T.C. 53 (1980), *Hager et al. v. Commr.*, 76 T.C. 759 (1981).

2. See *Oakes v. Comm.*, 44 T.C. 524 (1965); *Audano v. U.S.*, 428 F.2d 251 (CA-5, 1970).

3. IRC Sections 1245, 1250.

4. IRC Section 162. Can a sale-leaseback result in a deductible loss? Yes, says the Tax Court, if there is a bona fide sale and not an exchange of like-kind property. But, in the favorable case of *Leslie, Co. v. Comm.*, 64 T.C. 247 (1975), the IRS has non-acquiesced. Nonacq. 1978-47, I.R.B. 5.

5. IRC Sections 641, 652, 662.

6. *Van Zandt v. Comm.*, 341 F.2d 440 (CA-5, 1965) aff'g. 40 T.C. 824, cert. den. 382 U.S. 814.

7. *Oakes v. Comm.*, 44 T.C. 524 (1965).

8. See Rev. Rul. 55-540, 1955-2 C.B. 39. In *Servousek v. Comm.*, T.C. Memo 1977-105, the Tax Court allowed a rent deduction on a gift-leaseback of a medical building. In that case a taxpayer (1) gave up all beneficial control over the property; (2) paid a reasonable rent; (3) had a business purpose for the lease (he needed the building for his practice); and (4) retained no equity in the property during the lease period. See also *Lerner v. Comm.*, 71 T.C. No. 24 (1978). *May v. Comm.*, 76 T.C. No. 2 (1981).

   For an example of how *not* to arrange a gift-leaseback, see *Frank Lyon Co. v. U.S.*, 38 A.F.T.R. 2d 76-5019 (8th Cir. 1976); *Hilton v. Comm.*, 74 T.C. 305 (1980).

9. IRC Sections 167, 162; Reg. §1.162-4.

10. See Rev. Rul. 55-540, 1955-2 C.B. 39; Rev. Proc. 75-21, 1975-1 C.B. 715, as modified by Rev. Proc. 79-48, 1979-2 C.B. 529.

Figure 26.1

YOUR ODDS IN THE CIRCUITS

Second, Eighth and Ninth Circuits	Third and Seventh Circuits	Fourth Circuit	Fifth Circuit	Circuits That Have Not Ruled on Gift Leasebacks
New York, Vermont, Connecticut, North Dakota, South Dakota, Nebraska, Minnesota, Iowa, Missouri, Arkansas/Montana, Washington, Oregon, Idaho, Nevada, California, Arizona, Alaska, Hawaii, and Guam	Pennsylvania, New Jersey, Delaware, and the Virgin Islands/Wisconsin, Illinois, and Indiana	West Virginia, Virginia, Maryland, North Carolina, South Carolina	Mississippi, Louisiana, Texas	All others
Courts should side with the taxpayer if 1. T.P. doesn't maintain control over property (satisfied by independent trustee). 2. Rental payments are reasonable and terms of rent reduced to writing. 3. Leaseback has a business purpose.	Courts will side with taxpayer if Eighth and Ninth Circuit tests are met.	Courts are tougher here than in Eighth, Ninth, Third and Seventh Circuits, but deduction still possible where grantor gives up control and title to property is placed in valid irrevocable trust.	Taxpayers have consistently failed in attempts to obtain rental deductions. (This Ct. looks at the purpose of the arrangement as well as the arrangement itself and this Circuit has demanded that the T.P. show a business reason for *both* the lease-back and the gift itself.) But this court has not held that all intra-family trust lease-backs are economic nullities	Taxpayers likely to face litigation but likelihood of success is highest if 1. independent trustee used 2. arm's-length lease signed after negotiation with trustee 3. duration of trust exceeds length of lease
See *Quinlivan v. Comm'r*, 599 F.2d 269 (CA-8, 1979); *Brooke v. Comm'r*, 468 F.2d 1155 (CA-9, 1972); *Rosenfeld v. Comm'r*, 83-1 USTC ¶9341 (CA-2, 1983).	See *Brown v. Comm'r*, 180 F.2d 926 (CA-3, 1950); see also *S. Kemp v. Comm'r*, 168 F.2d 598 (CA-7, 1948).	See *Perry v. U.S.*, 520 F.2d 235 (CA-4, 1975), cert. den.	See *Van Zandt v. Comm'r*, 341 F.2d 440 (CA-5, 1965), cert. den. See also *Butler*, 65 T.C. 327 (1975).	Although there are cases on gift leasebacks in these circuits (cited below), none of these met all the tests set forth by the Tax Court, so it is not known how an Appeals Court in one of these circuits would react to a properly structured arrangement. See *Duffy v. U.S.*, 487 F.2d 282 (CA-6, 1973).

nor has it held that "economic reality" was unattainable with trust lease-backs. It appears that the Fifth Circuit is placing undue weight on the origin of the trustee's title in the property, a factor which is not otherwise considered relevant in cases dealing with rental payment deductability. See *Van Zandt v. Comm'r*, 341 F.2d 440 (CA-5, 1965), cert. den. See also *Butler*, 65 T.C. 327 (1975).

Chapter 27

SECTION 303 STOCK REDEMPTION

WHAT IS IT?

Section 303 of the Internal Revenue Code establishes a way for a corporation to make a distribution in redemption of a portion of the stock of a decedent that will not be taxed as a dividend. A Section 303 partial redemption can provide cash and/or other property from the corporation without resulting in dividend treatment and provides cash for the decedent shareholder's executor to use to pay death taxes and other expenses.

WHEN IS THE USE OF SUCH A DEVICE INDICATED?

1. When there is a desire to keep control of a close or family corporation within the decedent-shareholder's family after death.

2. When the corporation's stock is a major estate asset and a forced sale or liquidation of the business in order to pay death taxes and other costs is a threat.

3. Where a tax-favored withdrawal of funds from the corporation at the death of the stockholder would be useful.

4. When a redemption of Section 306 stock is desirable.

WHAT ARE THE REQUIREMENTS?

1. The redeemed stock must be included in the decedent's gross estate for federal estate tax purposes.[1]

2. The value for federal estate tax purposes of all stock of the corporation that is included in determining the value of the decedent's gross estate must be *more than* 35 percent of the excess of (1) the value of the gross estate over (2) the sum allowable as a deduction under Code sections 2053 (estate expenses, indebtedness, and taxes) and 2054 (losses).

3. Only an amount equal to the total of (a) all estate, inheritance, legacy, and succession taxes (including generation-skipping transfer taxes) and interest thereon imposed by reason of decedent's death, and (b) funeral and administration expenses (whether or not claimed as a deduction on the federal estate tax return) can be redeemed and receive favorable income tax treatment (i.e., avoid dividend treatment). Any excess will be taxed under the rules of Code Section 302.[3] This means any balance may be taxed as a dividend to the "seller," the executor or heir from whom the stock is being redeemed, or the balance may qualify for favorable tax treatment (no realization of taxable gain) if within the purview of Code section 302.

4. A redemption under Section 303 will qualify for favorable tax treatment only to the extent that the interest of a shareholder whose stock is redeemed is reduced either directly or indirectly through a binding obligation to contribute toward the payment of the decedent's administration expenses and death taxes.

In a hypothetical situation, assume the gross estate is $1,250,000; administrative and funeral costs are $250,000, and there are no other deductible expenses. To qualify for a Section 303 redemption, the value of the stock in question must *exceed* $350,000 (i.e., must be more than 35% of ($1,000,000 − $250,000)).

HOW IT IS DONE — EXAMPLES

The Section 303 stock redemption is relatively simple: The corporation redeems stock from the party who receives it at the death of the decedent-stockholder in question. Usually, the recipient of the stock will be the decedent-shareholder's personal representative, that is, the decedent's executor or administrator. Sometimes the seller will be a direct heir, surviving spouse, or trustee or an irrevocable trust created by the decedent. The redemption is protected under Section 303, however, only if it is from a stockholder who is obligated to pay death taxes, funeral, or administration expenses or whose share of the decedent's estate is reduced by these expenses.

Stock may not be redeemed from any stockholder who acquired his stock by purchase or gift (if the donor was not the decedent).[4] For example, if a father wills stock to his son and his son later sells or gives the stock to his brother, the brother's stock is not eligible for a Section 303 stock redemption in the father's estate. Also, Section 303 is not applicable where stock is redeemed from a stockholder who has acquired the stock from the executor in satisfaction of a specific monetary bequest.[5]

Without adequate prior planning, there may be insufficient funds in the corporation to effect a Section 303 redemption. Generally speaking, cash will be needed if the main purpose of a Section 303 redemption is to provide liquidity. A method of funding that will guarantee the necessary cash on the insured's death is the purchase of life insurance on the stockholder by the corporation.

The life insurance used to fund the Section 303 redemption should be a typical key man policy. The corporation should be the applicant, owner, premium payor, and beneficiary. (In the case of an uninsurable stockholder, a sink-

Tools and Techniques

Figure 27.1

DETERMINATION OF WHETHER ESTATE QUALIFIES FOR SECTION 303 STOCK REDEMPTION

FEDERAL ESTATE TAX VALUE OF CORPORATE STOCK
IN GROSS ESTATE . . . . (1) $600,000

GROSS ESTATE LESS ALLOWABLE DEDUCTIONS . . . . (2) $1,000,000
(Gross Estate less Allowable Deductions)

35% OF GROSS ESTATE LESS ALLOWABLE DEDUCTIONS . . . . (3) $350,000

QUALIFIES IF (1) IS GREATER THAN (3)

REDEMPTION UNDER SECTION 303 PROTECTED TO EXTENT OF

FUNERAL AND ADMINISTRATION EXPENSES $47,000

FEDERAL ESTATE AND GENERATION-SKIPPING TAXES $119,800

STATE DEATH TAXES $33,200

GENERATION SKIPPING TRANSFER TAXES $0

INTEREST COLLECTED AS PART OF ABOVE TAXES $0

MAXIMUM ALLOWABLE SECTION 303 REDEMPTION $200,000

(The foregoing computer printout was furnished courtesy of NumberCruncher Software)

---

ing fund can be established by using fixed or variable annuities, mutual funds, or other securities.)

For example, assume Aaron, a widower who dies in 1988, owns 75 percent of a corporation. His son Joshua owns the remaining 25 percent. Aaron's stock is valued at $600,000. His gross estate less allowable deductions under Code sections 2053 and 2054 is $1,000,000. Assume he has minimal estate liquidity. The family corporation is in the 34 percent federal income tax bracket. Aaron is in the 28 percent income tax bracket. The corporation would purchase $200,000 of life insurance on Aaron's life. (This assumes Aaron's estate and inheritance taxes and other death related expenses will approximate $200,000.)

Step 1: At Aaron's death, his stock will pass to his estate. *Step 2:* The corporation would then receive the insurance proceeds on Aaron's life. *Step 3:* The corporation would use the life insurance proceeds to pay Aaron's estate for stock qualifying for the Section 303 redemption. *Step 4:* The estate would transfer $200,000 worth of stock to the corporation. *Step 5:* Aaron's estate will use the cash to pay federal and state death taxes and administrative and funeral expenses.

WHAT ARE THE TAX IMPLICATIONS?

1. The amount paid to the estate should not be treated as a dividend distribution. Instead, it will be treated as the

"exchange price" for the stock and will generally result in no gain being recognized at all by the estate if the basis for the stock has been "stepped up" by reason of being included in the shareholder's estate, unless the stock was gifted to the decedent within one year of his death and the property passes from the donee-decedent back to the donor or the donor's spouse.[6] However, to the extent the price paid to the estate exceeds the estate's basis, it will pay a tax on any such gain. Although the stock sold is a capital asset, since passage of the 1986 Tax Reform Act, there will not be any deduction from income for any part of the gain, and it will, therefore, be taxed at ordinary income tax rates.

Under the step-up-in-basis rules, a redemption in accordance with Section 303 typically results in no adverse income tax consequences to the shareholder from whom the corporation made the redemption (generally the executor of the estate).

The favorable treatment occurs because the basis of the stock in the executor's hands (say $10 a share) is "stepped up" to the stock's fair market value for federal estate tax purposes (say $26 a share) and the $26 a share price paid to the executor by the corporation to redeem the stock is generally equal to the stock's basis, i.e., the $26 a share fair market value for federal estate tax purposes. Thus, the amount realized on the "sale" is exactly equal to the seller's basis and so there is no taxable gain for income tax purposes. In some cases the value per share paid by the corporation is greater than the value of the stock per share for federal estate tax purposes; when that happens, a capital gain results.

2. The insurance premiums paid on the life of the insured stockholder are not income tax deductible by the corporation.[7]

3. When the proceeds of the key man life insurance are paid to the corporation at the death of the stockholder, they will be received free of federal income taxes (with the possible exception of any corporate level alternative minimum tax).[8]

4. Section 303 redemptions are specifically exempt from attribution (constructive ownership) problems which helps to make redemptions from family corporations possible without the threat of dividend treatment.

IMPLICATIONS AND ISSUES IN COMMUNITY PROPERTY STATES

In order to qualify (aggregate) an ownership interest in two or more corporations for purposes of meeting the "more than 35 percent of adjusted gross estate" test, there must be at least 20 percent in value of each corporation included in the decedent's estate. In determining the 20 percent stock ownership by decedent, the surviving spouse's half of stock constituting community property may be included by treating it as if it had been included in determining the value of the gross estate of the decedent.

QUESTIONS AND ANSWERS

Question — Is cash the only property that may be distributed by the corporation?

Answer — No. If the need for liquidity exists, cash is generally the most practical type of property, but Section 303 does not require that the corporation make its purchase of the decedent's stock in cash. The corporation can distribute property "in kind." For instance, the corporation might distribute income-producing assets such as rental property (e.g., an apartment house, office building, or parking lot) in return for the stock it receives. The corporation would not generally recognize gain as a result of the redemption with the most notable exceptions being recapture of depreciation[9], liability in excess of basis[10], and the excess of the value distributed over the amount qualifying under Section 303(a)[11].

Question — Do the funds received in the redemption have to be used to pay estate settlement costs?

Answer — No, the funds received in the redemption do not have to be used directly to pay estate settlement costs. Often, an estate will already have sufficient cash. The estate's settlement costs (exclusive of debts) only serve as a measure of the amount which can be redeemed. As long as the requirements for Section 303 are met, the corporation can redeem the permitted number of shares regardless of whether or not the executor actually needs the cash for liquidity purposes.

Question — Is an agreement necessary for Section 303 redemptions?

Answer — Generally, an agreement is unnecessary in the case where the executor will acquire the controlling interest in the corporation. However, an agreement would be advantageous to a minority stockholder. This would provide assurance that his estate will benefit by a Section 303 redemption. (Quite often, however, a complete redemption is preferable to a partial redemption. This is particularly true in the case of the death of a minority shareholder because of the relatively weak voting control position the survivors of such a shareholder will have.) Specific permission should be granted by the stockholder in his will allowing his or her executor to effect the redemption.

Question — Can a Section 303 stock redemption be effected without a majority stockholder's losing control?

Answer — It is possible to effect a 303 stock redemption without losing corporate control or diluting stock interest. Where there is a nonvoting class of stock outstanding, it is permissible for the corporation to redeem only the nonvoting stock.[12]

Generally, only one class of stock (common) is outstanding. There are two or perhaps three ways to accomplish the 303 redemption without creating voting or control problems. Recapitalization is the first method. If a corporation has only one class of stock outstanding, a shareholder may exchange a portion of his or her voting common stock for nonvoting preferred stock of equal value. The new preferred stock is then redeemed under Section 303. This creates no adverse effect on the voting control of the corporation.

A second method of overcoming voting and control problems is the issuance of a preferred stock dividend prior to the death of a decedent-stockholder. A preferred stock dividend is declared on the common stock. This entails no recapitalization and, normally, the dividend is tax free. Then the preferred stock is redeemed pursuant to Section 303.

A third possible means of taking money out of a closely held corporation through section 303 without a relative loss of control was suggested by a ruling which allowed the company to issue a stock dividend of nonvoting stock and to redeem the newly issued stock from the estate without creating a taxable distribution. The approval for such a stock dividend followed by a redemption should be obtained from corporate shareholders.[13]

229

It does not matter, for Section 303 redemption purposes, that the new preferred stock under either of the above-described methods is "Section 306 stock," the sale or redemption of which ordinarily results in ordinary income to the seller (see Chapter 23). Under the stepped-up basis rules, the regulations make it clear that "a distribution in redemption of stock will qualify under Section 303, notwithstanding the fact that the stock redeemed is Section 306 stock to the extent that the conditions of Section 303 are met."[14]

Question — How is it possible to improve the chances of meeting Section 303 tests?

Answer — Lifetime gifts of personal insurance or other property (except the stock in question) to the surviving shareholder's family may reduce the gross estate of the stockholder (but only to the extent such gifts are not made within three years of the stockholder's death). Gifts of assets within 3 years of death are brought back into the gross estate for purposes of Code Section 303 and its tests.

A sale by the stockholder to the corporation of a personally owned life insurance policy on the stockholder's life or a contribution to the capital of the corporation should make qualification for a 303 redemption easier. This is because the stockholder's gross estate may not be significantly changed. The value of his business interest relative to his personal estate should be increased. (This may also make it easier to qualify for an installment payout of estate taxes attributable to the business.) Another technique to accomplish the same result is the purchase by the corporation of new key man insurance coverage.

Question — Can a 303 redemption be effected at any time?

Answer — The proceeds must be received after the decedent's death and no later than: (1) three years and 90 days from the due date of the federal estate tax return; or (2) 60 days after a tax court decision in a contest of estate tax liability has become final; or (3) the time permitted for the payment of estate tax installments where the executor has elected and the estate qualifies for a deferred payment of estate taxes attributable to the business under Section 6166 (up to 15 years).

However, where a distribution is made more than four years after the decedent's death, the amount of protected distribution is limited to the lesser of: (a) the amount of taxes, funeral, and administrative expenses remaining unpaid at that time, or (b) the taxes and expenses that are actually paid within one year of the Section 303 payment to the stockholder.

Question — If there is more than one class of stock outstanding, can the aggregate value of all classes be taken into account in meeting the "more than 35 percent test?

Answer — Yes, all types of stock can be added together in meeting the "more than 35 percent" test or the corporation can redeem solely preferred stock if so desired.[15]

Question — May stock of two or more corporations be aggregated for purposes of meeting the "more than 35 percent of adjusted gross estate" tests?

Answer — Only if 20 percent or more in value of the outstanding stock of *each* corporation is included in the decedent's gross estate.[16]

Question — Are the constructive ownership (attribution) rules a problem?

Answer — No, to the extent that stock is redeemed under Section 303, these rules can be ignored.

Question — Assume the executor needs cash quickly and before an IRS audit a Section 303 redemption takes place. At the audit of the estate tax return: (a) the IRS increases the valuation on the stock; (b) the IRS decreases the valuation; or (c) for some other reason the redemption does not qualify under Section 303. How can dividend treatment be avoided?

Answer — Arrange for the first contingency by providing that the purchase price and the number of shares redeemed will be adjusted so that the corporation will pay no more, and no less, than the value of the stock is finally determined for federal estate tax purposes. Alternatively, a contingency agreement that voids the purchase and sale could be arranged in the event that the "more than 35 percent" test is not met.

Question — Can the corporation issue notes instead of cash to buy the stock?

Answer — Yes. The stock can be purchased in exchange, not only for cash, but also for property including notes. The redemption rules are met when the notes are delivered, not when they are actually paid. However, the notes should have a fairly short (5 years or less) maturity date. Stock of the corporation making the distribution does not qualify as "property".[17]

Question — Does the money received by the seller of the redeemed stock have to be applied toward death taxes and other estate expenses?

Answer — Technically, no. But in essence, distributions are shielded from dividend treatment only to the extent a shareholder's interest is reduced (directly or through a binding obligation to contribute) by federal and state death taxes and administration and funeral expenses.

Question — Can the corporation redeem stock other than that held by the executor at the time of the stockholder's death?

Answer — Yes, subject to the limitations discussed directly above; if for any reason stock was included in the decedent-stockholder's gross estate, it can be redeemed even if it is in the hands of someone other than the estate's executor at the time of the redemption.[18] For example, if a mother purchased stock with her own funds and held it jointly with her daughter when she died, the entire value of the stock would be in the mother's estate but the daughter would become the owner of the stock. A 303 redemption would be permissible to the extent the daughter's interest had to bear a portion of her mother's estate's taxes and estate settlement costs. The corporation could purchase (redeem) the stock directly from the daughter.

Likewise (subject to the limitation discussed above regarding an obligation for taxes and expenses), where the stock transferred is considered included in the decedent's estate because of a transfer with a retained life estate, a transfer taking effect at death or a revocable transfer,[19] the corporation could purchase the stock under Section 303 from the new owner. The same result occurs where the stock is placed into a revocable trust. Since the stock would be included in the decedent-stockholder's estate, a redemption from the trustee would be allowed (again, assuming the share of the estate going into the trust bears a direct or indirect burden to pay death taxes or administration costs or is reduced by such amounts).

Question — Will life insurance owned by the corporation to fund the Section 303 redemption cause or aggravate an accumulated earnings tax problem?

Answer — In general, if in any tax year the corporation's taxable income is retained for the purpose of paying insurance premiums (or for any other purpose) in excess of the amount of the accumulated earnings credit ($250,000, except for "service" corporations, which are allowed only $150,000) the corporation should be prepared to show that such excess retentions are necessary to meet reasonable needs of the business; such excess retentions that are beyond reasonable business needs may attract the tax. Where an uncommitted key individual life insurance policy (of the appropriate amount and type) is used to shift the risk of the loss of a key person's services, it will generally not cause or aggravate an accumulated earnings tax problem

Likewise, even though death proceeds do increase earnings and profits (to the extent they exceed premiums paid), they should not, per se, cause or aggravate an accumulated earnings tax problem. Term, whole life, or a similar low cash value policy should be used. Furthermore, the redemption should be effected, wherever possible, in the same fiscal year that death occurs.

Note: The Internal Revenue Code provides that "the reasonable needs of the business" include the "Section 303 redemption needs of the business." However, the Internal Revenue Service's position is that this provision applies only to amounts accumulated in the year of death and thereafter.

Many authorities are suggesting that a third party — such as an irrevocable trust—own the life insurance. At the shareholder's death, the proceeds would be paid to the policy owner who could then make a fully secured loan to the corporation. The corporation could then redeem the stock under Code Section 303. The advantage of this technique is that the insurance proceeds don't "swell" the value of the corporation for estate tax purposes.

Question — If closely held stock is left to a specific legatee under the terms of a deceased stockholder's will, and there is a provision in the will which states that estate and inheritance taxes will be paid out of the residue of the estate, can there be a Section 303 redemption?

Answer — No. There cannot be a Section 303 redemption because the specific legatee will not bear any portion of paying the taxes. The redemption will qualify under Section 303 only to the extent that the interest of the redeemed shareholder is reduced directly or through a binding obligation to contribute to the payment of death taxes or funeral or administration costs.

ASRS, Sec. 43.

Footnote References

Section 303 Stock Redemption

1. IRC Section 303(a).
2. IRC Section 303(b)(2)(A).
3. IRC Section 303(a).
4. Reg. §1.303-2(f).
5. Reg. §1.303-2(f).
6. Reg. §1.303-1; IRC Sec. 1014(e).
7. IRC Section 264(a)(1).
8. IRC Section 101(a)(1).
9. IRC Sections 1245, 1250.
10. IRC Section 311(c).
11. IRC Section 311(d)(2)(C).
12. Reg. §1.303-2(c)(1).
13. Rev. Rul. 87-132, 1987-50 I.R.B. 4.
14. IRC Section 306(b)(5).
15. Reg. §1.303-2(c)(1).
16. IRC Section 303(b)(2)(B).
17. Rev. Rul. 65-289, 1965-2 C.B. 86; IRC Sections 303(a), 317.
18. Reg. §1.303-1.
19. IRC Sections 2036-2038.

Chapter 28

SPLIT INTEREST PURCHASE OF PROPERTY (Split)

WHAT IS IT?

A "Split" is an arrangement under which two parties agree to purchase an asset. One party (usually a parent) purchases a life estate (the right to receive the income from the property or the right to use, possess, and enjoy the property itself for as long as the life tenant lives). The second party (usually a son or daughter or grandchild of the life tenant) purchases a remainder interest (the right to the property, whatever it is worth, when the first party's interest terminates. If the first party purchased a life interest, by definition his interest terminates when he dies). Each party to the Split pays the actuarial value of the interest purchased.

There are many estate planning advantages to a Split. Two major tax advantages are that: (1) upon the life tenant's death, none of the property should be in his estate for estate, inheritance, or generation skipping tax purposes since he never owned the right to transfer an interest at his death, and (2) the life tenant's estate is depleted at no gift, estate, or generation skipping transfer tax cost by the amount of his contibution to the Split.

A Split is one of the more important value shifting vehicles available after the Tax Reform Act of 1986, the Omnibus Budget Reconciliation Act of 1987, and the Technical and Miscellaneous Revenue Act of 1988.

WHEN IS THE USE OF SUCH A DEVICE INDICATED?

1. When it is desirable to reduce a client's estate tax or avoid a generation skipping transfer tax. A split could save hundreds of thousands or even millions of dollars. There is no federal estate or generation skipping transfer tax because, at death, there is no transfer.

2. When a client would like to improve current income but lower current income taxes. If a Split is used to purchase income producing investment property, the client's income is enhanced by the remainderman's investment. Yet, it may be possible to amortize the client's investment and therefore shield a significant portion of investment income (from the Split or other investment income) from income tax.

3. When the client wants to transfer substantial wealth without the imposition of a gift tax. The Split is in all respects a bona fide arms' length transaction between the two parties (life tenant and remainderman) and between them and the third party from whom the property is purchased. Assuming no fraud, the property is purchased for its fair market value and each of the buyers is paying his actuarially fair share of the purchase price. There is, therefore, no gift involved.

4. When it is important to keep property within a family, but the client wants to enjoy it or needs to use it or receive its income for life, a Split may be strong protection against a will contest or an election against the will. Split property passes by contract and should not be part of the probate estate. So generally a disgruntled heir would have no right to property purchased through a Split. Likewise, a Split offers protection against the claims of a client's creditors and because it does not pass through probate affords the parties privacy.

5. When it is desirable to avoid ancillary administration, the Split is useful since at the termination of the first party's interest, the remainderman automatically by contract becomes full and complete owner of the property. This means the cost of multiple probates is avoided.

6. When a low risk highly reliable and relatively simple wealth shifting tool is desired for assets to be purchased in the future. The Split is both a "freezing" and "eliminating" device that has not been adversely affected by recent tax law changes and is unlikely to be challenged by the IRS if arranged properly. (See the discussion of Code section 2036(c) in Appendix B.)

WHAT ARE THE REQUIREMENTS?

Ownership of property is bifurcated into two parts: the first part, a "life estate," is the right to use, possess, or enjoy the property and the income it produces for as long as the holder of that life estate lives. The second part is the "remainder interest," the balance of the interest in the property not owned by the life tenant. When the life tenant dies, the holder of the remainder interest receives by contract all of the interest in the property.

Each party must pay his proportionate share of the cost based on government valuation tables illustrating the actuarial value of life and remainder interests. (See explanation at pages 390-391.) As explained below, it is essential that the life tenant not make a gift to the remainderman to enable him to purchase his portion of the Split.

The life tenant should be entitled to the exclusive use and benefit of any income from the property from the date of its purchase until the date he dies. Correspondingly, the life tenant should pay all expenses and charges (accordingly to state law) that are properly chargeable to a life tenant. The life tenant can not use the property as collateral or otherwise

Tools and Techniques

encumber it without the express written permission of the remainderman. The life tenant must not abuse his interest or in any way endanger the remainderman's interest.

A Split cannot be sold by the life tenant without the written consent of the remainderman. If it is sold, as explained below, the parties must share the proceeds according to the actuarial interests they had on the date of sale or exchange (presumably using whatever actuarial tables are in effect at that time).

HOW IT IS DONE—AN EXAMPLE

Your client is a divorced 50 year old real estate developer who is about to purchase a $1,000,000 office building. He is already in a 50 percent estate tax bracket and in the top income tax bracket. He has a daughter to whom he wants to shift wealth but he has already fully utilized his annual exclusion and his unified credit. He would like to increase his spendable income but at the same time begin to shift wealth to his daughter who is a successful women's clothing designer. If he purchases the building in his own name, he knows that half its value would be lost in federal estate taxes alone when he dies. He expects the building to appreciate by at least 13 percent per year.

The 50 year old father purchases a life estate in the building. He must pay, according to the actuarial tables, 84.743 percent of the $1,000,000 fair market value, $847,430. His daughter must pay the balance, 15.257 percent of the $1,000,000 fair market value, $152,570. (Note that her age is not relevant).

If the client lives his full life expectancy (33.1 years, according to the IRS life expectancy tables), the property will have grown to a value of $57,134,243 if the client's 13 percent growth rate projections are realized. If the property were

included in his estate, at a 50 percent estate tax bracket, the federal estate tax (assuming a 50 percent marginal rate) would be $28,567,122. But because none of it will be in the client's estate, it will all escape federal estate tax with a resulting savings of $28,567,122 (plus state death tax, probate, and other estate settlement expenses). The daughter receives property worth $57,134,243 at a cost of $152,570. See Figure 28.1.

WHAT ARE THE TAX IMPLICATIONS?

1. Assuming the asset in question is purchased from a third party seller (and the purchase price is therefore presumably the fair market value, and both purchasers' contributions to the purchase price were computed using the IRS valuation tables, there is no gift, and so there should be no gift tax. Both the father and the daughter in the example above have paid the full value of what they own.

2. Since the father owns no property interest at death, he has no property interest that falls within the ambit of the federal estate tax. There has been no transfer at death from father to daughter so there can be no argument by the Service that there was a transfer with a retained life estate. (See the discussion of Code section 2036(c) in Appendix B.)

A tax trap to avoid in this area is a gift from the father to the daughter to enable her to purchase the property. If the parent makes the gift that enables the child to purchase the remainder interest, the IRS will probably collapse the transaction and argue that the real substance of the situation is a gift with a retained life estate.[1] Aside from potential gift tax liability, this would mean the entire date of death value of the property would be in father's estate.

Figure 28.1

SPLIT INTEREST PURCHASE*	
INPUT: VALUE OF PROPERTY PURCHASED	$1,000,000
INPUT: AFTERTAX GROWTH RATE ON PROPERTY	0.130
INPUT: LIFE TENANT (CLIENT)'S AGE	50
VALUE OF LIFE INTEREST	$847,430
VALUE OF REMAINDER INTEREST	$152,570
LIFE TENANT'S ANNUAL AMORTIZATION DEDUCTION	$25,602
LIFE TENANT'S PRE-TAX RETURN ON INVESTMENT	0.184
INPUT: # OF YEARS UNTIL SALE (OR DEATH OF CLIENT)	33.1
INPUT: ASSUMED VALUE IN THAT YEAR	$57,134,243
REMAINDERMAN'S RETURN ON INVESTMENT	0.196

*Courtesy NumberCruncher Software

This problem could be avoided in a number of ways: (1) the gift could come from a relative other than the "splitting" parent; (2) an irrevocable trust which already holds assets for the child could split purchase the property with the parent (assuming the trust contains, or could be amended to add, powers authorizing the trustee to enter into a Split); (3) the adult child could borrow money from a relative or a bank to contribute to the Split. As a last resort, the parent could sign as a guarantor (but not "co-signer") of the child's note.

If the child lacks sufficient funds to pay his or her share, it is clear that the parent can not safely make a gift of the child's share. But can the parent safely lend the child the money if the loan is fully secured and bears interest at a fair market rate and under "third party" type terms? (This seems to pass the "smell test" if in fact the parties honor the loan.) Could a parent co-sign a loan for a child? (We feel this may be too close to the edge and at the least invites IRS scrutiny).

To be sure that no unintentional gift is made, be sure that neither party pays more than his share of the initial purchase price. A gift is made from parent to child if the parent pays too much. A gift is made from child to parent if the child pays too much.

If either party makes improvements to the property that enhance its value or extend its useful life, and the contribution is more than the contributing party's actuarially proper share, the IRS will claim a gift has been made.[2] Debt should be allocated proportionately between the life tenant and the remainderman. Financing used to purchase the property must be arranged in an actuarially correct manner.

3. The remainderman's basis will be the amount he pays.

There will be no step-up in basis at death since the Split property will not be in the estate of the life tenant. Consider that (a) the estate tax rates, if nothing is done, start at 37%, while the maximum income tax rates, when fully phased in, are 33%; (b) many assets are not depreciable by the remainderman in any event (such as land or a vacation home) and so basis is not an issue unless or until the asset is sold; and (c) no income tax gain is reported in any event until the remainderman chooses to sell it. In other words, using a Split, any gain can be deferred indefinitely or recognized (reported), at the discretion of the remainderman who, at the life tenant's death, can choose to sell it at any time. If there is no Split, federal and state taxes (plus administrative costs) will be due within 9 months of the parent's death. There would be no choice and little potential for "timing" the tax.

4. If the Split asset is depreciable, tax law requires the life tenant to depreciate the property using the entire basis. In other words, in spite of the Split, the deduction is computed just as if the life tenant were the absolute owner of the property. At the life tenant's death, any depreciation deductions remaining are allowed to the remainderman. (Regulation 1.167(h)-1(a)).

5. If the Split asset is an income producing investment, the life tenant can amortize the cost of the life estate. In the example above, the father has purchased an asset which diminishes in value to zero by the date of his death. Tax law allows a recovery of capital in the form of an amortization deduction as long as the property purchased is held for the production of income.[3]

This amortization deduction is available even if the property itself is not depreciable. A purchaser of a life estate may amortize the purchaser's capital investment over his life expectancy.[4] The point is that even if the father and the daughter had purchased intangible assets, such as stocks or bonds, the father could amortize the cost of the $847,430 life estate he purchased in our example and deduct, on a straight line basis, that amount over his actuarial life expectancy according to IRS tables. Since the tables project 33.1 years, he could deduct $25,602 a year. This amortization deduction could be used to offset income produced by the Split property itself or from other investment income.

Taking this concept one step further may prove most advantageous. Consider a Split involving the purchase of tax free municipal bonds. Even though the actual income generated would be tax free, since the life tenant's interest is diminishing, he is still allowed to recover his cost through a yearly amortization deduction.

6. If the parties to the Split sell the property during their lifetimes, the parent (in our example the father) will have to report gain equal to the difference between the amount he realizes on the sale (the portion of the sales proceeds allocable to the life estate at the time of the sale, according to IRS actuarial tables then in effect) and his adjusted basis. Note that the older the parent at the time of the sale, the smaller the value of the life estate. This translates into a lower amount received, which in turn means the gain reportable by the parent is lower. This lower amount payable to the parent is consistent with the major objective of the Split: a low risk, low cost method of "intentionally defunding" the parent's estate and shifting future wealth to a younger generation.

ISSUES AND IMPLICATIONS IN COMMUNITY PROPERTY STATES

If a husband and wife in a community property state use community funds to purchase the life estate, and an adult child purchases the remainder interest, it is possible to significantly increase the value of the life estate merely by providing that the remainder would not vest until the second spouse dies. The advantage of increasing the value of the life estate is that

Tools and Techniques

the value of the remainder interest (the amount the child must pay) is significantly reduced. For instance, if both a husband and wife are 60 years old, under government valuation tables (see the series of tables in Appendix B titled "Present Worth of $1 Due at Death of Survivor of Two Persons"), the remainder interest would have a value of 13.843 percent of the purchase price if the "last spouse to die" (joint life) Split concept was used. Under a typical first to die Split, the remainderman would have to pay about 25 percent of the purchase price. (See Figure 28.2.)

There are three other advantages to this "last spouse to die" Split: (1) The larger the amount paid by the spouses, the more they "intentionally defund" (at no gift tax cost) their estates; (2) the more the spouses pay for their joint life interest, the larger their amortization deduction; and (3) upon death of the first spouse, the surviving spouse will obtain a step-up in the basis of the split interest property, thereby increasing the amortization deduction that can be taken.

QUESTIONS AND ANSWERS

Question — Can a Split be for a term of years rather than a life estate?

Answer — Yes. The result of a Split for a term of years may be advantageous. Figure 28.3 shows the purchase of $1,000,000 property in which a 50 year old parent bought the right to the property for 15 years (assume he wanted income only until his pension began at age 65). His child purchased the remainder interest. The value of the term interest is $760,608. The child's portion is $239,392.

Figure 28.3 shows that the father's investment of $760,608 could be amortized over the 15 year period. This would provide the father with an annual deduction of $50,707 ($760,608/15). Assuming the investment generated nine percent on $1,000,000, it would produce $90,000 a year. But because of the amortization deduction of $50,707, the annually taxable amount to the father would be only $39,293. In effect, by creating a Split term of years, the father has created a super tax shelter.

As with any transaction which provides tax advantages, there are costs. The Split for a term of years has two major potential disadvantages: (1) at the end of the term, the parent loses the property and any income it produces (not a problem at all if shifting wealth and income was the major objective and the parent can afford

Figure 28.2

SPLIT INTEREST PURCHASE
JOINT LIFE INTEREST

INPUT:	VALUE OF PROPERTY PURCHASED	$1,000,000
INPUT:	AFTERTAX GROWTH RATE ON PROPERTY	0.050
INPUT:	LIFE TENANT (CLIENT)'S AGE	60
INPUT:	AGE OF SECOND SPOUSE	60
INPUT:	JOINT LIFE REMAINDER INTEREST FACTOR-TABLE A(2)	0.13843
INPUT:	JOINT LIVES ACTUARIAL LIFE EXPECTANCY-TABLE VIA	18.7
	LIFE TENANT'S SHARE OF PURCHASE PRICE	$861,570
	REMAINDERMAN'S SHARE OF PURCHASE PRICE	$138,430
	LIFE TENANT'S ANNUAL AMORTIZATION DEDUCTION	$46,073
	LIFE TENANT'S PRE-TAX RETURN ON INVESTMENT	0.112
INPUT:	# OF YEARS UNTIL SALE (OR DEATH OF CLIENT)	18.7
INPUT:	ASSUMED VALUE IN THAT YEAR	$2,490,232
	REMAINDERMAN'S RETURN ON INVESTMENT	0.167
INPUT:	ASSUMED VALUE OF INVESTMENT AT DEATH	$2,490,232
INPUT:	COMBINED FEDERAL & STATE DEATH TAX BRACKET	0.550
	TAX SAVINGS-COMPARED WITH SOLE NAME INVESTMENT	$1,369,628

Illustration Courtesy of NumberCruncher Software

Figure 28.3

	SPLIT INTEREST PURCHASE TERM OF YEARS	
INPUT:	VALUE OF PROPERTY PURCHASED	$1,000,000
INPUT:	YEARS TERM INTEREST RUNS	15
INPUT:	RATE OF RETURN ON PROPERTY.	0.090
	VALUE OF TERM INTEREST	$760,608
	VALUE OF REMAINDER INTEREST	$239,392
	ANNUAL INCOME FROM PROPERTY	$90,000
	ANNUAL AMORTIZATION DEDUCTION.	$50,707
	ANNUALLY TAXABLE AMOUNT	$39,293
	TERM OWNER'S PRE-TAX RETURN ON INVESTMENT	0.185

Illustration Courtesy of NumberCruncher Software

both financially and psycologically to do without both the capital and the income it produces); and (2) if the parent dies before the term expires, the actuarial value of his interest (the present value of the right to the income from the property for the balance of the term) will be included in his estate.

This potential problem could be negated (a) to the extent the $600,000 unified credit equivalent sheltered it; (b) if the right to the income for the term of years remaining at the parent's death was left in a qualifying manner to a surviving spouse (the marital deduction would eliminate federal estate tax); or (c) if the right to income were left to a charity in a qualifying manner (the charitable deduction would eliminate any estate tax).

Question — Could parties other than a parent and a child employ the Split technique?

Answer — Yes. The "POST-DEATH SHIFT" proves there is life to estate planning in the hereafter. Consider, for example, the purchase of split interests between a marital trust (which buys a life interest) and a CEBT (credit equivalent bypass trust) (which purchases a remainder interest). Assume the husband's will established a Q.T.I.P. marital trust with several million dollars. Assume the CEBT was funded with $600,000 and allows the trustee discretion to "spray" both principal and income to the spouse or other heirs of the decedent.

If the trustee of the Q.T.I.P. trust does nothing, the entire value of the assets in the trust will be in the wife's estate at her death. Instead, the trustee purchases a life interest in property based on the age of the surviving spouse. The balance of the cash to buy the asset is obtained from the CEBT, which purchases a remainder interest.

There are several advantages to this "MARITAL-BYPASS SPLIT" technique: First, the surviving spouse's income is increased by the return on the investment made by the trustee of the by-pass trust. Second, there would be an intentional defunding of the Q.T.I.P. trust. So, at the wife's death, the cash used to purchase the Split property would be removed from her gross estate. Third, none of the Split property itself would be in the surviving spouse's estate. (It is important that the trustee be given a general investment power authorizing investments in both terminable interests and other property. It is even more important that the power be stated in such a manner that it is permissive rather than mandatory. If the trustee were required to invest in a terminable interest (which the life estate clearly is), the IRS would disallow the marital deduction.[5] But as long as the husband's will does not require that the trustee of the marital trust purchase a life estate (or term of years), the result should be no different than if the surviving spouse (or the trustee on her behalf) decides to purchase an annuity.)

This MARITAL-BYPASS SPLIT technique could be turbocharged by a split purchase of tax free municipal bonds. The surviving spouse's net income is enhanced because even though the income from the municipal bonds is tax free (beware 1986-TRA AMT implications of certain otherwise tax free bonds), the trust would be allowed an amortization deduction (in spite of the general disallowance of the deduction for expenses incurred in connection with the purchase or carrying of tax free municipal bonds under Code section 265 since the amortization deduction is neither an expense nor interest).

Question — What is the best—or worst—property to use in a Split?

Tools and Techniques

Answer — Most authorities think that the best property to use in a Split is an income producing appreciating asset that does not have a limited useful life. A good example is land or other rental real estate. In the case of land, the Split in essence makes what is otherwise non depreciable into a depreciable asset. The amortization deduction shelters a portion of the income from the land if it is purchased for investment use and creates a tax shelter for both income and estate tax purposes.

Tax free municipal bonds which throw off high amounts of nontaxable income are good assets to purchase in a Split because of the life (or term) tenant's amortization deduction (resulting in a net shelter).

Closely-held stock is typically difficult to value accurately and usually does not pay a steady income. The IRS could claim that a true life estate has not been purchased because the interest purchased pays no income. But consider the purchase of closely held stock that has recently been valued for income, gift, or estate tax purposes. If the IRS has recently agreed that the price claimed by the taxpayer is correct (or the price has been agreed upon by both the IRS and the taxpayer either in or out of court), such stock would be ideal for a Split.

There would be significant estate planning utitilty to a "buy-sell Split": Instead of buying a decedent's stock in the normal outright manner, a surviving shareholder would purchase a life estate (or term of years). Children working with him in the business would purchase a remainder interest.

First, this would give the surviving shareholder an amortization deduction for his payment (in effect making the buy-out at least partially tax deductible).

Second, there would be no estate tax payable upon the surviving shareholder's death with respect to the stock. It would belong to the children working in the business without generating any federal estate tax.

Third, there would be no possibility of an election against the will or a will contest enabling a nonworking child, spouse, or other relative to obtain the stock. Because this is a more aggressive use of the Split, it is recommended that the stock at least pay some dividends after the Split.[6]

Question — How can a Split be unwound if the parties want to get out of it?

Answer — One of the major advantages of a Split as opposed to other estate freezing devices is that it can be severed at any time. For instance, assume a 60 year old father buys a life interest in $1,342,444 of securities for $1,000,000. His son would pay $342,444, the actuarial value of the right to the securities at the projected death of a 60 year old. Now assume that 5 years later the father and son decide to sell the securities. They would split the proceeds according to the actuarial values of their respective interests. The father, now age 65, would have a life interest that has reduced to about 68 percent of the proceeds. The son's interest would have increased to 32 percent.

Question — What are the downside risks and disadvantages of a Split?

Answer — A Split is a relatively new concept that has not been judicially tested. Obviously (as is the case with any tool or technique), it is not appropriate in every situation or in the case of every asset.

Assumptions and expectations of the parties entering into the Split may not be realized. For example, will the asset yield, appreciation rate, income and estate tax rates of the parties be as expected? What alternative investment opportunities exist for the remainderman (could the child do better investing elsewhere?)? Will amortization or depreciation deductions be available? And if so, to what extent will the client be able to utilize them under existing tax laws? Will the actuarial tables or life expectancy tables be changed? And if so, will those changes be retroactive, or will there be grandfathering of existing law?

Question — Is a Split a useful device for an elderly client?

Answer — The older the client, the less effective the Split, in most cases. This is because a very old person has a relatively short life expectancy, and therefore the value of his life interest is low relative to the purchase price. This makes the child's interest more valuable (some spell this EXPENSIVE). For instance, if the father were 90 years old, his portion of the purchase price is about 28 percent. That makes the child's (or grandchild's) portion of the purchase price about 72 percent. Because of the confiscatory nature of the generation-skipping transfer tax, it might still pay to arrange a Split with an adult grandchild even under these conditions. If necessary, the grandchild's father could give or lend cash to the grandchild who could split purchase assets with his or her grandfather. Not incidentally, the poorer the health of the life tenant, the more mathematically feasible and attractive the Split is. (The government's actuarial tables MUST be used unless the life tenant's death is probable within 12 months of the Split).

One solution to the problem of affordability on the part of the child or grandchild is to structure the life income interest as a "LAST TO DIE" (joint life) Split. In other words, income would be retained until the last of two individuals died. For example, assume a 65 year old client. His life interest is worth $679,700, about 68 percent of the full value of the $1,000,000 property to be purchased. This means his child would have to pay about 32 percent, $320,300. (This is about twice as much as the child would have had to pay if the Split had been done just 10 years earlier).

Now assume the father and mother, both age 65, purchase a "LAST TO DIE" (joint life) Split, which means they retain an interest in the property until the second of them dies. The value of the income interest is obviously larger, which makes the remainder interest much smaller. In fact, if you refer to table A(2) reproduced in Appendix B, you'll see that the value of the child's remainder interest drops from 32.03 percent to 19.181 percent. So to purchase his share of a $1,000,000 property, the child would have to pay only $191,810. If the father were age 52 and the mother were age 50, the value of the remainder interest would drop to only 7.233 percent of the fair market value of the property. So the child would pay only $73,330 to purchase his actuarial share of a $1,000,000 property. (See the example of a joint life split at Figure 28.2.)

Question — What if only one spouse (e.g., H) enters into a Split with his child, using community property funds?

Answer — One-half of the purchased item would be W's community property interest. H can dispose only of his separate property and one-half of the community property. Upon H's death, W would not get a stepped-up basis as to her one-half interest in the property, because at least one-half of the property would not have been includible in determining the value of the decedent's

(H's) gross estate for federal estate tax purposes, H's remainder interest having gone to the child under the Split.

Another potential problem would arise if the child were to pay the actuarially determined amount of the remainder interest in the entire property. The IRS could deem that a gift had been made to both parents. This could result in gift tax to the child because he paid too much for his remainder interest (he should have paid only the value of H's remainder interest, not also the value of W's remainder interest that H could not dispose of).

The solution to these problems is to have both H and W participate in the Split.

Footnote References

Split Interest Purchase of Property

1. *Gordon v. Comm.*, 85 TC 309 (1985).
2. *Penn v. Comm.*, 16 TC 1497 (1951), aff'd 199 F.2d 210 (8th Cir. 1952), cert. den. 344 U.S. 927 (1953).
3. IRC Section 167(a)(2); Reg. §1.167(a)-3; *Bell v. Harrison*, 212 F.2d 253 (7th Cir. 1954).
4. *Keitel v. Comm.*, 15 BTA 903 (1929); *Manufacturers Hanover Trust Co. v. Comm.*, 431 F.2d 664 (2nd Cir. 1970).
5. Reg. §20.2056(b)-1(f).
6. Oshins, "GRITS and Splits: Turning the Tables on the IRS and Insuring the Victory," *Journal of the American Society of CLU and ChFC,* November 1987, page 84.

Chapter 29

SURVIVOR'S INCOME BENEFIT PLAN

WHAT IS IT?

A Survivor's Income Benefit (S.I.B.) (often called a Death Benefit Only, "D.B.O.") is an agreement between a corporation and an employee. The corporation agrees that if the employee dies before retirement it will pay a specified amount (or an amount determinable by a specified formula) to the spouse of the employee or another designated class of beneficiary such as children. Typically, the amount may be a multiple of salary such as 2, 3 or 5 times the average base pay in the 3 years preceding death.[1]

A Survivor's Income Benefit Plan should not provide for (or be linked in any way with a plan that provides) retirement benefits of any kind.

WHEN IS THE USE OF SUCH A DEVICE INDICATED?

1. When additional income is desired for the family of an individual in a high estate tax bracket.

2. When an employer would like to provide a selected employee or employees with an impressive fringe benefit over and above qualified retirement plan security.

3. When a client presently covered under a split-dollar arrangement is experiencing rapidly increasing P.S. 58 costs (usually between age 60 and 65—see See Figure 17.3 in chapter 17). The split-dollar plan could be converted into a survivor's income benefit so that the security could be continued without the income tax burden.

4. When a corporation would like to provide an immediate death benefit for the family of a young employee which could later be coupled (by changing the S.I.B. to a nonqualified deferred compensation plan) with a retirement benefit.

HOW IT IS DONE — AN EXAMPLE

Nina Wasserman is a 35-year-old senior executive of Ship Shape Model Corporation (S.S.M.). In order to encourage her to give her ultimate effort for S.S.M., the corporation makes a legally binding promise to her that, "If Nina should die while an executive of S.S.M., S.S.M. will pay her children, Ross and Michelle, a death benefit equal to 3 times the average annual base compensation she received for the 3 years prior to her death—up to a maximum of $500,000. The payments will be made in equal annual installments over a 10-year period." In this example, assume payments would be $50,000 a year. Assume also that S.S.M. is in a 40 percent combined federal and state corporate tax bracket.

S.S.M. could finance its obligation by purchasing a $500,000 policy on Nina's life. The policy would be owned by and payable to S.S.M. at Nina's death. S.S.M. could use the cash proceeds to purchase $500,000 of tax-free municipal bonds. Assuming the bonds earned only 8 percent, the net income from the bonds would be $40,000 a year. This means corporate cash inflow would be $40,000. Outflow, after the corporation's $20,000 tax deduction (40% of $50,000) would be $30,000 ($50,000 – $20,000). Its net positive inflow each year is therefore $10,000. In 10 years the corporation will add $100,000 to its surplus. At the end of the payout period, S.S.M. has the $500,000 of bonds, and it has accumulated $10,000 a year for 10 years. At 8 percent this $10,000 annual amount would grow to $156,455 by the end of the 10th year. This will probably be enough to reimburse the business for its costs, the use of its money, and any administrative expenses it may have incurred.

WHAT ARE THE TAX IMPLICATIONS?

The Employer's Tax Position

1. Premiums the corporation pays on the life insurance policy covering the insured-employee are not deductible. But the TRA '86 bracket drop from 46 percent substantially reduced the corporate cost for nondeductible premiums.

2. Proceeds received by the corporation at the employee's death are income tax free. Proceeds may be subject to the corporate alternative minimum tax (AMT) as an adjustment for book income in years 1987 through 1989, and adjusted current earnings in later years. But, at worst, this possible tax on proceeds will not exceed 10 percent (of the difference between book and taxable income) with respect to the book income adjustment and 15 to 17 percent with respect to the adjustment for adjusted current earnings. If any AMT is payable with respect to the book income adjustment, it can be carried forward *indefinitely* and used as a credit against regular corporate tax in future years. However, the credit is not available with respect to proceeds taxable by reason of the adjustment for adjusted current earnings.

3. Payments made by the corporation to the designated beneficiaries are deductible if—and to the extent—such payments represent reasonable compensation for services the employee rendered and the plan serves a valid business (as opposed to a shareholder) purpose.

Tools and Techniques

The Employee's Tax Position

1. If the plan is properly drafted, under most circumstances none of the death benefit of an S.I.B. will be includible in the covered employee's estate (see the questions and answers below).

2. Payment of premiums by the corporate employer will not be income to the employee.

3. It is the position of the Internal Revenue Service that when an employee and his employer enter into a D.B.O. plan, a transfer occurs between the employee and his beneficiary. That transfer becomes completed for gift tax purposes when the employee dies, the benefit is payable, and the gift becomes capable of valuation. The gift qualifies for the gift tax annual exclusion.

   Where the beneficiary is the surviving spouse, assuming the value of the benefit qualifies for the unlimited marital deduction, the ruling has no practical effect (for federal purposes). Be sure to check state law implications.

   The IRS position should be considered where the benefit is payable to someone other than the surviving spouse. It has long been our position that the ruling should not survive judicial testing. A recent Tax Court case[2] upholds our view that coverage under a D.B.O. does not constitute a "transfer of an interest in property" by the covered employee, and therefore there can be no gift.

The Beneficiary's Tax Position

Payments received from the corporation by beneficiaries will be treated the same as salary; i.e., each payment will be taxed as deferred salary. Up to $5,000 of the death benefit paid to beneficiaries can be excludable from their gross income (see Chapter 6).

IMPLICATIONS AND ISSUES IN COMMUNITY PROPERTY STATES

In community property states, it may be necessary to determine whether the employee's spouse has any community property interest in the survivor's income benefit. This becomes important upon the divorce of the employee and the spouse. As previously stated, if a survivor's income benefit plan is properly drafted, none of the death benefits should be includable in the employee's estate for federal estate tax purposes, although state laws may vary on this issue. This is because courts have consistently found that the decedent had no interest in the payments at the time of his death.

This may also be the case upon a divorce after an employee has entered into a survivor's income benefit plan. As of the date of the divorce, the employee would have no interest which could be includable in his estate, and thus there may not be any interest which can be divided in a divorce proceeding.

However, many courts and the IRS generally find that the promise of the employer to pay a death benefit to a specified beneficiary in return for the employee's promise to continue working is a transfer by the employee of a property right. Community property states typically provide that a spouse may not make a gift of community personal property or dispose of community personal property without a valuable consideration, unless he or she obtains the written consent of the other spouse. The employee's employment, by its very nature in a community property state, is generating a community property interest in the spouse through salary and other employment benefits.

In a divorce proceeding, although an employee may be performing some services in return for the employer's promise to pay a stated amount to a named beneficiary at the time of the divorce proceeding, it does not follow that there are current property interests which can be divided equally between the spouses. The employee has no current right to any benefit, nor is there any assurance that he will ever have a named beneficiary receive a benefit. The survivor's income benefit is subject to many contingencies, among them the employee's continuing to work for the employer. Assuming the employee's spouse is the beneficiary of the survivor's income benefit plan, the spouse has obtained a benefit during the term of the marriage; i.e., if the employee were to die during the marriage, the spouse would receive the survivor's income benefit.

If the employee's spouse contends that there is an interest which can be valued and divided upon a divorce, the question of whether any value can be attributed to the survivor's income benefit may be solved differently in the various community property states. California, for example, has found that a non-vested benefit from a pension plan is not a mere expectancy, but is a contingent property right. Although we are not familiar with any case actually valuing a survivor's income benefit under this theory, it may be possible that California courts would attempt to value the survivor's income benefit and divide that value in the divorce proceedings. The value would probably be very low because of the substantial discounts for the many contingencies involved in this type of an arrangement.

As one can imagine, severe problems of valuation and the proportion of benefits to pay to a former spouse could arise in the event the employee were to remarry and continue working for the same employer. What portion of the survivor's income benefit is attributable to the employee's employment while married to his first spouse and what portion is attributable to the portion of his employment while married to his second spouse? With vexing problems like this, coupled with the employee's lack of right to a benefit prior to his death, it is likely that a court will put little or no value on the survivor's income benefit plan in the event of a divorce.

In most instances, the employee's spouse will be his or her beneficiary under the survivor's income benefit plan. In this instance, upon his or her death, there will be no controversy over the community property issue, unless he or she had previous marriages. In the event of a divorce, the community property issue may arise, even though the spouse is designated as the beneficiary, but the result is quite uncertain.

QUESTIONS AND ANSWERS

Question — What circumstances would cause death benefits to be includible in the employee's estate?

Answer — The promise of the employer to pay a death benefit to the specified beneficiary in return for the employee's promise to continue working has been considered to constitute a transfer by the employee of a property right.

If the agreement gives the employee the right to change the beneficiary, that retention of the power to designate who will enjoy the "transfer" will cause estate tax inclusion.[3]

If the beneficiary's right to receive the death benefit is conditioned on surviving the employee and the employee retained a right to direct the disposition of the property (for example, where the death benefit is payable to the employee's spouse, but if the spouse does not survive the employee, the death benefit is payable to the employee's estate), that reversionary interest may cause inclusion.[4]

If the beneficiary is a revocable trust established by the employee, the right to alter, amend, or revoke the transfer by changing the terms of the trust would cause inclusion.[5] Another problem relates to an employee who is also a controlling (more than 50 percent) shareholder. Does such an individual, by virtue of his or her voting power, have the right to alter, amend, revoke, or terminate the agreement? (Probably, the answer is, "Yes.")

If the employee already has post-retirement benefits, such as a nonqualified deferred compensation agreement that pays a retirement benefit, the IRS could claim that the pre-retirement survivor's death benefit and the post-retirement deferred salary plans should be considered as one plan. This would cause the present value of the death benefit to be treated for estate tax purposes as if it were a joint and survivor annuity; the present value of the death benefit would be includible in the deceased employee's estate.[6]

If the death benefit is payable to a trust over which the employee had a general power of appointment, the IRS might argue that he had a power of appointment over the death proceeds.[7]

If the death benefit is funded with life insurance on the employee's life and the employee owned the policy or had veto rights over any change in the beneficiary,

the IRS would probably attempt to include the policy proceeds because of the employee's incidents of ownership.[8]

Question — If proceeds are payable to the employee's spouse, will they qualify for the unlimited marital deduction?

Answer — Yes—if for any reason the IRS successfully maintains that the S.I.B. generated a taxable transfer (either during life or at death), there should be no adverse gift or estate tax consequence if the spouse of the employee is named outright beneficiary. It is also possible that the employer could pay S.I.B. payments to a "Q.T.I.P." (Qualified Terminable Interest Property) trust established by the employee (see chapter 30). This would secure the marital deduction—if one were needed—and in any case assure that the principal would pass upon the surviving spouse's death to the party designated by the decedent.

However, if the S.I.B. were not included in the employee's estate for tax purposes, the payment could not result in a marital deduction.

Question — Is a D.B.O. "funded" for ERISA purposes?

Answer — Although the Dependahl case[9] stated that D.B.O.s did not qualify for various exemptions from ERISA, at first impression it appeared that the Court improperly interpreted both facts and ERISA law in its desire to assist employees who seemed to have been terminated for malicious and unjustifiable reasons.

It now appears that the company involved in this case sent a letter each year to the executives covered by its D.B.O. plan. Those letters advised the participants of the annual status of "their" insurance policies. The obvious implication is that the participants could look to the policies for their families' security under the D.B.O. plan. This fact was not contained in the Court's opinion and may well have been the key reason the Court reached the conclusion the plan was "funded" for ERISA purposes.

The Department of Labor issued an Advisory Opinion subsequent to the Dependahl case which states that life insurance is not considered a "plan asset" if:

1. it is owned by and payable to the corporation;
2. it is under total control of the corporation;
3. it is subject to the claims of the corporation's creditors;
4. no participant has a preferred claim against the policies;
5. the policies are not formally tied to the plan; and
6. there will be no representation to any participant or beneficiary that the policies would be used solely to provide plan benefits or represent security for the payment of benefits or that plan benefits would be limited by the amount of the insurance proceeds received by the corporation.

In light of *Dependahl* and the Department of Labor Advisory Opinion in the appendix, the use of the phrase "to fund" (or "to informally fund") should be avoided in discussing the use of life insurance policies to support the plan in any documentation associated with the plan (i.e., corporate resolutions, plan document, SEC annual report disclosure statements).

Part of the corporate resolution authorizing the plan and the purchase of the supporting policies might better read as follows:

> RESOLVED: that in order for the X-ON Corporation to support its financial obligations under the Death Benefit Only plan and to insure itself against all other financial losses which would be incurred in the event of a pre- or postretirement death of *(Name of Executive)*, the vice-president of the Corporation is hereby authorized to enter into a contract of *(Description of Life Insurance Contract)* life insurance with the _____ Life Insurance Company for coverage of $____ insuring the life of *(Name of Key Executive)*.

Question — Is a voluntary D.B.O. plan the answer to the estate tax question?

Answer — If a death benefit is not made under a contract or plan but is purely voluntary on the employer's part, it will not be includable in the employee's estate.[10] An employer could adopt a program that is something less than a legally binding commitment giving rise to "hopes and expectancies, not enforceable obligations with respect to a death benefit."

Voluntary benefits are not includable in the employee's estate because neither the employee nor the employee's beneficiary possessed any right to compel the employer to pay the benefit, and therefore there was no transfer.

The problem here is a practical one. The benefit provides no peace of mind—nor financial security in an economic sense—except to the extent the employee can rely on the willingness and ability of the employer to pay a substantial sum of money after the employee's death.

Question — What is the formula for a successful D.B.O. plan?

Answer — An employer may offer a plan under which benefits are payable only to "eligible beneficiaries." This class would be determined by the employer and might include spouses and/or children of employees. No benefit would be payable if the employee is not survived by an eligible beneficiary. The employee would have no right to select or change the beneficiary. (More information on D.B.O. plans is available in our book, *The Tools and Techniques of Employee Benefits and Retirement Planning.*)

ASRS, Sec. 64.

Footnote References

Survivor's Income Benefit Plan

1. Some insurance carriers offer a coverage known as group survivors' income benefit insurance, commonly written as a supplement to group life insurance. Under this coverage, the employee has no choice of beneficiary, benefits are paid only if there is a survivor who qualifies, and a lump-sum payment of the commuted value of benefits is not available.

2. See *Estate of Anthony DiMarco*, 87 TC No. 39 (1986), which holds that Rev. Rul. 81-31 is inconsistent with the Code and regulations. Rev. Rul. 81-31, 1981 C.B. 475. See also GCM 39159 (March 31, 1984), which rejects a proposal to ease the IRS position. It concludes that an employee covered by a D.B.O. plan will be deemed to have made a gift in the year of death, even where mandatory, nonnegotiated death benefits are involved. The Service argues that the employee's agreement "to perform services forms the basis for concluding that he has made an indirect transfer of the benefit to the beneficiary."

Almost all of the cases and ruling on point conclude that for estate tax purposes, at the time the employer agrees to establish a D.B.O. plan in consideration of the employee's direct (or indirect) promise to remain as an employee of the business, the employee is gratuitously transferring a property interest to the named beneficiary. This is in direct contradiction to the IRS "gift at death" argument.

The IRS conclusion that there was a completed gift in the "calendar quarter of death" is based on the premise that:

• A property interest was created when the employee agreed to continue working in return for his employer's promise to pay the death benefit;

• The property interest was transferred gratuitously by the employee—during his lifetime; and

• Because the gift was not susceptible to valuation until death, it, therefore, did not become complete until the calendar quarter in which the employee died.

It is true that it would be difficult to precisely ascertain the amount of death benefit until death occurs, because in this situation the amount was payable only if the employee was

• still employed at death and

• still married at the time of death.

The amount payable could not be determined without reference to the employee's salary at the time of death. But even a property interest that is difficult or "impossible" to value precisely can have a value.

Furthermore, the completeness of a gift depends on whether or not the donor has so parted with dominion and control as to leave no power to change its disposition. If the decedent-employee ever did have the power to change the beneficiary, that right ceased at the time the agreement was entered into. Clearly, no gratuitous transfer was made—as the IRS contends—"in the calendar quarter of death." (The IRS is attempting—without the aid of law—to create a new type of taxable transfer—a "post mortem gift.") No right to any benefit accrues until the employee dies (even an instant before that moment, he or she could be fired and lose all rights to benefits). Therefore, how can a gift be made of a property right one never owned?

How can there ever be a gift—where the employee voluntarily gives up dominion and control irrevocably—if the employee never had dominion and control over either the property or the person who will succeed in ownership?

Clearly the IRS is using "leap in faith" logic to terrorize taxpayers and their advisers. Many editions ago we stated that this ruling should be struck down in court as being absurd, frivolous, and dilatory. The *DiMarco* case did just that.

3. IRC Sec. 2036; Rev. Rul. 76-304, 1976-2 C.B. 269.

4. IRC Sec. 2037; *Estate of Fried v. Comm.*, 54 T.C. 805 (1970), aff'd., 445 F.2d 979 (2nd Cir. 1971), cert. den., 404 U.S. 1016 (1972); Rev. Rul. 78-15, 1978-1 C.B. 289.

5. IRC Sec. 2038.

6. IRC Sec. 2039; *Estate of Fusz v. Comm.*, 46 T.C. 214 (1966).

7. IRC Sec. 2041.

8. IRC Sec. 2042.

9. *Dependahl v. Falstaff Brewing Corp.*, 491 F. Supp. 1188 (E.D. Mo. 1980), aff'd in part, 653 F.2d 1208 (8th Cir.), cert. den.; Dept. of Labor Advisory Opinion 81-11A. See also *Belka v. Rowe Furniture Corp.*, 571 F. Supp. 1249 (D. Md. 1983), where the court found a plan to be exempt from ERISA funding requirements where less than 5 percent of total employees were participants, and where participants' compensation averaged $55,000.

10. *Edith L. Courtney v. U.S.*, 84-2 USTC §13,580 (N.D. Ohio, 1984).

Chapter 30

TRUST — CRUMMEY

WHAT IS IT?

A Crummey trust is a popular device used in making gifts that qualify for the annual exclusion from gift tax (under IRC §2503) while still permitting the management of property by a trustee during those periods of time when the trust beneficiary is not yet in a good position to manage them. Most other forms of gifts that qualify for the annual exclusion require an immediate or at least very early (age 18, 21, or 25) distribution of the assets to the beneficiary.

With a Crummey trust, each time a contribution is made, the beneficiary has a temporary right to demand withdrawal from the trust. If the demand right is not exercised, the annual transfer for that year remains in the trust for management by the trustee. If the demand is made, the trustee must deliver the funds to the beneficiary. However, the beneficiary generally will recognize that such a withdrawal may affect the grantor's decision as to future transfers to that trust and may therefore not make a demand.

A Crummey trust is irrevocable. The trust instrument can include virtually any trust terms that meet the tax and non-tax objectives of the grantor. The trust instrument need not require current income distribution and may allow discretionary accumulation of income.

The name "Crummey trust" comes from the name of a party to a lawsuit, *Crummey v. Commissioner*, 397 F.2d 82 (9th Cir. 1968).

WHEN IS THE USE OF SUCH A DEVICE INDICATED?

Because the right of withdrawal is not usually exercised, a Crummey trust may be used to accumulate income for a period prior to distribution or to have the trustee use the funds (income and/or principal) for some purpose desired by both the trust grantor and the beneficiary. Paying premiums of life insurance on the life of the grantor is a typical use. This type of trust is often created for a child of the grantor, since it can allow the discretionary payment of income and can continue after the child reaches age 21.

As an irrevocable trust, a Crummey trust can save estate taxes by removing assets from the grantor's estate. Income taxes can be saved by transferring assets and the resulting income from the grantor to persons (including the trust) in lower tax brackets.

WHAT ARE THE REQUIREMENTS?

1. Each time a contribution is made to a Crummey trust, the beneficiary must have a right to demand withdrawal of an amount equal to the value of the gift. Frequently, the withdrawal right may be dependent upon the donor also specifying that the withdrawal right will apply to the gift, e.g., "This gift is made subject to the right of withdrawal provided in . . . ." This permits one trust to be able to receive both annual exclusion "Crummey gifts" as well as other gifts that the donor can be assured will not be removed by the beneficiary.

    However, in order for the annual exclusion to be permitted, the withdrawal right cannot be illusory. Implicit in every Crummey trust is the notion that the beneficiary will not exercise the right to withdraw and the gifts to the trust will remain in the trust until termination. However, the right to withdraw must be real and legally possible.

    The exclusion is allowed under a number of circumstances that may be surprising. An example is a gift in trust in which the beneficiary given the right to withdraw is an infant.

2. For an adult beneficiary to have an effective demand right, he must have effective notice of the demand right.[1] The IRS rulings have emphasized the importance of giving effective notice of the annual trust contributions that are subject to withdrawal, at least to adult beneficiaries. In several cases the IRS has implied that notice may be necessary even for minor beneficiaries.[2] Although this notice is typically made in writing to have evidence that the requirement was met, it seems that even oral notice is adequate.

    With regard to the frequency of notice, it is most common to give notice of each transfer that is subject to the withdrawal power. However, a "once only" notice may be sufficient. Such a notice alerts the beneficiary that the trust has received a gift that gives rise to the withdrawal power. The notice typically states that later contributions may be made that will give rise to additional withdrawal rights. Such a "once only" notice may be sufficient if the original notice states than an annual notice would be given if requested by the beneficiary, thereby putting the burden on the beneficiary to inquire about future annual contributions.[3]

3. In order for the demand right to be effective, an adequate amount of time must be allowed for the exercise of the power of withdrawal, especially if the exercise of the power would require a step such as appointing a guardian for a minor beneficiary. The IRS has not drawn a clear line between reasonable and unreasonable time

Tools and Techniques

limits. However, the IRS has disapproved a three-day period as not a sufficient duration,[4] but Crummey withdrawal periods of as little as thirty days after an addition to the trust have been deemed effective.[5]

4. An important feature of a Crummey trust is that it allows the grantor to make gifts that qualify for the annual exclusion from gift tax under IRC §2503. In order to qualify for the annual exclusion, a gift must be one of a "present interest." (A beneficiary must receive the immediate, unfettered, and ascertainable right to use, possess, or enjoy the money or other property placed into the trust for that year.) A "future interest" does not qualify. When a trust has no provisions for a current withdrawal of the gift, at least a portion of each gift is a future interest. It is the right of the beneficiary to withdraw the transferred asset that meets the requirement to make the gift eligible for the annual exclusion.

5. The beneficiary of a Crummey trust must be able to actually receive property if he exercises a demand right. The gift will be eligible for the annual exclusion only to the extent the trust has assets sufficient to satisfy the beneficiary's demand rights.[6]

6. Where a beneficiary is a minor, and is therefore unable to make an effective withdrawal, he will be deemed to have a present interest in the gift if a guardian can make a legally effective demand on his behalf. While the trust need not provide for the appointment of a guardian, it may be a good idea to include such a provision.

7. A recent Technical Advice Memorandum indicates that the IRS will allow the annual exclusion only where the beneficiary has a true and continuing interest in the trust, beyond the temporary power to demand a portion of the property contributed to the trust, or where the beneficiary has actually exercised the power.[7] From this IRS memorandum it appears that the beneficiary must be a beneficiary of the trust, not just a beneficiary of the withdrawal right. The goal of IRS in this memorandum is to prevent the naming of many potential beneficiaries (e.g., a number of friends) so as to increase the total annual exclusion right available while reserving the real intended benefit of the trust to a few people (e.g., one's children).

HOW IS IT DONE?

Harry and Donna Bradley would like to make gifts that will qualify for the annual exclusion to each of their two children and four grandchildren. Their annual exclusion amount for gifts to these donees would be $120,000 per year. (The husband and wife can give $10,000 apiece to each of the six individuals.) However, the Bradleys would prefer not to make outright gifts, especially not to the grandchildren.

The Bradleys would instead prefer to have a trust that would continue until their youngest child reaches the age of 35. At that time the trust would be distributed equally to the children and grandchildren. They decide that the trust will not make any distributions of current income.

A Crummey trust would meet all the Bradleys' requirements. The trust they create can have all the desired terms plus Crummey powers of withdrawal in all of the children and grandchildren. Separate shares are required if the trust is to be exempt from generation-skipping tax.

ISSUES AND IMPLICATIONS IN COMMUNITY PROPERTY STATES

1. A couple owning community property can give $20,000 per recipient without any need for gift splitting because each spouse owns half the community property.

2. Because of the nature of community property (the fact that each spouse owns a one-half interest in each community asset), it is unusual in a community property state for a Crummey irrevocable insurance trust that benefits the surviving spouse as to the entire trust to be created.

   In a separate property jurisdiction, the typical terms of such a trust might provide that at the death of the insured spouse (e.g., the husband) the proceeds of an insurance policy (purchased with funds given by the husband) will benefit the wife in the form of a life interest in the proceeds. After her death, the proceeds would be available to be lent to her estate (or to purchase assets from her estate) to provide funds to pay estate taxes then due.

   In a community property state, on the other hand, the wife usually is the grantor as to one-half the gifts used to pay the insurance premium, and it would not be appropriate to give the wife a life interest in the entire policy proceeds, for that would be a transfer with a retained interest, includible in the wife's estate as to the one-half purchased with her share of the community property gift.

   However, careful drafting can provide her with a life estate in the one-half of the proceeds produced by the husband's share of the community property gifts used to pay the premium. Further, even in a community property state, one spouse may have separate property already, or a "split" of community property can be achieved to produce separate property. With a trust funded by such separate property gifts, the other spouse can have a life estate in all of the policy proceeds without making them subject to estate tax in her or his estate.

WHAT ARE THE GIFT TAX AND ESTATE TAX IMPLICATIONS?

1. For the grantor/donor, a Crummey trust is an effective way to make a gift that qualifies for the annual exclu-

sion from gift tax while avoiding the early distribution requirements of other forms of gifts that permit the donor to take advantage of the $10,000 per donee per year exclusion from gift tax. The gifts are also free from estate tax at the death of the grantor if the trust is properly drafted.

With a consistent gift program over a reasonable period of time to a reasonably large group of donees, a large value of assets can be transferred without application of any federal gift or estate tax. Thus, the transfer tax problem may be solved for the grantor.

2. However, a second gift tax aspect arises when the beneficiary permits a lapse of his power to remove from the trust the contribution made by the grantor. This lapse of the withdrawal right was not often a problem when annual gifts from each donor were limited to $3,000, since IRC §2514(e) excludes from gift tax gifts that result from lapse of a power to withdraw assets from the trust up to the greater each year of $5,000 or 5% of the trust corpus. If each of two grantors gave $2,500 for a total of $5,000, the *de minimis* protection of IRC §2514(e) kept the lapse of the beneficiary's power from being a gift subject to gift tax.

However, §2514(e) no longer provided sufficient protection when the annual exclusion amount was increased to $10,000 in 1981, at which time gifts in excess of $5,000 began to be made to Crummey trusts. Unless the trust was quite large, even the 5% aspect of this so-called "five and five" rule did not give enough protection, and the lapse of the withdrawal power caused a taxable gift to the remaindermen of the trust. Since the (possibly unknown) remaindermen did not have a power to withdraw the gift from the trust, the beneficiary made a future interest gift, which did not qualify for the annual exclusion.

3. This taxable gift by the trust beneficiary has two negative aspects. One is that the beneficiary had made a transfer subject to gift tax and would use up some of his unified transfer credit or have an actual gift tax to pay.

The other negative aspect is that, since the beneficiary usually had some continuing right in the trust (e.g., a life estate), the property subject to the lapsed power would be included in his estate for estate tax purposes as a transfer in which an interest had been retained.[8]

The gift tax problem resulting from the lapse of a power relating to trust property in excess of $5,000 or 5% of the trust corpus can be resolved through good tax planning. By reserving in the beneficiary a power that keeps the lapse from being a completed gift (e.g., the power to direct where the trust property will go upon lapse of the withdrawal power), no gift tax is due. However, the estate tax problem is not avoided and the technically incomplete gift is included in the beneficiary's taxable es-

tate. Since most Crummey trusts are intended to be paid out during the beneficiary's lifetime, this is not a great problem for most people.

4. Many trusts will direct the trustee to keep separate those portions of the property over which a withdrawal right has lapsed that are within the "five and five" rule from those portions that exceed the "five and five" limit. The portion within the "five and five" rule can avoid estate tax at the death of the beneficiary. (See Questions and Answers concerning the generation-skipping transfer tax.) The other portion (amounts in excess of the "five and five" limit) will be subject to estate tax at the death of the beneficiary who retains the power of appointment over the gift (in order to avoid the gift tax upon lapse). Careful record keeping is important if a portion of the trust is intended to pass free of both estate tax and generation-skipping transfer tax at the death of the beneficiary.

5. Regardless of how much of the gift is within or in excess of the "five and five" rule, the portion of the trust over which the beneficiary has a right of withdrawal at his death (e.g., the amount subject to the Crummey withdrawal where the withdrawal period had not lapsed) is included in his estate for estate tax purposes. This is because the beneficiary had the power to appoint (or transfer out) the property to himself and thus had a "general power of appointment" as described in IRC §2041. If the beneficiary lives past the point at which the removal power terminates, then the property that was subject to the withdrawal power can no longer be taken out and thus may escape taxation in the beneficiary's estate.

QUESTIONS AND ANSWERS

Question — How should the beneficiaries be notified of the annual withdrawal right?

Answer — The basic requirement is that actual notice must be made in a timely manner. In order to show compliance it may be best to give written notice to all beneficiaries (and to the natural guardian of any minor) at least 30 days before the end of the withdrawal period (which is typically December 31).

Question — Is it sufficient if the beneficiaries are just given notice at the time the trust is created?

Answer — It appears that a "once only" notice may be adequate as long as it indicates that later contributions will give rise to additional withdrawal rights in future years. Such notice should put the burden on the beneficiary to inquire about any future annual contributions.

Question — What is the maximum number of annual exclusion gifts I can make with a Crummey trust?

Answer — This is an area in which there has been a great deal of speculation. Some Crummey trusts have included withdrawal powers for individuals who have no beneficial interest in the trust other than the right to withdraw. Theoretically an annual exclusion would be available for each individual with a withdrawal power.

However, a new Technical Advice Memorandum (T.A.M. 8727003) disallowed a number of exclusions where the beneficiaries' interests included only the withdrawal power. The IRS indicated that annual exclusions will be allowed only for gifts to beneficiaries who hold other beneficial interests in the trust or who have actually exercised their powers.

In light of this rule, it would be prudent to include withdrawal powers only for individuals who have a beneficial interest in the trust. The number of annual exclusions available should therefore be limited to the persons who have some rights in the trust other than merely a power to withdraw.

Question — If a beneficiary of a Crummey trust does not exercise the withdrawal power, he is considered to have made a gift to the remaindermen of the trust. Since part of this gift may be taxable, how do we know what is subject to gift tax and what is not?

Answer — For those older trusts in which only gifts of $5,000 or less to the trust were envisioned, there is often no continuing power in the beneficiary to affect the disposition of the gifts after they come into the trust. In this circumstance, any amounts subject to the Crummey withdrawal power in excess of $5,000 will be subject to a taxable gift upon lapse of the power. The exception to this is that if the total trust principal at the time of the gift is in excess of $100,000, then the alternate exception of 5% of the trust corpus under IRC §2514(e) would apply and that is the amount that would not be subject to gift tax.

Question — What should be done with an older trust which relies only on the "five and five" power to avoid a gift by the beneficiary because of the lapse of the withdrawal and as to which the donors now wish to make larger gifts?

Answer — Many practitioners are looking for ways to abandon such older trusts. Some wise practitioners included a provision for some third person to have a power to "kick out" assets. Many persons are arranging to have such a power exercised so that they may start out fresh with a new trust with more effective terms.

In some other cases, some grantors are buying from the trusts insurance policies on their lives (particularly when they cannot get new coverage) and making gifts of those policies to new Crummey trusts.

Question — Can one give an insurance policy directly to the trust as opposed to giving cash to pay for the policy?

Answer — Yes, an insurance policy can be given to the trust and generally will be valued at the interpolated terminal reserve value (usually very close to the cash surrender value) plus any unearned premium at the time of the gift. In those circumstances where the insured is no longer insurable, it may be that the value of the policy is greater than the interpolated terminal reserve value.

One negative aspect of making a gift of the policy itself is that the "transfers within 3 years of death rules"[9] now still bring back an insurance policy into one's estate if it is given within three years of death.

Question — Is there a way to avoid the three-year rule and still give an insurance policy?

Answer — No, there is really no way that is effective. Some people have given money to the trust and then let the trust purchase the policy from the insured. This triggers the "transfer for value" rule. Policy proceeds will then be taxed as ordinary income to the extent that they exceed the purchase price of the policy.

Question — How does one avoid the three-year rule and still give an insurance gift?

Answer — Where the donor is still insurable, it may well be that buying a new policy can actually be advantageous since the newer policies give a generally higher effective rate of return (with some unique exceptions). If this is the case, then the donor can give money to the trust and then let the trustee buy the policy. As long as the trustee is not required to purchase insurance with the funds contributed by the grantor and there is no other basis for saying that the grantor's gift of cash was really a gift of an insurance policy, the transfers within three-years of death rule can be avoided.

Question — If a person wants to cash in an insurance policy and buy a new one, are there any income tax aspects to the transaction?

Answer — Yes, to the extent that the insurance policy sale results in receiving more dollars than had been paid in net premiums, the "cashing in" of the policy can result in taxable income.

Question — The generation skipping tax applies to current gifts to grandchildren. Is it possible to draft a Crummey trust which will be able to avoid such a tax?

Answer — Yes, if separate shares are created. The annual exclusion is available for gift tax purposes, with respect to all power holders who have a beneficial interest in the trust. However, TAMRA '88 provides that a nontaxable gift which is a direct skip to a trust for the benefit of an individual has an inclusion ratio of zero (i.e., it is not subject to generation-skipping transfer tax) only if (1) during the life of such individual no portion of the trust corpus or income may be distributed to or for the benefit of any other person, and (2) the trust would be included in such individual's estate if such individual were to die before the trust terminated. A Crummey power can be used in conjunction with each such separate share to create an annual exclusion for generation-skipping transfer tax purposes.

However, a Crummey power will not satisfy the additional requirement which applies to the $2 million per grandchild exemption (which is available before 1990) that all of the income of the trust must be distributed at least annually to the grandchild once he has reached 21.

Question — Is it possible to use a Crummey trust to benefit my children and avoid both gift tax now and generation skipping tax at my children's deaths?

Answer — Generally, no. In order to obtain both the annual exclusion for gift tax purposes and a zero inclusion ratio for generation-skipping transfer tax purposes, separate trusts (or shares of trusts) must be used. Such separate trusts must benefit only one individual, and consequently, could not benefit both children and grandchildren.

Question — Is there a limit as to the amount that can be accumulated in the Crummey trust in order to escape gift tax or estate tax?

Answer —There is no limit that is based upon the value in the trust. The only limit is on the available gift tax exclusion each year and the number of donees who have rights under the trust.

If a couple had 20 grandchildren, they could be making a gift of $10,000 apiece to each grandchild from each grandparent each year, for a total of $400,000 which could be given annually to the trust without any gift tax. Obviously, this can build up substantially if the gift program extended over many years. A long-term planning program and good longevity permit the transfer of many millions of dollars of assets where there are large families or other large groups of beneficiaries. Thus, Crummey trusts can be a very significant planning tool in attempting to minimize transfer taxes.

Question — Can the donor be the trustee of the Crummey trust?

Answer — It is possible in certain very restricted circumstances to have the donor act as trustee. However, this requires a severe restriction of powers of the trustee and it is far better to have both no opportunity for the IRS to attach the transfer as being one that is included in the donor's estate and also to avoid subjecting property to management under very restricted circumstances. The more flexibility that can be given to a competent trustee, the better the trustee can manage the property.

Footnote References

Trust — Crummey

1. Revenue Ruling 81-7, 1981OICB 474; IRS Letter Rulings 7946007, 7947066.
2. IRS Letter Ruling 8019038.
3. Malcolm A. Moore, 22nd Annual Philip Heckerling Institute on Estate Planning, "Tax Consequences and Uses of 'Crummey' Withdrawal Powers: An Update," Paragraph II B 4d (iii).
4. Revenue Ruling 81-7, 1981-1.
5. IRS Letter Rulings 8103074, 8006048, 8004172.
6. IRS Letter Ruling 8103074.
7. TAM 8727003.
8. IRC Section 2036.
9. IRC Section 2035.

Tools and Techniques

Chapter 31

TRUST — GRANTOR RETAINED INCOME (GRIT)

WHAT IS IT?

A Grantor Retained Income Trust (GRIT), as its name implies, is an irrevocable trust into which the grantor places assets and retains the income (or the use of the propety) for a fixed period of years. Principal, at the end of the specified period of years, will pass to a noncharitable beneficiary, such as a child or grandchild of the grantor. Essentially, the grantor is making a future interest gift of the right to trust assets to the remainderman.

If the grantor survives the term selected, significant estate, gift, and generation-skipping transfer tax savings, as well as other transfer cost reductions, may be realized. A GRIT is one of the more important value-shifting vehicles available after the Tax Reform Act of 1986, the Omnibus Budget Reconciliation Act of 1987 (OBRA), and the Technical and Miscellaneous Revenue Act (TAMRA) of 1988. (See page 477 et seq. for a discussion of the impact of Code section 2036(c) on GRITs and other planning devices.)

WHEN IS THE USE OF SUCH A DEVICE INDICATED?

1. A GRIT is particularly useful where the client is single and has a substantial estate upon which federal estate taxes are certain to be paid. Wealthy widows or widowers or divorced individuals can use a GRIT as a "marital deduction substitute."

2. A married couple with an estate in excess of the couple's combined unified credit equivalent can use a GRIT to eliminate or reduce taxes on the death of the second spouse to die. The larger and more rapidly appreciating these estates are, the more effective a GRIT would be.

3. A GRIT is effective where income producing property is located in more than one state and unification and probate savings are desired. The GRIT would serve to transfer ownership in a manner that would avoid ancillary administration.

4. A GRIT will protect assets from a will contest, public scrutiny, or an election against the will if the grantor survives the trust term.

5. A GRIT is a useful technique when a client wants to purchase a tangible asset such as a work of art, retain the right to display it in his own home, but keep it in his family without the payment of transfer taxes.

6. A GRIT can serve as an alternative to a recapitalization that has the added advantages of gift tax leverage and possible estate tax savings (see the Question & Answer on this area below).

7. When the client is young enough to have a high probability of outliving the income term that is needed to obtain a low present value gift to the remainderman.

8. When the client has assets so substantial that a significant portion can be committed to a remainderman without compromising his own personal financial security.

9. When the client has a high risk-taking propensity and strong incentive to achieve gift and estate tax savings (rather than taking a safer but more costly approach of making an immediate gift).

WHAT ARE THE REQUIREMENTS?

1. An irrevocable trust must be established. The trust must provide that the grantor retains the right to enjoy trust income or possess trust property for a specified number of years (there is no limit to how few or how many years). As you will note below, the longer the specified term of the trust, the greater the value of the retained income interest and therefore the lower the taxable gift the grantor is making to the ultimate beneficiaries.

2. Evidence should be obtained of the value of the assets placed in the GRIT. It is recommended that one or more qualified appraisers value the property shortly before it is placed into trust.

3. The grantor should be given a mandatory income interest. The trust should specifically provide that the trustee has no discretion to withhold income from the grantor (or possession of the trust property from the remaindermen). Income should be paid annually or more frequently.

4. The grantor should be given an income interest only. The trustee should be specifically prohibited from making distributions of principal to the grantor.

5. The trustee should be prohibited from making discretionary allocations of receipts and disbursements. The trust should provide that the trustee must follow state law "principal and interest" allocation rules.

6. The grantor should be authorized to compel the trustee to make any nonproductive property productive by investment in income-producing assets.

7. If the asset placed into the GRIT is a home in which the grantor resides, a written lease should be entered into after the specified term expires. That lease should require the grantor to pay a fair market rental to the remainderman. Terms of the lease should be strictly enforced by the remainderman.[1]

Tools and Techniques

8. The trustee should be someone other than the grantor or the grantor's spouse.

HOW IT IS DONE — AN EXAMPLE

Assume a widow in a year when she is in a 50% estate tax bracket. She places $2,757,000 of publicly traded securities into an irrevocable trust. The trust provides that she will receive all income generated by the trust assets for a 16 year term.

The present value of her right to income from the trust for 16 years is $2,156,977. This is measured by the 10% actuarial tables in the government's regulations. Since the entire value of the assets placed in trust is $2,757,000 and the income interest retained by the grantor is $2,156,977, the value of the future interest gift being made at that point to the remainderman is the difference, $603,000. This entire amount of $603,000 is a taxable gift, since the gift tax annual exclusion is allowed only for gifts of a present interest. Of course, $600,000 can be sheltered by the unified credit equivalent, which means that the widow who places $2,757,000 into a GRIT will pay a gift tax on only $3,000.

If the $2,757,000 property appreciates at an after-tax rate of 6%, the property will be worth $7,003,050 by the end of the 16 year term.

Should the widow die before the term expires, the trust assets would be included in her estate at their date of death value. So there would be no federal death tax savings.

But if the widow survived the 16 year period (no matter by how short a period of time), none of the trust assets would be in her estate. At a 50% estate tax bracket, the savings would be $3,501,875 (50% of $7,003,750). Furthermore, since the property would not pass through probate, probate costs on $7,003,750 would be avoided.

WHAT ARE THE TAX IMPLICATIONS?

1. If the grantor outlives the specified term, none of the trust's assets will be included in the grantor's estate. This is because the grantor has retained no interest in trust assets at death. Code Section 2036 (retained life estates) applies only if the grantor retained the right to possess or enjoy the property or the income it produces (a) for life, or (b) for a period not ascertainable without reference to the grantor's death, or (c) for any period which does not, in fact, end before the grantor's death.

   Generally, safety from Section 2036(c) (see page 477 et seq.) requires that GRITs created after June 20, 1988 meet the following safe harbor rules: (1) the grantor's income interest should be determined solely by reference to property held in the trust, (2) the period for which income is retained should not exceed 10 years, and (3) the grantor may not be a trustee of the trust. It appears that a GRIT holding only publicly traded securities of a large company, will be safe from the reach of Section 2036(c) even if it does not meet the safe harbor rules, since 2036(c) requires that the decedent must own a 10% or greater interest in the enterprise for the code section to apply (a test not likely to be met even by most extremely wealthy clients).

2. The gift to the remainderman is valued using Table B,[2] reproduced in Appendix B, at Figure B.4a. (This table will soon be updated by the IRS to reflect current interest assumptions.)

3. The gift to the remainderman is a gift of a future interest. It therefore cannot qualify for the annual gift tax exclusion.

4. If the grantor lives beyond the specified term, there is no further transfer tax since the gift was complete upon the funding of the trust.

5. The taxable portion of post-'76 gifts is considered an "adjusted taxable gift." Since the entire present value of the gift to the remainderman is taxable, that amount ($603,000 in the example above) is considered an adjusted taxable gift. This will push up the rate at which the other assets in the grantor's estate, if any, will be taxed.

   But in the example we've been using above, an asset worth $7,003,750 will have been transferred at an extremely low transfer tax cost. This results in a significant "leveraging of the unified credit" since, in the example above, the $600,000 credit equivalent sheltered $2,757,000 of assets.

   Perhaps more importantly, 100% of post-gift appreciation in the property's value escapes estate, gift, and generation-skipping transfer tax. This makes a GRIT an excellent "estate freezing" device with respect to post-transfer appreciation.

6. At the grantor's death beyond the specified term of years, no step-up in basis will be allowed. The remainderman would therefore have a carryover basis in the property. In other words, the remainderman would carry over a portion of the grantor's basis.

   Basis is fractionalized.[3] The grantor takes a percentage equal to his original present value interest percentage. In the example avove, the grantor would take about 78% of the basis. The remainderman would therefore receive about 22% of the basis. So if the widow's original basis in the example above was $1,000,000, the donee's basis would be $217,629 (.217629 × $1,000,000).

   This would obviously result in a substantial gain if the remainderman disposes of the property. But the income tax rate on the gain will probably be well below the federal estate tax and GST tax rates that could have been imposed had the property been included in the widow's estate at her death. Furthermore, the potential for significant tax deferral exists; if the $2,757,000 of assets had been retained by the widow, an estate tax would have been due on it 9 months after her death. But if a GRIT is used, tax (probably at a much lower rate) could be deferred for much longer. In fact, tax would be imposed only if and when the remainderman disposes of the property.

7. If the grantor dies before the specified term expires, the date of death value of the property will be includible in the grantor's gross estate.[4] If there is an estate tax inclusion, (a) there would be no adjusted taxable gift[5], and (b) the unified credit utilized in making the gift would be restored to the estate. Note that if the spouse of the grantor "split the gift," the unified credit of the nongrantor spouse would not be restored. This could be solved if both spouses in fact are grantors. In other words, have each spouse create a separate GRIT.

It is appropriate for a beneficiary to purchase insurance on the life of the grantor and carry that life insurance during the period of time in which the death of the grantor would cause estate tax inclusion. The insurance proceeds, received estate tax free, could then be used to purchase assets from the grantor's estate and thereby provide estate liquidity.

8. If appreciated property is transferred to a GRIT, the tax on any gain will eventually be paid by (a) the grantor, or (b) the trust, or (c) the beneficiaries. If the trustee sells appreciated property within 2 years of its transfer to the trust, the grantor is taxable on the gain. This is not, however, a disadvantage, since the purpose of the trust is to "defund" the grantor's estate and shift as much wealth as possible to the remainderman with minimal gift taxes.

IMPLICATIONS AND ISSUES IN COMMUNITY PROPERTY STATES

Assume a husband and wife transfer community property to a GRIT. Each reserves the right to income as to his or her one-half community property interest for, say, 12 years. If the wife dies before the 12 years have expired, but the husband survives the 12 year term, (a) the wife's one-half community property interest would be in her gross estate, but (b) the husband's one-half community property interest would escape estate taxation at his death.

QUESTIONS AND ANSWERS

Question — What makes a GRIT work so well?

Answer — GRITs are based on two basic principles: the first principle is that the regulations made it possible and profitable to "turn the tables"—that is, the actuarial tables—on the IRS. The 10% term interest tables used prior to TAMRA '88 made an interest income more valu-

able than in prior years. But this made the value of any interest which follows the income interest lower. The result was a greatly reduced cost of making a remainder interest gift. Whether or not this valuation advantage will be available once new valuation tables or formulas are released remains to be seen.

The second principle that makes a GRIT work is that the federal estate tax doesn't reach a property interest unless the decedent owned it when he died or unless he held a "string," a property right strong enough to cause it to be pulled back into his estate. In a GRIT, once the grantor lives longer than the specified term, he neither owns the property in the trust nor holds any property interest. It therefore escapes estate taxation. (See the discussion of Code section 2036(c) beginning at page 477.)

Question — What are the downside risks, costs, or disadvantages of a GRIT?

Answer — The GRIT is the closest thing to a "no lose" situation; it is a "what have we got to lose?" technique.

If the client doesn't use a GRIT and purchases property in his sole name, the property and any growth on the property will be in his estate.

If the client who sets up a GRIT dies during the specified term, the result is that the property plus any appreciation will be includible in his estate (the same result as if the client had done nothing).

There are, of course, costs involved in a GRIT. These include:

(a) Attorney fees and the other transaction costs, such as appraisal fees and property titling costs of establishing the GRIT.

(b) Forfeiture of the ability to shift income during the specified income term (and the eventual estate tax on the consequent addition to the grantor's estate of property purchased by the after-tax net on that income). But, looking at it another way, the grantor has—before and after the GRIT—the same income and therefore the same income tax, but with a potential of substantial estate tax savings.

(c) Lost opportunity cost. The GRIT is an irrevocable trust. So, once assets are placed into the trust, the grantor is precluded from taking other planning measures.

(d) If the grantor does die during the specified income term, his executor may be liable for tax on the includible assets—but the property itself might not be available to pay that tax. (Solutions to this issue are discussed further below.)

Question — Assume a husband makes a large transfer to a GRIT. To reduce the potential gift tax on the value of the remainderman's interest, his wife consents to "split" the gift and use her unified credit to reduce or eliminate the gift tax. If the husband dies before the specified term expires, will the wife's unified credit be restored?

Answer — No. Although the husband's unified credit is restored if he dies within the specified income term, his wife's unified credit is not restored. A potential solution to this inequity is for the husband to make a gift to his wife. She then could make her own actual contribution to the GRIT. (Obviously, the IRS could consider this a step transaction, but this logic presumes that the gift to the wife (assuming the facts indicate it was an outright and unconditional gift) was per se a transfer to an agent of the husband. This presumption is at odds with the trend of constitutional and even tax law, i.e., recognition of a female as an independent person and the trend of antipathy to sexual bias.)

Question — What are the best assets to place into a GRIT?

Answer — Land, vacation property, such a condominium; tangible personal property (such as art or sculptures); closely held stock; or other assets with substantial appreciation potential—all would be suitable property to place into a GRIT. The very best assets are those producing minimal income but which will have high appreciation over the trust term.

If the GRIT is to last beyond the statutory safe harbor limit of 10 years to escape the ambit of Code Section 2036(c), the property placed in the trust must be publicly held stock of a large corporation, i.e., a property interest so large that the client can't possibly own the 10 percent interest in the enterprise required for 2036(c) inclusion.

Question — What happens if the IRS—many years after the GRIT is funded—claims that the true value of the property at the time it was placed into the trust was significantly greater than what the grantor claimed?

Answer — If the IRS successfully argues that the gift value of the remainder was understated, (a) additional gift taxes (plus interest) may be due, or (b) more of the client's unified credit may have to be utilized, and (c) if the grantor's death occurred after the specified term of years, the adjusted taxable gift component would be greater than reported. In summary, proper valuation is important but not critical.

Note that the statute of limitations barring the IRS from revaluing a gift (and therefore increasing the rate of tax on gifts the grantor makes in future years) doesn't apply if the grantor didn't pay a gift tax because of the unified credit.[6] Likewise, the IRS claims that if the unified credit prevented liability for a gift tax, it is not barred from revaluing the gift—even after the normal statute of limitations expires—for purposes of increasing the amount of adjusted taxable gifts for estate tax purposes.

In fact, the Service goes so far (too far in author's opinion) as to say that even if a gift tax was paid and the statute of limitations had run,[7] that it still had the right to revalue post-1976 taxable gifts.

The key to avoiding the entire valuation issue is to begin (before funding the trust) with strong authoritative evidence that the value claimed by the grantor at the time of transaction was in fact sound. This extra effort may be most important if the GRIT in fact achieves its major objective—to avoid estate taxation on rapidly appreciating property. Why? Because (a) if the grantor does survive the specified term, and (b) if the property has in fact appreciated substantially, there will be an "adjusted taxable gift." The IRS will argue "if the property at death was worth $ X, how could it have been worth $ Y only a few years later?" Obviously the IRS would argue, "The adjusted taxable gift the grantor made had to be much larger than he claimed." Absent strong evidence to the contrary, the estate would be at a disadvantage and probably would end up paying a much higher rate on the assets actually in the grantor's taxable estate.

Question — If closely held stock or some other nonincome producing asset is placed in the GRIT, can the IRS claim that its actuarial income-remainder interest valuation tables cannot be used because those tables presume an income flow which does not in fact occur?

Answer — The regulations specifically allow the use of the IRS actuarial tables even though the property produces no income, if the property has a "use value." Examples of property which have a use value include a house, a painting, or other work of art.[8]

The Service in the past has disallowed the use of its own actuarial tables for purposes of valuing a property interest where the use of the tables would be unrealistic or unreasonable.[9] The Service has also disallowed the use of its own tables where the stock placed into the trust (a) never paid a dividend and (b) was subject to a shareholders' agreement that made it impossible to be sold (or exchanged) and replaced with income producing property.[10]

The potential IRS attack (that the value of the gifted interest is not susceptible of valuation by generally accepted valuation principles, or that there is no assurance that a completed gift has in fact been made) can be eliminated by (1) giving the trustee the power to sell any asset placed into the trust and reinvesting the net proceeds in income producing property[11], and (2) forbidding the trustee from investing in "wasting" or nonproductive assets, and (3) requiring state law rather than trustee discretion to control the allocation of principal and income.[12]

Question — Is there an "escape mechanism" that could redirect the remainder interest if the grantor dies during the term? For instance, is there a way to provide that if the grantor's estate has to include GRIT assets, funds in the GRIT return to the grantor's estate rather than going to the remainderman?

Answer — A reversion to the grantor (or better yet to a revocable trust he established during his lifetime to avoid probate), conditioned on his death within the specified term, would create the funds to pay the estate tax. It might also result in a reduction in the value of the taxable gift to the remainderman. (The right to income for the specified term plus the potential right to receive the property back has a greater worth—and therefore the interest retained by the grantor is worth more—and therefore the taxable gift of the remainder is worth less and generates less of a gift tax.) For details on this modified GRIT technique, see Appendix B, "USING THE VALUATION TABLES."

An alternative would be for the grantor to retain a testamentary general power of appointment with a gift in default of appointment to the grantee.[13]

This power would be exerciseable only if the grantor dies during the term. This means that it would not cause estate tax inclusion but would keep the trust's assets out of the probate estate. This power is in essence a contingent power of appointment exercisable only during the specified term of years. (Although there is a contingency, because it is not an event within the grantor's power, the IRS could not claim the gift as incomplete; the grantor has divested himself of dominion and control in both form and substance and has given up all "economic benefit" (except for the value of the possible power of appointment).[14]

Like the "reversion to my estate" technique, the "power of appointment" technique increases the value of the retained interest of the grantor and therefore reduces the gift of the remainder interest.

If a client is older (and it is therefore more likely he will not outlive a specified term), the additional retained value resulting from the reversion increases significantly and therefore substantially reduces the taxable gift. For instance, under tables in effect at this printing, a 70-year-old who sets up a GRIT which lasts for 10 years has retained an interest with an actuarial value of 61.4457. But if the same person retains a reversion that brings GRIT assets back into his estate if he dies within the ten years, the value jumps to 78.0526. The older the client, the better the retention technique works.

The problem with the "power of appointment" technique is that it does not provide a source of funds with which to pay the estate tax. Therefore, the "reversion to my estate" technique is preferable.

Question — Is there a cutoff age after which the GRIT no longer is mathematically logical?

Answer — Since the GRIT is a "little to lose—a lot to gain" tool, even clients in their 80s may want to use a GRIT. For instance, under tables in effect at this printing, the value of the income interest retained in a five year GRIT is .379079 of the principal. Some clients—especially those who are in very good health—may want to gamble with a GRIT. For example, if the 80-year-old client opted for a ten year term, the value of the income interest jumps to .614457 of the funds placed in the GRIT (and therefore the taxable gift to the remainderman drops accordingly).

For clients with a slightly lower risk taking propensity, consider staggered terms. For instance, the 80-year-old client could transfer half the property into a five year GRIT and half the property into a ten year GRIT.

Question — Are there problems with using closely held stock with a GRIT?

Answer — The major problem with using a GRIT which holds closely held stock is caused by the interplay of Code sections 2036(b) and 2035. If voting control is retained over the stock placed into the GRIT, it is obvious that the death of the grantor while that right is retained will cause estate tax inclusion of all of the trust's assets.

But what is not obvious (but is nevertheless true), is that trust assets will be included in the grantor's estate unless the grantor lives for more than three years after the trust terminates in favor of the remainderman beneficiary. The choice is then (a) to extend the risk for three extra years and keep voting control only until the trust term ends or (b) give up voting control from the time the stock goes into the GRIT.

To avoid an IRS argument that the GRIT assets can't be valued and therefore the actuarial table can't be used, it is best to use closely held stock which has at least a modest dividend history or to pay at least some modest dividend. Another solution to thwart an IRS attack is to give the grantor the right to demand that trust assets be made income producing. (But if the grantor has the right to receive income and chooses not to exercise that right, has he made a gift to the remainderman of the income he could have taken but didn't?)

Question — It was stated above that there was an advantage to using the following provision: "If the grantor dies before the specified term of years expires, the grantor retains the right to have the property revert to his estate." If such a provision is advantageous, how do you calculate the value of the taxable gift he has made and the value of the interest he has retained?

Answer — Where a grantor retains the right to have property revert to his estate if death occurs within the specified term period, he increases the value of the interest he has retained and therefore reduces the value of the taxable gift he is making to the remainderman. This is because

Tools and Techniques

the donee has been given the right to receive the trust principal—but only if the grantor survives the trust term. There is no downside cost since the trust property will be taxed in the grantor's estate either way if he does not survive the term. But if the property reverts to his estate, it can then be available to help pay the estate tax—or better yet it can be paid outright, to a QTIP trust, or in some manner that will qualify for the estate tax marital deduction and therefore eliminate the estate tax.

If this reversion provision is incorporated into the GRIT, there are two rights involved: The first is the right to the income for a period lasting until the first to occur of (a) the end of the specified term of years or (b) the prior death of the grantor. The second right is the right to receive the principal of the trust if the grantor dies before the end of the specified period of years.

The value of the gift is found by (a) computing the present value of the remainder interest (the gift to the remainderman) and then (b) multiplying that value by the probability that the grantor will survive the trust term. Tables and government regulations are used[15] to compute the probability that the grantor will survive the trust term. The computation process is shown in Appendix B, "Using the Valuation Tables." Chart 1 illustrates that, using tables in effect on the date of this printing, an individual can establish a GRIT for five years, place $966,000 into it, and not exceed the $600,000 unified credit equivalent. If the term of years is extended through 30, the individual could place $10,455,000 into the GRIT and pay no gift tax because of the unified credit equivalent.

Chart 1	
Approximate Amounts That Can Be Given Through A GRIT Without Exceeding The $600,000 Exemption Equivalent Of The Unified Credit	
Term of Years Income Retained	**Maximum Gift**
5	$ 966,000
10	1,556,000
15	2,505,000
20	4,030,000
25	6,500,000
30	10,455,000

Chart 2 provides the same term of years but assumes the GRIT will end at the earlier of the specified term or the grantor's death and will revert to the grantor's estate if death occurs within the specified term. Note that if the GRIT lasts for five years or the grantor's earlier death, the maximum amount jumps to $1,010,000. If the term of years the grantor retains income is increased to 30, as much as $26,360,000 could be placed into the GRIT and no gift tax would be payable because of the unified credit equivalent!

Chart 2	
Approximate Amounts That Can Be Given Through A GRIT Ending At Earlier Of Term Or Grantor's Death Without Exceeding The $600,000 Exemption Equivalent Of The Unified Credit	
Term of Years Income Retained	**Maximum Gift**
5	$ 1,010,000
10	1,740,000
15	3,100,000
20	5,790,000
25	11,625,000
30	26,360,000

If a 50 year old places $26,360,000 into a 30 year GRIT which will return to his estate and pass to a surviving spouse if he dies within the 30 years, at a 4% net after-tax return, the money will grow to $85,495,958. The potential estate tax savings at a 50% estate tax bracket is $42,747,979. His probability of surviving the 30 years and thus achieving the estate tax savings is 39.7%, according to government tables. The gift tax costs (assuming no prior taxable gifts) is zero.

The illustration at Figure 31.1 shows just how valuable this gift tax leverage can be for estate tax savings purposes.

Question — Are there special provisions that should be inserted into the GRIT?

Answer — It is extremely important to document the "completeness" of the transfer at the date the trust is funded. Specifically, the trust must provide that the donor has given up all dominion and control over the property.

The grantor must specifically give up any power to revoke the gift of the remainder. The trust should also forbid the grantor to change any beneficial interests in the remainder. Therefore, the grantor can retain no power of appointment.

The grantor should not be named as trustee. An unrelated, independent trustee should be selected.

The trust should specifically deny the grantor any control over the manner or time in which the beneficiaries will enjoy the trust corpus (otherwise, that corpus will be pulled back into the grantor's estate).

Creditors of the grantor should be specifically prohibited from access to any portion of trust corpus. Since the law of the state in which a trust is created will control what part of trust assets, if any, can be reached by creditors, planners should consider state law implications. In most states if the grantor has retained only an absolute right to income, and all income must be paid out annually or more frequently, and the grantor has given up any power to revoke or otherwise control the

Figure 31.1

```
        GRANTOR RETAINED INCOME TRUST (G.R.I.T.)
        ENDING AT EARLIER OF TERM OR GRANTOR'S DEATH

INPUT:   NUMBER OF YEARS TRUST RUNS ..............................        20
INPUT:   VALUE OF CAPITAL PLACED INTO TRUST ......................  $5,790,000
INPUT:   GRANTOR'S CURRENT AGE (NEAREST BIRTHDAY)................        50
         GRANTOR'S AGE WHEN TRUST TERM ENDS ....................        70

         PROBABILITY OF GRANTOR SURVIVING...............20 YEARS        .697

         VALUE OF NONTAXABLE INTEREST RETAINED BY GRANTOR ....  $5,190,413

         TAXABLE GIFT (PRESENT VALUE OF REMAINDER INTEREST) ....   $599,587

INPUT:   AFTER-TAX AT WHICH PROPERTY GROWS ......................       .040
         VALUE OF G.R.I.T. PROPERTY AT END OF 20 YEARS ............ $12,686,603

INPUT:   COMBINED FEDERAL AND STATE DEATH TAX BRACKET.........       .600

         POTENTIAL DEATH TAX SAVINGS .............................   17,611,962
```
Illustration Courtesy of NumberCruncher Software

disposition of the remainder, creditors should not be able to touch any of the remainder (nor should the IRS be able to subject it to estate tax) once the grantor outlives the income term.

Question — What are the implications of providing in the trust instrument that, regardless of how long an income term the grantor had retained, at his death all income rights terminate (a "self-cancelling" provision)?

Answer — Two potential problems with a "cancel upon death" provision in a GRIT are (1) such a provisions would make the grantor's life interest worth less and therefore make the gift of the remainder interest worth more, and (2) the IRS might attempt to couple section 2035 (certain gifts made within three years of death) with section 2036 (retention of a life estate) because of the reference to an income interest which ends upon the grantor's death. (This second problem is not as likely as the first.)

Question — Is there a gift tax problem related to the use of nonproductive property in a GRIT?

Answer — The IRS has long held that the "use of valuable property...is itself a legally protectible property interest." This was the impetus in the famous Dickman case that held that intra-family interest-free demand loans result in taxable gifts equal to the value of the use of the loaned money. This broad reading of the gift tax law has now been extended. A recent IRS Technical Advice Memorandum (TAM) stated that the failure of the owner of a grantor retained income trust to exercise a power to compel the trustee to sell nonproductive property and replace it with property that will normally produce income will result in a gift to the remaindermen in any year the trust is not reasonably productive of income.[16]

This gift is by definition one of a future interest and therefore will not qualify for the gift tax annual exclusion.

A problem may result where a grantor contributes S corporation stock to a GRIT. If he has the power to make the trust income producing and to substitute productive assets but doesn't, the IRS may argue that the income he could have taken but didn't is in essence a future interest gift to the remaindermen.

How far the IRS will be able to take this argument remains to be seen. But the very existence of this avenue of attack indicates prudence in funding GRITs and suggests that whenever possible income producing assets or "use" property (property such as art that has an "income value" by virtue of its use by the grantor) be used and that the grantor be given specific powers to demand that trust assets be made productive at any time during the retained income period.

SUMMARY

A GRIT is the latest generation of "money value of time" value-shifting techniques that include "Splits".

A grantor who establishes a GRIT retains the right to all income in the irrevocable trust that lasts for a fixed term of years (or the prior death of the grantor). At the termination of the trust, principal passes to beneficiaries specified in the trust (or the grantor's estate if the grantor does not survive the trust term). If the grantor survives the trust term, all trust principal (including appreciation) can be excluded from federal estate tax (but see pages 477 et seq. for an analysis of the impact of Code section 2036(c) on GRITS) at little or no gift tax cost and result in significant probate savings as well.

Tools and Techniques

Footnote References

Trust—Grantor Retained Income (GRIT)

1. *Estate of Barlow v. Comm.*, 66 TC 333 (1970).
2. Reg. §§20.2031-7(f), 25.2512-5(f).
3. *Hunter v. Comm.*, 44 TC 109 (1965); Rev. Rul. 77-413, 1977-2 CB 298; Reg. §1.61-6(a).
4. IRC Section 2036(a)(1); *Estate of Fry v. Comm.*, 9 TC 503 (1947).
5. IRC Section 2001(b).
6. Rev. Rul. 84-11, 1984-1 CB 201.
7. IRC Section 2504(c).
8. Reg. §25.2512-5(c).
9. But see the IRS position in Rev. Rul. 77-195, 1977-1 CB 295.
10. *Stark v. U.S.*, 345 F. Supp. 1263 (W.D. Mo. 1972), aff'd *per curiam*, 477 F.2d 131 (8th Cir.), *cert. denied*, 414 U.S. 975 (1973).
11. *Rosen v. Comm.*, 397 F.2d 245 (4th Cir. 1968).
12. Rev. Rul. 62-13, 1962-1 CB 181.
13. Johanson, *The Record*, New York City Bar Association, Fall/Winter, 1986.
14. Let. Rul. 8546001; *Trever v. Comm.*, 40 BTA 1241 (1939).
15. Reg. §25.2512-5(f), Table LN, reproduced in Appendix B.
16. TAM 8801008.

Chapter 32

TRUST — INTERVIVOS

WHAT IS IT?

An *inter vivos* (living) trust is a relationship, created during the lifetime of the grantor (the person establishing the trust), in which one party (the trustee) holds property for the benefit of another (the beneficiary).

It can be established for a limited period of time or it can continue after the death of the grantor. It may be revocable or irrevocable.

A revocable living trust is one created by the grantor during his lifetime in which the grantor retains the right to revoke the trust, change its terms, or regain possession of the property in the trust.

An irrevocable living trust is created when the grantor has relinquished title to property placed in the trust and has given up all right to revoke, amend, alter, or terminate the trust.

WHEN IS THE USE OF SUCH A DEVICE INDICATED?

Revocable Living Trust

1. Where the grantor wishes someone else to accept management responsibility.

2. Where the grantor wishes to assure continuity of management and income flow in the event of death or disability.

3. Where the grantor wishes to secure investment advice.

4. Where the grantor wishes to protect against his own incapacity or the incapacity (physical, mental, or legal) of beneficiaries.

5. Where the grantor desires privacy in the handling and administration of his assets during lifetime or at death.

6. Where the grantor wishes to minimize estate administration costs and delay at death.

7. Where payment of insurance proceeds to a testamentary trustee does not qualify for the life insurance exemption under the state's death tax laws.

Irrevocable Living Trust

1. In addition to the reasons stated above with regard to revocable living trusts, an irrevocable trust is indicated where the grantor wishes to obtain federal income and estate tax savings (and is prepared to possibly incur a federal gift tax).

    Both the revocable and irrevocable trusts have disadvantages. For example, a revocable living trust generates trustee's fees during the grantor's lifetime to the extent that property is managed by the trustee. Furthermore, there are current legal drafting and advisory fees and all amounts in the revocable trust will be included in the grantor's estate for death tax purposes.[1]

    An irrevocable trust also generates trustee's fees. A gift tax is often incurred, and an income tax return must be filed for the trust annually. The grantor gives up the right to regain the trust property during the term of the trust and consequently has lost considerable flexibility.

WHAT ARE THE REQUIREMENTS?

1. In order for a trust to exist, there must be trust property (also known as trust principal, *res* or corpus).

2. There must be the following parties, although in some jurisdictions it is possible for the same individual to hold all these positions:

    (a) a grantor, sometimes referred to as a settlor—any person who transfers property to and dictates the terms of a trust;

    (b) a trustee—a party to whom property is transferred by the grantor, who receives legal title to the property placed in the trust, and who generally manages and distributes income according to the terms of a formal written agreement (called a trust instrument) between the grantor and the trustee;

    (c) a beneficiary—a party for whose benefit the trust is created and who will receive the direct or indirect benefit of the use of income from and/or principal of the trust property, as follows:

      (1) income beneficiary—the beneficiary who receives income, generally for life or for a fixed period of years or until the occurrence or nonoccurrence of a particular event;

      (2) remainderman—the ultimate beneficiary of trust property, who can also be for the specified period of time the income beneficiary.

3. The grantor must be legally competent.

HOW IT IS DONE — AN EXAMPLE

Russ Miller, a successful real estate broker, feels that if his wife survives him, she will be able to handle the assets in his estate and properly manage them. However, he is afraid that if his spouse predeceases him, his children will be un-

Tools and Techniques

able to properly manage the assets left to them. His estate is not subject to significant estate taxes.

Russ makes his life insurance proceeds and/or other assets payable to his wife, if she survives him. However, if Russ's wife predeceases him, those assets are payable to a trust at Russ's death. This type of *inter vivos* trust is revocable since Russ can always revoke the trust and repossess the property. Often, such a trust is known as a "contingent" trust, since it will take effect only in the event of the contingency that the grantor's wife predeceases him.

Under different circumstances, an irrevocable living trust would be indicated. For example, if Russ were in a high income tax bracket, as well as a high estate tax bracket, he might consider transferring assets to an irrevocable trust for the benefit of his wife or children. The trust could accumulate income during Russ's life or distribute that income to, or use it for the benefit of, his children (but not for Russ's own benefit). At Russ's death, the trust could provide income to his wife for life and at her death, provide income and eventually principal for his children.

WHAT ARE THE TAX IMPLICATIONS?

Revocable Living Trust

1. For federal income tax purposes, all income is taxed to the grantor at the grantor's tax rate, since he is considered owner of the trust corpus.[2]

2. No gift tax is generated by establishing a revocable trust since the gift is not completed until the trust becomes irrevocable.[3]

3. Since the grantor has not irrevocably disposed of any assets, the entire trust corpus will be included in the grantor's estate for federal estate tax purposes.[4]

Irrevocable Living Trust

1. The trust corpus will not be includible in the estate of the grantor, if:

(a) the grantor does not retain either a lifetime interest in the income of the trust or the right to use or enjoy the trust property;

(b) the grantor does not retain the right to designate who will presently or ultimately receive the trust principal or income;

(c) the grantor does not retain the right to change the trustee.[5]

(d) the grantor does not retain, for himself or his estate, a reversionary (right to regain trust assets) interest; and

(e) the grantor does not retain the right to alter, amend, or revoke the trust.[6]

2. The income earned by an irrevocable trust will not be taxed to the grantor of the trust unless:

(a) The trust income is, in the discretion of the grantor or a nonadverse party or both, or may be:

(1) distributed to the grantor or the grantor's spouse;

(2) accumulated for future distribution to the grantor or the grantor's spouse;

(3) applied to pay premiums on insurance on the life of the grantor or the grantor's spouse.[7]

(b) The income is used to support a person whom the grantor is legally obligated to support or is or may be used in the discharge of any legal obligations of the grantor.[8]

(c) The grantor or the grantor's spouse retains a reversionary interest.

The reversionary interest rule applies only if the value of the interest that may return to the grantor or his spouse exceeds five percent of the value of the trust. This interest is measured at the time the trust is created.

Under the actuarial table in use as of this printing, Table B of Gift Tax Regulation Section 25.2512-5 (reproduced in Appendix B at Figure B.4a), it appears that a trust lasting 32 or more years and then reverting to the grantor or the grantor's spouse will not be considered a grantor trust, since the actuarial value of the right to receive the property back is .047362, less than 5% of the value of the corpus. TRA '86 didn't eliminate short term trusts, but it did limit their utility. Young individuals who can afford to do without income and principal for very long periods of time can still take advantage of the income shifting potential.

An exception to the reversionary interest rule applies if the grantor retains a reversionary interest that takes effect only upon the death of a minor beneficiary (under age 21) who is a lineal descendant of the grantor. The beneficiary must be given the entire present interest in the trust or a trust portion for this exception to apply. This exception to the reversionary interest rule allows the grantor to recover property placed in trust for a beneficiary if that child or grandchild dies before reaching age 21.

(d) the power to control beneficial enjoyment of (the right to decide who will receive or when they will receive) trust principal or income.[9]

Income that is not taxed to the grantor will be taxed either to the trust or to the beneficiary(ies) of the trust or both.[10] Distributed income will be taxed directly to the recipient beneficiary and be subject to the "kiddie tax" rules, if paid to a child under age 14 (see chapter 11).

However, if the income is accumulated for future distribution, such income, when eventually distributed to the beneficiary may be taxed to that beneficiary as though it had been distributed each year although it was, in fact, being accumulated by the trust. The recipient beneficiary will receive credit for the taxes paid by the trust each year as it was accumulating income. (During the accumulation period, the trust paid tax on the income earned each year.) This concept is known as the "throwback rule."[11]

Where a beneficiary of a trust was under 21 years of age during the accumulation period, any income accumulated for his benefit during the years before reaching age 21 will not be subject to the throwback rules (i.e., the income will be taxed to the trust in the year accumulated).[12] In addition, capital gains are not subject to the throwback rule.

Where a gift is made into an irrevocable trust in which the donor retains for life the right to the income, the trust assets will be brought back into the donor's gross estate at death.[13] However, the gift of the remainder interest is still subject to gift taxes, and nonpayment of any taxes due will result in interest and penalties accruing. Some gifts made without the use of trusts (e.g., the gift by deed of a remainder interest in real property with the grantor retaining a legal life estate) are also within this rule relating to retention of use or benefits of property.

3. When a grantor transfers property to an irrevocable trust, the transfer is a completed gift for gift tax purposes. Unless the transfer is incomplete because of a reserved power, or for some other reason, the transfer is subject to the federal gift tax.[14] If the gift is large enough, a gift tax will be payable.

Generally, a gift in trust is not considered to be a "present interest" gift and will therefore not qualify for the $10,000 per donee annual gift tax exclusion. However, if drafted in a manner that gives the beneficiary an immediate, unfettered, and ascertainable right to use, possess, or enjoy the property or income interest transferred, the income interest can qualify for the annual exclusion.

4. When a grantor transfers appreciated property to an irrevocable trust and that property is sold at a gain by the trustee within two years of the grantor's transfer, the gain is taxed to the trust at the grantor's tax bracket.[15]

5. When a grantor is willing to make a nonreversionary transfer, trusts can result in significant long term income tax savings, even after TRA '86. For instance, if a parent in 1988 transfers property producing $10,000 a year of income to an irrevocable trust, which in turn pays out the income to a child 14 or older, the family unit could save as much as 18% a year (if parents' top bracket is 33% and the child's bracket is 15%). In this example, the tax saving would be $1,875 a year. The additional $75 in saving comes because of the standard deduction the child receives, which eliminates the tax on the first $500 of unearned income. The illustration at Figure 32.1 shows the effect of this saving compounded over a 4-year period and then over two succeeding 5-year periods.

Actually, the advantage could be increased. Each child could receive up to $500 of unearned income and pay no tax. If the $10,000 were divided and $2,500 were paid to each of four children, only $8,000 ($2,000 × 4) would

Figure 32.1

POST TRA '86 INCOME SHIFTING — CHILD 14 OR OVER			
INPUT:	AMOUNT OF INVESTMENT		$100,000
INPUT:	RATE OF RETURN ON INVESTMENT		0.100
INPUT:	YEARS INVESTMENT LASTS		4
INPUT:	PARENT'S COMBINED (FEDERAL AND STATE) TAX BRACKET		0.33
INPUT:	CHILD'S COMBINED (FEDERAL AND STATE) TAX BRACKET		0.15
INPUT:	TRUST'S COMBINED (FEDERAL AND STATE) TAX BRACKET		0.15

	PARENT	CHILD	TRUST
INTEREST INCOME	$10,000	$10,000	$10,000
TAX	$3,300	$1,425	$1,485
AFTER-TAX INCOME	$6,700	$8,575	$8,515
ANNUAL ADVANTAGE		$1,875	$1,815
TOTAL SAVINGS OVER 4 YEARS		$9,572	$9,266
TOTAL SAVINGS OVER 9 YEARS		$28,008	$28,917
TOTAL SAVINGS OVER 14 YEARS		$57,698	$57,653

Tools and Techniques

be subject to tax in a 15% bracket. This would result in a tax of only $1,200, instead of the $3,300 that probably would have been paid by the parents. The annual saving would be $2,100 a year!

6. Generation-skipping transfer taxes (GSTT) will be imposed on certain transfers going to an individual two or more generations below that of the grantor. (These direct skips, taxable transfers, and taxable terminations are discussed in detail in Appendix B.)

ISSUES AND IMPLICATIONS IN COMMUNITY PROPERTY STATES

In dealing with community property, the inter vivos trust would have two grantors, the husband and the wife. For a revocable trust, where the grantors intend to retain the beneficial ownership of the property, care must be taken to ensure that accidental gifts under state gift tax law are not made by giving either spouse ownership rights over the other spouse's half of the property. The unlimited gift tax marital deduction eliminates a federal gift tax problem on interspousal gifts. Thus, if the trust is revoked, the property should be clearly indicated as being returned to the husband and wife, as co-owners, and not to one spouse or the other.

Is the character of community property altered by transfer to a revocable trust? If the transfer is simply by husband and wife to trustee, and each retains a right to revoke, and the instrument specifically provides that the character of the property remains community in the trust and also if it is withdrawn from the trust, and state law recognizes the ability of the parties to achieve the intended result, the character of the property will remain unchanged. This means that, upon the death of the first spouse, the decedent's one-half and the surviving spouse's one-half interest in the trust will receive a new basis equal to fair market value at death or the alternate valuation date, and only the decedent's one-half of the property in the trust will be included in his estate. There will be no gift at the time the trust is created and there will be no gift upon the death of the first spouse unless, at that time, the trust becomes irrevocable. This is avoided by language that divides the trust into two trusts upon death of one of the donors; the trust in which the decedent's one-half is placed becomes irrevocable and the other remains revocable. This is the kind of a revocable trust most frequently used as an effective planning device.

Much care must be taken in determining the source and nature of title holding of property before taking the position that it is community property, as one may when the property is transferred to a trust which indicates that it is held as community property. Taxable gifts under state law may result if the property is the separate property of either spouse or is joint tenancy real property originally acquired with the separate property of one spouse. Although the unlimited marital deduction for federal gift tax purposes reduces the gift tax risks, there still may be state gift tax implications.[16] In addition, it could well inspire litigation in the event of a dissolution if there was not a clear intent between the parties that a gift take place.

Where insurance has been purchased with community property (and therefore belongs one-half to each spouse), care must be taken that the terms of a trust, becoming irrevocable at the death of the insured, do not result in a taxable gift by the surviving spouse of all or part of the survivor's half interest in the insurance proceeds. Such gifts are usually to the remaindermen of the trust and not subject to the marital deduction.

As noted in the discussion of "flower bonds", such bonds may be used to pay estate tax at par only to the extent they are owned by the decedent. Where a community property couple has placed some or all of their assets in a revocable trust to avoid probate, it is difficult to arrange that bonds be purchased as the separate property of the ill or older spouse unless the trust provides for the holding of the separate property of such grantor-spouse. For such circumstances, many community property estate planners now draft such trusts so as to have specific provisions for the holding of the separate property of each spouse, as well as community property, even though the spouses may only have community property at the time of the creation of the estate plan.

Great care must be taken in the drafting of the provisions regarding the division of property at the death of one community property owning spouse so as to avoid unintended gifts by the surviving spouse. At times, such trusts may be intended to benefit the survivor more if he or she agrees to have his or her property also be managed and distributed according to the terms of the trust. Such "election" provisions may also result in gifts by the surviving spouse and, if used, should be drafted carefully by an experienced estate planner.

The marital deduction rules make it important that all pre-1982 inter vivos trusts be examined carefully and revisions considered to take advantage of the very important new provisions which make it possible to have completely tax-free interspousal transfers. Chapter 33, on the Marital Deduction, reviews this in more detail.

Community property and separate property states generally have similar rules as to how long property can be held in trust and as to other trust law matters. However, property rights are different as to separate and community property, and estate plans involving trusts must be reviewed and probably revised when one moves from a separate property state to a community property state and vice versa.

QUESTIONS AND ANSWERS

Question — When is income taxable to the trust, and when is it taxable to trust beneficiaries?

Answer — Income from a revocable trust will be taxed to the grantor. For an irrevocable trust, the trust will be taxed on income that is accumulated for future distribution to someone other than the grantor pursuant to the terms of the trust instrument. The trust will also be taxed on income that the trustee has discretion to accumulate or distribute, but that is not paid or credited to a beneficiary during the taxable year.

A trust beneficiary will be taxed on income that is distributed to him or that should have been distributed to him during the taxable year (assuming the trust is a nongrantor trust). Where a trust pays income to a beneficiary under age 14, trust income in excess of the first $1,000 will be taxed to that child but at the child's parents' top bracket.[17] Alternatively, if an election is made by a parent to claim interest and dividend income on the parent's return, the income will be taxed to the parent. (To qualify for this election the child must have gross income for the taxable year only from interest and dividends and that income must be more than $500, but less than $5,000.) This election is unavailable if the child has made an estimated tax payment or if backup withholding has occurred.

Question — Are life insurance premiums paid by the trust on insurance owned by the trust considered a payment of income to the beneficiary or a type of accumulation?

Answer — A purchase of life insurance by a trust constitutes a type of accumulation; therefore, the trust will pay income taxes on income used to pay insurance premiums.[18] However, if the income is or may be used to pay premiums on the life of the grantor or the grantor's spouse, that income will be taxed to the grantor at the grantor's tax bracket.

Question — If a grantor places insurance policies on his or her own life into an irrevocable life insurance trust, will the proceeds escape estate taxation if the grantor is the trustee?

Answer — The results on this issue vary. The regulations take the position that an insured who has the power to change the beneficial ownership of a policy or its proceeds or change the time of manner of enjoyment has an "incident of ownership" even if only acting as trustee and can receive no personal benefit from the trust.[19]

A number of cases have held that if the decedent-insured was not the grantor of the trust, the proceeds will not be includible in his estate unless he possessed, at the time of his death, the power to benefit himself or his estate by exercising (either directly or indirectly) an "incident of ownership."[20]

Other cases and a revenue ruling, however, followed the reasoning of the regulations and held that mere possession of the power to change the beneficial ownership of a policy or its proceeds is an incident of ownership regardless of the fact that the insured can act only as

trustee and in no way can receive a personal economic benefit from the trust.[21]

The IRS abandoned the ruling just described and may not include a policy in an insured-trustee's estate as long as (1) the insured holds only trustee powers and cannot exercise rights for his own personal benefit, and (2) the insured-trustee did not transfer a policy on his life to the trust, and (3) the insured-trustee did not pay premiums to maintain the policy on his life held by the trust, and (4) there is no indirect attempt to accomplish any of these.[22]

Generally, the best course of action is for the insured to retain no incidents of ownership either personally or as trustee. This is best accomplished by naming someone other than the insured as trustee (or contingent trustee).

Note that where life insurance is transferred by gift to a trust within three years of the transferor's death, the "gifts within three years of death" rule must be considered. Essentially, this rule includes in an insured's gross estate all gifts of life insurance made by him within three years of death.[23] The "gifts within three years of death" rule applies only to transfers with strings attached under IRC Secs. 2036, 2037, 2038, or 2042 (except for determining the applicability of some special provisions, e.g., special use valuation of property, estate tax deferral, etc.). Gifts of money to pay premiums should not be affected by the three-year rule if the gifts of cash are unrestricted and could be used by the trustee for purposes other than the purchase of life insurance.

Question — How can an irrevocable life insurance trust be used to help provide estate liquidity to an insured's estate for estate settlement costs?

Answer — An irrevocable life insurance trust can supply the requisite liquidity to the estate by having the trustee use trust assets and/or income to purchase insurance on the lives of certain individuals. Although income which is or may be used to purchase life insurance on the life of the grantor or the grantor's spouse will be taxed to the grantor as "owner" of the property producing that income, such property will not be, per se, includible in the grantor's estate for federal estate tax purposes.

The trustee would be the owner and beneficiary of the insurance. Under the terms of the trust instrument the trustee would be given authority to purchase assets from or lend money to the estate of the deceased insured.

Question — When life insurance proceeds become payable to a trust at the death of an insured, are the proceeds taxable for income tax purposes?

Answer — No. Providing that neither the grantor nor the trust purchased an existing policy in such a way as to come within the "transfer for value" rule, the proceeds become

Tools and Techniques

part of the corpus of the trust and are received income tax free. Any interest earned on the proceeds as part of the corpus, however, will be taxable as income to the trust or its beneficiaries.

Question — Does the transfer of an existing life insurance policy to a trust cause a taxable gift to be made?

Answer — It depends. A transfer to a revocable trust is not deemed to be a completed gift. A transfer to an irrevocable trust, on the other hand, is a completed gift for gift tax purposes, subject to the "gifts within three years of death" rule. This assumes that the policyowner retains no reversionary interest in the trust and retains no economic rights in the trust.

Question — If an irrevocable trust is funded with income producing property and the income generated from that trust is used to pay premiums on a policy insuring the grantor's life, are the proceeds automatically includible in the grantor's gross estate for estate tax purposes?

Answer — No. Although the income used would be chargeable to the grantor, the proceeds would escape estate taxation if the insured-grantor retains no incidents of ownership in the policy, and does not retain any of the powers proscribed under Code sections 2035-2038.

ASRS, Sec. 48.

Footnote References

Trusts—Inter Vivos

1. IRC Section 2038.
2. IRC Section 671.
3. *Burnet v. Guggenheim*, 288 U.S. 280 (1933).
4. IRC Section 2038.
5. Rev. Rul. 79-353, modified by Rev. Rul. 81-51.
6. IRC Sections 2035-2038.
7. IRC Section 677(a)(3).
8. *Helvering v. Stuart*, 317 U.S. 154 (1942).
9. IRC Sections 674, 675.
10. IRC Sections 641, 652, 662; Reg. §1.641(a)-2.
11. IRC Section 667; Regs. §§1.668(a)-1A, 1.668(b)-4A.
12. IRC Section 665(b).
13. IRC Section 2036(a)(1).
14. *Burnet v. Guggenheim*, 288 U.S. 280 (1933). See generally regulations under IRC Section 2511.
15. IRC Section 644(a)(1).
16. IRC Section 2523.
17. IRC Sections 641, 652, 662; Reg. §1.641(a)-2.
18. IRC Section 641; Reg. §1.641(a)-2.
19. Reg. §20.2042-1(c)(4).
20. See *Skifter's Estate v. Comm.*, 468 F.2d 699 (CA-2, 1972); *Freuhauf's Estate v. Comm.*, 427 F.2d 80 (CA-6, 1970).
21. *Estate of Lumpkin v. Comm.*, 474 F.2d 1092 (CA-5, 1973); *Terriberry v. U.S.*, 517 F.2d 286 (CA-5, 1975), cert. denied 424 U.S. 977; Rev. Rul. 76-261, 1976-2 C.B. 276.
22. Rev. Rul. 84-179, 1984-53 IRB 7, revoking Rev. Rul. 76-261, 1976-2 C.B. 276.
23. IRC Section 2035.

Chapter 33

TRUST — MARITAL DEDUCTION

WHAT IS IT?

The marital/non-marital trust (also commonly referred to as the "A-B trust" or more currently sometimes the "A-B-Q" trust) is an arrangement designed to give the surviving spouse full use of the family's economic wealth, while at the same time minimizing, to the extent possible, the total federal estate tax payable at the deaths of both spouses.

For the period from 1948 through 1981, marital deduction trust planning focused on having the maximum portions of the property of the first spouse to die made available to support the surviving spouse without being subjected to death tax again at the survivor's death. This planning concept was based on the fact that all of the property of the first spouse to die, less approximately one-half of his or her separate property if it passed to the surviving spouse, was subject to tax at the death of the first to die. Literally millions of estate plans were written on this principle.

Now married couples can eliminate federal estate taxes entirely at the death of the first spouse to die through a carefully considered plan capitalizing on the marital deduction coupled with the unified credit. The term "federal estate tax" as used in this chapter means the tax imposed by Chapter 11 of the Internal Revenue Code, and does not deal with the 15% estate tax on "unreasonable accumulations" in retirement plans as discussed in Chapter 22 of this book. If it is desired to achieve the avoidance of federal estate tax at the first death, the great majority of all pre-1982 estate plans must be revised. All previously un-planned estates must still be brought within this planning concept, usually using a trust arrangement to avoid "overqualification" of the estate for the marital deduction because of "underutilization" of the unified credit in the estate of the first spouse to die.

Historical Perspective

The marital deduction concept was enacted into law in 1948 to give separate property states most of the advantages of community property.

Prior to 1948, there was great discontent in separate property states over what was perceived as an unfair advantage for estate tax purposes that was afforded to community property estates. For example, if Sam and Sarah lived in a separate property state[1], only Sam worked and they accumulated $400,000, upon Sam's death, the entire $400,000 was subject to estate tax. However, for Cal and Cassie, who lived in a community property state, if only Cal worked and they accumulated $400,000, half of it was considered to be owned by Cassie and therefore only Cal's half ($200,000) was taxed at his death.

In 1948, the concept of the marital deduction was introduced. The essence of it was that, if the spouse who owned separate property died (Sam in the above example), his estate could receive a deduction for up to one-half of the estate if he left it to his surviving spouse in such a way that it would be taxed in her estate. Thus, for a couple owning separate property, if the first spouse to die owned $400,000, $200,000 could escape tax at his death by going to the surviving spouse and thus qualifying for the marital deduction. This put the separate property estate generally in the same position for estate tax purposes as the community property estate, where half of the property was already exempt as being owned by the surviving spouse.

For many years after the introduction of the marital deduction, it was argued by many legislators that there should be no estate tax on any of the property—not just half of it—going to a surviving spouse. This concept was accepted in a limited fashion in the 1976 Tax Reform Act by permitting a minimum deduction of $250,000 regardless of the size of the estate and even permitting a marital deduction for community property estates to the extent that the surviving spouse owned less than $250,000 of community property.

The totally tax-free interspousal transfer idea was fully accepted in the 1981 Economic Recovery Tax Act (ERTA)[2], which permits a deduction for unlimited amounts of estate passing by lifetime gift or at death to a surviving spouse. Further, the qualifying rules were relaxed to permit a deduction not only for property passing directly to the surviving spouse or in a trust which will go to the survivor's estate or which is subject to the survivor's right to say where it goes at his or her death, but also the Executor may now elect to take a marital deduction where a right to all income is given to the survivor, even though the property goes to the children or someone else at the survivor's death.

There remains, however, the intent that the property must be included in the spouse's estate for estate tax purposes if it is to be exempt from tax under the marital deduction at the first spouse's death.

As the original marital deduction concept was the foundation stone for post-1948 planning for separate property estates, *the unlimited marital deduction concept, coupled with a judicious use of the unified credit, has dominated spousal estate planning in the 1980s and will in all probability continue to do so.*

Past (Pre-1982) and Current
Planning Techniques

The pre-1982 marital trust (or portion) was designed to qualify for the federal estate tax marital deduction. This was a deduction allowed for the net value of property passing at death from one spouse to his or her surviving spouse in a qualifying manner to the extent such gifts did not exceed the greater of $250,000 or 50 percent of the decedent's adjusted gross estate.[3] That property, to the extent it is owned by the surviving spouse or forms part of the corpus of the marital trust at the death of the surviving spouse, will generally be taxable at his or her death for federal estate tax purposes. The trust used to hold the marital deduction assets was also known as the "A" or "wife's" trust.

The pre-1982 family (or "bypass" or "B") trust was designed to hold assets for the economic well-being of the surviving spouse in a manner which would permit the corpus of such trust to pass free of federal estate taxes (i.e., bypass) at the death of the surviving spouse. In the typical situation, it was this bypass trust which was primarily responsible for minimizing the overall impact of death taxes upon the deaths of both spouses and therefore maximizing the amount passing to surviving children. Many clients still have this outdated arrangement.

The "no-tax-on-transfers-between-spouses" marital deduction should have triggered a review and a change in most plans and must be considered in dealing with unplanned estates.

Some couples may prefer to have some tax paid at the death of the first spouse to die (since some of the taxed portion will be taxed at the lowest federal estate tax rates (37% for deaths after 1986) instead of being shifted to the surviving spouse's estate and added "on top" of the assets the survivor already owns). However, the desire to pay an "up front" tax will be an exception. Since the tax at the top rate will be only 50% after 1992, the difference in rate is not great. Further, the surviving spouse may use up the additional assets received or give them away. The majority of "younger" couples may well decide to accept some possible penalty in estate tax rate in order to avoid tax altogether at the death of the first spouse to die. This is obviously an important decision which the estate planner must review at length with the husband and wife.

If the decision is made to avoid tax altogether at the death of the first spouse to die, then the decision must be made as to how much of the estate should be subject to the surviving spouse's power to say where it goes at the survivor's death.

For pre-1982 deaths, in order to obtain the marital deduction, it was necessary to give the property outright to the surviving spouse or in a trust which the survivor could give to a new spouse or otherwise do with as he or she pleased at death. Particularly for second marriages, where there were children of the first marriage from whom the property could be diverted by the use of the marital deduction, the decision to use the marital deduction was often a very difficult one.

For post-1981 deaths, under estate plans executed after September 13, 1981, the marital deduction can also be obtained by putting qualifying property into a qualified terminable interest property (QTIP) trust, a trust which provides for all of the income to go to the survivor and which is not subject to any contingencies (e.g. remarriage) or powers in anyone else to defeat the survivor's right to the income. The executor may elect to have all or a portion of such a qualifying trust be subject to the marital deduction. The assets in the QTIP trust or portion of it elected to pass tax free under the marital deduction will be included in the survivor's taxable estate.

For separate property estates where it is desired that *all* of the marital deduction property or *none* of it should be subject to the survivor's power of disposition at death, it will be satisfactory to have only one marital deduction or "A" Trust, since the same rules will pertain to all of the property.

However, for many estates, it may be desirable to limit the spouse's ability to divert all of the marital trust assets (to a new spouse or friend and away from the children) but to provide for such a power as to a portion of the estate. Particularly for community property, where the survivor already owns half, it may be very helpful to obtain the marital deduction for all of the estate in excess of the exemption (with the exempt portion going to the bypass (or "B") trust to avoid tax at the survivor's death), but to still provide that some of the deducted property will ultimately go to the children (or to the brothers or sisters of the first spouse to die if there are no children).

These "deducted" assets can be set aside for the ultimate use of the children by putting a portion of the assets into a trust (perhaps called Trust "Q") which will provide income to the survivor but go to the children at the survivor's death. The rest of the assets deducted as a marital deduction would go to the "A" or marital trust, which will be controllable by the survivor as to its disposition.

Thus, we may often provide a formula which will put into the "B" or family trust the amount of the effective exemption ($600,000 for deaths after 1986) at the death of the first spouse. Even though this trust can provide for income to the survivor (and if desirable, can even give to the survivor some limited power of disposition to other people and/or the power to take out each year the greater of $5,000 or 5% of the trust principal), property in this trust will escape taxation at the survivor's death. Obviously, the formula to achieve this is very important.

If it is decided to have a zero estate tax at the first death, and if it is desired that the spouse have disposition powers over all or none of the other assets, all of the other assets can go to the marital or "A" trust.

However, if it is desired that the survivor have a power of disposition over only a portion of the assets, then the portion subject to the power can go into the typical marital or

"A" trust, and the balance can go into a QTIP trust. Both trusts will qualify for the marital deduction and be included in the survivor's estate at death. Either or both of these trusts can provide for invasion of principal for the benefit of the survivor, but only the "A" trust will be subject to a power of disposition at the survivor's death.

Often the revocable A-B or A-B-Q trust takes the form of a life insurance trust coupled with a "pourover will." Here a revocable ("I can tear it up and forget about it") insurance trust is created during the grantor's lifetime. The trustee is named as the beneficiary of life insurance policies issued on the grantor's life. The grantor's will contains a provision to the effect that the grantor's residuary estate, what is left after payments of debts, expenses, taxes and specific bequests, is to be "poured over" into the living trust. (Think of a funnel. Life insurance passes outside of the funnel directly to the "pool of assets" at the bottom while noncontractual [probate] assets pass through the grantor's will into the top of the funnel and flow down to join the life insurance.)

The trust instrument provides that upon receiving the insurance proceeds from the insurance company and the residuary estate property from the pourover will provisions, the total principal will then be divided into two or three parts: a portion will go to the marital or "A" trust, a portion to the family or "B" trust, and if appropriate, a portion will go to the QTIP trust, which latter will qualify for the marital deduction but be distributed at the survivor's death as provided in the trust instrument (e.g. to the children).

The use of the trust can provide flexibility while achieving the long term goals of the family and minimizing death taxes.

WHEN IS THE USE OF SUCH A DEVICE INDICATED?

1. When it is the desire of the spouses that the survivor have full economic benefit of the family's wealth and that the aggregate death taxes payable at the deaths of both spouses be reduced. Where an individual leaves all of his property to his spouse, his estate may be "overqualified" for the marital deduction, as discussed below. Too much property may pass to the surviving spouse and thus be needlessly taxed at the surviving spouse's death. The reason for this result is that the spouse has "ownership" of all of the family wealth and therefore it is taxable for federal estate tax purposes at his death. If the surviving spouse merely had the "benefit" of all of the family wealth (i.e., an A-B or A-B-Q trust arrangement), only the portion that qualified for the marital deduction at the death of the first spouse to die would be subject to federal estate taxes at the survivor's subsequent death.

In order to maximize the utility of this technique, the A-B or A-B-Q trust device can be designed to pass to the A trust or to the A and Q trusts together exactly enough property to reduce the federal estate tax in the estate of the first spouse to die to the lowest desired amount—even to zero. Any additional property subject to tax at the decedent's death and passing to the trust would automatically pass into the B (family or nonmarital) trust (portion) and escape death taxation at the death of the second spouse to die.

2. The overqualification problem referred to above results in passing more to the surviving spouse in property interests qualifying for the marital deduction than is necessary to keep the federal estate tax at the decedent's death to the minimum. Overqualification results in wasting (in whole or in part) the decedent's unified credit. For couples with estates over $600,000 (the amount of estate that can have its tax "paid for" by the unified credit), wasting the unified credit of the first to die will likely result in a larger-than-necessary estate tax falling on the surviving spouse's estate at her later death. (An example later in the chapter illustrates the point.) A properly designed A-B or A-B-Q trust could eliminate or minimize this problem.

3. Where the couple plan to set up "generation-skipping trusts" (see Appendix B) for the children, the $1,000,000 exclusion from generation-skipping transfer tax of the first spouse to die can be lost if the property passes outright to the surviving spouse, or in any form of marital deduction trust other than a qualified terminable interest property trust (QTIP trust).

4. Favorable state inheritance tax treatment may be obtained. Rather than giving property outright to a spouse, if property is placed in a "marital trust", even if the spouse has a general power of appointment over the assets in that trust, the laws of some states exclude such property for state death tax purposes from the estate of the holder of the power of appointment. For example, in Pennsylvania, even though a surviving spouse could reduce the property in a marital trust subject to a general power of appointment to his or her own possession, it will not be subject to state inheritance tax at the death of such spouse. Thus, from a death-tax viewpoint, in some states it is preferable to leave a surviving spouse's assets in trust coupled with a general power of appointment over such assets, rather than leave the same amount outright, all other things being equal.

Some other states also provide a form of tax-free interspousal transfer. Such provisions parallel to a substantial degree the new post-1981 federal estate tax marital deduction rules.

5. When management of trust property is needed for the beneficiaries.

269

Tools and Techniques

6. Where it is desired to avoid probate. In addition to the tax reductions and management benefits described above, a person's estate can avoid the expense and delay of probate by transferring the title of the person's assets to a revocable inter vivos trust during the person's lifetime, which trust would also contain the tax minimization provisions. Since the property is already transferred before the person's death, there is no need for the Court to take charge and transfer the title and therefore no probate proceedings are required.

WHAT ARE THE REQUIREMENTS?

Property which passes outright to the surviving spouse can qualify for the federal estate tax marital deduction. It is also possible to qualify certain types of trusts for the marital deduction. There are three types of trusts which will qualify for the marital deduction—the "power of appointment" trust, the "estate" trust, and the QTIP trust.

1. Power of Appointment Trust—Requirements

   (a) The surviving spouse must be entitled to all of the income produced by the assets of the trust (note that the law states "all of the income" not "all of the net income").

   (b) The income produced by the trust must be payable at least annually.

   (c) The surviving spouse must be given a general power of appointment[4] (during lifetime, at death, or both) exercisable in favor of the spouse or the spouse's estate.

   (d) The power must be exercisable by the surviving spouse in all events.

   (e) No person may have any power to appoint any part of the trust assets to any person other than the surviving spouse.[5]

   An estate owner can give property in trust subject to a power of appointment but require that—to exercise the power—the donee's will (or a different instrument) must make specific reference to such power. This is important because in some states, such as Pennsylvania, a residuary clause will exercise a general power of appointment automatically unless there is a specific stated intention not to exercise it. In other words, absent the requirement that the donee of a power must specifically refer to it in states such as Pennsylvania, the donee is deemed to have exercised the power in favor of his or her residuary legatee.

   The trust property will qualify for the marital deduction if the spouse is given the power to appoint by will alone (i.e., a testamentary power of appointment). He or she does not have to be given the power to withdraw the principal during lifetime (i.e., an inter vivos power of appointment).[6]

A trust should not contain a specific provision authorizing investment in unproductive property or permitting the retention of unproductive assets unless the spouse is given a right to demand that the trust be made income-producing.[7]

Prior to 1982, this was the most commonly used type of trust.

2. Estate Trust—Requirements

   (a) The trust must provide for income to the surviving spouse for life (payable to her or accumulated for her benefit).

   (b) The remainder of the trust (both principal and any accumulated income) must be payable to the surviving spouse's estate at his or her death.

An estate trust falls outside the terminable interest rules because no interest passes to anyone other than the spouse and her estate.[8] This will enable the trustee to accumulate income or invest in non-income-producing property. However, accumulations will be taxed as part of the surviving spouse's estate at his or her death along with the original corpus. In addition, for federal income tax purposes the accumulations will be subject to the throwback rule.

The estate marital trust is indicated where (a) there is a need or desire to invest in non-income-producing property, (b) the survivor will not need trust assets or income during his or her lifetime, and (c) the property placed into the trust is not likely to appreciate substantially in value.

3. QTIP (Qualified Terminable Interest Property) Trust—Requirements

   (a) The same requirements regarding "all income to the surviving spouse" apply here as they do in the power of appointment trust. Thus, the survivor must receive all of the current beneficial interest in the trust.

   (b) However, this trust need not have any power in the surviving spouse to appoint or control the disposition of the property.

With this type of trust, the trustor can be certain that, at the death of the survivor, the property will go to the children or wherever the trustor decides (and not to the survivor's new spouse, which may be the case with the power of appointment trust or the estate trust).

4. Other General Requirements

   Assets in the marital trust must pass to or be held for the benefit of the decedent's surviving spouse—the person who is married to the decedent at his or her death.[9] Although this requirement appears simple to determine, it has been the cause of extensive litigation because of the increasing frequency of divorce and persons living together without formal marriage that are now prevalent in our society.

Furthermore, the decedent's spouse must survive the decedent. In the event of a common accident (such as a plane crash) when it is impossible to ascertain who dies first, the Uniform Simultaneous Death Act (the law in most states) would raise a presumption that neither spouse survived the other and therefore, would defeat the marital deduction. The application of such act can be overcome by inserting into the documents creating the marital trust a survivorship clause which creates a presumption that for purposes of the marital deduction, the spouse is deemed to survive if it is not possible to establish the order of deaths.[9a]

HOW IT IS DONE — AN EXAMPLE

Although there are a number of ways to accomplish the same objective, the life insurance trust/pourover will combination is one of the most popular. In this arrangement an individual establishes a trust during lifetime and names the trust as beneficiary of his or her insurance policies. When the grantor dies, the insurance maintained on his or her life is paid directly to the trust. The grantor's other assets pass through probate and are "poured over" by will into the trust. The one pourover trust is then split into two or three parts and different trusts are created; the "A" or appointment trust, a "B" or family (also called nonmarital or bypass) trust, and, in some cases, the "Q" or QTIP trust.

A — The Survivor's Property Trust or Power of Appointment Trust

The A trust, or power of appointment trust, used to be the primary vehicle for receiving the marital deduction assets before the advent of the QTIP trust, and is still used by some practitioners for that purpose. Where the QTIP trust is used for the marital deduction instead, Trust A often will hold the surviving spouse's property, particularly in community property states, in order to provide unified management of the assets under the umbrella of the estate planning trust.

Trust A would provide that all income from the trust be paid to the surviving spouse during his or her lifetime. Where Trust A is used as a marital deduction trust, the pourover trust in many cases would contain a funding formula to ensure that the power of appointment trust, together with any QTIP trust, would receive just enough property to reduce the federal estate tax at the death of the grantor to zero.

The formula for trust division, in some cases such as very elderly couples with relatively large estates, may be drafted so as to pay some estate tax at the first death with the property being taxed in relatively low tax brackets. For deaths after 1992, however, the lowest estate tax bracket will be 37% and the highest will be only 50%, a rather narrow spread on which

to decide to pay tax at the death of the first spouse to die. In addition, if the clients wish to permit payment of some estate taxes at the first death, this is generally better arranged by having the marital deduction property pass to a QTIP trust, since a QTIP trust allows the decision as to the amount of tax to pay to be deferred until the death of the first spouse to die. At that time, the planner and the family can better assess whether the surviving spouse's financial security may be impaired by early payment of death taxes.

The surviving spouse will be given the right to designate by will or other written instrument who will receive the corpus of the marital trust and such appointment may be made to anyone he or she chooses, including his or her estate. The surviving spouse may also be given the right to withdraw any part of the corpus of the appointment trust during lifetime. At the surviving spouse's death, if the surviving spouse fails to exercise his or her power of appointment, the remaining corpus in the appointment trust will pass to the next takers under the trust.

Since this type of trust, prior to 1982, was generally the only type of trust (other than the estate trust described above) to qualify for the marital deduction, it was often referred to as the "marital" trust. For deaths after 1981, however, the QTIP type of trust will also qualify for the marital deduction. Therefore, references to the trusts will now more often stress the "appointment" power in this type of trust, and the QTIP factor in the type of trust newly qualified for the marital deduction.

B — The Bypass Trust

The second trust, the "B" or bypass nonmarital (family) trust is designed to receive property that is not allocated to the power of appointment trust or the QTIP trust. An amount equal to the credit equivalent is placed in this trust. The Trustee may be directed to distribute the net income of this trust to the surviving spouse during his or her lifetime, or the income may be accumulated or directed to other persons in order to reduce the overall income tax effect on the family. Since the life estate terminates at the death of the surviving spouse, there will be no transfer of property that is includible in the estate of the life tenant (the surviving spouse) which is subject to the federal estate tax at death.[10] Thus, this trust "bypasses" the survivor's taxable estate and is therefore often called a CEBT, Credit Equivalent Bypass Trust.

The surviving spouse can be given a "limited" or "special" power of appointment under this family trust. For example, a surviving spouse might be given the right to appoint, at his or her death, all or any part of the assets in the family trust to a limited class of beneficiaries,[11] such as the children of the grantor. This means that the surviving spouse can distribute the assets in this trust only to the specified children,

Tools and Techniques

but can do so in any proportion he or she desires. A power of appointment will be classified as a "limited" or "special" power and will not subject the corpus of the trust to federal estate taxes at the death of the holder so long as the power cannot be exercised in favor of the holder of the power, his or her estate, his or her creditors, or the creditors of his or her estate.

The bypass trust can also provide a noncumulative right of withdrawal. Typically, this provision states that if the A and Q trusts are depleted, the surviving spouse is given the right to make limited withdrawals from the bypass or family trust. Usually, the surviving spouse is provided with a "non-cumulative" (use it or lose it) right to withdraw each year the greater of (a) 5 percent of the corpus of the trust or (b) $5,000.[12] Such a power will not cause the entire corpus of the family trust to be includible in the surviving spouse's estate (although the amount subject to withdrawal in the year of the surviving spouse's death will be included in the estate).

At the death of the surviving spouse, the family or bypass trust can continue to function for the benefit of the grantor's family, generally his or her children. The most common dispositive provision requires that the corpus of this trust be divided into separate equal trust funds for the benefit of the grantor's children, who will receive the net income currently and will have the right to demand distributions from principal at stated ages.

Often, rather than having all of the income from the family or bypass trust pass to the surviving spouse for life, a greater degree of flexibility may be obtained by utilizing a "spraying" or "sprinkle" clause. This provision authorizes the trustees (other than a trustee who is a beneficiary), at their discretion, to spray or sprinkle the net income of the bypass trust among the surviving spouse and the grantor's children in any way the trustees determine. The trustees can thus apportion the trust's income among the beneficiaries having the greatest need.

Alternatively, since for federal income tax purposes the trust is a separate taxable entity, the trustees could be given the right to apportion the net income of the trust among the trust and the beneficiaries after giving consideration to their relative income tax brackets. Net income generated by the trust is determined substantially in accordance with the same rules applicable to individuals, with certain important differences. Although the taxable income of the trust is subject to the federal income tax, in arriving at taxable income the trust receives a deduction for distributions made or required to be made to beneficiaries during its taxable year to the extent such distributions do not exceed "distributable net income" as that term is defined in the Code.[13] By deflecting income to beneficiaries with little or no personal income, the overall income tax for the family can be reduced. However, unearned income of a child under age 14 in excess of $1,000 per year will be taxed at the parent's highest marginal rate (the "kiddie tax").

In addition to income tax savings, the estate tax at the survivor's death may be reduced by use of a "sprinkling" or "spray" provision. Instead of the nonmarital income being paid to the surviving spouse, it may be accumulated in the nonmarital trust and pass, free of estate tax, at the survivor's death. Meanwhile, the survivor has been permitted to invade the appointment trust (or the QTIP trust, if one exists) and consume some of the principal of those trusts (instead of using the income which has been accumulated in the nonmarital trust) and thus the appointment trust, and any QTIP trust which would be taxed at the survivor's death, would be reduced and the estate tax lowered.

The "sprinkle" or "spray" clause should be avoided where the bypass trust will be a recipient of stock in an S corporation. Only certain types of trusts are permitted to own S corporation stock, and a major requirement of such trusts is that the trust benefit only a single individual, and that such individual receive all the income from the trust on an annual basis.[14]

Q — The QTIP Trust

When it is desired that an amount of estate in excess of the effective exemption amount (which exempt amount goes to the "bypass" or family trust) should produce a marital deduction at the death of the first spouse to die but should not be subject to the power of appointment in the surviving spouse, a QTIP trust may be created in planning for post-1981 deaths.

By providing the opportunity for a marital deduction, placing assets in this trust can result in zero estate tax at the death of the first spouse to die to the extent that the trustee or executor elects to take the marital deduction.

All of the income of this trust must be paid, at least annually, to the surviving spouse. No provision for invasions of the trust can be made for anyone other than the surviving spouse or the marital deduction will be lost. Likewise, it would be lost if there were any condition (e.g. remarriage) or power in anyone else which could prevent the surviving spouse from receiving all the trust income.

The principal of this trust may usually be invaded for the benefit of the surviving spouse but the trust terms may provide for first using up all or part of the marital or appointment trust before invading this trust.

To the extent that the trustee has elected to take a marital deduction at the first spouse's death for assets going into that trust (usually 100%), the QTIP (Q) trust will be included in the estate of the surviving spouse.[15] Thus, the marital deduction has merely deferred the tax on any assets in this trust which are not used up for the benefit of the surviving spouse.

Any assets remaining in this trust at the survivor's death will be distributed as the grantor decided, often subject to a non-general power in the surviving spouse as to the method of distribution among the children of the marriage.

HOW DO THE MECHANICS OF THE A-B OR A-B-Q TRUST PLAN WORK?

First, an inter vivos (living) trust instrument can be drafted creating the different trusts to be used—(the A or appointment trust, the B or bypass (family) trust and, when desired, the Q, QTIP trust.) Although the trust will come into being during the grantor's lifetime, it will not become operative until it is funded (until assets are placed into the trust) at the grantor's death (or prior to death if it is desired to use this living trust to avoid probate of the trust assets).

The trust is revocable because the grantor possesses the power to alter, amend, or revoke the trust until his or her death. Most states allow a grantor to name the trustee as beneficiary of his life insurance proceeds and obviates the need to transfer any other property to the trust during his or her lifetime.[16] But, if insurance is for some reason unavailable, many states recognize a trust funded with a nominal corpus such as $100, or even less.

Generally, however, the grantor will provide in his will that his probate property, after payment of settlement costs and any specific bequests or devises, will be added (poured over) to the trust. Where liquid assets may be insufficient to pay death costs and administration expenses, a useful provision in the inter vivos trust is to permit the trustee to make cash available to the estate executor through loans or the purchase of estate assets.

Alternatively, this same marital deduction arrangement can be created in a testamentary trust (i.e., one contained in the decedent's will).

The essential provision in the A-B or A-B-Q trust is known as the marital deduction formula. All property included in the decedent's probate estate or made payable to the inter vivos trust will be divided in accordance with the formula clause in the trust agreement. Such a clause might provide that the power of appointment and/or QTIP trust is to be funded in an amount equal to the amount necessary to maximize the marital deduction; or an amount required to reduce the federal estate tax payable to zero, or any other specified portion of the estate. The division of the marital deduction assets between the power of appointment "A" trust and the "Q" trust could be whatever the grantor desires (e.g., half of the separate property going to the "A" trust, and the other half going to the "Q" trust). In any event the funding clause would also provide that the amount of any such marital portion should be reduced by any property passing directly to the surviving spouse as a result of the grantor's death (e.g., a specific gift of personal effects, life insurance or jointly owned property).

The net balance of the trust corpus, after allocation of the marital deduction amount and after settlement costs are paid, is then allocated to the family ("B") trust.[17] Thus, the A-B/A-B-Q trust is really two or three trusts in one, administered under one trust agreement by the same trustees.

Why is the A-B/A-B-Q trust arrangement such an important estate planning tool? To fully appreciate the implications and tax savings potential, it is necessary to examine a typical estate.

A common arrangement is one where the testator leaves all of his property to his spouse (either by will, by jointly owning all assets with the spouse, or a combination of the two) and therefore overqualifies for the marital deduction and wastes the Unified Credit available at the death of the first spouse to die. As a result, when the settlement of both estates is considered, federal estate taxes may be higher than if other arrangements were made.

Example: Sam Kartman dies in 1987 and leaves his entire estate of $1,300,000 to his wife, Anne, if living, otherwise to their son, Myron. Sam's primary objectives are to retain control of the estate during his lifetime, to provide an adequate income for his wife after his death, and to minimize his estate settlement costs. Assuming Anne dies in 1995, and that she does not consume any of the principal of the estate, and further assuming that the value of the estate increases at the average rate of 7 percent a year, Figure 33.1 shows how much is paid in federal estate tax in each estate and how much after tax goes to Myron at Anne's death.

A Typical Pre-1981 A-B Trust

Prior to 1981, the typical trust to avoid additional taxes over the death of a husband and wife was to pass to the surviving wife outright or in trust an amount equal to the then marital deduction (the greater of one-half of the separate property or $250,000). This essentially resulted in equalizing the estates taxable at each death (assuming the couple's assets were acquired from the husband's earnings), at least for larger estates. The concept of equalizing the estates is still probably the most economical method of minimizing the taxes over the deaths of both husband and wife where the estates of the husband and wife will be over the available equivalent exemptions. In other cases, however, the tax burden will be greater.

If Sam had a trust designed to equalize the estates (e.g., by giving to Anne under the marital deduction one-half of his assets), Figure 33.2 shows how much would be paid in federal estate tax in each estate and how much would pass to Myron on Anne's death (same assumptions as stated in the previous example).

A Typical Post-1981 A-B or A-B-Q Trust to Reduce the Tax at the First Death to Zero

If Sam had wished to be certain that no federal tax were paid at his death, regardless of the size of his estate, he could

273

Figure 33.1

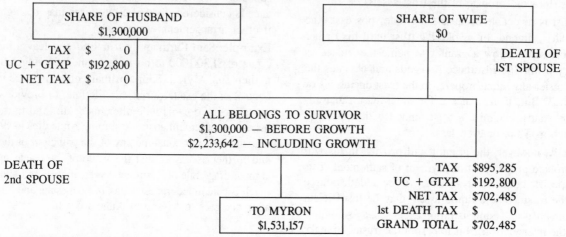

1. Sam's Entire Estate Passes to Anne

Note: The values in the chart below are shown net of debts, and funeral and administration expenses have been ignored. Also, it is assumed that upon Sam's death there has not been any depletion of property, and any possible credit for federal estate taxes on prior transfers has not been taken into account. The state death tax credit is assumed to equal the state death tax paid at the second death, and thus is not shown either as a debit or credit at the second death.

RESULT IF ALL TO SPOUSE: TODAY: $1,300,000/AT DEATH: $1,300,000
SAM KARTMAN & ANNE KARTMAN-DOD 1987, GROWTH 7%, 8 YRS/DT

SHARE OF HUSBAND	SHARE OF WIFE
$1,300,000	$0

TAX $ 0
UC + GTXP $192,800
NET TAX $ 0

DEATH OF
1ST SPOUSE

ALL BELONGS TO SURVIVOR
$1,300,000 — BEFORE GROWTH
$2,233,642 — INCLUDING GROWTH

DEATH OF
2nd SPOUSE

TAX $895,285
UC + GTXP $192,800
NET TAX $702,485
1st DEATH TAX $ 0
GRAND TOTAL $702,485

TO MYRON
$1,531,157

VIEWPLAN ESTATE FORECAST MODEL
Chart Courtesy of ViewPlan, Inc.

Observation: Since the marital deduction is taken on the whole $1,300,000 of adjusted gross estate at Sam's death, his unified credit of $192,800 is wasted. At Anne's death, the total net property of $1,300,000, plus the effect of inflation, is subject to federal estate taxation. Thus, the marital deduction portion passes tax free in Sam's estate, but is taxed in Anne's estate. The Unified Credit which was wasted at Sam's death results in the equivalent amount of property ($600,000 as of 1987), plus inflation on that sum, being needlessly taxed at Anne's death. This is a principal factor in diminishing the estate going to Myron, their only child.

have provided for an amount of marital deduction to go to Anne which would exactly equal the amount of deduction needed to reduce his federal estate tax to zero. This is called the "zero tax marital deduction." In that event, Figure 33.3 shows the amount of federal tax that would be paid in each estate and how much would pass to Myron upon Anne's death.

Comparison of Plans

Savings in federal estate taxes generally occur at the survivor's death. The federal estate tax payable in Sam's estate is the same in his overqualified arrangement (example 1) as it is in the Post-1981 A-B (or A-B-Q) trust arrangement (example 3)—in both cases it is $-0-. Actually, the savings in federal estate taxes occur in Anne's estate. The trust arrangement accomplishes this because the equivalent exemption

amount at Sam's death is never taxed in either estate. The savings afforded by example 2 (equalizing the estates) over the Post-1981 A-B trust example comes from the fact that having some of the property taxed in Sam's estate means that it is taxed at lower brackets, and all the increase in value after Sam's death is removed from Anne's estate. However, the amount paid in taxes is gone, and is not available to provide benefit to the survivor (or growth for the estate). The taxable amounts for each plan are illustrated in Figure 33.4.

Although it is not apparent from Figure 33.4, the second arrangement is "optimum" for the first spouse's death (zero estate tax then, regardless of the size of the estate), but it theoretically results in more overall tax if the spouse does not use up some of the estate or give some of it away during her lifetime.

Figure 33.2

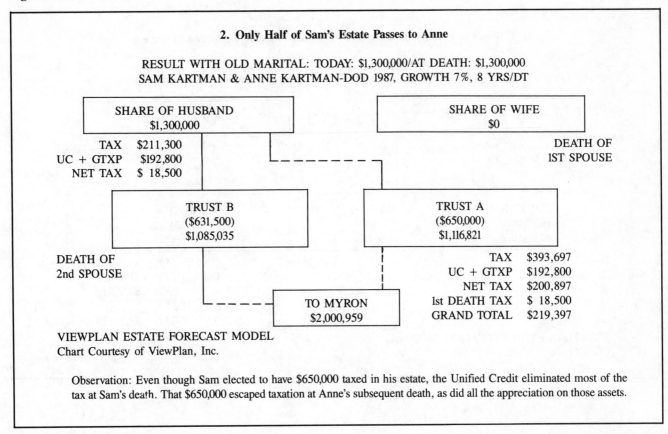

2. Only Half of Sam's Estate Passes to Anne

RESULT WITH OLD MARITAL: TODAY: $1,300,000/AT DEATH: $1,300,000
SAM KARTMAN & ANNE KARTMAN-DOD 1987, GROWTH 7%, 8 YRS/DT

SHARE OF HUSBAND	SHARE OF WIFE
$1,300,000	$0

TAX $211,300
UC + GTXP $192,800
NET TAX $ 18,500

DEATH OF
1ST SPOUSE

TRUST B	TRUST A
($631,500)	($650,000)
$1,085,035	$1,116,821

DEATH OF
2nd SPOUSE

TAX $393,697
UC + GTXP $192,800
NET TAX $200,897
1st DEATH TAX $ 18,500
GRAND TOTAL $219,397

TO MYRON
$2,000,959

VIEWPLAN ESTATE FORECAST MODEL
Chart Courtesy of ViewPlan, Inc.

Observation: Even though Sam elected to have $650,000 taxed in his estate, the Unified Credit eliminated most of the tax at Sam's death. That $650,000 escaped taxation at Anne's subsequent death, as did all the appreciation on those assets.

Electing to Pay Some Tax

As can be seen from the comparison in Figure 33.4, there can be some tax saving by paying tax early, where property is increasing in value. For example, if an asset now worth $100,000 is projected to be worth $500,000 at the second death, it is usually much more economical to pay the tax based on the current $100,000 value than on the $500,000 it will be worth later.

The drawback to the "old A-B" arrangement (Figure 33.2) is that the tax is *forced* to be paid at the first death. However, if a QTIP trust is used, the executor will have a right to elect how much of the property over the amount sheltered by the unified credit will be subject to tax—none of it, all of it, or any amount in between! Thus, the QTIP allows you to keep your options open, and decide at death how much, if any, tax to pay. If the loss of the funds used to pay the taxes will not impair the surviving spouse's security, substantial saving could be realized by paying some tax early.

If Sam Kartman had an estate of $2,500,000, and an insurance policy on his life of $300,000, his executor might elect to use that available cash to pay some tax at his death. Figure 33.5 shows a comparison of the results where no tax is paid, where all the tax is paid (no marital deduction is taken), and where the executor uses the $300,000 of cash to pay the tax.

Observation: Although many practitioners have abandoned the concept of insuring each spouse in favor of having "survivor insurance," which pays only at the death of the survivor, Figure 33.5 shows the benefits of having some cash available at the first death. Thus, insurance on each spouse's life is still a viable consideration.

Another reason for paying tax early may be to preserve the $1,000,000 generation skipping exemption of the first spouse to die. In a typical optimum marital deduction arrangement where only $600,000 goes to the bypass trust, the executor will almost certainly allocate $600,000 of the decedent's generation skipping exemption to that trust. The amounts passing under the marital deduction generally "belong" to the surviving spouse for generation skipping purposes and the remaining $400,000 of the decedent's exemption could be lost.

It is possible to override this loss of the $400,000 of exemption by using a QTIP trust, but in many cases this can be done only by a complex arrangement of having two or three separate QTIP trusts. This could saddle the trustee (who is often the surviving spouse) with an accounting nightmare that would continue throughout his or her remaining life.

What may be a better arrangement for a spouse who has his full unified credit available is to simply provide that $1,259,600 goes to credit shelter or bypass trusts. This will

Tools and Techniques

Figure 33.3

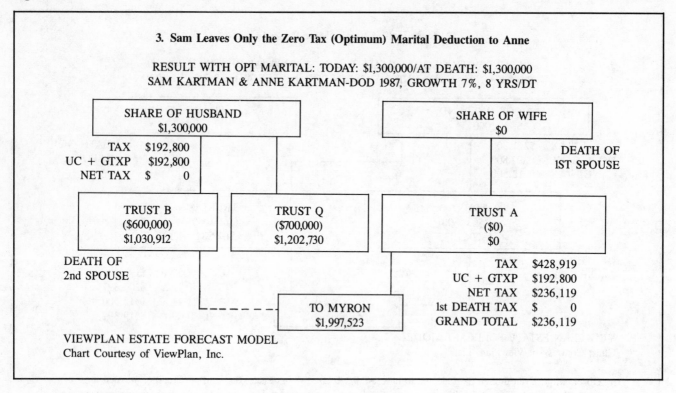

3. Sam Leaves Only the Zero Tax (Optimum) Marital Deduction to Anne

RESULT WITH OPT MARITAL: TODAY: $1,300,000/AT DEATH: $1,300,000
SAM KARTMAN & ANNE KARTMAN-DOD 1987, GROWTH 7%, 8 YRS/DT

| SHARE OF HUSBAND $1,300,000 | | SHARE OF WIFE $0 |

TAX $192,800
UC + GTXP $192,800
NET TAX $ 0

DEATH OF 1ST SPOUSE

| TRUST B ($600,000) $1,030,912 | TRUST Q ($700,000) $1,202,730 | TRUST A ($0) $0 |

DEATH OF 2nd SPOUSE

TO MYRON $1,997,523

TAX $428,919
UC + GTXP $192,800
NET TAX $236,119
1st DEATH TAX $ 0
GRAND TOTAL $236,119

VIEWPLAN ESTATE FORECAST MODEL
Chart Courtesy of ViewPlan, Inc.

Figure 33.4

COMPARISON OF TAXES BETWEEN RESULTS

SAM KARTMAN & ANNE KARTMAN-TODAY: $1,300,000/AT DEATH: $1,300,000
DOD 1987, GROWTH 7%, 8 YRS/DT

	All to Sps	Opt Marital	Old Marital
Death of HUSB			
Taxable estate after MD	$0	$600,000	$650,000
Tax On Estate	$0	$192,800	$211,300
Less UC + GTXP	$192,800	$192,800	$192,800
Net Tax	$0	$0	$18,500
Death of WIFE			
Taxable estate	$2,233,642	$1,202,730	$1,116,821
Tax On Estate	$895,285	$428,919	$393,697
Less UC + GTXP	$192,800	$192,800	$192,800
Net Tax	$702,485	$236,119	$200,897
GRAND TOTAL OF TAXES BOTH DEATHS	$702,485	$236,119	$219,397
SAVINGS OVER BOTH DEATHS*		$466,365	$483,088

*Without Considering Alternate Use of Funds Paid For Taxes

VIEWPLAN ESTATE FORECAST MODEL
Chart Courtesy of ViewPlan, Inc.

Figure 33.5

COMPARISON OF TAXES — ZERO TAX AT FIRST DEATH VS $300,000 TAX

SAM KARTMAN & ANNE KARTMAN — $2,500,000/$2,500,000
DOD 1987, GROWTH 7%, 8 YRS/DT

	Zero Tax Paid	Max Tax Paid	Elect Tax Pd
Death of HUSB			
Taxable estate after MD	$600,000	$2,500,000	$1,353,488
Tax On Estate	$192,800	$1,025,800	$492,800
Less UC + GfTxPd	$192,800	$192,800	$192,800
Net Tax	$0	$833,000	$300,000
Death of WIFE			
Taxable estate	$3,264,554	$0	$1,969,920
Tax On Estate	$1,408,077	$0	$767,264
Less UC + GfTxPd	$192,800	$192,800	$192,800
Net Tax	$1,215,277	$0	$574,464
GRAND TOTAL OF TAXES BOTH DEATHS	$1,215,277	$833,000	$874,464
SAVINGS OVER ZERO TAX ALTERNATIVE*			$340,813

*Without Considering Alternate Use of Funds Paid For Taxes

VIEWPLAN ESTATE FORECAST MODEL
Chart Courtesy of ViewPlan, Inc.

result in $259,600 of tax being due at the decedent's death, leaving the full $1,000,000 remaining, to which the generation skipping exemption may be allocated. Although this may require the creation of a separate trust to hold the $259,600 to be used in payment of the tax, that trust will disappear after the taxes are paid, leaving only the bypass and one QTIP trust for the trustee to administer during the surviving spouse's lifetime. An easy way to provide liquidity for payment of that $259,600 tax is by life insurance.

WHAT ARE THE TAX IMPLICATIONS?

1. For a typical revocable intervivos trust, no gift tax is payable upon creation of the trust since the grantor, at all times, has retained the right to terminate the trust.[18]

2. After death, the assets which qualify for the marital deduction (the assets actually going into the appointment and/or "Q" trust) are includible in the decedent's gross estate for federal estate tax purposes, but since they qualify for the marital deduction, they are not subject to estate tax.[19] In many situations the assets of these trusts will be minimal since the available credit will reduce the marital deduction amount and property passing outside the will may be sufficient to satisfy the marital deduction remaining. For example, if the decedent's adjusted gross estate is $900,000, the optimum marital deduction as of 1987 is $300,000 ($900,000 less the then effective exemption of $600,000 = $300,000). If the decedent left $350,000 worth of life insurance proceeds to his wife, she would already have received more than the maximum allowable marital deduction. It is important to remember that the marital deduction portion, which is established by formula, can be given outright to the surviving spouse instead of in trust.

3. Assets which are not used to fund the marital deduction trusts ("A" and "Q") are, by formula, placed into the family or bypass trust. The value of these assets is includible in the grantor's estate for federal estate tax purposes, but the available Unified Credit will actually result in zero tax. Further, since his or her surviving spouse receives no more than the income (and perhaps certain limited powers of appointment) from the trust, at his or her death these assets will not be taxed again.[20]

4. During the grantor's lifetime, income produced by any of the assets transferred to a revocable inter vivos trust will be taxed to the grantor since no irrevocable gift had been made and the grantor remained the owner of trust assets and income for both estate and income tax purposes. At the grantor's death, the income produced by trust assets will be taxable to the trust or to the income beneficiary depending on whether the income is accumulated by the trust or paid out to the income beneficiary.[21] Except for certain allowances made for accumulation of income for children under age 21, accumulated income

Tools and Techniques

is taxable to the income beneficiary in the year of distribution. However, the beneficiary will receive a credit for taxes paid by the trust when a distribution from the trust is made. This is known as the "throwback" rule.[22]

IMPLICATIONS AND ISSUES IN COMMUNITY PROPERTY STATES

Where the draftsman is dealing with community property, it should be noted that one-half of the property already belongs to the surviving spouse, and will not be subject to the "pour over" provisions of the will of the first spouse to die, unless the first spouse specifically indicates his or her desire to effect distribution of both halves of the community, *and* the surviving spouse acquiesces freely in that distribution.

To the extent the surviving spouse elects to retain his or her community half of the property outside the trust, then a problem of split ownership and management arises, with the survivor owning one-half of the assets, and the trustee of the trust owning the other half. If the surviving spouse does allow his or her half of the community property to pass to the trust, it would typically go into the "A" or power of appointment trust, so the survivor retains control over how the assets are distributed during lifetime or at death.

The marital deduction rules under the Economic Recovery Tax Act of 1981 apply to community property as well as separate property states, so community property state couples may also elect to defer the payment of any federal estate tax until the survivor's death.

Where a marital deduction is used, it will reduce the tax at the first spouse's death, but it may increase the tax at the second death if the surviving spouse does not use up the marital deduction portion during his or her lifetime, and result in somewhat higher overall taxes for both estates. However, most couples would prefer to minimize the tax at the first spouse's death in order to leave more assets available for the survivor's support, and take the risk of having slightly higher overall taxes.

In both community and common law states, holding property in joint tenancy (tenancy by the entirety) with right of survivorship will result in the property going outright to the surviving spouse, regardless of the provisions of the decedent's will. The marital deduction provisions may be drafted to reduce the marital deduction by the value of the assets passing outside the trust and thus still result in the optimum marital deduction amount passing to the spouse, so long as the assets passing outside the will do not exceed the optimum marital deduction amount. However, holding large amounts of property in joint tenancy can defeat the trust planning to a very significant degree since such holdings can be more than the optimum marital deduction and reduce the first to die spouse's estate to under $600,000 (thus resulting in a portion of the unified credit being wasted).

In many instances, a couple living in a community property state may have separate property as well as community property, and both kinds of property must be considered in determining the amount which will be optimum for the marital deduction. Typical pecuniary formula clauses to be used where there may be both separate and community property are shown in Figures 33.6 and 33.7 (for A-B-Q and A-B trusts, respectively).

The laws in Louisiana are unique and particular care should be taken to obtain counsel knowledgeable in Louisiana law and general tax law if a couple settle in or has community property located in Louisiana.

In any event, it is very important for persons who have an estate plan drafted with only separate property in mind to have the plan reviewed and most probably redrafted upon becoming a resident of a community property state.

QUESTIONS AND ANSWERS

Question — What are the disadvantages of an A-B/A-B-Q trust?

Answer — First, if the trust is an inter vivos trust and is currently "funded" (properties placed in the trust during the lifetime of the grantor), then trustee's fees must be paid. This fee can often be minimized if the grantor serves as his own trustee, which is permissable in some jurisdictions, or reserves the right and obligation to administer trust assets during lifetime—unless disabled.

Second, after the death of the grantor the surviving spouse cannot have full control of the assets which have been placed in the nonmarital trust(s). However, it is permissible to give the surviving spouse the right to invade principal at his or her own discretion to the extent of a noncumulative right to withdraw up to 5 percent of the corpus or $5,000 annually, whichever is greater.[23] If the surviving spouse is the trustee and if such spouse needs funds for his or her support, education, or maintenance, in addition to the income of the nonmarital trust and $5,000 or 5 percent of the trust's capital, then the trustee can be authorized to invade principal for such purposes. This use of an ascertainable standard would prevent him or her from being taxed on the trust property.[24]

Furthermore, the trustee (assuming the trustee was an independent party) may be given a power in its sole and absolute discretion to distribute principal to the surviving spouse for any reason satisfactory to the trustee. However, here the surviving spouse has no right to demand a distribution of principal. A further power that can be given to the surviving spouse is the right to appoint by deed or by will to and among a specified class of individuals (but this class must exclude the spouse, his or her estate, his or her creditors, and the creditors of his or her estate).[25] For example, the grantor could

Figure 33.6

CLAUSE — OPTIMUM MARITAL DEDUCTION — A-B-Q TRUST
(SEPARATE PROPERTY AND COMMUNITY PROPERTY STATE)

3. Upon the death of the first Trustor to die, and after making any payments or distributions pursuant to the preceding paragraphs, the Trustee shall divide the remaining trust estate into three parts which shall be separate trusts, hereinafter called Trust "A", Trust "B" and Trust "Q", respectively.

Trust "A" shall include the surviving Trustor's separate property received from any source, and the surviving Trustor's share of the community property of the Trustors.

Trust "Q" shall receive a marital deduction amount described as: An amount equal to the maximum marital deduction (allowable in determining the federal estate tax payable by reason of the deceased Trustor's death), minus the value for federal estate tax purposes of all items in the deceased Trustor's gross estate for federal estate tax purposes which qualify for said deduction and which pass or have passed in a form which qualifies for the federal estate tax marital deduction from the deceased Trustor to the surviving Trustor, by right of survivorship with respect to jointly owned property, under settlement arrangements relating to life insurance proceeds, or otherwise than under this paragraph. The words "pass or have passed" shall have the same meaning as such words shall have under the provisions of the Internal Revenue Code in effect at the time of the deceased Trustor's death. Provided however, that the marital deduction amount as determined above shall be reduced by an amount, if any, needed to increase the taxable estate of the first Trustor to die to the largest amount that will, after allowing for the unified credit and any other allowable credits and other factors, not result in a federal estate tax being imposed on the estate of the first Trustor to die. The amount determined under this Paragraph shall be computed on the basis the Executor will elect to qualify Trust "Q" for the marital deduction, whether or not the Executor does make such election.

In making the computations necessary to determine the amount of this pecuniary estate tax marital deduction gift, values as finally determined for federal estate tax purposes shall control. The selection of assets in making distributions in satisfaction of the marital deduction bequest shall not be subject to question by any beneficiary and no adjustment shall be made to compensate for a disproportionate allocation of unrealized gain for federal income tax purposes. Only assets which qualify for the estate tax marital deduction, or proceeds of such assets, shall be placed in Trust "Q".

An election may be made to have all or a portion of the property designated as going to Trust "Q" qualify for the marital deduction for federal estate tax purposes, such election to be made by the executor of the estate of the first Trustor to die (or such other person as shall have a right to make such election within the scope of Section 2056 of the Internal Revenue Code and other relevant sections and regulations). Such election shall be made (or not made) at the sole and absolute discretion of such executor (or other person as described above) on the basis of achieving the greatest reduction of tax at the death of the first Trustor to die which is consonant with the overall benefit to the income beneficiaries and remaindermen of this trust. The decision shall not be subject to question by any beneficiary, and the executor (or other person as described above) shall not be liable for any loss or expense to any person by virtue of making or not making such election.

In the event that any of the assets designated for distribution to Trust "Q" are not elected to qualify for the marital deduction, then, all the foregoing notwithstanding, those assets shall not be distributed to Trust "Q" but shall, instead, be distributed to Trust "Q-1", containing provisions identical to Trust "Q" hereof. Any such assets (for which no election to qualify for the marital deduction is made) which have already been transferred to Trust "Q" shall be removed from Trust "Q" and placed in Trust "Q-1".

The balance of the trust estate, after the distributions to Trust "A", Trust "Q" and Trust "Q-1" described above, shall constitute Trust "B". Provided however, in the event that any of the assets designated for distribution to Trust "B" is property which has been disclaimed by the surviving Trustor, those assets shall not be distributed to Trust "B" but shall, instead, be distributed to Trust "B-1", containing provisions identical to Trust "B" hereof except that the surviving Trustor shall have no power of appointment (either under said trust or under Paragraph NN of this trust). For all other purposes of this trust, Trust "B" and Trust "B-1" shall be considered as one trust.

Said trusts shall be held, administered and distributed as hereinafter provided:

*The above clause envisions taking the optimum marital deduction. However, it would be possible to provide for less than the optimum marital deduction to pass to the survivor's trust, e.g. one-half of the decedent's separate property or any other fraction or portion of the estate.

Tools and Techniques

Figure 33.7

CLAUSE — OPTIMUM MARITAL DEDUCTION — A-B TRUST
(SEPARATE PROPERTY AND COMMUNITY PROPERTY STATE)

3. Upon the death of the first Trustor to die, and after making any payments or distributions pursuant to the preceding paragraphs, the Trustee shall divide the remaining trust estate into two parts which shall be separate trusts, hereinafter called Trust "A" and Trust "B", respectively.

Trust "A" shall include the surviving Trustor's separate property received from any source, and the surviving Trustor's share of the community property of the Trustors.

In addition, Trust "A" shall receive a marital deduction amount described as: An amount equal to the maximum marital deduction (allowable in determining the federal estate tax payable by reason of the deceased Trustor's death), minus the value for federal estate tax purposes of all items in the deceased Trustor's gross estate for federal estate tax purposes which qualify for said deduction and which pass or have passed in a form which qualifies for the federal estate tax marital deduction from the deceased Trustor to the surviving Trustor, by right of survivorship with respect to jointly owned property, under settlement arrangements relating to life insurance proceeds, or otherwise than under this paragraph. The words "pass or have passed" shall have the same meaning as such words shall have under the provisions of the Internal Revenue Code in effect at the time of the deceased Trustor's death. Provided however, that the marital deduction amount as determined above shall be reduced by an amount, if any, needed to increase the taxable estate of the first Trustor to die to the largest amount that will, after allowing for the unified credit and any other allowable credits and other factors, not result in a federal estate tax being imposed on the estate of the first Trustor to die.

In making the computations necessary to determine the amount of this pecuniary estate tax marital deduction gift, values as finally determined for federal estate tax purposes shall control. The selection of assets in making distributions in satisfaction of the marital deduction bequest shall not be subject to question by any beneficiary and no adjustment shall be made to compensate for a disproportionate allocation of unrealized gain for federal income tax purposes. Only assets which qualify for the estate tax marital deduction, or proceeds of such assets, shall be placed in Trust "A" pursuant to this marital deduction bequest.

The balance of the trust estate, after the distributions to Trust "A" described above, shall constitute Trust "B". Provided however, in the event that any of the assets designated for distribution to Trust "B" is property which has been disclaimed by the surviving Trustor, those assets shall not be distributed to Trust "B" but shall, instead, be distributed to Trust "B-1", containing provisions identical to Trust "B" hereof except that the surviving Trustor shall have no power of appointment (either under said trust or under Paragraph NN of this trust). For all other purposes of this trust, Trust "B" and Trust "B-1" shall be considered as one trust.

Said trusts shall be held, administered and distributed as hereinafter provided:

*The above clause envisions taking the optimum marital deduction. However, it would be possible to provide for less than the optimum marital deduction to pass to the survivor's trust, e.g. one-half of the decedent's separate property or any other fraction or portion of the estate. Further, by not using a QTIP trust, the trustor has given up both control over the ultimate disposition of the assets qualifying for the marital deduction and also the opportunity to take advantage of the full amount of the trustor's exemption from Generation Skipping Tax in most cases.

---

state that his or her spouse has the right to appoint by will to and among the grantor's children, parents, or siblings.

Question — What functions does the trustee have in the A-B/A-B-Q trust?

Answer — The trustee will serve as the recipient of life insurance payable to it as well as property "poured over" from the decedent's will. The trustee will be the legal owner of the corpus assets of both trusts and manage the trusts in accordance with the provisions of the trust agreement. The trust agreement can be either extremely flexible or severely restrictive, depending on the objectives of the grantor.

The trustee's primary duties are twofold: (1) to manage and invest the trust corpus in such a manner as to generate income for the beneficiaries; and (2) to preserve the corpus. In many instances a corporate fiduciary may be indicated, either as sole or cotrustee if the estate is sizeable or if conflicts in interest are likely to arise between individual trustees.

Question — What are the different ways to write provisions that qualify for the maximum or optimum marital deduction?

Answer — The first is for the testator to leave a specific dollar amount bequest; however, this technique is not recommended since it is impossible, in most cases, to arrive at a dollar amount that will exactly equal the desired marital deduction at the time of the grantor's death with any degree of accuracy.

The second way is use of a funding formula which is geared to the marital deduction provisions of the Internal Revenue Code. Either a pecuniary formula bequest or a fractional share bequest is the formula clause to use. A pecuniary formula bequest is used where the testator wants his widow to receive a fixed dollar amount (a general legacy). An example of such a clause follows:

"If my wife, Deborah, survives me, I give, devise, and bequeath to my trustees (in trust "A" or trust "Q") an amount exactly sufficient—and no larger—to reduce the federal estate tax due at my death to the lowest possible amount, after taking into consideration all other property passing to my wife or which has passed to my wife and which qualifies for the marital deduction and after allowance of all applicable credits except the credit for property received by me from a transferor who died within two years after my death."[26]

Under this clause the property qualifying for the marital deduction is paid to the marital ("A" and/or "Q") trusts. The remainder of the property after satisfying the marital deduction is bequeathed to the family trust.

Instead of a fixed amount, the testator may want to give his widow a fractional share of the estate. Here, the sum which goes to the widow may fluctuate after the decedent's death and, in essence, she receives a share in the residue. In this case, the clause (the fractional share bequest) should read somewhat as follows:

"If my wife, Deborah, survives me, I give, devise, and bequeath to my trustees (in trust A or trust Q) the following fractional share of my residuary estate (before such estate is diminished by the payment therefrom of estate, inheritance, or death taxes):

(a) The numerator of the fraction shall be exactly sufficient—and no larger—to reduce to the lowest possible amount the federal estate tax due at my death, after taking into consideration all other property passing to my wife or which has passed to my wife and which qualifies for the marital deduction and after allowance of all applicable credits except the credit for property received by me from a transferor who died within two years after my death.

(b) The denominator of the fraction shall be the value of my residuary estate, before it is diminished by the payment therefrom of estate, inheritance, or death taxes."

IT IS IMPORTANT TO NOTE THAT MANY OTHER PROVISIONS ARE REQUIRED, IN ADDITION TO THE FUNDING FORMULA, IN ORDER TO OBTAIN THE MARITAL DEDUCTION.

Question — Which type of funding formula is preferable?

Answer — This depends upon the circumstances. The most important thing to look at is the type of assets the grantor owns.

If there is a probability of a substantial increase in value during the period of settlement of the trust or estate, then the pecuniary formula clause may have some benefit if it gives the residual amount (after the marital deduction) to the bypass trust. Under these circumstances, any increase in the size of the estate can be shifted to the bypass trust and thus reduce taxation at the survivor's death.

If there is a possibility that the estate may drop in value, then it may be wise to use a pecuniary formula clause that specifies the exact amount to go to the bypass trust and lets the residue go to the marital deduction trust.

In any use of a pecuniary formula clause, it is possible to recognize an income tax where assets that have increased in value since the date of death are used to satisfy distribution to a trust. In these circumstances a gain can be recognized and taxed.

A fractional share clause avoids the problem of any recognition of income tax gain upon transfer of assets to a trust to fund a bequest. Additionally, it shifts any increase or decrease proportionately to both the marital deduction trust and the bypass trust.

However, with the fractional share clause, the executor cannot pick and choose the assets to be placed in the bypass trust, and thus there may be less opportunity for post-mortem planning.

Question — What are some of the advantages of an estate trust over a power of appointment trust?

Answer — Under the estate trust, it is not necessary that all of the income be paid out to the surviving spouse. Instead, some of the income can be accumulated and kept in the trust. Where there is concern for use of income and a great deal of income available, an estate trust may provide more protection for the survivor.

Additionally, the estate trust may in some cases make it easier to retain assets that are not producing income for the trust.

Question — What are the advantages of having the marital deduction pass to a QTIP trust?

Answer — Many advantages exist. One important one is giving the trustee the power to determine how much of the trust is to be taxed at the death of the first spouse to die. Under the QTIP provisions, it is possible to arrange to

Tools and Techniques

have additional estate tax, so that there will be a tax to pay that is larger than the unified credit. This may be helpful in having the tax paid early and therefore having this additional property out of the way of inflation for the survivor's lifetime.

A second important benefit of a QTIP trust is that the trustor can be certain that, at the death of the survivor, the property will go where the trustor wanted the property to go and not merely to the survivor's new friend or new spouse (as is the case under the power of appointment trust where the surviving spouse must be given a power to appoint the property at the survivor's death).

Where it is desirable to give the surviving spouse some control over the disposition of assets, e.g., among the mutual issue of the decedent and survivor, the QTIP trust permits the modification of the disposition by the survivor if the trustor wants that to happen.

Last, the QTIP trust is the only optimum marital arrangement by which the grantor's full $1,000,000 exemption from the generation-skipping transfer tax can be preserved for the next generation, with the property still benefiting the surviving spouse during the survivor's lifetime.

Question — Can an A-B/A-B-Q trust be set up in an individual's will?

Answer — Yes. This is called a testamentary (as contrasted to an inter vivos) trust. Rather than have a separate trust instrument and a separate will, the two are combined into the will document. The provisions of the testamentary trust are generally the same as the inter vivos trust provisions.

Question — Are there any drawbacks to setting up the A-B/A-B-Q trust in the will rather than as an inter vivos document?

Answer — Use of a testamentary trust will *require* a probate at the grantor's death. Often there is a delay in probating a will. If the trust were part of the will, it would not function until the will was probated. Thus, if life insurance were payable to a testamentary trust, there could be a delay in getting funds into that trust.

Some states for inheritance tax purposes will tax insurance payable to a testamentary trust as opposed to proceeds payable to an inter vivos trust. This will unnecessarily cause additional costs to the estate.

ASRS, Sec. 51, ¶280.

Footnote References

Trusts—Marital Deduction

1. All states except California, Arizona, Nevada, Louisiana, Idaho, Texas, New Mexico, Washington, and, most recently, Wisconsin.

2. Section 403 of the Act, modifying IRC Sections 2056 (estate tax) and 2523 (gift tax).

3. IRC Section 2056, prior to ERTA.

4. Reg. §20.2041-1(c).

5. Reg. §20.2056(b)-5.

6. Reg. §20.2056(b)-5(a)(4).

7. Reg. §20.2056(b)-5(f)(4).

8. *Comm. v. Ellis*, 252 F.2d 109 (CA-3, 1958), Rev'g in part, 26 T.C. 694.

9. Reg. §20.2056(a)-1.

9a. TAMRA '88 imposed yet another requirement for obtaining the marital deduction: The surviving spouse must be a citizen of the United States, or the amount included in the gross estate must pass to the surviving spouse outside of probate through a "qualified domestic trust" prior to the date the estate tax return is filed. The major requirements of a qualified domestic trust are that (1) the trust allows only individuals who are also U.S. citizens as trustees, (2) the surviving spouse must be entitled to all trust income and that income must be paid annually or more frequently, and (3) the trust must meet certain requirements (to be issued in regulations) assuring the government that it can collect an estate tax at the death of the surviving spouse. Act Sec. 5033, adding IRC Secs. 2056(d) and 2056A, effective for estates of decedents dying after November 11, 1988.

TAMRA '88 also changed the estate tax law to allow a marital deduction with respect to property situated in the United States to estates of nonresidents (even though they are not U.S. citizens) if their surviving spouses are U.S. citizens. Act Sec. 5033(c), adding IRC Sec. 2106(a)(3), effective for estates of decedents dying after November 11, 1988.

10. Rev. Rul. 66-86, 1966-1 C.B. 216.

11. Reg. §20.2041-1(c).

12. IRC Section 2041(b)(2); Reg. §20.2041-3(d)(3).

13. IRC Sections 651, 661.

14. Additional requirements must be met in order for a trust to qualify as a "Qualified Subchapter S Trust," as outlined in IRC Section 1361(d).

15. IRC Section 2044. The property in the trust includible in the surviving spouse's estate under section 2044 is considered property acquired from a decedent, and thus in the hands of the one to whom the property passes from the surviving spouse has a basis equal to the fair market value of the property at the date of the surviving spouse's death or alternate valuation date (see the discussion of basis in Appendix B). IRC Sections 1019(b)(10) and 2044(c), as added by the Technical Corrections Act of 1982.

16. It is extremely important to check the applicable state law to be sure that merely naming a trust as life insurance beneficiary will serve as adequate corpus.

17. See Rev. Proc. 64-19, 1964-1 C.B. 682.

18. Regs. §§25.2511-2(b), 25.2511-2(c).

19. IRC Section 2056.

20. *Estate of Milner v. Comm.*, 6 T.C. 874 (1946).

21. IRC Sections 641, 652, 662.

22. IRC Sections 665-669.

23. IRC Section 2041(b)(2); Reg. §20.2041-3(d)(3).

24. Reg. §20.2041-1(c)(2).

25. Reg. §20.2041-1(c)(1).

26. Certain additional provisions must be added to this "funding" formula in order to guarantee the marital deduction. See, e.g., Rev. Proc. 64-19, 1964-1 C.B. 682.

Chapter 34

TRUST — SECTION 2503(c)

WHAT IS IT?

A Section 2503(c) trust is a gift tax tool that enables a grantor to make a gift to a minor in trust and still obtain the $10,000 annual gift tax exclusion.[1] The use of this irrevocable funded trust for gifts to minors eliminates many of the following practical objections to outright gifts:

1. Brokers are reluctant to deal in securities owned by minors since minors may disaffirm either a purchase of stock that subsequently falls in value or a sale of stock that later rises in value.

2. Property titled in a minor's name is, to a large extent, "frozen". It is difficult to sell or exchange that property since a minor's signature on a real estate deed gives the buyer no assurance of permanent title.

3. Guardianship must be used to avoid many of the objections of an outright transfer to a minor, but a guardian must generally post bond and account periodically to a local Orphans' (sometimes called Surrogate's or Probate) Court.

WHEN IS THE USE OF SUCH A DEVICE INDICATED?

When your client wishes to make a gift to minor children and:

1. When the grantor's income tax bracket is high and the donee's income tax bracket is relatively low. Significant income shifting, and therefore income tax saving, is still possible, once the child reaches age 14.

2. When the grantor owns an asset which is likely to appreciate substantially over a period of time but does not want the appreciation includible in his or her gross estate.

3. When use of the $10,000 gift tax annual exclusion is necessary or desirable.

WHAT ARE THE REQUIREMENTS?

1. A gift to a minor through a Section 2503(c) trust will not be considered a gift of a future interest (so the gift will qualify for the $10,000 annual gift tax exclusion) if the income and principal may be expended by or on behalf of the beneficiary at any time prior to the time the beneficiary reaches age 21. (Regardless of when a person becomes an adult under state law, the "magic" age is still 21 for Section 2503(c) purposes.)

2. Unexpended income and principal must be payable to the beneficiary when that individual reaches age 21.

3. If the child dies before age 21, trust corpus must go to the minor's estate or appointee under his or her will.[2]

4. Even if the minor is legally unable to exercise a power or to execute a will because he or she is under legal age, this fact will not cause the transfer to fail to satisfy the above conditions. Furthermore, it is permissible to provide that the trust will continue beyond the donee's 21st birthday, as long as anytime after reaching age 21, the donee can obtain the property in the trust at his or her whim. Thus, the trust property does not have to be forced on a trust beneficiary upon reaching age 21.[3]

HOW IT IS DONE — AN EXAMPLE

Jeff Mandell transfers stock in his closely held corporation to three trusts for his three minor boys. Assuming the trusts qualify under Section 2503(c), the irrevocable transfer of stock annually to the trusts will be considered gifts of a present interest. This will allow Jeff to obtain the $10,000 annual exclusion per donee ($20,000, assuming his wife joins in the gift) and therefore, minimize or eliminate any gift taxes.

Gifts, to the extent they qualify for the annual exclusion (without taking gift splitting into account), reduce the value of Jeff's estate and the income from any dividends paid on the stock is taxed currently either to the trust, if accumulated, or to the children, if distributed. Such a trust is often used to start children on a life insurance program by providing the trust with sufficient cash each year to pay premiums for the insurance on the boys' lives. Alternatively, trust income could be used to purchase nonnecessaries or be accumulated and used to help provide nonnecessaries when the children reach college age.

WHAT ARE THE TAX IMPLICATIONS?

1. If the income of the trust is distributed each year, it is taxable to the recipient.[4] To the extent income is accumulated, it will be taxed to the trust.[5] Eventually, when a distribution of income accumulated in a prior year is made, the beneficiary will pay tax on the distribution as though the income had been distributed annually; however, the beneficiary will receive credit for any taxes paid by the trust.[6] (This is the so called "throwback" rule.)

The throwback rule is not applicable to accumulations due to sales of capital assets or to accumulations for beneficiaries made during the years they were under age 21, since Section 2503(c) requires that the property and any accumulated income pass to the donee at age 21.

2. Gifts to the trust constitute a present interest. Therefore, the annual gift tax exclusion of $10,000 applies as long as the conditions mentioned above are met.

3. Appreciation on property from the date it is placed in trust will be removed from the grantor's gross estate. (However, the entire value of the 2503(c) trust will be includible in the grantor's estate if the grantor is the trustee at the time of his or her death.)

Generally, the gross estate of a decedent does not include the value of transfers, other than transfers of life insurance, made by a decedent within three years of his death.[7]

To the extent the transfers exceed or otherwise do not qualify for the $10,000 annual exclusion, they do not result in estate tax savings. This is because the taxable portion of any gift is added back in the estate tax computation as an "adjusted taxable gift" at the date of gift value (less a credit for any gift tax paid on the transfer). Nevertheless, a benefit from the gift does result because the property brought back into the computation as an adjusted taxable gift is valued as of the date of the gift. Post-transfer appreciation is excluded.

For instance, if a single individual gives his brother $210,000 worth of stock, $200,000 would, after the donor's death, be considered an adjusted taxable gift in his estate ($10,000 qualifies for the gift tax annual exclusion). That would be true even though the stock had appreciated in value to $300,000 by the time of the donor's death. The appreciation in value, $100,000 ($300,000-$200,000) would never enter the estate tax computation.

Transfers made within three years of death of interests in property otherwise included in the gross estate under Sections 2036, 2037, 2038 or 2042 are included in the gross estate at their date of death values. An unfavorable aspect of the law is that a transfer of insurance by the insured within three years of death continues to be includible in the gross estate.

IMPLICATIONS AND ISSUES IN COMMUNITY PROPERTY STATES

Where community property is the subject of a gift into a 2503(c) trust, each spouse is considered as being the grantor of one-half, by reason of the community ownership. For that reason, it is important that neither spouse be named as the trustee or successor trustee of the trust in order to avoid the problem of having the trust property included in the grantors' estates (see second question and answer below). In some states, if one spouse transfers community real or personal property to a trust for the benefit of a third party, such spouse must obtain the written consent of the nondonor spouse prior to such transfer or the gift could be entirely set aside.

QUESTIONS AND ANSWERS

Question — If it is likely that the grantor will make only one gift and that gift will be a relatively modest amount of marketable securities and there is little likelihood that further gifts will be made in subsequent years, should a Section 2503(c) trust be used?

Answer — No. Generally, the complexities and expenses of creating such a trust contra-indicate its use for small gifts or "single shot" gifts. In this type of situation, the use of the Uniform Gifts to Minors Act (UGMA) or the Uniform Transfers to Minors Act (UTMA) might be a more appealing alternative. However, where it seems likely that additional gifts will be made in future years, and a substantial amount of valuable property will ultimately be transferred to the minor, additional flexibility is called for and indicates the use of a trust.

The type of property in question may affect which device will be used. For example, the Internal Revenue Service has held that stock in an S corporation may be held by a custodian under the Uniform Gifts to Minors Act.[8] However, if a gift of stock in an S corporation is made to a Section 2503(c) trust, the corporation's election may be automatically terminated, since generally a trust may not be a shareholder of an S corporation.[9] The law does allow a trustee to be an S corporation shareholder, but only if (a) the grantor is treated for income tax purposes as the owner of trust property (a so-called "grantor trust"), or (b) the trust was created primarily to vote stock (a so-called "voting trust"), or (c) the trust receives the stock under a will (a so-called "testamentary trust" and it holds S corporation stock only up to a maximum of 60 days after the stock is transferred to the trust), or (d) a "Section 678" trust (see last question and answer).

One reason a trust is often used instead of the Uniform Gifts to Minors Act is custodianship: the U.G.M.A. provides that only one person may be custodian and specifies how a successor custodian may be named. But if a trust is created, the grantor may designate a line of succession of trustees and may provide for two or even more trustees to act together.

Question — Are there any adverse tax consequences if the donor acts as the trustee of a Section 2503(c) trust?

Answer — Yes. If the donor acts as trustee and dies in that capacity before the child has reached age 21, the assets in the trust may be includible in his estate (the same result occurs if the donor appoints himself as custodian under the Uniform Gifts to Minors Act or the Uniform Transfers to Minors Act and dies while serving in that capacity before the custodianship ends). The same result occurs where the grantor dies while serving as successor trustee or custodian.

For example, where the husband is appointed successor trustee upon the death of his wife, the corpus is taxed in the grantor-trustee's estate because of the trustee's power to "alter, amend, revoke or terminate" the trust. Even if the only power retained is the ability to advance principal to the beneficiaries from time to time in the discretion of the trustee, the grantor, as trustee, has the power to accelerate the termination date. In essence, this is the power to terminate the trust and, therefore, adverse estate tax consequences occur if the grantor is the trustee or one of the trustees (or the custodian in case of a Uniform Gifts to Minors Act or Uniform Transfers to Minors Act).[10]

Question — If a father places dividend-bearing securities into a 2503(c) trust for his minor son using an independent bank as trustee, what types of expenditures of income would cause the income to be taxed to the father?

Answer — If the income is or may be used to pay premiums on a life insurance policy on the life of either the grantor or the grantor's spouse, or if it is used for the support of a minor whom the grantor is legally obligated to support, then such income will be taxed to the grantor (father).[11] Note that the use of capital to pay premiums would not cause the grantor to be subject to income tax on trust income.

Question — In addition to giving the donee the continuing right to compel distribution upon reaching 21 is there any other arrangement which can avoid a mandatory distribution of principal and income to the donee child at age 21?

Answer — Yes. The donee can be given a right during a *limited period* of time to compel immediate distribution of the trust corpus by giving written notice to the trustee which, if not exercised, will permit the trust to continue by its own terms.

Question — What is a 2503(b) trust?

Answer — A 2503(b) trust is one which requires a mandatory distribution of income to the trust beneficiary on an annual or more frequent basis. All or portions of gifts to such trusts will qualify as gifts of a present interest and thus are eligible for the $10,000 annual gift tax exclusion. For example, if the trust provides income for life to the donee to be distributed at least annually and if the donee is age eleven, then based on tables published by the IRS,[12] the amount of the gift which will be considered as a present interest would be $9,845.30 (the actuarial value of such income interest).

In some respects a 2503(b) trust is more flexible than either a 2503(c) trust or a custodianship account since a 2503(b) trust does not require distribution of principal and unexpended income at age 21 or sooner. Furthermore, a 2503(b) trust can last for the lifetime of the beneficiary or for any lesser period of time. Also, unlike the case with a 2503(c) trust or a custodianship, under a 2503(b) trust, the principal does not ever have to be paid over to the income beneficiary. Trust principal can go to a donee specified by the grantor of the trust or can go to a person specified by the income beneficiary.

As income is earned by a 2503(b) trust, it must be distributed to the trust beneficiary. However, it can be deposited in a custodial account and used for the benefit of the minor or left to accumulate in the custodial account until the minor reaches majority. At that time, the accumulated income will be turned over to the beneficiary. Each year, as it is earned, the income of the trust will be taxed to the minor except to the extent it has been used to discharge a support or other legal obligation of a grantor-parent.

If the minor is under age 14, income will be taxed to the minor, but (with respect to unearned income in excess of $1,000) at the parents' top bracket. If the minor is 14 or older, all income (earned and unearned) is taxed to the minor at the minor's bracket.

Figure 34.1 illustrates that a $2,000 annual contribution to a 2503(c) trust will be worth $59,689 in 18 years. Had the same parents or grandparents set aside the same $2,000 and received the same 6% return, their tax rate would have cut down the return to $47,477 over the same period of time. The 2503(c) trust yields a $12,212 advantage.

For gift tax purposes, the entire amount placed into such a trust is treated as a gift. The gift is divided into two portions: an income portion and a principal (remainder) portion. The income portion will qualify for the $10,000 annual exclusion while the balance is considered a future interest gift and will not qualify for the exclusion.[13] To protect the annual exclusion for the income portion, the trust instrument should specifically deny the power of the trustee to invest in non-income producing property.

Question — Is it possible to make a gift into a trust which can retain the property for a child past age 21 and still have the entire gift qualify for the annual exclusion?

Answer — Yes; based on the *Crummey*[14] case, if the donee has an immediate, unfettered, and ascertained legal right at the time the gift is made to take out the amount put in, then the gift will be considered a present interest gift and qualify for the annual gift tax exclusion.

Ordinarily, failing to exercise a power to take property out of a trust (where the trust goes on under some cir-

Tools and Techniques

Figure 34.1

```
╔══════════════════════════════════════════════════════════════════════╗
         2503(c) TRUST INCOME-SHIFTING WORKSHEET
```

INPUT:	ANNUAL CONTRIBUTION	$2,000
INPUT:	RATE OF RETURN	0.060
INPUT:	DONOR'S TAX RATE	0.330
INPUT:	BENEFICIARY'S AGE (FIRST YEAR)	1
INPUT:	BENEFICIARY'S AGE AT TERMINATION	18
INPUT:	BENEFICIARY'S TAX RATE AFTER AGE 21 (IF APPLICABLE)	0.15
	FUTURE VALUE OF TRUST AMOUNT	$59,689
	FUTURE VALUE (CONTRIBUTION INVESTED OUTSIDE TRUST)	$47,477
	TAX ADVANTAGE OF USING A 2503(c) TRUST	$12,212
	ADDITIONAL PERCENTAGE RETURN DUE TO 2503(c) TRUST	0.257

cumstances to someone else) is a gift by the donee to the extent of the value which goes to someone else. However, there is a specific exception[15] which ignores the gift consequence to the donee where the power is to appoint (i.e., to give) to oneself no more than the greater of $5,000 or 5 percent of the trust corpus. To come within this rule, this type of trust gives the beneficiary the right to remove only this "5 and 5" amount each year (on a non-cumulative basis). However, the $5,000 limit is less than the amount of the new annual exclusion of $10,000 (or the $20,000 that a husband and wife can give).

There may be other persons (e.g. grandparents, uncles, aunts, etc.) who would like to make gifts to the trust. It is most probable that Crummey trusts can deal with these large gift potentials, and still not have a gift when the donee does not exercise his power by giving the donee a power to appoint the trust at his death to anyone other than himself (or his estate, creditors or estate creditors). This will bring the non-appointment trust assets into the donee's taxable estate, but that is not usually an unacceptable condition.

Note that gifts to grandchildren may be subject to generation-skipping transfer tax. See Appendix B.

Question — Is a 2503(c) trust a good receptacle for holding stock in an S corporation?

Answer — A 2503(c) trust is not an eligible shareholder of S corporation stock. A QSCT or a Section 678 trust is a better vehicle for this purpose.

The Economic Recovery Tax Act of 1981 (ERTA) made a modification of a simple trust eligible to hold S corporation stock. This modified conventional trust is called the QSCT, the Qualified S Corporation Trust.

Specifically, a QSCT is defined in the Internal Revenue Code as one that:

1. owns stock in one or more S corporations (and may hold other types of assets)

2. actually distributes all of its income to one individual (who must be a United States resident or United States citizen)

3. has trust terms requiring that

    (a) there can be only one beneficiary at any given time

    (b) if corpus is distributed during the term of the trust, it can be distributed only to the individual who is at that time the current income beneficiary

    (c) if an income beneficiary dies, the income interest itself will end at that death or upon the earlier termination of the trust

    (d) if the trust ends before the income beneficiary dies, all the assets of the trust must be distributed to that income beneficary

4. requires an election to be made by the income beneficiary (or the income beneficiary's legal representative) to have the QSCT qualify as such. (Once that election is made, it is irrevocable and can be revoked only if the IRS consents.) That election must be made by each income beneficiary as he or she becomes one. Separate elections must be made if the stock of more than one S corporation is held in the trust.

If the requirements described above are met, the income beneficiary of a QSCT (which can be set up during the grantor's lifetime or by will) is treated as the owner of the stock. The consequence is that any income, as well as any gains or losses, passes directly from the S corporation to the minor beneficiary.

What are the advantages of a QSCT? A gift of S corporation stock can be made to a minor through the trust without incurring the disadvantages of outright ownership. This enables an individual to split income among family members while at the same time eliminating the gift from inclusion in his gross estate. So both income shifting and wealth transfers are possible through the QSCT.

Unlike a custodianship, a QSCT can continue beyond age 18 (or 21) and can last as long as the grantor directed it to last. This means that if the minor dies before the trust terminates, the trust can continue for the lives of a number of successive income beneficiaries and does not have to force trust assets into the estate of the deceased income beneficiary.

The Nongrantor-Owner (Section 678) Trust

The QSCT is not the only new alternative to outright and UGMA or UTMA gifts. ERTA made "a nongrantor-owner trust" an eligible S corporation stock shareholder. The criterion for favorable tax treatment under this type of trust (Section 678 governs, and therefore these nongrantor-owner trusts have come to be called "Section 678 trusts") is that the beneficiary must have unrestricted power "exercisable solely by himself to vest the corpus or the income therefrom in himself." In other words, the beneficiary will be taxed on the income from the S corporation held by the trust if he has the right to take both income and corpus whenever he wants. There must be no restrictions on the beneficiary's right to exercise a withdrawal power.

A Section 678 trust can be created by a parent or grandparent who transfers S corporation stock to it for the benefit of a minor. The minor would be given an unrestricted power to withdraw income or corpus for his own benefit.

How are gifts to QSCTs and Section 678 trusts taxed for gift tax purposes? The answer is that from a gift standpoint, a contribution to either trust will be considered a complete gift. Such gifts can qualify for the $10,000 annual present-interest gift tax exclusion either by meeting the requirements of Section 2503(c) or by including a Crummey withdrawal power.

Estate Tax Implications

Will the property in a QSCT or Section 678 trust be includible in the estate of a beneficiary? The answer in the case of a QSCT beneficiary is that if the beneficiary is given only income rights, assets remaining in the trust at the time of the beneficiary's death will not be includible in his or her estate.

Just the opposite applies in the case of a Section 678 trust. Inclusion is a certainty since, by definition, the beneficiary must be given a general power of appointment (the power of withdrawal) over all or a portion of the trust. Property subject to that power at the time of the beneficiary's death will be includible in his or her estate.

The QSCT and the Section 678 trust offer two new ways to shift both business-generated income and wealth to minors at minimal gift tax cost.

Question — What are the disadvantages of a 2503(c) trust?

Answer — There are four "costs":

1. Expenses entailed in drafting ($500-$2,000).

2. Expenses involved in filing tax returns and estimated quarterly payments (cost depends on complexity of returns and time entailed).

3. A section 2503(c) trust can have only one beneficiary; this means money can't be transferred from the fund of a child who "goes astray" to the fund of a child who "who has seen the light."

4. The 2503(c) trust is irrevocable; the grantor must relinquish total control to obtain tax savings.

ASRS, Sec. 51, ¶230.2(d).

Footnote References

Trust—Section 2503(c)

1. Section 441a of P.L. 97-34, Economic Recovery Tax Act of 1981.
2. Reg. §25.2503-4.
3. Rev. Rul. 74-43, 1974-1 C.B. 285.
4. IRC Sections 652, 662.
5. IRC Section 641; Reg. §1.641(a)-2.
6. IRC Section 668; Regs. §§1.668(a)-1A to 1.668(b)-4A.
7. IRC Section 2035.
8. TIR No. 113, Nov. 26, 1958.
9. Regs. §§1.1371-1(a), 1.1371-1(d).
10. IRC Section 2038; Rev. Rul. 59-357, 1959-2 C.B. 212; Rev. Rul. 70-348, 1970-2 C.B. 193.
11. IRC Section 677.
12. Reg. §25.2512-9(f). This table is due to be revised pursuant to a direction under the 1988 Technical and Miscellaneous Revenue Act. See page 391.
13. *Herr v. Comm.*, 35 T.C. 732 (1961), aff'd. 303 F.2d 780(3rd Cir. 1962), acq. 1968-2 C.B. 2. See also *Pettus v. Comm.*, 54 T.C. 112 (1970); *Estate of David H. Levine v. Comm.*, 526 F.2d 717 (2nd Cir. 1976),rev'g. 63 T.C. 136.
14. *Crummey v. Comm.*, 397 F.2d 82 (9th Cir. 1968). See chapter 30 on Crummey trusts.
15. IRC Section 2514.

Chapter 35

UNIFORM GIFTS (TRANSFERS) TO MINORS ACT

WHAT IS IT?

The Uniform Gifts to Minors Act (UGMA) provides that an adult, while he or she is alive, may make a gift of certain types of property, such as securities, money, or a life insurance (or annuity) contract to a minor by having it registered in the name of, and/or delivering it to, the donor or another adult person or trust company as custodian for the minor.

Many states have amended their Acts to expand the types of property which can be the subject of a custodial gift to include real property, personal property and intangibles, and a few states permit transfers to custodians from other sources, such as trusts and estates, as well as lifetime gifts.

Following the expansive approach taken by these states, the National Conference of Commissioners on Uniform State Laws in 1983 approved the Uniform Transfers to Minors Act (UTMA). UTMA allows any kind of property, real or personal, tangible or intangible, to be made the subject of a custodial gift, and in addition permits transfers from trusts, estates, guardianships, and from other third parties indebted to a minor who does not have a conservator. At this writing over one-half the states have replaced their UGMA with the UTMA. Most of the rest will no doubt soon fall in line.

Under both the UGMA and the UTMA, the minor acquires both legal and equitable title to the subject matter of the gift.

Custodial gifts avoid many of the problems and expenses of other methods of transferring property to a minor such as outright gifts, trusts, or guardianship arrangements.

WHEN IS THE USE OF SUCH A DEVICE INDICATED?

1. When a parent would like to gift money or property for a child's benefit without giving it to him or her outright and without having to set up a trust.

2. When a parent would like to shift some of the income tax burden from his or her high tax bracket to a minor child's lower bracket.

3. When the $10,000 annual gift tax exclusion is desired.

4. When a parent would like to reduce his or her potential estate tax burden by shifting future appreciation in the value of an asset to a child.

5. Where the donor does not object to the donee's receiving the property outright upon reaching the age of majority (18 to 21, depending on state law).

WHAT ARE THE REQUIREMENTS?

1. Property must be transferred to a custodian who holds it as "custodian for (name of minor) under the (your state's) Gifts (or Transfers) to Minors Act."[1]

2. If there are two or more children to whom a parent wishes to make gifts, a custodian must be appointed for each child.[2]

3. Once made, a custodial gift is irrevocable.[3]

4. The property must be distributed to the child when he or she reaches the age of twenty-one.[4] (This age has been reduced in many states to a lower statutory age of majority. In some states the age at which the child receives the property can be extended by the donor. In New York, for example, the age of majority under the act is 18, but the donor may provide that the custodianship will last until the beneficiary reaches age 21.[5])

HOW IT IS DONE — AN EXAMPLE

Tony Arcangelo transfers his 10 shares of IBM stock to Mrs. Arcangelo as custodian for their son, Fred, by having the stock registered as follows: "Ginny Arcangelo as custodian for Fred Arcangelo under the *Pennsylvania* Uniform Gifts to Minors Act." Such a gift is a present interest gift and would allow Mr. Arcangelo to obtain the $10,000 annual gift tax exclusion. The future appreciation in the value of the stock also would be out of Mr. Arcangelo's estate. Any gift tax paid would be removed from the estate and any dividend income would be taxed to Fred.

WHAT ARE THE TAX IMPLICATIONS?

1. Income from any custodial property will be taxed to the minor whether distributed or not, except to the extent it is used to discharge a legal obligation of some other person (e.g., a parent's obligation to support a child). Where income produced by a custodial gift relieves an individual such as a parent of legal obligation, the income is taxed to that person.[6]

2. The gift is one of a present interest and qualifies for the $10,000 annual gift tax exclusion.[7] The exclusion will be allowed even if state law has lowered the age of majority to 18 and custodial property will be distributed to the donee at that age. Note that there is a growing trend in state divorce courts to assume that a financially well off parent has a legal duty to send children to college, even if they are, under state law, adults. We suggest that cus-

Tools and Techniques

todial income be accumulated until the child reaches college age. Income can then be paid out, semester by semester, in a series of unconditional checks. The child should deposit those checks in his own account and use the funds as needed.

3. The value of property transferred will be included in the estate of a deceased minor-donee. So if the donee dies, assets in the custodial account will be includible in his or her estate.

4. Custodial property will be included in the estate of the donor if the donor appoints himself or herself as custodian and dies while serving in that capacity.[8] Likewise, if the donor's spouse dies while serving as custodian and the donor becomes successor and then the donor dies, the value of the property transferred will be includible in the donor's estate.

5. State gift taxes must be considered. Many states have annual exclusions less than the federal $10,000 exclusion. Some states do not have gift taxes, although nearly all have some form of estate or inheritance tax.

IMPLICATIONS AND ISSUES IN COMMUNITY PROPERTY STATES

Where community property is the subject of a gift under the Uniform Gifts to Minors Act, each spouse is considered to be the donor as to one-half the value of the property given. Thus, in the example given above, Mrs. D'Ignazio would not be a good choice for custodian, since if she were to die, one-half of the gift made to Fred from their community property would be included in her estate on the basis of the rules relating to revocable trusts.

The same problems as discussed in chapter 33 may arise if one spouse gives community property without the written consent of the nondonor spouse.

Typically, in community property states, a brother or sister of the parents may be a good choice for acting as custodian.

QUESTIONS AND ANSWERS

Question — What types of property can be transferred to a custodian for the benefit of a minor?

Answer — In most states money, securities (stocks, bonds, evidence of indebtedness, certificate of interest or participation in an oil, gas mining title or lease), life or endowment insurance policies, and annuity contracts may be the subject of a gift under the Uniform Gifts to Minors Act.[9] Since the laws of different states vary, it's important to check your own state's laws.

There is a caveat with respect to gifts of insurance. Gifts of insurance are still included in the decedent's gross estate at their date of death value, regardless of the value of the policy, if the policy is transferred by the insured within three years of his death.

Under UTMA, any type of property interest may be transferred, including real property, tangible personal property, patents, royalties, etc.

Question — Who may be a custodian?

Answer — An adult person (age 21 or in some states 18), a trust company, or bank with trust powers.[10] A bank or trust company may now commingle such custodial property held for a minor under the Uniform Gifts to Minors Act in a common trust fund held by the bank or trust company in its capacity as trustee, executor, administrator, or guardian.[11]

Question — What use may be made of custodial property?

Answer — Under UGMA, the custodian may use the custodial property for the support, maintenance, education, and benefit of the minor to the extent that the custodian in his or her discretion deems suitable and proper.[12]

Under UTMA, Section 14 custodial property may be expended for the use and benefit of the minor, a more expansive use of custodial property than under UGMA.

Question — May there be one custodial account for two or more minors?

Answer — No, a separate custodial account must be established for each beneficiary. Only one custodian can be appointed for each account.[13] However, any number of separate gifts may be made.

Question — Who receives the custodial property if a minor dies?

Answer — Custodial property passes to the administrator or executor of the minor's estate.[14]

Question — Where a life insurance policy on a minor's life is placed in custodianship account, may the custodian be the beneficiary?

Answer — No. The beneficiary must be the minor or in the event of his or her death, the minor's estate must be the beneficiary.[15]

Question — If a custodian dies before the minor is legally an adult, how is a successor custodian appointed?

Answer — The guardian of the child is generally appointed successor custodian.[16] In some states a custodian can designate a successor custodian by executing and dating an instrument before a subscribing witness other than the successor. If there is no such successor designated before the death or incapacity of the custodian and the minor has no guardian and is age 14 or older, the minor can name a successor. The law of the state involved should be reviewed. Under UTMA, a transferor may nominate a successor custodian in his will.

Question — Must the custodian under the Uniform Gifts to Minors Act file an income tax return?

Answer — No fiduciary return is required by the custodian. This factor, as well as the fact that no trust agreement is required, makes the custodianship perhaps the least expensive and administratively the simplest method of transferring property to a minor.

ASRS, Sec. 48.

Footnote References

Uniform Gifts to Minors Act

1. 20 Pa. S. Section 5303(a). (Citations are to Pennsylvania Statutes.)
2. 20 Pa. S. Section 5303(b).
3. 20 Pa. S. Section 5304(a).
4. 20 Pa. S. Section 5305(d).
5. N.Y. E.P.T.L. Section 7-4.11.
6. Rev. Rul. 56-484, 1956-2 C.B. 23.
7. Rev. Rul. 56-86, 1956-1 C.B. 449, Rev. Rul. 59-357, 1959-2 C.B. 212.
8. Rev. Rul. 57-366, 1957-2 C.B. 618.
9. 20 Pa. S. Section 5302.
10. 20 Pa. S. Sections 5302, 5303.
11. IRC Section 584(c)(1).
12. 20 Pa. S. Section 5305(b).
13. 20 Pa. S. Section 5303(b).
14. 20 Pa. S. Section 5305(b).
15. 20 Pa. S. Section 5305(h).
16. 20 Pa. S. Section 5308(d).

Chapter 36

WILLS

WHAT IS A WILL?

A will is the legal expression of declaration of an individual's wishes as to the disposition of his property after death. Revocable during the individual's lifetime, a will is not operative until death and is applicable to the situation which exists at death.

WHEN IS THE USE OF SUCH A DEVICE INDICATED?

1. The most important reason for creating a will is to provide the testator ("testatrix" is the feminine form; either form means the one who makes or executes the "will and testament") with an opportunity to control the passing of his property and thereby to avoid "intestacy." Without a will the decedent's assets will pass by the laws of intestate succession of the state in which the decedent resides or in which his property is located.

   The principle of the intestate succession laws is to distribute the decedent's property as the government believes the decedent would have wanted had a will been executed.

   Typically the rules for distribution of separate property are as follows:

   A. Should the decedent die intestate with a spouse but no children, the spouse takes the entire estate.

   B. If a spouse and children survive, each takes some portion of the estate.

   C. If only the decedent's children survive, they take the entire estate.

   D. If no spouse or children survive, the estate goes to the decedent's parents, and if they do not survive, then to decedent's siblings or their heirs.

   E. The next level of intestate takers are the decedent's grandparents and their heirs (the aunts, uncles, and cousins of decedent).

   F. If none of the decedent's heirs survive, the next takers are the issue of decedent's pre-deceased spouse.

   G. If none of the above survive, the estate goes to the next of kin.

   H. The state is the final taker.

   While the rules above are typical, the laws in a particular state may have some variation. The above rules generally apply in the nine community property states (California, Arizona, Nevada, New Mexico, Washington, Louisiana, Idaho, Texas and, by a recent law change, Wisconsin) as to separate property; but if the property is held as community property, even where there are children, all community property goes to the surviving spouse in the absence of a will.

   Louisiana has unique rules which limit what a spouse may do with property, in some circumstances forcing the transfer of property to a certain person (usually the surviving spouse) regardless of the terms of the will.

   Be certain to remember that real property in a particular state is subject to the rules of that state. Therefore, for example, a will dealing with oil interests or other interests in land located in Louisiana is subject to the laws of Louisiana, even though the testator is a resident of New Jersey.

2. As described above, without a valid will the decedent's property goes to his relatives as provided by statute. By making a will a person can pass property in a different manner than that provided by statute. With a will, property generally can be left to one or more relatives, of any degree, or friends or charities to the exclusion of others.

   However, many states have laws which require the spouse and/or children to take some share of the estate. Property can be willed to non-relatives such as friends or charities, subject to rules in certain states that require some rights to pass to the spouse or children.

3. In a will the testator can name the "personal representative" of the estate. A person or institution can be named to act as executor ("executrix" is the feminine form) and be appointed to carry out the directions in the will and to dispose of the property according to the testamentary provisions.

   The named personal representative may often be a relative or close friend. But, if the estate is large or complicated, the testator should consider appointing either a professional or an institution accustomed to dealing with assets and with the sometimes complicated rules of probate. If the testator feels it wise to name a person who has no experience in probating a will but who may be well acquainted with the testator's personal affairs, an alternative is to suggest that the executor hire a specified attorney to assist with the probate.

   The will may provide that the executor need not be bonded, which can save money for the estate, but which gives up some protection. If there is no valid will or if no executor is named or if the named executor for any reason fails to qualify or ceases to act, the court will appoint an "administrator" ("administratrix" is the feminine form) to administer the estate.

4. A will can set out the terms of a trust in which the named trustee can manage assets on behalf of the beneficiaries for many years after the death of the testator. This may be especially appropriate in order to manage assets for the benefit of the testator's minor children. Such a trust is referred to as a "testamentary" trust since it is created through the decedent's last will and testament and comes into being at the probate of the will.

The terms of a testamentary trust are very important. Sometimes people have such trusts terminate when a child reaches age 18 or 21. Such an early distribution, at a time before the child has had the experience of handling large sums of money, often results in the child's not going to college and also losing all of the inheritance.

5. When there are minor children, the will can nominate a guardian of both the "person" and the "estate" of each child. State laws generally require a court to give significant weight to such a nomination by a parent who has custody of a child. Without such a provision, the court names the guardian upon the death of the parent(s) based on available information and often depending on who volunteers.

6. A will allows the testator to make alternative provisions in case some of the heirs predecease him. For instance, if a child dies, the testator may want to leave that share to the child's siblings, or perhaps to the child's issue.

7. Some types of property are not affected by the provisions in a will. Assets held in joint tenancy or tenancy by the entirety pass by right of survivorship to the remaining joint tenant(s). Policies of life insurance, IRAs, and certain other assets pass by contract to the person(s) named in beneficiary designations.

8. Even where an individual has a living trust which holds most of his assets in order to avoid probate, it is still very important to have a will which will "pour over" into the previously established trust any assets which were not already transferred to the trust.

9. A will can also be important in order to name an executor where a personal representative is needed to make elections for generation skipping, QTIP, or other purposes.

10. The majority of states provide that if a spouse or child is not named in a will, such a person is deemed to be a "pretermitted heir." Regardless of what the will says, such person will take the share of the estate that would be given to that person under the state's rules of intestacy. Thus it is wise to mention all such persons in the will so that they cannot claim to be pretermitted heirs left out of the will only because they were overlooked by the testator.

WHAT ARE THE REQUIREMENTS?

1. The general rule is that any person 18 or more years of age who is of sound mind may make a will.[1] While this is the general rule, a few states have a different minimum age requirement.

2. The law ordinarily requires less mental capacity to make a will than to make a contract. An individual can make a will even if he is sick, elderly, weak, or of low mental capacity. In general, most states require that the testator know (1) the nature and extent of his property and (2) the natural objects of his bounty.

3. Except where a "holographic will" (one written entirely in the testator's handwriting) or an oral ("nuncupative") will is allowed, wills must meet certain legal requirements. Typically, an attested will must be in writing, signed by the testator (or in the testator's name by some other person in the testator's presence and at his direction), and must be witnessed by at least two persons.[2] Some states still require three witnesses while at least one, Pennsylvania, requires no witnesses at the time the will is signed.

4. Approximately half of the states recognize a holographic or handwritten will.[3] A will which is not effective under other provisions may be effective as a holographic will, whether or not witnessed, if it is dated and the signature and the material provisions are in the handwriting of the testator.[4] In some states, having printed or typed material on the holographic will can invalidate it.

5. Less than half of the states recognize oral (nuncupative) wills. This is a will declared or dictated by the testator during the last illness, before a sufficient number of witnesses, and later reduced to writing. In some states such wills are valid only under certain circumstances. For instance, they may be valid only to transfer a limited amount of personal property.[5]

HOW ARE THE TERMS OF A WILL DECIDED?

John Lee is preparing for his retirement and has decided to "get his affairs in order." He knows that without a will, his spouse and his children will each receive a portion of his estate. Since John's wife is a wealthy woman in her own right, as the recipient of the estate of her parents, John would rather leave his assets to the children. The children are not experienced in dealing with assets and his wife deals well with assets.

John has three children. The youngest has been estranged from the family for many years. John makes a will leaving all of his assets in a trust for the benefit of his two other children, one-half to each. He names his eldest child as executor of the estate and the second child as the successor executor. John's wife was named as the trustee of the trust for the two older children.

John realizes that certain of his assets, his life insurance and his IRA account, will not pass by his will. He has named his two eldest children as equal beneficiaries of those assets. To avoid his wife and estranged child taking intestate shares as pretermitted heirs, his will names them but leaves nothing to them.

John has made his decisions on the basis of need and degree of positive feelings he has for each beneficiary. His exclusion of his wife does not indicate a lack of feeling for her (a fact he may wish to communicate in the will) but a recognition that she does not need his assets for her security and also that adding more to her estate would increase the share which would ultimately be paid in death taxes.

By leaving the funds for the two older children in trust with his wife as trustee, he has provided good management to protect the trust assets for the children. The trust terms also provide John's wife with latitude as to the distribution of the assets as between the children and how and when they will receive the assets. Thus, John has not deprived his wife of some continuing parental control.

Although some people would "always leave things equally to the children," John has recognized the estrangement of the one child and has made the difficult but perhaps logical decision to leave the assets to the children who are still close to the family. In making such decisions, there is simply no "right way" that can always be applied to distributing assets; the decisions must be made on the basis of what is important to each testator and the circumstances of the persons and organizations he wishes to benefit.

HOW IS A WILL CHANGED OR REVOKED?

A will may be changed by writing a separate document which is not intended to be a new will but which is meant to change a provision of an existing will. Such a document is called a "codicil."

A new will, to the extent that it does not state that it is revoking all prior wills, may often merely change the terms of an existing will. In other words, the unrevoked prior will(s) remain valid to the extent not inconsistent with a later will. For this reason, it is good practice to make clear in a will that it is intended to revoke all prior wills, if that is the testator's goal.

Generally, a codicil must follow the same rules as a will in order to be valid.

Revocation of a will also may occur by destroying a will or defacing it with the intent to revoke. Sometimes the issue of the testator's intent (e.g., if the will is burned together with other papers or trash, was there an intention to revoke the will?) will result in expensive litigation. A specific statement of revocation in a new will (or writing "Revoked" across an old will and signing and dating that revocation) often may achieve the testator's goals more effectively.

WHAT ARE THE DEATH TAX IMPLICATIONS?

At death, estate tax is imposed on property which is transferred to the beneficiaries. However, each U.S. resident now has a credit, the unified credit, which eliminates the tax on the first $600,000 in estate assets.

Therefore, if an estate is valued at less than $600,000 and no taxable gifts were made after 1976, no estate tax will be owed. (The amount of the "credit sheltered" estate gradually increased from $175,625 in 1981 to the maximum of $600,000 in 1987 and thereafter.)

While many states have abolished their state death taxes (except for a "credit estate tax," i.e., an estate tax sufficient to absorb the credit allowed against the federal estate tax for state death taxes actually paid) the majority do still have death taxes. Such a state death tax may be due even though there is no federal estate tax to pay.

If the decedent's assets are valued in excess of $600,000, federal estate tax will be owed unless a deduction can be taken. The most common deductions are the marital deduction (discussed in Chapter 33, Trust-Marital Deduction) and the charitable deduction (discussed in Chapter 2, Charitable Contribution).

Other deductions generally available include the following:

A. Debts of the decedent;

B. Administration expenses;

C. Casualty losses to estate assets;

D. Funeral expenses; and

E. Until 1992, a special deduction for certain stock sold to an Employee Stock Ownership Plan (ESOP).

If a married individual wishes to minimize taxes at his death, he should be certain to have a will that provides for all assets in excess of $600,000 to pass to his spouse or to a trust for the benefit of the spouse, so a marital deduction can be taken for those assets. The taxable estate will thus be reduced to the value which can be "sheltered" by the decedent's unified credit.

However, if all of the assets are left to a spouse, there will be a 100% marital deduction and no assets will be available to take advantage of the unified credit (which is a "use it or lose it" benefit). The result will be that all of the assets will be taxed at the death of the surviving spouse and the unified credit of the first-to-die spouse will be wasted. This is reviewed in more detail in Chapter 33, relating to the marital deduction.

Generally, unless the will provides otherwise, estate taxes are apportioned among all beneficiaries of the estate (although in a few states death taxes are paid from the residue).[6] Alternatively, the testator may want to provide that taxes should be paid from the residue (assets not specifically disposed of elsewhere in the will) so that the recipients of specific gifts will not be responsible for the tax on the gift(s) they receive.

Tools and Techniques

For example, if the will provides for taxes to be paid from the residue, Susie, the distributee of the decedent's Rolls Royce, will not have to make an out of pocket payment for her share of estate taxes, providing that there are sufficient assets in the estate residue to pay such taxes.

WHAT ARE THE INCOME TAX IMPLICATIONS?

For income tax purposes a probate estate is a separate taxable entity. A Federal fiduciary income tax return (Form 1041), and often a state income tax return, must be filed annually during the period of administration if sufficient income ($600 or more for the federal return) is received during a 12 month period.

No income tax is recognized solely as the result of a death. As a matter of fact there may be a tax benefit at death, since most of the assets in the decedent's gross estate receive a new income tax basis equal to the fair market value of each asset at the time of the decedent's death. Assuming the asset increased in value or is worth more than its basis in the decedent's hands during lifetime, it receives a "step-up" in basis. The taxable gain inherent in the asset disappears. Thus, an asset could be sold immediately after death and there would be no income tax to pay. For example, assume, 20 years before his death, a client purchased stock for $20 a share. If it was valued in his estate at $80 a share, that $80 would become the new basis for purposes of determining gain if his beneficiary sold it.

One exception to this rule is that type of asset which would have been subject to income tax if the decedent had received it. Unpaid fees due to a doctor or lawyer who reports his income on a cash basis, or notes resulting from the sale of property reported on the installment method would be examples of these. These assets are generally termed "income in respect of decedent" and they retain whatever income tax basis the testator had in them.

ISSUES & IMPLICATIONS IN COMMUNITY PROPERTY STATES

Assets held as community property are owned equally by the spouses. At death, each spouse has testamentary power of distribution over his or her half of the community assets. Thus there is no certainty that the survivor will receive the decedent's one-half share of the community assets, but the absence of a will generally will produce that result.[7]

In common law (non-community property) states, the surviving spouse may sometimes be protected against disinheritance through laws of forced shares, dower, or curtesy.

In a community property state, the will of the deceased spouse may affect the survivor's half of the community property. For example, the decedent's will may purport to give all of the community property assets (the shares of both husband and wife) to a trust for the benefit of the surviving spouse and the children. If so, the survivor must elect whether to take under the will (thus assenting to the decedent's disposition of the survivor's one-half community property interest) or to take his or her one-half of the community property outright (denying the decedent's power to dispose of the survivor's community property interest) which will often require the survivor to give up rights conditionally given by the will in the decedent's share of community property assets.

QUESTIONS AND ANSWERS

Question — All of my client's assets are held in joint tenancy or in a manner in which a beneficiary is designated (e.g., IRAs). Does my client need a will?

Answer — While the assets currently owned by the client will pass to the survivors or beneficiaries without probate, at some time the client may acquire additional assets which are titled in another manner. The named joint tenant(s) or beneficiary/ies might predecease the client. A will is always valuable to prevent against intestacy.

Question — Is it difficult to change a will as circumstances change?

Answer — A will can be amended or revoked at any time during the lifetime of the testator. It is possible to revoke a will in full and to create a new will, or to revoke only a portion of the will and add new provisions by means of a codicil. The will itself can provide for changing circumstances by making provisions for successor beneficiaries and/or executors in the event of the death of any named beneficiaries and/or executors.

Question — Can the imposition of estate taxes at death be avoided by having assets pass outside the will?

Answer — The gross estate includes all assets owned by the decedent at death. This includes assets held in the decedent's name, assets transferred to a revocable trust by the decedent, the decedent's interest in joint tenancy assets, proceeds of life insurance from policies owned by the decedent, and the value of most retirement plans (IRAs, for example). Even assets outside the United States are subject to federal estate tax for a U.S. citizen. Unless a will employs tax avoidance devices such as the marital or charitable deductions, the will really has no effect on the amount of estate tax that is owed.

However, some state death taxes are inheritance taxes, which vary the amount of deduction and tax rate based upon the relationship of the recipient to the testator. To the extent that the will provides a different distribution of property than would an intestacy, the amount of inheritance tax to be paid may be changed. The other form of death tax, called an estate tax, is a tax based in general on the total value of the assets in the estate, rather than how much is inherited by each person and the relationship of that person to the testator. Two areas where even estate taxes are affected by who is the recipient of a bequest or devise include gifts made to spouses (which may result in a marital deduction) and transfers to charities (which may qualify for a charitable deduction).

Question — Does a client with a modest estate need a will?

Answer — There are many reasons almost every adult should have a will. Even though an estate is modest, it can be important to name a guardian for both the person and the estate of the client's children. A client may have very strong feelings that a close friend is the best person to care for the children and if those wishes are not expressed, the children may end up in the custody of relatives or others who would not have been chosen to deal with the children and/or their assets. In some cases a client may wish to leave the personal custody of a child to one person and leave the management of the child's assets to another.

Question — Suppose a client planned to avoid probate by putting assets in a revocable intervivos trust (a "living trust"). Can the client change the disposition of assets in the trust by changing his will?

Answer — As long as the client has actually placed the assets in the intervivos trust, his will will not have any effect on these assets unless the trust provides for amendment or exercise of a power of appointment to be made by a will. When a living trust is used, generally the will is only a "pour-over will" which directs to the trust any assets not already placed in the trust. The revocable trust can be changed by a written amendment in the form set out in the trust for such changes.

In order to avoid the question of whether the trust terms are to be changed or a power of appointment exercised inadvertently by a will, the majority of planners provide that changes in a trust can be made only by an instrument in writing other than a will.

Question — Can probate be avoided through an intervivos trust?

Answer Yes, but only if the title of assets has been transferred from your client's name to that of the trustee of the trust. Failure to make the transfers will leave assets subject to a will and subject to the costs and delays of going through a probate in order to get into the trust.

Question — Is it expensive to have assets subject to probate?

Answer — Probate fees vary from state to state. In some states, they can be as high as a flat 5% of all probate property — plus additional fees for "extraordinary work" (preparing tax returns, some sales of property, fighting will contests, etc.). Both the executor and the attorney for the estate are entitled to a fee for their services.

Question — Assume a trust is desired to protect a client's children. Will it cost more to use a testamentary trust included as part of his will or more if a "intervivos trust" is used as a separate instrument?

Answer — There are at least three cost aspects to consider. One is the cost of going through probate, which is required for a testamentary trust but which can be avoided if assets are transferred before death to an intervivos trust. A different aspect is that many states require regular accounting to be made to the court by testamentary trusts, giving possibly better supervision but resulting in added attorney fees and court costs for each accounting. Lastly, the legal fees for drafting an intervivos trust may be greater since its use requires two documents (the trust and a "pour-over" will) and often some documentation to transfer title of assets.

Question — Is there any benefit to having property go through probate as opposed to having assets transferred to an intervivos trust prior to death?

Answer — Going through probate involves stricter supervision of the management and disposition of assets. To the extent that a client is concerned that the trustee who administers the trust may not carry out the trust terms in exactly the manner desired, the probate procedure may have some substantial benefit.

Another benefit of probate is that it has a "cut-off period" for creditors. As part of the probate process, a notice of the death is given to all creditors.[8] After notice, creditors have a specified period of time in which to file their claims and those creditors who do not make their claims within that time are thereafter cut off. With an intervivos trust, generally these claims are not cut off. For example, suppose a doctor were to die and a malpractice claim developed ten months after his death. That claim might well be cut off by a proper probate, but it would not be cut off with regard to any assets held in an intervivos trust at his death. Those assets have not gone through the "cleansing action" of probate. Some states, such as California, are considering a similar termination of creditors' rights for assets held in intervivos trusts.

Question — What things should an estate planner examine in reviewing a will?

Answer — See "How to Review a Will: A Checklist for the Estate and Financial Planner" in Appendix E.

Footnote References

Wills
1. Uniform Probate Code §2-501.
2. Uniform Probate Code §2-502.
3. Dan E. McConaughey, *Wills,* 18 (1984).

Tools and Techniques

4. Uniform Probate Code §2-503.

5. Dan E. McConaughey, *Wills,* 22 (1984).

6. Uniform Probate Code §3-916.

7. Robert J. Lynn, *Introduction to Estate Planning,* 2nd Ed., 23 (1978).

8. Notice is usually given by publication. However, in a very recent case, the United States Supreme Court has struck down as unconstitutional an Oklahoma statute that bars claims presented more than two months after notice by publication. The Court held that such notice does not necessarily satisfy the requirement of due process, that if a creditor's identity is known or reasonably ascertainable, the creditor must receive actual notice. *Tulsa Professional Collection Services, Inc. v. Pope, No. 86-1961, 4-19-88, rev'g and remanding 733 P.2d 396.*

THE UNAUTHORIZED PRACTICE OF LAW

It is sometimes difficult to draw the boundaries of professional responsibility in an area as complex and sophisticated as estate planning. Special skills and learning are necessary prerequisites not only to the attorney but also to a CPA, CFP, ChFC, CLU, trust officer, or other individual serving a client in an advisory capacity.

Yet it is clear that regardless of how knowledgeable an advisor is, only the attorney may practice law. The practice of law is regulated and limited for a number of reasons:

First, the public needs and deserves protection against advice by self-styled advisors who have been neither trained nor examined (nor licensed) by recognized educational or governmental authorities.

Second, many non-lawyers who are highly skilled in specific areas such as tax law may lack the broader viewpoint and depth of a lawyer.

Third, the lawyer-client relationship is one of confidentiality, relative objectivity, and impartiality. Even the most ethical sales person or trust officer cannot claim objectivity; his or her job is to sell a given investment, contract, or the use of a particular financial institution. This does not imply that the CFP, CLU, ChFC, or trust officer or CPA does not have highly important tasks to perform as a member of the estate planning team. On the contrary, it is often that individual who motivates the client to take action—and follows through to make sure the plan is implemented.

Were this the only responsibility and utility of those members, their positions on the "team" would be secure. But, in reality, each of those individuals can perform a function that serves as a valuable complement to the attorney's task. In fact, the attorney should not be "practicing" life insurance, providing trust services, or replacing the accountant. The very idea of an estate planning team implies that each member serves the client with his or her own special and essential skills. When any member of the team usurps the province of the other, it is the client who loses.

Returning to the topic of the unauthorized practice of law, the central issue must be: What is it? Clearly, the preparation of instruments and contracts by which legal rights are secured constitutes an invasion of the attorney's province. So, the non-attorney who drafts a will or a trust for a client is patently guilty of the unauthorized practice of law. But what of the person who reviews a will or trust and advises clients as to the desirability in their circumstances of specific clauses or instruments? Does every discussion of a legal principle constitute unauthorized practice? Is the recognized subject matter expert excused from the proscription against unauthorized practice? What if no fee is charged for the rendering of advice? Does long-time custom and tradition offer a valid reason for practice by non-lawyers?

A working knowledge of the tax law is essential to professionals in the life insurance, trust, and accounting disciplines. Generally, the protection of the public can be achieved without hampering or unduly burdening professionals with impractical and technical restrictions which have no reasonable justification. To say that non-attorneys cannot discuss any pertinent legal principles with a client would be so unrealistic and narrow as to be absurd.

But what can be safely discussed—and what cannot? Essentially, where a statute or legal interpretation has become so well-known and settled that no further legal issue is involved, there should be no problem in suggesting its simple application to the situation at hand. This is known as the "general-specific" test; no violation arises from the sharing of legal knowledge which is either generally informatory or, if specific, is so obvious as to be common knowledge. It is only when legal rules (which are general in nature) are applied to specific factual situations that the line is crossed. Providing advice involving the application of legal principles to a specific situation is the crux of the "general-specific" test.

A second criterion is known as the "complexity" theory. This involves the non-attorney answering difficult or complex questions of law. One court stated the theory this way "practicing as an attorney. . .is the giving of advice or the rendition of any sort of service. . .when the giving of such advice or the rendition of such service requires the use of any degree of legal knowledge or skill."

But perhaps the court should have gone beyond the questions of difficulty or complexity of subject matter into the issue of whether judgement was exercised by the non-attorney and relied on by the client. When basic legal principles are applied to specific and actual facts or the resolution of controversial or uncertain questions of law is required in an actual case, the practice of law is involved.

No safety can be found in an argument that the non-lawyer is both a specialist and an acknowledged expert in the field. The rationale for this seemingly harsh stand is that the interest of the public is not protected by narrow specialization of a person who lacks the broad perspective and orientation of a licensed attorney. That dimension of skill and knowledge comes only from a thorough understanding of legal concepts, processes, and the interaction of all the branches of law. In other words, the rules may have been learned by the non-lawyer but often the full meaning and import of the rule and its components—and the impact of that rule on other seemingly unrelated rules—may not be fully understood by even

Tools and Techniques

a highly competent specialist who is not also a licensed attorney.

Charging fees for legal advice seems important only where such fees were charged. Most courts have had little trouble finding violations where clients relied on advice or were provided with legal services regardless of whether or not fees were charged. Likewise, practices of the past provide little defense in the present. Recent decisions indicate that even custom and tradition long acquiesced in by the Bar does not make proscribed activities any less the practice of law.

Tools and Techniques is not designed to help the non-lawyer eliminate the need for an attorney. To the contrary, it is a text designed for all the members of the estate planning team to help delineate the large number of alternative solutions to general problem areas. Definitive solutions, i.e., the choice of which specific tools or techniques to use in a given case or the decisions as to how they should be used must be considered only by the client, together with his or her attorney. Likewise, the drafting or adopting of instruments needed to execute the techniques or utilize the tools discussed below is exclusively the province of the lawyer.

Every member of the estate planning team is obligated to be aware of these tools and techniques, to understand their limitations as well as their problem-solving potential, and to be knowledgeable enough to discuss them in general terms with clients and their other advisors.

THE FIRST INTERVIEW

Often, in order to encourage cooperation and full disclosure of pertinent data, it is necessary or helpful to explain to a client what estate planning is, who should be concerned with estate planning, how the federal estate tax laws work, and the mistakes that are commonly made because of a lack of proper planning. Ralph Miller, in his California law practice, to help his clients prepare for the interview, gives them an "Optional Checklist for Discussion." This extensive checklist is reproduced elsewhere in Appendix A. Finally, the delicate subject of anatomical gifts is discussed from the perspective of the estate planner.

WHAT IS ESTATE PLANNING?

A. The process of planning the accumulation, conservation, and distribution of an estate in the manner which most efficiently and effectively accomplishes your personal tax and nontax objectives. Every estate is planned — either by you or by the state and federal governments.

B. "Controlled estate planning" is a systematic process for uncovering problems and providing solutions in clients' L.I.V.E.S.:

1. Lack of liquidity

2. Improper disposition of assets

3. Inflation (need to diversify and "inflation-proof" portfolio)

4. Inadequate income or capital at retirement/death/disability

5. Value — need to stabilize and maximize value of business and other assets

6. Excessive transfer costs

7. Special problems

Tools and Techniques

Appendix A
The First Interview

WHO NEEDS ESTATE PLANNING?

More sophisticated planning than a simple will is indicated for:

1. Individuals with estates exceeding the unified credit equivalent.
    1982-$225,000   1983-$275,000   1984-$325,000   1985-$400,000   1986-$500,000
    1987 and later years-$600,000

2. Individuals in income tax brackets in excess of 15 percent.

3. People with:

    a. Children who are minors.

    b. Children (or spouses or other dependants) who are exceptionally artistic or intellectually gifted.

    c. Children (or spouses or other dependants) who are retarded, emotionally disturbed, or physically handicapped.

    d. Spouses (or children or other dependants) who can't or don't want to handle money, securities or a business.

    e. Closely held business interests.

    f. Property in more than one state.

    g. Charitable objectives.

    h. Special property such as fine art, a coin, gun, or stamp collection.

    i. Pets.

WHAT ARE THE TOOLS OF PROPERTY TRANSFER?

A. Lifetime transfers by gift or sale; gifts may be outright or in trust

B. Transfers at death
   1. Will
   2. Intestacy
   3. Operation of law

C. Methods of transfer
   1. Will — key vehicle of testamentary transfer
      a. Definition: Legal declaration of what a person wants done with his property or estate upon his death
      b. What a will can and should do
         (1) Distribute property according to your wishes
         (2) Make gifts of specific property to whomever you wish, including friends, charity, or devoted employee
         (3) Name executor of choice and direct that executor serve without bond
         (4) Nominate guardian of minors and incompetents
         (5) Designate source for payment of taxes
         (6) Use marital deduction most effectively
         (7) Denote appropriate procedure for disposition of estate in the event of a common disaster
      c. Limitations on disposition by will or trust
         (1) Extent to which you can disinherit spouse
         (2) Duration of trust
         (3) Prohibitions on appointment of minor or incompetent as executor
      d. Validity of will
         (1) Execution
            (a) Signing
            (b) Witnessing
      e. Revocation of will
         (1) By declaration in later will
         (2) Codicil
         (3) Execution of later will wholly inconsistent with former will
         (4) Intentional destruction of will
         (5) Operation of law
      f. Grounds to contest will in our state
         (1) Improper execution
         (2) Lack of testamentary capacity
         (3) Undue influence in making will
         (4) Fraud
         (5) Forgery
         (6) Revocation by testator or operation of law
      g. Taking "against the will" (Right of election)

Tools and Techniques

2. Intestate succession as a means of transferring property
   a. Who can inherit
   b. Statutory scheme
   c. Family allowances
   d. Problems inherent in allowing state law to control dispositive scheme
3. Operation of law as a means of transferring property
   a. Contracts
      (1) Insurance
      (2) Antenuptial and postnuptial agreements
      (3) Jointly held property
4. Disclaimers
   a. Defined — unqualified refusal to accept bequest or gift
   b. Must be in writing and received by transferor, his legal representative or holder of legal title to property
   c. Refusal received within 9 months of date when transfer creating the interest was made or, if later, day the person reaches 21 years of age
   d. The disclaimant never accepted the interest or any of its benefits
   e. Without direction by disclaimant, interest then passes to spouse of the decedent or person other than disclaimant
   f. Disclaimed interest in property is undivided portion of the interest
   g. A power over property may be disclaimed under above rules

D. Estate administration — What it is and how it works

1. Probate process
   a. Definition of probate — the process of proving:
      (1) the last will
      (2) the testator's intention
   b. What is probate versus nonprobate property
   c. Steps in settling an estate
      (1) Proving the will
         (a) Determine existence of will
            (i) Examine safe deposit boxes
            (ii) Search valuable papers
         (b) Deposit original will for probate
         (c) Locate witnesses to attest to validity of signature
         (d) Self-proving (notarized) wills
         (e) Appointment of executor — grant of Letters Testamentary
      (2) When there is no will
         (a) Petition court for appointment of administrator of estate
         (b) Grant of Letters of Administration
         (c) Necessity to post bond
      (3) Basic duties of personal representative (executor or administrator)
         (a) Assemble property of estate
         (b) Safeguarding and interim management of property
         (c) Advertise estate in legal and nonlegal newspapers
         (d) Locate and communicate with beneficiaries

        (e) Pay debts and expenses of estate

        (f) Make interim distributions to beneficiaries where indicated

        (g) Prepare inventory of estate

        (h) File and pay state inheritance or estate tax

        (i) File Federal estate tax return if necessary

        (j) Make final accounting

        (k) Distribution of net estate

        (l) Closing of estate and discharge of personal representative

E. How property can be owned
   1. Distinction between "real" and "personal" property
   2. Kinds of personal property
      a. Tangible
      b. Intangible
   3. Undivided interest in property
      a. Tenancies in common
      b. Joint tenancies with right of survivorship
         (1) Advantages
         (2) Disadvantages
         (3) Federal taxation of jointly held property with right of survivorship
      c. Tenancies by the entirety
      d. Community property interests
      e. Other property interests
         (1) Distinction between legal and equitable ownership
         (2) Distinction between present and future rights
         (3) Distinction between vested and contingent remainders

F. Trusts
   1. Definition of trust — legal fiduciary arrangement with respect to property
   2. Five necessary elements
      a. Creator
      b. Trust property or res
      c. Trustee
      d. Beneficiaries
      e. Terms of trust or trust instrument
   3. Types of trusts
      a. Intervivos
         (1) Revocable
         (2) Irrevocable
      b. Testamentary
   4. Duration of trusts: rule against perpetuities

G. Fiduciaries
   1. Types of fiduciaries
      a. Personal representative
         (1) Executor
         (2) Administrator

      b. Trustee

      c. Guardian

2. Fiduciary duties and responsibilities — duty to:

      a. Give undivided loyalty to the beneficiary

      b. Not delegate responsibilities to others which trustee can perform

      c. Keep accounts and to furnish information to beneficiaries (make full disclosure)

      d. Maintain and preserve trust property

      e. Make trust productive

      f. Pay income to beneficiaries when the trust instrument so provides

      g. Keep trust property separate (not commingle assets unless so instructed by trust instrument)

      h. Deal impartially with beneficiaries when more than one exists

      i. Communicate with other trustees and to act in concert with other trustees

      j. Not to self-deal or profit at beneficiaries' expense

      k. Enforce claims of trust, compromise and defend claims against trust

3. Powers of a trustee — Trustees' powers are limited by

    (a)   the terms of the trust,

    (b)   the law of the state in which the trust is being administered, and

    (c)   those necessary or appropriate powers that are not expressly forbidden by the terms of the trust.

          The trustee may be given absolute discretion to make decisions and exercise judgments without leave of court as long as the act is not illegal.

HOW DO THE FEDERAL ESTATE TAX LAWS WORK?

A. Your gross estate — all property owned at your death and transferred by reason of your death (with special exceptions and limitations) is subject to tax. This includes:

1. Property owned at death.
2. Property passing under state laws to your surviving spouse (or children).
3. Certain gifts made within 3 years of your death.
4. Gifts where you have retained certain rights or interests.
5. Gifts which don't take effect until your death.
6. Gifts which you can revoke, alter, amend or terminate.
7. Annuities.
8. Jointly owned property — except to the extent your survivor can prove contribution. (Only 50 percent of the estate tax value of jointly held property owned solely by husband and wife is includible.)
9. Property over which you possess certain powers.
10. Life insurance you own or which is payable to or for the benefit of your estate.
11. Marital deduction property in which you have a qualifying income interest.

B. Deductions — your gross estate may be reduced by:

1. Funeral expenses.
2. Administrative costs.
3. Debts and mortgages.
4. Certain taxes payable at your death.
5. Certain losses.
6. A "marital deduction" for property passing to your surviving spouse in a qualifying way.
7. A charitable deduction.
8. A deduction of 50 percent of certain proceeds from a sale of "qualified employer securities" to an ESOP or EWOC.

C. After allowable deductions are taken, certain taxable gifts made during your lifetime are added back and estate tax rates are applied. Gift taxes which would have been paid if rates in effect at your death had been in effect at time of gifts, on the gifts added back, reduce the tax otherwise payable.

D. Then the following credits reduce the estate tax:

1. Unified credit.
2. State death tax credit.
3. Foreign death taxes.
4. Estate tax on prior transfers.

E. A 15 percent additional estate tax is imposed on an "excess retirement accumulation" in qualified pension and profit sharing plans (including HR-10 plans), tax-sheltered annuities, and IRAs.

F. The remaining amount is the net estate tax — generally payable in cash within nine months from the date of your death.

The worksheet on the following page may be useful in understanding the operation of the federal estate tax law.

FEDERAL ESTATE TAX LAW
HOW IT WORKS

G. The Computation

(1) Start with: **Gross Estate** $_____

     Subtract:

     (a) Funeral expenses $_____

     (b) Administrative expenses   _____

     (c) Debts   _____

     (d) Taxes   _____

     (e) Losses   _____

(2) Result: **Adjusted Gross Estate** $_____

     Subtract:

     (a) Marital Deduction $_____

     (b) Charitable Deduction   _____

     (c) ESOP Deduction   _____

(3) Result: **Taxable Estate** $_____

(4) Add: **Adjusted Taxable Gifts**
(Taxable portion of Post '76 gifts) $_____

(5) Result: **Tentative Tax Base** $_____

(6) Compute: **Tentative Tax** $_____

(7) Subtract: Gift taxes which would have been payable on gifts made after 1976 if tax rate schedule in effect at decedent's death had been applicable $_____

(8) Result: **Tax Payable Before Reduction for Credits** $_____

(9) Subtract:

     (a) Unified Credit $_____

     (b) State Death Tax Credit   _____

     (c) Credit for Foreign Death Taxes   _____

     (d) Credit for Tax on Prior Transfers   _____

(10) Add: **15% Excess Accumulations Tax** $_____

(11) Result: **Net Federal Estate Tax Payable** $_____

THE TEN MOST COMMON ESTATE PLANNING MISTAKES

(And How To Avoid Them)

by Stephan R. Leimberg, Esq.
Copyright © 1988 by Stephan R. Leimberg, Esq.

This entire commentary is devoted to the types of problems that can cost you and your family tens of thousands of dollars and unbelievable heartache. Since only a fool learns from his own mistakes, this commentary is dedicated to the wise man (and woman) who can profit from the lessons so many have expensively learned the hard way.

Here are ten areas of common (and serious) mistakes that can be easily solved with the assistance of a financial services professional. Have you made one or more of these mistakes? If you haven't checked, how do you know?

Mistake 1: Improper Use of Jointly-Held Property

If used excessively or used by the wrong parties (especially by unmarried individuals) the otherwise "poor man's will" becomes a poor will for an otherwise good man or woman. In short, jointly held property can become a nightmare of unexpected tax and nontax problems including:

A. When property is titled jointly there is the potential for both federal and state gift tax.

B. There is the possibility of double federal estate taxation; if the joint ownership is between individuals other than spouses, the entire property will be taxed in the estate of the first spouse to die — except to the extent the survivor can prove contribution to the property. Then, whatever the survivor receives and does not consume or give away will be included (and taxed a second time) in the survivor's gross estate.

C. Once jointly owned property with right of survivorship has passed to the survivor, the provisions of the decedent's will are ineffective. This means the property is left outright to the survivor who is then without the benefit of management protection or investment advice.

D. The surviving spouse can give away or at death leave the formerly jointly owned property to anyone she wants regardless of the desires of the deceased spouse. In other words, holding property jointly equates to a total loss of control since the surviving spouse can ignore the decedent's wishes as to the ultimate disposition of the property. This loss of control can be especially horrendous when the joint owners are not related.

E. Since the jointly held property passes directly to the survivor (who then could possibly squander, gamble, give away, or lose the property to creditors), the decedent's executor could be faced with a lack of adequate cash to pay estate taxes and other settlement expenses.

F. A well drawn estate plan is designed to avoid double taxation — often by passing at least a portion of the estate into a CEBT (Credit Equivalent Bypass Trust). In this manner up to $600,000 can be sheltered from federal estate tax at both the first decedent's death and then again (since the surviving spouse has only an income interest) escape estate tax at the death of the surviving spouse. But holding property in joint tenancy thwarts that objective. Instead of going to a bypass trust to avoid a second tax, the property goes directly to the survivor and will be taxed at the survivor's death. So the credit of the first spouse to die is wasted.

Mistake 2: Improperly Arranged Life Insurance

A. The proceeds of life insurance are often payable to a beneficiary at the wrong time (before that person is emotionally or physically or legally capable of handling it) or in the wrong manner (outright instead of being paid over a period of years or paid into trust).

B. There is inadequate insurance on the life of the key person in a family (the "breadwinner") or the key person in a corporation (the "rainmaker").

C. Often, no contingent (backup) beneficiary has been named. The "Rule of Two" should be applied here: In any dispositive document there should be — for every name in the document — at least two backups.

D. The proceeds of the policy are includible in the gross estate of the insured because the policy was purchased by the insured and then transferred within three years of the insured's death. The solution is to have the ultimate beneficiary, acting without direction from the insured and using her (or its) own money, purchase and own the insurance from its inception. That party should also be named beneficiary.

E. When the policyowner of a policy on the life of another names a third party as beneficiary, at the death of the insured, the proceeds are treated as a gift to the beneficiary from the policy owner. For example, if a wife purchases a policy on her husband's life but names her children as beneficiaries, at the husband's death she is making a gift in the amount of the proceeds to the children.

F. If a corporation names someone other than itself (or its creditor) as the beneficiary of insurance on the life of a key employee, when the proceeds are paid, the IRS will argue that the proceeds are not income tax free and should be treated as either dividends if paid to or on be-

Tools and Techniques

half of a shareholder or compensation if paid to an employee who is not a shareholder (assuming the premiums were never reported as income or there was no split dollar agreement or no "P.S. 58" income reported). Worse yet, if the insured owned more than 50 percent of the corporation's stock, he is deemed to have incidents of ownership (that means federal estate tax inclusion of the proceeds) in the policy on his life. So, for example, the same $1,000,000 proceeds could be taxed as a dividend for income tax purposes ($280,000 income tax) and also be taxed as an asset in the estate for estate tax purposes ($550,000 maximum tax).

G. Whenever life insurance is paid to the insured's estate, it is needlessly subjected to the claims of the insured's creditors and in many states unnecessarily subjected to state inheritance tax costs. Probate costs are increased without reason and the proceeds are then subjected to the potential for an attack on the will or an election against the will.

H. If a life insurance policy — or any interest in a life insurance policy — is transferred for any kind of valuable consideration in money or money's worth, the proceeds may lose their income tax free status. For example, if a child buys the $1,000,000 term insurance policy owned on her father's life from his corporation or business partner, when she receives the proceeds, the entire $1,000,000 will be subject to ordinary income tax ($280,000).

I. Where a husband is required by a divorce decree or separation agreement to purchase or maintain insurance on his life, he will receive no income tax deduction for premium payments if he owns the policy — even if his ex-wife is named as irrevocable beneficiary. No alimony deduction is allowed on the cash values in a policy the husband is required to transfer to his ex-wife under a divorce decree. The safest way to assure a deduction is for the husband to increase his tax deductible alimony and for the ex-wife to purchase new insurance on his life which she owns and on which she is the beneficiary. It is extremely important for each spouse recently divorced to immediately review his or her own life, health and disability insurance situation.

Mistake 3: Lack of Liquidity

A. Most people don't have the slightest idea of how much it will cost to settle their estates or how quickly the taxes and other expenses must be paid. Worse yet, they don't realize that a forced (fire) sale of their most precious assets, highest income producing property, or loss of control of their family business will result from an insufficiency of cash. (If you haven't checked, how do you know your executor will have enough cash to avoid a forced sale?)

B. Liquidity demands have increased significantly in the last few years and should be revisited by those who have not done a "what if ..." hypothetical probate. Among the expenses that demand cash from the estate's executor are:

1. Federal Estate Taxes
2. State Death Taxes
3. Federal Income Taxes (including taxes on pension distributions)
4. State Income Taxes (including taxes on pension distributions)
5. Probate and Administration Costs
6. Payment of Maturing Debts
7. Maintenance and Welfare of Family
8. Payment of Specific Cash Bequests
9. Funds to Continue Operation of Family Business, Meet Payroll and Inventory Costs, Recruit Replacement Personnel, and Pay for Mistakes While New Management is Learning the Business
10. Generation Skipping Transfer Tax (55%)
11. Excise Tax on Excess Pension Accumulations (15%)

Most larger estates will be subjected to almost all of these taxes and costs.

Mistake 4: Choice of the Wrong Executor

A. Naming the wrong people to administer the estate can be disastrous. The person who administers the estate must — with dispatch — often without compensation, with great personal financial risk, and without conflict of interest:

1. Collect all assets
2. Pay all obligations
3. Distribute the remaining assets to beneficiaries

Although this three step process seems simple, in reality these tasks are highly complex, time consuming, and in some cases technically demanding. Is the named executor capable?

B. Selection of a beneficiary as an executor can result in a conflict of interest. That person may be forced to choose between his interest and that of the other beneficiaries. This problem can be solved by adding an independent third party such as a bank trust department to serve alone or together with a family member.

C. Selection of a business associate may result in a conflict of interest. If the executor's job is to decide whether or not to sell the business interest or the task is to obtain the highest possible sales price, the executor will be responsible for the course of action that will best serve the beneficiaries' interests. Yet that may be diametrically opposed to his own. He may be selling himself out of a job or demanding a higher price for the business than he is willing to pay.

D. Sometimes the selected executor has neither the time nor the inclination to devote to the sometimes long and drawn out process of estate administration. Does the executor even live in the state of the testator?

E. The appointment of executors who do not know or get along well with the family members they are to serve sometimes results in chaos.

Mistake 5: Will Errors

A. One of the greatest mistakes is dying without a valid will. This results in "intestacy" which is another way of saying that the state will force its own will upon the heirs it chooses.

B. Too many wills have not been updated. A will should be reviewed at least:

1. At the birth, adoption, or death of a child

2. Upon the marriage, divorce, or separation of anyone named in the will

3. Upon every major tax law change

4. Upon a move of the testator to a new state

5. On a significant change in income or wealth of either the testator or a beneficiary

6. On any major change in the needs, circumstances, or objectives of the testator or the beneficiaries

Mistake 6: Leaving Everything to Your Spouse

A. Many people feel that there will be no federal estate tax because of the unlimited estate tax marital deduction and so they leave their entire estates to their spouses. But upon the death of the surviving spouse, everything that he or she received (assuming it has not been consumed or given away) is then piled on top of the assets that spouse owns. It is then that the "second death wallop" occurs with federal estate tax starting at a minimum of 37 percent on taxable amounts in excess of $600,000 and reaching up to a confiscatory maximum of 60 percent. The solution can be simple: The establishment of a CEBT (credit equivalent bypass trust). Up to $600,000 of assets can be left to a trust that provides income to the surviving spouse as well as other financial security but will not be taxed in her estate no matter when she dies or no matter how large trust funds grow. The balance of the estate can go in trust or outright to the surviving spouse. If that amount together with the surviving spouse's own assets doesn't exceed $600,000, this portion will also pass estate tax free when the surviving spouse dies.

B. Some individuals leave huge amounts outright to a surviving spouse, amounts that they themselves have never managed (few people have ever managed huge amounts at one time let alone managed spouses at any time). Often the survivor doesn't have the slightest training or experience in handling and investing a large stock portfolio, real estate holdings, or running a family business.

Mistake 7: Improper Disposition of Assets

A. An improper disposition of assets occurs whenever the wrong asset goes to the wrong person in the wrong manner or at the wrong time. Leaving an entire estate to surviving spouse or leaving a large or complex estate outright to a spouse unprepared or unwilling to handle it is a good example. Leaving a sizeable estate outright to a teenager is another.

B. "Equal but inequitable" distributions are common. If an estate is divided equally among four children who have drastically different income or capital needs, an equal distribution can be very unfair. Consider, for example, four children, the oldest of which is a brilliant and financially successful medical doctor and the youngest of which has serious learning disabilities and is still in junior high school. Think of a family with a physically handicapped child and three healthy children with no physical problems. Obviously, their needs and circumstances are not the same. Should each child receive an equal share? The proper solution may be a "sprinkle" provision in a trust that empowers the trustee to provide extra income or principal to a child that needs more in a given year.

C. Obvious examples of improper dispositions include the gift of a high powered sports car to a child, or to a senior citizen who no longer drives. "That can't happen in my estate," many people would be tempted to say. But upon the death of a primary beneficiary at the same time or soon after the testator, quite often there is no secondary beneficiary, or the second beneficiary who is named shouldn't receive the asset in the same manner as the primary beneficiary. The solution is to consider a trust or custodial arrangements and to provide in the will or other dispositive instruments for young children and legally incompetent people. Consider also the importance of a well considered "common disaster" or "simultaneous death" provision so that the asset avoids needless second probates and double inheritance taxes and goes to the right person in the right manner.

Mistake 8: Failure to Stabilize and Maximize Value

A. Many business owners have not stabilized the value of their businesses in the event of the disability or death of key personnel. What economic "shock absorbers" have been put in place to cushion the blow caused if a key employee was lured away by competition at the wrong time? Who will pay for the fixed expenses of the practice or business if the key employee is not there to generate income? Key employee life and disability insurance coupled with good business overhead coverage will certainly help.

B. Buy-sell agreements are essential to a business that is to survive the death of one of its owners. Yet many businesses have no such agreement. Or the agreement isn't

Tools and Techniques

in writing. Or the price (or price setting mechanism) doesn't reflect the current value of the business. Or the agreement isn't properly funded. So there is no guarantee that the heirs will receive the price they are entitled to — or no assurance that the surviving owners will have the cash they need to buy out the heirs (especially the dissident ones who want to tell them how to run their company).

C. Wills, trusts, life insurance contracts, HR-10 (Keogh) plans, IRAs, tax deferred annuities, without "backup" beneficiaries mean that money that could otherwise pass outside of the probate estate may instead be subjected unnecessarily to such costs and risks. The value of all those instruments and wealth transfer tools can be enhanced at no cost by merely naming secondary beneficiaries.

Mistake 9: Lack of Adequate Records

A. It can drive your executor crazy — and cost thousands of dollars of expenses — if estate and financial documents are hard to find. Take out a safe deposit box. Tell your executor where it is and make sure your executor has or can get the key and has access to it. Put all your important documents in that box. Each year, put an updated list of the names and phone numbers of advisors your family can count on in the box. Check with your attorney on the rules that apply at death: some safe deposit boxes are "frozen" (the state requires that the bank seal the box from entry until the inheritance tax examiner can inventory the contents) and there can be lengthy delays in getting to the papers in the box.

B. It is possible for an executor to obtain new copies of old income tax returns from the IRS — but why put the executor to the trouble and expense? Be sure to keep tax returns and records at least six years.

C. Many survivors have never been told what the decedent's goals were, what assets they can rely on for income or capital needs, or how best to utilize the available resources. Most widows or surviving children never had a meaningful discussion with the decedent about their financial security if...

Mistake 10: Lack of a "Master Strategy" Game Plan

A. Do it yourself estate and financial planning is the closest thing to do it yourself brain surgery. Few people can do it successfully. Yet, even do it yourself planning — from taking courses or reading books or listening to radio shows on the subject — is preferable to no planning. Actually, an intelligent layman can learn and do quite a bit if the time is taken at least once a year to quantify in dollar terms financial needs and objectives ("here's what we must have and here's what we'd like to have"), current financial status (here's where we are), and a game plan for getting to the goal in the most efficient and effective way. Using the right team of CPA, attorney, life insurance agent, trust officer, and other financial services professionals to conduct an annual "Financial Firedrill" to help formulate and execute that plan can make all the difference.

The Bottom Line

The key principle in my book, *Keeping Your Money* (see "Introduction and Bibliography"), is that **you can't eliminate the big mistakes in your estate plan until you've identified them.** Every family (and single person) — every year — should stage a "financial firedrill." Become informed. Educate yourself now. Educate your survivors — before they *are* the survivors! Teach them how to handle money and make decisions. Show them, by example, how to read the bottom line on where their financial security stands.

A "financial firedrill" means that, with the assistance of competent financial services professionals, you annually measure your needs. Establish an order of priorities and then develop and put into effect plans to make certain that you are on target to meet your financial security needs.

RALPH GANO MILLER   CLIENT_____
MILLER, EWALD & MONSON,
A Professional Law Corporation

OPTIONAL CHECKLIST FOR DISCUSSION

As an option in preparing for our meeting, you may wish to review the following, which covers many of the specific areas of potential benefit and some of the areas of unique problems that relate to various circumstances in which clients find themselves. By reviewing the list and checking off those items which relate to your circumstances, we will be able to focus more clearly on your particular concerns at our estate planning conference. This will also provide you an opportunity to consider beforehand the matters which will come under discussion.

Please do not delay your meeting because of the fact that you have not had a chance to review the checklist, since there will be an opportunity in our discussions to cover any area in which you have an interest.

Checklist Index

CHECKLISTS FOR VARIOUS CIRCUMSTANCES

Please do recognize that the comments in this checklist are necessarily incomplete and that many important areas of potential benefit and detriment have not been covered. Therefore, you should not take any actions on the basis of the material in these lists without consultation with one of the attorneys in our office or with some other attorney.

Copyright 1988
Ralph Gano Miller
113o8803

Appendix A
The First Interview

Checklists For Various Circumstances   Ralph Gano Miller
_____

i. HOW TO USE THE CHECKLISTS

    To save you time, you will probably wish to review only
those aspects of the checklist which actually relate to your
circumstances, since some aspects are redundant. Using the list
of topics below, check the ones which relate to your circumstances, or to areas in which you might be interested (such as
incorporating a business which presently might be held as a
sole proprietorship).

    In every case, you will wish to review either Checklist A
or B (depending on your marital status). In addition, as an
example, if you have an incorporated business or professional
practice, you may wish to review the following additional areas:

    Owners of Private Corporations
    Professionals

    Once you have determined the topics you wish to review, you
can then turn to the appropriate page for each topic as shown
below and check off the individual items of interest which are
listed under that topic. Please also use the check-off boxes
at the bottom of each page of the checklists to indicate those
pages which you wish to review at our conference.

    In reviewing specific areas of potential benefit or prob-
lems, please note that those which relate to non-tax matters
(N), estate, gift or generation-skipping tax (E) or income or
payroll tax (I) are indicated by the letter next to the check-
off box to provide an easier means of identifying those areas
which are of special interest to you.

    The references to chapters after the heading of each item
are to chapters of the current edition of Tools and Techniques
of Estate Planning, a copy of which is enclosed. You may not
find it convenient to browse through the book before your first
appointment, but it may prove to be helpful to have as an addition to your library in your continued planning for your estate.

                          Checklist Index

                CHECKLISTS FOR VARIOUS CIRCUMSTANCES

Tools and Techniques   314

Checklists For Various Circumstances   Ralph Gano Miller
_____

A.   ALL HUSBANDS AND WIVES WITH SOME ESTATE

AREAS OF POSSIBLE BENEFIT

[ ]N*   (1) Avoidance of Probate: Use of a trust to both
            avoid the cost of probate and to eliminate the very
            substantial delays and restrictions of probate can be
            a benefit to even a very small estate. Although this
            course of planning is usually very beneficial, it may
            not apply to the extent that there are many potential
            liabilities of the decedent (e.g., a physician or
            engineer or attorney with no malpractice coverage or
            coverage which may be inadequate) which might be
            "scraped off" through the probate creditors-claim
            process. For some professionals or businesses, the
            unavailability of adequate malpractice coverage is
            probably the only strong argument for not avoiding
            probate. However, even for these persons, an inter-
            vivos trust will provide a means of keeping "safe from
            creditors" assets such as insurance and retirement
            plan proceeds from being mixed with other assets in a
            probate estate. For most estates, avoidance of
            probate (and conservatorship) is a major benefit to
            consider.

[ ]N   (2) Providing Assistance with Asset Management: Use
            of a trust may also provide financial planning assis-
            tance to a child or a spouse who is not experienced in
            handling funds and also delays distribution of trust
            principal until the beneficiary gains more experience
            in managing assets. Gifts outright to a child (which
            usually will be held by a court appointed guardian),
            being distributed at age 18 or 21 may also destroy
            planning for college. This problem may be avoided by
            a trust to provide for education and living expenses
            and distribution of the proceeds at later dates (e.g.,
            one-third each at ages 25, 30 and 35).

[ ]N   (3) Durable Power of Attorney: Like most states,
            California now permits one to give to another person a
            power of attorney which will be valid even if the per-
            son giving it becomes incompetent. This can aid
            greatly in the proper use of funds and avoid a con-
            servatorship of the estate in some situations for a
            period of time.

[ ]N   (4) Health Care Power of Attorney: California now
            also allows one to designate a person who will have
            the power to make health care decisions, often per-
            mitting the avoidance of a conservatorship of the per-
            son.

* The letters N, I or E after each check-
off box indicates whether the specific
item is more related to non-tax matters
(N), income or payroll tax (I) or estate
gift or generation-skipping tax (E).

ALL HUSBANDS AND WIVES WITH SOME ESTATE

Checklists For Various Circumstances   Ralph Gano Miller
_____

[ ]N   (5) "Pull the Plug" Directive: Those persons who want
        to do so now may have a directive created, strictly
        adhering to state requirements, which may direct a
        physician to not sustain their life when there is no
        reasonable expectation that they may regain the use of
        their faculties.

[ ]N   (6) Anatomical Gift Control: In the absence of
        direction from the decedent, executors of estates have
        the power to make gifts of parts or all of the
        decedent's body. The decedent may prevent this or at
        least control such distributions by a direction signed
        before death.

[ ]N   (7) Clarification of Property Rights Through Property
        Agreement (Appendix D): The actual ownership of prop-
        erty acquired before and during marriage is usually of
        importance, and often can be difficult to trace for ei-
        ther estate or income tax purposes or for marital rights
        purposes. A brief agreement can set forth the nature of
        the assets and avoid possible confusion. This can be
        particularly important for people living in a community
        property state in order to receive a new stepped-up in-
        come tax basis (at one spouse's death) on both halves of
        property which they considered community property but
        which was titled as joint tenancy property.

[ ]N   (8) Provision of Liquidity Through Insurance (Chapter
        17): Where liquidity is important, it can be provided
        by life insurance, something which has become a "better
        buy" item in recent years.

[ ]E   (9) Full Use of Unified Transfer Credit (Appendix D,
        Section I and Appendix D, Part A): Since every citizen
        or resident has the Unified Transfer Credit available to
        offset either gift tax during his or her lifetime or
        estate tax at death (see also Chapter 11), most estate
        planning for married couples since 1981 has been focused
        on the maximum use of the credit at the death of the
        first spouse to die so that, at the death of the second
        spouse, certain assets that have been already taxed and
        set aside (nearly always in a trust) will not be subject
        to tax again at the survivor's death.

[ ]E   (10) Measured Use of The Marital Deduction (Chapter
        29): Property left to a surviving spouse or to a mari-
        tal deduction trust that qualifies for the new marital
        deduction (provided by the Economic Recovery Tax Act of
        1981 [ERTA]) will be subject to a marital deduction and
        thus not subject to tax at the death of the first
        spouse. A great bulk of estate planning for spouses now
        calls for a measured amount of property to be taxed so
        as to result in a tax equal to the remaining Unified
        Transfer Credit, with the balance of the property sub-
        ject to the marital deduction and thus, deferred as to
        estate tax until survivor's death.   The property that
        has been taxed (with the tax offset by the Unified
        Transfer Credit) can escape taxation at the death of the
        surviving spouse.

        ALL HUSBANDS AND WIVES WITH SOME ESTATE - Cont.

Most estate plans executed before 1982 did not contain provisions which meet the criteria of the present law.

With proper planning, the surviving spouse may now have all of the assets available without any reduction for taxes to be paid to the Federal government (i.e., having a zero net estate tax to pay) and thus have a more financially secure position for the remainder of her or his life.

[ ]E   (11) Use of Annual Gift Tax Exclusion (Chapter 11): Outright gifts and other gifts qualifying as "present interests" with values up to $10,000 can be made to each person in the world each year without creating any taxable gifts.

Where financial security permits, a program of annual gifts of $10,000-or-less can greatly reduce the amount of tax to be paid at the death of anyone. Currently, such gifts may be made even a few minutes before death and thus may also be a part of death-bed tax planning.

[ ]E   (12) Taxable Gifts of Appreciating Property (Chapter 11): Where financial security permits, gifts made now of property which is expected to increase in value can be good planning even though a gift tax results.

Use of the Unified Transfer Credit to offset such gift tax will essentially reduce the amount of credit left available for offsetting estate tax at death. However, gifting an asset now which is worth $100,000 is much better than having that same asset included in one's estate if it is then expected to be worth $500,000.

If the gift is community property, it is divided between the two spouses. Where the property given is separate property, the availability of gift "splitting" (Chapter 11) permits the same result.

[ ]E   (13) Sales to Next Generation of Appreciating Property: Future appreciation in a property may be avoided by a sale of the entire property to the persons who would otherwise inherit it. The potential estate tax benefits here must be weighed against the income taxes paid by the seller which would have never been paid if the property were retained until death.

[ ]E   (14) Gifts of Insurance: A transfer of insurance, either outright or through the use of non-revocable trusts, may be an example of a gift with a high potential for appreciation since, for gift tax purposes, the gift is measured only by the value of the property at the time of the gift (usually the "interpolated terminal reserve value", approximately the same as the cash surrender value of the policy). Regardless of the gift value, the entire face amount of the policy will be paid over to the donee(s) at the insured's death. Besides being extremely effective in transferring values without

ALL HUSBANDS AND WIVES WITH SOME ESTATE - Cont.

significant transfer tax, such planning can often be done without any significant impairment of the financial security of the donors.

[ ]E   (15) <u>Private Annuities</u> (Chapter 21): (The 1988 Technical Corrections Act created a floating rate at 120% of the mid-term Applicable Federal Rate.) Although an increase in 1983 from six percent to ten percent in the effective rate used in computing private annuities probably makes such annuities less useful than before, they still can play a significant role in some areas of planning.

[ ]E   (16) <u>Sales of Remainder Interests in Property</u>: Prior to December 17, 1987, sales to the next generation of remainder interests (use of the property after the donor's death) in property constituted a very feasible planning technique. The Budget Reconciliation Act of 1987 has generally taken this planning tool from us. However, the creation of remainder interests upon the acquisition of assets (e.g., real property) can still be a very useful technique.

[ ]E   (17) <u>Freezing Values of Assets</u> (Chapters 9 & 23): Partnership "freezes" and corporate arrangements with different classes of stock can in many circumstances shift the increase in value from one generation to the next. The Budget Reconciliation Act of 1987 effectively stopped this transfer tax minimization technique for all transfers after December 17, 1987.

[ ]E/N (18) <u>Use of Generation Skipping Trusts</u> (Appendix D): Although changes in tax law in 1976 (modified by the Tax Reform Act of 1986) added the generation skipping tax to the Internal Revenue Code, thus restricting what had been almost an open field for delaying tax through successive generations, it still left some very significant areas of benefit which should be considered. The 1986 TRA Amendments substantially enhanced those areas of benefit.

Up to $1,000,000 per donor ($2,000,000 for a married couple with proper planning) can now benefit the children and go to their children (the grandchildren of the donors) without any tax at the death of each child or his spouse or anyone else in his generation. All larger estates should consider the possible use of this planning technique, including its use in relation to property that may be inherited by the client.

Apart from the estate tax benefits, this type of trust can also provide lifetime financial assistance and a measure of security to a child who is not "money wise".

[ ]E/N (19) <u>Special Limited Exclusion From Generation Skipping Tax</u>: Although the new generation skipping tax will apply to gifts made directly to grandchildren, there is a limited exception of up to $2,000,000 <u>per grandchild</u> for any such gifts made during lifetime if those gifts are made before 1990. For larger estates, where gifts away of assets are feasible in view of the donors' financial security, gifts to grandchildren may be considered.

ALL HUSBANDS AND WIVES WITH SOME ESTATE - Cont.

[ ]I   (20) Income Tax Benefits From Charitable Gifts: Where
the spouses have no children or where the children are
already financially secure, consideration may be given
to a transfer to a charity currently (providing a
current income tax deduction) of the right to a property
after the death of both spouses (done strictly according
to IRS rules). For some, the income tax benefit is
outweighed by the restrictions on selling or borrowing
on the property. In some cases, the most appropriate
charity may be a private foundation. Not only is a
charitable deduction available for the value of the
remainder interest transferred but the foundation, using
its income tax-free status, can liquidate assets with a
very low income tax basis in relation to their value and
avoid all tax on the gain.

POTENTIAL PROBLEMS

[ ]N   (1) Possible Estate Liabilities: To the extent that
the decedent has a large amount of potential liabilities
(e.g., an anesthesiologist or civil engineer or tax
shelter attorney who has neglected to carry professional
liability insurance or a businessman who has found
himself saddled with large debts), probate may be of
some benefit in that most states provide a creditors
claim period which cuts off liabilities to those
creditors that do not file their claims in the proper
way within that period.

       Differences in state laws affect this, but there are
some circumstances where most of the assets, if not all
of the assets, should be subjected to probate in order
the "cleanse" them of potential liabilities of the decedent. The availability of adequate professional or
business liability insurance is a factor to be considered in determining whether to have assets (other than
insurance or retirement fund benefits) be probated.

[ ]N   (2) Diversion of Assets to Replacement Spouse: Children are often unintentionally deprived of security and
benefits where assets are held in joint tenancy with a
surviving spouse or left outright to a surviving spouse
and that surviving spouse remarries. Without a trust to
protect the children, there is no way to be certain that
the children will receive any benefits, particularly if
the survivor remarries and is subject to pressure to
prove his or her love and devotion to a new spouse by
joint tenancy ownership or a new will.

[ ]N   (3) Distributions to Children at Early Ages: An estate
built with great care and effort may be wasted, with
little or no real benefit to the next generation, by
leaving the property outright to a child who has no experience or ability in managing the assets. Early distributions also usually have a very adverse effect on
educational planning.

[ ]N   (4) Loss of Mental Capacity: If no trust has been created to hold the assets and provide a successor trustee
to manage the assets, or where no one has been given a

ALL HUSBANDS AND WIVES WITH SOME ESTATE - Cont.

Checklists For Various Circumstances   Ralph Gano Miller

durable power of attorney, incapacity may cause serious disruption of a business and also payment of normal expenses of living. In this circumstance, a relatively cumbersome and expensive court conservatorship of the estate is the only way to provide some management for the assets.

[ ]N   (5) _Spouse's and Children's Ignorance of Estate Affairs_: Failure to provide information as to the existence and/or location of assets may seriously disrupt the process of garnering the estate assets and properly managing them.

[ ]N   (6) _Lack of Liquidity_: Although liquidity may not be required with current planning techniques at the first spouse's death for estate tax, it may well be required for other purposes, particularly if the decedent was in business or farming. Further, for larger estates, at the death of the second spouse, there may be a need to either have cash liquidity or liquidate many of the estate assets in order to pay death taxes.

Although it is now possible to have a zero estate tax liability at the death of the first-to-die spouse, there are circumstances where it may be beneficial to have funds available at the first death to pay estate taxes on assets at that time and avoid the increase in value which may take place during the lifetime of the surviving spouse.

[ ]E   (7) _Having an Estate Plan Which Does Not Qualify For the New Marital Deduction_ (Chapter 29): Many pre-1982 estate plans now result in payment of substantial federal estate tax at the death of the first spouse to die. The "totally tax-free transfer to a surviving spouse" simply doesn't happen under many pre-1982 estate plans, including some plans which use trusts to reduce estate taxes.

[ ]E   (8) _Loss of Unified Transfer Credit (UTC)_: (Chapter 29): The most frequently encountered estate "problem" for married couples is that of the first spouse to die leaving all assets outright to a surviving spouse.

The Economic Recovery Tax Act of 1981 (ERTA) provided for a deduction for estate tax purposes as to any assets left to a surviving spouse. Thus, the decedent leaving all assets to a surviving spouse has no tax to pay (since all the tax will be deferred until the survivor's death) and thus, loses the advantage of the unified transfer credit to reduce the overall estate and gift taxes on the estates of the two spouses. This is true regardless of whether the decedent had separate property or community property. See Chapter 29 for a description of the use of a trust to create sufficient tax and take advantage of the UTC so that the property in that trust, taxed at the first spouse's death and segregated until the survivor's death, can avoid tax at the survivor's death.

ALL HUSBANDS AND WIVES WITH SOME ESTATE - Cont.

[ ]E/N (9) <u>New Generation Skipping Laws</u> The Tax Reform Act of 1986 abolished the prior generation skipping laws and instituted new rules for deaths and gifts after September 25, 1985. Many trusts which were drafted with the prior rules in mind do not now meet the requirements of the new law and should be reviewed. Also, direct gifts to grandchildren can now trigger not only death taxes but also generation skipping taxes, and should be reevaluated.

[ ]E   (10) <u>State Inheritance Taxes</u>: Not all state laws follow the current federal tax rules allowing a total marital deduction for gifts to surviving spouses. Planning must also consider the applicable laws of the state since such inheritance taxes can be significant.

  California, Florida, Nevada and a number of other states have no inheritance or other death tax which would cause a higher overall death tax. Some states do have a "pick-up" tax which takes advantage of the federal credit for state death taxes and lets them share some of the federal estate tax.

[ ]E   (11) <u>Gifts with Retained Interests</u> (Appendix B): Where the donor retains an interest in a property (either technically as by retaining a life estate in property deeded to someone else or practically as by continuing to live in and make use of a house given to someone else), the property will be brought back into the donor's estate for estate tax purposes.

[ ]E   (12) <u>Custodianship Gifts</u> (Chapter 32): A typical example of retained right is the donor who makes a gift to a child and appoints himself or herself as the custodian of the gift until the child reaches maturity. Such gifts will be brought back into the taxable estate of the donor if he or she is the custodian of the gift.

[ ]E   (13) <u>State Gift Taxes</u>: As with inheritance taxes, state gift tax laws often differ from federal laws, and many states have lower or no amounts of gifts which are excluded from gift tax and there may well be no marital deduction available for certain gifts in certain states. State gift taxes can be very substantial. As with inheritance taxes, a number of states (California, Florida, Nevada and several others) have no gift taxes which cause any additional tax to be paid.

[ ]E   (14) <u>Accidental Gifts</u>: Although planned giving can be a most effective way of reducing transfer taxes, care should be taken to not create unintended taxable gifts.

  Except as between husband and wife, nearly every creation of a co-ownership with any other person (e.g., putting a stock or piece of real property in joint tenancy with someone) creates a taxable gift. Obtaining competent tax advice is the only way to avoid such gifts.

  The Tax Act of 1984 focused on interest-free loans or below-market-rate loans and created new and dangerous areas of potential unintended taxable gifts (Chapter 16).

  ALL HUSBANDS AND WIVES WITH SOME ESTATE - Cont.

Checklists For Various Circumstances   Ralph Gano Miller

[ ]E   (15) <u>Insurance Gifts Within Three Years of Death</u> (Chapter 17): Tax law changes in 1981 abolished the Three-Year Contemplation Of Death Rule with regard to most gifts but not with regard to insurance and certain other gifts. Thus, either direct or indirect gifts of insurance within that period can result in the taxability of the insurance proceeds in the donor's estate. Community property rules may often present unique problems in identifying the donor of insurance (Chapter 17).

[ ]E   (16) <u>Lack of a Qualifying Marriage</u>: The increasing frequency of absence of a formal marriage makes this a very real danger for couples who in other times would have married. Depending on state law, either a formal or a common law marriage can qualify for the marital deduction, but there must be a "marriage". Documentation for a marriage or a divorce in foreign countries must be examined by a competent attorney. California and several other states do not recognize "common law" marriages (those based on people living together).

[ ]E/I (17) <u>Failure to be Aware of Law Changes</u>: Although laws sometimes change in regard to wills and trusts, the changes are much more frequent with regard to estate, gift, and income taxes. Ignorance of such changes can have very adverse effects on an estate plan.

[ ]E/I (18) <u>Property Tax Reassessment at Death</u>: Where state law (e.g., Proposition 13 in California) has prevented valuation increases for property tax purposes, death can lift the barrier to such increases in valuation and also to tax increases. Some exceptions to such increases often do exist and estate planning must be done with property tax matters in mind.

[ ]E/I (19) <u>Retirement Plan Beneficiary Designation Forms</u>: Where benefits built up in a qualified retirement plan are planned to be transmitted at death, this is accomplished not by one's will or trust but by using a beneficiary designation form created for such a purpose. In those circumstances where there is a gift to anyone other than the surviving spouse of a participant (perhaps a gift over to a trust in the event the spouse does not survive or disclaims the gift), great care must be taken to see that the laws created by the Retirement Equity Act of 1984 are not violated. This law generally restricts all transfers of benefit from a qualified plan other than in the form of annuity payments. Further, any spouse of at least one year has an immediate right to half of the value in the plan to be left to her or him in the form of an annuity. Beneficiary designation forms must be carefully reviewed to spot any violations of this very surprising law.

ALL HUSBANDS AND WIVES WITH SOME ESTATE - Cont.

Checklists For Various Circumstances   Ralph Gano Miller

B. SINGLE PERSONS

AREAS OF POSSIBLE BENEFIT

(1) Implications for the Single Client: With the exception of a marital deduction, all the potential benefits described in the checklist for "Husbands and Wives" are available to a single person. This group includes persons who have never married, those who have had an annulment or divorce and also survivors of marriage, both with and without children. However, the marital deduction is available only to the extent that there is an existing spouse who receives a lifetime gift or assets transmitted at death.

With the possible exception of the annuity (discussed below), there are few unique estate planning benefits available for a single person, although income taxation rules may from time to time give some advantage to a single person as compared to one who is married.

[ ]N   (2) Use of Annuities: For those persons who truly have no financial responsibility for anyone else, the purchase of commercial annuities may have some application in increasing the cash available each month during the person's lifetime. However, the need for protection of purchasing power from inflation often argues against putting the majority of one's assets into such investments. Certain annuities provide some degree of protection from inflation.

[ ]I   (3) Use of Charitable Remainders (Chapter 2): Where the single person has no need for concern over leaving assets to children or other persons, consideration should be given to obtaining a current income tax deduction by giving to a charity the right to use property after the single person's death. Although the flexibility of sale and/or consumption of the asset is lost, the income is retained and income tax lessened because of the deduction.

POTENTIAL PROBLEMS

(1) Implications for the Single Client: All the potential problems with regard to the above "All Husbands and Wives With Some Estate" apply to the single person. The exception is that there is no accidental loss of unified credit by leaving all the assets to a surviving spouse since the marital deduction does not apply to a single person.

[ ]N   (2) Difficulty in Finding Conservator of Person or Estate: For those single persons who have no children, it is often much more difficult to find someone in whom they have enough confidence to make decisions regarding their person and all their assets when the single person is no longer able to make such decisions well.

SINGLE PERSONS

Tools and Techniques

Checklists For Various Circumstances   Ralph Gano Miller

[ ]N   (3) <u>The Lee Marvin Syndrome</u>: Unmarried persons who
        have a live-in companion but no written agreement as to
        ownership of property or rights to income have a sub-
        stantial exposure to lawsuits that may drastically re-
        duce assets that would otherwise go to the beneficiaries
        of their estate plan. A written property agreement can
        solve this problem.

[ ]N   (4) <u>Heirs' Lack of Knowledge of Estate</u>: Assets of a
        single person are frequently never all found since the
        executor, often an unrelated person and often a corpor-
        ate fiduciary, may never have been given information as
        to the existence or location of assets.

[ ]N   (5) <u>Single Parent Finding Guardian For Children</u>: Fail-
        ure to direct some thought and effort toward the often
        difficult question of finding a suitable guardian for
        the children of a single parent often results in not
        only not finding a suitable guardian but also often
        causes the single parent to delay having a will or trust
        drafted.

[ ]E   (6) <u>No Easy Way to Defer Estate Taxes</u> (Chapter 29):
        Without a valid surviving spouse, estate taxes must be
        faced and the single person's estate must be prepared to
        bear the brunt of such taxes.

SINGLE PERSONS - Cont.

C. PERSONS WITH POTENTIAL INHERITANCE

AREAS OF POSSIBLE BENEFIT

[ ]N   (1) Avoidance of Probate And/Or Conservatorships for
          Parents: Probate of a parent's estate and particu-
          larly that of the surviving parent, puts the burden of
          such delays and costs directly on the client. Use of
          a trust will permit the avoidance of such a probate.
          It also permits the avoidance of what may be an ex-
          pensive and cumbersome conservatorship (or guardian-
          ship) proceeding where the parent is not managing as-
          sets well.

[ ]E   (2) Generation Skipping Trust (Appendix D): Where
          the client has an expectation of an inheritance, there
          should be a discussion of the possibility of receiving
          such inheritance in the form of a trust which typi-
          cally gives the client as trustee the control over and
          all the benefits from the assets to be inherited, but
          also permits the avoidance of the additional genera-
          tion skipping tax on up to $2,000,000 ($1,000,000 per
          donor) of the property for estate tax purposes.

               Further, until 1990 there is an additional exemp-
          tion from generation skipping tax in the amount of
          $2,000,000 per grandchildren for intervivos gifts to
          grandchildren.

POTENTIAL PROBLEMS

[ ]N   (1) Reduction of Parental Control Over Children:
          Direct gifts to clients' children from the clients'
          parents may often interfere significantly with par-
          ental control, particularly as to education of the
          client's children. Use of a trust may avoid this
          problem and still provide the benefit the grandparents
          desire.

[ ]N   (2) Dissipation of Estate by Parent's New Spouse:
          Where the parent leaves all assets to a new spouse
          with the intent that she or he will leave it to the
          children of the prior marriage, the children often
          never receive any of the assets. Use of a trust by
          the parent to control the assets would avoid this
          problem. Often such a trust can be best created be-
          fore the death of either parent.

[ ]E   (3) Loss of Generation Skipping Exemption: There is
          an exception from generation skipping tax of
          $1,000,000 per donor, or $2,000,000 for a couple.
          However, without proper planning, the exemption of
          both parents and particularly that of the first parent
          to die can be lost. This is a very important aspect
          if generation skipping for an inheritance is planned.

PERSONS WITH POTENTIAL INHERITANCE

[ ]E   (4) <u>Accidental Application of Generation Skipping Tax</u> (Appendix D, Section 3): Planning in which the parent of the client plans to benefit both the client and the client's children may often unwittingly cause application of the generation skipping tax, resulting in the effective inclusion in the client's estate of assets which will really go on to benefit the next generation. Under some circumstances, the Unified Transfer Credit of the child will be unavailable to pay some of the tax and the 55% generation skipping tax may apply (50% after 1992).

PERSONS WITH POTENTIAL INHERITANCE - Cont.

D. PERSONS MOVING FROM OTHER STATES OR COUNTRIES

AREAS OF POSSIBLE BENEFIT

[ ]E   (1) Gifts to Permit Both Spouses to Use Unified Transfer Credit: Where one spouse has more property (because of state laws or inheritance) than the other spouse, gifts to the spouse with the smaller estate should be considered in order to be certain that such spouse has sufficient estate to take advantage of the full amount of the Unified Transfer Credit ($600,000 of estate) and/or generation skipping exclusions ($1,000,000 of estate). Where the spouse with the larger amount of assets is unwilling to make outright gifts to the other spouse, consideration may be given to having the other spouse purchase and continue to own life insurance on his or her life in an amount which will take advantage of the opportunity to pass assets tax free because of the Unified Transfer Credit.

[ ]E   (2) Change of Residence to Avoid State Death Taxes or Even U.S. Estate Taxes: Since many states (e.g., Florida, Nevada, California, etc.) now have no additional death taxes beyond what the federal estate tax would be, changing one's residence to one of those states may avoid significant death taxes. For those persons willing to give up U.S. citizenship, death taxes may be reduced substantially on property outside the country.

[ ]E   (3) Possibility of Non-Residents Making Gifts Before Becoming Residents: In some circumstances, non-residents (e.g., an exile from San Salvador temporarily living in the U.S. but who is as yet not a U.S. resident) may be able to make gifts without being subject to U.S. gifts taxes. In some such cases, planning may include gifts to family members made before becoming a resident of the U.S.

[ ]I   (4) Ownership Change to Community Property (Appendix D, How Basis is Determined): Where one spouse has separate property (è.g., acquired through earnings in a separate property state or from inheritance) that has increased in value, consideration should be given to changing that property to community property. If the property is left as separate property and the non-owning spouse dies, the property will retain its present income tax basis. If the property is changed to community property, in a properly conceived estate plan, it is possible that the death of either spouse will provide the survivor with a new and increased income tax basis for the property equal to the fair market value of the property at the time of the death of the first spouse to die.

POTENTIAL PROBLEMS

[ ]N   (1) Ancillary Probate: If a person retains ownership of real property in another state, there will probably have to be two probates, one for the state of residence and another for the state in which the retained real

PERSONS MOVING FROM OTHER STATES OR COUNTRIES

property is located. Use of a trust to hold such out-of-state property can usually avoid this costly and cumbersome circumstance.

[ ]N   (2) <u>State Law Differences for Execution and Administration of Wills and Trusts</u>: A will drafted in one state may simply not be valid in another state since the formalities required of such a document and the rules for inheritance, qualification of executors, etc., are controlled by the law of each state. The will must be examined by an attorney in the state in which the clients are currently residents.

[ ]X   (3) <u>Surviving Spouse's Rights Differ From State to State</u>: State laws also differ as to what rights the spouses have in property acquired during marriage (e.g., community property spouses each having a half interest in earnings during the marriage), rights in separate property at the death of a spouse, and also intestacy rules (which operate in the absence of a valid will). All of these differences may be magnified in comparing the laws of different countries.

[ ]N   (4) <u>Real Property in Other States Usually Subject to that State's Laws</u>: Even though the residence of the owners was considered in drafting their wills, laws of the location of the property will usually apply -- including the aspect of the validity of the form of the will, rights of surviving spouses and the rules of intestacy.

[ ]N   (5) <u>Foreign Residents</u>: For those persons who have previously lived in or who are currently residents of or perhaps even have property in other countries, there must be an examination of the law of the other country to see if a will must be drafted in accordance with its laws in order to be effective as to assets in that country.

[ ]E   (6) <u>Accidental Gifts Prior to 1982</u> (Chapter 11): Transfers of ownership between husband and wife prior to 1982 may very well have resulted in taxable gifts for federal estate tax purposes and for a state's gift tax purposes even though no gift was intended. Putting separate property (e.g., which was inherited or which was earned in a separate property state) of one spouse into co-ownership with the other in many cases resulted in taxable gift, and ERTA did not wipe out such prior gift tax liabilities. Such transfers should be reviewed to determine if any gift tax liability exists or if any steps should be taken to currently record the circumstances which argued against the transaction having been considered a gift.

[ ]E   (7) <u>Possibility of Two State Death Taxes Applying</u>: By having indicia of residence (e.g., drivers license, lodge membership, income tax filings, etc.) in two or more states, it is possible to be subject to state death tax in each state.

PERSONS MOVING FROM OTHER STATES OR COUNTRIES - Cont.

Checklists For Various Circumstances   Ralph Gano Miller

[ ]E   (8) Different U.S. Estate and Gift Tax Rules for Non-Residents: Foreign citizens who are not U.S. residents do not have all of the estate tax benefits of U.S. citizens in relation to federal estate and gift tax and also often with regard to state gift and death taxes. Such non-citizens with significant assets must have their estate plans prepared by an attorney who is aware of the impact of such differences on estate planning.

PERSONS MOVING FROM OTHER STATES OR COUNTRIES - Cont.

Checklists For Various Circumstances   Ralph Gano Miller

E. OWNERS OF PRIVATE CORPORATIONS

AREAS OF POSSIBLE BENEFIT

[ ]N' (1) Shield Against Corporate Liabilities (Chapter 13):
Wherever the business activity has some potential financial dangers, a business operated through a properly
organized and operated corporation with sufficient
capital may protect the other assets of a client.

[ ]N   (2) Pooling of Capital for Business (Chapter 13):
Issuance of shares to various persons permits the pooling of capital and thus raising of more funds than would
otherwise be available to any individual proprietor for
the capital needs of a business activity.

[ ]N   (3) Maintaining Value of Business -- Buy and Sell
Agreement (Chapter 1): Often the most important aspect
of estate planning is preserving the values built up in
the private corporation, and executing a proper buy and
sell agreement may be an effective way of doing this in
many situations which involve private corporations.

[ ]N   (4) Capitalization to Permit Retention of Control: In
circumstances where gifts of stock to family members are
contemplated, consideration might be given early to
issuance of both voting and non-voting stock.

[ ]N   (5) Use of a Voting Trust to Permit Retention of Control: Where issuance of non-voting stock is not practical, the possibility of maintaining control is feasible
in some circumstances by the use of a voting trust.

[ ]E   (6) Early Gifts of Stock Within Family: Where it is
likely the corporation will appreciate in value, gifts
of stock at an early stage of the corporation's growth
may permit the transfer of a much larger part of the
future value without there being any significant gift
tax consequences.

[ ]E   (7) Capitalization to Permit Easier Corporate Freeze --
A Lost Planning Tool: When an increase in the value of
a corporation is a very significant possibility,
consideration was previously given early to issuance of
both preferred stock (which can be recovered by the
corporation at stated prices) and common stock (to be
given to the next generation) which will not have such
restrictions, and thus will have the major potential for
increase in value. Unfortunately, the Budget
Reconciliation Act of 1987 introduced a new code section
[IRC §2036(c)] which specifically thwarts such attempts
to shift a disproportionate share of potential increase
in value to future generations.

[ ]E   (8) Corporation May Qualify More Assets for Estate Tax
Deferral (Chapter 8): All of the "business assets" in a
going business corporation may qualify at a client's
death to meet the minimum percentage limits in order to

OWNERS OF PRIVATE CORPORATIONS

achieve deferral of the related estate tax over a period of as long as 14 years and with some of the tax bearing interest at a very low rate. Although the 1984 Tax Act eliminated the value of "passive assets" in considering the value to be ascribed to a business for this purpose, holding assets in a corporation may still result in a larger amount qualifying for deferral of tax than if such assets were owned by an individual proprietor.

[ ]I   (9) Retaining Rights at Original Incorporation of Business (Chapter 13): As opposed to putting all the assets of a business into the corporation in exchange for stock, when forming a corporation consideration should be given to taking back a note in place of some of the stock so that some money or other assets can be later drawn out of the corporation against such note without recognition of income tax.

[ ]I   (10) Fringe Benefit Planning: The following are some of the most typically used fringe benefit planning techniques:

> (a)   group term life insurance (Chapter 17)
>
> (b)   medical reimbursement plans (Chapter 18)
>
> (c)   disability insurance deductibility
>
> (d)   cafeteria plans
>
> (e)   split-dollar insurance coverage (Chapter 17)
>
> (f)   education costs
>
> (g)   financial counseling
>
> (h)   prepaid group legal services
>
> (i)   dependent care assistance
>
> (j)   auto and travel costs

[ ]I   (11) Use of High Profile Qualified Retirement Plans (Chapters 7, 12 & 22): Pension and profit sharing plans, both for corporations and for individual proprietors and partners, now are recognized by tax experts as probably the most effective tax shelter for those persons in a business or profession.

[ ]I   (12) Use of Dividends Received Deduction: When investment of corporate funds is considered, the deduction afforded corporations of 80% (70% in some circumstances) of any dividends received should be taken into consideration.

[ ]I   (13) Use of Corporation's Initial Low Income Tax Rate (Chapter 13): Tax rates as low as 15% for income tax purposes makes the corporation a very useful tool for building capital for some businesses or professions. However, the Budget Reconciliation Act of 1987 ordained

OWNERS OF PRIVATE CORPORATIONS - Cont.

that all "personal service corporations" (e.g., those to practice law, medicine, or consulting using shareholders as employees) do not have the advantage of the lower corporate tax rate after 1987. Thus, all income of such corporations will be taxed at the 34% rate.

[ ]I (14) Electing Subchapter "S" Status (Chapter 27): Where circumstances warrant, the corporation may be shifted to being taxed like a partnership through election into "S" status, thus having the income taxed at the shareholder's own individual rate. The ability to make this election is subject to a number of important rules. The effect of the Tax Reform Act of 1986 in making individual income tax rates lower than corporate rates at levels over $75,000 is now a strong argument for electing the "S" corporation status.

[ ]I (15) Shifting Income to Low Tax Bracket Family Members (Chapter 27): The Subchapter "S" election described above also permits the shifting of income to other family members (unless under age 14) by giving them ownership of stock. This will be of more benefit if income taxes are raised above the 1988 limit of 28%/33%.

[ ]I (16) Using an ESOP to Defer or Avoid Gain on Sale (Chapter 7): The 1984 Tax Reduction Act (TRA) rules now permit deferral of gain on a sale of the corporation stock in certain circumstances by the use of an Employee Stock Ownership Plan as the buyer and the reinvestment of sale proceeds in domestic stock on the open market. This is a new and potentially important benefit for many clients.

[ ]I (17) Using an ESOP to Redeem Stock With Pre-Tax Dollars (Chapter 7): The installation of an ESOP can provide the means in some circumstances to redeem stock by making deductible contributions to a qualified plan. In some circumstances this can also provide for acquisition of the stock in conjunction with a bank loan and the repayment of that loan with tax deductible funds contributed to the ESOP.

[ ]E (18) Using an ESOP to Obtain Deduction for 50% of Value of Stock: A benefit provided by the 1986 TRA is permitting an owner of corporate stock to have his trustee or executor sell the stock to the corporation's ESOP and receive an estate tax deduction equal to 50% of the value of the stock! This extraordinary benefit expires after 1991. Some limitations were imposed by the Budget Reconciliation Act of 1987.

[ ]I (19) Non-Cash Deductions Through Use of ESOP (Chapter 7): Where taxable income may be high and cash resources low, the installation of the ESOP can provide for cash-free deductions by having the corporation issue stock to the ESOP. However, this planning also shifts some stock ownership to the employees of the corporation.

[ ]I (20) Lifetime Stock Redemptions to Remove Cash: Where some shareholders are not related, it may be possible to

OWNERS OF PRIVATE CORPORATIONS - Cont.

redeem stock of certain shareholders with the recognition of gain as a sale instead of dividend treatment. This will be of significant benefit if and when preferential treatment is reinstated for long-term capital gains.

[ ]I (21) Avoiding Tax on Underlying Gains: Even though the corporation may contain assets (e.g., unrecognized receivables, appreciated inventory, fixed assets which have been depreciated, etc.), that would normally produce income to the corporation when sold, under many circumstances all of the assets may be sold together through a sale of the corporation's stock, and thus a gain avoided at the corporation's level until the asset is sold or converted to cash. The selling shareholder, however, recognizes the gain which may exist with regard to his stock. However, item (29) below regarding the loss of the General Utilities Doctrine should be reviewed.

[ ]I (22) Stock Redemption at Death to Pay Death Taxes (Chapter 26): Special rules permit redemption of stock under Section 303 in an amount equal to the total of both federal and state death taxes without having the redemption treated as a dividend.

[ ]I (23) Total Stock Redemption at Death of Community Property Shareholder (Appendix D - Basis): By holding property in community property form, the death of one spouse gives the surviving spouse an income tax basis in both halves of the stock equal to the then fair market value. The corporation can then be liquidated and no gain is recognized at the shareholder level.

However, after 1988 the 1986 Tax Reform Act now requires corporations which have not elected Subchapter S status under certain specific rules to recognize any gain inherent in the assets upon liquidation (e.g., a building worth $100,000 with a cost basis to the corporation of only $30,000), as noted also in item (29) below.

[ ]I (24) Shifting of Income Between Tax Years (Chapter 13): By having a fiscal year of the corporation that overlaps the owner-employee's usual December 31st taxable year (e.g., having a January 31st year end for the corporation), it is possible to shift income from one year to the next. Holding back salary payments during the year and making them in January of the succeeding year may shift income from one taxable year of the owner-employee to his next taxable year, without creating any taxable income for the corporation. Generally, this is now possible only for non-Subchapter S corporations which are not personal service corporations.

[ ]I (25) $50,000 Borrowable From Qualified Retirement Plan (Chapter 22): Under the restrictions imposed by the Tax Equity and Fiscal Responsibility Act (TEFRA), the amount of money that can be borrowed by a participant from a corporate qualified plan is limited to $50,000. However,

OWNERS OF PRIVATE CORPORATIONS - Cont.

that is much better than the circumstance of Keogh plans, for individual proprietors and partners, which do not permit any borrowing.

[ ]I   (26) Full Deduction for California Income Tax Purposes of Plan Contributions: Several states restrict the deduction allowed for contributions allowed to non-corporate retirement plans (Keogh plans). Some states, like California, have recently conformed to federal law and now permit a full deduction. However, this can be an important reason for using a corporation in those states which have income tax rules which restrict such deductions.

[ ]I   (27) $5,000 Death Benefits: Up to $5,000 may be received by corporate employees including owner-employees under a valid written contract as a death benefit. This amount is free of income tax to the recipient but deductible to the corporation.

[ ]I   (28) Rollover of Qualified Plan Account to IRA on Retirement or Death of Spouse (Chapter 14): Recognition of income tax can be avoided by a "terminating" qualified retirement plan participant or spouse of a deceased participant by transferring -- under certain conditions -- the plan proceeds to an Individual Retirement Account.

[ ]I   (29) Loss of the General Utilities Doctrine: After 1988 liquidation of corporations other than subchapter S corporations will result in recognizing a tax at the corporate level on the excess of value of any assets over the corporation's income tax basis in them. E.g., a real property owned by the corporation with a corporate tax basis (cost less depreciation) of $20,000 but which is worth $100,000 at time of liquidation, will result in a corporate tax on the $80,000 difference. Even some subchapter S corporations can recognize all or part of this corporate gain upon liquidation under the "built in gain" rules.

    Prior to 1989, the General Utilities court case had crystallized the rule that no corporate tax was recognized upon many liquidations. TRA'86 legislated a reversal of this doctrine.

POTENTIAL PROBLEMS

[ ]N   (1) Wrong Choice of Form of Buy-and-Sell Agreement (Chapter 1): Whether you use a stock redemption agreement or a cross purchase agreement depends on several factors which should be reviewed with a competent advisor to avoid loss of potential benefits.

[ ]N   (2) Buy-In Problems Created by High Stock Values: Where future shareholders may not have much capital and where the corporation has accumulated a great deal of fair market value, many qualified prospective co-shareholders may be preempted from buying into the corporation. An example of this might be a large medical radiology group that over the years has accumulated in the

OWNERS OF PRIVATE CORPORATIONS - Cont.

operating corporation a very large amount of value related to accounts receivable and to the radiology equipment used in the practice. For a bright young doctor, it may simply cost too much to consider buying into such a corporation.

[ ]N   (3) Cash Problems in Redeeming Shares: The same problem as described above of accumulating too much in the way of asset values in a corporation may make the redemption of shares a very difficult problem.

[ ]N   (4) Piercing of Corporate Veil by Creditors (Chapter 13): Inadequate capitalization or failure to follow corporate procedures may result in a corporation failing to provide a shield for shareholders as to any liability for corporate debts.

[ ]N   (5) Securities Law Problems (Chapter 13): Failure to observe legal requirements in creating a corporation may cause adverse civil results and even criminal penalties. The incorporation should be done by an experienced and competent attorney.

[ ]E   (6) Corporate Owned Insurance on Life of Majority Shareholder (Chapter 17): Ownership by the corporation of insurance on the majority shareholder may result in that insurance being included in the taxable estate of the client-shareholder.

[ ]E   (7) Stock Valuation Problems (Appendix B): The various methods approved by the courts for valuation of corporations should be reviewed with a competent tax attorney in determining the value which estate tax authorities will place on the corporate stock. The client may be unpleasantly surprised to learn of the high value which will be assigned to a corporate ownership.

[ ]E   (8) Loss of Estate Tax Exclusion of Pension and Profit-Sharing Benefits (Chapter 22): For deaths after 1984, except for some unusual circumstances, the exclusion previously available for values in qualified corporate retirement plans (as well as those of partnerships and individual proprietors) is no longer allowed. Many estate plans require important revisions because of this change in the law.

[ ]I   (9) Double Taxation of Dividends: (Chapter 13): Where a corporation accumulates earnings, it pays income tax on them (unless it has elected to be taxed under Subchapter S). However, when the dividends are paid to the shareholder, the corporation receives no deduction or offset against taxable income but the shareholder is subject to income tax on the dividends received. For this reason, very few large dividends are paid to shareholders of privately owned non-subchapter S corporations.

[ ]I   (10) Real Property Owned by Corporation: In many planning circumstances where the business activity itself is in a corporation, the ownership of the building in which the business is carried on is maintained outside the

OWNERS OF PRIVATE CORPORATIONS - Cont.

corporation. Failure to do this may cause recognition of gain at both corporate and individual levels, in those circumstances where either the business or the real property are to be sold separately or where non-subchapter S corporations (and even some "S" corporations) liquidate after 1988.

[ ]I   (11) Corporation Ignored as Sham by Taxing Authorities (Chapter 13): Failure to observe the requirements for corporate meetings, salary arrangements, separation of ownership as between shareholder and corporation, etc., may result in all the corporate income being taxed to the individual shareholders.

[ ]I   (12) Possible Dividend Treatment for Payments or Benefits to Shareholder (Chapter 13): Certain salary payments and other payments to or for the benefit of shareholders (e.g., personal use of a corporate auto) may be challenged by the IRS and denied as deductions to the corporation on the basis that they are "dividends".

[ ]I   (13) Special IRS Scrutiny For Corporate Partners (Chapter 13): The 1982 TEFRA rules gave IRS a new tool to use against those corporations which are partners of a partnership, e.g., medical or legal "incorporated partnerships". Corporations in this situation should review IRC Code Section 269A with competent tax counsel to see if changes in the form of business or practice should be considered.

[ ]I   (14) Limitation on Accumulation of Corporate Earnings (Chapter 13): Accumulation of corporate earnings beyond $250,000 ($150,000 for service corporations in many professional areas) may result in an additional tax ranging from 27-1/2% to 38-1/2%. Avoidance of such tax on such accumulations requires a showing that the earnings are required to be retained for the "reasonable needs of the business".

[ ]I   (15) Extra Tax on "Incorporated Pocketbooks" (Chapter 13): Where 60% of the corporate income is from rents, royalties, dividends, interest and certain personal service income (with some very significant exceptions), a large extra income tax may apply.

[ ]I   (16) No More No/Low Interest Loans From Corporation: The 1984 Tax Act rules now cause a recognition of income, as a dividend, where a corporate owner has a loan from his corporation at no interest or at a rate lower than market. Since it is a dividend, the corporation gets no deduction.

[ ]I   (17) Higher Payroll Taxes Through 1989: Income received as salary by a shareholder-employee is subject to social security tax paid by both the corporation and the employee. Until 1990, the total of these taxes is more than the self-employment tax which an individual proprietor or partner would pay on such earned income.

OWNERS OF PRIVATE CORPORATIONS - Cont.

Checklists For Various Circumstances   Ralph Gano Miller
_____

[ ]I   (18) <u>Possible Second Tax on Liquidations:</u> Under the
        1986 Tax Reform Act for C-type corporation liquidations
        after 1988, the corporation will be taxed to the extent
        that any assets have a value in excess of the
        corporation's basis in them (e.g., a building with
        $100,000 which has a tax basis of only $30,000).
        Certain Subchapter S corporations can avoid this
        corporate level of tax, which is in addition to the tax
        on the shareholder to the extent that the net pro- ceeds
        from the liquidation exceed his or her basis in the
        corporate stock.

OWNERS OF PRIVATE CORPORATIONS - Cont.

Checklists For Various Circumstances   Ralph Gano Miller

F.   INDIVIDUAL PROPRIETORS

AREAS OF POSSIBLE BENEFIT

[ ]N   (1)   <u>No Corporate Creation or Operation Costs</u>: The individual proprietorship is the simplest form of doing business and avoids legal fees for incorporation as well as those for subsequent annual meetings, etc.

[ ]I   (2)   <u>Only One Level of Income Taxation</u>: By avoiding the corporation, one avoids the taxation of income at the corporate level and its subsequent second taxation where the payment to the shareholder is deemed to be a dividend, as opposed to being an expense deductible to the corporation (e.g., salary). One also avoids the corporate tax (which is in addition to the shareholder tax) on appreciation at the time of the sale of the business (followed by a liquidation).

[ ]I   (3)   <u>Assets Removable From Business Without Tax</u>: Unlike the corporation or certain partnership circumstances, the individual proprietorship allows the taxpayer to remove assets or add assets without the recognition of any gain for income tax purposes.

[ ]I   (4)   <u>Avoidance of Social Security Tax for Family Employees</u>: Payments of salary to spouses or children permits shifting of income from an individual proprietor to other persons in the family without payment of social security taxes. This is becoming more important as social security taxes are increasing.

[ ]I   (5)   <u>Lower Employment Tax Rates Through 1989</u>: A benefit which will cease by 1990 is that the total amount of self employment tax paid by an individual proprietor is currently less than the total of the employer's and the employee's portions of social security tax.

[ ]I   (6)   <u>Ability to Produce Losses Which Can Offset Salary or Other Taxable Income</u>: Where the business is actively pursued by the owner (and thus is not a "passive" activity) and produces a tax loss, the amount of the loss can be used to reduce the amount of ordinary taxable income. However, if the taxpayer does not materially participate in an active business or the activity is considered passive, then any loss will be considered a passive loss and can only offset passive income. Passive income does not include portfolio income (e.g., interest, dividends). The 1986 Tax Reform Act defers the deduction from losses from "passive" activities. Tax shelters were the target of this legislation. "Material participation" by the individual is now required in order to have the loss be currently applied to offset other income of the individual.

POTENTIAL PROBLEMS

[ ]N   (1)   <u>Lack of Shield Against Liabilities</u> (Chapter 13): Unlike a corporation, the individual proprietor is liable for all debts of the business.

INDIVIDUAL PROPRIETORS

[ ]N   (2) <u>No Ability to Borrow From Keogh Plan</u> (Chapter 12):
        Unlike a corporate plan, the individual proprietor can-
        not borrow from his Keogh plan.

[ ]N   (3) <u>More Difficult to Give Some of Business and Retain
        Control</u>: Unlike a corporate circumstance, it is very
        difficult to give interests in the individual propri-
        etorship without having to deal with the possibility of
        some control shifting to the donee.

[ ]I   (4) <u>All Inherent Gain in Assets Recognized on Sale of
        Business</u>: Sale of an individual proprietorship will
        result in the recognition of gain taxed as ordinary
        income with regard to sale of accounts receivable,
        inventory and other assets which have a value in excess
        of income tax basis. This problem should not be
        significant after 1987 when the tax rates for ordinary
        income and capital gain are equalized (although many
        economists still argue loudly for reduced or no taxation
        of capital gains).

[ ]I   (5) <u>Lack of Corporate Fringe Benefits</u>: The various
        corporate fringe benefits described above for corpora-
        tions generally do not apply to an individual propri-
        etorship.

[ ]I   (6) <u>Low Keogh Plan Deduction Limit For Some State In-
        come Taxes</u>: Some states permit only a small income tax
        deduction for contributions to Keogh plans. Recently,
        some states, e.g., California, now permit the full
        deduction for such contributions.

[ ]I   (7) <u>All Income Taxable at Individual Rates</u>: None of
        the income developed by an individual proprietorship
        will be taxed at the often lower corporate rates or on
        the tax return of other family members. However, after
        1987 the highest individual rate is presently lower than
        the highest corporate rate.

[ ]I   (8) <u>No Use of ESOP Available</u>: Unlike the corporation,
        the sale of an individual proprietorship may not have
        the gain deferred by sale to an ESOP and investment in
        corporate common stock nor is there available the 50%
        estate tax deduction for sale of corporate stock to an
        ESOP which a corporation would make possible.

[ ]I   (9) <u>No Shifting of Income Between Tax Years</u>: All of
        the income earned in a taxable year will be subject to
        tax in that year as opposed to the circumstances of a
        corporation with a fiscal year different from that of
        its shareholder-employee.

[ ]I   (10) <u>All Business Earnings Subject to Self-Employment
        Tax</u>: Unlike the corporation, where retained income may
        be subject only to income tax and not social security
        tax, earnings of an individual proprietor business are
        generally subject to both income tax and self-employment
        tax.

INDIVIDUAL PROPRIETORS - Cont.

Checklists For Various Circumstances   Ralph Gano Miller

[ ]N   (11) <u>No Pooling of Capital For Business Purposes</u> (Chapter 13): Since no other persons may be involved in the proprietorship, the individual may supply only his own or borrowed funds.

[ ]N   (12) <u>Difficult to Create Market-At-Death For Business</u> (Chapter 1): Although buy-and-sell agreements may, under unusual circumstances, be created for individual proprietorships, the lack of a partner or other shareholders as a potential ready buyer is a disadvantage in creating a market for the business.

[ ]E   (13) <u>Fewer Assets May Qualify For Estate Tax Deferral</u> (Chapter 8): In determining whether or not an estate meets the percentage requirements necessary to qualify for deferral of a portion of the estate tax, only those assets of an individual proprietorship which can be shown to relate directly to the business may be included in determining such percentages.

[ ]I   (14) <u>No Shifting of Income to Other Persons</u>: Under the 1986 TRA, income in excess of $1,000 shifted to children under age 14 will be taxed at their parents' top marginal rate. Unlike a partnership or a Subchapter "S" corporation, the individual proprietorship income cannot be shifted to other persons. Under the 1986 TRA, income in excess of $1,000 shifted to children under age 14 will be taxed at their parents' top marginal rate.

INDIVIDUAL PROPRIETORS - Cont.

G. PARTNERS

AREAS OF POSSIBLE BENEFIT

[ ]N   (1) <u>Pooling of Capital for Business</u>: Like a corporation, the assets of more than one person may be combined
to meet the capital needs of the business.

[ ]N   (2) <u>Market   For   Business   --   Buy-and-Sell   Agreement</u>
(Chapter 1): The existence of partners often creates a
market for business interests which does not exist for
an individual proprietorship.

[ ]N   (3) <u>Some Protection From Liability Available Through</u>
<u>Limited Partnerships</u>: Although the general partner(s)
will always be liable for all debts and other liabilities of the partnership, a limited partnership may be
created which will limit both the liability and control
of a limited partner.

[ ]E   (4) <u>Reduced Value of Certain Partnerships For Estate</u>
<u>Tax Purposes</u> (Chapter 9): The family partnership was a
vehicle often used for attempting to "freeze" the value
of real property and other assets including business
interests. This estate planning technique was stopped
by the Budget Reconciliation Act of 1987 for any form of
doing business.

        However,   certain   partnerships   which   have
restrictions on withdrawal of assets after death of a
partner can still be a very effective vehicle for
reducing value of a partner's interest in a partnership.

[ ]I   (5) <u>Some Removal of Assets From Business or Even Liqui-</u>
<u>dation Without Tax</u>: Unlike a corporation, under proper
circumstances, assets may be removed from a partnership
or the partnership may be liquidated without the recognition of any gain for income tax purposes. Gain may be
recognized without competent advice.

[ ]I   (6) <u>Only One Level of Income Tax</u>: Like an individual
proprietorship, there is no double taxation of income
(at both the corporate and an individual level). This
benefit is really often a detriment where lower corporate income tax rates might otherwise apply (e.g., the
15% corporate rate for the first $50,000 of income each
year for corporations which are not "personal service
corporations").

[ ]I   (7) <u>Some Shifting of Income to Other Family Members</u>
(Chapter 9): By observing the relevant rules, some income may be shifted to other family members by giving
interests in the ownership of the partnership.

[ ]I   (8) <u>Special Allocations of Income Between Partners May</u>
<u>be Possible</u> (Chapter 9): With a partnership agreement
drafted by an attorney with experience in dealing with
such "special allocations", it may be possible to allocate income and even income tax deductions among the
partners in such a way as to optimize income tax planning.

PARTNERS

[ ]I   (9) <u>Losses May Be Available to Offset Personal Income</u>:
         Like an individual proprietorship, losses from active
         general partnerships flow through to the taxpayer and
         may offset personal income, e.g., salary, interest,
         etc. However, losses from passive activities and
         activities in which the partner does not materially
         participate can only offset passive income. Passive
         income does not include portfolio income (e.g.,
         interest, dividends).

POTENTIAL PROBLEMS

         (1-10) The numbered items listed for the potential prob-
         lems of individual proprietors also apply to partner-
         ships:

[ ]N   (11) <u>Possible Liability For Actions of Partners</u>: Cer-
         tain actions of a partner in relation to a general part-
         nership may result in liability for all the other part-
         ners.

[ ]I   (12) <u>Tax Due on Certain Removals of Assets From Busi-
         ness</u>: Certain assets, e.g., accounts receivable which
         have not been taken into income or highly appreciated
         inventory, may result in the recognition of income if
         withdrawn from the partnership under some circumstances.

[ ]I   (13) <u>Greater Tax Shelter Audit Potential</u>: Because the
         partnership has been used so frequently for tax shel-
         ters, the IRS now seems to view all partnerships with
         more suspicion.

[ ]I   (14) <u>Disposition of Certain Partnership Interests May
         Trigger Recognition of Gain</u>: Where the income tax basis
         of the partner has been significantly reduced (as by
         depreciation expense), it may become impossible to even
         give away a partnership interest without the recognition
         of a large amount of gain.

[ ]I   (15) <u>Accidental Loss of Right to Partnership Deductions</u>:
         In attempting to deal with certain sophisticated tax
         shelter partnerships, the 1984 Tax Act imposed rules on
         all partnerships which may cause a partner's share of
         expense to be capitalized as opposed to being available
         to offset income.

[ ]I   (16) <u>Limited Partnerships Targeted by 1986 Tax Reform
         Act</u>: TRA'86 disallowed current deduction of all
         "passive losses". All limited partners are considered
         as not "materially participating" and therefore all
         losses from limited partnerships cannot be taken cur-
         rently but must be deferred until there is "passive
         income" (which excludes dividends, interest and certain
         other income) against which the passive loss can be
         offset.

PARTNERS

[ ]I (17) <u>Inactive General Partners Not Allowed Current</u>
<u>Partnership Loss Deductions</u>: In focusing on "passive
income" as a likely way to deal with tax shelters,
TRA'86 requires that there be "material participation"
in the activity in order for even a general partner to
currently deduct the loss from the partnership. A lower
standard of "active participation" is required for real
estate rental activity.

PARTNERS - Cont.

Checklists For Various Circumstances   Ralph Gano Miller
_____

H. BUSINESS PERSONS IN GENERAL

AREAS OF POSSIBLE BENEFIT

[ ]N   (1) Creating and Maintaining Market For Business (Chap-
        ter 1): Whether the business is in a corporate, part-
        nership or individual proprietorship form, planning can
        be 'done to create a market for the business whether that
        may be by creating a buy-and-sell agreement or whether
        it is accumulating information on other prospective pur-
        chasers of the business.

[ ]E   (2) Sharing of Name Goodwill Within Family (Chapter
        11): It may be possible to bestow benefits onto family
        members by permitting the use of a business name without
        the actual recognition of a gift or the application of a
        gift tax.

[ ]E   (3) Personal Financial Guarantees For Family Members
        (Chapter 11): Like the use of a family name, personal
        financial guarantees may currently permit the bestowing
        of real benefits on a family member or other person
        without the actual recognition of a gift or the applica-
        tion of a gift tax.

[ ]E   (4) Special Use (Low) Valuation For Estate Tax (Appen-
        dix B): Unlike investments in cash, securities or in-
        vestment real property, certain assets involved in a
        business (such as real property used for business) or
        farming may be subject to special rules which will
        permit use of lower values for estate tax purposes.

[ ]E   (5) Deferral and Installment Payments For Estate Tax
        (Chapter 8): Again, unlike investments in cash, secur-
        ities or investment real property, investment of the
        assets in an active business may permit the payment of
        related estate tax over a period as long as 14 years and
        at a very low interest rate for a portion of the tax.

POTENTIAL PROBLEMS

[ ]N   (1) Heirs Ignorant of Market For Business (Chapter 1):
        Preservation of estate values argues strongly for commu-
        nicating to spouse and heirs any plans for the business
        and especially potential markets for the sale of the
        business.

[ ]N   (2) Lack of Instruction to Heirs as to Disposition or
        Continuation of Business: Often only the family member
        active in the business knows whether it should be con-
        tinued or sold upon his death. Failure to communicate
        to other family members on this point may result in a
        tragically wrong decision as to the disposition or con-
        tinuation of the business.

[ ]N   (3) Lack of Successor Management (Chapter 1): Exis-
        tence of a buy-and-sell agreement may provide for some
        successor management that otherwise would not be

BUSINESS PERSONS IN GENERAL

available for the business. The universal dislike for thinking of one's own death often results in no planning in this important area for maintenance of the value of the business.

[ ]N (4) <u>Lack of Cash Reserves at Owner's Death</u> (Chapter 17):   Failure to provide for cash availability (e.g., through insurance) at the death of the person on whom the business depends often results in the complete collapse of the business.

BUSINESS PERSONS IN GENERAL - Cont.

Appendix A
The First Interview

Checklists For Various Circumstances   Ralph Gano Miller

I. RANCHER OR FARMER

AREAS OF POSSIBLE BENEFIT

[ ]E (1) Special Use (Low) Valuation For Estate Tax (Appendix B): Ranches and farms actually worked by the client are subject to very favorable rules for valuation as farm land rather than their value for use as shopping centers, subdivisions, etc.

[ ]E (2) Deferral and Installment Payments For Estate Tax (Chapter 8): Ranchers and farmers are particularly favored in the application of rules for the deferral of tax and payment (at low interest rates to some degree) over a period as long as 14 years.

[ ]I (3) No Income Recognized Until Sale of Product: Special cash basis rules for farmers permit the reaping of crops without the recognition of the income until the time the crops are actually sold and value received by the seller.

[ ]I (4) Some Greater Flexibility For Cash Deduction: Although the 1984 Tax Reduction Act placed some restrictions on the deductibility of farm payments, the farmer generally has more flexibility in this regard than the average business man.

[ ]I (5) Avoidance of Income Tax at Death on Some Products: Certain crops and livestock may receive a new income tax basis at death so as to prevent any recognition of gain upon their being sold.

POTENTIAL PROBLEMS

[ ]N (1) Liquidity Problems of Land Ownership (Chapter 17): Typically, a farmer or rancher has the greatest need for liquidity (often in the form of insurance) since so much of the total value of the farm is in the form of land that may not be readily saleable without destroying the farm as a viable unit.

[ ]N (2) Loss of Political Power: Because efficiency of operation and a number of other factors have drastically reduced the number of farmers in relation to the rest of the nation, the formerly very impressive political power of the American farmer or rancher has deteriorated greatly. This fact, combined with increasing free world trade in agriculture, has resulted in vast reductions in income to be received from farming.

[ ]E (3) Loss of Special Use Valuation and of Deferral of Estate Tax (Chapter 8 & Appendix B): Changing the farm operation to a cash rent basis can cause loss of these particularly important estate tax benefits.

RANCHER OR FARMER

Checklists For Various Circumstances   Ralph Gano Miller
_____

J.   **PROFESSIONALS**

    <u>General Comment</u> - Usually the term "professional" is applied to those persons who have met certain educational goals and who usually perform services for others, e.g., Architects, Dentists, Doctors, Engineers, Lawyers, etc.

    Although many of these people work for large companies as employees, a large proportion work essentially for themselves, as individual proprietors, partners and in corporate form. Thus, the professional should review the appropriate checklists for Individual Proprietorships, Partners, or Owners of Private Corporations, or perhaps that of the Corporate Executive where the category may be appropriate (usually thought of as applying to highly paid employees of large corporations).

    Over the years, many professionals have incorporated for income tax benefit reasons. The 1982 TEFRA rules were designed in part to remove incentives for such incorporations. However, there are many benefits of incorporation still available and the professional who is not yet incorporated should review the possible benefits and detriments listed in the checklist for Owners of Private Corporations to determine if his estate might be improved by incorporating.

    Below are listed some specific areas of possible benefit or problems which generally apply to professionals, regardless of the form in which they practice their profession:

AREAS OF POSSIBLE BENEFIT

[ ]N   (1) <u>Cost Savings Available From Professional Groups</u>: Frequently, membership in professional groups may provide medical or insurance coverage at lower rates than are generally available.

[ ]N   (2) <u>Market For Business/Practice Enhanced by Professional Group</u>: Some groups provide special services for retirees or estates of deceased members in finding a purchaser for the practice or business. Although professional goodwill may often die with a practitioner, in many cases such services can be very beneficial.

POTENTIAL PROBLEMS

[ ]N   (1) <u>Licensing Limitation on Marketability of Business or Practice</u>: Most states limit the practice of many professions only to those persons who are licensed by the state. Upon the death of someone practicing one of these professions, there is only the limited market of state licensees to whom the practice or business may be transferred. Such restrictions on marketability obviously will reduce the value that will be received from such a sale.

PROFESSIONALS

Tools and Techniques

Checklists For Various Circumstances   Ralph Gano Miller

[ ]N   (2)   <u>Licensing Restrictions on Transfers to Family Members</u>:   The same license restrictions typically often prevent shifting the value of the business or profession to the next generation over a period of years.

[ ]N   (3)   <u>Personal Liability Even Where Corporate Form Used</u>: Except for those professionals who perform work for the benefit of large corporations as opposed to benefiting the public, there is always some personal exposure of a professional who performs services for another person or entity. Although a corporation can shield the owner-employee from liability caused by the acts of other persons, each individual is still liable for his or her own acts regardless of the fact that the business may be carried on in a corporate form.

[ ]I   (4)   <u>No Low Corporate Tax Rates</u>:   For professionals who use the corporate form, after 1987 there will be the corporate disadvantage that income left in the corporation cannot be taxed at only 15% or 25% rates for lower levels of income. These lower corporate tax rates will not be available to such corporations. Professionals should remember this recent kick in the financial teeth when incumbent members of Congress ask for their support.

PROFESSIONALS - Cont.

K. CORPORATE EXECUTIVES

AREAS OF POSSIBLE BENEFIT

[ ]N   (1) Sick Pay - Disability Pay: Executives working for
        large corporations whose welfare and profitability does
        not depend solely on their efforts have a very real
        benefit in the contract provisions usually available for
        continuation of pay regardless of whether they may be
        sick or disabled. Agreements to spread compensation
        over future years often produce income tax benefits for
        the employee. Typically, this is available in and fea-
        sible for large corporations where the lack of current
        deductibility for such future payments is not the sig-
        nificant problem that it is for the smaller, private
        corporations.

[ ]I   (2) Income Tax Benefits Allowed to All Corporate Em-
        ployees (Chapter 13): The various possible benefits
        described in the Owners of Private Corporations check-
        list are all available to the extent that the corpora-
        tion is willing to tailor its decisions to benefit the
        corporate executive. Often the cost of including other
        employees of a large corporation may limit flexibility
        in benefits available to executives but they may still
        be very substantial.

[ ]I   (3) "Non-Qualified" Deferred Compensation (Chapter 3):
        The stability and good financial position of many large
        corporations permit many executives to enter, reasonably
        worry-free, into agreements which defer some portion of
        their compensation to future years (usually after a
        planned retirement date) when income tax can be expected
        to have less impact. Additionally, many such arrange-
        ments provide the equivalent of accumulation of "effec-
        tive interest" (in the form of increase of the compensa-
        tion based on how long it is deferred) which is not
        taxed until it is received.

[ ]I   (4) Incentive Stock Options: The 1981 ERTA provisions
        created a new type of "Incentive Stock Option" which is
        better than previously available options, and may both
        defer taxation and shift such benefits from ordinary
        income rates to capital gain rates. Strict rules must
        be adhered to in issuing such options. After 1987,
        capital gains and ordinary income will be taxed at the
        same rates.

[ ]I   (5) Regular and Restricted Stock Options: Although
        they may not qualify for the special tax benefits
        afforded incentive stock options, options to buy stock
        of a very successful business may be very valuable. By
        having certain restrictions on such options, in some
        instances the amount of gain recognized may be substan-
        tially reduced without a proportionate reduction in real
        value to the corporate employee.

CORPORATE EXECUTIVES

[ ]I   (6) "Phantom Stock" Plans: Contracts can provide both current income based upon the equivalent of ownership of stock and also future payment for equity which would be equal to the amount which stock might have appreciated.

[ ]I   (7) Education: Any company employee can receive tax-free, under many circumstances, education which is related to the business and designed to improve existing skills or to qualify a person for an existing job even though these expenses are all paid for and deducted by the employer company.

[ ]I   (8) Professional and Business Club Dues: Like education, if these are really related to the business, they may be received tax-free by an individual and can be deducted by the corporation. However, a greater scrutiny is being directed at such benefits.

[ ]I   (9) Death Benefits Over the $5,000 Limit: In addition to the $5,000 of death benefits allowed tax-free to all employees, some large companies also have practices of making greater payments which may be considered gifts to the employees. However, the IRS frequently does not quietly accept the concept of seeing a deductible expense result in no taxable income to the employee.

[ ]I   (10) Expense Accounts: Like the private corporation, travel and entertainment expenses paid for by the employee may be reimbursed to the executive tax-free (20% not deductible by the corporation in some cases), to the extent that may be shown that they are required for a company to carry out its business. More strict substantiation of such expenses has been required in recent years.

[ ]I   (11) Company Lodging: A long line of cases show that there may be a reasonable deduction for the corporation to provide an employee with lodging where it is in the best interests of the company that he live on the corporate premises or close to such premises. Each case must be examined on its own merits.

[ ]I   (12) Additional Executive "Perks" and Benefits: Many other additional executive perquisites are frequently offered, including housing aid, company cars, country club dues, tickets for various performances, sabbatical leaves, and similar niceties. In 1981, the IRS was given an 18-month delay in its advice on regulating and possibly taxing such fringe benefits. The deadline passed for 1984 with some decisions made but without the great crackdown that IRS envisioned. However, new laws were passed as part of the 1984 Tax Act which restricted greatly the possibility of receiving significant benefits without the recognition of income. Some benefits may well end up as a basis for income recognition by the recipients.

CORPORATE EXECUTIVES - Cont.

Checklists For Various Circumstances   Ralph Gano Miller

POTENTIAL PROBLEMS

[ ]N   (1) Possibility of Being Lulled into a False Sense of
Security and High Spending Habits: Since most of us
prefer to ignore unpleasant things, many executives who
have relied upon retirement based on time spent with the
employer have not felt it necessary to put aside funds
for retirement and often find that a change in corporate
structure may cut off their plans for relying on corporate funding for retirement.

[ ]N   (2) Non-Diversification of Assets Through Investment in
Company Stock: Often executives show their loyalty and
find some job leverage by investing all of their available funds in stock of the employer corporations. This
may be increased by the existence of an employer "stock
savings plan" which invests in stock of the employer.
Employees of companies like Sears have done well with
such circumstances, but many others would have done much
better to diversify their asset holdings.

[ ]N   (3) Directing Available Cash Into Tax Shelters With
Little/No Real Value: Where the executive feels frustrated that all of his earnings are taxable as ordinary
income and that he has no "tax benefits", he often suc-
cumbs to the thought of reducing current income tax by
putting his or her cash into "tax shelters". With the
exception of certain investments in real property and
occasionally oil programs on a diversified basis, most
such "investments" do not produce real assets which provide security for retirement or for the family in the
event of death of the executive.

        Further, under the 1986 Tax Reform Act, most tax
shelters will not be effective in providing current
deductions against salary income. An exception is
"actively" managed real property producing losses up to
$25,000. Even this exemption is phased out as the
taxpayer's adjusted gross income increases from $100,000
to $150,000, at which level no rental property losses
are allowed regardless of how actively the properties
are managed by the taxpayer.

[ ]E   (4) Forced Migrancy Can Cause Asset Title Problems:
Company mandated moves between separate property and
community property states can cause accidental gifts
between spouses (not taxable if made after 1981 for federal tax purposes) and confusion with title which should
be reviewed with competent tax counsel.

[ ]I   (5) Loss of Deduction For Unreimbursed Travel and Entertainment Expenses: The 1984 Tax Act now requires a
substantiation of all such expenses. For the executive
who plans to deduct on his own return such expenses
which are not reimbursed by his employer, if he has a
tax return preparer do his return, the preparer will
require a written certificate from the executive that
adequate records exist. Further, the 1986 TRA permits
such deductions only when they, together with other
"miscellaneous" deductions, exceed 2% of adjusted gross
income.

CORPORATE EXECUTIVES - Cont.

Checklists For Various Circumstances   Ralph Gano Miller
_____

[ ]I   (6) Recognition of Income From "Perks" and Discounts:
        The 1984 Tax Act also restricted greatly the scope of
        benefits which can be received tax free by the employee.
        Those benefits which create no additional cost for the
        employer, like filling empty airline seats with employ-
        ees or their relatives, may continue to be tax-free (in
        a more scrutinized form), but those which actually cost
        the employer are now subjected to rules which reduce
        benefits usually afforded tax free to executives.

[ ]I   (7) New "Golden Parachute" Excise Tax: The 1984 Tax
        Act also focused on payments or property transfers that
        are contingent on a change in ownership or control of a
        corporation or its assets and, for large payments (over
        300% of certain salary limits), a 20% excise tax is im-
        posed on the recipient - in addition to income tax!

CORPORATE EXECUTIVES - Cont.

L. PERSONS PLANNING FOR RETIREMENT

AREAS OF POSSIBLE BENEFIT

[ ]N/I (1) Build Up of Assets in Qualified Plan (Chapter 13):
Using the income-tax-free provisions of a qualified retirement plan permits a much more rapid build up of assets to provide financial security for retirement than
would the same amount paid out as additional current
salary.

[ ]N   (2) Receipt of Social Security Payments Before Actual
Retirement: Although the relatively vague social security (SS) eligibility rules may sometimes prevent it,
some persons upon reaching age 62 or 65 have shifted
their earnings to future years (e.g., to age 70 when
earnings do not inhibit SS payments) by deferred compensation arrangements with employers or by shifting
income to a corporation or pension plan in order to be
able to draw the social security benefits for which they
paid over past years.

[ ]I   (3) Stretching Qualified Plan Benefits Over Retirement
Period (Chapter 13): Where the plan rules permit,
electing to receive plan benefits over a period of time
may often provide a larger total retirement benefit by
postponing the recognition of income tax until payments
are received, and thus permitting a large amount of such
benefits still in the plan to continue tax-free production of income for future payments to the retired employee. Generally payment from such plans must start on
April 1 of the year after the participant reaches
age 70-1/2.

[ ]I   (4) Qualifying for "Lump Sum Averaging" for Qualified
Plan Payments (Chapter 13):   Some plans may require a
"lump sum" distribution of plan assets. Meeting certain
requirements can permit the availability of certain
rules of income taxation which, for smaller and medium
size plan benefits which are paid out as "lump sums",
can result in significantly lower income taxes than
otherwise would result. Very strict rules must be observed.

[ ]I   (5) Use of Deferred Compensation Program to Reduce Income Taxes: Where the employer makes it feasible and
one's financial stability and budget permits, shifting
some current compensation to future years after retirement may both reduce income tax overall and also, under
some circumstances, permit an employee who does not retire at 65 to begin to receive Social Security (SS) payments. Local SS offices are looking more closely at
such arrangements, however.

[ ]I   (6) Use of Corporation to Receive Income Produced After
Retirement: Many employers, particularly those with
significant pension benefits, may permit an employee to
"retire" and to stay on as a consultant without significant employee benefits. Using a corporation to provide

PERSONS PLANNING FOR RETIREMENT

such consulting services may often reduce income tax and
sometimes make social security payments currently available.
Social Security offices now actively seek to
restrict such practices.

[ ]I   (7) Use of Sale of Residence Rules: Where retirement
plans may call for sale of the taxpayer's residence,
care should be taken to come within the rules which permit
a taxpayer who has reached age 55 to postpone the
recognition of gain on up to $125,000 of sale proceeds.

POTENTIAL PROBLEMS

[ ]N   (1) Loss of Insurance or Medical Benefits Previously
Provided by Employment: Failure to review company insurance
programs may result in loss of life insurance or
medical coverage which might have been assumed before
retirement by the employee at lower group rates not usually
available to individuals.

[ ]N   (2) Failure to Create Estate For Retirement: Although
this problem may not be solvable in some circumstances,
it can be avoided in many circumstances with good planning
and will power.

[ ]N   (3) Stagnation of Physical and Mental Abilities:
Studies consistently show that continued mental abilities
and physical capacities can be maintained where
activity is continued as opposed to cessation of physical
and mental effort upon retirement. Planning for
continued activity in an area where one has the opportunity
to find satisfaction will not only improve financial
circumstances but also lead to a longer and fuller
life.

[ ]I   (4) Failure to Qualify Lump Sum Retirement Plan Benefit
for "Lump Sum Averaging": Failure to follow strict
rules (e.g., permitting only one "averaging" after age
59-1/2) can cause retirement benefit payments to be
taxed at regular ordinary income tax rates.

[ ]I   (5) Requiring Sale of Company Stock Held in Retirement
Plan: Lack of good tax advice can lose a tax benefit to
those persons who are retiring from employment which
included a qualified retirement plan which, in the retiree's
account, contained stock contributed by the employer
or purchased by the plan. Correct treatment will
permit the acquisition of such stock and taxation only
at the price at which it was acquired by the plan. Sale
of the stock by the plan before distribution will result
in loss of the benefit.

[ ]I   (6) New Penalty Excise Tax on "Excess Distributions":
After 1986, annual payments from retirement plans in
excess of $150,000 ($112,500 if "grandfathering" is
elected) are subject to a new excise tax of 15%.
Amounts held in plans as of 8/1/86 (if at least
$562,500) can be elected to be exempt from such new tax
but any taxpayer making such election to "grandfather"
these amounts will have to use the lower annual limit of

PERSONS PLANNING FOR RETIREMENT - Cont.

$112,500* on non-exempt payments. A lump sum total of five times the annual amount is also exempted from this new excise tax. Distributions from IRA, Keogh plans and corporate plans are lumped together for these calculations.

[ ]E   (7) New Penalty Estate Tax on "Excess Accumulations": For deaths after 1986, an accompanying new estate tax (not subject to any credits or deductions other than a modified marital deduction) will be applied to all plan accumulations which are in excess of the amount needed to fund for the participant's lifetime, payments equal to the new annual limit ($150,000/$112,500*). This tax, at a 15% rate, is intended to prevent people from avoiding the new penalty excise tax on distributions by permitting funds to build up in retirement plans. Estates of married persons with large amounts in retirement plans previously could have a zero estate tax to pay at the first spousal death. This new penalty estate tax now can cause an estate tax to be payable at the death of the first spouse to die. This tax is another kick by the Democratic Congress at those persons who prefer to fund their own retirement as opposed to relying upon the Social Security rules and payments dictated by Congress.

* For 1988, and until changed, the $112,500 figure has been adjusted for cost of living to $117,529.

PERSONS PLANNING FOR RETIREMENT - Cont.

Checklists For Various Circumstances   Ralph Gano Miller

M. PERSONS PLANNING FOR MARRIAGE

AREAS OF POSSIBLE BENEFIT

[ ]N (1) Entering Into Premarital Agreement Clarifying Title Holding: Hindsight clearly shows the advantage to both parties of facing the question of property rights and laying out in a clear agreement any understandings with regard to change of ownership of property. Listing the property belonging to each person at the beginning of the marriage has much merit and little real detriment.

[ ]N (2) Entering Into Premarital Agreement Clarifying Ownership of Earnings and Retirement Plan Rights: Not only should the separate property or community property rights of each party in the earnings of either party be clarified before the marriage but, particularly where there may be retirement plans, the separate property aspects of rights generated before the marriage should be clarified. The increasing importance of private retirement plan rights to many people argues for maintaining them as separate property until it is certain that the new marriage will be a stable one.

[ ]N (3) Executing New Will After or In Contemplation of Marriage: By executing a will which recognizes either an impending marriage or one that has just occurred, the new spouse will not be in the position of being a "pretermitted heir" and thus the testamentary scheme will not be disrupted by the laws of intestacy which favor such "pretermitted heirs".

[ ]N (4) Use of Trust to Avoid Probate as to Prenuptial Agreement Assets: Where a spouse-to-be has been given certain rights, e.g., life estate, in specific assets in place of other marital rights, it may serve both purposes of avoiding probate and that of avoiding future creditors of the donor by placing that asset or set of assets into an irrevocable trust.

[ ]E (5) Ability to Defer Estate Tax With Marital Deduction (Chapter 29): The existence of a formal marriage permits the deferral of estate tax by an arrangement which benefits the new spouse at least during her or his lifetime. The "Q-Tip" trust will permit the assets to avoid taxation at the death of the owning spouse as long as the income is paid to the new spouse. At the new spouse's death, the assets can thereafter go to the children of the prior marriage or to anyone else. This may often permit a business, which could not currently provide the funds for estate tax without causing its collapse, to mature and be in a position where cash reserves may be developed for payment of estate tax at the death of the second spouse and thus preserving the asset for the children of the first marriage.

Obviously, for the presently single person who wants to provide a benefit for a "live-in partner", marriage can provide a totally estate tax-free transition at his death.

PERSONS PLANNING FOR MARRIAGE

Checklists For Various Circumstances   Ralph Gano Miller

[ ]E   (6) The Ability to Make Tax-Free Gifts by Deferral Un-
         til Marriage: Gifts in large amounts which would pro-
         duce a gift tax if given to a "friend" or "live-in part-
         ner" can be transferred totally free of gift tax if
         given to a person with whom there has been a formal mar-
         riage.

[ ]E   (7) Creating Estate Tax Deductible Liability in Place
         of Marital Right of Spouse: In some states, the amount
         that would be automatically given under state laws to a
         spouse would not result in any deduction for estate tax
         purposes. Many such rights can be replaced with a clear
         liability which, when reduced to a proper contract, may
         result in a deductible liability for the estate of the
         deceased spouse.

POTENTIAL PROBLEMS

[ ]N   (1) Ineffective Termination of Prior Marriages: In
         order for the marital deduction to be available, there
         must be a real marriage. The failure to properly termi-
         nate a prior marriage will prevent the next marriage
         from being effective.

[ ]N   (2) Lack of New Estate Plan: Failure to execute a will
         or trust which recognizes the new marriage may give the
         new spouse rights, as a pretermitted heir, which divert
         assets from the children of a prior marriage. E.g., in
         California, half of the separate property of a wife will
         go to her new husband as a pretermitted heir if he is
         not recognized in her will, and thus the child of the
         wife from a former marriage will receive only half of
         the assets of the mother.

[ ]N   (3) Failure to Recognize the Possible Automatic Pay-
         ments "to Spouse": Many company death benefits, salary
         continuation rights and pension benefits may be paid
         automatically "to the spouse of the employee" where
         there has been a failure to properly designate the em-
         ployee's intended objects of his bounty, e.g., his
         mother or his children from a former marriage.

[ ]E   (4) Making Significant Gifts Before Marriage (Chapter
         11): Since the marital deduction does not apply to
         gifts made other than to spouses, gifts made before mar-
         riage are only subject to the $10,000 exclusion, with
         the excess being subject to gift tax.

[ ]N   (5) Failure to Deal With Rights in Retirement Plans:
         Where either or both of the spouses have rights that
         have been built up in retirement plans, failure to deal
         with such rights by a written agreement may have a very
         bad result in the event of a divorce or a death.

PERSONS PLANNING FOR MARRIAGE - Cont.

Checklists For Various Circumstances _____ Ralph Gano Miller

[ ]E (6) <u>Automatic Right of New Spouse to Half of Retirement
      Plan Benefits</u>: Now, upon one year of marriage, the
      participant's spouse receives the equivalent of the
      right to half of the pension benefits. Without a
      specific manner of written approval of the new spouse,
      the participant cannot direct all of his plan benefit to
      the children of his prior marriage or to anyone else!
      Without the prescribed form of written approval from the
      new spouse, existing designation of persons other than
      the spouse are invalid as to the spouse's half! This is
      very important for persons about to marry.

PERSONS PLANNING FOR MARRIAGE - Cont.

Checklists For Various Circumstances   Ralph Gano Miller

N. PERSONS PLANNING FOR SEPARATION OR DIVORCE

POSSIBLE AREAS OF BENEFIT

[ ]N   (1) Use of Alimony and/or Child Support Trust to Insure Payment: Putting assets into a separate non-revocable trust, at the time of the divorce, may insure actual payment of such amounts as compared to the possible results of leaving the assets in the hands of the other spouse.

[ ]N   (2) Use of Insurance Trust to Insure Premium Payment: Life insurance may be a most important asset in many instances, and both the ability of the other spouse to cancel the policy and the failure of the other spouse to make premium payments can be avoided by placing into an nonrevocable trust both the policy and assets which will produce income to make the premium payments.

[ ]I   (3) Avoiding Income Tax on Division of Pension Plan Benefits: Proper planning and a tolerant employer can result in the division of retirement benefits upon divorce without the often premature recognition of income tax caused by the actual distribution of such assets.

[ ]I   (4) Arranging Deductibility of Some Legal Costs: Certain aspects of a divorce, e.g., advice in regard to taxation, may be deductible. Identifying these amounts and limiting other areas of cost may result in significant income tax savings.

[ ]I   (5) Qualifying Alimony For Deductibility: The 1984 Tax Act set some new requirements for deductibility of alimony which should be reviewed and observed in arranging alimony payments so that the desired deductibility can be provided. Where there is only a single income earner, such deductibility can result in an overall larger amount available to both persons after income taxes.

[ ]I   (6) Providing For Children as Income Tax Exemptions: The existing rules for this area were modified by the 1984 Tax Act so as to provide a definite means of shifting such exemptions in the manner the parties desire. Such rules must be observed closely in the child support agreement and they may even be drafted in such a way as to help enforce child support payments.

[ ]I   (7) Contribution to IRA Based on Alimony Receipt: Under the rules of the 1984 Tax Act, amounts received which qualify for alimony may now be the basis for a deductible payment into an IRA.

PERSONS PLANNING FOR SEPARATION OR DIVORCE

Checklists For Various Circumstances   Ralph Gano Miller
_____

POTENTIAL PROBLEMS

[ ]N (1) <u>Failure to Change Estate Plan</u>: Divorce does not
      necessarily change the effect of a will or trust, and
      such plans should be reviewed in contemplation of or
      promptly after any divorce or separation in order to
      carry out the intentions of the client.

[ ]N (2) <u>Loss of Medical Plan Coverage</u>: Where one spouse's
      employment provides medical plan benefits for both
      spouses and possibly for children, most divorce or legal
      separation circumstances will terminate such protection
      for the non-employed family members where the employee
      works for a small company. However, under the Con-
      solidated Omnibus Budget Reconciliation Act (COBRA),
      employers of 20 or more employees must provide, at 2%
      over cost, coverage for dependents of terminated em-
      ployees where there has been a separation or divorce.

[ ]N (3) <u>Loss of Life Insurance Coverage</u>: As with the med-
      ical plan coverage described above, divorce or legal
      separation often destroys possible life insurance pro-
      tection previously afforded.

[ ]I (4) <u>Recognition of Income Tax on Retirement Plan Divi-
      sion</u>: Division of retirement plan rights, which result
      in distribution of the assets to the participant or the
      spouse, will result in current income tax, a circum-
      stance that may well be avoided by seeking an arrange-
      ment for division of the retirement benefits or other
      available means of preventing receipt and current income
      tax recognition. The 1984 Retirement Equity Act
      addressed a portion of this problem, but actions which
      are not founded on good tax advice can still result in
      the unnecessary recognition of gain. A properly drawn
      Qualified Domestic Relations Order (QUADRO) can shift
      benefits to a non-participant spouse without forcing
      recognition of income tax. Even where assets are
      distributed from a qualified plan to the spouse of the
      participant, income tax may be deferred by reinvesting
      such distribution in an Individual Retirement Account
      within 60 days of its receipt.

PERSONS PLANNING FOR SEPARATION OR DIVORCE - Cont.

ANATOMICAL GIFTS

Why Talk About It?

Perhaps one of the most emotionally charged issues which should be discussed between a planner and a client is the making of anatomical gifts.

One way or another, the issue must be faced. If a client wants to make a gift he should know how to do it. Conversely, if a client is strongly against a gift of one or more organs, as estate planners we have a duty to protect them against the violation of their desires by others after they die.

What Is It?

The Uniform Anatomical Gifts Act (UAGA) has been enacted in every state. The purpose of this Act is to encourage various types of organ donations and to avoid inconsistency among the various jurisdictions.

The UAGA provides that any person over 18 may donate his or her entire body or any one or more of its parts. The donee can be any hospital, physician, medical or dental school, or various organ banks or storage facilities. Organ gifts can be made for education, research, therapy, or transplants. These gifts become effective at death and can be made by will.

How Does It Work?

There are two ways a gift can be made under the UAGA. One is that the donor can designate a specific individual to receive the gift. For instance, the person might specify that one of his eyes be given to a blind sister. A hierarchy of donees can be established and various body parts can be specified to go to specific donees.

A second way the UAGA works is to allow persons other than the decedent to have the power to make the gift. In other words, various family members can donate a person's body or organs. If there is no actual knowledge that the decedent does not want to make an anatomical gift, his or her spouse, adult children, parents and siblings can make a donation. The UAGA establishes a priority system of relatives starting with the deceased's spouse and moving down from closest to furthest relatives who can make, or refuse to allow, anatomical gifts. The gifts can be made by these third parties unless (1) there is actual knowledge that the decedent would not want to make an anatomical gift, or (2) unless someone in the same or higher "class" opposes the gift. Donations can be authorized by third parties either before or after an individual's death.

Because of the possibility that an ill-intentioned relative would use anatomical gifts to obtain postmortem revenge, a person's intention regarding such gifts should be clearly specified one way or the other.

What Are the Requirements?

The UAGA requires that gifts must be made in writing by the donor and attested to by at least two witnesses. The donor must be of sound mind at the time of the writing (although there is no procedure for proving legal capacity in a manner similar to that used in probate). When gifts are made by family members, a written document is not a legal requirement and a telegram or tape recording may satisfy statutory formalities.

Many states provide for the making of anatomical gifts through a donation or a taped telephone conversation noted on a driver's license. But most authorities feel that because of the wide variety and the potential for problems with regard to revoking gifts made in such a way, it is better to either make or object to an anatomical gift through a document other than a driver's license.

When Is the Client Dead?

The Uniform Anatomical Gifts Act does not provide for a specific definition of death. Most states define death as a "total and irreversible loss of brain function" and require the opinion of at least two physicians. The UAGA forbids the physician who certifies death to participate in any organ removal or transplant procedures.

What Must the Estate Planner Do to Meet a Client's Wishes?

Regardless of the estate planner's personal feelings about anatomical gifts, the client's wishes should be honored. Likewise, regardless of the wishes of family members, the client's desires regarding anatomical gifts should be met if possible. Estate planners should explain to clients that a traditional funeral service is possible in most cases (check with local clergy) even if an entire body is left for medical research. This will alleviate a great deal of the tension regarding anatomical gifts. You might also point out that the anatomical gift is a "postself" device, a way to continue to have meaning beyond the event of your physical death.

Documents meeting the requirements of the Uniform Anatomical Gifts Act should be prepared separate and apart from the will. A codicil to the decedent's will would be useful to state the client's intentions regarding anatomical gifts in a way that does not disclose the other provisions of the will. If at all possible the client should designate a specific donee such as a family member or medical institution (and there should be "backup" donees in case the primaries can't or won't accept the gift for any reason).

Tools and Techniques

What Should the Estate Planner Do Where a Client Feels Strongly about Not Making an Anatomical Donation?

If a client does not want a gift of his body parts to be made, such desires should be clearly and strongly expressed. Prepare a "nonconsent" document and if the client feels quite strongly about not wishing to make an anatomical gift, consider providing in the will that any bequests made to an individual who consents to an anatomical gift will be void.

The discussion of anatomical gifts is one more facet of the uncomfortable—but highly important—nontax aspects of estate planning. It's part of the process by which the estate planner learns not only to face facts but to face a face.

DATA GATHERING AND ANALYSIS

There is no question that the most important skill of an estate planner is the ability to understand who his or her client is, where that client stands in relation to the objectives (realized or subconscious) he or she may have, and what things have to be done to move the client closer to the realization of these goals. Knowledge of the client, the objects of the client's bounty, the client's property, and the relation of each to the others is essential to the estate planner in utilizing this skill.

An ability to gather accurate, comprehensive, and useful information is most efficiently developed through the use of a data gathering system. Each question in the pages that follow is designed to help the attorney, the CPA, the trust officer or life underwriter obtain comprehensive and useful information in a logical, orderly manner.

The reason for some questions will be apparent—the justification for others will be less obvious but equally important. Not every question should be asked of every client or prospective client. Nor are the forms and questions meant to be used "as is" in every case. They are meant only as a starting place—to be adapted to suit each professional's needs and method of operation. Some will use only a few pages—others will ask almost every question and use almost every page. It is important to recognize that the data gathering and worksheet forms in TOOLS AND TECHNIQUES must be used carefully and selectively, and modified to both the needs of the planner and the circumstances of the client.

FORMS

Sample Information Request Letter

Many estate planners and conservationists prefer to obtain as much knowledge as possible about a potential client before their initial interview. This saves the time of all concerned. If handled properly, pre-interview data gathering helps prepare both the client and the estate planner for the interview and involves the client in the planning process.

The sample information request letter reiterates the "when and where" of the first meeting. A controllable atmosphere, such as the professional's office, is usually a much better location for data gathering than a client's home or office.

The client is asked to complete as much of the data gathering form as possible in advance of the first meeting and mail it back to the planner. Note that these are simple "non-threatening" questions, but are necessary for a multiplicity of reasons.

Data Gathering Forms

Page 366—The Cover Page

There is a reason for every page and every line of the data gathering forms. A client notes immediately that his or her file is considered personal and confidential. The client also notes that it will probably take a number of interviews to complete the initial process and then the case will be reviewed at specified times. The use of the forms indicates to the client that the planner has an organized, systematic and professional approach to estate planning.

Pages 367-368—Family Information

Here, the client is asked to print or type information about family members. Note that Question 7 is designed to list not only the names and addresses of children but also their spouse's names, as well as the names and ages of any grandchildren.

Supplementary pages may have to be added where the client or his children have large families. It may also be helpful, where grandchildren are no longer living with their parents, to list their addresses and, if appropriate, the names of their spouses. Whenever possible, obtain social security and telephone numbers.

Often a client will be providing financial support for individuals outside his or her immediate family. Their names and relationship, as well as their addresses, are essential if the client wishes to provide for them either during or after his death. Likewise, clients will often want to provide financial assistance to a charitable organization. Formal names, addresses, and other vital information about such charities should be stated on this page (or on attached supplementary pages).

Page 369

A simple stick diagram of the client's family, his (or her) parent's family, and spouse's parent's family is an invaluable tool when Seniors, Juniors, and third and fourth generation children have the same names. Such a diagram also helps to understand who's who if your client has been divorced, remarried, and has children by both marriages.

Pages 370-371—Advisors

Here, a client is forced to think about who has been—or has to be—selected to care for both the person and the property of children (or grandchildren) who are minors. A client must also select an individual or corporate ficuciary (or more than one of each or combination of both) to serve as a personal representative after his or her death. Alternates for both primary guardian(s) and executor(s) are essential as backups in the event the primary is ineligible, incapacitated, or for any other reason fails to qualify or ceases to act.

It is important that each member of the estate planning team locate other members of the team and inform them of progress and problems in planning the client's estate. Cooperation between the members of the team will assure the client of the best possible coordination of planning.

Page 372—Checklist of Documents

This list outlines the key documents that are of use to the estate planner. In various situations special documents such as contracts, leases, or other agreements should be added. But generally, those shown will provide adequate information for the first interview.

Pages 373-380—Alternative Form for Community Property Residents

An alternative data gathering form which will be particularly useful to residents of community property states can be found beginning on page 373. Community property planners (and common law planners who have had clients move to or from community property states) should notice a number of questions in the forms pertaining to "changes of state of residence during marriage." Problems of the peripatetic client are becoming more acute every day. The final page of the alternative forms dealing with inheritance tax information will be particularly useful in community property states.

SAMPLE INFORMATION REQUEST LETTER

Dr. Allen A. Murphy
6061 Kathleen Drive
Bala Cynwood, PA   19010

Dear Dr. Murphy:

I'm looking forward to meeting with you and your wife on Wednesday, June 16, at 2 p.m. in my office.

As I promised on the phone, I have enclosed the first several pages of a comprehensive data form we'll be using in creating an estate conservation plan. Please complete as much as you can and mail it to me in the enclosed envelope.

Also enclosed you will find a list of documents we will need. I would appreciate if you would send me photocopies of the documents in advance of our meeting or, if you prefer, you can bring them with you on Wednesday. (We can probably save a great deal of time if I can study these papers in advance of our meeting.)

Please feel free to call me if you have any questions.

Sincerely yours,

Charles McClu

CMcC/dl
Enc.

PERSONAL AND CONFIDENTIAL FILE

of

<u>Dr. Allen A. Murphy</u>

Initial Interview: <u>9/11/82</u>

Interviewer: <u>Charles McClu</u>

**Dates of
subsequent
interviews or
review:**

_____

_____

_____

_____

PLEASE COMPLETE (print or type) **AND RETURN IN THE ENCLOSED ENVELOPE:**

			Birthdate	Soc. Sec. No.
1.	Full name	Dr. Allen Albert Murphy	9/11/30	158-43-0865
2.	Nicknames	Al		
3.	Spouse's name	Stephanie Louise Murphy	1/1/33	158-20-3621
4.	Nicknames	Stephie		

5. Home address: 6061 Kathleen Drive   Home phone: El 3-5424
   Bala Cynwood
   PA 19010

6. Business address: 2700 Bryn Mawr Ave.   Bus. phone: La 5-9500
   Hill Hill
   PA 19101

7.

	Children (and Spouses)	Address	Phone	Birthdate
a.	Kathleen	same as above	see above	7/6/62
b.	Christopher	"	"	9/1/64
c.	Charles	"	"	11/15/66
d.	Lawrence	"	"	6/2/70

Names and Ages of Grandchildren

a.   b.   c.   d.

Tools and Techniques

8.	Parent's Names	Address	Age	Phone Number
Yours:	a. _Deceased_			
	b. _Deceased_			
Your Spouse's:	a. _William Lamont_	_872 W. Overbrook St._	_67_	_Lo 6-1276_
	b. _Mary Lamont_	_same as above_	_66_	_Lo 6-1276_

9. Dependants (other than children)/Relationship

William Lamont	_Father-in-law_	_see above_	_67_	_"_
Mary Lamont	_mother-in-law_	_see above_	_66_	_"_

10. Beneficiaries (other than those listed above):

Tools and Techniques   368

11. Please sketch a family tree showing any brothers and sisters:

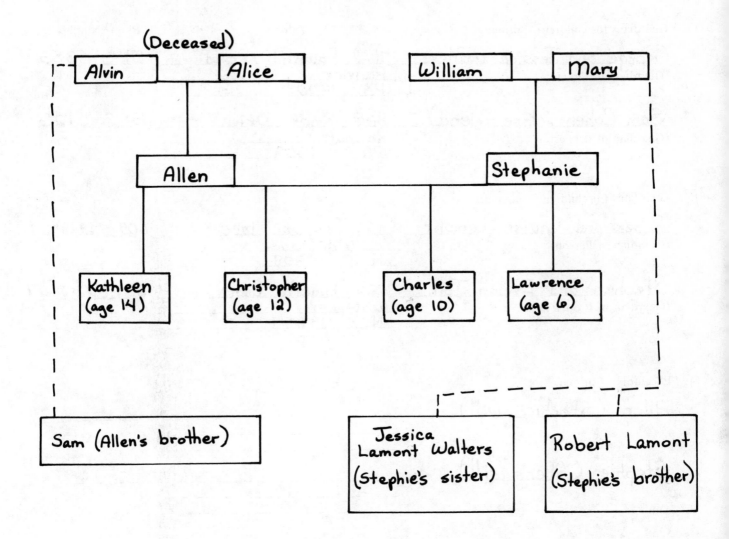

Advisors

		Address	Phone Number
12.	Guardians for children primary:		

George and Jessica Walters
(Guardian of Person)

767 Fawnhill Road
Radnor
PA   19008

EI 3-5353

Sam Cohen (close friend)
(Guardian of Property)

868 Knox Drive
Radnor
PA   19008

EI 3-5126

13.   Guardians for children   alternate:

Robert and Louise Lamont
(Guardian of Person)

121 Peyton Place
N. Wildwood
N. J. 19808

609-522-8707

Stephen and Evelyn Toll
(Guardian of Property)

222 Fayette Lane
Wildwood
N. J. 19807

609-522-7604

14.   Executors   primary:

Allen (Stephie's will)

Stephie (Allen's will)

15.   Executors   alternate:

Sam Cohen

see above

Sam Cohen

see above

16.   Accountant:

Frank Vallei, CPA

#1 Bala Avenue
Bala Cynwood
PA 19010

Mo 4-3874

Address   Phone Number

17. Attorney — personal:

Robert P. Krauss   1401 Walnut Street   Lo 8-5700
Philadelphia
PA 19102

Attorney — business:

Robert P. Krauss   see above   "

18. Banker/Trust Officer:

Allen Gart (Vice Pres. and Senior Trust Officer)   Girand Trust Co.   Lo 8-4858
Girand Plaza
Philadelphia, PA 19101

19. Insurance advisor:

20. Investment advisor broker:

Donald Rahill / Bob Eclair   Newbuilder & Co.   Lo 7-6000
121 Rothschild Bldg.
Philadelphia, PA 19010

21. Other information not listed above:

Allen's doctor - Dr. Alton Blake

Tools and Techniques

CHECKLIST OF DOCUMENTS TO BRING TO INTERVIEW

Present Wills   _____

Personal Income Tax Returns: Last 3 Years (federal and state)   _____

Business Tax Returns: Last 3 Years (include P&L and balance sheets)   _____

Life/Health/Disability Insurance Policies   _____

Employee Benefit Plan Descriptions (Pension, Profit Sharing, Group Insurance, etc.)   _____

Business Buy-Sell Agreements and Employment Contracts   _____

Pre or Post-Nuptual Agreements and Divorce Decrees/Property Settlements   _____

Trust Documents — created by you or by others for your (or your family's) benefit   _____

Gift Tax Returns   _____

Homeowner's Policy and Personal Property Floaters   _____

Deeds to Real Estate   _____

Other documents to bring _____   _____

                              _____   _____

                              _____   _____

RALPH GANO MILLER   Client _____

INFORMATION AND DOCUMENTS

FOR ESTATE PLANNING

PLEASE BRING WITH YOU COPIES OF:

Present Wills, if any

Deeds to real property (for title purposes) and any information regarding title to property, cost and present fair market value.

Manner of title holding of any stock (how the ownership appears on the certificates) and value of each stock.

Last three years' income tax returns.

Any available financial statements.

Copies of any gift tax returns filed.

If you feel appropriate, photos or a snapshot of yourself and spouse.

IF IN BUSINESS:

Any partnership agreements.

Any corporate minute books.

Any buy-and-sell agreements.

Last three years' income tax returns (partnership or corporation).

FILLING OUT INFORMATION SHEETS

It is most helpful (as well as cost-saving for you) if you can fill out the attached forms and bring them with you when you come in. However, please do not delay your appointment for lack of answers to the questions, since we can often assist you with troublesome items at the conference.

RALPH GANO MILLER   Page 1

CONFIDENTIAL DATA FOR

_____

FAMILY INFORMATION

Full Legal Name	Relation	Birthdate	H&W - Birthplace Children-Addresses
_____	Husband	_/_/_	_____
_____	Wife	_/_/_	_____
_____	Child Phone _____	_/_/_ Add.	_____
_____	Child Phone_____	_/_/_ Add.	_____
_____	Child Phone _____	_/_/_ Add.	_____
_____	Child Phone _____	_/_/_ Add.	_____
_____	Child Phone _____	_/_/_ Add.	_____

Other Dependents (Describe)_____

Adopted Children? ( ) Yes ( ) No   Who?_____

Marriage Date _____ Where _____

Previous marriages for either spouse? Yes ( ) No ( ) If Yes, list on back
dates of Marriage term and full name of prior spouse(s) and nature of termination,
(e.g. divorce, death).

Residence Address _____ Years there___ Phone_____

Previous Residence Address_____Years there _____

Any changes of State of residence during marriage? ( ) Yes ( ) No. If Yes,
give dates on back -- Year you came to California _____

Husband's Parents, brothers and sisters	Age	Name and age of spouse (for bro. or sis.)	City and State of residence	Health	Estimated Net Worth
*(F) _____	__	_____	_____	___	_____
*(M) _____	__	_____	_____	___	_____
*( ) _____	__	_____	_____	___	_____
*( ) _____	__	_____	_____	___	_____
*( ) _____	__	_____	_____	___	_____

Wife's Parents, etc.

*(F) _____	__	_____	_____	___	_____
*(M) _____	__	_____	_____	___	_____
*( ) _____	__	_____	_____	___	_____
*( ) _____	__	_____	_____	___	_____
*( ) _____	__	_____	_____	___	_____

*(F) - Father; (M)-Mother, (B)-Brother, (S)-Sister

RALPH GANO MILLER   Page 2

MISCELLANEOUS INFORMATION

Husband's Occupation _____

Husband's Employer _____

Address _____ Phone _____

Number of Years _____ Title _____ Dept. _____

Husband's Previous Occupation _____

Wife's Occupation _____

Wife's Employer _____

Address _____ Phone _____

Husband's Social Security Number _____ Wife's _____

Employer ID Number (for corporation or partnership, if any) _____

If you own your own business, do you have information on prospective purchasers
in the event of your death or on other aspects of disposition of the business? If
yes, who knows the location of this information?

_____

Has Social Security status been reviewed lately: ( ) Yes   ( ) No.

Armed Service: Branch _____ Serial No. _____

        Current Status _____ Disability _____

Husband and wife both U.S. Citizens? ( ) Yes   ( ) No.   If not, describe:

_____

Life Insurance Agent _____

Casualty Insurance Agent _____

Accountant _____

Investment Advisor _____

Personal Physician _____

Business Associates _____

_____

Safe Deposit Box No. _____ Location _____

        In whose names? _____

Is there a homestead filed on your home? ( ) Yes   ( ) No

Tools and Techniques

PLANNING INFORMATION

Do you have a pre or post-nuptial agreement? ( ) Yes ( ) No. If so, bring in.

Have either of you created a living trust?   ( ) Yes ( ) No If yes:

     Who created?   ( ) Husband   ( ) Wife   ( ) Both

     Who is the Trustee? _____

     Who are the beneficiaries?_____

Have you ever made a gift under the Uniform Gift to Minors Act? ( ) Yes ( ) No

     If Yes, Who is the custodian?_____

     Who are the donees? _____

     What was given? _____

Have either of you ever made gifts in excess of $10,000 to any person (including

     your spouse) in any one year? If so, describe_____

     _____

Are you or any member of your immediate family beneficiaries of a trust?

     ( ) Yes ( ) No. If so, who? _____

Do either of you expect to receive gifts or inheritances? ( ) Yes ( ) No.

     If so, Who? _____ How much? _____

     From Whom? _____

Describe any health problems or special needs of individual family members:

     _____

     _____

What is your estimate of the emotional maturity of your children? _____

     _____

     _____

Compare, in terms of your own priorities, the importance of adequate funds in order to do the following (indicate ranking by first, second, etc.):

     Enjoy a comfortable retirement   _____
     Take care of selves and family dur-
      ing a period of long term disability   _____
     Provide College educations for all children   _____
     Take care of your family in the event of your
      death   _____
     Any others that are important to you (specify)   _____

     _____   _____
     _____   _____
     _____   _____

PLANNING INFORMATION - CONTINUED

If your children are minors (under age 18), please indicate your first and second choices of guardian for the children if something should happen to the two of you:

First Choice _____
Relationship _____
Address _____
City, State _____
_____

Second Choice _____
Relationship _____
Address _____
City, State _____
_____

Which Bank or other corporate fiduciary might you wish to name as Executor or Trustee under your documents (recognizing that such institution may well be named only in an alternate capacity) _____

If your immediate family (e.g. spouse, children, grandchildren, etc.) were all to be deceased, to whom would you wish your property to pass (for example, you might want to have it go one-half to the heirs of each of you, or to a charity or charities, etc.): _____

_____

For older clients, would you want to designate a conservator of your person and estate in the event of your inability to manage your property? If so, who?

_____

Do you have any preference as to funeral and/or burial arrangements, or wish to place a limit on costs? If so, please fill out the following:

Religious Services, if any _____

Disposition of Body (e.g. specify burial or cremation, any preference for undertaking arrangements, particularly if you have made any such arrangements, and with whom) _____
_____
_____

Location of Interment _____

Limitation on Overall Cost (e.g. not to exceed $_____) _____
_____

RALPH GANO MILLER

SUPPLEMENTAL SCHEDULE "I"
LIFE INSURANCE

Company	Policy #	Issue Date	Owner*	Type**	Primary Beneficiary	Secondary Benefi-ciary, if any	Amount of Premium	Cash Value	Amount of Loan	Face Amount
On Life of Husband:										
On Life of Wife:										

*Unless otherwise indicated, insurance is usually owned by the insured; ownership by a spouse or someone else may sometimes reduce death taxes and therefore your agent may have arranged for an ownership other than by the insured
** e.g. Whole Life, Term, Endowment, Annuity, etc.

Tools and Techniques

378

HEALTH INSURANCE

MEDICAL EXPENSE

| MEDICAL EXPENSE POLICY NUMBERS |
| NAME OF INSURANCE COMPANY OR SERVICE TYPE PLAN |
| INSURED |
| OWNER OF POLICY |
| TYPE OF CONTINUANCE OR RENEWAL PROVISION |
| TERMINATION DATE FOR CHILD COVERAGE |
| BASIC HOSPITAL |
| ROOM RATE |
| NO. OF DAYS |
| HOSPITAL EXTRAS |
| OTHER BENEFITS |
| SURGICAL |
| MAXIMUM |
| TYPE OF SCHEDULE |
| MAJOR MEDICAL |
| DEDUCTIBLE |
| COINSURANCE |
| INSIDE LIMITS |
| OVERALL MAXIMUM |

DISABILITY INCOME

| DISABILITY INCOME POLICY NUMBERS |
| NAME OF INSURANCE COMPANY |
| INSURED |
| OWNER OF POLICY |
| TYPE OF CONTINUANCE OR RENEWAL PROVISION |
| DEFINITION OF DISABILITY |
| MONTHLY DISABILITY INCOME |
| ACCIDENT |
| SICKNESS |
| PARTIAL DISABILITY |
| ACCIDENT |
| SICKNESS |
| WAITING PERIOD |
| ACCIDENT |
| SICKNESS |
| BENEFIT PERIOD |
| ACCIDENT |
| SICKNESS |
| SUPPLEMENTARY BENEFITS |

Tools and Techniques

RALPH GANO MILLER

INHERITANCE TAX INFORMATION

1.   Did either of you own any real or personal property at date of marriage? If Yes, list below and attach real property tax bill for year of marriage, if available.

General Description of each asset   Approximate market value at mar.

_____
_____
_____
_____

2.   Husband's occupation at date of marriage _____
Husband's net worth at date of marriage _____
Wife's occupation at date of marriage _____
Wife's net worth at date of marriage _____

3.   If either of you have received any real or personal property after date of marriage by gift, bequest, devise or joint tenancy survivorship, list:

General Description of Each Asset	Full name and relationship of person rec'd from	Date rec'd	Approx. value on date rec'd

If California Inheritance Tax determination was made, Name of Estate _____
_____ Court Case No. (if any) _____ County _____

If Received by Gift, State of residence of donor*s) at date of gift: _____
_____

4.   Have any assets listed under 1 or 3 been transferred to anyone else (including spouse)? If Yes, for any such assets sold, give:

Asset	Date of Sale	Proceeds Received	Subsequent disp. of proceeds

For any such assets transferred without full consideration, give:

Asset	Date of Transfer	Names & addresses of persons transferred to	Consideration if any

5.

States in which you have resided after marriage, including California	Combined net worth upon taking up residence in each state (all assets, including cash)

6.   Does net worth at date of last arrival in California include any separate property of either of you? If Yes, state source and value:
_____
_____

7.   Trace subsequent disposition of combined net worth of spouses after last arrival in California _____
_____
_____
_____

8.   Did either of you receive damages or a settlement for personal injury after September 11, 1957? If Yes, show dates, amounts received and subsequent disposition: _____

9.   Have you ever obtained a legal separation (separate maintenance) or an interlocutory divorce? If Yes, attach copy of decree and any property settlement agreement _____ Date of reconciliation _____

10.   Give on attachment any additional information bearing upon the separate or community status of your property.

ANNUAL REVIEW CHECKLIST

Below you will find a number of questions. A positive answer to any of them may indicate a need to review your estate plan. Check the appropriate boxes and return to me.

Specific Bequests

☐ I would like to make specific bequests to individuals not presently included in my plans — or delete the names of one or more persons (or charities) currently named.

☐ I would like to change the amounts of some of the bequests I have made.

Changes in Valuation

☐ The value of my estate has changed more than 20 percent in the last two years.

Special Provisions for Children

☐ My health (my spouse's or children's health) has deteriorated substantially in the last year.

Newly Born or Adopted Children

☐ A child (grandchild) has been born (or adopted) since our last review.

Handicapped or Incompetent Children

☐ A child (grandchild or other dependent) has become handicapped or seriously injured since our last review.

Status of Family Marriages

☐ A member of the family has become divorced or separated since our last review.

Cancellation of Loans to
Children and Equalization of Inheritance

☐ I would like to discharge an obligation owed to me by cancelling the loan in my will.

☐ I would like to provide a clause to equalize any gifts made in the past (or to be made in the future) to certain children (grandchildren).

Life Insurance

☐ I have added (or dropped) more than $50,000 of life insurance since our last review.

☐ I have (or would like to) changed a beneficiary designation on an existing policy.

☐ I feel I may need more life insurance but I don't know how much to purchase or what type to consider.

Gifts to Minors

☐ I would like to make substantial gifts to minor children (grandchildren).

Gifts to Charities

☐ I would like to add (delete) one or more charitable beneficiaries.

☐ I would like to change the amount of my bequest to certain charities.

Business Interests

☐ I have entered into a stock (partnership) buy-sell agreement since our last review.

☐ My business situation has changed significantly since our last review.

Guardian, Executors and Trustees

☐ I would like to name a particular person as advisor to my executor and trustees.

☐ I would like to reconsider the designation of the guardians, executors, and trustees I have named.

Other

☐ I would like to review my estate plans for the following reasons.

☐ I'd like to know how the latest tax law affects my estate plan.

CHECKLIST OF INFORMATION TO KEEP IN SAFE DEPOSIT BOX

The following information or materials should be kept in your safe deposit box:

☐ (1) Birth certificates

☐ (2) Marriage certificates (including artifacts or documentation from any prior marriages or divorces)

☐ (3) Your will (and spouse's will) and trust agreements

☐ (4) Listing of life insurance policies or certificates

☐ (5) Your Social Security numbers

☐ (6) Military discharge papers

☐ (7) Bonds, stocks, and other securities

☐ (8) Real estate deeds

☐ (9) Business (Buy-Sell) Agreement

☐ (10) Automobile titles and insurance policies

☐ (11) Property insurance policies

☐ (12) Additional:

LIST numbers of all checking and savings accounts including bank addresses and location of safe deposit boxes:

_____   _____   _____

_____   _____   _____

LIST name, address, and phone number of fire and life insurance agent:

_____   _____   _____

LIST name, address, and phone number of accountant:

_____   _____   _____

LIST name, address, and phone number of (current or past) employer. State date when you retired if applicable. Include employee benefits booklets:

_____   _____   _____

_____   _____   _____

LIST all debts owed to *and* owed by you:

_____   _____   _____

_____   _____   _____

LIST the names, addresses, telephone numbers and birth dates of your children and other beneficiaries (including charitable beneficiaries):

_____   _____   _____

_____   _____   _____

_____   _____   _____

CHECKLIST OF EXECUTOR'S PRIMARY DUTIES

1. Probate of will.
2. Advertise Grant of Letters.
3. Inventory of safe deposit box.
4. Claim for life insurance benefits — obtain Form 712 from insurance company
     a. Consider mode of payment.
5. Claim for pension and profit-sharing benefits.
     a. Consider mode of payment.
     b. Obtain copies of plan, IRS approval and beneficiary designation.
6. Apply for lump sum Social Security benefits and V.A. benefits.
7. File Form 56 — Notice of Fiduciary Relationship.
8. Open estate checking and savings accounts.
9. Write to banks for date of death value.
10. Value securities.
11. Appraisal of real property and personal property.
12. Obtain 3 years of U.S. individual income tax returns and 3 years of cancelled checks.
13. Obtain 5 years financials on business interest plus all relevant agreements.
14. Obtain copies of all U.S. gift tax returns filed by decedent.
15. Obtain evidence of all debts of decedent and costs of administering estate.
16. Were any of decedent's medical expenses unpaid at death?
17. Has the estate received after death income taxable under Section 691 of the IRC?
18. Prepayment of state inheritance tax — check state law to determine if permissible and advantages and if so, the applicable deadlines.
19. Consider requesting prompt assessment of decedent's U.S. income taxes.
20. File personal property tax returns — due February 15 of each year estate in administration.
21. File final U.S. and state individual tax return (IRS Form 1040) — due April 15 of the year after the year in which death occurs and gift tax returns — due by time estate tax return due.
22. Is the estate subject to ancillary administration?
23. Are administration expenses and losses to be claimed as an income or estate tax deduction?
24. Obtain alternate valuation date values for federal estate tax return.
25. Payment of U.S. estate tax with flower bonds — must be tendered to Federal Reserve with Form within 9 months of death.
26. Consider election of extension of time to pay U.S. estate or generation skipping transfer tax (Sections 6161 or 6166) — must be filed on or before due date of U.S. estate tax returns including extensions.
27. Consider election to defer payment of inheritance tax on remainder interests — where permitted, determine deadline for election.
28. Consider election for special valuation of farm or business real estate under IRC Section 2032A — must be made with timely filed U.S. estate tax return.
29. Elect (or do not elect) to qualify certain terminable interest property for marital deduction.
30. Ascertain if credit for tax on prior transfers is allowable.
31. File inheritance and federal estate tax return — federal due within 9 months of death — extensions may be requested — check local state law for due date and possible extensions.
32. File inventory — check local state law for requirements and due date.
33. Consider requesting prompt assessment of U.S. estate tax return.

Tools and Techniques

34. Apply for U.S. I.D. number if estate will file U.S. income tax returns.

35. File U.S. Fiduciary Income Tax Return (Form 1041) — choice of fiscal year.

36. Consider redemption under IRC Section 303.

37. Apply for tax waivers.

38. File account or prepare informal family agreement.

39. Prepare audit notices and statement of proposed distribution.

40. File schedule of distribution if applicable.

APPENDIX B

VALUATION OF ASSETS FOR FEDERAL ESTATE TAX PURPOSES

INTRODUCTION

Valuing property for Federal Estate Tax purposes is a most complex and often uncertain process. Frequently the taxpayer's valuation has differed widely from the value established by the Internal Revenue Service. Courts will then be asked to resolve the valuation question.

Thus value is a variable, upon which reasonable minds can and will continue to differ. But value is not determined by a mere flip of the coin. The use of careful and thorough appraisals by qualified experts, documentation of sales of similar property recently sold, and well drawn arms-length restrictive agreements (such as a buy-sell arrangement) have proved effective tools in substantiating favorable values.

GENERAL VALUATION RULES

The Internal Revenue Code says very little about how to value items includable in the gross estate for federal estate tax purposes. Although the Code speaks of the "value" of the gross estate, there is no place in the Code where the word "value" is defined.

The general rule: "Value" is "fair market value," "the price at which the property would change hands between a willing buyer and a willing seller, neither being under any compulsion to buy or to sell and both having reasonable knowledge of relevant facts. . ." Thus, the value a particular person would place on property may vary greatly from the measure of worth placed on that same item by the Government. In fact, it is neither necessary that there be an established market for an item, nor that there be the "willing buyer and seller" spoken of in the Regulations. In the absence of an actual sale, the value is based on a hypothetical sale.

Generally, when an organized market does in fact exist, the market price will prevail. The ignorance of a material fact by the buying public or its inability to properly assess the significance of certain events does not form a basis for reducing the price indicated on the organized market. The contrary result applies in the absence of an established market. A purchase or sale is not regarded as determinative of value in situations in which one of the parties was ignorant of a material fact.

The following external factors have had varying effects on the probative value of sales: (a) the frequency of sales (the courts tend to disregard isolated or sporadic sales); (b) the relationship between the buyer and the seller (it is unusual for sales between parents and children or employers and employees to be given great weight in the light of their almost definitional unequal bargaining positions); (c) offers to purchase or sell (offers as opposed to options present little evidence of value).

Not only should all the factors affecting value be considered, but there should be sound reasoning for the relative weight given to each one.

DETERMINING VALUE

The Internal Revenue Service would likely consider all the facts and circumstances which a hypothetical buyer and seller would consider. The derived price at which the property would have changed hands between parties "X" and "Y" thus determines the Service's valuation. By this rule, a forced sale—or a sale outside of regular business channels—would not be determinative of the value.[1] Thus, generally, the Service's position is that the price at which the item or a comparable item would have been sold at retail is determinative.

Value is basically a question of fact in those situations where there is an established market for identical property. But valuation problems become essentially problems of evidential proof (and often, opinion) where:

1. There are different markets for the same property, such as in the case of a property with both wholesale and retail markets.

2. The appraisal of the worth must be made on the basis of comparison with somewhat similar property (which properties should be selected?; how comparable is it?). What is derived is at best an opinion based upon fact.

3. The property in question is unique, such as a patent or copyright. Here, the data must be analyzed (is the examiner capable of making an adequate analysis?), and an opinion must be formulated as to how much the potential anticipated benefits are worth.

Since in practice valuation problems are frequently viewed by the Service and the courts as problems of negotiation and compromise, the appraiser's object should be to derive a fair and sound value which, if litigated, would be sustained by the court. Evidence and proof secured in the form of expert advice through appraisal, promptly after death, would likely have a greater probative value than evidence obtained at a later date. (As to the valution of specific types of property, one must turn to the regulations, rulings and court decisions.)

Tools and Techniques

DATE ASSETS ARE VALUED

Generally, federal estate taxes are based either on the fair market value of the transferred property as of the date the decedent died or the value of the property six months after the date of the decedent's death (alternate valuation date).[2] Once selected for valuation purposes—date of death or alternate valuation—such date applies to all assets in the estate.

If the alternate valuation date is selected and if the property is distributed, sold, exchanged, or otherwise disposed of within six months of the decedent's death, it will be valued as of that date, not the six month date.[3] Certain types of property diminish in value as time goes on; for example, the present value of an annuity reduces each time a payment is made. Any such property interest or estate whose value is affected by the mere passing of time is valued as of the date the decedent died.[4]

VALUATION OF REAL PROPERTY

Because of the uniqueness of land, the value of any real property as of a given date may be subject to widely differing opinions. Absent a market for such property, the greater of (a) the highest price available or (b) the salvage value will control. Where there is a market for real property, the basic factors that affect valuation are:

1. The nature and condition of the property, its physical qualities and defects, and the adequacy of inadequacy of its improvements.

2. The size, shape, and location of the property.

3. The actual and potential use of the property and how the trends of development and economic conditions (such as population growth) affect it.

4. How suitable the property is for its actual or intended use.

5. Zoning restrictions.

6. Size, age, and condition of the buildings (degree of deterioration and obsolescense).

7. The market value of other properties in the area in which the property is located.

8. The value of net income received from the property. Rentals are often capitalized and then adjusted for depreciation. (See discussion of capitalization of income, below.) The same principle can be applied to gross rents. This method, however, must be adjusted to account for operating costs.

9. The value accepted by state probate courts for purposes of state death taxes, if based on appraisals made by qualified real estate experts.

10. Prices at which comparable property in the same area was sold at a time near the applicable valuation date (providing it was an arms-length transaction for the best price obtainable). Usually more than one "comparable property" sale will be used, especially where the property to be valued is a personal residence or undeveloped acreage.

11. How much, taking depreciation into account, would it cost to duplicate the property? The cost or value of land would have to be separated from the total value. The cost of reproducing the building, using present cost figures, would have to be estimated, and then the loss in value due to depreciation would have to be subtracted from the total of the other two figures.

12. Unusual facts.

In the event of a sale of real property within a reasonable period of time after the decedent's death, in such a manner as to insure the highest possible price, the amount received will usually be accepted as its value. Unaccepted offers to purchase the property will also be considered. What of a sale at auction? Usually, this price will be accepted only if it appears that there was no other method that would have obtained a higher price.

Land does not have to produce income or have an active market to attain substantial value. Where lands are in or adjacent to a settled community, owners frequently hold such lands in anticipation of realizing their true value from future sales. For example, a home at the edge of an expanding shopping center might be worth far more to the shopping center developer than it would to a potential buyer in the residential market.

SPECIAL VALUATION OF CERTAIN FARM AND BUSINESS REAL PROPERTY

An executor may elect to value qualifying real property on the basis of its actual "special" use rather than its "highest and best" use. This rule, especially useful where the price of farmland is artificially increased by, or has not kept up with, the price per acre of encroaching housing developments, enables the executor to value the farmland at its value for farming purposes. The maximum reduction of the decedent's gross estate under this provision is $750,000.

The following are the qualification requirements:

1. On the date of the decedent's death, the property must be involved in a "qualified use". That term is defined by Code section 2032A(b)(2) as use as a farm for farming purposes or in a trade or business other than farming.

2. The value of the qualified property (less debts or unpaid mortgages) in the decedent's estate must equal at least 50% of the decedent's gross estate (less debts or unpaid mortgages).

3. At least 25% of the gross estate (less debts and unpaid mortgages on all property in the gross estate)

Figure B.1

Determination of Whether Estate Qualifies for Current Use
Valuation of Farm Real Estate or Business Real Estate
(Husband's)(Wife's) Estate When (He)(She) Dies (First)(Second)

(1)   Gross estate (Form 102, line 1)* .... $ _____

Less

(2)   Unpaid mortgages or indebtedness on property included in estate at gross value
(Fact Finder, pp. 4, 5, 6, 20) .... $ _____

Equals

(3)   Adjusted value of gross estate .... $ _____

(4)   50% of adjusted value of gross estate .... $ _____

(5)   25% of adjusted value of gross estate .... $ _____

(6)   Value of real and personal property of
farm or closely held business
(Fact Finder, pp. 4 & 5) .... $ _____

Less

(7)   Unpaid mortgages or indebtedness on farm
or closely held business real or personal
property included in estate at gross value
(Fact Finder, pp. 4, 5, 6, 20) .... $ _____

Equals

(8)   Adjusted value of real and personal property
of farm or closely held business .... $ _____

(9)   Qualified real property (Form 101) .... $ _____

Less

(10)   Unpaid mortgages or indebtedness on qualified
real property included in estate at gross value
(Fact Finder, pp. 4, 5, 20) .... $ _____

Equals

(11)   Adjusted value of qualified real property .... $ _____

REAL PROPERTY OF FARM OR CLOSELY HELD BUSINESS QUALIFIES FOR CURRENT-USE VALUATION IF LINE 8 EQUALS OR EXCEEDS LINE 4 **AND** LINE 11 EQUALS OR EXCEEDS LINE 5.

This also assumes that (a) the decedent was a U.S. citizen or resident, (b) the real property passes to a qualified heir, and (c) for 5 out of the last 8 years before the decedent's death, the real property was used in the farm or closely held business, and the decedent or a family member materially participated in the farm or business operation.

---

* The full highest and best-use value and not the current-use value is used in determining the value of the gross estate for the 50% and 25% tests.

© 1983 by The American College as part of **Advanced Estate Planning I and II courses.**

FORM 108B

Tools and Techniques

must be qualified farm or closely held business real property.

4. Such property must pass to a "qualified heir." This term is defined at section 2032A(e) to include the decedent's immediate family plus his ancestors or lineal descendants, his spouse or the spouse of a descendant, or a lineal descendant of a grandparent.

5. The real property must have been owned by the decedent or a member of his family and used as a farm or in a closely held business for an aggregate of five years or more of the eight year period ending on the date of the decedent's death. During this period the decedent or a member of his family must have been a material participant in the operation of the farm or other business.

If the above conditions are met, the property qualifies for the special valuation rule.

Then if the executor elects to apply section 2032A, the value for a farm is determined as follows:

A. Average annual gross cash rental for comparable land.

B. Average annual state and local real estate taxes for such comparable land.

C. Average annual effective interest rate for all new Federal Land Bank Loans.

Formula: $\dfrac{A-B}{C}$ = value for section 2032A purposes.

This formula provides that the income that is to be capitalized is the average annual gross cash rental income (for five years prior to the decedent's death) less the average annual state and local real estate taxes (for the same five year period) for that comparable land.

"Comparable land" is (1) land used for farming purposes and (2) must also be located in the same vicinity as the farmland to be valued. If there is no comparable land, or if the executor chooses to have the farm valued in the manner of a qualifying closely-held business, other factors are applied.

The executor may not use cash rentals from the farm to be valued. The rentals used from comparable farmland must have been the result of arms' length bargaining.

The capitalization rate, the average annual effective interest rate on new Federal Land Bank loans, is the average billing rate charged on new agricultural loans to farmers in the farm credit district in which the qualified property is located. These amounts are published by the IRS according to the Federal Land Bank district in which property is located. A reproduction of the relevant parts of the latest ruling on this topic follows.

In order to determine the special use value of a farm under the formula method the average annual effective interest rates on new Federal Land Bank loans to be used for estates of decedents dying in 1986 are as follows:

Federal Land Bank District in Which Property is Located	Interest Rates Year of Death '86
Baltimore	12.82%
Columbia	12.14%
Texas	11.71%
Louisville	12.86%
Jackson	12.30%
Omaha	12.99%
Sacramento	12.31%
St. Louis	12.65%
St. Paul	12.46%
Spokane	12.51%
Springfield	12.20%
Wichita	12.77%

These are the states within each Federal Land Bank district:

District	States
Baltimore	Delaware, District of Columbia, Maryland, Pennsylvania, Virginia, West Virginia.
Columbia	Florida, Georgia, North Carolina, South Carolina.
Texas	Texas.
Louisville	Indiana, Kentucky, Ohio, Tennessee.
Jackson	Alabama, Louisiana, Mississippi.
Omaha	Iowa, Nebraska, South Dakota, Wyoming.
Sacramento	Arizona, California, Hawaii, Nevada, Utah.
St. Louis	Arkansas, Illinois, Missouri.
St. Paul	Michigan, Minnesota, North Dakota, Wisconsin.
Spokane	Alaska, Idaho, Montana, Oregon, Washington.
Springfield	Connecticut, Maine, Massachusetts, New Hampshire, New Jersey, New York, Rhode Island, Vermont.
Wichita	Colorado, Kansas, New Mexico, Oklahoma.

The following example calculates the interest rate of 9.66% for the Baltimore District for decedents dying in 1981:

Figure B.2

Special Use (2032A) Valuation							
Input:	**Capitalization Rate** **0.090**						
	Years Prior To Death		*Gross Rent Comparable Land*		*Real Estate Taxes*	*Capitalized Value*	
Input:	1987	Input:	$120,000	Input:	$5,000	$1,277,778	
	1986		$90,000		$4,500	$950,000	
	1985		$80,000		$4,000	$844,444	
	1984		$70,000		$3,500	$738,889	
	1983		$60,000		$3,000	$633,333	
	Totals		$420,000		$20,000		
	Five Yr. Average		$84,000		$4,000		
	Special (Current) Use Value					$888,889	

1. Billed interest rates for 1980, based on monthly interest rates received from Federal Land Bank:

(Jan.-Feb.)	9.85%
(Mar.-Apr.)	10.75%
(May-June)	12.00%
(Jul.-Nov.)	11.00%
(Dec.)	12.00%

   Average billing rate for 1980 (weighted average based on number of months each rate is in effect)

   11.02%

2. Adjustment to reflect 5% stock purchase requirement:

   11.60%

3. Average annual effective interest rate, calculated for each year in same manner as 1 and 2 above:

1976 —	9.08%
1977 —	8.95%
1978 —	8.95%
1979 —	9.73%
1980 —	11.60%

   48.31% ÷ 5 = 9.66%

   Calculations 1 and 2 are based on Reg. §20.2032A-4(e) and calculation 3 is based on Code Sec. 2032A(e)(7)(A).

If there is no comparable land, or if the executor elects to have the farm valued in the manner of a qualifying closely held business, then the following factors shall apply.

1. The capitalization of income that the property can be expected to yield for farming or closely held business purposes over a reasonable period of time under prudent management using traditional cropping patterns for the area, taking into account soil capacity, terrain configuration and other factors.

2. The capitalization of the fair rental value of the land for farmland or closely held business purposes.

3. Assessed land values in a state which provides a differential or use value assessment law for farmland or real estate owned by a closely held business.

4. Comparable sales of other farms or closely held business land in the same geographical area far enough removed from a metropolitan or resort area so that nonagricultural use is not a significant factor in the sales price.

5. Any other factor which fairly values the farm or closely held business value of the property.

If a farm or a closely held business qualified for the special valuation rules and its value so determined is used for federal estate tax purposes, then an additional estate tax will be imposed if within 10 years after the decedent's death and before the death of the qualified heir, the qualified heir who receives such property disposes of any interest in that property, other than to a qualified family member, or ceases to use that property in the manner in which it was used to qualify for this special tax treatment.

Generally, the additional tax imposed shall be the excess of the tax that would have been imposed on the property if it was valued at its best use over the tax imposed because the property was valued at its "qualified use" value.

If the additional tax is imposed, it is due six months after the date of the disposition of the property or the cessation of its use as a farm or as part of the closely held business. The qualified heir who received such property is personally liable for the additional tax imposed.

If within ten years after the death of the decedent, but before the death of the qualified heir to whom the property passed, the property is disposed of to non-family members or ceases to be used for farming or other closely held busi-

Tools and Techniques

ness purposes, all the tax benefits obtained by virtue of the reduced valuation will be recaptured. There is also a provision allowing for a partial recapture of the tax benefits obtained if the qualified heir disposes of a portion of the property or ceases to use a portion of the property for farming or for the closely held business.

VALUATION OF LIFE INSURANCE

Proceeds of life insurance on the life of the decedent receivable by or for the benefit of his estate will be taxed in the insured decedent's estate.[5] In addition, where the decedent held incidents of ownership, such ownership will invoke taxation.[6] The amount includible is the amount receivable by the beneficiary. This includes dividends and premium refunds. In determining how much is includible, no distinction is made between an ordinary life policy, a term policy, group insurance, or an accidental death benefit.

If a settlement option is elected, the amount that would have been payable as a lump sum is the amount includible. If the policy did not provide for a lump sum payment, the amount includible is the commuted amount used by the insurance company to compute the settlement option payments.

The value of an unmatured policy owned by a decedent on the life of another is included in the policy owners' gross estate where he predeceases the insured.

1. If a new policy is involved, the gross premium paid would be the value.

2. If the policy is paid-up or a single premium policy, its value is its replacement cost, that is, the single premium which that company would have charged for a comparable contract of equal face value on the life of a person who was the insured's age (at the time the decedent-policyholder died).

3. If the policy is an established whole life policy, the value is found by adding any unearned portion of the last premium to the interpolated terminal reserve.

4. If the policy is a term policy, the value is the unused premium.

VALUATION OF U.S. GOVERNMENT BONDS

Series E bonds are valued at their redemption price (market value) as of the date of death since they are neither negotiable nor transferable and the only definitely ascertainable value is the amount at which the Treasury will redeem them.

Certain U.S. Treasury Bonds (so-called "flower bonds") owned by a decedent at the date of death and forming part of his gross estate, may be redeemed at par value if used to pay federal estate taxes. These bonds are valued at the higher of the market price or par value.[7]

Even if such bonds are not used to pay estate taxes, the courts have often held that where the bonds could have been used for the payment of estate taxes, to that extent they will be valued at the higher of the market or par value.[8] Where the bonds could not be applied to pay the estate tax, their value is market (the mean quoted selling price).

VALUATION OF HOUSEHOLD AND PERSONAL EFFECTS

The general rule for valuing household property and personal effects such as watches, rings, etc., is: the "willing buyer-willing seller" rule. A room by room itemization is typical, especially where household goods include articles of artistic or intrinsic value such as jewelry, furs, silverware, paintings, engravings, antiques, books, statuary, oriental rugs, coin or stamp collections.

In other than community property states, "household goods" and like personalty acquired by and used by husband and wife during marriage are generally presumed to be the property of the husband. Therefore, in the absence of sufficient evidence to rebut this presumption, household goods and personal effects would be includible in the husband's estate.

VALUATION OF ANNUITIES, LIFE ESTATES, TERMS FOR YEARS, REMAINDERS AND REVERSIONS

Commercial annuities (annuities under contracts issued by companies regularly engaged in their sale) are valued by reference to the price at which the company issues comparable contracts. A retirement income policy, from the point in time that there is no longer an insurance element, is treated as a contract for the payment of an annuity.

Where the annuity is non-commercial, such as a private annuity, the present value of future payments determines its fair market value. Likewise, for gift and estate tax purposes, the fair market value of life estates, terms for years, remainders, and reversions is their present value.

An annuity is defined as a systematic liquidation of principal and interest. Payments might be made for the life of the annuitant (life annuity) or over a period of years (term certain).

A life estate is a disposition of property in which the primary beneficiary receives distributions of only income. Payments might be made for the life of the recipient or could be based on the life of a third party but the income beneficiary of a life estate receives no right to enjoy the principal. In other words, a life estate is the right of a person for his life, or for the life of another person, to receive the income from or the use of certain property. An example would be, "I give my home to my wife for life." The wife's interest would be a life estate. At her death, the property would go to some other party, called a "remainderman," or revert to the grantor.

In the case of a term certain arrangement, the present value of income for a given number of years is found in a like manner.

A remainder (the beneficiary gets the principal after a third party has enjoyed the income for life, or for a given period of time) is actuarially equivalent to a "reversion". An example of a remainder would be "to my son John, for life, remainder to Mary." Instead of coming back to the grantor (a reversion) the property "remains" away from the grantor and goes instead to Mary. Mary is said to have a remainder interest. An example of a reversion is where the principal (after a given beneficiary has enjoyed an income for life or for a given period) "reverts" to the grantor. If the grantor dies before the person enjoying the lifetime interest, his right to "will" that reversion to his heirs, who will some day receive the principal, is valued under the same rules as annuities, remainders, and life estates.

Changes Made By TAMRA '88

One of the most significant changes made by the 1988 legislation (TAMRA '88) was to change the means by which annuities, life estates, terms for years, reversions, and remainders are valued. To better understand the changes made, let us first consider the valuation procedure.

The first step in valuing an annuity based on a life (or on the joint lives of two or more people), a life estate, or a reversion or remainder based on a life (or joint lives) is to convert one of the unknowns (the length of the lifetime involved) to a known (life expectancy). This is done by means of a mortality table, which, based on a study of the longevities of a large number of people over a selected period of time, indicates the expectancy of life (in years) for a mythical individual who represents the average experience at each age of life.

The second step is to determine a proper interest rate (the second unknown) that should be attributed to the interest being valued. When that interest rate is determined, a valuation table can be constructed which converts the two factors to be applied, life expectancy and the rate of interest, into one factor to be applied to the amount of the periodic payment, to determine the present worth or value of the property interest.

The valuation tables in this appendix (Tables A and B at Figure B.4a, and Tables LN and A(2)) are products of the law as it existed prior to TAMRA '88. Those tables are now used only in cases where the date as of which the valuation is to be made occurs before May 1, 1989.

Under pre-TAMRA law, the mortality table used as the basis of the valuation tables was specified in the regulations but not in the Internal Revenue Code. Now the Code specifies that (1) within three months after enactment, the Treasury must prescribe initial tables based on the same mortality experience as used for purposes of federal estate tax valuation on November 10, 1988, (2) before December 31, 1989, the Treasury must revise the initial tables to take into account the most recent mortality experience available as of the time of such revision; and (3) the tables must be revised at least once every ten years thereafter to take into account the most recent mortality experience available as of the time of the revision.

Under pre-TAMRA law, valuation tables prescribed by the Treasury remained constant for years at a time. From 1970 until 1983, valuation tables based on a six percent interest rate were used. From 1983 until 1989, unisex tables based a ten percent interest rate were used (see Figure B.4a). Now the Code provides that the valuation tables must be based on an interest rate (rounded to the nearest 2/10ths of one percent) equal to 120 percent of the federal midterm rate in effect for the month in which the valuation date falls.

Once the mortality table upon which valuation is based is determined, it is possible, of course, to construct a series of valuation tables on that base assuming a whole array of possible interest rates. Perhaps this is what the Treasury will ultimately provide under the new law. Another possibility is that we will no longer have valuation tables, but formulas for determining values. Subsection (e) of the newly added Code section 7520 notes cryptically, "For purposes of this section, the term 'tables' includes formulas." What we will *not* have is a relatively stable valuation table upon which to base our planning.

For the sake of completeness, two qualifications need to be added to this explanation of the new law respecting valuation. First, these new valuation provisions do not apply to interests valued with respect to qualified plans (including tax sheltered annuities and IRAs) or in other situations specified in Treasury regulations. Second, if an income, estate, or gift tax charitable contribution is allowable for any part of the property transferred, the taxpayer may elect to use such federal midterm rate for either of the two months preceding the month in which the valuation date falls. However, if a transfer of more than one interest in the same property is made with respect to which the taxpayer could use the same interest rate, such interest rate is to be used with respect to each such interest.[9]

VALUATION OF LISTED STOCKS

Where a stock has an established market and quotations are available to value the stock as of the date in question, the fair market value per share on the applicable valuation date governs for both gift and estate tax purposes.

The FMV is based on selling prices when there is a market for the stock or bond. This would be the mean between the highest and lowest quoted selling price on the valuation date. If there were no sales on the valuation date, but there were sales on dates within a reasonable period both before and after the valuation date, the FMV is determined by taking a weighted average of the means between the highest and lowest sales on the nearest date before and the nearest date after the valuation. The average is then weighted inversely by the respective number of trading days between the selling date and the valuation date.

Where there is a large block of stock which could not be marketed in an orderly manner, the block might depress the market because it could not be converted to cash as readily as could a few shares. Therefore, selling prices and bid and asked prices may not reflect fair market value. Sometimes it may be necessary to value this type of stock as if it were closely held and not actively traded. If this can be established, a reasonable modification of the normal basis for determining FMV can be made. In some cases, a "blockage" discount is determined by the effect that block would have had on the market if it were sold over a reasonable period of time and in a prudent manner.[10] A similar situation occurs where sales at or near the date of death are few or of a sporadic nature and may not indicate a fair market value.[11]

The converse of the "blockage" situation above is where the block of stock to be valued represents a controlling interest (either actual or effective) in a going business. Here, the price of normally traded shares may have little relation to the true value of the controlling lot. The large block could have the effect of increasing value because of its element of control.

VALUATION OF CORPORATE BONDS

The valuation of bonds is similar to that of listed common stock. The means of the selling prices on or near the applicable valuation date, or, if there were no sales, the means of bona fide asked prices weighted inversely to the number of trading days from the valuation date will determine the fair market value of the bonds.

In the absence of sales or bid and asked prices, the value must be determined by:

(1) Ascertaining the soundness of the security.
(2) Comparing the interest yield on the bond in question to yields on similar bonds.
(3) Examining the date of maturity.
(4) Comparing prices for listed bonds of corporations engaged in similar types of business.
(5) Checking the extent to which the bond is secured.
(6) Weighing all other relevant factors including the opinion of experts, the good will of the business, the industry's economic outlook, the company's position in the industry and its management.

VALUATION OF STOCK OF CLOSELY HELD CORPORATIONS

There are at least seven situations in which the estate planner must value a business or professional practice. Valuation plays a critical role when a planner needs to

- plan for a client's estate liquidity
- establish a price for buy-sell purposes (should a buy-out be necessitated by death, disability or other health problems, retirement, or lifetime termination of relationship (e.g., sale of an interest in the business or practice to a third party)
- properly recognize the business's or practice's worth in a client's prenuptial or postnuptial agreement
- apportion assets in a marital dissolution
- ascertain the worth of the business or practice as loan collateral
- perform a "fiscal checkup" to test the financial health of a client's business or practice, detect adverse financial trends, or uncover opportunities (for instance. a doctor might find that patients are getting older and the business or practice should try to attract younger people or can profitably move into a new area of specialty)
- prepare an estate tax valuation

In the settlement of many estates, the valuation of closely held corporate stock can be a most difficult, time-consuming, and costly problem, especially when a confrontation arises between the Executor and the Internal Revenue Service. But careful use of a properly drafted restrictive business agreement can help alleviate and control the problem.

What exactly is "closely held stock"? Various criteria have been used to define such stock. Some of these are: (a) the number of stockholders; (b) restrictions imposed on a shareholder's ability to transfer the stock; (c) absence of exchange listing or regular quotation in the "over-the-counter" market; (d) an irregular, limited history of sales or exchanges.

For general purposes, however, stock can be considered "closely held" where there is some question as to whether its value can be found solely by reference to an established market. The problem of valuing closely held stock is compounded because, by definition, such stock is seldom traded.

The relevant Internal Revenue Code Sections and Regulations[12] are of little help. They are so vague and general that their application to a specific valuation question is of minimal planning value.

Valuing Stock for Estate Planning Purposes

Basic factors to consider. The fair market value of a closely held corporation is determined in the same manner as stock in a professional practice. Reg. §20.2031-3; Rev. Rul. 80-202, 1980-2 CB 363. In determining the value of a closely held business, Rev. Rul. 59-60, 1959-1 CB 237, the master guideline for valuing all businesses, requires that eight factors must be considered:

- *Nature of the business and the history of the enterprise from its inception.* This factor measures the risk, stability, depth of management of the business, and the diversity of its operations. With respect to the valuation of a professional practice, the appraiser should review the stability of the practice's financial history, its growth patterns, changes in ownership, market share, marketing approach, and "product" breakdown. For example, is this a law practice that does 70 percent negligence and personal injury work, 20 percent financial and estate planning, and 10 percent real estate? Significant events should be emphasized and events not likely to recur should be eliminated.

- *Economic outlook in general and for the specific industry in particular.* Here, the appraiser must evaluate the "industry" outlook and the position of the practitioner with reference to his competition. The appraiser should consider the cyclical nature of the practitioner's business, the direction of the national economy, and any unique elements in the professional's practice position.

- *Book value of the stock and the financial condition of the business.* The appraiser here must consider the asset value of the professional's practice. Note that the professional's statements are historical-cost based; they should be adjusted to reflect fair market value. Depreciation as recorded under generally accepted accounting principles need not bear any relationship to economic depreciation and the true net value of the assets under consideration.

- *Earnings capacity of the company.* The earnings of a professional practice have been held by many valuation authorities to be the essence of its fair market value, since "everyone knows that the value of shares in a . . . company depends chiefly on what it will earn." (Judge Learned Hand in *Borg v. International Silver*, 11 F.2d 147 (1925).) What is at issue is earnings *capacity*, future income potential, not net income. Adjustments should be made for salaries, travel, and entertainment expenses, nonrecurring items, and potential legal and tax liabilities. In a corporate setting, note that loans to shareholders may represent disguised dividends; loans from shareholders may represent equity rather than debt.

- *Dividend paying capacity.* The emphasis again is on *capacity*, not actual payout. With the professional corporation, the appraiser should focus on cash flow projections and relate dividend capacity to earnings capacity, with due consideration for the need to reinvest in the professional's practice.

- *Goodwill or intangible values.* Goodwill has been extensively discussed above. In its simplest form, goodwill is the excess earnings of the practice over the normal return on tangible assets. Note that the normal return should be the "fair rate of return" earned by comparable practitioners. Tangible assets should be valued at their fair market value rather than at historically based book value.

- *Sales of the stock and the size of the block to be valued.* Here, recent sales are most important. Has the interest in the practice been sold to insiders? What percentage of the practice has been sold? Have there been any recent events since the sale that would affect significantly the value of the practice?

- *The market price of stock of corporations engaged in the same or a similar line of business having their stock traded in a free and open market.* This factor is extremely difficult to apply to professional practices. Few professional practices exist as public corporations. Those that do rarely are comparable to closely held professional practices. A publicly held practice by definition has a value premium for marketability.

The following discussion summarizes four often-used approaches to business valuation: (1) book value, (2) comparable company, (3) capitalization of income, and (4) going concern value.

(1) Book Value

Book value (essentially assets minus liabilities) is a particularly good place to begin the process of valuing a closely held corporation in each of the following situations:

(1) Where the business in question is primarily an asset holding company—such as an investment company.

(2) Where the company is in the real estate development business and assets are the major profit making factor.

(3) Where one person is the sole or major driving force since such businesses are typically worth only their liquidation value upon the death, disability, or termination of employment of such a person.

(4) Where the liquidation of the corporation is in process or imminent at the valuation date. The impact of sacrifice sales and capital gains taxation must often be considered since the true value of a liquidating business is only the amount available to shareholders after all expenses and taxes.

(5) Where the business is highly competitive but only marginally profitable. Past profits thus become an unreliable tool to measure potential future earnings.

(6) Where the assets or the business itself is relatively new.

(7) Where some form of merger is likely to occur with another firm.

(8) Where the business is experiencing large deficits.

Book value must be adjusted since the assets of most businesses are usually carried on the company's books at historical cost rather than fair market value.

Tools and Techniques

Adjustments are recommended in the following cases:

(1) When assets are valued at cost. For instance, the primary assets of a closely held investment company consist of marketable securities. These are typically carried on the company's books at cost. Likewise, land is an asset most companies will carry at cost but which may be worth considerably more on the open market. The result is a book value which bears little or no relationship to the true present worth of the business.

(2) When assets have been depreciated at a rate in excess of their true decline in economic value. A good example is the operating company (one which produces or sells products or services to the public) that has purchased machinery or equipment originally costing $1,000,000 but which, on the company's books, has been depreciated down to $300,000. The equipment may be worth a lot more or a lot less than either its cost or the $300,000 figure at which it is presently carried.

(3) When items such as potential lawsuits or unfavorable long-term leases have not been shown in the footnotes of the firm's balance sheet.

(4) When one or more assets with significant economic value have been completely "written off"—thus reflecting a book value far below the price which they should realistically bring.

(5) When the business has carried assets such as franchises and goodwill on the books at a nominal cost.

(6) When the business experiences difficulty in collecting its accounts receivable.

(7) When the firm's inventory includes goods that are either obsolete or for some other reason are not readily marketable.

(8) Where the working capital or liquidity position of the business is poor (low current assets relative to current liabilities).

(9) Where the firm is burdened with a substantial amount of long-term indebtedness.

(10) Where the retained earnings are high only because they have been accumulated over a long period of time. Such a business may have poor current earnings and the outlook for increased earnings in the future may be dim.

After the adjustments described above have been made, the value of any other class of stock with a priority as to dividends, voting rights, or preference to assets in the event of a sale or liquidation must be subtracted. For example, the owner of common stock can't realize the value of the assets until owners of preferred stock have been satisfied.

Once the adjusted book value has been determined for the entire business, it is then necessary to divide the book value by the number of shares outstanding to determine the value per share.

Book value should rarely be used as the only means of valuing a closely-held business. It should be used in conjunction with or as a means of testing the relevancy of the capitalization of earnings and other methods. (Be sure not to "double count" an asset when combining two or more methods).

Book value should not be used when capital plays a minor role in profit making or where you are valuing the stock of a party who does not have the voting power to force liquidation, since in that case book values have little relevance.

Book Value Calculation

Input:	"Adjusted" Asset Value of Common Stock		$500,000
Input:	Total Adjusted Liabilities	$100,000	
Input:	Par Value of Preferred Stock	$50,000	
	Total Deductions	$150,000	
	Adjusted Book Value of Entire Business		$350,000
Input:	Number of Common Shares Outstanding		1,000
	Value Per Share of Common Stock ..		$350.00

(2) Valuation By Reference To Comparable (Traded Securities) Companies

A business can sometimes be valued by reference to the value of a comparable company if the stock of that second company is listed, and actively traded, on a securities exchange or on the over-the-counter (OTC) market.

The price per share of the publicly traded stock is divided by its earnings per share. The resulting ratio is then applied to the earnings per share of the business to be valued in order to arrive at the market value per share.

Comparable traded securities research should start with federal government publications such a the *Standard Industrial Classification* manual (which categorizes industries), the *S.E.C. Directory of Companies Required to File Annual Reports* (which, as its name implies, lists companies which must file reports under various S.E.C. acts), the U.S. Department of Commerce, *Census of Business* (which is a compilation of statistics and ratios on various businesses), Dun & Bradstreet's *Dun's Review* (which gives key operating and financial ratios), Moody's *Investors Service and Manual* (which provides a detailed description of many publicly held corporations), and Standard & Poor's *Corporation Records* (which provides financial and operating ratios for many corporations).

Be sure to check trade magazines for the industry in question. Many associations also provide detailed information for members of their industry.

In searching for comparable companies look for similarities in product line, service, size, marketing and geographic area, growth, profitability, overhead, and competitive position. Examine balance sheets and income statements (use the ratios template) to compare ratios and trends. Seldom, if ever, will a perfect match be found and many adjustments may have to be made even after a "close fit" is found.

This technique has a number of shortcomings: first, it is difficult to use. Second, an enormous expenditure of time and effort is required to compile accurate and adequate information concerning the business to be valued, the comparable business or businesses, and then to analyze and evaluate the data.

The larger the closely-held business, the more likely this approach will be appropriate since the size, corporate capital structure, earnings, liabilities, rate of growth, and diversification are more likely to be comparable to a publicly traded company.

Value Per Share of Closely Held Stock

Input:	Per Share Market Price of Similar Publicly Traded Company	$45.00
Input:	Earnings Per Share of Similar Publicly Traded Company	$4.50
Input:	Earnings Per Share of Business to be Valued	$14.00
	Computed Price/Earnings Ratio	10.00
	Equivalent Capitalization Rate	0.10
	Value Per Share of Closely Held Business	$140.00

(3) Capitalization of Income

No formula exists that applies to all assets and that will be accepted by both the IRS and the courts. Converting the projected flow of income from a business or asset into its present value, i.e., "capitalizing the income," provides a simple, reasonably accurate, and commonly accepted way of estimating fair market value.

The concept of income capitalization is simple: determine what amount of income is realistic and proper under the circumstances and then apply a capitalization rate that meets the same criterion. In essence the capitalization rate is the desired rate of return; the rate of return an investor would be willing to accept for the given level of risk. A high risk investment would equate to a high capitalization rate (which in turn results in a lower value). The asset or business is then presumed to be worth the result when adjusted earnings are divided by the capitalization rate.

The GraphPAK graph at Figure B.3 illustrates the valuation of a business generating adjusted earnings of $100,000 a year using five different capitalization rates.

Transforming theory into practice is often complex and frustrating. The brief comments below, pertaining to "adjusting" the earnings and selecting the appropriate rate of return may help:
(A) Adjustments to income (in the case of a business, use five year average after-tax profits):
(1) Add back excessive salaries
(2) Reduce earnings if salaries were too low
(3) Add back bonuses paid to stockholder-employees
(4) Add back excessive rents paid to shareholders
(5) Reduce earnings where rents paid to shareholders were below what was reasonable in the market
(6) Eliminate non-recurring income or expense items
(7) Adjust for excessive depreciation
(8) Adjust earnings for major changes in accounting procedures, widely fluctuating or cyclical profits, or abnormally inflated (or deflated) earnings.
(9) If there has been a strong upward or downward earnings trend, "weight the average" to obtain a more realistic appraisal of the company's prospects.
(B) Determine the capitalization rate (this is the amount that is divided into adjusted earnings). The result is the same as multiplying the reciprocal of the rate, (the result of dividing the number one by 5). In other words, you obtain the same result by multiplying $100,000 of income by 5 as you do if you divide the income by .20.

In deciding on a capitalization rate, consider the following:
(1) A smaller capitalization rate will result in a higher value. A higher capitalization rate results in a lower value. You can check this by examining the value of a business with an adjusted after tax income of $50,000 a year capitalized at 6 percent (that is, divided by .06), $833,333 and comparing the result with one capitalized at 15 percent (i.e. divided by .15), $333,333.
(2) Stable businesses with large capital asset bases and established goodwill should be less risky investments and you should use a lower capitalization rate than if you were valuing a small business with little capital, financial history, or management depth.

Assign a high capitalization rate to a personal business that depends on the presence of only one or two key people. an investor purchasing this type of business would want a high rate of return as a reward for that risk. (Another way to say the same thing is that such an investor would not make the investment unless a rapid return of capital through a high income stream was expected.)

Tools and Techniques

Figure B.3

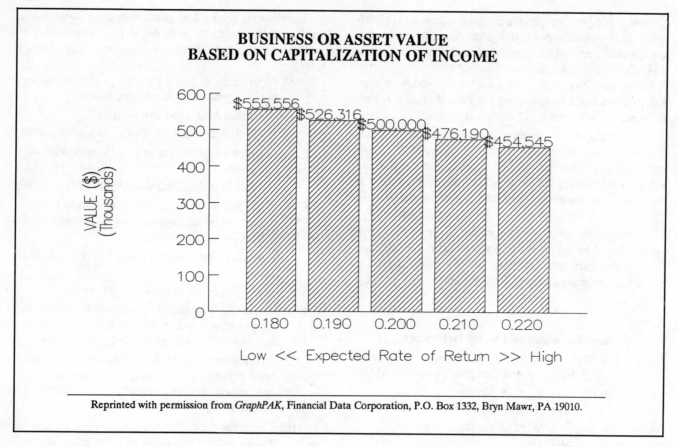

BUSINESS OR ASSET VALUE
BASED ON CAPITALIZATION OF INCOME

Reprinted with permission from *GraphPAK*, Financial Data Corporation, P.O. Box 1332, Bryn Mawr, PA 19010.

It is important to note that there are no "correct" or "official" rates. Even the IRS Uses different rates at different times and under different circumstances. It is for this reason that the capitalization of income template provides ten automatic options (which you can change to provide an infinite number of variations).

(4) Valuation of a Business As a "Going Concern"

A closely-held business should (and often does) produce an income in excess of the amount that could be expected from the mere employment of the capital its shareholders have invested. That additional amount of income is derived from an intangible value in the business, a value in excess of the total value of the tangible assets.

By capitalizing this "earnings attributable to intangibles," i.e., by dividing the additional profits generated by the firm's goodwill, by an appropriate rate, it is possible to estimate goodwill value. If this amount is then added to book (net tangible asset) value, the total business value can be found.

Some of the elements that may comprise a firm's goodwill include:

(1) Location of the business

(2) Reputation of the business

(3) Public recognition of the company's name

(4) Lists of customers and prospects owned by the business

(5) Management effectiveness and depth

(6) Sales, operations, and accounting skills

(7) Employee morale

(8) Position of the business relative to competitors

(9) Other factors that generate income in excess of that amount which could be expected after multiplying the value of tangible assets by a reasonable rate of return.

Note that goodwill does not include the portion of profits attributable to the corporation's ownership of patents, copyrights, formulas, or trademarks, even though they are intangible, since these are all specifically identifiable.

Goodwill, as in the case with other valuation formulas and procedures, should be used only as a guideline and not as the sole determinate of value. Goodwill has minimal relevance to the valuation of most investment companies since they usually do not have large amounts of intangibles. Officially the IRS does not give strong credibility to goodwill (although the service still insists that goodwill must be taken into account in the valuation process).

Caution: Before using this table, be sure to read the explanation of the changes made in the valuation of annuities, life estates, etc. by 1988 legislation, at page 391.

TABLE LN

(1) Age X	(2) lx	(1) Age X	(2) lx
0	100,000	56	84,142
1	97,998	57	83,103
2	97,876	58	81,988
3	97,792	59	80,798
4	97,724	60	79,529
5	97,668	61	78,181
6	97,619	62	76,751
7	97,573	63	75,236
8	97,531	64	73,631
9	97,494	65	71,933
10	97,460	66	70,139
11	97,430	67	68,246
12	97,401	68	66,254
13	97,367	69	64,160
14	97,322	70	61,984
15	97,621	71	59,715
16	97,181	72	57,360
17	97,083	73	54,913
18	96,970	74	52,363
19	96,846	75	49,705
20	96,716	76	46,946
21	96,580	77	44,101
22	96,438	78	41,192
23	96,292	79	38,245
24	96,145	80	35,285
25	96,000	81	32,323
26	95,859	82	29,375
27	95,721	83	26,469
28	95,586	84	23,638
29	95,448	85	20,908
30	95,307	86	18,282
31	95,158	87	15,769
32	95,003	88	13,407
33	94,840	89	11,240
34	94,666	90	9,297
35	94,482	91	7,577
36	94,285	92	6,070
37	94,073	93	4,773
38	93,843	94	3,682
39	93,593	95	2,786
40	93,322	96	2,068
41	93,028	97	1,511
42	92,712	98	1,087
43	92,368	99	772
44	91,995	100	542
45	91,587	101	375
46	91,144	102	257
47	90,662	103	175
48	90,142	104	117
49	89,579	105	78
50	88,972	106	52
51	88,315	107	34
52	87,605	108	22
53	86,838	109	14
54	86,007	110	0
55	85,110		

Tools and Techniques

Comparison Chart

"MULTIPLIER" (MULTIPLY THIS TIMES EARNINGS)			CAPITALIZATION RATE (DIVIDE THIS OR INTO EARNINGS)
LOW	28.6	=	3.5%
RISK	25	=	4 %
	20	=	5 %
	16.67	=	6 %
	14.29	=	7 %
	12.5	=	8 %
	11.11	=	9 %
	10	=	10 %
	9.09	=	11 %
	8.33	=	12 %
	7.69	=	13 %
	7.14	=	14 %
	6.67	=	15 %
	6.25	=	16 %
	5.88	=	17 %
	5.56	=	18 %
	5.26	=	19 %
	5	=	20 %
	4	=	25 %
HIGH	3.33	=	30 %
RISK	2.86	=	35 %

Going Concern Value

Input:	Average Annual Earnings	$100,000
Input:	Average Annual Asset Value	$500,000
Input:	Estimated Capitalization Rate	0.200
Input:	Rate of Return on Tangible Assets	0.16

Option	Return On Tangible Assets	Earn From Tangible Assets	Earn From Intangible Assets	Goodwill Value	Total Business Value
1	0.160	$80,000	$20,000	$100,000	$600,000
2	0.170	$85,000	$15,000	$75,000	$575,000
3	0.180	$90,000	$10,000	$50,000	$550,000
4	0.190	$95,000	$5,000	$25,000	$525,000
5	0.200	$100,000	$0	$0	$500,000

A reduction in value is often allowed because the shares being valued represent a "minority" interest in the business. Courts tend to aggregate the lack of marketability inherent in a closely held corporation with the minority interest principle although the "minority interest" discount arises because such shares have no power to force dividends, compel liquidation, or to control corporate policy. This in turn limits the potential market for such stock to the remaining (an usually controlling) shareholders and reduces the price at which such shares would be purchased.

Conversely, where the shares in question represent a "controlling" interest, the I.R.S. will generally attempt to increase the stock's value. "The size of the block of stock itself is a relevant factor to be considered. Although it is true that a minority interest in an unlisted corporation's stock is more difficult to sell than a similar block of listed stock, it is equally true that control of a corporation, either actual or in effect, representing as it does an added element of value, may justify a higher value for a specific block of stock."

Discount For Loss of Key Employee

Both the IRS and the courts have long recognized that the loss of a manager, scientist, salesperson, or other key individual will almost always have a serious effect on the earning power and sometimes on the very stability of a business. Although the principle applies in publicly-held businesses, it is particularly true in a closely-held corporation where profits are dependent on the ability, initiative, judgment, or business connections of a single person or small group of owner-employees. A discount in valuation may therefore be appropriate. (This same concept may also be used in determining the amount of key employee insurance a corporation should own.)

There is no universally recognized and accepted formula for computing the economic effect of the loss of a key person. One used in several court cases utilizes a discount approach: a percentage discount is taken from the going-concern value of the business.

Some authorities feel that if the business will survive the death of the key employee, and in time a competent successor can be found, a discount factor of from fifteen to twenty percent should be used. Where the business is likely to fail, or be placed in serious jeopardy upon the death (or disability) of the key employee, a discount of from twenty to forty-five percent is more appropriate. The exact discount factor should be arrived at through consultation with the officers of the company and the firm's accounting and legal advisers.

Some questions that should be answered in the process of determining the factor (or range of factors) to be used include:

(1) How long will it take for a new person to reach the efficiency of the key individual?

(2) How much will it cost to locate and situate a replacement? Will the new employee demand more salary? How much will it cost to train the new person?

(3) What mistakes is a replacement likely to make during the "break in" period and how much are those mistakes likely to cost the company?

(4) What proportion of the firm's current net profits are attributable to the key employee?

(5) Is the employee engaged in any projects which, if left unfinished at death or disability, would prove

costly to the business? How costly? Would a potentially profitable project have to be abandoned or would a productive department have to be closed?

(6) Would the employee's death result in the loss of clientele or personnel attracted to the business because of his or her personality, social contacts, or unique skills, talents, or managerial ability?

(7) What effect would the key employee's death have on the firm's credit standing?

(8) What proportion of the firm's actual loss is it willing to self insure, if any?

There are a number of ways—other than the approach used in the template—to value a key person's contribution to a corporation's profits. One way is to measure the number of working years remaining to the executive (say 10). Estimate the annual loss of earnings attributable to that person (say $30,000 per year). Then discount (see present value templates) the value of that annual loss (for example, at ten percent). This will result in the present value of the key person's services, about $113,000.

Alternatively, the goodwill template could be adjusted to measure the goodwill produced through the efforts of the management team and this total would then further be apportioned (perhaps by relative salaries) among the key employees.

For instance, assume a firm had an average annual asset value of $450,000 and an average annual earnings after taxes of $75,000. If ten percent were thought to be a fair rate return on tangibles, then $45,000 ($450,000 x .10) of the $75,000 would be attributable to tangibles. The remaining $30,000 would be attributable to goodwill. Assume sixty percent of this, $18,000, could reasonably be allocated to management. If it takes five years to replace the entire management team, then $18,000 should be multiplied by five, or a total of $90,000. If the executive in question drew eighty percent of the total salares of the management team, then that person's worth would approximate $72,000 ($90,000 x .80).

Most shareholders of closely held corporations restrict the marketability of co-shareholder's stock through "purchase options" or mandatory buy-sell agreements. If the terms of such agreement definitely fix the values of the shares in question, it is not necessary to examine either book value or earnings. The price fixed in the restrictive agreement will serve as the shares' market value, but to "peg" the value of such stock for federal estate tax purposes:

1. The agreement as to per share value must be made at arm's length and must have been fair and adequate at the time the agreement was executed.

2. The agreement must be binding during the lifetime of the stockholder; that is, he must be obligated to offer the stock to the corporation or other shareholders (a "first offer" commitment) at the speci-

Key Employee Valuation		
Input: Fair Market Value of Business with Key Employee $750,000		
Input: Discount Percent (%) without Employee		
Discount Percent	Value W/O Key Employee	Value of Key Employee
0.16	$630,000	$120,000
0.17	$622,500	$127,500
0.18	$615,000	$135,000
0.19	$607,500	$142,500
0.20	$600,000	$150,000
0.21	$592,500	$157,500
0.22	$585,000	$165,000
0.23	$577,500	$172,500
0.24	$570,000	$180,000

fied offer price before offering it to an outsider if he wishes to dispose of his stock during his lifetime.

3. The agreement must be "binding" at death—his executor must be legally obligated to sell the shares to the corporation at the price fixed by the agreement. Furthermore, the price stated in the agreement must either be fixed, (e.g., fixed dollar price or book value on the repurchase date) or determinable according to the formula.

The Treasury believes that taxpayers in general tend to keep values low and therefore restrictions which tend to limit the value of family owned closely held stock will be closely scrutinized to determine whether the agreement is a bona fide arms length business arrangement and not just a device to pass the decedent's shares for less than adequate consideration.[13]

VALUING A PROFESSIONAL PRACTICE
This section explains why estate planners must be able to value professional practices and discusses

- how a professional practice differs from a typical business, and why these differences are important
- considerations in valuing goodwill
- how to value a professional's stock for buy-sell purposes
- a shortcut approach to valuing a professional practice
- how to use the "prior transactions," "capitalization of billings," and "excess earnings" valuation methods
- rough rules of thumb

Tools and Techniques

A Complex Task

Valuation of a manufacturing business is difficult enough; the valuation of a professional practice, with its many intangible factors, is more complex still. Productivity, goodwill, and the multitude of other factors that affect a professional practice are difficult to quantify. Rules of thumb may differ widely from one appraiser to another and from one group of professionals to another. Some variables may have greater weight for some buyers than for others. For example, a young doctor seeking to purchase a practice may wish to buy one for about the same costs he'd incur if starting from scratch. Conversely, many hospitals purchase the practices of retiring staff physicians to help insure that the practice will continue to fill hospital beds. The hospital might pay more for the practice if the doctor typically referred patients to it, or if the practice might otherwise be sold to a competing hospital.

The questions asked and the methods used differ depending on the purpose of the valuation and the type of practice in question. For instance, valuations for divorce, one of the most common reasons a professional practice is valued, will emphasize the practitioner's age and health, experience, length of practice, financial success, skills, and reputation. The value of the goodwill these factors might generate could be more important to the divorce court than the factors leading to strong marketability which would be important for estate tax purposes. Factors established by statute and case law, which tend to vary widely from state to state, must also be taken into account. For example, some states give more weight than others to minority interests or lack of marketability discounts with reference to professional corporations.

Why a Professional Practice is Different

A professional practice differs from other businesses mainly because of:

Expertise. The expertise — or, more important, the *perceived* expertise — of the professionals involved is of paramount importance in determining the fees that can be charged and the income that can be earned from the practice. The education, training, and experience a professional brings to his practice, and the "consumer's" dependence on the delivery of the practitioner's services, are extremely important economic factors which must be considered in determining value. For example, a patient needing brain surgery typically does not shop for a bargain price.

Entry barriers. Higher education, licensing, and certification requirements all serve to slow or limit entrants into professional practice. If, for any reason, licensing or certification is lost, the practitioner can no longer practice. If a professional dies or is permanently disabled, his family members cannot continue to operate the practice unless they are duly licensed and certified in the same profession.

Professional goodwill. Reputation and recommendations are the life blood of the professional practice. Although some professionals obtain significant business from "walk-in" traffic due to location or advertisement, most depend mainly on referrals from peers and the recommendation of present clients to bring in new business. This is particularly true with respect to specialists. For this reason, trust, respect, and "liking" of the practitioner — by peers as well as patients or clients — are crucial to the success of the practice.

Nontransferability. Substitution may be difficult or impossible. Professional skills are to some extent unique and not interchangeable. Consider the relationship between psychiatrist and patient: If the psychiatrist is ill for three weeks and unable to work, an attorney-spouse can't "run the store."

Continuing education. In most professions, information becomes outdated, and the professional must engage in continuous education. This may be through formal course work or by keeping up with professional journals and magazines.

Why The Differences Are Important

Most businesses have as part of their value an asset called "goodwill." This can be defined as the quantified expectation of future profits from some source other than mere dollars at work. For instance, if a firm enjoys $80,000 of earnings on a $60,000 capital investment which can reasonably be expected to return 20% ($12,000) at a given risk level, then $68,000 of income ($80,000-$12,000) is attributable to something other than capital. This business-oriented goodwill is an asset of the business that generates value over and above the entity's net asset value.

In a professional practice there are two types of goodwill: business-oriented (stemming from the entity) *and* professional (originating from the individual).

Business-oriented goodwill is attributable to the elements of a professional practice that are similar to those of a regular business: location, operating systems, staff, and patient or client base. Business-oriented goodwill can have significant transferable value, value that can be sold to another licensed practitioner.

Professional goodwill, on the other hand, depends on the unique characteristics of the particular practitioner. At the professional's death, disability, or retirement, that portion of the practice income attributable to professional goodwill will generally leave with the individual. Much of this personal goodwill, however, can be transferred in a sale to another practitioner by creating a well-organized transition in which the departing professional lends credibility to the entering professional.

Valuing Business-Oriented Goodwill and Future Income Flow

Although many sources are available to provide information for valuing a practice's transferable business-oriented goodwill and its likely future earnings, the most accurate source will typically be the firm's own CPA. The CPA should examine ten factors.

Projected earnings. Projected earnings are normally an extension of past earnings. Financial statements and tax returns (specifically income statements, balance sheets, and cash flow statements) should be examined and adjusted to determine:

- *The level of gross income.* Net income figures may be misleading, since principals may be taking profits in the form of perquisites and benefits as well as salaries. The CPA should determine how salaries compare to the "norm" for services performed. Are they too high? Alternatively, if they are lower than comparable payments to similar professionals, does this indicate cash flow or earnings problems?

- *Earnings trend.* At least five years should be reviewed. Measure each year's amount as a percent of a "base" year. A business "trending up" indicates the likely presence of growing goodwill. However, the CPA must also consider whether there are unusual or nonrecurring factors that artificially inflate or deflate income. Large pension contributions, malpractice claims, fees or court costs, and salary structures should be studied particularly carefully. The inability of one or more professionals to work during the period examined would obviously have a strong impact on earnings. Did the professional, out of choice, work 40 hours a week or only 20?

Competition. An increased demand for established practices is typically reflected in an increase in prices. This has occurred in a number of professions due, in large part, to the increase in the number of newly licensed professionals — e.g., dentistry. An appraiser must also consider the number of other practitioners in the area, how thoroughly their practices saturate the market, and the price trend for services similar to those being valued.

Size of patient or client base. The greater the number of satisfied current patients or clients, the greater the likelihood that a large number of referrals will be made to the practice. More emphasis should be given to this factor when selling the entire practice than when valuing the practice for purposes of appointing assets in a divorce or legal separation. The distribution of the client base should also be evaluated. Consider whether the clients are repeaters, recent additions, referrals from prior clients, young or old, etc. How many patients or clients are seen each day?

Payment sources. How the professional is paid greatly influences both the level and the stability of the practice's income. Measure how likely the practice is to be paid for services rendered, and how soon. Government programs typically pay less per procedure than the usual fee, so the source of payment may also indicate how much will be paid. Questions that should be asked by an appraiser include:

- Is the practice dependent on any particular group of patients or clients for a significant portion of its income?

- What percentage of patients pay bills through private insurance, Medicare, Medicaid, other sources?

- What is the aging of the professional's accounts receivable? Are monthly bills paid in 30, 60, 90 days, etc.? (This is a good indication of the financing needs and efficiency of the practice's collection procedures.)

Practitioner's workload. Income figures alone do not tell how many hours it took to generate a given level of profit. A practice that took 40 hours of work to generate a given amount of earnings is worth more than one that took 70 hours to develop the same earnings. Factors that must be considered in this area include:

- Is the practice a "personal" type or "mass production" type? How much time spent with the patient or client was due merely to the practitioner's work style?

- Does the practitioner spend time on administrative or other problems which could be handled more efficiently and at lower cost by an office manager or other staff?

Fee structure. A great deal can be ascertained by examining the practice's fee structure. A professional who has been consistently and *successfully* charging above-average fees probably has developed significant professional goodwill. If fees are average or below average, perhaps there is an uncovered problem or a potential to increase revenues. An appraiser should ascertain:

- How do this practitioner's fees compare with fees charged in the community by other practitioners of similar reputation and skill?

- When was the last time fees were raised?

- How often have fees been raised in the last five years, and for what reasons?

- Was there measurable resistance to the last increase in fees (a significant drop-off in then current or prospective patients or clients)? Would there be a sizable loss of patients or clients if a fee increase was instituted? How large an increase would the market bear?

- Is billing computerized and how well is the system working?

Staff strength. Second only to the principal(s) in importance to the value of a professional practice is the quality and depth of the staff. Staff includes non-owner professionals (who may or may not carry clientele away if they leave), paraprofessionals, and clerical employees. Questions that should be asked by an appraiser in this area are:

- How long have the various individuals been with the practice; would they be likely to stay if the owner-

Tools and Techniques

professional(s) were to die or the practice were sold? What patients or clients (or essential skills) would nonowners take with them if they left? What costs would be involved in recruiting replacements and training them?

- What duties do the nonowners in the practice perform? What percentage of the total practice can be performed without the owner-professional?

- How well are nonowners compensated compared to similar employees in similar practices?

- Are there enforceable employment contracts, covenants not to compete, or special fringe benefits that would tie key employees to the practice even if new ownership takes over?

Location of the practice. In general, practices located in economically vibrant and growing communities are more valuable than those in unattractive and depressed areas, but this is not always true. For example, a dentist may have a higher volume of business in an area where preventive tooth care has not been stressed; a criminal attorney may have more potential business in the inner city than in a suburb.

Ironically, a practice producing a high income isn't necessarily more valuable in a community where there is a shortage of professionals; it would be relatively easy for a new practitioner to take advantage of the demand. Conversely, in a community saturated by and long-settled with professionals, start-up time and expense would be high for a new practitioner; so the value of an established practice with a full appointment book and a well-trained staff would therefore be higher.

Physical and mental health of the professional. Particularly in marital distribution situations, the professional's health is a dominant valuation factor. Significant professional goodwill may exist if the professional is in good health and can repeat or improve upon his past earnings record. But what if past earnings were generated by years of 80-hour weeks which are no longer feasible? A surgeon who has a blood-pressure problem, or worse yet, an alcohol or other drug problem, may not be capable of sustaining the workload that "built the business."

Age of the professional. Age is another factor that should be given great weight in a valuation for divorce or separation purposes. Age, aside from its tangential relationship to health, can be used to indicate how long a past flow of earnings can reasonably be projected into the future. Although it is logical to project the earnings of a young practitioner for a longer time than a practitioner only a few years from retirement, an appraiser must consider that the earnings of a younger practitioner are lower and less certain.

Shortcut approach to buy-sell valuations. Since nonprofessionals cannot generally hold stock in a professional corporation and since most states require that such stock be bought back by the corporation or its surviving shareholders within a relatively short period of time after the transfer of

interest, it is essential that a fully funded buy-sell agreement be utilized to protect the interests of all parties. Quite often the parties to such an agreement are unwilling to hire an independent appraiser to value their stock according to the appropriate sophisticated methods. For this reason, a quick and relatively inexpensive method of determining value is often desired, such as the "one times annual net income" formula all too often used for solo private practices.

Although there is no universal rule or perfect formula for arriving at a price, the simplified worksheet shown in Figure B.4 provides a quick way to "guesstimate" the worth of a physician's practice; it can be easily modified to apply to other professional practices.

Warning: Remember that the guidelines in the worksheet are only that; they will vary depending on the circumstances. Be sure to review the list of assumptions accompanying the worksheet. Note that a solo practice is almost always worth less than one where two or more professionals work together. This is why many practitioners bring in one or more associates well before they retire and negotiate a buyout that will effect a long and smooth transition period. This worksheet should be considered only a starting place for a full valuation.

Valuation Methods

Prior transactions method. Perhaps the most reliable method of valuing a practice, when it is available, is to ascertain the price it sold for in a previous transaction. This assumes, of course, that there was a recent sale or exchange and that it was at arm's length. Consideration should also be given to the magnitude of prior transactions — e.g., the purchase of greater than 50% of a practice creates a control premium, whereas the purchase of less than a 50% interest should involve a minority discount.

Capitalization of billings method. A practice can be valued by dividing the net income by the cost of capital. For example, using this formula, if the practice produced an adjusted net income after the owner's salary of $100,000, and it was assumed that capital should be "costed" at 20% (i.e., a buyer with a similar risk opportunity would demand a 20% return on his investment), the practice would be worth $500,000 ($100,000 divided by 20%).

Another traditional way of arriving at a practice value is by using a multiple of gross billings. The formula for determining the multiple to use is: net income percentage divided by capitalization rate equals percentage of billing factor. For example, assume the firm in our prior example billed $500,000 during the year. Since its adjusted net income was $100,000, its net income percentage on billings was 20% ($500,000 ÷ by $100,000). Given the 20% capitalization rate, its value is $500,000, or 100% of billings (20% ÷ 20% = 1 or 100%). If the same firm billed only $400,000 but still nettled $100,000 (a percentage of billing factor of 25%), it

Figure B.4

> ## Worksheet for Valuing a Physician's Practice
> ### WORKSHEET ASSUMPTIONS
>
> *ACCOUNTS RECEIVABLE.* Sellers sometimes exclude accounts receivable from the sale of the practice to keep the sales price down or to simplify the process; the selling professional collects the revenue from the receivables and the buyer doesn't have to worry about the collectibility or the trouble of collection. Conversely, the purchaser may want a practice with accounts receivable to maintain contact with the patients or clients (similar to purchasing a customer list).
>
> Bills outstanding for more than one year are considered uncollectible; those that have been turned over to collection agencies are not considered as part of accounts receivable. Accounts receivable within 30 days of billing are considered worth between 80% and 90% of their face value. Between 30 and 60 days, the value drops to between 50% and 80%; while in most practices, accounts receivable are worth little after 60 days, *unless* a government agency or private insurer will pay the claim.
>
> *Practice point.* It is imporatant to view accounts receivable in perspective. Has the professional been "cleaning out" his accounts receivable and living off previous work he's now collecting for? Has he imposed fee increases which create the impression of a constant level of patient volume which is in reality decreasing? Has the professional done a good job of collecting and reporting accounts receivable? In many cases, poor bookkeeping or collection procedures understate the true value of the practice. For instance, a practice may be building its patient volume but, because of inefficiencies or poor pricing of services, hasn't generated a representative cash flow.
>
> *BUILDINGS/LAND.* The fair market value of the real estate owned by the practice must be used rather than the book value.
>
> *EQUIPMENT/FURNISHINGS.* A potential purchaser views equipment as capital that will have to be replaced. Equipment depreciates rapidly, partially due to wear and partially to obsolescence caused by the introduction of more effective or efficient (less labor intensive) or easier to use technology.
>
> Some appraisal experts suggest that each item be priced between original cost and present book value. This worksheet suggests that equipment less than five years old be listed at 40% of its cost and older equipment at about 20% of cost. Where appropriate, use an actual fair market value appraisal; for example, certain furniture–say, an antique desk–may have value in excess of its original cost.
>
> *DRUGS/SUPPLIES.* Most physicians have at least a two-month supply of drugs and other supplies. Divide the annual supply cost by six. Unused disposables are typically worth their cost less 10% to 20%, although a buyer may not choose to use what is currently in inventory, further reducing the practice value.
>
> *GOODWILL.* Various methods of determining goodwill are discussed throughout this reading. The worksheet rule of thumb–25% of annual gross–can be used as an alternative to another commonly used guideline, $3 to $5 per record of regularly seen patients. Note that these are "quick guess" guidelines; they should not substitute for appropriate financial analysis and evaluation.
>
> *Value of Accounts Receivable*
>
> | Age | Percent of Face Value | Example | Your Figures |
> |---|---|---|---|
> | Input: 0-30 days | 80-90% | $ 20,000 | $_____ |
> | Input: 31-60 days | 50-60% | 50,000 | _____ |
> | Input: 61 days or more | 0 unless insurance | 5,000 | _____ |
>
> *Buildings and Land*
>
> | | | | |
> |---|---|---|---|
> | Input: Market value of building and land | | 1,000,000 | _____ |
>
> *Equipment and Furnishings*
>
> | Age | Percent of Face Value | Example | Your Figures |
> |---|---|---|---|
> | Input: Less than 5 years | 40% of cost | $ 30,000 | _____ |
> | Input: 5 years or more | 20% of cost | 4,000 | _____ |
> | Input: Drugs, supplies (last 2 month's bills) | | 12,000 | _____ |
> | Input: Cash and market value of invested securities | | 10,000 | _____ |
> | Input: Goodwill (25% of annual gross) | | 200,000 | _____ |
> | Total estimate of practice assets | | $1,331,000 | $_____ |
>
> *Liabilities*
>
> | | Example | Your Figures |
> |---|---|---|
> | Input: Balance owed on equipment and furnishings | $ 5,000 | _____ |
> | Input: Salaries, bonuses, severance pay due | 60,000 | _____ |
> | Input: Taxes due | 40,000 | _____ |
> | Input: Accounts payable | 23,000 | _____ |
> | Input: Insurance premiums due | 70,000 | _____ |
> | Input: Mortgage balance | 80,000 | _____ |
> | Input: Other liabilities | 3,000 | _____ |
> | Total estimate of practice liabilities | $ 281,000 | _____ |
> | Total estimate of practice assets | $1,331,000 | _____ |
> | Total estimate of practice liabilities | 281,000 | _____ |
> | Estimate of value practice | $1,050,000 | _____ |

Tools and Techniques

would be worth *more* than 100% of the billings. Using the formula, we get a 125% multiple: 25% ÷ by 20% = 1.25 or 125%. Thus, the practice's value, on these facts, would still be $500,000 (i.e., $400,000 X 125%).

Excess earnings method. This is another simple, widely-used — and often court-blessed — method of quantifying the value of intangible assets. Essentially, earnings (pretax, *including* the professional owner's salary and fringe benefits) are adjusted as discussed above. Then the earnings in excess of that which is earned by similar professionals in similar types of practices are computed and that excess is "capitalized" (divided by a percentage to arrive at the capital it would take to produce it annually). The result is the estimated value of the goodwill in the practice. This would be added to the fair market value of tangible assets to arrive at a total value.

For example, assume Doctor Know's average compensation for the last five years — after appropriate adjustments and weighting for its upward trend — was $180,000, but that similar physicians earned only $120,000 during the same period. This indicated that the difference, about $60,000 a year, is due to something other than return on tangible assets.

Excess earnings for most professional practices are capitalized at rates between 20% and 100%. The wide variation is a result of varying risk levels and differing ages of the professionals in question; the median capitalization rate is 33 1/3%. Here are the goodwill values of Doctor Know's practice at various capitalization rates:

Rate	Adjusted Excess	Value
20%	$60,000	$300,000
25%	$60,000	$240,000
33%	$60,000	$180,000
50%	$60,000	$120,000
100%	$60,000	$ 60,000

This brings up the question asked at the beginning of the discussion on valuations of businesses: what is meant by a "capitalization rate" and how does the appraiser know what capitalization rate to use? The capitalization rate is the projected cost of capital. But there is no fixed and certain answer to the question of "What is the right rate to use?" A good appraiser will consider such things as (1) how many more productive years the professional has, (2) where on the income-producing cycle the professional was as of the valuation date (highest income-producing years for most professionals occur between ages 45 and 55), and (3) changes in the profession, the economy, and in government regulation. For instance, skyrocketing malpractice costs are rapidly changing the practicing environment, causing many professionals to drastically change the way they work.

Most appraisers working with professional corporations will be conservative and use relatively high capitalization rates, 50% to 100% (meaning a low multiplier). *Reason:* It is more difficult to maintain "excess earnings" than earnings

produced by passive income investments and, further, total earnings have been used as a base. If pretax earnings after reduction for owner's compensation and benefits is used as the base, a 20% or 40% capitalization rate (and thus a higher multiple) would be more appropriate. The table below sets out various capitalization rates and their related multipliers for determining value using the excess earnings method.

Capitalization Rate/Value	
Capitalization Rate	Value (multiply adjusted excess by this rate)
3.5%	28.57/1
4.0%	25.00/1
5.0%	20.00/1
6.0%	16.67/1
7.0%	14.29/1
8.0%	12.50/1
9.0%	11.11/1
10.0%	10.00/1
11.0%	9.09/1
12.0%	8.33/1
13.0%	7.69/1
14.0%	7.14/1
15.0%	6.67/1
16.0%	6.25/1
17.0%	5.88/1
18.0%	5.56/1
19.0%	5.26/1
20.0%	5.00/1
25.0%	4.00/1
30.0%	3.33/1

Caveat: As is the case with any valuation method, the excess earnings concept has its limitations. Goodwill can be understated, because even a practice without excess earnings may have considerable worth as a going concern. On the other hand, goodwill can be overstated, because the excess earnings method does not consider whether or not the practice is marketable. Third, many subjective judgments are required (such as the appropriate weight to give the trend of earnings, the adjustments to make to earnings, and the capitalization rate to use).

Rough Rules of Thumb for Valuations

Almost all tax practitioners and financial planners use rules of thumb (often called SWAGs, scientific wild asset guesses) that they've developed as the byproduct of practical experience. SWAGs lie between calculations and pure conjecture and serve as starting places in the valuation process, later to be abandoned or modified. They can also be used where

Figure B.4a

Caution: Before using this table, be sure to read the explanation of the changes made in the valuation of annuities, life estates, etc. by 1988 legislation, at page 391.

Life Estate, Remainder, and Annuity Interests
(Taken from Estate Tax Reg. §20.2031-7 and Gift Tax Reg. §25.2512-5)

TABLE A.—SINGLE LIFE, UNISEX, 10 PERCENT SHOWING THE PRESENT WORTH OF AN ANNUITY, OF A LIFE INTEREST, AND OF A REMAINDER INTEREST

(1) Age	(2) Annuity	(3) Life estate	(4) Remainder
0	9.7188	.97188	.02812
1	9.8988	.98988	.01012
2	9.9017	.99017	.00983
3	9.9008	.99008	.00992
4	9.8981	.98981	.01019
5	9.8938	.98938	.01062
6	9.8884	.98884	.01116
7	9.8822	.98822	.01178
8	9.8748	.98748	.01252
9	9.8663	.98663	.01337
10	9.8565	.98565	.01435
11	9.8453	.98453	.01547
12	9.8329	.98329	.01671
13	9.8198	.98198	.01802
14	9.8066	.98066	.01934
15	9.7937	.97937	.02063
16	9.7815	.97815	.02185
17	9.7700	.97700	.02300
18	9.7590	.97590	.02410
19	9.7480	.97480	.02520
20	9.7365	.97365	.02635
21	9.7245	.97245	.02755
22	9.7120	.97120	.02880
23	9.6986	.96986	.03014
24	9.6841	.96841	.03159
25	9.6678	.96678	.03322
26	9.6495	.96495	.03505
27	9.6290	.96290	.03710
28	9.6062	.96062	.03938
29	9.5813	.95813	.04187
30	9.5543	.95543	.04457
31	9.5254	.95254	.04746
32	9.4942	.94942	.05058
33	9.4608	.94608	.05392
34	9.4250	.94250	.05750
35	9.3868	.93868	.06132
36	9.3460	.93460	.06540
37	9.3026	.93026	.06974
38	9.2567	.92567	.07433
39	9.2083	.92083	.07917
40	9.1571	.91571	.08429
41	9.1030	.91030	.08970
42	9.0457	.90457	.09543
43	8.9855	.89855	.10145
44	8.9221	.89221	.10779
45	8.8558	.88558	.11442
46	8.7863	.87863	.12137
47	8.7137	.87137	.12863
48	8.6374	.86374	.13626
49	8.5578	.85578	.14422
50	8.4743	.84743	.15257
51	8.3874	.83874	.16126
52	8.2969	.82969	.17031
53	8.2028	.82028	.17972
54	8.1054	.81054	.18946

TABLE A.—SINGLE LIFE, UNISEX, 10 PERCENT SHOWING THE PRESENT WORTH OF AN ANNUITY, OF A LIFE INTEREST, AND OF A REMAINDER INTEREST—Continued

(1) Age	(2) Annuity	(3) Life estate	(4) Remainder
55	8.0046	.80046	.19954
56	7.9006	.79006	.20994
57	7.7931	.77931	.22069
58	7.6822	.76822	.23178
59	7.5675	.75675	.24325
60	7.4491	.74491	.25509
61	7.3267	.73267	.26733
62	7.2002	.72002	.27998
63	7.0696	.70696	.29304
64	6.9352	.69352	.30648
65	6.7970	.67970	.32030
66	6.6551	.66551	.33449
67	6.5098	.65098	.34902
68	6.3610	.63610	.36390
69	6.2086	.62086	.37914
70	6.0522	.60522	.39478
71	5.8914	.58914	.41086
72	5.7261	.57261	.42739
73	5.5571	.55571	.44429
74	5.3862	.53862	.46138
75	5.2149	.52149	.47851
76	5.0441	.50441	.49559
77	4.8742	.48742	.51258
78	4.7049	.47049	.52951
79	4.5357	.45357	.54643
80	4.3659	.43659	.56341
81	4.1967	.41967	.58033
82	4.0295	.40295	.59705
83	3.8642	.38642	.61358
84	3.6998	.36998	.63002
85	3.5359	.35359	.64641
86	3.3764	.33764	.66236
87	3.2262	.32262	.67738
88	3.0859	.30859	.69141
89	2.9526	.29526	.70474
90	2.8221	.28221	.71779
91	2.6955	.26955	.73045
92	2.5771	.25571	.74229
93	2.4692	.24692	.75308
94	2.3728	.23728	.76272
95	2.2887	.22887	.77113
96	2.2181	.22181	.77819
97	2.1550	.21550	.78450
98	2.1000	.21000	.79000
99	2.0486	.20486	.79514
100	1.9975	.19975	.80025
101	1.9532	.19532	.80468
102	1.9054	.19054	.80946
103	1.8437	.18437	.81563
104	1.7856	.17856	.82144
105	1.6962	.16962	.83038
106	1.5488	.15488	.84512
107	1.3409	.13409	.86591
108	1.0068	.10068	.89932
109	.4545	.04545	.95455

TABLE B.—TABLE SHOWING THE PRESENT WORTH AT 10 PERCENT OF AN ANNUITY FOR A TERM CERTAIN, OF AN INCOME INTEREST FOR A TERM CERTAIN AND OF A REMAINDER INTEREST POSTPONED FOR A TERM CERTAIN

(1) Number of years	(2) Annuity	(3) Term certain	(4) Remainder
1	.9091	.090909	.909091
2	1.7355	.173554	.826446
3	2.4869	.248685	.751315
4	3.1699	.316987	.683013
5	3.7908	.379079	.620921
6	4.3553	.435526	.564474
7	4.8684	.486842	.513158
8	5.3349	.533493	.466507
9	5.7590	.575902	.424098
10	6.1446	.614457	.385543
11	6.4951	.649506	.350494
12	6.8137	.681369	.318631
13	7.1034	.710336	.289664
14	7.3667	.736669	.263331
15	7.6061	.760608	.239392
16	7.8237	.782371	.217629
17	8.0216	.802155	.197845
18	8.2014	.820141	.179859
19	8.3649	.836492	.163508
20	8.5136	.851356	.148644
21	8.6487	.864869	.135131
22	8.7715	.877154	.122846
23	8.8832	.888322	.111678
24	8.9847	.898474	.101526
25	9.0770	.907704	.092296
26	9.1609	.916095	.083905
27	9.2372	.923722	.076278
28	9.3066	.930657	.069343
29	9.3696	.936961	.063039
30	9.4269	.942691	.057309
31	9.4790	.947901	.052099
32	9.5264	.952638	.047362
33	9.5694	.956943	.043057
34	9.6086	.960857	.039143
35	9.6442	.964416	.035584
36	9.6765	.967651	.032349
37	9.7059	.970592	.029408
38	9.7327	.973265	.026735
39	9.7570	.975696	.024304
40	9.7791	.977905	.022095
41	9.7991	.979914	.020086
42	9.8174	.981740	.018260
43	9.8340	.983400	.016600
44	9.8491	.984909	.015091
45	9.8628	.986281	.013719
46	9.8753	.987528	.012472
47	9.8866	.988662	.011338
48	9.8969	.989693	.010307
49	9.9063	.990630	.009370
50	9.9140	.991481	.008519
51	9.9226	.992256	.007744
52	9.9296	.992960	.007040
53	9.9360	.993600	.006400
54	9.9418	.994182	.005818
55	9.9471	.994711	.005289
56	9.9519	.995191	.004809
57	9.9563	.995629	.004371
58	9.9603	.996026	.003974
59	9.9639	.996387	.003613
60	9.9672	.996716	.003284

more precise methods are deemed impractical. The following rough rules of thumb are suggested for valuing various professions:

- *Medical:* Net asset value plus 20% to 40% of annual revenue for goodwill (referral practices would be worth less, continuing client base practices worth more).

- *Veterinary:* Net asset value plus 60% to 90% of annual revenue for goodwill.

- *Legal:* Because client's files can't be sold (lawyers are ethically precluded from selling their law practices), personal goodwill typically does not enter into the valuation process. Therefore, net asset value is often the major

Tools and Techniques

value determinant. In the case of distribution upon divorce, if there is a buy-sell agreement, the price set in the agreement is usually considered merely an indication of value and is certainly rebuttable. Remember that work-in-progress fees are not reflected in the records of a law firm. So, even if the firm's accounting records are accurate and nonfraudulent, a firm that takes no retainers and sends no bills but has many contingent fee arrangements, can easily be undervalued. Conversely, fees contingent on events that may not occur must be discounted.

- *Accounting:* Net asset value plus a goodwill payment of from 80% to 130% of annual revenue (paid out over time). Another common method uses 20% of projected fees for five years, discounted for both attrition and the time value of money. According to the CPA Handbook, a third commonly used formula is 40% of gross receipts for the prior three years and a percentage of average annual fees as follows: 100% for clients served over four years, 75% for clients served from three to four years, 50% for clients served from two to three years, and 25% for clients served from one to two years.

- *Dental:* Net asset value plus 30% to 40% of annual revenues for goodwill.

- *Engineering/Architecture:* Net asset value plus 25% to 50% of annual revenues for goodwill (firms with few continuing clients would, of course, have little if any goodwill).

Data Needed in the Valuation Process

Valuation experts should review each of the following:

- Last five years' profit and loss statements and balance sheets (certified financial statements by an independent CPA firm are preferable). Five years is a common time frame because it (1) minimizes the possibility of "valuation planning," (2) covers a complete business cycle, (3) examines good as well as bad times, (4) permits discounting or elimination of "aberration years," and (5) illustrates the stability and trend of profits. Graphs are particularly useful in identifying and illustrating aberration years or the direction and velocity of a profit trend.

- Last five years' federal income tax returns.

- Any business leases.

- Last five years' fee schedules.

- Brochures on the firm.

- Articles of incorporation and by-laws, and minutes of board of directors' meetings for the last five years.

- Last five years' appointment books.

- State employment research data (particularly information from state professional licensing department).

- Demographic and practice economics information available from state or county professional societies (such as the state or local medical or bar association).

- Studies published in professional journals such as the

American Medical Association's "Socioeconomic Characteristics of Medical Practice" (published annually), or by the American Bar Association, or in private publications such as "Medical Economics," or, for the legal profession, "Corporate Law Department Surveys and Survey of Law Form Economics" (Altman-Weil Management Consultants, Inc., published annually) and "Compensation of Attorneys" (Steven Langer and Associates).

Conclusion

The valuation of a professional practice is an art, not a science. Many variables must be considered and evaluated. The quality of evaluation will be, in part, a function of the appraiser's skill in applying experienced judgment and subjectivity to the objective facts that are gathered.

Two computer programs specifically dedicated to business valuation are "Business Valuation" (Aardvark, (414) 225-7500) and "The Value Planner" (Alcar, Inc. (312) 967-4200). Simpler, and less expensive, Lotus-based valuation projections can be found in "NumberCruncher I" estate planning software (800-654-2227).

References

Valuing Small Business and Professional Practices, Dow Jones-Irwin, Homewood, Illinois, 1986, is an excellent text in the business valuation area. Other helpful references are:

Advanced Sales Reference Service, The National Underwriter Company, Cincinnati, Ohio.

Estate Valuation Handbook, Wiley Law Publications, New York, 1983.

"New Warnings on Stock Valuation," *CLU Journal,* May 1985, 60.

NumberCruncher-I Software, Financial Data Corporation, Box 1332, Bryn Mawr, PA 19010. 1-800-654-2227.

"Present Value Analysis in Estate Planning after ERTA," *CLU Journal,* May 1985, 52.

The Professional Handbook of Business Valuation, Addison-Wesley Publishing Co., Reading, Massachusetts.

Footnote References

Valuation of Assets for Federal Estate Tax Purposes.

1. Reg. Section 20.2031-1(b); Reg. Section 25.2512-1.
2. IRC Sections 2031(a); 2032(a)(1)(2).
3. IRC Section 2032(a)(1).
4. IRC Section 2032(a)(3).
5. IRC Section 2042(1).
6. IRC Section 2042(2).
7. Rev. Rul. 69-489, 1969-2 CB 172.
8. *Bankers Trust Company v. U.S.*, 284 F.2d 537 (CA-2 1960), cert. denied.
9. TAMRA '88, Sec. 5031; IRC Section 7520.
10. See *Estate of David Smith*, 57 TC 650 (1972), acq. 1974-2 CB 4.
11. Reg. Section 20.2031-2(e).
12. IRC Sections 2031 and 2512. Regs. Sections 20.2031-1(b), 2(b), 2(f) and 25.2512-2.

13. The broad and ambiguous ambit of Code section 2036(c) is specifically designed to reach property interests shifted in an indirect manner from one party to another. Many authorities think that a fixed price is a red flag that will not only fail as an estate value determinant for the interest retained by the decedent-shareholder, but will also trigger inclusion of any appreciation ending up in the hands of another shareholder. For example, if a fixed price of $10 a share was used for stock which appreciated to a value of $16 a share between the 1989 date of execution and the 1996 date of the shareholder's death, the IRS might include both the $10 a share actually received (using Code section 2033) and the $6 a share transferred by virtue of the buy-sell's fixed price (using Code section 2036(c)). Formula-set prices which are realistic and continually update the purchase price to an arm's length figure are much more likely to escape the reach of Code section 2036(c). (See the detailed explanation of section 2036(c) beginning at page 477.)

USING THE VALUATION TABLES

Caution: Before using any of the valuation tables in this appendix, be sure to read the explanation of the changes made in the valuation of annuities, life estates, etc. by 1988 legislation, at page 391.

BASIC GUIDELINES

Until the tables (or formulas) mandated by Congress in TAMRA (Technical and Miscellaneous Revenue Act of 1988) are effective and available, tables A, B, and LN, above, will be used to compute the present value of annuities, life estates, terms for years, remainders, and reversions.

Here are the basic guidelines for using these tables:

1. Use Table A to compute the present value of an annuity, life estate, remainder, or reversion which is dependent on the continuation or termination of one person's life.

   An annuity is defined as a periodic payment. That payment can extend for a specific period of time regardless of outside events (for instance the annuity can last for "a period certain" of 10 years) or it can run for a specified life or lives.

   A life estate is the right of a person to use property or receive the income from property for his life or for the life of some other person.

   A remainder is the right to use, possess, and enjoy property when the prior owner's interest ends. A remainder interest is valued by subtracting the present value of any prior interest from the fair market value of the property.

   A term for years is a right to the income from property or the right to use property that is limited to a specified period of time. It is not dependent on some outside measurement such as the life of one or more persons.

   A reversion is the future right the transferor of property has retained to regain possession of the property in question. It is the fixed right to future possession and enjoyment that was never sold or given away.

2. Use Table B to compute the present value of an annuity term for years, remainder, or reversion dependent on a term certain.

3. Use age at a person's nearest birthday.

4. To compute the present value of an annuity which is payable annually at the end of each year and lasting for the life of one person, multiply the amount payable annually by the figure in column 2 of Table A opposite the appropriate age in column 1.

   For instance, if the annuity is $10,000 a year and it is payable for the life of a person age 41, you would multiply 10,000 by 9.1030. This results in a present value of $91,030 ($10,000 × 9.030).

5. To compute the present value of an annuity which is payable annually at the end of each year and lasting for a definite number of years, multiply the amount payable annually by the figure in column 2 of Table B opposite the appropriate number of years (the duration of the annuity). For instance, if the annuity is $10,000 a year for 5 years, you would multiply 10,000 by 3.7908. This results in a present value of $37,908 ($10,000 × 3.7908).

6. If an annuity is payable at the end of some period other than annually, the result of the calculation in (5) and (6) above must be multiplied by a further factor.

   A. If the annuity is payable for life, multiply by:

      1.0244 for semiannual payments

      1.0368 for quarterly payments

      1.0450 for monthly payments

      1.0482 for weekly payments

   B. If the annuity is payable for a definite number of years, multiply by the same factors as above.

7. If the first payment of an annuity payable for the life of an individual is payable at the *beginning* (or some payment period other than at the end) of the annual payment period, you must add:

   A. The first payment to

Tools and Techniques

B. The present value of the annuity computed as if payments were made at the end of the year (or other payment period). For instance, if payments of $50 a month were to be made for the life of a 50 year old person, the present value of the annuity would be $5,363.39. You would (a) add the first payment of $50 to (b) the result of multiplying $50 × 12 × 8.4743 (see Table A) and then the factor for monthly payments, 1.0450.

8. If the first payment of an annuity payable for a definite number of years were made at the *beginning* of the annual (or some other period), you multiply the factor from Table B by the appropriate following factor:

1.100 for annual payments

1.0744 for semiannual payments

1.0618 for quarterly payments

1.0534 for monthly payments

1.0502 for weekly payments

For instance, if a $50 annuity were payable each month for 300 months, to compute the value of the annuity, you would multiply $50 × 12 × 9.0770 (see Table B) × 1.0534 = $5,737.03.

9. If the interest to be valued is the right to receive only the income or only the right to use nonincome producing property for life, you multiply the fair market value of the property by the appropriate figure in column 3 of Table A. Use the number of years nearest to the actual age of the measuring life. For instance, if a 31 year old person has been given the right to the income from $50,000 for as long as he lives, to value that right, go to Table A, column 3, find the factor opposite age 31, and multiply it by $50,000. The result is $47,627 ($50,000 × .95254).

10. If the interest to be valued is the right to receive only income or only the right to use nonincome producing property, for a term of years, use column 3 of Table B.

11. A remainder and reversion interest have the same value. The present value of a remainder or reversion interest which takes effect after another person's death is found by multiplying the value of the property by the appropriate figure in column 4 of Table A. Use the age nearest to the actual age of the measuring life. For instance, if an individual will receive property worth $50,000 at the death of another person age 31, you would multiply the $50,000 by .04746, the present value factor for the life of a 31 year old. The result is $2,373 ($50,000 × .04746).

12. To determine the present value of a remainder interest which takes effect at the end of a definite term of years, you should use column 4 of Table B.

13. Where more than one life is involved in the valuation, or the valuation depends upon both a life and a term certain, a special factor must be computed from the values of lx that are set forth in column 2 of Table LN. However, if a special factor is required in the case of an actual decedent, the Commissioner will furnish the factor to the executor upon request. The request must be accompanied by a statement of the date of birth of each person, the duration of whose life may affect the value of the interest, and by copies of the relevant instruments. Special factors are not furnished for prospective transfers. Reg. §20.2031-7(e).

USE OF TABLE LN IN COMPUTING VALUE OF REVERSION IN MODIFIED GRIT

Table LN is used in the computation of the probability of the grantor's surviving the term of a GRIT that lasts for a specified period of time or the earlier death of the grantor. An irrevocable trust is established, and the trustee is directed to pay to the grantor the income from the trust for a specified number of years. When the term expires (or, if earlier, when the grantor expires), the grantor's interest terminates.

The value of the retained interest is usually found by multiplying the appropriate annuity factor by the number of years the trust will run. But where the grantor's interest includes the right of his estate to receive the trust principal upon death before the expiration of the specified term, the value of the retained interest is greater than the mere right (the present value) to receive income for that period of time.

Conceptually, the present value of a vested remainder interest in trust assets is multiplied by the probability that the grantor will survive the term of the trust. This results in the value of the contingent remainder interest. The aggregate value of (a) the right to receive income for a term certain, and (b) the right to receive the entire trust property if the grantor dies during the term certain must be computed through the use of probability tables (Table LN) from Treasury Regulations §§20.2031-7(f) or 25.2512-5(f).

The formula that must be used is

$$1-[(Lx/Ly)/1.1^n]$$

Lx (age at beginning of term) and Ly (age at end of term) are found in the LN table. Use the grantor's age to the nearest birthday. N is the remaining term (technically, the number of whole and part years stated as a fraction using days remaining in the term certain).

The contingent remainder technique makes a significant difference in the gift tax implications. The additional value attributable to this interest increases the value of what the grantor retains and therefore lowers the gift tax value of the gift. This means the grantor can — with no significant additional gift tax cost — (a) use a much shorter term than would otherwise be feasible, or (b) make a much larger gift.

The older the client the greater the chance of death during the trust term, and therefore the greater the value of the retained interest (which in turn lowers the actuarial value of the gift and therefore the gift tax). This makes the GRIT an attactive estate planning vehicle for the estate of an elderly client.

A comparison illustrates how effective the technique can be. Suppose the client is 80. He sets up an irrevocable trust that lasts for five years and then pays assets over to his children. If he retains no reversionary interest, the gift is about 62 percent of the value of the assets he places in the trust. If he puts $1,000,000 in the trust, his gift is $620,921. If he retains the right to dispose of the assets in the trust upon his death within the five-year term, his gift drops to about 36.7 percent. His gift would be about $368,000 instead of about $621,000.

Figure B.5

FORMULA TO VALUE REMAINDER INTEREST WHERE DEATH MAY OCCUR PRIOR TO EXPIRATION OF INCOME INTEREST

LX Grantor's age to nearest birthday beginning of term	80	35285
LY Grantor's age to nearest birthday at end of term	85	20908
Number of years in term		5
Percentage value of remainder interest $\left(\dfrac{20908}{35285}\right)\big/ 1.1^5$		.368
Value or remainder interest		$367,925
Formula $(Lx/Ly)/1.1^n$		
LN Factor - age 85		20908
LN Factor - age 80		35285

Illustration Courtesy of NumberCruncher Software

Tools and Techniques

Caution: Before using this table, be sure to read the explanation of the changes made in the valuation of annuities, life estates, etc. by 1988 legislation, at page 391.

Table A(2)
The Present Worth of $1.00 Due at the Death of the Survivor of Two Persons
Interest at 10 Percent

Older	Younger	Present Worth	Older	Younger	Present Worth	Older	Younger	Present Worth
0	0	.00162	8	4	.00153	12	2	.00165
1	0	.00115	8	5	.00160	12	3	.00173
1	1	.00101	8	6	.00168	12	4	.00181
2	0	.00117	8	7	.00175	12	5	.00190
2	1	.00105	8	8	.00184	12	6	.00199
2	2	.00109	9	0	.00157	12	7	.00209
3	0	.00122	9	1	.00140	12	8	.00219
3	1	.00109	9	2	.00146	12	9	.00230
3	2	.00113	9	3	.00153	12	10	.00241
3	3	.00118	9	4	.00160	12	11	.00253
4	0	.00126	9	5	.00167	12	12	.00265
4	1	.00114	9	6	.00175	13	0	.00189
4	2	.00118	9	7	.00183	13	1	.00165
4	3	.00123	9	8	.00192	13	2	.00172
4	4	.00129	9	9	.00201	13	3	.00180
5	0	.00132	10	0	.00165	13	4	.00189
5	1	.00118	10	1	.00146	13	5	.00198
5	2	.00123	10	2	.00152	13	6	.00208
5	3	.00129	10	3	.00159	13	7	.00218
5	4	.00134	10	4	.00167	13	8	.00229
5	5	.00140	10	5	.00175	13	9	.00240
6	0	.00137	10	6	.00183	13	10	.00252
6	1	.00124	10	7	.00192	13	11	.00264
6	2	.00129	10	8	.00201	13	12	.00277
6	3	.00134	10	9	.00210	13	13	.00290
6	4	.00140	10	10	.00220	14	0	.00198
6	5	.00147	11	0	.00172	14	1	.00172
6	6	.00153	11	1	.00152	14	2	.00179
7	0	.00144	11	2	.00159	14	3	.00187
7	1	.00129	11	3	.00166	14	4	.00196
7	2	.00134	11	4	.00174	14	5	.00206
7	3	.00140	11	5	.00182	14	6	.00217
7	4	.00146	11	6	.00191	14	7	.00227
7	5	.00153	11	7	.00200	14	8	.00239
7	6	.00160	11	8	.00210	14	9	.00251
7	7	.00168	11	9	.00220	14	10	.00263
8	0	.00150	11	10	.00231	14	11	.00276
8	1	.00134	11	11	.00241	14	12	.00290
8	2	.00140	12	0	.00181	14	13	.00303
8	3	.00146	12	1	.00159	14	14	.00318

Table A(2)
The Present Worth of $1.00 Due at the
Death of the Survivor of Two Persons
Interest at 10 Percent

Older	Younger	Present Worth	Older	Younger	Present Worth	Older	Younger	Present Worth
15	0	.00207	17	7	.00256	19	10	.00321
15	1	.00178	17	8	.00269	19	11	.00338
15	2	.00186	17	9	.00283	19	12	.00355
15	3	.00195	17	10	.00297	19	13	.00373
15	4	.00204	17	11	.00312	19	14	.00391
15	5	.00214	17	12	.00328	19	15	.00410
15	6	.00225	17	13	.00345	19	16	.00429
15	7	.00237	17	14	.00361	19	17	.00449
15	8	.00249	17	15	.00378	19	18	.00469
15	9	.00261	17	16	.00395	19	19	.00489
15	10	.00274	17	17	.00413	20	0	.00250
15	11	.00288	18	0	.00232	20	1	.00213
15	12	.00302	18	1	.00199	20	2	.00222
15	13	.00317	18	2	.00207	20	3	.00233
15	14	.00332	18	3	.00217	20	4	.00245
15	15	.00347	18	4	.00228	20	5	.00257
16	0	.00215	18	5	.00240	20	6	.00271
16	1	.00185	18	6	.00252	20	7	.00285
16	2	.00193	18	7	.00265	20	8	.00300
16	3	.00202	18	8	.00279	20	9	.00316
16	4	.00212	18	9	.00294	20	10	.00333
16	5	.00223	18	10	.00309	20	11	.00351
16	6	.00234	18	11	.00325	20	12	.00369
16	7	.00246	18	12	.00341	20	13	.00388
16	8	.00259	18	13	.00359	20	14	.00407
16	9	.00272	18	14	.00376	20	15	.00427
16	10	.00286	18	15	.00394	20	16	.00447
16	11	.00300	18	16	.00412	20	17	.00468
16	12	.00315	18	17	.00431	20	18	.00489
16	13	.00331	18	18	.00449	20	19	.00510
16	14	.00347	19	0	.00241	20	20	.00532
16	15	.00363	19	1	.00206	21	0	.00259
16	16	.00379	19	2	.00215	21	1	.00220
17	0	.00224	19	3	.00225	21	2	.00230
17	1	.00192	19	4	.00236	21	3	.00241
17	2	.00200	19	5	.00248	21	4	.00253
17	3	.00210	19	6	.00261	21	5	.00266
17	4	.00220	19	7	.00275	21	6	.00281
17	5	.00231	19	8	.00290	21	7	.00296
17	6	.00243	19	9	.00305	21	8	.00311

Tools and Techniques

Table A(2)

**The Present Worth of $1.00 Due at the
Death of the Survivor of Two Persons**

Interest at 10 Percent

Older	Younger	Present Worth	Older	Younger	Present Worth	Older	Younger	Present Worth
21	9	.00328	23	4	.00271	24	20	.00628
21	10	.00345	23	5	.00285	24	21	.00656
21	11	.00364	23	6	.00301	24	22	.00685
21	12	.00383	23	7	.00317	24	23	.00715
21	13	.00403	23	8	.00334	24	24	.00747
21	14	.00423	23	9	.00352	25	0	.00299
21	15	.00444	23	10	.00371	25	1	.00251
21	16	.00465	23	11	.00392	25	2	.00262
21	17	.00487	23	12	.00413	25	3	.00275
21	18	.00509	23	13	.00434	25	4	.00289
21	19	.00532	23	14	.00457	25	5	.00305
21	20	.00555	23	15	.00480	25	6	.00322
21	21	.00579	23	16	.00503	25	7	.00339
22	0	.00268	23	17	.00527	25	8	.00358
22	1	.00227	23	18	.00551	25	9	.00378
22	2	.00237	23	19	.00577	25	10	.00399
22	3	.00249	23	20	.00603	25	11	.00421
22	4	.00262	23	21	.00629	25	12	.00444
22	5	.00276	23	22	.00657	25	13	.00468
22	6	.00290	23	23	.00686	25	14	.00492
22	7	.00306	24	0	.00288	25	15	.00517
22	8	.00323	24	1	.00243	25	16	.00543
22	9	.00340	24	2	.00254	25	17	.00570
22	10	.00358	24	3	.00266	25	18	.00597
22	11	.00378	24	4	.00280	25	19	.00624
22	12	.00398	24	5	.00295	25	20	.00653
22	13	.00418	24	6	.00311	25	21	.00683
22	14	.00440	24	7	.00328	25	22	.00714
22	15	.00462	24	8	.00346	25	23	.00746
22	16	.00484	24	9	.00365	25	24	.00779
22	17	.00507	24	10	.00385	25	25	.00814
22	18	.00530	24	11	.00406	26	0	.00310
22	19	.00554	24	12	.00428	26	1	.00259
22	20	.00578	24	13	.00451	26	2	.00271
22	21	.00604	24	14	.00474	26	3	.00284
22	22	.00630	24	15	.00498	26	4	.00299
23	0	.00278	24	16	.00523	26	5	.00315
23	1	.00235	24	17	.00548	26	6	.00333
23	2	.00245	24	18	.00574	26	7	.00351
23	3	.00258	24	19	.00600	26	8	.00371

Table A(2)

The Present Worth of $1.00 Due at the
Death of the Survivor of Two Persons

Interest at 10 Percent

Older	Younger	Present Worth	Older	Younger	Present Worth	Older	Younger	Present Worth
26	9	.00391	27	22	.00775	29	5	.00348
26	10	.00413	27	23	.00811	29	6	.00368
26	11	.00436	27	24	.00848	29	7	.00388
26	12	.00460	27	25	.00886	29	8	.00410
26	13	.00485	27	26	.00926	29	9	.00434
26	14	.00511	27	27	.00968	29	10	.00458
26	15	.00537	28	0	.00335	29	11	.00484
26	16	.00564	28	1	.00277	29	12	.00512
26	17	.00592	28	2	.00289	29	13	.00540
26	18	.00620	28	3	.00304	29	14	.00570
26	19	.00650	28	4	.00320	29	15	.00600
26	20	.00680	28	5	.00337	29	16	.00631
26	21	.00712	28	6	.00356	29	17	.00663
26	22	.00744	28	7	.00376	29	18	.00696
26	23	.00778	28	8	.00397	29	19	.00730
26	24	.00813	28	9	.00419	29	20	.00765
26	25	.00849	28	10	.00443	29	21	.00802
26	26	.00887	28	11	.00468	29	22	.00840
27	0	.00322	28	12	.00494	29	23	.00880
27	1	.00268	28	13	.00522	29	24	.00921
27	2	.00280	28	14	.00550	29	25	.00964
27	3	.00294	28	15	.00579	29	26	.01008
27	4	.00309	28	16	.00608	29	27	.01055
27	5	.00326	28	17	.00639	29	28	.01103
27	6	.00344	28	18	.00670	29	29	.01153
27	7	.00363	28	19	.00702	30	0	.00362
27	8	.00384	28	20	.00736	30	1	.00295
27	9	.00405	28	21	.00771	30	2	.00308
27	10	.00428	28	22	.00807	30	3	.00324
27	11	.00452	28	23	.00845	30	4	.00341
27	12	.00477	28	24	.00884	30	5	.00360
27	13	.00503	28	25	.00924	30	6	.00380
27	14	.00530	28	26	.00967	30	7	.00401
27	15	.00558	28	27	.01011	30	8	.00424
27	16	.00586	28	28	.01056	30	9	.00448
27	17	.00615	29	0	.00348	30	10	.00474
27	18	.00645	29	1	.00286	30	11	.00501
27	19	.00676	29	2	.00299	30	12	.00530
27	20	.00708	29	3	.00314	30	13	.00560
27	21	.00741	29	4	.00330	30	14	.00591

Tools and Techniques

Table A(2)

The Present Worth of $1.00 Due at the
Death of the Survivor of Two Persons

Interest at 10 Percent

Older	Younger	Present Worth	Older	Younger	Present Worth	Older	Younger	Present Worth
30	15	.00622	31	24	.00998	32	32	.01499
30	16	.00655	31	25	.01045	33	0	.00408
30	17	.00688	31	26	.01095	33	1	.00325
30	18	.00722	31	27	.01147	33	2	.00339
30	19	.00758	31	28	.01201	33	3	.00356
30	20	.00795	31	29	.01257	33	4	.00375
30	21	.00834	31	30	.01314	33	5	.00395
30	22	.00874	31	31	.01374	33	6	.00418
30	23	.00915	32	0	.00392	33	7	.00442
30	24	.00959	32	1	.00315	33	8	.00467
30	25	.01004	32	2	.00328	33	9	.00495
30	26	.01051	32	3	.00345	33	10	.00523
30	27	.01100	32	4	.00363	33	11	.00554
30	28	.01151	32	5	.00383	33	12	.00587
30	29	.01204	32	6	.00405	33	13	.00620
30	30	.01258	32	7	.00428	33	14	.00655
31	0	.00377	32	8	.00453	33	15	.00691
31	1	.00305	32	9	.00479	33	16	.00728
31	2	.00318	32	10	.00507	33	17	.00766
31	3	.00334	32	11	.00536	33	18	.00805
31	4	.00352	32	12	.00567	33	19	.00846
31	5	.00371	32	13	.00600	33	20	.00888
31	6	.00392	32	14	.00633	33	21	.00933
31	7	.00415	32	15	.00668	33	22	.00979
31	8	.00438	32	16	.00703	33	23	.01027
31	9	.00464	32	17	.00740	33	24	.01078
31	10	.00490	32	18	.00777	33	25	.01130
31	11	.00519	32	19	.00816	33	26	.01186
31	12	.00548	32	20	.00857	33	27	.01243
31	13	.00580	32	21	.00899	33	28	.01304
31	14	.00612	32	22	.00943	33	29	.01366
31	15	.00645	32	23	.00989	33	30	.01430
31	16	.00679	32	24	.01037	33	31	.01497
31	17	.00714	32	25	.01087	33	32	.01565
31	18	.00750	32	26	.01140	33	33	.01636
31	19	.00787	32	27	.01195	34	0	.00424
31	20	.00826	32	28	.01252	34	1	.00335
31	21	.00866	32	29	.01311	34	2	.00349
31	22	.00908	32	30	.01372	34	3	.00367
31	23	.00952	32	31	.01434	34	4	.00386

Table A(2)
The Present Worth of $1.00 Due at the
Death of the Survivor of Two Persons
Interest at 10 Percent

Older	Younger	Present Worth	Older	Younger	Present Worth	Older	Younger	Present Worth
34	5	.00408	35	10	.00558	36	14	.00723
34	6	.00431	35	11	.00591	36	15	.00764
34	7	.00456	35	12	.00626	36	16	.00805
34	8	.00482	35	13	.00662	36	17	.00848
34	9	.00510	35	14	.00700	36	18	.00892
34	10	.00540	35	15	.00739	36	19	.00939
34	11	.00572	35	16	.00779	36	20	.00987
34	12	.00606	35	17	.00820	36	21	.01037
34	13	.00641	35	18	.00863	36	22	.01090
34	14	.00678	35	19	.00907	36	23	.01145
34	15	.00715	35	20	.00953	36	24	.01203
34	16	.00753	35	21	.01002	36	25	.01264
34	17	.00793	35	22	.01052	36	26	.01328
34	18	.00834	35	23	.01105	36	27	.01395
34	19	.00876	35	24	.01161	36	28	.01466
34	20	.00921	35	25	.01219	36	29	.01539
34	21	.00967	35	26	.01280	36	30	.01615
34	22	.01015	35	27	.01344	36	31	.01693
34	23	.01066	35	28	.01411	36	32	.01774
34	24	.01119	35	29	.01480	36	33	.01857
34	25	.01174	35	30	.01552	36	34	.01943
34	26	.01232	35	31	.01626	36	35	.02032
34	27	.01293	35	32	.01703	36	36	.02122
34	28	.01357	35	33	.01782	37	0	.00478
34	29	.01422	35	34	.01863	37	1	.00368
34	30	.01491	35	35	.01946	37	2	.00382
34	31	.01561	36	0	.00460	37	3	.00401
34	32	.01633	36	1	.00357	37	4	.00422
34	33	.01708	36	2	.00371	37	5	.00446
34	34	.01785	36	3	.00390	37	6	.00472
35	0	.00442	36	4	.00410	37	7	.00499
35	1	.00346	36	5	.00433	37	8	.00528
35	2	.00360	36	6	.00458	37	9	.00560
35	3	.00378	36	7	.00484	37	10	.00593
35	4	.00398	36	8	.00513	37	11	.00629
35	5	.00420	36	9	.00543	37	12	.00666
35	6	.00444	36	10	.00575	37	13	.00706
35	7	.00470	36	11	.00610	37	14	.00747
35	8	.00497	36	12	.00646	37	15	.00789
35	9	.00527	36	13	.00684	37	16	.00832

Table A(2)
The Present Worth of $1.00 Due at the Death of the Survivor of Two Persons
Interest at 10 Percent

Older	Younger	Present Worth	Older	Younger	Present Worth	Older	Younger	Present Worth
37	17	.00876	38	19	.01002	39	20	.01089
37	18	.00922	38	20	.01055	39	21	.01146
37	19	.00970	38	21	.01109	39	22	.01205
37	20	.01020	38	22	.01167	39	23	.01268
37	21	.01073	38	23	.01227	39	24	.01334
37	22	.01128	38	24	.01290	39	25	.01404
37	23	.01186	38	25	.01357	39	26	.01477
37	24	.01246	38	26	.01427	39	27	.01554
37	25	.01310	38	27	.01501	39	28	.01636
37	26	.01377	38	28	.01578	39	29	.01720
37	27	.01448	38	29	.01659	39	30	.01808
37	28	.01522	38	30	.01743	39	31	.01900
37	29	.01598	38	31	.01830	39	32	.01995
37	30	.01678	38	32	.01920	39	33	.02093
37	31	.01761	38	33	.02013	39	34	.02194
37	32	.01846	38	34	.02109	39	35	.02298
37	33	.01935	38	35	.02208	39	36	.02405
37	34	.02025	38	36	.02309	39	37	.02516
37	35	.02119	38	37	.02413	39	38	.02628
37	36	.02215	38	38	.02520	39	39	.02743
37	37	.02313	39	0	.00518	40	0	.00539
38	0	.00498	39	1	.00390	40	1	.00402
38	1	.00379	39	2	.00405	40	2	.00417
38	2	.00394	39	3	.00425	40	3	.00437
38	3	.00413	39	4	.00447	40	4	.00460
38	4	.00435	39	5	.00472	40	5	.00486
38	5	.00459	39	6	.00500	40	6	.00514
38	6	.00485	39	7	.00529	40	7	.00544
38	7	.00514	39	8	.00560	40	8	.00576
38	8	.00544	39	9	.00594	40	9	.00611
38	9	.00576	39	10	.00629	40	10	.00648
38	10	.00611	39	11	.00668	40	11	.00687
38	11	.00648	39	12	.00708	40	12	.00729
38	12	.00687	39	13	.00750	40	13	.00773
38	13	.00728	39	14	.00794	40	14	.00819
38	14	.00770	39	15	.00840	40	15	.00865
38	15	.00814	39	16	.00886	40	16	.00913
38	16	.00859	39	17	.00934	40	17	.00963
38	17	.00905	39	18	.00983	40	18	.01014
38	18	.00953	39	19	.01035	40	19	.01068

Table A(2)
The Present Worth of $1.00 Due at the Death of the Survivor of Two Persons
Interest at 10 Percent

Older	Younger	Present Worth	Older	Younger	Present Worth	Older	Younger	Present Worth
40	20	.01124	41	19	.01101	42	17	.01022
40	21	.01183	41	20	.01159	42	18	.01077
40	22	.01245	41	21	.01220	42	19	.01134
40	23	.01310	41	22	.01284	42	20	.01194
40	24	.01379	41	23	.01352	42	21	.01258
40	25	.01451	41	24	.01423	42	22	.01324
40	26	.01528	41	25	.01499	42	23	.01394
40	27	.01609	41	26	.01579	42	24	.01469
40	28	.01693	41	27	.01663	42	25	.01547
40	29	.01782	41	28	.01752	42	26	.01630
40	30	.01875	41	29	.01845	42	27	.01718
40	31	.01971	41	30	.01942	42	28	.01811
40	32	.02070	41	31	.02042	42	29	.01908
40	33	.02173	41	32	.02147	42	30	.02009
40	34	.02280	41	33	.02255	42	31	.02115
40	35	.02390	41	34	.02367	42	32	.02224
40	36	.02503	41	35	.02483	42	33	.02338
40	37	.02620	41	36	.02603	42	34	.02456
40	38	.02739	41	37	.02726	42	35	.02578
40	39	.02861	41	38	.02852	42	36	.02704
40	40	.02985	41	39	.02981	42	37	.02833
41	0	.00560	41	40	.03112	42	38	.02966
41	1	.00413	41	41	.03247	42	39	.03102
41	2	.00429	42	0	.00583	42	40	.03242
41	3	.00450	42	1	.00425	42	41	.03384
41	4	.00473	42	2	.00441	42	42	.03530
41	5	.00499	42	3	.00462	43	0	.00606
41	6	.00528	42	4	.00486	43	1	.00437
41	7	.00559	42	5	.00513	43	2	.00453
41	8	.00592	42	6	.00543	43	3	.00475
41	9	.00628	42	7	.00575	43	4	.00499
41	10	.00666	42	8	.00609	43	5	.00527
41	11	.00707	42	9	.00646	43	6	.00557
41	12	.00751	42	10	.00685	43	7	.00590
41	13	.00796	42	11	.00727	43	8	.00625
41	14	.00843	42	12	.00772	43	9	.00663
41	15	.00892	42	13	.00819	43	10	.00704
41	16	.00941	42	14	.00868	43	11	.00748
41	17	.00992	42	15	.00918	43	12	.00794
41	18	.01045	42	16	.00969	43	13	.00843

Tools and Techniques

Table A(2)
The Present Worth of $1.00 Due at the Death of the Survivor of Two Persons
Interest at 10 Percent

Older	Younger	Present Worth	Older	Younger	Present Worth	Older	Younger	Present Worth
43	14	.00893	44	10	.00723	45	5	.00555
43	15	.00944	44	11	.00768	45	6	.00587
43	16	.00997	44	12	.00816	45	7	.00622
43	17	.01052	44	13	.00866	45	8	.00659
43	18	.01109	44	14	.00918	45	9	.00699
43	19	.01168	44	15	.00971	45	10	.00743
43	20	.01230	44	16	.01026	45	11	.00789
43	21	.01295	44	17	.01082	45	12	.00838
43	22	.01364	44	18	.01140	45	13	.00890
43	23	.01437	44	19	.01201	45	14	.00943
43	24	.01514	44	20	.01266	45	15	.00998
43	25	.01596	44	21	.01333	45	16	.01055
43	26	.01682	44	22	.01405	45	17	.01112
43	27	.01774	44	23	.01480	45	18	.01172
43	28	.01870	44	24	.01560	45	19	.01235
43	29	.01972	44	25	.01644	45	20	.01301
43	30	.02077	44	26	.01734	45	21	.01371
43	31	.02188	44	27	.01829	45	22	.01445
43	32	.02303	44	28	.01930	45	23	.01523
43	33	.02422	44	29	.02036	45	24	.01605
43	34	.02546	44	30	.02146	45	25	.01693
43	35	.02674	44	31	.02261	45	26	.01786
43	36	.02806	44	32	.02381	45	27	.01885
43	37	.02942	44	33	.02506	45	28	.01990
43	38	.03082	44	34	.02636	45	29	.02100
43	39	.03226	44	35	.02770	45	30	.02215
43	40	.03373	44	36	.02909	45	31	.02335
43	41	.03524	44	37	.03053	45	32	.02461
43	42	.03678	44	38	.03200	45	33	.02591
43	43	.03835	44	39	.03351	45	34	.02727
44	0	.00629	44	40	.03507	45	35	.02868
44	1	.00450	44	41	.03666	45	36	.03013
44	2	.00466	44	42	.03828	45	37	.03164
44	3	.00487	44	43	.03994	45	38	.03319
44	4	.00513	44	44	.04163	45	39	.03478
44	5	.00541	45	0	.00654	45	40	.03642
44	6	.00572	45	1	.00462	45	41	.03809
44	7	.00606	45	2	.00478	45	42	.03981
44	8	.00642	45	3	.00500	45	43	.04156
44	9	.00681	45	4	.00526	45	44	.04335

Table A(2)

The Present Worth of $1.00 Due at the Death of the Survivor of Two Persons

Interest at 10 Percent

Older	Younger	Present Worth	Older	Younger	Present Worth	Older	Younger	Present Worth
45	45	.04517	46	39	.03606	47	32	.02620
46	0	.00679	46	40	.03778	47	33	.02762
46	1	.00474	46	41	.03954	47	34	.02910
46	2	.00491	46	42	.04135	47	35	.03064
46	3	.00513	46	43	.04320	47	36	.03224
46	4	.00540	46	44	.04509	47	37	.03389
46	5	.00569	46	45	.04701	47	38	.03559
46	6	.00602	46	46	.04896	47	39	.03735
46	7	.00638	47	0	.00706	47	40	.03915
46	8	.00676	47	1	.00487	47	41	.04101
46	9	.00717	47	2	.00503	47	42	.04291
46	10	.00762	47	3	.00526	47	43	.04486
46	11	.00810	47	4	.00553	47	44	.04685
46	12	.00860	47	5	.00584	47	45	.04888
46	13	.00914	47	6	.00617	47	46	.05094
46	14	.00969	47	7	.00654	47	47	.05303
46	15	.01025	47	8	.00693	48	0	.00732
46	16	.01083	47	9	.00736	48	1	.00500
46	17	.01143	47	10	.00781	48	2	.00516
46	18	.01205	47	11	.00830	48	3	.00539
46	19	.01269	47	12	.00883	48	4	.00567
46	20	.01337	47	13	.00937	48	5	.00598
46	21	.01409	47	14	.00994	48	6	.00633
46	22	.01485	47	15	.01052	48	7	.00670
46	23	.01566	47	16	.01112	48	8	.00710
46	24	.01651	47	17	.01173	48	9	.00754
46	25	.01742	47	18	.01237	48	10	.00801
46	26	.01839	47	19	.01303	48	11	.00851
46	27	.01941	47	20	.01373	48	12	.00905
46	28	.02050	47	21	.01447	48	13	.00962
46	29	.02164	47	22	.01526	48	14	.01020
46	30	.02284	47	23	.01609	48	15	.01080
46	31	.02409	47	24	.01697	48	16	.01141
46	32	.02540	47	25	.01791	48	17	.01204
46	33	.02677	47	26	.01891	48	18	.01269
46	34	.02818	47	27	.01997	48	19	.01337
46	35	.02966	47	28	.02110	48	20	.01409
46	36	.03118	47	29	.02228	48	21	.01486
46	37	.03276	47	30	.02353	48	22	.01566
46	38	.03439	47	31	.02483	48	23	.01652

Tools and Techniques

Table A(2)
The Present Worth of $1.00 Due at the Death of the Survivor of Two Persons
Interest at 10 Percent

Older	Younger	Present Worth	Older	Younger	Present Worth	Older	Younger	Present Worth
48	24	.01742	49	15	.01107	50	5	.00627
48	25	.01839	49	16	.01170	50	6	.00663
48	26	.01943	49	17	.01235	50	7	.00702
48	27	.02053	49	18	.01302	50	8	.00745
48	28	.02170	49	19	.01371	50	9	.00791
48	29	.02293	49	20	.01445	50	10	.00840
48	30	.02422	49	21	.01524	50	11	.00894
48	31	.02558	49	22	.01607	50	12	.00950
48	32	.02700	49	23	.01694	50	13	.01010
48	33	.02848	49	24	.01788	50	14	.01072
48	34	.03002	49	25	.01888	50	15	.01135
48	35	.03163	49	26	.01995	50	16	.01199
48	36	.03329	49	27	.02109	50	17	.01265
48	37	.03502	49	28	.02229	50	18	.01334
48	38	.03680	49	29	.02357	50	19	.01406
48	39	.03864	49	30	.02491	50	20	.01482
48	40	.04054	49	31	.02632	50	21	.01562
48	41	.04249	49	32	.02779	50	22	.01647
48	42	.04449	49	33	.02934	50	23	.01737
48	43	.04654	49	34	.03094	50	24	.01834
48	44	.04863	49	35	.03262	50	25	.01936
48	45	.05077	49	36	.03435	50	26	.02047
48	46	.05295	49	37	.03616	50	27	.02164
48	47	.05516	49	38	.03802	50	28	.02289
48	48	.05741	49	39	.03995	50	29	.02421
49	0	.00760	49	40	.04193	50	30	.02560
49	1	.00513	49	41	.04397	50	31	.02706
49	2	.00529	49	42	.04608	50	32	.02859
49	3	.00553	49	43	.04823	50	33	.03019
49	4	.00581	49	44	.05043	50	34	.03186
49	5	.00613	49	45	.05268	50	35	.03361
49	6	.00648	49	46	.05498	50	36	.03542
49	7	.00686	49	47	.05731	50	37	.03730
49	8	.00727	49	48	.05968	50	38	.03925
49	9	.00772	49	49	.06209	50	39	.04126
49	10	.00821	50	0	.00789	50	40	.04333
49	11	.00872	50	1	.00526	50	41	.04547
49	12	.00928	50	2	.00542	50	42	.04767
49	13	.00986	50	3	.00566	50	43	.04993
49	14	.01046	50	4	.00594	50	44	.05225

Table A(2)
The Present Worth of $1.00 Due at the Death of the Survivor of Two Persons
Interest at 10 Percent

Older	Younger	Present Worth	Older	Younger	Present Worth	Older	Younger	Present Worth
50	45	.05461	51	34	.03278	52	22	.01727
50	46	.05703	51	35	.03459	52	23	.01822
50	47	.05948	51	36	.03648	52	24	.01924
50	48	.06199	51	37	.03844	52	25	.02033
50	49	.06453	51	38	.04047	52	26	.02149
50	50	.06710	51	39	.04257	52	27	.02274
51	0	.00818	51	40	.04473	52	28	.02407
51	1	.00539	51	41	.04697	52	29	.02548
51	2	.00555	51	42	.04928	52	30	.02697
51	3	.00579	51	43	.05164	52	31	.02853
51	4	.00608	51	44	.05407	52	32	.03017
51	5	.00642	51	45	.05655	52	33	.03190
51	6	.00678	51	46	.05909	52	34	.03370
51	7	.00718	51	47	.06168	52	35	.03558
51	8	.00762	51	48	.06431	52	36	.03754
51	9	.00809	51	49	.06699	52	37	.03957
51	10	.00860	51	50	.06971	52	38	.04169
51	11	.00915	51	51	.07246	52	39	.04388
51	12	.00973	52	0	.00848	52	40	.04614
51	13	.01034	52	1	.00552	52	41	.04847
51	14	.01098	52	2	.00568	52	42	.05088
51	15	.01162	52	3	.00593	52	43	.05336
51	16	.01228	52	4	.00622	52	44	.05590
51	17	.01296	52	5	.00656	52	45	.05850
51	18	.01366	52	6	.00694	52	46	.06116
51	19	.01440	52	7	.00735	52	47	.06388
51	20	.01517	52	8	.00779	52	48	.06665
51	21	.01600	52	9	.00828	52	49	.06947
51	22	.01687	52	10	.00880	52	50	.07233
51	23	.01780	52	11	.00936	52	51	.07524
51	24	.01879	52	12	.00996	52	52	.07817
51	25	.01985	52	13	.01059	53	0	.00879
51	26	.02098	52	14	.01123	53	1	.00565
51	27	.02219	52	15	.01190	53	2	.00581
51	28	.02348	52	16	.01258	53	3	.00606
51	29	.02485	52	17	.01327	53	4	.00636
51	30	.02629	52	18	.01399	53	5	.00671
51	31	.02780	52	19	.01474	53	6	.00709
51	32	.02938	52	20	.01553	53	7	.00751
51	33	.03105	52	21	.01638	53	8	.00796

Tools and Techniques

Table A(2)
The Present Worth of $1.00 Due at the
Death of the Survivor of Two Persons
Interest at 10 Percent

Older	Younger	Present Worth	Older	Younger	Present Worth	Older	Younger	Present Worth
53	9	.00846	53	49	.07197	54	35	.03753
53	10	.00899	53	50	.07498	54	36	.03964
53	11	.00957	53	51	.07804	54	37	.04183
53	12	.01018	53	52	.08113	54	38	.04411
53	13	.01083	53	53	.08426	54	39	.04648
53	14	.01149	54	0	.00911	54	40	.04893
53	15	.01217	54	1	.00579	54	41	.05147
53	16	.01287	54	2	.00594	54	42	.05409
53	17	.01358	54	3	.00619	54	43	.05679
53	18	.01431	54	4	.00650	54	44	.05956
53	19	.01508	54	5	.00685	54	45	.06241
53	20	.01589	54	6	.00724	54	46	.06533
53	21	.01675	54	7	.00767	54	47	.06831
53	22	.01767	54	8	.00814	54	48	.07136
53	23	.01864	54	9	.00864	54	49	.07447
53	24	.01968	54	10	.00919	54	50	.07764
53	25	.02080	54	11	.00978	54	51	.08085
53	26	.02200	54	12	.01041	54	52	.08411
53	27	.02329	54	13	.01107	54	53	.08740
53	28	.02466	54	14	.01175	54	54	.09072
53	29	.02611	54	15	.01245	55	0	.00943
53	30	.02765	54	16	.01316	55	1	.00592
53	31	.02926	54	17	.01388	55	2	.00607
53	32	.03096	54	18	.01463	55	3	.00633
53	33	.03274	54	19	.01541	55	4	.00664
53	34	.03461	54	20	.01624	55	5	.00700
53	35	.03656	54	21	.01712	55	6	.00740
53	36	.03859	54	22	.01806	55	7	.00783
53	37	.04071	54	23	.01906	55	8	.00831
53	38	.04290	54	24	.02012	55	9	.00883
53	39	.04518	54	25	.02127	55	10	.00939
53	40	.04754	54	26	.02250	55	11	.00999
53	41	.04997	54	27	.02382	55	12	.01064
53	42	.05249	54	28	.02524	55	13	.01131
53	43	.05507	54	29	.02673	55	14	.01201
53	44	.05773	54	30	.02832	55	15	.01272
53	45	.06046	54	31	.02998	55	16	.01345
53	46	.06325	54	32	.03174	55	17	.01419
53	47	.06610	54	33	.03358	55	18	.01495
53	48	.06900	54	34	.03551	55	19	.01575

Table A(2)
The Present Worth of $1.00 Due at the Death of the Survivor of Two Persons
Interest at 10 Percent

Older	Younger	Present Worth	Older	Younger	Present Worth	Older	Younger	Present Worth
55	20	.01659	56	4	.00677	56	44	.06321
55	21	.01749	56	5	.00714	56	45	.06630
55	22	.01845	56	6	.00755	56	46	.06948
55	23	.01947	56	7	.00799	56	47	.07274
55	24	.02056	56	8	.00848	56	48	.07608
55	25	.02174	56	9	.00901	56	49	.07949
55	26	.02300	56	10	.00958	56	50	.08297
55	27	.02436	56	11	.01020	56	51	.08651
55	28	.02581	56	12	.01086	56	52	.09010
55	29	.02735	56	13	.01155	56	53	.09374
55	30	.02898	56	14	.01227	56	54	.09742
55	31	.03070	56	15	.01300	56	55	.10113
55	32	.03251	56	16	.01373	56	56	.10486
55	33	.03441	56	17	.01449	57	0	.01009
55	34	.03640	56	18	.01527	57	1	.00619
55	35	.03849	56	19	.01608	57	2	.00634
55	36	.04067	56	20	.01694	57	3	.00659
55	37	.04295	56	21	.01786	57	4	.00691
55	38	.04532	56	22	.01884	57	5	.00728
55	39	.04777	56	23	.01988	57	6	.00770
55	40	.05032	56	24	.02099	57	7	.00815
55	41	.05295	56	25	.02219	57	8	.00865
55	42	.05568	56	26	.02349	57	9	.00919
55	43	.05849	56	27	.02488	57	10	.00978
55	44	.06139	56	28	.02637	57	11	.01041
55	45	.06436	56	29	.02795	57	12	.01109
55	46	.06741	56	30	.02963	57	13	.01180
55	47	.07053	56	31	.03140	57	14	.01253
55	48	.07372	56	32	.03327	57	15	.01327
55	49	.07698	56	33	.03523	57	16	.01402
55	50	.08030	56	34	.03729	57	17	.01479
55	51	.08368	56	35	.03944	57	18	.01558
55	52	.08710	56	36	.04170	57	19	.01641
55	53	.09057	56	37	.04406	57	20	.01729
55	54	.09406	56	38	.04651	57	21	.01822
55	55	.09759	56	39	.04905	57	22	.01922
56	0	.00976	56	40	.05169	57	23	.02028
56	1	.00605	56	41	.05443	57	24	.02142
56	2	.00621	56	42	.05726	57	25	.02265
56	3	.00646	56	43	.06019	57	26	.02397

Tools and Techniques

Table A(2)
**The Present Worth of $1.00 Due at the
Death of the Survivor of Two Persons**
Interest at 10 Percent

Older	Younger	Present Worth	Older	Younger	Present Worth	Older	Younger	Present Worth
57	27	.02540	58	9	.00937	58	49	.08449
57	28	.02693	58	10	.00997	58	50	.08829
57	29	.02855	58	11	.01062	58	51	.09216
57	30	.03028	58	12	.01131	58	52	.09611
57	31	.03210	58	13	.01203	58	53	.10011
57	32	.03402	58	14	.01278	58	54	.10416
57	33	.03604	58	15	.01354	58	55	.10825
57	34	.03816	58	16	.01431	58	56	.11238
57	35	.04039	58	17	.01509	58	57	.11653
57	36	.04272	58	18	.01589	58	58	.12071
57	37	.04515	58	19	.01674	59	0	.01078
57	38	.04768	58	20	.01763	59	1	.00645
57	39	.05032	58	21	.01858	59	2	.00659
57	40	.05306	58	22	.01959	59	3	.00685
57	41	.05589	58	23	.02068	59	4	.00718
57	42	.05884	58	24	.02184	59	5	.00756
57	43	.06188	58	25	.02309	59	6	.00800
57	44	.06501	58	26	.02445	59	7	.00847
57	45	.06824	58	27	.02591	59	8	.00898
57	46	.07155	58	28	.02748	59	9	.00955
57	47	.07495	58	29	.02914	59	10	.01016
57	48	.07843	58	30	.03091	59	11	.01082
57	49	.08199	58	31	.03278	59	12	.01153
57	50	.08563	58	32	.03475	59	13	.01227
57	51	.08934	58	33	.03683	59	14	.01303
57	52	.09310	58	34	.03902	59	15	.01381
57	53	.09692	58	35	.04131	59	16	.01459
57	54	.10079	58	36	.04372	59	17	.01538
57	55	.10468	58	37	.04623	59	18	.01620
57	56	.10861	58	38	.04885	59	19	.01706
57	57	.11257	58	39	.05157	59	20	.01797
58	0	.01043	58	40	.05441	59	21	.01894
58	1	.00632	58	41	.05735	59	22	.01997
58	2	.00646	58	42	.06040	59	23	.02107
58	3	.00672	58	43	.06355	59	24	.02225
58	4	.00705	58	44	.06681	59	25	.02353
58	5	.00742	58	45	.07016	59	26	.02492
58	6	.00785	58	46	.07360	59	27	.02641
58	7	.00831	58	47	.07714	59	28	.02801
58	8	.00882	58	48	.08077	59	29	.02972

Table A(2)
The Present Worth of $1.00 Due at the
Death of the Survivor of Two Persons
Interest at 10 Percent

Older	Younger	Present Worth	Older	Younger	Present Worth	Older	Younger	Present Worth
59	30	.03154	60	10	.01035	60	50	.09357
59	31	.03345	60	11	.01103	60	51	.09779
59	32	.03548	60	12	.01175	60	52	.10209
59	33	.03762	60	13	.01251	60	53	.10646
59	34	.03987	60	14	.01329	60	54	.11090
59	35	.04223	60	15	.01408	60	55	.11539
59	36	.04471	60	16	.01487	60	56	.11992
59	37	.04730	60	17	.01568	60	57	.12451
59	38	.05000	60	18	.01651	60	58	.12912
59	39	.05282	60	19	.01738	60	59	.13377
59	40	.05574	60	20	.01831	60	60	.13843
59	41	.05878	60	21	.01929	61	0	.01150
59	42	.06194	60	22	.02034	61	1	.00671
59	43	.06521	60	23	.02146	61	2	.00685
59	44	.06859	60	24	.02266	61	3	.00711
59	45	.07206	60	25	.02397	61	4	.00744
59	46	.07564	60	26	.02538	61	5	.00784
59	47	.07932	60	27	.02690	61	6	.00829
59	48	.08310	60	28	.02854	61	7	.00878
59	49	.08698	60	29	.03029	61	8	.00932
59	50	.09094	60	30	.03215	61	9	.00990
59	51	.09498	60	31	.03412	61	10	.01054
59	52	.09910	60	32	.03620	61	11	.01123
59	53	.10329	60	33	.03839	61	12	.01197
59	54	.10753	60	34	.04070	61	13	.01275
59	55	.11182	60	35	.04313	61	14	.01354
59	56	.11615	60	36	.04568	61	15	.01434
59	57	.12052	60	37	.04835	61	16	.01515
59	58	.12491	60	38	.05114	61	17	.01597
59	59	.12933	60	39	.05404	61	18	.01682
60	0	.01114	60	40	.05706	61	19	.01770
60	1	.00658	60	41	.06020	61	20	.01864
60	2	.00672	60	42	.06347	61	21	.01964
60	3	.00698	60	43	.06685	61	22	.02070
60	4	.00731	60	44	.07035	61	23	.02184
60	5	.00770	60	45	.07395	61	24	.02306
60	6	.00814	60	46	.07767	61	25	.02439
60	7	.00862	60	47	.08149	61	26	.02583
60	8	.00915	60	48	.08542	61	27	.02739
60	9	.00973	60	49	.08945	61	28	.02906

Tools and Techniques

Table A(2)

The Present Worth of $1.00 Due at the Death of the Survivor of Two Persons
Interest at 10 Percent

Older	Younger	Present Worth	Older	Younger	Present Worth	Older	Younger	Present Worth
61	29	.03085	62	7	.00893	62	47	.08576
61	30	.03276	62	8	.00948	62	48	.08999
61	31	.03477	62	9	.01008	62	49	.09433
61	32	.03690	62	10	.01073	62	50	.09879
61	33	.03915	62	11	.01144	62	51	.10335
61	34	.04152	62	12	.01219	62	52	.10801
61	35	.04402	62	13	.01298	62	53	.11277
61	36	.04664	62	14	.01379	62	54	.11759
61	37	.04939	62	15	.01461	62	55	.12249
61	38	.05225	62	16	.01543	62	56	.12746
61	39	.05525	62	17	.01626	62	57	.13248
61	40	.05836	62	18	.01712	62	58	.13754
61	41	.06160	62	19	.01802	62	59	.14266
61	42	.06497	62	20	.01897	62	60	.14780
61	43	.06847	62	21	.01998	62	61	.15298
61	44	.07209	62	22	.02106	62	62	.15817
61	45	.07582	62	23	.02221	63	0	.01225
61	46	.07967	62	24	.02346	63	1	.00697
61	47	.08363	62	25	.02481	63	2	.00710
61	48	.08771	62	26	.02628	63	3	.00736
61	49	.09190	62	27	.02786	63	4	.00770
61	50	.09619	62	28	.02958	63	5	.00811
61	51	.10058	62	29	.03140	63	6	.00857
61	52	.10506	62	30	.03335	63	7	.00908
61	53	.10962	62	31	.03541	63	8	.00964
61	54	.11425	62	32	.03759	63	9	.01025
61	55	.11895	62	33	.03990	63	10	.01092
61	56	.12370	62	34	.04233	63	11	.01164
61	57	.12849	62	35	.04489	63	12	.01241
61	58	.13333	62	36	.04758	63	13	.01321
61	59	.13821	62	37	.05040	63	14	.01404
61	60	.14312	62	38	.05335	63	15	.01487
61	61	.14804	62	39	.05643	63	16	.01571
62	0	.01187	62	40	.05964	63	17	.01655
62	1	.00684	62	41	.06298	63	18	.01742
62	2	.00697	62	42	.06646	63	19	.01833
62	3	.00724	62	43	.07007	63	20	.01929
62	4	.00757	62	44	.07381	63	21	.02032
62	5	.00798	62	45	.07767	63	22	.02141
62	6	.00843	62	46	.08165	63	23	.02258

Table A(2)
The Present Worth of $1.00 Due at the Death of the Survivor of Two Persons
Interest at 10 Percent

Older	Younger	Present Worth	Older	Younger	Present Worth	Older	Younger	Present Worth
63	24	.02385	64	0	.01263	64	40	.06213
63	25	.02522	64	1	.00710	64	41	.06567
63	26	.02671	64	2	.00722	64	42	.06936
63	27	.02833	64	3	.00748	64	43	.07319
63	28	.03007	64	4	.00783	64	44	.07717
63	29	.03194	64	5	.00824	64	45	.08128
63	30	.03393	64	6	.00871	64	46	.08553
63	31	.03603	64	7	.00923	64	47	.08992
63	32	.03827	64	8	.00980	64	48	.09445
63	33	.04063	64	9	.01042	64	49	.09910
63	34	.04312	64	10	.01110	64	50	.10390
63	35	.04575	64	11	.01183	64	51	.10881
63	36	.04851	64	12	.01262	64	52	.11384
63	37	.05140	64	13	.01344	64	53	.11897
63	38	.05443	64	14	.01428	64	54	.12420
63	39	.05760	64	15	.01513	64	55	.12951
63	40	.06090	64	16	.01598	64	56	.13491
63	41	.06434	64	17	.01684	64	57	.14038
63	42	.06792	64	18	.01772	64	58	.14591
63	43	.07164	64	19	.01863	64	59	.15151
63	44	.07550	64	20	.01961	64	60	.15715
63	45	.07949	64	21	.02065	64	61	.16284
63	46	.08361	64	22	.02176	64	62	.16856
63	47	.08785	64	23	.02294	64	63	.17431
63	48	.09223	64	24	.02423	64	64	.18005
63	49	.09673	64	25	.02562	65	0	.01302
63	50	.10136	64	26	.02714	65	1	.00722
63	51	.10610	64	27	.02879	65	2	.00734
63	52	.11094	64	28	.03056	65	3	.00760
63	53	.11588	64	29	.03246	65	4	.00795
63	54	.12091	64	30	.03449	65	5	.00837
63	55	.12602	64	31	.03664	65	6	.00885
63	56	.13120	64	32	.03892	65	7	.00937
63	57	.13644	64	33	.04134	65	8	.00995
63	58	.14174	64	34	.04389	65	9	.01059
63	59	.14709	64	35	.04658	65	10	.01128
63	60	.15249	64	36	.04941	65	11	.01203
63	61	.15792	64	37	.05238	65	12	.01283
63	62	.16337	64	38	.05549	65	13	.01367
63	63	.16884	64	39	.05874	65	14	.01453

Tools and Techniques

Table A(2)
The Present Worth of $1.00 Due at the
Death of the Survivor of Two Persons
Interest at 10 Percent

Older	Younger	Present Worth	Older	Younger	Present Worth	Older	Younger	Present Worth
65	15	.01539	65	55	.13297	66	29	.03347
65	16	.01625	65	56	.13858	66	30	.03558
65	17	.01712	65	57	.14428	66	31	.03782
65	18	.01801	65	58	.15004	66	32	.04019
65	19	.01894	65	59	.15588	66	33	.04271
65	20	.01992	65	60	.16178	66	34	.04538
65	21	.02097	65	61	.16774	66	35	.04819
65	22	.02210	65	62	.17373	66	36	.05115
65	23	.02330	65	63	.17975	66	37	.05427
65	24	.02460	65	64	.18578	66	38	.05753
65	25	.02601	65	65	.19181	66	39	.06095
65	26	.02756	66	0	.01341	66	40	.06452
65	27	.02923	66	1	.00735	66	41	.06825
65	28	.03104	66	2	.00746	66	42	.07214
65	29	.03298	66	3	.00772	66	43	.07619
65	30	.03504	66	4	.00807	66	44	.08040
65	31	.03724	66	5	.00850	66	45	.08476
65	32	.03957	66	6	.00898	66	46	.08927
65	33	.04204	66	7	.00951	66	47	.09394
65	34	.04464	66	8	.01010	66	48	.09876
65	35	.04740	66	9	.01075	66	49	.10373
65	36	.05029	66	10	.01146	66	50	.10885
65	37	.05334	66	11	.01222	66	51	.11411
65	38	.05652	66	12	.01304	66	52	.11950
65	39	.05986	66	13	.01389	66	53	.12502
65	40	.06334	66	14	.01477	66	54	.13064
65	41	.06697	66	15	.01564	66	55	.13638
65	42	.07077	66	16	.01652	66	56	.14221
65	43	.07471	66	17	.01740	66	57	.14813
65	44	.07880	66	18	.01830	66	58	.15413
65	45	.08304	66	19	.01924	66	59	.16022
65	46	.08742	66	20	.02023	66	60	.16637
65	47	.09195	66	21	.02130	66	61	.17259
65	48	.09662	66	22	.02243	66	62	.17886
65	49	.10144	66	23	.02365	66	63	.18517
65	50	.10639	66	24	.02496	66	64	.19149
65	51	.11148	66	25	.02640	66	65	.19781
65	52	.11669	66	26	.02796	66	66	.20412
65	53	.12202	66	27	.02966	67	0	.01381
65	54	.12744	66	28	.03150	67	1	.00747

Table A(2)

**The Present Worth of $1.00 Due at the
Death of the Survivor of Two Persons**

Interest at 10 Percent

Older	Younger	Present Worth	Older	Younger	Present Worth	Older	Younger	Present Worth
67	2	.00757	67	42	.07348	68	14	.01524
67	3	.00784	67	43	.07764	68	15	.01614
67	4	.00819	67	44	.08196	68	16	.01704
67	5	.00862	67	45	.08644	68	17	.01794
67	6	.00911	67	46	.09108	68	18	.01886
67	7	.00965	67	47	.09588	68	19	.01982
67	8	.01025	67	48	.10085	68	20	.02084
67	9	.01091	67	49	.10597	68	21	.02192
67	10	.01163	67	50	.11125	68	22	.02307
67	11	.01241	67	51	.11668	68	23	.02432
67	12	.01324	67	52	.12226	68	24	.02566
67	13	.01411	67	53	.12796	68	25	.02713
67	14	.01500	67	54	.13379	68	26	.02874
67	15	.01589	67	55	.13973	68	27	.03049
67	16	.01678	67	56	.14578	68	28	.03239
67	17	.01767	67	57	.15193	68	29	.03443
67	18	.01858	67	58	.15817	68	30	.03661
67	19	.01953	67	59	.16450	68	31	.03893
67	20	.02054	67	60	.17091	68	32	.04139
67	21	.02161	67	61	.17740	68	33	.04401
67	22	.02275	67	62	.18394	68	34	.04678
67	23	.02398	67	63	.19053	68	35	.04971
67	24	.02532	67	64	.19715	68	36	.05280
67	25	.02677	67	65	.20378	68	37	.05605
67	26	.02836	67	66	.21040	68	38	.05946
67	27	.03008	67	67	.21700	68	39	.06304
67	28	.03195	68	0	.01422	68	40	.06678
67	29	.03396	68	1	.00759	68	41	.07069
67	30	.03610	68	2	.00768	68	42	.07478
67	31	.03838	68	3	.00795	68	43	.07904
67	32	.04080	68	4	.00830	68	44	.08348
67	33	.04337	68	5	.00874	68	45	.08808
67	34	.04609	68	6	.00924	68	46	.09285
67	35	.04896	68	7	.00979	68	47	.09778
67	36	.05199	68	8	.01040	68	48	.10289
67	37	.05517	68	9	.01107	68	49	.10816
67	38	.05851	68	10	.01180	68	50	.11361
67	39	.06201	68	11	.01259	68	51	.11921
67	40	.06566	68	12	.01344	68	52	.12496
67	41	.06949	68	13	.01433	68	53	.13085

Tools and Techniques

Table A(2)
The Present Worth of $1.00 Due at the
Death of the Survivor of Two Persons
Interest at 10 Percent

Older	Younger	Present Worth	Older	Younger	Present Worth	Older	Younger	Present Worth
68	54	.13687	69	25	.02749	69	65	.21555
68	55	.14302	69	26	.02912	69	66	.22281
68	56	.14928	69	27	.03089	69	67	.23005
68	57	.15566	69	28	.03282	69	68	.23727
68	58	.16214	69	29	.03488	69	69	.24446
68	59	.16872	69	30	.03710	70	0	.01504
68	60	.17538	69	31	.03945	70	1	.00782
68	61	.18214	69	32	.04196	70	2	.00790
68	62	.18896	69	33	.04463	70	3	.00816
68	63	.19584	69	34	.04745	70	4	.00852
68	64	.20276	69	35	.05043	70	5	.00896
68	65	.20970	69	36	.05359	70	6	.00948
68	66	.21663	69	37	.05690	70	7	.01004
68	67	.22355	69	38	.06039	70	8	.01067
68	68	.23043	69	39	.06404	70	9	.01137
69	0	.01463	69	40	.06786	70	10	.01212
69	1	.00771	69	41	.07186	70	11	.01295
69	2	.00779	69	42	.07605	70	12	.01383
69	3	.00806	69	43	.08041	70	13	.01475
69	4	.00841	69	44	.08496	70	14	.01569
69	5	.00885	69	45	.08967	70	15	.01662
69	6	.00936	69	46	.09457	70	16	.01755
69	7	.00992	69	47	.09963	70	17	.01847
69	8	.01054	69	48	.10488	70	18	.01941
69	9	.01122	69	49	.11030	70	19	.02038
69	10	.01196	69	50	.11591	70	20	.02141
69	11	.01277	69	51	.12167	70	21	.02252
69	12	.01364	69	52	.12760	70	22	.02369
69	13	.01454	69	53	.13368	70	23	.02495
69	14	.01546	69	54	.13990	70	24	.02633
69	15	.01638	69	55	.14625	70	25	.02783
69	16	.01730	69	56	.15273	70	26	.02948
69	17	.01821	69	57	.15933	70	27	.03127
69	18	.01914	69	58	.16604	70	28	.03323
69	19	.02010	69	59	.17286	70	29	.03533
69	20	.02113	69	60	.17979	70	30	.03757
69	21	.02222	69	61	.18681	70	31	.03997
69	22	.02339	69	62	.19391	70	32	.04252
69	23	.02464	69	63	.20108	70	33	.04523
69	24	.02600	69	64	.20830	70	34	.04810

Table A(2)

The Present Worth of $1.00 Due at the Death of the Survivor of Two Persons

Interest at 10 Percent

Older	Younger	Present Worth	Older	Younger	Present Worth	Older	Younger	Present Worth
70	35	.05114	71	4	.00862	71	44	.08779
70	36	.05435	71	5	.00907	71	45	.09273
70	37	.05773	71	6	.00959	71	46	.09786
70	38	.06128	71	7	.01017	71	47	.10318
70	39	.06501	71	8	.01080	71	48	.10871
70	40	.06891	71	9	.01151	71	49	.11442
70	41	.07300	71	10	.01228	71	50	.12033
70	42	.07728	71	11	.01312	71	51	.12642
70	43	.08174	71	12	.01402	71	52	.13269
70	44	.08640	71	13	.01496	71	53	.13914
70	45	.09122	71	14	.01591	71	54	.14574
70	46	.09624	71	15	.01686	71	55	.15250
70	47	.10143	71	16	.01780	71	56	.15939
70	48	.10682	71	17	.01873	71	57	.16644
70	49	.11239	71	18	.01967	71	58	.17361
70	50	.11815	71	19	.02065	71	59	.18093
70	51	.12408	71	20	.02170	71	60	.18836
70	52	.13018	71	21	.02280	71	61	.19592
70	53	.13644	71	22	.02399	71	62	.20358
70	54	.14285	71	23	.02526	71	63	.21133
70	55	.14941	71	24	.02665	71	64	.21916
70	56	.15610	71	25	.02816	71	65	.22703
70	57	.16292	71	26	.02983	71	66	.23494
70	58	.16987	71	27	.03165	71	67	.24286
70	59	.17694	71	28	.03363	71	68	.25076
70	60	.18412	71	29	.03575	71	69	.25865
70	61	.19141	71	30	.03803	71	70	.26650
70	62	.19879	71	31	.04046	71	71	.27431
70	63	.20625	71	32	.04305	72	0	.01590
70	64	.21377	71	33	.04581	72	1	.00805
70	65	.22133	71	34	.04872	72	2	.00811
70	66	.22891	71	35	.05181	72	3	.00836
70	67	.23649	71	36	.05508	72	4	.00873
70	68	.24405	71	37	.05853	72	5	.00918
70	69	.25158	71	38	.06215	72	6	.00970
70	70	.25907	71	39	.06595	72	7	.01028
71	0	.01547	71	40	.06993	72	8	.01093
71	1	.00794	71	41	.07410	72	9	.01165
71	2	.00801	71	42	.07847	72	10	.01243
71	3	.00827	71	43	.08303	72	11	.01329

Tools and Techniques

Table A(2)

The Present Worth of $1.00 Due at the Death of the Survivor of Two Persons

Interest at 10 Percent

Older	Younger	Present Worth	Older	Younger	Present Worth	Older	Younger	Present Worth
72	12	.01420	72	52	.13514	73	19	.02118
72	13	.01516	72	53	.14176	73	20	.02224
72	14	.01613	72	54	.14855	73	21	.02336
72	15	.01709	72	55	.15550	73	22	.02456
72	16	.01804	72	56	.16261	73	23	.02585
72	17	.01898	72	57	.16987	73	24	.02726
72	18	.01993	72	58	.17728	73	25	.02880
72	19	.02092	72	59	.18483	73	26	.03050
72	20	.02197	72	60	.19252	73	27	.03235
72	21	.02309	72	61	.20034	73	28	.03438
72	22	.02428	72	62	.20828	73	29	.03656
72	23	.02556	72	63	.21632	73	30	.03890
72	24	.02696	72	64	.22445	73	31	.04140
72	25	.02849	72	65	.23264	73	32	.04406
72	26	.03017	72	66	.24087	73	33	.04690
72	27	.03201	72	67	.24913	73	34	.04990
72	28	.03401	72	68	.25738	73	35	.05310
72	29	.03616	72	69	.26563	73	36	.05647
72	30	.03848	72	70	.27385	73	37	.06004
72	31	.04094	72	71	.28204	73	38	.06378
72	32	.04357	72	72	.29016	73	39	.06772
72	33	.04636	73	0	.01633	73	40	.07185
72	34	.04933	73	1	.00816	73	41	.07619
72	35	.05247	73	2	.00821	73	42	.08073
72	36	.05579	73	3	.00846	73	43	.08548
72	37	.05930	73	4	.00882	73	44	.09044
72	38	.06298	73	5	.00928	73	45	.09559
72	39	.06685	73	6	.00981	73	46	.10095
72	40	.07091	73	7	.01040	73	47	.10652
72	41	.07516	73	8	.01105	73	48	.11230
72	42	.07962	73	9	.01178	73	49	.11829
72	43	.08428	73	10	.01258	73	50	.12450
72	44	.08914	73	11	.01345	73	51	.13090
72	45	.09419	73	12	.01438	73	52	.13751
72	46	.09944	73	13	.01535	73	53	.14431
72	47	.10488	73	14	.01634	73	54	.15128
72	48	.11054	73	15	.01731	73	55	.15842
72	49	.11639	73	16	.01827	73	56	.16573
72	50	.12245	73	17	.01923	73	57	.17320
72	51	.12870	73	18	.02019	73	58	.18083

Table A(2)
The Present Worth of $1.00 Due at the Death of the Survivor of Two Persons
Interest at 10 Percent

Older	Younger	Present Worth	Older	Younger	Present Worth	Older	Younger	Present Worth
73	59	.18862	74	25	.02910	74	65	.24343
73	60	.19656	74	26	.03081	74	66	.25231
73	61	.20464	74	27	.03268	74	67	.26124
73	62	.21285	74	28	.03473	74	68	.27019
73	63	.22119	74	29	.03694	74	69	.27916
73	64	.22961	74	30	.03931	74	70	.28813
73	65	.23812	74	31	.04183	74	71	.29709
73	66	.24668	74	32	.04453	74	72	.30600
73	67	.25527	74	33	.04741	74	73	.31481
73	68	.26388	74	34	.05046	74	74	.32345
73	69	.27249	74	35	.05370	75	0	.01720
73	70	.28108	74	36	.05712	75	1	.00837
73	71	.28965	74	37	.06074	75	2	.00840
73	72	.29817	74	38	.06455	75	3	.00864
73	73	.30657	74	39	.06855	75	4	.00900
74	0	.01677	74	40	.07276	75	5	.00946
74	1	.00826	74	41	.07716	75	6	.01000
74	2	.00830	74	42	.08179	75	7	.01060
74	3	.00855	74	43	.08663	75	8	.01128
74	4	.00891	74	44	.09168	75	9	.01203
74	5	.00937	74	45	.09694	75	10	.01285
74	6	.00991	74	46	.10241	75	11	.01375
74	7	.01050	74	47	.10809	75	12	.01471
74	8	.01117	74	48	.11399	75	13	.01572
74	9	.01191	74	49	.12012	75	14	.01673
74	10	.01272	74	50	.12646	75	15	.01774
74	11	.01360	74	51	.13302	75	16	.01872
74	12	.01455	74	52	.13978	75	17	.01969
74	13	.01554	74	53	.14675	75	18	.02067
74	14	.01654	74	54	.15390	75	19	.02168
74	15	.01753	74	55	.16123	75	20	.02274
74	16	.01850	74	56	.16873	75	21	.02388
74	17	.01946	74	57	.17641	75	22	.02509
74	18	.02043	74	58	.18426	75	23	.02639
74	19	.02143	74	59	.19228	75	24	.02782
74	20	.02250	74	60	.20046	75	25	.02938
74	21	.02362	74	61	.20880	75	26	.03111
74	22	.02483	74	62	.21728	75	27	.03300
74	23	.02613	74	63	.22589	75	28	.03507
74	24	.02754	74	64	.23462	75	29	.03729

Tools and Techniques

Table A(2)
The Present Worth of $1.00 Due at the Death of the Survivor of Two Persons
Interest at 10 Percent

Older	Younger	Present Worth	Older	Younger	Present Worth	Older	Younger	Present Worth
75	30	.03969	75	70	.29496	76	34	.05147
75	31	.04225	75	71	.30429	76	35	.05480
75	32	.04498	75	72	.31360	76	36	.05832
75	33	.04789	75	73	.32281	76	37	.06204
75	34	.05098	75	74	.33186	76	38	.06596
75	35	.05426	75	75	.34068	76	39	.07009
75	36	.05774	76	0	.01763	76	40	.07442
75	37	.06141	76	1	.00847	76	41	.07897
75	38	.06528	76	2	.00848	76	42	.08375
75	39	.06934	76	3	.00873	76	43	.08875
75	40	.07361	76	4	.00908	76	44	.09398
75	41	.07809	76	5	.00955	76	45	.09943
75	42	.08280	76	6	.01009	76	46	.10510
75	43	.08772	76	7	.01070	76	47	.11100
75	44	.09286	76	8	.01138	76	48	.11714
75	45	.09821	76	9	.01214	76	49	.12351
75	46	.10379	76	10	.01297	76	50	.13012
75	47	.10958	76	11	.01389	76	51	.13696
75	48	.11561	76	12	.01487	76	52	.14402
75	49	.12186	76	13	.01589	76	53	.15130
75	50	.12834	76	14	.01692	76	54	.15879
75	51	.13504	76	15	.01794	76	55	.16647
75	52	.14196	76	16	.01893	76	56	.17435
75	53	.14908	76	17	.01991	76	57	.18242
75	54	.15640	76	18	.02090	76	58	.19068
75	55	.16391	76	19	.02191	76	59	.19914
75	56	.17161	76	20	.02298	76	60	.20778
75	57	.17949	76	21	.02412	76	61	.21660
75	58	.18755	76	22	.02534	76	62	.22560
75	59	.19579	76	23	.02665	76	63	.23476
75	60	.20420	76	24	.02808	76	64	.24405
75	61	.21279	76	25	.02965	76	65	.25346
75	62	.22153	76	26	.03139	76	66	.26296
75	63	.23042	76	27	.03330	76	67	.27254
75	64	.23943	76	28	.03538	76	68	.28217
75	65	.24855	76	29	.03763	76	69	.29184
75	66	.25775	76	30	.04006	76	70	.30154
75	67	.26700	76	31	.04264	76	71	.31125
75	68	.27630	76	32	.04540	76	72	.32095
75	69	.28562	76	33	.04835	76	73	.33056

Table A(2)

**The Present Worth of $1.00 Due at the
Death of the Survivor of Two Persons**

Interest at 10 Percent

Older	Younger	Present Worth	Older	Younger	Present Worth	Older	Younger	Present Worth
76	74	.34002	77	37	.06264	77	77	.37601
76	75	.34925	77	38	.06661	78	0	.01848
76	76	.35822	77	39	.07079	78	1	.00865
77	0	.01806	77	40	.07518	78	2	.00865
77	1	.00856	77	41	.07980	78	3	.00888
77	2	.00857	77	42	.08465	78	4	.00924
77	3	.00880	77	43	.08973	78	5	.00970
77	4	.00916	77	44	.09504	78	6	.01025
77	5	.00963	77	45	.10057	78	7	.01087
77	6	.01017	77	46	.10634	78	8	.01156
77	7	.01079	77	47	.11234	78	9	.01235
77	8	.01147	77	48	.11859	78	10	.01320
77	9	.01225	77	49	.12507	78	11	.01414
77	10	.01309	77	50	.13181	78	12	.01516
77	11	.01402	77	51	.13878	78	13	.01621
77	12	.01502	77	52	.14598	78	14	.01727
77	13	.01605	77	53	.15341	78	15	.01831
77	14	.01710	77	54	.16105	78	16	.01933
77	15	.01813	77	55	.16890	78	17	.02033
77	16	.01914	77	56	.17695	78	18	.02132
77	17	.02012	77	57	.18521	78	19	.02234
77	18	.02111	77	58	.19367	78	20	.02343
77	19	.02213	77	59	.20233	78	21	.02458
77	20	.02321	77	60	.21119	78	22	.02580
77	21	.02435	77	61	.22024	78	23	.02712
77	22	.02557	77	62	.22949	78	24	.02856
77	23	.02689	77	63	.23890	78	25	.03015
77	24	.02833	77	64	.24846	78	26	.03191
77	25	.02991	77	65	.25816	78	27	.03385
77	26	.03166	77	66	.26796	78	28	.03597
77	27	.03358	77	67	.27785	78	29	.03826
77	28	.03568	77	68	.28781	78	30	.04072
77	29	.03795	77	69	.29782	78	31	.04336
77	30	.04040	77	70	.30787	78	32	.04617
77	31	.04301	77	71	.31796	78	33	.04918
77	32	.04580	77	72	.32803	78	34	.05238
77	33	.04878	77	73	.33804	78	35	.05578
77	34	.05194	77	74	.34790	78	36	.05939
77	35	.05531	77	75	.35753	78	37	.06320
77	36	.05887	77	76	.36691	78	38	.06722

Tools and Techniques

Table A(2)
The Present Worth of $1.00 Due at the Death of the Survivor of Two Persons
Interest at 10 Percent

Older	Younger	Present Worth	Older	Younger	Present Worth	Older	Younger	Present Worth
78	39	.07145	79	0	.01889	79	40	.07658
78	40	.07590	79	1	.00874	79	41	.08132
78	41	.08058	79	2	.00873	79	42	.08630
78	42	.08550	79	3	.00895	79	43	.09152
78	43	.09065	79	4	.00931	79	44	.09698
78	44	.09604	79	5	.00977	79	45	.10268
78	45	.10166	79	6	.01032	79	46	.10862
78	46	.10751	79	7	.01095	79	47	.11481
78	47	.11361	79	8	.01165	79	48	.12126
78	48	.11996	79	9	.01244	79	49	.12796
78	49	.12656	79	10	.01331	79	50	.13492
78	50	.13341	79	11	.01426	79	51	.14214
78	51	.14051	79	12	.01529	79	52	.14961
78	52	.14784	79	13	.01636	79	53	.15732
78	53	.15542	79	14	.01743	79	54	.16525
78	54	.16321	79	15	.01849	79	55	.17341
78	55	.17121	79	16	.01952	79	56	.18179
78	56	.17943	79	17	.02052	79	57	.19039
78	57	.18787	79	18	.02152	79	58	.19922
78	58	.19651	79	19	.02255	79	59	.20827
78	59	.20537	79	20	.02363	79	60	.21753
78	60	.21444	79	21	.02479	79	61	.22702
78	61	.22372	79	22	.02602	79	62	.23672
78	62	.23319	79	23	.02734	79	63	.24663
78	63	.24285	79	24	.02879	79	64	.25670
78	64	.25268	79	25	.03038	79	65	.26694
78	65	.26265	79	26	.03215	79	66	.27731
78	66	.27274	79	27	.03410	79	67	.28780
78	67	.28293	79	28	.03624	79	68	.29839
78	68	.29321	79	29	.03854	79	69	.30906
78	69	.30356	79	30	.04103	79	70	.31980
78	70	.31396	79	31	.04368	79	71	.33060
78	71	.32440	79	32	.04653	79	72	.34143
78	72	.33486	79	33	.04957	79	73	.35221
78	73	.34526	79	34	.05279	79	74	.36287
78	74	.35551	79	35	.05623	79	75	.37330
78	75	.36555	79	36	.05988	79	76	.38349
78	76	.37533	79	37	.06373	79	77	.39340
78	77	.38484	79	38	.06780	79	78	.40304
78	78	.39407	79	39	.07208	79	79	.41241

Table A(2)

The Present Worth of $1.00 Due at the
Death of the Survivor of Two Persons

Interest at 10 Percent

Older	Younger	Present Worth	Older	Younger	Present Worth	Older	Younger	Present Worth
80	0	.01931	80	40	.07722	80	80	.43104
80	1	.00883	80	41	.08201	81	0	.01972
80	2	.00880	80	42	.08706	81	1	.00891
80	3	.00902	80	43	.09234	81	2	.00887
80	4	.00937	80	44	.09787	81	3	.00909
80	5	.00984	80	45	.10365	81	4	.00943
80	6	.01039	80	46	.10967	81	5	.00990
80	7	.01102	80	47	.11594	81	6	.01046
80	8	.01173	80	48	.12248	81	7	.01109
80	9	.01253	80	49	.12929	81	8	.01180
80	10	.01340	80	50	.13636	81	9	.01261
80	11	.01437	80	51	.14369	81	10	.01349
80	12	.01541	80	52	.15128	81	11	.01447
80	13	.01650	80	53	.15912	81	12	.01553
80	14	.01759	80	54	.16719	81	13	.01663
80	15	.01866	80	55	.17549	81	14	.01773
80	16	.01969	80	56	.18402	81	15	.01882
80	17	.02071	80	57	.19279	81	16	.01986
80	18	.02171	80	58	.20179	81	17	.02088
80	19	.02274	80	59	.21102	81	18	.02189
80	20	.02383	80	60	.22048	81	19	.02293
80	21	.02499	80	61	.23017	81	20	.02402
80	22	.02622	80	62	.24009	81	21	.02518
80	23	.02755	80	63	.25022	81	22	.02642
80	24	.02900	80	64	.26054	81	23	.02775
80	25	.03060	80	65	.27104	81	24	.02920
80	26	.03238	80	66	.28168	81	25	.03081
80	27	.03434	80	67	.29246	81	26	.03260
80	28	.03649	80	68	.30334	81	27	.03456
80	29	.03881	80	69	.31433	81	28	.03673
80	30	.04132	80	70	.32540	81	29	.03907
80	31	.04399	80	71	.33655	81	30	.04159
80	32	.04686	80	72	.34775	81	31	.04429
80	33	.04993	80	73	.35892	81	32	.04718
80	34	.05319	80	74	.36996	81	33	.05027
80	35	.05666	80	75	.38079	81	34	.05355
80	36	.06034	80	76	.39138	81	35	.05705
80	37	.06423	80	77	.40169	81	36	.06077
80	38	.06834	80	78	.41174	81	37	.06470
80	39	.07267	80	79	.42152	81	38	.06885

Tools and Techniques

Table A(2)

**The Present Worth of $1.00 Due at the
Death of the Survivor of Two Persons**

Interest at 10 Percent

Older	Younger	Present Worth	Older	Younger	Present Worth	Older	Younger	Present Worth
81	39	.07322	81	79	.43030	82	37	.06514
81	40	.07782	81	80	.44024	82	38	.06932
81	41	.08266	81	81	.44985	82	39	.07374
81	42	.08777	82	0	.02012	82	40	.07838
81	43	.09311	82	1	.00899	82	41	.08327
81	44	.09871	82	2	.00894	82	42	.08843
81	45	.10455	82	3	.00915	82	43	.09383
81	46	.11065	82	4	.00949	82	44	.09949
81	47	.11701	82	5	.00996	82	45	.10540
81	48	.12364	82	6	.01052	82	46	.11157
81	49	.13053	82	7	.01115	82	47	.11800
81	50	.13771	82	8	.01187	82	48	.12471
81	51	.14515	82	9	.01268	82	49	.13170
81	52	.15285	82	10	.01358	82	50	.13897
81	53	.16081	82	11	.01457	82	51	.14651
81	54	.16901	82	12	.01564	82	52	.15433
81	55	.17746	82	13	.01675	82	53	.16240
81	56	.18614	82	14	.01787	82	54	.17073
81	57	.19506	82	15	.01897	82	55	.17930
81	58	.20421	82	16	.02002	82	56	.18812
81	59	.21362	82	17	.02105	82	57	.19718
81	60	.22326	82	18	.02207	82	58	.20649
81	61	.23315	82	19	.02311	82	59	.21606
81	62	.24328	82	20	.02420	82	60	.22588
81	63	.25363	82	21	.02537	82	61	.23595
81	64	.26418	82	22	.02660	82	62	.24628
81	65	.27493	82	23	.02793	82	63	.25684
81	66	.28583	82	24	.02939	82	64	.26761
81	67	.29688	82	25	.03100	82	65	.27859
81	68	.30805	82	26	.03280	82	66	.28974
81	69	.31935	82	27	.03477	82	67	.30105
81	70	.33074	82	28	.03695	82	68	.31251
81	71	.34223	82	29	.03930	82	69	.32409
81	72	.35378	82	30	.04184	82	70	.33580
81	73	.36532	82	31	.04456	82	71	.34762
81	74	.37675	82	32	.04747	82	72	.35951
81	75	.38797	82	33	.05058	82	73	.37141
81	76	.39895	82	34	.05389	82	74	.38321
81	77	.40967	82	35	.05742	82	75	.39481
81	78	.42011	82	36	.06117	82	76	.40618

Table A(2)

The Present Worth of $1.00 Due at the Death of the Survivor of Two Persons

Interest at 10 Percent

Older	Younger	Present Worth	Older	Younger	Present Worth	Older	Younger	Present Worth
82	77	.41728	83	34	.05421	83	74	.38934
82	78	.42813	83	35	.05777	83	75	.40131
82	79	.43872	83	36	.06154	83	76	.41306
82	80	.44906	83	37	.06554	83	77	.42454
82	81	.45908	83	38	.06976	83	78	.43578
82	82	.46873	83	39	.07421	83	79	.44676
83	0	.02052	83	40	.07890	83	80	.45751
83	1	.00907	83	41	.08384	83	81	.46793
83	2	.00900	83	42	.08904	83	82	.47798
83	3	.00920	83	43	.09450	83	83	.48764
83	4	.00955	83	44	.10022	84	0	.02091
83	5	.01001	83	45	.10619	84	1	.00914
83	6	.01057	83	46	.11243	84	2	.00906
83	7	.01121	83	47	.11893	84	3	.00926
83	8	.01193	83	48	.12572	84	4	.00960
83	9	.01275	83	49	.13279	84	5	.01006
83	10	.01365	83	50	.14015	84	6	.01062
83	11	.01466	83	51	.14779	84	7	.01126
83	12	.01574	83	52	.15570	84	8	.01199
83	13	.01687	83	53	.16389	84	9	.01281
83	14	.01800	83	54	.17233	84	10	.01373
83	15	.01911	83	55	.18103	84	11	.01474
83	16	.02017	83	56	.18997	84	12	.01583
83	17	.02121	83	57	.19918	84	13	.01697
83	18	.02223	83	58	.20863	84	14	.01812
83	19	.02327	83	59	.21835	84	15	.01924
83	20	.02437	83	60	.22833	84	16	.02031
83	21	.02554	83	61	.23858	84	17	.02135
83	22	.02678	83	62	.24909	84	18	.02238
83	23	.02811	83	63	.25985	84	19	.02343
83	24	.02957	83	64	.27084	84	20	.02453
83	25	.03119	83	65	.28204	84	21	.02570
83	26	.03298	83	66	.29343	84	22	.02694
83	27	.03497	83	67	.30499	84	23	.02828
83	28	.03716	83	68	.31670	84	24	.02974
83	29	.03952	83	69	.32857	84	25	.03136
83	30	.04208	83	70	.34057	84	26	.03316
83	31	.04481	83	71	.35270	84	27	.03515
83	32	.04774	83	72	.36493	84	28	.03735
83	33	.05087	83	73	.37718	84	29	.03973

Tools and Techniques

Table A(2)
The Present Worth of $1.00 Due at the Death of the Survivor of Two Persons
Interest at 10 Percent

Older	Younger	Present Worth	Older	Younger	Present Worth	Older	Younger	Present Worth
84	30	.04230	84	70	.34507	85	25	.03152
84	31	.04504	84	71	.35751	85	26	.03333
84	32	.04799	84	72	.37006	85	27	.03533
84	33	.05115	84	73	.38265	85	28	.03753
84	34	.05450	84	74	.39515	85	29	.03992
84	35	.05809	84	75	.40749	85	30	.04250
84	36	.06189	84	76	.41959	85	31	.04526
84	37	.06592	84	77	.43145	85	32	.04823
84	38	.07017	84	78	.44307	85	33	.05140
84	39	.07466	84	79	.45444	85	34	.05478
84	40	.07939	84	80	.46558	85	35	.05838
84	41	.08437	84	81	.47641	85	36	.06221
84	42	.08962	84	82	.48686	85	37	.06627
84	43	.09512	84	83	.49693	85	38	.07055
84	44	.10090	84	84	.50662	85	39	.07507
84	45	.10692	85	0	.02130	85	40	.07984
84	46	.11322	85	1	.00921	85	41	.08485
84	47	.11979	85	2	.00912	85	42	.09015
84	48	.12666	85	3	.00931	85	43	.09570
84	49	.13380	85	4	.00965	85	44	.10152
84	50	.14125	85	5	.01011	85	45	.10761
84	51	.14898	85	6	.01067	85	46	.11396
84	52	.15699	85	7	.01131	85	47	.12060
84	53	.16528	85	8	.01204	85	48	.12753
84	54	.17383	85	9	.01287	85	49	.13475
84	55	.18264	85	10	.01379	85	50	.14227
84	56	.19171	85	11	.01481	85	51	.15008
84	57	.20104	85	12	.01592	85	52	.15819
84	58	.21063	85	13	.01707	85	53	.16657
84	59	.22050	85	14	.01823	85	54	.17522
84	60	.23064	85	15	.01936	85	55	.18414
84	61	.24105	85	16	.02045	85	56	.19332
84	62	.25173	85	17	.02149	85	57	.20278
84	63	.26268	85	18	.02253	85	58	.21250
84	64	.27387	85	19	.02358	85	59	.22250
84	65	.28528	85	20	.02468	85	60	.23279
84	66	.29689	85	21	.02585	85	61	.24335
84	67	.30869	85	22	.02709	85	62	.25421
84	68	.32065	85	23	.02843	85	63	.26533
84	69	.33279	85	24	.02989	85	64	.27670

Table A(2)
The Present Worth of $1.00 Due at the Death of the Survivor of Two Persons
Interest at 10 Percent

Older	Younger	Present Worth	Older	Younger	Present Worth	Older	Younger	Present Worth
85	65	.28831	86	19	.02372	86	59	.22434
85	66	.30014	86	20	.02482	86	60	.23476
85	67	.31216	86	21	.02599	86	61	.24547
85	68	.32436	86	22	.02724	86	62	.25648
85	69	.33675	86	23	.02857	86	63	.26776
85	70	.34930	86	24	.03004	86	64	.27931
85	71	.36203	86	25	.03166	86	65	.29110
85	72	.37489	86	26	.03348	86	66	.30313
85	73	.38780	86	27	.03548	86	67	.31536
85	74	.40064	86	28	.03770	86	68	.32778
85	75	.41332	86	29	.04009	86	69	.34041
85	76	.42579	86	30	.04269	86	70	.35321
85	77	.43801	86	31	.04546	86	71	.36621
85	78	.44999	86	32	.04844	86	72	.37936
85	79	.46175	86	33	.05163	86	73	.39257
85	80	.47328	86	34	.05503	86	74	.40574
85	81	.48450	86	35	.05865	86	75	.41874
85	82	.49535	86	36	.06250	86	76	.43154
85	83	.50581	86	37	.06659	86	77	.44411
85	84	.51591	86	38	.07090	86	78	.45644
85	85	.52560	86	39	.07545	86	79	.46856
86	0	.02167	86	40	.08025	86	80	.48046
86	1	.00927	86	41	.08530	86	81	.49207
86	2	.00917	86	42	.09063	86	82	.50330
86	3	.00936	86	43	.09623	86	83	.51415
86	4	.00969	86	44	.10210	86	84	.52464
86	5	.01015	86	45	.10823	86	85	.53473
86	6	.01071	86	46	.11464	86	86	.54424
86	7	.01135	86	47	.12133	87	0	.02202
86	8	.01208	86	48	.12832	87	1	.00934
86	9	.01292	86	49	.13561	87	2	.00922
86	10	.01385	86	50	.14321	87	3	.00940
86	11	.01488	86	51	.15110	87	4	.00973
86	12	.01600	86	52	.15928	87	5	.01019
86	13	.01716	86	53	.16776	87	6	.01075
86	14	.01833	86	54	.17650	87	7	.01139
86	15	.01948	86	55	.18552	87	8	.01213
86	16	.02057	86	56	.19481	87	9	.01296
86	17	.02162	86	57	.20438	87	10	.01390
86	18	.02266	86	58	.21421	87	11	.01494

Tools and Techniques

Table A(2)

The Present Worth of $1.00 Due at the Death of the Survivor of Two Persons

Interest at 10 Percent

Older	Younger	Present Worth	Older	Younger	Present Worth	Older	Younger	Present Worth
87	12	.01607	87	52	.16027	88	4	.00977
87	13	.01725	87	53	.16882	88	5	.01022
87	14	.01843	87	54	.17765	88	6	.01078
87	15	.01958	87	55	.18676	88	7	.01143
87	16	.02068	87	56	.19614	88	8	.01216
87	17	.02174	87	57	.20581	88	9	.01300
87	18	.02278	87	58	.21576	88	10	.01395
87	19	.02384	87	59	.22600	88	11	.01499
87	20	.02495	87	60	.23654	88	12	.01613
87	21	.02612	87	61	.24738	88	13	.01732
87	22	.02737	87	62	.25853	88	14	.01851
87	23	.02870	87	63	.26996	88	15	.01967
87	24	.03017	87	64	.28167	88	16	.02078
87	25	.03180	87	65	.29363	88	17	.02185
87	26	.03361	87	66	.30583	88	18	.02289
87	27	.03562	87	67	.31825	88	19	.02395
87	28	.03785	87	68	.33088	88	20	.02507
87	29	.04025	87	69	.34372	88	21	.02624
87	30	.04286	87	70	.35675	88	22	.02748
87	31	.04564	87	71	.37000	88	23	.02882
87	32	.04863	87	72	.38341	88	24	.03029
87	33	.05184	87	73	.39691	88	25	.03192
87	34	.05525	87	74	.41036	88	26	.03374
87	35	.05889	87	75	.42368	88	27	.03575
87	36	.06277	87	76	.43679	88	28	.03798
87	37	.06687	87	77	.44967	88	29	.04039
87	38	.07121	87	78	.46233	88	30	.04301
87	39	.07579	87	79	.47479	88	31	.04580
87	40	.08062	87	80	.48704	88	32	.04881
87	41	.08570	87	81	.49899	88	33	.05202
87	42	.09107	87	82	.51059	88	34	.05545
87	43	.09670	87	83	.52180	88	35	.05911
87	44	.10261	87	84	.53266	88	36	.06300
87	45	.10879	87	85	.54312	88	37	.06713
87	46	.11525	87	86	.55300	88	38	.07149
87	47	.12199	87	87	.56211	88	39	.07609
87	48	.12904	88	0	.02235	88	40	.08094
87	49	.13639	88	1	.00939	88	41	.08606
87	50	.14405	88	2	.00927	88	42	.09146
87	51	.15201	88	3	.00944	88	43	.09712

Table A(2)
The Present Worth of $1.00 Due at the
Death of the Survivor of Two Persons
Interest at 10 Percent

Older	Younger	Present Worth	Older	Younger	Present Worth	Older	Younger	Present Worth
88	44	.10307	88	84	.54001	89	35	.05931
88	45	.10929	88	85	.55082	89	36	.06322
88	46	.11579	88	86	.56104	89	37	.06736
88	47	.12258	88	87	.57048	89	38	.07174
88	48	.12968	88	88	.57917	89	39	.07637
88	49	.13708	89	0	.02266	89	40	.08124
88	50	.14480	89	1	.00944	89	41	.08638
88	51	.15282	89	2	.00931	89	42	.09181
88	52	.16115	89	3	.00948	89	43	.09751
88	53	.16978	89	4	.00980	89	44	.10349
88	54	.17869	89	5	.01026	89	45	.10974
88	55	.18788	89	6	.01082	89	46	.11628
88	56	.19735	89	7	.01146	89	47	.12311
88	57	.20711	89	8	.01219	89	48	.13026
88	58	.21715	89	9	.01304	89	49	.13771
88	59	.22750	89	10	.01399	89	50	.14548
88	60	.23814	89	11	.01504	89	51	.15356
88	61	.24910	89	12	.01619	89	52	.16195
88	62	.26037	89	13	.01738	89	53	.17065
88	63	.27194	89	14	.01858	89	54	.17962
88	64	.28379	89	15	.01975	89	55	.18889
88	65	.29590	89	16	.02087	89	56	.19844
88	66	.30827	89	17	.02194	89	57	.20828
88	67	.32086	89	18	.02299	89	58	.21841
88	68	.33367	89	19	.02406	89	59	.22885
88	69	.34670	89	20	.02517	89	60	.23960
88	70	.35995	89	21	.02635	89	61	.25067
88	71	.37342	89	22	.02759	89	62	.26205
88	72	.38707	89	23	.02893	89	63	.27374
88	73	.40083	89	24	.03040	89	64	.28572
88	74	.41456	89	25	.03203	89	65	.29797
88	75	.42815	89	26	.03385	89	66	.31049
88	76	.44155	89	27	.03587	89	67	.32324
88	77	.45473	89	28	.03810	89	68	.33622
88	78	.46769	89	29	.04052	89	69	.34943
88	79	.48046	89	30	.04314	89	70	.36287
88	80	.49303	89	31	.04595	89	71	.37655
88	81	.50532	89	32	.04896	89	72	.39043
88	82	.51725	89	33	.05219	89	73	.40442
88	83	.52881	89	34	.05563	89	74	.41840

Tools and Techniques

Table A(2)

The Present Worth of $1.00 Due at the
Death of the Survivor of Two Persons
Interest at 10 Percent

Older	Younger	Present Worth	Older	Younger	Present Worth	Older	Younger	Present Worth
89	75	.43225	90	25	.03213	90	65	.29988
89	76	.44592	90	26	.03395	90	66	.31253
89	77	.45937	90	27	.03597	90	67	.32543
89	78	.47262	90	28	.03821	90	68	.33856
89	79	.48568	90	29	.04064	90	69	.35194
89	80	.49855	90	30	.04327	90	70	.36556
89	81	.51115	90	31	.04608	90	71	.37943
89	82	.52340	90	32	.04910	90	72	.39352
89	83	.53528	90	33	.05234	90	73	.40774
89	84	.54682	90	34	.05580	90	74	.42196
89	85	.55797	90	35	.05949	90	75	.43606
89	86	.56852	90	36	.06341	90	76	.44997
89	87	.57828	90	37	.06757	90	77	.46369
89	88	.58726	90	38	.07197	90	78	.47720
89	89	.59565	90	39	.07662	90	79	.49054
90	0	.02296	90	40	.08151	90	80	.50371
90	1	.00949	90	41	.08668	90	81	.51661
90	2	.00935	90	42	.09213	90	82	.52916
90	3	.00951	90	43	.09786	90	83	.54136
90	4	.00983	90	44	.10387	90	84	.55321
90	5	.01029	90	45	.11016	90	85	.56469
90	6	.01084	90	46	.11673	90	86	.57557
90	7	.01149	90	47	.12360	90	87	.58563
90	8	.01222	90	48	.13079	90	88	.59492
90	9	.01307	90	49	.13828	90	89	.60359
90	10	.01402	90	50	.14611	90	90	.61182
90	11	.01508	90	51	.15424	91	0	.02325
90	12	.01624	90	52	.16269	91	1	.00954
90	13	.01744	90	53	.17144	91	2	.00939
90	14	.01865	90	54	.18048	91	3	.00954
90	15	.01983	90	55	.18982	91	4	.00986
90	16	.02096	90	56	.19944	91	5	.01031
90	17	.02203	90	57	.20936	91	6	.01087
90	18	.02309	90	58	.21957	91	7	.01151
90	19	.02415	90	59	.23010	91	8	.01225
90	20	.02527	90	60	.24094	91	9	.01310
90	21	.02644	90	61	.25210	91	10	.01405
90	22	.02769	90	62	.26359	91	11	.01512
90	23	.02903	90	63	.27540	91	12	.01628
90	24	.03050	90	64	.28750	91	13	.01750

Appendix B
Valuation of Assets

Table A(2)
The Present Worth of $1.00 Due at the
Death of the Survivor of Two Persons
Interest at 10 Percent

Older	Younger	Present Worth	Older	Younger	Present Worth	Older	Younger	Present Worth
91	14	.01872	91	54	.18127	92	2	.00942
91	15	.01990	91	55	.19066	92	3	.00957
91	16	.02103	91	56	.20035	92	4	.00989
91	17	.02211	91	57	.21034	92	5	.01034
91	18	.02317	91	58	.22062	92	6	.01089
91	19	.02424	91	59	.23123	92	7	.01153
91	20	.02536	91	60	.24215	92	8	.01227
91	21	.02653	91	61	.25341	92	9	.01313
91	22	.02778	91	62	.26500	92	10	.01408
91	23	.02912	91	63	.27691	92	11	.01515
91	24	.03059	91	64	.28912	92	12	.01632
91	25	.03222	91	65	.30162	92	13	.01754
91	26	.03404	91	66	.31440	92	14	.01877
91	27	.03607	91	67	.32742	92	15	.01996
91	28	.03831	91	68	.34070	92	16	.02110
91	29	.04074	91	69	.35424	92	17	.02219
91	30	.04338	91	70	.36802	92	18	.02325
91	31	.04620	91	71	.38207	92	19	.02432
91	32	.04923	91	72	.39636	92	20	.02544
91	33	.05248	91	73	.41078	92	21	.02662
91	34	.05595	91	74	.42522	92	22	.02786
91	35	.05965	91	75	.43954	92	23	.02920
91	36	.06359	91	76	.45370	92	24	.03067
91	37	.06776	91	77	.46766	92	25	.03230
91	38	.07218	91	78	.48142	92	26	.03413
91	39	.07684	91	79	.49502	92	27	.03615
91	40	.08176	91	80	.50846	92	28	.03840
91	41	.08694	91	81	.52164	92	29	.04084
91	42	.09242	91	82	.53449	92	30	.04348
91	43	.09817	91	83	.54698	92	31	.04631
91	44	.10422	91	84	.55914	92	32	.04935
91	45	.11053	91	85	.57093	92	33	.05261
91	46	.11714	91	86	.58212	92	34	.05608
91	47	.12404	91	87	.59249	92	35	.05979
91	48	.13127	91	88	.60206	92	36	.06374
91	49	.13881	91	89	.61101	92	37	.06793
91	50	.14667	91	90	.61951	92	38	.07236
91	51	.15486	91	91	.62749	92	39	.07704
91	52	.16335	92	0	.02352	92	40	.08198
91	53	.17217	92	1	.00958	92	41	.08718

445

Tools and Techniques

Table A(2)
The Present Worth of $1.00 Due at the Death of the Survivor of Two Persons
Interest at 10 Percent

Older	Younger	Present Worth	Older	Younger	Present Worth	Older	Younger	Present Worth
92	42	.09268	92	82	.53926	93	29	.04092
92	43	.09845	92	83	.55203	93	30	.04357
92	44	.10452	92	84	.56447	93	31	.04640
92	45	.11086	92	85	.57655	93	32	.04945
92	46	.11750	92	86	.58804	93	33	.05271
92	47	.12443	92	87	.59868	93	34	.05619
92	48	.13169	92	88	.60852	93	35	.05992
92	49	.13927	92	89	.61773	93	36	.06388
92	50	.14717	92	90	.62650	93	37	.06808
92	51	.15540	92	91	.63473	93	38	.07252
92	52	.16394	92	92	.64221	93	39	.07721
92	53	.17280	93	0	.02376	93	40	.08216
92	54	.18196	93	1	.00961	93	41	.08738
92	55	.19141	93	2	.00945	93	42	.09290
92	56	.20115	93	3	.00960	93	43	.09870
92	57	.21120	93	4	.00991	93	44	.10479
92	58	.22155	93	5	.01036	93	45	.11115
92	59	.23223	93	6	.01091	93	46	.11781
92	60	.24323	93	7	.01155	93	47	.12477
92	61	.25457	93	8	.01229	93	48	.13206
92	62	.26624	93	9	.01315	93	49	.13967
92	63	.27824	93	10	.01411	93	50	.14761
92	64	.29055	93	11	.01518	93	51	.15587
92	65	.30316	93	12	.01636	93	52	.16445
92	66	.31605	93	13	.01759	93	53	.17336
92	67	.32920	93	14	.01882	93	54	.18256
92	68	.34260	93	15	.02002	93	55	.19206
92	69	.35627	93	16	.02116	93	56	.20185
92	70	.37021	93	17	.02225	93	57	.21196
92	71	.38442	93	18	.02331	93	58	.22236
92	72	.39887	93	19	.02438	93	59	.23310
92	73	.41349	93	20	.02551	93	60	.24417
92	74	.42812	93	21	.02669	93	61	.25558
92	75	.44265	93	22	.02793	93	62	.26732
92	76	.45702	93	23	.02927	93	63	.27941
92	77	.47120	93	24	.03074	93	64	.29181
92	78	.48519	93	25	.03237	93	65	.30450
92	79	.49903	93	26	.03420	93	66	.31749
92	80	.51272	93	27	.03623	93	67	.33074
92	81	.52616	93	28	.03848	93	68	.34426

Table A(2)
The Present Worth of $1.00 Due at the
Death of the Survivor of Two Persons
Interest at 10 Percent

Older	Younger	Present Worth	Older	Younger	Present Worth	Older	Younger	Present Worth
93	69	.35805	94	15	.02006	94	55	.19261
93	70	.37211	94	16	.02121	94	56	.20245
93	71	.38646	94	17	.02230	94	57	.21260
93	72	.40107	94	18	.02337	94	58	.22306
93	73	.41585	94	19	.02444	94	59	.23386
93	74	.43066	94	20	.02557	94	60	.24498
93	75	.44537	94	21	.02675	94	61	.25644
93	76	.45993	94	22	.02799	94	62	.26826
93	77	.47430	94	23	.02933	94	63	.28041
93	78	.48850	94	24	.03080	94	64	.29288
93	79	.50254	94	25	.03243	94	65	.30566
93	80	.51645	94	26	.03426	94	66	.31873
93	81	.53012	94	27	.03629	94	67	.33208
93	82	.54346	94	28	.03855	94	68	.34569
93	83	.55647	94	29	.04099	94	69	.35958
93	84	.56916	94	30	.04364	94	70	.37375
93	85	.58151	94	31	.04648	94	71	.38822
93	86	.59325	94	32	.04953	94	72	.40297
93	87	.60415	94	33	.05280	94	73	.41789
93	88	.61423	94	34	.05629	94	74	.43285
93	89	.62368	94	35	.06002	94	75	.44772
93	90	.63268	94	36	.06399	94	76	.46244
93	91	.64115	94	37	.06821	94	77	.47698
93	92	.64886	94	38	.07266	94	78	.49135
93	93	.65572	94	39	.07736	94	79	.50558
94	0	.02398	94	40	.08233	94	80	.51968
94	1	.00964	94	41	.08756	94	81	.53355
94	2	.00947	94	42	.09309	94	82	.54710
94	3	.00962	94	43	.09891	94	83	.56032
94	4	.00993	94	44	.10501	94	84	.57323
94	5	.01037	94	45	.11140	94	85	.58581
94	6	.01093	94	46	.11808	94	86	.59779
94	7	.01157	94	47	.12506	94	87	.60891
94	8	.01231	94	48	.13238	94	88	.61920
94	9	.01317	94	49	.14001	94	89	.62886
94	10	.01413	94	50	.14798	94	90	.63807
94	11	.01521	94	51	.15628	94	91	.64676
94	12	.01639	94	52	.16489	94	92	.65467
94	13	.01762	94	53	.17383	94	93	.66171
94	14	.01886	94	54	.18307	94	94	.66787

Tools and Techniques

Table A(2)
**The Present Worth of $1.00 Due at the
Death of the Survivor of Two Persons**
Interest at 10 Percent

Older	Younger	Present Worth	Older	Younger	Present Worth	Older	Younger	Present Worth
95	0	.02417	95	40	.08246	95	80	.52244
95	1	.00967	95	41	.08771	95	81	.53648
95	2	.00949	95	42	.09326	95	82	.55021
95	3	.00964	95	43	.09908	95	83	.56361
95	4	.00994	95	44	.10521	95	84	.57671
95	5	.01039	95	45	.11161	95	85	.58949
95	6	.01095	95	46	.11831	95	86	.60167
95	7	.01158	95	47	.12531	95	87	.61298
95	8	.01233	95	48	.13265	95	88	.62346
95	9	.01318	95	49	.14030	95	89	.63330
95	10	.01414	95	50	.14830	95	90	.64270
95	11	.01523	95	51	.15662	95	91	.65156
95	12	.01641	95	52	.16527	95	92	.65965
95	13	.01765	95	53	.17424	95	93	.66685
95	14	.01889	95	54	.18351	95	94	.67317
95	15	.02010	95	55	.19309	95	95	.67859
95	16	.02125	95	56	.20296	96	0	.02433
95	17	.02235	95	57	.21316	96	1	.00969
95	18	.02342	95	58	.22366	96	2	.00951
95	19	.02449	95	59	.23450	96	3	.00965
95	20	.02562	95	60	.24566	96	4	.00996
95	21	.02680	95	61	.25718	96	5	.01040
95	22	.02805	95	62	.26905	96	6	.01096
95	23	.02938	95	63	.28127	96	7	.01160
95	24	.03085	95	64	.29380	96	8	.01234
95	25	.03248	95	65	.30665	96	9	.01319
95	26	.03431	95	66	.31979	96	10	.01416
95	27	.03635	95	67	.33321	96	11	.01525
95	28	.03860	95	68	.34691	96	12	.01643
95	29	.04105	95	69	.36089	96	13	.01767
95	30	.04370	95	70	.37515	96	14	.01892
95	31	.04654	95	71	.38973	96	15	.02014
95	32	.04960	95	72	.40458	96	16	.02129
95	33	.05288	95	73	.41963	96	17	.02239
95	34	.05638	95	74	.43472	96	18	.02346
95	35	.06011	95	75	.44972	96	19	.02453
95	36	.06409	95	76	.46458	96	20	.02566
95	37	.06831	95	77	.47927	96	21	.02684
95	38	.07278	95	78	.49379	96	22	.02809
95	39	.07749	95	79	.50818	96	23	.02943

Table A(2)
The Present Worth of $1.00 Due at the
Death of the Survivor of Two Persons
Interest at 10 Percent

Older	Younger	Present Worth	Older	Younger	Present Worth	Older	Younger	Present Worth
96	24	.03089	96	64	.29458	97	7	.01161
96	25	.03253	96	65	.30748	97	8	.01235
96	26	.03436	96	66	.32069	97	9	.01321
96	27	.03639	96	67	.33417	97	10	.01417
96	28	.03865	96	68	.34794	97	11	.01526
96	29	.04110	96	69	.36199	97	12	.01645
96	30	.04376	96	70	.37634	97	13	.01770
96	31	.04660	96	71	.39100	97	14	.01895
96	32	.04966	96	72	.40595	97	15	.02017
96	33	.05295	96	73	.42110	97	16	.02132
96	34	.05645	96	74	.43630	97	17	.02242
96	35	.06019	96	75	.45142	97	18	.02350
96	36	.06417	96	76	.46640	97	19	.02457
96	37	.06840	96	77	.48120	97	20	.02570
96	38	.07288	96	78	.49585	97	21	.02688
96	39	.07760	96	79	.51037	97	22	.02813
96	40	.08258	96	80	.52477	97	23	.02947
96	41	.08784	96	81	.53896	97	24	.03093
96	42	.09339	96	82	.55283	97	25	.03257
96	43	.09923	96	83	.56638	97	26	.03440
96	44	.10537	96	84	.57965	97	27	.03643
96	45	.11179	96	85	.59259	97	28	.03869
96	46	.11850	96	86	.60494	97	29	.04115
96	47	.12552	96	87	.61641	97	30	.04381
96	48	.13287	96	88	.62704	97	31	.04665
96	49	.14055	96	89	.63704	97	32	.04972
96	50	.14857	96	90	.64659	97	33	.05301
96	51	.15691	96	91	.65561	97	34	.05651
96	52	.16559	96	92	.66385	97	35	.06026
96	53	.17458	96	93	.67119	97	36	.06425
96	54	.18388	96	94	.67762	97	37	.06848
96	55	.19349	96	95	.68315	97	38	.07296
96	56	.20340	96	96	.68781	97	39	.07769
96	57	.21362	97	0	.02447	97	40	.08268
96	58	.22416	97	1	.00971	97	41	.08795
96	59	.23504	97	2	.00953	97	42	.09352
96	60	.24625	97	3	.00967	97	43	.09937
96	61	.25781	97	4	.00997	97	44	.10552
96	62	.26973	97	5	.01042	97	45	.11195
96	63	.28199	97	6	.01097	97	46	.11868

Tools and Techniques

Table A(2)

The Present Worth of $1.00 Due at the Death of the Survivor of Two Persons

Interest at 10 Percent

Older	Younger	Present Worth	Older	Younger	Present Worth	Older	Younger	Present Worth
97	47	.12571	97	87	.61946	98	29	.04119
97	48	.13308	97	88	.63022	98	30	.04385
97	49	.14077	97	89	.64035	98	31	.04670
97	50	.14881	97	90	.65004	98	32	.04977
97	51	.15717	97	91	.65920	98	33	.05306
97	52	.16587	97	92	.66756	98	34	.05657
97	53	.17489	97	93	.67503	98	35	.06032
97	54	.18421	97	94	.68157	98	36	.06432
97	55	.19385	97	95	.68720	98	37	.06856
97	56	.20378	97	96	.69194	98	38	.07304
97	57	.21404	97	97	.69614	98	39	.07778
97	58	.22461	98	0	.02460	98	40	.08278
97	59	.23552	98	1	.00973	98	41	.08805
97	60	.24676	98	2	.00954	98	42	.09363
97	61	.25837	98	3	.00968	98	43	.09949
97	62	.27032	98	4	.00998	98	44	.10565
97	63	.28263	98	5	.01043	98	45	.11209
97	64	.29527	98	6	.01098	98	46	.11883
97	65	.30822	98	7	.01162	98	47	.12588
97	66	.32148	98	8	.01236	98	48	.13326
97	67	.33503	98	9	.01322	98	49	.14097
97	68	.34885	98	10	.01418	98	50	.14902
97	69	.36297	98	11	.01527	98	51	.15741
97	70	.37739	98	12	.01647	98	52	.16612
97	71	.39213	98	13	.01772	98	53	.17516
97	72	.40717	98	14	.01897	98	54	.18451
97	73	.42241	98	15	.02019	98	55	.19417
97	74	.43770	98	16	.02135	98	56	.20413
97	75	.45292	98	17	.02246	98	57	.21441
97	76	.46801	98	18	.02353	98	58	.22501
97	77	.48292	98	19	.02461	98	59	.23595
97	78	.49768	98	20	.02573	98	60	.24723
97	79	.51231	98	21	.02692	98	61	.25886
97	80	.52684	98	22	.02816	98	62	.27086
97	81	.54115	98	23	.02950	98	63	.28321
97	82	.55516	98	24	.03097	98	64	.29589
97	83	.56885	98	25	.03260	98	65	.30889
97	84	.58225	98	26	.03443	98	66	.32220
97	85	.59534	98	27	.03647	98	67	.33579
97	86	.60784	98	28	.03873	98	68	.34967

Table A(2)
The Present Worth of $1.00 Due at the
Death of the Survivor of Two Persons
Interest at 10 Percent

Older	Younger	Present Worth	Older	Younger	Present Worth	Older	Younger	Present Worth
98	69	.36385	99	10	.01420	99	50	.14923
98	70	.37833	99	11	.01529	99	51	.15763
98	71	.39314	99	12	.01648	99	52	.16636
98	72	.40825	99	13	.01774	99	53	.17543
98	73	.42357	99	14	.01900	99	54	.18479
98	74	.43896	99	15	.02022	99	55	.19447
98	75	.45427	99	16	.02138	99	56	.20446
98	76	.46944	99	17	.02248	99	57	.21477
98	77	.48445	99	18	.02356	99	58	.22539
98	78	.49931	99	19	.02464	99	59	.23636
98	79	.51405	99	20	.02577	99	60	.24767
98	80	.52868	99	21	.02695	99	61	.25934
98	81	.54311	99	22	.02820	99	62	.27137
98	82	.55723	99	23	.02954	99	63	.28375
98	83	.57104	99	24	.03100	99	64	.29648
98	84	.58457	99	25	.03263	99	65	.30952
98	85	.59778	99	26	.03447	99	66	.32288
98	86	.61041	99	27	.03651	99	67	.33652
98	87	.62215	99	28	.03877	99	68	.35045
98	88	.63304	99	29	.04123	99	69	.36469
98	89	.64328	99	30	.04389	99	70	.37923
98	90	.65309	99	31	.04674	99	71	.39411
98	91	.66236	99	32	.04981	99	72	.40929
98	92	.67085	99	33	.05311	99	73	.42469
98	93	.67841	99	34	.05662	99	74	.44015
98	94	.68505	99	35	.06038	99	75	.45555
98	95	.69076	99	36	.06438	99	76	.47081
98	96	.69557	99	37	.06863	99	77	.48591
98	97	.69983	99	38	.07312	99	78	.50086
98	98	.70358	99	39	.07786	99	79	.51570
99	0	.02471	99	40	.08287	99	80	.53044
99	1	.00975	99	41	.08815	99	81	.54496
99	2	.00956	99	42	.09373	99	82	.55919
99	3	.00969	99	43	.09960	99	83	.57311
99	4	.00999	99	44	.10577	99	84	.58676
99	5	.01044	99	45	.11222	99	85	.60010
99	6	.01099	99	46	.11898	99	86	.61284
99	7	.01163	99	47	.12604	99	87	.62470
99	8	.01237	99	48	.13343	99	88	.63570
99	9	.01323	99	49	.14116	99	89	.64605

Table A(2)

**The Present Worth of $1.00 Due at the
Death of the Survivor of Two Persons**

Interest at 10 Percent

Older	Younger	Present Worth	Older	Younger	Present Worth	Older	Younger	Present Worth
99	90	.65597	100	30	.04393	100	70	.38013
99	91	.66535	100	31	.04679	100	71	.39507
99	92	.67394	100	32	.04986	100	72	.41032
99	93	.68160	100	33	.05316	100	73	.42579
99	94	.68833	100	34	.05667	100	74	.44134
99	95	.69412	100	35	.06044	100	75	.45682
99	96	.69899	100	36	.06444	100	76	.47217
99	97	.70331	100	37	.06869	100	77	.48736
99	98	.70711	100	38	.07319	100	78	.50241
99	99	.71068	100	39	.07794	100	79	.51734
100	0	.02483	100	40	.08295	100	80	.53218
100	1	.00977	100	41	.08824	100	81	.54681
100	2	.00957	100	42	.09384	100	82	.56115
100	3	.00970	100	43	.09972	100	83	.57518
100	4	.01000	100	44	.10590	100	84	.58893
100	5	.01044	100	45	.11236	100	85	.60239
100	6	.01100	100	46	.11913	100	86	.61525
100	7	.01164	100	47	.12620	100	87	.62723
100	8	.01238	100	48	.13361	100	88	.63833
100	9	.01324	100	49	.14134	100	89	.64878
100	10	.01421	100	50	.14943	100	90	.65881
100	11	.01530	100	51	.15785	100	91	.66830
100	12	.01650	100	52	.16660	100	92	.67698
100	13	.01776	100	53	.17569	100	93	.68474
100	14	.01902	100	54	.18507	100	94	.69155
100	15	.02024	100	55	.19478	100	95	.69741
100	16	.02141	100	56	.20479	100	96	.70235
100	17	.02251	100	57	.21512	100	97	.70672
100	18	.02359	100	58	.22577	100	98	.71057
100	19	.02467	100	59	.23677	100	99	.71419
100	20	.02580	100	60	.24811	100	100	.71775
100	21	.02698	100	61	.25981	101	0	.02493
100	22	.02823	100	62	.27188	101	1	.00978
100	23	.02957	100	63	.28430	101	2	.00958
100	24	.03103	100	64	.29706	101	3	.00971
100	25	.03267	100	65	.31015	101	4	.01001
100	26	.03450	100	66	.32355	101	5	.01045
100	27	.03654	100	67	.33724	101	6	.01101
100	28	.03881	100	68	.35123	101	7	.01165
100	29	.04126	100	69	.36552	101	8	.01239

Table A(2)
The Present Worth of $1.00 Due at the
Death of the Survivor of Two Persons
Interest at 10 Percent

Older	Younger	Present Worth	Older	Younger	Present Worth	Older	Younger	Present Worth
101	9	.01325	101	49	.14153	101	89	.65139
101	10	.01422	101	50	.14963	101	90	.66150
101	11	.01532	101	51	.15806	101	91	.67108
101	12	.01652	101	52	.16684	101	92	.67985
101	13	.01777	101	53	.17594	101	93	.68769
101	14	.01904	101	54	.18535	101	94	.69457
101	15	.02027	101	55	.19507	101	95	.70049
101	16	.02143	101	56	.20511	101	96	.70548
101	17	.02254	101	57	.21547	101	97	.70990
101	18	.02362	101	58	.22614	101	98	.71379
101	19	.02470	101	59	.23717	101	99	.71744
101	20	.02583	101	60	.24854	101	100	.72104
101	21	.02701	101	61	.26027	101	101	.72437
101	22	.02826	101	62	.27237	102	0	.02504
101	23	.02960	101	63	.28483	102	1	.00980
101	24	.03107	101	64	.29763	102	2	.00959
101	25	.03270	101	65	.31076	102	3	.00973
101	26	.03453	101	66	.32421	102	4	.01002
101	27	.03657	101	67	.33795	102	5	.01046
101	28	.03884	101	68	.35199	102	6	.01102
101	29	.04130	101	69	.36633	102	7	.01165
101	30	.04397	101	70	.38100	102	8	.01240
101	31	.04683	101	71	.39600	102	9	.01326
101	32	.04991	101	72	.41132	102	10	.01423
101	33	.05321	101	73	.42687	102	11	.01533
101	34	.05673	101	74	.44249	102	12	.01653
101	35	.06049	101	75	.45806	102	13	.01780
101	36	.06450	101	76	.47349	102	14	.01906
101	37	.06876	101	77	.48877	102	15	.02030
101	38	.07326	101	78	.50390	102	16	.02146
101	39	.07802	101	79	.51893	102	17	.02258
101	40	.08304	101	80	.53386	102	18	.02365
101	41	.08834	101	81	.54860	102	19	.02473
101	42	.09394	101	82	.56303	102	20	.02586
101	43	.09983	101	83	.57716	102	21	.02705
101	44	.10602	101	84	.59103	102	22	.02830
101	45	.11249	101	85	.60459	102	23	.02964
101	46	.11927	101	86	.61756	102	24	.03110
101	47	.12635	101	87	.62964	102	25	.03274
101	48	.13377	101	88	.64084	102	26	.03457

Table A(2)
The Present Worth of $1.00 Due at the Death of the Survivor of Two Persons
Interest at 10 Percent

Older	Younger	Present Worth	Older	Younger	Present Worth	Older	Younger	Present Worth
102	27	.03661	102	67	.33873	103	4	.01004
102	28	.03888	102	68	.35282	103	5	.01047
102	29	.04134	102	69	.36723	103	6	.01103
102	30	.04401	102	70	.38196	103	7	.01167
102	31	.04687	102	71	.39704	103	8	.01241
102	32	.04995	102	72	.41244	103	9	.01327
102	33	.05326	102	73	.42807	103	10	.01425
102	34	.05678	102	74	.44378	103	11	.01535
102	35	.06056	102	75	.45944	103	12	.01655
102	36	.06457	102	76	.47496	103	13	.01782
102	37	.06883	102	77	.49034	103	14	.01909
102	38	.07334	102	78	.50558	103	15	.02033
102	39	.07811	102	79	.52071	103	16	.02150
102	40	.08313	102	80	.53575	103	17	.02261
102	41	.08844	102	81	.55060	103	18	.02369
102	42	.09405	102	82	.56515	103	19	.02477
102	43	.09995	102	83	.57940	103	20	.02591
102	44	.10615	102	84	.59338	103	21	.02709
102	45	.11263	102	85	.60706	103	22	.02834
102	46	.11942	102	86	.62015	103	23	.02968
102	47	.12652	102	87	.63234	103	24	.03114
102	48	.13396	102	88	.64365	103	25	.03278
102	49	.14173	102	89	.65430	103	26	.03461
102	50	.14985	102	90	.66452	103	27	.03665
102	51	.15830	102	91	.67420	103	28	.03892
102	52	.16709	102	92	.68306	103	29	.04139
102	53	.17622	102	93	.69098	103	30	.04406
102	54	.18565	102	94	.69794	103	31	.04693
102	55	.19540	102	95	.70393	103	32	.05001
102	56	.20546	102	96	.70897	103	33	.05332
102	57	.21585	102	97	.71344	103	34	.05685
102	58	.22655	102	98	.71736	103	35	.06063
102	59	.23761	102	99	.72106	103	36	.06465
102	60	.24901	102	100	.72469	103	37	.06892
102	61	.26078	102	101	.72805	103	38	.07344
102	62	.27292	102	102	.73182	103	39	.07821
102	63	.28542	103	0	.02518	103	40	.08324
102	64	.29826	103	1	.00982	103	41	.08856
102	65	.31144	103	2	.00961	103	42	.09418
102	66	.32493	103	3	.00974	103	43	.10009

Table A(2)
The Present Worth of $1.00 Due at the Death of the Survivor of Two Persons
Interest at 10 Percent

Older	Younger	Present Worth	Older	Younger	Present Worth	Older	Younger	Present Worth
103	44	.10631	103	84	.59625	104	20	.02595
103	45	.11280	103	85	.61009	104	21	.02714
103	46	.11961	103	86	.62334	104	22	.02838
103	47	.12672	103	87	.63568	104	23	.02972
103	48	.13418	103	88	.64713	104	24	.03119
103	49	.14197	103	89	.65791	104	25	.03282
103	50	.15011	103	90	.66826	104	26	.03466
103	51	.15858	103	91	.67807	104	27	.03670
103	52	.16740	103	92	.68705	104	28	.03897
103	53	.17655	103	93	.69508	104	29	.04144
103	54	.18601	103	94	.70213	104	30	.04412
103	55	.19579	103	95	.70820	104	31	.04699
103	56	.20587	103	96	.71331	104	32	.05008
103	57	.21629	103	97	.71784	104	33	.05339
103	58	.22703	103	98	.72183	104	34	.05692
103	59	.23813	103	99	.72557	104	35	.06071
103	60	.24957	103	100	.72924	104	36	.06474
103	61	.26138	103	101	.73264	104	37	.06901
103	62	.27357	103	102	.73644	104	38	.07354
103	63	.28612	103	103	.74125	104	39	.07832
103	64	.29901	104	0	.02532	104	40	.08336
103	65	.31224	104	1	.00984	104	41	.08869
103	66	.32580	104	2	.00963	104	42	.09432
103	67	.33966	104	3	.00976	104	43	.10025
103	68	.35382	104	4	.01005	104	44	.10647
103	69	.36830	104	5	.01049	104	45	.11298
103	70	.38311	104	6	.01104	104	46	.11981
103	71	.39827	104	7	.01168	104	47	.12694
103	72	.41377	104	8	.01242	104	48	.13441
103	73	.42950	104	9	.01328	104	49	.14222
103	74	.44532	104	10	.01426	104	50	.15038
103	75	.46109	104	11	.01536	104	51	.15888
103	76	.47673	104	12	.01658	104	52	.16772
103	77	.49223	104	13	.01785	104	53	.17690
103	78	.50759	104	14	.01912	104	54	.18639
103	79	.52285	104	15	.02036	104	55	.19620
103	80	.53803	104	16	.02154	104	56	.20632
103	81	.55302	104	17	.02266	104	57	.21678
103	82	.56772	104	18	.02374	104	58	.22756
103	83	.58212	104	19	.02482	104	59	.23869

Tools and Techniques

Table A(2)
The Present Worth of $1.00 Due at the Death of the Survivor of Two Persons
Interest at 10 Percent

Older	Younger	Present Worth	Older	Younger	Present Worth	Older	Younger	Present Worth
104	60	.25017	104	100	.73419	105	35	.06081
104	61	.26203	104	101	.73762	105	36	.06484
104	62	.27427	104	102	.74146	105	37	.06913
104	63	.28687	104	103	.74630	105	38	.07367
104	64	.29982	104	104	.75170	105	39	.07845
104	65	.31311	105	0	.02552	105	40	.08351
104	66	.32673	105	1	.00988	105	41	.08885
104	67	.34066	105	2	.00966	105	42	.09450
104	68	.35490	105	3	.00978	105	43	.10044
104	69	.36946	105	4	.01007	105	44	.10669
104	70	.38436	105	5	.01051	105	45	.11322
104	71	.39962	105	6	.01105	105	46	.12006
104	72	.41522	105	7	.01169	105	47	.12721
104	73	.43107	105	8	.01243	105	48	.13471
104	74	.44700	105	9	.01330	105	49	.14254
104	75	.46290	105	10	.01428	105	50	.15073
104	76	.47867	105	11	.01538	105	51	.15927
104	77	.49430	105	12	.01660	105	52	.16814
104	78	.50980	105	13	.01788	105	53	.17736
104	79	.52521	105	14	.01916	105	54	.18688
104	80	.54054	105	15	.02041	105	55	.19673
104	81	.55569	105	16	.02159	105	56	.20690
104	82	.57056	105	17	.02271	105	57	.21740
104	83	.58512	105	18	.02379	105	58	.22822
104	84	.59943	105	19	.02488	105	59	.23941
104	85	.61344	105	20	.02601	105	60	.25095
104	86	.62686	105	21	.02720	105	61	.26287
104	87	.63936	105	22	.02845	105	62	.27517
104	88	.65097	105	23	.02978	105	63	.28784
104	89	.66191	105	24	.03125	105	64	.30087
104	90	.67240	105	25	.03288	105	65	.31424
104	91	.68235	105	26	.03472	105	66	.32794
104	92	.69145	105	27	.03676	105	67	.34196
104	93	.69959	105	28	.03904	105	68	.35629
104	94	.70674	105	29	.04151	105	69	.37096
104	95	.71289	105	30	.04419	105	70	.38597
104	96	.71807	105	31	.04706	105	71	.40136
104	97	.72266	105	32	.05015	105	72	.41710
104	98	.72669	105	33	.05347	105	73	.43310
104	99	.73047	105	34	.05702	105	74	.44920

Table A(2)
The Present Worth of $1.00 Due at the
Death of the Survivor of Two Persons
Interest at 10 Percent

Older	Younger	Present Worth	Older	Younger	Present Worth	Older	Younger	Present Worth
105	75	.46526	106	9	.01331	106	49	.14294
105	76	.48121	106	10	.01429	106	50	.15117
105	77	.49703	106	11	.01541	106	51	.15974
105	78	.51272	106	12	.01663	106	52	.16866
105	79	.52833	106	13	.01792	106	53	.17792
105	80	.54388	106	14	.01921	106	54	.18749
105	81	.55926	106	15	.02047	106	55	.19740
105	82	.57436	106	16	.02165	106	56	.20762
105	83	.58918	106	17	.02278	106	57	.21817
105	84	.60375	106	18	.02387	106	58	.22906
105	85	.61802	106	19	.02495	106	59	.24031
105	86	.63170	106	20	.02609	106	60	.25192
105	87	.64446	106	21	.02728	106	61	.26392
105	88	.65631	106	22	.02852	106	62	.27630
105	89	.66750	106	23	.02986	106	63	.28906
105	90	.67824	106	24	.03132	106	64	.30218
105	91	.68842	106	25	.03296	106	65	.31565
105	92	.69774	106	26	.03479	106	66	.32947
105	93	.70608	106	27	.03684	106	67	.34360
105	94	.71339	106	28	.03912	106	68	.35805
105	95	.71969	106	29	.04159	106	69	.37285
105	96	.72499	106	30	.04428	106	70	.38801
105	97	.72968	106	31	.04715	106	71	.40356
105	98	.73381	106	32	.05025	106	72	.41948
105	99	.73768	106	33	.05358	106	73	.43569
105	100	.74147	106	34	.05713	106	74	.45200
105	101	.74496	106	35	.06093	106	75	.46829
105	102	.74885	106	36	.06498	106	76	.48448
105	103	.75375	106	37	.06928	106	77	.50055
105	104	.75920	106	38	.07382	106	78	.51650
105	105	.76757	106	39	.07863	106	79	.53239
106	0	.02585	106	40	.08370	106	80	.54824
106	1	.00992	106	41	.08905	106	81	.56392
106	2	.00969	106	42	.09472	106	82	.57935
106	3	.00981	106	43	.10068	106	83	.59453
106	4	.01010	106	44	.10695	106	84	.60948
106	5	.01053	106	45	.11350	106	85	.62415
106	6	.01108	106	46	.12037	106	86	.63823
106	7	.01171	106	47	.12755	106	87	.65137
106	8	.01245	106	48	.13508	106	88	.66361

Table A(2)

The Present Worth of $1.00 Due at the Death of the Survivor of Two Persons

Interest at 10 Percent

Older	Younger	Present Worth	Older	Younger	Present Worth	Older	Younger	Present Worth
106	89	.67518	107	22	.02862	107	62	.27756
106	90	.68631	107	23	.02995	107	63	.29042
106	91	.69689	107	24	.03141	107	64	.30365
106	92	.70659	107	25	.03304	107	65	.31724
106	93	.71527	107	26	.03488	107	66	.33118
106	94	.72290	107	27	.03693	107	67	.34544
106	95	.72946	107	28	.03921	107	68	.36003
106	96	.73498	107	29	.04168	107	69	.37498
106	97	.73988	107	30	.04438	107	70	.39030
106	98	.74417	107	31	.04726	107	71	.40603
106	99	.74819	107	32	.05036	107	72	.42216
106	100	.75214	107	33	.05370	107	73	.43860
106	101	.75575	107	34	.05726	107	74	.45517
106	102	.75973	107	35	.06107	107	75	.47173
106	103	.76475	107	36	.06512	107	76	.48821
106	104	.77029	107	37	.06944	107	77	.50456
106	105	.77877	107	38	.07400	107	78	.52083
106	106	.79212	107	39	.07881	107	79	.53705
107	0	.02631	107	40	.08391	107	80	.55326
107	1	.00998	107	41	.08928	107	81	.56932
107	2	.00973	107	42	.09497	107	82	.58515
107	3	.00984	107	43	.10095	107	83	.60075
107	4	.01013	107	44	.10724	107	84	.61617
107	5	.01056	107	45	.11382	107	85	.63137
107	6	.01110	107	46	.12071	107	86	.64598
107	7	.01173	107	47	.12792	107	87	.65964
107	8	.01247	107	48	.13548	107	88	.67237
107	9	.01333	107	49	.14339	107	89	.68445
107	10	.01431	107	50	.15165	107	90	.69613
107	11	.01543	107	51	.16026	107	91	.70726
107	12	.01666	107	52	.16923	107	92	.71752
107	13	.01796	107	53	.17854	107	93	.72672
107	14	.01926	107	54	.18817	107	94	.73482
107	15	.02053	107	55	.19813	107	95	.74179
107	16	.02172	107	56	.20841	107	96	.74766
107	17	.02285	107	57	.21904	107	97	.75286
107	18	.02395	107	58	.22999	107	98	.75744
107	19	.02504	107	59	.24132	107	99	.76171
107	20	.02618	107	60	.25301	107	100	.76586
107	21	.02737	107	61	.26508	107	101	.76969

Table A(2)

The Present Worth of $1.00 Due at the Death of the Survivor of Two Persons

Interest at 10 Percent

Older	Younger	Present Worth	Older	Younger	Present Worth	Older	Younger	Present Worth
107	102	.77385	108	34	.05739	108	74	.45858
107	103	.77901	108	35	.06121	108	75	.47545
107	104	.78468	108	36	.06528	108	76	.49224
107	105	.79334	108	37	.06960	108	77	.50894
107	106	.80695	108	38	.07418	108	78	.52556
107	107	.82699	108	39	.07901	108	79	.54216
108	0	.02702	108	40	.08412	108	80	.55878
108	1	.01005	108	41	.08951	108	81	.57529
108	2	.00979	108	42	.09522	108	82	.59159
108	3	.00989	108	43	.10123	108	83	.60767
108	4	.01016	108	44	.10754	108	84	.62364
108	5	.01059	108	45	.11415	108	85	.63947
108	6	.01113	108	46	.12108	108	86	.65477
108	7	.01176	108	47	.12832	108	87	.66911
108	8	.01250	108	48	.13591	108	88	.68248
108	9	.01336	108	49	.14385	108	89	.69520
108	10	.01433	108	50	.15216	108	90	.70757
108	11	.01545	108	51	.16082	108	91	.71947
108	12	.01669	108	52	.16983	108	92	.73049
108	13	.01799	108	53	.17920	108	93	.74046
108	14	.01931	108	54	.18889	108	94	.74928
108	15	.02059	108	55	.19891	108	95	.75690
108	16	.02179	108	56	.20926	108	96	.76332
108	17	.02293	108	57	.21995	108	97	.76901
108	18	.02403	108	58	.23098	108	98	.77399
108	19	.02513	108	59	.24238	108	99	.77869
108	20	.02627	108	60	.25416	108	100	.78323
108	21	.02747	108	61	.26632	108	101	.78731
108	22	.02872	108	62	.27889	108	102	.79184
108	23	.03005	108	63	.29186	108	103	.79733
108	24	.03151	108	64	.30521	108	104	.80303
108	25	.03314	108	65	.31893	108	105	.81197
108	26	.03497	108	66	.33300	108	106	.82601
108	27	.03702	108	67	.34741	108	107	.84642
108	28	.03930	108	68	.36216	108	108	.87924
108	29	.04179	108	69	.37727	109	0	.02812
108	30	.04448	108	70	.39276	109	1	.01012
108	31	.04737	108	71	.40868	109	2	.00983
108	32	.05048	108	72	.42503	109	3	.00992
108	33	.05382	108	73	.44172	109	4	.01019

Tools and Techniques

Table A(2)

The Present Worth of $1.00 Due at the
Death of the Survivor of Two Persons
Interest at 10 Percent

Older	Younger	Present Worth	Older	Younger	Present Worth	Older	Younger	Present Worth
109	5	.01062	109	40	.08429	109	75	.00279
109	6	.01116	109	41	.08970	109	76	.00279
109	7	.01178	109	42	.09543	109	77	.00279
109	8	.01252	109	43	.10145	109	78	.00279
109	9	.01337	109	44	.10779	109	79	.00279
109	10	.01435	109	45	.11442	109	80	.00279
109	11	.01547	109	46	.12137	109	81	.00279
109	12	.01671	109	47	.12863	109	82	.00279
109	13	.01802	109	48	.13626	109	83	.00279
109	14	.01934	109	49	.14422	109	84	.00279
109	15	.02063	109	50	.15257	109	85	.00279
109	16	.02185	109	51	.16126	109	86	.00279
109	17	.02300	109	52	.17031	109	87	.00279
109	18	.02410	109	53	.17972	109	88	.00279
109	19	.02520	109	54	.18946	109	89	.00279
109	20	.02635	109	55	.19954	109	90	.00279
109	21	.02755	109	56	.20994	109	91	.00279
109	22	.02880	109	57	.22069	109	92	.00279
109	23	.03014	109	58	.23178	109	93	.00279
109	24	.03159	109	59	.24325	109	94	.00279
109	25	.03322	109	60	.25509	109	95	.00279
109	26	.03505	109	61	.26733	109	96	.00279
109	27	.03710	109	62	.27998	109	97	.00279
109	28	.03938	109	63	.29304	109	98	.00279
109	29	.04187	109	64	.30648	109	99	.00279
109	30	.04457	109	65	.32030	109	100	.00279
109	31	.04746	109	66	.33449	109	101	.00279
109	32	.05058	109	67	.34902	109	102	.00279
109	33	.05392	109	68	.36390	109	103	.00279
109	34	.05750	109	69	.37914	109	104	.00279
109	35	.06132	109	70	.39478	109	105	.00279
109	36	.06540	109	71	.41086	109	106	.00279
109	37	.06974	109	72	.42739	109	107	.00279
109	38	.07433	109	73	.44429	109	108	.00279
109	39	.07917	109	74	.46138	109	109	.00279

COMPUTING THE FEDERAL ESTATE TAX

GENERAL

Basically, the federal estate tax is computed in six stages:

(1) The *gross estate* is the total of all property in which the decedent had an interest and which is required to be included in the estate.

(2) The *adjusted gross estate* is determined by subtracting allowable funeral and administration expenses (as well as certain debts, taxes, and losses) from the gross estate. The calculation of the adjusted gross estate is primarily for the purpose of determining whether or not Section 303 redemption and/or 6166 installment payout tests can be met.

(3) The *taxable estate* is determined by subtracting from the adjusted gross estate any allowable marital deduction or charitable deduction or ESOP deduction.

(4) The *federal estate tax payable before credits* is determined as follows: (a) the *tentative tax base* is calculated by adding to the taxable estate any "adjusted taxable gifts" (essentially, this means the taxable portion of post-1976 gifts that were not already included in the decedent's gross estate); (b) the "unified rate schedule" (applicable to both estate and gift taxes) is then applied to determine the tentative tax; (c) the aggregate amount of gift tax which would have been payable with respect to gifts made by the decedent after 1976 if the tax rate schedule (IRC Sec. 2001 (c)) as in effect at the decedent's death had been applicable at the time of such gift is then subtracted from the tentative tax to arrive at the estate tax payable before credits.

(5) To determine *net federal estate tax*, the estate tax payable before credits is reduced, dollar-for-dollar, by subtracting the amount of any allowable:

(a) unified credit

(b) state death tax credit

(c) credit for foreign death taxes

(d) credit for tax paid on prior transfers

(6) Any tax imposed on "excess accumulations" is added to the tax as above computed. The tax is 15 percent of the excess of a participant's interest in all qualified plans and IRAs at death over the present value of an annuity for a term certain with annual payments equal to the limitation on excess distributions (currently $150,000) and payable for a period equal to the life expectancy of the participant immediately before death.

The resulting federal estate tax is imposed on the decedent's estate and is usually payable by the decedent's executor on the date the return is due, i.e., within nine months of the decedent's death.

Each stage mentioned above will now be examined in more detail. The form at Figure B.6 may be useful in following the flow of dollars from the gross estate to the net federal estate tax payable. References to the applicable line of such form will be made throughout the text. Section references in the headings are to Code sections.

ASCERTAINING THE GROSS ESTATE (LINE 1)

The total of the value of the following (as of the appropriate valuation date) equals the gross estate for federal estate tax purposes:

(1) property owned outright;

(2) certain property transferred gratuitously within three years of death and gift taxes paid on all gifts made within three years of death;

(3) certain lifetime transfers where the decedent retained the income or control over the income from the property transferred;

(4) certain gratuitous lifetime transfers where the transferee's possession or enjoyment of the property is conditioned on surviving the decedent;

(5) gratuitous lifetime transfers over which the decedent retained the right to alter, amend, or revoke the gift;

(6) annuities or similar arrangements purchased by the decedent and payable for life to both the annuitant and to a specified survivor (joint and survivor annuities);

(7) certain jointly held property where another party will obtain the decedent's interest at death by survivorship;

(8) general powers of appointment (a power so large that it approaches actual ownership of the property subject to the power);

(9) life insurance in which the decedent possessed incidents of ownership (economic benefits in the policy) or which was payable to or for the benefit of the decedent's estate.

(10) QTIP in the estate of the surviving spouse.

(1) Property Owned Outright (§2033)

All property owned by an individual at the time of death valued on the applicable valuation date is includible in the

Tools and Techniques

Figure B.6

	STAGE 1	(1)	Gross Estate	_____
minus		(2)	Funeral and administration expenses (estimated as _____ % of _____)	_____
		(3)	Debts and taxes	_____
		(4)	Losses	_____
			Total deductions	_____
equals	STAGE 2	(5)	Adjusted gross estate	_____
minus		(6)	Marital deduction	_____
_____		(7)	Charitable deduction	_____
		(8)	Deduction for sales to ESOP	_____
			Total deductions	_____
equals	STAGE 3	(9)	Taxable estate	_____
plus		(10)	Adjusted taxable gifts (post-1976 lifetime taxable transfers not included in gross estate)	_____
equals		(11)	Tentative tax base (total of taxable estate and adjusted taxable gift)	_____
compute		(12)	Tentative Tax	_____
minus		(13)	Gift taxes which would have been payable on post-1976 gifts	_____
equals	STAGE 4	(14)	Estate tax payable before credits	_____
minus		(15)	Tax credits	
			(a) Unified credit _____	
			(b) State death tax credit _____	
			(c) Credit for foreign death taxes _____	
			(d) Credit for tax on prior transfers _____	
			Total reduction _____	
equals	STAGE 5	(16)	Net federal estate tax payable	_____
plus	STAGE 6	(17)	15% tax on excess accumulations from qualified plans and IRAs	_____
equals		(18)	**TOTAL ESTATE TAX**	$_____

©1988 Stephan R. Leimberg, Esq.

computation of the gross estate. This section of the tax law causes property to be includible if (a) it was beneficially owned by the decedent at the time of his death and (b) it was transferred at death by the decedent's will or by state intestacy laws. But because the tax is levied on the transmission of property at death, the measure of that inclusion is the extent to which the property interest passes from the decedent to an heir, legatee, or devisee. Regardless of how much the decedent owned during lifetime, property interests are includible only to the extent such rights are passed on to some other party at the estate owner's death.

All types of property owned by a decedent outright at death, whether real or personal property (both tangible and intangible) are includible. This means that intangible personal property such as stocks, bonds, mortgages, notes, and other amounts payable to the decedent are includible in the gross estate, as well as tangible personal property such as a decedent's jewelry and other personal effects.

However, decedent must possess more than the bare legal title to property before it can be includible in the estate. For example, if under state law the decedent was the trustee of property or was a "strawman" owner and had no beneficial interest in the property, no part of such property would be includible in the estate. So if the president of a corporation signed as owner of a life insurance policy on his life but all premiums were paid by the corporation, the policy was carried and treated as a corporate asset on its books, and the corporation was named beneficiary, the proceeds should not be includible as insurance in his estate (he would be considered a mere nominal owner).

Furthermore, the decedent's gross estate will include the value of his or her share of certain property held in concert with others. For instance, if an individual holds property as a tenant in common with another person, the decedent's share will be includible as property owned at death. Similarly, the value of the decedent's share of community property will be included in his or her estate.

It is important to note that no inclusion is required for property in which the decedent's interest was obtained from someone else and was limited to lifetime enjoyment; i.e., an interest that terminated at the decedent's death and that the decedent had no right to transmit at death will not be included. So if Brett gives Eric the right to live in Brett's home in Miami for as long as Eric lives (and nothing more), the value of that home will not be includible in Eric's estate. On the other hand, if Brett had given Eric's wife, Pat, the house in Miami for her lifetime and the remainder to Eric, and Eric dies before Pat, Eric's gross estate will include the value of his remainder interest, since it does not terminate at his death. An interest will be includible even if it is limited, contingent, or extremely remote as long as it does not end when the decedent dies. (Of course, the contingency or remoteness of the interest will affect its valuation.)

The right to future income earned but not received prior to a decedent's death is a property interest that will be includible in the decedent's estate. Future income rights include bonuses, rents, dividends, interest payments and the decedent's share of any post-death partnership profits earned but not yet paid at death. The right of a life insurance agent to receive renewal commissions is a prime example of entitlement to future income. Such rights, as of the date of death or the alternate valuation date, whichever is applicable, are generally considered property owned outright and must be included in the decedent's gross estate. The income tax term for such right is "income in respect of a decedent" and a special income tax deduction to the extent of the estate tax attributable to the "income in respect to a decedent" is allowed under IRC Section 691.

(2) Certain Property Transferred Gratuitously Within Three Years of Death (§2035)

The general rule is that gifts (transfers for less than full and adequate consideration in money or money's worth) made within 3 years of death are not, with certain exceptions, includible regardless of the size of the gift or the manner in which it is made. There are two major classes of exemptions:

The first class of exceptions to that general rule is a transfer of an interest in property which is included in the value of the gross estate under section 2036 (transfer with retained life estate), 2037 (transfer taking effect at death), 2038 (revocable transfer), 2042 (life insurance) or would have been included under any of such sections if such interest had been retained by the decedent. For example, inclusion is still required to the extent the transfer by the insured was "with respect to a life insurance policy."

When testing to see if a decedent's estate qualifies for a Section 303 stock redemption, a 6166 installment payout of estate tax, or special use valuation under Code Section 2032A (the second class of exceptions), property given away within 3 years of death may be brought back into the gross estate. Even though, for purposes of computing the estate tax, a transfer within 3 years of death would not be brought back, it would be "brought back" in to see if the decedent's estate would qualify under the 303 (or 6166 or 2032A) tests. In qualifying for the section 6166 election, the "more than 35% of adjusted gross estate" requirement (see chapter 8) is met only if the estate meets such requirement both with and without application of the three-year inclusion rule of section 2035.

(3) Gratuitous Lifetime Transfers Where the Decedent Retained the Income or Control over the Income (§2036)

If an estate owner, during lifetime, transferred property as a gift, the value of that property will be includible in the

Tools and Techniques

donor's gross estate if the donor retained, for the donor's life (or for a period incapable of being determined without referring to the date of the donor's death or for a period that does not in fact end before the donor's death):

(a) a life estate;

(b) the possession, enjoyment, or right to income from the property; or

(c) the right to specify who will possess or enjoy either the property itself or the income it produces.

For example, Carolyn transfers stock in Texas Electric Company to a trust. She provides that the income from the trust is payable to herself for life and that the corpus will then pass to her daughter. The Texas Electric Company stock would be includible in Carolyn's estate, since she has retained a life estate.

The rationale for including this type of lifetime transfer is that the right to enjoy or control property or designate who will receive the property or its income is characteristic of ownership. Therefore, a transfer subject to this type of retained right is—to an important degree—essentially an incomplete disposition. Since the donee's possession or enjoyment of the property cannot begin until the decedent dies and "transfers" the retained interest, the donor will continue to be treated as owning the property.*

(4) Gratuitous Lifetime Transfers Conditioned On Surviving the Decedent (§2037)

Property must be included in a decedent's gross estate if the lifetime gift the decedent made is contingent on the donee's surviving the decedent. If the donee can obtain possession or enjoyment through ownership only by being alive at the time the donor dies, and the donor retained a significant (more than 5? chance) right to regain the property personally (either while living or through the right to dispose of it by will or intestacy at death), the value of the property transferred (not the value of the interest retained) will be includible. This is often called the "But if...back to..." Code section. Why? Because it will not be operative unless the transferring document provides wording to the effect of: *"But if the donee does not survive the donor, the property comes back to the donor."*

The right to regain the property is called a "reversionary interest." To cause inclusion, the actuarial value of the transferor's reversionary interest must be significant. Stated more precisely, the right to regain the property (or the right to dispose of it) must be worth actuarially more than 5 percent of the property's value.

For example, during his lifetime, Stuart transferred property to his wife, Mona, for her lifetime. Upon Mona's death, the property was to return to Stuart if he was living. If he was not living, the property was to go to Stuart's daughter, Ellen. Stuart dies before Mona. Stuart's daughter can obtain the possession or enjoyment of the property only if she survives Stuart. If she is not alive at the time Stuart dies, neither she nor her heirs will receive any interest in the property. Stuart retained a reversionary interest under the original transfer. If Stuart's reversion is worth more than five percent (5?) of the value of the property he placed in trust, the value of the remainder interest will be includible in Stuart's estate. Such a transfer is includible because it is considered to be, in substance, a substitute for disposing of the property by will.

(5) Gratuitous Lifetime Transfers in Which the Decedent Retained the Right to Alter, Amend, or Revoke the Gift (§2038)

If the decedent made a transfer of property during lifetime but retained a power (alone or together with others) to alter, amend, revoke, or terminate the gift, the value of property subject to that power (not the entire value of the transfer of property) will be included in the gross estate.

The courts have interpreted this provision broadly and the mere power retained by the donor to vary the timing of when a beneficiary will receive an interest (even if the beneficiary cannot forfeit the interest) will cause inclusion. Furthermore, if the donor has retained any of such forbidden powers, inclusion is required even if the donor holds those powers in his or her capacity as trustee and cannot regain the property or personally benefit from it in any way. (The capacity in which the power is held is irrelevant.) The provision is so broad that the mere retention and possession of such power is all that is required; the donor-decedent does not have to have the physical or mental capacity to use it.

(6) Annuities or Similar Arrangements Purchased by the Decedent and Payable for Life to Both the Annuitant and Specified Survivor (§2039)

If there is an annuity (or similar payment) payable as a result of the recipient's surviving the decedent and if the payment is made under a contract that also provided the decedent with a payment (or a right to a payment) for life (or for a period which did not in fact end before death or for a period which cannot be ascertained without referring to death), the present value of that income right is includible in the decedent's gross estate. For example, Steve purchased an annuity that would pay him $20,000 a year for life and upon his death would pay his wife, Jayne, $10,000 a year for as long as she lives. If Steve died before Jayne, the present value of future annuity payments to Jayne would be includible in his gross estate. Using the government valuation tables reproduced here in Appendix B (Figure B.4a), if Jayne were age 55 when Steve died, the annuity would have a present value at that time of $80,046.

This inclusion provision applies not only to commercial joint and survivor annuities but also to certain other types of payments made under a contract or agreement to the survivor(s) of the decedent.

The general rule stated above is subject to three qualifications. First, contracts (such as a life annuity) that provide payments to the decedent and end at death are not subject to this provision since they are not capable of "death time" transmission; i.e., there is no transferable interest.

Second, to the extent the survivor or anyone other than the decedent furnished part of the original purchase price, that portion of the survivor's annuity will not be included in the decedent's gross estate. So if the survivor paid one-third of the initial premium, only two-thirds of the value of survivor's income interest would be includible. If the decedent's employer furnished all or part of the purchase price, that contribution is treated as if it were made by the decedent.

Where the death proceeds of a life insurance policy are taken under a settlement option, they are considered life insurance proceeds rather than an annuity and are not taxed according to annuity rules.

(7) Jointly Held Property Where Another Party Will Obtain the Decedent's Interest at His or Her Death by Survivorship (§2040)

There are two rules that affect the estate taxation of property held jointly with the right of survivorship. The first is the "50-50 rule." It provides that only 50 percent of certain property titled and held jointly by the decedent and spouse with rights of survivorship, or as tenants by the entirety, will be includible in the decedent's estate—regardless of the size of his or her contribution (in fact, even if contribution of more than half can be proven by the survivor, this rule must be used).

For example, if Stan and his wife, Shelley, purchase 100 shares of AT&T for $50,000 and hold the property as joint tenants with rights of survivorship, even if the entire contribution was made by Stan from his salary, only 50% will be included in his estate. If the stock is worth $120,000 at that time, $60,000 will be included in his estate.

This 50-50 rule applies to both real and personal property regardless of how it was acquired or when it was purchased. But it can be used only in the case of a joint tenancy between spouses (and only between spouses) or a tenancy by the entirety.

The "percentage-of-contribution rule" (also known as the "consideration-furnished rule") is the second rule that affects the estate taxation of property held jointly with the right of survivorship and is used where the 50-50 rule does not apply. Essentially, this provision measures the estate tax includibility of jointly held property with survivorship rights by referring to the portion of the purchase price attributable to the decedent's contribution.

Actually, the rule is that jointly held property is includible in the estate of the first joint owner to die, except to the extent the survivor can prove contribution (out of funds other than those acquired by gift from the decedent). So if the survivor can prove contribution of one-third of the original purchase price, only two-thirds of the value of the jointly held property will be includible in the decedent's estate. If the survivor can prove contribution of two-thirds of the original purchase price, only one-third would be includible in the decedent's estate.

Assume Stan and his son Bill purchased 200 shares of stock for $100,000. Bill contributes $60,000. At Bill's death, 60 percent of the value of the stock at that time is includible in Bill's estate. If the stock has an estate tax value of $120,000, $72,000 (.60 x $120,000) would be includible.

(8) General Powers of Appointment (§2041)

When a power of appointment (the right to say who is to receive property in trust) is so extensive that it approaches actual ownership of the affected property, property subject to the power will be includible in the gross estate of the person who holds the power. Such property will be includible in a decedent's gross estate regardless of whether the power could be exercised at death or only during lifetime.

Inclusion of property over which a decedent held a general power of appointment will be required in certain circumstances even if the power is "released" (formally given up) or in some cases if the power is allowed to "lapse" (fails through the lack of use).

Likewise, the lifetime exercise or release of a general power is often treated as if the decedent made a lifetime transfer of the property subject to the power. So if the exercise (or release) is made within three years of the decedent's death, it will (to the extent that a gift tax return was required to be filed) be brought back into the computation of the gross estate.

(9) Life Insurance in Which the Decedent Possessed Incidents of Ownership or Which Was Payable to or for the Benefit of the Decedent's Estate (§2042)

If a decedent dies possessing any incidents of ownership in a life insurance policy on his life, regardless of the identity of the beneficiary, the proceeds will be includible in the decedent's gross estate. The term "incidents of ownership" refers to the right to benefit from the policy (or decide who is to enjoy the benefit) in an economic sense. For example, if an insured had the right to name a policy beneficiary, surrender a policy, or borrow its cash value, the insured would be enjoying the economic benefits of a policy.

Almost any meaningful ownership attribute in the policy held by the decedent will cause the entire proceeds to be includible in the gross estate. This is true regardless of how

Tools and Techniques

the decedent obtained the ownership rights or whether the use of such powers could directly or indirectly benefit the decedent. Mere possession of the ownership right at death (not the capacity to utilize the power) is all that is required to cause inclusion.

A decedent's gross estate will also include the proceeds of any policy payable to his executor or for the benefit of the decedent's estate—whether or not the decedent had retained any incidents of ownership in the policy at death. Therefore naming the insured's estate or executor either the direct or indirect beneficiary (such as naming a trustee beneficiary and requiring the use of trust assets to satisfy estate obligations) will cause inclusion of the proceeds—even if the insured possessed none of the incidents of ownership in the policy.

Corporate owned life insurance is includible in a decedent's estate if he owned more than 50 percent of the corporation's stock at his death, but only to the extent it is payable to a party other than the corporation or its creditors. Assume Chuck Heikenen owned 60 percent of the CH Corporation. The corporation owned a $1,000,000 policy on Chuck's life. If the $1,000,000 were payable to the corporation, it would push up the value per share of the stock included in Chuck's estate. But if the $1,000,000 were payable to Chuck's brother, the entire $1,000,000 would be includible. (The IRS would probably also claim that the distribution constituted either a dividend or deferred compensation. A 28 percent income tax would be applied to the $1,000,000 in addition to any federal tax.)

(10) Assets Which Have Qualified for QTIP (Qualified Terminable Interest Property) Treatment and Must Be Included in the Surviving Spouse's Estate (§2044)

If a marital deduction (either gift or estate tax) was allowed for the transfer of property in which the decedent had a qualifying income for life, such property must be included in the decedent's gross estate. For instance, if $1,000,000 deduction was allowed at Sam's death to his estate for property left to his wife, Sadie, at Sadie's death the value of such property at the time of her death will be included in her estate.

So if an election to have qualified terminable interest property qualify for the estate tax marital deduction (or the gift tax marital deduction) is made, the value of that property in the estate of the first spouse to die (or for gift tax purposes) will be included in the estate of the surviving spouse — unless that spouse made a lifetime transfer of his or her "qualifying income interest for life" (which would have resulted in a gift subject to gift tax).

The Date Assets Are Valued. Generally, federal estate taxes are based on the fair market value of the transferred property as of (a) the date the decedent died, or (b) an "alternate valuation date," six months after the date of the decedent's death. (This optional valuation date is designed to alleviate hard-

ship where there is a sudden and sharp decline in the value of the estate's assets). The executor can choose either date but must value all assets using the chosen date. The election must be made at the time a timely return is filed. Generally this means within nine months of the decedent's death but could be longer if the time to file is extended by the IRS.

If property is distributed, sold, exchanged or otherwise disposed of within six months after the decedent's death and the alternate valuation date is elected, the asset disposed of will be valued as of the disposition date. Certain types of property diminish in value as time goes on; for example, the present value of an annuity reduces each time a payment is made. Any such property interest (where the value is affected by the mere passing of time) is valued as of the date the decedent died (even if the alternate valuation date is selected). An adjustment to the value of such asset is then made for any difference in value due to factors other than the mere lapse of time.

The alternate valuation election is available only in those situations in which such an election will result in a reduction of the federal gross estate size *and* in a reduction of federal estate tax liability. In other words, both the total property value in the gross estate and the federal estate tax liability must be reduced below the date of death values in order for the alternate valuation date to be elected.

This provision prevents a "no cost" step-up in basis and thwarts the executor who might intentionally value property high in order to obtain a higher income tax basis, while knowing there would be no additional estate tax to pay because of the unlimited marital deduction or because the unified credit would absorb any estate tax otherwise payable.

DETERMINING THE ADJUSTED GROSS ESTATE (LINE 5)

Once the gross estate is calculated, certain deductions are allowed in arriving at the adjusted gross estate.

Deductions allowed fall into three categories:

(1) funeral and administrative expenses;

(2) debts (including certain taxes); and

(3) casualty and theft losses.

Funeral expenses, subject to certain limitations, are deductible (see line 2). Such expenses would include interment, burial lot or vault, grave marker, perpetual care of the grave site, and transportation of the person bringing the body to the place of burial. Deductions are generally limited to a "reasonable" amount.

Administrative expenses encompass those costs of administering property that are includible in the decedent's gross estate. Essentially this means the expenses incurred in the collection and preservation of probate assets, in the payment of estate debts, and in the distributing of probate assets to estate beneficiaries. Such expenses include court costs, accounting fees, appraisers' fees, brokerage costs, executors' commissions, and attorneys' fees. These vary widely from location to location and depend on the size of the estate and the complexity of the administration problems involved.

Deductions cannot exceed the amount allowed by the laws of the jurisdiction under which the estate is being administered.

Certain administration costs may be deducted from either the federal estate tax return (Form 706) or from the estate's income tax return (Form 1041). The estate's executor has the option of electing either one (but not both).

Generally, the executor will elect to deduct attorneys' fees and executors' commissions from the return in which the tax rates are higher. This will result in an overall tax saving, but note that a deduction on the income tax return, as opposed to the estate tax return, or vice versa, may result in favoring one beneficiary or group of beneficiaries over another.

Bona fide debts, including mortgages and other liens, that were (a) personal obligations of the decedent at the time of death (together with any interest accrued to the date of death), and (b) founded on adequate and full consideration in money or money's worth are deductible (line 3). Mortgages are deductible if the decedent was personally liable and the full value of the property was includible in the estate. But if the decedent had no personal liability for the payment of the underlying debt and the creditor would look only to encumbered property for payment, the mortgage would result in a reduction in the value of the property subject to the mortgage.

In the case of community property, only those claims and expenses that were the decedent's personal obligations are deductible in full. This means an allocation of claims and expenses must be made. Since only one-half of the total community property is includible, only half of any obligation attributable to community property is deductible.

Certain taxes unpaid at the time of the decedent's death are considered debts. Three common deductible taxes are:

(1) income taxes unpaid but reportable for some tax period prior to the decedent's death;

(2) gift taxes that were not paid on gifts the decedent made sometime prior to death; and

(3) property taxes that accrued but remained unpaid at the time of the decedent's death.

Casualty and theft losses incurred by the estate are deductible if the loss arose from fire, storm, shipwreck (or other casualty), or theft.

To be deductible, the loss must have occurred during the time the estate was in the process of settlement and before it was closed. Such deductions are limited in two respects: the deduction is reduced (1) to the extent that insurance or any other compensation is available to offset the loss, and

(2) to the extent that a loss is reflected in the alternate valuation (an executor can elect to value assets in the estate either on the date of death or at the alternate date).

At the executor's option, losses may be deducted from either the estate tax return or the estate's income tax return. Typically, they will be taken on the return which produces the highest deduction.

DETERMINATION OF TAXABLE ESTATE (LINE 8)

The adjusted gross estate may be reduced by (1) a marital deduction, (2) a charitable deduction, (3) a deduction for sales of certain securities to an ESOP or EWOC.

A marital deduction (line 6) is allowed for property that (a) is included in the decedent's gross estate, and (b) passes at the decedent's death to a surviving spouse, (c) "in a qualifying manner" (in a manner that gives the surviving spouse control and enjoyment essentially tantamount to outright ownership or that meets the requirements of "qualified terminable interest (QTIP)" property, as defined below).

The maximum amount allowable as a marital deduction for federal estate tax purposes is the net value of the property passing to the surviving spouse in a qualifying manner. Otherwise, there is no limit to the marital deduction. An individual could conceivably transfer his entire estate to his (or her) spouse's estate tax free.

Under prior law most "terminable interests" (where the surviving spouse's interest would cease upon the occurrence or nonoccurrence of a particular event and the children or some other party would receive the marital property) would not qualify for the marital deduction.

Most terminable interests can qualify for the marital deduction if the executor makes the appropriate QTIP election in a timely manner. A qualifying terminable interest is one which (a) passes from the decedent, (b) gives the surviving spouse a lifetime income payable at least annually, and (c) the decedent's executor makes an irrevocable election on his estate tax return.

The election is really the price of qualifying what under prior law would not have qualified. For instance, an individual can now provide, "income to my wife for life. At her death the principal goes to my children." The election would obligate the wife's estate to pay the appropriate estate tax on the interest as if she were the ultimate recipient instead of the children. In other words, the value of the principal is included in the estate of the life tenant. (Her executor is, however, entitled to recover from the person who receives the principal the share of estate taxes generated in her estate by the inclusion of that property—unless in her will she choses to exonerate that individual.)

A charitable deduction (line 7) is allowed for the fair market value of any type of gift to a "qualified charity" at a de-

Tools and Techniques

cedent's death. The deduction is limited to the net value of the property includible in the gross estate that is transferred to the charity. In other words, a decedent could conceivably leave his or her entire estate to charity and receive a deduction for the entire amount.

A deduction is allowed (line 8) to an estate which sells employer securities to an ESOP (Employee Stock Ownership Plan) or EWOC (Eligible Worker-Owned Cooperative).

This temporary provision (the deduction does not apply to any sale after December 31, 1991) was designed to encourage transfer of employer securities to ESOPs. Tax law permits a deduction equal to 50 percent of the proceeds received from a qualified sale of employer securities (but limited to 50 percent of the taxable estate and in no event to exceed a maximum estate tax reduction of $750,000).

The deduction will not be available unless

(1) the decedent directly owned employer securities immediately before death;

(2) after the sale the employer securities are allocated to plan participants or set aside for future allocation;

(3) the securites were not "publicly traded";

(4) the securities were listed as securities on the decedent's estate tax return; *and*

(5) certain holding period requirements are met.

No deduction is allowed in the case of securities acquired with assets transferred from another plan of the employer. Certain excise taxes are imposed on an ESOP or EWOC for a failure to satisfy the allocation and holding period requirements.

ESTATE TAX PAYABLE BEFORE CREDITS (LINE 13)

Once the taxable estate (Line 9) is found, adjusted taxable gifts are added to arrive at the tentative tax base. Adjusted taxable gifts are defined as the taxable portion of all post-1976 gifts. A gift is taxable to the extent it exceeds any allowable (a) annual gift tax exclusion, (b) gift tax marital deduction (similar to the estate tax marital deduction but for lifetime gifts to a spouse), (c) gift tax charitable deduction. Gifts that for any reason have already been includible in a decedent's gross estate (i.e., a gift with a retained life estate) are not considered adjusted taxable gifts.

Adding adjusted taxable gifts to the taxable estate makes the estate tax computation part of a unified transfer tax calculation. The process uses a cumulative approach, with "death time" dispositions merely being the last in a series of gratuitous transfers. The net effect of adding in adjusted taxable gifts is to subject the taxable estate at death to rates that are higher than if the computation did not consider lifetime gifts.

When adjusted taxable gifts (line 10) are combined with the taxable estate, the result is the "tentative tax base", the amount upon which the tax rates are based.

At this point, the "tentative tax" (line 12) is computed by applying the appropriate rates (see the Unified Rate Schedule for Estate and Gift Taxes, reproduced in Appendix C) to the tentative tax base. These rates are progressive. The tax on a tentative tax base of $1,000 is $180. On $100,000, the tax is $23,800. On $1 million, the tentative tax is $345,800.

The 55 percent top federal estate and gift tax rate (and also generation skipping transfer tax flat rate) remains in effect until 1993 (see rate schedules in Appendix C). Effective at that time, for decedents dying and for gifts made after December 31, 1992, the maximum gift and estate (and the flat generation skipping transfer tax) rate drops to 50 percent.

The advantage of the unified credit and graduated rates is lost to estates in excess of $10,000,000. This is accomplished in the following manner: The gift and estate tax liability for taxable transfers in excess of $10,000,000 is increased by imposing an additional 5 percent add-on tax on the excess of (a) the taxable transfer over (b) $10,000,000.

Until 1993

This 5 percent add-on tax ends when cumulative transfers reach $21,040,000. At that point, the 55 percent rate becomes applicable to additional amounts. So a taxable estate of $3,000,000 or more is taxed at 55 percent on any amount in excess of $3,000,000 plus a 5 percent add-on tax for the taxable estate exceeding $10,000,000 but not exceeding $21,040,000.

For example, assume an individual who died in 1988 has a taxable estate of $25,000,000. The tentative tax would be $13,390,800. This is $1,290,800 on the first $3,000,000 plus a 55 percent tax rate applied to the next $22,000,000, a tax of $12,100,000. This is further increased by a 5 percent add-on tax on $11,040,000 ($21,040,000 - $10,000,000). The total tentative tax would therefore be $13,942,800. (Note that if the flat 55 percent rate were applied to the entire $25,000,000 estate, the tax would total $13,750,000. If the $192,800 credit, which is phased out by operation of the five percent add-on tax, is then added, the result is $13,942,800.) The computation is shown in Figure B.7.

1993 and Later Years

If the decedent dies or the gift is made after December 31, 1992, the 5 percent additional tax ends when cumulative transfers reach $18,340,000. At that point, the 50 percent rate becomes applicable to additional amounts. The computation, using the same example as in Figure B.7, is shown at Figure B.8.

Figure B.7

COMPUTING THE ESTATE OR GIFT TAX
UNTIL 1993

Step 1: State taxable gift/tentative tax base	$25,000,000
Step 2: Find tax from table on amounts up to $3,000,000	$1,290,800
Step 3: Compute the amount over $3,000,000	$22,000,000
Step 4: Compute tax on Step 3 amount at 55%	$12,100,000
Step 5: State amount of gift or estate over $10,000,000 but not over $21,040,000	$11,040,000
Step 6: Compute tax on Step 5 amount at 5 percent	$552,000
Total Tax	$13,942,800

(The five percent rate adjustment does not affect the maximum federal estate tax rate for purposes of computing the generation skipping transfer tax (GST tax). That remains at 55 percent for generation skipping transfers made before 1993, and 50 percent after that date.)

Since the taxable portion of gifts made after 1976 have already been added back in as adjusted taxable gifts, the gift tax generated (or that would have been generated) by such gifts is subtracted at this point (line 13).

DETERMINING THE NET FEDERAL ESTATE TAX PAYABLE

Certain tax credits are allowed as a dollar-for-dollar reduction of the estate tax. These credits (line 15) are (a) the uni-

fied credit, (b) the state death tax credit, (c) the credit for foreign death taxes, and (d) the credit for taxes on prior transfers.

A unified credit is allowed against the estate tax otherwise payable. The term "unified credit" was adopted because that credit is used as an offset against gift as well as estate taxes. However, to the extent the unified credit has been used against gift taxes, the credit available against the estate tax is lowered. No refund is available if the credit exceeds the estate tax.

Note that the required computation process has the effect of reducing the credit by requiring the "add back" of adjusted taxable gifts. In other words, although the $121,800 unified credit in the example below does not appear to be reduced by $1,800 (the tax on a $10,000 gift which was not paid only

Figure B.8

COMPUTING THE ESTATE OR GIFT TAX
1993 AND LATER

Step 1: State taxable gift/tentative tax base	$25,000,000
Step 2: Find tax from table on amounts up to $2,500,000	$1,025,800
Step 3: Compute the amount over $2,500,000	$22,500,000
Step 4: Compute tax on Step 3 amount at 50%	$11,250,000
Step 5: State amount of gift or estate over $10,000,000 but not over $18,340,000	$8,340,000
Step 6: Compute tax on Step 5 amount at 5 percent	$417,000
Total Tax	$12,692,800

Tools and Techniques

because the decedent used $1,800 of credit), the effect is the same because of the adding back of the $10,000 worth of adjusted taxable gifts. Stated another way, adding back $10,000 of adjusted taxable gifts "restores" the $1,800 of unified credit.

For example, assume a widow died in 1988 with a $900,000 taxable estate. In 1977 she made only one taxable gift of $10,000 (after utilizing the annual exclusion). The widow paid no gift tax because $1,800 of her unified credit was applied to offset the $1,800 gift tax liability. These facts resulted in the following estate tax liability (ignoring other tax credits):

Taxable Estate	$900,000
Adjusted taxable gifts	10,000
Total	$910,000
Tax on $910,000	310,700
Less: gift taxes paid on lifetime transfers	–0–
Less: unified credit for 1988	192,800
Tax due	$117,900

Year	Unified Credit	Exemption Equivalent
1981	$ 47,000	$175,625
1982	62,800	225,000
1983	79,300	275,000
1984	96,300	325,000
1985	121,800	400,000
1986	155,800	500,000
1987 and later years	192,800	600,000

The second credit allowed against the estate tax is for any death taxes paid to a state because of property includible in the decedent's gross estate. This includes estate, inheritance, legacy, or succession taxes. The maximum credit allowable is the lower of (a) the death tax actually paid to the state, or (b) the ceiling amount provided in the maximum credit table reproduced in Appendix C. Note that the IRS table used to calculate the state death tax credit is based on the taxable estate (line 9) rather than the tentative tax base (line 11).

A credit for foreign death taxes, the third credit available, is intended to prevent double taxation. It is allowed for death taxes paid to a foreign country or a United States possession on property that is (a) included in the decedent's gross estate, and (b) situated (and subject to tax) in that country or possession. The credit is available only to United States citizens or resident aliens.

Finally, where a prior decedent (the transferor) transferred property (which was taxed at death) to the decedent and the property is includible in the present decedent's estate, a credit will be allowed for all or part of the estate tax paid by the transferor's estate on the transferred property. The present decedent must have received the property prior to death. The transferor must have died within ten years before or two years after the present decedent.

As long as the property was includible in the transferor's estate and passed from the transferor to the present decedent, the method of transfer is irrelevant; it can be by will, by intestacy, by election against the will, by lifetime gift, as life insurance proceeds, or as joint property with right of survivorship.

Interestingly enough, the law arbitrarily assumes that property that was in the transferor's estate and that was transferred to the present decedent is subject to double taxation (and is therefore entitled to the credit). There is no requirement that the property actually be in existence at the present decedent's death or if in existence subject to federal estate tax at that time.

The credit is the lower of:

(1) the federal estate tax attributable to the transferred property in the transferor's estate, or

(2) the federal estate tax attributable to the transferred property in the estate of the present decedent.

The credit is reduced every two years, and at the end of ten years after the transferor's death no credit is allowable. For example, between years two and four only 80 percent of the credit is allowable.

DETERMINING EXCESS RETIREMENT ACCUMULATIONS TAX (ERAT)

After the net federal estate tax (line 16) has been determined, the tax on any "excess retirement accumulation" must be computed. The ERAT is equal to 15 percent of the individual's "excess retirement accumulation." This is defined as the excess of

A. The decedent's interest in all qualified retirement plans and IRAs

over

B. The present value of an annuity for a term certain, with annual payments equal to the limitation on distributions in effect for the year in which death occurs, and payable for a term certain equal to the individual's actuarial life expectancy immediately before his death.

For instance, assume a 65 year old who had $3,000,000 in his pension when he died and a maximum permissable retirement payout of $150,000 a year. Multiplying $150,000 by the annuity factor obtained from Table A (Figure B.4a) for a decedent 65 years old as of date of death (6.7970—the appropriate factor until new tables or formulas mandated under TAMRA '88 are effective), the maximum present value in this hypothetical is determined to be $1,019,550. The "excess" ($3,000,000-$1,019,550) would be $1,980,450. The 15% tax imposed on that amount would be $297,068.

This tax is not eligible to be offset by any marital deduction, charitable deduction, unified credit, or IRD (Code section 691) income tax deduction. It could easily push a decedent's estate up to a 70% federal death tax bracket in 1987 (55% estate tax plus 15% additional tax) or 65% in 1988 and later years (50% estate tax plus 15% additional tax).

EXAMPLES

Examples of the estate tax computation process utilizing some of the Advanced Estate Planning Course I forms prepared by The American College and used in its Advanced Estate Planning courses can be found at Figures B.9 through B.13. These are:

Example

(1) Estate tax computation — No lifetime gifts
(2) Estate tax computation — Life gift, no gift tax
(3) Comparison to Example 2 — Same facts except no lifetime gift
(4) Estate tax computation — Lifetime gift, gift tax
(5) Comparison to Example 4 — Same facts except no lifetime gift

PAYMENT OF THE ESTATE TAX

As mentioned above, the estate tax is due at the time the return is to be filed nine months after the decedent's death. A return must be filed if the gross estate exceeds certain limits. These limits are called "exemption equivalents" because they are roughly equal to the exemption from taxation provided by the unified credit.

Year	Unified Credit	Exemption Equivalent
1981	$ 47,000	$175,625
1982	62,800	225,000
1983	79,300	275,000
1984	96,300	325,000
1985	121,800	400,000
1986	155,800	500,000
1987 and later years	192,800	600,000

It is important to note that these threshold amounts are lowered by the total of any adjusted taxable gifts (which have not been included in the gross estate). Therefore, in some estates filing will be required even if the taxable estate is far less than the exemption equivalent.

The "reasonable cause" extension. As stated previously, the tax is due 9 months from the date of the decedent's death. But an executor or administrator can request that the IRS grant an extension of time for paying the tax—up to 12 months from the date fixed for the payment—if there is reasonable cause. Furthermore, the IRS could, at its discretion, upon the executor's showing of reasonable cause, grant a series of extensions which—in total—could run as long as 10 years from the due date of the original return. There is no definition of reasonable cause in the Internal Revenue Code or Regulations. However, the Regulations give illustrative examples of situations where reasonable cause will be found:

(a) a substantial portion of the estate consists of rights to receive future payments such as annuities, accounts receivable, or renewal commissions and the estate cannot borrow against these assets without incurring substantial loss;

(b) the gross estate is unascertainable at the time the tax is normally due because the estate has a claim to substantial assets that cannot be collected without litigation; or

(c) an estate does not have sufficient funds to pay claims against the estate (including estate taxes when due) and at the same time provide a reasonable allowance during the period of administration for decedent's surviving spouse and dependent children because the executor, despite reasonable efforts, cannot convert assets in his or her possession into cash.

The "up to 14-year closely held business interest" extension: Under IRC Section 6166, an executor may elect to pay estate tax attributable to a closely held business in 14 annual installments if the interest in the closely held business exceeds 35 percent of the adjusted gross estate. This extension is explained in detail in chapter 8.

---

*Code section 2036 is extremely broad and encompasses direct and indirect transfers of future appreciation coupled with retention of an income interest. More precisely, if a person holds a substantial interest in an enterprise and, in effect, transfers (after December 17, 1987) property having a disproportionately large share of the potential appreciation in that person's interest in the enterprise while retaining a share in the income of or rights in the enterprise, then the retention of those interests is treated as if the person had retained the enjoyment of the transferred property as well. In other words, both interests (with certain adjustments) are includible in the person's gross estate. (See the explanation of section 2036(c) beginning at page 477.)

Tools and Techniques

Figure B.9

Example 1

Herb Stevens, recently divorced, dies in 1988. His gross estate is $940,000. Funeral and administrative costs total $25,000. Debts and taxes total $15,000. He made no taxable gifts during his lifetime. The estate tax liability would be computed as follows:

Determination of Cash Requirements

Herb Stevens

	(1)	Gross Estate		$940,000
Minus	(2)	Funeral and Administration Expenses	25,000	
		(Estimated as _____ % of _____)		
	(3)	Debts and Taxes	15,000	
	(4)	Losses	0	
		Total Deductions	40,000	
Equals	(5)	Adjusted Gross Estate		$900,000
Minus	(6)	Marital Deduction	0	
	(7)	Charitable Deduction	0	
	(8)	Deduction for sales to ESOP	0	
		Total Deductions	0	0
Equals	(9)	Taxable Estate		$900,000
Plus	(10)	Adjusted Taxable Gifts (Post '76 Lifetime Taxable Transfers not included in Gross Estate)		0
Equals	(11)	Tentative Tax Base (Total of Taxable Estate and Adjusted Taxable Gifts)		$900,000
Compute	(12)	Tentative Tax	306,800	
Minus	(13)	Gift Taxes Payable on Post '76 Gifts	0	
Equals	(14)	Tax Payable Before Credits		$306,800
Minus	(15)	Tax Credits		
		(a) Unified Credit	192,800	State death tax payable 27,600
		(b) State death tax credit	27,600	
		(c) Credit for tax on prior transfers	0	
		(d) Credit for foreign death taxes	0	
		Total Reduction	220,400	
Equals	(16)	Net Federal Estate Tax Payable		$86,400
Plus	(17	Tax on Excess Accumulations from Qualified Plans and IRAs		0
Plus	(18)	Total Cash Bequests		0
Equals	(19)	Total Cash Requirements (sum of 2, 3, State Death Tax Payable, 16, 17 & 18)		$191,000

© 1987 by The American College as part of Advanced Estate Planning Courses I and II

Figure B.10

Example 2

Mary Joe Murphey, a single woman, has a gross estate of $1,000,000 at the time of her death in 1989. Assume funeral and administrative expenses are $60,000 and debts and taxes total $40,000. She made no gifts prior to 1977 but made a $100,000 taxable gift to her niece in December of 1977. Her gift tax liability was $23,800 on the gift but this was entirely offset by the gift tax credit. Her estate would be computed as follows:

Determination of Cash Requirements Mary Jo Murphey — Gift of $100,000

	(1)	Gross Estate		$1,000,000
Minus	(2)	Funeral and Administration Expenses (Estimated as _____ % of _____)	60,000	
	(3)	Debts and Taxes	40,000	
	(4)	Losses	0	
		Total Deductions	100,000	
Equals	(5)	Adjusted Gross Estate		$ 900,000
Minus	(6)	Marital Deduction	0	
	(7)	Charitable Deduction	0	
	(8)	Deduction for Sales to ESOP	0	
		Total Deductions	0	0
Equals	(9)	Taxable Estate		$ 900,000
Plus	(10)	Adjusted Taxable Gifts (Post '76 Lifetime Taxable Tranfers not included in Gross Estate)		$ 100,000
Equals	(11)	Tentative Tax Base (Total of Taxable Estate and Adjusted Taxable Gifts)		$1,000,000
Compute	(12)	Tentative Tax	345,800	
Minus	(13)	Gift Taxes Payable on Post '76 Gifts	0	
Equals	(14)	Tax Payable Before Credits		$ 345,800
Minus	(15)	Tax Credits (a) Unified Credit (b) State death tax credit (c) Credit for tax on prior transfers (d) Credit for foreign death taxes Total Reduction	192,800 27,600 _____ _____ 220,400	State Death Tax Payable 27,600
Equals	(16)	Net Federal Estate Tax Payable		$125,400
Plus	(17)	Tax on excess accumulations from Qualified Plans and IRAs		0
Plus	(18)	Total Cash Bequests		0
Equals	(19)	Total Cash Requirements (sum of 2, 3, State Death Tax Payable, 16, 17 and 18)		$ 253,000

Tools and Techniques

Figure B.11

Example 3

If no gift had been made, Mary Jo's Federal estate tax liability is slightly less than it would have been if she gave away the $100,000. (Because her taxable estate is higher, the credit for state death taxes is increased, which in turn lowers the Federal estate tax liability. But the total liability need ($253,000 including funeral and administrative expense, Federal and state taxes, and the Federal gift tax) is the same, because of the increase in state death taxes):

Determination of Cash Requirements

Mary Jo Murphey — No Gift

	(1) Gross Estate		$1,100,000
Minus			
	(2) Funeral and Administration Expenses	60,000	
	(Estimated as _____ % of _____)		
	(3) Debts and Taxes	40,000	
	(4) Losses	0	
	Total Deductions	100,000	
Equals			
	(5) Adjusted Gross Estate		$1,000,000
Minus			
	(6) Marital Deduction	0	
	(7) Charitable Deduction	0	
	(8) Deduction for Sales to ESOP	0	
	Total Deductions	0	0
Equals			
	(9) Taxable Estate		$1,000,000
Plus			
	(10) Adjusted Taxable Gifts (Post '76 Lifetime Taxable Transfers not included in Gross Estate)		0
Equals			
	(11) Tentative Tax Base (Total of Taxable Estate and Adjusted Taxable Gifts)		$1,000,000
Compute			
	(12) Tentative Tax	345,800	
Minus			
	(13) Gift Taxes Payable on Post '76 Gifts	0	
Equals			
	(14) Tax Payable Before Credits		$ 345,800
Minus			
	(15) Tax Credits		State Death
	(a) Unified Credit	192,800	Tax
	(b) State death tax credit	33,200	Payable 33,200
	(c) Credit for tax on prioer transfers	_____	
	(d) Credit for foreign death taxes	_____	
	Total Reduction	226,000	
Equals			
	(16) Net Federal Estate Tax Payable		$ 119,800
Plus			
	(17) Tax on excess accumulations from Qualified Plans and IRAs		0
Plus			
	(18) Total Cash Bequests		0
Equals			
	(19) Total Cash Requirements (sum of 2, 3, State Death Tax Payable, 16, 17 & 18)		$ 253,000

Tax savings can be realized by making a gift large enough — even after credits — to generate a gift tax. The savings results from being able to exclude the gift tax paid from the estate tax calculation (assuming the donor lives more than three years after the gift is made, since the tax on a gift made within 3 years of death is brought back into the gross estate — even if the gift itself is not brought back into the computation).

Figure B.12

Example 4

Bob Hopkins, a single individual, owned property worth $2,300,000 (before the gift). He gave a taxable gift of $1,000,000 (the annual exclusion is ignored), to his friend, Flicka. The gift tax was $345,800. Bob made the gift in December 1977 and took a credit of $30,000, so the tax actually paid was $315,800. Assuming funeral and administrative costs of $100,000 and debts and taxes of $150,000, the computation of estate tax liability if he died in 1989 would be:

Determination of Cash Requirements

Bob Hopkins

	(1)	Gross Estate		$ 984,200
Minus				
	(2)	Funeral and Administration Expenses	100,000	
		(Estimated as _____ % of _____)		
	(3)	Debts and Taxes	150,000	
	(4)	Losses	0	
		Total Deductions	250,000	
Equals				
	(5)	Adjusted Gross Estate		$ 734,200
Minus				
	(6)	Marital Deduction	0	
	(7)	Charitable Deduction	0	
	(8)	Deduction for Sales to ESOP	0	
		Total Deductions	0	0
Equals				
	(9)	Taxable Estate		$ 734,200
Plus				
	(10)	Adjusted Taxable Gifts (Post '76 Lifetime Taxable Transfers not included in Gross Estate)		$1,000,000
Equals				
	(11)	Tentative Tax Base (Total of Taxable Estate and Adjusted Taxable Gifts)		$1,734,200
Compute				
	(12)	Tentative Tax	661,190	
Minus				
	(13)	Gift Taxes Payable on Post '76 Gifts	315,800	
Equals				
	(14)	Tax Payable Before Credits		$ 345,390
Minus				
	(15)	Tax Credits		State Death Tax
		(a) Unified Credit	192,800	
		(b) State death tax credit	19,642	Payable 19,642
		(c) Credit for tax on prior transfers	___	
		(d) Credit for foreign death taxes	___	
		Total Reduction	212,442	
Equals				
	(16)	Net Federal Estate Tax Payable		$ 132,948
Plus				
	(17)	Total Cash Bequests		0
Equals				
	(18)	Total Cash Requirements (sum of 2, 3, State Death Payable, 16, and 17)		$ 402,590

Tools and Techniques

Figure B.13

Example 5

But if Bob had retained the $1,000,000, the computation would have resulted in an increased liability (funeral, administrative expenses, debts, and taxes are assumed to remain the same for illustrative purposes):

Determination of Cash Requirements

Bob Hopkins

	(1)	Gross Estate		$2,300,000
Minus				
	(2)	Funeral and Administration Expenses	100,000	
		(Estimated as _____ % of _____)		
	(3)	Debts and Taxes	150,000	
	(4)	Losses	0	
		Total Deductions	250,000	
Equals				
	(5)	Adjusted Gross Estate		$2,050,000
Minus				
	(6)	Marital Deduction	0	
	(7)	Charitable Deduction	0	
		Total Deductions	0	0
Equals				
	(8)	Taxable Estate		$2,050,000
Plus				
	(9)	Adjusted Taxable Gifts (Post '76 Lifetime Taxable Transfers not included in Gross Estate)	0	
Equals				
	(10)	Tentative Tax Base (Total of Taxable Estate and Adjusted Taxable Gifts)		$2,050,000
Compute				
	(11)	Tentative Tax	805,300	
Minus				
	(12)	Gift Taxes Payable on Post '76 Gifts	0	
Equals				
	(13)	Tax Payable Before Credits		$ 805,300
Minus				

(14) Tax Credits
  (a) Unified Credit — 192,800
  (b) State death tax credit — 103,200 State Death Tax Payable 103,200
  (c) Credit for tax on prior transfers — _____
  (d) Credit for foreign death taxes — _____

Total Reduction — 296,000

Equals				
	(15)	Net Federal Estate Tax Payable		$ 509,300
Plus				
	(16)	Total Cash Bequests		0
Equals				
	(17)	Total Cash Requirements (sum of 2, 3, State Death Tax Payable, 15 & 16)		$ 862,500

Two reasons for the increased liability are (1) the $315,800 gift tax would not be removed from the gross estate and (2) $1,315,800 more property is subject to state death taxes. This is an important reason for lifetime gifts in states with no state gift tax. The difference would be even more dramatic if the estate had grown at 10 percent or more each year.

SECTION 2036(c):
A CLEAR AND PRESENT DANGER TO WEALTH RETENTION

By Stephan R. Leimberg, JD, CLU, of The American College
and
Howard Zaritsky, Esq., of Zaritsky and Zaritsky
and
William J. Wagner, JD, LLM, of The National Underwriter Company

The authors wish to express their appreciation to Lawrence Brody, Esq., of Bryan, Cave, McPheeters, and McRoberts, St. Louis, Mo., and to Eric Johnson, JD, LLM, Assistant Professor of Taxation at The American College, Bryn Mawr, Pa., for their assistance.

PART I - THE LAW

Many estate planners have long felt that the unlimited marital deduction eliminated any federal estate tax at the death of a client (no matter how wealthy) who was willing to leave his estate to a surviving spouse. For many years emphasis in planning has been placed on saving taxes at the death of the client's surviving spouse. But Code Section 2036(c) may mean that hundreds of thousands or even millions of federal estate tax dollars will now have to be raised at the death of the first spouse to die (even though the assets that generated those awesome tax burdens may no longer be available to the client's estate). The resulting drain for those unprepared for this horrendous liquidity demand will be disastrous for many survivors and many closely held businesses.

The snake in the grass that's forcing the change bites almost anyone of wealth with a closely held business who wants to keep that business in the family, as well as successful investors seeking continued financial security for their heirs. The snake without the C is OBRA '87, (Omnibus Budget Reconciliation Act of 1987), the 1987 Tax Act that should rattle your most successful clients.[1] Additional fangs have been added by the Technical and Miscellaneous Revenue Act of 1988 (TAMRA '88).[2]

What is the impact of Section 2036(c), the anti-freeze provision of OBRA '87, on such tools and techniques as

(a) recapitalizations?

(b) intrafamily installment sales?

(c) self-canceling installment notes (SCINs)?

(d) private annuities?

(e) buy-sell agreements?

(f) grantor retained income trusts (GRITs)?

(g) remainder interest transactions (RITs)?

(h) split interest purchases of property (SPLITs)?

(i) debt unrelated to gifts or sales of stock?

(j) stock options or stock owned by an ESOP?

Before we state our opinion on the impact of 2036(c) on each of these freezing techniques and on other common estate and business planning transactions, as well as outline what other authorities are saying, let's first review what this new provision was intended to do and what it says.

The Objectives

We have to start with the definition of the term "estate freeze." Traditionally, it is a technique by which the client converts a "growth" interest in a business or other enterprise into an interest that has little or no growth potential. In the most familiar type of freeze the client recapitalizes a corporation by exchanging common stock worth $XXX for a combination of common and preferred stock of the same value; then the client gives or sells the common stock to his children.

Alternatively, several levels of partnership interests are established. Some levels carry income while others represent the value of future growth in the partnership. The income interests are retained while the growth interests are given away or sold to family members. As the list of techniques above indicates, there have been many other ways of freezing the growth in an enterprise and shifting the estate tax on wealth.

The major federal estate tax objective of an estate freeze is to shift the federal estate tax on a business's future appreciation from the client to one or more other family members. Other objectives of an estate freeze are to:

(a) transfer the future growth in the business to a younger generation;

(b) remove the asset from the client's estate for state death tax purposes;

(c) remove the asset from the client's estate for probate purposes;

(d) escape the reach of creditors with respect to the "growth" interest;

(e) thwart or discourage an attack on or an election against the client's will to reach the given stock or other property;

(f) retain, to whatever extent possible and consistent with the achievement of the objectives above, income from or control over the business;

(g) provide an incentive for a younger generation family member to stay with and work for a family business.

Congress, in its never ceasing quest to raise revenues without increasing taxes, intended to treat the traditional corporate recapitalization followed by a gift of common stock (and the traditional partnership restructuring followed by a gift of the growth interest) as if it were a gift with a retention by the client of an interest for life (or at least until the time of certain later transfers of either the common or preferred stock, or corresponding partnership interests). It is now clear that Congress intended to treat other estate freezing techniques similarly. The rationale of this treatment is that the retention of substantial rights (such as the right to a disproportionate interest in the income of the corporation) in an enterprise is equivalent to the retention of the enjoyment of the capital of that enterprise, including the capital represented by some other family member's equity. Giving away growth while keeping the income is equated with keeping the growth, even if the income retained is not tied or related to the growth interest given away.

Of course, the Code has provided for many years that if you give something away but keep a "string," a right to the income from the asset or a similarly important property right, the estate tax value of the asset will be in your estate. So, in the past, if the IRS could find a string, they hanged the client. Now, a vapor string will do. Furthermore, certain transfers, lapses, or terminations with respect to an income or growth interest involved in an estate freeze will result in the estate tax value of the growth interest being treated as a gift for gift tax purposes.

Effective Dates

Generally, the rules described below apply to estates of decedents dying *after* December 31, 1987. Transfers completed *before* December 18, 1987 are protected from inclusion.[3] But there is no transitional rule for transactions in progress on December 17th. Note that it may be possible to inadvertently "ungrandfather" a freeze accomplished prior to December 18, 1987 by engaging in a new transaction which falls within the scope of the new statute. However, with respect to property transferred before December 18, 1987, the failure thereafter to exercise a conversion right, to pay dividends, or to exercise other rights to be specified in regulations is not treated as an additional transfer occurring on or after December 17, 1987.[4]

The gift tax freeze provisions apply to transfers made *after* June 20, 1988.[5] However, neither the estate or gift tax provisions apply to transfers completed after December 17, 1987 and before January 1, 1990 if either (1) before January 1, 1990,

steps are taken to remove the transaction from Section 2036(c)'s scope, or (2) on January 1, 1990 (or at the original transferor's death, if earlier), the original transferor and his spouse own no interest in the enterprise.[6]

An Overview

Let's take a quick look (in very general terms) at what the new law says:

If a person has a *substantial interest* in an *enterprise* and, in effect, *transfers* property having a *disproportionately large share* of the potential appreciation in his interest, while retaining an interest in the income from or voting or other rights in the enterprise, and the retention is for life, then the person is treated as if he had retained a life estate in the property transferred.[7] This retained life estate will cause the property given away to be included in the client's gross estate. However, certain transfers, lapses, or terminations with respect to either the retained life estate or the property given away will result in the estate tax value of the property given away being treated as a gift for gift tax purposes (rather than including such property in the client's estate).[8]

Key Words and Phrases

The key words above are, of course, those in italic print.

"Substantial Interest"

An interest will not be considered substantial unless the client, directly or indirectly, holds 10 percent or more of the income stream, voting power, or both,[9] taking into account interests held by "family members" (collateral relatives such as a brother or sister don't count).[10]

So if a client gives common stock to her youngest son, that stock will be included in her estate if she owned 2 percent of the voting common stock, 3 percent of the nonvoting stock, and her daughter owned 14 percent of the corporation's voting stock. The mother will be deemed to own stock actually owned by the daughter. But if neither the daughter nor any family member other than the son owned stock, Section 2036(c) would not apply.

A married couple is treated as one person, except as otherwise provided in regulations.[11] The House Committee Report for TAMRA '88 indicate that it is intended that the spousal rule be interpreted to prevent inclusion of the property in both spouses' estates. Examples given by the committee indicate an intention to include growth property in the surviving spouse's estate, at least where the surviving spouse holds or receives income or rights in the enterprise at the decedent spouse's death. For example, if a parent owning all of the stock of a corporation gives common stock to a child and thereafter leaves preferred stock to his wife at death, the common stock would be included only in the surviving spouse's estate. Also, if the decedent spouse leaves property with a disproportionately large share of appreciation in an enterprise to a person other than his spouse, and the surviving spouse retains income or rights in the same enterprise, the growth property would be included in the surviving spouse's estate.

If a client gives all the common stock he owns to his son and at death gives all of his preferred stock to his daughter, he has retained the preferred stock and therefore the common stock will be included in his estate. But what if the wife (who owns no stock) dies before the client. The stock owned by the son may be included in the estate of the first spouse to die even though she owns neither common or preferred stock. If so, will it be included a second time when the husband dies? Regulations are needed to prevent double inclusions of property in both spouses' estates. However, it is clear that the statute will be applied regardless of which spouse owns the income property.

The IRS could reasonably interpret the new statute to mean that, because a husband and wife are one person, that person does not die until they have both died. In that case the interest given away during life should be included only in the estate of the surviving spouse. Alternatively, because treating a husband and wife as a unit was intended only to prevent one spouse from defeating the new rule by giving preferred stock (or other similar interests) to the other spouse, it could argue that the common stock (or similar interest) should be included in the estate of the initial preferred stockholder, regardless of which spouse dies first. However, the committee report indicates an intent to include growth property in the surviving spouse's estate, at least where the surviving spouse holds or receives income or rights in the enterprise at the decedent spouse's death.

If the statute is interpreted by the IRS to read that the growth property will be included only once, in the estate of the spouse actually making the growth property transfer, then planners should advise the client to have the younger (healthier) spouse make the gift of the growth property. Assuming that person lives to live expectancy, the tax will have been delayed as long as possible.

Tiered entities such as trusts, corporations, and partnerships are included under the "directly or indirectly" wording. For instance, assume a client owns 2 percent of the voting common stock and 4 percent of the nonvoting preferred stock of a corporation. The remaining stock of the corporation is owned by an irrevocable trust of which the trustee is the Overflowing Bank and Trust Company and the beneficiaries are the client's two children. If the client gives her common stock to her granddaughter, it will be included in the client's estate since she indirectly owns the stock owned by her children, who in turn indirectly own the stock actually held by the trust.

Consider a sale, rather than a gift, to a family member or to a trust for family members. Section 2036(c), after amendment by TAMRA '88, no longer treats certain consideration between family members as a gift.[12] In lieu of the full and adequate consideration test of Section 2043 applying, if a member of the transferor's family provides in a bona fide sale consideration in money's worth for an interest in the enterprise, and it can be shown to the satisfaction of the IRS that the consideration originally belonged to that family member and was never received or acquired (directly or indirectly) from the transferor for less than full and adequate consideration, a portion of the enterprise is not includable under 2036(c). That portion is:

$$
\begin{array}{c}
\text{Portion of enterprise} \\
\text{that would have been} \\
\text{included under 2036(c)} \\
\text{(including the value of} \\
\text{the retained interest)}
\end{array}
\times
\dfrac{
\begin{array}{c}
\text{Amount of} \\
\text{consideration received}
\end{array}
}{
\begin{array}{c}
\text{Portion of enterprise that} \\
\text{would have been includible} \\
\text{immediately after the} \\
\text{disproportionate transfer} \\
\text{(including value of} \\
\text{retained interest)}
\end{array}
}
$$

A sale to a trust for family members may be advantageous. Consider a client (or a surviving spouse) with very high basis common stock. Assume a recapitalization and an exchange of that stock for common and preferred stock. What if the common stock were sold to a CEBT (Credit Equivalent Bypass Trust) and the preferred stock were retained? Alternatively, assume common stock were contributed to a personal holding company in return for its preferred stock. Then the common stock of that holding company were purchased for cash by a trust (perhaps a CEBT) for the client's children.

Assume two brothers each holding less than 10 percent but more than 5 percent of the voting power of a corporation. Would the stock of one be attributed to the other (and therefore cause each brother to have a substantial interest) if both brothers were to place their stock into a voting trust? The answer should be, No. On their face, the 2036(c) rules do not apply to any of these transactions. But care is suggested in advising clients to do something clearly outside of the legislative intent of the new rules and which may be caught by regulations.

Section 2036(c) may require inclusion of the common stock even if the retention of the right to vote stock is held by the client merely as a trustee or other fiduciary.

The statute requires that the client must own a substantial interest and then states that there is such a substantial interest if that person holds 10 percent or more of the voting power or income stream. It does not define what is meant by an "income stream," but does provide that the estate freeze provisions do not apply solely by reason of "qualified debt," "startup debt," or certain agreements for the sale or lease of property to be used in the enterprise or the providing of services.[13]

Tools and Techniques

"Qualified debt" means:

(1) true indebtedness that unconditionally requires fixed payment(s) not to extend beyond 15 years (30 years, if secured by real property) from the date of issue (unless the debt is payable on demand and issued for cash for normal business use),

(2) interest dates are fixed and interest rates are fixed or set relative to a specified market rate,

(3) such debt is not by its terms subordinated to general creditors,

(4) such debt does not grant voting rights or limit others' voting rights (except where the indebtedness is in default), and

(5) such debt is not convertible into an interest in the enterprise which is not qualified debt.

"Startup debt" may qualify under relaxed rules if:

(1) the payment of a sum certain is required with respect to true indebtedness,

(2) the debt was received in exchange for cash to be used in the active conduct of a trade or business,

(3) the creditor does not *at any time* (a) transfer any other property, any customers, or any business opportunities to the enterprise, or (b) hold any other interest in the enterprise (including an interest as an officer, director, or employee),

(4) any original transferees actively participate in the enterprise,

(5) such debt does not grant voting rights or limit others' voting rights (except where the indebtedness is in default), and

(6) such debt is not convertible into an interest in the enterprise which is not qualified debt.

It is not yet clear whether private annuities or self-canceling installment notes would fit within a safe harbor for debt.

An agreement for the sale or lease of property to be used in the enterprise or the providing of services will not of itself subject a transaction to the estate freeze provisions provided the agreement is entered into at arm's length and for fair market value, the agreement makes no changes in interests in the enterprise, and the agreement is not contingent on profits. For this purpose, the term of an agreement to provide services (for example, as a consultant or director) cannot extend beyond three years, including any period which may be extended at the service provider's option.

The IRS has been given authority to issue regulations which will deal with debt and agreements for the sale or lease of property to be used in the enterprise or the providing of services. Such regulations may provide circumstances under which the safe harbors, above, become unsafe by reason of other aspects of an estate freeze transaction. Such regulations could also extend additional safe harbors. It is clear that Con-

gress intended for income interests to be interpreted quite broadly to include interest on debt, consultant's or director's fees, or even royalties or rents, except where the retained interest provides a limited possibility for subsequent transfer of appreciation.

Generally, the statute requires that the 10 percent or more (substantial) interest be held prior to the gift or sale to a family member. Therefore, Section 2036(c) should not apply if before the transaction the client does not own the requisite 10 percent or more interest (directly or indirectly). For instance, assume a client owns 14 percent of both the common and preferred stock of a corporation. No other family member owns any interest in the business. He gives 5 percent of both the common and preferred stock to his niece leaving him with only 9 percent. The stock he gives the niece will not be in his estate (because it is not a disproportionate transfer). If he makes a gift of only common stock at a later date to his son, that common stock should not be included in his estate (the interest held is less than 10%). Timing (and attention to step transaction regulations) will be important.

"Voting power" is a term that is not defined in the Conference Report Explanation.[14] It will probably include the power to vote: (a) whether exercisable alone or in conjunction with other persons; (b) regardless of the capacity in which the decedent held that voting power (so the right to vote stock as a trustee, co-trustee, or corporate officer would fall within the definition); (c) where there was any type of agreement with the decedent, express or implied, that the shareholder or other holder of a power to vote stock either will vote that stock in a specified manner or will not vote the stock (for instance, a voting trust); and (d) where the decedent had retained the power to obtain the right to vote the stock (for instance, if he could appoint himself as trustee of a trust holding the stock). Hopefully, rights to vote, or to limit others' voting rights, where qualified or startup debt (see above) is in default will not be treated as voting power.

Transfers

The antifreeze provision will not apply unless there has been a transfer. But any transfer counts (even one which does not appear to be a transfer but is "in effect" a transfer in which an interest in an enterprise is shifted from the client to others). Note that sales to non-family members aren't counted.[15] But sales to family members are treated as if they were gifts for purposes of this provision. Even though for income tax purposes the transaction may be treated as a sale requiring the reporting of gain by the seller client, and for gift tax purposes no gift tax would be payable, for estate tax purposes a sale to a family member (even though for full and adequate consideration) is treated as a transfer without consideration. So a client can't escape the reach of this Code section by selling rather than giving away his interest to family members. If a client sells his common stock to a family member for adequate and full consideration in cash but keeps all the preferred stock, the common stock will be in the seller's gross estate (subject to the offset relating to sales to family members in which no part of the consideration directly or indirectly was received or acquired from the client).[16]

An option or other agreement to buy or sell property at its fair market value at the time the option is exercised is not of itself a transfer subject to the estate freeze provisions.[17] Such option or agreement would not generally permit the transfer of appreciation prior to its exercise. However, once exercised, the transaction must be examined to see if it falls within the estate freeze provisions.

"Enterprise"

Not only businesses (corporate, partnership, or sole proprietorship) but any other property which may produce income or gain can be considered an "enterprise."[18] This implies that artwork, a vacation home, as well as other investments could be considered, for purposes of this Code section, an enterprise. Perhaps the only asset that could not be treated as an enterprise is cash itself (although cash equivalents such as money-market funds and bank accounts are certainly income-producing enterprises).

Will a client's investment in publicly traded stock, such as AT&T, be considered an enterprise? Even if it were, few clients would have the requisite "10 percent or more" interest in the income stream or voting power to make that interest "substantial." But if the client were to put the AT&T stock into a partnership or personal holding company, the new entity probably would be considered an enterprise.

Disproportionately Large Share

The disproportionately large share test is met if: the share of potential appreciation attributable to the transferred property divided by the value of the transferred property *is greater than* the potential appreciation attributable to the retained interest divided by the value of the retained interest.[19]

The relative values of the two types of property in question are irrelevant; inclusion will be required even if the value of the retained preferred stock is worth one thousandth the value of the common stock.

Could it be argued (successfully) in the case of preferred stock that can be converted into common stock at a bargain price under given conditions, that the growth potential of the preferred makes it impossible for the appreciation potential in the gratuitously transferred common stock from being "disproportionate"? (If the concept is viable, will the IRS thwart this technique by claiming that the client's failure in any given year to convert the preferred stock to common is a gift if the common stock increases in value beyond the preferred?)

In the "before and after" ratio, it is only the disproportionate share (as a percentage of the growth interest) that will

be includable. For instance, before the gift, a client owns 100 percent of the stock of a corporation. She recapitalizes the business into common and preferred stock. She then gives 49 percent of the common stock to her son. She keeps all of the preferred stock. To the extent she has not given away proportionately equal interests of growth and income, the common stock will be includable in her estate. In this case, since she has given away none of the income interest, all of the common stock will be includable in her estate.

If she had given away 48 percent of the preferred stock at the same time she gave away the 49 percent interest in the common stock, the share of the growth given away is larger than the share of income retained and so the "disproportionately large" test is met. But only the 1 percent differential (i.e., one percent of the common stock) will be includable.

There is no "threshold test" in terms of the extent of the disproportion between the income property and the growth property. This will create boundless confusion and is inherently unfair. For instance, assume a client who is living in the warmth and sunshine of Florida owns all the common stock of a company located in Maine. His son recently took over as chief operating officer of the business. Over the last 30 years, the father gave the son $20,000 a year of common stock currently worth several million dollars. The father now needs retirement income and the son wants to oblige by either providing his father with a modest "salary" or paying preferred stock dividends. To the extent reasonable salary would satisfy the need, there would be no problem with Section 2036(c), assuming the agreement to provide services was not treated as a retained interest in the corporation (for example, the salary will not trigger 2036(c) inclusion if the agreement falls within a safe harbor). But if the father were to receive preferred stock dividends, the common stock owned by the son would be included in the father's estate, regardless of how modest the value of the preferred stock in relation to the company's total value.

Note that there are no "lookbacks" to see if the corporation or other enterprise has increased or decreased in value. The "disproportionately large" test is applied only at the date the growth interest is transferred (in spite of the fact that upon turning over the reins of a business to a junior generation many enterprises experience tremendous plunges - or increases - in value).

Gift Tax

As first enacted by OBRA '87, the estate freeze provisions could be avoided if the client with the retained income or voting interest disposed of the retained interest more than three years before death. Thus, considerable opportunity existed to transfer substantial amounts of appreciation while avoiding Section 2036(c). Additionally, it was perceived that including appreciating property in the transferor's estate after the transferee had disposed of the property would result

Tools and Techniques

in including more appreciation in the transferor's estate than was intended under Section 2036(c).

As a result of these and other considerations, Congress added provisions in the Technical and Miscellaneous Revenue Act of 1988 (TAMRA '88) which would impose (in addition to the gift tax on a transfer of the preferred stock) a gift tax on the common stock previously transferred regardless of how long ago it was transferred or how much gift tax was paid at that time.[20] This gift tax (imposed on the client) would apply regardless of whether it is the client (or the client's spouse) who transfers all his preferred stock or if it is the donee of the common stock who transfers all the common stock to a person outside of the family. In essence, the Act "accelerates" the tax that would be payable under 2036(c) if either the retained income interest or the transferred growth interest are transferred (or retransferred, as the case may be) before the client dies. The gift tax provisions are effective where the original transfer of growth property occurs after June 20, 1988.[21]

For instance, a client who owns all the preferred stock and all the common stock of a corporation gives his common stock to his daughter but keeps all the preferred stock. If the father transfers the preferred or the daughter gives away or sells the common stock to someone outside the family, the client (the original transferor) is treated as if he had made a gift with respect to the common stock at that time.

Where the client transfers part of his income interest, or the donee-owner of the growth interest transfers less than all of his interest to someone outside the client's family, a portion of the common stock will be includable. For instance, in the example above, if only one half of the client's preferred stock were given away or sold before the client's death, he would be treated as if he had made a gift of half of the common stock actually owned by his daughter. Then, at his death, the other half of the common stock would be includable in his estate. If the gift occurred within three years of death, gift tax attributable to the transfer would also be included in his estate.

The gift tax on the growth property would be based on its value at the time of the gift of the preferred stock rather than at the time the growth property was originally given. In other words, the client who made the gift of the common stock would be deemed to be making a second taxable transfer of that stock (just as if he had died on the day he transferred the preferred stock). The value of the common stock would be ascertained on that day in the same manner as if he had died but special use valuation and the alternate valuation date could not be used. To the extent of this "cosmic gift," no amount would be included in the client's estate (probably on the theory that two bites at the apple are sufficient, or the more likely reality that there would be nothing left to tax).

No credit is allowed under the estate tax for the gift tax that may have been previously paid or the unified credit uti-

lized in the original transfer of the common stock. So, for example, if the common stock was worth $1,000,000 when given and the client paid a gift tax at a 50 percent rate 10 years before his death, and the stock is worth $3,000,000 at his death when he is still in the 50 percent bracket, he would be deemed to have made a second transfer worth $3,000,000 at an estate tax cost of $1,500,000 (in addition to the original $500,000 gift tax). However, the amount of a gift deemed made because of a subsequent transfer by the original transferor or the transferee would be reduced by taxable gifts attributable to the original transfer, and adjusted to take into account previous deemed gifts. This would eliminate the potential double gift tax on gifts. Also, to the extent that transferred property is subject to the deemed gift tax, it is not included in the client's estate. The amount of a deemed gift is also reduced to the extent that the client fails to exercise his right to recover taxes on the deemed transfer from the actual maker of the gift. However, this reduction merely eliminates another possible double gift tax situation because the failure to exercise such a right is itself a gift.

The second transfer rule applies to terminations, lapses, and other changes in interests in the income property of the original transferor or the growth property of the original transferee (including family members of the original transferor receiving their interests from such transferee). Thus, the termination of an income interest in a GRIT (grantor retained income trust) would be covered unless the GRIT falls within the safe harbor for certain GRITS. (In general, a GRIT is not subject to Section 2036(c) if (1) the grantor's income interest is determined solely by reference to property held in the trust, (2) the grantor's income period does not exceed 10 years, and (3) the grantor is not a trustee of such trust.)

The House Committee Report to TAMRA '88 indicates that with respect to debt which is subject to Section 2036(c), a deemed gift is made when the debt is fully retired. It is not yet clear whether private annuities or self-canceling installment notes would fit within a safe harbor for debt and thus possibly avoid both a deemed gift upon termination of the interest and inclusion in the client's estate of transferred property.

The rule deeming a gift whenever the original transferor or transferee later transfers an interest in the enterprise would not apply if the transferee transferred the interest back to the transferor. But this transfer would trigger the normal gift tax. To the extent that the fair market value of the property transferred back to the transferor exceeds consideration paid by the original transferor in exchange for such property, the amount of property subject to Section 2036(c) is reduced. However, such property would be included in the original transferor's estate if retained until death or treated as a gift if given away.

A transfer of property would not result in a deemed gift for Section 2036(c) purposes, if the transferor or transferee retained a continuing direct or indirect interest in the transferred property. For example, if a client made a contribution of property to a wholly owned personal holding company, no deemed gift would be made. However, the House Committee Report to TAMRA '88 indicates that the lapse or termination of a transferred growth interest (as part of a continuing interest in transferred property) results in a deemed gift to the extent that the lapse or termination restores the proportionality of the appreciation potential which existed prior to the original transfer.

Recapitulation

To recapitulate, all four of the following conditions must be present before 2036(c) will apply:

(1) The *"substantial interest"* test: The decedent or his family must hold a substantial interest in an enterprise.

(2) The *"transfer of appreciation"* test: The decedent must have *transferred* (after December 17, 1987) property having a disproportionately large share of the potential appreciation in that person's interest in the enterprise.

(3) The *"retention of income"* test: The decedent must have *retained* at the time of the property transfer a share of the income or the rights in the enterprise.

(4) The *"second transfer"* or *"held at death"* tests: If the original transferor transfers his income interest or the original transferee transfers the growth interest to a person outside of the family, a gift tax is imposed on the amount of the growth property deemed given in the second transfer. To the extent not already deemed given away, the growth interest is included in the decedent's estate because of the income interest held by the decedent at the time of his death.

If any *one* of these four conditions is *not* met, no inclusion is possible under 2036(c). If all four conditions are met: the entire value of what was given away, valued at the time of a second transfer, will be deemed a gift; or the entire value of what was given away, valued at the client's date of death or alternate valuation date, will be includable in his estate. Such values are subject to the "differential" and "offset" rules, below.

A More Complete Look at Section 2036(c)

At this point it is important to restate Code section 2036(c) more completely and in more detail:

If a person, or an entity in which that person has an interest, or that person's "family" (i.e., spouse, lineal descendant of the person or his spouse, that person's parent or grandparent, or any of their spouses)

(a) holds a "substantial interest" (direct or indirect ownership of 10 percent or more of the voting power or income stream or both in the enterprise) in

(b) any "enterprise" (a business or other property which may produce income or gain) and

(c) in effect "transfers" (passes to or confers ownership on another) by any means or in any manner

(d) after December 17, 1987

(e) property having a "disproportionately large share of potential appreciation" (any share of appreciation in the enterprise greater than the share of appreciation represented in the property retained by the transferor) of that person's interest in the enterprise while

(f) retaining a share of the income of or voting, liquidation, or conversion rights in the enterprise,

then the retention of the retained interest is treated as a retention of the enjoyment of the transferred property — but only if the decedent held the retained interest

(a) for his or his spouse's life, or

(b) for a period which is not ascertainable without reference to his or his spouse's death, or

(c) for a period which does not in fact end before his or his spouse's death.

Inclusion is mandated unless before death the client transfers all his income interest or if the donee of the growth interest transfers all his growth interest to a person outside of the client's family — in which case a gift is deemed made of the growth interest at the time of the second transfer. As noted above, a limited opportunity exists to remove a transaction from the scope of Section 2036(c) before January 1, 1990.

Note that there is no exemption for annual exclusion gifts. If 2036(c) requires the inclusion in a decedent's gross estate of an asset transferred by gift, the taxable portion of the gift will then be "washed out" of the "adjusted taxable gifts" category.

Transfers Within 3 Years of Death

The release or transfer, within three years of death, of the interest in the enterprise retained by the client — for example, by a gift of preferred stock — will trigger the "transfers within 3 years of death" rule of Section 2035. If the preferred stock was given away by the client within 3 years of death and before June 21, 1988, the common stock was includable in his gross estate (as was any gift tax paid on the gift).[22] However, a transfer of the preferred stock by the client within 3 years of death (or even if not within three years of death) and after June 20, 1988 will result in a deemed gift of the common stock at the time of the transfer of the preferred stock and the common stock is not included in the client's estate (although any gift tax paid on a gift within three year of death will continue to be included in the gross estate).[23]

Prior to enactment of the "deemed gift upon a second transfer" provisions of TAMRA '88, a client who lived for

Tools and Techniques

more than 3 years after such a transfer avoided the sweep of Code section 2036(c). For instance, assume a client recapitalized his corporation, received common and preferred stock, gave the common stock to his children, and then, four years before his death (and before June 21, 1988) gave away the preferred stock. Since he gave away the retained interest more than 3 years prior to his death, Section 2035 would not apply and therefore 2036(c) would not cause inclusion. Note that the preferred stock was an adjusted taxable gift to the extent it exceeded or didn't qualify for the annual exclusion but was not includable in the client's gross estate.

TAMRA '88 effectively blocks this strategy by imposing a gift tax on the common stock previously transferred if in a second transfer the client transfers all his preferred stock or if the donee of the common stock transfers all the common stock to a person outside of the client's family.

Death of Transferee Before Transferor

If a child who is the recipient of common stock held until death dies before the transferor client, the common stock will be includable in that person's estate. But will it be includable again under Section 2036(c) when the client dies? Probably, unless it has already been deemed a gift under the second transfer provisions. (Had the father died first, followed by the child, the stock would have been taxed twice so we feel that it will likely be includable in the transferor's gross estate at his or her later death, unless already deemed given away). If the child transfers the common stock to someone not a member of the client's family at his death, the common stock may be included in the child's estate and the transfer of the common stock could also be deemed a gift by the client at the same time.

Offsets and Other Adjustments

Section 2036(c)(5) provides an "offset" which it calls "appropriate adjustments" for the value of the retained interest, extraordinary dividends, and changes in capital structure which occur after the initial transfer. Although adequate and full consideration paid by a client's children will not take a transaction out of Section 2036(c), it appears that the amount they pay the client can be used as an offset against the amount includable. Section 2036(c)(2)(B) provides that if it can be shown that the consideration was the original transferee's (e.g., children's) own property and had not been given (directly or indirectly) to the children by the original transferor (client), a portion of the property which otherwise would be included in the client's estate under Section 2036(c) is excluded by reason of the consideration. The portion to be excluded is determined by multiplying the amount otherwise includable under Section 2036(c) by a fraction: the denominator of which is such consideration, and the numerator of

which is the value of the enterprise (including the retained interest) which *would* have been includible in the estate under 2036(c) immediately after the transfer.

For example, if a parent owning all of the preferred and common stock of a corporation worth $3 million sells all of the common stock to a child for $1 million of cash (earned solely by the child), at death two-thirds of the corporation is includible in the parent's estate ($1 million divided by $3 million equals an exclusion ratio of one-third). If, at the parent's death, the corporation is worth $9 million and the preferred stock is worth $1 million, $6 million is includible in the parent's estate; $1 million of preferred stock owned outright, and $5 million of common stock deemed owned under Section 2036(c). (The $5 million is determined by offsetting the $6 million includible with the $1 million preferred stock retained.) Of course, the $1 million consideration (plus any appreciation thereon) will *also* be included in the parent's estate if held at death.

This "offset" may not be as kind to the taxpayer as it appears. The family unit may fare better if the client makes a gift: First, if the client invests the after income tax proceeds of a sale to his son, those after tax proceeds will be in his estate — together with any appreciation on that money. Second, the property actually sold (as adjusted for offsets) will be subject to estate tax in the client's estate. In the case of a gift, the gift tax will reduce rather than increase the client's taxable estate (and therefore reduce the tax) and there will be no income tax to pay until and unless the donee chooses to sell it (with a step-up in basis at the client's death because of the 2036(c) inclusion). On the other hand, the initial capitalization of a new business corporation or partnership should not be affected by Section 2036(c) if the client's interest is "qualified debt" or "startup debt."

What 2036(c) Means

Assume a client owns 100 percent of both the common and preferred stock of the XYZ corporation. She transfers the common stock to her daughter but retains the preferred stock for as long as she lives. Because of the retention of the preferred stock, the value of the common stock will be in her estate. However, if before the client's death she transfers the preferred stock, or her daughter transfers the common stock to someone not a member of the client's family, the client is deemed to make a gift of the common stock at that time (and the common stock is not included in her estate).

Likewise, if a client forms a multilevel partnership in which one interest carries with it only growth while the other provides only income and the interest which carries appreciation is given away while the interest which provides income is retained, the transferred interest will be in the client's estate. However, if before the client's death she transfers the income interest, or her daughter transfers the growth interest to someone not a member of the client's family, the client is deemed to make a gift of the growth interest at that time (and the growth interest is not included in her estate).

In essence the IRS will be imposing a real tax on a phantom transfer; a tax that could conceivably be five or six times the value of the real gift itself!

As discussed in Part II, Section 2036(c) will affect many tools and techniques of estate planning other than those described above.

"Differential Rule"

Note that only the disproportionate (differential) portion will be includable: For instance, assume a client owns 100 shares of common stock and 100 shares of preferred stock. He transfers 80 of the 100 shares of common stock and 20 of the 100 shares of preferred stock. The client's share in the appreciation given away (80 percent) is greater than the client's share of the appreciation retained (20 percent). So a disproportionately large share of appreciation has been given away while a share of the income (80 percent) has been retained. But the property which carries appreciation is disproportionately large only with respect to a 60 percent differential (80 percent transferred minus 20 percent retained). So only that portion, 60 shares (60 percent of the 100 common shares), is included in his estate under 2036(c).

Section 2036 does not deal with valuation. It deals solely with inclusion.

Part II
IMPACT OF SECTION 2036(c) ON VARIOUS TOOLS AND TECHNIQUES OF ESTATE PLANNING

Recapitalizations

It should be obvious at this point that 100 percent of the common stock will be included in the gross estate of a client who owns 100 percent of the common stock of a corporation, recapitalizes, and gives the common stock to his children while retaining the preferred stock.

But many not-so-obvious traps are inherent in other common recapitalization situations. For instance, assume a client owns 60 percent of the single class of common stock of a corporation. The other 40 percent is owned by his son. In a tax free recapitalization the client exchanges all his common stock for voting preferred stock. Sixty percent of the growth was in effect transferred to the son, who now consequently owns the right to 100 percent of the corporation's growth. The retention of the preferred stock by the client will cause 60 percent of the common stock actually owned by the son to be included in the client's estate.

What if a new enterprise is formed and the parties, upon the inception of the business, take common and preferred?

An earlier House version of TAMRA '88 said that a parent's interest in an enterprise should be measured both before and after the transfer. But the final version of the law dropped this requirement. This should allow any form of capitalization on new enterprises, so long as the parent has not transferred a controlled enterprise to the new venture. Thus, for example, if parent's contributions to the truly new enterprise to be operated by the child is 10,000 shares of an NYSE listed stock, the parent should be able to receive preferred stock without triggering Section 2036(c).

In the appropriate situation, reversing the traditional recapitalization, that is, retaining the common stock and transferring the preferred stock, may be a means of avoiding Section 2036(c). If high (but reasonable) dividends are paid on the preferred stock, substantial wealth can be transferred to a family member safely because the transfer of preferred stock would not generally be considered transfer of a growth interest under Section 2036(c).

Installment Sales

An installment sale of stock or of property to be used in the enterprise will generally not be treated as a retained interest in the income stream of the enterprise under Code section 2036(c) if certain safe harbors are met. With respect to the interest retained by the client, the statute does not define what is meant by an "income stream," but does provide that the estate freeze provisions do not apply solely by reason of "qualified debt," "startup debt," or certain agreements for the sale of property to be used in the enterprise.[24]

"Qualified debt" means:

(1) true indebtedness that unconditionally requires fixed payment(s) not to extend beyond 15 years (30 years, if secured by real property) from the date of issue (unless the debt is payable on demand and issued for cash for normal business use),

(2) interest dates are fixed and interest rates are fixed or set relative to a specified market rate,

(3) such debt is not by its terms subordinated to general creditors,

(4) such debt does not grant voting rights or limit others' voting rights (except where the indebtedness is in default), and

(5) such debt is not convertible into an interest in the enterprise which is not qualified debt.

"Startup debt" may qualify under relaxed rules if:

(1) the payment of a sum certain is required with respect to true indebtedness,

(2) the debt was received in exchange for cash to be used in the active conduct of a trade or business,

(3) the creditor does not *at any time* (a) transfer any other property, any customers, or any business op-

Tools and Techniques

portunities to the enterprise, or (b) hold any other interest in the enterprise (including an interest as an officer, director, or employee),

(4) any original transferees actively participate in the enterprise,

(5) such debt does not grant voting rights or limit others' voting rights (except where the indebtedness is in default), and

(6) such debt is not convertible into an interest in the enterprise which is not qualified debt.

An agreement for the sale of property to be used in the enterprise will not of itself subject a transaction to the estate freeze provisions provided the agreement is entered into at arm's length and for fair market value, the agreement makes no changes in interests in the enterprise, and the agreement is not contingent on profits.

The IRS has been given authority to issue regulations which will deal with debt and agreements for the sale of property to be used in the enterprise. Such regulations may provide circumstances under which the safe harbors, above, become unsafe by reason of other aspects of an estate freeze transaction. These regulations could also provide additional safe harbors. It is clear that Congress intended for income interests to be interpreted quite broadly to include debt, except where the retained interest provides a limited possibility for subsequent transfer of appreciation.

Thus, if a client owned both common stock and corporate notes and he gave the common stock to his son, the nature of the retained debt owed to the client by the corporation determines whether the client has retained an interest in the income of the corporation which will cause the common stock to be included in his estate. The regulations ought to provide that a sale of part or all of the client's interest in the business in return for "pure debt" installment payments should not be considered a retained interest in the enterprise. Such debt should provide that the amount of income the client can receive is based on fixed criteria such as a fixed rate of return on the amount owed to the client by the corporation and not how much profit the corporation does or does not earn or what the corporation is or is not worth.[25]

Use of the business's stock as collateral for the debt should not change this result. But if the seller retains any type of "equity kicker," the result is likely to be disastrous. For instance, if in addition to normal interest payments the seller has retained the right to extra payments measured and triggered by how profitable the enterprise is, the seller client will be considered to have retained an interest in the enterprise.

Debt which is treated as an interest in an enterprise under Code section 2036(c) will result in the transferred growth interest being either (1) treated as a deemed gift when the debt is retired, or (2) included in the decedent's estate if he dies before the debt is retired.

Assume, upon retirement, a client, instead of exchanging common stock for common and preferred, receives common and the corporation's note. He gives away the common stock to his son. Assume the note is an installment note which is still held by the date the client dies (10 years later) and has not been fully paid by the corporation. If the note represents a true debt interest, it should be irrelevant that it runs for the client's life. However, note that generally qualified debt is limited in duration to 15 years.

Furthermore, section 2036(c) should not apply to any sale to another family member of a transferor's entire interest in an enterprise. Section 2036(c) applies only to transfers in which the transferor retains some interest in the enterprise after the transfer. The personal debt of another family member cannot be viewed as an interest in the enterprise itself, absent some special arrangement, such as a corporate guaranty, or perhaps debt tied to the enterprise's income. Therefore, any form of installment sale between family members, if the selling family member retains no other interest in the enterprise, should preclude application of Section 2036(c).

Self-Canceling Installment Note

This is in essence an installment sale in which payments end at the earlier of (a) a fixed term of years or (b) the death of the seller. Self-canceling installment notes cannot be qualified debt or startup debt under the safe harbor rules of Section 2036(c), because they do not have a fixed maturity date nor do they unconditionally require payment of principal on a specified date. The possible discharge of the notes constitutes a prohibited condition. Thus, self-canceling installment notes should be permissible under Section 2036(c) only when they relate to the sale of publicly traded assets, or when the seller retains no other interest in the enterprise and the sale is between family members, rather than between an individual and the enterprise itself.

Private Annuities

When one party sells property to another in return for the buyer's promise to pay the seller a specified stream of income lasting for the life of the seller (and/or the seller's spouse), the transaction is termed a private annuity (assuming the buyer is not in the business of selling annuities). In the traditional private annuity the stream of income is not dependent on how well or how poorly the transferred property produces income or grows in value. In other words, because the classic private annuity is merely an unsecured promise of a child (or grandchild) to pay income to a parent (or grandparent), the seller has not retained any share of the income of the enterprise. The purchaser's obligation is personal and not related to the income the property itself produces. Furthermore, the promise to pay is not secured by the transferred property (or by any other property). For these reasons, we feel that the seller has not retained an interest in the enterprise, and therefore Section 2036 should not apply to the typical private annuity.

It is true that private annuity sales cannot be qualified debt or startup debt under the safe harbor rules of section 2036(c), because: they do not have a fixed maturity date, they do not unconditionally require payment of principal on a specified date, and they are not assured of being paid off in 15 or 30 years. Therefore, private annuities are outside the reach of 2036(c) when they relate to the sale of publicly traded assets, or when the seller sells his entire interest in the enterprise and the sale is between family members. At this point we do advise caution with respect to private annuities between an individual and the enterprise itself.

If the seller's income is measured by or dependent on the income produced by the property or by growth in the value of the property, the anti-freeze provision would apply (perhaps this is redundant since the IRS and the courts have long held that this would result in inclusion under Section 2036(a) where trusts were used and the annuity payments were tied directly to the asset sold).[26] This will make it difficult in some cases (but not impossible) to sell property to minor children through a private annuity and escape the scope of Section 2036(c). Specifically, if the children are totally dependent on the income from the transferred property to make payments and they have no outside source of income or capital, it is possible for the IRS to claim that the seller's income is in reality inextricably tied to the success of the enterprise in spite of the terms of the agreement. If the children had a source of income or capital that could not be traced back to a gift from either parent, chances of the taxpayer's success are significantly improved.

Buy-Sell Agreements

A buy-sell agreement is a restriction on the right to transfer an interest in a business or other financial enterprise. It is clear that Section 2036(c) will not be applied to such an agreement when it exists solely between unrelated individuals. Full and adequate consideration (the fair market value of the business) will be paid for the interest and since that sale will take place between nonfamily members the price paid will take the transaction out of the "sales to family members are treated as gifts" category.

The traditional intrafamily buy-sell should also escape the reach of Section 2036(c) since there will be no disproportionate shifting of appreciation to the buyer, even in the case where stock is sold in return for installment payments (assuming the installment obligation is treated as qualified debt). (Nor does the existence of Section 2036(c) in any way affect the ability of a properly drawn buy-sell agreement to fix the value of the stock for federal estate tax purposes since, according to the Conference Report Explanation, the statute "only makes certain property includable in the estate; it does not affect the valuation of such property for estate tax purposes.")[27]

Section 2036(c)(7)(A)(iii) provides that an option or other buy-sell agreement exercisable at fair market value at time of exercise is not subject to Section 2036(c) solely by reason of such right because such an option does not have the potential for avoiding transfer tax. But will a buy-sell agreement that fixes the value of the interest at a price which is fair and adequate, as of the date the agreement is signed, escape Section 2036(c) inclusion? Arguably, such an agreement or option has the potential to transfer appreciation. Hopefully, the normal guidelines for fixing the price of a closely-held business for estate tax purposes which permit a fair and adequate price determined as of the date the agreement is signed will be permitted under Section 2036(c). (However, such guidelines place additional requirements on such options or buy-sell agreements.)

Has the seller retained the requisite interest in the enterprise when, in order to completely terminate his interest in a closely held corporation and receive sale or exchange treatment in a stock redemption, he waives family attribution rules? We think not, since at that point (assuming all the requirements for successfully waiving family attribution have been met) the seller's only interest in the business is as a creditor. Since qualified debt interests (that by definition are not tied in any way to the profits produced or the growth in value of the business) will not be considered "a retained interest in the enterprise," a waiver of family attribution should not trigger Section 2036(c).

Buy-sell agreements should not be subject to Section 2036(c) as a rule where the transaction is motivated by a business intent rather than a donative consideration. But, in our opinion, there are situations which could bring a buy-sell within the reach of the anti-freeze rules.

For example, where a lifetime transfer of stock by gift or by sale is made simultaneously with or is coupled to the price established in the buy-sell, the transaction as a totality is suspect. In other words, clients should make lifetime gifts well before or well after the execution of buy-sell agreements. This is so the IRS can't successfully argue that the lifetime transfer coupled with the buy-sell mechanism constituted a unified plan to freeze the growth in the client's estate and shift it to the natural objects of his bounty.

A second situation which some commentators feel will fall within the ambit of Section 2036(c) is in the case of a stock redemption where the selling shareholder owns both common and preferred stock before the sale of stock to the corporation. For instance, assume the client owns 80 percent of the common and 80 percent of the preferred stock of a corporation. His daughter owns the remaining 20 percent of the outstanding common stock. The corporation redeems his

Tools and Techniques

common stock and pays him cash equal to the stock purchased by the business. If the client's transfer of common stock to the corporation is considered as if it were a transfer to the corporation's (now) sole common stock shareholder, his daughter, the transaction would fall under 2036(c) even though there was no direct gift to a family member and the cash received in the sale of the stock was a fair payment. Eighty percent of the common stock owned by the daughter would be includable in the father's estate.

Grantor Retained Income Trusts (GRITs)

A grantor retained income trust, as its name implies, is created when a grantor establishes an irrevocable trust for others (who will eventually receive the principal) but retains for a specified period of time the income of the trust. In essence, the client has made a gift of the right to the principal at a specified time in the future to the selected remaindermen. It appears that the purpose of a GRIT is the exact thing Section 2036(c) was designed to prevent; the transfer of potential appreciation coupled with the retention of income.

However, with respect to GRITs created *before June 21, 1988*, if the grantor survives the specified term, Section 2036(c) should not apply because the transferor grantor did not retain an interest for life, for a period not ascertainable without reference to his death, or for a period which does not in fact end until after his death. Any interest the client may have retained was retained at the inception of the trust and lapses (not by transfer or release at the termination of the trust) when the term expires (or in the case of some GRITs at the earlier of (a) the specified term or (b) the death of the grantor). Therefore, we think that Section 2035, which encompassed only the release or transfer of an interest retained under 2036(c), cannot apply since the GRIT does not fall under 2036(c) if the grantor survives the term even by one day and there has not been the requisite release or transfer. However, some commentators have expressed concern over whether the grantor would have to live three years beyond the trust term to avoid 2036(c).

With respect to GRITs created *after June 20, 1988*, the lapse of the term of years with respect to the income interest of a GRIT used in an estate freeze is treated as a transfer which will result in the estate tax value of the growth interest being treated as a gift for gift tax purposes *unless* the GRIT falls within the safe harbor for certain "statutory" GRITS.[28] In other words the ultimate transfer of the grantor's income interest (at the end of the trust's term) is considered a second transfer (the first was the transfer of the growth in the form of the remainder interest). That second transfer is treated as a gift to the extent of the full value of the amount includable under 2036(c) less any amount that had already been includible under 2036(c).

In general, under TAMRA '88 safe harbor rules, a GRIT is not subject to Section 2036(c) if (a) the grantor's income interest is determined solely by reference to property held in the trust, (b) the grantor's income period does not exceed 10 years, and (c) the grantor is not a trustee of such trust.[29] Used in conjunction with the unified credit this statutory GRIT (depending on the effect of newly mandated valuation tables) can keep a million dollars out of a client's estate.

Whether the grantor survives the term of years or dies during such term, the GRIT which does not come within the safe harbor will be caught by Section 2036(c), either as a deemed gift of the remainder interest upon lapse of the term or through inclusion of the growth interest in the decedent's estate at death. Even the statutory GRIT which qualifies for the safe harbor will be included in the grantor's estate (under Section 2036(a)) if the grantor dies during the income term.

Conservative planners who want an escape hatch at death should consider a GRIT clause providing that if GRIT funds are included for any reason in the grantor's estate, GRIT assets will be diverted to the grantor's estate. This would make such funds available to pay estate taxes. Alternatively, the assets could be diverted to a marital trust and thus avoid an estate tax. Perhaps the best approach is to insure the contingency with life insurance owned by and payable to the estate's beneficiaries, who could then use the estate tax free money to purchase other assets from the decedent's estate and thereby provide the estate with cash to pay estate taxes generated by GRIT assets.

Even if a GRIT were covered by Section 2036(c), it should only be so affected if the GRIT holds an interest in a closely-held enterprise. If the GRIT is funded with cash and/or marketable securities, and the trustee is directed to invest only in such assets, the trust itself should not be considered a "new enterprise" and therefore the GRIT should be exempt from Section 2036(c). However, caution is in order because Section 2036(c) does not define what is meant by an enterprise and committee reports do not provide clear guidance.

Remainder Interest Transactions (RITs)

A person can sell (or give) to another the right to receive property at some time in the future. That future interest transfer can be set up to take place at the seller's death. In other words, the client sells the buyer (typically a family member) the right to possess the property at the seller's death, no matter how soon or how far away in time that occurs. The seller retains the right to use, possess, or enjoy the property as long as he lives. Typically, property or a business interest is transferred in exchange for cash or property with a value equal to the actuarial value of the buyer's right to receive the property when the seller dies.

The RIT falls squarely within the reach of Section 2036(c). Assuming family members are involved on both sides of the transaction, the price paid for the property given up, even if it is a full and fair consideration for all other purposes, will be disregarded. There has been a transfer. The new owner has the right to all of the appreciation. The seller holds a share of the income since he has kept all of the income.[30]

TAMRA '88 may leave the case for RITS almost as strong as it was prior to the enactment of Section 2036(c). As discussed earlier, whenever an asset is included in the transferor's gross estate under Section 2036(c), the deceased transferor's estate receives proportionate credit for the independent consideration paid by the transferee. To ascertain the amount excludable under the "independent consideration" rule, multiply the date-of-death value of the interest otherwise includable under Section 2036(c) by a fraction. The fraction is:

$$\text{Portion of enterprise that would have been included under 2036(c) (including the value of the retained interest)} \times \frac{\text{Amount of consideration received}}{\text{Portion of enterprise that would have been includible immediately after the disproportionate transfer (including value of retained interest)}}$$

For example, if the actuarially correct amount to purchase a $1 million interest was, say, $250,000 and that much was in fact paid by the client's child from independent funds, one-fourth of the assets otherwise includable under 2036(c) could be excluded. To make this technique viable, the client would also have to consume or give away the consideration he's received. Thus, a RIT can be an effective means of removing at least a portion of an asset from an estate in exchange for payment for the actuarial value of the remainder. It may thus have regained some of its validity and usefulness after TAMRA '88. (The Act specifically removes independent consideration from Code section 2043 and may therefore have obviated a *Gradow* type problem.)

It appears that the major defense to this strong IRS case is that (if the facts support it) the seller held less than a 10 percent interest in the enterprise. Otherwise, at least for estate tax purposes, where the parties involved are all family members, RITs are dead (but there are many important non estate tax reasons why RITs may still be indicated). However, if the RIT is between unrelated parties, it should still result in federal estate tax savings.

Split Purchases (SPLITs)

Two parties can split the purchase of an asset purchased from a third party in many different ways. There are multiple advantages if the older generation client purchases a life interest and the younger generation child or grandchild purchases a remainder interest. Each party pays the actuarial share of the total purchase price for the interest he or she is acquiring.

SPLITs presuppose that the property is purchased from an independent third party at its full and fair market value. The transaction also presupposes that each party used his or her own money and that the remainderman did not acquire his or her interest by gift from the life tenant. If this is the case, even if there was a transfer from the client taking into consideration the "in effect" wording of the transfer language, the client would not have held a 10% interest in the enterprise at the time of the transfer. Language which would have treated a person as owning a substantial interest in an enterprise if such person owns the requisite 10% interest either before or after the transfer was eliminated in the final version of TAMRA '88. Consequently, such a transaction should not be caught by 2036(c). However, the IRS may argue that there is a deemed 10% ownership just prior to the deemed transfer. In a similar situation, a startup business, Congress created an exception for qualified startup debt. Similarly to the SPLIT, no interest is held in a startup business until it is created. An exception would not have been necessary unless there would otherwise have been a deemed 10% interest in the enterprise prior to any deemed transfer. Caution may be in order.

Irrevocable Life Insurance Trusts

In the traditional irrevocable life insurance trust, the insured transfers to the trustee all of the incidents of ownership over one or more policies of insurance on the insured's life. When the insured dies, the proceeds are held in trust for the benefit of the insured's family, often including both the surviving spouse and children. In order to avoid current gift taxes on transfers to such trusts, the spouse and children are often given some form of short-term (Crummey) demand power that will qualify transfers to the trust for the gift tax annual exclusion.

While a life insurance policy may well be an enterprise under Section 2036(c), life insurance trusts would initially seem to be outside of Section 2036(c), because the transferor/insured must part with all incidents of ownership over the insurance policy. Thus, the transferor seemingly retains no interest in the enterprise to trigger Section 2036(c). However, remember that Section 2036(c) treats the transferor as holding any interest granted to his or her spouse. Both parties are treated as one if the transferor used either the marital deduction or annual exclusion to make the transfer without tax. Thus, if the insured/grantor gives his or her spouse a demand power in a life insurance trust, and if the spouse is a beneficiary of the life insurance trust (even after the insured's death), Section 2036(c) may well apply to such trusts.

The IRS may not adopt this reasoning, but it seems that they certainly have the legal authority to do so. This can be avoided with new insurance trusts merely by refraining from giving the spouse any present interest demand power, so that the interest is not transferred to the spouse through use of the annual exclusion with respect to the spouse. However, what about existing life insurance trusts in which the spouse had a demand power? We can only wait until the IRS issues regulations to decide what to do with these trusts.

Nonqualified Deferred Compensation

The statute provides that an agreement for the providing of services will not of itself subject a transaction to the estate freeze provisions provided the agreement is entered into at arm's length and for fair market value (determined at the time services are provided), the agreement makes no changes in interests in the enterprise, and the agreement is not contingent on profits. For this purpose, the term of an agreement to provide services (for example, as a consultant or director) cannot extend beyond three years, including any period which may be extended at the service provider's option.[31] Thus, a contract providing for employment at will would qualify assuming the first three requirements are met. Apparently, except as otherwise provided in regulations, a contract for the providing of services which does not meet these requirements may be treated as a retained interest in the income of the enterprise.

The typical nonqualified deferred compensation plan should be able to fall within this safe harbor test. However, assume a situation where a client gives some common stock to his children over a period of years. At retirement he exchanges the remaining (controlling) common stock he holds and in return receives cash. He now holds no stock and his children own all the outstanding common stock. During retirement he begins to receive payments under the corporation's nonqualified deferred compensation (salary continuation) plan for key executives. Even if the nonqualified compensation was provided under a contract for the providing of services which qualified for the safe harbor above, it is unclear whether the deferring of the compensation will qualify for the safe harbor or be treated as a retained interest in the income of the corporation. Our opinion is that if income is deferred under a contract which otherwise qualifies for the safe harbor the deferred income should also qualify for the safe harbor. However, if the nonqualified compensation was provided under a contract for the providing of services which does not qualify for the safe harbor above, it is very likely that the deferring of the compensation will be treated as a retained interest in the income of the corporation. Apparently, if an employment contract is treated as a retention of an income interest in an enterprise, such contract (or retained interest) would not terminate until all deferred compensation under such contract has been received.

At what point in time should a contract for the providing of services be tested to see if it is in compliance with the safe harbor? It would seem that the appropriate time would be any time that a transfer is made which might be subject to Section 2036(c).

Debt Unrelated to Gifts or Sales of Stock

Assume a client has made gifts of common stock or a growth interest in a business over a number of years to his children and grandchildren. Assume further that these gifts were all within the gift tax annual exclusion limits and therefore no gift tax was payable nor were the gifts considered "adjusted taxable gifts" (and therefore would have no adverse estate tax impact).[32] If the client made loans to the business, the client will not be considered to have retained an income interest in the enterprise solely by reason of having retained "qualified debt."[33]

"Qualified debt" means:

(1) true indebtedness that unconditionally requires fixed payment(s) not to extend beyond 15 years (30 years, if secured by real property) from the date of issue (unless the debt is payable on demand and issued for cash for normal business use),

(2) interest dates are fixed and interest rates are fixed or set relative to a specified market rate,

(3) such debt is not by its terms subordinated to general creditors,

(4) such debt does not grant voting rights or limit others' voting rights (except where the indebtedness is in default), and

(5) such debt is not convertible into an interest in the enterprise which is not qualified debt.

What if a client lends money to his son's recently formed business to help his son's business handle cash flow demands during its early years. "Startup debt" may qualify under relaxed rules if:

(1) the payment of a sum certain is required with respect to true indebtedness,

(2) the debt was received in exchange for cash to be used in the active conduct of a trade or business,

(3) the creditor does not *at any time* (a) transfer any other property, any customers, or any business opportunities to the enterprise, or (b) hold any other interest in the enterprise (including an interest as an officer, director, or employee),

(4) any original transferees actively participate in the enterprise,

(5) such debt does not grant voting rights or limit others' voting rights (except where the indebtedness is in default), and

(6) such debt is not convertible into an interest in the enterprise which is not qualified debt.

The IRS has been given authority to issue regulations which will deal with debt. Such regulations may provide circumstances under which the safe harbors, above, become unsafe by reason of other aspects of an estate freeze transaction. Such regulations could also extend additional safe harbors. It is clear that Congress intended for income interests to be interpreted quite broadly to include interest on debt except where the retained interest provides a limited possibility for subsequent transfer of appreciation.

Ideally, when the regulations are issued, they should provide that indebtedness will be treated as income from the enterprise only when it is a substitute for a previously owned property that evidenced the right to the enterprise's income or if it is of a duration that evidences an interest other than debt.

Stock Options (or Stock Owned by an ESOP)

Some authorities think that ESOPs can trigger the 2036(c) inclusion in the following circumstances: The client owns the majority of the voting common stock of a corporation to which he, from time to time, makes working capital loans. All employees are covered by an ESOP which owns a large interest in the client's corporation. Assume further that one or more family members work for the corporation and therefore have interests in stock owned by the ESOP. These authorities think that if the corporation still owes the client money (other than qualified debt) at the time of his death, that will cause the stock owned by those family members (including a son or daughter-in-law working in the business) to be included in the client's estate. Our opinion is that this is an absurd result that would strongly discourage family corporations. It is also our opinion that if this is what Congress actually said (we doubt it) that they certainly did not know what they had done. We don't feel that a reasonable reading of the statute would require this result.

What about the case where a client grants family members options to purchase stock? Assume that the options give those family members, say, eight years to purchase common stock at its date-of-grant per share value. Obviously, the grant is a transfer of potential appreciation. Apparently, such an option may be subject to Section 2036(c). However, the grant of an option exercisable at fair market value at time of exercise is not subject to Section 2036(c) solely by reason of such right because such an option does not have the potential for avoiding transfer tax.[34]

Limited Partnerships

Should Section 2036(c) apply upon a transfer by a father, who was a general partner, of a limited partnership interest to his son? Only after the appreciation potential and values of the respective partnership interests are calculated can it be determined whether a disproportionately large share of appreciation has been transferred to the son. This is so because Committee Reports indicate that a disproportionately large share of appreciation has been transferred if the potential appreciation attributable to the transferred partnership interest divided by the value of such partnership interest is greater than the potential appreciation attributable to the retained partnership interest divided by the value of the such partnership interest. By both definition and design, in a limited partnership, the general partner retains management powers greater than that given to the limited partners. This adds value to the general partnership interest. However, a limited partner's liability is limited to his investment in the partnership. This adds value to the limited partnership interest. These and other factors, such as income and liquidation rights, will determine the respective values of the general and limited partnership interests. Potential appreciation attributable to the respective partnership interests must be determined under the partnership agreement. Obviously, the determination of whether a disproportionate share of appreciation has been transferred is not simple.

Nonvoting Common Stock

Many companies have both voting and nonvoting common stock but no preferred. The gift (or sale to a family member) of nonvoting stock coupled with a retention of the voting common stock should fall within the statute. Committee Reports indicate that a disproportionately large share of appreciation has been transferred if the potential appreciation attributable to the transferred stock divided by the value of the transferred stock is greater than the potential appreciation attributable to the retained stock divided by the value of the retained stock. Both the transferred and retained stock share equally in appreciation potential. However, the voting stock is worth more than the nonvoting stock because of the voting right. When the appreciation potential is divided by the value of the respective voting and nonvoting stock, it is clear that a disproportionately large share of appreciation has been given to the transferred nonvoting stock.

Sale (or Gift) and Leaseback

A sale (or gift) of property such as an office building to a child or other family member followed by a leaseback of the same property is a common estate planning tool which is used to shift the burden of income tax to one or more lower bracket individuals and divide wealth as well. Quite often a professional, such as a physician, will give his children the building in which his practice is located and then his professional corporation will lease back the building. Executed properly, payments made after the signing of an arms' length lease and in return for a fair rental should be tax deductible to the client. Generally, to be respected for tax purposes: (1) the transfer and the leaseback had to be at arms' length, (2) the corporation rather than the client leased back the building, and (3) the sale was to a trust for the client's child or children.

Section 2036(c)(7) provides further that an agreement for the lease of property to be used in the enterprise will not of itself subject a transaction to the estate freeze provisions provided the agreement is entered into at arm's length and for fair market value, the agreement makes no changes in interests in the enterprise, and the agreement is not contingent on profits. The IRS has been given authority to issue regulations which will deal with agreements for the lease of property to be used in the enterprise. Such regulations may provide circumstances under which the safe harbor becomes unsafe by reason of other aspects of an estate freeze transaction. Such regulations could also extend additional safe harbors. It is clear that Congress intended for income interests to be interpreted quite broadly to include rent except where the retained interest provides a limited possibility for subsequent transfer of appreciation.

Tax Apportionment

The Technical and Miscellaneous Revenue Act of 1988 addresses several tax apportionment problems not addressed when Section 2036(c) was first enacted. Concern was raised over who would bear the burden of the tax imposed under Section 2036(c). The Act answers some of the questions by adding new Section 2207B which provides that (1) a client's estate can recover the proportionate share of taxes (including penalties and interest) attributable to property included in a client's estate under Section 2036(c) from the persons receiving such property (unless the client specifically provides otherwise by will or revocable trust) and (2) a client may recover from all original transferees the proportionate share of taxes (including penalties and interest) attributable to property for which a gift is deemed made under Section 2036(c). However, no right of recovery is permitted against a charitable remainder trust.

Return To First Death Focus May Be Needed

If the IRS succeeds in including property under Section 2036(c) in the estate of the first spouse to die, almost by definition it will not qualify for the marital deduction, regardless of how much of the client's estate is left to a surviving spouse. Committee reports indicate an intention to include growth property in the surviving spouse's estate, but only where the surviving spouse holds or receives income or rights in the enterprise at the decedent spouse's death in a manner that qualified for either the marital deduction or the annual gift tax exclusion. Clearly, "second to die" insurance or a policy covering the younger healthier spouse would be indicated in such cases.

Don't overlook the liquidity crunch that may occur if the 2036(c) transferee is also a "skip" person.[35] For example, if the recipient of a client's common stock is his granddaugh-

ter, a GST tax will be payable on top of the estate tax. (The value of the GST will be reduced by any consideration paid by the granddaughter.[36] So if the client sold, rather than gave her the stock, both the "anti-freeze" estate tax statute and the GST tax statute would apply, but both would allow the amount paid by the granddaughter to, in effect, offset the respective taxes.)

PART III — PLANNING STRATEGIES

What Strategies Will Still Work?

(1) The "reverse freeze": Give away preferred stock and keep the common. Pay a high but reasonable dividend on the (nonvoting) noncumulative preferred. This avoids Section 2036(c) since the client by definition is not giving away the "growth" part of the business. At the same time, if the dividend is significant (say, 14 percent or greater), the amount of wealth that can be shifted from parent to child is considerable.

(2) Divide a partnership into two portions, growth and income, and give away the "income" interest. That interest would have a priority right to the annual profits of the business, limited to a specified preference amount. (However, the family partnership rules of Section 704(e) should be kept in mind.) Using the same reasoning as above, there should be no inclusion of the given interest.

(3) Recapitalize in the normal manner and give away (or sell) to a family member equal portions of preferred and common stock. For instance, 2036(c) would not apply if a client gave his son 30 percent of the common stock and 30 percent of the preferred stock of the corporation. (If he gave 70 percent of the common stock and only 30 percent of the preferred stock, 40 percent of the common stock would be in the client's estate).

(4) "Water down the common": Pay significant dividends on the common stock given away or sold to a younger generation. The greater the dividends paid, the less valuable the common stock that will be included in the client's estate. This concept will make sense as long as income tax rates are lower than estate tax rates.

(5) Sell to Non-Family Members. Sell disproportionate interests to nonfamily members for full and adequate consideration. Then make gifts of the net proceeds and have the donees invest those dollars.

(6) Sell to a family member under an installment sale (keeping in mind what is qualified debt). Retain only that one interest in the enterprise and terminate all relationships with the business.

(7) Utilize aggressive valuation techniques to obtain minority and lack of marketability discounts or to lower the value

for gift tax purposes. However, lowering the value of the transferred interest could increase exposure to transfer of a disproportionately large share of appreciation by increasing the share of appreciation factor with respect to the transferred stock (potential appreciation is divided by the value of the interest — reducing the value of the interest without reducing the appreciation potential results in a larger share of appreciation borne by such interest). Qualified short term GRITs will work and, hopefully, so will SPLITs.

(8) Divert the client's efforts and customers of the client's present business to a new business owned by the client's children and/or grandchildren. Consider the use of an S corporation totally owned by the client's children. The client would own no stock, hold no debt, nor have any legal connection to the new business, either as employee or director.

(9) If, for nontax reasons, a client has deliberately (or inadvertently) fallen within the scope of 2036(c), life insurance to pay the additional tax should be purchased on his life. It can be paid for by the corporation through a split dollar or salary bonus to a child working in the business. Alternatively, the client can make annual exclusion gifts to an irrevocable life insurance trust with Crummey withdrawal powers. The trustee could purchase the insurance and use it to purchase assets from the client's estate at his death. That would provide the executor with cash to pay the tax without increasing the size of the tax itself.

(10) Plan a Section 303 partial stock redemption. At the very least, this would provide additional liquidity to pay some of the Section 2036(c) tax. To the extent Section 303 applies, any gain on the sale would be income tax free. Fund the redemption with sufficient life insurance (perhaps paid for through a split dollar or salary bonus arrangement) and have the policy owned by an irrevocable trust to keep the life insurance out of the client's estate. The trust could lend the corporation sufficient cash to affect the stock purchase. The corporation could pay the trust interest on the fully secured loan and pay back the principal from future earnings and profits over a period of years.

(11) A "Cryogenic Superfreeze" should work for clients who don't need to retain the income from the transferred property. Recapitalize in the classic manner. Then have the client transfer the income interest to some family member other than the client's spouse. Then transfer the growth interest. Alternatively (and perhaps better yet), give away the single class of common stock to the children.

(12) The "Only If QTIP Trust" may provide a partial answer for some clients. Transfer the common stock to a trust for the client's children. Provide income to the children until the client's death. Provide further that at the client's death, the income from the assets in the trust would pass to the client's surviving spouse in a manner that would qualify trust assets for the marital deduction under the QTIP rules, ONLY IF (and only to the extent) the assets in that trust were for any reason includable in his estate at death. The client would have no ability to alter the disposition of the trust property. Neither would he have the reserved power to name new beneficiaries or to change the interests of the beneficiaries. This should not be considered an incomplete gift nor should it be considered a reserved power under Code section 2038.

The Baby and The Bath Water

It is important that planners focusing on the possible adverse estate tax implications of Section 2036(c) not abandon familiar and long tested tools and techniques merely because the federal estate tax savings will not be realized. This article began with many reasons for an estate freeze. All but one can still be accomplished — including significant state death tax savings in many states — using traditional estate capping methods.

Ill Wind Windfalls

Since it's an ill wind that blows no man good, even Section 2036(c) can have some benefits to some clients. For instance, the inclusion of a business interest will make it easier to qualify for (a) a Section 303 stock redemption, (b) Section 2032A special use valuation, (c) Section 6166 extension of time to pay estate taxes. Basis of property included because of 2036(c) will typically be stepped up to its federal estate tax value. This in turn may make a Section 303 redemption an effective way to remove significant amounts of income from the corporation at no income tax cost.[37] A step up in basis may save considerable income tax for the heirs. In fact, if it is anticipated that the client's estate, including the 2036(c) assets, wouldn't greatly exceed the $600,000 unified credit equivalent, it may pay to deliberately fall within 2036(c) to gain what may be a sizable step-up in basis at no meaningful estate tax cost.

Consider the implications if the overall value of the enterprise drops in value after the gift of the appreciation interest (as has been the case with many farming corporations). If Section 2036(c) applies, the common stock will be included in the transferor's gross estate at its date of death value. But full credit will have been given for the gift taxes paid on the initial transfer. In this situation the 2036(c) inclusion is actually beneficial.

Closing Thoughts

It is important to note that there are many authorities who feel that Code Section 2036(c) is far more pervasive and insidious than we have indicated.

We think this tax may be unconstitutional:

(a) it only impacts on family owned enterprises;

(b) it applies transfer tax law even when there is no transfer; and

(c) it treats family members as if they had made a gift even when they have in fact paid full and adequate consideration and the IRS taxes them accordingly for income tax purposes.

If anything violates the "equal protection" provision of the Constitution, this law (if read as broadly as some commentators say it will be) does. Likewise, it does not apply to transfers; it applies to transactions. It therefore is a "direct" tax which is applied on a transactional basis rather than according to the population (supposedly Congress can not assess a tax against property or persons directly except on a population basis).[38]

Congress has given the Treasury Department the power to "prescribe such regulations as may be necessary or appropriate to carry out the purposes of this subsection, including such regulations as may be necessary or appropriate to prevent avoidance of the purposes of this subsection through distributions or otherwise".[39] To give the IRS such sweeping powers to interpret (and expand) what is already an overly broad, often vague, and certainly significant statute amounts to a delegation of legislative power to an executive body.

There is a quote from Charles Dickens' *Oliver Twist* that is seeming more and more appropriate:

"IF THE LAW SUPPOSES THAT, THE LAW IS A ASS, A IDIOT!"

At the very least, OBRA '87 (with amendments by TAMRA '88) has hatched an overly broad, imprecise, and unclear snake to be aware of and watch constantly. There are many unanswered questions that will have to await further technical corrections, regulations, and litigation.

What is certain is that Section 2036(c) will significantly affect anyone of wealth who desires to shift that wealth to his beneficiaries rather than the IRS, and may, if other authorities are correct about its true scope, strike a venomous blow at the capitalistic system.

It imposes a tax even though

(1) an asset, such as stock, has been given away with no strings attached;

(2) both the gift and estate tax systems supposedly tax only transfers without adequate and full consideration, yet Section 2036(c) applies even if there has been a sale to a family member for full value;

(3) this Code section flies against the face of the reality of the marketplace; it assumes appreciation can be guaranteed and that values never go down; it ignores the fact that in an exchange of like values the accumulated income from the frozen interest is economically equivalent to the potential appreciation in the growth interest;

(4) the potential for growth is a carrot often given (or sold) to family members to induce them to remain in a family owned business in return for the risk taking and forfeiture of alternative employment opportunities; it should be governmental policy to assist rather than penalize the family businesses which contribute so much to the stability of our economy.

The effective use of irrevocable life insurance trusts and other tools and techniques of estate planning will become more important than ever, now that it is more difficult to shift wealth by other conventional means.

Footnote References

Section 2036(c)

1. P.L. 100-203 (December 22, 1987). The tax provisions are contained in Titles IX and X, and are popularly known as the Revenue Act of 1987.

2. P.L. 100-647 (November 10, 1988).

3. OBRA '87, Section 10402.

4. TAMRA '88, Section 3031(h)(5).

5. TAMRA '88, Section 3031(h)(2).

6. TAMRA '88, Section 3031(h)(4).

7. I.R.C. Section 2036(c)(1).

8. I.R.C. Section 2036(c)(4), as amended by TAMRA '88 (eff. 6-21-88).

9. I.R.C. Section 2936(c)(3)(A).

10. I.R.C. Section 2036(c)(3)(B) defines "family" to include the individual's spouse, any lineal descendants of the individual or the individual's spouse, any parent or grandparent of the individual, and any spouse of any of the foregoing.

11. I.R.C. Section 2036(c)(3)(c).

12. I.R.C. Section 2036(c)(2), as amended by TAMRA '88, Sec. 3031(g)(1).

13. I.R.C. Section 2036(c)(7).

14. Rights in the enterprise include, but are not limited to, voting rights, conversion rights, liquidation rights, warrants, options and other rights of value. Conference Reports, Revenue Act of 1987.

15. I.R.C. Section 2036(a) specifically exempts transfers in the case of a bona fide sale for an adequate and full consideration in money or money's worth from the application of the retained life estate rules.

16. Note that an appropriate adjustment to reflect the consideration received in the sale is allowed as an offset. This is discussed later in connection with I.R.C. Section 2036(c)(2).

17. I.R.C. Section 2036(c)(7)(A)(iii).

18. Enterprise is not defined in the Code. Under the House Report of the Bill, it was limited to business; under the Conference Report, it includes a business or other property which may produce income or gain.

19. Disproportionate large share is again a term that is not statutorily defined. Both the House Report and the Conference Report make it clear that it is only that portion of what was given away in excess of what was retained that is subject to the new rules.

20. I.R.C. Section 2036(c)(4).

21. TAMRA '88, Section 3031(h)(2).

22. I.R.C. Section 2035(c)(4), prior to amendment by TAMRA '88.

23. I.R.C. Sections 2035(c)(4)(B), 2035(c).

24. I.R.C. Section 2036(c)(7).

25. I.R.C. Section 1361(c)(5)(B) provides this safe harbor for debt and recognizes that other relationships may also qualify as debts.

26. *Greene v. United States*, 237 F.2d 848 (7th Cir. 1956); *Estate of Bergan*, 1 T.C. 543 (1943).

27. Conference Reports, Revenue Act of 1987.

28. I.R.C. Section 2036(c)(4)(D)(iv).

29. I.R.C. Section 2036(c)(6).

30. The RIT was already suspect under prior law as it related to the 3 year rule. *Gradow v. United States*, 87-1 USTC 97,929 (Cl. Ct. 1987); and *United States v. Allen*, 293 F.2d 916 (10th Cir. 1961).

31. I.R.C. Section 2036(c)(7).

32. I.R.C. Section 2001(b) defines adjusted taxable gifts as taxable gifts made by decedent after December 31, 1976, other than gifts that are includable in the gross estate of the decedent.

33. I.R.C. Section 2036(c)(7).

34. I.R.C. Section 2036(c)(7)(A)(iii).

35. I.R.C. Section 2613(a) defines a skip person, generally, as a person assigned to a generation which is 2 or more generations below the generation assignment of the transferor.

36. I.R.C. Section 2624(d).

37. I.R.C. Section 303(a) permits a redemption of stock in certain closely held corporations to be treated as an exchange to the extent of the sum of estate and inheritance taxes and the funeral and administration expenses of the estate. This is particularly helpful in family corporations in which a redemption of stock cannot qualify as a complete termination of interest because of the family attribution rules. The redemption nevertheless reduces the corporation's earnings and profits ratably. I.R.C. Section 312(n)(7).

38. U.S. Constitution, article I, section 9. The federal income tax is exempt from this provision by the sixteenth amendment.

39. I.R.C. Section 2036(c)(8).

1980 COMMISSIONERS STANDARD
ORDINARY MORTALITY TABLE
(Life expectancy, years)

Age	Male	Female	Age	Male	Female	Age	Male	Female	Age	Male	Female
0	70.83	75.83	25	47.84	52.34	50	25.36	29.53	75	8.31	10.32
1	70.13	75.04	26	46.93	51.40	51	24.52	28.67	76	7.84	9.71
2	69.20	74.11	27	46.01	50.46	52	23.70	27.82	77	7.40	9.12
3	68.27	73.17	28	45.09	49.52	53	22.89	26.98	78	6.97	8.55
4	67.34	72.23	29	44.16	48.59	54	22.08	26.14	79	6.57	8.01
5	66.40	71.28	30	43.24	47.65	55	21.29	25.31	80	6.18	7.48
6	65.46	70.34	21	42.31	46.71	56	20.51	24.49	81	5.80	6.98
7	64.52	69.39	32	41.38	45.78	57	19.74	23.67	82	5.44	6.49
8	63.57	68.44	33	40.46	44.84	58	18.99	22.86	83	5.09	6.03
9	62.62	67.48	34	39.54	43.91	59	18.24	22.05	84	4.77	5.59
10	61.66	66.53	35	38.61	42.98	60	17.51	21.25	85	4.46	5.18
11	60.71	65.58	36	37.69	42.05	61	16.79	20.44	86	4.18	4.80
12	59.75	64.62	37	36.78	41.12	62	16.08	19.65	87	3.91	4.43
13	58.80	63.67	38	35.87	40.20	63	15.38	18.86	88	3.66	4.09
14	57.86	62.71	39	34.96	39.28	64	14.70	18.08	89	3.41	3.77
15	56.93	61.76	40	34.05	38.36	65	14.04	17.32	90	3.18	3.45
16	56.00	60.82	41	33.16	37.46	66	13.39	16.57	91	2.94	3.15
17	55.09	59.87	42	32.26	36.55	67	12.76	15.83	92	2.70	2.85
18	54.18	58.93	43	31.38	35.66	68	12.14	15.10	93	2.44	2.55
19	53.27	57.98	44	30.50	34.77	69	11.54	14.38	94	2.17	2.24
20	52.37	57.04	45	29.62	33.88	70	10.96	13.67	95	1.87	1.91
21	51.47	56.10	46	28.76	33.00	71	10.39	12.97	96	1.54	1.56
22	50.57	55.16	47	27.90	32.12	72	9.84	12.26	97	1.20	1.21
23	49.66	54.22	48	27.04	31.25	73	9.30	11.60	98	0.84	0.84
24	48.75	53.28	49	26.20	30.39	74	8.79	10.95	99	0.50	0.50

TABLE V
ONE LIFE–EXPECTED RETURN MULTIPLES

Age	Multiples (Life Expectancy)	Age	Multiples (Life Expectancy)	Age	Multiples (Life Expectancy)
5	76.6	42	40.6	79	10.0
6	75.6	43	39.6	80	9.5
7	74.7	44	38.7	81	8.9
8	73.7	45	37.7	82	8.4
9	72.7	46	36.8	83	7.9
10	71.7	47	35.9	84	7.4
11	70.7	48	34.9	85	6.9
12	69.7	49	34.0	86	6.5
13	68.8	50	33.1	87	6.1
14	67.8	51	32.2	88	5.7
15	66.8	52	31.3	89	5.3
16	65.8	53	30.4	90	5.0
17	64.8	54	29.5	91	4.7
18	63.9	55	28.6	92	4.4
19	62.9	56	27.7	93	4.1
20	61.9	57	26.8	94	3.9
21	60.9	58	25.9	95	3.7
22	59.9	59	25.0	96	3.4
23	59.0	60	24.2	97	3.2
24	58.0	61	23.3	98	3.0
25	57.0	62	22.5	99	2.8
26	56.0	63	21.6	100	2.7
27	55.1	64	20.8	101	2.5
28	54.1	65	20.0	102	2.3
29	53.1	66	19.2	103	2.1
30	52.2	67	18.4	104	1.9
31	51.2	68	17.6	105	1.8
32	50.2	69	16.8	106	1.6
33	49.3	70	16.0	107	1.4
34	48.3	71	11.6	108	1.3
35	47.3	72	14.6	109	1.1
36	46.4	73	13.9	110	1.0
37	45.4	74	13.2	111	.9
38	44.4	75	12.5	112	.8
39	43.5	76	11.9	113	.7
40	42.5	77	11.2	114	.6
41	41.5	78	10.6	115	.5

Tools and Techniques

FORMS FOR ANALYZING ASSETS AND FOR DETERMINING FEDERAL ESTATE TAX, CASH NEEDS, AND CAPITAL AND INCOME AMOUNTS

(These forms were used by the late Herbert Levy in his private practice.)

The form titled "Analysis of Assets" (following page) is used to analyze the assets of the husband and the wife. It has the flexibility to indicate that in the estate of the second to die you can include any assets which the second to die would expect to receive from the estate of the first to die. Thus, for example, if real estate is owned jointly and would all be included in the estate of the first to die, the value of that real estate would be set forth in the column marked "Joint" across from the line titled "Real Estate" and that same amount would appear in the column marked "Probate" for the analysis of the assets in the estate of the second to die at the line marked "Real Estate". The space on the form for "notes" would cross-reference the fact that it is the same property.

The Analysis of Assets form can also be used in a manner which would merely show the assets owned by each of the two people outright before either dies and the interest that each has in jointly held property to the extent that the interest would be taxable in that person's estate if that person dies first.

The columns marked "Probate" and "Joint" specifically categorize the property. The columns marked "Life Insurance" and "Other" have specific purposes. The life insurance column is to clearly set forth and segregate life insurance which would be includable in an estate (but not in the probate estate) and the column marked "Other" would be used for property being taxed but which is not subject to probate nor is jointly held property, such as power of appointment property or Section 2035 property which has been added back because a gift of life insurance was made within three years of death.

The columns are all totalled and the totals carried over to a form which shows the federal estate tax computation. The first two columns on the federal estate tax computation would be the computation for a person dying first followed by the spouse dying second. The next two columns would be a reverse computation, that is, the spouse who is deemed to die second would now die first and the spouse who was deemed to die first would now die second. This gives you, on one piece of paper before any planning suggestions are made, the federal estate tax consequences, regardless of the order of deaths. The total cash needs of the estate are set forth on a separate page specifically for that purpose. This schedules out not only the federal estate tax but also the state death taxes, administration expenses, liabilities and cash bequests which all are a drain on estate liquidity.

The summary page is designed to show the total passing for the next generation under a present plan or alternate plans. The total assets of the second to die should not include any assets that were included in the estate of the first to die. Thus, for example, jointly held property would be eliminated from the line called "Total Assets of the Second to Die". Without such an elimination, we would be duplicating certain property, and the results would be fallacious.

The balance of the form attempts to show how much money would be available on an annual income basis to the surviving spouse after computing productive assets available to that survivor from various sources.

Tools and Techniques

ANALYSIS OF ASSETS

_____ DIES FIRST

DESCRIPTION	PROBATE	JOINT	LIFE INS.	OTHER
REAL ESTATE	_____	_____	_____	_____
STOCKS & BONDS (PUBLIC)	_____	_____	_____	_____
STOCKS & BONDS (PRIVATE)	_____	_____	_____	_____
MORTGAGES, NOTES & CASH	_____	_____	_____	_____
INSURANCE — DECEDENT OWNED	_____	_____	_____	_____
MISCELLANEOUS PROPERTY	_____	_____	_____	_____
SECTION 2035 PROPERTY & GIFT TAX	_____	_____	_____	_____
SECTION 2036-2038 PROPERTY	_____	_____	_____	_____
POWER OF APPOINTMENT PROPERTY	_____	_____	_____	_____
ANNUITIES — SECTION 2039	_____	_____	_____	_____
INHERITANCES NOT YET RECEIVED	_____	_____	_____	_____
TOTAL	_____	_____	_____	_____

NOTES:

_____ DIES SECOND

DESCRIPTION	PROBATE	JOINT	LIFE INS.	OTHER
REAL ESTATE	_____	_____	_____	_____
STOCKS & BONDS (PUBLIC)	_____	_____	_____	_____
STOCKS & BONDS (PRIVATE)	_____	_____	_____	_____
MORTGAGES, NOTES & CASH	_____	_____	_____	_____
INSURANCE — DECEDENT OWNED	_____	_____	_____	_____
MISCELLANEOUS PROPERTY	_____	_____	_____	_____
SECTION 2035 PROPERTY & GIFT TAX	_____	_____	_____	_____
SECTION 2036-2038 PROPERTY	_____	_____	_____	_____
POWER OF APPOINTMENT PROPERTY	_____	_____	_____	_____
ANNUITIES — SECTION 2039	_____	_____	_____	_____
INHERITANCES NOT YET RECEIVED	_____	_____	_____	_____
TOTAL	_____	_____	_____	_____

NOTES:

CLIENT: _____ DATE: _____ FILE NO: _____

FEDERAL GROSS ESTATE:

  PROBATE PROPERTY

  JOINT PROPERTY

  LIFE INSURANCE

  OTHER PROPERTY

TOTAL FED. GROSS ESTATE

LESS: ADM. EXP. (%)

  DEBTS

ADJUSTED GROSS ESTATE

LESS: MARITAL DED. (M.D.)

  CHARITABLE CONTR.

PLUS: ADJ. POST 1976 GIFTS

FEDERAL ESTATE TAX BASE

TAX ON ESTATE TAX BASE

LESS: UNIFIED CREDIT

  STATE DEATH TAX CR.

  OTHER CREDITS

  GIFT TAX PD. CR.

FEDERAL ESTATE TAX

15% EXCESS ACCUMULATED TAX

NOTES:

Tools and Techniques

CASH NEEDS OF ESTATE

FEDERAL ESTATE TAXES _____ _____ _____ _____ _____

STATE DEATH TAXES _____ _____ _____ _____ _____

DEBTS & ADMIN. EXP. _____ _____ _____ _____ _____

CASH BEQUESTS _____ _____ _____ _____ _____

TOTAL CASH NEEDS OF ESTATE _____ _____ _____ _____ _____

LESS: PROBATE PROPERTY (_____) (_____) (_____) (_____) (_____)

SURPLUS (DEFICIT) _____ _____ _____ _____ _____

CLIENT: _____ DATE _____ FILE NO. _____

SUMMARY

TOTAL ASSETS OF 1st TO DIE _____ _____ _____

TOTAL ASSETS OF 2nd TO DIE _____ _____ _____

CASH NEEDS OF 1st TO DIE (_____) (_____) (_____)

CASH NEEDS OF 2nd TO DIE (_____) (_____) (_____)

BALANCE AFTER 2nd TO DIE _____ _____ _____

ADD LIFETIME GIFTS _____ _____ _____

TOTAL TO NEXT GENERATION _____ _____ _____

SURPLUS PROBATE ASSETS AFTER FIRST TO DIE _____ _____ _____

ADD: ASSETS OF SURVIVOR _____ _____ _____

    M.D. ASSETS TO OR FOR SURVIVOR _____ _____ _____

    NON. M.D. ASSETS FOR SURVIVOR _____ _____ _____

    NON TAXED ASSETS TO OR FOR SURVIVOR _____ _____ _____

LESS: NON-PRODUCTIVE ASSETS (_____) (_____) (_____)

TOTAL PRODUCTIVE ASSETS AFTER FIRST SPOUSE DIES ════════ ════════ ════════

INVESTMENT RETURN AT _____ % _____ _____ _____

ADD: QUAL. RETIREMENT PLAN PAYMENT _____ _____ _____

    DEFERRED COMPENSATION _____ _____ _____

    TAXABLE ANNUITY PAYMENT _____ _____ _____

    SOCIAL SECURITY PAYMENT _____ _____ _____

TOTAL PROJECTED ANNUAL INCOME TO
    SURVIVING SPOUSE ════════ ════════ ════════

NOTES:

Tools and Techniques

This form allows for inclusion of an inflation factor in estimating estate costs where the second spouse to die is assumed to survive 10 years.

RALPH GANO MILLER, APLC

Net Value of
Estate Assets

SPH $_____

SPW $_____

CP $_____

Tot. $_____

Type of Plan:

( ) Simple Wills (all to surviving spouse)

( ) A B Trust to equalize estates and avoid "double tax"

( ) Optimum Martial Deduction (A-B or A-B-C Trust)

Death H in 19 _____ , W 10 yrs later

****

Death of Husband (H)

1. H's Adjusted Gross Estate (AGE) .... $_____

    Less Marital Deduction (MD) .... _____

    Taxable Estate .... $_____

    Federal Tax on Base Rate .... _____ =

                Marg Rate .... _____ @____% _____

                Total Tentative Tax .... _____

2. State Death Tax Credit:

        Base Rate _____ = _____

        Marg. Rate _____ @____ _____

        Total .... − _____

3. Unified Credit .... − _____

4. Total Tax .... $_____

Death of Wife (W)

1. Wife's adjusted gross estate .... $_____

    Plus Husband's MD .... _____

    Less Tax at H's death .... _____

    Wife's total AGE .... _____

    Increased by inflation

        @ _____/yr for 10 yrs =

        W's new AGE .... _____

2. W's New AGE .... $_____

    Federal Tax on Base Rate .... _____ =

                Marg Rate .... _____ @___% _____

                Total Tentative Tax .... _____

3. State Death Tax Credit:

        Base Rate _____ = _____

        Marg. Rate _____ @____ _____

        Total .... − _____

3. Unified Credit .... − 192,800

4. Total Tax .... $_____

TOTAL TAX OVER BOTH DEATHS:

    Tax at H's death .... $_____

    Tax at W's death .... _____

           TOTAL .... _____

THE GENERATION-SKIPPING TRANSFER TAX:
AN EXPLANATION AND ANALYSIS
by Stephan R. Leimberg

PRIOR LAW

Under prior law a generation-skipping transfer (GST) provided for the splitting of wealth between two or more generations of beneficiaries, both younger than the grantor's generation. For instance, a father could have left property in trust with income to his son and the remainder to his grandson. The generation-skipping transfer tax (GST tax) was essentially the same tax that would have been imposed on the son's estate had the property been left directly to the son and from him to the grandson.

The GST tax was imposed because many individuals would give the beneficiary in the next generation (the son in the example above) broad powers that provided him with significant rights but deftly avoided taxation. For instance, a grandfather could give his son a life income coupled with one or more of the following powers:

• the right to capital or income for his health, education, maintenance, or support

• the right to invade capital under *5 and 5* powers

• special powers to appoint to his (the son's) children

• a discretionary right in the trustee to invade capital for the son's benefit

None of these powers would cause the son's estate to be taxable, yet the son had significant beneficial enjoyment. This perceived evasion of transfer tax at the *skipped-generation* level (that is, when the son died and the trust property skipped taxation in his estate) was the reason for creating the GST tax.

No tax was imposed, however, if the skip was direct; that is, if the grandfather left the entire amount directly to his grandson. No tax was imposed if the younger generation (the son in the example above) merely had a management right over trust assets or a limited power to appoint the trust assets among the lineal decendants of the grantor.

NEW LAW

General Rules

Current law imposes a flat rate tax equal to the highest current estate or gift tax bracket on every generation-skipping transfer (55 percent until 1993). Essentially the GST law will affect transfers to grandchildren or others in the grandchildren's or younger generations. The tax applies to transfers in trust or arrangements having substantially the same effect as a trust, such as transfers involving life estates and remainders, estates for years, and insurance and annuity contracts.

Every individual is allowed to make aggregate transfers of up to $1 million either during lifetime or at death, that will be wholly exempt from the GST tax.

Perhaps the most significant departure from prior law is that the GST tax now will be applied to direct generation-skipping transfers (so-called *direct skips*), such as where a grandparent leaves property or an interest in property directly to a grandchild or other individual two or more generations below the transferor. This imposes a tax where none previously existed. The tax is imposed, not at the death of a skipped generation member (the grandchild's parent), but much sooner; that is, at the death of the grandparent, as an *additional* tax to the normal federal estate tax (or as an additional tax on top of the gift tax in the case of lifetime transfers). As discussed in more detail below, there is a $2 million-per-grandchild tax exemption on direct skips. This limited exemption expires on January 1, 1990.

Essentially the GST tax rate is equal to the maximum estate tax rate (55 percent until 1993 and 50 percent after 1992) on estates of decedents dying at the time the *taxable distribution*, *taxable termination*, or *direct skip* is made. Technically, the *applicable rate* is the maximum federal estate tax rate multiplied by a fraction that the Code calls an *inclusion ratio*. This inclusion ratio is described below.

The *taxable amount*, which is the amount multiplied by the applicable rate mentioned in the preceding paragraph, depends on whether the transfer is considered a taxble distribution, a taxable termination, or a direct skip.

Taxable Distribution

A taxable distribution is any distribution of income or corpus from a trust to a *skip person* or *skip beneficiary* (essentially a person two or more generations below the transferor's generation) that is not otherwise subject to estate or gift tax. For instance, a distribution from a trust to a grandson of the grantor would be to a skip person. Likewise, if a mother creates a trust providing distributions of income or principal to her daughter or granddaughter at the discretion of the trustee, a distribution from that trust to the granddaughter is a taxable distribution. A transfer to a trust would be considered a transfer to a skip person if all interests in the trust were held by skip persons.

The taxable amount in the case of a taxable distribution is the net value of the property received by the distributee less any consideration he paid. In other words, the taxable amount is what the distributee received, reduced by (1) any expenses incurred by him in connection with the determina-

Figure B.14

THE NEW TAX ON GENERATION-SKIPPING TRANSFERS

TRA'86 Act Sections	Internal Revenue Code Sections	Effective Date
1431, 1432, 1433	2601, 2602, 2603, 2604, 2611, 2612, 2613, 2621, 2622, 2623, 2624, 2631, 2641, 2642, 2651, 2652, 2653, 2654, 2661, 2662, 2663, 164, 303, 2032A, 2515, 6166	Generally the new rules apply to any generation-skipping transfer made after October 22, 1986. Any inter vivos transfer made between (and including) September 26, 1985, and October 22, 1986 will be subject to the new generation-skipping rules.

In order to permit a reasonable period for individuals to re-execute their wills to conform to the extension of the generation-skipping transfer tax to direct transfers, certain delays in effective dates to the tax have been allowed. These very limited exceptions include

- a generation-skipping transfer under a trust that was irrevocable on September 25, 1985, but only to the extent that the transfer is not attributable to corpus that was added to the trust after September 25, 1985

- a generation-skipping transfer direct skip under any will executed prior to October 22, 1986 where the testator dies before January 1, 1987

- if a person is mentally incompetent for the purposes of making dispositions of property on October 22, 1986 and does not regain competency before death, any generation-skipping transfer under (1) a trust to the extent the trust consists of property included in the decedent's gross estate (except for property the decedent transferred after date of enactment during his lifetime), or (2) a direct skip occurring by reason of the death of such person

---

tion, collection, or refund of the GST tax, and (2) any consideration paid for the distribution. The transferee is obligated to pay the GST tax in a taxable distribution. If the trust itself pays the tax for the transferees, the payment will be treated as an additional taxable distribution.

The tax levied upon a taxable distribution is *tax inclusive*. That means the property subject to tax includes (1) the property and (2) the GST tax itself.

Example: If a trustee makes a distribution of $10,000 of trust income to a grandchild in 1989, the tax would be $5,500 (if paid by the grandchild). The grandchild will net $4,500.

Taxable Termination

A taxable termination is essentially the termination by death, lapse of time, release of a power, or otherwise of an interest in property held in a trust resulting in *skip beneficiaries* holding all the interests in the trust. For instance, if Alan leaves a life income to his son, Sam, with a remainder to his granddaughter, Gina, the son's death terminates his life interest in trust property and it then passes to Gina, the skip beneficiary. A taxable termination occurs on the date

of the son's death. A taxable termination cannot occur as long as at least one non-skip person has an interest in the property. A taxable termination cannot occur if a skip person could not ever receive a distribution after the termination. Furthermore, there is no taxable termination if an estate or gift tax is imposed on the non-skip individual (the son in this example) at termination.

The taxable amount in the case of a taxable termination is the value of all property involved less (1) a deduction for any expenses, debts, and taxes generated by the property, and (2) any consideration paid by the transferee. If one or more taxable terminations with respect to the same trust occur at the same time as a result of the death of an individual, the executor may elect to value all the taxable termination property under federal estate tax alternate valuation rules. The trustee (broadly defined to mean the person in actual or constructive possession of the GST property) is responsible for the payment of the tax in a taxable termination (or in a direct skip from a trust).

The tax payable upon a taxable termination is tax inclusive. The tax is imposed as if a transfer were made one generation down and at that individual's death the tax was levied. The transfer is tax inclusive because, as with the taxable distribution, the property subject to the transfer includes the generation-skipping tax itself.

Example: Assume $1 million is placed into an irrevocable trust for the benefit of the grantor's daughter for life with remainder to his granddaughter. At the daughter's death in 1989, a taxable termination occurs. The tax is 55 percent of $1 million, or $550,000. It must be paid out of property passing to the granddaughter. Therefore, the granddaughter nets only $450,000.

Direct Skips

A direct skip is a transfer subject to an estate or gift tax made to a skip person.

A gift from an individual to his grandchild is a direct skip. A direct skip can also occur when an individual makes a transfer to a trust if all the beneficiaries of the trust are skip persons. Therefore, an individual who creates an irrevocable trust for the benefit of his grandchildren would be making a direct skip upon funding the trust.

Why an *additional* tax on direct skips? Under prior law planners avoided the GST tax by suggesting that an individual skip directly from himself to his grandchild. In other words, if the son was affluent and could afford to be entirely bypassed (and in fact was), then under prior GST law the GST tax could not be imposed. The direct skip provision precludes this tactic. The tax will now be imposed even if the son in our example receives no interest whatsoever. Note that in the case of a transfer to grandchildren (of the grantor, the grantor's spouse, or the grantor's former spouse), a person will not be considered a skip person if, at the time of the transfer, his parent (the grantor's child or the grantor's spouse's or former spouse's child) is dead. Instead of treating that person as a grandchild, that person will be treated as a child. His children (the grantor's great grandchildren) will then be treated as if they were the grantor's grandchildren.

The taxable amount in the case of a direct skip is the value of the property or interest in property (including the current right to receive income or corpus or power of appointment) received by the transferee, reduced by any consideration paid by the transferee. The transferor (the decedent in the case of a death time transfer or the donor in the case of a lifetime transfer) is responsible for payment of the GST tax in the case of a direct skip.

The tax in a direct skip is *tax exclusive*. In other words, the tax is paid by the transferor or the estate and the taxable amount does not include the amount of generation-skipping tax. Here the tax is similar to that which would have applied had the transfer been made to a member of the skipped generation who then immediately used the property (net of the transfer tax) to make a second gift to the ultimate recipient (typically the grantor's grandchild) and to pay the gift tax. Note that the amount of the gift tax is not included in the taxable value of the gift. Therefore, the tax can be no higher than the gift tax that would have been paid by the intervening generation level (the grantor's son or daughter in most cases) had that individual been in the top gift tax bracket and made a gift to the skip beneficiary.

Example: A grandfather makes a lifetime gift of $1 million to his granddaughter in 1989. Assume no exemptions are claimed. The grandparent must pay a generation-skipping tax of $550,000. But the tax is paid, not out of the gift, but out of additional assets of the grandparent. The grandchild will therefore net the full $1 million.

Exemptions and Exclusions

There is a very important provision dealing solely with direct skips to grandchildren. Prior to January 1, 1990, a transfer will not be considered a direct skip and will escape the GST tax to the extent that aggregate transfers from such transferor to such grandchildren do not exceed $2 million. This per-grandchild exemption is in addition to the $1 million-per-donor exemption.

If, under gift tax law, each spouse is treated as having made half of the gift, GST law will likewise recognize gift splitting. This means a married couple during lifetime could (and should) make up to $4 million of direct generation-skipping transfers to grandchildren in addition to the $1 million exemption without the imposition of a GST tax. (But there would be a currently payable gift tax that must be considered.) A transfer in trust will not qualify for the $2 million exemption unless (1) during the life of such individual no portion of the trust corpus or income may be distributed to or for the benefit of any other person, (2) the trust would be included in such individual's estate if such individual were to die before the trust terminated, and (3) all of the income of the trust must be distributed at least annually to the grandchild once he has reached 21.

Certain transfers are excluded from the definition of the term generation-skipping transfer. Transfers excluded from the definition include

- certain transfers that, if made by gift, would qualify as gift tax free under the Code provisions as direct payments made for the donee's educational or medical expenses or pass gift tax free under the annual exclusion rules. Transfers in trust will not qualify for this exemption unless (1) no portion of the trust's income or principal can be distributed to or used for the benefit of anyone other than the grandchild as long as the grandchild is alive, and (2) if the grandchild dies prior to the termination of the trust, the assets of the trust must be includible in the grandchild's estate.
- certain transfers that have already been subjected to the GST tax in which the transferee was in the same or lower generation as the present transferee.

507   **Tools and Techniques**

Unless the governing instrument directs otherwise (by specific reference to the GST tax), the GST tax is charged to the property constituting the tranfer.

Property subject to the GST tax must be valued as of the time of the generation-skipping transfer. However, where the tax involves a direct skip (for example, from grandparent to grandchild), if the property is included in the transferor's estate, its value for GST tax purposes is the same as its value for federal estate tax purposes, including elections for the alternate valuation date or special-use valuation.

Computing the Tax

A $1 million exemption is allowed in computing the tax actually payable. Because married individuals making a lifetime transfer can elect to treat the transfer as if made one-half by each, the $1 million exemption can be doubled to $2 million. To understand how this exemption works and how the tax is actually calculated, it is first necessary to examine the "inclusion ratio."

The inclusion ratio procedure is in two parts. Compute the *applicable fraction* as follows:

1. State the portion of the $1 million GST tax exclusion allocated to the trust or direct skip (every individual is allowed a GST tax exemption of $1 million). This exemption may be allocated by that individual (or the executor) among any property that is transferred. If this allocation is not made on or before the estate tax return is due, it will be made automatically under statutory provisions. Once made, the allocation is irrevocable. $ _____

2. (a) State the value of the property transferred to the trust (or involved in the direct skip). $ _____

   (b) State the total of any federal estate or state death tax actually recovered from the trust attributable to such property. $ _____

   (c) State the amount of any charitable deduction allowed under estate or gift tax law with respect to the property. $ _____

   (d) Add (b) and (c). $ _____

3. Subtract (d) from (a). $ _____

4. Divide the line 1 exemption by line 3. This is the "applicable fraction." $ _____

Once you have computed the applicable fraction, you then find the inclusion ratio. The inclusion ratio is the excess (if any) of 1 over a fraction; the numerator is #1 above, and the denominator is #3 above.

After computing the inclusion ratio, you then multiply that number by the maximum federal estate tax rate to arrive at the applicable rate.

The total GST tax due is determined by multiplying the taxable amount by the applicable rate. (See Figure B.15.)

A credit for state death taxes will be allowed against the GST tax if the transfer (other than a direct skip) occurs at the same time and as a result of an individual's death. The credit is the lower of (a) the amount of any GST tax actually paid to a state under its laws or (b) 5 percent of the GST tax payable to the federal government.

The worksheet at Figure B.16, courtesy of NumberCruncher I (Financial Data Corporation, P. O. Box 1332, Bryn Mawr, PA 19010; 1-800-654-2227) illustrates the entire process.

Figure B.17 shows the impact of the GST tax when the taxable event occurs, not at the time assets are placed into the trust, but at a later date (20 years in this example).

Special Provisions

The new law contains special provisions for the following:

- QTIP property (see Commentary below)
- taxation of multiple skips
- basis adjustments (A basis step-up similar to the step-up allowed under Code Sec. 1014 for property passing at death will be provided with respect to that portion of the property that is actually subject to the GST tax.)
- disclaimers (A disclaimer that results in property passing to a person at least two generations below that of the original transferor will result in a GST tax. For instance, assume a daughter disclaimed a bequest from her mother. As a result of that disclaimer, certain property passes to the mother's granddaughter. The GST tax would be imposed on the transfer—in addition to the federal estate tax.)
- administration
- return requirements (The GST tax return must be filed by the person liable for the payment of the generation-skipping tax. In the case of a direct skip, the return must be filed on or before the due date of the applicable gift or estate tax return. In other cases, the GST tax return must be filed on or before the 15th day of the 4th month after the close of the taxable year in which the transfer occurs.)

Generation assignments are as follows:

- Adoption and half blood are treated as full blood.
- Once married, the couple is in the same generation.
- A nonlineal descendant born more than 12½ years after the transferor is born is in a younger generation. If the difference in birth dates is not more than 37½ years, the

Figure B.15

COMPUTING THE GENERATION SKIPPING TRANSFER TAX

Step 1	List	Value of property transferred	$4,000,000
Step 2	List	Exemption allocated to transfer	$1,000,000
Step 3	List	State & fed tx paid on transfer	$600,000
Step 4	List	Gift or estate tax charitable deductions allowed on transfer	$0
Step 5	Add	Steps 3 and 4	$600,000
Step 6	Subtract	Step 5 from Step 1	$3,400,000
Step 7	Divide	Step 2 by Step 6 This is the "applicable fraction"	0.2941
Step 8	Subtract	Step 7 from one (1) This is the "inclusion ratio"	0.7059
Step 9	Multiply	Step 8 by 55% until 1993 — 0.3882	
	Multiply	Step 8 by 50%—1993 on — 0.3529 This is the "Applicable rate"	
Step 10		Assuming no "per grandchild amount" and no growth GST tax if death prior to 1993	$1,552,941
		GST tax if death 1993 or beyond	$1,411,765

This computation assumes:
- (A) Transfer of $4,000,000
- (B) Federal and state death taxes of $600,000
- (C) No charitable deductions
- (D) No per grandchild exclusion
- (E) Use of full $1,000,000 exemption.

---

nonlineal descendant is assigned to the first younger generation.

Multiple-trust skips are taxed more than once. But if a direct skip is directly to a great grandchild, two taxes are not imposed.

Section 303 was expanded so that protected redemptions that can be made safely now include purchases of stock to pay a GST tax.

Furthermore, Code Section 6166, which allows for installment payments of federal estate tax, was expanded to include deferral of the tax generated under a GST because of direct skips resulting at death.

COMMENTARY

Note that the generation-skipping tax may be imposed *in addition to* any estate or gift tax that may also be due because of the transfer. It appears that in many cases the total cost of making a property transfer can exceed the value of the gift.

Example 1: Assumume a grandfather in a 55 percent gift tax bracket makes a gift in 1989. Assume the value of his gift is $2 million, and it is made to a *non*vested trust for his grandchild. (Because the gift is nonvested, it will *not* qualify for the $2 million-per-grandchild exclusion.) Assume he doesn't allocate any of his $1 million generation-skipping transfer tax exemption to the gift (or has already used the exemption). The generation-skipping transfer tax is $1,100,000 ($2,000,000 x .55). For gift tax purposes, the amount of the gift to the grandson includes the amount of the generation-skipping transfer tax. In other words, the gift is $3,100,000 ($2,000,000 actual gift plus $1,100,000 GST tax). The gift tax on the total deemed gift is $1,705,000 ($3,100,000 x .55). The total tax therefore is $2,805,000, which exceeds the value of the gift actually made by over 40 percent.

Example 2: Assume a father in a 55 percent federal estate tax bracket establishes a testamentary trust that provides, "to my son for life, then to my grandson." Assume he has already used his $1 million exemption. He leaves $5 million, and the federal estate tax is $2,750,000 ($5,000,000 x .55). That leaves $2,250,000 to provide income for his son. Assume that during the son's lifetime there is no appreciation in the trust. At the son's death, a generation-skipping transfer tax is levied at 55

509

Tools and Techniques

Figure B.16

GENERATION SKIPPING TRANSFER TAX WORKSHEET

Step 1	List	Value of property transferred	
Step 2	List	Exemption allocated to transfer	_____
Step 3	List	State & fed tx paid on transfer	_____
Step 4	List	Gift or estate tax charitable deductions allowed on transfer	_____
Step 5	Add	Steps 3 and 4	_____
Step 6	Subtract	Step 5 from Step 1	_____
Step 7	Divide	Step 2 by Step 6 This is the "applicable fraction"	_____
Step 8	Subtract	Step 7 from one (1) This is the "inclusion ratio"	_____
Step 9	Multiply Multiply	Step 8 by 55% if GST before 1993 Step 8 by 50% if GST in 1993 or later This is the "applicable rate"	_____ _____
Step 10	Subtract	Any applicable "per grandchild" amount from step 1 and multiply by Step 9; this is GST tax payable	before 1993 $ _____ 1993 or later $ _____

---

percent and amounts to $1,347,000 ($2,250,000 x .55). The total tax on the $5 million is therefore $4,097,000 ($2,750,000 plus $1,347,000), which means that the grandchildren receive $903,000—from a $5 million gift!

Under prior law, generation-skipping distributions of trust income were not subject to the GST tax. But under current law, these income distributions will be subjected to the tax regardless of whether they are made from income or from corpus. Recipients of income subject to the GST tax may take an income tax deduction (similar to the IRD deduction under Code Section 691) for the GST tax imposed on the distribution.

When all or a portion of a person's $1 million exemption is allocated to a GST in computing the applicable fraction, this has the effect of exempting from the GST tax all future appreciation on the property designated to be exempt. For example, assume a divorced man transfers $1 million in trust for his children and grandchildren. To eliminate the GST tax he allocates his entire $1 million exemption to the trust and avoids any GST tax. All the property in that trust will always be exempt from the GST tax no matter how much it appreciates. (If asset values are rapidly increasing, the more quickly the allocation is made, the better.) But if the individual had allocated only half of his exemption, one-half of all future distributions from the trust to his grandchildren would be subject to the tax as taxable distributions, and one-half of the value of the assets remaining in the trust would be subject to the GST tax when his children die (as taxable terminations). When selecting assets that will be protected by the $1 million exclusion, assets most likely to appreciate should be used. This is because once assets are protected by the exemption, any growth in the value of the assets is beyond the

scope of the GST tax. Therefore, it would make great sense to include life insurance on the grantor's life among these assets.

Part of the $1 million exemption can be allocated to offset any GST tax when the transferor's surviving spouse dies if the property qualifies under estate or gift tax QTIP rules.

When both the client and the client's children have large estates, immediate consideration should be given to using the $2 million ($4 million if split with donor's spouse during lifetime) per-grandchild direct-skip exemption since it will be available only until January 1, 1990. Note that to qualify for the exemption, the bequest must *vest* in the grandchild. Obviously, an outright gift will meet this test. But if the transfer is made in trust, it will not vest unless the trust provides that if the grandchild does not survive long enough to receive the property, it will pass to the grandchild's estate or to the person specified in a general power of appointment held by the grandchild. TAMRA '88 provides that all income from the trust must be paid to the grandchild when he reaches age 21. Since these are not typical trust provisions, clients with large estates should immediately consult with competent counsel.

Whenever possible, direct skips in excess of a protective exemption should be avoided since (1) the tax is an extra tax, (2) it is imposed at the same time as the estate or gift tax and therefore may create or aggravate a liquidity problem, and (3) together with the estate or gift tax it could exceed 100 percent of the gift's value.

Since irrevocable trusts created before September 26, 1985, are completely exempt from the GST tax system (but only to the extent no additions are made to the trust from that date), it is important not to taint such trusts by adding new property

Figure B.17

PROJECTING THE ULTIMATE GST TAX

Initial value of assets		$4,000,000
Less		
Federal and state death taxes		$600,000
Equals		
Net value of assets		$3,400,000
Input: Assumed growth rate (net after tax)	.06	
Input: Years until taxable event	20	

		Future Value	GST Tax
At	.040	$7,449,819	$2,629,348
At	.050	$9,021,212	$3,183,957
At	.060	$10,904,261	$3,848,563
At	.070	$13,156,927	$4,643,621
At	.080	$15,847,254	$5,593,149

Courtesy of Financial Data Corporation — 1-800-654-2227

---

to them. Not only would this create a tax where none existed, but it would also create an administrative nightmare tracking and allocating pre- and post- September 26 assets and appreciation.

Split purchases and other "early on" wealth-shifting devices must be considered in all large estates.

Use of a QTIP trust allows a special election. That election by the executor of the transferor's estate (or by the donor-spouse in the case of a lifetime gift) will enable a transfer from client to QTIP trust to generation-skipping beneficiary in order to make full use of the $1 million exclusion available to *each* spouse. Conversely, the use of the typical power-of-appointment marital trust followed by a generation-skipping gift in default of appointment will probably be charged *solely* to the surviving spouse. Since the surviving spouse will be treated as a transferor, there will be no opportunity to use the deceased grantor's exclusion.

Whenever possible, transfer assets from a super rich spouse to a less wealthy spouse. This is because the $1 million exemption is not freely transferable between spouses. But a transfer to a less wealthy spouse doubles the advantage of the $1 million exemption since both spouses can take advantage of it. This is similar to the rationale for making transfers to a spouse in order to achieve the full benefit of both spouses' unified credits.

Direct skips should be made as quickly as possible. The $2 million-per-grandchild exclusion will be available only until 1990. At the very least, gifts equal to the husband and wife's unified credits should be made.

Direct skips in excess of GST tax exemptions should be avoided. Even though the direct-skip tax rate (like the gift tax rate) is essentially lower, it is a pay now tax. It transfers the time-value-of-money advantage to the IRS rather than to the client. Typically, it is better to defer and pay a larger tax much later.

Annual Exclusion Exemption Modified

Under prior law, a life insurance trust or other trust could be created in a manner that would provide an exemption from the GST tax; all that was necessary was that the transfer qualify as "nontaxable" for gift tax purposes. This meant that if the gift in trust qualified for the gift tax annual exclusion it would automatically be exempted from the GST tax. A trust could be set up for the lifetime of the insured's children with the remainder at their deaths passing to the insured's grandchildren. Crummey powers to each beneficiary multiplied the GST tax exemption at no practical cost.

TAMRA '88 effectively eliminated this technique with respect to all post March 31, 1988 transfers by allowing the GST tax exclusion only for (1) transfers made directly for the benefit of the transferor's grandchild which also (2) forbid distributions of either income or principal during the grandchild's life to *anyone* (including other grandchildren) other than the grandchild (or for the grandchild's benefit), and (3) the trust must require that if the grandchild dies prior to the termination of the trust, the trust's assets must be payable to the grandchild's estate. The transfer of property must still meet annual gift tax exclusion requirements or qualify under the educational/medical exclusion provision of the gift tax law.

So where, for instance, the insured-transferor's trust provides with respect to transfers made after March 31, 1988

Tools and Techniques

(even if the trust itself was irrevocable before that date), "all assets in this trust go to my granddaughter on her 35th birthday," the gift tax exclusion will not double as a GST tax exclusion unless the trust also provides a direct (no intervening estate) skip and (for instance) provides: "(1) during my granddaughter's life, none of the income or principal can be distributed to or used to benefit anyone other than my granddaughter, and (2) if my granddaughter dies before this trust terminates, the assets in the trust at that time will be includible in her gross estate." Only if the trust contains both these two highly restrictive provisions would annual exclusion gifts also protect against the GST tax.

Although it may be possible to (a) draft an irrevocable life insurance trust with several grandchildren as beneficiaries, and (b) divide the trust into as many separate shares as there are beneficiaries, and (c) provide in the trust that if any beneficiary dies, that person's share of trust assets would be in that person's estate, and (d) give that person a Crummey power, although this would avoid both gift tax and the GST tax, few clients would want to give up so much flexibility.

These changes are obviously much more than a mere "technical correction," and require an immediate review of any transfer in trust that falls under the GST tax.

Greater emphasis should now be placed on protecting irrevocable life insurance trusts from the GST tax by advising clients to consider allocating a portion of the $1,000,000 exemption to each transfer made to the trust. Keep in mind that the use of a portion of the $1,000,000 exemption to shield, say, twenty $50,000 annual premiums protects not only that $1,000,000, but also the future trust corpus generated by the policy proceeds created by those premium payments. Leveraging the $1,000,000 exemption this way (for as long as this technique lasts) may be the single most effective long run means of keeping wealth within the family.

COMPUTING THE FEDERAL GIFT TAX

This article will present an overview of the federal gift tax law and basic planning considerations in the following order:

(1) Purpose, Nature, and Scope of Gift Tax Law

(2) Advantages of Lifetime Gifts

(3) Technical Definition of a Gift

(4) Gratuitous Transfers That Are Not Gifts

(5) Exempt Gifts

(6) Requirements for a Completed Gift

(7) Valuation of Property for Gift Tax Purposes

(8) Computing the Tax on Gifts

(9) Reporting of Gifts and Payment of the Tax

(10) Relationship of the Gift Tax System to the Income Tax System

(11) Determination of the Basis of Gift Property

(12) Relationship of the Gift Tax System to the Estate Tax System

(13) Factors to Consider in Selecting Appropriate Subject of a Gift

(1) PURPOSE, NATURE, AND SCOPE OF GIFT TAX LAW

Purpose

If an individual could give away his entire estate during lifetime without the imposition of any tax, a rational person would arrange affairs so that at death nothing would be subject to the federal estate tax. Likewise, if a person could, freely and without tax cost, give income-producing securities or other property to members of his family, the burden of income taxes could be shifted back and forth at will to lower brackets, and income taxes would be saved.

The federal gift tax was designed to discourage taxpayers from making such inter vivos (lifetime) transfers and—to the extent that this objective was not met—to compensate the government for the loss of estate and income tax revenues.

Nature

The gift tax is an excise tax, a tax levied not directly on the subject of the gift itself or on the right to receive the property, but rather on the right of an individual to transfer money or other property to another. (The tax is imposed only on transfers by individuals, but certain transfers involving corporations are treated as indirect transfers by corporate stockholders.)

The gift tax is based on the value of the property transferred.

The gift tax is computed on a progressive schedule based on cumulative lifetime gifts. In other words, the tax rates are applied to total lifetime taxable gifts (all gifts less the exclusions and deductions described in Section 8) rather than only to taxable gifts made in the current calendar year.

Scope

The Internal Revenue Regulations summarize the comprehensive scope of the gift tax law by stating that "all transactions whereby property or interests are gratuitously passed or conferred upon another, regardless of the means or device employed, constitute gifts subject to tax." Almost any transfer or shifting of property or an interest in property can subject the donor (the person transferring the property or shifting the interest) to potential gift tax liability to the extent that the transfer is not supported by adequate and full consideration in money or money's worth, i.e., to the extent that the transfer is gratuitous.

Direct and indirect gifts, gifts made outright and gifts in trust (of both real and personal property) can be the subject of a taxable gift. The gift tax is imposed on the shifting of property rights, regardless of whether the property is tangible or intangible. It can be applied even if the property transferred (such as a municipal bond) is exempt from federal income or other taxes.

The broad definition includes transfers of life insurance, partnership interests, royalty rights, and gifts of checks or notes of third parties. Even the forgiving of a note or cancellation of a debt may constitute a gift.

Almost any party can be the donee (recipient) of a gift subject to tax. The donee can be an individual, partnership, corporation, foundation, trust, or other "person." (A gift to a corporation is typically considered a gift to the other shareholders in proportion to their proprietary interest. Similarly, a gift to a trust is usually considered to be a gift to the beneficiary[ies] in proportion to their interest.)

In fact, a gift can be subject to the tax (assuming the gift is complete) even if the identity of the donee is not known at the date of the transfer and cannot be ascertained.

(2)
ADVANTAGES OF LIFETIME GIFTS

Nontax-Oriented Advantages

Individuals give property away during their lifetimes for many reasons. Although a detailed discussion of the nontax motivations for lifetime giving is beyond the scope of this article, some of the reasons include (a) privacy that would be impossible to obtain through a testamentary gift, (b) potential reduction of probate and administrative costs, (c) protection from the claims of creditors, (d) the vicarious enjoyment of seeing the donee use and enjoy the gift, (e) the corresponding opportunity for the donor to see how well—or how poorly—the donee manages the business or other property, and (f) provision for the education, support, and financial well-being of the donee.

Tax-Oriented Advantages

The unification of the estate and gift tax systems attempted to impose the same tax burden on transfers made during life as at death. The disparity of treatment between lifetime and "deathtime" transfers was minimized through the adoption of a single unified estate and gift tax rate schedule. Both lifetime and "deathtime" gifts are subject to the same rate schedule and are taxed cumulatively, so that gifts made during lifetime push up the rate at which gifts made at death will be taxed.

Although at first glance it seemed that unification eliminated the advantage of inter vivos gifts, there are still some significant advantages.

First, an individual can give up to $10,000 gift tax free every year to each of an unlimited number of donees. This means that a person desiring to make $10,000 gifts to each of his four children and four grandchildren could give a total of $80,000 each year without gift tax liability. (This $10,000 annual gift tax exclusion is described in greater detail in Section 8.)

Since an individual's spouse can also give such gifts, up to $20,000 per year of money or other property, multiplied by an unlimited number of donees, can be transferred gift tax free. In the example above, the donor and spouse together could give up to $160,000 annually on a gift tax-free basis. In fact, one spouse can make the entire gift if the other spouse consents; the transaction can then be treated as if both spouses made gifts. This is known as "gift splitting." Split-gift provisions are also covered in Section 8.

Gift tax free transfers can translate into significant federal estate tax savings. Consider the estate tax savings potential if the amount given to the donees over the life expectancy of the donor is invested (in life insurance, annuities, mutual funds, etc.). Figure B.18, courtesy of the Financial Data Corporation, producer of The Financial and Estate Planner's NumberCruncher and Financial Planning Tool Kit Computer Software, illustrates the potential estate or generation-skipping transfer tax savings possible if a 40-year-old donor split gifts to five donees over his life expectancy.

A second tax incentive for making an inter vivos as opposed to testamentary ("deathtime") gift is that if a gift is made more than 3 years prior to a decedent's death, the amount of any gift tax paid on the transfer is not brought back into the computation of the gross estate. In the case of a sizable gift, avoidance of the "gross up rule" can result in meaningful tax savings. ("Gross up rule" means that all gift tax payable on taxable gifts made within 3 years of death are included in calculating the value of the gross estate even if the gift itself is not added back.) For example, if an individual

Figure B.18

ESTATE TAX OR GST TAX ADVANTAGE OF THE GIFT TAX ANNUAL EXCLUSION	
INPUT: DONOR'S AGE	40
INPUT: DONEES' ANNUAL AFTER-TAX RETURN ON GIFTS	0.060
INPUT: AMOUNT OF UNUSED ANNUAL EXCLUSION	$20,000
INPUT: NUMBER OF DONEES	X 5
	$100,000
DONOR'S LIFE EXPECTANCY (YEARS)	X 42.5
TOTAL AMOUNT OF GIFTS	$4,250,000
INPUT: DONOR'S PROJECTED ESTATE TAX OR GST TAX BRACKET	X 0.55
POTENTIAL ESTATE TAX OR GST TAX SAVINGS	$2,337,500
PROJECTED VALUE OF GIFTS AT LIFE EXPECTANCY	$18,164,489
POTENTIAL ESTATE TAX OR GST TAX SAVINGS IF ANNUAL GIFTS INVESTED BY DONEES AT COMPOUND INTEREST	$9,990,469

makes a $1 million taxable gift, the $345,000 gift tax payable on that transfer will not be brought back into the estate tax computation if the gift was made more than 3 years before the donor's death.

Third, when a gift is made more than 3 years prior to the donor's death, any appreciation accruing between the time of the gift and the date of the donor's death escapes estate taxation. This may result in a considerable estate tax (as well as probate and inheritance tax) saving. If a father gives his daughter stock worth $100,000 and it grows to $600,000 by the date of the father's death 5 years later, only the $100,000 value of the stock at the time of the gift enters into the estate tax computation.

Furthermore, the $500,000 of appreciation does not enter into the computation of an "adjusted taxable gift" and thus does not push up the decedent's marginal estate tax bracket. An excellent example of both advantages is the gift of life insurance to an adult beneficiary or to an irrevocable trust for adult or minor beneficiaries more than 3 years prior to the insured's death.

A $1,000,000 death benefit could be removed from a donor's estate at the cost of only the gift tax on the value of the policy at the time of the transfer (in the case of a whole life policy, usually roughly equivalent to the policy cash value plus unearned premiums at the date of the gift). If the insured lives for more than 3 years after the transfer and the premiums are present interest gifts of $10,000 a year or less, there would be no estate tax inclusion and none of the "appreciation" (the difference between the death benefit payable and the adjusted taxable gift if any at the time the policy was transferred) would be in the insured's estate.

Fourth, even after TRA '86 there are often strong income tax incentives for making an inter vivos gift. This advantage derives from moving taxable income from a high-bracket donor to a lower-bracket age 14 or over donee. For example, shifting $10,000 of annual income—through the transfer of income-producing securities, real estate, or other property—results in an immediate and annually recurring $2,100 savings if the property is given by a 40 percent bracket parent to a child in a 20 percent state and federal combined income tax bracket. The year-in year-out income tax savings may far exceed the estate tax savings, as Figure B.19 illustrates.

Fifth, gifts of the proper type of assets more than 3 years prior to death may enable a decedent's estate to meet the mathematical tests for a Section 303 stock redemption, a Section 6166 installment payout of taxes, and the 2032A special-use valuation of farms and certain other business real property.

Sixth, no gift taxes have to be paid until the transferor makes *taxable* gifts in excess of the unified credit in the year of the gift. The "exemption equivalent for 1982 was $225,000. In 1983 it was $275,000. In 1984 it was $325,000. It increased to $400,000 in 1985 and to $500,000 in 1986. In 1987 and later years it became $600,000. Only taxable gifts in excess of a donor's unused exemption equivalent will cause a loss of income and/or capital because of gift taxes paid.

(3)
TECHNICAL DEFINITION OF A GIFT

Elements of a Gift

Under common law, a gift is defined simply as a voluntary transfer without any consideration. But for tax law purposes, neither the Code nor the Regulations specifically define

Figure B.19

POST TRA '86 INCOME SHIFTING — CHILD 14 OR OVER			
INPUT: AMOUNT OF INVESTMENT			$100,000
INPUT: RATE OF RETURN ON INVESTMENT			0.100
INPUT: YEARS INVESTMENT LASTS			4
INPUT: PARENT'S COMBINED (FEDERAL AND STATE) TAX BRACKET			0.40
INPUT: CHILD'S COMBINED (FEDERAL AND STATE) TAX BRACKET			0.20
INPUT: TRUST'S COMBINED (FEDERAL AND STATE) TAX BRACKET			0.15
	PARENT	CHILD	TRUST
INTEREST INCOME	$10,000	$10,000	$10,000
TAX	$4,000	$1,900	$1,485
AFTER-TAX INCOME	$6,000	$8,100	$8,515
ANNUAL ADVANTAGE		$2,100	$2,515
TOTAL SAVINGS OVER 4 YEARS		$10,721	$12,839
TOTAL SAVINGS OVER 9 YEARS		$31,369	$40,074
TOTAL SAVINGS OVER 14 YEARS		$64,622	$79,894

Tools and Techniques

what is meant by the term "gift." However, the regulations dealing with the valuation of gifts provide that

> Value of property transferred
>
> minus
>
> Consideration received
>
> equals
>
> Gift

in cases where property is transferred for less than adequate and full consideration in money or money's worth.

Note that this definition focuses on whether the property was transferred for adequate and full consideration in money or the equivalent of money, rather than turning on whether the transferor intended to make a gift. This is because Congress did not want to force the IRS to have to prove something as intangible and subjective as the state of mind of the transferor. This does not negate the importance of donative intent, but, instead of probing the transferor's actual state of mind, an examination is made of the objective facts of the transfer and the circumstances in which it was made.

Certain factors are examined by courts to determine if there was an "intent" to make a gift:

(1) Was the donor competent to make a gift?

(2) Was the donee capable of accepting the gift?

(3) Was there a clear and unmistakable intention on the part of the donor to absolutely, irrevocably, and currently divest himself of dominion and control over the gift property?

Assuming that these three objective criteria are met, three other elements must be present. There must be

(1) an irrevocable transfer of the present legal title to the donee so that the donor no longer had dominion and control over the property in question;

(2) a delivery to the donee of the subject matter of the gift (or the most effective way to command dominion and control of the gift); and

(3) acceptance of the gift by the donee.

Although all these requirements must be met before a gift is subject to tax, the essence of these tests can be distilled into the following factors (state law is examined to determine the presence or absence of these elements):

(1) There must be an "intention" by the donor to make a gift.

(2) The donor must deliver the subject matter of the gift.

(3) The donee must accept the gift.

Adequate and Full Consideration in Money or Money's Worth Defined

Sufficiency of Consideration Test

Since the measure of a gift is the difference between the value of the property transferred and the consideration received by the transfer, a $100,000 building that is transferred from a mother to her daughter for $100,000 in cash clearly does not constitute a gift. However, the mere fact that consideration has been given does not pull a transaction out of the gift tax orbit; to be exempt from the tax the consideration received by the transferor must be equal in value to the property transferred. This is known as the "sufficiency of consideration test." If the daughter in the example above had paid $60,000, the excess value of the building, $40,000, would not be removed from the scope of the gift tax. To escape the gift tax, there must be "adequate and full consideration" equal in value to the property transferred.

Effect of Moral, Past, or Nonbeneficial Consideration

Consideration is not "in money or money's worth" when the consideration is moral consideration, past consideration, or consideration in the form of a detriment to the transferee that does not benefit the transferor. The classic example is the case where a man transferred $100,000 to a widow when she promised to marry him. (Upon remarriage she would forfeit a $100,000 interest in a trust established for her by her deceased husband; the $100,000 from her fiance was to compensate her for the loss.) The Supreme Court held that the widow's promise to marry her fiance was not sufficient consideration because it was incapable of being valued in money or money's worth. Nor was her forfeiture of $100,000 in the trust sufficient consideration, since—although the widow did in fact give up something of value—the benefit of that value did not go to the transferor, her fiance.

Consideration in Marital Rights and Support Rights Situations

Two issues often arise in connection with the consideration question: (1) Does the relinquishment of marital rights constitute consideration in money or money's worth? (2) Does the relinquishment of support rights constitute consideration in money or money's worth?

The Code is specific in the case of certain property settlements. It provides that transfers of property or property interests made under the terms of a written agreement between spouses in settlement of marital or property rights are deemed to be for an adequate and full consideration. Such transfers are therefore exempt from the gift tax—whether or not the agreement is supported by a divorce decree—if the spouses enter into a final decree of divorce within 2 years after entering the agreement. So, for example, if a husband agrees to give his wife $10,000 as a lump-sum settlement on divorce in exchange for her release of all marital rights she may have in his estate, the $10,000 transfer is not subject to the gift tax if the stated requirements above are met. But even in a case where the 2-year requirement was not met, a taxpayer has successfully argued that the transfer was not made voluntarily and was therefore not a gift.

A spouse's relinquishment of the right to support constitutes consideration that can be measured in money or money's worth. Likewise, a transfer in satisfaction of the transferor's minor children's right to support is made for money's worth. (But most transfers to (or for the benefit of) adult children are generally treated as gifts unless—for some reason—state law requires the transferor to support that child.)

Transfers Pursuant to Compromises or Court Orders

Consideration is an important factor where a transfer is made pursuant to compromises of bona fide disputes or court orders. Such transfers are not considered taxable gifts because they are deemed to be made for adequate and full consideration. For example, if a mother and daughter are in litigation and the daughter is claiming a large sum of money, a compromise payment by the mother to the daughter is not a gift. However, in an intrafamily situation in which the court is not convinced that a bona fide arm's-length adversary proceeding was present, the gift tax will be imposed. For example, in a case where a widow "settled" with a son who threatened to "break" his father's will, the gift tax was levied.

Likewise, the gift tax can be applied even in the case of a transfer made pursuant to (or approved by) a court decree if there is not an adversary proceeding. For instance, if an incompetent's property was transferred to his mother, the transfer would be a gift even though it was approved by court decree (assuming the incompetent had no legal duty to care for the parent).

Types of Gifts

Direct Gifts

Cash or tangible personal property is the subject of most transfers that can be reached by the gift tax law. Generally, delivery of the property itself effectuates the gift. In the case of corporate stock, a gift occurs when endorsed certificates are delivered to the donee or his agent or the change in ownership is delivered to the corporation or its transfer agent. Real property is typically given by the delivery of an executed deed.

If a person purchases a U.S. savings bond but has the bond registered in someone else's name and delivers the bond to that person, a gift has been made. If the bonds are titled jointly between the purchaser and another, no gift occurs until the other person has cashed in the bond or has the bond reissued in his name only. See Section 6, "Requirements for a Completed Gift."

Income that will be earned in the future can constitute a gift presently subject to tax. For example, an author can give his right to future royalties to his daughter. Such a gift is valued according to its present value; i.e., the gift is not considered to be a series of year-by-year gifts valued as the income is paid, but rather a single gift valued on the date the right to future income is assigned. Current valuation will be made even if, for some reason, the payments are reduced substantially or even if they cease. No adjustment is required—or allowed—if the actual income paid to the donee is more or less than the valuation.

Forgiving a debt constitutes a gift in nonbusiness situations. For example, if a father lends his son $100,000 and later cancels the note, the forgiveness constitutes a $100,000 gift. However, if the father lends the son $100,000 and the initial agreement is that no interest be charged and that the loan is repayable immediately upon the father's demand, no gift is made.

Some forgiveness of indebtedness, however, constitutes income to the benefited party. If a creditor tore up a debtor's note in return for services rendered by the debtor, the result would be the same as if the creditor compensated the debtor for the services rendered and then the debtor used the cash to satisfy the debt. The debtor realizes income and does not receive a gift.

Payments in excess of one's obligations can be gifts. Clearly a person does not make a gift when he pays his bills. Therefore when a person pays bills or purchases food or clothing for his wife or minor children, he is not making gifts. Courts have allowed considerable latitude in this area. But if a father gives his minor daughter a $50,000 ring, the IRS may claim the transfer goes beyond his obligation of support. Payments made in behalf of adult children are often considered gifts. For example, if a father pays his adult son's medical and hospital bills, living expenses, and mortgage payments, or gives an adult child a monthly allowance, the transfer is a gift subject to tax.

In another situation, the taxpayer, pursuant to an agreement incorporated in a divorce decree, created two trusts for the support of his minor children. He put a substantial amount of money in the trusts, which provided that after the children reached 21 they were to receive the corpus. The court measured the economic value of the father's support obligation and held that the excess of the trust corpus over that value was a taxable gift. Only the portion of the transfer required to support the children during their minority was not subject to the gift tax.

Indirect Gifts

Indirect gifts, such as the payment of someone else's expenses, are subject to the gift tax. For instance, if a person makes payments on an adult son's car or pays premiums on a life insurance policy his wife owns on his life, such payments are gifts.

The shifting of property rights alone can trigger gift tax consequences. In one case an employee gave up his vested rights to employer contributions in a profit-sharing plan. He was deemed to have made a gift to the remaining participants in the plan. Similarly, an employee who has a vested right to an annuity is making a gift if he chooses to take—irrevocably—a lesser annuity coupled with an agreement that payments will be continued to his designated beneficiary. No gift occurs until the time the employee's selection of the survivor annuity becomes irrevocable.

Tools and Techniques

Third-party transfers may be the medium for a taxable gift. For example, if a father gives his son $100,000 in consideration of his son's promise to provide a lifetime income to the father's sister, the father has made an indirect gift to his sister. Furthermore, if the cost of providing a lifetime annuity for the sister is less than $100,000, the father also has made a gift to his son.

The creation of a family partnership may involve an indirect gift. The mere creation or existence of a family partnership (which is often useful in shifting and spreading income among family members and in reducing estate taxes) does not, per se, mean a gift has been made. But if the value of the services of some family member partners is nil or minimal and earnings are primarily due to assets other than those contributed by the partners in question, the creation of the partnership (or the contribution by another partner of assets) may constitute a gift.

At the other extreme, in cases where new partners are to contribute valuable services in exchange for their share of the partnership's earnings and where the business does not contain a significant amount of capital assets, the formation of a family partnership does not constitute a gift.

Transfers by and to corporations are often forms of indirect gifts. Technically, the gift tax is not imposed upon corporations. But transfers by or to a corporation are often considered to be made by or to corporate stockholders. The regulations state that if a corporation makes a transfer to an individual for inadequate consideration, the difference between the value of the money or other property transferred and the consideration paid is a gift to the transferee from the corporation's stockholders. For example, a gratuitous transfer of property by a family-owned corporation to the father of the shareholders of a corporation could be treated as a gift from the children to their father.

Generally, a transfer to a corporation for inadequate consideration is a gift from the transferor to the corporation's other shareholders. For example, a transfer of $120,000 by a father to a corporation owned equally by him and his three children is treated as a gift of $30,000 from the father to each of the three children. (The amount of such a gift is computed after subtracting the percentage of the gift equal to the percentage of the transferor's ownership.)

A double danger lies in corporate gifts. The IRS may argue that (1) in reality the corporation made a distribution taxable as a dividend to its stockholders and (2) that the shareholders in turn made a gift to the recipient of the transfer. Since any distribution from a corporation to a shareholder generally constitutes a dividend to the extent of corporate earnings and profits, the IRS could claim that a transfer was first a constructive dividend to the shareholders and then a constructive gift by them to the donee. For example, if a family-owned corporation sold property with a fair market value of $450,000 for $350,000 to the son of its shareholders,

the transaction could be considered a $100,000 constructive dividend to the shareholder-parents, followed by a $100,000 constructive gift by them to their son.

Life insurance—or life insurance premiums—can be the subject of an indirect gift in three types of situations: (1) the purchase of a policy for another person's benefit, (2) the assignment of an existing policy, and (3) payment of premiums. (The first two of these three situations are discussed directly below. Premium payments are discussed in Section 7.)

If an insured purchases a policy on his life and

(1) names a beneficiary(ies) other than his estate, and
(2) does not retain the right to regain the policy or the proceeds or revest the economic benefits of the policy (i.e., retains no reversionary interest in himself or his estate); and
(3) does not retain the power to change the beneficiaries or their proportionate interests (i.e., makes the beneficiary designation irrevocable)

he has made a gift measurable by the cost of the policy. All three of these requirements must be met, however, before the insured will be deemed to have made a taxable gift.

If an insured makes an absolute assignment of a policy or in some other way relinquishes all his rights and powers in a previously issued policy, a gift is made. It is measurable by the replacement cost (in the case of a whole life policy equal to the interpolated terminal reserve plus unearned premium at the date of the gift).

This can lead to an insidious tax trap. Assume a wife owns a policy on the life of her husband. She names her children as revocable beneficiaries. At the death of the husband, the IRS could argue that the wife has made a constructive gift to the children. In this example the gift is equal to the entire amount of the death proceeds. It is as if the wife received the proceeds to which she was entitled and then gave that money to her children.

An extension of this reasoning, which was actually (and successfully) applied by the IRS, is a case where the owner of policies on the life of her husband placed the policies in trust for the benefit of her children. Because she reserved the right to revoke the trust at anytime before her husband died, she had not made a completed gift—until his death. It was not until his death that she relinquished all her powers over the policy. When the husband died the trust became irrevocable, and therefore the gift became complete. The value of the gift was the full value of the death proceeds rather than the replacement value of the policy when it was placed in trust.

Deemed Gifts

In order to expand the scope of estate tax Code section 2036(c) (explained at page 477), the gift tax law was amended by TAMRA '88 to create a new category of gift, the "deemed gift."

Under the deemed gift rules, the original transferor of a transfer subject to Code section 2036(c) will be treated as making a gift to the original transferee if either (a) the original transferor transfers his retained (income) interest or (b) the original transferee transfers the transferred (growth) interest to a person other than the original transferor or a member of the original transferor's family.

The amount of the deemed gift is the amount that would have been includible in the original transferor's estate under 2036(c) had he died at the date of the deemed gift. But once the deemed gift has been made (and therefore becomes taxable), section 2036(c) no longer will apply. In other words, nothing will be included in the original transferor's estate to the extent of the deemed gift. The amount of the deemed gift is reduced by (1) any prior deemed gifts of the same property, (2) any taxable gifts made with respect to the original transfer, and (3) any consideration paid by the original transferor in return for a retransfer of the growth property.

For example, assume a father owns 100 percent of both the common and the preferred stock of a corporation. The father gives his son the common stock but keeps the preferred stock. He later gives the preferred stock to his nephew (or the son gives his common stock to his cousin). The father will be treated for gift tax purposes as if he had made a gift of common stock. The value of the gift is the fair market value of the common stock at the time of the later transfer—less the fair market value of the common stock when it was originally transferred to the son.

(4)
GRATUITOUS TRANSFERS THAT ARE NOT GIFTS

A number of common situations do not attract the gift tax because they do not involve gifts in the tax sense. These situations fall into three basic categories: (A) where property or an interest in property has not been transferred, (B) certain transfers in the ordinary course of business, and (C) sham gifts.

The Requirement That Property or an Interest in Property Be Transferred

(1) Gratuitous Services Rendered

The gift tax is imposed only on the transfer of "property" or "an interest in property." Although the term "property" is given the broadest possible meaning, it does not include services that are rendered gratuitously. Regardless of how valuable the services one person renders for the benefit of another person, those services do not constitute the transfer of property rights and do not, therefore, fall within the scope of the gift tax.

Difficult questions often arise in this area. For example, if an executor performs the multiplicity of services required in the course of the administration of a large and complex estate, the services are clearly of economic benefit to the estate's beneficiaries. Yet since services are just that, they do not constitute a transfer of property rights. If the executor formally waives the fee (within 6 months of appointment as executor) or fails to claim the fees or commissions by the time of filing and indicates through action (or inaction) that he intends to serve without charge, no property has been transferred.

Conversely, once fees are taken (or if the fees are deducted on an estate, inheritance, or income tax return), the executor has received taxable income. If he then chooses not to (or neglects to) actually receive that money and it goes to the estate's beneficiaries, he is making an indirect (and possibly taxable) gift to those individuals.

(2) Interest-Free Loans

Does the right to use property (such as money) at no charge constitute a gift of property? Yes, the Code treats interest-free and below market rate loans as taxable gifts. It imposes a gift tax on the value of the right to use the borrowed money, the so-called "foregone interest" (see Chapter 16), generally the going rate of interest the money could earn in the given situation. (By this reasoning, giving someone the use of real estate or other property—such as a vacation home or car—at little or no rent would seem to be a gift, but the IRS has been focusing on property interest transfers rather than permitted-use cases.)

(3) Disclaimers (Renunciations)

Generally, a potential donee is deemed to have accepted a valuable gift unless he expressly refuses it. But in some cases an intended donee may decide (for whatever reason) that he does not want or does not need the gift. If he disclaims the right to the gift (refuses to take it), it will usually go to someone else as the result of that renunciation.

By disclaiming, the intended transferee is in effect making a transfer to the new recipient subject to the gift tax—unless the disclaimer meets certain rules.

A disclaimer that meets those rules is called a "qualified disclaimer" and is treated for gift tax purposes as if the property interest went directly from the original transferor to the person who receives it because of the disclaimer. In other words, the disclaimant is treated as if he made no transfer of property or an interest in property to the person to whom the interest passes because of the disclaimer. This makes the qualified disclaimer an important estate-planning tool.

There are a number of requirements for a qualified disclaimer of gifted property:
(1) The refusal must be in writing.
(2) The writing must be received by the transferor, his legal representative, or the holder of the legal title to the property no later than 9 months after the later of (a) the date on which the transfer creating the in-

Tools and Techniques

terest is made (date of death) or (b) the date the person disclaiming is 21.

(3) The person disclaiming must not have accepted the interest or any of its benefits.

(4) Because of the refusal, someone other than the person disclaiming receives the property interest. The person making the disclaimer cannot in any way influence who is to be the recipient of the disclaimer.

(4) Promise to Make a Gift

Although income that will be earned in the future can be the subject of a gift, the promise to make a gift in the future is not taxable—even if the promise is enforceable. This is because a mere promise to make a transfer in the future is not itself a transfer. The IRS agrees—as long as the gift cannot be valued. But if the promise is enforceable under state law, the IRS will attempt to subject it to the gift tax when it becomes capable of valuation.

Transfers in the Ordinary Course of Business

(1) Compensation for Personal Services

Situations often arise in business settings that purport to be gifts from corporate employers to individuals. The IRS often claims that such transfers are, in fact, compensation for personal services rather than gifts. The IRS argues that the property transfers constitute income to the transferee rather than a gift by the transferor. In these cases the focus changes to the effect on the transferee: Has the transferee received taxable income or has he received a tax-free gift?

A payment may be taken out of the normal gift tax rules (and thus be considered taxable income to the recipient) by the Regulations, which state that "the gift tax is *not* applicable to...ordinary business transactions." An ordinary business transaction, defined as a sale, exchange, or other transfer of property (a transaction which is bona fide, at arm's length, and free from donative intent) made in the ordinary course of business, will be considered as if made for an adequate and full consideration in money or money's worth.

A situation will be considered an ordinary business transaction and not be classified as a tax-free gift to the recipient if it is "free from donative intent." This means that donative intent becomes quite important. The taxpayer-recipient, of course, would like to have the transaction considered an income tax-free gift. The IRS would reap larger revenues if the transfer were considered compensation and therefore were taxable income.

When will a payment will be considered a tax-free gift (to the recipient—the donor must still pay any gift taxes) rather than taxable income? A gift is deemed to have been made if the donor's dominant reason for making the transfer was detached and disinterested generosity (for example where an employer makes flood relief payments to his employees because of a feeling of affection, charity, or similar impulses)

rather than consideration for past, present, or future services of the recipient employees.

A transfer is not a gift if the primary impetus for the payment is (a) the constraining force of any legal or moral duty or (b) anticipated benefit of an economic nature.

Among the factors typically studied in examining the donor's intent are

(1) the length and value of the employee's services

(2) the manner in which the employer determined the amount of the reputed gift

(3) the way the employer treated the payments in corporate books and on tax returns, i.e., was the payment deducted as a business expense? (The corporation's characterization of payment is often persuasive where the corporation makes a payment or series of payments to the widow of a deceased employee. The employer generally prefers to have such payments taxed as compensation to the employee's survivors so that the corporation can deduct payments as compensation for past services of the employee.)

In one case a business friend gave the taxpayer a car after the taxpayer had furnished him with the names of potential customers. The car was not a gift but was intended as payment for past services as well as an inducement for the taxpayer to supply additional names in the future. In another case, however, the employer had made a payment of $20,000 to a retiring executive when he resigned. After examining the employer's esteem and kindliness, and the appreciation of the retiring officer, the court stated that the transfer was a non(income) taxable gift. Another court, in a similar case, came to the same conclusion when it found payments were made "from generosity or charity rather than from the incentive of anticipated economic benefit."

This type of issue—gift or compensation—is settled on a case-by-case basis after an analysis of the circumstances evidencing motive or intent. Usually the intrafamily transfer will be considered a gift even if the recipient rendered past services. Transfers to persons outside the family will usually be considered compensation.

(2) Bad Bargains

A bad bargain is another "ordinary course of business" situation; a sale, exchange, or other property transfer made in the ordinary course of business is treated as if it were made in return for adequate and full consideration in money or money's worth. This assumes the transaction is (a) bona fide, (b) at arm's length, and (c) not donative in intent.

There are a number of court-decided examples of "bad bargains" that have not resulted in gift tax treatment. In one case, certain senior executive shareholders sold stock to junior executives at less than fair market value pursuant to a plan arranged to give the younger executives a larger stake in business profits. The court noted that the transfers were for less than adequate consideration but stated that "the pertinent inquiry for gift tax purposes is whether the transaction is a genuine business transaction, as distinguished, for example, from the marital or family type of transaction." Bad bargains, sales for less than adequate money's worth, are made every day in the business world for one reason or another; but no one would think for a minute that any gift is involved, even in the broadest sense of the term "gift."

Another example of a "no-gift" situation would be where a group of businessmen convey real estate to an unrelated business corporation with the expectation of doing business with that corporation sometime in the future.

But the "ordinary course of business" exception has its limits; no protection from the gift tax law would be afforded where the transferor's motive was to pass on the family fortune to the following generation. In one case a father transferred property to his children at a price below the fair market value. In return he received noninterest-bearing notes rather than cash, and in the children's behalf he continued to make certain payments with respect to the property. The court found these actions showed that in reality he was not dealing with his children at arm's length. It is possible that the same result could occur if the father employed the son at a wage of $50,000 a year but the son rendered services worth only $20,000 a year. The IRS could claim that the $30,000 difference constituted a gift.

Sham Gifts

It is often advantageous—for income or estate tax purposes—to characterize a transaction as a gift. The taxpayer's goal is to shift the burden of income taxes from a high- to a relatively lower-bracket age 14 or older relative. But if the transfer has no real economic significance other than the hoped-for tax savings, it will be disregarded for tax purposes; i.e., if the transaction does not have meaning—apart from its tax sense—it will not be considered a gift by the IRS or by the courts and will therefore not shift the incidence of taxation. For example, a well-known golfer contracted with a motion picture company to make a series of pictures depicting his form and golf style. In return the golfer was to receive a lump sum of $120,000 plus a 50 percent royalty on the earnings of the picture. But before any pictures were made he sold his father the right to his services for $1. The father, in turn, transferred the rights to the contract to a trust for his son's three children. The court held that the entire series of transactions had no tax effect and that the income was completely taxable to the golfer.

Assignments of income

Assignment of income questions are among the most common and also confusing in the tax law because they often involve inconsistent property, gift, and income tax results. For example, a person could agree to give his son one-half of every dollar he earned in the following year. The agreement

might be effective for property law purposes, and the son could have an enforceable legal right to half his father's income. Gift tax law might also recognize the transfer of a property right, and the present value of a father's future income could be subject to the gift tax. Yet for income tax purposes the father would remain liable for taxes on the entire earnings.

A general agent for a life insurance company assigned renewal commissions to his wife. The wife had a property law right to the commissions. The present worth of the renewals the wife would receive was treated as a gift. Yet, the general agent was subject to income tax on the commissions as they were paid. In a similar case a doctor transferred the right to accounts receivable from his practice to a trust for his daughter. Again, the court held that as the trustee received payments from the doctor's patients, those sums were taxable to the doctor even though he had made an irrevocable and taxable gift to the trust.

Gifts of income from property meet a similar fate. For example, if a person assigns the right to next year's rent from a building to her daughter or next year's dividends from specified stock to her grandson, the transfers will be effective for property law purposes and will generate gift taxes. But the income will be taxable to the donor for income tax purposes.

Gifts of property, however, produce a more satisfactory result to the donors; if the tree (property) is given away, the fruit (income) it bears will be taxable to the tree's new owner. Thus if the donor in the examples above had given the building and the stock, gifts equal to the value of those properties would be made; and the income produced by those assets would be taxed to her daughter and grandson respectively. Likewise, if stock that cost the donor $1,000 is transferred to a donee at a time when it is worth $2,500 and is later sold by the donee for $3,500, the donee takes the donor's cost ($1,000) as his basis, and is taxed on the gain ($2,500).

(5)
EXEMPT GIFTS

A few types of gratuitous transfers are statutorily exempted from the gift tax. A qualified disclaimer, described above, is a good example. Certain transfers of property between spouses in divorce and separation situations are further examples.

Tuition paid to an educational institution for the education or training of an individual is exempt from the gift tax regardless of the amount paid or the relationship of the parties; no family ties must exist for this unlimited exclusion to apply. This means parents, grandparents, or even friends can pay private school or college tuition for an individual without fear of incurring a gift tax.

Still another exempt transfer is the payment of medical care. A donor, any donor, can pay for the medical care of a donee without making a gift. This allows children or other

Tools and Techniques

relatives—or friends—to pay the medical expenses of needy individuals (or anyone else) without worrying about incurring a gift tax.

(6)
REQUIREMENTS FOR A COMPLETED GIFT

A completed transfer is necessary before the gift tax can be applied. The phrase "completed transfer" implies that the subject of the gift has been put beyond the donor's recall, i.e., that he has irrevocably parted with dominion and control over the gift. There would be no completed gift if the donor had the power to change the disposition of the gift and thus alter the identity of the donee(s) or amount of the gift. More technically stated, if the donor can (alone or in conjunction with a party who does not have a substantial amount to lose by the revocation) revoke the gift, it is not complete.

Parting with dominion and control is a good test of completeness, but in a number of cases it is difficult to ascertain just when that event occurs. Some of the more common problem areas are (a) incomplete delivery situations, (b) cancellation of notes, and (c) incomplete transfers to trusts.

When Delivery is Complete

Incomplete delivery situations involve transfers where certain technical details have been omitted or a stage in the process has been left uncompleted. For example, no gift is made at the moment the donor gives the donee a personal check or note; the transfer of a personal check is not complete and taxable until it is paid (or certified or accepted) by the drawee or it is negotiated for value to a third person. For instance, if a check is mailed in December, received in late December, but not cashed until January of the following year, no gift is made until that later year. This is because typically the maker of a check is under no legal obligation to honor the check until it is cashed (presented for payment or negotiated to a third person for value). Likewise, a gift of a negotiable note is not complete until it is paid.

An individual on his deathbed will sometimes make a gift *causa mortis* (in anticipation of his imminent death) and then quite unexpectedly recover. Assuming that the facts indicate (1) the transfer was made in anticipation of death from a specific illness and that (2) the gift was contingent on the occurrence of the donor's death, neither the original conveyance nor the return of the property to the donor is subject to the gift tax if the transferor recovers and the transferee returns the property. A gift *causa mortis* is therefore incomplete as long as the donor is alive but becomes complete at the donor's death.

A gift of stock is completed on the date the stock was transferred or the date endorsed certificates are delivered to the donee (or his agent) or to the corporation (or its tranfer agent).

Transfer of U.S. government bonds is governed by federal rather than state law. Even if state law requirements for a valid

gift are met, for tax purposes no completed gift has been made until the registration is changed in accordance with federal regulations. For example, if a grandmother purchases a U.S. savings bond that is registered as payable to her and to her two children as co-owners, no gift is made to the grandchildren until one of them surrenders the bond for cash.

The creation of a joint bank account (checking or savings) constitutes a common example of an incomplete transfer. Typically, the person making a deposit can withdraw all of the funds or any portion of them. Therefore the donor has retained a power to revoke the gift and it is not complete. When the donee makes a withdrawal of funds from the account (and thereby eliminates the donor's dominion and control), a gift of the funds occurs.

A similar situation occurs in the case of a joint brokerage account; the creation and contribution to a joint brokerage account held in "street name" is not a gift until the joint owner makes a withdrawal for his personal benefit. At that time the donee acquires indefeasible rights and the donor parts irrevocably with the funds. Conversely, if a person calls her broker and says, "Buy 100 shares of Texas Oil and Gas and title them in joint names—mine and my husband's—with rights of survivorship," the purchase constitutes a gift to her husband. He has acquired rights that he did not have before to a portion of the stock. (No gift tax would be due in this case due to the unlimited gift tax marital deduction described below.)

Totten trusts (bank savings accounts where the donor makes a deposit for the donee—"Joanne Q. Donor in trust for James P. Donee"—and retains possession of the savings book) are typically revocable transfers. Here again, because the donor can recover the entire amount deposited, no gift occurs until the donee makes a withdrawal of funds.

Some property cannot conveniently be delivered to the intended donee; farm property is a good example. Where it would be difficult or impossible to make physical delivery of the gift, a gift will usually be considered completed where the delivery is as complete as possible. In one case a father owned cattle he wished to give his minor children. The court held that the gift was complete when he branded the livestock with each child's initials even though he kept the cattle with others he owned. The court held that the father was acting as the natural guardian of the children and had done everything necessary to make a completed gift.

Real estate is transferred by executing a deed in favor of the donee. But if the donor retains the deed, does not record it, makes no attempt to inform the donee of the transfer, and continues to treat the property as his own, no transfer occurs.

Cancellation of Notes

In many cases a transfer of property will be made and then the transferor will take back installment notes from the donee. The transaction will not be characterized as a sale until the transferee pays off the notes. But if the transferor forgives the notes, the forgiveness would be a gift.

Cancellation of notes is a frequently used technique for two reasons. First, it provides a simple means of giving gifts to a number of donees of property which is not readily divisible. Second, by forgiving the notes over a period of years, the donor could maximize the use of the $10,000 annual exclusion and unified credit discussed below in Section 8. A good example is a situation where the donor deeds real estate to her sons and takes back notes payable serially on an annual basis. Each son is required to pay his mother $10,000 per year. But when the notes become due, the donor marks the note "cancelled by gift." The gift would occur in the year each note was cancelled—as long as there is no preestablished and predetermined plan for the donor to forgive notes on a systematic basis in future years.

Note that although the annual exclusion would eliminate the gift tax consequences, in this example there is an income tax liability since the donor is actually selling the real estate to her sons. The difference between the donor's basis (cost plus or minus appropriate adjustments) and the amount she'll realize on the sale is taxable (under the installment sales rules since the notes are payable over more than one tax year).

Incomplete Gifts in Trust

Donors will sometimes transfer property to a trust but retain the right to revoke the transfer. When property is transferred to such a revocable trust, that transfer is not a completed gift. Only when the donor relinquishes all his retained control over the transferred property (i.e., when the trust becomes irrevocable) is a completed gift made.

Tax liability is measured by the value at the moment the gift becomes complete rather than at the time of the transfer. This can have harsh tax consequences. For example, if the donor retains the power to alter the interests of the trust beneficiaries, even if he cannot exercise any powers for his own benefit, the transfer is not complete.

Assume, for instance, that the donor transfers stock to a trust for his two children and three grandchildren. The income of the trust is payable to the donor's children for as long as they live. Then the remainder is payable to his grandchildren or their estates. If the donor retains the power to vary the amount of income his children will receive or reach into corpus to enhance their security, the gift is incomplete. But the gift will be complete when the donor relinquishes control. If that happens when the stock has substantially increased in value, as is often the case, the gift tax payable by the donor may also substantially increase.

GRITs (Grantor Retained Income Trusts) are based on the fact that gift tax liability is measured by the property's value at the moment the gift becomes complete. By making a gift to an irrevocable nonreversionary trust, but reserving the income for a specified period of years, an individual reduces the value of the gift.

When the property is ultimately transferred, many years after the grantor contributed the property to the trust, it may have appreciated significantly. In essence this "leverages" the annual exclusion and the unified credit, since the date of transfer value is typically much greater than the value of trust assets at the inception of the trust.

(7)
VALUATION OF PROPERTY FOR GIFT TAX PURPOSES

Valuation is the first step in the gift tax computation process. Only after the property is valued can the applicable annual exclusion and various deductions be applied in arriving at the amount of the taxable gift and the ultimate gift tax. (See "Valuation of Assets," this appendix.)

The value of the property on the date the gift becomes complete is the amount of the gift. Value, for gift tax purposes, is defined as "the price at which the property would change hands between a willing buyer and a willing seller, neither being under any compulsion to buy or to sell, and both having reasonable knowledge of relevant facts."

Although the provisions of the gift tax law on valuation parallels the estate tax law in many respects, there is one major difference: property transferred during lifetime is valued for gift tax purposes on the date the gift is made. No alternate valuation is allowed.

There are certain valuation problems unique to the gift tax law. These include problems associated with (1) indebtedness with respect to transferred property, (2) restrictions on the use or disposition of property, (3) transfers of large blocks of stock, (4) valuation of mutual fund shares, and (5) valuation of life insurance and annuity contracts.

Indebtedness with Respect to Transferred Property

Generally, when the subject of a gift is encumbered or otherwise subject to an obligation, only the net value of the gift—the value of the property less the amount of the obligation—is subject to the gift tax. Under this rule, which assumes the donor is *not* personally liable for the debt, the amount of the gift is the donor's equity in the property.

However, if the donor is personally liable for the indebtedness—which is secured by a mortgage on the gift property—a different result occurs. In this case the amount of the gift may be the entire value of the property, unreduced by the debt. The reason for the difference is that where a solvent donor makes a gift subject to a debt and the creditor proceeds against the pledged property, the donee is, in effect, paying the donor's personal debt. In some cases this makes the donee a creditor of the donor. If the donee can then collect from the donor the amount he has paid to the

Tools and Techniques

donor's creditor, the donee has received the entire value of the gift rather than merely the equity.

For example, assume the donor transfers a $100,000 building subject to a $40,000 mortgage on which he is personally liable. If the donor's creditors collect the $40,000 by proceeding against the pledged building and the donee is subrogated to that creditor's rights against the donor-debtor (i.e., the donee now stands in the shoes of the creditor), the donee can collect an additional $40,000 from the donor.

A third possibility is that the donor-debtor is personally liable for the indebtedness secured by a mortgage on the gifted property, but the donee has no right to step into the creditor's shoes and recover the debt from the donor. In this case the amount of the gift is merely the amount of the donor's equity in the property. In the example above, that amount would be $60,000 ($100,000 fair market value minus $40,000 of indebtedness).

Where the donee has no right to proceed against the donor and recover the debt, actual facts must determine the result. If the donor in fact pays off the liability after transferring the mortgaged property to the donee, he is making an additional gift. But if the donee pays off the liability (or if the mortgagee forecloses), the gift was only the donor's equity.

Among the obligations that could be imposed upon a donee is a requirement that the donee pay the gift tax. This is called a "net gift." The donor has primary liability to pay the gift tax, and the donee is only secondarily liable. The donor could—expressly or by implication—require the donee to pay the donor's gift tax liability. If the donee is required to pay the gift tax imposed on the transfer (or if the tax is payable out of the transferred property), the value of the donated property must be reduced by the amount of the gift tax. But the gift tax computation is based on the value of the property transferred. Obviously, the two figures—the net amount transferred and the tax payable on the transfer—are interdependent. Fortunately, there is a Revenue Ruling formula for making the computation.

An example of a net gift and the formula are illustrated in the NumberCruncher printout below:

TRUE TAX ON A NET GIFT

INPUT: YEAR OF GIFT		1988
INPUT: TAXABLE GIFT		$1,000,000
GIFT TAX ON GIFT		$345,800
UNIFIED CREDIT		- $192,800
TENTATIVE TAX		$153,000

TRUE TAX ON NET GIFT EQUALS:

$$\frac{\text{TENTATIVE TAX}}{(1.00 + \text{RATE OF TAX})} \quad \$110,072$$

It is important to note that, for income tax purposes, there are net gift cases which state that the donor must recognize gain where the donee pays the tax or where payment is made from the gifted property. Gain is realized by the donor for income tax purposes to the extent the gift tax paid by the donee exceeds the donor's basis for the property. It is as if the donor sold the property for an amount equal to the gift tax, realized again, and then gave the remaining value of the gift property to the donee.

Restrictions on the Use or Disposition of Property

Value is affected by restrictions placed on the donee's use or ability to dispose of the property received. The general rule is that most restrictive agreements do not fix the value of such property but often have a persuasive effect on price. For example, a donor gives stock to his daughter subject to an agreement between the corporation and its shareholders. Under that agreement, the corporation is entitled to purchase those shares at their book value, $30 per share, upon the retirement or death of the stockholder.

Does the existence of a restrictive agreement fix the value of the shares at book value? After all, in the example, no buyer would pay more than $30 a share while the restriction is operative. But if the stock has "use values" other than sale values (for example, if the stock paid dividends of $10 a year) it may have a fair market value in excess of $30. On one hand, the corporation's option right to purchase the stock at $30 a share limits the fair market value, but on the other hand "use values," such as the right to receive dividends, increase the fair market value.

How much the use values increase the fair market value is largely dependent on how much time is likely to pass before the corporation has an opportunity to exercise its option and on the probability of the corporation's exercising its option at that time.

In the example above, a court would probably state that the existence of a restrictive agreement would not fix the purchase price, since the circumstances requiring purchase (retirement or death) do not exist at the date of the gift. But the existence of the agreement itself is likely to have a depressing effect on the market value of the stock and result in a discounted gift tax value.

Transfers of Large Blocks of Stock

Another principle that applies to some degree to both lifetime and "deathtime" gifts is the so-called blockage rule. The blockage rule is not based on forced sale value. Instead, it attempts to value gifts of large blocks of stock based on the price the property would bring if the stock was liquidated in a reasonable time in some way outside the usual marketing channels. The marketability (and therefore the value) of a massive number of shares of stock may have a lower value than the current pershare market value of the same stock because of the depressive effect if the block is dumped on the market all at once. The utility of blockage evaluation is diminished and may be inapplicable when a large block is divided among a number of donees or when gifts are spread over a number of tax years.

Valuation of Mutual Fund Shares

Mutual fund shares are valued at their net asset value, the price of the fund net of any "load" charge.

Valuation of Life Insurance and Annuity Contracts

When a life insurance policy is the subject of a gift, the value is the policy's replacement value: the cost of similar or comparable policies issued by the same company.

If the policy is transferred immediately (within the first year) after its purchase, the gift is equal in value to the gross premium paid to the insurer.

If the policy is paid up at the time it is assigned (or is a single-premium policy), the amount of the gift is the amount of premium the issuing company would charge for the same type of single-premium policy of equal face amount on the insured's life, based on the insured's age at the transfer date. (Impaired health of the insured is not considered by the Regulations, but it is possible that the IRS would argue that the adverse health of the insured at the time of the gift may affect evaluation.)

If the policy is in a premium-paying stage at the time it is transferred, the value of the gift is generally equal to (a) the interpolated terminal reserve plus (b) unearned premiums on the date of the gift.

Except in the early years of most contracts, the interpolated terminal reserve is roughly equivalent to the policy's cash value. In special conditions—such as where the interpolated terminal reserve does not approximate the policy's true value (for example, if the insured donor was terminally ill and had only 1 or 2 months to live)—the value of a premium-paying policy may be more than the sum of the interpolated terminal reserve plus unearned premiums as of the date of the gift. (Unearned premiums are defined as the proportionate part of the last premium paid that is attributable to the remainder of the period for which the premium was paid.)

Mr. Martin owned an ordinary life policy on his partner's life to fund a cross-purchase agreement. The policy was 9 years and 4 months old at the time of Mr. Martin's death. The gross annual premium was $2,800, and Mr. Martin died four months after the most recent "premium due" date. Assuming no accrued dividends or policy loans, the policy would be valued as follows:

Terminal reserve at end of 10th year	$14,601
Terminal reserve at end of 9th year	12,965
Increase (10th year)	$ 1,636

Portion of year between death of Mr. Martin and last preceding premium due date is 4/12 (1/3) of a year.

1/3 of increase in reserve (1/3 of $1,636)	$ 545
+	
Terminal reserve — end of 9th year	12,965
=	
Interpolated terminal reserve at date of Martin's death	13,510
+	
2/3 of gross premium	1,874
Total value of insurance policy	$15,384

The interpolated reserve method will be allowed as long as the contract is not an unusual contract and this method does not develop an amount that varies greatly from the true value of the contract.

Premiums paid by (or on behalf of) the donor after the transfers are also gifts. Therefore, when an owner of a life insurance policy irrevocably assigns that policy to another person or a trust, each premium he pays subsequent to the transfer is considered a gift to the new policy owner (or the beneficial owner[s] of the trust's assets).

Usually the premium payor and the donor are the same. However, the IRS has stated that if an employee assigns his group life insurance policy to an irrevocable trust he had established for his family, a cash premium paid by the employer is deemed to be a gift of the amount of the premium. The deemed gift is from the employee to the beneficiaries of the trust. But (in a rather poorly considered and not widely accepted ruling) the assignment of the group term coverage itself was held not to be a taxable gift because the coverage had no ascertainable value.

A "split-dollared policy" is often assigned to a trust. If an insured-employee assigns the right to name the beneficiary of the proceeds in excess of the cash surrender value of a life insurance policy under an employer-pay-all plan to an irrevocable trust, a gift is made annually; the yearly tax liability of the employee is the greater of (a) the "P.S. 58" cost of the insurance coverage or (b) the difference between the net premium and the annual increase in cash surrender values.

(8)
COMPUTING THE TAX ON GIFTS

Gift tax rates are applied to a net figure, "taxable gifts." Before the tax on a transfer is computed, certain reductions are allowed. These reductions may include

(1) "gift splitting"

(2) an annual exclusion

Tools and Techniques

(3) a marital deduction

(4) a charitable deduction

Gift Splitting

The tax law permits a married donor—with the consent of the nondonor spouse—to elect to treat a gift to a third party as though each spouse has made half of the gift. The election must be made on the applicable gift tax return of the donor spouse.

Gift splitting is an artificial mechanism: even if one spouse makes the entire gift, the single transfer is treated for tax computation purposes as though each spouse made only one-half of the gift. This means that the rate of tax that each will pay is separately calculated by reference to his own particular prior gifts.

Furthermore, if a nondonor spouse has agreed to treat half of the donor spouse's gift as if made by the nondonor spouse, it will have a direct effect on the future gift tax and estate tax that spouse will eventually have to pay if the gift exceeds the annual exclusion. Even though such spouse did not *actually* make half the gift, it will, nevertheless to the extent it exceeds the $10,000 annual exclusion, become an "adjusted taxable gift" to be added to all other gifts deemed to have been made for purposes of calculating the future gift tax bracket and to be added to the taxable estate at the nondonor spouse's death.

Gift splitting, which applies only to gifts by a married donor to a third party and only with respect to noncommunity property, was introduced into the tax law to equate the tax treatment of common-law taxpayers with that of community-property residents. When one spouse earns a dollar in a community-property state, fifty cents is deemed to be owned by the other spouse automatically and immediately. Therefore, if the couple gave that dollar to their daughter, each spouse would be treated as having given only fifty cents.

Gift splitting places the common-law resident in the same relative position. For example, if a married individual in a common-law state gives his son a gift worth $20,000 and the requisite gift splitting election is made, for purposes of the gift tax computation that individual is considered to have given only $10,000. His spouse is treated as if she gave the other $10,000—even if, in fact, none of the gift was her property.

If the spouses elect to "split" gifts to third parties, all gifts made by either spouse during that reporting period must be split.

The privilege of gift splitting is available only with regard to gifts made while the couple is married. Therefore, gifts the couple makes before they are married may not be split even if they are later married during the same calendar year. Likewise, gifts made after the spouses are legally divorced or one spouse dies may not be split. But gifts made before one spouse dies may be split even if that spouse dies before signing the appropriate consent or election; the deceased spouse's executor can make the appropriate election or consent.

The Annual Exclusion

Purpose of the Exclusion

A *de minimis* rule is one that is instituted primarily to avoid the bother of administrative record keeping. The annual gift tax exclusion is a classic example of such a rule. It was instituted to eliminate the need for a taxpayer to keep an account of or report numerous small gifts. Congress intended that the amount of the annual exclusion be set large enough so that no reporting would be required in the case of wedding gifts or other occasional gifts or relatively small amounts.

Effect of Gift Splitting Coupled with Exclusion

Generally, the annual exclusion allows the donor to make, tax free, up to $10,000 worth of gifts (other than "future-interest gifts" as they are defined below) to any number of persons or parties each year. Since an exclusion of up to $10,000 is allowed per donee per year, the total maximum excludible amount is determined by multiplying the number of persons to whom gifts are made by $10,000. For example, if an unmarried individual makes cash gifts this year of $2,000, $8,000, and $16,000 to his brother, father, and son, respectively, the $2,000 gift would be fully excludible, the entire $8,000 gift to his father would be excludible, and $10,000 of the $16,000 gift to his son would be excludible.

If the same individual is married and his spouse consents to splitting the gift, each spouse is deemed to have made one-half of the gift. This means that both spouses can maximize the use of their annual exclusions. Assuming the nondonor spouse made no gifts, the computation at Figure B.20 shows that none of the $26,000 of gifts would be subject to tax.

Present versus Future Interest

An annual exclusion is allowed only for "present-interest gifts" and is denied to "gifts of future interests." A present interest is one in which the donee's possession or enjoyment begins at the time the gift is made. A future interest refers to any interest or estate in which the donee's possession or enjoyment will not commence until some period of time after the gift is made. More technically, "future interest" is a legal term, and includes reversions, remainders, and other interests or estates, whether vested or contingent, and whether or not supported by a particular interest or estate, which are limited to commence in use, possession, or enjoyment at some future date or time."

An easy way to distinguish between a present interest (which qualifies for the gift tax annual exclusion) and a future interest (which does not qualify for the gift tax exclusion) is to ascertain:

Figure B.20

Donee	Amount of Gift to Donee	Treated as if Donor Gave	Exclusion	Subject to Tax	Treated as if Nondonor Spouse Gave	Exclusion	Subject to Tax
Brother	$ 2,000	$ 1,000	$ 1,000	—	$ 1,000	$ 1,000	—
Father	$ 8,000	$ 4,000	$ 4,000	—	$ 4,000	$ 4,000	—
Son	$16,000	$ 8,000	$ 8,000	—	$ 8,000	$ 8,000	—
Totals	$26,000	$13,000	$13,000	—	$13,000	$13,000	—

At the moment of the gift, did the donee have an immediate, unfettered, and actuarially ascertainable legal right to use, possess, or enjoy the property in question? If the answer is "Yes," the gift is a present interest. If the answer is "No," the gift is a future interest gift.

Clearly, the outright and unrestricted gift of property to a donee (even a minor) that passes legal and equitable title qualifies as a present-interest gift.

A single gift can be split into two parts: one a present interest that qualifies for the annual exclusion and the other a future interest that does not. For example, a widowed donor creates a trust this year and places income-producing property in the trust. The income is payable annually to the donor's son for life. At the son's death, the remainder is payable to the donor's grandson. The gift to the son of the right to receive income annually for life is a present-interest gift since he has unrestricted right to its immediate use, possession, or enjoyment. If the son is 30 years old at the time of the gift and $100,000 is placed into the trust, the present value of that gift would be worth $95,543 ($100,000 times .95543, which is the present value of the stream of income produced by $100,000 of capital and payable annually for the life of a 30-year-old male, according to tables in government regulations — Figure B.3). Of the $95,543, $10,000 would be excludible.

If the donor was married and the appropriate election and consent were filed, each spouse could claim a $10,000 exclusion even though only the donor placed property in the trust. No exclusion is allowed with respect to the ultimate gift of the corpus to the grandson, since his possession or enjoyment may not commence for some time in the future.

Assume the donor and his spouse had provided that their son was to receive income for 10 years and then the principal was to pass to another beneficiary, a grandson. If the donor had placed only $1,000 in the trust, the exclusion for the gift of the income interest would be $614.46 ($1,000 times .614457, the actuarial factor from the government's table representing the present value of $1 payable each year for only 10 years). Gift splitting with a spouse would not increase the amount of the exclusion. Each spouse would be allowed a $307.23 exclusion.

No exclusion would be allowed for the gift of the future interest (remainder) that passes to the grandson at the end of 10 years, even though he has an interest that cannot be forfeited. This is because he does not have the right to immediate possession or enjoyment; any delay (no matter how unlikely or how short) in the absolute and immediate right of use, possession or enjoyment, is fatal to the gift tax exclusion.

Note that if the trustee in either situation above had been given the power or discretion to accumulate the income, rather than distribute it, the donor's son would not have received the unfettered and immediate use of the income, and it would be impossible to ascertain the present value of the income interest. For example, assume the trustee is directed to pay the net income to the son for as long as he lives, but is authorized to withhold payments of income during any period he deems advisable and add such payments to corpus. In this case, even the income interest would be a gift of a future interest. No annual exclusion would be allowed.

Where a trustee is required by the trust agreement to accumulate income for a time (or until the occurrence of a specified event), the income interest is a future interest.

The number and amount (or availability) of exclusions depends on the identity of the donee(s), the type of asset involved, and restrictions, if any, placed on the asset.

Summary of Rules for Ascertaining the Amount and Availability of the Gift Tax Annual Exclusion

These rules regarding the annual exclusion can be summarized as follows:

(1) A gift in trust is a gift to a trust's beneficiaries and not to the trust in determining the number of annual exclusions to which a donor is entitled.

(2) The value of an income interest in a trust qualifies for the exclusion if the trustee is required to distribute trust income at least annually—even if the value of the remainder interest does not qualify.

(3) The gift of an interest that is contingent upon survivorship is a gift of a future interest. (If a gift in trust is made with income going to the grantor's son for life, then income to the grantor's daughter for

Tools and Techniques

life, the gift to the son will qualify but the daughter's interest will not.)

(4) A gift is one of a future interest if enjoyment depends on the exercise of a trustee's discretion. (The nature of the interest must be present as of the date of the gift and is not, for example, determined by what the trustee may subsequently do or not do in the exercise of a discretionary power.)

(5) A gift must have an ascertainable value to qualify for the exclusion. (The exclusion will be denied if the donor or anyone else can divert the income from the beneficiary.)

Identity of Donees

When a gift is made in trust, the beneficiaries of the trust (and not the trust itself) are considered the donees. For instance, if there are three life income beneficiaries, up to three annual exclusions could be obtained. Conversely, if five trusts were established for the same beneficiary, only one exclusion is allowed. (Technically, the actuarial value of each gift in trust to that beneficiary would be totaled. That per donee total is then added to direct gifts the donor made to that beneficiary to ascertain whether and to what extent an annual exclusion remains and is allowable for the present transfer.)

A transfer to a corporation is treated as a gift to its shareholders. Therefore, separate exclusions should be allowed with respect to each shareholder regarded as a donee.

Transfers to two or more persons as joint tenants with right of survivorship, tenants by the entireties, or tenants in common are considered multiple gifts. Each tenant is deemed to receive an amount equal to the actuarial value of his interest in the tenancy. If, for example, one person has a one-half interest in a tenancy in common, a cash gift of $6,000 to the tenancy would be treated as a $3,000 gift to that person. This would be added to other gifts made directly by the same donor to determine how much of the exclusion will be allowed. In all probability, gifts to partnerships should follow the same rules: a gift to a partnership should be treated as if made to each partner in proportion to his partnership interest.

Note that a joint gift, in which neither party can sever his interest without the other's consent, will be considered a future interest gift and not qualify for the annual exclusion. For instance, if Herb gives Diana and Laura joint ownership in a policy on his life, Herb has made a future interest gift to each daughter.

Gifts to Minors

Outright gifts to minors pose no particular qualification problem. The IRS states in a Revenue Ruling that "an unqualified and unrestricted gift to a minor, with or without the appointment of a guardian, is a gift of a present interest." But there are, of course, practical problems involved, especially with larger gifts. Although minors can buy, sell, and deal with some limited types of property, such as U.S. sav-

ings bonds, gifts of other types of property create difficulties. For example, some states do not give minors the legal capacity to purchase their own property, care for it, or sell or transfer it. Some states forbid the registration of securities in a minor's name, and a broker may be reluctant to deal in securities titled in a minor's name. In many states a minor has the legal ability to disaffirm a sale of stock sold at a low price that later rises in value. Furthermore, a buyer receives no assurance of permanent title when a minor signs a real estate deed.

Legal guardianship of the minor is not a viable answer in many situations. Since guardianship laws are rigid, a guardian must generally post bond, and periodic and expensive court accounting is often required. Most importantly, a parent may not want to give a legal minor control over a large amount of cash or other property.

To minimize these and other practical problems involved with most large gifts to minors, such transfers are generally made in trust or under some type of guardianship or custodian arrangement. An incredible amount of litigation developed over whether such gifts qualified for the annual exclusion. Section 2503 of the Internal Revenue Code provides clear and precise methods of qualifying gifts to minors for the exclusion. There are three basic means of qualifying "cared-for gifts" to minors under Section 2503: (1) a Section 2503(b) trust, (2) a Section 2503(c) trust, or (3) the Uniform Gifts to Minors Act (or the Uniform Transfers to Minors Act).

Section 2503(b) Trust. To obtain an annual exclusion for gifts to a trust, an individual can establish a trust which requires that income *must* be distributed at least annually to or for use of the minor beneficiary. The trust agreement would state how income is to be used and would give the trustee no discretion as to its use. The minor would receive possession of the trust principal whenever the trust agreement specifies. A distribution does not have to be made by age 21; corpus may be held for as long as the beneficiary lives—or for any shorter period of time. In fact, the principal can actually bypass the income beneficiary and go directly to the individuals whom the grantor—or even the named beneficiary—has specified. The trust agreement can also control the dispositive scheme if the minor dies before receiving trust corpus. Trust assets do not have to be paid to the minor's estate or appointees.

Mandatory payment of income to (or in behalf of) beneficiaries seems onerous—especially while the beneficiary is a minor. But such income could be deposited in a custodial account and used for the minor's benefit or left to accumulate in a custodial account until the minor reaches majority (at which time the inexpended amount would be turned over to the beneficiary).

Although the entire amount of property placed in a 2503(b) trust would be considered a gift, for exclusion purposes it would be split into two parts: income and principal. The value of the income—measured by multiplying the amount of the gift by a factor that considers both the duration over which the income interest will be paid and the discounted worth of $1 payable over the appropriate number of years—would be eligible for the annual exclusion. The balance of the gift would not qualify for the annual exclusion.

For example, assume a donor places $10,000 into a Section 2503(b) trust that is required to pay his 10-year-old daughter all income until she reaches age 25. The present value of the income the daughter would receive over those 15 years is $7,606.08 ($10,000 × .760608). If the income were payable for her entire life, the present value would jump to almost $9,857.

It is important to note that, according to at least one Revenue Ruling, the annual exclusion would be denied for a 2503(b) trust that permits principal to be invested in nonincome-producing securities, nonincome-producing real estate, or life insurance policies (since they do not produce taxable income).

Section 2503(c) Trust. The Section 2503(b) trust described above has the advantage of not requiring distribution of principal at the minor's reaching age 21, but it does require a current (annual) distribution of income. The Section 2503(c) trust requires the distribution of income and principal when the minor reaches 21. But it does not require the trustee to distribute income currently.

Certain requirements make it possible for a donor to obtain the exclusion by a gift to a minor under Section 2503(c): the trust must provide (1) the income and principal may be expended by or on behalf of the beneficiary and (2) to the extent not so expended income and principal will pass to the beneficiary at 21 or (3) if the beneficiary dies prior to that time, income and principal will go to the beneficiary's estate or appointees under a general power of appointment. (The annual exclusion will not be lost merely because local law prevents a minor from exercising a general power of appointment.)

A substantial amount of flexibility can be built into the 2503(c) trust. Income that has been accumulated as well as any principal in the trust can be paid over to the donee when he reaches age 21. This may be indicated if the sums involved are not substantial. But the donor may want the trust to continue to age 25 or some other age. It is possible to provide continued management of the trust assets and at the same time avoid forfeiting the annual exclusion by giving the donee, at age 21, a right for a limited but reasonable period to require immediate distribution by giving written notice to the trustee. If the beneficiary fails to give written notice, the trust can continue automatically for whatever period the donor provided when he established the trust. Some states have lowered the age of majority from 21 to age 18 or some inbetween age. A trust can provide that the distribution can be made between

the age of majority and age 21 without jeopardizing the Section 2503(c) exclusion. (The rule is that age 21 is the maximum rather than the minimum age at which the right to trust assets must be made.)

A 2503(c) trust has a number of advantages over the type of custodianship found in the Uniform Gifts to Minors Act or Uniform Transfers to Minors Act arrangements, as shown in Figure B.21.

Uniform Gifts (Transfers) to Minors Act. The Uniform Gifts to Minors Act or the Uniform Transfers to Minors Act (reference to either Act herein is simply to the Uniform Act—see chapter 35 for background) provides an alternative to the Section 2503(c) trust. The Uniform Act is frequently utilized for smaller gifts because of its simplicity and because it offers the benefits of management, income and estate tax shifting, and the investment characteristics of a trust with little or none of the setup costs.

The Uniform Act is also indicated over a trust if the gift consists of stock in an S corporation. That's because, generally speaking, a trust (other than a voting or "grantor" trust) cannot hold S corporation stock without causing a loss of the election privilege. The result might be double taxation of corporate profits and forfeiture of the privilege of passing through profits (and losses) to shareholders. (See the discussion of QSCTs and Section 687 Trusts in Chapter 25.)

The original Uniform Gifts to Minors Act was approved in 1956 and provided for gifts of money and securities to minors. In 1966, the Uniform Act was revised to accommodate gifts of life insurance policies and annuity contracts. Over the years between 1956 and 1984, all states adopted one or other of the Uniform Acts or variations thereof. Most states from time to time added to the kinds of property that could be given under the Act. In 1983, the National Conference of Commissioners on Uniform State Laws, concerned about the lack of uniformity among the states with respect to the Uniform Gifts to Minors Act, yielded to the expansive approach taken by most of the states and approved the Uniform Transfers to Minors Act.

The 1983 Act accommodates gifts, lifetime and testamentary, of any interest in property. At this writing, about three-fifths of the states have replaced their Uniform Gifts to Minors Act with the Uniform Transfers to Minors Act. The listing at Figure B.22, taken from TAXATION FOR FINANCIAL PLANNING, a loose-leaf monthly reference service published by The National Underwriter Company, shows the kinds of property that could be given under the Uniform Act in effect in each of the states at the end of 1987. Generally, the indication for a state that "any interest in property" can be given is an indication that that state has adopted the 1983 Act. By way of example, in Pennsylvania, a state which has a variation of the original Uniform Gifts to Minors Act, a custodianship gift may be made as follows:

Figure B.21

Factor	Trust	UGMA	UTMA
Type of property	Donor can make gifts of almost any type of property	Type of property must be permitted by appropriate statute. Gift of real estate may not be permitted	Donor can make gifts of almost any type of property
Dispositive provisions	Donor can provide for disposition of trusts trust assets if donee dies without having made disposition	Disposition must follow statutory guideline	Disposition must follow statutory guideline
Investment powers	Trustee may be given broad virtually unlimited investment powers	Custodian limited to investment powers specified by statute	Custodian limited to investment powers specified by statute
Time of distribution of assets	Trust can continue automatically even after beneficiary reaches age 21. Trustee can make distribution between state law age of majority and age 21	Custodial assets must be paid to beneficiary upon reaching statutory age	Custodial assets must be paid to beneficiary upon reaching statutory age

(1) if the subject of the gift is a security in registered form, by registering it in the name of the donor, other adult person, or trust company, followed in substance by the words "as custodian for _____ under the Pennsylvania

Name of Minor

Uniform Gifts to Minors Act";

(2) if the subject of the gift is a security not in registered form, by delivering it to a guardian of the minor or a trust company, accompanied by a statement of gift in the following form or substance, signed by the donor and the person designated as custodian "Gift under Pennsylvania Uniform Gifts to Minors Act — I, _____, hereby deliver to _____

Name of Donor   Name of Custodian

as custodian for _____ as custodian

Name of Minor

for the Pennsylvania Uniform Gifts to Minors Act, the following security(ies): [insert an appropriate description of the security or securities delivered sufficient to identify it or them]

_____

(Signature of Donor);

(3) if the subject of the gift is money, by paying or delivery it to a broker or a bank, for credit to an account in the name of the donor, another adult person, an adult member of the minor's family, a guardian of the minor, or a bank with trust powers, followed in substance by the words "as custodian for _____

Name of Minor

under the Pennsylvania Uniform Gifts to Minors Act";

(4) if the subject of the gift is a life or endowment insurance policy or an annuity contract the donor shall cause the ownership of such policy or contract to be recorded on a form satisfactory to the insurance company or fraternal benefit society, in the name of the donor, another adult person, a guardian of the minor, or a bank with trust powers, followed in substance by the words, "as custodian for_____under the

Name of Minor

Pennsylvania Uniform Gifts to Minors Act," and such policy or contract shall be delivered to the person in whose name it is thus registered as custodian.

The Effect of Type of Asset

The type of asset given and restrictions placed on that asset may prevent the donor from obtaining the annual exclusion.

An outright "no strings attached" gift of life insurance will qualify for the annual exclusion. Life insurance (and annuity policies) are subject to the same basic test as any other type of property in ascertaining whether the interest created

Figure B.22

```
┌─────────────────────────────────────────────────────────────────────────────────┐
│                                                                                   │
│   Kinds of Property That Can Be Given Under the     California. Any interest in property. Prob. C. §§3900-
│   Uniform Gifts To Minors Act and the Uniform       3925.
│   Transfers To Minors Act In the Various States
│                                                     Colorado. Any interest in property. CRS (1973) 11-50-
│   Note: Gifts of money and securities can be made under   101 to 11-50-126.
│   the Uniform Gifts To Minors Act in all states. Under
│   the Act: A "security" includes any note, stock, treasury   Connecticut. Securities, life insurance policies, annuity
└─────────────────────────────────────────────────────────────────────────────────┘
```

Kinds of Property That Can Be Given Under the Uniform Gifts To Minors Act and the Uniform Transfers To Minors Act In the Various States

Note: Gifts of money and securities can be made under the Uniform Gifts To Minors Act in all states. Under the Act: A "security" includes any note, stock, treasury stock, bond, debenture, evidence of indebtedness, [certificate of interest or participation in an oil, gas or mining title or lease or in payments out of production under such a title or lease,] collateral trust certificate, transferable share, voting trust certificate or, in general, any interest or instrument commonly known as a security, or any certificate of interest or participation in, any temporary or interim certificate, receipt or certificate of deposit for, or any warrant or right to subscribe to or purchase, any of the foregoing. The term does not include a security of which the donor is the issuer. The donor cannot serve as custodian if the gift is of a security not in registered form. A security is in "registered form" when it specifies a person entitled to it or to the rights it evidences and its transfer may be registered upon books maintained for that purpose by or on behalf of the issuer. A few states have modified the foregoing definition of a "security"; those modifications have *not* been included in this table.

The Uniform Transfers To Minors Act allows for the transfer in custodianship of any kind of property, real or personal, tangible or intangible.

"Custodial property" under the Act includes the property interests listed below, the income from such interests, and the proceeds from any disposition of those interests.

Statutory citations are to the whole Act.

Alabama. Any interest in property. Code of Ala. (1975) §§35-5A-1 to 35-5A-24.

Alaska. Securities, life insurance policies, annuity contracts, money. AS §§45.60.011 to 45.60.101.

Arizona. Securities, life insurance policies, annuity contracts, money. ARS §§44-2071 to 44-2080.

Arkansas. Any interest in property. AS §§50-933 to 50-956.

California. Any interest in property. Prob. C. §§3900-3925.

Colorado. Any interest in property. CRS (1973) 11-50-101 to 11-50-126.

Connecticut. Securities, life insurance policies, annuity contracts, money, Connecticut real estate, general and limited partnership interests, tangible personal property, proceeds of life insurance and endowment policies and annuity contracts. CGSA §§45-101 to 45-109.

Delaware. Any interest in property. 12 Del. Code (Rev. 1974) §§4501-4511.

District of Columbia. Any interest in property. DCC §§21-301 to 21-324.

Florida. Any interest in property. FSA §§710.101-710.126.

Georgia. Securities, life insurance policies, annuity contracts, money. GC (1981) 44-5-110 to 44-5-124.

Hawaii. Any interest in property. L. 1985, Act 91, §§1-24, eff. 7-1-85.

Idaho. Any interest in property. IC §§68-801 to 68-825.

Illinois. Any interest in property. SHA ch. 110-1/2, ¶¶251-274.

Indiana. Securities, money, life or endowment insurance policies, annuity contracts, and proceeds of a life or endowment insurance policy or of an annuity contract. IC 1971, §§30-2-8-1 to 30-2-8-10.

Iowa. Any interest in property. ICA §§565B.1 to 565B.26.

Kansas. Any interest in property. KSA 38-1701 et seq.

Kentucky. Any interest in property. KRS §§385.012-385.242.

Louisiana. Any interest in property. LRS 9:751-9:773.

Maine. Securities, life insurance policies, annuity contracts, money. 33 MRSA §§1001-1010.

TAXATION FOR FINANCIAL PLANNING
© 1988 The National Underwriter Company

[5-88]

---

is "present or future," even though the ultimate obligation under a life insurance policy—payment of the death benefit—is to be discharged in the future. A policy does not have to have cash value at the time of the gift to make the transfer one of a present interest. But the annual exclusion would be lost

if the donor prevented the donee from surrendering the policy or borrowing its cash value or limited the donee's right to policy cash values in any way.

When a life insurance policy is transferred or otherwise assigned to a trust, will the transfer of policy cash values con-

Tools and Techniques

Figure B.22 (con't.)

Maryland. Securities, life insurance policies, annuity contracts, real estate, tangible personal property, money, and any other type of property. ACM, ET, §§13-301 to 13-310.

Massachusetts. Any interest in property. ALM c. 201A, §§1-24.

Michigan. Securities, money, life insurance and annuities. MCLA §§554.451 to 554.457.

Minnesota. Any interest in property. MSA §§527.21 to 527.44.

Mississippi. Securities, life insurance policies, annuity contracts, money. MC §§91-19-1 to 91-19-19.

Missouri. Any interest in property. VAMS §§404.005 to 404.094.

Montana. Any interest in property. MCA §§72-26-501 through 72-26-803.

Nebraska. Securities, life insurance policies, annuity contracts, money. RSN §§38-1001 to 38-1010.

Nevada. Any interest in property. NRS 167.010 et seq.

New Hampshire. Any interest in property. RSA §§463-A:1 through 463-A:26.

New Jersey. Any interest in property. NJSA 46:38A-1 to -57.

New Mexico. Securities, life insurance policies, annuity contracts, money. NMSA 1978, 46-7-1 to 46-7-10.

New York. Securities, life insurance policies, annuity contracts, money, interests as a limited partner, interests in real property, interests in tangible personal property. EPTL §§7-4.1 to 7-4.13.

North Carolina. Any interest in property. GS §§33A-1 to -24.

North Dakota. Any interest in property. NDCC §§47-24.1-01 to 47-24.1-22.

Ohio. Any interest in property. RC §§1339.31 to .39.

Oklahoma. Any interest in property. 58 OS §§1201-1226.

Oregon. Any interest in property. ORS°126.805 to 126.880.

Pennsylvania. Personal property in any form including, without limitation, securities, interests in partnerships, money, life or endowment insurance policies, annuity contracts, tangible personal property, interests in real property located in Pennsylvania. 20 Pa. CSA §§5301-5310.

Rhode Island. Any interest in property. GLRI §§18-7-1 through 18-7-26.

South Carolina. Securities, life insurance policies, annuity contracts, money, real estate, tangible personal property, any other type of property. CLSC (1976) §§20-7-140 to 20-7-240.

South Dakota. Any interest in property. SDCL §§55-10A-1 to -26.

Tennessee. Securities, life insurance policies, annuity contracts, money. TCA §§35-7-101 to -110.

Texas. Money, securities, life or endowment insurance policies and proceeds, annuity contracts and proceeds, real property, tangible personal property. VTCA, Property Code, Ch. 141.

Utah. Securities, money, life insurance policies, endowment policies, annuity contracts, interests in real property located in Utah, tangible personal property, interests in a limited partnership. UCA §§75-5-601 to 75-5-609.

Vermont. Securities, money, life insurance policies, annuity contracts. 14 VSA §§3201-3209.

Virginia. Securities, money, annuities, life insurance. Code of Va. §§31-26 to 31-36.

Washington. Any property. RCW §§11.93.010-11.93.920.

West Virginia. Any interest in property. WVC §§36-7-1 to 36-7-24.

Wisconsin. Securities, life insurance policies, annuity contracts, money. WSA 880.61-880.71.

Wyoming. Any interest in property. 34-13-114 to -137.

[5-88]

TAXATION FOR FINANCIAL PLANNING

stitute a present interest? The answer depends on the terms of the trust. Generally, the gift will be one of a future interest, since beneficiaries are not usually given an immediate right to possession or enjoyment of the policy values or other items constituting trust corpus. For example, a trust

will typically provide no payments to beneficiaries unless they survive the insured. Furthermore, there is generally no actuarially sound method of making an allocation between the value of a present interest and future interest. Unless the given beneficiary's present interest can be ascertained, no exclusion is allowed. (A related attack used by the IRS is that insurance is nonincome-producing property. This concept is discussed further below.)

Premium payments will usually be considered present- or future-interest gifts depending on the classification of the policy itself; if the assignment of the policy was considered a present interest, premiums paid by the donor after the transfer will qualify for the annual exclusion. For instance, if a person makes an absolute assignment of a policy on his life to his daughter but continues to pay premiums, premiums paid subsequent to the transfer would be present-interest gifts. Conversely, if the gift of the policy was a future interest, premium payments made by the donor after the transfer may also be considered future-interest gifts.

A gift in trust of a life insurance policy or of premiums can be made a present interest by inserting a "Crummey" power (named after the major case in this area). A Crummey power gives the named individual(s) an immediate, unfettered, and actuarially ascertainable right—in short, the absolute right to withdraw a specified amount or portion of the assets contributed to the trust. This withdrawal right (essentially, a general power of appointment over a specified amount or portion of each year's contribution to the trust) makes the gift in trust of a life insurance policy or of premiums qualify for the gift tax annual exclusion.

Clearly, an outright gift of nonincome-producing property will qualify for the gift tax exclusion. Will the same property qualify if placed in a trust? The IRS uses three arguments to disallow annual exclusions:

(1) the right to income (which is the only current right given to a life beneficiary) from a gift of nonincome-producing property is a future interest since its worth is contingent upon the trustee's converting it to income-producing property;

(2) it is impossible to ascertain the value of an income interest in property that is not income-producing at the time of the gift; and

(3) if a gift tax exclusion *is* allowable, the exclusion must be limited to the actual income produced by the property (or expected to be produced) multipled by the number of years over which the income beneficiary is expected to receive the income—discounted to its present value.

Nondividend-paying stock is a good example of property that may not qualify for the gift tax exclusion when it is placed into a trust. The IRS has been successful in a number of cases in disallowing an exclusion for gifts in trust of stock in closely held corporations paying no dividends. Gifts in trust of life insurance policies pose the same problem: a mother assigns policies on her life to a trust created to provide financial protection for her daughter. Upon the mother's death, the policy proceeds will be reinvested and the daughter will receive the net income of the trust for life. Will the mother be allowed the exclusion for the present value of her daughter's income interest? The Regulations answer in the negative since the daughter will not receive income payments until her mother dies.

But even these last two types of property can qualify for the annual exclusion if the beneficiary is given the power to require the trustee to make assets in the trust income-producing. Consider, however, the potential adverse implications of that power if the beneficiary chooses to exercise it.

Gift Tax Marital Deduction

An individual who transfers property to a spouse is allowed an unlimited deduction (subject to certain conditions) known as the gift tax marital deduction (M.D.).

The purpose of the gift tax marital deduction is currently to enable spouses to be treated as an economic unity.

Requirements to Qualify for Gift Tax Marital Deduction

For a gift to qualify for the gift tax marital deduction, the following conditions must be satisfied: (1) The donor's spouse must be a United States citizen or resident at the time the gift is made. (The donee-spouse need not be either a resident or citizen.) (2) The recipient of the gift must be the spouse of the donor at the time the gift is made. (3) The property transferred to the donee-spouse must not be the type of terminable interest that will disqualify the gift for the marital deduction.

Most of the qualifications above are self-explanatory. The terminable interest rule for marital deduction gifts is similar to the rule employed for estate tax purposes. Essentially, the effect of these rules is that generally no marital deduction will be allowed where (a) the donee-spouse's interest in the transferred property will terminate upon the lapse of time or at the occurrence or failure of a specified contingency (b) where the donee-spouse's interest will then pass to another person who received his interest in the property from the donor-spouse and (c) who did not pay the donor full and adequate consideration for that interest.

The exception is for a gift of "QTIP" assets. (In the past a gift—or bequest—of a terminable interest in property—one which could end for example at a spouse's death and therefore escape taxation—would not have been eligible for the gift (or estate) tax marital deduction.)

Current law now provides that if a donor spouse gives a donee spouse a "qualifying income interest for life," it will qualify for a gift (or estate) tax marital deduction. To qualify,

(1) the surviving spouse must be entitled to all the income from the property (and it must be payable annually or more frequently), and

(2) no person can have a power to appoint any part of the property to any person other than the surviving spouse, and

Tools and Techniques

(3) the property must be taxable at the donee-spouse's death (in the case of a bequest the first decedent's executor makes an irrevocable election that the property remaining at the surviving spouse's death is taxable in her estate).

The Gift Tax Charitable Deduction

A donor making a transfer of property to a qualified charity may receive a charitable deduction equal to the value of the gift (to the extent not already excluded by the annual exclusion). The net effect of the charitable deduction—together with the annual exclusion—is to avoid gift tax liability on gifts to qualified charities. There is no limit on the amount that can be passed, gift tax free, to a qualified charity.

The gift tax deduction is allowed for all gifts made during the calendar year by U.S. citizens or residents if the gift is to a qualified charity. A qualified charity is defined as (a) the United States, a state, territory, or any political subdivision or the District of Columbia if the gift is to be used exclusively for public purposes; (b) certain religious, scientific, or charitable organizations; (c) certain fraternal societies, orders, or associations; (d) certain veterans' associations, organizations, or societies.

Technically the charitable deduction is limited. A charitable deduction is allowed only to the extent that each gift exceeds the annual exclusion. For example, during the calendar year a single client makes total gifts of $51,000: $26,000 to his daughter and $25,000 to The American College. After taking annual exclusions, gifts qualifying for the charitable deduction would amount to $16,000 (the gift of $26,000 to the daughter less the $10,000 annual exclusion) and $15,000 (the $25,000 gift to The American College less the $10,000 annual exclusion). Therefore the client's charitable deduction would be limited to $15,000. The reason for the rule is this: If the annual exclusion were already deducted, the allowance of a charitable deduction equal to the total amount of the gift would result in an extra $10,000 exclusion. The operation of these rules is illustrated below.

In certain cases a donor will transfer a remainder interest to a qualified charity. A personal beneficiary will be given all or part of the income interest in the transferred property, and the charity will receive the remainder at the termination of the income interest. Where a charitable remainder is given to a qualified charity, a gift tax deduction is allowable for the present value of that remainder interest only if at least one of the following conditions is satisfied:

(1) the transferred property was either a personal residence or a farm; or
(2) the transfer was made to a charitable remainder annuity trust; or
(3) the transfer was made to a charitable remainder unitrust; or
(4) the transfer was made to a pooled income fund.

The terms "charitable remainder annuity trust," "charitable remainder unitrust," and "pooled income fund" are de-fined in essentially the same manner as they are for estate and income tax purposes.

Calculating Gift Tax Payable

The process of computing the gift tax payable begins with ascertaining the amount of taxable gifts in the current reporting calendar year. In order to find the amount of taxable gifts, it is first necessary to value all gifts made. If appropriate, the gift is then "split," annual exclusions and marital and charitable deductions are applied. An example and computation format will illustrate the process.

Assume a single donor in the last month of 1989 makes certain outright gifts: $160,000 to his son, $125,000 to his daughter, $8,000 to his grandson, and $25,000 to The American College (a total of $318,000).

Computing Taxable Gifts

Step 1	*List* total gifts for year		$318,000
Step 2	*Subtract* one-half of gift deemed to be made by donor's spouse (split gifts)	$ 0	
	Gifts deemed to be made by donor		$318,000
Step 3	*Subtract* annual exclusion(s)	$38,000	
	Gifts after subtracting exclusion(s)		$280,000
Step 4	*Subtract* marital deduction	$ 0	
Step 5	*Subtract* charitable deduction	$15,000	
	Taxable gifts		$265,000

Note that, although there were four donees, the annual exclusion was $38,000 and did not total four times $10,000, or $40,000. This is because the annual exclusion is the lower of (a) $10,000 or (b) the actual net value of the property transferred. In this example the gift to the grandson was only $8,000, which limits the annual exclusion to that amount.

A slight change in the fact pattern above will illustrate the computation where the donor is married and his spouse consented to split their gifts to third parties. In this case, only half the gifts made by the donor would be taxable to the donor (half the gifts made by the donor's spouse to third parties would also be included in computing the donor's total gifts).

A separate (and essentially identical) computation is made for the donor's spouse. That computation would show (a) the other half of the husband's gifts to third parties plus (b) half of the wife's actual gifts to third parties (since all gifts must be split if any gifts are split).

Computing Taxable Gifts

Step 1	*List* total gifts for year		$318,000
Step 2	*Subtract* one-half of gift deemed to be made by donor's spouse (split gifts)	$159,000	
	Gifts deemed to be made by donor		$159,000
Step 3	*Subtract* annual exclusion(s)	$ 34,000	
	Gifts after subtracting exclusion(s)		$125,000
Step 4	*Subtract* marital deduction	$ 0	

Appendix B
Computing the Federal Gift Tax

Step 5   *Subtract* charitable deduction $ 2,500

Taxable gifts $122,500

(The calculation on the wife's return would parallel this return.)

Note that in this example the annual exclusions were computed *after* the split and each donor's exclusions would be:

(a)	Gift to son	$10,000
(b)	Gift to daughter	10,000
(c)	Gift to grandson	4,000
(d)	Gift to The American College	10,000
		$34,000

The charitable deduction for each spouse would be $2,500 [{$25,000 divided by 2} less $10,000].

If the married donor in the fact pattern directly above had also made an outright gift of $200,000 to his wife, the computation would be as follows:

Computing Taxable Gifts

Step 1   *List* total gifts for year $518,000

Step 2   *Subtract* one-half of gift deemed to be made by donor's spouse (split gifts) $159,000

Gifts deemed to be made by donor $359,000

Step 3   *Subtract* annual exclusion(s) $ 44,000

Gifts after subtracting exclusion(s) $315,000

Step 4   *Subtract* marital deduction $190,000

Step 5   *Subtract* charitable deduction $ 2,500

Taxable gifts $122,500

When the total value of taxable gifts for the reporting period is found, the actual tax payable is computed using the following method:

Computing Gift Tax Payable

Step 1   Compute gift tax on all *taxable* gifts regardless of when made (use unified rate schedule) $ _____

Step 2   Compute gift tax on all *taxable* gifts made prior to the present year's gift(s) (use unified rate schedule) $ _____

Step 3   Subtract Step 2 result from Step 1 result $ _____

Step 4   Enter gift tax credit remaining $ _____

Step 5   Subtract Step 4 result from Step 3 result to obtain *gift tax payable* $ _____

For instance, a widow gives $1,400,000 to her daughter and $100,000 to The College for Financial Planning in 1989. Both transfers are present-interest gifts. If she had made no previous taxable gifts in the current or prior years or quarters, the computation would be as follows:

Computing Taxable Gifts

Step 1   *List* total gifts for year $1,500,000

Step 2   *Subtract* one-half of gift deemed to be made by donor's spouse (split gifts) $ 0

Gifts deemed to be made by donor $1,500,000

Step 3   *Subtract* annual exclusion(s) $20,000

Gifts after subtracting exclusion(s) $1,480,000

Step 4   *Subtract* marital deduction $ 0

Step 5   *Subtract* charitable deduction $90,000

Taxable gifts $1,390,000

To find the gift tax payable on this amount, the procedure would be as follows:

Computing Gift Tax Payable

Step 1   Compute gift tax on all *taxable* gifts regardless of when made ($1,390,000) $508,500

Step 2   Compute gift tax on all *taxable* gifts made prior to the present gift(s) $ 0

Step 3   Subtract Step 2 results from Step 1 result $508,500

Step 4   Enter gift tax (unified) credit remaining (1987) $192,800

Step 5   Subtract Step 4 result from Step 3 result to obtain *gift tax payable* $315,700

The Step 1 entry, $508,500, is found by using the unified rate schedule for estate and gift taxes. Note that the unified rate table is used regardless of when the gifts were made.

If the donor in the example above had made $100,000 of additional taxable gifts in 1984 (a total of $1,490,000), the computation would be as follows:

Computing Gift Tax Payable

Step 1   Compute gift tax on all *taxable* gifts regardless of when made ($1,490,000) $551,500

Step 2   Compute gift tax on all *taxable* gifts made prior to the present gift(s) $23,800

Step 3   Subtract Step 2 result from Step 1 result $527,700

Step 4   Enter gift tax credit remaining (1987) $169,000

Step 5   Subtract Step 4 result from Step 3 result to obtain *gift tax payable* $358,700

This illustrates the cumulative nature of the gift tax (the $100,000 prior taxable gifts pushed the present $1,390,000 of taxable gifts into a higher bracket) and the progressive rate structure.

What if $200,000 of taxable gifts were made in 1984? The tax computation would be as follows:

Tools and Techniques

Computing Gift Tax Payable

Step 1	Compute gift tax on all *taxable* gifts regardless of when made ($1,590,000)	$596,300
Step 2	Compute gift tax on all *taxable* gifts made prior to the present gift(s)	$ 54,800
Step 3	Subtract Step 2 results from Step 1 result	$541,500
Step 4	Enter gift tax (unified) credit remaining (1987)	$138,000
Step 5	Subtract Step 4 result from Step 3 results to obtain *gift tax payable*	$403,500

This assumes that the $200,000 taxable gifts made in 1984 used up a credit equal to the $54,800 tax it generated.

Note that gift tax rates will remain at a high of 55 percent until 1993, when they are sceduled to drop to 50 percent. The five percent add-on tax (see last table in Appendix C) applies to ultra-large gifts.

Credits

A unified credit can be applied against the tax on gifts made either during lifetime or at death or part can be applied against each. The gift tax credit, which provides a dollar-for-dollar reduction of the tax otherwise payable, is as follows:

Donors Making Gifts in	Receive a Credit of
1982	$ 62,800
1983	79,300
1984	96,300
1985	121,800
1986	155,800
1987 and later years	192,800

In the example directly above since the taxable gifts in prior years used up part of the available credit, to that extent they are not available to reduce the tax liability for the present gifts.

Note also that the utility of both graduated rates and the unified credit is lost where ultra-large gifts have been made (see Unified Rate Schedule for Estate and Gift Taxes in Appendix C).

(9)
REPORTING OF GIFTS AND PAYMENT OF THE TAX

Future-Interest Gifts

A gift tax return is required for a gift of a future interest regardless of the amount of the gift. For example, if an individual transfers $100,000 to an irrevocable trust payable to the grantor's wife for life and then to the grantor's son, a gift tax return would be required regardless of the value of the son's remainder interest.

The term "future interest" is defined the same as for annual exclusion purposes: a gift in which the donee does not have the unrestricted right to the immediate use, possession, or enjoyment of the property or the income from the property.

Present-Interest Gifts

No gift tax return is due (if no future interest gifts are made) until present-interest gifts made to one individual exceed $10,000. At that point, a return must be filed on an annual basis when a gift to one person in one year exceeds $10,000 even if no gift tax would be due (e.g., if gift splitting provisions eliminated the tax). For example, if a married woman gave $15,000 to her son, the transfer would be tax free. However, a gift tax return would be required because it exceeded the annual exclusion limit (and because the gift was split). A return must be filed where a couple elects to split gifts.

A gift tax return must be filed and the gift tax due, if any, on reported gifts must be paid by April 15 of the year following the year in which the taxable gifts were made. When an extension is granted for income tax return filing, that automatically extends the time limit for gift tax return filing.

Gifts to Charities

No return must be filed and no reporting is required for charitable contributions of $10,000 or less in value—unless a noncharitable gift is also made. In that case, the charitable transfer must be reported at the same time the noncharitable gift is noted on a gift tax return. If the value of the charitable transfer exceeds $10,000, the general rule is that the transfer must be reported on a gift tax return for that year.

If a split-interest gift is made to a charity (where there are charitable and noncharitable donees of the same gift), the donor will not be able to claim a charitable deduction for the entire value of the transfer. In this case the donor must file and report the transfer subject to the filing requirements discussed above. For example, if an individual establishes a charitable remainder trust with the income payable to his daughter for life and the remainder payable to charity at her death, a gift tax return would have to be filed.

Liability for Payment—Net Gift

The donor of the gift is primarily liable for the gift tax. However, if the donor for any reason fails to pay the tax when it falls due, the donee becomes liable to the extent of the value of the gift. This liability begins as soon as the donor fails to pay the tax when due.

If a donor makes a gift and the donee decides, voluntarily, to pay the gift tax out of the property just received, the gift tax value of the gift is the entire fair market value of the property. In other words if the donee is not obligated by the terms of the gift to pay the gift tax but chooses to pay it anyway, he must pay a tax based on the full fair market value of the property received based on the donor's gift tax bracket.

Conversely, if the terms of the gift obligate the donee to pay the gift tax, the value of the gift (and therefore the amount of the gift tax liability) is reduced. If a gift is made subject to an express or implied condition at the time of transfer that the gift tax is to be paid by the donee or out of the property transfered, the donor is receiving consideration (taxable as income) in the amount of the gift tax to be paid by the donee.

The value of the "net gift' is measured by the fair market value of the property passing from the donor less the amount of any gift tax paid by the donee. In computing the donee's gift tax liability, you must use the donor's unified credit.

The formula used to compute the donee's tax is:

tentative tax ÷ (1.00 + donor's gift tax bracket)

For instance, assume a retired, 66 year old, single donor living almost entirely from the income of $4,000,000 worth of tax-free municipal bonds who made no prior gifts made a gift in 1988 of property worth $1,000,000. The gift was made to his niece on the condition that she pay the federal gift taxes. As the NumberCruncher printout below illustrates, the tentative tax on a gift of $1,000,000 is $153,000. But the gift tax actually payable is $110,072.

True Tax on a Net Gift

Input:	Year of Gift	1988
Input:	Taxable Gift	$1,000,000
	Gift Tax on Gift	$345,800
	Unified Credit . . . . −	$192,800
	Tentative Tax	$153,000

True Tax on Net Gift Equals:

Tentative Tax ÷ (1.00 + Rate of Tax)	$110,072

Note that the formula is not applicable if the gift is split between the donor and spouse, each of whom is in a different gift tax bracket because either or both have made prior taxable gifts. Quite often, however, you can determine the correct tax bracket by inspection and adjusting for the bracket differential by computing the tentative tax in the correct lower bracket. In other situations you'll have to make trial computations using first the bracket indicated by the tentative taxable gift and then later using the next lower bracket.

Time Tax Is Due

Generally, the gift tax must be paid at the same time the return is filed. However, reasonable extensions of time for payment of the tax can be granted by the IRS—but only upon a showing of "undue hardship." This means more than in-convenience. It must appear that the party liable to pay the tax will suffer a "substantial financial loss" unless an extension is granted. (A forced sale of property at a sacrifice price would be an example of a substantial financial loss.)

(10)
RELATIONSHIP OF THE GIFT TAX SYSTEM TO THE INCOME TAX SYSTEM

When the gift tax law was written, one of the principal purposes was to complement the income tax law by discouraging taxpayers from making gifts to reduce their taxable incomes. It is true that to some extent the gift tax does supplement the income tax system and there is some overlap. However, it is important to note that the tax treatment accorded a given transaction when the two taxes are applied will not necessarily be consistent.

A lack of consistency between the gift and income tax systems forces the practitioner to examine four different issues:

(1) Is the transfer one upon which the gift tax will be imposed?

(2) Will the transfer constitute a taxable exchange subject to the income tax?

(3) If the transfer was made in trust, will the income from the transferred property be taxable to the donor, or will the incidence of taxation be shifted to the recipient of the property (the trust or its beneficiaries)?

(4) If the income is taxable to the beneficiary, will it be taxable at the parent's rate or at the beneficiary's tax bracket (as it would be if (a) the income were earned income no matter what the beneficiary's age, or (b) the beneficiary were age 14 or older no matter whether the income was earned or unearned)?

In summary, the treatment of a transaction for gift tax purposes is not necessarily consistent with the income tax consequences. Therefore it is important not to place undue reliance upon the provisions and interpretations of the income tax law when determining probable results or potential interpretations of the gift tax system (or vice versa).

(11)
DETERMINATION OF THE BASIS OF GIFT PROPERTY

When property is transferred from a donor to a donee and the donee later disposes of the property through a sale or other taxable disposition, gain or loss depends on the donee's basis. In return, the donee's basis is "carried over" from the donor; i.e., the donor's cost basis for the gift property immediately prior to the gift becomes the donee's cost basis for that property.

Tools and Techniques

For example, if an individual has paid $10 a share for stock and transfers it when it is worth $20, and the donee sells it when it is worth $30, the donee's cost basis for that property is the donor's $10 cost. The gain, therefore, is the difference between the amount realized by the donee, $30, and the donee's adjusted basis, $10.

An addition to basis is allowed for a portion of any gift tax paid on the transfer from the donor to the donee. The basis addition is for that portion of the tax attributable to the "appreciation" in the gift property (the excess of the property's gift tax value over the donor's adjusted basis determined immediately before the gift). This increase in basis may be added to the donee's carryover basis for the property.

Stated as a formula, the basis of gifted property is the donor's basis increased as follows:

$$\frac{\text{NET APPRECIATION IN VALUE OF GIFT}}{\text{AMOUNT OF GIFT}} \times \text{GIFT TAX PAID}$$

This means the basis carried over from the donor is increased by only the gift tax on the net appreciation in the value of the gift. For example, an individual bought stock worth $40,000 and gave it to his daughter when it was worth $100,000. If the donor paid $18,000 in gift taxes at the time of the gift, the daughter's basis would be

a. Donor's basis $40,000

plus

b. Gift tax on "net appreciation in value" (here, the difference between the $100,000 value of the gift at the time of transfer and the donor's cost, $40,000)

$$\frac{\$60,000}{\$100,000} \times \$18,000 = \qquad 10,800$$

equals

c. Daughter's basis $50,800

(12)
RELATIONSHIP OF THE GIFT TAX SYSTEM TO THE ESTATE TAX SYSTEM

We are operating under a unified estate and gift tax system. The unification correlates the estate and gift tax laws in three essential ways:

(1) Lifetime gifts and testamentary transfers are taxed by using the same tax rates (so-called unified tax rates), rather than separate and different rates.

(2) There is a single unified tax credit that can be applied to lifetime and "deathtime" gifts. The unified tax credit replaces what was previously a specific estate tax exemption and a specific gift tax exemption.

(3) The estate tax imposed at death is found by adding the taxable portion of gifts made during lifetime (after 1976) to the taxable estate (any gift tax paid on post-1976 transfers can be subtracted to arrive at the estate tax liability) to arrive at the tentative tax base.

For these reasons, there are many correlations between the two tax systems. Like the income tax law, however, the gift tax law is not always consistent with the estate tax law.

When a gift is made, certain issues must be considered. In spite of the lifetime transfer, will the transferred property be included among the other assets in the donor's gross estate upon his death? Will the property a donor transfers during lifetime be subjected first to a gift tax and later included in the donor's gross estate? For example, if a donor gives a policy of insurance on his life to his son, the transfer would be considered a taxable gift and if the donor dies within 3 years after making the gift, the transferred property would be includible in his gross estate.

Likewise, if the donor transfers property but retains a life interest, both gift and estate taxes will be payable. Although the gift tax paid on post-1976 transfers may be subtracted in arriving at the estate tax liability, because of the "time value" of money—i.e., the donor's loss of the use of gift taxes paid—the net result is less favorable than a mere washout (i.e., it is in essence a prepayment of the death tax).

(13)
FACTORS TO CONSIDER IN SELECTING APPROPRIATE SUBJECT OF A GIFT

Gift tax strategy must be part of a well-planned and carefully coordinated estate-planning effort. This in turn requires careful consideration as to the type of property to give. There are a number of strategies and factors that must be examined in selecting the types of property that are appropriate for gifts.

Some of the general considerations in planning gift tax property include:

(1) Is the property likely to appreciate in value? Other things being equal, planners generally try to pick property that will appreciate substantially in value from the time of the transfer. The removal from the donor's estate of the appreciation in the property (as well as the income from the property) should save a meaningful amount of estate taxes.

The best type of property will have a low gift tax value and a high estate tax value. Life insurance, for example, is property with a low present value but a high appreciation potential. If held until the date the insured dies, its appreciation in value is guaranteed.

(2) Is the donee in a lower income tax bracket than the donor? Income splitting between the donor and a donee age 14 or older can be obtained by transferring high income-producing property to a family member in a lower bracket. High income-producing property is best for this purpose. High-dividend participating preferred stock in a closely held business or stock in a successful S corporation is a good example of high income-producing property.

Conversely, if the donor is in a lower bracket than the donee (for instance, if the parent who is retired makes a gift to a financially successful middle-aged child), the use of low-yield growth-type property may be indicated. Typically, gifts to children under age 14 should emphasize growth.

(3) Is the property subject to indebtedness? A gift of property subject to indebtedness that is greater than its cost to the donor may result in a taxable gain. A gift of such property causes the donor to realize capital gain on the excess of the debt over basis. For example, the gift of a building that cost the donor $10,000, appreciated to $100,000, and was mortgaged to $70,000 would result in an income tax gain to the donor on the difference between the debt outstanding at the time of the transfer and the donor's basis (assume $70,000 and the donor's basis, $10,000). In this example, the gain would be $60,000. It would be realized at the time the gift became complete.

(4) Is the gift property's cost basis above, below, or approximately the same as the property's fair market value? Income tax law forbids the recognition of a capital loss if the subject matter of the gift has a cost basis above the property's present fair market value. Neither the donor nor the donee can recognize a capital loss with respect to such property. Furthermore, if the gift property's cost basis is above present fair market value, there will be no gift tax addition to basis because that addition depends on appreciation at the time of the transfer. Since there is no appreciation, no gift tax addition would be allowed.

Conversely, if the donor's cost basis for income tax purposes is very low relative to the fair market value of the property, it might be advantageous to retain the property until death because of the "stepped-up basis" at death rules. (This is especially true if inclusion of the property will generate little or no gift tax because it will pass to a surviving spouse and qualify for a marital deduction or if the asset owner is "sheltered" by the unified credit.) The result of the stepped-up basis provision is that a portion of the future capital gain would be avoided in the event the property is later sold by the estate or heir. But if the property should be sold, it may pay to transfer it first to a low-bracket age 14 or over family member by gift; that individual could then sell it and realize a lower tax. For instance, on a $10,000 gain, a father in a 28% bracket would pay $2,800 in tax. If, instead, he gave the stock to his college age daughter, who was in a 15% bracket, she'd pay (slightly less than) $1,500 in tax, a $1,300 ($2,800-$1,500) saving.

A third possibility is that the donor's cost basis is approximately the same or only slightly below fair market value. Again, the rules providing for a gift tax addition to basis are of little help. The addition to basis is limited to gift tax allocable to appreciation in the property at the time of the gift. One further factor that should be considered is the likelihood that the donee will want or need to sell the property in the foreseeable future. If this is not likely, the income tax basis (except for depreciable property) will be relatively meaningless.

Tools and Techniques

HOW BASIS IS DETERMINED

WHAT BASIS IS AND WHY IT IS IMPORTANT

Basis is the starting point in any computation used to determine how much gain (or loss) is incurred upon a sale of property. Gain, for example, is found by the following formula:

Amount realized − Adjusted basis = Gain

Therefore, the higher the basis, the lower the reportable gain on a sale of an asset.

Basis is also the key factor in determining the allowable depreciation deduction that may be taken on buildings and other business or investment assets that wear out over time. Again, a high basis is advantageous since depreciation, the recovery of capital over a given useful life through annual deductions or amortization, the recovery of cost in equal annual increments, depends directly on how much capital—that is, how much investment—the taxpayer has in the property.

Basis, therefore, is what a person or other taxpayer "paid" for property. For instance, if property is acquired through a purchase, usually the basis of that asset is its cost. In a loose sense basis can be thought of as the actual or constructive cost of property for tax purposes (although technically the term, basis, has broader implications).

BASIS AT DEATH

Assets owned by a decedent receive a new federal income tax basis equal to the property's fair market value for federal estate tax purposes.[1] When the fair market value of the asset is higher than the pre-death basis, the old basis is "stepped-up" to the fair market value. Thus, if a father bought a farm for $5,000 and it was valued at $50,000 for federal estate tax purposes when he died and left it to his son, the son (or the father's estate) might have to pay an estate tax, but the son could then sell the farm for its $50,000 value without having to pay any income tax. This is because the $5,000 basis is "stepped up" to $50,000. Using the formula above, when the new adjusted basis of $50,000 is subtracted from the amount realized on the sale, $50,000, there is no gain. This concept is particularly important in buy-sell agreements where stock is purchased at a shareholder's death at a pre-arranged price or under a pre-arranged formula.

NO STEP-UP IN BASIS WHERE DECEDENT HAD ACQUIRED PROPERTY BY GIFT WITHIN A YEAR OF DEATH IF PROPERTY IS LEFT TO DONOR OR DONOR'S SPOUSE

Under prior law, some owners of appreciated property transferred that property to a dying individual and had then received a step-up in basis when the property was left to them under the decedent's will or by intestacy.

Current law contains a provision intended to prevent the avoidance of income taxes on appreciated property by such transfers to dying donees. The law currently provides that if (a) the decedent had received appreciated property by gift during the one-year period ending on the date of death and (b) that property was acquired from the decedent by (or passes from the decedent to) the donor of that property (or to the donor's spouse), the basis of that property in the donor's hands (or in the hands of the donor's spouse) is the adjusted basis of the property in the hands of the decedent immediately before death. In short, the old trick wouldn't work any more.

For example, assume a daughter transferred property with a $10,000 cost and $100,000 fair market value to her mother within one year of the mother's death. Assume the mother left the property to her daughter. The mother's basis would not be stepped up. Rather, it would remain the same as it was in the mother's hands just before she died. In most cases, this means that the daughter will receive the same basis (with adjustments for any gift taxes she paid upon the gift to the mother) as she had before she made the gift.

There is a solution: If the donee-decedent lives for more than one year after receiving the gift, or if the gift is left to anyone other than the donor or the donor's spouse, the property will receive a stepped up basis. So the property could be left to grandchildren in this example and it would receive a $100,000 basis.

EFFECT OF STEP-UP BASIS RULES ON STOCK REDEMPTIONS AND CROSS PURCHASE AGREEMENTS

As noted in the chapter on Section 303 Stock Redemptions, there are specific rules as to the non-recognition of income tax gain upon the redemption of stock to pay death taxes in certain situations.

Stock includible in the decedent's estate receives a new basis equal to its value at death (or the alternate valuation date if elected). This is usually close to the redemption value,

Tools and Techniques

particularly if the stock redemption is promptly carried out. Typically, no or little gain is recognized by the estate or other seller of the stock upon the redemption.

OVERALL EFFECT

The step-up in basis rule has an effect on all tax planning that relates to the sale of assets after death or assets which might be held until death.

There is an incentive for the owner of property with a very low income tax basis, in relation to its market value, to hold the property until death so that the estate can sell it without any income tax on the appreciation in value.

However, inflation is becoming a greater factor in planning and the wise estate planner will take into consideration the probable future increase in value, with possible concurrent increase in death taxes (consider the implications of both the unified credit and the unlimited marital deduction), and balance this against a current sale. This is particularly appropriate to consider where the sale would be to a person who would eventually recieve the property upon the owner's death.

POSSIBLE FUTURE TAX ON APPRECIATION

Informal discussion with Treasury Department officials and a review of the Department's consistent efforts to tax property which has appreciated and is held at death leads to the conclusion that there may be future efforts to tax such appreciation.

Therefore, clients should be urged to keep accurate records with regard to the cost of assets, including such items as purchase price, improvements, depreciation, etc.

IMPLICATIONS AND ISSUES IN COMMUNITY PROPERTY STATES

Stepped-up basis focuses attention on the manner of holding title to property between spouses.

If property is held by spouses in a community property state as the separate property of one spouse, it will all be included in the spouse's estate and receives a new basis at death. The entire property can go to the surviving spouse under the marital deduction rules and will not be subject to tax. Thus, the entire property gets a new stepped-up basis even though it may escape estate tax entirely.

If the property is held as community property, only one-half of the property is included in the estate of the first spouse to die but, equalizing the basis with the separate property arrangement, both halves receive a new income tax basis.[2]

However, this step-up in basis does not occur if the property is held in joint-tenancy or tenancy-in-common.

Take the example of a husband and wife purchasing property using funds earned while residents of a community property state. They want to hold the property in some form of co-ownership. The cost of the property was $1,000 and, at the date-of-death of the first spouse to die, the value is $10,000.

The couple has three different ways to take the property in co-ownership:

1. As joint-tenancy (or tenants by the entirety);
2. As tenants in common; or
3. As community property.

Note the significant difference in income tax basis in Situation II, Figure B.23.

Thus, with the reinstatement of the stepped-up basis rule, where property has been paid for with community property earnings or if the contribution to the acquisition was otherwise equal, it again affords a significant advantage as to federal income tax to hold such property in community property as opposed to either joint-tenancy (known as tenancy by the entirety in some states as applied to spouses) or tenancy-in-common.

Unfortunately, the state income tax rules of the community property states, such as California, which adopted the carry-over basis concept, have not all yet been repealed. Therefore, as to state income tax, one must look at the basis rules of the particular state to determine what the basis of property of a decedent will be for that state's income tax.

In California, when and if such repeal of carryover basis is enacted, there will most probably not be the step-up in basis for both halves of community property. This was a hotly disputed question in California courts and in the legislature and it is very probable that the ultimate rule will be that only one-half of community property will receive the stepped-up basis for California income tax purposes.

However, federal income tax is much more important than state income tax for most returns and therefore the double step-up in federal income tax basis of property held as community property will continue to be a very important tax planning consideration.

QUESTIONS AND ANSWERS

Question — Does property receive a new income tax basis equal to fair market value when it is given away during one's lifetime?

Answer — No. In general, the donee retains the donor's basis, increased by the amount of gift tax (or a part thereof) paid with respect to the gift. (See "Computing the Federal Gift Tax," section (ll), this appendix.) However, if such basis is greater than the fair market value of the property at the time of the gift, then for purposes of de-

Figure B.23

Situation I — Property sold for $10,000 prior to death of either spouse					
Plan:	**#1**		**#2**	**#3**	
	Tenants by the Entirety		**Tenants in Common**	**Community Property**	
Sales price of property	$10,000		$10,000	$10,000	
Tax basis of spouses:					
Husband's half	$500		$500	$500	
Wife's half	500		500	500	
Total Basis		1,000	1,000	1,000	
		$ 9,000	$ 9,000	$ 9,000	

Situation II — Property sold for $10,000 after death of husband				
Plan:				
Sales price of property	$10,000	$10,000	$10,000	
Tax basis of spouses:				
Husband's half	$5,000	$5,000	$5,000	
Wife's half	500	500	5,000	
Total Basis	5,500	5,500	10,000	
Taxable gain on sale	$ 4,500	$ 4,500	$—0—	

termining loss, upon the donee's sale of the property, the basis is such fair market value.[3] If the property is given in trust, the donee's basis is the donor's basis increased or decreased by any gain or loss the donor recognized on the transfer under the law applicable in the year of the transfer.[4] Where property is transferred between spouses, or between former spouses if the transfer is incident to the divorce, the transferee's basis is the same as the transferor's basis.[5]

Property which is given away, but for some reason is brought back into the donor's estate for death tax purposes will receive a new basis equal to the fair market value at the time of death. Thus, having a gift brought back into the estate may be good for the donee (who gets a new basis) but bad for the estate (which has to pay death taxes on a larger estate).

Question — If a property is sold with the seller taking back a note and the installment basis of recognizing gain is elected, does the note receive a new basis if the seller dies owning the note?

Answer — No. The gain which is inherent in the note will still be recognized.[7] Thus, a sale of the property before death will result in the gain being recognized, either during the seller's lifetime or after his death.

Question — If, instead of selling an asset such as stock, the shareholder enters into a buy-sell agreement, does the stock receive a stepped-up basis?

Answer — Yes. In general, the stock receives a new basis if it is still held by the shareholder at death as long as there is not a binding executed contract that did not depend on death.

However, entering into a contract of sale that calls for payment of a purchase price and the delivery of an asset upon completion of the payment will generally be treated as if the stock were sold and a note taken back. Gain will still be recognized to the extent there is any payment yet to be made on the purchase of the asset.

Question — If an attorney (or other taxpayer) reporting on the cash basis for income tax purposes dies with clients owing money for services rendered, do these debts receive a stepped-up basis?

Answer — No. Such amounts, which would have been income to the decedent if he had lived, are termed "income in respect of a decedent"[8] and do not receive a stepped-up basis at death. They will be taxed to the taxpayer's estate as income, just as they would have been if he had received them during his lifetime.

Question — Does the person's estate which receives such "income in respect of a decedent" receive any deductions for the estate tax paid on such amounts included in the estate?

Answer — Yes. There is an income-tax deduction for a portion of the estate tax paid on such amounts of "income in respect of a decedent".[9]

Tools and Techniques

Question — If an estate is so small that no estate tax is payable or if no tax is payable because of the unlimited estate tax marital deduction, does the property still receive a stepped-up basis?

Answer — Yes. Regardless of the size of the estate or whether or not a federal estate tax is payable, a stepped-up (or stepped-down if the property has decreased in value below the original cost) basis will apply. Payment of estate tax is not a condition for receiveing a new income tax basis.

Question — If a Personal Representative elects to use the alternate valuation date (six months after death) for valuing property for estate tax purposes, does that affect the stepped-up basis rule?

Answer — Yes. If the alternate valuation date is elected for federal estate tax purposes,[10] the fair market value of the property on that six-months-after-death date will be the new income tax basis of the property.[11]

Question — How is basis adjusted in a generation-skipping transfer?

Answer — Very similarly to the basis adjustment allowed when a gift tax is paid on a transfer. The transferee's basis is increased—but not beyond the fair market value of the property transferred—by an amount equal to that portion of the GST tax imposed on the transfer generated by the potential gain in the property immediately prior to the transfer.

Basis Adjustments for Taxable Distributions or Direct Skips

Fair market value of transferred property	$1,000,000
Adjusted basis of transferred property immediately before GS transfer	$600,000
GST tax imposed on transfer	$500,000
Increase in transferee's basis	$200,000
Transferee's new BASIS	$800,000

If the GST tax is imposed because of a taxable termination that occurs at the same time as, and as the result of, an individual's death, the property's basis is stepped up similar to the normal step-up in basis of property at death (with certain limitations).

Footnote References
How Basis is Determined

1. I.R.C. Section 1014
2. I.R.C. Section 1014(b)(6)
3. I.R.C. Section 1015(a), (d)
4. I.R.C. Section 1015(b)
5. I.R.C. Section 1015(e)
6. I.R.C. Section 1014(b)(2), (3), (9)
7. I.R.C. Section 691(a)(4)
8. I.R.C. Section 1014(c) and I.R.C. Section 691
9. I.R.C. Section 691(c)
10. I.R.C. Section 2032
11. I.R.C. Section 1014(a)(2)

FIGURING COMPOUND INTEREST
AND ANNUITY VALUES

The two tables that follow on the next two pages enable the estate planner to make various projections in actual cases. They show the compound interest and annuity functions at interest rates of 5 and 10 percent.

There are three functions which can be used for compound interest computations:

1. Amount of $1 (what a dollar will be worth at some date in the future if the deposit is made immediately).

   For Example, if $1,000 is invested today and grows at a rate of 10 percent per year compounded annually, it will be worth $1,948.72 in 7 years. (Go to Form A on the following page. Find 7th year. Look under "Amount of 1" column. The value is 1.948717 multiplied by $1,000.)

2. Amount of $1 per period (what a series of $1 deposits will be worth at some date in the future if the deposits are made at the end of each period).

   For example, if $1,000 is invested at the end of each year for 10 years and the return has been 10 percent interest compounded annually, the value of the fund is $15,937. (Go to Form A. Find 10 years. Look under the "Amount of 1 per Period" column. The value is 15.937,425. Multiply this by $1,000.)

3. Sinking fund payment (how much you need to deposit at the end of each period to have a given sum of money at a specified point in the future).

   For example, you'll need $100,000 in 5 years to pay off a debt. If you can earn 10 percent compounded annually on your money, you must deposit $16,379.74 each year for 5 years. (Go to Form A. Find 5 years. Look under the "Sinking Fund Payment" column. The value is .1637974808. Multiply that figure by $100,000.)

There are three functions which enable annuity computations:

1. Present worth of $1 (the value of $1 today if it will not be received until some time in the future).

For example, you are owed $1,000 and it will be paid to you in 10 years. Assuming a 5 percent interest rate, the present value of that debt is $613.91. (Go to Form B. Find 10 years. Look under the "Present Worth of 1" column. The value is 0.613,913. Multiply that by $1,000.)

2. Present worth of $1 per period. (How much is a future stream of dollars—payable at the end of each year—worth today?)

   For example, suppose you were to receive $1,000 at the end of each year for the next 20 years. Assuming 10 percent interest, that stream of dollars would be worth $8,513.56 today. (Go to Form A. Find 20 years. Look under the "Present Worth of 1 per Period" column. The value is 8.513,564. Multiply that by $1,000.)

3. Periodic payment to amortize $1. (What mortgage payment must be made each year to pay off a given loan? In other words, you have a dollar now. What annuity do you have to pay each year—given a certain number of years—to pay off the loan?)

   For example, what is the annual payment needed to pay off a $100,000 loan over 10 years if a 10 percent interest rate is payable on the unpaid balance? Assuming payments are made annually at the end of each year and interest is compounded annually, the amount is $16,274.54. (Go to Form A. Find 10 years. Look under the "Periodic Payment to Amortize 1" column. The value is 0.1627453949. Multiply that by $100,000.)

There is one measurement function: total interest (how much interest is paid over a given period of time where a loan is amortized by regular periodic payments).

For example, assume you were going to borrow $100,000 over 10 years at 10 percent interest. The total interest you'd pay on such a loan is $62,745. (Go to Form A. Find 10 years. Look under the "Total Interest" column. The value is 0.627,454. Multiply that by $100,000.)

Figuring Compound Interest and Annuity Values 10 percent

	Amount of 1	Amount of 1 Per Period	Sinking Fund Payment	Present Worth of 1	Present Worth of 1 Per Period	Periodic Payment to Amortize 1	Total Interest
	What a single $1 deposit grows to in the future. The deposit is made at the beginning of the first period.	What a series of $1 deposits grow to in the future. A deposit is made at the end of each period.	The amount to be deposited at the end of each period that grows to $1 in the future.	What $1 to be paid in the future is worth today. Value today of a single payment tomorrow.	What $1 to be paid at the end of each period is worth today. Value today of a series of payments tomorrow.	The mortgage payment to amortize a loan of $1. An annuity certain, payable at the end of each period worth $1 today.	The total interest paid over the term on a loan of $1. The loan is amortized by regular periodic payments.
YEAR							
1	1.100 000	1.000 000	1.000 000 0000	0.909 091	0.909 091	1.100 000 0000	0.100 000
2	1.210 000	2.100 000	0.476 190 4762	0.826 446	1.735 537	0.576 190 4762	0.152 381
3	1.331 000	3.310 000	0.302 114 8036	0.751 315	2.486 852	0.402 114 8036	0.206 344
4	1.464 100	4.641 000	0.215 470 8037	0.683 013	3.169 865	0.315 470 8037	0.261 883
5	1.610 510	6.105 100	0.163 797 4808	0.620 921	3.790 787	0.263 797 4808	0.318 987
6	1.771 561	7.715 610	0.129 607 3804	0.564 474	4.355 261	0.229 607 3804	0.377 644
7	1.948 717	9.487 171	0.105 405 4997	0.513 158	4.868 419	0.205 405 4997	0.437 838
8	2.143 589	11.435 888	0.087 444 0176	0.466 507	5.334 926	0.187 444 0176	0.499 552
9	2.357 948	13.579 477	0.073 640 5391	0.424 098	5.759 024	0.173 640 5391	0.562 765
10	2.593 742	15.937 425	0.062 745 3949	0.385 543	6.144 567	0.162 745 3949	0.627 454
11	2.853 117	18.531 167	0.053 963 1420	0.350 494	6.495 061	0.153 963 1420	0.693 595
12	3.138 428	21.384 284	0.046 763 3151	0.318 631	6.813 692	0.146 763 3151	0.761 160
13	3.452 271	24.522 712	0.040 778 5238	0.289 664	7.103 356	0.140 778 5238	0.830 121
14	3.797 498	27.974 983	0.035 746 2232	0.263 331	7.366 687	0.135 746 2232	0.900 447
15	4.177 248	31.772 482	0.031 473 7769	0.239 392	7.606 080	0.131 473 7769	0.972 107
16	4.594 973	35.949 730	0.027 816 6207	0.217 629	7.823 709	0.127 816 6207	1.045 066
17	5.054 470	40.544 703	0.024 664 1344	0.197 845	8.021 553	0.124 664 1344	1.119 290
18	5.559 917	45.599 173	0.021 930 2222	0.179 859	8.201 412	0.121 930 2222	1.194 744
19	6.115 909	51.159 090	0.019 546 8682	0.163 508	8.364 920	0.119 546 8682	1.271 390
20	6.727 500	57.274 999	0.017 459 6248	0.148 644	8.513 564	0.117 459 6248	1.349 192
21	7.400 250	64.002 499	0.015 624 3898	0.135 131	8.648 694	0.115 624 3898	1.428 112
22	8.140 275	71.402 749	0.014 005 0630	0.122 846	8.771 540	0.114 005 0630	1.508 111
23	8.954 302	79.543 024	0.012 571 8127	0.111 678	8.883 218	0.112 571 8127	1.589 152
24	9.849 733	88.497 327	0.011 299 7764	0.101 526	8.984 744	0.111 299 7764	1.671 195
25	10.834 706	98.347 059	0.010 168 0722	0.092 296	9.077 040	0.110 168 0722	1.754 202
26	11.918 177	109.181 765	0.009 159 0386	0.083 905	9.160 945	0.109 159 0386	1.838 135
27	13.109 994	121.099 942	0.008 257 6423	0.076 278	9.237 223	0.108 257 6423	1.922 956
28	14.420 994	134.209 936	0.007 451 0132	0.069 343	9.306 567	0.107 451 0132	2.008 628
29	15.863 093	148.630 930	0.006 728 0747	0.063 039	9.639 606	0.106 728 0747	2.095 114
30	17.449 402	164.494 023	0.006 079 2483	0.057 309	9.426 914	0.106 079 2483	2.182 377

FORM A

Figuring Compound Interest and Annuity Values 5 percent

	Amount of 1	Amount of 1 Per Period	Sinking Fund Payment	Present Worth of 1	Present Worth of 1 Per Period	Periodic Payment to Amortize 1	Total Interest
	What a single $1 deposit grows to in the future. The deposit is made at the beginning of the first period.	What a series of $1 deposits grow to in the future. A deposit is made at the end of each period.	The amount to be deposited at the end of each period that grows to $1 in the future.	What $1 to be paid in the future is worth today. Value today of a single payment tomorrow.	What $1 to be paid at the end of each period is worth today. Value today of a series of payments tomorrow.	The mortgage payment to amortize a loan of $1. An annuity certain, payable at the end of each period worth $1 today.	The total interest paid over the term on a loan of $1. The loan is amortized by regular periodic payments.
YEAR							
1	1.050 000	1.000 000	1.000 000 0000	0.952 381	0.952 381	1.050 000 0000	0.050 000
2	1.102 500	2.050 000	0.487 804 8780	0.907 029	1.859 410	0.537 804 8780	0.075 610
3	1.157 625	3.152 500	0.317 208 5646	0.863 838	2.723 248	0.367 208 5646	0.101 626
4	1.215 506	4.310 125	0.232 011 8326	0.822 702	3.545 951	0.282 011 8326	0.128 047
5	1.276 282	5.525 631	0.180 974 7981	0.783 526	4.329 477	0.230 974 7981	0.154 874
6	1.340 096	6.801 913	0.147 017 4681	0.746 215	5.075 692	0.197 017 4681	0.182 105
7	1.407 100	8.142 008	0.122 819 8184	0.710 681	5.786 373	0.172 819 8184	0.209 739
8	1.477 455	9.549 109	0.104 721 8136	0.676 839	6.463 213	0.154 721 8136	0.237 775
9	1.551 328	11.026 564	0.090 690 0800	0.644 609	7.107 822	0.140 690 0800	0.266 211
10	1.628 895	12.577 893	0.079 504 5750	0.613 913	7.721 735	0.129 504 5750	0.295 046
11	1.710 339	14.206 787	0.070 388 8915	0.584 679	8.306 414	0.120 388 8915	0.324 278
12	1.795 856	15.917 127	0.062 825 4100	0.556 837	8.863 252	0.112 825 4100	0.353 905
13	1.885 649	17.712 983	0.056 455 7652	0.530 321	9.393 573	0.106 455 7652	0.383 925
14	1.979 932	19.598 632	0.051 023 9695	0.505 068	9.898 641	0.101 023 9695	0.414 336
15	2.078 928	21.578 564	0.046 342 2876	0.481 017	10.379 658	0.096 342 2876	0.445 134
16	2.182 875	23.657 492	0.042 269 9080	0.458 112	10.837 770	0.092 269 9080	0.476 319
17	2.292 018	25.840 366	0.038 699 1417	0.436 297	11.274 066	0.088 699 1417	0.507 885
18	2.406 619	28.132 385	0.035 546 2223	0.415 521	11.689 587	0.085 546 2223	0.539 832
19	2.526 950	30.539 004	0.032 745 0104	0.395 734	12.085 321	0.082 745 0104	0.572 155
20	2.653 298	33.065 954	0.030 242 5872	0.376 889	12.462 210	0.080 242 5872	0.604 852
21	2.785 963	35.719 252	0.027 996 1071	0.358 942	12.821 153	0.077 996 1071	0.637 918
22	2.925 261	38.505 214	0.025 970 5086	0.341 850	13.163 003	0.075 970 5086	0.671 351
23	3.071 524	41.430 475	0.024 136 8219	0.325 571	13.488 574	0.074 136 8219	0.705 147
24	3.225 100	44.501 999	0.022 470 9008	0.310 068	13.798 642	0.072 470 9008	0.739 302
25	3.386 355	47.727 099	0.020 952 4573	0.295 303	14.093 945	0.070 952 4573	0.773 811
26	3.555 673	51.113 454	0.019 564 3207	0.281 241	14.375 185	0.069 564 3207	0.808 672
27	3.733 456	54.669 126	0.018 291 8599	0.267 848	14.643 034	0.068 291 8599	0.843 880
28	3.920 129	58.402 583	0.017 122 5304	0.255 094	14.898 127	0.067 122 5304	0.879 431
29	4.116 136	62.322 712	0.016 045 5149	0.242 946	15.141 074	0.066 045 5149	0.915 320
30	4.321 942	66.438 848	0.015 051 4351	0.231 377	15.372 451	0.065 051 4351	0.951 543

FORM B

Tools and Techniques

CHOOSING AN ENTITY — A CHECKLIST OF ISSUES TO CONSIDER

PROPRIETORSHIP

(1) One person owner
(2) Few employees
(3) Relatively low income
(4) Relatively low start up costs
(5) No double tax on business earnings
(6) Not possible to "time" or "split" income
(7) Administration of estate difficult
(8) Valuation freezing techniques not available

PARTNERSHIP

(1) Sharing of net profits
(2) Presence of loss sharing
(3) Pass through of losses
(4) Avoidance of double taxation on profits
(5) Relatively low start up costs
(6) Relatively economical operation costs
(7) Taxable years must match those of partners
(8) No restrictions on who can invest or number of investors
(9) Easy to convert to another form of entity
(10) No accumulated earnings tax
(11) No personal holding company tax
(12) Unlimited personal liability
(13) Subject to "at risk" limitations
(14) Losses not deductible in excess of basis
(15) Interest deduction limits at personal level
(16) Equity received for services creates income
(17) On contribution of encumbered property, generally, only liabilities assumed by other partners in excess of contributing partner's basis is taxable
(18) Income splitting — wealth shifting potential
(19) IRS can reallocate income if member of family renders services without reasonable compensation
(20) Partners who render services are treated as employees for certain fringe benefit purposes but tax law typically precludes nontaxable fringe benefits for most partners

CORPORATION — "C"

(1) Limited liability to creditors
(2) Shareholder-employees can exclude certain fringe benefits from income
(3) Income trapped at corporate level
(4) Reasonableness of compensation an issue
(5) Accumulated earnings and alternative minimum tax liability
(6) Losses trapped at corporate level
(7) Passive loss rules avoided at corporate level and deductions at corporate rates
(8) Flexibility in terms of numbers of shareholders
(9) Can have more than one class of stock
(10) Stock can be used as compensation
(11) Ability to form subsidiaries

Tools and Techniques

(12) Must be adequately capitalized

(13) Decision making centralized through management structure

(14) Possible to retain earnings without tax at personal level

(15) Dividends received exclusion

(16) 34 percent flat rate on certain professional service corporations

(17) Subject to double taxation upon liquidation

CORPORATION — "S"

(1) Restrictions on who can hold stock

(2) Limits on number of investors

(3) Only one class of stock (common) allowed

(4) No subsidiaries possible

(5) Some states do not recognize pass through of income or losses

(6) Limited liability

(7) Decision making centralized through management structure

(8) Pass through of income, losses, and credits

(9) Difficult to do estate planning since spray or sprinkle trust can't own S stock

(10) Limits on type of business an S corporation can be

(11) Potential for accidental or nonvoluntary termination of S election

A Comparison of Splits, Gifts, GRITs, and RITs

RELATIVE ODDS OF AVOIDING FEDERAL ESTATE TAX INCLUSION

Splits   HIGH   (This assumes the remainderman does *not* acquire his contribution from the life or term tenant.) Net after-tax income received by life or term tenant will be includible to extent not consumed or given away.

Gifts   HIGH   (Only adjusted taxable gifts enter the estate tax computation.) The future income stream produced by the gift is removed from the donor's estate.

GRITs   LOW/HIGH   (If death occurs within the term the grantor has retained the right to income, inclusion is certain. But if death occurs beyond that point, it is likely there will be no inclusion assuming the trust meets 2036(c) safe harbor rules or if grantor didn't own 10% or more of voting power or income of enterprise prior to inception of GRIT. Net after-tax income received by the life or term tenant will be includible to the extent not consumed or given away.)

RITs   LOW   (Intra-family sales of remainder interests may save federal estate tax and may save state death taxes in full unless (1) the purchaser furnished full and adequate consideration in money or money's worth for the purchaser's interest, (2) it can be proven to the satisfaction of the IRS that the consideration belonged to the purchaser and wasn't received or acquired from the transferor, and (3) the *Gradow* holding can be overcome. In this case, at least a partial freeze may be possible. The value of the remainder interest on the date of the seller's death will be includible. Net after-tax income received by life or term tenant seller will be includible to the extent not consumed or given away.)

RELATIVE ABILITY TO "DEFUND" CLIENT'S ESTATE

Splits   VERY HIGH   (Neither the value of the appreciated property nor the amount of the life or term tenant's contribution to the purchase will be in his estate. Since there is no gift, the life tenant's annual exclusions and unified credit remain intact and can be used to offset otherwise taxable gifts and are therefore available to further defund the estate.)

Gifts   LOW/HIGH   (A gift removes from the gross estate (a) the property itself, (b) future appreciation on the property, and (c) income from the property. But depending on the size of the gift, some or all of the client's annual exclusion and unified credit must be used to offset otherwise taxable gifts and are therefore not available to further defund the estate.)

GRITs   LOW   (Assuming the grantor outlives the specified term and either the trust meets the 2036(c) safe harbor rules or the grantor didn't own 10% or more of enterprise's voting power or income rights prior to inception of the GRIT, the following are removed from his estate: (a) the property itself and (b) all appreciation. Net after-tax income received and not consumed or given away by the grantor will be in his estate. Since, by definition, the GRIT involves a future interest gift to the remainderman, to the extent used to offset this taxable gift, the unified credit will not be available to further defund the estate.)

RITs   LOW   (Both the asset itself and any appreciation could be partially removed from the client's estate if the 3 conditions mentioned above can be met. To the extent consumed or given away, the aftertax sales proceeds are not includible in the client's estate. Because there is no gift, neither the gift tax annual exclusion nor the unified credit have been used. Therefore, both are available to help defund the client's estate.) Note that for state death tax and probate cost purposes, significant savings may be available.

Appendix B
A Comparison of Splits, Gifts, GRITs, and RITs

RELATIVE COST OF TECHNIQUE IN TERMS OF UNIFIED CREDIT

Splits — VERY LOW — (Since there is no gift, there is no gift tax to offset. Therefore the use of this device does not use up any of the unified credit.)

Gifts — HIGH — (To the extent the value of the gift exceeds the annual exclusion or for any reason does not qualify as a present interest gift, the unified credit must be used to offset what would otherwise be a gift tax.)

GRITs — MODERATE — (Since the gift to the remainderman is a future interest gift and therefore is taxable, the unified credit is used. But because the gift is not the entire value of the property but merely the value of the remainder interest, the use of the unified credit can be leveraged. This leverage can be multiplied if the grantor retains an income interest lasting for the lesser of (a) the specified term or (b) the grantor's lifetime. But if death occurs prior to the end of the specified period of time, assets in the trust revert to the grantor's estate. This contingency significantly reduces the value of the remainderman's interest (and therefore the taxable gift is reduced).)

RITs — VERY LOW — (By design in the sale of a remainder interest there is no gift. Therefore, no utilization has been made of the unified credit.)

RELATIVE IMPORTANCE OF PROPER VALUATION TO FEDERAL ESTATE TAX SUCCESS

Splits — LOW — (It is assumed that a split interest transaction involves a purchase at arms' length from a third party for the property's fair market value and that the appropriate government tables have been used to determine the respective payments. If these guidelines have been met, a later valuation challenge should not raise any significant estate tax problems.)

Gifts — LOW — (If the Service determines that the gift was undervalued, the result will be an increase in adjusted taxable gifts — typically resulting in a greater use of the unified credit.)

GRITs — LOW — (If the Service determines that the gift was undervalued, the result will be an increase in adjusted taxable gifts — typically resulting in a greater use of the unified credit.)

RITs — HIGH — (In an intra-family sale, if the remainderman is able to prove that — at the time of the sale — the price paid was an adequate and full consideration for the property interest purchased and none of the purchase price came from the donor (directly or indirectly), the transfer might partially fall outside the ambit of Code Section 2036(c). Therefore, the porton of the federal estate tax value (attributable to consideration actually paid would not be included in the decedent's gross estate. Proper valuation is essential to save state death taxes (which may be considerable).)

RELATIVE PROBABILITY OF FEDERAL ESTATE TAX SAVING SUCCESS BASED ON CURRENT LAW AND CASES

Splits — HIGH — (The life tenant does not own an interest at death. Since there has been no gratuitous transfer with retained life estate, there should be no Section 2036 inclusion.)

Gifts — VERY HIGH — [Once the gift is made (with the exception of certain gifts made within 3 years of death), it is highly likely that it will escape the ambit of the federal estate tax.]

GRITs — HIGH — (Assuming the grantor outlives the specified term, there is a high likelihood that there will be no federal estate tax inclusion.)

RITs   UNCERTAIN   (Assuming the remainderman paid consideration that is adequate and full at the time of purchase and could prove that none of the purchase price was received or acquired from the seller, the issue of the (poorly reasoned) *Gradow* case and the relevance of its holding would be raised by the IRS. But since Congress clearly took this issue outside of Code Section 2043, the author feels RITS may have new life as a partial freeze.)

ADVANTAGEOUS BASIS TO ULTIMATE RECIPIENT OF PROPERTY

Splits   VERY LOW   (Remainderman's basis is price paid for remainder interest.)

Gifts   LOW   (The donee takes the donor's basis plus a step-up for gift taxes paid on the appreciated portion of the gift.)

GRITs   VERY LOW   (Remainderman receives a fractionalized portion of the grantor's basis.)

RITs   VERY LOW   (The remainderman's basis is the price paid for the remainder interest.)

RELATIVE AMOUNT OF MONEY ULTIMATE RECIPIENT OF PROPERTY MUST HAVE TO MAKE TRANSACTION WORK

Splits   MODERATE   (Must have or obtain enough cash to purchase remainder interest.)

Gifts   NONE   (Unless "net gifts" requires donee to pay gift tax.)

GRITs   NONE   (Remainderman has no outlay.)

RITs   MODERATE   (Remainderman must have sufficient funds to purchase remainder interest.) Installment sale, self-canceling installment note, or private annuity may make it possible to "annualize" what would otherwise be a lump-sum payment requirement. Gift from the life tenant to finance the remainder interest would definitely cause the remainder interest transaction to be categorized as a gift with a retained life estate. Even, an indirect "old and cold" gift or other transfer for less than full and adequate consideration to the remainderman from the life tenant would cause 2036(c) to apply. Assuming the transaction makes sense to accomplish other objectives (or if estate tax inclusion is unimportant), gifts by the seller that qualify for the annual exclusion or that are within the client's unified credit limits may help the remainderman considerably at no additional cost.

PROBABILITY THAT THE DEVICE WILL SHIFT INCOME

Splits   NONE   [In fact, the life or term tenant may be receiving more aftertax income after the transaction than before. But the remainderman receives no income (and therefore no income shift is possible) until after the life (or term) tenant's interest expires.]

Gifts   HIGH   (Subject to expanded grantor trust and under age 14 "kiddie tax" rules, a gift will shift income from donor to donee but at the cost of both the property and its income.)

GRITs   NONE   (By definition, the grantor retains income and therefore no shift occurs until the specified term ends and the property itself belongs to the remainderman.)

RITs   NONE   (Again, by definition, all income (or all rights to possess or enjoy the property) is retained. In the case of a RIT, income rights continue until the life tenant's death. So no lifetime income shifting is possible.)

PROBABILITY THAT THE CLIENT WILL RECEIVE A DEPRECIATION OR AMORTIZATION DEDUCTION

Splits   HIGH   (Even if the property itself is a nondepreciable asset such as land, if it is held for investment purposes, an amortization deduction is allowed based on the life tenant's basis since the life tenant's interest has (like the life tenant himself) a limited life (amortization is subject to the 2 percent floor on the deductibility of miscellaneous itemized expenses). Although there appears to be no Code provision barring both amortization of a life estate and a depreciation deduction if the property is depreciable, the double writeoff is an aggressive position.)

Gifts   NONE   (If the property is depreciable, that deduction can be taken by the property's new owner, the donee.)

GRITs   NONE   (Since the trust is, by definition, a grantor trust, the grantor will, however, be entitled to any depreciation deductions inherent in the property.)

RITs   NONE   (Although the transaction itself does not produce or result in any new depreciation deductions, any depreciation inherent in the property can still be taken by the life tenant (up to the basis retained and not sold by the life tenant).)

IMPACT OF LIFE EXPECTANCY ON SUCCESS POTENTIAL OF DEVICE

Splits   HIGH   (A split interest purchase is particularly attractive where the client's life expectancy is short. Where the client's life expectancy is longer than what could be predicted from the government's tables, the remainderman may have paid too much. But if the property appreciates at a rate in excess of the government's presumed rate of 10 percent, or if certainty of obtaining the property is important to the remainderman, a split may still be indicated.)

Gifts   HIGH   (An outright gift is particularly attractive where the client's actual life expectancy is substantially greater than the expectancy projected in government tables. This is because after the gift, none of the appreciation enters into the estate tax computation. If the client's life expectancy is short, a gift is often contraindicated since the loss of a stepped up basis must be weighed against a small possibility of substantial postgift appreciation. Little leveraging of the annual exclusion and unified credit is likely when the client has a less than normal life expectancy.)

GRITs   HIGH   (A GRIT is particularly attractive where a client has an actual life expectancy in excess of the life expectancy projected under government tables. Conversely, if the client is likely to die within the specified term, the odds of estate tax inclusion and therefore failure to accomplish a major planning objectives are high.)

RITs   HIGH   (A remainder interest transaction is particularly attractive where a client has a life expectancy lower than the life expectancy projected under government tables. Conversely, if the client lives significantly longer than the projected life expectancy, the remainderman will mathematically have paid too much. But if property appreciates at a rate in excess of the interest rate assumed in the government's tables (or formulas) or if certainty of receiving the property (i.e., protection against loss of the property to a surviving spouse or other beneficiary through a contest of an election against the will, or to creditors) is important to the remainderman, these factors may outweigh the mathematics.)

APPENDIX C

INCOME TAX RATE SCHEDULES

	Taxable Years Beginning in 1987	Taxable Years Beginning in 1988
STANDARD DEDUCTION:		
Married, filing jointly	$3,760	$5,000
Married, filing separately	1,880	2,500
Single	2,540	3,000
PERSONAL EXEMPTION:	$1,900	$1,950

SCHEDULE X — SINGLE INDIVIDUALS AND CERTAIN MARRIED INDIVIDUALS LIVING APART

Taxable Years Beginning in 1987

Taxable Income	Tax on Lower Amount	Tax Rate on Excess
$ -0- to $ 1,800	$ -0-	11 %
1,800 to 16,800	198	15
16,800 to 27,000	2,448	28
27,000 to 54,000	5,304	35
54,000 to	14,754	38.5

Taxable Years Beginning in 1988

Taxable Income	Tax on Lower Amount	Tax Rate on Excess
$ -0- to $17,850	$ -0-	15%
17,850 to 43,150	2,678	28
43,150 to	9,762	*

SCHEDULE Y(J) — JOINT RETURNS AND SURVIVING SPOUSES

Taxable Years Beginning in 1987

Taxable Income	Tax on Lower Amount	Tax Rate on Excess
$ -0- to $ 3,000	$ -0-	11 %
3,000 to 28,000	330	15
28,000 to 45,000	4,080	28
45,000 to 90,000	8,840	35
90,000 to	24,590	38.5

Taxable Years Beginning in 1988

Taxable Income	Tax on Lower Amount	Tax Rate on Excess
$ -0- to $29,750	$ -0-	15%
29,750 to 71,900	4,463	28
71,900 to	16,265	*

* The tax rate for this and higher taxable incomes will be 33% and will remain at that rate until the taxpayer's personal exemptions have been recaptured; when the exemptions have been recaptured, the rate on additional income drops to 28%.

Tools and Techniques

SCHEDULE Y(S) — MARRIED FILING SEPARATELY

Taxable Years Beginning in 1987

Taxable Income	Tax on Lower Amount	Tax Rate on Excess
$ -0- to $ 1,500	$ -0-	11 %
1,500 to 14,000	165	15
14,000 to 22,500	2,040	28
22,500 to 45,000	4,420	35
45,000 to	12,295	38.5

Taxable Years Beginning in 1988

Taxable Income	Tax on Lower Amount	Tax Rate on Excess
$ -0- to $14,875	$ -0-	15%
14,875 to 35,950	2,231	28
35,890 to	8,132	*

SCHEDULE Z — HEAD OF HOUSEHOLD

Taxable Years Beginning in 1987

Taxable Income	Tax on Lower Amount	Tax Rate on Excess
$ -0- to $ 2,500	$ -0-	11 %
2,500 to 23,000	275	15
23,000 to 38,000	3,350	28
38,000 to 80,000	7,550	35
80,000 to	22,250	38.5

Taxable Years Beginning in 1988

Taxable Income	Tax on Lower Amount	Tax Rate on Excess
$ -0- to $23,900	$ -0-	15%
23,900 to 61,650	3,585	28
61,650 to	14,155	*

TAX RATE SCHEDULE FOR ESTATES AND TRUSTS

Taxable Years Beginning in 1987

Taxable Income	Tax on Lower Amount	Tax Rate on Excess
$ -0- to $ 500	$ -0-	11 %
500 to 4,700	55	15
4,700 to 7,550	685	28
7,550 to 15,150	1,483	35
15,150 to	4,143	38.5

Taxable Years Beginning in 1988

Taxable Income	Tax on Lower Amount	Tax Rate on Excess
$ -0- to $ 5,000	$ -0-	15%
5,000 to 13,000	750	28
13,000 to 26,000	2,990	33
26,000 to	7,280	28

TAX RATE SCHEDULE FOR CORPORATIONS

Tax Years Ending Before 7-1-87

Taxable Income	Tax on Lower Amount	Tax Rate on Excess
$ -0- to $ 25,000	$ -0-	15%
25,000 to 50,000	3,750	18
50,000 to 75,000	8,250	30
75,000 to 100,000	15,750	40
100,000 to	25,750	46
1,000,000 to 1,405,000	-0-	5

Tax Years Ending After 6-30-87

Taxable Income	Tax on Lower Amount	Tax Rate on Excess
$ -0- to $ 50,000	$ -0-	15%
50,000 to 75,000	7,500	25
75,000 to 100,000	18,750	34
100,000 to 335,000	34,000	39
335,000 to	130,650	34

For taxable years beginning before and including July 1, 1987, the tax rates are blended between the old and new ates. Thus, the top tax rate (disregarding the surtax) was 40% for a calendar year corporation in 1987 (one half of 46% and 34%).

* The tax rate for this and higher taxable incomes will be 33% and will remain at that rate until the taxpayer's personal exemptions have been recaptured; when the exemptions have been recaptured, the rate on additional income drops to 28%.

Appendix C
Income Tax Rate Schedules

5 Year Averaging

Net Lump Sum Taxable Amount	Tax 1987	Effective Tax Rate*	Tax 1988	Effective Tax Rate*
$ 10,000	$ 550	.06	$ 750	.08
20,000	1,140	.06	1,500	.08
30,000	2,940	.10	3,300	.11
40,000	4,740	.12	5,100	.13
50,000	6,540	.13	6,900	.14
75,000	10,890	.15	11,250	.15
100,000	16,720	.17	16,398	.16
150,000	31,770	.21	30,393	.20
200,000	49,270	.25	44,398	.22
250,000	66,770	.27	60,110†	.24
300,000	85,320	.28	76,610†	.26
500,000	162,320	.32	140,000†	.28
1,000,000	354,820	.35	280,000†	.28
2,000,000	739,820	.37	560,000†	.28
3,000,000	932,320	.37	840,000†	.28
4,000,000	1,124,820	.37	1,120,000†	.28
5,000,000	1.894,820	.38	1,400,000†	.28

Note that if you were age 50 before January 1, 1986, and you receive a distribution in 1987 or a later year, you may elect to use 10 year averaging using the tax rates in effect in 1986 instead of 5 year averaging with current rates. Income averaging for lump sum distributions is discussed in more detail in Chapter 22.

*Effective tax rates rounded.

†These amounts reflect the phase-out of the 15% tax bracket for high-income taxpayers under Code section 1 (g). (Section 402(e) (1) (B) currently provides that the amount of tax applicable to lump sum distributions is to be determined using the unmarried individuals tax rate in section 1 (c); no reference is made to section 1 (g). However, section 111A(b) (10) of the Technical Corrections Bill of 1988, if enacted, would amend section 402(e) (1) (B) to take into account the phase-out of the 15% bracket.)

Tools and Techniques

UNIFIED RATE SCHEDULE FOR ESTATE AND GIFT TAXES
(IRC Sec. 2001(c))
(for decedents dying and gifts made in years *1977-1981*)

If the amount with respect to which the tentative tax to be computed is:

The tentative tax is:

Not over $10,000 . . . . 18% of such amount.

Over $10,000 but not over $20,000 . . . . $1,800 plus 20% of the excess of such amount over $10,000.

Over $20,000 but not over $40,000 . . . . $3,800 plus 22% of the excess of such amount over $20,000.

Over $40,000 but not over $60,000 . . . . $8,200 plus 24% of the excess of such amount over $40,000.

Over $60,000 but not over $80,000 . . . . $13,000 plus 26% of the excess of such amount over $60,000.

Over $80,000 but not over $100,000 . . . . $18,200 plus 28% of the excess of such amount over $80,000.

Over $100,000 but not over $150,000 . . . . $23,800 plus 30% of the excess of such amount over $100,000.

Over $150,000 but not over $250,000 . . . . $38,800 plus 32% of the excess of such amount over $150,000.

Over $250,000 but not over $500,000 . . . . $70,800 plus 34% of the excess of such amount over $250,000.

Over $500,000 but not over $750,000 . . . . $155,800 plus 37% of the excess of such amount over $500,000.

Over $750,000 but not over $1,000,000 . . . . $248,300 plus 39% of the excess of such amount over $750,000.

Over $1,000,000 but not over $1,250,000 . . . . $345,800 plus 41% of the excess of such amount over $1,000,000.

Over $1,250,000 but not over $1,500,000 . . . . $448,300 plus 43% of the excess of such amount over $1,250,000.

Over $1,500,000 but not over $2,000,000 . . . . $555,800 plus 45% of the excess of such amount over $1,500,000.

Over $2,000,000 but not over $2,500,000 . . . . $780,800 plus 49% of the excess of such amount over $2,000,000.

Over $2,500,000 but not over $3,000,000 . . . . $1,025,800 plus 53% of the excess of such amount over $2,500,000.

Over $3,000,000 but not over $3,500,000 . . . . $1,290,800 plus 57% of the excess of such amount over $3,000,000.

Over $3,500,000 but not over $4,000,000 . . . . $1,575,800 plus 61% of the excess of such amount over $3,500,000.

Over $4,000,000 but not over $4,500,000 . . . . $1,880,800 plus 65% of the excess of such amount over $4,000,000.

Over $4,500,000 but not over $5,000,000 . . . . $2,205,800 plus 69% of the excess of such amount over $4,500,000.

Over $5,000,000 . . . . $2,550,800 plus 70% of the excess over $5,000,000.

(See following page for rates in succeeding years.)

UNIFIED RATE SCHEDULE FOR ESTATE AND GIFT TAXES
(for decedents dying and gifts made in years *following 1981)*

For 1982

In the case of decedents dying and gifts made in 1982, the following substitution should be made in the rate schedule:

Over $2,500,000 but not over $3,000,000	$1,025,800, plus 53% of the excess over $2,500,000.
Over $3,000,000 but not over $3,500,000	$1,290,800, plus 57% of the excess over $3,000,000.
Over $3,500,000 but not over $4,000,000	$1,575,800, plus 61% of the excess over $3,500,000.
Over $4,000,000	$1,880,800, plus 65% of the excess over $4,000,000.

For 1983

In the case of decedents dying and gifts made in 1983, the following substitution should be made in the rate schedule:

Over $2,500,000 but not over $3,000,000	$1,025,800, plus 53% of the excess over $2,500,000.
Over $3,000,000 but not over $3,500,000	$1,290,800, plus 57% of the excess over $3,000,000.
Over $3,500,000	$1,575,800 plus 60% of the excess over $3,500,000.

For 1984 through 1992*

In the case of decedents dying and gifts made in 1984 through 1992, the following substitution should be made in the rate schedule:

Over $2,500,000 but not over $3,000,000	$1,025,800, plus 53% of the excess over $2,500,000.
Over $3,000,000	$1,290,800 plus 55% of the excess over $3,000,000.

For 1993 and later years*

In the case of decedents dying and gifts made in 1993 and later years, the following substitution should be made in the rate schedule:

Over $2,500,000	$1,025,800, plus 50% of the excess over $2,500,000.

*In the case of decedents dying and gifts made after 1987, the tentative tax as determined above is increased by an amount equal to 5 percent of so much of the amount with respect to which the tentative tax is computed as exceeds $10,000,000 but does not exceed $21,040,000 ($18,340,000 in the case of decedents dying and gifts made after 1992). See immediately succeeding pages and the table ULTRA LARGE ESTATES at the end of Appendix C for more information on this add-on tax.

UNIFIED GIFT AND ESTATE TAX RATE SCHEDULE IN THE CASE OF DECEDENTS DYING AND GIFTS MADE IN 1984-1992			
(A)	(B)	(C)	(D)
Amount subject to tentative tax		Tax on amount in Column A*	Tax rate on excess over amounts in Column A*
exceeding	but not exceeding		Percent
$ —	$ 10,000	$ —	18
10,000	20,000	1,800	20
20,000	40,000	3,800	22
40,000	60,000	8,200	24
60,000	80,000	13,000	26
80,000	100,000	18,200	28
100,000	150,000	23,800	30
150,000	250,000	38,800	32
250,000	500,000	70,800	34
500,000	750,000	155,800	37
750,000	1,000,000	248,300	39
1,000,000	1,250,000	345,800	41
1,250,000	1,500,000	448,300	43
1,500,000	2,000,000	555,800	45
2,000,000	2,500,000	780,800	49
2,500,000	3,000,000	1,025,800	53
3,000,000	—	1,290,800	55
*Before credits and phase-out of graduated rates.			

TRANSFERS MADE BEFORE 1993

The advantage of the unified credit and graduated rates is lost to estates (or for taxable gifts) in excess of $10,000,000. This is accomplished in the following manner: the gift and estate tax liability for taxable transfers in excess of $10,000,000 is increased by imposing an additional 5 percent tax on the excess of

(a) the taxable transfer

over

(B) $10,000,000

This 5 percent add-on tax ends when cumulative transfers reach $21,040,000. At that point the 55 percent rate becomes applicable to additional amounts. So a taxable estate of $3,000,000 or more is taxed to 55 percent on any amount in excess of $3,000,000 plus a 5 percent add-on tax for the taxable estate exceeding $10,000,000 but not exceeding $21,040,000.

For example, assume an individual who dies in 1988 has a taxable estate of $25,000,000. The tentative tax would be $13,390,800. This is further increased by a 5 percent add-on tax on $11,040,000 ($21,040,000 - $10,000,000), $552,000. The total tentative tax would total $13,750,000. If the $192,800 credit that is phased out by operation of the 5 percent add-on tax is then added, the result is $13,942,800.)

UNIFIED GIFT AND ESTATE TAX RATE SCHEDULE IN THE CASE OF THE DECEDENTS DYING AND GIFTS MADE IN 1993 AND THEREAFTER			
(A)	(B)	(C)	(D)
Amount subject to tentative tax		Tax on amount in Column A*	Tax rate on excess over amounts in Column A*
exceeding	but not exceeding		Percent
$ —	$ 10,000	$ —	18
10,000	20,000	1,800	20
20,000	40,000	3,800	22
40,000	60,000	8,200	24
60,000	80,000	13,000	26
80,000	100,000	18,200	28
100,000	150,000	23,800	30
150,000	250,000	38,800	32
250,000	500,000	70,800	34
500,000	750,000	155,800	37
750,000	1,000,000	248,300	39
1,000,000	1,250,000	345,800	41
1,250,000	1,500,000	448,300	43
1,500,000	2,000,000	555,800	45
2,000,000	2,500,000	780,800	49
2,500,000	—	1,025,800	50

*Before credits and phase-out of graduated rates.

TRANSFERS MADE IN 1993 AND LATER YEARS

The advantage of the unified and graduated rates is lost to estates (or for taxable gifts) in excess of $10,000,000. This is accomplished in the following manner: the gift and estate tax liability for taxable transfers in excess of $10,000,000 is increased by imposing an additional 5 percent tax on the excess of

(a) the taxable transfer

over

(b) $10,000,000

This 5 percent add-on tax ends when cumulative transfers reach $18,340,000. At that point the 50 percent rate becomes applicable to additional amounts. So a taxable estate of $2,500,000 or more is taxed at 50 percent on any amount in excess of $2,500,000 plus a 5 percent add-on ta[x] taxable estate exceeding $10,000 but not [exceeding] $18,340,000.

For example, assume an individual who dies i[n] a taxable estate of $25,000,000. The tentative tax $12,692-800. This is $1,025,800 on the first $2,50[0,000] a 50 percent tax rate applied to the next $22,500[,000] of $11,250,000. This is further increased by a 5 pe[rcent] on tax on $8,340,000 ($18,340,000 - $10,000,000) The total tentative tax would therefore be $12,692[,800] that if a flat 50 percent rate was applicable to th[e es-] tate, the would total $12,500,000. If the $192,00[0 that] is phased out by operation of the 5 percent add-o[n is] added, the result is $12,692,800.)

Tools and To

MAXIMUM CREDIT TABLE FOR STATE DEATH TAXES

The amount of any state death taxes paid may be subtracted from the federal estate tax as determined under the preceding table, provided, however, that the maximum to be subtracted may not exceed the maximum determined under the following table:*

If the taxable estate is:	The maximum tax credit shall be:
Not over $150,000	8/10ths of 1% of the amount by which the taxable estate exceeds $100,000.
Over $150,000 but not over $200,000	$400 plus 1.6% of the excess over $150,000.
Over $200,000 but not over $300,000	$1,200 plus 2.4% of the excess over $200,000.
Over $300,000 but not over $500,000	$3,600 plus 3.2% of the excess over $300,000.
Over $500,000 but not over $700,000	$10,000 plus 4% of the excess over $500,000.
Over $700,000 but not over $900,000	$18,000 plus 4.8% of the excess over $700,000.
Over $900,000 but not over $1,100,000	$27,600 plus 5.6% of the excess over $900,000.
Over $1,100,000 but not over $1,600,000	$38,800 plus 6.4% of the excess over $1,100,000.
Over $1,600,000 but not over $2,100,000	$70,800 plus 7.2% of the excess over $1,600,000.
Over $2,100,000 but not over $2,600,000	$106,800 plus 8% of the excess over $2,100,000.
Over $2,600,000 but not over $3,100,000	$146,800 plus 8.8% of the excess over $2,600,000.
Over $3,100,000 but not over $3,600,000	$190,800 plus 9.6% of the excess over $3,100,000.
Over $3,600,000 but not over $4,100,000	$238,800 plus 10.4% of the excess over $3,600,000.
Over $4,100,000 but not over $5,100,000	$290,800 plus 11.2% of the excess over $4,100,000.
Over $5,100,000 but not over $6,100,000	$402,800 plus 12% of the excess over $5,100,000.
Over $6,100,000 but not over $7,100,000	$522,800 plus 12.8% of the excess over $6,100,000.
Over $7,100,000 but not over $8,100,000	$650,800 plus 13.6 of the excess over $7,100,000.
Over $8,100,000 but not over $9,100,000	$786,800 plus 14.4% of the excess over $8,100,000.
Over $9,100,000 but not over $10,100,000	$930,800 plus 15.2% of the excess over $9,100,000.
Over $10,100,000	$1,082,800 plus 16% of the excess over $10,100,000.

* This table resembes the table contained in IRC Section 2011(b), but it is not the same. The table in the Code is based on the *adjusted taxable estate*, defined as the taxable estate reduced by $60,000. This table is a modification of that table and can be used directly from the *taxable estate*. Note that the state death tax credit column in the computer printout, following, is likewise based on the *taxable estate*.

STATE DEATH TAX CREDITS AND TENTATIVE TAXES ON ESTATES AND GIFTS BY THOUSAND DOLLAR INCREMENTS

USING THE COMPUTER PRINTOUT

(1) **To find the State Death Tax Credit:** Work from the **"Taxable Estate"** column (#1). The figures in column 2 show the maximum state death tax credit allowable for taxable estates of the size shown opposite in column 1. *Example:* Herb Stevens has a taxable estate of $400,000. Herb's maximum state death tax credit is $6,800. The $6,800 amount is found in the computer printout in column 2 (State Death Tax Credit) opposite the $400,000 amount in column 1 (Taxable Estate).

(2) **To find the Tentative Gift or Estate Tax:** Work from the **"Tentative Tax Base"** column (#3). The figures in column 4 show the tentative tax (either gift or estate) for tentative tax bases shown opposite in column 3. *Example:* Sam Shepard's tentative tax base is $400,000. His tentative tax is $121,800. The $121,800 amount is found in the computer printout in column 4 (Tentative Tax) opposite the $400,000 amount in column 3 (Tentative Tax Base).

(3) This computer printout shows the tentative tax on tentative tax bases from $1,000 to $2,000,000 in $1,000 intervals, and from $2,000,000 to $2,500,000 in $100,000 intervals. For tentative tax bases over $2,500,000, see the unified rate schedule.

Tools and Techniques

1 TAXABLE ESTATE	2 STATE DEATH TAX CREDIT	3 TENTATIVE TAX BASE	4 TENTATIVE TAX
61,000	0	1,000	180
62,000	0	2,000	360
63,000	0	3,000	540
64,000	0	4,000	720
65,000	0	5,000	900
66,000	0	6,000	1,080
67,000	0	7,000	1,260
68,000	0	8,000	1,440
69,000	0	9,000	1,620
70,000	0	10,000	1,800
71,000	0	11,000	2,000
72,000	0	12,000	2,200
73,000	0	13,000	2,400
74,000	0	14,000	2,600
75,000	0	15,000	2,800
76,000	0	16,000	3,000
77,000	0	17,000	3,200
78,000	0	18,000	3,400
79,000	0	19,000	3,600
80,000	0	20,000	3,800
81,000	0	21,000	4,020
82,000	0	22,000	4,240
83,000	0	23,000	4,460
84,000	0	24,000	4,680
85,000	0	25,000	4,900
86,000	0	26,000	5,120
87,000	0	27,000	5,340
88,000	0	28,000	5,560
89,000	0	29,000	5,780
90,000	0	30,000	6,000
91,000	0	31,000	6,220
92,000	0	32,000	6,440
93,000	0	33,000	6,660
94,000	0	34,000	6,880
95,000	0	35,000	7,100
96,000	0	36,000	7,320
97,000	0	37,000	7,540
98,000	0	38,000	7,760
99,000	0	39,000	7,980
100,000	0	40,000	8,200
101,000	8	41,000	8,440
102,000	16	42,000	8,680
103,000	24	43,000	8,920
104,000	32	44,000	9,160
105,000	40	45,000	9,400
106,000	48	46,000	9,640
107,000	56	47,000	9,880
108,000	64	48,000	10,120
109,000	72	49,000	10,360
110,000	80	50,000	10,600

1 TAXABLE ESTATE	2 STATE DEATH TAX CREDIT	3 TENTATIVE TAX BASE	4 TENTATIVE TAX
111,000	88	51,000	10,840
112,000	96	52,000	11,080
113,000	104	53,000	11,320
114,000	112	54,000	11,560
115,000	120	55,000	11,800
116,000	128	56,000	12,040
117,000	136	57,000	12,280
118,000	144	58,000	12,520
119,000	152	59,000	12,760
120,000	160	60,000	13,000
121,000	168	61,000	13,260
122,000	176	62,000	13,520
123,000	184	63,000	13,780
124,000	192	64,000	14,040
125,000	200	65,000	14,300
126,000	208	66,000	14,560
127,000	216	67,000	14,820
128,000	224	68,000	15,080
129,000	232	69,000	15,340
130,000	240	70,000	15,600
131,000	248	71,000	15,860
132,000	256	72,000	16,120
133,000	264	73,000	16,380
134,000	272	74,000	16,640
135,000	280	75,000	16,900
136,000	288	76,000	17,160
137,000	296	77,000	17,420
138,000	304	78,000	17,680
139,000	312	79,000	17,940
140,000	320	80,000	18,200
141,000	328	81,000	18,480
142,000	336	82,000	18,760
143,000	344	83,000	19,040
144,000	352	84,000	19,320
145,000	360	85,000	19,600
146,000	368	86,000	19,880
147,000	376	87,000	20,160
148,000	384	88,000	20,440
149,000	392	89,000	20,720
150,000	400	90,000	21,000
151,000	416	91,000	21,280
152,000	432	92,000	21,560
153,000	448	93,000	21,840
154,000	464	94,000	22,120
155,000	480	95,000	22,400
156,000	496	96,000	22,680
157,000	512	97,000	22,960
158,000	528	98,000	23,240
159,000	544	99,000	23,520
160,000	560	100,000	23,800

1 TAXABLE ESTATE	2 STATE DEATH TAX CREDIT	3 TENTATIVE TAX BASE	4 TENTATIVE TAX
161,000	576	101,000	24,100
162,000	592	102,000	24,400
163,000	608	103,000	24,700
164,000	624	104,000	25,000
165,000	640	105,000	25,300
166,000	656	106,000	25,600
167,000	672	107,000	25,900
168,000	688	108,000	26,200
169,000	704	109,000	26,500
170,000	720	110,000	26,800
171,000	736	111,000	27,100
172,000	752	112,000	27,400
173,000	768	113,000	27,700
174,000	784	114,000	28,000
175,000	800	115,000	28,300
176,000	816	116,000	28,600
177,000	832	117,000	28,900
178,000	848	118,000	29,200
179,000	864	119,000	29,500
180,000	880	120,000	29,800
181,000	896	121,000	30,100
182,000	912	122,000	30,400
183,000	928	123,000	30,700
184,000	944	124,000	31,000
185,000	960	125,000	31,300
186,000	976	126,000	31,600
187,000	992	127,000	31,900
188,000	1,008	128,000	32,200
189,000	1,024	129,000	32,500
190,000	1,040	130,000	32,800
191,000	1,056	131,000	33,100
192,000	1,072	132,000	33,400
193,000	1,088	133,000	33,700
194,000	1,104	134,000	34,000
195,000	1,120	135,000	34,300
196,000	1,136	136,000	34,600
197,000	1,152	137,000	34,900
198,000	1,168	138,000	35,200
199,000	1,184	139,000	35,500
200,000	1,200	140,000	35,800
201,000	1,224	141,000	36,100
202,000	1,248	142,000	36,400
203,000	1,272	143,000	36,700
204,000	1,296	144,000	37,000
205,000	1,320	145,000	37,300
206,000	1,344	146,000	37,600
207,000	1,368	147,000	37,900
208,000	1,392	148,000	38,200
209,000	1,416	149,000	38,500
210,000	1,440	150,000	38,800

1 TAXABLE ESTATE	2 STATE DEATH TAX CREDIT	3 TENTATIVE TAX BASE	4 TENTATIVE TAX
211,000	1,464	151,000	39,120
212,000	1,488	152,000	39,440
213,000	1,512	153,000	39,760
214,000	1,536	154,000	40,080
215,000	1,560	155,000	40,400
216,000	1,584	156,000	40,720
217,000	1,608	157,000	41,040
218,000	1,632	158,000	41,360
219,000	1,656	159,000	41,680
220,000	1,680	160,000	42,000
221,000	1,704	161,000	42,320
222,000	1,728	162,000	42,640
223,000	1,752	163,000	42,960
224,000	1,776	164,000	43,280
225,000	1,800	165,000	43,600
226,000	1,824	166,000	43,920
227,000	1,848	167,000	44,240
228,000	1,872	168,000	44,560
229,000	1,896	169,000	44,880
230,000	1,920	170,000	45,200
231,000	1,944	171,000	45,520
232,000	1,968	172,000	45,840
233,000	1,992	173,000	46,160
234,000	2,016	174,000	46,480
235,000	2,040	175,000	46,800
236,000	2,064	176,000	47,120
237,000	2,088	177,000	47,440
238,000	2,112	178,000	47,760
239,000	2,136	179,000	48,080
240,000	2,160	180,000	48,400
241,000	2,184	181,000	48,720
242,000	2,208	182,000	49,040
243,000	2,232	183,000	49,360
244,000	2,256	184,000	49,680
245,000	2,280	185,000	50,000
246,000	2,304	186,000	50,320
247,000	2,328	187,000	50,640
248,000	2,352	188,000	50,960
249,000	2,376	189,000	51,280
250,000	2,400	190,000	51,600
251,000	2,424	191,000	51,920
252,000	2,448	192,000	52,240
253,000	2,472	193,000	52,560
254,000	2,496	194,000	52,880
255,000	2,520	195,000	53,200
256,000	2,544	196,000	53,520
257,000	2,568	197,000	53,840
258,000	2,592	198,000	54,160
259,000	2,616	199,000	54,480
260,000	2,640	200,000	54,800

1 TAXABLE ESTATE	2 STATE DEATH TAX CREDIT	3 TENTATIVE TAX BASE	4 TENTATIVE TAX
261,000	2,664	201,000	55,120
262,000	2,688	202,000	55,440
263,000	2,712	203,000	55,760
264,000	2,736	204,000	56,080
265,000	2,760	205,000	56,400
266,000	2,784	206,000	56,720
267,000	2,808	207,000	57,040
268,000	2,832	208,000	57,360
269,000	2,856	209,000	57,680
270,000	2,880	210,000	58,000
271,000	2,904	211,000	58,320
272,000	2,928	212,000	58,640
273,000	2,952	213,000	58,960
274,000	2,976	214,000	59,280
275,000	3,000	215,000	59,600
276,000	3,024	216,000	59,920
277,000	3,048	217,000	60,240
278,000	3,072	218,000	60,560
279,000	3,096	219,000	60,880
280,000	3,120	220,000	61,200
281,000	3,144	221,000	61,520
282,000	3,168	222,000	61,840
283,000	3,192	223,000	62,160
284,000	3,216	224,000	62,480
285,000	3,240	225,000	62,800
286,000	3,264	226,000	63,120
287,000	3,288	227,000	63,440
288,000	3,312	228,000	63,760
289,000	3,336	229,000	64,080
290,000	3,360	230,000	64,400
291,000	3,384	231,000	64,720
292,000	3,408	232,000	65,040
293,000	3,432	233,000	65,360
294,000	3,456	234,000	65,680
295,000	3,480	235,000	66,000
296,000	3,504	236,000	66,320
297,000	3,528	237,000	66,640
298,000	3,552	238,000	66,960
299,000	3,576	239,000	67,280
300,000	3,600	240,000	67,600
301,000	3,632	241,000	67,920
302,000	3,664	242,000	68,240
303,000	3,696	243,000	68,560
304,000	3,728	244,000	68,880
305,000	3,760	245,000	69,200
306,000	3,792	246,000	69,520
307,000	3,824	247,000	69,840
308,000	3,856	248,000	70,160
309,000	3,888	249,000	70,480
310,000	3,920	250,000	70,800

1 TAXABLE ESTATE	2 STATE DEATH TAX CREDIT	3 TENTATIVE TAX BASE	4 TENTATIVE TAX
311,000	3,952	251,000	71,140
312,000	3,984	252,000	71,480
313,000	4,016	253,000	71,820
314,000	4,048	254,000	72,160
315,000	4,080	255,000	72,500
316,000	4,112	256,000	72,840
317,000	4,144	257,000	73,180
318,000	4,176	258,000	73,520
319,000	4,208	259,000	73,860
320,000	4,240	260,000	74,200
321,000	4,272	261,000	74,540
322,000	4,304	262,000	74,880
323,000	4,336	263,000	75,220
324,000	4,368	264,000	75,560
325,000	4,400	265,000	75,900
326,000	4,432	266,000	76,240
327,000	4,464	267,000	76,580
328,000	4,496	268,000	76,920
329,000	4,528	269,000	77,260
330,000	4,560	270,000	77,600
331,000	4,592	271,000	77,940
332,000	4,624	272,000	78,280
333,000	4,656	273,000	78,620
334,000	4,688	274,000	78,960
335,000	4,720	275,000	79,300
336,000	4,752	276,000	79,640
337,000	4,784	277,000	79,980
338,000	4,816	278,000	80,320
339,000	4,848	279,000	80,660
340,000	4,880	280,000	81,000
341,000	4,912	281,000	81,340
342,000	4,944	282,000	81,680
343,000	4,976	283,000	82,020
344,000	5,008	284,000	82,360
345,000	5,040	285,000	82,700
346,000	5,072	286,000	83,040
347,000	5,104	287,000	83,380
348,000	5,136	288,000	83,720
349,000	5,168	289,000	84,060
350,000	5,200	290,000	84,400
351,000	5,232	291,000	84,740
352,000	5,264	292,000	85,080
353,000	5,296	293,000	85,420
354,000	5,328	294,000	85,760
355,000	5,360	295,000	86,100
356,000	5,392	296,000	86,440
357,000	5,424	297,000	86,780
358,000	5,456	298,000	87,120
359,000	5,488	299,000	87,460
360,000	5,520	300,000	87,800

Tools and Techniques

1 TAXABLE ESTATE	2 STATE DEATH TAX CREDIT	3 TENTATIVE TAX BASE	4 TENTATIVE TAX
361,000	5,552	301,000	88,140
362,000	5,584	302,000	88,480
363,000	5,616	303,000	88,820
364,000	5,648	304,000	89,160
365,000	5,680	305,000	89,500
366,000	5,712	306,000	89,840
367,000	5,744	307,000	90,180
368,000	5,776	308,000	90,520
369,000	5,808	309,000	90,860
370,000	5,840	310,000	91,200
371,000	5,872	311,000	91,540
372,000	5,904	312,000	91,880
373,000	5,936	313,000	92,220
374,000	5,968	314,000	92,560
375,000	6,000	315,000	92,900
376,000	6,032	316,000	93,240
377,000	6,064	317,000	93,580
378,000	6,096	318,000	93,920
379,000	6,128	319,000	94,260
380,000	6,160	320,000	94,600
381,000	6,192	321,000	94,940
382,000	6,224	322,000	95,280
383,000	6,256	323,000	95,620
384,000	6,288	324,000	95,960
385,000	6,320	325,000	96,300
386,000	6,352	326,000	96,640
387,000	6,384	327,000	96,980
388,000	6,416	328,000	97,320
389,000	6,448	329,000	97,660
390,000	6,480	330,000	98,000
391,000	6,512	331,000	98,340
392,000	6,544	332,000	98,680
393,000	6,576	333,000	99,020
394,000	6,608	334,000	99,360
395,000	6,640	335,000	99,700
396,000	6,672	336,000	100,040
397,000	6,704	337,000	100,380
398,000	6,736	338,000	100,720
399,000	6,768	339,000	101,060
400,000	6,800	340,000	101,400
401,000	6,832	341,000	101,740
402,000	6,864	342,000	102,080
403,000	6,896	343,000	102,420
404,000	6,928	344,000	102,760
405,000	6,960	345,000	103,100
406,000	6,992	346,000	103,440
407,000	7,024	347,000	103,780
408,000	7,056	348,000	104,120
409,000	7,088	349,000	104,460
410,000	7,120	350,000	104,800

1 TAXABLE ESTATE	2 STATE DEATH TAX CREDIT	3 TENTATIVE TAX BASE	4 TENTATIVE TAX
411,000	7,152	351,000	105,140
412,000	7,184	352,000	105,480
413,000	7,216	353,000	105,820
414,000	7,248	354,000	106,160
415,000	7,280	355,000	106,500
416,000	7,312	356,000	106,840
417,000	7,344	357,000	107,180
418,000	7,376	358,000	107,520
419,000	7,408	359,000	107,860
420,000	7,440	360,000	108,200
421,000	7,472	361,000	108,540
422,000	7,504	362,000	108,880
423,000	7,536	363,000	109,220
424,000	7,568	364,000	109,560
425,000	7,600	365,000	109,900
426,000	7,632	366,000	110,240
427,000	7,664	367,000	110,580
428,000	7,696	368,000	110,920
429,000	7,728	369,000	111,260
430,000	7,760	370,000	111,600
431,000	7,792	371,000	111,940
432,000	7,824	372,000	112,280
433,000	7,856	373,000	112,620
434,000	7,888	374,000	112,960
435,000	7,920	375,000	113,300
436,000	7,952	376,000	113,640
437,000	7,984	377,000	113,980
438,000	8,016	378,000	114,320
439,000	8,048	379,000	114,660
440,000	8,080	380,000	115,000
441,000	8,112	381,000	115,340
442,000	8,144	382,000	115,680
443,000	8,176	383,000	116,020
444,000	8,208	384,000	116,360
445,000	8,240	385,000	116,700
446,000	8,272	386,000	117,040
447,000	8,304	387,000	117,380
448,000	8,336	388,000	117,720
449,000	8,368	389,000	118,060
450,000	8,400	390,000	118,400
451,000	8,432	391,000	118,740
452,000	8,464	392,000	119,080
453,000	8,496	393,000	119,420
454,000	8,528	394,000	119,760
455,000	8,560	395,000	120,100
456,000	8,592	396,000	120,440
457,000	8,624	397,000	120,780
458,000	8,656	398,000	121,120
459,000	8,688	399,000	121,460
460,000	8,720	400,000	121,800

1 TAXABLE ESTATE	2 STATE DEATH TAX CREDIT	3 TENTATIVE TAX BASE	4 TENTATIVE TAX	1 TAXABLE ESTATE	2 STATE DEATH TAX CREDIT	3 TENTATIVE TAX BASE	4 TENTATIVE TAX
461,000	8,752	401,000	122,140	511,000	10,440	451,000	139,140
462,000	8,784	402,000	122,480	512,000	10,480	452,000	139,480
463,000	8,816	403,000	122,820	513,000	10,520	453,000	139,820
464,000	8,848	404,000	123,160	514,000	10,560	454,000	140,160
465,000	8,880	405,000	123,500	515,000	10,600	455,000	140,500
466,000	8,912	406,000	123,840	516,000	10,640	456,000	140,840
467,000	8,944	407,000	124,180	517,000	10,680	457,000	141,180
468,000	8,976	408,000	124,520	518,000	10,720	458,000	141,520
469,000	9,008	409,000	124,860	519,000	10,760	459,000	141,860
470,000	9,040	410,000	125,200	520,000	10,800	460,000	142,200
471,000	9,072	411,000	125,540	521,000	10,840	461,000	142,540
472,000	9,104	412,000	125,880	522,000	10,880	462,000	142,880
473,000	9,136	413,000	126,220	523,000	10,920	463,000	143,220
474,000	9,168	414,000	126,560	524,000	10,960	464,000	143,560
475,000	9,200	415,000	126,900	525,000	11,000	465,000	143,900
476,000	9,232	416,000	127,240	526,000	11,040	466,000	144,240
477,000	9,264	417,000	127,580	527,000	11,080	467,000	144,580
478,000	9,296	418,000	127,920	528,000	11,120	468,000	144,920
479,000	9,328	419,000	128,260	529,000	11,160	469,000	145,260
480,000	9,360	420,000	128,600	530,000	11,200	470,000	145,600
481,000	9,392	421,000	128,940	531,000	11,240	471,000	145,940
482,000	9,424	422,000	129,280	532,000	11,280	472,000	146,280
483,000	9,456	423,000	129,620	533,000	11,320	473,000	146,620
484,000	9,488	424,000	129,960	534,000	11,360	474,000	146,960
485,000	9,520	425,000	130,300	535,000	11,400	475,000	147,300
486,000	9,552	426,000	130,640	536,000	11,440	476,000	147,640
487,000	9,584	427,000	130,980	537,000	11,480	477,000	147,980
488,000	9,616	428,000	131,320	538,000	11,520	478,000	148,320
489,000	9,648	429,000	131,660	539,000	11,560	479,000	148,660
490,000	9,680	430,000	132,000	540,000	11,600	480,000	149,000
491,000	9,712	431,000	132,340	541,000	11,640	481,000	149,340
492,000	9,744	432,000	132,680	542,000	11,680	482,000	149,680
493,000	9,776	433,000	133,020	543,000	11,720	483,000	150,020
494,000	9,808	434,000	133,360	544,000	11,760	484,000	150,360
495,000	9,840	435,000	133,700	545,000	11,800	485,000	150,700
496,000	9,872	436,000	134,040	546,000	11,840	486,000	151,040
497,000	9,904	437,000	134,380	547,000	11,880	487,000	151,380
498,000	9,936	438,000	134,720	548,000	11,920	488,000	151,720
499,000	9,968	439,000	135,060	549,000	11,960	489,000	152,060
500,000	10,000	440,000	135,400	550,000	12,000	490,000	152,400
501,000	10,040	441,000	135,740	551,000	12,040	491,000	152,740
502,000	10,080	442,000	136,080	552,000	12,080	492,000	153,080
503,000	10,120	443,000	136,420	553,000	12,120	493,000	153,420
504,000	10,160	444,000	136,760	554,000	12,160	494,000	153,760
505,000	10,200	445,000	137,100	555,000	12,200	495,000	154,100
506,000	10,240	446,000	137,440	556,000	12,240	496,000	154,440
507,000	10,280	447,000	137,780	557,000	12,280	497,000	154,780
508,000	10,320	448,000	138,120	558,000	12,320	498,000	155,120
509,000	10,360	449,000	138,460	559,000	12,360	499,000	155,460
510,000	10,400	450,000	138,800	560,000	12,400	500,000	155,800

Tools and Techniques

1 TAXABLE ESTATE	2 STATE DEATH TAX CREDIT	3 TENTATIVE TAX BASE	4 TENTATIVE TAX
561,000	12,440	501,000	156,170
562,000	12,480	502,000	156,540
563,000	12,520	503,000	156,910
564,000	12,560	504,000	157,280
565,000	12,600	505,000	157,650
566,000	12,640	506,000	158,020
567,000	12,680	507,000	158,390
568,000	12,720	508,000	158,760
569,000	12,760	509,000	159,130
570,000	12,800	510,000	159,500
571,000	12,840	511,000	159,870
572,000	12,880	512,000	160,240
573,000	12,920	513,000	160,610
574,000	12,960	514,000	160,980
575,000	13,000	515,000	161,350
576,000	13,040	516,000	161,720
577,000	13,080	517,000	162,090
578,000	13,120	518,000	162,460
579,000	13,160	519,000	162,830
580,000	13,200	520,000	163,200
581,000	13,240	521,000	163,570
582,000	13,280	522,000	163,940
583,000	13,320	523,000	164,310
584,000	13,360	524,000	164,680
585,000	13,400	525,000	165,050
586,000	13,440	526,000	165,420
587,000	13,480	527,000	165,790
588,000	13,520	528,000	166,160
589,000	13,560	529,000	166,530
590,000	13,600	530,000	166,900
591,000	13,640	531,000	167,270
592,000	13,680	532,000	167,640
593,000	13,720	533,000	168,010
594,000	13,760	534,000	168,380
595,000	13,800	535,000	168,750
596,000	13,840	536,000	169,120
597,000	13,880	537,000	169,490
598,000	13,920	538,000	169,860
599,000	13,960	539,000	170,230
600,000	14,000	540,000	170,600
601,000	14,040	541,000	170,970
602,000	14,080	542,000	171,340
603,000	14,120	543,000	171,710
604,000	14,160	544,000	172,080
605,000	14,200	545,000	172,450
606,000	14,240	546,000	172,820
607,000	14,280	547,000	173,190
608,000	14,320	548,000	173,560
609,000	14,360	549,000	173,930
610,000	14,400	550,000	174,300
611,000	14,440	551,000	174,670
612,000	14,480	552,000	175,040
613,000	14,520	553,000	175,410
614,000	14,560	554,000	175,780
615,000	14,600	555,000	176,150
616,000	14,640	556,000	176,520
617,000	14,680	557,000	176,890
618,000	14,720	558,000	177,260
619,000	14,760	559,000	177,630
620,000	14,800	560,000	178,000
621,000	14,840	561,000	178,370
622,000	14,880	562,000	178,740
623,000	14,920	563,000	179,110
624,000	14,960	564,000	179,480
625,000	15,000	565,000	179,850
626,000	15,040	566,000	180,220
627,000	15,080	567,000	180,590
628,000	15,120	568,000	180,960
629,000	15,160	569,000	181,330
630,000	15,200	570,000	181,700
631,000	15,240	571,000	182,070
632,000	15,280	572,000	182,440
633,000	15,320	573,000	182,810
634,000	15,360	574,000	183,180
635,000	15,400	575,000	183,550
636,000	15,440	576,000	183,920
637,000	15,480	577,000	184,290
638,000	15,520	578,000	184,660
639,000	15,560	579,000	185,030
640,000	15,600	580,000	185,400
641,000	15,640	581,000	185,770
642,000	15,680	582,000	186,140
643,000	15,720	583,000	186,510
644,000	15,760	584,000	186,880
645,000	15,800	585,000	187,250
646,000	15,840	586,000	187,620
647,000	15,880	587,000	187,990
648,000	15,920	588,000	188,360
649,000	15,960	589,000	188,730
650,000	16,000	590,000	189,100
651,000	16,040	591,000	189,470
652,000	16,080	592,000	189,840
653,000	16,120	593,000	190,210
654,000	16,160	594,000	190,580
655,000	16,200	595,000	190,950
656,000	16,240	596,000	191,320
657,000	16,280	597,000	191,690
658,000	16,320	598,000	192,060
659,000	16,360	599,000	192,430
660,000	16,400	600,000	192,800

Tools and Techniques

Appendix C
State Credit and Tentative Taxes

1 TAXABLE ESTATE	2 STATE DEATH TAX CREDIT	3 TENTATIVE TAX BASE	4 TENTATIVE TAX
661,000	16,440	601,000	193,170
662,000	16,480	602,000	193,540
663,000	16,520	603,000	193,910
664,000	16,560	604,000	194,280
665,000	16,600	605,000	194,650
666,000	16,640	606,000	195,020
667,000	16,680	607,000	195,390
668,000	16,720	608,000	195,760
669,000	16,760	609,000	196,130
670,000	16,800	610,000	196,500
671,000	16,840	611,000	196,870
672,000	16,880	612,000	197,240
673,000	16,920	613,000	197,610
674,000	16,960	614,000	197,980
675,000	17,000	615,000	198,350
676,000	17,040	616,000	198,720
677,000	17,080	617,000	199,090
678,000	17,120	618,000	199,460
679,000	17,160	619,000	199,830
680,000	17,200	620,000	200,200
681,000	17,240	621,000	200,570
682,000	17,280	622,000	200,940
683,000	17,320	623,000	201,310
684,000	17,360	624,000	201,680
685,000	17,400	625,000	202,050
686,000	17,440	626,000	202,420
687,000	17,480	627,000	202,790
688,000	17,520	628,000	203,160
689,000	17,560	629,000	203,530
690,000	17,600	630,000	203,900
691,000	17,640	631,000	204,270
692,000	17,680	632,000	204,640
693,000	17,720	633,000	205,010
694,000	17,760	634,000	205,380
695,000	17,800	635,000	205,750
696,000	17,840	636,000	206,120
697,000	17,880	637,000	206,490
698,000	17,920	638,000	206,860
699,000	17,960	639,000	207,230
700,000	18,000	640,000	207,600
701,000	18,048	641,000	207,970
702,000	18,096	642,000	208,340
703,000	18,144	643,000	208,710
704,000	18,192	644,000	209,080
705,000	18,240	645,000	209,450
706,000	18,288	646,000	209,820
707,000	18,336	647,000	210,190
708,000	18,384	648,000	210,560
709,000	18,432	649,000	210,930
710,000	18,480	650,000	211,300

1 TAXABLE ESTATE	2 STATE DEATH TAX CREDIT	3 TENTATIVE TAX BASE	4 TENTATIVE TAX
711,000	18,528	651,000	211,670
712,000	18,576	652,000	212,040
713,000	18,624	653,000	212,410
714,000	18,672	654,000	212,780
715,000	18,720	655,000	213,150
716,000	18,768	656,000	213,520
717,000	18,816	657,000	213,890
718,000	18,864	658,000	214,260
719,000	18,912	659,000	214,630
720,000	18,960	660,000	215,000
721,000	19,008	661,000	215,370
722,000	19,056	662,000	215,740
723,000	19,104	663,000	216,110
724,000	19,152	664,000	216,480
725,000	19,200	665,000	216,850
726,000	19,248	666,000	217,220
727,000	19,296	667,000	217,590
728,000	19,344	668,000	217,960
729,000	19,392	669,000	218,330
730,000	19,440	670,000	218,700
731,000	19,488	671,000	219,070
732,000	19,536	672,000	219,440
733,000	19,584	673,000	219,810
734,000	19,632	674,000	220,180
735,000	19,680	675,000	220,550
736,000	19,728	676,000	220,920
737,000	19,776	677,000	221,290
738,000	19,824	678,000	221,660
739,000	19,872	679,000	222,030
740,000	19,920	680,000	222,400
741,000	19,968	681,000	222,770
742,000	20,016	682,000	223,140
743,000	20,064	683,000	223,510
744,000	20,112	684,000	223,880
745,000	20,160	685,000	224,250
746,000	20,208	686,000	224,620
747,000	20,256	687,000	224,990
748,000	20,304	688,000	225,360
749,000	20,352	689,000	225,730
750,000	20,400	690,000	226,100
751,000	20,448	691,000	226,470
752,000	20,496	692,000	226,840
753,000	20,544	693,000	227,210
754,000	20,592	694,000	227,580
755,000	20,640	695,000	227,950
756,000	20,688	696,000	228,320
757,000	20,736	697,000	228,690
758,000	20,784	698,000	229,060
759,000	20,832	699,000	229,430
760,000	20,880	700,000	229,800

Tools and Techniques

TAXABLE ESTATE	STATE DEATH TAX CREDIT	TENTATIVE TAX BASE	TENTATIVE TAX	TAXABLE ESTATE	STATE DEATH TAX CREDIT	TENTATIVE TAX BASE	TENTATIVE TAX
761,000	20,928	701,000	230,170	811,000	23,328	751,000	248,690
762,000	20,976	702,000	230,540	812,000	23,376	752,000	249,080
763,000	21,024	703,000	230,910	813,000	23,424	753,000	249,470
764,000	21,072	704,000	231,280	814,000	23,472	754,000	249,860
765,000	21,120	705,000	231,650	815,000	23,520	755,000	250,250
766,000	21,168	706,000	232,020	816,000	23,568	756,000	250,640
767,000	21,216	707,000	232,390	817,000	23,616	757,000	251,030
768,000	21,264	708,000	232,760	818,000	23,664	758,000	251,420
769,000	21,312	709,000	233,130	819,000	23,712	759,000	251,810
770,000	21,360	710,000	233,500	820,000	23,760	760,000	252,200
771,000	21,408	711,000	233,870	821,000	23,808	761,000	252,590
772,000	21,456	712,000	234,240	822,000	23,856	762,000	252,980
773,000	21,504	713,000	234,610	823,000	23,904	763,000	253,370
774,000	21,552	714,000	234,980	824,000	23,952	764,000	253,760
775,000	21,600	715,000	235,350	825,000	24,000	765,000	254,150
776,000	21,648	716,000	235,720	826,000	24,048	766,000	254,540
777,000	21,696	717,000	236,090	827,000	24,096	767,000	254,930
778,000	21,744	718,000	236,460	828,000	24,144	768,000	255,320
779,000	21,792	719,000	236,830	829,000	24,192	769,000	255,710
780,000	21,840	720,000	237,200	830,000	24,240	770,000	256,100
781,000	21,888	721,000	237,570	831,000	24,288	771,000	256,490
782,000	21,936	722,000	237,940	832,000	24,336	772,000	256,880
783,000	21,984	723,000	238,310	833,000	24,384	773,000	257,270
784,000	22,032	724,000	238,680	834,000	24,432	774,000	257,660
785,000	22,080	725,000	239,050	835,000	24,480	775,000	258,050
786,000	22,128	726,000	239,420	836,000	24,528	776,000	258,440
787,000	22,176	727,000	239,790	837,000	24,576	777,000	258,830
788,000	22,224	728,000	240,160	838,000	24,624	778,000	259,220
789,000	22,272	729,000	240,530	839,000	24,672	779,000	259,610
790,000	22,320	730,000	240,900	840,000	24,720	780,000	260,000
791,000	22,368	731,000	241,270	841,000	24,768	781,000	260,390
792,000	22,416	732,000	241,640	842,000	24,816	782,000	260,780
793,000	22,464	733,000	242,010	843,000	24,864	783,000	261,170
794,000	22,512	734,000	242,380	844,000	24,912	784,000	261,560
795,000	22,560	735,000	242,750	845,000	24,960	785,000	261,950
796,000	22,608	736,000	243,120	846,000	25,008	786,000	262,340
797,000	22,656	737,000	243,490	847,000	25,056	787,000	262,730
798,000	22,704	738,000	243,860	848,000	25,104	788,000	263,120
799,000	22,752	739,000	244,230	849,000	25,152	789,000	263,510
800,000	22,800	740,000	244,600	850,000	25,200	790,000	263,900
801,000	22,848	741,000	244,970	851,000	25,248	791,000	264,290
802,000	22,896	742,000	245,340	852,000	25,296	792,000	264,680
803,000	22,944	743,000	245,710	853,000	25,344	793,000	265,070
804,000	22,992	744,000	246,080	854,000	25,392	794,000	265,460
805,000	23,040	745,000	246,450	855,000	25,440	795,000	265,850
806,000	23,088	746,000	246,820	856,000	25,488	796,000	266,240
807,000	23,136	747,000	247,190	857,000	25,536	797,000	266,630
808,000	23,184	748,000	247,560	858,000	25,584	798,000	267,020
809,000	23,232	749,000	247,930	859,000	25,632	799,000	267,410
810,000	23,280	750,000	248,300	860,000	25,680	800,000	267,800

1 TAXABLE ESTATE	2 STATE DEATH TAX CREDIT	3 TENTATIVE TAX BASE	4 TENTATIVE TAX	1 TAXABLE ESTATE	2 STATE DEATH TAX CREDIT	3 TENTATIVE TAX BASE	4 TENTATIVE TAX
861,000	25,728	801,000	268,190	911,000	28,216	851,000	287,690
862,000	25,776	802,000	268,580	912,000	28,272	852,000	288,080
863,000	25,824	803,000	268,970	913,000	28,328	853,000	288,470
864,000	25,872	804,000	269,360	914,000	28,384	854,000	288,860
865,000	25,920	805,000	269,750	915,000	28,440	855,000	289,250
866,000	25,968	806,000	270,140	916,000	28,496	856,000	289,640
867,000	26,016	807,000	270,530	917,000	28,552	857,000	290,030
868,000	26,064	808,000	270,920	918,000	28,608	858,000	290,420
869,000	26,112	809,000	271,310	919,000	28,664	859,000	290,810
870,000	26,160	810,000	271,700	920,000	28,720	860,000	291,200
871,000	26,208	811,000	272,090	921,000	28,776	861,000	291,590
872,000	26,256	812,000	272,480	922,000	28,832	862,000	291,980
873,000	26,304	813,000	272,870	923,000	28,888	863,000	292,370
874,000	26,352	814,000	273,260	924,000	28,944	864,000	292,760
875,000	26,400	815,000	273,650	925,000	29,000	865,000	293,150
876,000	26,448	816,000	274,040	926,000	29,056	866,000	293,540
877,000	26,496	817,000	274,430	927,000	29,112	867,000	293,930
878,000	26,544	818,000	274,820	928,000	29,168	868,000	294,320
879,000	26,592	819,000	275,210	929,000	29,224	869,000	294,710
880,000	26,640	820,000	275,600	930,000	29,280	870,000	295,100
881,000	26,688	821,000	275,990	931,000	29,336	871,000	295,490
882,000	26,736	822,000	276,380	932,000	29,392	872,000	295,880
883,000	26,784	823,000	276,770	933,000	29,448	873,000	296,270
884,000	26,832	824,000	277,160	934,000	29,504	874,000	296,660
885,000	26,880	825,000	277,550	935,000	29,560	875,000	297,050
886,000	26,928	826,000	277,940	936,000	29,616	876,000	297,440
887,000	26,976	827,000	278,330	937,000	29,672	877,000	297,830
888,000	27,024	828,000	278,720	938,000	29,728	878,000	298,220
889,000	27,072	829,000	279,110	939,000	29,784	879,000	298,610
890,000	27,120	830,000	279,500	940,000	29,840	880,000	299,000
891,000	27,168	831,000	279,890	941,000	29,896	881,000	299,390
892,000	27,216	832,000	280,280	942,000	29,952	882,000	299,780
893,000	27,264	833,000	280,670	943,000	30,008	883,000	300,170
894,000	27,312	834,000	281,060	944,000	30,064	884,000	300,560
895,000	27,360	835,000	281,450	945,000	30,120	885,000	300,950
896,000	27,408	836,000	281,840	946,000	30,176	886,000	301,340
897,000	27,456	837,000	282,230	947,000	30,232	887,000	301,730
898,000	27,504	838,000	282,620	948,000	30,288	888,000	302,120
899,000	27,552	839,000	283,010	949,000	30,344	889,000	302,510
900,000	27,600	840,000	283,400	950,000	30,400	890,000	302,900
901,000	27,656	841,000	283,790	951,000	30,456	891,000	303,290
902,000	27,712	842,000	284,180	952,000	30,512	892,000	303,680
903,000	27,768	843,000	284,570	953,000	30,568	893,000	304,070
904,000	27,824	844,000	284,960	954,000	30,624	894,000	304,460
905,000	27,880	845,000	285,350	955,000	30,680	895,000	304,850
906,000	27,936	846,000	285,740	956,000	30,736	896,000	305,240
907,000	27,992	847,000	286,130	957,000	30,792	897,000	305,630
908,000	28,048	848,000	286,520	958,000	30,848	898,000	306,020
909,000	28,104	849,000	286,910	959,000	30,904	899,000	306,410
910,000	28,160	850,000	287,300	960,000	30,960	900,000	306,800

Tools and Techniques

1 TAXABLE ESTATE	2 STATE DEATH TAX CREDIT	3 TENTATIVE TAX BASE	4 TENTATIVE TAX
961,000	31,016	901,000	307,190
962,000	31,072	902,000	307,580
963,000	31,128	903,000	307,970
964,000	31,184	904,000	308,360
965,000	31,240	905,000	308,750
966,000	31,296	906,000	309,140
967,000	31,352	907,000	309,530
968,000	31,408	908,000	309,920
969,000	31,464	909,000	310,310
970,000	31,520	910,000	310,700
971,000	31,576	911,000	311,090
972,000	31,632	912,000	311,480
973,000	31,688	913,000	311,870
974,000	31,744	914,000	312,260
975,000	31,800	915,000	312,650
976,000	31,856	916,000	313,040
977,000	31,912	917,000	313,430
978,000	31,968	918,000	313,820
979,000	32,024	919,000	314,210
980,000	32,080	920,000	314,600
981,000	32,136	921,000	314,990
982,000	32,192	922,000	315,380
983,000	32,248	923,000	315,770
984,000	32,304	924,000	316,160
985,000	32,360	925,000	316,550
986,000	32,416	926,000	316,940
987,000	32,472	927,000	317,330
988,000	32,528	928,000	317,720
989,000	32,584	929,000	318,110
990,000	32,640	930,000	318,500
991,000	32,696	931,000	318,890
992,000	32,752	932,000	319,280
993,000	32,808	933,000	319,670
994,000	32,864	934,000	320,060
995,000	32,920	935,000	320,450
996,000	32,976	936,000	320,840
997,000	33,032	937,000	321,230
998,000	33,088	938,000	321,620
999,000	33,144	939,000	322,010
1,000,000	33,200	940,000	322,400
1,001,000	33,256	941,000	322,790
1,002,000	33,312	942,000	323,180
1,003,000	33,368	943,000	323,570
1,004,000	33,424	944,000	323,960
1,005,000	33,480	945,000	324,350
1,006,000	33,536	946,000	324,740
1,007,000	33,592	947,000	325,130
1,008,000	33,648	948,000	325,520
1,009,000	33,704	949,000	325,910
1,010,000	33,760	950,000	326,300

1 TAXABLE ESTATE	2 STATE DEATH TAX CREDIT	3 TENTATIVE TAX BASE	4 TENTATIVE TAX
1,011,000	33,816	951,000	326,690
1,012,000	33,872	952,000	327,080
1,013,000	33,928	953,000	327,470
1,014,000	33,984	954,000	327,860
1,015,000	34,040	955,000	328,250
1,016,000	34,096	956,000	328,640
1,017,000	34,152	957,000	329,030
1,018,000	34,208	958,000	329,420
1,019,000	34,264	959,000	329,810
1,020,000	34,320	960,000	330,200
1,021,000	34,376	961,000	330,590
1,022,000	34,432	962,000	330,980
1,023,000	34,488	963,000	331,370
1,024,000	34,544	964,000	331,760
1,025,000	34,600	965,000	332,150
1,026,000	34,656	966,000	332,540
1,027,000	34,712	967,000	332,930
1,028,000	34,768	968,000	333,320
1,029,000	34,824	969,000	333,710
1,030,000	34,880	970,000	334,100
1,031,000	34,936	971,000	334,490
1,032,000	34,992	972,000	334,880
1,033,000	35,048	973,000	335,270
1,034,000	35,104	974,000	335,660
1,035,000	35,160	975,000	336,050
1,036,000	35,216	976,000	336,440
1,037,000	35,272	977,000	336,830
1,038,000	35,328	978,000	337,220
1,039,000	35,384	979,000	337,610
1,040,000	35,440	980,000	338,000
1,041,000	35,496	981,000	338,390
1,042,000	35,552	982,000	338,780
1,043,000	35,608	983,000	339,170
1,044,000	35,664	984,000	339,560
1,045,000	35,720	985,000	339,950
1,046,000	35,776	986,000	340,340
1,047,000	35,832	987,000	340,730
1,048,000	35,888	988,000	341,120
1,049,000	35,944	989,000	341,510
1,050,000	36,000	990,000	341,900
1,051,000	36,056	991,000	342,290
1,052,000	36,112	992,000	342,680
1,053,000	36,168	993,000	343,070
1,054,000	36,224	994,000	343,460
1,055,000	36,280	995,000	343,850
1,056,000	36,336	996,000	344,240
1,057,000	36,392	997,000	344,630
1,058,000	36,448	998,000	345,020
1,059,000	36,504	999,000	345,410
1,060,000	36,560	1,000,000	345,800

1 TAXABLE ESTATE	2 STATE DEATH TAX CREDIT	3 TENTATIVE TAX BASE	4 TENTATIVE TAX	1 TAXABLE ESTATE	2 STATE DEATH TAX CREDIT	3 TENTATIVE TAX BASE	4 TENTATIVE TAX
1,061,000	36,616	1,001,000	346,210	1,111,000	39,504	1,051,000	366,710
1,062,000	36,672	1,002,000	346,620	1,112,000	39,568	1,052,000	367,120
1,063,000	36,728	1,003,000	347,030	1,113,000	39,632	1,053,000	367,530
1,064,000	36,784	1,004,000	347,440	1,114,000	39,696	1,054,000	367,940
1,065,000	36,840	1,005,000	347,850	1,115,000	39,760	1,055,000	368,350
1,066,000	36,896	1,006,000	348,260	1,116,000	39,824	1,056,000	368,760
1,067,000	36,952	1,007,000	348,670	1,117,000	39,888	1,057,000	369,170
1,068,000	37,008	1,008,000	349,080	1,118,000	39,952	1,058,000	369,580
1,069,000	37,064	1,009,000	349,490	1,119,000	40,016	1,059,000	369,990
1,070,000	37,120	1,010,000	349,900	1,120,000	40,080	1,060,000	370,400
1,071,000	37,176	1,011,000	350,310	1,121,000	40,144	1,061,000	370,810
1,072,000	37,232	1,012,000	350,720	1,122,000	40,208	1,062,000	371,220
1,073,000	37,288	1,013,000	351,130	1,123,000	40,272	1,063,000	371,630
1,074,000	37,344	1,014,000	351,540	1,124,000	40,336	1,064,000	372,040
1,075,000	37,400	1,015,000	351,950	1,125,000	40,400	1,065,000	372,450
1,076,000	37,456	1,016,000	352,360	1,126,000	40,464	1,066,000	372,860
1,077,000	37,512	1,017,000	352,770	1,127,000	40,528	1,067,000	373,270
1,078,000	37,568	1,018,000	353,180	1,128,000	40,592	1,068,000	373,680
1,079,000	37,624	1,019,000	353,590	1,129,000	40,656	1,069,000	374,090
1,080,000	37,680	1,020,000	354,000	1,130,000	40,720	1,070,000	374,500
1,081,000	37,736	1,021,000	354,410	1,131,000	40,784	1,071,000	374,910
1,082,000	37,792	1,022,000	354,820	1,132,000	40,848	1,072,000	375,320
1,083,000	37,848	1,023,000	355,230	1,133,000	40,912	1,073,000	375,730
1,084,000	37,904	1,024,000	355,640	1,134,000	40,976	1,074,000	376,140
1,085,000	37,960	1,025,000	356,050	1,135,000	41,040	1,075,000	376,550
1,086,000	38,016	1,026,000	356,460	1,136,000	41,104	1,076,000	376,960
1,087,000	38,072	1,027,000	356,870	1,137,000	41,168	1,077,000	377,370
1,088,000	38,128	1,028,000	357,280	1,138,000	41,232	1,078,000	377,780
1,089,000	38,184	1,029,000	357,690	1,139,000	41,296	1,079,000	378,190
1,090,000	38,240	1,030,000	358,100	1,140,000	41,360	1,080,000	378,600
1,091,000	38,296	1,031,000	358,510	1,141,000	41,424	1,081,000	379,010
1,092,000	38,352	1,032,000	358,920	1,142,000	41,488	1,082,000	379,420
1,093,000	38,408	1,033,000	359,330	1,143,000	41,552	1,083,000	379,830
1,094,000	38,464	1,034,000	359,740	1,144,000	41,616	1,084,000	380,240
1,095,000	38,520	1,035,000	360,150	1,145,000	41,680	1,085,000	380,650
1,096,000	38,576	1,036,000	360,560	1,146,000	41,744	1,086,000	381,060
1,097,000	38,632	1,037,000	360,970	1,147,000	41,808	1,087,000	381,470
1,098,000	38,688	1,038,000	361,380	1,148,000	41,872	1,088,000	381,880
1,099,000	38,744	1,039,000	361,790	1,149,000	41,936	1,089,000	382,290
1,100,000	38,800	1,040,000	362,200	1,150,000	42,000	1,090,000	382,700
1,101,000	38,864	1,041,000	362,610	1,151,000	42,064	1,091,000	383,110
1,102,000	38,928	1,042,000	363,020	1,152,000	42,128	1,092,000	383,520
1,103,000	38,992	1,043,000	363,430	1,153,000	42,192	1,093,000	383,930
1,104,000	39,056	1,044,000	363,840	1,154,000	42,256	1,094,000	384,340
1,105,000	39,120	1,045,000	364,250	1,155,000	42,320	1,095,000	384,750
1,106,000	39,184	1,046,000	364,660	1,156,000	42,384	1,096,000	385,160
1,107,000	39,248	1,047,000	365,070	1,157,000	42,448	1,097,000	385,570
1,108,000	39,312	1,048,000	365,480	1,158,000	42,512	1,098,000	385,980
1,109,000	39,376	1,049,000	365,890	1,159,000	42,576	1,099,000	386,390
1,110,000	39,440	1,050,000	366,300	1,160,000	42,640	1,100,000	386,800

Tools and Techniques

1 TAXABLE ESTATE	2 STATE DEATH TAX CREDIT	3 TENTATIVE TAX BASE	4 TENTATIVE TAX
1,161,000	42,704	1,101,000	387,210
1,162,000	42,768	1,102,000	387,620
1,163,000	42,832	1,103,000	388,030
1,164,000	42,896	1,104,000	388,440
1,165,000	42,960	1,105,000	388,850
1,166,000	43,024	1,106,000	389,260
1,167,000	43,088	1,107,000	389,670
1,168,000	43,152	1,108,000	390,080
1,169,000	43,216	1,109,000	390,490
1,170,000	43,280	1,110,000	390,900
1,171,000	43,344	1,111,000	391,310
1,172,000	43,408	1,112,000	391,720
1,173,000	43,472	1,113,000	392,130
1,174,000	43,536	1,114,000	392,540
1,175,000	43,600	1,115,000	392,950
1,176,000	43,664	1,116,000	393,360
1,177,000	43,728	1,117,000	393,770
1,178,000	43,792	1,118,000	394,180
1,179,000	43,856	1,119,000	394,590
1,180,000	43,920	1,120,000	395,000
1,181,000	43,984	1,121,000	395,410
1,182,000	44,048	1,122,000	395,820
1,183,000	44,112	1,123,000	396,230
1,184,000	44,176	1,124,000	396,640
1,185,000	44,240	1,125,000	397,050
1,186,000	44,304	1,126,000	397,460
1,187,000	44,368	1,127,000	397,870
1,188,000	44,432	1,128,000	398,280
1,189,000	44,496	1,129,000	398,690
1,190,000	44,560	1,130,000	399,100
1,191,000	44,624	1,131,000	399,510
1,192,000	44,688	1,132,000	399,920
1,193,000	44,752	1,133,000	400,330
1,194,000	44,816	1,134,000	400,740
1,195,000	44,880	1,135,000	401,150
1,196,000	44,944	1,136,000	401,560
1,197,000	45,008	1,137,000	401,970
1,198,000	45,072	1,138,000	402,380
1,199,000	45,136	1,139,000	402,790
1,200,000	45,200	1,140,000	403,200
1,201,000	45,264	1,141,000	403,610
1,202,000	45,328	1,142,000	404,020
1,203,000	45,392	1,143,000	404,430
1,204,000	45,456	1,144,000	404,840
1,205,000	45,520	1,145,000	405,250
1,206,000	45,584	1,146,000	405,660
1,207,000	45,648	1,147,000	406,070
1,208,000	45,712	1,148,000	406,480
1,209,000	45,776	1,149,000	406,890
1,210,000	45,840	1,150,000	407,300

1 TAXABLE ESTATE	2 STATE DEATH TAX CREDIT	3 TENTATIVE TAX BASE	4 TENTATIVE TAX
1,211,000	45,904	1,151,000	407,710
1,212,000	45,968	1,152,000	408,120
1,213,000	46,032	1,153,000	408,530
1,214,000	46,096	1,154,000	408,940
1,215,000	46,160	1,155,000	409,350
1,216,000	46,224	1,156,000	409,760
1,217,000	46,288	1,157,000	410,170
1,218,000	46,352	1,158,000	410,580
1,219,000	46,416	1,159,000	410,990
1,220,000	46,480	1,160,000	411,400
1,221,000	46,544	1,161,000	411,810
1,222,000	46,608	1,162,000	412,220
1,223,000	46,672	1,163,000	412,630
1,224,000	46,736	1,164,000	413,040
1,225,000	46,800	1,165,000	413,450
1,226,000	46,864	1,166,000	413,860
1,227,000	46,928	1,167,000	414,270
1,228,000	46,992	1,168,000	414,680
1,229,000	47,056	1,169,000	415,090
1,230,000	47,120	1,170,000	415,500
1,231,000	47,184	1,171,000	415,910
1,232,000	47,248	1,172,000	416,320
1,233,000	47,312	1,173,000	416,730
1,234,000	47,376	1,174,000	417,140
1,235,000	47,440	1,175,000	417,550
1,236,000	47,504	1,176,000	417,960
1,237,000	47,568	1,177,000	418,370
1,238,000	47,632	1,178,000	418,780
1,239,000	47,696	1,179,000	419,190
1,240,000	47,760	1,180,000	419,600
1,241,000	47,824	1,181,000	420,010
1,242,000	47,888	1,182,000	420,420
1,243,000	47,952	1,183,000	420,830
1,244,000	48,016	1,184,000	421,240
1,245,000	48,080	1,185,000	421,650
1,246,000	48,144	1,186,000	422,060
1,247,000	48,208	1,187,000	422,470
1,248,000	48,272	1,188,000	422,880
1,249,000	48,336	1,189,000	423,290
1,250,000	48,400	1,190,000	423,700
1,251,000	48,464	1,191,000	424,110
1,252,000	48,528	1,192,000	424,520
1,253,000	48,592	1,193,000	424,930
1,254,000	48,656	1,194,000	425,340
1,255,000	48,720	1,195,000	425,750
1,256,000	48,784	1,196,000	426,160
1,257,000	48,848	1,197,000	426,570
1,258,000	48,912	1,198,000	426,980
1,259,000	48,976	1,199,000	427,390
1,260,000	49,040	1,200,000	427,800

1 TAXABLE ESTATE	2 STATE DEATH TAX CREDIT	3 TENTATIVE TAX BASE	4 TENTATIVE TAX
1,261,000	49,104	1,201,000	428,210
1,262,000	49,168	1,202,000	428,620
1,263,000	49,232	1,203,000	429,030
1,264,000	49,296	1,204,000	429,440
1,265,000	49,360	1,205,000	429,850
1,266,000	49,424	1,206,000	430,260
1,267,000	49,488	1,207,000	430,670
1,268,000	49,552	1,208,000	431,080
1,269,000	49,616	1,209,000	431,490
1,270,000	49,680	1,210,000	431,900
1,271,000	49,744	1,211,000	432,310
1,272,000	49,808	1,212,000	432,720
1,273,000	49,872	1,213,000	433,130
1,274,000	49,936	1,214,000	433,540
1,275,000	50,000	1,215,000	433,950
1,276,000	50,064	1,216,000	434,360
1,277,000	50,128	1,217,000	434,770
1,278,000	50,192	1,218,000	435,180
1,279,000	50,256	1,219,000	435,590
1,280,000	50,320	1,220,000	436,000
1,281,000	50,384	1,221,000	436,410
1,282,000	50,448	1,222,000	436,820
1,283,000	50,512	1,223,000	437,230
1,284,000	50,576	1,224,000	437,640
1,285,000	50,640	1,225,000	438,050
1,286,000	50,704	1,226,000	438,460
1,287,000	50,768	1,227,000	438,870
1,288,000	50,832	1,228,000	439,280
1,289,000	50,896	1,229,000	439,690
1,290,000	50,960	1,230,000	440,100
1,291,000	51,024	1,231,000	440,510
1,292,000	51,088	1,232,000	440,920
1,293,000	51,152	1,233,000	441,330
1,294,000	51,216	1,234,000	441,740
1,295,000	51,280	1,235,000	442,150
1,296,000	51,344	1,236,000	442,560
1,297,000	51,408	1,237,000	442,970
1,298,000	51,472	1,238,000	443,380
1,299,000	51,536	1,239,000	443,790
1,300,000	51,600	1,240,000	444,200
1,301,000	51,664	1,241,000	444,610
1,302,000	51,728	1,242,000	445,020
1,303,000	51,792	1,243,000	445,430
1,304,000	51,856	1,244,000	445,840
1,305,000	51,920	1,245,000	446,250
1,306,000	51,984	1,246,000	446,660
1,307,000	52,048	1,247,000	447,070
1,308,000	52,112	1,248,000	447,480
1,309,000	52,176	1,249,000	447,890
1,310,000	52,240	1,250,000	448,300

1 TAXABLE ESTATE	2 STATE DEATH TAX CREDIT	3 TENTATIVE TAX BASE	4 TENTATIVE TAX
1,311,000	52,304	1,251,000	448,730
1,312,000	52,368	1,252,000	449,160
1,313,000	52,432	1,253,000	449,590
1,314,000	52,496	1,254,000	450,020
1,315,000	52,560	1,255,000	450,450
1,316,000	52,624	1,256,000	450,880
1,317,000	52,688	1,257,000	451,310
1,318,000	52,752	1,258,000	451,740
1,319,000	52,816	1,259,000	452,170
1,320,000	52,880	1,260,000	452,600
1,321,000	52,944	1,261,000	453,030
1,322,000	53,008	1,262,000	453,460
1,323,000	53,072	1,263,000	453,890
1,324,000	53,136	1,264,000	454,320
1,325,000	53,200	1,265,000	454,750
1,326,000	53,264	1,266,000	455,180
1,327,000	53,328	1,267,000	455,610
1,328,000	53,392	1,268,000	456,040
1,329,000	53,456	1,269,000	456,470
1,330,000	53,520	1,270,000	456,900
1,331,000	53,584	1,271,000	457,330
1,332,000	53,648	1,272,000	457,760
1,333,000	53,712	1,273,000	458,190
1,334,000	53,776	1,274,000	458,620
1,335,000	53,840	1,275,000	459,050
1,336,000	53,904	1,276,000	459,480
1,337,000	53,968	1,277,000	459,910
1,338,000	54,032	1,278,000	460,340
1,339,000	54,096	1,279,000	460,770
1,340,000	54,160	1,280,000	461,200
1,341,000	54,224	1,281,000	461,630
1,342,000	54,288	1,282,000	462,060
1,343,000	54,352	1,283,000	462,490
1,344,000	54,416	1,284,000	462,920
1,345,000	54,480	1,285,000	463,350
1,346,000	54,544	1,286,000	463,780
1,347,000	54,608	1,287,000	464,210
1,348,000	54,672	1,288,000	464,640
1,349,000	54,736	1,289,000	465,070
1,350,000	54,800	1,290,000	465,500
1,351,000	54,864	1,291,000	465,930
1,352,000	54,928	1,292,000	466,360
1,353,000	54,992	1,293,000	466,790
1,354,000	55,056	1,294,000	467,220
1,355,000	55,120	1,295,000	467,650
1,356,000	55,184	1,296,000	468,080
1,357,000	55,248	1,297,000	468,510
1,358,000	55,312	1,298,000	468,940
1,359,000	55,376	1,299,000	469,370
1,360,000	55,440	1,300,000	469,800

Tools and Techniques

1 TAXABLE ESTATE	2 STATE DEATH TAX CREDIT	3 TENTATIVE TAX BASE	4 TENTATIVE TAX
1,361,000	55,504	1,301,000	470,230
1,362,000	55,568	1,302,000	470,660
1,363,000	55,632	1,303,000	471,090
1,364,000	55,696	1,304,000	471,520
1,365,000	55,760	1,305,000	471,950
1,366,000	55,824	1,306,000	472,380
1,367,000	55,888	1,307,000	472,810
1,368,000	55,952	1,308,000	473,240
1,369,000	56,016	1,309,000	473,670
1,370,000	56,080	1,310,000	474,100
1,371,000	56,144	1,311,000	474,530
1,372,000	56,208	1,312,000	474,960
1,373,000	56,272	1,313,000	475,390
1,374,000	56,336	1,314,000	475,820
1,375,000	56,400	1,315,000	476,250
1,376,000	56,464	1,316,000	476,680
1,377,000	56,528	1,317,000	477,110
1,378,000	56,592	1,318,000	477,540
1,379,000	56,656	1,319,000	477,970
1,380,000	56,720	1,320,000	478,400
1,381,000	56,784	1,321,000	478,830
1,382,000	56,848	1,322,000	479,260
1,383,000	56,912	1,323,000	479,690
1,384,000	56,976	1,324,000	480,120
1,385,000	57,040	1,325,000	480,550
1,386,000	57,104	1,326,000	480,980
1,387,000	57,168	1,327,000	481,410
1,388,000	57,232	1,328,000	481,840
1,389,000	57,296	1,329,000	482,270
1,390,000	57,360	1,330,000	482,700
1,391,000	57,424	1,331,000	483,130
1,392,000	57,488	1,332,000	483,560
1,393,000	57,552	1,333,000	483,990
1,394,000	57,616	1,334,000	484,420
1,395,000	57,680	1,335,000	484,850
1,396,000	57,744	1,336,000	485,280
1,397,000	57,808	1,337,000	485,710
1,398,000	57,872	1,338,000	486,140
1,399,000	57,936	1,339,000	486,570
1,400,000	58,000	1,340,000	487,000
1,401,000	58,064	1,341,000	487,430
1,402,000	58,128	1,342,000	487,860
1,403,000	58,192	1,343,000	488,290
1,404,000	58,256	1,344,000	488,720
1,405,000	58,320	1,345,000	489,150
1,406,000	58,384	1,346,000	489,580
1,407,000	58,448	1,347,000	490,010
1,408,000	58,512	1,348,000	490,440
1,409,000	58,576	1,349,000	490,870
1,410,000	58,640	1,350,000	491,300

1 TAXABLE ESTATE	2 STATE DEATH TAX CREDIT	3 TENTATIVE TAX BASE	4 TENTATIVE TAX
1,411,000	58,704	1,351,000	491,730
1,412,000	58,768	1,352,000	492,160
1,413,000	58,832	1,353,000	492,590
1,414,000	58,896	1,354,000	493,020
1,415,000	58,960	1,355,000	493,450
1,416,000	59,024	1,356,000	493,880
1,417,000	59,088	1,357,000	494,310
1,418,000	59,152	1,358,000	494,740
1,419,000	59,216	1,359,000	495,170
1,420,000	59,280	1,360,000	495,600
1,421,000	59,344	1,361,000	496,030
1,422,000	59,408	1,362,000	496,460
1,423,000	59,472	1,363,000	496,890
1,424,000	59,536	1,364,000	497,320
1,425,000	59,600	1,365,000	497,750
1,426,000	59,664	1,366,000	498,180
1,427,000	59,728	1,367,000	498,610
1,428,000	59,792	1,368,000	499,040
1,429,000	59,856	1,369,000	499,470
1,430,000	59,920	1,370,000	499,900
1,431,000	59,984	1,371,000	500,330
1,432,000	60,048	1,372,000	500,760
1,433,000	60,112	1,373,000	501,190
1,434,000	60,176	1,374,000	501,620
1,435,000	60,240	1,375,000	502,050
1,436,000	60,304	1,376,000	502,480
1,437,000	60,368	1,377,000	502,910
1,438,000	60,432	1,378,000	503,340
1,439,000	60,496	1,379,000	503,770
1,440,000	60,560	1,380,000	504,200
1,441,000	60,624	1,381,000	504,630
1,442,000	60,688	1,382,000	505,060
1,443,000	60,752	1,383,000	505,490
1,444,000	60,816	1,384,000	505,920
1,445,000	60,880	1,385,000	506,350
1,446,000	60,944	1,386,000	506,780
1,447,000	61,008	1,387,000	507,210
1,448,000	61,072	1,388,000	507,640
1,449,000	61,136	1,389,000	508,070
1,450,000	61,200	1,390,000	508,500
1,451,000	61,264	1,391,000	508,930
1,452,000	61,328	1,392,000	509,360
1,453,000	61,392	1,393,000	509,790
1,454,000	61,456	1,394,000	510,220
1,455,000	61,520	1,395,000	510,650
1,456,000	61,584	1,396,000	511,080
1,457,000	61,648	1,397,000	511,510
1,458,000	61,712	1,398,000	511,940
1,459,000	61,776	1,399,000	512,370
1,460,000	61,840	1,400,000	512,800

Tools and Techniques

1 TAXABLE ESTATE	2 STATE DEATH TAX CREDIT	3 TENTATIVE TAX BASE	4 TENTATIVE TAX
1,461,000	61,904	1,401,000	513,230
1,462,000	61,968	1,402,000	513,660
1,463,000	62,032	1,403,000	514,090
1,464,000	62,096	1,404,000	514,520
1,465,000	62,160	1,405,000	514,950
1,466,000	62,224	1,406,000	515,380
1,467,000	62,288	1,407,000	515,810
1,468,000	62,352	1,408,000	516,240
1,469,000	62,416	1,409,000	516,670
1,470,000	62,480	1,410,000	517,100
1,471,000	62,544	1,411,000	517,530
1,472,000	62,608	1,412,000	517,960
1,473,000	62,672	1,413,000	518,390
1,474,000	62,736	1,414,000	518,820
1,475,000	62,800	1,415,000	519,250
1,476,000	62,864	1,416,000	519,680
1,477,000	62,928	1,417,000	520,110
1,478,000	62,992	1,418,000	520,540
1,479,000	63,056	1,419,000	520,970
1,480,000	63,120	1,420,000	521,400
1,481,000	63,184	1,421,000	521,830
1,482,000	63,248	1,422,000	522,260
1,483,000	63,312	1,423,000	522,690
1,484,000	63,376	1,424,000	523,120
1,485,000	63,440	1,425,000	523,550
1,486,000	63,504	1,426,000	523,980
1,487,000	63,568	1,427,000	524,410
1,488,000	63,632	1,428,000	524,840
1,489,000	63,696	1,429,000	525,270
1,490,000	63,760	1,430,000	525,700
1,491,000	63,824	1,431,000	526,130
1,492,000	63,888	1,432,000	526,560
1,493,000	63,952	1,433,000	526,990
1,494,000	64,016	1,434,000	527,420
1,495,000	64,080	1,435,000	527,850
1,496,000	64,144	1,436,000	528,280
1,497,000	64,208	1,437,000	528,710
1,498,000	64,272	1,438,000	529,140
1,499,000	64,336	1,439,000	529,570
1,500,000	64,400	1,440,000	530,000
1,501,000	64,464	1,441,000	530,430
1,502,000	64,528	1,442,000	530,860
1,503,000	64,592	1,443,000	531,290
1,504,000	64,656	1,444,000	531,720
1,505,000	64,720	1,445,000	532,150
1,506,000	64,784	1,446,000	532,580
1,507,000	64,848	1,447,000	533,010
1,508,000	64,912	1,448,000	533,440
1,509,000	64,976	1,449,000	533,870
1,510,000	65,040	1,450,000	534,300

1 TAXABLE ESTATE	2 STATE DEATH TAX CREDIT	3 TENTATIVE TAX BASE	4 TENTATIVE TAX
1,511,000	65,104	1,451,000	534,730
1,512,000	65,168	1,452,000	535,160
1,513,000	65,232	1,453,000	535,590
1,514,000	65,296	1,454,000	536,020
1,515,000	65,360	1,455,000	536,450
1,516,000	65,424	1,456,000	536,880
1,517,000	65,488	1,457,000	537,310
1,518,000	65,552	1,458,000	537,740
1,519,000	65,616	1,459,000	538,170
1,520,000	65,680	1,460,000	538,600
1,521,000	65,744	1,461,000	539,030
1,522,000	65,808	1,462,000	539,460
1,523,000	65,872	1,463,000	539,890
1,524,000	65,936	1,464,000	540,320
1,525,000	66,000	1,465,000	540,750
1,526,000	66,064	1,466,000	541,180
1,527,000	66,128	1,467,000	541,610
1,528,000	66,192	1,468,000	542,040
1,529,000	66,256	1,469,000	542,470
1,530,000	66,320	1,470,000	542,900
1,531,000	66,384	1,471,000	543,330
1,532,000	66,448	1,472,000	543,760
1,533,000	66,512	1,473,000	544,190
1,534,000	66,576	1,474,000	544,620
1,535,000	66,640	1,475,000	545,050
1,536,000	66,704	1,476,000	545,480
1,537,000	66,768	1,477,000	545,910
1,538,000	66,832	1,478,000	546,340
1,539,000	66,896	1,479,000	546,770
1,540,000	66,960	1,480,000	547,200
1,541,000	67,024	1,481,000	547,630
1,542,000	67,088	1,482,000	548,060
1,543,000	67,152	1,483,000	548,490
1,544,000	67,216	1,484,000	548,920
1,545,000	67,280	1,485,000	549,350
1,546,000	67,344	1,486,000	549,780
1,547,000	67,408	1,487,000	550,210
1,548,000	67,472	1,488,000	550,640
1,549,000	67,536	1,489,000	551,070
1,550,000	67,600	1,490,000	551,500
1,551,000	67,664	1,491,000	551,930
1,552,000	67,728	1,492,000	552,360
1,553,000	67,792	1,493,000	552,790
1,554,000	67,856	1,494,000	553,220
1,555,000	67,920	1,495,000	553,650
1,556,000	67,984	1,496,000	554,080
1,557,000	68,048	1,497,000	554,510
1,558,000	68,112	1,498,000	554,940
1,559,000	68,176	1,499,000	555,370
1,560,000	68,240	1,500,000	555,800

Tools and Techniques

Taxable Estate	State Death Tax Credit	Tentative Tax Base	Tentative Tax
1,561,000	68,304	1,501,000	556,250
1,562,000	68,368	1,502,000	556,700
1,563,000	68,432	1,503,000	557,150
1,564,000	68,496	1,504,000	557,600
1,565,000	68,560	1,505,000	558,050
1,566,000	68,624	1,506,000	558,500
1,567,000	68,688	1,507,000	558,950
1,568,000	68,752	1,508,000	559,400
1,569,000	68,816	1,509,000	559,850
1,570,000	68,880	1,510,000	560,300
1,571,000	68,944	1,511,000	560,750
1,572,000	69,008	1,512,000	561,200
1,573,000	69,072	1,513,000	561,650
1,574,000	69,136	1,514,000	562,100
1,575,000	69,200	1,515,000	562,550
1,576,000	69,264	1,516,000	563,000
1,577,000	69,328	1,517,000	563,450
1,578,000	69,392	1,518,000	563,900
1,579,000	69,456	1,519,000	564,350
1,580,000	69,520	1,520,000	564,800
1,581,000	69,584	1,521,000	565,250
1,582,000	69,648	1,522,000	565,700
1,583,000	69,712	1,523,000	566,150
1,584,000	69,776	1,524,000	566,600
1,585,000	69,840	1,525,000	567,050
1,586,000	69,904	1,526,000	567,500
1,587,000	69,968	1,527,000	567,950
1,588,000	70,032	1,528,000	568,400
1,589,000	70,096	1,529,000	568,850
1,590,000	70,160	1,530,000	569,300
1,591,000	70,224	1,531,000	569,750
1,592,000	70,288	1,532,000	570,200
1,593,000	70,352	1,533,000	570,650
1,594,000	70,416	1,534,000	571,100
1,595,000	70,480	1,535,000	571,550
1,596,000	70,544	1,536,000	572,000
1,597,000	70,608	1,537,000	572,450
1,598,000	70,672	1,538,000	572,900
1,599,000	70,736	1,539,000	573,350
1,600,000	70,800	1,540,000	573,800
1,601,000	70,872	1,541,000	574,250
1,602,000	70,944	1,542,000	574,700
1,603,000	71,016	1,543,000	575,150
1,604,000	71,088	1,544,000	575,600
1,605,000	71,160	1,545,000	576,050
1,606,000	71,232	1,546,000	576,500
1,607,000	71,304	1,547,000	576,950
1,608,000	71,376	1,548,000	577,400
1,609,000	71,448	1,549,000	577,850
1,610,000	71,520	1,550,000	578,300

Taxable Estate	State Death Tax Credit	Tentative Tax Base	Tentative Tax
1,611,000	71,592	1,551,000	578,750
1,612,000	71,664	1,552,000	579,200
1,613,000	71,736	1,553,000	579,650
1,614,000	71,808	1,554,000	580,100
1,615,000	71,880	1,555,000	580,550
1,616,000	71,952	1,556,000	581,000
1,617,000	72,024	1,557,000	581,450
1,618,000	72,096	1,558,000	581,900
1,619,000	72,168	1,559,000	582,350
1,620,000	72,240	1,560,000	582,800
1,621,000	72,312	1,561,000	583,250
1,622,000	72,384	1,562,000	583,700
1,623,000	72,456	1,563,000	584,150
1,624,000	72,528	1,564,000	584,600
1,625,000	72,600	1,565,000	585,050
1,626,000	72,672	1,566,000	585,500
1,627,000	72,744	1,567,000	585,950
1,628,000	72,816	1,568,000	586,400
1,629,000	72,888	1,569,000	586,850
1,630,000	72,960	1,570,000	587,300
1,631,000	73,032	1,571,000	587,750
1,632,000	73,104	1,572,000	588,200
1,633,000	73,176	1,573,000	588,650
1,634,000	73,248	1,574,000	589,100
1,635,000	73,320	1,575,000	589,550
1,636,000	73,392	1,576,000	590,000
1,637,000	73,464	1,577,000	590,450
1,638,000	73,536	1,578,000	590,900
1,639,000	73,608	1,579,000	591,350
1,640,000	73,680	1,580,000	591,800
1,641,000	73,752	1,581,000	592,250
1,642,000	73,824	1,582,000	592,700
1,643,000	73,896	1,583,000	593,150
1,644,000	73,968	1,584,000	593,600
1,645,000	74,040	1,585,000	594,050
1,646,000	74,112	1,586,000	594,500
1,647,000	74,184	1,587,000	594,950
1,648,000	74,256	1,588,000	595,400
1,649,000	74,328	1,589,000	595,850
1,650,000	74,400	1,590,000	596,300
1,651,000	74,472	1,591,000	596,750
1,652,000	74,544	1,592,000	597,200
1,653,000	74,616	1,593,000	597,650
1,654,000	74,688	1,594,000	598,100
1,655,000	74,760	1,595,000	598,550
1,656,000	74,832	1,596,000	599,000
1,657,000	74,904	1,597,000	599,450
1,658,000	74,976	1,598,000	599,900
1,659,000	75,048	1,599,000	600,350
1,660,000	75,120	1,600,000	600,800

1 TAXABLE ESTATE	2 STATE DEATH TAX CREDIT	3 TENTATIVE TAX BASE	4 TENTATIVE TAX
1,661,000	75,192	1,601,000	601,250
1,662,000	75,264	1,602,000	601,700
1,663,000	75,336	1,603,000	602,150
1,664,000	75,408	1,604,000	602,600
1,665,000	75,480	1,605,000	603,050
1,666,000	75,552	1,606,000	603,500
1,667,000	75,624	1,607,000	603,950
1,668,000	75,696	1,608,000	604,400
1,669,000	75,768	1,609,000	604,850
1,670,000	75,840	1,610,000	605,300
1,671,000	75,912	1,611,000	605,750
1,672,000	75,984	1,612,000	606,200
1,673,000	76,056	1,613,000	606,650
1,674,000	76,128	1,614,000	607,100
1,675,000	76,200	1,615,000	607,550
1,676,000	76,272	1,616,000	608,000
1,677,000	76,344	1,617,000	608,450
1,678,000	76,416	1,618,000	608,900
1,679,000	76,488	1,619,000	609,350
1,680,000	76,560	1,620,000	609,800
1,681,000	76,632	1,621,000	610,250
1,682,000	76,704	1,622,000	610,700
1,683,000	76,776	1,623,000	611,150
1,684,000	76,848	1,624,000	611,600
1,685,000	76,920	1,625,000	612,050
1,686,000	76,992	1,626,000	612,500
1,687,000	77,064	1,627,000	612,950
1,688,000	77,136	1,628,000	613,400
1,689,000	77,208	1,629,000	613,850
1,690,000	77,280	1,630,000	614,300
1,691,000	77,352	1,631,000	614,750
1,692,000	77,424	1,632,000	615,200
1,693,000	77,496	1,633,000	615,650
1,694,000	77,568	1,634,000	616,100
1,695,000	77,640	1,635,000	616,550
1,696,000	77,712	1,636,000	617,000
1,697,000	77,784	1,637,000	617,450
1,698,000	77,856	1,638,000	617,900
1,699,000	77,928	1,639,000	618,350
1,700,000	78,000	1,640,000	618,800
1,701,000	78,072	1,641,000	619,250
1,702,000	78,144	1,642,000	619,700
1,703,000	78,216	1,643,000	620,150
1,704,000	78,288	1,644,000	620,600
1,705,000	78,360	1,645,000	621,050
1,706,000	78,432	1,646,000	621,500
1,707,000	78,504	1,647,000	621,950
1,708,000	78,576	1,648,000	622,400
1,709,000	78,648	1,649,000	622,850
1,710,000	78,720	1,650,000	623,300

1 TAXABLE ESTATE	2 STATE DEATH TAX CREDIT	3 TENTATIVE TAX BASE	4 TENTATIVE TAX
1,711,000	78,792	1,651,000	623,750
1,712,000	78,864	1,652,000	624,200
1,713,000	78,936	1,653,000	624,650
1,714,000	79,008	1,654,000	625,100
1,715,000	79,080	1,655,000	625,550
1,716,000	79,152	1,656,000	626,000
1,717,000	79,224	1,657,000	626,450
1,718,000	79,296	1,658,000	626,900
1,719,000	79,368	1,659,000	627,350
1,720,000	79,440	1,660,000	627,800
1,721,000	79,512	1,661,000	628,250
1,722,000	79,584	1,662,000	628,700
1,723,000	79,656	1,663,000	629,150
1,724,000	79,728	1,664,000	629,600
1,725,000	79,800	1,665,000	630,050
1,726,000	79,872	1,666,000	630,500
1,727,000	79,944	1,667,000	630,950
1,728,000	80,016	1,668,000	631,400
1,729,000	80,088	1,669,000	631,850
1,730,000	80,160	1,670,000	632,300
1,731,000	80,232	1,671,000	632,750
1,732,000	80,304	1,672,000	633,200
1,733,000	80,376	1,673,000	633,650
1,734,000	80,448	1,674,000	634,100
1,735,000	80,520	1,675,000	634,550
1,736,000	80,592	1,676,000	635,000
1,737,000	80,664	1,677,000	635,450
1,738,000	80,736	1,678,000	635,900
1,739,000	80,808	1,679,000	636,350
1,740,000	80,880	1,680,000	636,800
1,741,000	80,952	1,681,000	637,250
1,742,000	81,024	1,682,000	637,700
1,743,000	81,096	1,683,000	638,150
1,744,000	81,168	1,684,000	638,600
1,745,000	81,240	1,685,000	639,050
1,746,000	81,312	1,686,000	639,500
1,747,000	81,384	1,687,000	639,950
1,748,000	81,456	1,688,000	640,400
1,749,000	81,528	1,689,000	640,850
1,750,000	81,600	1,690,000	641,300
1,751,000	81,672	1,691,000	641,750
1,752,000	81,744	1,692,000	642,200
1,753,000	81,816	1,693,000	642,650
1,754,000	81,888	1,694,000	643,100
1,755,000	81,960	1,695,000	643,550
1,756,000	82,032	1,696,000	644,000
1,757,000	82,104	1,697,000	644,450
1,758,000	82,176	1,698,000	644,900
1,759,000	82,248	1,699,000	645,350
1,760,000	82,320	1,700,000	645,800

Tools and Techniques

1 TAXABLE ESTATE	2 STATE DEATH TAX CREDIT	3 TENTATIVE TAX BASE	4 TENTATIVE TAX
1,761,000	82,392	1,701,000	646,250
1,762,000	82,464	1,702,000	646,700
1,763,000	82,536	1,703,000	647,150
1,764,000	82,608	1,704,000	647,600
1,765,000	82,680	1,705,000	648,050
1,766,000	82,752	1,706,000	648,500
1,767,000	82,824	1,707,000	648,950
1,768,000	82,896	1,708,000	649,400
1,769,000	82,968	1,709,000	649,850
1,770,000	83,040	1,710,000	650,300
1,771,000	83,112	1,711,000	650,750
1,772,000	83,184	1,712,000	651,200
1,773,000	83,256	1,713,000	651,650
1,774,000	83,328	1,714,000	652,100
1,775,000	83,400	1,715,000	652,550
1,776,000	83,472	1,716,000	653,000
1,777,000	83,544	1,717,000	653,450
1,778,000	83,616	1,718,000	653,900
1,779,000	83,688	1,719,000	654,350
1,780,000	83,760	1,720,000	654,800
1,781,000	83,832	1,721,000	655,250
1,782,000	83,904	1,722,000	655,700
1,783,000	83,976	1,723,000	656,150
1,784,000	84,048	1,724,000	656,600
1,785,000	84,120	1,725,000	657,050
1,786,000	84,192	1,726,000	657,500
1,787,000	84,264	1,727,000	657,950
1,788,000	84,336	1,728,000	658,400
1,789,000	84,408	1,729,000	658,850
1,790,000	84,480	1,730,000	659,300
1,791,000	84,552	1,731,000	659,750
1,792,000	84,624	1,732,000	660,200
1,793,000	84,696	1,733,000	660,650
1,794,000	84,768	1,734,000	661,100
1,795,000	84,840	1,735,000	661,550
1,796,000	84,912	1,736,000	662,000
1,797,000	84,984	1,737,000	662,450
1,798,000	85,056	1,738,000	662,900
1,799,000	85,128	1,739,000	663,350
1,800,000	85,200	1,740,000	663,800
1,801,000	85,272	1,741,000	664,250
1,802,000	85,344	1,742,000	664,700
1,803,000	85,416	1,743,000	665,150
1,804,000	85,488	1,744,000	665,600
1,805,000	85,560	1,745,000	666,050
1,806,000	85,632	1,746,000	666,500
1,807,000	85,704	1,747,000	666,950
1,808,000	85,776	1,748,000	667,400
1,809,000	85,848	1,749,000	667,850
1,810,000	85,920	1,750,000	668,300

1 TAXABLE ESTATE	2 STATE DEATH TAX CREDIT	3 TENTATIVE TAX BASE	4 TENTATIVE TAX
1,811,000	85,992	1,751,000	668,750
1,812,000	86,064	1,752,000	669,200
1,813,000	86,136	1,753,000	669,650
1,814,000	86,208	1,754,000	670,100
1,815,000	86,280	1,755,000	670,550
1,816,000	86,352	1,756,000	671,000
1,817,000	86,424	1,757,000	671,450
1,818,000	86,496	1,758,000	671,900
1,819,000	86,568	1,759,000	672,350
1,820,000	86,640	1,760,000	672,800
1,821,000	86,712	1,761,000	673,250
1,822,000	86,784	1,762,000	673,700
1,823,000	86,856	1,763,000	674,150
1,824,000	86,928	1,764,000	674,600
1,825,000	87,000	1,765,000	675,050
1,826,000	87,072	1,766,000	675,500
1,827,000	87,144	1,767,000	675,950
1,828,000	87,216	1,768,000	676,400
1,829,000	87,288	1,769,000	676,850
1,830,000	87,360	1,770,000	677,300
1,831,000	87,432	1,771,000	677,750
1,832,000	87,504	1,772,000	678,200
1,833,000	87,576	1,773,000	678,650
1,834,000	87,648	1,774,000	679,100
1,835,000	87,720	1,775,000	679,550
1,836,000	87,792	1,776,000	680,000
1,837,000	87,864	1,777,000	680,450
1,838,000	87,936	1,778,000	680,900
1,839,000	88,008	1,779,000	681,350
1,840,000	88,080	1,780,000	681,800
1,841,000	88,152	1,781,000	682,250
1,842,000	88,224	1,782,000	682,700
1,843,000	88,296	1,783,000	683,150
1,844,000	88,368	1,784,000	683,600
1,845,000	88,440	1,785,000	684,050
1,846,000	88,512	1,786,000	684,500
1,847,000	88,584	1,787,000	684,950
1,848,000	88,656	1,788,000	685,400
1,849,000	88,728	1,789,000	685,850
1,850,000	88,800	1,790,000	686,300
1,851,000	88,872	1,791,000	686,750
1,852,000	88,944	1,792,000	687,200
1,853,000	89,016	1,793,000	687,650
1,854,000	89,088	1,794,000	688,100
1,855,000	89,160	1,795,000	688,550
1,856,000	89,232	1,796,000	689,000
1,857,000	89,304	1,797,000	689,450
1,858,000	89,376	1,798,000	689,900
1,859,000	89,448	1,799,000	690,350
1,860,000	89,520	1,800,000	690,800

1 TAXABLE ESTATE	2 STATE DEATH TAX CREDIT	3 TENTATIVE TAX BASE	4 TENTATIVE TAX	1 TAXABLE ESTATE	2 STATE DEATH TAX CREDIT	3 TENTATIVE TAX BASE	4 TENTATIVE TAX
1,861,000	89,592	1,801,000	691,250	1,911,000	93,192	1,851,000	713,750
1,862,000	89,664	1,802,000	691,700	1,912,000	93,264	1,852,000	714,200
1,863,000	89,736	1,803,000	692,150	1,913,000	93,336	1,853,000	714,650
1,864,000	89,808	1,804,000	692,600	1,914,000	93,408	1,854,000	715,100
1,865,000	89,880	1,805,000	693,050	1,915,000	93,480	1,855,000	715,550
1,866,000	89,952	1,806,000	693,500	1,916,000	93,552	1,856,000	716,000
1,867,000	90,024	1,807,000	693,950	1,917,000	93,624	1,857,000	716,450
1,868,000	90,096	1,808,000	694,400	1,918,000	93,696	1,858,000	716,900
1,869,000	90,168	1,809,000	694,850	1,919,000	93,768	1,859,000	717,350
1,870,000	90,240	1,810,000	695,300	1,920,000	93,840	1,860,000	717,800
1,871,000	90,312	1,811,000	695,750	1,921,000	93,912	1,861,000	718,250
1,872,000	90,384	1,812,000	696,200	1,922,000	93,984	1,862,000	718,700
1,873,000	90,456	1,813,000	696,650	1,923,000	94,056	1,863,000	719,150
1,874,000	90,528	1,814,000	697,100	1,924,000	94,128	1,864,000	719,600
1,875,000	90,600	1,815,000	697,550	1,925,000	94,200	1,865,000	720,050
1,876,000	90,672	1,816,000	698,000	1,926,000	94,272	1,866,000	720,500
1,877,000	90,744	1,817,000	698,450	1,927,000	94,344	1,867,000	720,950
1,878,000	90,816	1,818,000	698,900	1,928,000	94,416	1,868,000	721,400
1,879,000	90,888	1,819,000	699,350	1,929,000	94,488	1,869,000	721,850
1,880,000	90,960	1,820,000	699,800	1,930,000	94,560	1,870,000	722,300
1,881,000	91,032	1,821,000	700,250	1,931,000	94,632	1,871,000	722,750
1,882,000	91,104	1,822,000	700,700	1,932,000	94,704	1,872,000	723,200
1,883,000	91,176	1,823,000	701,150	1,933,000	94,776	1,873,000	723,650
1,884,000	91,248	1,824,000	701,600	1,934,000	94,848	1,874,000	724,100
1,885,000	91,320	1,825,000	702,050	1,935,000	94,920	1,875,000	724,550
1,886,000	91,392	1,826,000	702,500	1,936,000	94,992	1,876,000	725,000
1,887,000	91,464	1,827,000	702,950	1,937,000	95,064	1,877,000	725,450
1,888,000	91,536	1,828,000	703,400	1,938,000	95,136	1,878,000	725,900
1,889,000	91,608	1,829,000	703,850	1,939,000	95,208	1,879,000	726,350
1,890,000	91,680	1,830,000	704,300	1,940,000	95,280	1,880,000	726,800
1,891,000	91,752	1,831,000	704,750	1,941,000	95,352	1,881,000	727,250
1,892,000	91,824	1,832,000	705,200	1,942,000	95,424	1,882,000	727,700
1,893,000	91,896	1,833,000	705,650	1,943,000	95,496	1,883,000	728,150
1,894,000	91,968	1,834,000	706,100	1,944,000	95,568	1,884,000	728,600
1,895,000	92,040	1,835,000	706,550	1,945,000	95,640	1,885,000	729,050
1,896,000	92,112	1,836,000	707,000	1,946,000	95,712	1,886,000	729,500
1,897,000	92,184	1,837,000	707,450	1,947,000	95,784	1,887,000	729,950
1,898,000	92,256	1,838,000	707,900	1,948,000	95,856	1,888,000	730,400
1,899,000	92,328	1,839,000	708,350	1,949,000	95,928	1,889,000	730,850
1,900,000	92,400	1,840,000	708,800	1,950,000	96,000	1,890,000	731,300
1,901,000	92,472	1,841,000	709,250	1,951,000	96,072	1,891,000	731,750
1,902,000	92,544	1,842,000	709,700	1,952,000	96,144	1,892,000	732,200
1,903,000	92,616	1,843,000	710,150	1,953,000	96,216	1,893,000	732,650
1,904,000	92,688	1,844,000	710,600	1,954,000	96,288	1,894,000	733,100
1,905,000	92,760	1,845,000	711,050	1,955,000	96,360	1,895,000	733,550
1,906,000	92,832	1,846,000	711,500	1,956,000	96,432	1,896,000	734,000
1,907,000	92,904	1,847,000	711,950	1,957,000	96,504	1,897,000	734,450
1,908,000	92,976	1,848,000	712,400	1,958,000	96,576	1,898,000	734,900
1,909,000	93,048	1,849,000	712,850	1,959,000	96,648	1,899,000	735,350
1,910,000	93,120	1,850,000	713,300	1,960,000	96,720	1,900,000	735,800

Tools and Techniques

1 TAXABLE ESTATE	2 STATE DEATH TAX CREDIT	3 TENTATIVE TAX BASE	4 TENTATIVE TAX	1 TAXABLE ESTATE	2 STATE DEATH TAX CREDIT	3 TENTATIVE TAX BASE	4 TENTATIVE TAX
1,961,000	96,792	1,901,000	736,250	2,011,000	100,392	1,951,000	758,750
1,962,000	96,864	1,902,000	736,700	2,012,000	100,464	1,952,000	759,200
1,963,000	96,936	1,903,000	737,150	2,013,000	100,536	1,953,000	759,650
1,964,000	97,008	1,904,000	737,600	2,014,000	100,608	1,954,000	760,100
1,965,000	97,080	1,905,000	738,050	2,015,000	100,680	1,955,000	760,550
1,966,000	97,152	1,906,000	738,500	2,016,000	100,752	1,956,000	761,000
1,967,000	97,224	1,907,000	738,950	2,017,000	100,824	1,957,000	761,450
1,968,000	97,296	1,908,000	739,400	2,018,000	100,896	1,958,000	761,900
1,969,000	97,368	1,909,000	739,850	2,019,000	100,968	1,959,000	762,350
1,970,000	97,440	1,910,000	740,300	2,020,000	101,040	1,960,000	762,800
1,971,000	97,512	1,911,000	740,750	2,021,000	101,112	1,961,000	763,250
1,972,000	97,584	1,912,000	741,200	2,022,000	101,184	1,962,000	763,700
1,973,000	97,656	1,913,000	741,650	2,023,000	101,256	1,963,000	764,150
1,974,000	97,728	1,914,000	742,100	2,024,000	101,328	1,964,000	764,600
1,975,000	97,800	1,915,000	742,550	2,025,000	101,400	1,965,000	765,050
1,976,000	97,872	1,916,000	743,000	2,026,000	101,472	1,966,000	765,500
1,977,000	97,944	1,917,000	743,450	2,027,000	101,544	1,967,000	765,950
1,978,000	98,016	1,918,000	743,900	2,028,000	101,616	1,968,000	766,400
1,979,000	98,088	1,919,000	744,350	2,029,000	101,688	1,969,000	766,850
1,980,000	98,160	1,920,000	744,800	2,030,000	101,760	1,970,000	767,300
1,981,000	98,232	1,921,000	745,250	2,031,000	101,832	1,971,000	767,750
1,982,000	98,304	1,922,000	745,700	2,032,000	101,904	1,972,000	768,200
1,983,000	98,376	1,923,000	746,150	2,033,000	101,976	1,973,000	768,650
1,984,000	98,448	1,924,000	746,600	2,034,000	102,048	1,974,000	769,100
1,985,000	98,520	1,925,000	747,050	2,035,000	102,120	1,975,000	769,550
1,986,000	98,592	1,926,000	747,500	2,036,000	102,192	1,976,000	770,000
1,987,000	98,664	1,927,000	747,950	2,037,000	102,264	1,977,000	770,450
1,988,000	98,736	1,928,000	748,400	2,038,000	102,336	1,978,000	770,900
1,989,000	98,808	1,929,000	748,850	2,039,000	102,408	1,979,000	771,350
1,990,000	98,880	1,930,000	749,300	2,040,000	102,480	1,980,000	771,800
1,991,000	98,952	1,931,000	749,750	2,041,000	102,552	1,981,000	772,250
1,992,000	99,024	1,932,000	750,200	2,042,000	102,624	1,982,000	772,700
1,993,000	99,096	1,933,000	750,650	2,043,000	102,696	1,983,000	773,150
1,994,000	99,168	1,934,000	751,100	2,044,000	102,768	1,984,000	773,600
1,995,000	99,240	1,935,000	751,550	2,045,000	102,840	1,985,000	774,050
1,996,000	99,312	1,936,000	752,000	2,046,000	102,912	1,986,000	774,500
1,997,000	99,384	1,937,000	752,450	2,047,000	102,984	1,987,000	774,950
1,998,000	99,456	1,938,000	752,900	2,048,000	103,056	1,988,000	775,400
1,999,000	99,528	1,939,000	753,350	2,049,000	103,128	1,989,000	775,850
2,000,000	99,600	1,940,000	753,800	2,050,000	103,200	1,990,000	776,300
2,001,000	99,672	1,941,000	754,250	2,051,000	103,272	1,991,000	776,750
2,002,000	99,744	1,942,000	754,700	2,052,000	103,344	1,992,000	777,200
2,003,000	99,816	1,943,000	755,150	2,053,000	103,416	1,993,000	777,650
2,004,000	99,888	1,944,000	755,600	2,054,000	103,488	1,994,000	778,100
2,005,000	99,960	1,945,000	756,050	2,055,000	103,560	1,995,000	778,550
2,006,000	100,032	1,946,000	756,500	2,056,000	103,632	1,996,000	779,000
2,007,000	100,104	1,947,000	756,950	2,057,000	103,704	1,997,000	779,450
2,008,000	100,176	1,948,000	757,400	2,058,000	103,776	1,998,000	779,900
2,009,000	100,248	1,949,000	757,850	2,059,000	103,848	1,999,000	780,350
2,010,000	100,320	1,950,000	758,300	2,060,000	103,920	2,000,000	780,800

1	2	3	4
TAXABLE ESTATE	STATE DEATH TAX CREDIT	TENTATIVE TAX BASE	TENTATIVE TAX
2,160,000	111,600	2,100,000	829,800
2,260,000	119,600	2,200,000	878,800
2,360,000	127,600	2,300,000	927,800
2,460,000	135,600	2,400,000	976,800
2,560,000	143,600	2,500,000	1,025,800

ULTRA LARGE ESTATES		
Tentative Tax Base	Tax-Transfer Before 1993	Tax-Transfer 1993 or Later
$ 3,000,000	$1,290,000	$1,275,800
5,000,000	2,390,000	2,275,800
10,000,000	5,140,800	4,775,800
15,000,000	8,140,800	7,525,800
20,000,000	11,140,800	10,192,800
30,000,000	16,692,800	15,192,800
40,000,000	22,192,800	20,192,900
50,000,000	27,692,800	25,192,800
75,000,000	41,442,800	37,692,800
100,000,000	55,192,800	50,192,800
200,000,000	110,192,800	100,192,800

Appendix D

COMPUTERS AND ESTATE PLANNING

Estate planning is multidimensional; it involves the interplay between "people" planning and "asset" planning. The accumulation, conservation, distribution of assets in a manner that most effectively and efficiently accomplishes a client's objectives can be accomplished only if both the planner and the client have established goals and have developed a system for achieving them.

Developing goals and the system that will achieve them requires facts and figures. The incredible array of possibilities is mind boggling.

"What if?" can be reduced to "here are our options" only after a laborious gathering, assembeling, and analysis of data. The mathematical multiplicity is obvious. Clearly, computers are an answer, but......

First, the planner has to be able to do—by hand—everything the computer can do. This is the only way the planner can tell if there is a mistake or if the neatly printed and handsomely packaged output is in fact "garbage in—garbage out".

Second, to understand how to modify a commercial product to suit your level of depth and presentation needs, you must have at least a basic understanding of how the software works or what assumptions the programmers have made.

Third, the planner has to understand that no software is a panacea or a replacement for thinking. Intelligence and a working knowledge of the estate and gift tax computational process is essential to proper utilization of commercially available computer software.

Financial Data Corporation (1-800-654-2227 or 215-525-6957, P.O. Box 1332, Bryn Mawr, PA 19010) has developed the financial and estate planner's **NumberCruncher**, a series of over 40 templates (a fancy word for computer files that do specific tasks and are not interrelated) using The Tools and Techniques of Estate Planning.

Some of the tasks **NumberCruncher I** will perform are:

Valuation: NumberCruncher I

1. Capitalizes income in order to value an asset or business
2. Computes value of closely held stock by comparison with public companies
3. Computes the book value per share of common stock
4. Computes the value of business as a going concern (good will valuation)
5. Computes the value of a key employee
6. Computes special use valuation for estate tax savings

Tools: NumberCruncher I

1. Computes the income tax deduction for contribution to uni or annuity remainder trusts (five separate programs)
2. Computes eligibility for and costs of a Section 6166 payout
3. Computes the income tax implications of a private annuity
4. Computes qualification for and protection under Section 303
5. Computes the payments required under a split purchase of assets (Split) and potential tax savings
6. Computes gift and estate tax implications of a GRIT

Techniques: NumberCruncher I

1. Computes the estate tax savings available through use of annual gift tax exclusion
2. Computes the after tax deduction cost of a gift to charity
3. Computes amount of stock that must be redeemed under a substantially disproportionate redemption
4. Computes the income tax deduction allowed to recipient of I.R.D. (691 income)

Tables: NumberCruncher I

1. Computes gift and estate taxes from taxable gifts or tentative tax bases
2. Computes income tax liability of policyowner under split dollar or qualified pension plan (P.S. 58 cost)
3. Computes income tax liability of policyowner under group term life insurance
4. Computes income tax, net income remaining, marginal tax brackets, and effective tax rates from taxable income of single, joint, head of household, trusts, estates, and corporations
5. Computes client's life expectancy according to IRS Table V

Time/Money: NumberCruncher I

1. Computes the future value of a stream of payments
2. Computes the present value of a series of payments
3. Computes the value of an ordinary annuity (an annuity in arrears)
4. Computes the net present value of a stream of income

Tools and Techniques

5. Computes the value of a lump sum

6. Computes the present value of a future lump sum

7. Computes the value of three funds at different rates of interest

8. Compares a taxfree investment with one that is fully taxable

9. Computes the internal rate of return of an investment

10. Computes rate of return on treasury bills

11. Calculates annual rate of return on investments

Included with the "NUMBERCRUNCHER I" disk is a comprehensive manual explaining in detail each of the computations. This software tracks extremely well with the chapters in "Tools and Techniques of Estate Planning."

Another excellent estate planning software program is the estate Forecast Model from ViewPlan, Inc. (1-800-826-2127 or in California, 1-800-352-6699, 2257 Boundary Street, San Diego, CA 92104). Whereas NumberCruncher concentrates on a number of the finer details of estate planning, the Estate Forecast Model is a graphics oriented package which can be used interactively with a client to show the results of different estate tax minimization techniques using trusts and gifts. The charts in Chapter 33 relating to the Marital Deduction were produced with the Estate Forecast Model.

The Estate Forecast Model is so easy to use that even computer novices can be productive almost immediately, and it is the only estate planning software which has been approved by the American Bar Association's Legal Technology Advisory Council.

There are, of course, many commercially available software products that do not do individual computations but are designed to "work up" an entire estate planning case. Here are some questions you should ask—and be able to answer — *before* you buy any software:

TRY BEFORE YOU BUY

Try before you buy is the most important rule of computer software selection. Get "hands-on" experience or talk—at length—to a user (with a sales or service operation similar to yours). Many software vendors will send you a demo disk, rent you the software with an option to buy, or arrange for a demonstration in your office. Don't buy until you (or someone you trust) try!

DECIDE WHAT IT IS YOU NEED, WANT, OR WISH

Before you begin your analysis, write up a job description. That's right—a job description. Buying software is like hiring a part-time employee; a good manager will write down exactly what it is that must be done (essential tasks with a very high importance level), what it is that you want—over and above the absolutely necessary (frills or conveniences

that it would be nice or neat to have), and then, a "wish list" (a low importance level).

DECIDE HOW MUCH YOU ARE WILLING TO PAY

The cash you pay for a computer program is only part of the cost; the more sophisticated the program, the more time it generally takes to input the data. Certain programs take so much familiarity that only an administrative assistant who works with the program all the time can run them. Others take so much expertise, you'll have to take *your* precious time to input data.

HOW TO COMPARE ESTATE PLANNING PROGRAMS

To fairly analyze any program and decide which of several is best for you, you've got to create some decision making device to objectively compare them.

Here are six categories of key decisions:

1. cost and compatibility
2. learning ease
3. using ease
4. backup
5. capacity
6. printing

Cost and Compatability

The question of cost is more difficult than merely comparing price. Assuming the software will work in your machine, the true cost of software includes the purchase price of any auxiliary software (as well as the installation cost of memory units or other hardware necessary to run the software) you need to drive the system. For example, if you need Lotus 1, 2, 3 to run the financial planning software, your computer must have a minimum of 192K of memory.

Learning Ease

A good software program will provide "tutorial aids," devices to guide you in the learning process. These include cassette tapes, tutorial disks, and carefully constructed user's manuals. Do these instructions put you at ease? Does the manual show you what the screen should look like at various points?

Another issue is "booting." Booting is what you have to do to get the program from the floppy disk to your monitor's screen. The best are those that just require you to insert the disks and turn on the machine.

Does the program define each new work or term? For instance, can you push a "help" key to find out what is meant by the term, "range" or the term, "cell"?

"Prompts" are clear precise statements from the machine to you stating what it wants next. The more the program prompts you, the better.

A sample case that walks you through the software—step-by-step—is an invaluable way to learn to apply the power you've purchased. Does the vendor provide at least one sample case?

Learning time is a key factor in comparing software. Ask the vendor how much time (assuming a working technical familiarity with the subject matter) it should take to learn to use the program. Then check with a user.

Using Ease

Will you receive fact finders or input sheets and (more importantly) is that fact finder coordinated with what you'll see on the monitor screens?

How much time does it take to enter the data (a) on a simple case, (b) on an average case, and (c) on a complex case? Obviously, the shorter, the better. (Of course, too little data makes the output meaningless while a program which requires too much information before it will run may require a greater time expenditure than it's worth.)

A "command module" is a group of signals you can give to the computer to tell it to perform various tasks (such as, I made a mistake and I want to correct or edit or review what I've just done). Some programs make you feel you are on a turnpike with no exits—going the wrong way. The more often the program gives you the ability to make changes or give the computer various commands (such as print only what I want printed), the more valuable it is.

"Defaults" are not problems; they are opportunities. A default is a built-in anticipation by the software vendor's programmer for normal responses. For instance, most parents will leave their estates in equal shares to their children. So, in default of your selecting an alternative, the program will assume each child receives an equal share. Well considered defaults save you time and are quite useful as long as you know what they are, how to override them, and have suitable alternatives when you need them.

"Saving" data is one of the most important functions of a program. What if you've spent 45 minutes inputting data and you hit the wrong key and it's all gone? A good program will make it very easy for you to store data on a disk. Some even remind you or do it for you automatically.

"Retrieving" data is the reverse of storing it. Once it's stored, how quickly and easily can you locate and bring back information that you've saved?

Check for "data entry redundancy." Do you have to enter the same information more than once? In other words, once you put in your client's name or age, will that data be automatically used in all relevant modules or do you have to reenter it as you go (for example) from the gift to the estate to the income tax module of the same program?

Will one change change all the numbers? Will the program alter all the linked computation if one number changes?

Is the user's manual more than just an operational guide? Does the manual describe how to use the software system's planning capacity as well?

How many alternatives will the program illustrate and can you see them all side by side?

Once you've entered all the data, how long does it take or how many steps are involved in the actual computational process? Some programs are practically instantaneous. Others take as long as 5 to 8 minutes after data are entered before you can see the results.

Perhaps the best way to test the using ease of a program before you buy it is to talk to someone who has been using it. If you don't know someone, ask the vendor for the number of two or three satisfied users. Ask what they *don't* like about the program as well as what they do like.

Backup

No matter how good the program is or how knowledgeable you are, sooner or later you are going to need help. *Before* you buy, be sure to ask:

Does the computer manual explain how it reached a given result—so that you can explain a discrepancy or make appropriate adjustments?

Does the vendor provide technical (computer-software) backup by phone? Is it toll free? Do you have to pay a fee? Who will you get to talk to (and will that person speak your language)?

How often is the program updated? What if you've just purchased the program and 2 months later the tax law changes? Do modifications occur through new disks, does the vendor modify your old disks, or will you have to make the changes? (Who pays the cost for all these changes?)

Does the company provide users with a newsletter sharing planning ideas as well as technical updates?

Capacity

Is the program capable of meshing with a data base or a mailing list, and does it have word processing capacities (or is it solely a number cruncher)?

Can you modify or supplement the final product? Do you have to take all the output exactly as it is given or can you insert your own paragraphs or pages when you want?

Will the program do graphics? (A Hewlett-Packard study claims that a chart is 114,000 times easier to understand than the same information presented as words and numbers. A study by the Wharton School of the University of Pennsylva-

Tools and Techniques

nia shows that graphics cuts decision time by 30 percent.) If the program will do graphics, is that capacity integrated with the main program or do you have to reenter the data? Can you create color graphics? If the program will not do graphics, will it integrate with another program that will?

Printing

Is the print menu flexible? How much control do you have over the formatting and physical appearance of the final product? Is the standard format "client presentable" or is it so unconventional or unprofessional that it can't be used "as is"? How long is a full report?

Can you print the input so that you have a record of what went into the end product?

Can you view the report on the screen prior to printing (so that you can detect and correct mistakes)?

Can you print only that portion of the report that you want or do you have to take the whole thing?

Does the program allow you to input new data or make calculations while it is printing?

Can you stop printing whenever you want and then restart? Do you have to go back to the beginning when you do restart?

Does the program allow you to select between single and continuous feed printing?

Does the program have to be specially configured to your printer or will it work in any printer? If modification is needed, will the vendor do it or assist you?

Will the program "batch process" and "batch print"? That is, will the program perform a series of computations and then print out a number of cases or alternatives—without your being there?

COMPARING ESTATE PLANNING SOFTWARE

When the estate planner looks for software, there are very specific issues that should be considered in the comparison process once the questions above (that apply to all software selection) have been answered. Grouped in terms of general categories, these include:

1. input
2. special computations

Input

Does the entry of data follow the same rules that apply to the estate, gift, or income tax returns? Is the same order and procedure used or is it necessary to learn a new process or make adjustments for a different end product because of different assumptions? For example, in doing estate tax computations, are assets on which there is a personal liability entered at gross and netted out later, or must you enter net equity?

How many assets and sources of income can you input? If there is a limit, does the screen tell you how many spaces are left?

Do the prompts speak English? That is, does the program use familiar or easily remembered symbols such as "J.S." to represent joint and survivor or "A.G.I." for adjusted gross income?

Special Computations

There are a number of special tasks or computations you may want a particular program to do.

An estate planner would find the following questions particularly useful:

Will the program calculate the sufficiency of income for survivors and compare income to cash requirements?

Does the machine do a 6166 qualification test? Will it do the payout calculation using the latest interest rates? How many businesses will the program handle, and can it combine proprietorships, partnerships, and corporations?

Does the program compute the actuarial value of life estates, annuities, term certain, or remainder interests? Does it have the latest tables?

Will the program do charitable remainder and lead trust calculations?

Can you use the program to compute qualification for "special use" valuation as well as the amount of property eligible?

Is the program capable of calculating private annuity and installment sale payments and tax implications under the latest valuation tables?

Will the software do gift tax computations? Are gift tax computations coordinated with estate tax calculations? Will the program handle adjusted taxable gifts as well as gifts includible in the gross estate?

Is the credit for tax on prior transfers factored into the computations?

Will the program do business valuations? Will it do weighted averages of earnings?

Does the program consider the state law of your client? What flexibility do you have if the client owns property in more than one state?

How many insurance policies can be handled? Does the program allow for variations in policy ownership, or beneficiary arrangements?

Will the software project the cash flow effects of a long-term disability for at least 10 years?

Can the program allocate investments to "risk categories" so that you can show the client how much or what percentage of assets is in high, moderate, or low risk investments or what amounts or percentage of the entire portfolio is liquid, semiliquid, or nonliquid?

Will the program illustrate the client's yield from the date of investment? Will it show income as a percent of current market value?

Is the program capable of displaying, on a month-to-month basis, all sources of income and disbursements and cash flow surplus (investable income) or deficit?

Can the program compare projected income at specified retirement ages to a client's stated objectives? Will it consider taxes and inflation and then compute the annual savings at given percentage returns to reach a specified objective?

Is the program capable of storing costs and tracing dates of purchases and sales?

Can a balance sheet be projected for at least 10 years to reflect retirement planning?

Does the income tax analysis consider all sources of income, adjustments, deductions, exemptions, and credits?

Will the program provide a step-by-step printout to show intermediate computations and values?

Can you input the dollar liquidity value of each item?

Can you write your own asset description (such as the "12th and Market" property)?

Can you enter assets in any order?

Can you input the growth rate of assets individually or must the same rate be applied to all assets? Can you assign a negative growth rate to a given asset?

Can you input a dollar amount or specify the percentage of probate estate to compute administrative expenses?

Can you specify the order of deaths? Can you vary the year of death for unified credit purposes?

Does the program give you flexibility in computing the marital deduction?

Can you input assets available to a family which will not have a federal estate or state death tax effect (such as life insurance owned by an irrevocable trust or by adult children)?

In reality, one software package generally can't provide all the tools a planner may need to both analyze the estate results and provide an interactive teaching tool for clients. That is why many planners use both the Estate Forecast Model and NumberCruncher, since NumberCruncher can provide the fine tuning the planner needs to make informed recommendations to the clients, and the Estate Forecast Model can use its graphics to help the clients picture the benefits of adopting an estate plan for themselves and their families.

CONCLUSION

These are only a few of the most essential of the many questions that you should ask before you buy. Note that the interplay of two factors should be key in your decision making process: First, ask yourself, for each of the questions above, *"How important is it to me that the program be able to accomplish a given task?"* Second, *"Does the program accomplish the task easily, quickly, and accurately?"*

Remember—*ignorance, aggravation,* or *misplaced trust* could *cost much more than the price you pay for the product itself!*

Tools and Techniques

KEEPING WEALTH IN THE FAMILY: THE ALMOST IMPOSSIBLE DREAM

Copyright ©1988 by Stephan R. Leimberg

INTRODUCTION

First of all, you may be saying, "I don't have any really wealthy clients, so why should I continue to read?" Trust me . . . just for another paragraph or two.

This is the tale of two men — one Mr. Paul Paris, the other Mr. Larry London. In age (45), health (excellent), hobbies, and especially in looks, Paul Paris and Larry London are identical. Among the many things they have in common, they both have been wise enough to use you as their advisor. Paul Paris has an estate currently worth $600,000 (well within the unified credit's protection). Larry London's estate is currently worth $1,200,000. Both men have children and each has a grandchild. Both are in business and both are remarried. But because of premarriage (antenuptial) agreements, neither man's estate will qualify for the marital deduction.

Look at Figures D.1 and D.3. Paul Paris's estate, worth $600,000 (completely estate tax free) today is growing at a 3 percent net rate together with a 4 percent average rate of inflation. The life expectancy of a 45-year-old, according to government tables, is about 38 years. In that length of time, at a 7 percent total growth assumption, wealth will double approximately every ten years. (You can approximate how quickly an estate will double in value by dividing the growth rate you are assuming into the number 72.) By the end of his life expectancy, at a mere 7 percent total growth assumption, Paul Paris's wealth will have grown to $7,847,563. Larry London's estate will be worth $15,695,126. The point is that many individuals who never thought of themselves as "wealthy" will be wealthy — at least for purposes of the federal estate tax. See Figures D.2 (related to Figure D.1) and D.4 (related to Figure D.3), which graphically illustrate this point.

Figure D.1

COMPUTING ESTATE TAX ON FUTURE TAXABLE ESTATE
PAUL PARIS'S ESTATE

Input:	Current taxable estate (tentative tax base)	$600,000
Input:	Number of years of assumed growth & inflation	38
Input:	Inflation rate 040	
Input:	Appreciation Rate 030	
	Combined appreciation and inflation rate	.070

Combined Rate	Taxable Estate 38 Years From Now	Estate Tax After Credit	Estate Remaining
.070	$7,847,563	$3,506,781	$4,340,781

Tools and Techniques

Figure D.2

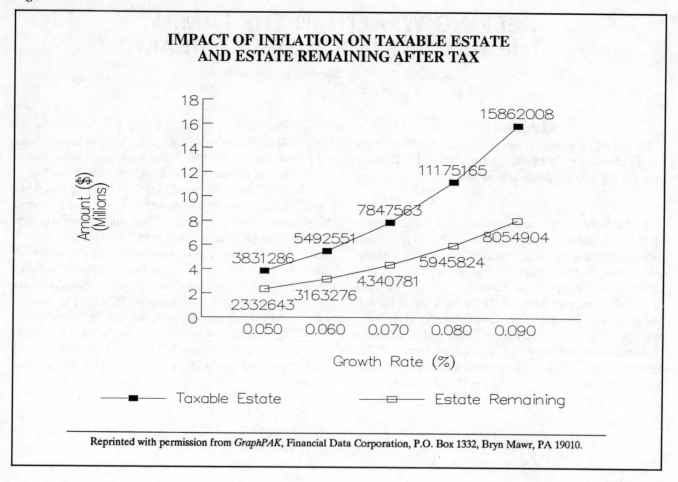

IMPACT OF INFLATION ON TAXABLE ESTATE
AND ESTATE REMAINING AFTER TAX

Reprinted with permission from *GraphPAK*, Financial Data Corporation, P.O. Box 1332, Bryn Mawr, PA 19010.

Figure D.3

COMPUTING ESTATE TAX ON FUTURE TAXABLE ESTATE
LARRY LONDON'S ESTATE

Input: Current taxable estate (tentative tax base) $1,200,000

Input: Number of years of assumed growth & inflation 38

Input: Inflation rate .... .040
Input: Appreciation Rate .... .030

Combined appreciation and inflation rate .... .070

Combined Rate	Taxable Estate 38 Years From Now	Estate Tax After Credit	Estate Remaining
.070	$15,695,126	$7,715,319	$7,979,807

Figure D.4

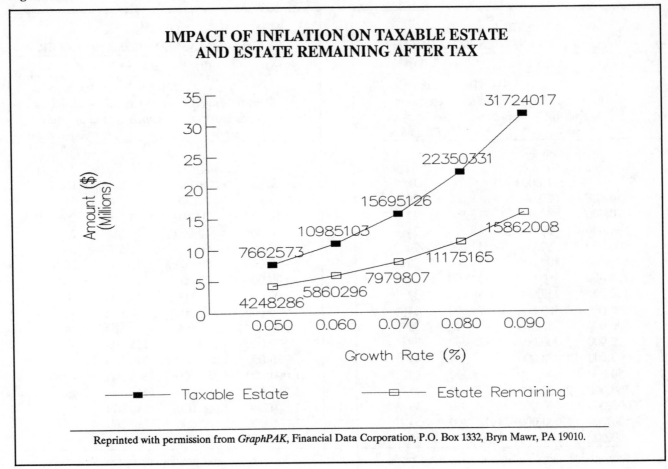

IMPACT OF INFLATION ON TAXABLE ESTATE
AND ESTATE REMAINING AFTER TAX

Reprinted with permission from *GraphPAK*, Financial Data Corporation, P.O. Box 1332, Bryn Mawr, PA 19010.

The discussion below pertains to five forces that will make it impossible for either Paul Paris or Larry London to keep the bulk of their hard-earned wealth within their families: (1) rate solidification; (2) five percent add-on estate tax; (3) section 2036(c) antifreeze; (4) generation skipping transfer tax; and (5) 15 percent excess accumulation tax.

Amazingly, most of these forces were not present a few years ago. *The point is that anyone who is or hopes to be wealthy must take immediate steps to understand and overcome these forces — or lose a great portion of a lifetime's efforts!*

FORCE 1 - RATE SOLIDIFICATION

The 55 percent top federal estate and gift tax rate is now frozen until 1993. Although it is supposed to drop at that time

to 50 percent, current budgetary problems make that wishful thinking. It is more likely that the transfer tax rates will be increased (or the unified credit decreased).

FORCE 2 - FIVE PERCENT ADD-ON ESTATE TAX

The advantage of the unified credit (currently $192,800) and graduated rates are lost to clients with estates in excess of $10,000,000. A five percent add-on tax is imposed on the amount of taxable estate in excess of $10,000,000 up to $21,040,000. (If death occurs in 1993 or a later year, the five percent add-on tax is imposed from $10,000,001 up to $18,340,000.)

Following are the rate tables for deaths occurring and gifts made (A) before 1993 and (B) ln 1993 and later years:

Tools and Techniques

TABLE A, TAXABLE TRANSFERS BEFORE 1993			
(A)	(B)	(C)	(D)
Amount subject to tentative tax		Tax on amount in Column A*	Tax rate on excess over amounts in Column A*
exceeding	but not exceeding		Percent
$ —	$ 10,000	$ —	18
10,000	20,000	1,800	20
20,000	40,000	3,800	22
40,000	60,000	8,200	24
60,000	80,000	13,000	26
80,000	100,000	18,200	28
100,000	150,000	23,800	30
150,000	250,000	38,800	32
250,000	500,000	70,800	34
500,000	750,000	155,800	37
750,000	1,000,000	248,300	39
1,000,000	1,250,000	345,800	41
1,250,000	1,500,000	448,300	43
1,500,000	2,000,000	555,800	45
2,000,000	2,500,000	780,800	49
2,500,000	3,000,000	1,025,800	53
3,000,000	—	1,290,800	55

*Before credits and phase-out of graduated rates.

TABLE B, TAXABLE TRANSFERS 1993 AND LATER			
(A)	(B)	(C)	(D)
Amount subject to tentative tax		Tax on amount in Column A*	Tax rate on excess over amounts in Column A*
exceeding	but not exceeding		Percent
$ —	$ 10,000	$ —	18
10,000	20,000	1,800	20
20,000	40,000	3,800	22
40,000	60,000	8,200	24
60,000	80,000	13,000	26
80,000	100,000	18,200	28
100,000	150,000	23,800	30
150,000	250,000	38,800	32
250,000	500,000	70,800	34
500,000	750,000	155,800	37
750,000	1,000,000	248,300	39
1,000,000	1,250,000	345,800	41
1,250,000	1,500,000	448,300	43
1,500,000	2,000,000	555,800	45
2,000,000	2,500,000	780,800	49
2,500,000	—	1,025,800	50

*Before credits and phase-out of graduated rates.

The worksheet at Figure D.5 illustrates the computation for the estate of a decedent dying before 1993 with a $25,000,000 taxable estate. Note that the result is the same as if a flat 55 percent rate were applied to the entire $25,000,000 and no unified credit were allowed. (You can check the worksheet result by applying a 55 percent tax to $25,000,000 ($13,750,000) and then adding the $192,800 unified credit for a total of $13,942,800.)

Figure D.5

ESTATE TAX COMPUTATION WORKSHEET TRANSFERS BEFORE 1993		
Step 1:	Compute tax on (up to) first $3,000,000 from Table A	$ 1,290,800
Step 2:	Compute tax on ($22,000,000) amount (if any) in excess of $3,000,000. ($25,000,000 minus $3,000,000) at a 55 percent rate	$12,100,000
Step 3:	Compute tax on amount over $10,000,000 but not over $21,040,000 at 5 percent. ($21,040,000 - $10,000,000) × .05..................................	$ 552,000
TOTAL TAX		$13,942,800

FORCE 3 - SECTION 2036(c) - "ANTIFREEZE"

Congress, in its never ceasing quest to raise revenues without increasing taxes, intended to treat the traditional corporate recapitalization followed by a gift of common stock as if it were a gift with a retention by the taxpayer of an interest for life (or at least until the time of certain later transfers of either the common or preferred stock, or corresponding partnership interests). It is now clear that Congress intended to treat other estate freezing techniques similarly. The Code has provided for many years that if you give something away but keep a "string"— i.e., a right to the income from the asset or a similarly important property right — the estate tax value of the asset you gave away will be in your estate. So, in the past, if the IRS could find a solid string, they hanged the taxpayer. Now, a vapor string will do. Furthermore, certain transfers, lapses, or terminations with respect to an income or growth interest involved in an estate freeze will result in the estate tax value of the growth interest being treated as a gift for gift tax purposes.

Generally, the section 2036(c) rules described below apply to estates of decedents dying after December 31, 1987. *There is an exception which applies to transfers completed before December 18, 1987.*

Let's take a quick look (in very general terms) at what section 2036(c) (the antifreeze provision) says:

If a person has a *substantial interest* in a *enterprise* and, in effect, *transfers* property having a *disproportionately large* share of the potential appreciation in his interest, while retaining an interest in the income from or rights in the enterprise, and the retention of the income is for life, then the person is treated as if he had retained a life estate in the property transferred. The result is that the value of the property given away will be includible in the person's estate. However, certain transfers, lapses, or terminations with respect to either the retained life estate or the property given away will result in the estate tax value of the property given away being treated as a gift for gift tax purposes (rather than including such property in the client's estate).

What 2036(c) Means

Assume a client owns 100 percent of both the common and preferred stock of the XYZ corporation. She transfers the common stock to her son but retains the preferred stock for as long as she lives. Because of the retention of the preferred stock, the value of the common stock she gave to her son will be in her estate. However, if before the client's death she transfers the income interest, or her son transfers the growth interest to someone not a member of the client's family, the client is deemed to make a gift of the growth interest at that time (and the growth interest is not included in her estate).

It is important to note that there are many authorities who think that Code section 2036(c) is far more pervasive and insidious than indicated here (see detailed three-part discussion of this topic beginning at page 477). Some say it may be unconstitutional. At the very least, it is a Code section that will drastically affect many classic wealth shifting tools and techniques. *Section 2036(c) is a force that will significantly and adversely affect anyone of wealth who desires to shift that wealth to his beneficiaries rather than to the IRS.*

FORCE 4 - THE GENERATION SKIPPING TRANSFER TAX

Whenever a person of wealth makes a large gift during lifetime or at death, either directly or in trust, to a grandchild or to a person in that or a lower generation, in addition to the other taxes mentioned in this list of horrors, the generation skipping transfer tax (GST tax) must be considered. The tax is imposed at a flat rate of 55 percent (50 percent in 1993 and later years) on the taxable transfer.

Figure D.6 illustrates the computation and the GST tax which, together with other taxes that may be imposed, is no less than "draconian." Keep in mind that where the transfer is to "my son for life and then to my grandchild," the GST tax is imposed, not on the value of what is put into the trust, but on the value of trust assets at the time the "skip" occurs, typically at the death of the client's child. Part II of Figure D.6 illustrates how much that tax can increase assuming even a modest growth of trust assets.

FORCE 5 - THE 15 PERCENT EXCESS ACCUMULATION TAX

Under TRA '86, a new (additional) estate tax was created to prevent avoidance of the lifetime tax imposed on those who take "excess distributions" from retirement plans. The deathtime tax is imposed in addition to any regular estate tax and is equal to 15 percent of a person's "excess retirement accumulation."

The term "excess retirement accumulation" is defined as the excess, if any, of

(1) the present value of the decedent's interests in all qualified retirement plans, tax sheltered (403(b)) annuities, and IRAs

over

(2) the present value of a single life annuity with annual payments equal to the annual ceiling of the greater of (a) $150,000 or (b) $112,000 (increased annually by an inflation index at the same time and in the same manner as the dollar limitation on annual benefits under a defined benefit pension plan) over a period equal to the life expectancy of the individual immediately before death.

In other words, as a general rule you add up amounts payable under qualified pension and profit sharing and other retirement plans, tax sheltered annuities, and IRAs. Then,

Tools and Techniques

Figure D.6

Part I
COMPUTING THE GENERATION SKIPPING TRANSFER TAX

Step 1	List	Value of property transferred	$3,000,000
Step 2	List	Exemption allocated to transfer	$1,000,000
Step 3	List	State & Fed tax paid on transfer	$600,000
Step 4	List	Gift or estate tax charitable deductions allowed on transfer	$0
Step 5	Add	Steps 3 and 4	$600,000
Step 6	Subtract	Step 5 from Step 1	$2,400,000
Step 7	Divide	Step 2 by Step 6	
		this is the "applicable fraction"	.4167
Step 8	Subtract	Step 7 from One (1)	
		this is the "inclusion ratio"	.5833
Step 9	Multiply	Step 8 by 55% unitl 1993	.3208
	Multiply	Step 8 by 50% - 1993 and on	.2917
Step 10		Assuming no "per granchild amount" and no growth GST tax if death prior to 1993	$962,500
		GST tax is death 1993 or beyond	$875,000

Part II
PROJECTING THE ULTIMATE GST TAX

	Initial value of assets		$3,000,000
Less			
	Federal and state death taxes		$600,000
Equals			
	Net value of assets		$2,400,000
Input:	Assumed growth rate (net after tax)		.06
Input:	Years until taxable event		38

		Future Value		GST Tax
At	.040	$10,653,152	. . . .	$3,107,169
At	.050	$15,325,145	. . . .	$4,469,834
At	.060	$21,970,206	. . . .	$6,407,977
At	.070	$31,390,251	. . . .	$9,155,490
At	.080	$44,700,662	. . . .	$13,037,693

you subtract an amount equal to the present value of a $150,000 annuity payable for the life of the client. Any excess is subject to a flat 15 percent tax. If the surviving spouse elects to treat the decedent's aggregate retirement plans as her own, the tax need not apply at the decedent spouse's death.

In the case of a 55-year-old person with a $3,000,000 accumulation and a life expectancy of 28.6 years (according to Table V of the government's tables), the excess accumulation tax would be $269,879, according to the IRS's latest pronouncements and tables current at the date of this printing (TAMRA '88 has mandated updated tables and formulas but they have not been released as of this printing). Remember, this tax is in addition to the regular estate tax! See Figure D.7 for the computation (which assumes no grandfathering of benefits).

Note these characteristics of the excess retirement accumulation tax:

(1) This tax cannot be eliminated by the charitable deduction even if a charity receives the entire amount.

(2) The unified credit cannot be used to reduce this tax. Neither can any other credit be used against this tax. For instance, the credit for taxes paid on prior taxable transfers is not allowed against this tax.

(3) The tax applies regardless of how many beneficiaries the decedent has who will receive these benefits. So it is not possible to conquer the tax by dividing the benefits.

(4) The tax is imposed regardless of the form (lump sum or annuity) of the distribution.

Only policy cash value immediately before death is subject to this tax. The "pure term insurance" portion of any

Figure D.7

```
EXCESS RETIREMENT ACCUMULATION WORKSHEET
(USING 20.2031 ANNUITY FACTORS)
```

Input:	Total amount payable at death...................................		$3,000,000
Input:	"Protected annual amount"	$150,000	
Input:	Age of decedent at death	55	
	Decedent's life expectancy	28.6	
	Current IRS discount rate	.100	
	Value of "protected annuity"		$1,200,690
	Excess amount subject to 15 percent tax		$1,799,310
	Excess accumultion tax		$269,897

death payment from a retirement plan owning a life insurance contract will not be part of the base subject to tax. (Technically, the law provides that only the death benefit that would have been payable the moment before death is subject to the tax.) This means insurance proceeds in excess of the cash surrender value are exempt.

A client may be eligible to protect some wealth if a special "grandfathering" provision is elected. But that provision is very limited, and many clients should not utilize it anyway.

TAXES IN TANDEM - A WORST CASE EXAMPLE

Many individuals use qualified pension and profit sharing plans and ESOPs as wealth building and then wealth shifting vehicles. But as the simplified "worst case" example at Figure D.8 illustrates, the combination of an estate tax on pension proceeds, in tandem with a generation skipping transfer tax (if the pension is paid to the client's grandchild), together with the 15 percent excise tax, can result in an inheritance of less than 10 cents on the dollar!

SOLUTIONS

There are solutions to the problems caused by the five forces discussed above. But they will take immediate action on the part of the client. More estates break up because people haven't done anything than break up because they have done something wrong.

The SuperTrust (irrevocable life insurance trust — see chapter 32) concept is more viable than ever as a wealth shifting device. It can enable incredible sums of wealth to pass free of federal estate tax, GST tax, and the 15 percent excise tax. There is no state death tax on the proceeds, nor is there a probate cost. Proceeds are both publicity and creditor free.

The choice of beneficiaries for wealthy individuals is now an easy one because of these five forces: Either do nothing and in essence name THE UNITED STATES TREASURY as a majority beneficiary of the estate, or take immediate and decisive action to reduce or eliminate the impact of these forces and keep the business and other assets in the family.

Tools and Techniques

Figure D.8

THE DISAPPERAING PENSION DEATH BENEFIT
CAPITAL PUNISHMENT BY CONFISCATION

Input:	Total value of all accumulations payable at death	$2,500,000
Input:	Participant's federal estate tax bracket	.55
Input:	GST tax rate if applicable (55% to 1993, then 50%)	.55
Input:	Particpant's age at assumed death.....................................	55
Input:	Assumed discount rate to compute life annuity.........................	.100
Input:	Maximum permissible annual retirement benefit........................	$150,000

Present value of $150,000 life annuity	$1,200,690
Initial value of participant's interest	$2,500,000

EST tax at .55 percent	$1,375,000	
Balance after federal estate tax		$1,125,000
GST tax .55 percent	$ 618,750	
Balance after GST tax		$ 506,250
15% excise tax on $1,299,310 excess	$ 194,897	
Balance after 15% excise tax		$ 311,354
Lump sum income tax on $506,250	$ 141,750	
Balance after lump sum income tax		$ 169,604
Cents per dollar received by heirs		$ .07

SELECTION OF EXECUTOR, TRUSTEE, AND ATTORNEY

Note: The pages appearing below, "How to Select an Executor, Trustee, and Attorney," by Stephan R. Leimberg and Charles K. Plotnick, are reproduced with the publisher's permission from THE HANDBOOK OF ESTATE PLANNING, edited by D. Larry Crumbley (Dow-Jones-Irwin, Inc.: Homewood, IL 60430), copyright 1988 by Dow Jones-Irwin.

2

How to Select an Executor, Trustee, and Attorney

Stephan R. Leimberg, Esq.
Professor of Taxation and Estate Planning,
The American College

Charles K. Plotnick, Esq.
Practicing Attorney

INTRODUCTION

Selecting the people to carry out the provisions of an estate plan is one of the most important and difficult tasks involved in the estate planning process. This chapter concerns three of the most essential parties in the estate planning process: the executor, the trustee, and the attorney. It will establish practical guidelines in the selection process from the point of view of the person who ultimately must make those choices, the client.

It is impossible to make a proper selection of any member of the estate planning team without understanding—in general terms—what it is that the individual should be doing and how that person interacts with others who have important roles to fulfill. For this reason, you'll find a brief discussion of the duties of the executor, trustee, and estate's attorney before the attributes and selection criteria of each are covered.

The authors are grateful for the significant assistance of Lawrence Brody, Esq., of Bryan, Cave, McPheeters and McRoberts in St. Louis, Missouri.

Tools and Techniques

PART I—SELECTING AN EXECUTOR

DUTIES OF THE EXECUTOR

An executor is the person (and/or institution) named in a valid will to serve as the personal representative of a testator when his or her will is being probated. Technically, this person is referred to as the "executor" if male and "executrix" if female but is commonly referred to as the executor or personal representative regardless of gender.

When death occurs, the executor must locate and probate the decedent's will (prove that it was the decedent's will and that it in fact was his or her last will). The executor must then collect the decedent's property; pay debts, taxes, and expenses; and distribute any remaining assets to the beneficiaries specified in the decedent's will.

An executor's responsibilities typically last from nine months to two or three years. In rare instances (such as when there is a contest of a will or the estate remains open for tax or other reasons) the executor's duties continue for a period of years.

ATTRIBUTES OF A GOOD EXECUTOR

When choosing an executor, the major attributes to consider are:

1. Sensitivity.
2. Competence.
3. An understanding of the needs and appreciation of the circumstances of the beneficiaries.
4. Knowledge of the nature, value, and extent of the decedent's assets.
5. Experience in the administration of estates.
6. Business and investment experience.
7. Familiarity with the decedent's business.
8. Ability to serve.
9. Willingness to serve.
10. Geographic proximity to the estate's beneficiaries and the estate's assets.
11. Lack of any conflict of interest.
12. Integrity and loyalty.

Sensitivity. Although the intangible attribute of "caring" both about the people involved and the performance of one's duties cannot be accurately or objectively measured, this single quality is perhaps the most important of all the factors in the selection process. It is always possible for the personal representative, if lacking knowledge in certain areas, to learn more about the subject or hire others with expertise.

The highest preference should be given to the identification of an individual who is willing and able to give concerned personal attention and extra effort to the psychological as well as financial needs and individual circumstances of the beneficiaries. Often this individual will be the beneficiary with the largest share of the estate and almost always will be a close relative or friend of the decedent.

Competence.   Competence encompasses both the legal ability to serve and the intellectual and emotional capacity to serve effectively.

Legal capacity entails U.S. citizenship and the satisfaction of state law requirements such as (*a*) age (21 or 18 in most states), (*b*) mental competency (generally, the same required to be a testator or in some states a higher capacity, the ability to contract), and (*c*) domicile (some states require that the executor be a domiciliary of the state in which the will is probated while others allow executors from other states but may require that an out-of-state executor post a bond).

Intellectual capacity in a general sense does not require that the executor be completely aware of all the decedent's personal affairs or the intricacy of the decedent's business. What is necessary is that the person selected has the ability to analyze the situation as quickly as possible under the circumstances, determine what facets of the estate administration can be handled within the bounds of the executor's personal knowledge and capabilities, and then secure the appropriate professional assistance in those areas in which the executor knows he or she lacks experience. In other words, the executor must have the ability to organize both facts and people and understand and follow through with what must be done.

Emotional capacity involves the ability to make a multitude of important decisions. Often these decisions (e.g., the selection of and negotiations with the estate's attorney and tax elections) must be made within a relatively short time span and yet may have tremendous financial significance to the estate and its beneficiaries. An intelligent individual capable of making quick, well-considered decisions will more than make up for an initial lack of experience.

An understanding of the needs and circumstances of the beneficiaries.   Personal knowledge of the beneficiaries, their ages, health conditions, income requirements, strengths, weaknesses, and eccentricities is extremely helpful to an executor. One child, for instance, may need immediate and continuing medical care, while another may be a highly successful surgeon. An elderly parent may need cash to meet the daily necessities of life or be so wealthy that a delay in the distribution of assets from a deceased child may have no adverse effect.

Knowledge of the nature, value, and extent of the decedent's assets.   If an executor is familiar with the specific assets that comprise the estate, that information can be of great use in performing each of the most essential of his or her duties. For example, if one of the principal assets of the estate is a business in which the executor was active in the management, the advantage to the estate of that experience and continuity could be quickly translated into dollars.

Many individuals invest in or amass collectibles for pleasure. An executor with expertise in this area would know how to safeguard, transport, insure, have appraised, and sell such items far more readily than an executor with no particular knowledge of the subject matter. This is particularly true with respect to large collections of art, precious gems, stamps, coins, and many other similar items.

One of the most troublesome responsibilities of an executor is also one that must be started early in the estate administration process—the discovery and assembly of all the decedent's assets. An executor who is privy to the extent of the estate and knows the location of all of the assets or the names of those persons who can help in this key part of the estate's probate will have a great advantage. This should simplify the tasks and enable the executor to realize a great deal more from those assets. Prior familiarity is of considerable benefit if the decedent's assets were varied and located in different states or overseas.

Experience at administering an estate.   Although death is a common occurrence, few individuals have experience in being executors. Obviously, if an individual has probated at least one or two estates, he or she is an ideal candidate. Note that this criterion emphasizes one of the major strengths of a corporate fiduciary vis-à-vis an individual. Few if any individuals have probated as many estates as a bank or trust company specializing in estate planning and administration. In ultra large or highly complex estates this consideration should be given high priority.

Business and investment experience and familiarity with the testator's investments and business.   Intelligence and emotional maturity may not be enough to successfully handle the administration of an estate. The brightest spouse or most intelligent child may lack the business or investment experience to handle a large corporation or a sizable stock and bond portfolio. The experience-tested executor clearly will have an edge in a case where significant business or investment decisions will have to be made.

Professional executors such as banks and trust companies are in the business of collecting, managing, and investing securities. They typically have separate departments to handle, analyze, and evaluate securities, supervise and sell real estate, and run businesses. To a lesser degree, professional advisors and associates (even friendly competitors in rare cases) who knew the operation of the decedent's business can provide invaluable service to the estate.

Obviously, a buy-sell agreement can incredibly simplify the task of an executor where a business interest comprises the bulk of an individual's estate. But where there is no such agreement, the executor must—at least temporarily—assume whatever role the decedent had in the business.

Depending on the circumstances and nature of the business, it could be either continued or terminated. But without knowledge of the details of the business or expertise in the specific area involved, the executor or administrator would obviously be working under a considerable handicap. Even a professional executor such as a bank or trust company may not have the requisite expertise if the decedent's business was in a specialized or personalized area in which particular or unique knowledge was necessary to survive in the marketplace.

Clearly, the executor who has an in-depth understanding of the inner workings of the decedent's business or profession has a tremendous edge over the neophyte. But although there is no substitute for experience, intelligent individuals who have the ability to obtain the necessary information and experience as well as the time and inclination to administer the estate can usually do a credible and often an outstanding job, if they are willing to put time and effort into the performance of their duties.

Consider also that individuals or banks with strong investment or business expertise can be named as coexecutors or can be hired on an hourly or annual retainer basis by the estate's executor. Certainly, any executor without extensive investment knowledge should secure the services of skilled advisors and investment personnel where appropriate. An executor who does nothing—to the detriment of the estate's beneficiaries—is just as liable to surcharge as the executor who makes a mistake of commission. So it is essential for a nonprofessional executor to secure competent advice when dealing with an estate largely composed of securities.

Ability and willingness to serve. It is extremely important in selecting a personal representative to consider the ability of the chosen person (or persons) to serve. The duties and responsibilities of an executor can amount to considerable time and effort, ranging from dozens of hours to hundreds and even thousands of hours. The decedent's heirs suffer the consequences if the designated executor is unable or unwilling to perform the necessary tasks.

Most laymen are under the impression that to name someone the executor of an estate is to bestow upon them a great honor. To the extent the term *executor* carries with it the ultimate in trust, this impression is justified. But with that honor, the personal representative must accept an awesome measure of responsibility and potential liability.

Tools and Techniques

An executor is considered a *fiduciary*. This means a potential lawsuit by beneficiaries for breach of confidentiality, conflicts of interest, failure to exercise due care or diligence or prudence, failure to properly preserve or protect estate assets, failure to file timely and proper tax returns or maintain adequate records, and the breach of the duty to make all major discretionary decisions personally and not to delegate such decisions. This responsibility and potential personal liability may drastically reduce the willingness of the nominee to accept the position. (For this reason, no one can be forced to accept the position of executor. And for that reason every will should provide at least one, and preferably more than one, backup executor in case the one named fails to qualify or ceases to act.)

Geographic proximity to the estate's assets and beneficiaries. Testators should consider, when selecting an executor, the physical distance the executor may have to travel and the time the executor may have to spend away from home. For example, New York state law may allow a son who lives in California to be the executor of his father's estate—but will the son be able to take the time away from his own job (not to mention his family) to serve properly? What expenses will be incurred out of the son's pocket or what nonreimbursable income will be lost by the son because he must be handling an estate on the opposite end of the continent? Quite often, the executor's fee or the size of the estate will be insufficient to economically justify the executor's expenditure of time. In such instances it may be preferable to appoint a local executor—perhaps a bank or a trust company—and to have the distant relative serve as an unofficial advisor to the executor or as a coexecutor.

Lack of a conflict of interest. An otherwise logical choice of a particular individual or individuals may fail to consider potential conflicts of interest. For example, an older child may well be qualified to manage her father's affairs. But will a conflict arise between the personal interest of that older child and a surviving parent or younger siblings? Such problems can easily occur when the executor makes decisions on where to take certain deductions or other tax-oriented elections.

The problem of a potential conflict of interest is particularly acute where a business associate is named as executor. It is imperative to consider in advance of such a nomination the effect that the associate's handling of the business ("to sell or not to sell," and if so, to whom and at what price?) will have on the testator's personal heirs. What if the most likely purchaser is the associate himself? How can the heirs be assured they have received a fair price for the business interest? Or how can they know the right decision was to sell rather than to retain the business? How do they know he did not pay himself an exorbitant salary (as well as an exorbitant executor's fee)? It is inevitable that doubt will linger when a partner or coshareholder is named as executor, regardless of how careful that person is to make decisions impartially and in the best interest of the beneficiaries.

Another area in which a conflict of interest can easily occur is where a client names the attorney who drafted the will as executor. In our opinion an attorney who unilaterally names himself or his law partner as attorney—without the knowledge or express direction of the client—has committed a breach of ethics and has clearly acted improperly.

If the attorney who drew the will is named as executor, then technically, he or she is not an employee or agent of the beneficiaries. That means they have no power to fire him as executor if he doesn't answer phone calls or if letters requesting information about the estate go unanswered. It will be difficult for beneficiaries to challenge his actions or lack of actions. If that person hires himself or his business partner as the estate's attorney, beneficiaries have little right to question the legality. Who, aside from the court upon final audit of the estate, can question the fee that such an executor pays himself as attorney? The appointment of attorney as executor reduces the checks and balances desirable in the probate of an estate and—aside from the other issues of competency, ability, and willingness to take the time away from the practice of law to do a proper job—creates inevitable conflict of interest.

There are, of course, exceptions to the general rule that the attorney who draws the will should not be named as the estate's executor. For instance, if the attorney is a close relative of the testator or the natural object of his bounty, it is proper and in most cases appropriate for that attorney to be named as executor. If the attorney is the one individual most familiar with the decedent's assets, family, and business, then the attorney may be a logical choice, but in this case it may be best to name the attorney as coexecutor with a family member.

The very possibility of a conflict of interest may put the potential executor in an uncomfortable and even dangerous situation. In many cases such an individual will injure his own interest in the attempt to bend over backwards to avoid the appearance of impropriety. Nevertheless, he will always be conscious of the likelihood of secondguessing by beneficiaries if they feel the apportionment of profits or proceeds was inadequate. Such an individual should, in many cases, properly and promptly refuse to serve as executor.

One possible solution to a potential conflict of interest is to name a business associate as an advisor or as coexecutor with a bank and to name some third coexecutor so there could not be a tie vote. In fact, wherever there is any potential for a conflict of interest a professional fiduciary should be considered. Impartiality is one of the major strengths of having a bank or trust company serve as executor.

Integrity and loyalty. These are among the duties owed by a fiduciary to the beneficiaries of the estate. But it is as essential that the testator have absolute trust in the honesty and loyalty of the executor for reasons that go beyond the obvious legal or ethical implications; an important part of the estate planning process is the peace of mind an individual obtains in knowing that his or her affairs are in order and that the financial security he has paid for during his lifetime will serve those he loves and wants to benefit in the years beyond his lifetime. For these reasons, it is essential that the testator have absolute trust that his will will be carried out as he intended to the best of the executor's ability.

Fees. Although fees are not among the listed attributes of a good executor, they are an important consideration in the selection process. The amount of fee a personal representative is entitled to may be determined by (1) the statutory law of the state where the estate is probated, or (2) local county rules or customs governing what the personal representative is entitled to charge for services rendered to the estate, or (3) in the case of professional executors such as banks or trust companies, an advertised fixed and scheduled fee (for a large estate the scheduled fee may possibly be lowered by negotiation, in which an attorney specializing in estate administration can be invaluable), or (4) provisions in the will or in separate contractual agreements between the testator and the nominated executor.

An executor is entitled to reasonable compensation for services rendered. Fees should not be determined solely on the basis of the monetary amount of the decedent's probate assets but should take into account the nature of the executor's tasks, the time spent, the complexity of the problems and decisions that have to be made, the professional background and competence of the executor, and the ultimate results and benefits obtained for the heirs.

There are valid tax and nontax reasons why an executor who is a relative or friend of the testator may or may not accept a fee. Although the selection process should encompass the likely course of action the executor will take in this regard, it is important that this factor not override or take the place of the other selection criteria.

In many cases testators expect that family members named as executors will charge no fees but that professional fiduciaries will. Although in many situations this assumption will be correct, this selection criterion should be tempered by considering the mistakes the nonprofessional may make that the professional would not and the opportunities the nonprofessional may miss that the professional would not.

Summary. The choice of executor(s) and backups (there should always be at least one and preferably two backups) is complicated by a combination of family, personal, tax, and nontax considerations both tangible and intangible. All of these must be considered and balanced, for the executor's tasks and responsibilities are often complex and their successful and prompt completion is always—from the heirs' viewpoint—crucial.

PART II—SELECTING A TRUSTEE

DUTIES OF THE TRUSTEE

A trustee is the person (and/or institution) named in a trust agreement to carry out the objectives and follow the terms of the trust. A trustee can be an individual (professional or nonprofessional) or a corporate fiduciary. It is also possible and common to appoint both individual and corporate trustees for reasons that will be discussed below.

It is useful in enumerating the duties and listing the attributes of a good trustee to consider the typical objectives that a trust is designed to accomplish. These goals include the following actions:

1. Reduce or eliminate income or estate or generation-skipping transfer taxes at the federal or state level.
2. Reduce or eliminate probate costs.
3. Provide a vehicle that will serve as a receptacle for both probate and nonprobate assets and facilitate attainment of other estate planning objectives through unified administration.
4. Provide for minor children in a manner more flexible and custom-tailored to the grantor's desires than the Uniform Gifts or Uniform Transfers to Minors Acts allow.
5. Provide for recipients who are legally of majority age but who lack the emotional or intellectual maturity or physical capacity or technical training to handle large sums of money or an investment portfolio or a family business.
6. Provide for individuals who have the capacity to handle large sums of money or an investment portfolio or a family business but choose not to make the necessary investment decisions or deal with the constant problems or devote the degree of attention required.
7. Postpone full ownership of trust assets until the beneficiaries of the trust have attained ages specified by the grantor or until events specified by the grantor have occurred.
8. Enable the investment of an asset that does not lend itself to fragmentation. This often occurs where the grantor desires to spread the beneficial ownership among a number of individuals. Life insurance policies and real estate are just two examples of assets that are difficult to split up or are worth substantially more if held together.

Tools and Techniques

9. Limit the parties who can obtain the assets and achieve particular dispositive objectives. For instance, where family control of a business or a specific asset is important, the grantor will want to limit the class of beneficiaries and prevent recipients from disposing of property to persons outside the family. A common example is the desire to protect assets from the consequence of an unsuccessful marriage.

The duties of the trustee may therefore include the satisfaction of a number of tax and nontax objectives that include but are not limited to the investment, management, and protection of trust assets and compliance with the dispositive intentions of the grantor.

To a great extent the selection process and decision criteria for selecting a trustee will follow the same pattern as in choosing an executor; premium will be placed on many of the same attributes. But there are several significant distinctions.

Unlike the role of the executor, which is typically concluded within a year or two, the trustee's responsibilities commonly last for at least one generation and often last beyond two or three generations. This fact should have a significant effect on the choice of trustee or on the decision to name both cotrustees and successor trustees (or to provide a mechanism for their appointment by a resigning trustee or by the beneficiaries).

A second distinguishing factor is that the choice of trustee, unlike the selection of the executor, is tax sensitive. In other words, there will be situations in which tax consequences will vary widely (results ranging from success to tax disaster) according to whether the grantor, the grantor's spouse, the beneficiaries, the grantor's business associates, the grantor's professional advisors, or a totally independent third party is named as trustee.

The decision is further complicated by a multiplicity of personal, family, business, investment, and nontax considerations—which must all be weighed by the grantor and the attorney drafting the trust. Quite often, a trade-off between flexibility and tax-saving objectives will be required. And even with the aid of skilled counsel, some compromise may be necessary.

ATTRIBUTES OF A GOOD TRUSTEE

When selecting a trustee, the major attributes to consider are:

1. Availability.
2. Impartiality and lack of conflict of interest.
3. Financial security.
4. Investment sophistication, policy, and track record.
5. Business sophistication.

6. Accounting and tax-planning expertise.
7. Recordkeeping and reporting ability.
8. Knowledge of and sensitivity to beneficiaries and their circumstances.
9. Fees.
10. Tax-neutral impact.
11. Decision-making abilities.
12. Competence.
13. Standard to which trustee will be held.
14. Integrity.
15. Flexibility to meet changing circumstances.
16. Willingness to serve throughout the term of the trust.
17. Experience as a trustee.
18. Neutral state law impact.

Availability. This criterion has two aspects, permanency and proximity. Corporate trustees are often considered because they possess one attribute that individuals (even individuals who are professional trustees) do not possess—perpetual existence, at least in the sense that a bank (or its successor) is likely to be in business during the entire term of the trust even if it lasts for generations, whereas individuals, even professional trustees, may with unpredictable frequency retire or make a career change or die or become disabled. Although banks may take holidays, they never take vacations. So to some extent it can be said that corporate fiduciaries have an availability advantage over individuals.

This perpetual-existence theory must be considered in perspective; only change lasts forever. The real issue is whether the trustee will be able to serve effectively long enough. The briefly considered answer to this question would still seem to give unparalleled advantage to a bank, especially when the possible senility or emotional instability or physical disability of an individual trustee is considered. It is particularly difficult to protect beneficiaries against these human frailties, since there is no automatic retirement mechanism for superannuated or mildly incompetent trustees.

But consider that with change in personnel at senior management, professional, and clerical levels, even if the same legal entity is involved, both the personalities and the principles on which money is managed and invested may have changed so drastically as to constitute a new entity for all practical purposes. Surely, in the time span of a trust running for two or more generations, turnover in most banks will effect a drastic if not revolutionary change in people dealing with and policies affecting trust beneficiaries. The bank that was so friendly and competent (perhaps because its senior management gave great priority to trust business in the years in which the trust was established) may be cold and less than satisfactory to a second generation of beneficiaries.

Tools and Techniques

Availability must also be considered in geographic terms. An individual trustee is likely—over a long period of time—to move from the city in which the trust or its beneficiary is located. Of course, although banks generally remain and in fact are becoming regional in scope, since beneficiaries often move (or perhaps did not live in the same city or state or country as the grantor to begin with), dealing with the bank selected by the grantor may no longer be convenient. Consider provisions giving beneficiaries the power to change from one corporate fiduciary to another. (See discussion below of removal and replacement of trustees.)

Impartiality and absence of a conflict of interest. How will the trustee react when faced with a choice that favors him at the expense of other beneficiaries—or favors others at his expense? What are the intra-family implications of those choices? For instance, will he alienate one family member by (even properly) denying a distribution, or ingratiate himself to another by being liberal in his policy of making distributions? Can he say no to one child and yes to another without causing a never-ending family feud? A trustee who is also a family member may be forced by conscience or by duty to make choices injurious to the harmony of family relationships.

Will the trustee (such as the grantor's spouse) be subject to the influence of one or more children (or a second spouse or lover) to make distributions that may not be in the best interest of other beneficiaries? Is the family member-trustee easily persuaded or likely to show favoritism? The remarriage of a spouse or child who is named as trustee may result in less than impartial decisions—especially where the trustee has been given discretionary powers over trust income or principal—even if the new spouse is not included in the class of possible recipients.

A child/trustee may take on the role of a parent to his or her remaining parent or siblings. This may be positive, but it also may result in an attempt to control the lives of family members through the family finances as if that person were a parent rather than a child.

An independent professional trustee is not subject to such problems. Since the choice between no and yes may be one of the most important duties of a trustee, this ability of a professional trustee to be objective and impartial should be given high preference in the decision-making process.

Conflict of interest can occur even where there is no issue of impartiality. For example, assume the grantor names his attorney as trustee. The attorney/trustee would most likely be objective and impartial as between the conflicting interests of family members. But consider these questions:

Once the grantor has died, who will negotiate with the attorney to ensure that fees are reasonable?

Who could fire the attorney (or trustee) if services were not performed properly or in a timely manner?

Can the attorney remain impartial as a trustee if he represents the business of one of the beneficiaries?

Is it appropriate for an accountant serving as trustee to continue in the dual capacity if he also represents a business owned by the trust?

What if there is an argument between the attorney/trustee and the grantor (or the trust's beneficiaries) that is entirely personal or is on the attorney/client level and has nothing to do with the relationship he has as a trustee?

Is it possible for an attorney/trustee to fairly represent the beneficiaries, the grantor, or cotrustees in a trust-related situation?

Will the attorney or accountant be willing to allocate appropriate time to the trust or will that person concentrate on obtaining and servicing professional clients (especially if the fees for serving as trustee are substantially lower than that charged in the professional's practice)?

Conflict of interest problems would plague a business associate or partner who was named trustee. For instance, if the trust held stock in one or more businesses in which the trustee was an officer or shareholder, his salary, or his stock interest would be affected by his actions taken as a trustee. What if the trustee was the art dealer for the trust of an artist who trusted him and had the highest degree of respect for the dealer's integrity, judgment, and marketing expertise? Assume the trust's assets consisted mainly of the artist's paintings. The dealer/trustee would be bound to obtain the highest price possible when selling trust assets. But as a dealer, he would want to pay the lowest possible price. Would it be appropriate to continue as trustee under those circumstances? It is risky to name anyone who is likely to buy or lease assets from or sell or lease assets to the trust or have any other dealings with trust property.

Some of these impartiality and conflict-of-interest problems can be overcome or minimized if anticipated in advance. But in most cases, if such problems can occur, they will. Often, the problem is not that an unethical transaction has occurred or an improper decision has been made. Rather, it is that the parties are uncomfortable merely because the beneficiaries know it could happen and the trustee knows the beneficiaries may distrust, second-guess, or sue him merely because they suspect a conflict of interest could have occurred or might occur.

Financial security. This refers to the security of the funds entrusted to the trustee and the "depth of the trustee's pockets" in the event of a successful malfeasance or misfeasance suit by beneficiaries. A nonprofessional trustee will not have an internal audit staff to review the acts of

Tools and Techniques

the person administering the trust. This lack of a system of checks and balances is one of the major shortcomings of an individual nonprofessional trustee. Conversely, banks and trust companies are audited both internally and (usually by the state) externally. All investments made by a corporate fiduciary must be approved by a trust investment committee, and the portfolio, which is typically diversified, is reviewed frequently.

If sued, will the fiduciary be available to answer for and be able to pay damages for a wrongful act? The answer is likely to be "no" with respect to an individual trustee but "yes" with respect to a corporate fiduciary. For example, in the event of an embezzlement or some other impropriety or breach of trust, the odds of a recovery from a bank or trust company are significantly higher than from an individual trustee merely because of the relative sizes of the fiduciary's own assets. Banks serving as trustees are required to meet minimum amounts of capitalization requirements.

An individual trustee can acquire physical security for trust assets by hiring safe deposit and other facilities. Banks and trust companies have such protection on site but of course build charges for their use into their fees.

Investment sophistication, track record, and investment policy. The trustee's ability to successfully invest and reinvest trust funds is one of the more important attributes to consider in the selection process. In this regard, many professional and even nonprofessional individuals have proved more astute or competent than their corporate counterparts. In some cases the grantor's opinion of a spouse or child as "financially inept" has proved to be an incorrect perception.

But the highly computerized and experienced investment departments of banks and professional individual fiduciaries do have an advantage over anyone who is not a professional investor. A further advantage of the professional trustee is that trust assets can be invested in a bank's common trust funds, which increases the safety of trust investments through diversity.

The ultimate decision in this category should not be made until the various track records are compared. The performance of commercial trust departments has varied considerably from bank to bank and from the investment returns of other investment managers.

Investment policy is an important consideration in the selection process. Corporate fiduciaries tend to be conservative. This may be either attractive or a drawback depending on how aggressive the grantor's own style or personal objectives are.

The investment decisions of an ultraconservative trustee may not be suited to the beneficiaries' risk-taking propensities or their growth and income objectives. But this in turn may be more in keeping with the grantor's long-range goals of restraining the lifestyle of income and principal recipients.

So the ultimate decision is not between professional and nonprofessional or between individual and corporate fiduciary; it must be made on the basis of the type of investment policy the grantor of the trust desires and the particular trustee that will come closest to matching that policy.

Business sophistication. Where one or more businesses are held in the trust, it is extremely important that the trustee have expertise in running that type of business. Even if the trustee should and will sell it, knowing when and how best to dispose of it is a very important skill. If the business is large or large relative to other trust assets, or if it is a specialized or personal service type of business, this may mean that a family member, business associate, professional advisor, or even a former competitor may have to be considered in spite of impartiality issues or potential conflicts of interest.

Typically, corporate fiduciaries do not continue businesses left in trust. The business is quickly sold and the proceeds are reinvested. In most cases that will be the appropriate course of action, since few banks have enough of the right type of personnel to continue the success of a growing business, and a failing business should usually be liquidated as quickly as possible. Nonprofessional individual fiduciaries rarely have the time to run a business even if they have the expertise and experience.

Accounting and tax planning expertise. Corporate fiduciaries have a definite advantage over nonprofessional individual trustees when considering the myriad accounting procedures, tax compliance, and tax planning opportunities that must be handled by a trustee. The level of sophistication, expertise, and experience that should be applied over the lifetime of any trust is one that few nonprofessionals can provide. This means that most family members will simply be incapable of fully understanding all of the problems that must be avoided and the availability and implications of the tax and property law elections that must be weighed. Even knowledgeable attorneys and accountants do not have the requisite practical day-to-day experience unless they practice solely in this field.

It is possible and in many cases appropriate for a trustee to hire agents for advice and assistance. Most trustees will communicate regularly with outside attorneys and accountants. But planning policy and decisions must be made by the trustee; these are among the duties that cannot be delegated. Thus, the trustee must have a working knowledge of the accounting laws and both federal and state tax laws (income, estate, gift, and generation-skipping). Will an untrained trustee know whom to call or if the advice received is both legally correct and practical? Will a nonprofessional understand the interplay between tax, trust, and property law well enough to interpret provisions in the trust and adequately inform beneficiaries about the tax and other legal effects of various choices?

Recordkeeping and reporting ability. A trust is a long-term arrangement under which accountings must be made periodically over many years to a number of parties that may include the grantor, the beneficiaries, the appropriate federal and state taxing authorities, and the supervising court. This requires regular statements of the receipts, disbursements, and assets of the trust in an intelligible form, and careful long-term record storage.

Knowledge of and sensitivity to beneficiaries and their circumstances. In some cases an understanding of the family involved and their special needs or desires and how they relate to the grantor's objectives should properly take priority over many of the other objectives on this list. If the financial encouragement of a handicapped child, for example, is not provided through the trust, the trust may fail in its purpose regardless of how much tax it saves or how closely the trustee meets both the letter of the law and the terms of the trust itself. *Sensitivity* here is therefore used interchangeably with *flexibility*. If flexibility in dealings with trust beneficiaries and a high degree of personal sensitivity are primary considerations, a nonprofessional trustee is indicated.

Fees. Corporate and other professional fiduciaries charge a fee for their services. Usually, this fee is based on a percentage of the income and principal of the trust. A distribution fee equal to a percentage of the principal disbursed from the trust is also often charged (upon termination or otherwise). Although this fee is typically set according to a standard schedule of fees, it may be possible to negotiate the fee in the case of a trust with a large amount of assets. This may be an amount agreed on or may be a flat hourly charge. Where trust assets consist solely of unfunded life insurance trusts, unimproved real estate, or closely held stock, the nonprofessional may be the best choice for a trustee. Likewise, trusts with assets of less than $200,000 in value are often discouraged from using corporate fiduciaries because of the fees.

Many individuals name their spouses or relatives or close friends or even trust beneficiaries because they will serve as a personal favor or as an accommodation and will not charge a fee to act as a trustee. This may be an economic necessity where the value of trust assets is small and payment of the minimum fees to the corporate fiduciary would significantly reduce the income and principal of the trust. But in most cases, the fee saved by using a nonprofessional amounts to a false economy.

There is a further aspect with respect to fees and the selection of a trustee; in selecting a relative who is also a beneficiary, will the fees charged be understood by and acceptable to other beneficiaries, or will such fees—even if reasonable for the services performed—be resented and cause conflict?

Tax-neutral impact. A revocable trust has a neutral impact on taxes at both federal and state levels. As long as the grantor has reserved the right to revoke the trust at any time, in most situations he will be treated as if he had not established a trust and had remained as the outright owner of the property in the trust. So with respect to a revocable trust, it does not matter for tax purposes who is selected as trustee. For example, the grantor will be taxed on the income of a revocable trust whether he names himself, his spouse, a beneficiary, a friend, a business associate, a professional whom he employs, or an independent corporate or other professional fiduciary.

But if one of the major reasons for establishing an irrevocable trust is to save taxes (federal and state income, estate, or generation-skipping transfer), the identity of the trustee is a very tax-sensitive decision: Inclusion of the trust's assets in income (or in the gross estate or in the generation-skipping tax base) will result if the wrong party is selected as trustee. The potential for adverse tax results increases significantly when the trustee is given discretionary powers over the income or principal of the trust if the trustee or a cotrustee is the grantor, his or her spouse, a family member (or some combination of them), or if one or more of these people becomes a trustee under a successor provision in the trust.

Consequently, the adverse tax consequences can be avoided very simply by providing that these individuals may not become a trustee or by specifying that if such a person is a trustee, he or she may not participate in a decision that will result in the to-be-avoided tax result. For example, a surviving spouse/trustee would be prohibited from exercising a broad discretionary power over principal in her own favor if the objective of the trust was to prevent inclusion of assets in her estate. But it is obvious that favorable tax results are obtained at the cost of a loss of flexibility.

The following commentary summarizes the major income and estate tax consequences of powers held by various parties. It emphasizes that before naming the grantor or anyone with an interest in the trust as trustee, consideration must be given to these implications.

I. Powers to affect beneficial enjoyment.
    A. Power to distribute income to the grantor or the grantor's spouse.
        1. Grantor as trustee.
            a. Grantor taxed on the income of the trust since the grantor will be treated as the owner of trust assets.
            b. Assets in the trust includable in the grantor's gross estate.
        2. Nonadverse party as trustee.
            a. Grantor taxed on the income of the trust.

Tools and Techniques

         b. Assets in the trust not includable in the grantor's gross estate.

    3. Adverse party as trustee.

         a. Grantor not taxed on trust income.

         b. Assets in the trust not includable in grantor's gross estate.

B. Power to distribute income to beneficiaries other than the grantor or the grantor's spouse without the restriction of an ascertainable standard.

    1. Grantor as trustee.

         a. Grantor taxed on the income of the trust since the grantor will be treated as the owner of the trust.

         b. Assets in the trust includable in the gross estate of the grantor if the power can be exercised by the grantor alone or with any other party (adverse or not).

    2. Nonadverse party as trustee.

         a. Grantor taxed on the income of the trust since the grantor will be treated as the owner of the trust (unless the power is limited to withholding distributions temporarily during legal disability).

         b. Assets in the trust not includable in the estate of the grantor unless the grantor has retained the right to substitute himself as trustee.

    3. Independent party as trustee.

         a. Grantor not taxed on the income of the trust.

         b. Assets in the trust will generally not be includable in the grantor's gross estate unless the grantor can substitute himself as beneficiary.

C. Power—subject to an ascertainable standard—to distribute income to beneficiaries other than the grantor or the grantor's spouse.

    1. Grantor as trustee.

         a. Grantor taxed on the income of the trust since the grantor will be taxed as the owner of the trust (unless the power can be exercised only with the consent of an adverse party).

         b. Assets in the trust will generally not be includable in the grantor's gross estate since the power can only be exercised pursuant to ascertainable standards.

2. Person other than the grantor (or the grantor's spouse) as trustee.
   a. Grantor not taxed on the income of the trust.
   b. Assets in the trust will generally not be includable in the grantor's estate unless the grantor can substitute himself as trustee.

D. Power—subject to an ascertainable standard—to distribute principal to a beneficiary or class of beneficiaries.
   1. Grantor as trustee.
      a. Grantor not taxed on the income of the trust.
      b. Assets in the trust will generally not be included in the grantor's estate because exercise of the power is limited by an ascertainable standard.
   2. Person other than grantor as trustee.
      a. Assets in the trust will generally not be included in the grantor's estate because exercise of the power is limited by an ascertainable standard.

E. Power to distribute principal to a current income beneficiary.
   1. Grantor as trustee.
      a. Grantor not taxable on the income of the trust.
      b. Assets in the trust will be includable in the grantor's gross estate unless the power is limited by an ascertainable standard.
   2. Person other than grantor as trustee.
      a. Grantor not taxable on the income of the trust.
      b. Assets in the trust will not be includable in the grantor's gross estate unless the grantor can substitute himself as trustee.

F. Power to distribute or accumulate income for a current income beneficiary.
   1. Grantor as trustee.
      a. Income of the trust not taxable to the grantor.
      b. Assets in the trust will be includable in the grantor's estate unless the power can be exercised only pursuant to an ascertainable standard.
   2. Person other than grantor as trustee.
      a. Income of the trust not taxable to the grantor.
      b. Assets in the trust will not be includable in the grantor's estate unless the power can be

Tools and Techniques

exercised without an ascertainable standard and the grantor can substitute himself as the trustee.

G. Power to make mandatory distributions of income or principal to specified beneficiaries other than the grantor or the grantor's spouse.
   1. Grantor as trustee.
      a. Income of the trust not taxable to the grantor unless trust income is used to discharge his legal obligations.
      b. Assets in the trust will not be included in the grantor's gross estate because the grantor has retained no power to affect beneficial enjoyment of trust property.
   2. Person other than grantor as trustee.
      a. Income of the trust not taxable to the grantor unless trust income is used to discharge his legal obligations.
      b. Assets in the trust not includable in the grantor's gross estate.

II. Administrative powers.
   A. Power to allocate receipts between principal and income.
      1. Grantor as trustee.
         a. Grantor not taxable on the income of the trust.
         b. Assets of the trust will not be includable in the grantor's estate unless the power can be exercised by the grantor in a nonfiduciary capacity either alone or in conjunction with another person.
      2. Person other than grantor as trustee.
         a. Grantor not taxable on the income of the trust.
         b. Assets of the trust will not be includable in the grantor's estate.
   B. Power to use trust income to pay premiums on insurance insuring the life of the grantor or the grantor's spouse.
      1. Grantor as trustee.
         a. Grantor is taxable on the income of the trust to extent the income is or may be used for the payment of life insurance premiums without the consent of an adverse party.
         b. Assets of the trust will not be includable in the grantor's gross estate assuming the trust both owns and is beneficiary of the policy proceeds.
      2. Nonadverse party as trustee.
         a. Grantor will be taxed on the income of the trust.

       b. Assets of the trust will not be includable in the gross estate of the grantor.

   3. Adverse party as trustee.

       a. Grantor will not be taxed on income of the trust.

       b. Assets of the trust will not be includable in the gross estate of the grantor.

C. Power to purchase, exchange, or otherwise deal with trust assets for less than adequate consideration.

   1. Grantor as trustee.

       a. Grantor will be taxed on income of the trust if he or a nonadverse party (or both) can exercise the power without the consent of an adverse party.

       b. Assets of the trust will be includable in the gross estate of the grantor.

   2. Nonadverse party as trustee.

       a. Grantor will be taxable on trust income if the nonadverse party can exercise the power without the consent of an adverse party.

       b. Assets in the trust will not be includable in the estate of the grantor unless the grantor can substitute himself as trustee.

   3. Adverse party as trustee.

       a. Grantor not taxed on the income of the trust.

       b. Assets in the trust will not be includable in the estate of the grantor unless the grantor can substitute himself as trustee.

D. Power to borrow trust income or principal without adequate interest or adequate security.

   1. Grantor as trustee.

       a. Grantor taxed on trust income if trust property can be loaned to grantor without adequate interest or security (income will not be taxed to grantor if approval of adverse party needed).

       b. Assets in trust will be includable in grantor's gross estate.

   2. Person other than grantor as trustee.

       a. Grantor not taxed on trust income if person other than grantor is trustee and that person has the power to make loans to anyone.

       b. Assets will not be included in grantor's gross estate unless he can substitute himself as trustee.

E. Power to vote the securities of a controlled corporation.

   1. Grantor as trustee.

       a. Grantor taxed on income of trust if (1) power can be exercised in a nonfiduciary capacity and (2) the stockholdings of the grantor and the trust are significant from the viewpoint of control.

       b. Assets in the trust must be included in the grantor's gross estate.

  2. Person other than grantor as trustee.

       a. Grantor taxed on trust income if power to vote securities held by person with nonadverse interest in a nonfiduciary capacity without consent of person in fiduciary capacity, assuming stockholdings of grantor and trust are significant from the viewpoint of control.

       b. Assets in the trust will not be included in the grantor's estate unless he has retained the power to substitute himself as trustee.

F. Power to reacquire trust principal by substituting property of equal value.

  1. Grantor as trustee.

       a. Grantor will be taxed on trust income if the power can be exercised by anyone in a nonfiduciary capacity without the consent of a person in a fiduciary capacity.

       b. Assets in the trust will be includable in the gross estate of the grantor.

  2. Persons other than the grantor as trustee.

       a. Grantor will be taxed on trust income if the power can be exercised by anyone in a nonfiduciary capacity without the consent of a person in a fiduciary capacity.

       b. Assets in the trust will not be includable in the grantor's gross estate unless he can substitute himself as trustee.

III. Powers over principal.

  A. Power to revoke the trust and revest the principal in the grantor or in grantor's spouse.

    1. Grantor as trustee.

       a. Grantor taxed on trust income unless power can be exercised only with consent of adverse party.

       b. Assets in trust includable in grantor's gross estate if power exercisable only by grantor alone or with any person whether or not adverse (unless the power can be exercised only with consent of all persons with a vested or contingent interest in the estate).

2. Nonadverse party as trustee.
   a. Grantor taxed on trust income unless power can be exercised only with consent of adverse party.
   b. Assets in trust not includable in grantor's estate unless power is exercisable by trustee and grantor can substitute himself as trustee.
3. Adverse party as trustee.
   a. Grantor not taxed on trust income.
   b. Assets in trust not includable in grantor's gross estate.

B. Power to terminate trust and distribute principal to beneficiaries.
   1. Grantor as trustee.
      a. Grantor not taxed on trust income if principal can be paid out only to income beneficiaries in same proportion as they currently receive income, or if principal can be paid out only with the approval of an adverse party.
      b. Assets in the trust are includable in the grantor's gross estate if the grantor can exercise the power alone or with any other person whether or not adverse.
   2. Adverse party as trustee.
      a. Grantor not taxed on trust income.
      b. Assets in trust not includable unless power exercisable by trustee and grantor can substitute himself as trustee.
   3. Nonadverse party as trustee.
      a. Grantor taxed on trust income unless approval of adverse party required or unless payment must be made to current income beneficiaries in proportion to income receipts.
      b. Assets in trust not includable unless power exercisable by trustee and grantor can substitute himself as trustee.
   4. Independent Trustee.
      a. Grantor not taxed on trust income if half or more of trustees are independent.
      b. Assets in trust not includable unless power exercisable by trustee and grantor can substitute himself as trustee.

IV. Powers to discharge legal obligations.
    A.   Power to discharge support obligation.
        1.   Grantor as trustee.
            a. Grantor not taxable on trust income merely because of the existence of the power unless he has the power in a nonfiduciary capacity or the power is to support his or her spouse. But the grantor will be taxed on the income to the extent it in fact is used to discharge the grantor's support obligation.
            b. Assets in the trust will be includable in the grantor's estate if trust income may be used to discharge the grantor's legal obligation.
        2.   Persons other than grantor as trustee.
            a. Grantor not taxable on income unless it is in fact used to discharge the grantor's legal obligation.
            b. Assets in the trust will not be included unless the grantor could substitute himself for the trustee.

Decision-making ability. The trustee selected must be able to make many decisions, some of great significance, over an extended period of time. This entails the need for emotional maturity and wisdom as well as knowledge.

Competence. A trustee must have the legal capacity to contract. This precludes the appointment of a minor or an incompetent adult. In many states a nonresident individual can act as a trustee (although as a practical matter, geographical considerations often contraindicate selecting a person who lives a considerable distance from the beneficiaries of the trust). Some states bar nonresident corporations from serving as trustees.

Skill to which trustees will be held. A trustee will be held to a high degree of skill and care. Under the "prudent man" rule, a trustee must use the same degree of care and skill that a person of ordinary prudence would exercise in dealing with his own property.

The Uniform Probate Code, adopted by many states, places a higher standard on professional trustees by providing that if the trustee has greater skill than that of a man of ordinary prudence, he is under a duty to exercise such skill.

Integrity. Honesty and loyalty are the watchwords of trusts. Vast sums of money and other assets are entrusted to fiduciaries who must exercise a high degree of care over trust property and act consistently on behalf of trust beneficiaries.

Flexibility to meet changing circumstances. Change in tax law and in the circumstances and goals of each of the beneficiaries is the only certainty. Since a trust is a mechanism specifically designed to meet that change, the trustee must be willing and able to change as well.

Willingness to serve throughout the term of the trust. An individual trustee could easily lose interest through the long years and even generations a trust may last. Corporate fiduciaries are more likely than individuals to continue for the full term.

Experience as a trustee. This is the most rare of all characteristics. Obviously, past experience in administering a trust is invaluable. Through experience, the fiduciary is more likely to appreciate the broad and complex multiplicity of laws involved, know who to call on for assistance, avoid many mistakes, and more efficiently administer and execute the terms of the trust.

Neutral state law impact. State trust laws must be considered in selecting a trustee. If state law trust requirements are not met, the trust will be invalid and provide none of any intended tax benefits. This is because federal law's recognition of a trust as a separate tax entity presupposes validity of the trust under state law.

When a beneficiary is named as trustee, the Doctrine of Merger must be considered. This doctrine holds that the trust as a separate entity ceases to exist when the legal title to the property held by the trustee is identical to the beneficial interest held by the beneficiary. For instance, if the grantor's son is both the sole trustee and the sole beneficiary, the trust will cease to exist.

COTRUSTEES

After considering each of the desirable characteristics of a good trustee, it will become obvious to most grantors that it is impossible to select a trustee that has all of the advantages and none of the disadvantages. Many grantors therefore attempt to obtain the strengths of both the corporate and the nonprofessional trustee by naming a cotrustee. Often, one or more family members and a corporate fiduciary are selected.

Combining the positive aspects of more than one trustee has a cost; certain drawbacks or issues must be considered. For instance, if two trustees are selected, what is the procedure if they do not agree on a given issue? If three or more are selected, will the majority rule? What responsibility does a dissenting trustee have for an action (or nonaction) taken by the majority?

REMOVAL AND SUCCESSION OF TRUSTEES

As part of the selection process itself, a grantor should think about the removal of current trustees and the appointment of successor trustees (typically, at least two should be named). The trust instrument itself should consider issues such as the following:

Tools and Techniques

Who, if anyone, should be given the power to remove trustees?

Should such a power be given to the grantor, the beneficiaries, the trustee(s), or an outside party?

How narrow or broad should a removal power be (i.e., under what circumstances should someone be able to remove a trustee)?

How often may a removal power be exercised?

How will succession be determined?

What restrictions will be placed on the successor trustee?

What are the various tax consequences of allowing the grantor or the beneficiaries to remove a trustee and without restriction appoint a new one?

Summary. The selection of a trustee is a most difficult one because of the longevity of most trusts, the complexity of the tax and other laws with which the trustee must comply, and the sensitivity a trustee must have to both the grantor's objectives and the beneficiary's needs and desires. For these reasons, one or more cotrustees (almost always professionals) is indicated where the terms of the trust are complex or the estate is large.

PART III—SELECTING AN ATTORNEY

DUTIES OF THE ATTORNEY

The duties of the attorney will depend on the client's stage in the estate planning cycle—accumulation, conservation, or distribution. In actuality it is sometimes difficult to know where one stage ends and another begins. Clearly, the attorney must be aware in each stage of the implications of what is done at that stage for the other two stages—and of the consequences to the client and his beneficiaries. For instance, it may be easier and less expensive in the planning stage of the cycle to draft a simple will than a series of more complex trusts. But the client's family may have fared better in the later stages had the attorney done a more extensive estate plan.

An estate planning attorney must gather data regarding the client and his family or other potential beneficiaries and their circumstances; the client's sources of wealth, income, liabilities, and expenses; and the client's financial goals and fears. The attorney must then assemble this data and relate each of these objective facts and subjective feelings to each other and be able to ascertain the client's current position and the extent of his weaknesses in the following areas:

1. Liquidity: Will the client during his lifetime and his executor at his death be able to pay taxes and other expenses without the need for a forced sale?
2. Disposition of assets: Are they going to the right person at the right time in the right manner?
3. Adequacy of capital and income: Does the client have enough capital and income in the event of death or disability, or at retirement, or for special family needs such as the care of a retarded or physically handicapped child, or for charitable bequests?
4. Stability and maximization of value: Has the client first put a floor under and then maximized the value of the assets he currently owns? For instance, the value of a business without adequate liability or fire insurance coverage has not been stabilized; the value of a partnership without a fully funded buy-sell plan has not been maximized.
5. Excessive transfer costs: Is the client paying too much in income taxes, or will the client's estate pay an unnecessary amount of estate or other death taxes or transfer costs?
6. Special needs: Does the client have special needs or desires that must be met, such as making gifts to a charity, supporting a poor relative, or protecting a spendthrift spouse?

An estate planning attorney must not only understand these problems and their solutions but also be able to communicate them to the client in a manner that will allow the client to make informed decisions.

Often the attorney must organize the entire estate planning team. Always the attorney should work with the client and the client's other professional advisors in establishing an order of priorities and responsibilities and make sure each aspect of the plan is completed in a timely manner.

Only the attorney can draft the appropriate documents. These range in complexity and length from a simple durable power of attorney, which may run four or five pages, to the recapitalization of the client's business and the complete restructuring of the nature of the client's estate plan, which may take hundreds of drafted pages.

ATTRIBUTES OF A GOOD ATTORNEY

Many of the same attributes important in the selection of an executor or trustee are also of key importance in the search for an attorney. For example, an attorney with business experience who is also familiar with the client's business can be invaluable. The major attributes that should be considered in the selection of an estate planning (or administration) attorney are competence, compassion, clarity, and affordability.

Tools and Techniques

Competence.   The level of competence necessary depends to a great extent on the nature and extent of the client's wealth and the complexity of the client's situation. Most general practitioners are competent to draft a power of attorney or simple will. This may be all that is necessary in smaller estates where all the parties involved including the beneficiaries are self-sufficient adults and there are no unusual assets, objectives, or problems.

But once the estate reaches the size at which federal estate taxes may be imposed, or if the client or any of the client's beneficiaries are under a legal, physical, mental, or emotional disability, or if there is any unusual fact pattern, it is best to find an attorney who specializes in estate planning and administration. The question is How do you find an attorney in the estate planning field, and then how do you ascertain his or her competence? Some of the ways to locate attorneys practicing in the estate planning field are discussed below.

1. Call the county or city estate planning council. Ask for a copy of the membership directory. This should contain lists of not only attorneys but also CPAs, CLUs, trust officers, and other key members of the estate planning team. This list, of course, does not ensure any specific level of competence, but most estate planning councils require peer nomination for entrance, and membership fees help eliminate those who do not spend substantial time in the practice of estate planning. More important, estate planning councils make continuing education and in-depth seminars available to their members. The best attorneys active in the estate planning and administration field tend to be members of an estate planning council.

2. Many states now certify attorneys in selective areas of practice. Texas, for example, examines an attorney through a rigorous additional state bar–administered examination in the estate planning area. Attorneys who have earned the right to specialize in estate planning through certification will usually signify that in their telephone book listings and on their business cards and stationery.

3. Trust officers are excellent sources for finding attorneys active in estate planning. Visit three or four banks with large trust offices. Ask for the two or three most competent attorneys. If the same name is mentioned favorably by more than one trust officer, he or she might be a good choice. CLUs, ChFCs, CFPs, and CPAs are also excellent sources for the names of competent attorneys who specialize in estate planning.

4. Attorneys who specialize in estate planning often lecture at business meetings or adult education courses. After attending one or two sessions, a person should find it easy to tell if the attorney can communicate complex legal matters effectively.

5. Practicing attorneys who teach estate planning in law schools, in the tax masters' programs at business schools, and especially those who

have taught the American College's estate planning courses for several years are excellent candidates.

6. Some attorneys write in professional journals such as *Taxation for Accountants, the Practical Lawyer, Estate Planning Magazine, The CLU Journal, Trusts and Estates Magazine,* or the *Journal of Accountancy.* Some write regular newspaper columns or do radio talk shows on estate planning.

7. Attorneys with an LLM (masters) in taxation generally have higher than average expertise in the estate planning area.

8. Friends and business associates may be able to provide referrals.

9. Bar association referral services and local law schools with tax masters programs are also good sources of estate planning attorneys.

Compassion. The single most important distinction between a truly good estate planning attorney and the average practitioner is not a superior knowledge of the tax law, nor is it the sense of combativeness that makes winners out of litigation attorneys: it is an attitude of being counselor rather than advocate. The estate planning attorney will be keenly sensitive to the importance of a client's business, for instance, not only as figures on a ledger sheet but also as a personification of the client and as part of a goal-striving behavior. Such an attorney will be extremely conscious of the circumstances, needs, hopes, and fears of the client and of his intended beneficiaries.

Clarity. An estate planning attorney must be able to communicate. Often, the attorney will captain the estate planning team. This means he or she must be able to request information from other professionals, explain to them what each member of the estate planning team is doing and what remains to be done. The attorney must also be able to communicate clearly with nonprofessionals, such as the client or the client's family, the nature and extent of problems the client may not have known existed.

Clarity encompasses not only transferring information but also the urgency of deciding and then acting. The estate planning attorney must be able to convey the importance of the client's doing certain things (such as signing a will, obtaining adequate amounts of life or disability insurance, or establishing a buy-sell agreement) now!

Affordability. Malpractice premiums for estate planning and administration attorneys are among the highest in the profession. This is indicative of the complexity of the practice and of the potential for making expensive mistakes. The point is, selecting the right attorney is a cost-saving factor. The lowest fee may be far from the least expensive.

Clients should demand a written and signed statement of the attorney's hourly fee or an estimate of the overall cost for planning or administering the estate—before allowing work to begin.

Tools and Techniques

There is one more important consideration involving the relationship of an attorney to the estate of a deceased person. In most cases the attorney who drafted a will or trust or other estate planning document should be employed to help execute it. That attorney will probably know the client and his intentions better than anyone else. But if the personal representative of a deceased person is not satisfied with the deceased person's attorney or if the decedent gave no indication of his or her choice of attorney for the estate, the personal representative should, in practically every instance, make his or her own independent selection of an attorney qualified in the area of administering the decedent's estate.

Since the executor has the full responsibility if something goes wrong, the executor has the right and responsibility to personally select the estate's attorney—regardless of which attorney drew the decedent's will. In fact, a number of states protect that right with specific legislation.

Summary. The selection of an attorney who specializes in estate planning should focus primarily on identifying someone who has competence, compassion, the ability to communicate clearly with other professionals and with clients, and who is willing to work at a price that is in line with a client's means.

HOW TO REVIEW A WILL:
A CHECKLIST FOR THE ESTATE AND FINANCIAL PLANNER

By Stephan R. Leimberg, Esq.
Copyright ©1988 by Stephan R. Leimberg

Note: A version of this article under the title "How To Review a Will" has appeared in the magazine *Financial Planning* in two parts, April and May, 1988.

INTRODUCTION

A will is the legal document that specifies how a person wants to dispose of the real and personal property he owns in his own name at the time of his death. Most mentally competent adults have the legal capacity to draw a will. But few persons are knowledgeable enough to do so properly. Only an attorney should draft a will and even most attorneys should not attempt to draw their own.

Despite this, every member of the estate planning team, including the financial planner, should know how to review a will.

First, it is necessary to coordinate the will properly with other dispositive documents such as employee benefit plans. For example, if the will is not synchronized with an executive's pension, group insurance, and 401(k) plan, there is no way to minimize overall death taxes and provide for a smooth and efficient estate administration.

Second, it is impossible to know if there will be appropriate liquidity unless the will and its various dispositive schemes are examined.

Third, wills become outdated, tax laws change (for instance, a marital deduction provision in a will drafted before September 13, 1981, may not qualify for the unlimited marital deduction), and the circumstances, needs, and desires of the parties are always in flux. The attorney who drafted the will may have died and it may have been many years since the will was revised or reviewed.

Every professional in the estate planning team must therefore be able to examine a will and spot — in general terms at least — what's wrong.

"What's wrong" with a given will is more often a question of what has been omitted or what has changed than what has been improperly drafted. "What's wrong" is even more often the failure of the draftsman to match the facts of the case or the circumstances or desires of the parties with the documents. "What's wrong" may be something the accountant, for instance, knows that no other professional knows. "What's wrong" may be that the will has not been updated for years and no longer addresses the current circumstances or client goals or latest tax law.

The following is a (by no means complete) checklist designed to give each member of the estate planning team the tools needed to examine a will:

INTRODUCTORY CLAUSE

Start with the introductory ("exordium") clause which should be the first paragraph in the will. The purpose of this preamble is to

(1) identify the testator, the person disposing of property at death;

(2) establish domicile, the county that will have legal jurisdiction for purposes of determining the validity of the will and interpreting will provisions, for purposes of state inheritance taxation (technically, what is said in a will about the testator's domicile is not dispositive but is evidence which will usually be considered even if subordinated to proof of facts to the contrary);

(3) declare that the document in question is intended to dispose of the testator's property at death and no matter how many wills have been written in the past, this is meant to be the last will; and

(4) revoke all prior wills. This is designed to nullify old and forgotten wills — and "codicils" (legally effective modifications of existing wills).

An example of this introductory clause is:
I, Edward Grieg, a resident of and domiciled in the city of Bryn Mawr in Montgomery County, Pennsylvania, declare this to be my last will. I revoke all wills and codicils made prior to this will.

Planners should check:

(1) Is the spelling of the client's name correct? Has the client's full name been used?

(2) Is the client "A/K/A" ("also known as"), i.e., is there some other name by which the client is known and should that name be listed?

(3) Is the domicile correct? For tax or other planning purposes, would it make sense to begin to document a different domicile? Will the will meet all the statutory requirements of the stated domicile? If the client spends a great deal of time in more than one residence, could the address mentioned in the will trigger a "double domicile" problem (e.g., where more than one state claims the decedent was a domiciliary of the state and therefore has the right to impose an inheritance tax)?

(4) Is there a reason prior wills and codicils should not be revoked? Instead of a new will, should the present document be a codicil making a small change but otherwise ratifying an existing will? For instance, if there is a potential for an attack on this will on the grounds of mental incompetency, fraud, or undue influence, a prior will providing a similar disposition will help prove the men-

Tools and Techniques

tal capacity of the testator and may discourage would-be contestants from attacking the current will. Conversely, if a beneficiary has been deleted, a new will should be drawn rather than a codicil to avoid the mention of the eliminated beneficiary.

After the introductory clause, the will can take either of two directions. It can (1) describe the steps that take place in administering the testator's estate (such as payment of debts and taxes and then payment of legacies) or it can (2) dispose of legacies first and describe obligations later. We will take the former approach in formulating this checklist.

DEBTS CLAUSE

The next clause usually pertains to the payment of debts, expenses, and costs. The purposes of this clause are:

(1) To state the source from which each debt will be paid. (This is an extremely important point because of the death tax implications. For instance, if a surviving spouse rather than some other beneficiary must pay debts, to that extent the marital deduction will be decreased and taxes may be increased. Furthermore, if the burden falls on the wrong person(s), the testator's goals may not be met.)

(2) To establish as debts items which might not otherwise be considered the testator's obligations.

An example of the payment of debts clause is:

I direct all of my debts (including any expenses of my last illness) and my funeral expenses be paid.

Planners should check:

(1) Does the testator have any rights to property held in the trust of another person (a so-called "power of appointment") and, if so, what effect does the debts clause have on that property? Does it expose that property to the claims of creditors?

(2) Will the beneficiaries receive more or less than the client intended when the will was drawn because of the operation of this provision? Has the size of the debt changed since the will was drawn? What will be the federal and state death tax impact of the clause?

(3) What is the effect of the Equal Rights Amendment in the state of domicile? In some states the will of a married woman should contain a direction to pay debts and taxes. Otherwise, the burden of her funeral and medical expenses will be placed on her surviving husband — thus barring a deduction for payment of those expenses by her estate.

(4) Did the will provide detailed funeral arrangements? Most authorities feel this is inadvisable since the will may not be found or may not be accessible in sufficient time after the testator's death. Should such provisions be placed in a "Letter of Instructions," an informal and nonlegal list of requests, suggestions, and recommendations that should not be placed in the will?

(5) Does the client intend that "payment of debts" include the mortgage on property left to a specific individual? In some states, absent an express direction to the contrary, when specific property is left to an individual (a "specific bequest"), any debt on that property will not be paid off. In other states, such a clause will require the executor to satisfy the mortgage. Does the named beneficiary of a life insurance policy that has been pledged as the collateral for a loan have the right to have the loan paid off because of the "pay my [just] debts" clause? The planner must check state law. In at least one state the answer depends on who the lender is. The result, absent specific direction to the contrary, is one way if the lender is the insurance company (the beneficiary takes only the net proceeds) and another (the beneficiary is entitled to have the estate pay off the debt out of other estate assets) if the creditor is an independent lending institution.

TAX CLAUSE

The clause pertaining to the payment of death taxes can either be stated next or appear after the provisions disposing of property.

The purpose of the tax clause is to establish the source for the payment of the federal estate tax, the state inheritance and estate tax, and any federal or state generation-skipping transfer tax.

This is an example of a tax clause:

I direct that all inheritance, estate, transfer, succession, legacy and other death taxes upon property required to be included in my taxable estate whether or not passing under this Will [except (1) transfer taxes levied pursuant to the provisions of Chapter 13 of the Internal Revenue Code of 1986, relating to "generation-skipping transfers", or any similar state law, and (2) taxes on property held in trust under the Will (or any revocable trust) of my spouse], and any interest and penalties thereon, shall be charged against and paid from my residuary estate passing under Article *FOURTH* of Part I of this my Will.

Planners should check:

(1) State "apportionment" statutes. If there is no tax clause in the will or if it does not adequately address the payment of a particular death tax, state law will allocate the burden of taxes among the beneficiaries. Many states require beneficiaries to pay a share of estate taxes unless the will provides otherwise. The result is often an inappropriate or unintended reduction of the shares of certain beneficiaries or adverse tax consequences. (For example, there may be a spiraling reduction of the estate tax marital deduction. The deduction is allowed only

for the net amount passing to the surviving spouse. If that amount is reduced by an estate tax burden, the tax increases — further reducing the amount passing to the spouse, etc.) An "anti-apportionment" tax clause may be the solution. For instance, suppose you wanted a child to receive $100,000 of your client's $2,000,000 estate free and clear. Without special provision, that child would be forced to pay his or her share of taxes, or 1/20 of the total federal and state death taxes. With a special tax clause, the child will receive the entire $100,000.

(2) Does the client expect or want property passing outside the probate estate to pay its share of tax if it in fact generates tax? For instance, assume $1,000,000 of pension proceeds (or life insurance) is payable to the client's two oldest children and $1,000,000 of cash is payable to the client's two youngest children. Who is to pay the tax on the $2,000,000? What if the $1,000,000 of pension proceeds (or life insurance) is state inheritance tax exempt but the cash is not? Unless the will provides to the contrary, estate taxes must be paid by recipients of property passing outside the will. The will should specify who pays taxes on both probate and nonprobate property.

(3) Assume a sizable amount of property will pass through a revocable living trust. Is the tax clause in that instrument coordinated with the tax clause in the will or are they incompatible? What if assets under the will are to "pour over" into a previously funded trust which itself will generate significant estate taxes. Is there (should there be) a will provision calling upon the trust to help the estate pay taxes? Does the trust have a provision recognizing and empowering a "call" on its assets to pay the probate estate's taxes?

(4) Who is to pay the tax on a generation-skipping transfer? Absent a contrary direction, the taxes will probably be payable from the assets of the fund subject to the tax. Some draftsmen specifically provide that such taxes are not to be imposed on the "skip person's" estate.

(5) Assume the facts indicate that very large taxable gifts have been made by the client. The taxable portion of these gifts — to the extent not included in the client's gross estate — will be considered "adjusted taxable gifts." They will increase the rate of federal estate tax payable on the taxable estate remaining. Will an unexpectedly high burden be placed on the assets remaining because of these prior gifts and should the tax clause take such gifts into account in apportioning the tax burden?

(6) Should certain beneficiaries be insulated from tax for either tax reasons or to accomplish the dispositive goals of the client or better meet the needs of the beneficiaries? For example, should a child to whom 2036(c) growth property (see page 477) has been given be exempted by the will from paying the estate tax on that property?

TANGIBLE PERSONAL PROPERTY CLAUSE

A clause pertaining to the disposition of tangible personal property is often next. The purposes of this clause are:

(1) to provide for who will receive personal property and the terms under which they will receive it; and

(2) to make special dispositions among the persons and the organizations of the testator's choice.

An example of the tangible personal property dispositive clause is:

I give to my daughter, Eva Grieg, all of my clothing, household furnishings, jewelry, automobiles, books, pictures, and all other articles of tangible personal property owned by me at the date of my death. If my daughter, Eva Grieg, does not survive me, I give the property mentioned above in equal shares to my grandchildren, Gretta and Gail Grieg or the survivor who is alive at the date of my death.

or

I give the Philadelphia Museum of Art my painting of "Helga" by Andrew Wyeth.

Planners should check:

(1) Does (or should) the client make specific bequests of all "intimate" items such as a watch or ring? Absent such provisions, if personal property has been left to several individuals, the result is often needless expense in determining who gets what or reducing the estate to cash (not to mention the potential for bitter intrafamily fights). If specific bequests have been made, has each item been described in enough detail so that there will be no confusion as to which diamond ring the testator meant? (Use the same description as is found in the insurance policy covering the loss or theft of the item).

(2) Has provision been made in case the item specifically left to a beneficiary is not owned by the decedent at death? For instance, what if one ring is sold and the proceeds are used to purchase a second. Does the named beneficiary receive the second ring?

(3) If the item specifically bequeathed has been lost, stolen, etc. and the loss has been covered by insurance, would the client want the named beneficiary to receive the insurance? In many states the bequest of an item of personal property does not — absent specific direction to the contrary — also pass the insurance covering the item.

(4) Does the client intend to pass — under the category of personal property — cash in a safe deposit box, travelers' checks, and cash found in his home or on his person? Does the client know that cash on deposit is typically not considered tangible personal property?

(5) If the client has property in many different places, consider allowing the executor — at the expense of the estate — to take possession of the property "as and where

Tools and Techniques

is" (a provision which will permit the beneficiary to receive the property free of delivery costs and protect the fiduciary and beneficiaries during administration from the risk that specific assets will be lost).

(6) The phrase "personal effects" may not encompass items of household use or even a car. Consider specific mention of items of tangible personal property.

(7) Is there a "catchall" phrase that passes the residue of tangible personalty? The phrase, "all other tangible personal property" should dispose of any residual property.

(8) Should the will confirm that certain property such as household furnishings, silverware, etc. belongs to someone else?

(9) Does this clause dispose of property by referring to an instrument outside the will? This "incorporation by reference" is not recommended since it often leads to litigation.

(10) The use of the term "contents" should be avoided. Personal property should not be described by its location.

General checkup of legacies:

(1) Has property been left outright to a minor who is legally incapable of handling it or to a person under a physical, mental, or emotional handicap who does not have the physical or intellectual capacity?

(2) Are all beneficiaries named alive? Are there "backup" beneficiaries (at least two) for each beneficiary? Are they the beneficiaries the client currently desires?

(3) Are any of the gifts conditioned on events or circumstances which are impossible, "against public policy," or in violation of the Constitution? For example, a bequest would be invalidated by the courts if it were made on the condition that the recipient first divorce her spouse.

(4) Are there gifts to "my issue" (which would unintentionally disinherit an adopted person)?

(5) Do gifts to charities meet state law requirements? Has the charity's full legal (corporate) name and address been stated? (The popular name is often different from the full legal name). Have you checked the IRS's "Cumulative List of Organizations" or obtained assurances from the charity itself to make sure the gift to the charity will qualify for a tax deduction? Has the client named a backup charity? Check to be sure the will specifies that taxes are to be paid from the portion of the residue not passing to charity. Otherwise, what should be a tax-free bequest must bear its portion of the total taxes. That reduces the charity's share and therefore increases taxes. This in turn creates a new cycle of problems.

(6) If someone is intentionally omitted, have you checked state law to see if such an omission is permissible? Are there defamatory statements in the will concerning an heir? (At the probate of the will, such statements may become libelous and expose the client's estate to an action for damages.)

(7) Does the will make so many specific bequests of cash that the residuary estate doesn't have enough left to pay estate taxes? Keep in mind that the IRS can attach the assets of any beneficiary for the unpaid estate tax. Check to be sure the executor will have a sufficient reserve of funds for paying estate tax and all the bequests to residuary beneficiaries.

(8) Note that a tangible personal property clause should nearly always be used where the residue of the estate will be paid to a trust. Few clients want trusts involved in handling personal effects such as jewelry, or household furniture, antiques, or cars.

DEVISES OF REAL ESTATE CLAUSE

The next clause pertains to "devises," testamentary grants of real property. The purposes of the devises clause are:

(1) to specify which real estate is to be disposed of under the will and to dispose of that real estate, and

(2) to handle the problems where the property has been sold or destroyed prior to the testator's death.

An example of a devise is:

I leave my residence located at 207 Rawles Run Lane, Bryn Mawr, Pa. to my daughter, Larrissa Grieg. If, at the time of my death, I am no longer using the property at 207 Rawles Run Lane as my residence, then this devise is to be void and of no effect; however, if I own any other real estate which I am using as my residence at that time, then, in such an event, I devise such other real estate to my daughter, Larrissa Grieg. If my daughter, Larrissa Grieg, does not survive me, this devise shall lapse and such real estate shall become part of my residuary estate.

SPECIFIC BEQUESTS OF INTANGIBLES AND CASH

After disposing of tangible personal property and real estate, the will may then cover specific gifts of intangibles (property where the item itself is evidence of value) such as gifts of cash or accounts receivable. An example of a gift of an intangible asset is:

I give 100 shares of Rohm and Haas stock to my niece, Danielle Green.

or

I give the sum of Five Thousand ($5,000) dollars to my sister, Sara Black, if she survives me.

Planners should check:

(1) Has provision been made in the event the primary beneficiary does not survive the decedent?

(2) Does the will spell out what gift, if any, is made if the decedent does not possess, at the time of death, the stock mentioned in the will? What if the stock had been sold but new stock was purchased with the proceeds?

RESIDUARY CLAUSE

The next clause is called the "residuary clause." The purposes of the residuary clause are to:

(1) transfer all assets not disposed of up to this point,

(2) (in some cases) provide a mechanism for "pouring over" assets from the will to a previously established (inter vivos) trust (if a pourover is made, it is important to review the trust as carefully as the will itself), and

(3) provide for an alternative disposition in case the primary beneficiary has died or the trust to which probate assets (assets passing under a valid will or by intestacy) were to be poured over was for some reason invalid, previously revoked, or never came into existence.

An example of a residuary clause is:

All the rest, residue, and remainder of the property which I own at the date of my death, real and personal, tangible or intangible, regardless of where it is situated, I leave to my daughter, Larrissa Grieg. But if Larrissa Grieg does not survive me, then I leave the said property in equal shares to my grandchildren, Ronald Reimus and Reginald Reimus or to the survivor of them.

Planners should check:

(1) Has a spouse been disinherited? If so, is the client aware of the "elective rights" (rights to a portion of the probate estate and perhaps certain other property owned by the decedent at death regardless of what the will provides) the surviving spouse has even if the will is valid? (It may be possible to control the surviving spouse to some degree by inserting a provision at least as attractive as the spouse's intestate share or by a provision reducing or eliminating the share of a person in whom the spouse is interested if he or she exercises his or her right of election. An alternative is a pre- or post-nuptial agreement).

(2) Has the client, inadvertently, exercised a "power of appointment" (a right to direct the disposition of property in a trust established by someone else)? In some states, a residuary clause automatically exercises a general power of appointment unless the trust requires that it must be specifically referred to in order to make a valid exercise or unless the will itself states that no exercise is intended.

(3) Is there a disposition to a young adult, minor, or a person legally, mentally, or emotionally incompetent that should be made in trust? Is there provision for the executor to retain the property during the minority of such a person or to use income or principal for that person's benefit? Has the right person been named as the custodian of a child's property and are there backups in case that person is unwilling or unable to serve?

(4) Is there a default provision in case a trust into which the residue was to have poured is for any reason revoked or never came into existence?

(5) If a child dies, will that child's share pass to the parties desired by the client?

(6) Does the will address the possibility of the birth of a child to the client (it's never too late)?

(7) Has the client, in lieu of leaving his residuary estate outright to his spouse, created a marital deduction formula disposition through a so-called formula clause?

Marital deduction formula clauses are very important to review and analyze. They are often found in the wills of clients who own assets of at least $600,000. Such clauses typically divide the client's estate into two parts, one "marital" and the other "nonmarital." The marital portion passes property to the client's surviving spouse as part of the marital deduction and may contain an outright or trust disposition. The nonmarital portion is designed to set aside property exempted from federal estate tax by reason of the client's available unified credit and passes property to persons other than the surviving spouse (or to a credit equivalent "bypass trust" for the benefit of the surviving spouse that will not be included in the spouse's estate on his or her death).

The language used in the formula typically takes the form of a fixed sum (a "pecuniary marital deduction") or a fraction of the client's residuary estate (a "fractional share marital deduction"). The formula clause (especially if it is a pecuniary one) will also have to contain a provision for funding the marital deduction when assets are distributed to it.

If the marital deduction clause directs that the property is to be held in trust, the surviving spouse must be entitled to all of the trust's net income in each year and no other person may be interested in the income or principal during the survivor's lifetime.

Any planner who regularly reviews client wills should familiarize himself with marital deduction requirements, or, at least, direct inquiries to persons who have expertise in this area.

POWERS CLAUSE

The next clause is often one pertaining to the powers of the executor (and trustee if the will establishes a "testamentary trust," a trust created at the testator's death under the will). The purposes of the powers clause are to:

(1) give the executor (and trustee) specific power and authority over and above those provided by state law to enable the executor to conserve and manage the property, and

Tools and Techniques

(2) limit, where desired and appropriate, the executor's power and authority (for instance, the client may not want the executor to make certain investments), and

(3) provide authority to continue a business (or handle other property with special management or investment problems) and the special flexibility necessary to accomplish that objective, and

(4) protect the executor against suit by other beneficiaries by specifying the powers necessary to accomplish the executor's role.

An (abbreviated) example of a powers clause is:

I authorize my executor (as well as any substitute executor) in his, her, or its discretion, with respect to all property, real and personal, in addition to the powers conferred by law, to:

1. retain assets
2. purchase investments
3. hold cash
4. vote and grant proxies
5. sell, exchange, or dispose of
6. distribute in cash or in kind
7. delegate to agents
8. assign or compromise claims
9. borrow funds
10. lease, manage, develop real estate
11. abandon property
12. make certain tax elections
13. receive and use employee benefits

Planners should check:

(1) Are there any assets or problems in this case which require special powers to fulfill the desires of the client or provide the executor with sufficient flexibility? (Beware of "boilerplate" clauses). Are there powers that should be added?

(2) Will any power adversely affect the estate tax marital deduction? For instance, a marital deduction trust, under Code Sec. 2056(b)(5) or (b)(7), must provide that the surviving spouse receive all income at least annually. Consider the impact of a power allowing the trustee under a testamentary trust to retain nonincome producing property. Unless the will/trust also contains a provision allowing the surviving spouse to demand that the trust assets be sold or made income producing, the marital deduction may be lost. Will such a power thwart other objectives of the testator? For instance, what if the unproductive property was stock in a family corporation? A sale of such stock would raise income but could cause the loss of family control of the corporation.

The draftsman might consider including a "savings clause" that would nullify any power, duty, or discretionary authority that might jeopardize the marital deduction.

(3) Will any of the powers granted cause a conflict of interest? For instance, if the executor is a bank, discretionary authority to invest in its own securities or common trust funds will cause a conflict that must be specifically "forgiven" by the will (assuming the client wants to do so).

(4) Is there specific authority for the executor to make distribution "in kind" (as opposed to selling estate assets and making the distribution in cash?) In some states absent specified power to do so, the executor may have no choice: the distribution must be made in cash.

APPOINTMENT OF FIDUCIARIES CLAUSE

The appointment of the executor, trustee of any testamentary trust, and guardian of any minor child, often comes toward the end of the will.

The purposes of the fiduciary appointment clause are:

(1) to name the individual(s) or corporate fiduciary or combinations of individual(s) and fiduciaries who will administer the testator's estate and any trust which the will creates;

(2) to give the executor the appropriate power to act on behalf of the estate and carry out the terms of the will;

(3) to specify if and how the executor is to be compensated;,

(4) state whether or not the executor is to post bond;

(5) to specify the authority of and decision making process for co-executors; and

(6) to name guardian(s) and successor guardian(s) of any minor child of the testator.

An example of the appointment clause is:

I appoint my nephew, Farnsworth Dowlrimple III, as the executor under this will. If for any reason he fails to qualify or ceases to act, I appoint the Left Bank and Trust of Overflow, Pa. as my executor. I confer upon my executor all the powers enumerated in clause _____ above. No executor shall be required to furnish any bond or other security in any jurisdiction. I direct the my nephew, Farnsworth, shall receive no compensation for his services as Executor and that the Left Bank and Trust of Overflow, Pa. be entitled to be compensated for its services as executor in accordance with its regularly adopted schedule of compensation in effect and applicable at the time of the performance of such services.

Planners should check:

(1) Does the client trust the individual who is currently named as executor and backup executor? Is that individual or corporate fiduciary legally qualified to act as executor? (Has the attorney who drew the will been named

as executor? Typically, absent special circumstances, this raises a number of ethical questions and raises the spectre of a conflict of interest.)

(2) Should the executor's bond be waived?

(3) Is the executor named willing to serve? (How recently has the client checked?)

(4) Is the guardian for minors willing to act? Is he or she able to act? Is that person suitable?

(5) Is a prolonged estate (or trust) administration anticipated? If so, consider giving executors (trustees) the power to appoint successors by filing an instrument with the probate or other appropriate court.

TESTATOR'S SIGNING CLAUSE

The next to the last clause in a will is typically the testator's signing or "testimonium" provision. The purposes of the testimonium clause are

(1) to establish that the document is intended to be the testator's last will,

(2) to meet statutory requirements that require the testator's signature at the logical conclusion of the will, and

(3) to state the date on which the will was signed.

An example of a testimonium clause is:

In witness of the above, I subscribe my name, this 11th day of September, 1988 at Bryn Mawr, Pennsylvania to this, my last will, which consists of 13 pages (each of which I have initialed at the bottom).

Planners should check:

(1) Is the will signed by the testator at its logical end? Is each page numbered? Is the page count correct?

(2) Are there duplicate or triplicate signed wills in existence? If the testator was given a signed duplicate which is not found at his death, it is possible that a presumption will arise that the testator destroyed it with the intention of revoking it. The potential for litigation is therefore increased significantly. The better practice is for only one original to be executed.

ATTESTATION CLAUSE

The final clause in a will is the "attestation" provision. The purposes of the attestation (often called the witness) clause are to:

(1) witness the testator's signing,

(2) comply with statutory requirements,

(3) underline the testamentary character of the document, and

(4) comply with state law requirements in cases where the testator signed by a mark (such as an "X") or where, at the testator's direction and on his behalf, the will was signed by someone else (as would be the case where the testator was physically incapable of signing but mentally competent).

An example of an attestation clause is:

This will was signed by Edward Grieg, the testator, and declared to be his last will in our presence. We, at his request and in his presence and in the presence of each other, state that we witnessed his signing and declaration and at his request we have signed our names as witnesses this 11th day of September, 1988.

Planners should check:

(1) Are there three witnesses to the testator's signing? Although most states require less, three witness will comply with the most stringent probate requirements of any state and as a practical matter provide stronger evidence of the competence and testamentary intent of the testator.

(2) Were any of the witnesses beneficiaries under the will? This is inadvisable for at least two reasons: First, the witnesses may become incompetent to testify as to the execution or validity of the will. Second, witnesses who are also beneficiaries may be prevented from receiving bequests under the will.

(3) Are the addresses of the witnesses stated? Although addresses may not be legally required, they make it easier to locate and identify witnesses when needed.

(4) Is the will "self proving"? I.e., in some states a notarized affidavit attached to the will signed by the witnesses (and in some states, the testator, also) which describes the circumstances of the execution of the will may permit the will to be admitted to probate without the requirement that the witnesses be found or appear before the court in the probate proceeding.

OTHER CLAUSES

There are, of course, many other clauses which should be considered in reviewing a will. Some additional points for the planner to check are:

(1) Is the federal estate tax marital deduction important? If so, consider that the Uniform Simultaneous Death Act, which applies in most states, presumes that the testator survives in the event of a simultaneous death involving the testator and a beneficiary. This would cause a loss of the estate tax marital deduction unless the will superseded state law by providing a "common disaster" clause. This provision makes the presumption that the testator's spouse is deemed to have survived.

(2) Does the will consider the possibility that one or more beneficiaries will disclaim? The will should state who will receive property if the named beneficiary renounces his or her interest. The transfer is then treated as if the decedent had left property directly to the ultimate recipient.

(3) Have the provisions in the will been coordinated with other dispositive instruments? For instance, is the will coordinated with all trusts, with employee benefit plans, buy-sell agreements, and life insurance beneficiary designations?

(4) Are the problems of minors, incompetents, and other beneficiaries with special needs or circumstances properly addressed in the will? In other words, is the right asset going to the right person at the right time and in the right manner?

Has the client considered the financial burden that may be placed on the guardians of minor children, and have appropriate financial provisions been made so that they can afford to raise both the client's children and their own? (Some may want to set up a special life insurance funded trust that, if necessary, can provide to the guardians needed dollars, but, if not, will go to the client's children later in life.)

(5) Is the client's spouse's will coordinated with the client's will?

(6) Is there a "spendthrift clause" to provide protection against the claims of creditors?

SUMMARY

Although only an attorney should draft a will, every member of the estate planning team should make it a practice to review a client's will on a regular basis. The nonattorney's role in the will review process should be thought of not as a replacement for or as a means of "second guessing" the attorney, but rather as a source of additional strength in the planning process. The estate planner can provide in that regard a valuable resource to ascertain how the client's total dispositive plan can most effectively and efficiently meet the current needs, circumstances, and goals of both the client and the client's beneficiaries.

DEATH-SENSITIZATION FOR THE ESTATE PLANNER

It is no wonder that CLUs, CPAs, trust officers, and attorneys involved in the estate-planning process spend so much time in tax planning and relatively minimal effort on "people" planning; pitifully little formal thought has been given — in or out of the classroom — to the human factor in the estate-planning process. It is fascinating that the subject of life — and death — appears so seldom in the curriculum of estate-planning courses given in law schools, in insurance training classes, or in estate-planning seminars and workshops.

Isn't it ironic that death, the very reason for the estate planner's existence, the "biological center of the personal service involved," is hardly ever discussed in texts on estate planning?

This commentary pertains to the psychological rather than the tax aspects of death, and is meant to serve as a compilation of some of the things the estate planner — both as a professional member of a human services team and as a person — should know about death and dying. Although the thoughts and words below have been synthesized from the works of a number of scholars, a special debt is owed to Dr. Elizabeth Kubler-Ross (On Death and Dying) and Thomas L. Shaffer (Death, Property, and Lawyers). The former is a psychiatrist and social scientist of extraordinary skill and sensitivity, whose books are based on the results of hundreds of actual interviews with dying patients and their families; the latter is the dean of Notre Dame Law School, who has written the most comprehensive text available to the estate-planning professional on the subject of death. One text that is not cited but should be read by every member of the estate-planning team is Widow, *by Lynn Caine. It is a frank, intimate, and shocking account of death from a widow's point of view.*

Why Should the Estate Planner Think About Death and Dying?

Reduction of Client's Anxiety

Many professionals, even those highly learned in the law, associate estate planning merely with dispositive and tax goals. A young attorney specializing in estate planning was introduced to a well-known and highly respected probate judge by one of the attorney's clients. The client spoke admiringly of the young man's talents as an estate planner and when the judge asked, "Young man, are you really that good?" the attorney quipped, "I guess I must be — it seems that once I draw a will, my clients seem to live forever." The judge retorted, "Well then how do you know what you are doing will work?" Although the judge's retort was clever, perhaps he missed the point. A client doesn't have to die for the estate-planning process to be successful. Estate planning can and should be an end in itself.

One of the most important goals of the estate-planning process is the reduction of fear and anxiety about death. That, in fact, is what the estate-planning experience (from the client's viewpoint) should be about, a personal reconciliation to death.

Properly handled, the estate planning experience can be one of great psychological satisfaction. In fact, that peace of mind is the only payoff the client himself receives from making a will. After all, will the client, by making a will, avoid family fights? Will the client, by a complex scheme of wills and trusts, save taxes? Shouldn't we examine just what it is the client wants out of the estate planning process?

Estate planning, in its broadest sense, presents an opportunity for a significant, growing, healthy encounter with one's own death. "Death is resented, perhaps, because the event itself cannot be controlled. Yet through planning, even though he cannot abolish death, the client can frustrate it by removing the worst consequences of its surprise."

Melville, in *Moby Dick*, wrote about the constructive nature and therapeutic effect on death anxiety of the will-making process:

> It may seem strange that of all men sailors should be tinkering at their last wills and testaments.... After the ceremony was concluded upon the present occasion, I felt all the easier; a stone was rolled away from my heart. Besides, all the days I should now live would be as good as the days that Lazarus lived.... I survived myself....

Free Client's Energy to Life-Related Matters

A second reason that the planning experience is an end unto itself is the relationship between death and life. Worrying about death and its consequences is emotionally expensive. Society's taboos regarding death generate delusions that in turn siphon off energy from the task of living. If the client spends energy maintaining the denial of mortality, that much less strength is available to be used in meaningful living.

An individual's values in life are affected strongly by the way he has (or has not) dealt with death and dying. Philosophers, psychiatrists, and religious scholars stress that death should be dealt with before it is imminent, because only by giving meaning to death can one give meaning to life. They explain that a human's mortality is a good thing, that only by the limited scope of one's time can existence be dramatic and intense. What is important is how (rather than how long) we live and that we maximize the creative possibilities of life.

How can an openness (between the professional and a client) about death enhance the client's ability to live well? By helping the client come to terms with death, and by helping him create an atmosphere in which he would be willing to die, it is easier for the client to learn to see his life in relationship with others in a clearer perspective and to make his lifetime interpersonal relationships more meaningful. In other words, we can show our client that rather than repress his fears of death he should "use as an antidote for death an extensive love of life." Estate planning, then, is to reduce our client's anxiety about death and free his emotional energies for life-oriented activities.

As practitioners in people-serving professions, our efforts have consequences beyond property distribution, beyond tax savings, and even beyond the financial security of our client's survivors. What we do affects not only those who survive the client, but also the client himself. A great deal of our efforts must be directed toward the psychological satisfaction of our client.

Additional Psychological Factors Encouraging Testamentary Process

What other factors concern an individual enough for him to pay money to have a will and trust drawn? Why does he purchase life insurance and reduce his current spendable income to pay premiums? Why does he make inter vivos gifts?

Basically, there are four additional reasons. One is that structuring the future and providing support for survivors is a moral imperative. (Just as it would be immoral to neglect predeath support duties, so would it be immoral to neglect postdeath obligations.)

A second powerful impetus is guilt. Many clients feel that money or other property will somehow make up for neglect. They attempt to pay back a wife or children in property for the time they were too busy at the office to take with their family.

Security devices such as wills, trusts, and life insurance provide a client with a means of doing something to stabilize the future of his family and rob death of its ability to threaten him with his own hungry children.

Perhaps the most powerful reason for the testamentary process is the step it enables a person to take toward immortality. Some have called this the concept of "postself." Essentially, it recognizes that individuals engage in cognitive and emotional maneuverings in the present so they can survive, continue to live, and have a measure of impact and influence after the event of their physical deaths.

The Estate Planner's Responsibility by Definition or Default

Why must the estate planner (in addition to other human services teams) be involved with the subjects of death and dying? Possibly the responsibility is his by definition — or perhaps the burden rests upon him by default. Social taboos have caused the dismissal of the subject of death from the public mind. This in turn shifts the weight to those of us who are forced by our relationship with the client to deal with their feelings about death and dying. Regardless of the reason, as advisers we must recognize that our clients — even those in the prime of life — have thoughts and reactions to death; and an essential part of the estate planning process relates to a healthy resolution of those feelings.

Resolution of Professional's Own Anxieties Necessary to His Utility

It is impossible for the estate planner to help his client until his own feelings and anxieties about death are first resolved. Not until the professional knows and can deal with his own fears and thoughts concerning death can he properly construct policies and priorities based on the needs and desires of his client — rather than his own defenses.

There are many thoughts embedded in the minds and hearts of clients that beg to be shared with another human being. But we often close off the openness necessary to the flow of such information because we are unwilling to talk directly about death. A discussion of death — even the very word — is kept to a bare minimum or surrounded with euphemisms by the attorney or trust officer in the will-making process or the insurance agent in the sales interview.

The feelings of the professional, however, do not go unnoticed or without effect. His values and attitudes are communicated (both verbally and nonverbally) to a client regardless of whether the estate planner intends such message or not. His annoyance, impatience, lack of interest, or personal anxiety affects his clients more than he realizes. Our method of handling our own feelings sometimes conveys that we cannot, do not want to, and are unwilling to listen to those of others.

Rewards of Openness to the Estate Planner and Client

Substantial rewards are available to both the estate planner and his client who are willing to talk about death and dying long before it happens. A healthy and strong individual is less frightened and better able to deal with the interpersonal and financial implications of death "when it is still miles away than when it is right in front of the door." It is also easier for the client's family to discuss such matters in times of relative health and well-being. Appropriate arrangements for children and others are more rationally made while the head of the household is still functioning. (The value of such predeath conversations seems obvious — yet we often postpone such talks to serve our own defenses rather than the best interests of the client and his family.)

The rewards to the estate planner are abundant. If we are strong enough to examine our own reactions more closely and take an honest look at ourselves, our own growth and maturity is nurtured. When we learn to listen, we reduce the powerlessness (and often frustration and anger) of those toward whom we profess to offer human caring.

Why the Word "Death" Is Unspoken

When the topic of death is raised — or when the professional must deal with a dying client — his concerns about his own mortality are raised toward consciousness. His childhood feeling about separation and death are reawakened. Talking about one's own death is even more sensitive and more terrible. Because it is an unknown, death is associated with a bad act, a frightening happening. We deny death by discussing it — if at all — in euphemistic language. Much of this extends from the societal taboo concerning the recognition of man's mortality.

The problem, of course, is not uniquely reserved to the estate planner. The medical profession offers a good example of the reluctance of other professionals to meet the problem. For instance, the physician often prefers not telling a patient he has cancer. And unless the patient is persistent, the doctor might disregard the patient's questions. Even those questions intuitively perceived as a "real wish to know" are often ignored: "No one wants to know he is dying." Professionals have difficulty stating a diagnosis to a patient. They tend to use a staccato, impersonal, medical textbook style.

The Estate Planning Interview — An Opportunity to Touch, to Feel, to Help

Coming to Grips with Life and Death

The estate planning interview is perhaps the first time in a client's life when he will be confronted with his property, his beloved ones, his mortality, and the relationship of each to the others. The impact of death must be discussed and met head on. He must recognize and internalize the possibility of unexpected sudden death and, in some cases, eventuality of rapidly approaching certain death. He must come face to face with the effects of the orphaning of his children, the potential for family strife, the problems inherent in projects left unfinished, and the psychological and financial burdens of liabilities outstanding. Additionally, the estate planning interview is an opportunity to come to grips with and eliminate the uncertainty involved in the mysterious machinery of probate.

The Process of Human Counseling

This reduction in tension and anxiety doesn't just happen: it must be part of a carefully thought out process on the part of the estate planner. The hoped-for result will not occur if the experts, the CPA, the CFP, the CLU, the ChFC, the attorney, or the trust officer, think of the estate-planning interview as a mental tug-of-war involving on the one side the estate planner, who knows or makes up the rules, and on the other the client, who becomes willing to accept those rules by dependence on the estate planner. This psychology can only result in an arrangement that the client will probably not understand or even want. How could he if he hasn't "bought into" the ultimate plan?

What must the professional do to involve the client and turn what might otherwise be a cold, impersonal gathering of data into an opportunity for human counseling? It is not so difficult a task for the estate planner to identify issues or face problems. What the estate planner needs to learn is how to face a face.

Listen to the client. Study not only what the client (and his family) says, but also what he doesn't say. Try to understand what the client's body language (the shrug of a shoulder, the positioning of the hands, the apparent physical tension on the face, the lifting of the eyebrows, or the fleeting frown) really means. Summarize what you have been told and reflect accurately on what you have seen, felt, and heard.

Be sensitive to the client's world. Accept his feelings and try to understand them. Communicate honestly — and humanly. Be open, involved, and willing to enter the client's world. The professional must want to be personally helpful. To do this he must be tuned in not only to the client's feelings but also to his own.

Objectives of the Estate Planning Interview

The goal of the estate planner should be to help his client come to his own realizations and conclusions. To accomplish this, he must find out how the client feels about life and death — and the values and relationships that death will affect or destroy. So he must search for feelings and attitudes as well as information. The failure of an estate planner is more often a failure of perception than a restricted range of information, an incomplete understanding of "people facts" rather than "fact facts."

More specifically, the estate planner must under stand his client's system of needs, his modes of expressing or revealing himself, his ideas about life, and his feelings and practices relating to his family and his career. There must also be an appreciation of the client's feelings about property, security, health, and perhaps most importantly, an ability to contemplate all of these things in relation to each other.

Tools and Techniques

The Role of Property in the Testamentary Process

It is extremely important that the estate planner have an understanding of the roles of property in the testamentary process: "Our clients' thoughts and emotions are deeper, more puzzling realities than taxation or legal rhetoric." Clients are people, complex, and worthy of behavioral examination.

At its simplest level, a client's thoughts about his property could be considered mere statements on a ledger. But on higher levels, property is both and expression and an extension of a client himself, a part of the way he defines himself. (We see this clearly when a person is stripped of his possessions. He is attacked at the deepest layers of his personality; there is less man left since something of himself has been taken away from him. The first day of basic training in the army, incarceration as a prisoner of war, and even routine hospital check-ins serve as examples of the loss of identity that is coupled with the loss that comes when clothing and other material possessions are taken away.)

The items on a person's desk, perhaps mementos of difficult business careers, are not significant for their economic values but are important because — like other property — they are an idiom of the owner's personality.

If we accept the premise that property represents and immortalizes a person, then when a person makes a gift (inter vivos or testamentary) he is really giving part of himself. He is giving his own nature and substance, since the property he gives is not inert but has the life and personification of the giver. His attitude toward giving, therefore, expresses the relationships between the people he loves and the things — the wealth and objects — he owns.

Property is used in the exercise of power, of love, of guilt, remorse, of hope, and resignation. A person's needs, feelings, thoughts, and actions grow and attach in different manners to different kinds of properties. A home, for example, represents a protective attachment to a person's family. A business may represent the continuation or perhaps completion of a personal project (goal-striving behavior).

The estate planner should incorporate the role of personification of property in the estate-planning process. He should understand that clients — in drawing wills — are interested as much in values and identifications in their property as they are in taxes. They are interested in the people they love.

What Is Death and What Does It Mean?

Death — Multifaceted Meanings and Effects

In the most general sense, death is the continuing and constantly accelerating process that begins the moment we are born. Perhaps that definition should set the stage for how we live: "We can realize that we might die at any moment and yet live as though we were never going to die."

Death attaches to each individual's soul, psyche, relationships, and property — but does so in different ways for different people. The meanings of the word "death" fluctuate, therefore, from person to person:

To some, death is the bringer of financial distress: With the extreme treatment and costs of hospitalization, financial burdens are added. Little luxuries at first and necessities later on may not be afforded any more. The immense sums that such treatment and hospitalization cost in recent years have forced many patients to sell the only possessions they had; they were unable to keep a house which they built for their old age, unable to send a child through college, and unable, perhaps, to make many dreams come true.

Death to many conjures up images of loss of dignity and independence. Guilt, anxiety, and fear color perceptions of dying. Death is frightening because it is uncertain, because it will sever important relationships (especially relationships that involve mutual obligations), and because it will cause experience to cease.

Social scientists, physicians, and philosophers have looked upon death as part of life. They have asked, if one is not able to die, is he really able to live?: "We die as we have lived. Death belongs to life as birth does. The walk is in the raising of the foot as in the laying of it down." Others have said that "death is an important interface — part of a larger process which is somehow related to what it is to be human."

Dying — How It Colors Perceptions of Death

We know much more about dying than we do about death. As estate planners, we are sometimes confronted with a client who has been told he has a limited time to live or who may even be on his deathbed. What are the feelings some of these people might experience? Some have said that dying is partially reliving the past, partially preoccupation with the illness, and partially just going on living. And death? Some say it is very much like rest: "In the end a dying man needs to die like a sleepy man needs to sleep."

Do dying and death represent failure? To many, they do. To others, the thoughts of dying and death generate fear of losing time, physical decay, the cessation of thought, and irreversibility, and the loss of pleasure. Still others view the process of dying as a deprivation, a threat, a punishment, and a devouring of their persons.

People who are dying experience a tremendous range of problems — from the purely practical (such as transportation to and from the hospital) to the deeply internal emotional experience, such as dealing with intense sadness, anger, and guilt. Perhaps worst of all is the loneliness: "He was ...interrupted, left dangling, perhaps to die alone .... It was the isolation, the exclusion we had forced upon him. We could not be with him — we could not even hear him." The vast change in life-styles makes dying alien and lonely, mechanical and dehumanizing.

Interaction between the Estate Planner and the Dying Client

There are a number of tools and techniques in use where members of the estate planning team are aware that death is impending:

Unlike the normal estate planning situation, however, deathbed estate planning by definition usually precludes detailed research and requires immediate decisions. The estate planner is likely to propose technically sound recommendations which may be personally unacceptable to the client and his family. They may not even be willing to listen to recommendations. Sometimes, the client or his family will make requests which are technically unsound or even illegal. These must, of course, be delicately rejected.

How much can be accomplished depends on a number of variables. Three of the most important are the client's state of mind, the emotional involvement of near relatives, and the relationship between the estate planner and the client.

If the client is physically, mentally, and emotionally able to assist, his cooperation can vastly increase the effectiveness of predeath planning. But, as will be further explained below, some persons lose all interest when they learn death is near. Often the client has been kept ignorant of the gravity of his situation by a well-intentioned physician or family member. This at least complicates, if not totally frustrates, the estate planner's ability to render meaningful service.

Family members are sometimes more emotionally crippled by the impending loss they will suffer than is the client himself. His spouse, children, or other close relatives may be incapable of making logical decisions or taking pragmatic action. The special taboos against mentioning a will or "getting things in order" have kept even estate planning specialists from being of much help when faced with their own dying parents.

A close relationship between the estate planner and the client gives the adviser perspective and insight into the client's personal objectives and his family's potential problems. Even more important, the adviser's role must be to provide emotional ballast, to objectively help his client and his client's family arrange a list of priorities and implementation procedures.

The Dying Client — Expressions of Grief

It is important for the estate planner to understand how grief is expressed by both the dying client and his survivors. How these individuals come to terms with impending death and move through the various stages of grief is thought to be strongly influenced by a person's basic personality. The leading authority feels there are essentially five stages through which a persons goes: denial, anger, bargaining, depression, and acceptance. (These stages can occur in any order at any time.)

Denial is a temporary defense. In the young there is the typical "It can't happen to me" reaction. Denial serves as a healthy way of dealing with the uncomfortable and painful fact of impending death.

An expression of anger, which can be directed without reason at doctors, friends, relatives, or estate planning advisers, is thought to vary in intensity with the dying client's early life experiences. It is yet another means of expressing powerful emotional trauma.

Bargaining ("Let me live one more year and I'll be good to my children, donate money to my religious organization, etc.") is an attempt on an emotional level to postpone what is inevitable on the intellectual and physical levels.

Depression is a reaction that is a common response to the actual loss of health or use of part of the body. It is a preparatory measure to the impending loss of life.

Acceptance is often (but not always) the final stage. At this point the dying client is void of feelings and expresses an increased desire and need for sleep. The dying person's family often needs more help, support, and understanding than the client.

Another authority suggests that the stages of grief are

(1) shock

(2) disorganization

(3) expression of volatile emotions

(4) guilt

(5) feelings of loss and loneliness

(6) periods of relief and reestablishment

Feelings expressed by a dying professor included panic (he was terrified that he had lost control of his fate, decisions were made without his knowledge or consent, and he gradually found himself passively accepting the decisions), anger (he felt dehumanized, an object instead of a person), the need to talk (he wanted to share his feelings and vent his frustrations), and deep depressions (he had feelings of guilt and inadequacy as a husband and father).

What the Estate Planner Can Do for the Dying Client

Although the estate planning process should give all clients a feeling of control, a sense of usefulness, and the satisfaction of completing unfinished business, this goal is particularly important in the case of a client who has been told — because of a particular medical condition such as cancer or a failing heart — that he or she has only a limited time to live.

The Importance of Providing the Client with Control

What should occur in the estate-planning process is a series of experiences that result in change through (the client's) choice. The professional can increase the client's dignity by empowering him with as much control as possible. But it is not enough to give the dying client a voice; he must also be given a listener. Only then can he be an active participant in decision making. Psychiatrists have found that hopelessness and depression are precipitated when individuals can't (or perceive they can't) act on their environment. Any actions the estate planner can take to bring the dying client into the problem-solving process will help relieve the client's feelings of helplessness and increase the quality of his remaining life.

A word of warning, however, is in order. Even for the health client, "the testamentary experience is death-confronting, novel, and taboo-defying." For the dying client, such experience could possibly be overwhelming. Obviously, a great deal of discretion must be exercised by all the parties involved.

Helping the Client to Feel Useful by Encouraging the Completion of Unfinished Business

By presenting the estate planning process as an unfinished project, the client is given a developmental task with which he is involved. He is given value and a meaningful tie to life. This final stage — even though quite possibly limited in terms of absolute time — may be relatively as important as all previous tasks in life.

Family, as well as members of the estate planning team, must interface with the dying person and his environment. They must help the client maintain his autonomy and dignity by encouraging him to participate — and thus help him to face death in his own way. This conceptualization allows family members to help the dying person complete his unfinished business in a meaningful way that will benefit all concerned.

"Death ceases to be an absurd and intolerable scandal only when a person knows he has given meaning to his life." So the estate planner confronted with a dying must do what he can do to give that person the sense of pride, a feeling of worth, and a knowledge he has resolved much of his unfinished business.

Development of a Support System of Advisers

The dying person and his survivors need large doses of supportive intervention which can best be accomplished by knowing his previous history of reactions to stress.

The nature of the client's response to grief will be largely determined by the quality of his lifetime personal relationships, and the use he makes of the defense mechanisms such as denial or anger and the retraction of his ego. Start where the client is — let him face impending death, denial, or acceptance, whichever he selects. Don't force him to behave according to your preconceptions or hustle him along a preplanned course.

In dealing with the dying client (or his family) proceed at the rate determined by the client's receptivity. Sense where the client is emotionally:

> Set your pace at the rate at which they are able to understand. Do the correct thing financially even if it may provoke angry confrontations at some subsequent date.... The widow will generally be more rational and receptive to good advice in approximately six to nine months after the death. Do not make brisk unexplained conclusions or assertions. Do not be provoked into anger. Be deliberate, correct, and extremely open and proper. Diplomacy, patience, genuineness, and warmness are essential. Take the time to be empathetic, to listen attentively, to have unconditional positive regard.... If you find yourself becoming very angry or acting abruptly, it is best to consider why this is so and excuse yourself from the ongoing exchange until you have better composure.

Strengthen the coping mechanisms whether they be made of denial or acceptance. Reduce anxiety and fear. Help the family to understand the feelings of the dying individual and help the family with their feelings.

Perhaps the most meaningful service is the opportunity the estate planner has to allow his client to share his feelings before death and to work through those feelings, rational or irrational.

The dying need reassurance they will not be left alone. If we, as estate planners, have the courage not to desert them, they offer us a gift in return — help in completing our own unfinished business.

Effect of Death on the Survivors

A breadwinner's death results in drastic changes in the life of the family. These include loss of security and an end to the survivors' dependence on the decedent. Survivors will be required to take over many of the decedent's roles and tasks, accept a strange new schedule, and shoulder what are sometimes actually (and are almost always perceived as) harsh and awesome new responsibilities. Especially for widows, this often means a sudden involvement in business and financial affairs.

In every substantial estate, the widow (if there is one) has major roles to perform. Yet in most situations she lacks even a modicum of previous exposure or training to function efficiently in handling legal, business, probate or taxation problems. Quite often she's never balanced a checkbook, let alone handled an $800,000 estate. She has not been shown how to do things which will be her certain responsibility. Nor has she been taught to avoid acts which she should not even attempt.

Ironically, at the very time the widow is first involved in these matters, she is in the worst possible frame of mind. She is depressed, unhappy and insecure, and her entire social life has changed. After the few days when her friends, relatives and close family are there to comfort her, they will return to their normal lives. The widow is left — alone and lonely. Confronting her with strange and complex legal duties is like throwing her into a pitch-black room. She loses all sense of direction, doesn't know where the light switch is and is afraid to move because all sorts of risks and impediments are there in the darkness.

How does the widow feel? One widow said, "I feel like one of those spiraled shells washed up on the beach. Poke a straw through the twisting tunnels inside and nothing is there — no flesh, no life. Whatever lived there has dried up and gone!"

And, although the male pronoun is commonly used to designate the breadwinner/decedent, it is quite often the *man* who survives. Studies show that a widower faces even more serious emotional problems than many widows do. Men seldom have a support system to hold them up — and *keep* them up.

The word "widow" is appropriate — it comes from Sanskrit and it means "empty." The shock of that emptiness is always immediately felt. Another widow said, "It took me some time to grasp the meaning of what happened. The word 'death' didn't mean anything to me. All I thought of was that it would be impossible for Marty to be here one day and gone the next. It was as if the earth had just opened up and swallowed him. My shock turned to panic; I felt lost. I didn't want to see or talk to anyone. The thought of going to bed frightened me because I would always wake up in the middle of the night trying to stifle a scream. I couldn't believe Marty was dead."

Years ago, we had the benefit of a socially accepted collection of rites and ceremonies to help survivors make the transition. In some societies, these rites were performed for weeks or even months after an individual's death. But today, we don't often have elaborate wakes, mourning clothes or annual remembrances. Many of society's rules, rites and ceremonies of the past are gone. And so survivors are not really sure how to cope with death — they have to make their own decisions at to what to do and how to react. This uncertainty produces anxiety.

Survivors experience guilt for what they did or did not do in life to or for the deceased, or simply embarrassment for having lived while the deceased died. Survivors may feel guilty because the death of the deceased has relieved them from heavy, emotionally and financially draining burdens. ("If he'd die already, the financial nightmare would end.")

At the same time, the bereaved may feel anger at being deserted and left to face life's problems. A young daughter, speaking of her father who had just died, told us, "I felt as though he didn't have the right to die. I wasn't ready for him to die."

Perhaps the most difficult of all emotions that survivors must overcome is a deep sense of loneliness and resentment at being left alone. There are 10 million widows in our country — one out of every 6 women over age 21. A study of over 1,700 widows showed that loneliness is the single most serious problem of widowhood. One of those widows said, "It's funny, but it's love and companionship that you miss. You don't get someone out of your system so easily after 26 years ...Being lonesome is a big void that can't be filled."

The second most serious problem of widowhood is the financial pressure of raising children without a father.

So besides their emotional problems, families are likely to have financial problems, or at least concern as to how they will pay current bills and continue to get along after the breadwinner's death. One widow said, "After my husband died, there was the emotional shock. The pain was so deep — so consuming — it seemed unendurable. But I learned to live with it. The economic shock was something else. It didn't strike as fast or hit as furious. It's the sort of thing you don't even notice at first. But after a while, the shock of your economic plight begins to creep into your consciousness like some black, oozing reality that you can't believe or escape. It's true ... money can't compensate two children for the loss of their father; money can't reach out in the night and caress you; money can't come home at night with a briefcase, a twinkle and a hug; but money can give you some peace of mind." And so survivors must be concerned, among other things, with the need for money — because, to the extent the decedent didn't provide it, his or her survivors have the problem of raising it — or doing without it. This in turn creates incredible psychological pressures.

Bereavement is not a commonplace occurrence in our lifetimes. The whirlwind shock of sudden change is a crisis with which many family members feel particularly unable to cope. Quite often a real, and almost always a perceived, imbalance exists between the difficulty and importance of the problems and the resources available to deal with them. Obviously, professional psychiatric and psychological help may be required.

Survivors must release their ties with the deceased. They must adjust to their new environment and form new relationships. The family must allow mourning to occur, relinquish the memory of the deceased as a force in family affairs and activities, and realign themselves in terms of readjusting responsibilities and needs.

It is particularly important that all (both children and adults) who are touched by the death of the decedent be given an opportunity to adequately work out their feelings about the event. You can expect problems to occur when a person of any age is unable to express grief or tries to hold back natural responses. Symptoms of the morbid and abnormal reactions which tend to occur when there is an unnatural delay include

- exhausting overactivity
- symptoms similar to those manifested in the last illness of the deceased, or the outbreak of other psychosomatic illnesses such as asthma or colitis (this is a combination of normal mourning and the "It should have been me" feeling)
- furious (and usually unreasonable) hostility toward specific persons (often including the estate's executor)
- agitated and acute depression (sometimes leading to suicidal thoughts)
- extreme and prolonged difficulty in sleeping
- preoccupation with the image of the deceased (you may find dozens of pictures of the deceased suddenly appear throughout the house)
- difficulty in continuing normal social interaction and a withdrawal of interest in the outside world

About the Will and Probate — What They Mean to the Survivors

The will and the probate process itself fulfill important functions in the process of emotional repair known as mourning. The will is the last communication of the deceased. It has unique emotional meanings because in it the decedent states many of his feelings about the bereaved. Of course, the decedent's thoughts are usually not implicit in the words used. But in terms of *who* receives property, *how* that property is to be received, and *when* it will be received, the testator has expressed approval (or disapproval), gratitude (or revenge), and confidence (or a lack of confidence). Likewise, the terms of a will may emphasize that the testator recognized one child's need or another child's deservingness. Or the testator may have favored a blood relative over someone who is loved but is not related (or vice versa).

It is important to recognize that what the testator meant to say when his will was written may not be how it is taken by the beneficiaries. A devoted but less needy son who gets less than a proportionate part of his father's estate may resent the injustice of being left less than his less worthy brother.

Choice of Executor — What It Means

A person is selected as an executor because of the testator's trust and confidence in that person. They may have had a close or very deep emotional relationship.

A bereaved executor, in performing his or her duties, facilitates the process of coming to terms with the testator's death.

By carrying out the wishes of the deceased the executor is retaining and strengthening his or her relationship with the deceased, but at the same time, while going through the stages of the probate process, the executor is gradually "letting go."

Of course, the opposite is true in some situations. For instance, assume a widow had always been dependent on her husband for every decision. If the couple's son or a bank is named as executor, the sense of helplessness precipitated by the loss of her husband is increased by the lack of control she continues to experience. Her helplessness may generate fear and distrust. The result may be that every move the executor makes may be questioned or viewed with suspicion.

What Can — and Should — the Executor Do?

One of the positive results of the estate planning process is to give survivors a feeling of control, a sense of usefulness and the satisfaction of completing the decedent's (and their own) unfinished business. Increase the family members' dignity by empowering them with as much control as possible. Keep in mind that it is not enough to give survivors a voice; you must also give them a listener. Only then can they be active participants in the decision-making process. Hopelessness and depression are precipitated and exacerbated when individuals can't (or perceive they can't) act on their environment.

Any steps taken to bring all family members into the decision-making process will relieve their feelings of helplessness. The death of a loved one will be experienced as less absurd, and may become more tolerable, if the family knows that the life of the deceased had meaning.

Accumulating an estate, buying life insurance, preparing the will and trust are all like buying a car, filling it with gas, and expecting that a wife or child who has never been in a car can get in and drive that vehicle in heavy traffic. We can't, of course, make survivors into mechanics, but we can help them learn where the steering wheel is, how to make the car go, how to put on the brakes and how to read road signs. The more that can be done to explain what comes next and how the family can take the wheel, the better off they will be.

Summary

As a member of the estate planning team, you must be extremely conscious of the trauma of the bereaved. Understanding the five stages of grief experienced by a dying person (denial, anger, bargaining, depression and acceptance) will help you understand what survivors experience. Every person will react to death differently than others. How the bereaved react is largely dependent on their relationship with the deceased, their emotional and financial dependence, the energy and time they have devoted to the deceased, and how many other important relationships they may have.

Death often results in drastic life-style changes. These are coupled with various physical symptoms of grief that can be normally anticipated, as well as abnormal reactions that occur when the mourning process is delayed or repressed.

Probate is an important part of the "letting go" process; it is also a means of completing the unfinished business of the deceased and at the same time a beginning of the family's taking control.

If the estate planner can serve as a neutral outsider who is not himself emotionally overinvolved, he can be of great assistance in listening to the client's family's concerns, their wishes, and needs.

Any steps an estate planner takes to bring the survivors into the probate process and give them control will help relieve their feelings of helplessness and help them readjust.

PROBATE — A PRIMER FOR THE COULD-BE EXECUTOR

Copyright ©1988 Charles K. Plotnick and Stephan R. Leimberg

Any adult could be an executor. But few of us would want to be if we knew the awesome, complex, and time-consuming responsibilities and potential liabilities the task entails.

GENERAL ROLE OF AN EXECUTOR

When a person dies, the law requires that his property must be collected. After debts, taxes, and expenses are paid, the remaining assets are distributed to whoever is entitled to that property. That distribution is determined by the person's will or the intestate laws of the state. It is the executor's or administrator's responsibility to collect the assets, to pay the death taxes, debts, and expenses of the decedent (the person who died), and to make the appropriate distribution of any remaining assets. The entire process by which these tasks are accomplished (with the guidance and supervision of the court system) is called "probate." The court that oversees the process is called the probate or orphans' or surrogates' court.

DISTINCTION BETWEEN EXECUTOR AND ADMINISTRATOR

An "executor" is the person appointed in the will of the decedent. If the decedent left no will, or if the will is invalid for some reason, then either the surviving spouse of the decedent, or one or more of the persons entitled to his or her estate, may be appointed as the "personal representative." That person is called the "administrator" of the estate.

It is this person who will "probate" the decedent's will; i.e., the will will be accepted as the decedent's, and as the decedent's *last* will. (Probate is used here in its most narrow sense.)

FUNERAL ARRANGEMENTS

Typically, the funeral will take place before the executor has been appointed. So the executor's only legal duty with respect to the funeral will be to pay the bill if it is reasonable.

APPOINTMENT OF THE PERSONAL REPRESENTATIVE

Even before the appointment of a personal representative of a decedent's estate, a determination has to be made as to where the deceased person was domiciled. A person's domicile is his permanent and principal home, the place to which he always intends to return. The difference between domicile and residence is that your residence is where you happen to be living. Domicile requires not only your presence, but also an intention to make it your permanent home.

The will must then be recorded in the office of the local register of wills of the county in which the decedent was domiciled. The register of wills will issue either "letters of administration" to the administrator or "letters testamentary" to the executor. These "letters" are proof of the legal authority of the personal representative to collect and deal with the assets of the decedent's estate. (To make things simpler, the register of wills gives the executor "short certificates," brief documents evidencing the fact that you are the executor or administrator of the decedent's estate.)

The executor or administrator is now the person who actually has title to the decedent's property and who acts on behalf of the estate.

EMPLOYMENT OF THE ATTORNEY FOR THE ESTATE

An executor is entitled to use any qualified attorney he or she would like. The term "qualified attorney" is stressed because of the complexity of handling an estate. Generally, an executor may use any attorney he feels is competent — even if the decedent named a different attorney in his will.

For both state law and federal tax purposes, the executor or administrator must keep informed as to exactly how the estate is being administered. He can't just close his eyes and shift all the responsibility to the attorney. In one case, a court held an administratrix responsible for the actions of her attorney where she had surrendered all her duties to the attorney and exercised no effective supervision whatsoever over his activities. The court felt that she did not exercise that degree of care, prudence, circumspection, and foresight that a prudent person would employ in matters of her own.

COLLECTING THE ASSETS

After the executor is appointed, the first thing he should do is to get together with the members of the decedent's family, assuming that they are the decedent's beneficiaries, and make sure that he has a clear understanding of the size and nature of the decedent's estate. The second step, if the size, nature, and complexity of the estate warrant, is to hire competent counsel. Once appropriate counsel has been employed the executor should take specific steps to safeguard and collect the decedent's assets as quickly as possible.

Tools and Techniques

It is extremely important that the executor take every possible measure to make certain that he has a complete inventory of all of the decedent's assets. In this regard, he should review the decedent's past income tax returns and cancelled checks to determine if there are any purchases, accounts, securities, or other assets of which the executor is not otherwise aware.

Prior income tax returns, for example, might list interest from bank accounts or dividends from securities of which the executor has no knowledge. From this information, the executor can trace the present location of the assets and determine whether those assets were still owned by the decedent at the time of his death. In addition, the executor must try to collect all outstanding claims that the decedent had against others at his death. In one case, a court even held the executor responsible for failing to make a claim that the estate was the beneficiary of — and therefore entitled to — monies from another state.

The executor should advertise the fact that he has been appointed executor so that creditors or other persons who might have an interest in the decedent's estate will have public notice of his death and thus have time to present any claims against the estate to the executor. The public notice also gives creditors warning that claims must be made before a certain date. If notice of one's appointment as executor is advertised, and the prescribed period of time elapses from the first date of publication, then the executor files his final account with the court. Only after that time elapses and the executor has accounted for what came into the estate, what went out, and what he paid to the beneficiaries can the executor be discharged of all responsibility for handling the estate. Since the "final account" will also be advertised, claims of creditors following the filing of the final account will not be allowed. The executor is then discharged from personal liability.

There is no special order in which the executor must collect the decedent's assets, but it is usually logical to file the appropriate claim form to collect the decedent's life insurance as soon as possible. There are also forms for collecting social security and veterans' administration benefits. Sometimes unpaid salary, as well as other fringe benefits, must be collected. Arrange to have the decedent's safe-deposit box opened and make a list of its contents.

It is important for the executor to open an estate checking account and a savings account. The executor can then take all the liquid assets and pass them through the checking account and savings account, if appropriate, in order to have an accurate accounting of the assets collected and bills paid.

The executor should give notice of the decedent's death to the banks where the decedent had his accounts. He should obtain from the banks letters giving the exact values of the accounts on the date of death, the dates that the accounts were opened, and the exact names on the accounts.

All securities in the decedent's name should be assembled, and the executor should maintain close contact with the decedent's broker to be certain that he has an accurate record of all the securities that the decedent owned, or had an interest in, at the time of his death. There are certain forms the executor must obtain to transfer title to stocks or bonds. The executor must also determine the value of the securities on the decedent's date of death according to the valuation method prescribed by the Internal Revenue Service.

If the decedent held real estate in his own name, the executor must be certain that the property is protected, that appropriate amounts of insurance are obtained or maintained, and that adequate safeguards are instituted to maintain the security of the property. If it is decided that the property should be sold, the executor is responsible for making sure that the sale is conducted properly and a fair price is received. Even if the executor makes a completely innocent mistake, it could cost him money. For example, one executor mistakenly obligated an estate to two real estate commissions. As a result, the court held that the executor was personally responsible for the amount of the overpayment.

It is also necessary for the executor to have court approval for the sale of real estate unless that power is specifically given to him in the will. In another case, the court found that even where the will gave the executor all the powers set forth in the general statutes of the state, which included the power to sell any property of the decedent without court approval, the executor still did not have the right to sell real estate without court approval.

As assets are collected, they should also be valued. This means an appraisal must be made of the real property and of any personal property that the decedent owned, such as jewelry, clothing, automobiles, and household furniture and effects. And, of course, a value has to be placed on any business interest of the decedent. In one recent case, the court felt that because the executor erred in calculating the value of the decedent's shares in a corporation, and thereby obtained a sales price below the value of the shares, the executor should be surcharged.

HANDLING THE BUSINESS

Where the executor finds a business among the decedent's assets, particular attention must be given to the books of the business. He should examine prior tax returns and take whatever action is necessary to ensure that the business is being run as efficiently as possible. A determination will have to be made as to whether the business should be continued or liquidated. In this regard, the executor can be guided by the decedent's instructions in his will, by the wishes of the family, or by whatever professional guidance the executor can obtain. If the decedent had any business agreements, such as a buy-sell agreement with a surviving partner, or with a surviving shareholder if the business is incorporated, or with the corporation itself, then the executor must comply with the provisions of the agreement.

Very serious problems can arise in trying to conserve the value of a decedent's business or real estate. If the decedent's business was a sole proprietorship, then it terminates on his death. A partnership also terminates, in effect, unless the proper predeath agreements have been made, such as buy-sell agreements that would enable the surviving partner or partners to continue the business. If the business is closed by any period of time following the decedent's death, its value as a going concern is greatly diminished. An interruption of the normal flow of business will result in the loss of customers and a large drop in the value for which the business might be sold. If the assets of the business are perishable, or have a time value, then the executor faces the problem of taking immediate action or having these business assets dissipated.

Unfortunately, the executor can be held personally responsible for negligence in the management of a decedent's business. In fact, the results in most cases where businesses are continued without court authorization are generally unfavorable to the personal representatives. The court in one such case held that the personal representative did not have the unqualified right to perpetuate a decedent's enterprise without approval of the court, and that any loss to the estate suffered by continuation of the business fell upon the representative.

INVESTING AND PROTECTING THE ASSETS

The executor should take steps to ascertain that the assets are properly invested, so that there will be no possibility of the executor's being held responsible for dissipating the assets or allowing their value to decrease unreasonably. In investing these assets, an executor is required to exercise the same degree of judgment that a reasonable person would exercise in the management of his own estate. In one case, the executrix held an estate balance of approximately $6,000 in a noninterest-bearing checking account for 3 years because of the need for ready cash and liquidity of funds. The court, however, felt that it would have been more prudent to invest the money and not permit it to remain idle. The executrix was consequently charged for failing to invest the funds.

Protection of assets is another responsibility of an executor, who must make certain that silverware, jewelry, and art objects are protected and insured, so that he will not be held responsible in the event of loss by theft, fire, or other unforeseen calamity.

The executor must try to obtain a fair price if he sells the assets. For example, the executor of the estate of a prominent painter sold paintings to an art dealer, and the dealer later resold the paintings at prices ranging from six to ten times what the dealer paid the estate for them. The court held the executor responsible for the loss to the estate.

What does an executor do when property is not in the decedent's name alone, but the decedent owns it jointly with his wife, or another family member, or even a business associate? Whenever property is held in joint names, the applicable state law will determine whether the decedent's interest in the property will be included as part of his estate to be administered by the executor or whether, in fact, the property will pass directly to the remaining joint owner or owners. For example, in most states, property owned jointly by husband and wife is owned as a joint tenancy with the right of survivorship (sometimes know as "tenancy by the entirety"). The right of survivorship means that upon the death of one of these joint owners the survivor owns all property rights to the exclusion of the executor.

However, property is sometimes owned by several persons "in common." In this situation, each person has an undivided right to a certain percentage of the property. Where the decedent owned a tenancy in common, the executor will represent the decedent's interests in his or her proportionate share of the property. In some cases, questions can be raised as to what exactly the decedent's interest is, and these cases require extreme caution on the part of the executor. There is also the problem of the responsibility for the taxes due on the decedent's interest in his share of the jointly held property.

PAYMENT OF TAXES, DEBTS, AND EXPENSES

A decedent's assets must often be converted into cash in order to pay expenses, debts, and taxes. Since no two decedents own exactly the same property, no two estates will be handled in an identical manner. There is very little demand for some of the personal property that people own. Therefore it is hard to realize cash from many of these assets. Of course, assets such as the proceeds of life insurance, certificates of deposits, and Treasury bills may be available to take care of the estate's liabilities. Listed securities can also be quickly converted to cash, but the market value at the time that funds are needed might preclude their sale at that time. Assets such as real estate and business interests are not readily convertible into cash, and it might take months, or even years in the case of business interests, to realize cash from these assets. Therefore the executor has to analyze the assets of the estate after they have been assembled, determine what amounts of cash will be needed to cover the debts, expenses, and taxes of the estate, and then develop a plan to make the necessary funds available when required.

Typical debts that the decedent might have outstanding at his death include outstanding loans, credit card balances, and day-to-day bills such as household bills, telephone, electric, gasoline, department store charges, and past taxes.

Common expenses are the costs of administering the estate. These include probate costs, legal fees, executor's or administrator's fees, fees for appraisers, costs included in selling real estate and personal property, costs arising on account of the decedent's last illness, and the costs involved in winding up the executor's business.

Numerous categories of taxes must be paid in the process of settling an estate. In many estates the executor must pay two categories of death taxes — state inheritance and estate taxes, and the federal estate tax. In addition, the executor is also responsible for the payment of unpaid income taxes, both federal and state, and any state personal property and real estate taxes that might be due on the personal and real property in the decedent's name.

State death taxes are typically paid by the executor out of the estate's assets. (Technically, the person receiving the property is taxed on his right to receive such assets.) The amount of the tax, which is on the transfer itself, usually depends on the relationship of the beneficiary or receiver of the property to the decedent. For example, in Pennsylvania property left to children, grandchildren, parents, or anyone in the family line is taxed to the recipient at the rate of 6 percent, while property left to all other beneficiaries is taxed at 15 percent. There are exceptions for certain types of property held jointly by husband and wife for which no tax is due. There are also specific exemptions, such as for the proceeds of life insurance paid to a named beneficiary, for charitable bequests, and for real estate located outside of the taxing state.

Where a decedent owns real estate located in a state different from that of his domicile at the time of death, the state in which the real estate is located has the right to tax the property. This often leads to problems, especially if those cases where two states are trying to tax the same property.

A federal estate tax return must be filed if the decedent's net assets exceed a specified amount at the time of his or her death. This amount was $275,000 in 1983, $325,000 in 1984, $400,000 in 1985, $500,000 in 1986, and $600,000 in 1987 and subsequent years. (It is important to remember that the decedent's estate for federal estate tax purposes may be different from the decedent's estate for state death tax purposes.) The federal estate tax is a graduated tax. Maximum estate tax rates are being reduced from 70 percent to 50 percent. The maximum rate if 55 percent from 1984 to 1987 and then will drop to 50 percent in 1988 and remain at that level thereafter. This 50 percent tax rate will apply to taxable bequests in excess of $2,500,000. There is also a unified credit that can be applied to the tax payable. The credit, which reduces the tax otherwise payable dollar for dollar, was $79,300 for 1983, $96,300 for 1984, $121,800 for 1985, and will be $155,800 for 1986 and $192,800 for 1987 and subsequent years.

Tax returns must, of course, accompany tax payments. The federal estate tax return is a long and highly complex form, requiring a great deal of time both in assembling the necessary information and in preparing the return. There are im-

portant questions that must be answered by the executor as well as available options that can result in considerable tax savings to the estate, and with which the executor must be familiar. Before listing the assets on the return, the executor must first decide on the value of the assets at the time of death. For cash or listed securities, the value of the asset is fixed. However, in determining the value of a business interest or of real estate, it is first necessary to have the properties in question appraised. Appropriate parallels should then be drawn between similar assets, so that a valuation can be arrived at that will keep taxes to a minimum, but will also be acceptable to the government as a fair representation of the market value of the properties as of the date of the decedent's death.

The executor has the choice of using the value of property as of the date of death or selecting the alternate valuation date value. This simply means valuing the assets in the estate at a date 6 months following the decedent's death. Alternate valuation would be advantageous in the event that the value of the property had fallen during that period, and this is a very important decision on the part of the executor.

There are also certain types of closely held business property and farm property that may qualify for specific tax advantages because of the nature of the property. The executor should be aware of these special elections as well as other important valuation rules and should use them to the best advantage of the estate and its beneficiaries.

Another very important tax-saving device is the marital deduction. Under prior law the estate of a decedent received a deduction for any property left to the decedent's spouse in a qualified manner in an amount equal to the greater of one-half of the decedent's adjusted gross estate or $250,000. Under current law, it is now possible to transfer an unlimited amount of money and/or property to a surviving spouse, outright or in trust, and not pay any federal estate tax. It is even possible to provide that the surviving spouse will receive only the income from that property, with the remainder passing at death to some third party, such as the couple's children. (Under prior law, this would have caused a loss of the marital deduction.) Prompt action on the part of the executor, though is essential if this enhanced flexibility is to be secured. Still other choices and elections must be made by executors to fully maximize the almost unlimited tax-saving potential of current law.

Federal estate taxes are due 9 months from the date of death. There are serious penalties if the return is not filed promptly or if an extension is not requested within a specified time period. In certain circumstances, there are options available to an executor that will extend the time period for the payment of all or a portion of the federal estate tax. If the estate qualifies, no payment of the tax is required for 4 years (although interest at an extremely favorable rate is payable during this time). The executor can then pay the tax due (plus interest) in up to ten annual installments. This can stretch out the payments for up to 14 years.

The executor is responsible for knowing all of these dates and taking advantage of all options and elections. Courts have held that where the untimely filing of federal estate tax returns resulted in a loss to the estate, the executor was personally responsible. There are many cases where beneficiaries have attempted to surcharge executors for their failure to take advantage of tax saving and expense-saving opportunities.

In many cases there are other taxes to be paid and other forms to be filed. For example, income taxes have to be paid on the income that the decedent earned prior to his death. Tax also has to be paid on the income generated from the assets in the estate. Options are available to the executor in regard to the timing of the estate's income tax return, and the executor should make this determination after a thorough review of the entire tax picture of the decedent, the estate, and the beneficiaries.

There is also a federal (and in some cases a state) gift tax, the returns for which would have been filed by the decedent in most cases. The executor should review any transfers made by the decedent prior to his death and make a determination as to whether any gift taxes are due. If so, the appropriate gift tax returns should be filed. Thus an executor has to be aware of the recent changes in the gift tax laws as well as the changes in the state and income tax provisions.

DISTRIBUTING REMAINING ASSETS

Once an executor has assembled the decedent's assets and paid appropriate debts, expenses, and taxes, he must distribute any remaining assets according to the decedent's will or under state intestacy laws. In the case of a very small estate where the spouse might be the executor and sole beneficiary, distribution can be accomplished by turning the property over to the beneficiary and accepting a "receipt and release" to the executor of any liability to the beneficiary. However, while this is certainly the most expedient and inexpensive way of concluding an estate, the executor may remain liable for any unpaid debts and for outstanding taxes and may be responsible for any number of other problems that might arise.

If the executor wishes to be formally discharged from his duties, responsibilities, and liabilities, then it is necessary to prepare a final account of administration. Unpaid credits and beneficiaries are given notice of the filing of the account. In the event that there are charitable gifts in the will, the notice must be sent to the attorney general or other appropriate official appointed to protect the interests of the charities. On the date of the audit, those persons having any objections appear and are given the right to a further hearing, if necessary, to present their position to the court. When the court is satisfied that all of the procedures in handling the estate have been complied with, then the account is approved, a formal schedule of distribution is presented and approved, and the executor distributes the assets to the beneficiaries and is discharged from his responsibilities. When trusts have been established in the decedent's will, assets are transferred from the executor to the trusts so that these trusts can be immediately implemented if assets have not already been so transferred.

Complications in making distribution often occur because the people mentioned in the decedent's will are not all available to take distribution, or assets that are supposed to pass to named beneficiaries are not in the decedent's estate at the time of his death, or are there in different form. For example, if a decedent leaves his estate equally to his two brothers, and subsequent to the writing of the will but prior to his death the two brothers die, with one leaving two children and the other survived solely by his wife, how should the executor distribute the proceeds? The answer would depend upon an interpretation of the decedent's will, or the law of the state of domicile, or perhaps a combination of both.

Further complications arise when a decedent has bequeathed specific assets that are no longer in his estate at the time of his death. For example, bequests of "all my money in my savings account at XYZ Bank to my brother" and "all of my stock certificates to my sister" would be complicated if, before his death, the decedent had closed out his bank account and used part of the funds to purchase securities and part to purchase an automobile. In any event, if the executor made distribution in any contested situation without court approval, the executor could be held personally responsible if it was later determined that the distribution was improper.

Of course, the executor must make distribution promptly, unlike the tardy executrix who one court felt unreasonably and intentionally withheld distribution of the funds to her sisters, under the will of their mother, and was charged with interest at the legal rate during the period of the delay.

SUMMARY

Being an executor is a serious business. In addition to having to understand incredibly complex state and federal tax laws, the executor must also be accountable to the decedent's family, his beneficiaries if they are not members of his family, his creditors, his business associates, various branches of government for the myriad of taxes for which the executor is responsible, and finally to the court for the proper performance of his duties. It is for these reasons that the use of a corporate fiduciary should be considered (as sole or coexecutor) by every estate owner.

INDEX

Tools and Techniques

Tools and Techniques

Tools and Techniques

Tools and Techniques

Tools and Techniques